Hello Everybody !
MACDONALD
Calling

LABOUR *in*
POWER
THIS TIME

RAMSAY
MACDONALD

RAMSAY MACDONALD

DAVID MARQUAND

JONATHAN CAPE
THIRTY BEDFORD SQUARE LONDON

FIRST PUBLISHED 1977
© 1977 BY DAVID MARQUAND

JONATHAN CAPE LTD, 30 BEDFORD SQUARE, LONDON WCI

BRITISH LIBRARY CATALOGUING IN PUBLICATION DATA

Marquand, David
Ramsay MacDonald.
Index.
ISBN 0–224–01295–9
941.083′092′4   DA 566.9.M25
MacDonald, James Ramsay

PRINTED IN GREAT BRITAIN BY THE ANCHOR PRESS LTD
AND BOUND BY WM BRENDON & SON LTD
BOTH OF TIPTREE, ESSEX

For Judith

Contents

CONTENTS

Illustrations

(Picture research by Robyn Wallis)

Preface

Ramsay MacDonald was, by any reckoning, a pivotal figure in the history of modern Britain. He was also a profoundly controversial figure; and many of the controversies he provoked during his life still help to shape political attitudes forty years after his death. But although a number of books have been written about him, ranging from the extravagantly eulogistic to the obsessionally hostile, most of them were published more than a generation ago, and none of their authors had access to his private papers or, for that matter, to the vast store of official material which is now available for research at the Public Record Office. Some of them contain valuable insights into his character, but none of them, it seems to me, gives an adequate account of his career.

In this book, I have tried to fill the gap: to give a fuller account of Mac-Donald's actions and motives than earlier writers were able to do and, in doing so, to provide the evidence for a more dispassionate assessment of his significance than was possible before the dust of old battles had begun to settle. I was invited to write it by Ramsay MacDonald's son, the Rt Hon. Malcolm Mac-Donald, and was given unrestricted access to Ramsay MacDonald's personal and official papers, most of which had never been examined by his family. In the course of my research, I received immense assistance and encouragement – as well as a great deal of personal kindness and hospitality – not only from Malcolm MacDonald, but from his brother, Mr Alister MacDonald, and from his sisters, Mrs Ishbel Peterkin and Mrs Sheila Lochhead. My debt to all of them is enormous, and it is pleasant to be able to acknowledge it at last. It is all the greater because none of them has sought to interfere in any way with my treatment of the subject, or even to suggest what sort of approach I ought to adopt.

That makes it all the more necessary for me to explain what my approach has been. I believe strongly that the past can have lessons for the present. But I do not believe that its lessons can be learned by forcing it on to a procrustean bed, shaped by present-day expectations and present-day assumptions. Hence, I have tried to depict MacDonald as a man of his own time, facing the problems of his own time and applying or failing to apply the solutions of his own time, and not as an exemplar or a warning for ours. I believe that when he is looked at in this way, without the hindsight which seems to me to mar many interpretations of the period, he emerges as a greater and, at the same time, as a more attractive, man than he has generally been thought to be; the hostile view of him which became almost universal, at any rate in the Labour movement, after the split in 1931 seems to me to emerge as myth rather than as history. But although I have tried to avoid the trap of hindsight, I have also tried to avoid the opposite trap of apologia, and to portray him 'warts and all'. If the warts are less obtrusive than in previous portraits, that is because, for nearly a generation after his death, they attracted so much attention that the face beneath was almost ignored.

In the course of what turned into a much bigger and more time-consuming undertaking than I foresaw when I began, I have accumulated a host of other debts, in addition to my debt to the MacDonald family. I should like, in particular, to thank the Warden and Fellows of St Antony's College, Oxford, for the award of a research fellowship which greatly facilitated the early stages of my research; the authorities at the Public Record Office who arranged with Malcolm MacDonald to sort and classify his father's papers before I had finished with them; Mrs Jane Hoare, of the Public Record Office, who actually sorted them, and without whose labours this book would still not be finished; Mrs Irene Wagner and the staff of the Labour Party Library at Transport House, for good-humoured advice and assistance stretching over a longer period than I care to remember; Dr J. R. van der Leeuw of the International Institute of Social History in Amsterdam who found valuable MacDonald material for me in the archives of the Labour and Socialist International; the Librarian and staff of the House of Commons Library, for their unfailing helpfulness at all hours of the day and night; and the Librarians and staffs of the Bodleian Library, the British Library, the British Newspaper Library, the Cambridge University Library and the London School of Economics Library.

In a different category, I should like to express my gratitude to the following friends, colleagues and acquaintances of MacDonald's, who gave me the benefit of their personal memories of him and some of whom also gave me access to important material concerning him: Mr Frank Barlow, Princess Marthe Bibesco, Lady Mairi Bury, Sir Neville Butler, Mr Sidney Campion, Mrs Grace Cooke, Dr Gertrude Cormack, Sir Patrick Dollan, Sir Patrick Duff, Captain Dunbar, Lord Elton, Mr Bill Gregory, Mrs M. A. Hamilton, Mr and Mrs Hett, Mrs Rose Hoenig, Mr Montgomery Hyde, Mr Francis Johnson, Mr A. B. Mackay, Mr Allan Maclean, Mr James Margach, Sir Alec Martin, Mr James Middleton, Mrs Lucy Middleton, Mr Rosslyn Mitchell, the Hon. Lily Montagu, Sir Oswald Mosley, Mrs Cecily Mure, Mrs Grace Paton, Miss Elizabeth Peterkin, Miss Marianne Peterkin, Lord Ponsonby, Lady Helen Roberton, Mr Kenneth Roberton, Mr and Mrs Sammon, Mr William Sims, Lord Stamford, Mr Ernest Stanford, the Rt Hon. John Strachey, the Rt Hon. G. R. Strauss, Mrs Margaret Sutherland, Mr James Welsh and Mr Len

Williams. In this connection, I am particularly grateful to Lady Mairi Bury and the Northern Ireland Public Record Office for giving me access to MacDonald's letters to Lady Londonderry.

I have also received an immense amount of help from friends and colleagues. Dr Henry Pelling gave me invaluable guidance to the source material for MacDonald's early life, and lent me his transcripts of MacDonald's letters to Keir Hardie and Bruce Glasier. Professor Arthur Marwick lend me transcripts of MacDonald's letters to Clifford Allen. Mr Martin Gilbert gave me access to the Churchill papers and entertained me at his home while I worked on them. Captain S. W. Roskill entertained me, both at his home and at Churchill College, Cambridge, and gave me valuable information about MacDonald's later years. Drs Janeway and Wrench, both of whom had consulted the MacDonald papers while these were in my custody, lent me their subsequent doctoral dissertations, to my great profit. At different stages my manuscript has been read, in whole or in part, by Lord Briggs, the Rt Hon. Roy Jenkins, Professor John Mackintosh, Dr Kenneth Morgan, Mr David Shapiro, Dr R. J. Skidelsky, Mr A. F. Thompson and Mr Philip Williams, all of whom generously spared the time from busy lives to correct inaccuracies and suggest improvements; the errors and infelicities that remain are, of course, my own. Not content with reading my manuscript, Dr Morgan also lent me transcripts of a number of important MacDonald letters. Last, but by no means least, Professor Anthony King and Dr Janet Morgan both undertook the labour of reading the proofs. To all of these, I am more grateful than I can say.

I should like to thank Miss Robyn Wallis for picture research; Mrs Anne Shotts for typing the final draft of most of my manuscript; my secretary, Mrs Jennifer Stringer, and my former secretaries, Mrs Pip Burton, Mrs Mary-Lou Clarke, Mrs E. F. Donoughue, Mrs Norma Nathan and Mrs Anne Smail, for typing preliminary drafts and other material; and Mrs Francis Cohen, Mr Graham Thomas and Mrs Marion Yass, for helping, at different stages, with some of the chores of research.

I wish to thank the following for permission to quote material in which they hold the copyright: Miss Polly Allen, Miss Ada Ammon, Lord Attlee, Lord Baldwin, Mrs Nancy Bargrave-Dean, the Beaverbrook Foundation, the British Library of Political and Economic Science, Lord Brockway, Lady Mairi Bury, Mrs Grace Cooke, Dame Isobel Cripps, Dr B. T. Davis, Mr H. R. Dunnico, Mrs Hope Pattison Dyson, Sir John Gilmour, Mr Malcolm Bruce Glasier, Lord Greenwood, Lord Henderson, Mrs Martha Hughes, Mrs Jessie Irvine, Lord Kahn, Mr Philip Leach, Mrs Stephen Lloyd, the Rt Hon. Malcolm MacDonald, Mrs Lucy Middleton, Mrs M. E. Nichol, the Oxford University Press, Brigadier A. W. Llewellen Palmer, Lord Parmoor, Mrs Helen Pease, Mr Nicholas Pease, Lord Ponsonby, Mr Kenneth Roberton, Mr Leslie Russell and the Society of Authors on behalf of the Bernard Shaw Estate (© Shaw texts, 1977. The Trustees of The British Museum, The Governors and Guardians of The National Gallery of Ireland, and Royal Academy of Dramatic Art). I should add that, in a manuscript note pasted into his diary, Ramsay MacDonald wrote that the contents were 'meant as notes to guide and revive memory as regards happenings and must on no account be published as they are'. Malcolm MacDonald has accordingly decided that, at least for the time being, the diary is not to be published *in extenso*. He has, however, imposed no restrictions on the use I have made of the diary and has given me permission to publish all the quotations from it which I wished to use and which I have included in this book; and I am particularly grateful for this. I should also add that extracts from Crown Copyright material are reproduced with the permission of the Controller of Her Majesty's Stationery Office. I also wish to thank the following for permission to reproduce illustrations: Fox Photos for nos 74 and 78; the Labour Party Photographic Library for nos 9, 23, 53, 64 and endpaper no. 1; Keystone View Co. for no. 77; the MacDonald Archives (P.R.O.) for nos 3–8, 10–12, 14–16, 21–2, 24–7, 29–31, 33–4, 36, 46–7, 49–51, 54, 61, 63, 68 and 70; the Mansell Collection for nos 1, 40, 52, 58 and 72; Mr W. Mure for no. 56; the Radio Times Hulton Picture Library for nos 2, 13, 28, 35, 37–9, 41, 43–5, 48, 62, 65–6, 69, 71, 73, 75–6 and endpapers 2–4; Sport and General Press Agency for nos 17, 32 and 68. Finally, I should like to make it clear that I have made every effort to trace all holders of copyright in material which I have quoted and in illustrations, and to apologize to those concerned where I have failed to do so.

A few outstanding debts remain to be acknowledged. The first is to my friend and publisher, Mr Graham Greene, who has shown me kindness and patience beyond any conceivable call of duty, and to all at Jonathan Cape who have been concerned with the production of this book. The second is to my teachers, Mr A. J. P. Taylor, Mr A. F. Thompson and Mr E. N. Williams, who cannot escape at least a partial responsibility for its appearance, even though they are in no way responsible for its contents. The third is to my parents, both of whom sat at MacDonald's feet fifty years ago and who, between them, taught me more about the atmosphere of that time than I have learned from any other source. The fourth is to my children, whose entire lives have been spent in MacDonald's shadow, with only intermittent protests on their part. The fifth, and greatest, is to my wife, whose advice and help have been invaluable, whose encouragement has been unwavering and to whom this book is dedicated.

August 1976   D.M.

CHAPTER 1

Lossiemouth

I

RAMSAY MACDONALD died a lonely and disappointed old man, worn out in body and mind. For six years, his former followers in the Labour Party had reviled him as a traitor; the Conservatives, who had once profited greatly from their association with him, had increasingly come to regard him as an encumbrance. By the end of his official life, it is doubtful if there was much enthusiasm for him even in the minuscule National Labour group, whose sole reason for existing was the fact that he led it: when Harold Nicolson, then a National Labour M.P., learned that MacDonald planned to stay in the House of Commons after leaving office, he noted disconsolately that his own reaction was one of 'blank horror, since we shall never get ahead with our group so long as the old man is with us'.[1] Death sometimes gives a spur to reassessment; MacDonald's was followed by a further fall in reputation. The war, which broke out only two years after he died, blotted out the successes of the previous twenty years and magnified the failures; policies which had once been supported by large popular majorities now seemed explicable only on the supposition that their authors had been unusually weak or foolish. In an influential study published in 1955, the historian C. L. Mowat wrote that from 1922 to 1939 Britain had been subjected to 'the rule of the pygmies':[2] like many good phrases, this summed up the mood of the time when it was coined. Few saw MacDonald as the most culpable of the pygmies, but few doubted that he was, so to speak, one of the most diminutive. The Right had never taken him to its heart, and had less sympathy for him now than formerly. Most people on the Left saw him at best as a skeleton in their collective cupboard, and at worst as a kind of archetype of the Lost Leader, cynically betraying his followers for the sake of an enemy ribbon.

Immediately before the war, Lord Elton — once a Labour candidate for Parliament and later a National Labour peer — published an admiring biography of MacDonald, which took his career to 1919.[3] Apart from that, his critics had the field almost to themselves. His character and motives were savagely attacked in a hostile life by his old P.P.S., L. MacNeill Weir; he appeared, thinly disguised, as the opportunistic hero of Howard Spring's novel, *Fame is the Spur*; with rare exceptions, the memoirs and biographies of other Labour politicians depicted him in a more or less hostile light.[4] Though his critics did not all take the same line, there was general agreement that he had, in some sense, 'gone wrong': that his actions in 1931 had been inconsistent, if not with his actual beliefs, then at least with what a self-respecting leader of the Labour Party ought to have believed; and that such a grave inconsistency could have been due only to grave weaknesses of character, or to an insecure grasp of socialist principles, or perhaps to both. Official Labour publications were less outspoken, but no more flattering. In 1946, the Labour Party brought out a pamphlet on its history from 1900 to 1945. The 1931 crisis was described in two hurried and embarrassed sentences; though MacDonald's re-election to the party leadership in 1922 was given a cursory acknowledgement, nothing was said about his achievements as leader, while the fact that he had been the party's secretary for its first twelve years was not even mentioned.[5] In 1950, a shorter pamphlet was published to mark the party's golden jubilee. This made it clear that MacDonald had been present at the conference which voted to set up the Labour Representation Committee in 1900, and then made no further reference to him.[6] So far as the party machine was concerned, he had become, in effect, a non-person.

The next twenty years brought a change of perspective. Labour historians discovered – or perhaps it would be more accurate to say that they rediscovered – that MacDonald had contributed more to the establishment and early growth of the Labour Party than a later generation had realized. Diplomatic historians discovered that he had frequently talked more sense about foreign policy than had most of his contemporaries. The 'pygmy' theory of inter-war British politics began to crumble, perhaps because it became increasingly apparent that post-war British Governments were not over-endowed with giants either; new interpretations of the period came out, which suggested both that MacDonald must have been a more formidable figure than had been supposed in the ten or fifteen years after his death, and that his actions in 1931 had more to be said for them.[7] Meanwhile, the Labour Party's attitude towards him showed signs of mellowing – a process which may have been accelerated and was certainly underlined when Harold Wilson, the first leader of the party who was too young to have played an active part in the politics of the early 1930s, paid him a warm and compassionate tribute at a lunch to commemorate the centenary of his birth.[8]

Yet the extent of the change should not be exaggerated. Old views of MacDonald seemed less plausible: no new view took their place. It is doubtful if many still see him as the scheming careerist portrayed by MacNeill Weir, or as the 'boneless wonder' which Winston Churchill once accused him of being. It is equally doubtful if many have a clear notion of how he should be seen instead. Labour people still find it hard to come to terms with him emotionally; to judge by their writings, he has baffled the historians of the 1960s and 1970s as successfully as he baffled his colleagues and opponents. He emerges from the literature of the last twenty years as a bundle of contradictory attributes rather than as a credible human being. The part he played in building up the Labour Party in its first few years is reasonably well established. Many of the most important questions raised by the rest of his career remain unanswered – sometimes because the facts are in dispute, more often because the question concerned still carries a strong emotional charge. His actions in 1931 provide the most obvious example. As will appear later, the full story of the crisis has not yet been told, but, in broad outline at least, there is no longer much doubt about what MacDonald did. His reasons for doing it, and even more the rights and wrongs of his behaviour, are still profoundly controversial, and are likely to remain so long after the last factual discoveries have been made. Less obviously, the same applies to a whole range of other episodes: to his attempts to devise an ideology and strategy for the Labour Party before 1914, for example; to his role during the wave of industrial disputes before and after the war; to his tactics as leader of the Opposition in 1922 and 1923 and between 1924 and 1929; to the economic policies of the second Labour Government in 1930 and 1931; to his foreign policy in the early 1930s. Each of these presents a historiographical puzzle; each is puzzling partly because it raises issues which, in one form or another, are as alive today as they were when MacDonald faced them.

For although he was unmistakably a product of his own time – a cultivated late Victorian in his literary tastes, a Gladstonian liberal internationalist in his foreign policy, an Edwardian revisionist in his social philosophy – he also belongs to ours. In the late 1950s or early 1960s, when the post-war international monetary order was still intact, it was possible to see the 1931 crisis as a remote and almost incomprehensible episode, with no relevance to a more enlightened age. It is difficult to see it in such a way after the sterling crises of the last fifteen years. The problems of low productivity and declining competitiveness, which absorbed an inordinate amount of ministerial time under the second Labour Government, have absorbed, if anything, even more ministerial time in the 1960s and 1970s. The vexed question of European security and disarmament, to which MacDonald devoted the lion's share of his energies at repeated intervals for more than ten years, presented many of the dilemmas which were to face post-war British Governments when they had to decide their attitude to European integration. The official case for building the Singapore base in 1924 was remarkably similar to the official case for staying east of Suez forty years later; the arguments for sticking to free trade in 1930 and 1931 were to be heard again from the opponents of the Common Market's agricultural policy in the early 1970s. As all these examples help to show, moreover, most of the really intractable problems with which MacDonald had to deal as prime minister can be seen as variations on the interwoven themes of declining economic and political power, dwindling freedom of action and sluggish adaptation to the forces which had made it dwindle. All three have sounded even more loudly in the last twenty-five years.

The same is true of his role in Labour history. He was, if not the chief architect of the 'Labour Alliance' of 1900, then at least its master builder. He created its organization; he made the famous deal with the Liberals which gave it its first significant foothold in the House of Commons; in its first few years, his was the most important single influence on its strategy and tactics. He played a dominant part in Labour politics throughout the tumultuous period which saw the Labour Party replace the Liberals as the main anti-Conservative force in Britain—for some of the time as party leader and for the rest of it as the leadership's foremost critic. He was the first Labour prime minister in British history and, as such, did much to determine who were to be the leading figures in Labour politics in the next generation: Attlee, Morrison, Cripps and Dalton all received their first ministerial offices from him. For nearly thirty years, he poured out a flood of articles, pamphlets and books which helped to shape the party's thinking; in a sense true of none of his successors, he not only led it but captured its imagination and seemed to embody its hopes. Partly because of all this, his career throws a peculiarly harsh and poignant light on the tensions which were built into the structure he did so much to create—notably, on the tension between the party's Utopian aspirations on the one hand and the realities of democratic politics on the other, and on the even more acute tension between its original role as the political arm of the trade unions and its later role as an actual or potential party of government. For no one voiced the party's aspirations more powerfully than he did: and part, at least, of the blame for its failure to marry aspiration to reality lies at his door. By the same token, no one did more to bring the unions into the 'Labour Alliance' after it had been formed, or to ensure that its strategy conformed to their requirements once they had joined it. Yet in the two great crises of his political life, in 1914 and again in 1931, it was the trade-union wing of the alliance that led the opposition to him. It can at least be argued, moreover, that the party was influenced as much by its later hostility towards him as by its earlier admiration: that it ruled out policies which might otherwise have been adopted and adopted policies which might otherwise have been rejected partly because it was haunted by his memory: and that it failed to learn the lessons of his leadership because his supposed treachery in 1931 provided a ready-made explanation of all that had gone wrong.

MacDonald was prime minister for a total of seven years, leader of the Opposition for six and a leading figure in British politics for twenty-five: an up-to-date account of his career is needed simply to fill a historiographical gap. It is needed even more because the British Labour movement—and hence modern British politics in general—cannot be fully understood without understanding him.

II

The story begins in a tiny 'but-and-ben' cottage in Lossiemouth—a small fishing port on the coast of Morayshire in north-east Scotland, about forty miles east of Inverness—where MacDonald was born on October 12th, 1866. Like Keir

Hardie and Ernest Bevin, he was illegitimate. For most of his life he was known as James Ramsay MacDonald; his birth certificate described him as 'James McDonald Ramsay, child of Anne Ramsay'. His father, whose name was not recorded, was probably a Highlander named John Macdonald, who had worked as a ploughman on the nearby farm of Claydale, where the young Annie Ramsay was for a time in service. The minute-book of the Kirk Session of the Alves Free Kirk makes the position as clear as it is ever likely to be:

14th Dec. 1866. Compeared of their own accord John Macdonald Foreman at Sweethillock, and with him Anne Ramsay residing at Lossiemouth, who being called acknowledged that she had borne a male child on the 12th of October last, and she now named as the father of her child John Macdonald, sometime fellow servant with her at Claydale. The said John Macdonald being present was asked by the Moderator to say whether he acknowledged the truth of the charge, to which he answered that he did. The parties were then solemnly addressed by the Moderator as to the evil of the sin they had committed and were exhorted to seek repentance and forgiveness and divine grace to guide them in time to come. They received the same in a becoming manner and professed their sorrow and their desire to be forgiven and led in the way of divine commandment. The Kirk Session were satisfied with the same, and considering that one of the parties resides at a distance agreed that they be now absolved from Church censure and be restored to Church privileges, which was done accordingly.[9]

With that, the elusive figure of John Macdonald fades away.

It seems fairly clear that he and Anne Ramsay had been engaged to be married, and that their engagement was broken off only at the last moment. But there are two versions of what happened. According to the first, the responsibility lay with Annie Ramsay herself. She and her lover are said to have had a violent quarrel not long before their wedding was due, in the course of which he threatened to desert her and their unborn child unless she did as he wished. But she was a girl of spirit and refused to be blackmailed. She is said to have retorted that she would be perfectly capable of bringing up her child on her own and to have defied Macdonald to carry out his threat.[10] According to the second version, the marriage was prevented by Annie's mother, Isabella. Bella Ramsay was a formidable woman, with no mean conception of her place in society. She had been married to a William Ramsay, who kept a baker's shop in Elgin, the county town of Morayshire, but at some time in the 1850s she and her husband had separated. She had then settled in Lossiemouth, where she earned her living as a seamstress, and brought up her four children singlehanded. Through all her misfortunes, she had preserved the memory of better days, fortified by the fierce family pride of the Scot. For she was an Allan by birth, and the Allans were small farmers whose gravestones in Spynie churchyard went back for a century and more. As such, she was a cut above the fishermen and farm labourers of

Lossiemouth among whom she was obliged to live.[11] Bella Ramsay, the second version runs, refused to allow her daughter to marry John Macdonald on the grounds that no mere ploughman could aspire to the hand of an Allan, and in spite of Annie's protestations she eventually succeeded in driving the young man away.[12]

The effect of all this on MacDonald can never be known with certainty. Even to his family and closest friends, he rarely spoke of the things that touched him most. In later life, it is true, he published a number of semi-autobiographical essays on Lossiemouth and his childhood there, but in spite of their undoubted biographical value the reader has the sense that, as so often with MacDonald's writings, the rich prose style and colourful imagery have become a veil for some fugitive inner reticence.[13] All the same, some facts are clear and some guesses can be made. The stigma attaching to illegitimacy may well have been less marked among the Morayshire peasantry than respectable middle-class Victorians would have liked. The report of the royal commission of 1867 on the employment of women, young persons and children in agriculture revealed that in that part of Scotland the illegitimacy rate was about fifteen per cent — the highest north of the border. The smaller farms were usually worked by young unmarried men and girls: in most districts a ploughman like John Macdonald would lose his job if he married, and become a day labourer, dependent on casual earnings. Perhaps because of this, the local clergy, as an Elgin solicitor put it in his evidence to the royal commission, had 'all but abandoned ecclesiastical discipline in cases of sexual immorality, and even if such discipline were attempted to be revived it would now be so little regarded as to be quite ineffectual'.[14] Even so, there can be little doubt that there was a stigma of some sort; and to a sensitive child it may well have seemed greater than it was. It is clear, moreover, that MacDonald's illegitimacy was well known: his mother never married, and was known as 'Miss' Ramsay to her dying day. It is clear too that those who knew him best — and few could claim to know him well — themselves sensed his inner reticence and believed that the scars left by his illegitimacy provided an important part of the explanation for it.

Beyond that, we can only speculate. Some of MacDonald's unhappier traits — his prickliness, his sensitivity to criticism, his suspiciousness and perhaps also his shyness and reserve — may well have been due, in part, to the circumstances of his birth. In spite of his charm and personal magnetism and his splendid assurance on a public platform, he never gave the impression of being at ease with himself or with the world, and it does not need much imagination to trace the uneasiness of the man back to the uneasiness of a fatherless child, uncertain of his identity and unsure where he belonged. But what was a handicap in some ways may well have been a source of strength in others. Lacking a secure identity, he made an identity for himself; belonging nowhere, he was determined to behave as though he could belong anywhere; lacking a father, a Freudian might conclude, he did his best to become the father of his people. Less fancifully, it is worth remembering that, although he had no father, he was the focus of his mother's undivided attention and that his grandmother helped to bring him up as well; the care which they must have lavished on him clearly compensated for much. Some, at least, of the driving force that took him to the top of politics in spite of greater obstacles than any other British prime minister has had to face must have been due to them; so must some of the courage and self-reliance that accompanied it.

Bella Ramsay is a shadowy figure. She is said to have been deeply religious and an ardent member of the Lossiemouth Free Kirk, with strong opinions on the theological controversies of the day. She is also said to have possessed a rich store of the ancient legends of the Laigh of Moray, which had been passed down by word of mouth from generation to generation, and which her children and grandchildren in turn learned at her knee.[15] Apart from that, however, little is known about her now. With Annie Ramsay we are on firmer ground. Until recently, she was still remembered in Lossiemouth. She was a handsome woman with strong features and great natural dignity: reserved and rather brusque on the surface, but warm-hearted and emotional beneath. She was also a stubborn woman, and she must have needed all her stubbornness. As well as the cares of motherhood, she had to cope with the burdens of the breadwinner. According to one account, she used to follow the herring fleet in the summer with the fisherwomen, helping to gut the catch at the ports along the coast where it was landed, and she worked in the fields in the autumn. It seems clear, however, that her main source of income was dressmaking. Like her mother, she was a skilled seamstress, and within living memory half the women in Lossiemouth wore her bonnets. She was a confirmed rebel, as well. One witness still remembers how, as a boy, he used to see fishermen 'spitting with rage, talking politics with Annie Ramsay'. When Ladysmith was relieved, during the Boer War, she pulled down her blinds and hung black crêpe on her front door; for her pains, she was burned in effigy on the bonfire celebrating the end of the siege.[16]

The second big influence on MacDonald's character was Lossiemouth itself, and if we are to have any hope of understanding him we must try to imagine what it must have been like to grow up there a century ago. It is a grey little town: squat, grey cottages huddled behind a spur of rock called the Coulard Hill; low, grey houses on the seaward side of the rock, facing out across the Moray Firth to Wick and the Arctic beyond. Though it has a certain gaunt charm, the town itself is not particularly remarkable. The setting is spectacular, and, for an imaginative child like the young MacDonald, evocative as well. To the north, across the Firth, there are the distant hills of Sutherland and Ross, where, a generation before MacDonald was born, the ancient culture of his father's people was destroyed in the Highland clearances. To the east, there is the sea and a broad sweep of yellow sand; to the south, the rolling farmland of the Laigh of Moray, with the peaks of the Cairngorms on the horizon. At Spynie, a mile or two inland from Lossiemouth, there is a ruined castle, which was once the palace of a medieval bishop. Burghead, a few miles along the coast, marked the furthest limit of the Romans' penetration northwards. About thirty miles away is Culloden Moor, where Bonnie Prince Charlie's doomed army made its last stand against Butcher Cumberland.

Even now, a southern visitor's first impression of the place is of an exhilarating, yet daunting, remoteness. After the crowded, gentle countryside of southern England, even the Laigh of Moray seems empty and unsubdued; the hills and moors inland seem to have more in common with Canada or Scandinavia than with the demure undulations of the home counties; Lossiemouth itself reminds one of a frontier outpost, isolated from its parent civilisation by the sea and the surrounding hills. When MacDonald was born there, it must have seemed more isolated still. For Morayshire was a conservative place, where memories and customs went back a long way. Older and less respectable beliefs still flourished alongside the dour teachings of the Kirk. Approaching deaths might still be heralded by the appearance of a 'dead candle' – a ghostly light which would issue mysteriously from a cottage where a death was imminent, and then wind its way slowly and ominously to the churchyard. The Kirk still dealt with 'charmers', whose noxious practices had to be curbed by the appropriate forms of ecclesiastical discipline. At Burghead on New Year's Day evil spirits were still warded off in the pagan ceremony of 'burning the clavie', in which an empty barrel would be covered in tar, set alight and paraded around the boundaries of the village, and then left to burn on a stone at the top of the nearest hill.[17]

As for centuries before, the storms that swept the Moray Firth were part of the texture of life. 'The unfortunate mariner that is overtaken by the storm and who, in hopes of saving his life, runs his ship ashore, or is driven on it by the tempest at low water, must inevitably perish,' wrote the minister of Drainie parish in 1845. 'From the violence of the surf which lashes this shallow coast in every northern storm, no ship can live, nor boat give aid or assistance. The decks are swept clear of every living soul, and the vessel itself, if it holds together, digs its own grave in the shifting sand.'[18] The social climate was almost as bleak. The old Calvinist assumptions that individual effort is the mark of salvation, and that the unfortunate probably deserve their misfortunes, still retained some of their old force. As late as the 1840s, the synods of Morayshire made no regular assessment for poor relief, and in Drainie parish church collections for charitable purposes averaged less than £28 a year – facts which appear to have given some satisfaction to the local minister, who wrote grimly that if all those who had applied for poor relief had been granted it, 'the rental of the parish in a short time would not suffice to satisfy the demand.'[19]

Compared with what it had been in the past, the pace of change was rapid. In the middle ages, the Laigh of Moray had been celebrated throughout Scotland for the length of its summers, the fertility of its soil and the prosperity of its inhabitants. Perhaps because of climatic changes, it had then fallen behind; and by the eighteenth century the county had become, in the terse phrase of the

Imperial Gazetteer of 1858, a 'laggard'. Green crops were unknown; potatoes were not cultivated; fencing and scientific manuring were unheard of; the staple diet consisted of oats, rye and barley, supplemented by nettles and mugwort. In the nineteenth century, however, there took place what the county historian called 'an enormous advance' in agriculture. Between 1857 and 1881 the arable acreage of the county trebled in extent, and great progress was made in the squaring-up of farms, the laying of drains and the use of artificial manures. Lossiemouth advanced as well. In the 1840s, a new harbour was built. In 1852 a railway to Elgin was opened to traffic. In 1863 a viaduct was built across the river Spey, linking the Morayshire railway system with Aberdeen and the south.[20] In 1861 the population of Lossiemouth was about 1,300, more than twice what it had been thirty years before, while that of the adjoining village of Branderburgh was 600. In the 1871 census, Lossiemouth and Branderburgh were classed together as a town, with a joint population of 2,600.

Thus it was in a vigorous and expanding community that MacDonald grew up. Yet the benefits of expansion were slow to trickle down to the poorest section of the community, and there is some evidence that the gap between farmers and farm labourers was widening rather than narrowing. During his childhood, MacDonald wrote years later, 'the larger farmers were turning the people off the land, and ... the good honest hatred the Scotsman has for landlords was being encouraged, and was taking firm root.'[21] In the 1860s a ploughman like John Macdonald would be paid around £20 a year in cash, with anything from another £10 to £20 a year in kind. A servant girl like the young Annie Ramsay could expect £7 or £8 a year.[22] Unmarried labourers lived either in the farmhouse, or in a special part of the farm buildings known as a 'bothy'; and according to the 1867 royal commission, the 'bothy plan' was becoming more general as agricultural techniques improved. What this meant for the Morayshire farm labourer can be inferred from the following extract from the commission's report:

As a general rule, the bothy consists of a portion of the farm buildings or steading formed into a single room of moderate size. It is supplied with no separate sleeping apartments and nobody is employed to clean it or to make the beds (and the bothy men if left to themselves will never attempt to keep it clean and tidy); a heap of coals will be seen in one corner and of firewood in another; it is furnished with no tables and no seats, so that on returning from work the only place the servants have to sit upon is their chests; and the flags with which it is paved are generally broken into small pieces by having the firewood chopped upon them. In a few cases I have met with bothies attached to the stables, where the ventilation (if indeed it can be so called) was of the worst description. I recollect two which consisted of portions of the stables in which cart horses were kept and were only separated from the stables themselves by thin wooden partitions, which were broken and defective in many places. These bothies had no means of obtaining air except what came through the stables; and the stables themselves were badly ventilated and contained several horses each ... There can be no question that a life in such bothies as I have last been describing must have the effect of making the men rude and boorish.[23]

In the circumstances, it is hardly surprising that the farmers should have complained of 'the unsettled condition of their servants, who, they say, are always desirous of "flitting" '.[24]

III

There was a third childhood influence on MacDonald as well. At first, he went to the Free Kirk school in Lossiemouth, perhaps at the wish of his grandmother who was anxious that he should imbibe the right theological doctrines. There he was taught, and mercilessly thrashed, by the same teacher who had previously taught James Barrie in another village school in northern Scotland.[25] But after a year or two the schoolmaster of the Free Kirk school was drowned, and MacDonald was sent to the parish school at Drainie, four miles across the fields from home. Chance rarely played a more important part in his career. In externals, Drainie school was unremarkable. It had one teacher, helped by a pupil teacher and a sewing mistress, about seventy pupils of both sexes and diverse ages, and two classrooms, one of thirty-three feet by seventeen and the other of fourteen feet by twelve-and-a-half.[26] What *was* remarkable was the quality of the teaching, and of the dominie, James Macdonald.

Not that he was viewed with unqualified approval by his superiors. The Inspectors, whose periodic reports have been preserved in the school log-book, had to admit that his results were more than satisfactory; but they could not say the same for his methods. In 1875, for example, they conceded that 'this school continues to be taught with the same tone and intelligence,' but added sternly that 'humming at work should be discontinued.' In 1878 it was the same story. The registers and log-book were correct; the master, pupil teacher and sewing mistress were all at their posts; and this time the work was proceeding 'quietly and earnestly'. But the 'schoolroom and offices were not as clean as might be expected and it is necessary to attend to these matters with care.' These admonitions were of no avail. Four years later, the Inspector once again admitted that the school was taught with 'great care' and that the results were 'very satisfactory'. The schoolroom, however, was still 'not as clean as could be wished'.[27] But, whatever the Inspectors may have thought of the dominie, at least one of his pupils was to acknowledge a lifelong debt to him. The dominie, MacDonald wrote years afterwards, belonged 'to that goodly company of schoolmasters, who teach without putting any goal except knowledge before their pupils, and who present knowledge to them as something which is pursued through a man's life'. For him, education was a serious business:

> The work done in the school was of an old order now. It was a steady hard grind to get at the heart of things. We turned everything outside in, pulled everything to pieces in order to put it together again, analysed, parsed, got firm hold of the roots, shivered English into fragments and fitted it together like a Chinese puzzle, all by the help of Bain's Sixteenpenny Grammar (which the dominie's pupils must remember as they do the Shorter Catechism), and wrestled with 'deductions'. Then every bolt in our intellect was tightened up. One of the dominie's generalizations was: 'You must master: that is education: when you have mastered one thing you are well on the way to master all things' ... Mental capacity and character are what he strove to produce in his boys. He was Calvinistic enough to see that he did not provide the armour for life's fight. That came from the Fates who give presents to life at birth. His work was to temper what was given.[28]

If MacDonald's adult memories are to be relied on, there was a good deal of tempering to be done. As a child, he had apparently been rather sickly, but by his schooldays he had grown into a high-spirited and adventurous boy – prone to days of truancy when the dominie blew his whistle in vain in the playground; adept at flicking peas at the occupants of the penitents' form when the Salvation Army held services in Lossiemouth; and a leader in the endemic warfare against the youth of the 'smug capital town' of Elgin.[29] But these exploits did not take up all his time. For a couple of weeks in the spring of 1880, when he was thirteen, he kept a diary, from which two extracts are worth quoting:

> April 6th. Tuesday. Towards evening heard thunder. A little shower of rain about 5 pm. Read in Isaiah 54 and Psalms 78. Taken as a whole, the day was good. Heard that Gladstone gained Midlothian.

> 7th Wednesday. Day fine, like one in summer. Had a splendid play at Cricket. Started a Cricket Club. I hope it shall prosper. Resigned the office of Secretary of the 'Thistle' of Stotfield. Was 3 in my reading class and 3 in my Latin. Read Isiah [sic] LXI, and Psalm LXXVIII 66–72, Psalm LXXIX 1–end, Hymn 56, 57 and 58.[30]

Gladstone and Isaiah – not a bad combination for a future Labour leader.

MacDonald was taught by the dominie for ten years altogether. His name first appears on the school register for the year 1875–6, and reappears every year until 1880–81. Then in July 1881 the pupil teacher was absent for a week taking examinations in Edinburgh; and 'J. Macdonald' was temporarily promoted to act in his place. By December 1881 the pupil teacher had left; and MacDonald's name was included in the list of the staff. Those laconic entries in the log-book of Drainie school mark one of the most decisive turning-points of

MacDonald's life. In the summer of 1881 he was nearly fifteen. He left school at the end of the summer term, and began work on a nearby farm. His appointment as a pupil teacher saved him from the fields, and from the common fate of his class. It also gave him an education superior to that of any Labour leader of his generation. For in those days, as he put it later,

> the Elementary School was not skimmed of its cream ... We stayed where we were taught the ABC until we passed into the University or the world. The machinery was as old as Knox; the education was the best ever given to the sons and daughters of men. So instead of going a few miles off by train for the higher wisdom, we got it from the dominie who also drove it into the heads of petticoated males that a-t was 'at' and c-a-t was 'cat'. Night after night and morning after morning we took the long walk with Latin books, or Greek or Euclid open in our hands, and we tramped to the rhythm of Amo, Amavi, Amatum, Amare or τύπτω τέτυφα τέτυμμαι.[31]

His four years as a pupil teacher were a time of rapid intellectual growth. A lifelong passion for English literature had already been kindled, partly by the Chambers Readers used at school, partly by the miscellaneous collection of church histories and sermons in Bella Ramsay's cottage, and most of all by the volumes of Burns, Dickens and Shakespeare borrowed from a consumptive watchmaker who had come home to Lossiemouth to die.[32] In adolescence, a different but equally characteristic interest developed alongside. The mid-nineteenth century was in many respects the heroic age of the natural sciences, above all of geology and biology. At some time in his teens MacDonald acquired a copy of Hugh Miller's *My Schools and Schoolmasters* and Orr's *Circle of the Sciences*;[33] for some years, science was the dominant intellectual passion of his life. During his last two years at Drainie he founded the 'Lossiemouth Field Club', whose members went on scientific excursions around the neighbourhood and read papers to each other on scientific subjects, and he wrote a large number of such papers himself. Some of the manuscripts still survive – among them, a painstaking description of the geological structure of the Coulard Hill, running to forty-four manuscript pages; a passionate attack on 'Cruelty to Animals', warning that 'Nero began his long list of cruelties by torturing flies and ended by murdering his mother;' and a vivid description of the prehistory of Lossiemouth, which is worth quoting at length:

> Have you ever thought how many forms of life since life's first dawn existed in this small spot where we now live, and how many changes it has undergone? Many thousands of years ago, where birds now fly, fish swam. Fish! but not the harmless looking fish we see lying in our quays today. These were terrible looking animals with thick fretted bony scales in some cases 1/8 of an inch in thickness, sharp barbarous looking spines, and teeth two inches long and more than an inch in diameter. But then came a change

and long ages after that we see huge monstrous reptiles basking in the sun exactly where our Coulard Hill now is. About this time our part of the world underwent a great volcanic outburst the remnants of which are to be seen in the igneous rocks occurring in isolated patches between the harbour and the western end of the Coulard Hill ... The scene is changed. We now gaze upon a vast plain of glaziers [sic] and icebergs. As they come crashing along they deeply scratch the cliffs to the west, drop a large conglomerate boulder near the lighthouse, and 4 or 5 on the northern brow of the Coulard Hill, and the Great Ice Age, like the Old Red Sandstone and the Oolite passes away.[34]

The Lossiemouth Field Club was not MacDonald's only public activity. He also joined the Mutual Improvement Society, at which the leading citizens of Lossiemouth took part in weekly debates as to whether Literature had done more for the world than Invention or whether the Cow was a more useful animal than the Horse.[35] Before long he had become its secretary, and a frequent participant in its debates. He does not seem to have trusted to extempore inspiration, however: and the tattered manuscripts of a few early speeches, evidently written during his schooldays at Lossiemouth, and presumably delivered to the Mutual Improvement Society, still survive among his papers. They provide an oddly touching glimpse of the adolescent MacDonald: rebellious, argumentative, a shade earnest. In the earliest of them, dated September 1883, for example, he defends the view that superstition is natural rather than acquired – deploying, for the purpose, a dialectical subtlety so tortuous that the argument is at times almost incomprehensible. Superstition, he says, is a 'great power damming back the flood of social progress and scientific research'. Its roots lie in 'too much fear or reverence', and it is as common today as it used to be. 'Silly stories' about 'witchcraft, ghosts and foresights' are only its 'extremities'. Properly considered, superstition

is a more real and formidable thing to cultured minds than these. What is an overscrupilous [sic] religion – Superstition; What is hero or saint worship – superstition; What is bigotry in any moral devise or thought – Superstition ...We can have an idea of the superstitions that led people to believe in a Hercules, a Jupiter & a Mars, but ... rest assured yet who choose to call yourselves unpolluted by superstition for your posterity who shall occupy a position as far in advance of you as ye do of these ancients will brand you as a most superstitious ancestry. Schoolboys will then regale each other with articles on the superstitions of the latter end of the 19th Century, and old men will pass judgement on you 'In all things I perceive ye are too superstitious![36]

His speeches were not always as philosophical as this. He was a keen politician, as well as a would-be scientist; and his politics were those of his community and class. During his last year at Lossiemouth the political power of the local land-lords was undermined by the effects of the 1884 Reform Act, and the political climate of the county was being rapidly transformed. The Reform Act extended the principle of household suffrage to the counties, and enfranchised at least a part of the agricultural working class. In doing so, it tripled the size of the electorate of Elgin and Nairn, and made it possible for the stubborn agrarian radicalism of the Morayshire farm labourer to become a factor in parliamentary elections. The results were dramatic. In the general election of 1885 C. H. Anderson, hitherto unknown in the constituency, stood as an 'Advanced Radical', with a platform whose main planks were the disestablishment of the Church of Scotland and opposition to the game laws. He won almost a third of the total vote and seriously alarmed the orthodox Liberal supporters of the sitting M.P., Sir George McPherson Grant.[37] The following year he was elected; and Grant lost his seat.[38]

The aspirations and resentments which lay behind this upheaval were echoed in the most outspoken of MacDonald's youthful manuscripts – a heavily ironic attack on the game laws, entitled 'Is game property?' The question is, of course, a rhetorical one; and the answer is not left in doubt:

> Our landlords, not content with merely compelling our farmers to supply them with 'meat, drink & clothing', also force them to feed and rear certain 'live stock' which shall eventually afford sport to Lord So-and-so and the Hon Sir This-and-that. Lately they have to a certain degree handed over hares and rabbits to the guns of their farmers, yet, as they hoped they (the farmers) would for this act of charity and benevolence protect all the winged game, since the Creator told our first parents that although Man was made superior to, and lord over, the beasts, yet there were to be certain winged creatures, certain fish and certain quadrupeds (I wonder if he also said bipeds) that were to be under no living person save landlords and – poachers, adding however that if poachers were to be caught they were to suffer more severely for that crime (?) than if they had killed their brother. And if this has been the case we must congratule [sic] the landlords for acting up to its utmost provision. If this has not been the case is there an epithet in the English language too strong to apply to these aristocratic tyrants who have been robbing the nation and its people, who have been drawing from the national resources these many years, for what? to fatten rabbits, hares and fowls.[39]

Attitudes like this were not a sign of originality in MacDonald; they were part of his heritage. But there is some evidence that by his late teens he was beginning to venture into less familiar territory. He is said to have subscribed to the land reformers' monthly, the *Christian Socialist*, and he also seems to have read Henry George's *Progress and Poverty*, which argued that private property in land was the source of economic inequality and injustice.[40] 'The land', he announced uncompromisingly in the course of another youthful essay, 'must be nationalised.'[41]

IV

He was soon to venture into unfamiliar territory in a more literal sense also. An entry in the log-book of Drainie school at the end of April 1885 notes curtly that 'J. Macdonald has passed well.' Shortly after it there is another entry, dated May 1st, which tells us that 'J. Macdonald left today with the permission of the School board.'[42] For some time he had been ransacking the advertisement columns of the *Scotsman* and applying for posts all over Britain, and in the end he found one, as assistant to a Bristol clergyman named Mordaunt Crofton, who was trying to set up a Boys' and Young Men's Guild at St Stephen's Church.[43] He left home in the early summer of 1885, wearing a new suit of clothes presented by the local draper and, it is said, with twenty-seven shillings in his pocket.[44]

CHAPTER 2

London

I

It is easy to imagine the mixture of excitement and apprehension which MacDonald must have felt when he arrived in Bristol, some time in the early summer of 1885. In Lossiemouth, he had been the dominie's prize pupil, a star of the Mutual Improvement Association, a 'lad o' pairts', who might have a golden future ahead of him. Now he was plunged into the anonymous hurly-burly of a busy commercial city, four hundred miles away from home and a world away from the close-knit, granite culture in which he had been brought up. That, in itself, would have made the time he spent with the Rev. Mordaunt Crofton and his Boys' and Young Men's Guild an important part of his growing up; and its importance did not end there. As we have seen, MacDonald had been influenced by Georgeite ideas before leaving home. Now he was able to take his political education a stage further. Bristol was one of the focal points of the socialist revival which took place in the 1880s among scattered groups of middle-class idealists and thoughtful working men. It had a flourishing tradition of working-class Radicalism: as long ago as 1872 George Odger, a member of the first provisional council of the International Workingman's Association, had won over a thousand votes in a 'test ballot' to select the Liberal parliamentary candidate. When MacDonald arrived there, it was one of the few provincial cities in England which could boast an active socialist organization. In February 1884 a 'pioneer class' which had been set up a few months before to discuss 'democratic and social reform schemes' formally reconstituted itself as the Bristol branch of the Democratic Federation — an extreme Radical sect which had recently been founded in London by the eccentric financier and Marxist convert, H. M. Hyndman. It drew up a manifesto calling for collective owner-ship of the means of production and distribution; and when the Democratic Federation changed its name to the Social Democratic Federation in October 1884, the Bristol branch followed suit.[1]

In 1885 the Bristol Social Democrats used to meet in St Philip's Coffee Tavern in West Street, at eight o'clock on Thursday evenings.[2] Soon after his arrival in Bristol MacDonald sought them out. He first heard of their existence, he wrote later, in an obscure little newspaper shop and was told that he might find them at a certain public meeting. He went to the meeting and introduced himself to two of their leaders, who invited him to join the group. As he remembered it years later, there was something almost sacramental about the ceremony. The socialists met in a small, dimly-lit upper room, rich with the smells of sawdust and steaming coffee, at the top of a long wooden staircase. The 'hard penitential forms' might have been designed to give the novice 'a sense of awe and expectation'; the coffee shop could have been a cathedral, whose 'odours were the smells of sacrifice being offered up by Demos'. After he had listened to a paper on Ruskin, the ceremony was completed, and MacDonald found himself a 'full-blown Social Democrat'.[3]

He still kept up his interest in science, particularly in geology, and even found time to write a treatise on the 'Geology of Bristol',[4] but for the next few months the coffee tavern in West Street was the centre of his life. He took a room in Franklyn Street, opposite the home of one of his new comrades, with whom he used to play cards in the evenings. After a while the branch appointed him as its librarian, and gave him the task of spending a £5 donation from the socialist evangelist, Edward Carpenter. According to the historian of Bristol socialism, he left the library 'a model of precision'. In October he lectured to the group on 'Malthusianism versus Socialism'. In a 'lucid and interesting manner,' we are told, 'the lecturer compared the two doctrines, and pointed to the powerlessness of Malthusianism to remove the evils by which we are surrounded, while by the adoption of Socialist principles the misery could be stamped out.'[5] He also took part in more controversial discussions. In London the S.D.F. was dominated by Hyndman's powerful and autocratic personality; the columns of its newspaper, *Justice*, preached a militant and dogmatic brand of Marxist socialism. The atmosphere in St Philip's Coffee Tavern was very different, for the Bristol socialists owed more to the gentle idealism of Edward Carpenter than they did to Hyndman or Marx and, as events were to show, they were shocked by the harsh conclusions which Hyndman deduced from his revolutionary principles. MacDonald shared their attitudes. In a discussion on the sales of *Justice*, he is recorded as making the characteristic suggestion that the Bristol branch should express its satisfaction at the improvement in the paper's 'tone', and also 'our desire that it should rise higher and higher in tone'.[6]

Before long, however, his political baptism came to an end. By the end of the year he was back in Lossiemouth. The reason is unknown — but whatever the reason it must have been disappointing to return home only a few months after setting out. The disappointment did not put an end to his interest in socialism. The winter of 1885 was a critical period in the history of the S.D.F., and he did his best to take part in the debates which accompanied the crisis. In the general election of November 1885, the S.D.F. ran three candidates: John Burns in Nottingham, another in Hampstead and a third in Kennington. Burns won almost 600 votes, but the other two candidates polled only 27 and 32 votes respectively. This was bad enough, and worse soon followed. In December, J. Hunter Watts, the S.D.F. treasurer, disclosed in a letter to the *Pall Mall*

B

Gazette that the S.D.F. candidatures had been financed with Conservative funds. The disclosure provoked a storm of protest from the S.D.F. rank and file. Hyndman treated it with bland disdain. An editorial in *Justice* claimed that Hunter Watts's allegations could not be proved – and argued that even if they could, socialists should be indifferent to the source of money which had made it possible to preach socialism in 'aristocratic Hampstead and genteel Kennington'.[7] These arguments did not mollify Hyndman's opponents. The S.D.F. lost a large proportion of its scanty membership; the Bristol branch, among others, disaffiliated itself altogether from the Federation; C. L. Fitzgerald, a former war correspondent who belonged to the S.D.F. executive council, resigned and set up a rival body called the Socialist Union.[8]

MacDonald watched these developments with outraged dismay. He drafted two letters on the 'Tory gold' scandal, both clearly intended for publication in *Justice*. In the first he conceded that 'it does not much matter whether we get money from Tories, Radicals or Liberals – three classes of Gentlemen who may be fused into one without hurting either much.' But he added that 'if it comes from a Tory for the purpose of splitting the Liberal vote in a constituency & to let in the Tory candidate or vice versa the taking of the money makes the recipient a Tory (or Liberal) dupe.' Socialists, he declared, should be 'moved by a spirit of fairness for if we are to be unscrupulous where are we to look for scruples?' In his second draft letter, written shortly after the general meeting of the S.D.F. in January 1886, he broadened the attack:

> Sir, if practical Socialism means an autocracy or the Government of a Cabal I for one will have nothing to do with it. Did I take my ideas of the movement from the organ which you proudly yet falsely call the only vigorous weekly organ of the proletariat in the English language I would have that erroneous impression. To read that paper one would think the SDF's hand was against all other Soc[ialist] societies in England and that its duty was to heap slander of all sorts upon them ... We have over and over again had to read arguments in favour of Socialism that never went deeper than calling an opponent an 'outrageous old hypocrite', 'a bloodsucker', 'ignorant', and many other epithets as delicious as the fumes of a Billingsgate market. Indeed, I have often been amazed at the expressiveness of the English language as shown in 'Justice'. Well, that could in a certain measure have been put up with, but when this last dishonour has fallen upon us we are obliged to speak and to act. It has been plainly shown in the history of the Federation that the great virtues it recognises are unscrupulousness, unfairness and slander. Be it so! I hope there may be many who can now see to what they have been trusting, and how they have been used, many who love the grand principles of Socialism more than the distorted doctrines of the Federation and who have the courage and manliness to act accordingly.

The draft ended, somewhat unconvincingly in the circumstances, with a hope that matters might be mended if only the executive would 'trust the branches with information'.[9]

The editors of *Justice* were not in the habit of publicizing revolts against their leadership, and neither of MacDonald's draft letters seems to have seen the light of day. But although his revolt must have seemed a trivial affair to the S.D.F. executive, it was an important milestone in his own political development. Hyndman's tactics in the 1885 election had been characteristically maladroit, but judged from a Marxist standpoint they were not immoral. To a consistent Marxist, MacDonald's appeal for scruples would have seemed naïve: scruples are presumably as out of place in the class war as in any other war. The same applied to the tone of *Justice*. A Marxist could argue that his most important task is to stiffen the fighting sinews of the proletariat for the coming revolution; and for this a certain crudity of language might well be appropriate. In denouncing the unscrupulousness of the S.D.F. and the Billingsgate language of *Justice*, MacDonald was in fact denouncing the entire revolutionary philosophy of the Federation. He had fired the first shot in a battle which was to last for the rest of his political life.

II

Early in 1886 MacDonald left Lossiemouth once again, this time for London. A friend there had written to tell him of a post which was vacant, and which might suit him. When he arrived he found that it had already been filled.[10] He could hardly have chosen a worse time for his misadventure. A severe trade depression had just reached its lowest point; all over the country, thousands were out of work; the problem of unemployment, in any case more noticeable in the 1880s than it had been for decades, now impinged more dramatically on the consciousness of middle-class England than at any time since the Chartist agitation almost fifty years before. MacDonald experienced the plight of the unemployed at first hand. He tramped the streets of London in search of work, eking out the few pounds he had somehow contrived to save at Bristol, living on oatmeal sent from home, an occasional threepenny beefsteak pudding, and hot water in place of tea or coffee. When he was almost at the end of his meagre resources he found a job addressing envelopes at the National Cyclists' Union in Fleet Street, at 10s. a week. But this was only a temporary refuge, and another period of unemployment followed, until he found a post as an invoice clerk in the city at 12s. 6d. a week, rising to 15s.[11] A letter to J. S. Lamb, dated May 25th, 1886, tells its own story:

My Dear Friend,
    I am perfectly ashamed of my seemingly ungrateful conduct to you after the great kindness you showed me so recently. And yet I assure you though

I never wrote you I thought much about you all. As I told you I was afraid the place I was last in was only temporary. The work finished when I was there 4 weeks. Now you will see a reason for my silence. Being out of work and a blank void before me I had little heart to write to anyone. I hope it is now all over. I have got a place which is to be permanent in a large warehouse in the city — Cooper, Box, & Co. My hours are from 8.30 AM to 9 PM or thereabouts with a dinner hour from 12 to 1 and from 1 to 2 alternately ...

Give my very best wishes to your mother, whose goodness to me I shall ever remember. I also hope your brother is getting on well at College, and that you yourself are moving ahead

With best regards

Yours very sincerely

JAS. R. MACDONALD.[12]

Meanwhile, he had achieved a minor prominence in the world of socialist politics and propaganda. While still at Lossiemouth, he had written a letter to the *Christian Socialist*, advocating the formation of a Socialist Union of Young Men.[13] In the May issue he followed it with an article on 'The Professors and Socialism' — a reply to a lecture on political economy which had recently been delivered by a Glasgow economist named Smart. Professors of political economy, MacDonald wrote briskly, were slowly realizing

> that their profession is endangered. They have begun to read Marx, and to discuss Lassalle and the tide of public opinion has dragged them on the public platform to do battle for their old-fashioned and dearly beloved notions of capital, wage funds and over-population. It makes one sad to see them sally forth, badly equipped and attended by the skeleton forms of starvation, the gaunt beings of vice, and the repulsive followers of crime: and yet sadder is it to see the noble efforts they make in tilting with a clumsy windmill which to their dim vision appears a formidable foe ... It cannot be expected that this lecturer could refrain from instructing his audience that under Socialism 'we should all be servants of the State, borrowing our capital from the State, paying our rent to the State'. Absurdities, like misfortunes, alas! never come singly. This simply means that we should be our own servants, that we should borrow from ourselves and that we should pay our rent to ourselves.[14]

For a time, MacDonald also played an active part in C. L. Fitzgerald's Socialist Union. Unlike the S.D.F., the Socialist Union took full account of the possibilities inherent in the parliamentary system. Its manifesto insisted on the 'absolute necessity' of making full use of the 'existing political machinery', and in a pregnant phrase called for the 'intelligent and early exercise of political power by the wealth producers'. For a few months in the summer and early autumn of 1886 it published a magazine called the *Socialist*, to whose managing and editing committee MacDonald belonged. During the summer he spoke for the Socialist Union at meetings of the Woolwich Labour League and the Kilburn Liberal Club, and in the August issue of the *Socialist* he published a spirited attack on conventional middle-class philanthropy, on the grounds that 'ladies from the West End' who went on occasional pilgrimages to Whitechapel or Seven Dials were 'but restoring in a very mean way the merest iota of the wealth they have filched'.[15] But these activities did not last for long. Unlike the S.D.F., the Socialist Union had no wealthy backer, and its superb grasp of political strategy was no substitute for a bank balance. For a while it boasted of branches in Cumberland, Carlisle, Scotland and South Wales, but by the end of the year it seems to have petered out.

MacDonald was still an active socialist. He was present in Trafalgar Square on the notorious 'Bloody Sunday' of November 13th, 1887, when a large crowd which had gathered to defend the right of free speech was broken up by soldiers and mounted police. Among his papers is a penny pamphlet published by the *Pall Mall Gazette*, entitled 'Remember Trafalgar Square: Tory Terrorism in 1887'. It is inscribed with the sardonic comment in pencil: 'I am well but very busy. Send this to anyone that would be interested to read. You will see what a nice Sunday we had here.'[16] He also took part in more sedate activities. In September 1887 he wrote home to a friend in Lossiemouth that

> Down here about the movement which I am more and more interested in moves on apace. The spirit of Socialism is abroad, not only stirring the lower ranks of labour to discontent, but moving those whose physical wants are all provided for and whose education and intellectual training are such as to preclude every idea of their being led away by any mere sentimental fad or impracticable scheme.

At meetings of the 'better kind of Socialist', he added smugly, 'Scotchmen reign supreme.'[17]

But for a while, in these early days in London, politics seems to have been a secondary interest. MacDonald had no intention of remaining an invoice clerk for the rest of his life: the road to the south had surely beckoned him to more purpose than that. Cooper, Box & Co gave him a modicum of economic security: on fifteen shillings a week, he boasted later, he was able to live 'like a fighting cock'.[18] It was up to him to put that security to good use. London had much to offer a determined and hard-working young man, anxious to better himself in the approved Victorian mode of self-help. MacDonald was more determined than most young men: then, as later, he must have been almost obsessively hard-working. During the lunch hours and in the evenings, he was his own master; and he took full advantage of both. In his lunch hours, he read at the Guildhall Library: a notebook dating from this period, with notes on Howell's *Conflicts between Capital and Labour* and a list of articles on geology, still survives among his papers.[19] After a while he began to attend evening classes in science at the Birkbeck Institute; and for a while, at least, science seems to have taken up more of his time than socialism. In the second half of 1887 and the first few months of 1888 he took courses on botany, agriculture, experimental physics and mathematics, filling pages of notes with a clear, round and rather immature script;[20] and with characteristic doggedness he set himself to win a science scholarship at the South Kensington Museum. When an analytical chemist with whom he had struck up a friendship offered him a post as his assistant, it must have seemed that the goal was within reach. But, not for the last time, he was placing a heavier strain on his nervous system than it could bear. A week or so before he was due to sit his examination, he broke down from systematic overwork. The exact nature of his breakdown is unknown. It was enough to prevent him from taking the scholarship, and to shatter his hopes of a scientific career.[21]

III

It was a cruel blow, but not a mortal one. Early in 1888, probably with the help of a reference from Liberal friends in Morayshire, he was engaged as private secretary by Thomas Lough—a tea merchant and Radical politician, who was at that time organizing secretary of the Home Rule Union.[22] MacDonald's salary was £75 a year, rising to £100.[23] After fifteen shillings a week this was affluence—and the job was more rewarding than the salary. Lough was born in Ireland in 1850, and had contested Truro in 1886. He was now the prospective Liberal candidate for West Islington, where he was elected in 1892. He had founded the Home Rule Union in 1887, and by 1888 more than sixty Liberal Associations were affiliated to it.[24] As his secretary, MacDonald had an entrée to the National Liberal Club, to the editorial offices of Liberal and Radical newspapers, and to comfortable Liberal drawing-rooms. He was well placed for making contacts in London Radical clubs, and with the Radical and labour politicians who were building up the Progressive party in the L.C.C. He also received an invaluable training in the mechanics of electioneering. He helped to organize Lough's campaign in Islington, and in the autumn of 1889 he went back to Scotland to help the 'Advanced Liberal' candidate—Seymour Keay—in a by-election in Moray and Nairn. Keay's programme was advanced, even by the standards of Morayshire Radicalism. It ranged from adult suffrage and payment of members, to home rule for Ireland and Scotland, and included such socialistic measures as state aid for fisheries, free education up to and including the university, and by implication, at least, nationalisation of the land. He was elected by 2,573 votes to his opponent's 2,044.[25] A card from P. Macdonell at the National Liberal Club suggests that MacDonald's part in the victory did not go unnoticed:

Dear Macdonald,

We all owe you great gratitude for the Elgin victory. It was not the candidate, I imagine, who won the election.[26]

MacDonald's interest in Scottish politics did not end there. In 1886 a Scottish Home Rule Association had been set up in Edinburgh, to press for home rule for Scotland on the lines which Gladstone's first Irish Home Rule Bill had proposed for Ireland. On March 6th, 1888, MacDonald took part in a meeting of Scotsmen resident in London which, on his motion, resolved itself into the London General Committee of the Scottish Home Rule Association, and which chose him as its honorary secretary.[27] The position was not an arduous one. The Scottish Home Rule Association was a radical body. The chairman of its London branch, and the chief parliamentary champion of the movement, was Dr G. B. Clark — Radical M.P. for Caithness and soon to be a member of Keir Hardie's Scottish Labour Party. R. Cunninghame Graham, the elegant and flamboyant Scottish laird who had recently been converted to socialism, also sat on the London executive. In spite of this, the Scottish home rule movement lacked the fire of its Irish counterparts; and at the London end it was almost languid. The only notable decision taken by the sub-committee was to send a message of support to Keir Hardie when he fought the famous Mid-Lanark by-election in April, on the ticket of Scottish home rule and Labour independence.[28] In March 1889, a thousand leaflets were printed, asking for help from the London Scottish community, but the executives had to admit that the response was disappointing. In 1888 subscriptions had brought in only a little more than £10, and in 1889 the figure was only sixteen shillings higher. In May 1890 a second honorary secretary was elected to serve alongside MacDonald; and thereafter MacDonald's attendance at committee meetings fell off.[29] He still supported the cause of Scottish home rule, and in 1892 there were rumours that he intended to stand as Home Rule candidate in Aberdeen.[30] But from 1890 onwards he no longer took much part in the work of the Association.

He cannot, in any case, have had much time to spare for it. He had found his feet in London by now, and he was absorbed by a number of new interests. He helped with a boys' club run by a doctor friend, named James Gwyther — taking part in amateur theatricals, supervising parties of boys on visits to the country and organizing entertainments for the old people in a workhouse.[31] He had joined the 'St Pancras Parliament', where aspiring North London politicians cut their debating teeth and learned something of parliamentary procedure; and, as an unidentified press-cutting in his papers makes clear, he had soon become one of its most prominent members. Mr MacDonald, wrote the author of the cutting, was

now below the gangway, now above it, sometimes he consults the Speaker and gets behind the chair, then he is in close 'confab' with the Clerk of the House; again he consults the leader of the Opposition, and anon he flits

across to have a chat with the Premier; in fact he beats Sir Boyle Roche's
bird hollow, for he is in half-a-dozen places at once. There is no rest for the
sole of his foot and little for the soul of his body; and wherever he 'lives
and moves and has his being' all the world may know it, on account of the
tie so flaringly red, a colour sacred to the cults of Socialism and Salvationism.
You may lose sight of him for a few minutes, but be patient and you will
see a red tie slowly wending its way round a corner of a seat below the
gangway, and in a minute or so you will discover Mr. MacDonald behind
it — the tie I mean.[32]

At some time in the late 1880s, he had also joined the Fabian Society, and by
1890 he had become sufficiently prominent to be invited to take Bernard Shaw's
place as a lecturer on 'the New Politics'.[33] Meanwhile, his position as Lough's
private secretary had brought him into contact with Sidney Webb, already one
of the leading architects of Fabian policy. Once or twice, he was even allotted
a minor part is one of the tortuous manœuvres by which Webb hoped to
advance the Fabian cause. Early in 1890, when Webb wanted to persuade Lough
to use his influence with T. P. O'Connor, the founder of the *Star*, to push the
paper in a Fabian direction, MacDonald was called in to help; a year later, when
Webb hoped to find a safe L.C.C. seat in Islington, MacDonald may once again
have been a valuable ally.[34] It was the beginning of a more fruitful relationship
than either was always willing to admit.

IV

MacDonald owed a great deal to Lough's committee-rooms and to the St
Pancras Parliament, and more still to the Fabian Society, but they fulfilled only
one side of his character. Then, as always, the dour, hard-working Lowland
Scot — the MacDonald of Bain's *Sixteenpenny Grammar*, so to speak — went
hand in hand with a brooding romantic, sceptical of, even hostile to, the values
of the workaday world in which the first MacDonald was determined to rise.
In the late 1880s and early 1890s this second MacDonald found one important
outlet in the Ethical movement — attending services at the South Place Ethical
Society and preaching at the East London Ethical Society, where, as the organizer of the occasion told him, the 'hymns used are "Hymns of Progress" '.[35] A
much more important outlet, however, was provided by a struggling socialist
sect called the Fellowship of the New Life. The Fellowship had been founded in
December 1883 by the disciples of an itinerant socialist sage named Thomas
Davidson. Davidson was a Scotsman by birth, but he emigrated in early manhood to the United States, and his teaching owed more to transatlantic thinkers
like Thoreau and Emerson than to any European socialist. The Fellowship
defined as its 'Object' the 'cultivation of a perfect character in each and all', and as

its 'Principle' the 'subordination of material things to spiritual'. The sole and essential condition of membership was to be 'a single-minded, sincere and strenuous devotion to the object and principle'. But there was some disagreement as to how these principles could best be realized. Almost immediately after the Fellowship had been set up, a group of dissident New Lifers seceded and formed themselves into the Fabian Society, and it is as the parent of the Fabian Society that the Fellowship has achieved its modest place in most histories of British socialism.[36]

In MacDonald's biography it deserves greater prominence. It would be easy to smile at the Fellowship's somewhat humourless concern with the moral perfection of its own members. It would also be foolish, for the New Lifers had put their finger on a genuine problem of socialist theory. Most socialists took it for granted that the socialist society of the future would be morally superior to the capitalist society against which they were struggling: indeed, that was one of the fundamental axioms of their creed. But how could a morally superior society come into existence without morally superior human beings to live in it? And how could morally superior human beings flourish in the morally inferior society of the present? These, in essence, were the Fellowship's questions. As MacDonald put it in its quarterly journal, *Seedtime*:

> Political change is not desirable for its own sake, but rather for its effect on human well-being. But human well-being is not a matter of machinery or condition merely. We know, indeed, that it cannot be served by a system of wage slavery any more than it can be served by a feudal system; but even where the economic hindrances are overcome the ideal humanity may be as far away as ever ... The individual is truly complete only in a perfect society, but to make society perfect requires the sympathetic and conscious efforts of the individual ... The Fellowship therefore aims at a reform of the ideals of individuals.[37]

He was to return to that theme again and again during the next forty years, and his career is incomprehensible unless due weight is given to it. It was the MacDonald of Lough's committee rooms who was to create the Labour Party machine: it was MacDonald the New Lifer who was to capture the imagination and loyalty of ordinary party members.

He came into contact with the Fellowship early in 1890. Edith Lees, the secretary, who was soon to marry Havelock Ellis, another Fellowship member, had heard him lecture on the movement for women's emancipation and had been greatly impressed by him. At the beginning of February, she asked him to give the same lecture at a Fellowship meeting. 'What I so distinctly like in your paper', she wrote eagerly, 'is that though you give woman her right place by the side of man through giving her equal opportunity yet you hold fast to those family ties which are the most sacred in life.' She had, however, one question. Suppose MacDonald 'married a woman in your first youth, before you knew

life at all & found you had married a vision & that in 6 years you were living a
cat & dog existence': surely in these circumstances it would be better, even from
the children's point of view, if the marriage tie were broken?[38] MacDonald's
answer is not known. He did, however, give his lecture to the Fellowship.
According to *Seedtime*, it consisted of an 'elaborate account of the growth of the
ideas, which are at the bottom of the modern movement for the political enfranchisement and the economic emancipation of women'. Women's grievances,
he argued, had a 'common origin with many other social grievances'; the
women's movement should therefore be seen as 'part of that stirring of revolt,
throughout society, against the old spirit of Individualism which is the special
characteristic of modern thought'.[39] That, too, was a theme to which he was to
return.

A closer association with the Fellowship soon followed. In the spring of 1891
some of the more enthusiastic members decided that it was time to put their
founder's communal principles into practice. A house was acquired, 29 Doughty
Street, near Mecklenburgh Square, in Bloomsbury, and a co-operative household of Fellowship members installed in it. Rooms were let by the night or the
week to friends seeking temporary lodgings near the centre of London; and there
was talk of providing a club room on the premises, to be available to Fellowship
members at a charge of five shillings a year. The residents included Sydney
Olivier, one of the original Fabian essayists and then an official at the Colonial
Office, an anarchist lady named Miss Henry, assorted Fellowship members and
a floating population of boarders. The moving spirits were MacDonald and
Edith Lees, and MacDonald was chosen as secretary.[40]

The charges were low. Olivier's account for the last quarter of 1891, which
has survived among MacDonald's papers, shows that he owed £1 for rent and
six shillings for his share of the 'deficit on service account'.[41] But it is hard to
tell how far the experiment was a success in other respects. A sympathizer called
Thomas Lulman wrote to MacDonald in March 1891, pointing out that 'the
danger will be when some new member is introduced who turns out to be
crotchety or irritating,' and advising the group to be 'New Life—orthodoxly
so—and then *not to discuss it*'. He thought MacDonald would make an 'excellent
paterfamilias', and advised him to adopt 'Comte's motto: "Conciliant en fait,
inflexible en principe" '.[42] There were times, however, when this was easier
said than done. In late September 1891, Edith Lees wrote to MacDonald in
exasperation:

Dear Old Fellow,
    For heaven's sake come home when you can—can it be that I have
turned man or what but I'm *choked* with women—Miss H. has almost
driven me *mad*—women, women everywhere & not a breath of peace—
Malatesta—teeth—boots—dress—legal marriage—good heavens!—I do
long for the gentle patter of your feet.[43]

Two days later she wrote again, in even greater exasperation:

> Miss Henry really is *awful!* —I hate the place without you & I'm already
> fagged out—fidget, fidget fidget & poor Ellen slept in her own room last
> night for the first time & caught 52 fleas: she is cursing roundly at co-
> operation. What did you go & tell Miss H. about that letter I wrote to you
> for? —I thought you were too Scotch — when she told me how furious you
> were etc etc etc I got angry & swore I hated the house & all in it as a dreary
> fag & a manufactory of melting tallow grease.[44]

Two days after that she was slightly more contrite. 'Thanks for your sermon-
ette ... ,' she wrote on September 29th. 'I must be left my wholesome likes &
dislikes — you are candidly one of my likes — I like you — so I shd. be *glad* for you
to take a real family share in all I have but I cd. not honestly say that to Olivier
or Miss H.'[45] But that, of course, was an implicit criticism of the whole arrangement.

In 1892 Edith Lees resigned her office as secretary of the Fellowship, and
MacDonald took it over in her place. She seems to have felt that there were
dangers in the change. 'Don't keep the secretaryship more than two years—,'
she wrote at the beginning of April; 'it will make you a mellow humbug &
though I've had a good many word fights with you I'd be sorry to see that.
Don't believe all the sweet girls tell you & don't forget that there are other slums
than in London & that "co-operative" houses are often built and run outside
Doughty St.'[46] Part of her advice was unnecessary: in fact, MacDonald kept the
secretaryship for only fifteen months, though he remained on the committee
until the Fellowship was wound up in 1898.[47] Whether her warning against the
'sweet girls' was equally unnecessary is harder to tell. The emancipated 'new
woman' was a familiar figure in politically advanced circles in the 1890s, and it
is clear from his correspondence that MacDonald, who was already strikingly
handsome, had no lack of feminine admirers. But it is not clear how far their
admiration was reciprocated. His most enthusiastic correspondent was a certain
'Mary', who began by addressing him as 'my dear MacDonald' and advanced
through 'My dear Mac' to 'my dear Jamie', but the tone of the decipherable
parts of her largely illegible letters suggests that she was the pursuer rather than
the pursued.[48] In July 1891, MacDonald's friend, Dr Gwyther, told him that
he was getting married, on the grounds that 'Society declines to sanction any
other relation between men and women.'[49] The news provoked a distinctly
mournful reaction, only partially concealed by tone of rather forced gaiety,
contained in a long, pencilled letter, which MacDonald presumably decided
would be better left unposted:

> You go away on Saturday don't you? Jolly time to you both! I may not see
> you until you return. I feel very queer in all this transformation. Born and
> brought up a bachelor as I was and surrounded in my youth (and the

accepted moralists have all told that the influences of youth are the best) by those to whom the marriage problem had never presented itself, this spectacle which I have been called upon to witness is at once confusing and appaling [sic]. My mind is continually reverting to a grove of trees. I see them green & flourishing, I see the leaves seared with the breath of autumn (love) I see them scattered in the wintry wind (marriage) I alone am ever green. Or when I am devotionally minded I think of the revival hymn which tells so pathetically of the wandering sheep and the cosy ninety and nine. But the ninety and nine seem to have wandered and I alone remain in the fold's safety and comfort. At such times I tremble when someone whispers in my ear 'not lost but gone before' and I bethink me of my principles as an advocate of the truth of the New Liberalism and a believer in the enunciation of Aristotle that the state exists for [the] good life and debate with myself whether I shall not draw out a bill to make such back-slidings penal. The party that has adopted Sunday closing cannot object to that humanitarian resolve.[50]

He struck a similar note in an unpublished novel, evidently written at about this time. The title has perished and only the second of what must have been two manuscript volumes survives. But it is at least clear that the plot was suitably tragic. A young socialist journalist named Graham, who comes from a fishing port in north-east Scotland, settles in Aberdeen, where he works as a leader-writer on the local Liberal newspaper, and becomes friendly with a circle of socialist artists and professional people. There he marries a servant girl, Jessie, who comes from his own village, and who has recently given birth to an illegitimate child. But Graham's capacity for feeling has been blunted by an unhappy love affair. When it is too late, he discovers that his affection for his wife was based on pity, not on love, and that he has nothing in common with her intellectually. The marriage turns out to be an empty shell, in spite of the enthusiasm of Graham's fellow socialists, who welcomed it on ideological grounds, and of the unselfish devotion of his wife, who looks up to him as her saviour. Then an emancipated schoolmistress appears: socialist, feminist, intel-lectually his equal. They collaborate on a book, and when the book is finished Graham and Jessie take the schoolmistress with them on a holiday by the Moray Firth. There Jessie commits suicide.[51]

It is easy to see why the novel was not published. There are some good touches, and some acute flashes of observation, but the style is derivative and the dialogue stiff and unnatural. It is hard to believe that a conversation like this one could ever have taken place, even among the most whisky-sodden of debauchees, even in the 1890s:

'We two are left alone – to love each other. Ah – ha – ha! And won't we love each other – I, the hawk; you the falcon? A – ha! Don't you feel that love already, Tam? It's like hell itself in me. Come you lazy dotard, kiss me.

When are we to be married? When are we to begin life together? Answer me, man. Have you lost your courage? Have you repented? Does the part of the falcon terrify you? Speak, you fool. Ah — ha — ha — a — a — a.'

'By the devil, I'll stick, to you — like a limpet. *I* can take the part of the falcon, my Juliet. I'll marry you now — here in your filth, you witch. You have ruined me and I long to wallow with you in the mire.'[52]

Yet the novel reveals a great deal of its author. First novels by lonely and sensitive young men are apt to be autobiographical, and MacDonald's was no exception. It provides important clues to his intellectual preoccupations and uncertainties when he wrote it; at a deeper level, it casts at least some light on the hidden recesses of his character. The basis of the plot is that Jessie has become a social outcast after giving birth to an illegitimate child. The relevance to MacDonald's own birth is obvious; and his treatment of Jessie is revealing in another and less obvious way as well. We see that her husband is deceiving himself when he thinks that he has made a great sacrifice in marrying her: in reality, she is not merely his equal, but his superior. She is, in fact, the one wholly attractive and admirable character in the book. Graham's middle-class socialist friends are depicted as crass and insensitive: they are governed by facile theories and blind to psychological realities. Genteel, middle-class social reformers are treated with a rather heavy-handed irony, and there is a distinct implication that their charitable exercises are a form of emotional self-indulgence, of dubious value to the supposed beneficiaries. Jessie, on the other hand, is sensitive and kind, with a wisdom that owes nothing to formal education. The portrait of Graham — the central character, whose career is in many ways a mirror of Graham's creator's — is of equal interest. He is an idealist, but he does not live up to his ideals. He is a leader-writer on a Liberal newspaper, though he is not a Liberal. He is a feminist, but he treats his wife like a servant and drives her to suicide. He is a socialist, but in the crisis of his emotional life he finds that socialism gives him no help.

It would be wrong to read too much into any of this. MacDonald's novel was clearly autobiographical, but it should not be seen as a disguised autobiography. Jessie's life-story has something in common with MacDonald's mother's, but it does not follow that she is a fictional Annie Ramsay. At certain points, Graham's career runs parallel to MacDonald's own, but it would be a mistake to assume that he is a self-portrait. All the same, one conclusion stands out. Socially, as well as in other respects, MacDonald had already travelled a long way from his grandmother's cottage, and had done so of his own volition and in the face of formidable obstacles. But the journey had been accompanied by more backward glances, and had left more emotional scars, than those who knew him only in his later years would ever have suspected.

CHAPTER 3

Dover, Southampton and Bayswater

I

ALTHOUGH MacDonald's novel found no publisher, he had better luck in other directions. Though there is no direct evidence, it seems clear that by now his work for Lough was becoming increasingly irksome, and that he had begun to look to journalism as a way of escape. It was not an easy one. A large part of his time in 1891 and 1892 must have been spent pestering newspaper offices with manuscripts; and the manuscripts had a distressing habit of coming back, accompanied by chilly or evasive replies. In August 1891 the *New Review* returned an article on the grounds that they were 'so full of papers already received that the writers are complaining of delay', and that they would have to wait so long to publish his article that 'in the meantime you may wish to get it in elsewhere.' In February 1892 the *British Weekly* said grudgingly that they would be willing to look at specimen paragraphs, but added that the sort of paragraph they wanted was much harder to write than he seemed to think. In January 1892 a contact on the *Daily Telegraph* returned a specimen article with the daunting comment: 'Perhaps you would not mind doing one on a lighter topic—say on the terrible mortality in London at the present time.'[1] Little by little, however, he made his way. Early in 1892 he left Lough, to rely entirely on the exiguous earnings of his pen. Though he had occasional windfalls—as when he won the first prize of £10 in a short-story competition held by the Dundee *People's Journal* with an arch essay in dialect humour entitled 'Lovers Twain'[2]—he faced a hard grind to make ends meet. There is no record of his total income from journalism, but the few monthly statements from the *Star* and the *Echo* which survive among his papers make it clear that they must have been pitifully small. In March and July 1892, for example, the *Star* paid him a guinea; in March the same year, his total earnings from the *Echo* amounted to thirty-six shillings.[3] For some time, at any rate, he must have been a long way from making up the £100 a year which he had given up when he left Lough.

He was, however, his own master; and it was not long before he was devoting a large part of his new freedom to labour politics. After he left Lough, there was talk of appointing him as secretary to the Fabian Society. Nothing came of it, but in the spring and early summer of 1892 he toured South Wales, the midlands and the north-east as a Fabian lecturer, speaking on the topics 'Why are the many poor?', 'Signs of the Times', and 'Fabian policy'.[4] It was an invaluable experience for a future Labour leader. Provincial Fabian societies were often more proletarian and more down-to-earth than the parent body in London. In the course of his travels, MacDonald was able to get a first-hand impression of the Labour and socialist movements at the grass roots.

They had developed a great deal in the seven years since he had first made his way, a raw 'Lossie loon' of eighteen, to the socialist meeting-place in the coffee tavern near Bristol prison. In the summer of 1885 the total membership of all the socialist societies in Britain cannot have been much more than a thousand. Many of the future leaders of British socialism were as yet unconverted. Sidney Webb had not yet attended his first Fabian meeting; Keir Hardie, although a stubborn champion of his fellow miners, was still a Liberal in politics. By 1892 much of this early obscurity had been dissipated. Socialists had been in the forefront of the great Dock Strike of 1889, and were leading the agitation for an eight-hour day. The 'new unions', which sought to organize the unskilled masses, were inspired largely by socialists; socialists were slowly gaining ground in the T.U.C. On a different plane, the collection of Fabian essays which had first been published in 1889 had been a best-seller of its kind, and had helped to popularize socialist teachings among the Radical intelligentsia. The socialist movement was still very much a stage army, richer in would-be officers and N.C.O.s than in private soldiers, but it was at least a noisy and demonstrative one, whose appearances were attracting increasing public attention.

Yet its strategy was uncertain. Hopes that London would see in 1889 what Paris had seen in 1789 had not been fulfilled, and all but the most hardened of Hyndmanites now accepted that Britain offered no hope of a socialist revolution. But if revolutionary tactics were to be abandoned, what should be put in their place? In 1886 the T.U.C. had set up a Labour Electoral Committee – later called the Labour Electoral Association – with the aim of increasing the unions' representation in the House of Commons by pressing labour candidates on local Liberal Associations. Should socialists follow the T.U.C.'s example, work within the existing party framework and try to push the Liberal Party along a socialist path? Or should they emulate the Irish home-rulers and try to set up an independent political party of their own? The Fabians mostly favoured the first course, and for a while in the early 1890s they pointed to the allegedly collectivist implications of the Newcastle programme which the Liberals adopted in 1891 as evidence of the advantages which that course could bring. As time went on, however, it became clear that the Labour Electoral Association was not achieving as much as had been hoped, and its failure struck a heavy blow at the Fabian argument. For local Liberal Associations were mostly middle-class in composition and laissez-faire in ideology; and as such, they were suspicious of the candidates whom the Labour Electoral Association urged upon them. This was true even in the north of England, where the working class was strongest and had the best claim to a more powerful voice in Parliament. Gradually socialists in the north of England deserted the Liberal Party for complete political independence, and by the early 'nineties the propaganda of the independents had generated the beginnings of a mass movement. In January 1893 the Independent Labour Party was set up at a conference in Bradford.

It was against this background that MacDonald's career took shape. Like the 'Lib-Labs' of the Labour Electoral Association, he had little confidence in the political skill of the independent socialists in the north of England; like the Fabians, he saw no reason of principle why socialism could not be ushered in under the aegis of the Liberal Party. Yet the I.L.P. — with its exalted nonconformist atmosphere and its insistence on moral regeneration as the complement of social reform — struck an emotional chord which the Fabians and the Lib-Labs could not touch. Moreover, the Fabians, for all their apparent political dexterity, lacked that nose for power which is the indispensable prerequisite for political leadership. MacDonald had other weaknesses; but not that. For him, the first goal of socialist politics was still what it had been for the Socialist Union as long ago as 1886: 'the early and intelligent exercise of political power by the wealth producers'. If labour could win a fair share of political power by working within the Liberal coalition, well and good. If not, a more aggressive strategy would have to be tried instead.

His first direct experience of the strengths and weaknesses of the Liberal-Labour approach came a few months after he left Lough. In July 1892 he visited Dover to support the Labour Electoral Association's candidate — a retired army officer named Major Edwards — in the general election. Dover was a safe Conservative seat; although there was no Liberal in the field, Edwards was soundly beaten. But MacDonald made a better impression than the candidate he had come to support, particularly on the local Liberals whom Edwards had abused as 'a set of old Tory grandmothers'. The local Liberal newspaper, the *Dover Express*, was distinctly cool towards Edwards, but thought that MacDonald's speech supporting him was 'a masterpiece of election oratory'.[5] Two weeks after the election Edwards gave up his candidature, and MacDonald was unanimously selected as his successor. The *Dover Express* commended the Labour Electoral Association on its choice. MacDonald, it wrote, was 'well in touch with all phases of public life'; he would come to Dover 'with such recommendations from public men of all classes on the Progressive side as will render it an easy task for every Liberal voter in Dover to adopt him'.[6] He was not quite twenty-six.

The enthusiasm of the *Dover Express* was not shared universally. The opening meeting of MacDonald's campaign was an exciting occasion — and not only because of the quality of the oratory:

A party of turbulent spirits which had been got together ... in a semi-intoxicated state took up a position in the front seats and throughout the proceedings were noisily demonstrative, shouting choruses, using coarse language and making themselves very objectionable ... The chairman's rising was the signal for loud hooting and some cheering. He announced the object of the meeting, and after a short speech, he proceeded to read the address amidst an almost indescribable din rendering it almost impossible to hear his voice beyond a yard or two ... Mr. MacDonald next rose to address the meeting and was received in the same manner as the other speakers, but with true Scotch sturdiness he stuck to his guns, and in a speech of over an hour's duration, during which he was subjected to continual interruptions, he explained the relationship of the Labour party to the Liberal party and the programme on which he should fight the next Parliamentary election ... In conclusion, Mr. MacDonald said that he had kept them rather long but he had done so mainly for the purpose of teaching certain interests in Dover a lesson, and if the same policy were adopted at every meeting he should do exactly as he had done that night.[7]

The interruptions did MacDonald more good than harm: even the local Conservative paper congratulated him on his 'pluck and temper'.[8] But the sequel was more embarrassing. Without consulting anyone, Major Edwards suddenly decided that it was time to carry the war into the enemy camp. The methods he chose were appropriate, but bizarre. On the evening after MacDonald's meeting he stationed himself at the back of the Town Hall, at a Church Congress meeting presided over by the Bishop of Manchester. When the bishop rose to deliver his address, Edwards burst out singing the popular song 'Ta-ra-ra-boom-de-ay'. He was forcibly ejected, and promptly brought an action for assault against the stewards – in order, as he claimed later, to test the right of private individuals to disrupt public meetings.[9] Dover Labour circles were thrown into disarray. The Labour Electoral Association promptly dissociated itself from Edwards's action; and one of MacDonald's more circumspect supporters, a clergyman named Garrett, wrote that 'it was such a stupid thing to do that I can find no excuse.'[10] In the end the storm blew over, but it must have left wounded feelings behind.

At the opening meeting of his campaign MacDonald announced that he would fight Dover 'as a Labour candidate', and denied that 'the Labour Party are a wing of the great Liberal Party'.[11] Though he added the significant qualification that the Liberal and Labour Parties should both be regarded as 'two separate wings, which would not be complete unless those two wings were put together, and then they would form a great Progressive party,'[12] he also made it clear that the Liberals would have to make substantial concessions before the 'completion' he envisaged became possible. In the autumn of 1892 he wrote a series of articles for the *Dover Express* which were reprinted as a pamphlet with the challenging title 'The New Charter: a programme of working-class politics'. Though the policies contained in it—the eight-hour day, old-age pensions, municipalization of ground rents and the abolition of the House of Lords—might have been accepted by some of the more Radical Liberal back-benchers, they would have won few supporters on the Liberal front bench. In any case, the policies set out in 'The New Charter' were of secondary importance: what mattered was its approach to the central question of parliamentary representation and political power. Labour, MacDonald insisted, was a separate interest and, as such, it had an intrinsic right to separate representation. For history showed that 'the power ruling in the State looks after its own interests'. The King had used his power to strengthen the royal prerogative; the landed aristocracy had been kind to landlords; the 'commercial classes' had used their power to cheapen production and open up foreign markets. Now it was the turn of the working class:

> Hitherto the working classes have been asked to use their votes mainly to help the social and financial ambitions of moneyed men, and the genuine representation of labour interests in the House of Commons has been ridiculously inadequate. It will serve no good purpose, either for Liberal or Tory, to tell the working-class voter that the interests of the wage earners are safe in the hands of employers. Railway directors are bad representatives of railway porters.

It followed that working-class interests could be represented properly only by a 'Labour Party'. And although the Labour Party would sympathize with the Liberals more than with the Conservatives, it would adopt 'no shibboleth which will tie us to the old parties'.[13] Labour, in other words, might ally itself with the Liberals if it decided that it would gain by doing so. But it would be an independent ally, not a subordinate, and it would negotiate from a position of strength. In June 1893, MacDonald told a rowdy audience in Dover market square that he was determined 'to arouse the labouring classes of Dover to a knowledge of their power'.[14] It was a fair summary of the central theme of his campaign.

II

A wide gulf still lay between his position and that of the I.L.P., and the events which bridged it must be examined with some care. In April 1894, the Liberals of Southampton—a two-member constituency, with one Liberal M.P. and one Conservative—began to look for a second parliamentary candidate. Southampton had a substantial working-class electorate, and in theory, at any rate, the local Liberal Association had a strong incentive to find a labour candidate to run in harness with the sitting Liberal M.P. The labour forces in the town, working theough the Gladstone Working Men's Liberal and Radical Club, secured MacDonald an invitation to address the Liberal Council at the end of

April. Two other would-be candidates were invited as well, however—a bacon-curer named Barnes, who sat on the Surrey county council, and R. G. Wilberforce, who had been Liberal candidate for the Farnham division of Hampshire.[15]

Barnes turned down the invitation, and on April 26th the Liberal Council selected Wilberforce by 94 votes to MacDonald's 65. But this result provoked an uproar from MacDonald's supporters. On April 27th they held a meeting at the Gladstone Club, at which they decided, as one of those present reported to MacDonald, that 'Wilberforce shall have plenty of petitions urging him to withdraw in your favour.'[16] Before Wilberforce could be considered as the official Liberal candidate he had to go before a mass meeting of the Liberal voters in the constituency. Before the meeting was held, he was persuaded to leave the race altogether. But when the Liberal Council met on May 10th to reconsider the situation, MacDonald's supporters were not informed of the meeting. By a large majority the Council decided to approach Barnes a second time, and deleted MacDonald's name from the list of candidates along with Wilberforce's. On May 21st Barnes appeared before the Council, and was duly selected.[17]

When MacDonald had first accepted the invitation to address the Liberal Council he had promised to abide by the result. He now declared that his promise was no longer binding, and that he would fight Southampton as a labour candidate, in opposition to the Liberals. He was still anxious for Liberal support, and his appeal was still sectional rather than ideological. On June 7th, he spoke at the Gladstone Liberal and Radical Club. The Liberal leaders, he declared, had admitted that labour had a right to more seats in Parliament. Every loyal Liberal in Southampton would therefore 'recognise the undoubted claims of labour to equal recognition with commercial claims'.[18] But by now he was on the verge of joining the I.L.P. The Labour Electoral Association, he told the readers of Seedtime, was 'gradually sinking into insignificance'. Local Liberal Associations were dominated by commercial interests; and labour candidates were repugnant to them. The I.L.P. was now in existence; that in itself would widen still further the gulf between labour and the Liberal Party. Above all, the I.L.P. had established itself as a mass movement, with its own drive and élan:

Paid secretaries, paid organisers, paid lecturers are at work in the North, marshalling and encouraging the forces of Independent Labour. Beginning with the shallow, optimistic man who could not see much difficulty in re-constructing English society tomorrow, the party is now having a substantial accession of clearer and more cautious heads, and still it has lost none of its 'go'. Nothing is too hard for the members in their virgin enthusiasm to do. They run their little prints, they sell their stock of pamphlets, they drop their pennies into the collecting box, they buy their I.L.P. tea and cocoa, etc, as though they were members of an idealist communist society.

It was true that the I.L.P. leadership was 'atrociously bad', and that its energies were apt to be wasted in 'levelling mountains that could be marched around'. But with all its faults, it occupied the decisive position in progressive politics.[19]

The logic seemed to point towards joining it; but a final, decisive feather had still to be placed in the scales. In June a by-election was held in the Attercliffe division of Sheffield. The Labour Electoral Association put forward a trade unionist who was well known in the town. He was turned down by the local Liberal Association. The I.L.P. then intervened, and ran a London journalist named Frank Smith. MacDonald went to Sheffield to help organize Smith's campaign.[20] When he got back to London, he decided to throw in his lot with the I.L.P. On July 15th, he made a formal application for membership in a letter to Keir Hardie, in which he admitted that the 'prophecies of the I.L.P. relating to Liberalism have been amply justified'.[21] Next day he wrote a much fuller letter to the secretary of the Southampton Labour Electoral Association, formally accepting his invitation to contest the seat in the labour interest, and setting out his own attitude to the Liberals in some detail:

> The fact that your town has two members gave the Liberals an opportunity of running a purely Labour candidate. They might have done this without much damage to themselves locally and they would certainly have won the gratitude of the Parliamentary leaders of their party. They decided otherwise. Two commercial men are to champion what was once a progressive cause ...
>
> Just at the time when your Liberal Council plunged you into your difficulties you were hearing of similar things in scores of other constituencies throughout the country. Mid-Lanark Liberals refused a Labour candidate; the Liberal Association of Newcastle-on-Tyne was scouring the face of the earth for a capitalist to oppose the nominee of the Trades Council; at Wigan Mr Aspinall who contested the constituency at the last election was being opposed by a Liberal candidate; at Huddersfield, Bradford, Manchester, Bolton, South Shields, Glasgow and elsewhere the same state of things existed; and to crown all came Attercliffe. In deference to such overwhelming evidence you had to make up your minds that local Liberal Associations had cast themselves adrift from the forward movement in politics, and that the decision of the Southampton Liberal Council was but part of a national policy which is compelling what was once the advanced wing of Liberalism to sever itself from an old alliance and form itself into an independent Labour party ...
>
> To go back to the Liberals, even if it were possible, would simply stultify ourselves; the further we go the wider will be the divergence between us, until at last the change, of which there is now ample evidence, which is breaking down the part[y] wall between Liberalism and Toryism

is accomplished and the political battle will be fought out by the 'interests' on the one side and the wage earners on the other ... Our movement is neither a party nor a class movement, but a national one, and as such it must be presented to Southampton.[22]

On July 17th his campaign as I.L.P. candidate for Southampton was officially inaugurated at an open-air meeting. His political apprenticeship was over at last.[23]

III

In the next few weeks, MacDonald and his supporters made determined efforts to win over the local Trades Council. At the beginning of July, the Amalgamated Society of Carpenters and Joiners had proposed that the Trades Council should convene a mass meeting of trade unionists, with a view to adopting MacDonald as their candidate, but the council had refused.[24] In August, the secretary of the Labour Electoral Association wrote to the Trades Council to ask whether it would be willing to hear an address from MacDonald. The suggestion was opposed by the president, H. G. Wilson, on the revealing grounds that 'they were there to propagate Trades Union principles and he did not see how they could give their support to a man who was not a Trades Unionist. There was an attempt on the part of a certain party outside to make the Council their cat's paw.'[25] In spite of Wilson's opposition to his candidature, MacDonald eventually appeared before the council towards the end of September. He made a powerful speech, pointing out that since the age of nineteen 'he had been identified with the cause of labour and had been in favour of a set of principles which had for their centre ... the welfare and improvement of the condition of the working classes with whose wants and aspirations he had an intimate acquaintance' and that the trade-union movement had 'at last come to cross the political movement which had been running on convergent lines'. But his candidature was not endorsed.[26]

For a while, in the early months of 1895, his chances brightened. In January, Barnes withdrew, and it seemed that there might be only one Liberal in the field after all. But the improvement did not last. In June, the languishing Rosebery Government at last succumbed to its own internal divisions and loss of morale. After a relatively trivial defeat in the House of Commons it dissolved Parliament and went to the country. The prospect of an I.L.P. victory was too much for the Southampton Liberals to stomach, and in July they selected H. G. Wilson, the Trades Council president, to run in harness with the sitting M.P., Sir Francis Evans. It was a smart move. 'Mr. Wilson', the Southampton Times observed blandly, 'is well known as a bona-fide working man; and in selecting him the Liberals of Southampton have given practical evidence of their sympathy with labour.'[27]

With two Liberals in the field the I.L.P. had no chance of winning a seat. It put up a gallant fight. On the eve of the poll, I.L.P. stalwarts took possession of the Kingsland Square and held it against all comers; on polling day MacDonald was carried around the town in a dog-cart decorated with the party colours, while the 'I.L.P. ladies', whose presence seems to have been one of the more agreeable features of the election, made a brave show in their red jerseys.[28] But these efforts were no match for those of the older parties. The main issue of the election was the local veto; and when polling day came the voters were left in no doubt as to what was at stake. A procession of Tory costermongers paraded around the town with the Unionist candidate, Tankerville Chamberlayne, at its head. The procession included a donkey painted blue and red, and a dog which had allegedly been trained to bark furiously whenever it heard a Liberal speech. A large tankard was hoisted on the top of a pole on the roof of Chamberlayne's carriage, while a Conservative supporter proclaimed periodically 'Vote for Chamberlayne and this,' or, less ambiguously, 'Vote for Chamberlayne and beer.'[29] The *Southampton Times* commented sourly that 'there was a large number of men who did no work on Tuesday, and many of them were so gloriously fuddled that they could hardly tell the difference between a rabbit and a barn-door fowl.'[30]

For MacDonald and the I.L.P. the result was a bitter disappointment. The Conservatives won both seats; the two Liberals came third and fourth respectively; and MacDonald's vote was less than a quarter of Wilson's. After a recount the figures were

Chamberlayne	5,924
Simeon	5,390
Evans	5,181
Wilson	4,178
MacDonald	867

An analysis of the cross-voting suggested that MacDonald had probably cost Evans his seat; but even that was not certain.[31]

The disappointment of the Southampton I.L.P. was as nothing compared to the indignation of the Southampton Liberals. In August two of them brought a petition against the result; and at the beginning of December Chamberlayne was unseated for infringing the Corrupt Practices Act. Southampton now faced a by-election, in which the I.L.P. might well hold the key to the result. If MacDonald stood again, the Conservatives might hold the seat. If he did not, the scales might be turned in favour of the Liberals. His first instinct was to fight. The Liberals, he wrote at the beginning of August, had 'kicked us out and slammed the door in our faces'. There could be 'no going back now — unless of course circumstances change greatly, and then the change will be not so much on our side (at least those of us who have not plunged into the excesses of the I.L.P.) as on the side of the Liberals.'[32]

By December, however, the 'change' had taken place. On December 16th a leading Southampton Liberal, named Dr Aldridge, wrote to the secretary of the local I.L.P., expressing the hope that 'we can again fight together [against] our common foe.'[33] Towards the end of the month, MacDonald accepted an invitation to meet Sir Francis Evans in London, together with the Liberal chief whip.[34] By December 30th, the secretary of the Southampton I.L.P. was writing to warn MacDonald against discussing the 'proposed Liberal compromise' with certain unreliable members of the local I.L.P. executive.[35] The following un-dated pencilled note, preserved among MacDonald's papers, makes it fairly clear what the basis of the 'proposed Liberal compromise' must have been:

No ILP candidate to come forward for the present vacancy at S.

No second Liberal candidate to run at the next General Election at S.

In the event of a Bye Election at S thro' the death or removal of a Tory no Liberal candidate to be brought forward.[36]

From MacDonald's point of view it was a notable coup. If the I.L.P. were to contest the by-election it would have no chance of winning. A non-aggression pact with the Liberals would give it a reasonable hope of victory in the future, at the cost of a modicum of self-restraint in the present. At I.L.P. headquarters matters were looked at in a less hard-headed fashion. At the beginning of January 1896, the party secretary, Tom Mann, was instructed to warn the Southampton branch against taking part in any conference with the Liberals. But his letter did not arrive until it was too late. On January 7th, the South-ampton I.L.P. decided to receive a deputation from the Liberal Association,[37] and on the 14th the conference took place. Next day, one of MacDonald's chief supporters in the Southampton party reported:

Dr Aldridge came before us last night & said that he came before us with proposals communicated to him by one of the highest authorit[ies] in our party (There followed 1.2.3.) which he thought the Liberal party might well accept. When it was pointed out to him that we had made no propos-als & that we wanted to hear what the Liberal party had to propose & that it was for us to accept or reject, he objected that the proposals came from our side, that they came from one high in authority on our side, from one who would carry the greatest weight & authority if we only knew his name, in fact he would give us his name – I knew the name that was coming only too well & being in the chair jumped up & stopped him – several of the committee here demanded the name, I was firm & refused to allow the name ... to be introduced into an official discussion, other mem-bers of the committee backed me up, the other members of the deputation saw the point & urged the Dr not to give the name & the Dr gave way on the point & so the situation was saved but God! it was a near thing & if I had not been in the Chair you would have been in a tight place to-day. Fancy your going & giving yourself away to Dr Aldridge like that, surely you must now confess you were a damned fool? ...

... Dr Aldridge ... also said he had a letter from Sir Francis Evans saying he would be only two [*sic*] pleased to run with you as the second candidate, for which the Dr got into trouble with the other members of the deputation. His idea was that you should be adopted as the second candidate & that we should become a wing of the Liberal party to fight for them from the present time onwards. The other members of the deputation did not expect as much, in fact did not think it desirable, but thought we might have a secret alliance to work together as allies, each with our own candidate, but of course withdrawing our candidate at this election & doing what we could to help them. I put it to Cheverton would he consider it a friendly action on our part & entitle us to expect no second Liberal candidate to be brought out against us if we retired our candidate & took no part in the fight? he asked if that would mean our preventing our members voting? I said that to do that would be taking part in the fight, what I meant by taking no part in the fight was – to have our members free to do what they liked. He said he should take that to be a friendly action & in his opinion sufficient to satisfy the Liberal party ...

I called upon Cheverton this morning & asked him – supposing you receive a reply from the Branch saying that they could make no terms with the Liberal party & declining to hold any further [illegible] with them, & yet afterwards they withdrew you & decided to take no part in the fight, would the deputation pledge themselves to me to use their utmost influence to prevent a second candidate being brought out? He said it was much better so ... & if we ran no candidate this time & remained neutral he pledged himself, & every member of the deputation, & also Sir Francis Evans that they would use their whole influence to prevent you being opposed by the Liberal party on another occasion. I said on these terms & on this understanding I would promise to do my best to keep the branch neutral this time (well knowing we could not fight) & that I [would] make sure I would manage it & that on this understanding they might now assume they would not be opposed by us.[38]

On the same day, the secretary of the Southampton I.L.P. wrote to Mac-Donald to tell him that a special meeting of the branch would be summoned in the latter part of the following week, and that since no correspondence was taken at special meetings it would be possible to settle the whole affair without reference to the N.A.C. and without reading Tom Mann's letter to the branch. 'If things go on as at present,' he concluded jubilantly, 'your success is assured when that day comes I will drink a glass of champagne.'[39] Early in February there was another intervention from I.L.P. headquarters but it too was frustrated.

Tom Mann wrote to the Southampton branch to ask whether it would like a different candidate. The secretary replied that the branch was satisfied with MacDonald.[40] Soon afterwards, the Southampton I.L.P. officially announced that it would not contest the by-election, but that it pledged itself to fight the next parliamentary vacancy in the town.[41] The by-election took place three weeks later. Sir Francis Evans recaptured the seat with a majority of 33, while a candidate run by the local S.D.F. polled only 274 votes.[42]

IV

Southampton showed that, in spite of his conversion to the I.L.P., MacDonald's conception of independent labour politics was still very different from that of the party leadership. As so often happened with him, the two sides of his nature pulled him in different directions. The strain of romantic idealism which had been attracted by the Fellowship of the New Life, and before that by the Bristol Social Democrats, responded to the intransigent message of the I.L.P.; the cautious pragmatism of the committee-man and the election agent pulled him back. He now accepted the basic strategy of the I.L.P. If Labour was to fight its way into the citadels of political power, it must fight independently. But for him independence was not an end in itself. Part of its purpose was to bludgeon the Liberals into conceding what they had refused to concede to persuasion; it did not imply isolation, or a squeamish refusal to engage in electoral horse-trading. He had abandoned the Fabian strategy of 'permeation', but he wished to reach the same goal by other means. In a Fabian Labour Party, or perhaps an Independent Fabian Party, both sides of his character might have been satisfied. As things were, he found himself in a no-man's-land between the two societies, and was wholly at ease in neither. The N.A.C.'s disapproval of his negotiations with the Southampton Liberals was fully equalled by the disapproval of the Fabian 'old gang', who looked upon him as an extreme and irresponsible I.L.P. '*frondeur*'.[43]

At first his relations with the Fabian leadership were cordial enough. He was elected to the executive of the Society in the spring of 1894. In March 1895, he was made chairman of a 'fresh activities' committee of the executive;[44] that autumn Beatrice Webb noted in her diary that he was 'one of a certain set of young people, all more or less devoted to the Fabian junta'.[45] By the spring of 1896 his devotion had worn off. For some months he was involved in a bitter struggle with the Webbs and the Webbian conception of Fabian politics. It centred around a legacy which had been left to the Society two years before by an eccentric businessman called Henry Hutchinson. Hutchinson left almost £10,000 to set up a charitable trust, whose president was to be Sidney Webb. Its object was to apply the money to the 'propaganda and other purposes of the [Fabian] Society and its Socialism'. Hutchinson's wishes were interpreted loosely, to say the least. At Webb's suggestion, the trustees decided to spend the money in three ways. Part went to the Fabian Society; part was to be spent on educational lectures in the provinces; the bulk was to be devoted to setting up a School of Economics and Political Science in London. These decisions encountered no serious opposition in the Fabian Society. So far from objecting to them, MacDonald accepted an appointment as a Hutchinson Trust lecturer.[46]

But he was soon dissatisfied by the limited scope of the Hutchinson Trust scheme. In April 1896 he sent Edward Pease, the Society's secretary, an elaborate plan for extending its activities, and evidently asked whether the Hutchinson trustees would be prepared to foot the bill. In February, however, the trustees had decided to make a capital grant of £1,500 towards a 'library of political science', to be associated with the new School of Economics.[47] They were therefor reluctant to spend more money on the Fabian Society proper. On April 8th, Pease wrote to MacDonald to say that 'we are now committed to a big scheme, & there would be difficulties in taking up anything else which involved much money'.[48] The following day he wrote again:

> Your Hutchinson Trust information is inaccurate; it comes I suppose from Clarke, who neglects his duty as a trustee. I hope you are not going to cause a rumpus. You were asked for suggestions, & your only one, I believe, was carried out. No other proposal has yet been made by yourself or anyone else. Do you want us to stop doing anything on the chance that you may hit on a good idea? I am not prepared to say what the Trustees may or may not do: but having started this school we are going on with it.[49]

Pease's hopes were disappointed. One of the noisiest 'rumpuses' in the Society's history soon followed. In the middle of April, MacDonald moved a resolution at the Fabian executive, demanding that the Hutchinson trustees should furnish it with a statement of the monies they had spent so far, and an estimate of their proposed expenditure in 1896.[50] The debate that followed was presumably acrimonious and certainly prolonged. It was adjourned until the following week, when MacDonald's resolution was passed.[51] Meanwhile, he had launched a direct attack on the Webbs. On April 18th, Beatrice noted in her diary that they had just received 'furious letters' from MacDonald, denouncing the 'abuse of the Hutchinson Trust in the proposal to contribute to the library of Political Science'. MacDonald, she commented, 'is a brilliant young Scot'; but she added that he was 'personally discontented because we refused to have him as a lecturer for the London school'. She recognized, however, that he had raised an issue of fundamental importance. MacDonald wanted the Society to appoint an organizer to establish Fabian branches in the provinces. Beatrice suspected that his real object was to set up I.L.P. branches with Fabian money. In any case she saw no value in provincial branches as such. 'Do we want to organise the unthinking persons into Socialistic Societies,' she asked, 'or to make the thinking persons socialistic? We believe in the latter process.'[52]

But it was not clear that the 'thinking persons' would agree. MacDonald had support from surprising quarters, including Pease's wife who deplored the way her husband 'blindly follows Webb'.[53] On June 5th, his plan was discussed by the executive. It fell into four parts. The Society was to spend an extra £500–£600 a year. Of this, £50 a year would go on educational lectures in London; £100 a year on advertising the Society in progressive journals; and £200 a year on provincial lectures on the lines of the existing Hutchinson Trust lectures. The remaining £200 a year was to be spent on a 'travelling Secretaryship or representative', whose job would be to bring Fabian influence to bear on 'active centres of Socialist work' in the provinces.[54] The essence of the plan was contained in this final proposal. The I.L.P. and S.D.F., MacDonald's resolution pointed out, 'are alive and doing work without us. The work is all the poorer for that and the ultimate influence and prospects of Socialism all the more uncertain.' Beatrice was wrong in thinking that he wanted merely to set up more I.L.P. branches. His aim was not so much to extend the I.L.P. as to Fabianize it. But the Fabians lacked the stomach for such a role. MacDonald's plan was accepted in principle and emasculated in practice. The Hutchinson trustees were persuaded to grant an extra £200 a year to the Society, but the money was earmarked for purely educational purposes. A travelling secretary was appointed, but only for an experimental period of three months. The following spring the experiment was allowed to lapse altogether.[55]

No sooner was this rumpus over, than it was followed by a still noisier one. In July 1896, the Second International held its Congress in London. Like the other bodies represented at the Congress, the Fabian Society had the right to submit a report on its activities. Its report was drafted by Bernard Shaw, and contained a coruscating statement of Fabian socialism – in a form which must have been calculated to cause the greatest possible offence to the greatest possible number of delegates. In the original draft Marx and Lassalle, the twin heroes of German socialism, were attacked as out of date; and the Fabian Society was committed to the heretical proposition that 'freedom to engage in industry independently of the State' stood on a par with freedom of speech and freedom of the press. Thanks to Henry Macrosty, one of MacDonald's allies on the executive, these sentiments were omitted from the final version.[56] But, even in its final form, the report was deeply offensive to the I.L.P. 'Frivolous' parliamentary candidatures were denounced, on the grounds that a third candidate without strong support might bring about the defeat of the 'better of the two candidates competing with him'. In such circumstances, the report continued uncompromisingly, the Fabian Society 'throws its weight against the third candidate, whether he calls himself a Socialist or not, in order to secure the victory to the better of the two candidates between whom the contest really lies'.[57]

An angry squabble followed. At a members' meeting early in July, a group of Fabians who also belonged to the I.L.P. tried to amend the report again, and voted against its adoption by the Society. Furious attacks were made on Shaw, causing particular anguish to a female supporter of the executive who was heard to cry out 'Cads, cads, cads; we don't want such people here,' and again, '*Our* Shaw, we are all so fond of him.' But the rebels were out-debated, or at least out-generalled, and wasted so much time moving obstructive amendments on unimportant clauses that, when the important sections of the report were reached, debate on them often had to be closured. In spite of a split among the executive members present at the meeting, the report was adopted with only six dissentients, and was duly published as Tract 70.[58] MacDonald had not been present at the meeting and was infuriated by the outcome – the more so since he had been told, how accurately it is impossible to tell, that Webb had sent out whips to his supporters in order to make sure of a victory for the 'old gang'.[59] At an executive meeting at the end of July, MacDonald proposed a motion declaring that it was 'unbecoming for individual members of the Executive to attempt to influence the opinion of meetings of members by the issue of whips'.[60] After discussion, his motion was withdrawn, but in September he sent in a requisition for a members' meeting to discuss the withdrawal of Tract 70. The meeting was held early in October. MacDonald moved that the tract be withdrawn, and was supported by Macrosty and Pete Curran. His motion was opposed by Shaw, Webb and Hubert Bland, and, after what Pease described years later as an 'excited discussion', it was defeated by 108 votes to 33.[61]

V

In spite of the energy he threw into his struggle with the Fabian leadership, the Hutchinson Trust and Tract 70 were far from the main stream of MacDonald's life in the summer of 1896. In May the previous year, he had been lying ill in St Thomas's hospital when a letter had arrived from an unknown sympathizer, enclosing a cheque for £1 as a contribution to his election fund at Southampton. It was signed 'M. E. Gladstone', and it came from a young social worker from Bayswater called Margaret Gladstone. MacDonald's letter acknowledging her cheque was recorded in a special notebook: 'First letter from J. R. MacDonald: May 29, 1895'. The note was soon followed by another: 'First saw him, Pioneer Club, June 13, 1895'. She had already heard a great deal about him from her Bayswater friends, the Montagus, in whose house a Lossiemouth friend of MacDonald's was employed as a governess, and had decided that he was the sort of person whom she would like to marry one day. Her first impressions, however, were unfavourable – largely, she confessed to him later, because she thought his red tie and curly hair looked 'horribly affected'. But her disapproval soon wore off. A few days later, she was introduced to him at a party given by the Montagus. By July, she was buying envelopes for the I.L.P.'s election campaign in Southampton.[62]

Her purchases had been preceded by a long process of self-discovery. The Gladstone family home at 17 Pembridge Square might have been in a different continent from the I.L.P. committee rooms in Southampton. At the end of the nineteenth century, as MacDonald remembered it later, Pembridge Square lay 'in the calm dignity of pillared porticoes, bow-windows, broad steps and massive front doors'; the houses breathed 'that air of detached independence which surrounds the English middle-class home of substantial possessions'.[63] It was the sort of place where Soames Forsyte might have been asked to dine. Yet he might not have felt altogether at home at No. 17. The Gladstones came of puritan stock from the Scottish border. Margaret's father, Dr John Gladstone, was one of the founders of the Y.M.C.A. as well as Professor of Chemistry at the Royal Institution and a Fellow of the Royal Society. He had contested York as a Liberal in 1868 and belonged to the London School Board. Margaret's maternal grandfather had been a Presbyterian minister; one of her uncles on her mother's side was the famous scientist, William Thomson, later Lord Kelvin. Her mother died soon after she was born; but she seems to have had a happy and secure childhood – in which science and religion both played a part. On Sundays Dr Gladstone used to hold a bible class in the living-room; and when Margaret went to her first Friday evening lecture at the Royal Institution, it was treated like a 'coming of age'.[64]

Other interests soon followed. Margaret was an attractive, light-hearted girl; but she had all the stubborn determination, as well as the intense religious feeling, of her puritan ancestors. She had no respect for middle-class convention, and she was certainly not prepared to wait meekly in her father's house till someone came to marry her. In May 1889 she became a Sunday-school teacher at St Mary Abbot's in Kensington, and before long she was helping in a boy's club connected with the church. Some time later she became secretary of the Hoxton and Haggerston Nursing Association, and in 1893 she started work as a charity organization visitor in Hoxton. Little by little her experiences as a social worker made her a socialist. In 1891 she heard Ben Tillett speak at a Unitarian Congress, and was distressed by the way the audience 'did not seem to be very warm to him'. In 1893 her conversion was completed, partly by the Fabian essays (which gave her 'rather clear and hopeful views about Socialism') and partly by her experiences in Hoxton. But she had not yet found herself emotionally. 'I wonder whether I shall meet him in this world,' she asked herself in her diary. 'I mean *my* him, my sir, my knight. If love lasts on to another world for those whose souls are married here, can we believe that God leaves some souls always unmarried?'[65]

Her first question, at any rate, had been answered by the summer of 1896. She and MacDonald used to meet at the Socialist Club in Bride Street, and at the British Museum, where they both had readers' tickets; and on June 15th she wrote him a long letter about herself, in answer to one from him which does not survive. It gives a more vivid impression of her character at the age of twenty-six, and of their courtship, than can be gleaned from any other source, and it is worth quoting at length:

> Thankyou for yr. letter of Wednesday. I do not think GOD will mock us by letting either of us make a mistake. Tennyson's Wages I have read, & written out on the blank page in yr. letter. I did not remember the poem; but if I had read it within the past few months it wd. have made me think of you.
>
> You touch a little on the practical side: perhaps I might do so too from my point of view.
>
> I have not much of the fever [? fear] of fight; my strength of will is needed more to keep me from fighting, & things I find hardest are such trivialities as meekly spending £3 or £4 on a new evening dress when I wd. rather give it to Tom Mann's election fund, or giving up a labour meeting to dine with a boring aunt & cousins. But I don't bother about these: I know they have to be done.
>
> My financial prospects I am very hazy about, but I know I shall have a comfortable income. At present I get £80 allowance (besides board & lodging, travelling & postage); my married sister has, I think about £500 all together. When my father dies we shall each have our full share, & I suppose mine will be some hundreds a year ... My ideal wd. be to live a simple life among the working people, spending on myself whatever seemed to keep me in best efficiency, & giving the rest to public purposes, especially Socialist propaganda of various kinds. I don't suppose I am a very good manager; but I don't think I am careless or extravagant about money. If I married & a fixed income made my husband & myself more free to do the work we thought right, I shd. think it an advantage to be used. But if you saw this differently, & led me to see as you did; and at the same time we thought that by marrying we cd. help each other to live fuller & better lives, I would give up the income & try to do my share of potboiling. I suppose I cd. do some work for which people would be willing to give money. Of course one ought to consider one's relations as well as oneself; but that is fortunately simple, as any who are worth considering wd. trust us to do what we thought right. I know your life is a hard one: I know there must be much apparent failure in it, I don't know whether I shd. have pluck & ability to carry me through anything worth doing: if you ever asked me to be with you it wd. be a spur to try my best – but there I am getting to the deeper [? water] & will stop.

The last sentence was crossed out, though only lightly; and in the second half of the letter, added the following morning, she confessed 'I think I hardly had any business to write that last sentence.' However, she continued, she wanted to make another suggestion as well, which she also had no business to make. So far, MacDonald had only seen her best side. If he cared to glance at it, she would send him the journal she had kept for the last eight or nine years, so as to give him a better idea of 'the "tout ensemble" '. 'I never expected anyone to see it — unless I married,' she wrote, '& have no right to treat even as much of my soul as appears therein lightly; but I trust you so absolutely that I shd. not mind your having read it if we each married someone else after.'[66] Her offer was taken up; and after this, their courtship proceeded rapidly. At first Margaret had addressed MacDonald as 'dear Mr. MacDonald'; by the end of June, she was addressing him as 'My *dear* Sir'. 'It is only just beginning to dawn on me a very little bit, since yr. last Sunday's letter, what a new good gift I have in your love ... ,' she wrote. 'But when I think how lonely you have been I want with all my heart to make up to you one tiny little bit for that. I have been lonely too — I have envied the veriest drunken tramps I have seen dragging about the streets if they were man & woman because they had each other ... This is truly a love letter: I don't know when I shall show it you: it may be that I never shall. But I shall never forget that I have had the blessing of writing it.'[67]

There were still some hurdles to be surmounted, however. MacDonald was painfully conscious of the social gulf between them, and nervous about facing her relatives; and on July 2nd she wrote to upbraid him:

My Dear Humbug (I am obediently dropping formalities. I know you're not a humbug, but if you will write a letter like one you must take the consequences), I feel so cocky after your letter received yesterday: I find I am much less narrow minded than you & I was afraid I was more so. What right have you to talk eloquently about having discovered humanity & then go & say it is wonderful that two poor little bits of humanity shd. care for each other because they happen to have had rather different circumstances? Not so very different after all, either, for in the most important things we have had the same — we are under the same civilisation — have the same big movements stirring around us — the same books to open our minds; & we both have many good true friends to help us along by their affection. I even have had all my life 'darned stockings'; perhaps you think some magic keeps them from going into holes in the station of life where it has pleased GOD to place me, but I can assure you I have spent many hours darning my own & my father's — badly too ...

... I don't mind how long you are making up yr. mind one way or the other — only I *would* like you to take me on my own merits & not on what my esteemed relations might think of you or what particular kind of summer holiday I had eight years ago. If you want it of course I will bring specimens of my relations to [illegible] or you can come to us & I'll have a selection for you to inspect — like animals at the zoo. But I can't introduce them to you without their having some idea of the relations between us, & I certainly at present don't relish the idea of this sort of thing.

'May I introduce you to Mr. M, who will condescend to marry me (or whom I will condescend to marry) if you speak respectfully to him.'

I [would] rather tell them straight out (I mean if we do settle anything definite) Here is the man I'm going to marry & take it all as a matter of course.[68]

They got engaged soon afterwards, on the steps of the British Museum. Margaret's relatives took the news better than she had feared – 'all very differently,' she told MacDonald happily, 'but all so kindly – not nasty & cantankerous & unsocialistic like you'. Her father, however, evidently felt that he ought to make some inquiries about his prospective son-in-law, and Margaret referred him to the Radical economist, J. A. Hobson, on the grounds that he knew MacDonald well and was a 'quiet bookwormy sort of person', whose judgment was likely to be respected.[69] She also wrote to Annie Ramsay to ask for her blessing, and to explain that she could not come to Lossiemouth as she had hoped to do because her grandmother was ill:

My dear Mrs. MacDonald,

Your son tells me that he has told you that we love one another, and that you send me kind thoughts and words. I thank you for them from the bottom of my heart. I never knew my mother, and I always hoped that if I ever married, my husband's mother would be living and would like me. That I shall like her I never feel any doubt; & if you need any promise that I will not try to take him away from you (I could not do it if I did try) here it is.

I cannot tell you how sorry I am that I am tied in London just at this time when I want to come to Lossiemouth and get to know you & his home. But if you could see my grandmother you would see how any excitement is utterly out of the question ... I have been wondering whether it would interest you at all to see the life she wrote of my grandfather who was a Presbyterian minister, of Montrose; and I am sending it to you ...

... There is one thing that I should be very glad if you would tell me, and that is by what name I am to call your son. I only know him as Mr. MacDonald & really don't know what Christian name he uses. Mine is Margaret.

He tells me that you asked him if I could cook and keep a house clean, & that he did not know. I have done a little both of cooking & of housework, but I have not had much practice, & I am afraid you would not think much of my performances, though I liked what I did of both. I often make butter when I am staying at a farmhouse which my grandmother goes to every summer & I always long to milk the cows there, but have never screwed up the courage to ask if I may.

I am nothing like so good as my mother must have been according to the accounts of her in the book; but nothing could help to make me better like your son's love, and if you will love me too it will help me. I am, if you will let me be, yours affectionately

MARGARET GLADSTONE.

Annie Ramsay's reply deserves quotation as well:

My Dear Margaret

Many thanks for the Book and letter i shall read it and return it my Dear gural i am sorry to here of your grandmothers illness i do hope she is better i now wat nursing is i nursed my Grandmother my Aunt and then My Dear Mother was confined to bed for 4 years & 6 months and a dear person in trouble she was but i trust your Granmother will soon get over this bad turn My Dear Gural you ask me for my Young Mans christian name it is Jamie Ramsay Macdonald we call him Ramsay My own name is Annie Ramsay My son is a good son to me and i trust if it please God that you and Ramsay be happy i trust god will go with you in all your ups and downs in life and I shall be verry glad to sea you in Lossiemouth My Dear Gural you spoke of milking cows i have Milked cows and made Butter and all that work but for the last 29 years i have been doing little but sowing in my dear little home Now my dear i will not forget to pray god for you as i have done for him in the past that god may be with you both and that you may be happy Ramsay will soon be Back to London and i will be all alone again with Much Love and i hopes you will writ me soon

from your frind
MRS A RAMSAY[70]

Margaret's grandmother died soon afterwards, and in late September Margaret visited Lossiemouth after all, MacDonald staying behind in London. 'Person,' she wrote exuberantly, 'I am using your red ink. And what is more, I am using your desk ... So if anything of your influence lingers about it this love letter of mine ought to be a very sweet one. But my dear Sir I don't think it will be very sweet, for the simple reason that I'm much too happy to tell you about it.'[71] The wedding took place in November, and after a short honeymoon the couple moved in to a flat at 3 Lincoln's Inn Fields. MacDonald had wanted a house in the suburbs, but Margaret had warned that if he found somewhere respectable to live, 'I should take a tent & pitch it in an East End slum & forsake you.'[72] Meanwhile, the following resolution had been forwarded on to them by the Long Eaton Trades Council: 'That this meeting of the Workingmen of Long Eaton congratulates Mrs J. R. Macdonald in having won the esteem of Comrade J. R. Macdonald which in due time matured into love and it further resolves that she is one in a thousand.'[73]

G

CHAPTER 4

Lincoln's Inn Fields

I

MARRIAGE meant even more to MacDonald than it does to most men. He came, he once wrote, 'of a people who were as ready to use their dirks as their tongues',[1] and the phrase may have revealed more than he intended. The world, for him, was a dangerous as well as a strenuous place, where injuries were to be expected and enemies lay in wait. In his later years, at any rate, his public speaking was often remarkably direct and spontaneous, in spite of the flowery language, but although he could give himself away on a public platform, he found it hard to drop his guard with individuals. Many public figures acquire a thick carapace, protecting them against insults and abuse: with him, it was as though one layer of skin were missing. As we have seen, the picture that emerges from the tantalizingly scanty evidence surviving from his early days in London is that of a taut and vulnerable young man, easily hurt and quick to take offence. These traits persisted. All his life, he was excessively sensitive to criticism, apt to think the worst of his critics and to brood over wounds which would have been better forgotten. Though Margaret was a downright and strong-minded woman, determined to speak the truth as she saw it and unwilling to stifle her opinions for the sake of a quiet life, she had an inner serenity that he lacked, and while she lived his earlier prickliness was less obtrusive. Above all, she gave him, for the first time in his life, a secure emotional anchorage. 'Weary and worn, buffeted and discouraged, thinking of giving up the thankless strife and of retiring to books and my own children and household shrines,' he wrote after her death, 'I would flee with her ... and my lady would heal and soothe me with her cheery faith and steady conviction, and send me forth to smite and be smitten.'[2] The phrases were, perhaps, a little histrionic, but they expressed a deeply felt emotion. For MacDonald, the fatherless child, a home and family could not be taken for granted. The clichés of domesticity were not clichés at all: they were a revelation.

Marriage made an important difference to his life in more mundane respects as well. Since leaving Lough, he had managed to keep his head above water financially, but it must have been a hard struggle. No doubt he would have survived in the twilight world of freelance journalism and political lecturing; conceivably, he might even have prospered. But he would have found it hard to prosper and at the same time to devote himself to socialist politics and propaganda. In spite of his journalistic and organizational talents, he had no formal professional or academic qualifications; though he could almost certainly have continued to earn a living as a freelance socialist journalist, it would always have been a precarious one. Margaret was not rich, but her private income was large enough to give him financial independence – an even more valuable asset for an aspiring politician in the days before members of Parliament were paid out of public funds than it is today. The exact nature of her marriage settlement is not clear, but a letter she wrote to MacDonald before their wedding gives a good indication of what its outlines must have been. He father, she wrote, had explained that her mother's marriage settlement was for £5,000, which brought in about £160 a year, and that he had left her £10,000 in his will; before he died, he was planning to give her an allowance of £300 a year.[3] On the assumption that his offer was carried out, and that the £300 a year from her father did not include the income from her mother's marriage settlement, Margaret's private income after her marriage must have been about £460 a year. Later documents in the MacDonald papers make it clear that the capital sum in her trust fund eventually amounted to more than £25,000.[4] These were not princely sums, but they gave MacDonald a degree of economic security unique in his generation of Labour leaders.

Not that the atmosphere at 3 Lincoln's Inn Fields was remotely luxurious. The flat was a hive of activity. There was a constant stream of visitors – Radical intellectuals like J. A. Hobson, Bayswater friends like the Montagus, Labour politicians from the provinces or the colonies, continental socialists like Eduard Bernstein or Jean Jaurès. Every three weeks or so, Margaret gave an At Home, where the young and unknown might find themselves rubbing shoulders with the notabilities of the socialist movement, foreign and domestic, over coffee and ham sandwiches. Soon there were children. Alister, the eldest, was born in 1898. Malcolm followed in 1901; Ishbel, the eldest daughter, in 1903; David in 1904; Joan in 1908; and Sheila in 1910. As well as bringing up a large and turbulent family, Margaret maintained her interest in social work and came to play an increasingly active part in the Labour movement. To give an idea of a few of her activities, after her marriage she belonged to the committees of the Women's Industrial Council and the National Union of Women Workers, busied herself with a multitude of welfare and charitable organizations in the East End and played a leading part in founding the Women's Labour League. But although she coped efficiently with an intimidating mass of public work, there was nothing intimidating about her personality. Her clothes were the despair of her friends, and slightly shocked her much more conventional husband. Once, her colleagues on some committee or other insisted on buying her a new blouse to wear on an important deputation. 'When she appeared and rose to address the powers who were to be persuaded to do righteously,' MacDonald wrote later, 'it was noticed that the new garment had been put on with its back to the front.

I could tell even more grievous tales than that.'[5] She ran her household with the same insouciance. In spite of the efforts of a daily and a char, one of MacDonald's secretaries remembered it years later as a chaos of improvisation:

> It was a big flat, I think on the third floor up a lot of steps. There was a large living room, and a little office where I had my cubby hole, and their bedroom, and the back bedroom for the boys which looked out on to the Holborn Empire – which gave them much pleasure ... They were very untidy – he wasn't, I think he wanted to be tidy, but she never. There was a great big arm-chair, an enormous one full of papers; and I think she kept all the clothes she ever had, because clearing up was rather difficult. You never knew where you might have to go ... I might have to take the baby up to the bath ... or attend to the little girl who was sitting on her pot, or if they were out to take garlands from an Indian visitor.[6]

Ishbel paints a similar picture:

> And did Malcolm say about the conferences that they used to have in our living room? We used to have to get the chairs all round in lines, and then we used to run up and down on the chairs before the conferences started ... I thought that all these delegates were 'delicates', you know, that they were all invalids; and I used to think how strong they looked, being delicate. But some of them were, being frail vegetarians ... I have been told that the only person who could concentrate at some of these committee meetings was my mother; and we used to be crawling around under their feet, under the table, while they were sitting on committee. Or we'd by crying in the corner. And my mother just went on with the business.[7]

When they were first married, MacDonald and Margaret were able to spend most of their evenings together, though, even then, it was a rare week when he had no engagements away from London; and she would sit sewing by the fireside, while he read aloud from Thackeray, Dickens, Scott, Carlyle or Ruskin.[8] As time went on, however, the demands of political life became heavier; and after a long search they bought a weekend cottage at Chesham Bois, in Buckinghamshire, as a refuge from the pressures of their London lives. MacDonald grew vegetables and standard roses in the garden, and they both spent long hours tramping through the Buckinghamshire countryside – hallowed ground to MacDonald because of its associations with Milton and John Hampden – accompanied by a gaggle of sometimes mutinous children. As Malcolm remembered them later, these expeditions had an educational purpose as well as a recreational one. MacDonald would tell the children about the trees and flowers that they passed, and talk about the historical associations of the neighbourhood. Perhaps because of this, Ishbel, who was eighteen months younger than Malcolm, seems to have taken a slightly more jaundiced view of the proceedings. One of her chief memories in later years was of a long walk in tight new boots,

which pinched her ankles. After a while, she plucked up courage to tell her
father that her boots were hurting. 'Oh,' he replied, 'think what a pleasure it will
be when you get them off.'[9]

Another link that bound MacDonald and Margaret together was their attitude
to religion. Curiously enough, they had both feared before their marriage that
this might be a source of strain. In one of her early letters to him, Margaret
wrote:

> You say the gulf between us is most apparent in our religion ... That point
> of religion was the only one about which I wondered whether it was worth
> while to make any explanation in sending you my diary. I have changed or
> developed in that as in other things; but I really know so little & care still
> less what my dogmatic beliefs are now that I left it. You told me you were
> a Unitarian. I daresay I am — I leave out the earlier sentences about Christ
> in the creed if I think about it. But I know that whatever I do believe is only
> a small & distorted part of the real truth, & it never has troubled me much
> what it was at any particular time, so long as I had a practical working faith,
> & thank GOD I can generally keep hold of something of that. I can worship
> just as well with R.C.s or Jews, as with any Protestant, so long as whoever
> they are they seem to be in earnest; & I can get spiritual good from the
> writings of Buddhists or Atheists or anyone who looks beyond the super-
> ficial life. I never now regularly read the Bible or kneel down regularly to
> pray, except in family prayers night & morning & I never have a notion
> what they are about though I have a sort of superstitious feeling that I like
> them to go on![10]

That described MacDonald's attitudes as well, and their family life after their
marriage was conducted in that spirit. On holidays in Lossiemouth they went
every Sunday to the Free Kirk, but in England the only trace of formal church-
going religion that could be detected in their behaviour was that on Sundays,
instead of reading adventure stories aloud to the children, as he liked to do on
weekday evenings when he had the chance, MacDonald would read from the
Bible or from popular science.

It was a revealing choice. Like many of his generation, brought up in the
aftermath of the Darwinian revolution, he spent a large part of his early manhood searching for a meeting-point between the religious inheritance he had
absorbed in childhood and the scientific attitudes he had learned in adolescence.
Darwin, it seemed, had cut the ground from under Biblical revelation and
Christian theology. In that case, what foundation was there for Christian
morality and ethics? MacDonald had already begun to grapple with questions
of this sort in his early days in London; and his attempts to answer them provide
one of the most important themes of the years immediately before and after his
marriage. By now he was playing a fairly prominent part in the Ethical movement. He once took the chair at the annual meeting of the Union of Ethical

Societies, and for a while he wrote regularly for Stanton Coit's paper, the *EthicalWorld*.[11] It was here, and in occasional lectures to Ethical Societies, even more than in his political writings, that his deepest beliefs were expressed; and the attitudes contained in them provide a revealing counterpoint to his politics, then and later.

As we have seen, he lived at the margin of several worlds, in none of which was he wholly at home. He was a Scot, living in London: working-class by origin, but middle-class by occupation: an I.L.P.–er on the executive of the Fabian Society. As we shall see, he was also a born negotiator, adept at finding common ground between opposing views. In his politics, he was, above all, a moderate – willing to see the good in everything, except extremism. In his religious writings, it was the same. Two things stand out from them: a longing for an exalted communion of feeling; and a revulsion from sharp doctrinal precision. He mourned the disappearance of 'the old austere heroism in worship, the simple Covenanter's psalm, the silent Quaker meeting'. Protestantism, he felt, had become 'as formal as the religion of Rome'; its true spirit was now to be found in the Ethical movement rather than in the churches. For the Ethical Societies insisted, above all, 'that all intellectual propositions regarding the nature of the good life should be held as an open question'; and the movement's underlying conception was that 'of man as a rational being, fighting out his spiritual battles within himself, aided neither by the prayers of a priest nor the communion of a church, excepting in so far as man can aid man to noble effort'. These propositions challenged the 'intellectual superstitions and the spiritual formalisms' of the present in precisely the way that the early Protestants had challenged the superstitions and formalisms of the sixteenth century.[12]

It followed that the Ethical movement should avoid anything that smacked of 'a Sinaitic set of commandments' or a 'levitical formulary of conduct'. Doctrinals and creeds, indeed anything 'purely intellectual', should be abandoned as a test of religious feeling. For the religious spirit was an 'indwelling impulse and if an attempt were made to put it into words it would slip away'. Thus dogma was the enemy of the aspirations it presumed to formalize:

> The dogmatists have fought every new truth: every inch of intellectual ground gained has been torn from them, until at last, Liberal theologians have taken courage & bowed to the necessity of applying the idea of evolution to their theologies by admitting that dogma must change with thought, that it is not final, that its content is in a state of flux and flow. This is the end. For a dynamic dogma is like a square circle ... Had it been that by some accident or other we were taught to describe the life of a tree in mathematical phraseology, the biologist's first victory would have been to get the mathematician to admit the existence of a biological mathematics, but his complete triumph would have been reached only when he got the mathematician to see that a biological mathematics was nonsense, that the

processes of his study were not the processes of biological phenomena & that the language of the two groups of sciences could not be interchanged. And so with the religious spirit. A creed can never express it; a theology can never illuminate & interpret it; a scientific treatment of it is error.[13]

He might have been describing the difference between the I.L.P. and the S.D.F. as he saw it.

II

Marriage did not cut down the range of MacDonald's political and journalistic activities. He was still actively nursing Southampton and fulfilling political engagements in a wide range of other places as well. He was still on the executive of the Fabian Society and, in spite of his struggle with the 'old gang', he contributed to an abortive volume of essays which was to have been called 'Studies in Democracy', while later in the decade he was asked to edit a volume of essays for the Society – a project which came to nothing, because of a dispute about who should be asked to publish it.[14] Meanwhile, he wrote regularly for the *New Age*, and contributed a number of articles to the *Dictionary of National Biography*.

In 1896 and the first part of 1897 he also took part in another, and more revealing, journalistic enterprise. During the early 'nineties he had become honorary secretary of a small discussion group of Radical and socialist journalists, economists and would-be politicians; it was called the Rainbow Circle because its first meetings were held in the Rainbow Tavern in Fleet Street. Its members included Herbert Burrows of the S.D.F.; Graham Wallas, the Fabian, later Professor of Political Science at the L.S.E.; Herbert Samuel, the rich young Liberal candidate for South Oxfordshire; J. A. Hobson; and William Clarke, a well-known Radical journalist, who had written one of the most penetrating of the original Fabian essays. Some of its members were Liberals; others had deserted the Liberal Party for independent socialist politics. But they were all convinced collectivists, of one school or another; and they all believed that the apparent disintegration of the Liberal Party, and the collapse of traditional laissez-faire liberalism, had left the forces of progress without an effective political focus.[15]

At first they confined themselves to writing papers and holding discussions, but gradually they found that they had enough in common to justify a more ambitious venture. Early in 1896, apparently at MacDonald's suggestion, the committee of the Rainbow Circle decided to publish a monthly review which would 'afford to the progressive movement in all its aspects – political, ethical, literary etc – a medium of expression such as the Whig movement had in the *Edinburgh Review* and the later Radical and Positivist movements found in the original *Fortnightly'*. The editors of the *Progressive Review* were to be Hobson and Clarke; Herbert Samuel and Russell Rea were directors of the company that published it; and MacDonald was chosen as secretary.[16] From the first, there were dissensions among the inner circle. Clarke was a gifted writer, but a difficult man. He was suspicious of Samuel as a 'man on the make', and feared that he would 'run the craft straight into the harbour of Haldane & Co'. This was objectionable, not merely because he believed that 'the Haldane–Webb–Buxton–Burns gang is played out as a political force & its ideas are dead or else all wrong,' but because he suspected Haldane and the 'Eighty Club gang' of jingoism:

> The real crux of politics is not going to be Socialism and anti-Socialism, but Jingoism and anti-Jingoism. It is well for the directors to know that Hobson & I take strong views on this, & that we are dead against Jingoism in every form (in the form of a huge navy & of an aggressive policy), & that we should make the P.R. anti-Jingo, as against men like Dilke ... who have supported these vile navy estimates.[17]

In spite of these divisions, the *Progressive Review* eventually appeared in October 1896. 'The great emotional product of our age', the opening editorial declared, 'is an ever-widening, ever-deepening dissatisfaction with many of the most distinctive features of our material and moral civilisation, especially as they are reflected in the lives of the poorer members of the working classes.' But that dissatisfaction had no political outlet. The Liberal Party had 'wellnigh done the work which it was fitted to accomplish by its traditional principles and its composition'; in the past it had had 'powerful watchwords and a well-defined policy. It now has no such watchwords, no such policy.' If the Liberal Party was to maintain its claim 'to be regarded as the progressive party of the future', the concept of Liberty must be redefined: 'it must no longer signify the absence of restraint but the presence of opportunity.'[18] The editorial left it unclear whether such a redefinition was to be expected; on the whole, the implication was that although the Liberals had fallen sadly from a state of grace, there was at least a faint chance that they might return to it, with suitable prodding. Meanwhile, the *Progressive Review* pledged itself to an austere political neutrality. The very facts which had made its publication necessary, it wrote gravely, 'preclude us from acting as the mouthpiece of or the advocate of either of the great political parties. Nor can we identify ourselves with the policy of any of the minor sects which claim to be the accredited representatives of progress, though the constructive character of much of our work will place us in closer sympathy with the more thoughtful and practical advocates of experimental collectivism ... than with any other school of politicians.'[19]

On the whole it lived up to its promise. Keir Hardie, leader of the most prominent of the 'minor sects' referred to in the opening editorial, published an article in the December issue, attacking the Liberal leadership for its hostility to the I.L.P. and arguing that the ineffectiveness of the recent Liberal Government proved the impotence of liberalism; Herbert Samuel replied on behalf of the Liberal Party. The contributors to the first volume included Sir Charles Dilke, Havelock Ellis, Eduard Bernstein, Haldane and the Webbs. The editors made a praiseworthy effort to keep their readers in touch with progressive politics on the continent and in North America. But like other left-wing periodicals, the *Progressive Review* discovered that the journalistic equivalent of plain living and high thinking does not attract readers. In March 1897 the circulation was still only seven hundred. This created bad blood within the company, for Clarke was convinced that all would be well if only those responsible for the business side conducted it as efficiently as he conducted the editorial side. Relations reached a breaking-point in July when a furious row broke out between MacDonald and Clarke. It ended in an undignified wrangle between MacDonald and the directors, in which the directors summarily terminated his engagement as secretary because he refused to resign, while he announced that he would take no notice of their decision since the meeting at which it was taken had been held improperly. Soon after the company was wound up. The last issue of the review appeared in September.[20]

III

As will appear later, one of the central themes of MacDonald's career as prime minister and as leader of the Opposition is to be found in his concern for, and knowledge of, foreign policy. The concern began early. He and Margaret were both passionately fond of foreign travel, and her private income made it possible for them to indulge their taste to the full. Their first big excursion was a visit to the United States, made just before the collapse of the *Progressive Review*; both because the visit gave him his first taste of foreign travel, and because it laid the foundations for a lifelong interest in American politics which was to be an important diplomatic asset thirty years later, MacDonald's reactions are of great interest.

He and Margaret sailed from Southampton on the *Paris* at the beginning of August 1897. They were shocked by the class divisions on board and the 'sickening atmospheres' in which the crew had to work, but otherwise the voyage passed pleasantly enough. MacDonald was delighted by the exuberant patriotism of the American passengers. 'The American Drakes and Raleighs', he wrote, 'are living now.' This mood survived even the customs examination at New York. The customs officers were 'civil', and even 'prepared to discuss Bryanism whilst they counted my shirts'. The porters, who could 'render you a service without being flunkies', made him feel that he ought to 'fly to a secluded spot and read Whitman from the beginning again'. But for the rest New York was disappointing:

It was dirty, disorganised, impressive only because of its fearful din. We had to look to our feet, so broken was the road and so bestrewn with filth. The house fronts were hidden by the dirty yellow lines and supports of the overhead railway. The horses were mean and miserable compared with our London drays; the vehicles were ramshackle; the drivers looked as though they had either seen their best days or had not been born to enjoy good ones. Even the finer buildings struck no awe in us. The huge piles of buildings were no more impressive than a six-foot man.[21]

Chicago was worse. MacDonald's indignation at the notorious Chicago stockyards equalled Upton Sinclair's ten years later. 'No one who goes to Chicago should, for any reason whatever, fail to see these shambles ... ,' he wrote indignantly. 'They are sickening beyond description. The men in them are more brutes than the animals they slaughter.' Unlike many British visitors, however – unlike the Webbs, for example, who visited the United States the following year – he saw beneath the faults. Chicago, he wrote, was at bottom a hopeful city: 'you may picture it as a foul depravity if you like, but by doing so you will confess that you do not understand it.'[22] He and Margaret became firm friends with Jane Addams, the pioneer social reformer who worked in the settlement at Hull House; and he paid a glowing tribute to the work she and her colleagues were doing. Above all he responded to the pulsating vitality of the place:

In Chicago everyone wears his hat at the back of his head, everyone speaks at the rate of 200 words a minute, everyone gulps down a stodgy American meal in five minutes, everyone smokes and chews. What a paltry rheumatic Briton one feels in the midst of these electric batteries. Every man you meet down town has in his head a scheme that is to lick creation. It will probably do nothing but burst himself, but people are accustomed to that out here, and think nothing of it. The economy of waste is the basis of American society. Put this man in a well-governed city of clean streets and honest officials, and he will be out of his element. Do not mistake him. He can govern a town as well as anybody, as the marvellous organisation of the World's Fair shows. At heart he is as sound as most of his critics. But he will not settle down to the civic virtues. The West is in his blood. He boasts that he has tried three systems of traction on his streets within ten years; that he can turn rivers upon their courses; that he can build the biggest buildings and pull them down at the quickest rate; that he has grown faster than anybody; that his is the sincerest reverence, as it is for the future and not for the past. He thinks in prairies that are bounded on all sides by the sky and domed above by the heavens. He is the pushfullest and roughest elbower in the world. When he leaves Chicago for ever, and goes to be with the gods, he will sit with Rudyard Kipling, and over their ambrosial feasts will tell of his Board of Trade operations, and Kipling will feel how unromantic and weak his dollar-a-word stories were.[23]

One of MacDonald's main interests was the state of progressive politics in America in the wake of William Jennings Bryan's revivalist campaign for the presidency the year before, and particularly the state of the Labour movement. He was shocked by the violence of American industrial relations, depressed by the political and industrial weakness of the American trade unions, and disappointed to find that the American socialists – partly because of the factiousness of the German immigrant groups in New York – had little influence on American public opinion. He was equally disappointed to find that American society seemed to be growing more stratified, that economic forces were proving stronger than 'the phrases of a Declaration of Independence' and that although there were fewer entrenched obstacles to social equality than in England, the classes did not in fact mix socially. But this, after all, was the turbulent America of the Populist revolt. MacDonald responded to its 'tremendous vitality', and caught the enthusiasm of the reformers 'girding up their loins preparatory to a great campaign against the enemies of the State'. He recognized that it was too soon to predict the final shape of American society: America, he wrote, was 'like a London alderman after a heavy meal. It is digesting.' He hoped that Bryan's campaign for the presidency was the beginning of a new epoch in American politics. Above all, he was encouraged by an apparently universal ferment of self-criticism. 'Every bookseller's stock we examined', he wrote, 'was rich in discussions of the spiritual needs of American society. The one drawback is that up to the present the movement has the suspicion of a class bias, that it is just a little self-conscious ... The moment it becomes fired with democratic enthusiasm it is to be part of the great living national forces of America.'[24]

IV

He returned to a Labour movement which was also beginning to behave more encouragingly than it had done for some time. As we have seen, MacDonald had thrown his lot in with the I.L.P. in 1894. In April 1896, he went to the annual conference as delegate from Southampton. He stood for the N.A.C., and was runner up with 39 votes.[25] In May he was co-opted on to the publishing committee; and when Caroline Martyn, one of the best-loved N.A.C. members, died suddenly at the end of July, MacDonald took her place on the council. At the annual conference in April 1897 he was re-elected on the first ballot. An equally important election came at the N.A.C. meeting a few days later, when he was chosen to serve on the parliamentary and publications sub-committees.[26] Increasingly, it was in the council sub-committees that the real work was done and the real power concentrated and it was in committee that MacDonald excelled. He was already a competent and vigorous speaker, but he was not yet the oratorical spell-binder that he later became, nor the idol of the rank and file.

By the end of the decade the I.L.P. was led, in effect, by four men: Keir Hardie, now in his prime as an agitator of genius and already the symbol of independent labour; Philip Snowden, a thin-lipped Yorkshireman, whose crippled body and biting invective gave him the delusive air of an English Robespierre; Bruce Glasier, a kindly former architect from Glasgow who edited the *I.L.P. News* and who acted as the peacemaker of the group; and MacDonald himself. Of the four, Hardie was pre-eminent in the public eye; to judge by the annual elections to the N.A.C. Snowden and Glasier also eclipsed MacDonald in popularity. MacDonald was re-elected year after year, but he never headed the poll, and in 1898 he was not even elected on the first ballot. At this stage, moreover, he does not seem to have played a prominent part at the annual conferences. His influence on the party's policy, however, became steadily more apparent.

At first his position on the central issues of party strategy and tactics differed significantly from that of the party leadership. In the 1895 elections the 28 I.L.P. candidates polled an average of only 1,500 votes apiece, and Keir Hardie lost his seat at West Ham. MacDonald blamed Hardie's attacks on the Liberals for the debacle. 'The party of progressive ideas', he wrote, 'is being so badly handled that it is almost suicide to join it.'[27] A year later he crossed swords with Hardie on a more fundamental question. In July 1896, he was one of the Fabian delegates to the London Congress of the Socialist International. One of the most important questions at the Congress was whether or not the anarchists should be represented. Hardie and Tom Mann voted in favour of seating the anarchist delegations: the Fabians and the S.D.F. voted with the continental Marxist parties against. MacDonald had a deep loathing for anarchism as a political movement. In his papers there is a curious fragment in his own handwriting, entitled, with heavy sarcasm, 'Whi i am Anarkist'. It purports to contain the anarchist creed, and starts as follows:

1. Bekase I am nobody but myself and nobody is me.
2. Bekase I beleeve in nuthin but voluntary taxashun and pa-ing nothink for alkinhole.
3. Bekase I have the inklinashun to marrie and kannot and bekase the other secks don't like me I am in faver of the State abolishing maridge. I am an ibsinite out and out.
4. Bekase I am not in faver of the State. The State cannot understand me even though it tryd. The Socialists thinks the State can but it Kan't.[28]

It can safely be assumed that he voted with the Fabians and the S.D.F. and against Hardie.

At this stage Hardie's opponents in the I.L.P. seem to have regarded him as at least a potential ally. In September 1896, John Gerrie, the leader of the anti-Hardie faction in the Aberdeen branch, wrote him a long letter appealing for support:

It is said that there is a 'slump' in Labour politics, a want of interest in any sort of politics, that makes it almost impossible to make any headway. A 'slump' if it does exist is not a bad thing if it has not been brought about by the action of our leaders. And even if it were so, it is not altogether an unmixed evil. For a movement like ours does not really make much progress when it is kept going on 'gas' & enthusiasm of the bad sort, & I fear the aerial and insane displays of our leaders during the past two years account for the inevitable 'slump' of wh. complaint is made. But now that we have got to the earth again, let us try to remain there till the next General Election at any rate. I'm going to have a try at it at all costs. As regards these leaders of ours I feel convinced in my own mind that they must go.[29]

There is no evidence that MacDonald agreed with Gerrie about the need to replace the party leadership (though Gerrie would presumably not have written to him in that spirit unless he had expected a sympathetic hearing), but he undoubtedly did agree that the I.L.P. had been too much inclined to ' "gas" sentimentalities', and that it was time to come down to earth with an immediate programme of limited reforms. The I.L.P., he declared in October 1896, had to 'convince the genuine progressist, who is not an out-and-out Socialist, that in our hands the minor (as we think) reforms are safe'.[30]

As time went on, however, the gulf between Hardie and MacDonald shrank. The main difference between them had lain in their respective attitudes to the Radical wing of the Liberal Party. In the early and middle 1890s, Hardie had seen the Liberal Party as a bankrupt force and had given the impression that for him one Liberal was as bankrupt politically as any other. MacDonald, by contrast, never altogether abandoned his old dream of a progressive coalition, embracing advanced Liberals as well as moderate socialists. He was prepared to fight the Liberals if he had to. After his return from the United States he threw himself into an energetic, though unsuccessful, campaign as I.L.P. candidate for South Hackney in the L.C.C. election—provoking fierce opposition from the local Liberals, who alleged that he had been selected 'in a small private room outside the division', and attacked him as a wrecker who might 'let in the enemy'. In his programme he demanded that the council should employ its own labour, insert fair-wages clauses into all contracts and 'accept responsibility for the provision of work for unemployed citizens who are neither criminals nor loafers'. The reason for his candidature, he explained, was that the South Hackney Liberal Association appeared to think that it had a 'right as a partisan body to both South Hackney seats' — a right which he would never concede.[31] But even when he was most critical of the Liberal Party, he took care to leave the door open to future co-operation with its Radical wing. In March 1897, for example, he wrote a long letter to the Bradford Observer, attacking the Halifax Liberals for their hostility to the I.L.P. at a current by-election. 'No one hates Toryism more than I do,' he exclaimed, 'and yet no one distrusts Liberalism more.' But he added characteristically that he had never been 'one of those ... members of the Independent Labour Party who regard "independent" as meaning "isolated". I have never been averse to talking over difficulties with the genuine Radicals still remaining in the Liberal Party. I have never given up hopes that a limited and temporary trial might be given to an electoral co-operation in certain favoured constituencies.'[32]

In the mid-1890s, Hardie's attitude had set the tone for the rest of the I.L.P. At the end of the decade, however, there was a distinct change of emphasis. At the N.A.C. meeting in July 1897, it was decided that, instead of concentrating on a few seats at the next general election, the I.L.P. would try to 'obtain the highest aggregate Socialist vote possible', by running candidates wherever the prospects were 'fairly satisfactory'. The rank and file proved, however, more cautious than the leadership. At the 1898 conference this section of the N.A.C. report was deleted, and the N.A.C.'s policy reversed.[33] In May 1898 the I.L.P. News commented on the 'enormous disadvantage our party and the cause of Socialism and Labour suffers by the absence of a single voice for Socialism in Parliament. A dozen or so energetic men in the next House of Commons would, in the opinion of many, at once lift the party into a position of influence and power.'[34] Later in the year the N.A.C. decided to fight only twenty-five seats; and in January 1899, Hardie and MacDonald published a joint article in the Nineteenth Century, setting out the new policy. The style and tone were unmistakably MacDonald's, and there can be little doubt that he was, in fact, the author.

The new policy had disturbing implications. If only twenty-five seats were to be contested, the I.L.P. might hold the balance between Liberals and Conservatives elsewhere. If those twenty-five seats were to be won, Liberal candidates would have to stand aside. The logic pointed to an arrangement between the Liberals and the I.L.P., of the sort which MacDonald had made at Southampton. But if such an arrangement were reached, what would become of the party's independence? These considerations were not stated openly in the Nineteenth Century article, but they were clearly present in the background; the result was a masterly demonstration of tightrope-walking. MacDonald and Hardie repeated the standard I.L.P. argument that 'Liberalism had done its work.' They reaffirmed that 'for the Independent Labour Party to give up its independence would be to give up its life.' But they interpreted independence in a remarkably modest way. The very fact that the I.L.P. had established itself as an independent force, they argued, meant that it could now identify itself with immediate reforms on which Radicals and socialists were in agreement, without fearing that it might be swallowed up in 'a shiftless opportunism'. From there it was a short step to claiming that 'in so far as co-operation with kindred sections is possible while retaining our freedom, there is no barrier to it in our methods or tradition.' Then followed an announcement that the I.L.P. would contest only twenty-five seats at the next election. The article ended with an adroit plea for Liberal neutrality in those seats, and a guarded hint that the I.L.P.

would support a Liberal Government in Parliament. 'This announcement', Hardie and MacDonald wrote, 'ought to satisfy those who are never tired of claiming that they go with us nine tenths of the way, for they must see that the conclusion from that is ... that they should stand aside in a number of constituencies, provided we keep to our own ground. It should be quite possible for them, knowing our intentions thus early, to make provision against a collision which must dissipate what little hope they have of a majority. To make that majority impossible is not our business. Should it be elected and attempt to pass measures of real benefit to the country, we, as an independent factor in the House, should be bound by our principles to support it.'[35]

The N.A.C. report to the 1899 conference warmly endorsed the *Nineteenth Century* article. The party was advised to fight only twenty-five seats at the next election; and an attempt to reject the advice was defeated by 59 votes to 50. The report stressed the need for caution in dealing with other parties. But it went out of its way to add that 'it is not alleged that such an alliance as is now in operation in France and Belgium between the Socialist and Radical parties is for ever impossible here.' 'When the Radical party has an organisation apart and separate from official Liberalism,' it pointed out, 'the situation will be to that extent changed.'[36]

In the spring and summer of 1899 it looked as though that day might not be long delayed. The Liberal Party was bitterly divided; its divisions seemed to reflect fundamental cleavages of doctrine as well as the jangling personal antipathies of a party which has been out of power too long. Others, besides the I.L.P. council, expected a Radical secession, and many Radicals seemed genuinely anxious for closer co-operation with Independent Labour. In July 1899, MacDonald wrote to Hardie:

> I met a Mrs. Cobb ... the other day & found her a strong sympathiser of ours ... She asked if we would be willing to attend a meeting which she would be prepared to get up at which leading Radical MPs would be present and 'have it out'. I replied that as I was an official of the ILP I could say nothing definite upon that point; that my personal feeling was that if there was to be no attempt at negotiation but simply an exchange of opinion either formal or informal, some typical ILP-ers should go ... the meeting is coming off on the 25th inst. I have seen the list of names & think it good. It includes C. P. Scott, Logan, Wedderburn, Harwood, G. W. E. Russell. Now, the question is, should I go to the meeting? It is to be informal, no resolutions are to be passed, no negotiations attempted. As I understand it, the purpose is to get an interchange of opinion upon whether it is likely that for any purpose there can be an independent co-operation between advanced & sturdy Radicals and ourselves.[37]

'Advanced and sturdy Radicals': here was the key. When necessary MacDonald was as happy to attack official Liberalism as were the rest of the I.L.P.

In October 1899, he was adopted as I.L.P. candidate for Leicester, and his adoption speech was largely devoted to an attack on the Liberal leadership on the grounds that it had been 'kept democratic' only by the threat of destruction.[38] But while official Liberalism was to be denounced, advanced Radicals were to be treated with wary cordiality. In February 1900, MacDonald stood once again for the L.C.C., this time as 'Labour and Progressive' candidate in Woolwich. Two seats were vacant; and the second 'Labour and Progressive' candidate was a local Radical. MacDonald was described in the local press as the 'nominee of the Labour Party'. At his adoption meeting—convened by the Plumstead Progressive Association—a motion was moved rejecting his candidature on the grounds that he 'came as an extreme Socialist, posing as an advocate of the claims of the working classes'. The motion was rejected, and a disgruntled Progressive promptly stood as an Independent.[39] At the I.L.P. conference a few weeks later MacDonald was denounced for having run in double harness with a Progressive.[40] But although he had not won the seat, he could at least argue that he had performed a valuable service in driving a wedge between the Radical and moderate wings of Woolwich Liberalism.

V

By now the prospects for co-operation between the I.L.P. and the Radical wing of the Liberal Party had improved still further. In the summer of 1899, the Liberal Party's internal conflicts were given new ferocity by the approach of an aggressive war against the Boer Republics in South Africa; in October the war broke out, and the shape of the political landscape for some years was determined by the ensuing divisions. These divisions cut across party lines, and even across ideological lines. Nonconformist businessmen found themselves co-operating with socialist agitators; Robert Blatchford, the editor of the *Clarion*, who had often criticised Hardie and the I.L.P. from an extreme socialist standpoint, found himself supporting a war which had been started by a Conservative Cabinet. The strength of these new alignments was felt particularly keenly by those opposed to the war. The 'pro-Boers' were in a minority. They were vilified on imperialist platforms and in the imperialist press; their meetings were broken up; sometimes they risked physical assault. Inevitably, their opposition to the war took on the character of a moral crusade, over-shadowing mundane concerns. The I.L.P. threw itself into this crusade with special fervour. 'On the Tory benches', the normally peaceable *I.L.P. News* wrote in a characteristic passage, 'sit the obscene pack yelping for more blood to appease its hungry malice.'[41] In such an atmosphere, I.L.P.-ers seemed to have more in common with an old-fashioned Gladstonian Radical like John Morley, who also opposed the war, than with collectivist neo-Radicals like Haldane who supported it—or than with the Fabian Society which was divided.

The position adopted by the Fabian Society had little effect on the rest of the Labour movement. It had a great effect on MacDonald, whose differences with the 'old gang' now came to a head. Intellectually, as well as emotionally, he abominated violence and detested war; the whole imperialist ethos by which this particular war was justified seemed to him to be based on a fallacy. The imperialists of the late nineteenth century claimed to carry with them the blessings of civilization and progress. For MacDonald, civilization was above all an organic growth, which could not be transplanted from one society to another. The 'lowest barbarian' had his own civilization: 'His resistance to civilization, as *we* understand it, is not simply that *he* does not understand it, but that he has a civilization of his own which he *does* understand.' Indeed, the very fact that Western imperialism rested on force proved the ineffectiveness of its civilizing mission. 'A system of government that, on the admission of everybody, would vanish within twenty-four hours after our troops are withdrawn,' MacDonald wrote of the British presence in Egypt, 'is a very artificial contribution to the civilization of the world.'[42]

Imperialist arguments were bad: imperialist motives were worse. 'Further extensions of Empire,' MacDonald warned in 1898, 'are only the grabbings of millionaires on the hunt.'[43] The Boer War, with its pervasive odour of trickery, corruption and demagogy, seemed to him a perfect example of what he had in mind. But the Fabian executive refused to condemn the war, partly because it had always regarded foreign affairs as lying outside the Society's province, and partly because some influential Fabians supported annexation. A special members' meeting was held at the beginning of December, at which S. G. Hobson moved a resolution condemning imperialism. Bernard Shaw, on behalf of the majority of the executive, moved what was in effect a pro-war amendment – exclaiming afterwards, in a letter to MacDonald:

Democratic sentiment be blowed! do you want to go back to the old Radicalism that always had a foaming bowl of virtuous indignation on tap, and never a practical suggestion? ... Radicalism we found to be sentiment without administration; and we opposed to it administration without sentiment. Now, if you can draft a resolution that will combine the two, let us have it by all means. I have done my best to avert the fight for which the democratic spirit and the large grasp of human ideas is always spoiling, and for which the jingo spirit is no doubt equally ready. If you won't take my way, and wont find a better way, then punch one another's heads and be damned. Only *do* remember, if you insist on discussing the rightness and wrongness of the war, that the Boers declared it, and that what forced them to declare it was the absolutely unanimous declaration of the English, Daily Chronicle and all, that the Outlanders must be enfranchised ... I dont believe that the causes of the war menace our democracy. Quite the contrary. I dont believe that the capitalists have created or could have created the situation they are now exploiting for all it is worth. I regard the Transvaal Republic as a relic of the order of things which we are making impossible; and I am quite ready for annexation provided we introduce our higher social organization there, just as I should be on the side of the Government if the manufacturers started a civil war against the Workmen's Compensation Act. In short I am not old Radical, but International Collectivist — if the name Imperialist is too connotative of Capitalism.[44]

MacDonald was not appeased. On January 12th, 1900, he persuaded the executive to hold a referendum to discover whether the Society wanted an 'official pronouncement on the War'. The results came in at the end of February. There were 217 votes in favour of a pronouncement, and 259 against. On April 20th the executive noted the collective resignation of thirteen members of the Society, of whom MacDonald was one.[45]

Meanwhile, he was playing a more active part in another realignment of forces, more far-reaching than any brought about by events in South Africa. For the I.L.P. the mid-1890s had been, in MacDonald's words, a time 'of fighting, of murmuring, of dreary desert trudging'.[46] By the end of the decade, Canaan at last came in sight. The I.L.P. was no nearer to establishing itself as a mass socialist party on the continental model. Instead it was able to buttress its weakness with the financial and numerical strength of the trade unions. At the Cardiff congress in 1895 the T.U.C. had changed its rules in order to strengthen the position of the large, anti-socialist unions and to prevent leading socialists, who were neither active workers nor full-time union officials, from attending Congress as delegates. But as time went on a combination of industrial reverses, unfavourable judicial decisions, and persistent socialist pressure slowly convinced the union leaders that if they were to protect the interests of their members they would have to play a more active and more independent part in parliamentary politics. A number of unions took steps to run candidates at the next general election. In 1898, the T.U.C. passed a resolution urging trade unionists to support the 'working-class Socialist parties', and elected a Parliamentary Committee less hostile to socialism than any of its predecessors had been. The culmination of this process came at Plymouth in 1899. The Railway Servants proposed a resolution requiring the Parliamentary Committee to call a conference of 'all the co-operative, socialistic and other working organisations', which would 'devise ways and means for securing the return of an increased number of labour members to the next Parliament'. It was carried on a card vote by 546,000 to 434,000.

It used to be thought that the Railway Servants' resolution was drafted at the *Labour Leader* offices, either by MacDonald or by MacDonald and Hardie in collaboration. Dr Pelling, however, has shown that it originated from the Doncaster branch of the union, and there is no evidence that it was stimulated from London.[47] But, even if MacDonald and Hardie cannot claim the credit for drawing up the resolution, it seems fairly clear that they must have been in touch with those who did. The N.A.C. report to the 1899 Leeds conference of the I.L.P., which met some months before the T.U.C., declared that the party was 'on the eve' of 'perhaps the greatest labour and democratic combination which has yet been witnessed', while, at a mass meeting in the Leeds Theatre Royal, MacDonald announced that 'the time was not far distant when the I.L.P., the trade-unionists and the co-operators would be working hand in hand for one common object.'[48] In any case, the significance of the Railway Servants' resolution lay less in what it said than in the opportunity which it created. MacDonald and Hardie exploited that opportunity with great tactical skill. By the end of November, they had drawn up a rough scheme, to be used as a basis for negotiations with the T.U.C. Parliamentary Committee. It contained three essential points. Candidates were to be run by trade-union, socialist and other labour bodies independently of the Liberal and Conservative parties; each party to the alliance would run its own candidates and find its own money; most important of all, a joint committee of the organizations concerned would be established to act as the 'political committee of the combined forces'.[49] At the beginning of December, representatives of the Fabian Society, the I.L.P., the S.D.F. and the Parliamentary Committee met together in London to prepare the resolutions and agenda for the conference envisaged in the Railway Servants' resolution. In essentials, the scheme prepared by Hardie and MacDonald was accepted, and by the end of the month MacDonald was sufficiently confident to ask the readers of the *Ethical World*: 'Are we really to witness the birth of a genuine Labour Party in the House of Commons? ... If the Conference should be a success, and a Labour Party spring out of it, it is only extending to Parliamentary contests a combination which has been found to be of considerable strength in municipal contests. But, as Parliament is infinitely greater than a municipal council, so this projected combination is infinitely greater than anything which has gone before it.'[50] Two months later the conference assembled in that 'cathedral of nonconformity',[51] the Memorial Hall in Farringdon Street.

On the surface, it was an unimpressive affair. There were only 129 delegates, representing a total membership of 570,000 – less than half the total represented at the T.U.C. But under the surface, the proceedings were as dramatic as any in recent British history. Four main tendencies were represented. There was an out-and-out Marxist contingent from the S.D.F. There was a group of Lib-Lab trade-union leaders, who probably expected the conference to fail, and who might not have been altogether displeased if it had. There was a group of more advanced trade unionists, who wanted a new party to emerge, but who resented socialist attempts to capture it and wished to keep it firmly under the thumb of the Parliamentary Committee. Finally, there was the I.L.P. Its chief representative was Hardie, whose generalship was decisive. On all the critical questions, the I.L.P.'s position was accepted. The conference set up a permanent organization to achieve the aims set out in the Railway Servants' resolution It rejected a suggestion that Labour candidates should come exclusively from the working class — thus administering, as MacDonald wrote shortly afterwards, 'a well-deserved rebuke to those who suppose that the Labour Movement is a Movement of trades and not of opinions ... [N]o worship of labour, and no desire to be out-and-out democratic, must ever obscure the fact that the Labour Movement is a Movement of opinion first and last.'[52] An S.D.F. resolution committing the new organization to the class war was rejected; a trade-union amendment which would have left future Labour M.P.s 'entirely free on all purely political questions' was withdrawn. The object of the new party was defined, in terms proposed by Hardie, as the establishment of 'a distinct Labour group in Parliament, who shall have their own Whips and agree upon their own policy'. The size of the executive committee of the new party was reduced from the eighteen originally proposed to twelve, but the socialist representation on it was reduced only from six to five. Lastly, but no less momentously, the conference agreed unanimously that the secretary of the new organization should be MacDonald.[53] At the age of thirty-three he was about to begin the most enduring part of his life's work.

CHAPTER 5

Building a party

I

THE Memorial Hall conference had not created a Labour Party: at most it had opened the door to one. Only time could tell whether the Labour movement would walk through it. That it did so in the end was due to the anonymous devotion of thousands of ordinary men and women and to the impersonal pressures of social and economic change. It was also due to MacDonald's drive, organizing ability and political flair. The new committee which had been set up at the Memorial Hall was, at most, a loose alliance of sovereign bodies, each jealous of its own autonomy and each suspicious of its new allies. As its secretary, MacDonald was the one man in the entire movement who had a greater personal stake in the alliance as such than in any one of its constituent parts. He alone was elected by the whole conference: he alone was forced by his position to think and plan in terms of the alliance as a whole. From the first, he threw himself into the task of welding it into a united party, and it soon became clear that he had the right combination of talents for the task. As the novelist Richard Whiteing put it, he was 'a Highlander by race, doubled with a Lowlander in his outlook on life':[1] he had the antennae necessary for political generalship, and at the same time the appetite for detail necessary for creating a party machine. Even in his early thirties, he also had a promise of the personal magnetism necessary for the leadership of men and women.

In part, this came from the fine features and splendid presence which made him, according to the *Labour Leader*, one of the two best-looking men in the I.L.P.[2] In part, it came from a more elusive quality. 'Mr Macdonald', the *Leicester Mercury* wrote at about this time, 'is a tall, strong, vigorous young man, and has evidently got a lot of fight in him. He appears to have a great deal of nervous electric energy as well as abundant muscular force. He stands upright with every inch of his measurement — with conscious power.'[3] This 'nervous electric energy' — the most mysterious and at the same time the most valuable attribute a political leader can possess — lasted to the end. In his later years, it was clouded by personal unhappiness and a kind of brooding melancholy, which made him seem aloof and unapproachable to all but a few intimates. But the clouds had not yet descended. The tensions left by his childhood and early manhood had not disappeared: nor had the faintly self-righteous truculence that accompanied them. In 1901 he was returned unopposed to the L.C.C. at a by-election for Central Finsbury. Within a few months, he had embarked on another bitter struggle with Sidney Webb, over the policy of the Technical Education Board of which Webb was chairman, and before long he had mustered enough support from the Progressive caucus on the board to drive Webb out of the chairmanship;[4] though Webb was a formidable opponent, adept at turning any compromise to his own advantage, it is hard to believe that the battle need have been fought with the ferocity which MacDonald brought to it. New enmities were prosecuted as ferociously. Early in 1905, the Countess of Warwick, a recent and glamorous aristocratic convert to socialism, who had had the temerity to align herself with the S.D.F., sent MacDonald an invitation to a dinner at Warwick House for Labour candidates and their wives, to 'talk over many mutual interests'. It was doubtful, he replied icily, whether

a talk over matters would be of very much value. You have very suddenly come amongst us from totally different circumstances and have taken sides instantly. Our people seem to be inclined to make full use of the advertisement which you undoubtedly give us, and, so far as I am concerned, I prefer to allow things to run their course. Far be it from me to put any obstacles in your way if you sincerely desire the good of our cause, but at the same time I have doubts as to the permanent good which can be done to a democratic movement by the exploitation of an aristocratic convert, and I am therefore compelled to refrain from joining in the process. I am sure you are perfectly well aware that the crowds who applaud you and the people who gather round your tables do so because you are a Countess and would neglect you if you were Mrs Smith. It may be, as some of my friends cynically say that there is a divine economy in these things and that we should exploit sycophancy. That however is not in accordance with my conception of the Socialist and Labour movement nor is it consistent either with your self respect or with my own. I also regret some of the methods which you have thought fit to adopt, but of course if our movement does not resent them — well I can but regret. I think you had better do your best honestly in accordance with the spirit of Socialism and not trouble about what I or anyone else thinks. In due course we shall all meet somewhere doing our work if we remain steadfast.[5]

But, although the old touchiness was still there, there was a gayer and more emollient side to MacDonald's character as well; and in these years it prevailed more frequently than before. In a letter to Margaret after the I.L.P. conference at York, in 1903, he wrote:

We stayed at a fine old hotel at York with rambling passages upstairs & downstairs; & as there was a crowd of us together (something like Leicester) we have had a very merry time of it ... At half past one this morning the innocent Jowett was shouldering the fire irons & marching around the room singing: 'We're all brothers', but as Mrs Hardie was there and Mrs Pankhurst had only just gone to bed it was not quite true.[6]

The picture of MacDonald joining in the high jinks of an I.L.P. conference at 1.30 in the morning squares badly with later Labour legend. But if that side of his character had not existed he would never have been able to pull his loose-knit new committee together or to turn it into an effective political machine. Even established political parties have to be persuaded rather than driven; and the Labour Representation Committee was very far from being an established party. Holding it together required, not only drive and organizing ability, but tact, understanding and the ability to do business with a wide variety of often prickly people. Sometimes, MacDonald's tact failed him. In the summer of 1904 he went on holiday to Italy to recover from an appendix operation, accompanied by Keir Hardie, who had had a similar operation the year before. In a letter to Bruce Glasier, Hardie complained sourly that 'Mac is not an ideal travelling companion … He wanted to see everything not so much I think from any real interest as to be able afterwards to talk at dinner tables about what he had seen'[7] – a complaint which has to be met alongside MacDonald's complaint that when he wanted to rest, Hardie wanted to 'go on the spree'.[8] On the whole, however, MacDonald's relations with the rest of the inner circle of the I.L.P. seem to have been reasonably harmonious; and, although he encountered some opposition from the T.U.C. old guard, it was directed against his policy, not against his personality. MacDonald was far from being a back-slapping extrovert, but as he was to show at more than one tense international conference in later years, he had an unusual capacity to see other people's points of view and find common ground with them. If he had not, the Labour Party might never have come into existence.

His political philosophy was an asset as well. The Memorial Hall conference had struck a precarious balance between the I.L.P. and the more advanced trade unions; and it was on the preservation of that balance that the success of their alliance would depend. For the most part, the trade unions represented at the conference saw it as a way of defending their interests, not as a way of changing society. Many of them were slow to shake off the habits of the old Labour Electoral Association; any prospect that the new alliance would be captured for socialism might send them back to the Liberal fold they had only just left. The I.L.P.'s position was very nearly the opposite. From its point of view, the purpose of the alliance was to harness the trade-union whale to the socialist minnow: it would be self-defeating if its only result was that the minnow was swallowed up. This balance of forces was carried through on to the committee. Even its name – 'Labour Representation Committee' rather than 'Labour Party' – implied a compromise between the thorough-going independence of the I.L.P. and the cautious attitudes of the older trade-union leaders. The same applied to its composition. The I.L.P. generally had a majority, just as it had had at the Memorial Hall; but that majority consisted in part of trade-union representatives who were socialists as well. This same balance was reflected in MacDonald's own person. He was a socialist, and a member of the I.L.P. council; his presence as secretary was, in itself, a tacit guarantee that socialism was not being submerged. But his conception of socialism — with its insistence on the slow and gradual processes of social evolution, and its conciliatory attitude to Liberalism and the Liberal Party — contained little to alarm a non-socialist trade-union leader. He was, in fact, not only the ideal secretary for the Labour Representation Committee, but the ideal apologist: uniquely qualified to interpret the socialist wing of the alliance to the trade-union wing, and to achieve a theoretical synthesis between the aims of the first and the day-to-day practices of the second.

II

For the time being, however, these qualifications had little scope. It was not at all clear that the committee would survive, still less that it would play a significant part in Labour politics. In May 1900, the total membership affiliated to it was 187,000;[9] with subscriptions fixed at ten shillings per thousand affiliated members, its income was exiguous. MacDonald was unpaid. Keir Hardie proposed that the secretary should receive a fee of £50 for the year, but the matter was deferred to a later date.[10] It was not until January 1901 that MacDonald received any payment for his services, and then it was only twenty guineas.[11] The committee had no office. It met in a small back room at the MacDonalds' flat in Lincoln's Inn Fields, in quarters so cramped that on at least one occasion a committee member had to sit out a meeting perched on the coal scuttle.[12] MacDonald's first act as secretary was to send out a circular to trade-union secretaries, urging them to put the advantages of affiliation to their organizations[13] but by September the total affiliated membership was still only 278,000.[14]

While it was still in this embryonic state, the committee was called upon to face its first big challenge. In September 1900, the Government went to the country. In the circumstances, the L.R.C. could feel moderately complacent about its performance. Two of its fifteen candidates were returned — Keir Hardie at Merthyr, and Richard Bell, the secretary of the Amalgamated Society of Railway Servants, at Derby. But they had both stood in two-member constituencies; Bell had faced only one Liberal opponent, while Hardie had been supported by one of the two Liberal candidates against the other. In Leicester, MacDonald was not so lucky. It too was a two-member constituency, but there were two Liberal candidates, one of whom was Henry Broadhurst, the veteran

Liberal-Labour leader who had represented the town since 1894. With two Liberal candidates in the field and no divisions in the Liberal camp to exploit, Mac-Donald could not expect to win the seat; in the special circumstances of the so-called 'Khaki election', his chances were minimal.

When the campaign began, the Unionist committee-rooms were decorated with coloured posters showing British soldiers under fire in South Africa; more galling still from MacDonald's point of view, Conservative womenfolk were out in force to rub home the moral. 'The lady in fine attire is no new thing in Parliamentary elections,' he wrote indignantly. 'This time she has been especially busy ... I have seen her push her way into shops and restaurants; I have seen her parade the streets smiling at every rake who looked into her eyes; I have seen her inhale with a smirk of pleasure the breathed fumes of beer and tobacco — and they went in twos and threes, poor miserable wretches, and voted for her and against themselves.'[15]

MacDonald could do little to counteract the smirking Conservative ladies, but he tried hard to counteract the patriotic coloured posters on the Unionist committee-rooms. The war was unnecessary, he argued in the opening speech of his campaign, but once it had started it had become 'too sacred a matter' for the platform. He intended to fight the election 'upon Leicester rather than Johannesburg, upon London rather than upon Pretoria ... upon the problems which faced the wage earners rather than upon the problems of the capitalists who did their mining for gold and diamonds in South Africa by black labour'.[16] Accordingly, he concentrated on the nationalization of the mines, the taxation of land values to finance old-age pensions, and the provision of low interest rates for local authorities which might wish to borrow money for working-class housing.[17] But, although he managed to sidestep the problems raised by the war, he could not sidestep the even more awkward problems raised by his Liberal opponents. In order to justify his candidature in the face of the obvious Liberal taunt that he would split the anti-Conservative vote, he was forced to draw his listeners' attention to the inadequacies of the Liberal Opposition in the House of Commons; before long, criticisms of the Liberal Party figured at least as prominently in his speeches as did attacks on the Government. After the results were declared on October 2nd, mutual bitterness between Liberalism and Labour reached a new height. Broadhurst held his seat with more than 10,000 votes; but Walter Hazell, the second Liberal candidate, was defeated — polling only 8,528 to the Conservative candidate's 9,066. MacDonald, with 4,164, had only just improved on the I.L.P.'s vote in 1895 and could plausibly be accused of having let the Conservative in.

The immediate consequence was to drive a further wedge between the Liberals and the I.L.P. Hazell sent round a pained circular to his supporters, alleging that there had been an alliance between 'the I.L.P., the Tories and the Publicans'. MacDonald immediately dispatched a still more pained letter of protest to Hazell, asking him what he meant by the circular and warning that any correspondence between them would be published.[18] Hazell replied blandly that if MacDonald remembered 'the many public house windows which contained arguments against the Liberals, and note the analysis of the voting, I think you will see that there are sufficient grounds for the statements which I made'. MacDonald thereupon returned to the charge with an even longer letter of protest, accusing Hazell of making accusations which were 'annoying, mean and untrue', and of doing so 'recklessly, without thought, without evidence, [and] without justification'.[19] In the long run, however, the more temperate reaction of the Liberal *Leicester Daily Post* turned out to be more significant as well. It compared Hazell's defeat to the last great Liberal setback in Leicester, about forty years before, when the Conservatives had won a seat at a by-election because two Liberal candidates had stood against each other. 'The lesson ... ', it wrote, 'had a salutary, if belated, effect. Thus menaced by the loss of both their seats by their fratricidal wrangles, the Liberals promptly closed up their ranks, and once again became thoroughly united.'[20]

III

Between 1900 and 1906, most of MacDonald's energies were absorbed by the wearing, repetitive and time-consuming tasks of party management. From the L.R.C.'s offices in the back room of his flat he created, out of nothing, the rudiments of an organization; he kept a watchful eye on developments in the constituencies, helping to promote Labour candidatures in suitable seats and keeping them out of unsuitable ones; he did his best to dig himself in as prospective Labour candidate for Leicester; from 1901 to 1904, as we have seen, he represented Central Finsbury on the L.C.C.; last, but by no means least, he maintained intermittent contact with prominent Liberals who might be of use to him or to his cause – notably, with George Cadbury, the pro-Boer chocolate-manufacturer and philanthropist, who owned the *Daily News* and who hoped for an alliance of all the progressive parties against the Unionists, and with Jesse Herbert, the private secretary to the Liberal chief whip, Herbert Gladstone. His activities as a journalist and publicist were equally impressive. He kept up a formidable output of articles and pamphlets, arguing the L.R.C.'s case on the issues of the day; and towards the end of the period under discussion he even found time to write an extended work of socialist theory. From 1901 to 1905 he also wrote a weekly column for Pethick-Lawrence's *Echo*.[21] It was called 'Work and the Workers' and signed: 'Spectator'. The true authorship was kept secret, and the opportunities it presented for political kite-flying were exploited to the full. As 'Spectator', MacDonald intervened assiduously in elections to the T.U.C. Parliamentary Committee, supporting candidates friendly to the L.R.C. and denigrating its opponents. When his committee was under attack, he sprang to its defence; when the cause of moderate socialism seemed to be in danger from the zealots of the S.D.F., he rushed to the attack. From time to time, he even found it possible to award a judicious pat on the back to the ubiquitous and indefatigable secretary of the L.R.C., to denounce his enemies and to expose their machinations against him.

Little by little his efforts began to bear fruit. At the beginning of 1901 – a year after its foundation – the L.R.C.'s total membership was still only 350,000. Its finances were still meagre, and its organization fragmentary. In the summer of 1901, however, its prospects were transformed by the Law Lords' judgment in the famous Taff Vale case between the Taff Vale railway and the Amalgamated Society of Railway Servants. The effect of its judgment was to make it possible for a trade union to be sued in the courts for damages caused by its members in pursuance of a trade dispute. At one blow, the unions lost the legal immunity which they thought they had enjoyed for the last thirty years. A more persuasive argument for increased labour representation would have been hard to find. 'Trade unionism is being assailed, not by what the law says of it, but by what judges think the law ought to say of it,' MacDonald wrote in his column in the *Echo*. 'That being so, it becomes necessary for the unions to place men in the House of Commons, to challenge the decisions which I have no doubt will follow this.'[22] In November, he sent out a circular on behalf of the L.R.C., arguing that no reform could be expected from the existing House of Commons, since both parties benefited from the unsatisfactory position in which the unions had been placed, and that the remedy lay in political action by the entire trade-union movement, acting in concert with other labour organizations.[23] Little by little the moral sank in. In the first six months of 1902 the membership of the L.R.C. rose by 238,000. By September 1902, it was more than 700,000.[24]

Membership was one essential ingredient of political strength; another was money. As early as August 1900, the Fabian Society had circularized the trade unions with a scheme to finance Labour members of Parliament, but at the I.L.P. conference in 1901 MacDonald had opposed the suggestion on the grounds that it was premature.[25] Here, too, Taff Vale changed the situation. In December 1901 the miners decided to institute a levy of 1s. a head to set up a Parliamentary Fund; and at its Birmingham Conference in 1902 the L.R.C. decided in principle to follow the miners' example. 'Hitherto Labour war chests have been left in the possession of the unions which filled them, and were only used for candidates connected with those unions … ,' MacDonald explained in a jubilant column in the *Echo*. 'Now we are to have a Trade Union levy paid into a common fund, and Labour candidates – not necessarily Trade Unionists – run from that fund … if the Committee responsible for drafting [the scheme] has enough statesmanship in it to steer clear of the difficulties, the next election will be unique in the annals of Labour.'[26] By July a scheme had been drawn up; and in September the L.R.C. sent out a circular commending it to affiliated organizations. The essential points were that the Parliamentary Fund was to be raised by a levy of 1d. per affiliated member per annum, which would yield £3,000 a year from a membership of 700,000; that M.P.s elected under L.R.C. auspices would receive £200 a year from the fund; and that the L.R.C. would help to pay the election expenses of its candidates.[27] If the scheme were approved at the 1903 conference – and it almost certainly would be – the L.R.C. would command financial resources on a different scale from those of its predecessors.

It remained to translate money and members into seats. Labour representation had been talked of for thirty years. Every attempt to secure it on a significant scale had foundered on the rock of Liberal opposition. Ever since the election MacDonald had recognized that this rock must somehow be removed: by displays of force at the constituency level, by diplomacy at the national level, by a combination of both. Not long after the election he and Pease had drawn up a memorandum for the L.R.C., arguing that its first task should be to win the seats it had just contested, and suggesting that the way to win them was to 'secure sufficient local importance for the combinations which ran our candidates to enable those committees at the next contest to compel Liberal Associations to stand aside'.[28] But this was only part of the answer. In October 1901, J. A. Hobson, MacDonald's old collaborator of Rainbow Circle days, published an article in the Echo, calling for a 'New Party' of pro-Boer Radicals, trade unionists and members of the I.L.P. In his reply, MacDonald dismissed Hobson's suggestion as premature; instead, he urged that Radicals and Labour men should arrange to help each other electorally 'by securing for each other opportunities of contesting seats unhampered by third candidates'.[29] At the same time, he kept in touch with Liberal Party headquarters. In March 1901, he had an interview with Jesse Herbert, of which we know only that Herbert remembered it afterwards 'with pleasure'.[30] The following year he sent Herbert a copy of the official report of the L.R.C. annual conference in Birmingham – no doubt drawing his attention to the resolution on the Parliamentary Fund.[31] In August 1902, his bargaining position was still further improved when David Shackleton, the Lancashire weavers' leader, was returned unopposed as L.R.C. candidate at a by-election for Clitheroe – the local Liberals having been persuaded by the strength and determination of the Labour forces in the constituency not to run a candidate.

At this point, however, MacDonald's interest in the outside world momentarily took precedence over Labour politics. In June 1902, the Boer War at last came to an end; and in August, MacDonald and Margaret went to South Africa to investigate the aftermath of the war at first hand. In the next four months, they travelled extensively – visiting Cape Town, Pretoria, Kimberley and the battlefields of Natal, crossing the veld in a three-day journey with a wagon and team of mules, and driving for four days in a Cape cart through the ostrich farms and vineyards of Oudtshoorn. They interviewed politicians, editors and former soldiers from the British and Boer communities; and they became friends with some of the leading Boer generals. Smuts, in particular, corresponded with

MacDonald for several years, while Margaret and Mrs Smuts kept each other up to date on their respective family histories.[32] From South Africa, MacDonald wrote a series of articles for the *Echo* and the *Leicester Pioneer*; when he got back to England they were expanded into a booklet called *What I Saw in South Africa*. Articles and booklet together provide an indispensable and moving glimpse of a side of his character which has often been misunderstood.

He had opposed the war, not because he was a pacifist, but because he thought it unnecessary and unjust. Yet his descriptions of the South African battlefields, of the cemeteries in the concentration camps, and the stench of putrefying flesh hanging over the veld, make it clear that his opposition was based on an emotional abhorrence for war as such, as well as on a reasoned conviction that this particular war should never have been fought. What struck him most were the trenches — sprawling across the plain 'like volcanic cracks ... They could be for nothing but war. They lie eloquent with wicked hate like a fragment of a shattered shell. You stand on the rugged edge and look down at their shadowy, jagged sides, and shiver as you would at a gallows tree.'[33] Worse even than the fact of violence was the irrationality that lay behind it. At one point, the MacDonalds drove across the Orange River Colony from Bethlehem to Lindley. MacDonald's description of the journey reveals even more about him than about the sights he described:

We outspanned for our morning meal in the garden of the General who had entertained us the previous evening in Bethlehem. His peach trees threw out scraggy blossoms from the thick, tall yellow reeds, the stumps of his gum trees stood rotting in the ground, his water dams were broken. His house, a substantial building of well-dressed stone, stood a grey ruin. When we walked up to what had been his front door, lizards scuttled away beneath the stones. Lying embedded in ashes was the iron framework of an upright grand piano, with its wires twisted over in an entangling mass. The iron handles lay where they had fallen in the fire. Picture nails, brass studs, all the little metal knick-knacks of the best room of a well-to-do Boer, lay in the ashes just where they had fallen, and, as though in grim irony, a copy of a *Royal Reader*, in English, fluttered only half-consumed in the kitchen doorway ...

That evening we outspanned on the edge of the Church Square of Lindley. It was dark when we got there, but against the sky we could see roofless houses around us ...

When I awoke next morning and looked out it was as though I had slept among some of the ancient ruins of the desert. Every house, without a single exception, was burnt; the church in the square was burnt ... Before the war, Lindley was an Arcadia embowered in trees. Now it lay shadeless on the yellow, parched veldt slope ... The place had stood practically untouched, although taken and retaken many times, until February, 1902, when a column entered it unmolested, found it absolutely deserted, and proceeded to burn it. The houses are so separated from each other by gardens that the greatest care must have been taken to set every one alight. From inquiries which I made from our officers and from our host, who was the chief intelligence officer for the district, there was no earthly reason why Lindley should have been touched.[34]

He had gone to South Africa suspecting that the war had settled nothing; what he saw there turned suspicion into certainty. Its only result, he wrote, was that 'for the present, the Dutch flags disappear from the old capitals and Downing Street appoints the man who is to try and govern the late Republics.'[35] On one of his first evenings in Cape Town he met the Malans and the De Villierses at dinner. His notebook contains a brief impression of the conversation:

> Full of recent reception of Boer Generals in Cape Town. Had drawn Africanders in C.T. together & given them hope & courage. Felt triumphant in defeat. The impressiveness of the pride of these people in the Generals & confidence in them. Feeling as though they were playing with us. Note two points (1) No sense of defeat (2) *No sense of beginning anew with us but rather with themselves — a united Africanderdom.*[36]

It was the same everywhere. The Boers had not been forced to surrender unconditionally; in their hearts they did not admit that they had been beaten. Thus conciliation was the only policy which had any hope of succeeding. The British authorities, headed by Lord Milner, were trying to force the Boers under a British yoke. That could only exacerbate tension. The only sensible policy was one of 'Union, not dominance'.[37] In practice, this meant that Milner should be recalled, that the peace terms should be interpreted generously, and that representative government should be restored as soon as possible. Above all, it meant that the two communities should recognize what they had in common. 'Dutch and English alike', MacDonald wrote hopefully, 'have suffered by the conduct of Downing Street, and have been maligned by partisan advocates; Dutch and English alike must dwell in South Africa and find in it their home.'[38] It is easy to see now that these comfortable assertions begged the really difficult questions. Few saw it then.

IV

However lacking in prescience MacDonald may have been about South Africa, he soon demonstrated considerable prescience nearer home. Soon after his return in late 1902 he put out feelers to Herbert, intimating that the L.R.C. would like an arrangement with the Liberal Party, allowing its candidates a straight fight with the Conservatives in a score or more constituencies. The fish nibbled; and early in February 1903, MacDonald and Herbert met to discuss the proposal.

In this discussion, MacDonald revealed formidable powers as a negotiator. He held one or two good cards – notably the Parliamentary Fund – but on the whole his hand was not a strong one. In effect, he was asking the Liberals to allow the L.R.C. to establish itself in Parliament, but he had little to offer in exchange. The L.R.C. had a large affiliated membership, but no one who knew the Labour movement would imagine that the trade unionists affiliated to it could be 'delivered' in a parliamentary election. Many were Liberals already: their votes would go to Liberal candidates without any special arrangement between the Liberals and the L.R.C. Others were Conservative, notably in Lancashire, but it was far from clear that Conservative working-men would vote for Liberal candidates merely because the L.R.C. asked them to. Yet all this was obscured in a tantalizing cloud of promises and threats. The L.R.C., MacDonald claimed, had a membership of a million and a political fund of £5,000 a year. Its candidates were 'in almost every instance earnest Liberals who will support a Liberal Government'. Liberal opposition to these candidates would 'not only lose the possible accession of the erstwhile Tory working man, but will inevitably estrange the hitherto loyal Liberal working man'.

Herbert said little, but it is clear that he was impressed. He asked MacDonald to send a list of the constituencies which the L.R.C. had in mind; and he sent Gladstone a report of his conversation which faithfully echoed MacDonald's most effective points:

> The LRC can directly influence the votes of nearly a million men. They will have a fighting fund of £100,000 … Their members are mainly men who have hitherto voted with the Liberal party. Should they be advised to vote against Liberal candidates, and (as they probably would) should they act as advised the Liberal party would suffer defeat not only in those constituencies where L.R.C. candidates fought, but also in almost every borough, and in many of the Divisions of Lancashire and Yorkshire. This would be the inevitable result of unfriendly action towards the L.R.C. candidates. They would be defeated, but so also should we be defeated.[39]

Shortly afterwards MacDonald discussed the proposed arrangement with Gladstone and in the next three months he had at least seven further meetings with Herbert.[40] Meanwhile, his hand was improved by two more L.R.C. victories at by-elections. In March 1903, Will Crooks was elected at Woolwich with a majority of more than 3,000 in a straight fight with a Conservative; though he had received some Liberal support, it was generally agreed that his vote was a Labour vote, which no Liberal could have polled. In July, there came an even more portentous victory, when Arthur Henderson, a former iron-moulder and Liberal election agent, was returned as L.R.C. member for Barnard

Castle, in County Durham, after a three-cornered fight in which the Liberal candidate was forced into third place.

The negotiations between MacDonald and the Liberals reached their climax two months later. At the beginning of September he went to Leicester for the annual conference of the T.U.C., and while he was there he was suddenly taken ill and admitted to Leicester Isolation Hospital. Soon afterwards Herbert was sent to Leicester to complete the negotiations; and it was in the faintly lugubrious atmosphere of the Isolation Hospital that agreement was reached on September 6th. As the historians of the L.R.C. point out, MacDonald and Herbert met to confirm an *entente* which had already been tentatively concluded.[41] The final product was not a full-scale alliance. In an undated note, probably written about three years later, MacDonald described the negotiations as follows:

> Before the General Election of 1906 I saw Mr. Gladstone, the Chief Liberal Whip, twice and his confidential secretary, Mr. Jesse Herbert, several times. There was no bargain struck. I told them what seats we were determined to fight. They were friendly & no doubt expected their friendship to influence our policy. They never asked that it should however. The impression they gave me was that they [agreed] that we should have a fair chance of representation. Their attitude no doubt did influence me in opposing wild-cat candidatures, & in one or two constituencies I told them there would be no Labour candidates because there was no Labour organisation. I repeat, however, that information was not given in any way as a *quid pro quo*. A case in point was Walsall when it was proposed to make Sir Arthur Hayter a peer. I said there would be no Labour candidate. There could have been none.[42]

On the whole, this seems to have been a reasonably accurate – if coyly phrased – description of what happened. The Liberal leaders were willing to do their best to dissuade local Liberal Associations from opposing Labour candidates, but they made it clear that once a Liberal candidate had been adopted they would have to support him. In any case MacDonald had made it clear from the first that he did not want an alliance; and he would have been in no position to conclude one even if he had. He had taken Hardie into his confidence, but he had not consulted his committee, much less obtained a mandate from it. The negotiations had been secret throughout, and the understanding which emerged from them was secret also. Even so, its effects were far-reaching. By the end of January 1904, MacDonald was able to write that the L.R.C. had adopted thirty-eight candidates in addition to its sitting M.P.s. Twenty-seven of them were in single-member constituencies, and of these seventeen had no Liberal opponents. Of the eleven who were standing in two-member constituencies, only one had two Liberal candidates to contend with.[43] An effective parliamentary Labour Party was still some way off. But after long and arduous struggles, the first lap of the journey was almost over.

1 Bella Ramsay's cottage, Lossiemouth

2 MacDonald at six, wearing his first suit of trousers

3 The pupil teacher — MacDonald in 1882

4 Four generations — Bella Ramsay (seated), Anne Ramsay (standing, left), MacDonald and Alister MacDonald as a child

5 Mother and son — Anne Ramsay and MacDonald in Lossiemouth

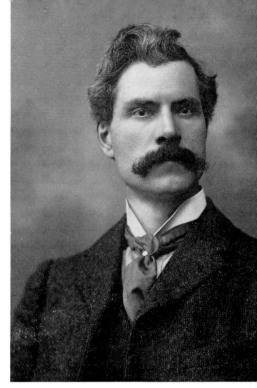

6 Margaret Gladstone at nineteen

7 Candidate for Leicester — MacDonald
   in 1899

8 MacDonald and Margaret Gladstone before their marriage, autumn, 1896

9 The I.L.P. council in 1899. *Back row, left to right:* MacDonald, J. Burgess, J. Parker, J. Penny, F. Littlewood. *Front row, left to right:* Bruce Glasier, Keir Hardie, H. Russell Smart, Philip Snowden

10 MacDonald with Hardie, Snowden and Bruce Glasier, early 1900s

V

So was the first lap of MacDonald's journey to its leadership. The election had shown that Labour could not expect to win a seat in Leicester against two Liberal opponents: it had also shown that Labour was strong enough to let in a Conservative candidate by splitting the anti-Conservative vote. The obvious moral was that Labour and the Liberals should divide the representation of the borough between them. But it was some time before this moral was accepted by the Leicester Liberal Association. There is some evidence that in the summer of 1901 MacDonald's supporters made an approach to the local Liberals, but it was rebuffed and no further moves were made until 1903.[44] Then the Liberals elected as president Alderman Wood, who claimed to have taken the position with the deliberate aim of improving relations between Liberalism and Labour. On February 20th, Wood told one of the leaders of the local I.L.P. that 'MacDonald must be the member for Leicester, & all his energies as President of the Liberal Association would be bent in that direction.' He even agreed to take out a £50 share in the chronically ailing I.L.P. paper, the *Leicester Pioneer*.[45]

It was some time before Wood's hints were followed up, but on March 12th MacDonald's candidature was formally ratified by the L.R.C. executive; and on April 24th he drafted the following letter to Wood:

> I have not written to you sooner because I wanted to talk matters over with one or two of my friends in Leicester. I find they are quite willing to accept the Derby situation & its consequences e.g.: independent candidatures, but both sides showing a friendly & helping feeling towards each other. The precise way of showing that relationship towards each other would be determined by the circumstances of the election, but in no case, of course, could it be such as would absolutely identify us with each other or make it absurd for us to claim a Trade Union support apart from party politics.[46]

The negotiations that followed hinged on the complex internal politics of the Liberal Association. Walter Hazell, the unsuccessful Liberal candidate in 1900, decided not to stand again. The Liberals had therefore to choose between finding a second candidate and giving MacDonald a clear run. Approaches were made to prominent Liberals outside the constituency, but without success. Meanwhile a former president of the Liberal Association, a Liberal Imperialist named Sir Israel Hart, announced his intention of standing.[47]

Hart's position was, however, a weak one; and it was not improved by bad tactics. He refused to let his name go forward to the Liberal caucus, following the normal selection procedure of the Liberal Party, because he was reluctant to promise that he would abide by the result. Instead he issued a manifesto, implying that he would stand as an Independent if the Liberals did not adopt him.[48] MacDonald, on the other hand, had 4,000 Labour votes behind him and

D

the intermittent support of Wood; better still, he had powerful backing from his friends at Liberal headquarters. From the beginning of June a series of letters in favour of MacDonald's candidature appeared in the *Leicester Daily Post*: it turned out later that they had been inspired by Wood. At about the same time Wood met Herbert Gladstone, who told him that he wanted to see the way opened for MacDonald.[49]

Labour could not yet afford to lower its guard or weaken its bargaining position. For a while, a second would-be Liberal candidate – a local councillor named Tudor Walters – appeared disconcertingly on the horizon. On June 18th, MacDonald's leading supporter had another long conversation with Wood, who

> began by confessing that he had not been so successful in his efforts of conciliation as he had hoped for. He wondered whether you could be induced to stand down for a while. I told him emphatically no … Later on he wondered in the event of an arrangement being come to whether you could not run in double harness … He said the expenses would only be half. I told him the expenses were no consideration with us. But our principles were that it would be impossible for you to go on their platforms but we would welcome them on ours … He candidly admitted that although they were going to call the executive together they had got no one to suggest … Of course there were some who were favourable to Sir Israel Hart but he would not assist Hart anyway. Then there had been considerable pressure put upon himself … he did not want to be put into the position but there might be certain circumstances under which he might feel it his duty etc. But again there was Walters who failing Wood would like the position and it appears from what Wood said that Walters has got the idea that we would support his candidature. But I told Wood plainly that Walters need not anticipate any support from the Labour Party … Wood then asked me, what my opinion was. Supposing that he was to consent, would his name be supported by us. I … replied that we would be sorry to have to oppose him.[50]

But it became increasingly clear that the leading Leicester Liberals had made up their minds in favour of doing a deal with MacDonald. At the end of June the *Leicester Daily Post* published a powerful leader in support of Labour's claim to the second seat. 'The paramount and pressing duty of every Progressive worthy of the name', it wrote, 'is to "go" for the only working political union that can enable Leicester to throw off its minority member.'[51] Some time later Walters was adopted as Liberal candidate for the Brightside division of Sheffield with the unofficial assurance that he would not be opposed by Labour.[52] Finally, on September 4th, the Liberal Thousand nominated Broadhurst as its sole candidate and passed a resolution moved by Walters, which recognized the 'friendly attitude of the L.R.C.' and pledged the Liberal Association to promote the return of 'two Progressive candidates' at the next election. Wood made a long speech commending his understanding with MacDonald, on the grounds that labour was under-represented in the House of Commons and that, in any case, Labour M.P.s could usually be relied upon to vote with the Liberals.[53]

VI

In a deeper sense than he could have realized, Alderman Wood had put his finger on one of the central themes of labour politics in these years and on one of MacDonald's most perplexing preoccupations as secretary of the L.R.C. The committee had been set up in order to strengthen labour's voice in the House of Commons. It had no hope of doing so unless it came to terms with the Liberals. Yet if it did come to terms with them, it risked losing its separate identity and frustrating what many of its supporters saw as its fundamental purpose. Thus MacDonald had to steer a careful, not to say circuitous, course between the perils of isolation and parliamentary impotence, and the less obvious but still graver perils of old-fashioned 'Liberal-Labourism'.

Friendship with the Liberals was one of the cornerstones of his political strategy; and he was prepared to go a great deal further than most of his I.L.P. colleagues in public recognition of the fact. At the Amsterdam Congress of the Second International in 1904, for example, he denounced the attempt of the German Social Democrats to prohibit collaboration between socialists and bourgeois radicals, on the grounds that the British Labour movement would take no notice of instructions from the International;[54] when he came home he published an article in a Liberal weekly arguing that labour might find it expedient to support a future Liberal Government in the House of Commons – a suggestion which led Bruce Glasier to 'marvel' at his lack of 'statesmanship'.[55] But if friendship with the Liberals was indispensable, so was independence of Liberalism. For, in his eyes, it was not enough that more Labour M.P.s should be sent to the House of Commons: it was also necessary that they should stand for something distinctive once they got there. Labour representation was not only a matter of class origin and trade-union affiliation; implicitly, at least, it was a matter of ideology. As he put it in a long and important article in the *New Liberal Review* in September 1903,

> If the new Labour movement were simply an attempt of Trade Unionists to use their political power for purely sectional ends – as we are told that teachers have done at School Board elections – it would be a menace to all the qualities that mark public life with distinction and honour. But when it was evident that the time had come to swing the united forces of Trade Unionism into politics, it was seen that those forces should accept allies, and take up a more commanding standpoint. Trade Unionism in politics

must identify itself with something higher and wider than Trade Union industrial demands. It must set those demands into a system of national wellbeing; the wage earner must become the citizen; the Union must become the guardian of economic justice. So soon as there is a Labour movement in politics, the very meaning of Labour representation must change. The Labour representative must then satisfy more tests than that he has been a manual labourer. The narrower view was all very well so long as Labour was a mere attachment of one or other existing political party, and the Labour political movement was only an attempt to thrust working-men candidates upon Liberal Associations. But that was not how the moving spirits of the new Labour movement regarded the work which lay before them. Labour politics to them was the political expression of the needs of the working class, not as a class but as the chief constituent of the nation. The Labour problem to them was, therefore, not merely the problem which is created every now and then when Trade Unionism and Capitalism clash, but the problem which presents itself to everyone who considers the conditions under which Labour lives, works, is paid, dies and is buried ... Thus ... the term Labour candidate no longer necessarily signifies a working man, but a candidate who may or may not be a working man, introduced to a constituency by organisations affiliated to the Labour Representation Committee, holding certain opinions in politics, and believing in the Labour Representation Committee's political method. The Committee takes its stand on opinion, not on social status.[56]

The L.R.C., in other words, was more than a trade-union pressure group on the lines of the old Labour Electoral Association. In embryo, at least, it was a political party in its own right, with its own ideology, its own distinctive position on the questions of the day and an ultimate responsibility to the nation as a whole.

These high and challenging formulations represented an aspiration, however, not a fact. The Parliamentary Committee of the T.U.C. still clung, in the main, to the 'narrower view'; so did many of the trade unionists on the L.R.C. executive itself. The chairman of the L.R.C. for the year 1902–3 was Richard Bell, the general secretary of the Railway Servants; and, so MacDonald wrote, Bell did not care 'what politics a [parliamentary] candidate professes, provided he is to vote with Mr. Bell on matters touching railway servants' interests'.[57] Though Bell had been elected to Parliament on the L.R.C. ticket, his behaviour as an M.P. was indistinguishable from that of his Lib-Lab colleagues. On three occasions during his term of office as chairman, he went out of his way to support Liberal candidates at by-elections; and his activities caused mounting resentment in the I.L.P. and among the socialist faction in the trade unions.

This resentment came to a head at the Newcastle conference of the L.R.C. in February 1903. A resolution was passed, debarring L.R.C. members of Parlia-

ment, parliamentary candidates or executive members from identifying themselves with, or promoting the interests of, 'any section of the Conservative or
Liberal Parties'.[58] But the Newcastle resolution did not solve the problem. In
September the Lib-Lab old guard counter-attacked. A motion was put before
the T.U.C. which would have made it impossible for MacDonald and many of
his I.L.P. colleagues to remain in the L.R.C.; and, although the resolution was
comfortably defeated, Congress reverberated with rumblings of discontent at
the machinations of 'middle-class Socialists'.[59] Not long after the T.U.C. dispersed, moreover, rumours of MacDonald's impending resignation appeared in
the press; and on October 21st he thought it necessary to deny them in his
column in the *Echo*.[60] At the beginning of November, this succession of pinpricks seems to have brought his patience to breaking point. He circulated a
memorandum to his colleagues in the I.L.P., in which he hinted that he might
have to give up his post in the L.R.C., and implied that its independence was in
danger. The response was immediate. Within a few days of each other, Snowden,
James Parker and Bruce Glasier all wrote, urging him to stay on.[61] Glasier was
particularly emphatic:

Regarding your private circular to us. We considered its statement: and we
all felt (1) That you must hold the fort in the LRC till after the general
election anyway. The Conference (LRC) will carry this with acclamation.
(2) Your position is very strong in the LRC and we feel that it would be a
pity to seem to yield to the narrower and feebler set who are against ILP.

In the end, there was no occasion for yielding. 1903 marked the high point
of Lib-Lab antipathy to the L.R.C. At the 1904 session of the T.U.C. it was
ruled that attempts to amend the constitution of an outside body – in other
words, of the L.R.C. – were out of order. In February 1905, a conference was
held at Caxton Hall, representing the Parliamentary Committee, the General
Federation of Trade Unions, and the L.R.C.; and at Caxton Hall it was agreed
that L.R.C. parliamentary candidates should be supported by all sections of the
Labour movement, while in return the L.R.C. agreed to support parliamentary
candidates sponsored by the Parliamentary Committee. Opposition to Mac-
Donald's position as secretary also died down. Nothing more seems to have been
heard of his resignation; and in February 1904 he was voted £150 for the year
1904–5 and empowered to appoint an assistant at a salary of £100 a year.[62] Soon
after, the committee moved out of its back room in the MacDonalds' flat, and
into more spacious quarters in Victoria Street. By April 1904, Bernard Shaw was
reporting that Sir Charles Dilke had complained that MacDonald had 'established a Reign of Terror on the Labour benches', and that as a result Bell and
Shackleton were 'afraid to move'.[63] By November, MacDonald felt able to
write, with pardonable smugness, 'Last year we heard a great deal about opposition to the secretary [of the L.R.C.] on the grounds that the office should be

held by a member of a trade union. This year I believe there is not a whisper of opposition.'[64]

But although the organizational identity of the L.R.C. was no longer in danger it faced a subtler danger of a non-organizational kind. Ten years earlier, when he had finally decided to throw in his lot with the I.L.P., MacDonald had looked forward to the disintegration of the Liberal Party and the emergence of a clear-cut political struggle between the 'interests' and the 'wage earners'. In the next few years it had looked as though his forecast was coming true. The ramshackle Liberal coalition had no coherent ideology to hold it together; and the sad record of the Rosebery Government – to say nothing of the disputes that reverberated through the party after that Government's fall – suggested that its disintegration would come sooner rather than later. After the turn of the century, however, the situation changed. The two classical battle-cries of nineteenth-century liberalism – religious equality and free trade – were suddenly given a new lease of life: the first by the 1902 Education Act which abolished the elected School Boards and made it possible for Church of England schools to be subsidized out of the rates; and the second when Joseph Chamberlain resigned from the Cabinet to campaign for a system of protective tariffs and imperial preference. So far from disintegrating, the crumbling Liberal coalition magically recovered its unity and fighting spirit; so far from emerging into the open, the clear-cut political struggle between 'interests' and 'wage earners' was postponed for a generation. In spite of its organizational independence, there was a real danger that the L.R.C. might diminish into the working-class tail of a revived and militant Liberal Party and that 'Lib-Labism' – having been expelled through the organizational door – might return through the ideological window.

MacDonald's response to this danger was characteristically complex. In common with the overwhelming majority of the Labour movement, he was strongly opposed to the 1902 Education Act – though, like Keir Hardie, on secularist, rather than nonconformist grounds. His attitude to free trade, however, showed a greater awareness of the shortcomings of the traditional Radicalism. The case against protection, as put forward by the Cobden Club and the Liberal leadership, he argued in the *New Liberal Review*, was hopelessly inadequate. It was not enough to point to the 'vast national wealth' which had been accumulated since the 1840s: ordinary people who were told that Britain's national income had now reached £1,750,000,000 a year thanks to free trade were less likely to utter 'a breathed thanksgiving that God is great and is growing greater' than to wonder where the money went and why the working-class voter saw so little of it. Instead of trying to refute Chamberlain by pointing to Britain's non-existent economic health, it was necessary to put forward an alternative cure for her sickness. MacDonald's cure was remarkably modern in tone. Britain's economic inefficiency was due to the dead weight of the aristocracy and to the deadening effect of the aristocratic idea. Rent bore more heavily on British industry than on its continental counterparts; Britain's 'caste differences' were directly hostile to economic progress. A positive attempt should be made to unite the 'industrious sections' of the community against the 'idle sections', by setting up conciliation machinery to adjust disputes between capital and labour, by founding a department of commerce and labour with funds to investigate industrial questions and by establishing technical laboratories in every big industrial centre.[65]

These proposals were coupled with a critique of the economic doctrines on which most free-traders based their case. 'Factory Laws, Fair Wages resolutions, Trade Unionism itself,' MacDonald pointed out in a booklet on *The Zollverein and British Industry*, 'are ... all Protection – not the Protection of Mr. Chaplin, the landlord, nor of Mr. Chamberlain, the demagogue, but the Protection of the Socialist.'[66] Free-traders were wrong to attack tariffs on the grounds that they encouraged the growth of trusts. In reality, trusts were objectionable only because they were privately owned and controlled, not because they prevented free competition. Considered purely as economic organizations, they pointed the way to Socialism:

Mr. Rockefeller not only owns the Standard Oil supplies: he controls the railways, the banks, the shops ... upon which his Trust depends. The Steel Corporation not only makes steel; it owns coal and iron fields, ore steamers, railways; it pays the engineers and sailors on Lake Erie, the railwaymen on the Erie and Pittsburgh mineral railway, as well as the operatives in Homestead. We oppose the Trust, not as an organisation, but because it is controlled by individuals for their own ends ... But the Trust points out the line of British advance. In this country, however, the introduction of the Trust should be marked by public ownership.[67]

Potentially, at least, it was a valuable insight – pointing the way to such developments as the Industrial Reorganisation Corporation of the 1960s and the National Enterprise Board of the 1970s. If it had been elaborated into a systematic analysis of how and where trusts should be encouraged and public ownership introduced, it might have furnished the starting-point for an economic strategy of democratic socialism to correspond with the political strategy already implied by the growth of the L.R.C. But, as so often happened with MacDonald's insights, it was left hanging in mid-air, a hint and not a policy. The tragedy was that there was no one else in the Labour movement to bring it down to earth.

VII

The dilemmas which MacDonald faced as secretary of the L.R.C. were reflected, at a more abstract level, in his approach to socialist theory. For although he was a shrewd tactician, skilled at the politics of manœuvre and compromise, it would be a mistake to picture him as an opportunist in the style of a Roosevelt or a

Lloyd George. Unlike many practical politicians, he was acutely conscious of the value of political theory, particularly to a party seeking change. Empirical methods, he pointed out, were of no value unless they were used 'as tests of ideal systems';[68] not all change was progressive, and only theory could determine which changes were desirable and which not. Unlike many British socialists, moreover, he was as conscious of the theoretical weakness of the British Labour movement in contrast with its continental counterparts. 'Every time I go abroad and see on the bookstalls evidence of intellectual and imaginative activity amongst foreign Socialists,' he wrote in March 1905, 'I am ashamed of our English movement.'[69] Tacitly, moreover, he realized that if the L.R.C. was to be transformed from a loose alliance into an effective political party, it would need an ideology capable of satisfying its socialist wing as well as its trade-union wing, and of reconciling each to the demands of the other. In a series of books and articles published before the First World War, he did his best to formulate such an ideology; and the MacDonald of the 1920s, to some extent even the MacDonald of the 1930s, can already be detected in these early attempts to construct a theoretical framework within which the 'Labour alliance' could find a justification and a rationale.

The most important of these early theoretical writings are *Socialism and Society*, first published in 1905, *Socialism and Government* (1909) and *The Socialist Movement* (1911). All three are marked by the preoccupations of the moment. But they are all designed to serve the same purpose, and they all outline essentially the same theoretical system. At the risk of running ahead of our narrative it is therefore convenient to treat them as a whole.

The starting-point of all three is a stark collectivism. 'Throughout our lives,' MacDonald wrote in *Socialism and Society*, 'we are but as men feasting at the common table of a bountiful lord, and when we carry in the dishes for the feast or gather up the crumbs from the board, we pride ourselves on our wealth and the magnificent reward which our labour has brought us.'[70] The sentiments are reminiscent of a Calvinist hymn, only in MacDonald's case the 'bountiful lord' was not the Almighty, but society. Man was a social animal, moulded by society and owing everything to society; without society to sustain him, even the most highly developed individual would be 'more helpless than the primitive savage catching fish with his shell hooks'.[71] It followed that society's claims on the individual were paramount and the individual's claims on society almost nonexistent. The state was not concerned 'with man as the possessor of rights, but with man as the doer of duties';[72] a 'right' which might prevent its possessor from doing his duties properly – like the right to get drunk – was no right at all. Indeed, the individual was to society what the cell was to the body. For society was not 'a mere collection of individuals like a heap of sand'. It was a 'unified and organised system of relationships, in which certain people and classes perform certain functions and others perform other functions,'[73] just as the functions of individual cells were differentiated in a biological organism.

MacDonald's organic metaphor was, of course, far from original. It has been applied to society by a wide range of political theorists, and it was especially popular at the end of the nineteenth century. But MacDonald rode it harder than most. In one striking passage in *Socialism and Society* he compared the arguments put forward by individualistic psychologists to the efforts which might be made by 'cell philosophers to prove that the body existed for them, and that the modifying and moving force in the organism was the individual cell'; in another, he compared the monarchs of the middle ages to a 'central nerve nucleus' and the barons to 'nerve fibres and ganglia'.[74] Above all, he pushed its evolutionary implications to their furthest limits. The 'boot and shoe operative of today' was 'as different from the boot and shoe operative of fifty years ago as the stomach of the bell animalcule is different from that of man,'[75] the 'horrors of child labour' were 'as much a "necessity" in the nature of things as the processes of organic evolution';[76] the complex social and economic developments which took place in the late middle ages were 'the response to a law of mutual aid as imperative as that law which determines that the bee must pack its cells as octahedrons and not as cubes'.[77]

It followed that Marx was wrong in thinking that socialism would come about through a revolutionary cataclysm, resulting from the breakdown of capitalism. Marx, MacDonald conceded, was ' "the father" of modern Socialism': he had laid down the broad outlines of the socialist state, and had established for ever that 'the distinguishing mark of Socialist opinion' was an insistence that capital should be subject to democratic control.[78] But Marx's children, like all children, had to 'fulfil the life which he imparted to them by wandering far from the parental roof'.[79] For Marx, in spite of his great achievements, had not absorbed the full implications of Darwinian biology; trapped, as he was, in Hegel's dialectic, he failed to realize that social evolution, like biological evolution, resulted from the slow emergence of higher forms of life out of lower forms, not from a clash between opposing forces. Hence his failure to predict the way in which British society was in fact to evolve in the late nineteenth century. In the 1840s, when Marx began his economic studies, it had looked as though Britain was on the verge of revolution. No revolution had come, and 'The Marxian today still wonders why England fell from grace. England did not fall from grace. Neither Marx nor Engels saw deep enough to discover the possibilities of peaceful advance which lay hidden beneath the surface.'[80]

The same was true of the Marxist concept of the class war. Socialism, Mac-Donald insisted again and again, was a matter of belief, not of class interest. Indeed, the working class did not have a single interest: it had a multiplicity of interests, some of them in conflict with each other. Workers were also consumers: and the interests of unionized workers who could join with their employers to force up prices might well conflict with the interests of workers in other industries who would have to buy the products of the first. Sometimes workers were employers as well: a factory worker who thought of himself as an exploited wage-earner during the day might become a capitalist employer in the evening, when he sat on the committee of his local co-operative society. It was true, of course, that the working class would be better off under socialism. But that did not prove the validity of the class war, for the same was true of the rest of the community – capitalists included.[81] At a deeper level, moreover, an appeal to class interest was bound, in practice, to become an appeal to personal interest; and, as such, it would run counter to the 'ideals of moral citizenship' which lay at the heart of the socialist creed. In reality, the key to social progress lay in intellectual and moral factors, not in economic ones:

Man is moved by his head as well as by his pocket. The richest possession of any man is an approving conscience ...

Economic needs may give volume and weight to the demand for change, but reason and intelligence, the maturing of the social mind, ideals of social justice grasped so firmly that they have become real existences for those who hold them, give that demand a shape, a policy a direction. Socialism, must, therefore recognise the intellectual as well as the economic movement. And if it over emphasises either side, let it be the former. For the pressure of economic need may exert itself in several conceivable directions, not every one of which opens the gateway to progressive advance. A consciousness of class disabilities may be either a motive for reactionary sycophancy or for revolutionary indignation. A man's poverty may make him a Socialist, but it is as likely to induce him to sell his birthright for a mess of pottage ...

... Socialism marks the growth of society, not the uprising of a class.[82]

The Marxist doctrines of revolution and class war were not merely mistaken. From the point of view of the modern, post-Darwinian socialist, they were dangerous as well. For the pace and direction of social change were governed by the 'General Will' of society, and the 'General Will' moved in its own good time and at its own pace. It could be prodded, but it could not be coerced; and if attempts were made to force it to accept changes for which it was not ready, the results would be disastrous. The 'General Will' consisted, MacDonald wrote in *Socialism and Government*, of society's 'inherited habits, modes of thought, axioms of conduct, traditions both of thought and of activity'; sometimes these could be modified quite rapidly, as they had been in the late middle ages and at the end of the eighteenth century, but they could not be ignored or over-ridden. Conservatives exaggerated the stability of the 'General Will'; 'individualist Radicals and those Socialists who cherish the errors of Radical politics have failed to understand its enormous capacity to resist change when an attempt is made to assault rather than persuade it. Thus, if we can conceive a social revolution to be even possible, the only result would be a furious reaction caused by the General Will becoming active in defence of the General Habit'.[83]

MacDonald's alternative to Marxism was implied by his critique of it. Capitalism would disappear, not because it was doomed to crisis and revolution, but because its success had created new problems, which could be solved only by socialism. As the national income grew, the disparity between wealth and poverty became more offensive; as competition was replaced by mono-poly, the public interest had to be safeguarded by controlling the machinery of production. Meanwhile, 'common needs, sacrificed by private interest ... assert themselves more and more through Factory Laws, experiments in municipal-ization, Sanitary Laws and so on.'[84] These and other reforms like them were socialist in effect even if not in avowed intention; through them, 'men of all classes' acquired a 'conception of society, of the community and the individual, formed on Socialist principles'.[85] Because of all this, socialists had an influence out of all proportion to their numbers, just as the Benthamites had had in the early nineteenth century. 'The men who specifically admitted that they were individualists and utilitarians, and who consciously applied their philosophy to legislation,' MacDonald pointed out in *Socialism and Government*, 'were, if brilliant in intellect and untiring in activity, very few. But the men who were responsible for the work of the legislative organ, both in and out of Parliament, could not help accepting the common-sense of Benthamism ... So it is always, and exactly the same thing is happening to-day with Socialism.'[86] The alterna-tive to revolution, in other words, was exhortation. The lectern was mightier than the barricades.

But how, in practice, should socialists bring their influence to bear? The Benthamites, after all, had not formed a distinct political party: if socialists were the Benthamites of the twentieth century, why should they not imitate the Benthamites' restraint? Why not rest content with influencing the Liberals, as the Benthamites had influenced the Whigs? And if 'permeation' of that sort was ruled out, what justification was there for the L.R.C. and the Labour Party? The 'Labour Alliance' was not explicitly socialist, any more than the Liberal Party was. If it was wrong for socialists to work with non-socialist Liberal politicians, why was it right for them to work with equally non-socialist trade-union leaders?

MacDonald's answers to these questions lacked philosophical precision. Even so, they provided a subtle and, if the premises were accepted, a convincing justification of his political strategy. 'The life of a party', he argued, 'is finite.'[87] A party's principles evolved in response to a particular set of circumstances. When the circumstances changed, the principles became obsolete. This had now happened to the Liberal Party. The historic principles of nineteenth-century liberalism – democracy, nationalism, free trade and religious equality – offered no answers to the social problems of the twentieth. As a result, the Liberal Party was in a state of decay, like an ageing biological organism, in which 'the hard structures of the body are hardened and thickened, the saps of life flow more and more slowly and suffer greater and greater impediments, until at length motion ceases altogether.'[88] Clearly, then, it would be a waste of time for socialists to work within the Liberal Party. The alternative was equally clear.

Though socialism was not a class creed and should not be promulgated in class terms, it was the working class which suffered most directly from the 'chaos' of capitalism, and the working class which was most sensitive to the need for greater 'mutual aid in society'.[89] Hence, it was the Labour movement which offered the most promising base for socialist politics.

This did not mean, however, that the Labour Party had to be explicitly socialist. Unlike continental parties, British parties expressed needs, not words; in Britain, therefore, 'Socialism cannot create for itself a political party founded on its dogmas – it can only hope to become the spirit of a party which may or may not profess the Socialist constructive ideas as guides in practical legislation.'[90] Nor did it mean that there was any 'profound gulf' between the Labour Party and the Liberals. For there were no 'gulfs' in evolution: 'Lower forms merge into higher forms, one species with another, the vegetable into the animal kingdom; in human history one epoch slides into another ... Socialism, the stage which follows Liberalism, retains everything of value in Liberalism by virtue of its being the hereditary heir of Liberalism.'[91]

MacDonald was trying to provide a rival attraction both to the S.D.F. on his left and to the increasingly socialistic 'New Liberals' on his right; he had to reassure doubting I.L.P.-ers, who were beginning to wonder whether the 'Labour Alliance' was socialist enough, without frightening off former 'Lib-Lab' trade unionists, who suspected that it was more socialist than they had intended it to be. It is hardly surprising that there should have been some soggy patches in his argument. He had put forward a theory of gradualism, but no strategy for gradualists. Like his Marxist rivals, he insisted that the distinguishing characteristic of socialism was public ownership. Yet he made no proposals as to how and when public ownership should be introduced, and offered no calculus by which priorities for public ownership could be determined. Though he insisted that socialism would come only through trial and error, and compared the socialist politician to a sailor who 'steers by certain marks and at certain points alters his course and follows new marks where the old can lead him no further',[92] his rejection of Marx's sociology and economics did not extend to Marx's historicism. For him, as for Marx, socialism was a goal in the future towards which history was inexorably moving, rather than a set of values to be applied to the changing problems of the present: thus his theory offered no more guidance to a socialist faced with the practical tasks of government than Marx's had done. In place of the revolutionary utopianism of Marx, he offered, in effect, evolutionary utopianism – a kinder, but not in practice a more useful, creed.

These were serious weaknesses. But although it is easy to see in retrospect that the Labour Party – and indeed, MacDonald himself – would have been better served by a more practical, more sceptical and less optimistic theory, it would be anachronistic to imagine that he could have produced such a theory at the time when he was writing. His theory was produced in and for the 1900s, not for the 1920s, and still less for the 1950s or the 1970s. Its most damaging weaknesses –

above all, its assumption that history obeys discoverable laws and moves towards a knowable goal, and its corresponding assumption that social change can
meaningfully be described as a movement from 'lower' stages to 'higher' stages
— were shared by most socialist thinkers of the time, and by many liberals and
radicals as well. Much the same applies to his failure to develop a strategy for
Labour in government. At the time he wrote, Labour had no hope of exercising
power. As a minor party, on the edge of the political stage, it could only consolidate its strength; keep its powder dry; and make the most of whatever
opportunities happened to come its way. MacDonald's theory was designed to
justify such a policy of principled opportunism, not to guide a hypothetical
Labour Government at some time in the remote future. The real criticism to be
made of him is not that his theories were ill-suited to the time when they were
produced, but that he failed to advance beyond them when times had changed.

VIII

Ever since Chamberlain's resignation in 1903, MacDonald and his opposite
numbers at the Liberal Party headquarters had had to reckon with the possibility
of an imminent general election. In spite of frequent false alarms, however, the
Unionists clung stubbornly to office, while Balfour, the prime minister, tried
unavailingly to bridge the gap between protectionists and free-traders in his own
ranks. The uncertainty, Jesse Herbert complained in a letter to MacDonald in
May 1905, was 'most trying. The ceaseless expectation, the confident assurances
that "it is coming", the secret communications that "it is certain next month"
have rubbed my nerves raw.'[93] Balm for Herbert's nerves was on its way. By
November 1905, it was clear that Balfour's attempts to unite his party had
failed. At the beginning of December he resigned, and the Liberals returned to
power after ten years in the wilderness. In the general election which followed
in January 1906 they won 401 seats to the Unionists' 157: one of the most
resounding victories in modern electoral history.

It was an equally resounding victory for MacDonald. Thanks largely to his
understanding with Herbert Gladstone, the L.R.C. shared to the full in the
Liberals' triumph. It had fifty candidates in the field. Of these, twenty-nine were
successful: and of the twenty-nine, only five had faced Liberal opposition.[94]
Leicester conformed to the national pattern. At MacDonald's adoption meeting, Alderman Wood declared that the Liberals 'had decided not only to run
one candidate, but they were going to take off their coats and work not only
for the return of their candidate, but also of their good friend Mr. MacDonald'.
MacDonald returned the compliment. 'He was on no account going to ask them
to plump on polling day,' he announced in the opening speech of his campaign:
'The Trades Council advised everybody influenced by the Labour movement
to vote for Mr. Broadhurst and him.'[95]

His campaign conformed to the national pattern in another sense as well. The 1906 election was fought on a medley of Radical issues: free trade, the 1902 Education Act, the iniquities of 'Chinese slavery' in the goldfields of the Rand. It was these issues which dominated the public debate; and it would have been impossible for the L.R.C.'s candidates to ignore them, even if they had wished to. But, on these issues, the L.R.C.'s position was indistinguishable from that of the Liberals: thus the effect of the election campaign was to blur the differences between the L.R.C. and its Liberal allies, and to accentuate the similarities. Leicester was no exception. In his election address, MacDonald advocated a sweeping programme of social reform: higher taxes on unearned incomes, 'drastic laws to deal with the land and other monopolies', old-age pensions, and the reversal of the Taff Vale judgment.[96] But in his speeches from the platform, this programme took second place to the fallacies of protection and the wickedness of the Government's South African policy:

> He had been across the veldt, he had seen the battlefields, the still open trenches, and it all came to Chinese labour. They were told it was going to release the slaves, the Uitlanders, to open up South Africa to a great flood of white men emigrants. They were told it was going to plant the Union Jack upon the land of the free. But the echoes of the muskets had hardly died out on the battlefields, the ink on the treaty was hardly dry, before the men who plotted the war began to plot to bring in Chinese slaves. (Cheers.) They could talk about their gold; their gold is tainted. (Hear, hear.) They could talk about employing white men; it was not true, and even if it were true, was he going to stand and see his white brothers degraded to the position of yellow slave drivers? No, he was not. (Loud and continued cheers.) These patriots! These miserable patriots! If they had had the custodianship of the opinions of the country 75 years ago, slavery in the colonies would have continued. When the North was fighting the South for the liberty of men, these men would have counted their guineas, would have told them how many white men had plied the lash in the southern states, and they would have said that for miserable cash, miserable trash, the great name of the country required to be bought and sold. Thank God there were no twentieth century Unionist imperialists in office then. (Loud cheers.)[97]

Speeches are made to be heard, not read; cold print cannot convey the emotional impact of a speech delivered to a packed hall, by a speaker in full command of himself and his audience. If we are to understand MacDonald's appeal as a platform speaker, however — and his career is incomprehensible if his appeal as a speaker is left out of account — we must picture the scene which took place at his adoption meeting in 1906: 'the tremendous gathering of supporters who filled every nook and cranny of the Temperence Hall'; the hour which the audience spent, before the meeting began, singing 'with great vigour and emphasis a number of popular political songs'; the 'enthusiastic cheers, which were renewed again and again' when MacDonald at last appeared on the platform.[98] Above all, we must picture his effect on his audience. 'As the speaker led them through the many intricate subjects with which he dealt they seemed to follow him with an almost breathless eagerness,' wrote the *Leicester Pioneer*. 'As he added fact to fact, and little by little completed the sequence of a practically faultless argument, one could almost feel the pent-up excitement of the audiences: and when the final climax came and the speaker had added the last link to his chain, there was such a round of cheers as could only have come from the throats of the British working men.'[99]

Applause at an election meeting is a notoriously unsafe guide to the subsequent verdict of the ballot box. But in the Radical dawn of 1906, both spoke with the same voice. Broadhurst won 14,745 votes, MacDonald 14,685 and the Conservative candidate 7,504. What was equally significant was that 13,999 votes had been cast both for Broadhurst and for MacDonald.[100] In electoral terms, at least, MacDonald's pact with the Liberals could not have been more triumphantly vindicated; and the problems which that fact implied for the future must have seemed remote and academic compared with the jubilation of the present.

CHAPTER 6

Parliamentary apprenticeship

I

'LOSSIEMOUTH is in a flutter of pride,' MacDonald wrote exuberantly in a letter to his wife at the end of January 1906. 'The wind has been so high that bonfires have been out of the question, except burning the bushes on the hill, but a banquet is now spoken about. The wind will not interfere with that.' In one respect, however, his elation was tempered by apprehension. 'I hear that there is a great log rolling going on about the leadership of the party,' he added, 'and I am rather afraid that personal jealousies combined with Trade Union exclusiveness may produce nasty feelings & unfortunate results ... There will be a fearful amount of work adapting the machine to the new circumstances, but so soon as our members settle down and hold their tongues, things will move all right I hope.'[1]

Some of his apprehension, at any rate, turned out to be unnecessary. The twenty-nine M.P.s elected under the L.R.C.'s auspices, together with one Miners' M.P. who joined them after the election, sat on the Opposition side of the House. At the beginning of the new Parliament, they elected Keir Hardie as their chairman – though only by a majority of one vote over the trade unionist, David Shackleton, and only after a show of hands and a previous ballot had both produced a head heat. At the same time, MacDonald was chosen as secretary of the parliamentary party and Arthur Henderson, the victor of the Barnard Castle by-election in 1903, as chief whip. Three days later, the annual conference of the L.R.C. agreed that the name 'Labour Representation Committee' should be changed to 'Labour Party'.[2] But in spite of these assertions of independence, the new party was a sedate and cautious body. Only a minority of the new Labour M.P.s acknowledged any debt to socialist theory. When they were asked to name the books which had influenced them most, the Bible, Ruskin, Carlyle and Dickens figured most prominently in their replies: only two of them mentioned Marx.[3] More than half of them belonged to the I.L.P., but only seven of them had been sponsored by it in the election. Most of them were trade unionists who had come to Westminster to win tangible benefits for their members and their class, not socialist evangelists who saw it as a stepping-stone to a new Jerusalem. They owed their seats, and their party its existence, to the ingrained parliamentarianism of the British working class as much as to its appetite for change; in spite of their lack of parliamentary experience and their weakness in the division lobbies, they were content – indeed anxious – to play the parliamentary game by the parliamentary rules.

This was to be MacDonald's greatest strength. The parliamentary game requires parliamentarians to play it; and although MacDonald's reputation as a debater was never as high as the reputation he was eventually to win as a platform speaker, he had a shrewder idea of how a minor party could best make an impact on parliamentary debates than had most of his colleagues. 'I am sometimes sorry when we are imagined to be men whose hair bristles and whose eyes flash when Satan, in the shape of a Liberal, or Beelzebub, in the shape of a Tory, gets up to address the House … ,' he wrote in the *Labour Leader* after he had been in Parliament for about fifteen months. 'The picture is not only inaccurate – it is mischievous. If it were true, we would be the weakest party in the House … Governments are not afraid of Socialist speeches; they are very much afraid of successful criticism in details.'[4] Labour, in other words, had to insinuate socialist ideas into the detailed discussion of practical problems, in such a way that even non-socialists might be coaxed along a socialist road, almost without realizing what was happening. It was a difficult role, perhaps an impossible one. But for a minority party which had eschewed non-parliamentary methods, it was the only role which offered much hope of influencing events; and the main significance of MacDonald's parliamentary activities during the next few years is to be found in his attempts to play it.

In his first session, he confined himself, perhaps deliberately, to questions on which there was no distinctively socialist case to make. 'Personally, I was very anxious that the first Session should be one of peace,' he wrote in an undated note, probably in the late summer or early autumn of 1906. 'We had to master the ways of the House, we had to win recognition, we had to feel at home before fighting.'[5] He made his maiden speech on March 5th. It was a vigorous attack on the examination syllabus for factory inspectors, charging that it discriminated against working-class candidates in favour of university graduates, and that it produced inspectors educated in generalities but lacking in technical expertise. To judge by an article he wrote afterwards in the *Leicester Pioneer*, he found making it a daunting experience. 'There is no crowded audience in front, no commanding rostrum from which to survey your listeners, no convenient desk or table for your notes …,' he complained. 'The eyes of your "Honourable Friends" dart critical glances of cold steel that strike through to your backbone. And, oh, the awful sense that every word and every sentence may be analysed, picked to pieces, or turned into a bludgeon to brain you by the next speaker!'[6] Even so, it was an effective performance, and in one passage, at any rate, he struck sparks. The two obligatory subjects, he pointed out, were English composition and arithmetic. Of the eight optional subjects, one was English literature from Shakespeare to Wordsworth – 'he was glad the Home Office had not abandoned hope of having poets among the manual workers' – another was

English history, a third general history and a fourth French, German or Italian.
As an alternative to a modern language, it was possible to offer higher mathematics. The result of all this was to make it impossible for a man with practical
experience to compete with young men just down from Oxford and Cambridge.
'He might say that when he was in Johannesburg he had met almost the whole
of Balliol University [*sic*], and the only justification given him was that under
the circumstances such as existed there, the administrators were said to require
a very general knowledge, and a general education. Every single one of those
gentlemen had been an absolute failure (Cries of "no!", "no!").'[7]

Once he had broken the ice, he became active in a number of parliamentary
good causes. As befitted an ardent walker, he gave enthusiastic support to a Right
of Way Bill, promoted by the Commons and Footpaths Preservation Society.[8]
Shortly after his election he had written to E. D. Morel of the Congo Reform
Society to ask whether the Labour Party could help to further its objects in the
House; and he soon became one of Morel's leading parliamentary allies.[9] In
April he moved the adjournment of the House in protest against the imposition
of martial law in Natal, following a native riot earlier in the year. In a colony
where there are 'ten natives to every white man', he declared, it was inevitable
that 'even the civil law was carried out with a certain amount of unpleasant
harshness.' Martial law, 'administered by a court composed exclusively of
Militia, without a single member of such a court being able to approach the
problem raised in an impartial way', was bound to be even harsher.[10] His chief
parliamentary interest in the 1906 session, however, was in education. The
Liberals had won the election partly because of the widespread nonconformist
revolt against the 1902 Education Act. Now they had to pay their debt: and they
brought in a Bill which laid it down that schools supported out of the rates
would henceforth be confined to providing non-denominational education –
'simple Bible reading', in the phrase of the day. But although this infuriated
the Church of England and the Unionist Party, it did not satisfy the most
thorough-going critics of the 1902 Act, who demanded, rather than non-
denominational education, full-scale secular education. The Labour Party was
committed to the 'secular solution'; and it was the 'secular solution' which
MacDonald advocated in the long and tedious debates on the Government's
Bill.

For him, secular education was more than a solution to a political problem.
The whole notion of religious education – whether denominational or non-
denominational – ran counter to the attitudes which had brought him into the
Ethical movement as a young man; and behind the debating skill exhibited in
his speeches on the Education Bill there lay a deep current of emotion. 'Simple
Bible reading', he pointed out, was not non-denominational at all: in the eyes of
many Roman Catholics and Anglicans it was 'rank Nonconformity, naked and
unashamed'. Thus it would perpetuate the religious strife it had been designed
to end. Worse still, it would cripple the religious feelings it was supposed to

foster. In his own schooldays, he declared, he had been 'told all about the Kings of Israel and the succession of the prophets, and when we studied the life of Paul we were told only of the number of places he visited, and the number of churches he founded'. From a religious point of view, such an education was 'practically barren', if not worse than barren. He supported the 'secular solution', not because he was a secularist, and not because he was a Roman Catholic or a High Churchman, but 'because I feel the very greatest sorrow and grief when I find that religion is becoming so much a formal affair, so much a thing of the lips, so much a thing of mere outward conduct, and so little of the real spirit. I oppose any attempt to teach this skeleton of religion in the name of religion, and to bolster up the idea that it is going to secure our children in their allegiance to a religious creed.'[11]

However outrageous the 'secular solution' might seem to the average Conservative, it was orthodoxy in the Labour movement. On a more minor educational issue, however, MacDonald provoked equally violent indignation from some of his fellow socialists. On May 21st, Sir John Brunner, Liberal M.P. for Northwich, brought in an Education Acts Amendment Bill to make it possible for children between the ages of thirteen and sixteen to attend a 'continuation school' for three evenings a week, as an alternative to leaving school at fourteen. The Bill was sponsored by a number of Radical and Labour M.P.s, among them Charles Masterman, Will Crooks and MacDonald; but at the beginning of June it was denounced in an S.D.F. circular as 'a wicked attempt to put back the age of leaving shool' and as a 'nefarious attack upon the interests of the children of our class'. The results were impressive. Between June 13th and July 6th, twenty-six I.L.P. branch secretaries, from districts as far apart as Cwmavon and Harrogate, wrote to protest against MacDonald's attitude. Some of their letters were reasonably friendly. Neath said they could not believe that he would support a Bill detrimental to the I.L.P., and asked courteously for an explanation; the secretary of the Altrincham branch said that he regretted having to criticize, but that he was bound by the resolution of his members; Oxford resolved unanimously that 'they had every confidence in the ability of those representing our movement in the House to deal with the question'. But this was not the characteristic note. In Deptford MacDonald was 'strongly condemned'; Eccles expressed 'surprise and indignation'; Tottenham 'censured' him; and Coatbridge 'instructed' him to take no further action.[12]

MacDonald's response was unusually accommodating. 'There has been a little storm raging about a little Education Bill which I backed ... ,' he wrote in the *Labour Leader* on August 10th. 'I still hold that the attack was an attempted assassination and not an honourable battle; but my comrades can always be assured ... that I value their confidence and esteem too much to stand obstinately to a Bill which is easily misunderstood and easily attacked.'[13] Accordingly, he withdrew his name from the Bill. It was a storm in a teacup, no doubt: but it was an ominous indication of the weather ahead.

II

MacDonald had fought two general elections unsuccessfully before his victory at Leicester in 1906, and had been trying actively to enter the House of Commons since 1892. Though the evidence is scanty, there can be no doubt that he relished the fact that he had arrived there at last, or that he derived great satisfaction from his work as an M.P. Unlike some of his Labour colleagues, he does not seem to have been put off by the rather ponderous atmosphere of the Palace of West-minster — even more reminiscent of an old-fashioned gentlemen's club in those days than it is today—and it is clear from his papers that he was soon on good terms with a number of ministers and Liberal backbenchers. Like most M.P.s with young children, however, he soon found that parliamentary life inter-fered badly with family life; and for him that was a heavy price. The 'At Homes' at Lincoln's Inn Fields had to be given up because his attendance at them could no longer be relied on;[14] and although he was now able to treat his children to strawberries and cream on the terrace, he saw less of them than before.[15] He saw less of Margaret as well, and that was even more irksome. 'My Dearest Missus of whom distance does not lend enchantment to the view ... ,' he exclaimed dolefully in a letter to her, written in the House of Commons at the beginning of August 1906. 'There is nothing doing here but ordinary work, work, work!'[16] That must have been a frequent mood by the end of a heavy session.

In those days, however, sessions were shorter than they are today; and in the autumn and winter of 1906 he and Margaret were able to spend four months on a long tour of Canada, Australia and New Zealand. They worked hard, studying the operation of the local legislatures, investigating the social and economic con-ditions and making contacts in the Labour and trade-union movements; and, after their return early in 1907, MacDonald published a short book entitled *Labour and the Empire*, based in part on the material he had gathered during their tour and calling for the adoption of an 'imperial standard' of human rights to be embodied in a declaration akin to the American Declaration of Independence.[17] But it was a holiday as well, with long walks in the Canadian Rockies, stops in Honolulu and Fiji, visits to the Australian deserts and the geyser regions of New Zealand, and a short stay in Ceylon on the way home. Before they left, Margaret had written to a friend, explaining that 'Our only chance of having three meals a day together and of discovering really how nice people we both are, is to run away together.' She returned, MacDonald wrote later, 'happy and buoyant and longing for the yoke of work'.[18]

In his case at any rate, the yoke was a good deal heavier in 1907 than it had been in 1906. 1906 had been a good year for the Labour Party. The Liberals had passed a Trades Disputes Act setting aside the Taff Vale judgment, a Workmen's Compensation Act and an Act making it possible for local authorities to provide school meals for needy children. The contents and scope of the first had been heavily influenced by the Labour Party, which had lobbied hard and successfully to change the Government's original proposals in a way that made them more favourable to the trade unions, and Labour M.P.s could claim much of the credit for the other measures as well. 1907 was doubly barren by contrast. No important law was passed, and a number of Labour measures fell by the way-side. The Government's only significant gesture in the direction of social reform was a promise to introduce old-age pensions the following year. Meanwhile, the boom which had accompanied the Liberals' arrival in office began to peter out. By the end of 1907 unemployment was significantly higher than it had been twelve months before; and by early 1908 it was clear that the country was in the grip of a severe trade depression.

Partly because of all this, the morale and cohesion of the parliamentary Labour Party sharply declined. As early as July 1906, Snowden was complaining that Hardie's chairmanship was a 'hopeless failure' and that there was 'intense dis-satisfaction amongst the ILP members'.[19] Similar noises came from Arthur Henderson,[20] while MacDonald was, if anything, more critical still. He had, he confessed to Bruce Glasier at the end of the 1906 session, voted for Hardie only 'with much reluctance'. Having done so, however, he had tried to ensure that the party co-operated loyally with its new chairman, and to that end he had arranged a daily meeting of the party officers at 2 p.m. Hardie had not bothered to attend; and although he had mended his ways for a while, after MacDonald had explained what was at stake, he had since 'dropped off until the daily meet-ing is now practically abandoned'.[21] By May 1907, MacDonald's complaints had become even more pained. The 'old resentment' against Hardie, he reported to Bruce Glasier, had now reappeared with the result that 'the elements of dis-cord are gathering in a most menacing way.'[22]

It soon became clear, however, that the elements of discord owed less to Hardie's inadequacies as chairman than to the structure of the party over which he had to preside. At the end of the session, Hardie gave up the chairmanship, with every appearance of relief, and left the country for a world tour lasting for the best part of nine months. His natural successor was David Shackleton, the runner-up in 1906, and probably the ablest trade unionist in the party. Much to MacDonald's dismay, however, Shackleton refused to stand; and after a certain amount of lobbying behind the scenes, Arthur Henderson was elected instead.[23] But, whereas Hardie had failed to win the confidence of the trade-union wing of the alliance, Henderson was soon at loggerheads with the I.L.P. 'Henderson', Bruce Glasier complained to MacDonald in October 1908, 'is not popular – he is reckoned perhaps quite unjustly as playing the Liberal game. Were he to resign and the rupture end there, I have no doubt that the movement would be inclined to rally afresh to the Party in the House.' There was no need for a 'display of heroics', he added a week later. All that was necessary was that Henderson 'should appear to lead the party as a fighting force, and he cannot do that if he is always side by side with Liberals on virtually Liberal platforms.'[24]

Against that drab background, however, MacDonald's parliamentary star continued to rise. As in his first session, many of his most effective speeches contained scarcely a trace of socialist ideology. In the debate on the address in 1907 he attacked a Conservative amendment in favour of imperial preference with arguments which could have been used by Gladstone;[25] in the debate on Haldane's Territorial and Reserve Forces Bill in April he attacked the Government's incipient militarism with arguments which would have given pleasure to Bright.[26] On other occasions, however, he struck a more distinctive note. In the spring of 1907, Asquith, the chancellor of the exchequer, brought in his second budget. It was a curiously double-edged measure. For the first time in British history, unearned incomes were taxed at a higher rate than were earned incomes. But instead of raising the tax on unearned income, Asquith lowered the tax on earned incomes below £2,000 a year. For a Government which wished to move to the left without alienating its wealthy supporters, it was a shrewd move. But MacDonald's reply was shrewd also. The working classes whose incomes averaged only £70 a year, he argued in the debates on the Finance Bill, paid a total of £48,000,000 a year to the national exchequer in indirect taxes – the equivalent of a direct tax of two shillings in the pound. Thus, the working-class taxpayer paid taxes 'upon life not upon property', whereas a wise Government would tax property rather than life. The way to do this was to take Asquith's own distinction between earned and unearned income to its logical conclusion and to treat all socially created income as unearned.[27]

It was an ingenious argument, but it was also a peripheral one. In the debates on Asquith's budget, MacDonald was confined to the role of a parliamentary sharpshooter, on the fringe of the battle. He could put a Labour gloss on Liberal proposals and introduce socialist arguments into the struggle between the two capitalist parties, but he could not decide what proposals were to be made or determine the framework within which the struggle was to be conducted. In the following session, however, he was able to play a more commanding role. In 1905 the Unionists had passed an Unemployed Workmen Act, setting up a central unemployed body for London and a number of 'distress committees' in the provinces. In many ways, it was a historic measure, for it recognized implicitly that the state had a duty to find work for its citizens. But the powers granted to the distress committees were hopelessly inadequate, and the responsibility for initiating schemes to provide work lay at the local level, not at the centre. In 1908 the Act was due to expire; and, in May 1907, MacDonald and Isaac Mitchell, the secretary of the General Federation of Trade Unions, were asked by the so-called Joint Board, representing the Labour Party, the T.U.C. Parliamentary Committee and the General Federation of Trade Unions, to draw up a Bill to replace it.[28] In July, MacDonald introduced a more radical Unemployed Workmen Bill on behalf of the Labour Party incorporating the results of his and Mitchell's labours. It contained only fourteen clauses, many of them clumsily drafted, and it has been accurately described as a 'manifesto rather than a Bill in the strict sense'.[29] All the same, it was a landmark in labour history. It made the local authorities responsible for finding work for the unemployed and for providing maintenance if no work could be found. There was to be an elaborate network of local unemployment committees and a national committee to co-ordinate their activities and to draw up national schemes for providing work. When unemployment reached 4 per cent, the schemes drawn up by the local committees were automatically to be financed out of national funds, and the national schemes were automatically to come into operation. Thus, the Bill proposed a deliberate national effort to counteract the trade cycle. More important still, it sought to introduce into British law the revolutionary principle that work was a right. It was known in the Labour movement as the 'right to work' Bill.[30]

In 1907, the Bill got no further than a first reading. In the autumn and winter, however, local 'right to work' committees were set up to promote the principles embodied in it; and in March 1908, no Labour member having been successful in the ballot for private members' Bills, it was reintroduced by the Liberal M.P., Philip Whitwell Wilson. Shortly before the second reading debate, Bruce Glasier wrote to MacDonald, urging him to 'make a great stand' for the Bill:

A pitched battle on this question would be immensely popular, while feebleness or compromise would have a ruinous effect upon our movement. The feeling, aspiration – whatever we call it – in favour of State provision of work for those who cannot get it otherwise, is, I think the most active sentiment among the people today. Everyone is now apprehensive about his future in respect to employment. Labourers, artisans, clerks, shopmen are all in dread of the loss of work. The awful state of matters on the Tyneside and in many other places has also deeply impressed the imaginations of the whole working class. I would give much to see you and all our men make a very passionate proclamation of the right of the workers to work. But whatever you do, fight, fight, fight – do not give way on any point to the Government.[31]

MacDonald needed no prompting. In his days as 'Spectator' he had devoted many of his *Echo* articles to unemployment; as secretary of the L.R.C. he had helped to organize a great demonstration of unemployed workers in Hyde Park in July 1905; as candidate and M.P. for Leicester he had been brought face to face with the problem of unemployment in the boot-and-shoe trade. In December 1905, he had been appointed to the central unemployed body for London, and until his resignation in October 1907, he had been excellently placed to observe the working of the 1905 Act at first hand.[32] His speech seconding the 'right to work' Bill on behalf of the Labour Party was the most effective he had yet made in the House of Commons.

He began by appealing straightforwardly to humanitarian sentiment. Unemployment, he declared in a passage obviously marked by his memories of his own early days in London, meant 'tramping the streets in rain and in sunshine going about cadging and losing one's humanity, going about from factory to factory and from workshop to workshop begging to be employed, and going home every day without anything found, feeling a horrible sense that one was abandoned by his neighbours'. If Opposition members wished to retain such experiences 'as a precious possession for the twentieth century', they should say so. If not, 'let them stop talking about the fearful damage that was going to be done by making it impossible for men to walk about the streets begging for work.' Humanitarian sentiment could not, however, answer the widespread belief that unemployment was caused by the laziness, fecklessness and immorality of the unemployed. MacDonald tried to answer it by arguing that, in reality, unemployment was inevitable under capitalism. Modern industry, he declared, 'required a surplusage of labour to carry it on'; worse still, 'It did not only require its 2 per cent always, but it also required its 10 per cent occasionally, so that whilst in the shady corner of the stage of life they had for ever the tragedy of unemployment being played, they had, periodically, right out in the full glare of the footlights, the same tragedy coming to disturb their consciences.' The conclusion was clear. 'If it was necessary for society that a section should be without work, was it not the duty of society to take care that that section should not be trodden down to destruction?' As for the widely held view that there was, by definition, no useful work for the unemployed to do, the Bill's purpose was not 'to put men to the same work they were doing now'. It was to find 'new work' and 'new markets' to absorb what that work produced.[33]

But where were these 'new markets' to come from? This was the most important question of all, for until it was answered the advocates of public works had no answer to the objection that all they were trying to do was to provide a less humiliating form of charity under another name. After all, the traditional argument ran, the unemployed would not have been without work in the first place if their labour had been in demand. And if their labour were not in demand, how could state spending on public works alter the situation? The question was not answered fully until Keynes published his *General Theory* nearly thirty years later, but MacDonald's old collaborator, J. A. Hobson, had already begun to sketch out the beginning of an answer in his theory that unemployment was caused by 'under-consumption'. Like many I.L.P.-ers, MacDonald had been strongly influenced by Hobson, but in the debate on the 'right to work' Bill he made scant use of Hobsonian theory. In the debate on the report of the royal commission on the poor law a year later, however, his debt to Hobson was more obvious. The suggestion that the state could not provide employment over and above what private employers could provide, he declared, was a profound mistake ... Take a case in point, namely afforestation. The virtue of afforestation is not merely that it puts a few men to work and gives an opportunity to local authorities and the State to find employment for casual labour ... The chief virtue is that it creates a new labour market, and in creating a new labour market it creates a new market of consumers. It creates a new economic demand.[34]

As with his earlier speculation on the growth of trusts, this was a hint, not a policy. If he had followed it up, Britain's history between the wars might have been much happier than it was. So might his own last years.

III

In spite of MacDonald's efforts, the 'right to work' Bill was refused a second reading by 267 votes to 118. Years later, however, J. R. Clynes, Labour M.P. for North-East Manchester since 1906, remembered that MacDonald's speech in the second reading debate gave him the reputation of a 'bitter and dour fighter', and created 'an unusual amount of interest in the House'.[35] But although MacDonald's stock was rising among his colleagues on the Labour benches in Parliament, he was beginning to encounter fierce opposition from some of his followers outside. Labour M.P.s, conscious of the difficulties faced by any minority party in the British House of Commons, could take a legitimate pride in their performance at Westminster. To a significant and growing minority of the I.L.P., however, that performance seemed less and less impressive, and parliamentary activity less and less rewarding. For the I.L.P. saw itself as the conscience and spearhead of the Labour movement. It had helped to set up the Labour Party, not merely to put more trade unionists in the House of Commons or even to win concessions from a capitalist Government, but as a stepping-stone to socialism. Now the party was in existence; socialism was as distant as ever; and some of the worse evils of capitalism seemed, if anything, even more obtrusive than before. Worse still, the party's electoral tactics seemed to be determined less by the requirements of socialist propaganda than by the convenience of Labour M.P.s who depended on Liberal votes for their seats. The 'Labour Alliance' still seemed sacrosanct to the leaders of the I.L.P., but to many ordinary members of the party it was beginning to look less like an alliance than a strait-jacket.

The conflict between these two attitudes revolved increasingly around the policy and personality of MacDonald. He was secretary of the Labour Party and, as such, uniquely identified with the restraints it imposed on the bodies affiliated to it. In 1906 he had succeeded Philip Snowden as chairman of the I.L.P., thus becoming the most conspicuous target for criticisms of the leadership. No matter how he had responded to his critics, these two facts would have guaranteed him a rough passage as the unemployment figures mounted, and as the hopes of 1906 gave way to the disillusionment and recrimination of 1907 and 1908. All too often he responded in a way that made his critics even more hostile to him than they had been before. Privately, he sometimes had more sympathy for them than might have been expected, and there were times when he was almost as exasperated with his trade-unionist colleagues as they were. But his private sympathy did not show in public. One of the classic tactics of the leader of a left-wing party faced with opposition from his own followers is to blur the issues at stake by using extreme language to disguise a moderate position. MacDonald came close to doing the opposite. In negotiation with other parties, he could be deft and accommodating. When his authority inside his own party was under attack, his instinctive reaction was to fight back first and ask questions afterwards: and he fought with all the passion of a sensitive introvert who had to screw himself up to a pitch of nervous tension to fight at all. For although he liked to picture himself as a seasoned political warrior who loved a battle,[36] the truth was more complicated. He was a brave man, morally as well as physically; and after twenty years in working-class politics he was used to hard knocks. But the knocks still hurt: and knocks from his own side hurt most of all. In the internal party struggles which faced him during his chairmanship of the I.L.P., moreover, his own leadership and reputation were not the only things at stake. It seemed to him, not wholly without reason, that his critics opposed not only the incidental details of his policy but the tacit compact with the trade unions, on which the Labour Party was based, and his fundamental commitment to parliamentary government itself. On these there could be no compromise. The criticisms of the Left were repaid with interest: and, as they mounted in intensity, his own position became correspondingly more stubborn and more provocative.

The revolt against the 'Labour Alliance' first came into the open in 1907. At the I.L.P. conference in April it was decided to tighten up the rules governing the selection of parliamentary candidates in order to conform to the requirements of the wider Labour Party. Branches wishing to nominate candidates were to communicate with the N.A.C., which was to maintain a list of suitable names. Once nominated, the candidate was to go before a selection conference representing all the societies affiliated to the Labour Party in the constituency concerned.[37] At the end of June, however, a by-election took place in Colne Valley. The Colne Valley Labour League, which was affiliated to the I.L.P., selected as its candidate a magnetic young mob orator named Victor Grayson, who had drifted into socialist politics and agitation after a brief period as a theological student at Manchester. Only a month before, the N.A.C. had turned down the League's application to nominate Grayson; to make matters worse, the conference which had selected him had represented only the local branches of the I.L.P., and not the other affiliated sections of the Labour Party. His candidature was undoubtedly irregular; and at the end of June an emergency sub-committee of the Labour Party Executive, consisting of MacDonald,

Shackleton, Pease and Walter Hudson, decided that the Labour Party should play no part in the election.[38]

Even so, Grayson was elected with a small majority after a passionate and tumultuous campaign. The I.L.P. council decided to pay him a maintenance allowance out of its own funds, equivalent to that paid to the other I.L.P. M.P.s from the Labour Party fund.[39] The proposal that the Labour Party should play no part in Grayson's campaign had come from Shackleton, and although MacDonald had not opposed it he had doubted its wisdom. Once Grayson was elected, he hoped that bygones would be allowed to be bygones. 'Henderson is insisting that none of our members shall stand sponsor for the foundling unless the said foundling says "I'm sorry" — which the foundling will not do ... ,' he reported gloomily to Bruce Glasier at the end of July. 'Shackleton is away and will not be back until Monday at 6 p.m. So Henderson and I shall be in charge and there will be deadlock, as my policy will be to accept the situation and try and not allow it to be repeated.' The wisest course, he added, was 'to get Grayson to join us, and that cannot be done by hectoring.'[40] Accordingly, he took the chair at a reception for Grayson and Pete Curran (the victor of the Jarrow by-election which had taken place just before that of Colne Valley), at which he declared that the Labour Party's refusal to help at Colne Valley had been due only 'to certain technical difficulties'; and that it made Grayson's victory 'all the more impressive'.[41] Grayson, for his part, agreed to the following statement, probably drawn up by MacDonald:

> I have been elected as an independent Socialist member of Parliament. I did not receive any assistance from the Parliamentary Labour Party, but during my election I stated repeatedly, & I think still, that all the good which the workers have had from this Parliament has been through the agency of the Labour Party & that sufficiently indicates what my action in the House is to be.[42]

But vague expressions of goodwill could not alter the facts. Grayson's election was an implicit threat to the 'Labour Alliance,' not primarily because of anything which Grayson himself might do, but because he had been elected at all. What Colne Valley had done, other I.L.P. branches might try to do: if they did, the Labour Party might dissolve into its constituent parts. Thus Grayson became a symbol of the growing tensions within the I.L.P.: a symbol of revolt and indiscipline to the leadership, and of socialist militancy to the Left.

At the I.L.P. conference in 1908 these tensions came to the surface more violently than ever before. A delegate from Tooting moved the reference back of the N.A.C. report, on the grounds that the council 'should make a special point of supporting men who were fighting as "clean Socialists"'. A delegate from New Mills demanded 'a clearing out of the Conservative cobwebs which had accumulated'. Jim Larkin, of Belfast, announced that 'he would not sink his Socialism inside the Labour Party', and ended his speech with the cry,

'Socialists for Grayson, the remainder for yourselves.' Grayson himself declared modestly that he regarded 'any innuendo that he was anywhere near the level of the average Labour candidate' as 'insinuations or misunderstandings almost approaching to insults'.[43] In the end, however, the conference was a victory for the leadership. The reference back of the N.A.C. report was defeated; and before the delegates dispersed they passed a vote of thanks to MacDonald amid what the official report described as 'a scene of the wildest enthusiasm, the delegates springing to their feet again and again'.[44] Paul Campbell, one of MacDonald's strongest supporters in the I.L.P., reported shortly afterwards:

> As for Ramsay — never did Chairman get such a splendid ovation as he at the end — It was something to remember for the rest of one's life — Snowden proposed the vote of thanks — & when Wallhead in seconding asked the Conference to respond in such a way as to condemn once & for all the 'dirty attacks' which have been made on J.R. — You should have heard the yell which rose from us all! Some of the Colne Valley crowd seemed appalled by the fierceness of the shout ... Ramsay has a stronger hold than ever upon the party. It was really a MacDonald conference.[45]

MacDonald himself was equally euphoric. 'I ruled like an autocrat,' he wrote in a letter to Margaret half-way through the Conference. 'The Colne Valley crowd is swamped.'[46]

His euphoria must have been short-lived. Constant criticism from the left wing of the I.L.P. was beginning to wear down his patience. 'I am afraid I am down in the dumps,' he had burst out in a letter to Bruce Glasier in May 1907. 'I am tired of all this bickering and suspicion, the horns of which creep up through Answers to Correspondence, special columns, *Justice*, etc., etc. ... Is it to be quite impossible to gain the confidence of our people for a sane laborious policy of reconstruction having for a background an active platform of idealism? I warn you most seriously that if that cannot be done, our party here will split.'[47] By 1908, he had become still more impatient. 'I find that critics of Parliamentary work do not appear to consider that it is necessary for them to understand the most rudimentary facts about that work ... ,' he wrote plaintively in a column in the *Leicester Pioneer* in April. 'I am tired of stage play. I am tired of tub-thumping. Cannot we be allowed to think and do in peace, and if in the end we do not carry out our pledges — kick us out?'[48] To make matters worse, the united front which the party leaders had managed to maintain in public concealed bitter internal divisions. Snowden and Bruce Glasier were at loggerheads over Glasier's editorship of the *Labour Leader*.[49] Hardie was suspicious of his colleagues' *penchant* for 'luncheons and confabbing with Cabinet Ministers'[50] and criticized MacDonald's unwillingness to make a 'show of fight'.[51] MacDonald and Snowden were as critical of Hardie as they had been two years earlier — MacDonald accusing him of vanity, showmanship and a refusal to consult his colleagues,[52] while Snowden wrote mysteriously that he knew of things which Hardie had done 'of which I have been ashamed for the sake of the movement'.[53] Glasier, for his part, thought that Snowden and MacDonald lacked the 'instinct of agitation' and believed that they went to too many 'rich parties'.[54]

The significance of these complaints can easily be exaggerated. The I.L.P. was a party of prima donnas. Its leaders lived on their nerves, addressing great meetings up and down the country, pouring out articles for the propagandist press, sleeping too little and working too much; friction was inevitable. Friction between MacDonald and Hardie, moreover, was almost certainly due to emotional factors, of which neither was fully aware, as much as to political disagreements. Though Hardie was only ten years older than MacDonald, their relationship was, in some respects, that of monarch and crown prince. Hardie saw himself as the grand old man of the Labour Party, as the founding father whose child showed a disturbing tendency to stray from the parental path. MacDonald was the up-and-coming young man, with a brisker, more business-like approach, exasperated by having to stand in the old man's shadow. But, although the charges which the I.L.P. leaders brought against each other should not be taken at face value, they should not be dismissed altogether. In the summer and autumn of 1908, at any rate, they reflected a deeper malaise in the party as a whole. The Labour Party Executive – knowing that most Labour M.P.s had been elected without Liberal opposition – was reluctant to make forays into Liberal territory for fear of provoking Liberal retaliation, and wiping out the gains Labour had won in 1906. To the left wing of the I.L.P., such considerations seemed little more than a camouflage for political cowardice.

Its suspicions were exacerbated by the revival of the old campaign, dormant since the late 'nineties, for 'Socialist Unity' between the I.L.P. and the S.D.F. Both parties were gaining new members,[55] to whom old quarrels meant nothing; the gulf between them was narrowing as the S.D.F. became more moderate. But 'Socialist Unity' was incompatible with the 'Labour Alliance.' In 1907, the S.D.F. changed its name to the Social Democratic Party, presumably implying that it now regarded itself as a direct competitor to the Labour Party; and on three occasions in 1908 the Labour Party refrained from fighting by-elections, only to find that the S.D.P. had nominated a candidate instead.[56] On each occasion the local branches of the I.L.P. were torn between loyalty to the Labour Party and the claims of 'Socialist Unity'; on each occasion they supported the S.D.P. candidate in defiance of Labour Party headquarters; on each occasion the gulf between the party leadership and the Left grew wider than before.

IV

Both sides saw the Newcastle by-election in September 1908 as the last straw. Newcastle was a two-member constituency, covered by the MacDonald–

Gladstone *entente*. The Labour Party held one seat, and the Liberals the other. Thus, if the Labour Party contested the by-election it might invite Liberal reprisals at the next general election. At the beginning of September, J. J. Stephenson of the Engineers was adopted as the Labour candidate. At that point the National Executive stepped in, and persuaded Stephenson to withdraw.[57] The S.D.P. thereupon put up a candidate, and the I.L.P. branches in Newcastle gave him their support. Their action provoked a storm of indignation from the party leadership. 'We cannot continue to have a nominal responsibility for the direction of the I.L.P. if our decisions are to be flouted in such a way ... ', wrote Snowden on September 16th. 'It means a split if we take definite action, and the retirement of ourselves from a directing influence in our movement, but I don't mind that at all.'[58] W. C. Anderson, one of MacDonald's staunchest supporters in the I.L.P., suggested that the N.A.C. should appeal to the annual conference for 'wider powers', and when circumstances demanded 'rigidly enforce these'. If the conference refused to grant them, he added darkly, the matter would be 'serious enough to warrant us individually and collectively declining to stand for [the] N.A.C.'[59]

MacDonald was more indignant still. Traces of rebellion were to be found even in his own constituency; the *Leicester Pioneer*, normally unshakeable in its loyalty to the party leadership, had openly sympathized with the S.D.P. candidature in Newcastle and was distinctly half-hearted in its eventual endorsement of the Executive's policy. 'A crisis is coming,' he wrote in an undated letter to his wife. 'I really cannot remain in the Party if this sort of thing is to be habitual.'[60] On September 21st, he wrote a long letter to his colleagues on the N.A.C., pointing out that the Newcastle branches had acted 'in the teeth of the decision of the National Labour Party Executive', and that

> As Secretary to the Labour Party I have been open to the most unjustifiable personal attacks for carrying out my official duties. I have refrained from asking the N.A.C. to defend me in any way, although it was by its pressure that I accepted this secretaryship in 1900 & in the full knowledge that I was, in consequence, making my bed of thorns. But I am of opinion that if the I.L.P. is to remain a national party with a national policy, & that if the N.A.C. (whoever be on it) is to be held in the least respect by the branches & the Party it must take some steps to assert itself.
>
> Two considerations are of importance. 1. The I.L.P. has joined the Labour Party and for it to pursue its course with absolute indifference regarding the decisions of that party is a piece of political cynicism which cannot be paralleled even in the most disgraceful dishonesties of either Liberalism or Toryism. 2. The N.A.C. has been asked by annual conferences to carry out the decisions of those conferences, one of which has been loyalty to the Labour Party ... The Labour Party Executive has therefore a perfect right to charge us with disloyalty ... If this spirit of self-will is not

curbed in the branches, no self-respecting member of the I.L.P. will continue to act as a member of the Labour Party Executive or as an official of
the Party, and we run the risk of being expelled from the Party by a vote
of the Annual Labour Party Conference.[61]

When the results at Newcastle were declared, the S.D.P. candidate came
bottom of the poll with less than 3,000 votes. MacDonald summed up his reaction in a scornful outburst in the *Labour Leader*. The S.D.P., he pointed out
savagely, had won only 600 more votes in 1908 than in 1895: at that rate it
would take 'about 2,000 years' for Newcastle to be won. The Social Democrats
had attacked and vilified the I.L.P. ever since its foundation, but their policy
of fighting elections which the I.L.P. had decided not to fight was 'more
diabolical'; altogether, they were still living 'as parasites on the Labour movement as Engels said they were doing in 1890'.[62] In an anonymous editorial in the
Socialist Review — a theoretical monthly which the I.L.P. had begun to publish
earlier in the year — he went further. It was, he warned, a mistake to imagine
that the only danger posed by episodes like the Newcastle by-election was that
the left wing of the I.L.P. might 'split off and attach itself to the Impossibilists'.
A much greater danger was the possible emergence of a 'Socialist-Radical group
as in France': and this might be encouraged by 'the secession of the Right
Socialist Wing, caused by incessant attacks, and by a feeling that, on the one
hand, it is not wanted, and that on the other, the regular Socialist movement is
to refuse to discipline itself into fighting efficiency'.[63]
    Veiled hints of resignation and secession could not, however, coerce the hard
core of the Left. For many left-wingers objected, not merely to the leadership's
policy, but to its position — perhaps to the fact that the party had to be led at all.
As one indignant correspondent put it, in a letter to MacDonald, 'Power is
being concentrated in a few hands — & these hands are getting very helpless &
these eyes very blind in consequence'.[64] On September 16th, the York branch
sent out a circular to other I.L.P. branches, declaring that the Labour Party's
by-election policy has raised 'considerable misgivings in the minds of all the
members of the I.L.P. in the country who wish the I.L.P. to be independent in
fact as well as in name'. It called for a special conference to discuss 'the whole
question of the I.L.P.'s relationship with the Labour Party', and demanded a
statement from the I.L.P. representatives on the Labour Party executive 'as to
the relations existing between the Labour Party and the Liberal Party — especially as regards election policy generally, and in two member constituencies in
particular'.[65] In October, tempers were inflamed still further by Victor Grayson's
suspension from the House of Commons. He had tried to raise the question of
unemployment at the beginning of a debate on the Government's licensing Bill,
and had refused to obey the Speaker's ruling that he was out of order. To
Snowden, Grayson's behaviour seemed in retrospect 'a piece of hypocritical
acting',[66] while MacDonald sneered at his attempt to emulate 'the dramatic

force of a Henry Irving'.[67] But to many of the rank and file, it seemed that Grayson had delivered a heroic blow for working-class interests against stifling and irrelevant parliamentary conventions. As the president of the Farsley I.L.P. wrote:

Hundreds of thousands of our fellow creatures are starving in the land due to unemployment and we are strongly of opinion that they should have received the first care.

The lives of these people are more important than all the other questions that Parliament is 'gassing' about, and we felt, and still feel, that considera-tion of the unemployed question should be given preference over all other business.

Comrade Grayson, by his theatrical, melodramatic protests, in defying the Speaker, 'badly chosen time & method false' notwithstanding – empha-sised the superlative importance of the unemployed question, and for that we thank and congratulate him.[68]

It was not clear whether the attitudes of the Farsley branch were shared by the rest of the party, and still less clear how they should be dealt with if they were. On November 3rd, R. C. Wallhead, national organizer of the I.L.P. scouts, reported that Grayson and his supporters were trying to set up a new party composed of dissident I.L.P. branches and the more moderate sections of the S.D.P., and that Grayson had boasted that he had 240 I.L.P. branches on his side.[69] Bruce Glasier, on the other hand, believed that the talk of 'branches being approached by Grayson with the object of creating a split is founded upon the mere braggadocio with which he has been regaling his friends', and doubted whether more than 20 I.L.P. branches supported him.[70] But, although no one knew how strong Grayson was, it seemed clear that he was spoiling for a fight. On November 18th, he refused to appear at a joint meeting with Keir Hardie at Holborn town hall.[71] Early in 1909 he was reported to have said that he would refuse to sign the Labour Party constitution even if the coming I.L.P. conference asked him to, and that he wished to provoke defections from the I.L.P. so as to set up a new Socialist Representation Party of his own.[72]

By now, MacDonald had nothing but contempt for Grayson,[73] but he was anxious that the leadership should not play into his hands by appearing to cling on to office. 'The Movement has turned after the sons and daughters of anarchy,' he wrote gloomily to Bruce Glasier at the end of December 1908, 'and I cannot help feeling that some of the local storm centres are caused by personal feelings of jealousy bred of disappointment and similar causes. I also suppose the rank-and-filer does appear to see a Junta and over-centralisation, and we had better devise some means of placing greater responsibility on local federations.' The composition of next year's N.A.C., he added, was 'exercising me a little. I am quite clear that if one or two of us were to stand aside it would tend to allay some of the honest suspicions that are held regarding our action.'[74] Though

11 MacDonald in 1900

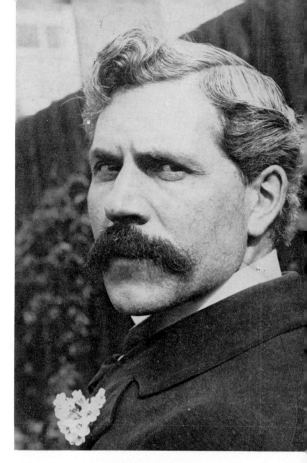

12 The MacDonalds at work,
Lincoln's Inn Fields, around 1903

13 Sidney and Beatrice Webb

14 MacDonald and Jim Middleton, around 1905

15 Addressing a march of unemployed workers from Leicester, Trafalgar Square, 1905

16 On the terrace of the House of Commons

17 Keir Hardie in bucolic mood

18 *Far left:* Ben Tillett
19 *Left:* Philip Snowden

20 *Far left:* Victor Grayson
21 *Left* Bruce Glasier

there is no direct evidence, it seems clear that he must have written in the same terms to Philip Snowden, who wrote back on February 5th, 1909:

Re. the N.A.C. At the present time my frame of mind is somewhat as follows. I want to retire and I should never have hesitated one moment but for the events of the last six months. I am half afraid my retiral may be misunderstood and construed wrongly. Moreover I am receiving a great many very urgent requests to stand from men whose friendship I highly value. So that at present I am simply allowing the thing to drift, and I tell those who write to me that they can nominate me if they wish and I will decide later. I think we had better let the question rest until the Conference and see how things turn. There might be developments which would necessitate us having a real stand-up fight, and if so I should want to be in it.

Moreover I do not agree with you that one only ought to retire. If for instance you stopped and I went the inference would be obvious—namely that I had funked. If you went and I stopped it would certainly give rise to statements that you were playing a move. Either we must both go or both stop; unless there should be developments at the Conference which could make it easy for one or the other to go.[75]

The conference was held at Edinburgh in April. When it began, Snowden's 'stand-up fight' duly took place. The opening shots were fired by the leadership. With great tactical skill, the rebels were exposed at their most vulnerable points, and voted down by heavy majorities. A motion affirming the I.L.P.'s loyalty to the Labour Party was carried with only ten dissentients. By 244 to 146 the conference rejected a suggestion that I.L.P. branches should be allowed to run parliamentary candidates independently of the N.A.C. and the Labour Party. A motion that no salaries should be paid to I.L.P. M.P.s who refused to sign the Labour Party constitution was carried by 332 to 64.[76] With these victories behind him, MacDonald then turned to the attack. On the second day of the conference, he delivered his valedictory address as chairman. It was a passionate and uncompromising statement of his conception of parliamentary socialism. The suggestion that strict observance of parliamentary procedure would somehow make it more difficult to solve the unemployment problem, he declared, was a 'purely fictitious one'. No Parliament could deal with unemployment without rules of procedure; and any rules of procedure would have to prescribe majority responsibility. 'Every facility given to a minority to impose its will upon the majority is a facility which any minority can use, and not simply a Labour or a Socialist minority. To protect the conditions and the existence of democratic government is just as essential to the building up of a Socialist state as is the solution of the problem of unemployment.' Everything depended on how the party expected socialism to come about:

Is it to be by a sudden change? A sudden change owing to force, or a sudden change owing to legislative action? To me, the first is quite unthinkable.

E

We can cut off kings' heads after a few battles ... and we can make similar superficial changes, by force; but nobody who understands the power of habit or custom in human conduct, who appreciates the fact that by far the greater amount of our social action is begun, controlled and specified by the system of social inter-relationships in which we live, move and have our being; and, still more, nobody who understands the delicate and intricate complexity of production and exchange which keeps modern Society going, will dream for a single moment of changing it by any act of violence...

Will, then, the change be brought about by a revolutionary Act of the Legislature? This is equally unthinkable to me, owing to the resistance of habits of thought and of action. Far be it from me to imply that this resistance amounts to immobility ... In every form of life there is ... an internal accumulation of forces making for change ... In Society today we are aware of this pent-up accumulation of forces. Capitalism violates our moral sense as well as our reason. It brings, decade after decade, its prolific crop of industrial failures, and those industrial failures present, not merely material, but also spiritual ugliness. Therein lies the hope and the promise of change which we desire, but we must work scientifically ... and no academic dogma, either regarding the way in which we are to define our Socialism or the way in which we should carry it out, should be allowed to stand in our path ... There is no finality in our formulae and modes of expression. Our cause, like the cause of knowledge itself, constantly leads us to new discoveries which require a re-statement of our creeds and a revision of our methods. Socialism shall prevail just as it is served by men who follow it, not as flatterers, but as counsellors, and who employ in its service, not their lips only, but their heads and their hearts.[77]

At that point, however, the tide suddenly and inexplicably turned. Grayson moved the reference back of the sections of the N.A.C. report dealing with his refusal to appear at Holborn Town Hall with Keir Hardie; and in a mood of good-natured tolerance, Grayson's motion was carried by more than twenty votes. It does not need much imagination to picture MacDonald's feelings at that moment. For two years the party had been seething with revolt aimed, not only against his policy, but against him personally. For a while it had looked as though the revolt was crushed: only that day the old guard had been triumphantly re-elected to the N.A.C., with MacDonald second in the poll. Now victory had been snatched out of his hands; the ground so painfully won in the first session of the conference turned out not to have been won at all. Only a few hours before, he had thrown himself into an important speech, with all the nervous tension that implied: the result was a humiliating slap in the face. When the figures were called up to him, he wrote later, he was dumbfounded:

What were we to do? Were we to smile, as we had done so often, and let the matter rest? It is just that smiling, however, that has been doing so much mischief. The minds of too many of our branches have become enervated and sloppy. For a long time it had been growing upon me that something would have to be done to compel branches to feel more responsible than they had been for some time. If we had said to the delegates: 'Brethren, your intentions are admirable but your way of showing your intentions is very wrong; we shall, however, take the will for the deed', nothing would have happened, and as soon as some obscure branch of the Social-Democratic party, or some villainous paragraph in 'Justice' prompted them, our easy-going branches would have started passing the usual resolutions and assuring us afterwards that they meant us no harm by their votes.

Quite clearly, the mistake of the delegates at Edinburgh could not be overlooked.[78]

That evening the N.A.C. met to decide what to do; and on the following day MacDonald announced its decision. A 'movement of irresponsibility' had grown up within the party; and because of it, the four national members of the N.A.C. —Hardie, Snowden, Glasier and MacDonald—could not see their way to remaining on the council for the next twelve months. The announcement was heard in 'stunned silence'. With ten dissentients, the conference expressed its confidence in the four and appealed to them to reconsider their decision; by a majority of 140 the paragraphs which had been referred back were reinstated. But it was of no avail. The old guard remained adamant; and the conference broke up with the delegates singing 'Will ye no' come back again?'[79]

In MacDonald's case, five years were to pass and a world war was to break out before the invitation was accepted.

CHAPTER 7

Leader bereaved

I

MACDONALD returned from Edinburgh to take part in one of the fiercest parliamentary struggles in recent British history. In 1908 Campbell-Bannerman had died, and Asquith had succeeded him as prime minister. Lloyd George, the leading champion of the radical wing of the Liberal Party, had moved from the Board of Trade to the Treasury. In April 1909, Lloyd George brought in the famous 'people's budget', which provided, among other things, for an increase in estate duty, a super-tax on incomes of more than £5,000 a year and a tax of 20 per cent on unearned increments in the capital value of land. Three months before, the Labour Party had held a special conference on taxation policy, designed to put pressure on the Government to make the taxation system more progressive. MacDonald had moved a resolution calling for a super-tax on large incomes, special taxes on state-conferred monopolies, increased estate and legacy duties and 'a really substantial beginning with the taxation of land values'. Now Lloyd George had moved a long way down Labour's path, and it seemed to MacDonald that the Labour Party had no alternative but to back him as strongly as it could. 'Of the Budget as a whole, I say "Bravo",' he wrote a week after its introduction. 'I am going to support it through thick and thin.'[1] If anything, second thoughts only intensified his enthusiasm. 'Mr. Lloyd George's Budget', he wrote early in the summer, 'classified property into individual and social, incomes into earned and unearned, and follows more closely the theoretical contentions of Socialism and sound economics than any previous Budget has done.'[2] By August he was writing that, even if it brought nothing to the exchequer and even if only a small proportion of the land in the country were subject to it, the budget would still be 'an epoch-making measure so long as the existence of unearned increment is recognised and the public right to property in it is enforced'.[3] He was equally emphatic in the House of Commons —pouncing eagerly on Balfour's argument, that it was unfair to single out the land for special burdens to which other forms of property were not subject, with the rejoinder that

> The right hon. Gentleman laid down the proposition, if I did not misunderstand him, that the community created all wealth. That is much too revolu-

tionary for me. I was perfectly amazed to hear the right hon. Gentleman express that Communist doctrine. Socialism is not in it ... It is not good enough to say that you should not tax land because you are not taxing anything else. We are beginning with land. We never concealed that, and the Leader of the Opposition has encouraged us to conceal it less than we ever did before, because he is not merely a follower of ours – he is a leader of ours.[4]

The finance Bill did not leave the House of Commons until the beginning of November, and was thrown out by the Lords four weeks later. At the beginning of December, the House of Commons passed a motion, moved by Asquith, declaring that the Lords had acted unconstitutionally; and, at the beginning of January 1910, Parliament was dissolved. The MacDonalds had, however, made plans some months before to visit India during the long recess, and they were reluctant to abandon them at the last moment. In August and September, MacDonald had a number of agitated discussions with the Liberal whips, who told him in confidence that they were expecting a general election early in the new year and urged him to cancel his visit.[5] In spite of some trepidations, however, he decided to reject their advice; and from late September until late December, he and Margaret were out of the country.[6]

It was a wise decision. The visit made a deep impression on him and laid the foundations of an involvement in Indian problems which lasted until well into the 1930s; the account of it which he published after his return, under the title *The Awakening of India*, reveals a great deal about the author as well as about the subject. For if the tangled problems of Indian administration and finance offered a challenge to MacDonald the pragmatist, the sights and smells of India, the heritage of the Indian past and, above all perhaps, the generous mysticism of the Hindu religion, appealed even more to MacDonald the romantic. He was particularly struck by the Holy city of Benares, where he and Margaret drifted down the river:

past places varying in their degrees of sacredness, past stairs which rise upwards in uninterrupted flights and others which are broken by shrines, by masses of bamboo rods bearing wicker-work baskets at their tips, by platforms where wise and holy men teach novices the way of life, and in the end we come to where the poor Hindu body seeks rest at last. All day long thin blue columns of smoke rise from this ghat; all day long they seem to be building piles of wood there; all day long processions come bearing gaily decorated burdens on their shoulders. The bodies wrapped up in white, or pink, or yellow cloth, lie with their feet in the water, waiting for the pyre.[7]

His attention was not, however, confined to the picturesque. 'India', he wrote, 'is the home of the poverty-stricken'; for days, the traveller 'sees nothing but thin bodies, toiling, toiling, toiling, trudging, trudging, trudging; or pinched bodies worshipping, worshipping, worshipping with a sadness that one sees in no other temples'.[8] And India's poverty was largely due to the British. In the first place, there were the direct costs of the Empire – the legacy of an epoch of 'bombastic Imperialism at the expense of India'. India contributed too much to the costs of Empire, while too little was spent on economic development which would benefit the Indians themselves.[9] But direct exploitation was only part of the reason for India's poverty. Much more important was the dislocation of the traditional economy of the Indian village, brought about by an individualistic capitalism which was proving 'even more destructive of the best that is in India ... than it has proved to be in the West'.[10]

Like Keir Hardie, however, who had visited India two years before, MacDonald saw no practical alternative to British rule for years to come. As its title implies, the main theme of *The Awakening of India* is the growth of Indian national self-consciousness. Of this MacDonald warmly approved. 'We can conceive of strenuous times when, with a hymn like "O God, our help in ages past" on their lips our people went out gladly to die,' he wrote enthusiastically. 'Some Indians are now living in that time.'[11] As time went on, he believed, Indian nationalism would gather strength. The educated Hindus who formed the spearhead of the nationalist movement were, he conceded, only a tiny minority as yet, but the few were 'becoming many. Every year adds to their numbers and their disappointments'.[12] But although he was fiercely critical of the narrow-minded British officials, who refused to mix socially with the Indians, and whose attitudes were driving the nationalists into increasing hostility to British rule, he did not believe that India would be ready for self-government in the foreseeable future. The 'warring elements' in Indian life needed 'a unifying and controlling power'. Britain was 'the nurse of India. Deserted by her guardian, India would be the prey of disruptive elements within herself as well as the victim of her own too enthusiastic worshippers to say nothing of what would happen to her from incursions from the outside.'[13] The right policy was slowly to develop parliamentary institutions; and thanks to the reforms which the Liberal Government had started to introduce, this was, in fact, the path India had now begun to take. For, although Lord Morley, the secretary of state, had denied that the Government's reforms would lead to parliamentary government, 'the intention of reformers is nothing, and the internal momentum of reforms is everything.'[14] What was needed was to give India 'wide liberty to govern herself in all her internal affairs' – a policy which would present great difficulties, but which offered 'the only way to abiding peace'.[15] Today, such conclusions seem tame, perhaps even timid. It is worth remembering that they seem so partly because of what MacDonald was later to do to put them into effect.

II

When the MacDonalds arrived back in England in late December, the election campaign, which did not formally begin until January 1910, was, for all practical purposes, under way. In Leicester, the result was scarcely in doubt. As in 1906, MacDonald faced only one Liberal candidate; as in 1906, he was comfortably elected, only a few hundred votes behind the Liberal. But the rest of the country spoke with a more uncertain voice. When the House of Commons assembled in February 1910, the Liberals had 275 seats – only two more than the Unionists. The Irish had 80; the Labour Party, its strength augmented by the miners' members, had 40. If the Irish abstained, the Labour Party might hold the balance. If it combined with the Irish and dissident Radical backbenchers, the Government might be severely shaken, perhaps even overthrown. On paper, Labour's position was stronger than ever before. In practice, it was to be a source of confusion, dissension and bitterness.

The confusion was due largely to the new problems created by the election results: the dissension and bitterness were exacerbated by the old problem of finding an acceptable chairman. Hardie had stayed in the chair for only two years. Henderson followed Hardie's precedent, and after two years as chairman he, in turn, retired. Thus the party's first task after the general election was to choose his successor. Even in 1908, MacDonald's name had been canvassed. By now, with the debate on the 'right to work' Bill to his credit, his standing in the party was higher. Unlike Hardie, he was acceptable to the non-socialist trade unions; unlike Henderson, he was a socialist, and a member of the I.L.P. There is little doubt that he believed himself, and was widely believed, to be the best candidate. Yet he was reluctant to throw his hat into the ring. The British Labour movement had traditionally been reluctant to combine symbolic authority with real power. Its 'chairmen' and 'presidents' were figureheads: power rested with 'secretaries', theoretically responsible to committees. The L.R.C., and later the Labour Party, followed this tradition. The chairman presided over the National Executive: it was MacDonald, the secretary, who controlled the machine. Under Hardie and Henderson, the parliamentary party had followed a similar pattern. Thus the temporary chairmanship of the parliamentary party would be a poor exchange for the permanent secretaryship of the party outside, while it would be difficult to persuade the party to allow both offices to be held at once or to make the parliamentary chairmanship permanent. Moreover, MacDonald believed in strong leadership. 'I do not care a dump about the chairmanship,' he told Hardie in a characteristic passage. 'I do want the Party however to be led. Let it be led to the devil if you like, but don't let it be the nerveless thing of last Session.'[16] But strong leadership was hardly compatible with a temporary chairmanship.

So he dithered—his uncertainties multiplied by a bitter squabble with Arthur Henderson, who had been in charge of the party offices while he had been away in India. Henderson believed, with what justification it is not clear, that MacDonald had looked upon his appointment as a personal insult, and, in a wounded letter to W. C. Robinson, declared that he felt the matter 'very much' and considered 'that in the interests of the harmonious working of the Committee it should be looked into'.[17] MacDonald, for his part, seems to have suspected that Henderson was trying to dislodge him from the secretaryship. Probably towards the end of January he wrote to Hardie that the assistant secretary, James Middleton, had told him that 'everything is arranged. I am to be *put* in the chair of the Party & asked to resign the Secretaryship which is then to be filled by Henderson.'[18] Hardie's reply was the reverse of reassuring:

As it happened, Henderson and I talked together for the best part of an hour ... Someone it appears told him that you said his appointment to act in your absence was an insult to you, & he is very wroth about this. Then he is angry about the payment offered him, & wants (a) to bring the matter before the Executive and (b) to tender his resignation in order to raise the whole question of your attitude to him ...

He also spoke about the Chairmanship & I at once suspected what you now tell me. You can however foil that by refusing nomination. I shd have advised that in any case. We are in for more criticism than ever in the new parliament ... and were you in the Chair this would concentrate itself on you which would not be good.[19]

Meanwhile, others had also begun to sniff out the ground. On February 1st, George Barnes—formerly the general secretary of the engineering union, and himself a candidate for the chairmanship in 1908—wrote to inquire about MacDonald's intentions, offering his support if it was required, but adding that he was not prepared to stand down for anyone else.[20]

In the midst of these preliminary soundings, MacDonald suffered two shattering emotional blows, in quick succession. On February 3rd, his youngest son, David, died of diphtheria. Meanwhile his mother had been taken seriously ill. A few days after David's death he hurried back to Lossiemouth, to find her in delirium. '[T]his is the most heartbreaking experience I have yet had,' he wrote in a letter to Margaret. 'I am sitting with mother & the poor thing is glaring at me with wild eyes telling me of the terrible things that have been done to her. They have ill-used her and beaten her and there are now evil persons about and holes in the wall through which light is coming. Death is terrible but oh nothing like this.'[21] On February 11th, she died. In the circumstances it is not surprising that MacDonald should have found it hard to make up his mind. He told Barnes that he had not committed himself one way or the other. 'I should be very unwilling to give up the secretaryship at the present time,' he added significantly, 'although being chairman of the Party in the House during these trying times has great attractions for me.'²² But the pressure on him continued to mount, and it came from a quarter particularly respected. On February 8th, David Shackleton wrote from the party conference at Newport:

> I am very sorry you will not be able to be with us this week. I can fully sympathise with you & Mrs. MacDonald in this dark hour. Time alone can make the cloud pass away. Have courage your little ones will give you comfort.
>
> Had you been here, it was my intention to have a talk with you about the Chairmanship. In my opinion you are the man for the post, & if you agree to accept, I shall be glad to move you for the position ...
>
> I have also given notice that at the Party Meeting I shall move (1) That a Vice-Chairman be not appointed but that the last preceding Chairman shall be Vice-Chairman by virtue of his position as an Ex-Chairman. (2) That whilst the Chairman should be elected annually he should be eligible for re-election similar [sic] to the Office of secretary & Whip.
>
> I have long felt that the position of Chairman should be of a more permanent character than it is at present.²³

This was an important development. MacDonald evidently agreed to let his name go forward, though he remained anxious about the secretaryship. On February 11th, Shackleton wrote that he was pleased 'to find that you do not refuse the suggestion I made'; and added that it had never occurred to him 'that you being Secretary of the National Party would make any bar to you accepting the Chairmanship of the Parliamentary Party'.²⁴ On February 15th, the *Daily Telegraph* printed a picture of MacDonald with the caption 'who has consented to accept nomination as leader of the Labour Party in the House of Commons', while the *Daily Chronicle* reported that at the party meeting that day, MacDonald would be proposed for the Labour Party chairmanship and that a proposition would probably be moved to enable the office to be held for more than two years. But the final outcome was as confusing as the events which had led up to it. 'I did my best to persuade them to appoint you,'²⁵ Shackleton assured MacDonald some months later, but on what basis remains unclear. In any case, he failed. On February 16th, the *Daily Chronicle* reported briefly that, at the Labour Party meeting the day before, George Barnes had been unanimously elected as chairman.

MacDonald's opinion of Barnes had never been high, and within a month of Barnes's election they found themselves on opposite sides on two critical questions of party tactics. During the general election campaign, Asquith had given the impression that if the Liberals won, the House of Lords would be summarily shorn of its veto. It soon became clear that this impression was false. The Cabinet decided that, before it tackled the Lords, the Budget must be passed a second time by the Commons. To the Irish, and to many Radical backbenchers, this seemed a gross betrayal of the Government's election pledges. John Redmond, the Irish leader, threatened that his party would oppose the Budget unless the Government postponed it, or gave a guarantee that the Lords would be dealt with before the year was up. Barnes – fearing that the Labour Party might be thought 'a mere drifting appendage'[26] to the Liberal Government – decided that he, too, should intervene. On February 17th, he issued a statement declaring that the Government's policy was unacceptable to the Labour Party.[27] The press buzzed with rumours of a revolt among the Radical backbenchers; and it seemed possible that the Government might be defeated. But Barnes had failed to discover whether the rest of the Labour Party agreed with him. In quick succession Snowden told the Press Association that Barnes's statement was only a personal opinion; Henderson announced that he would make no comment until he had heard Barnes's explanation for speaking in the name of the party; and MacDonald declared that he was 'as innocent as a new-born babe with regard to the statement made by Mr. Barnes'.[28] At the party meeting on February 21st, Barnes's policy was repudiated. As MacDonald put it in the *Labour Leader*:

> I moved in the Party meeting that the Party attack should be wider, more drastic and more determined than the mere Radical policy of veto first and veto only – with a dissolution at the end of a month or so. I wanted the Labour Party to declare that the Budget which had been passed by the old Parliament had been passed for good and all so far as the House of Commons is concerned, and should therefore be returned to the House of Lords without discussion or alteration. The Party agreed.[29]

The second question arose two weeks later. On March 7th, in the debate on the army estimates, MacDonald moved an amendment deploring the Government's administration of the so-called 'fair wages clause' in assigning contracts. Charles Mallett, the financial secretary to the War Office, made what Hardie called a 'Reactionary speech'[30] and what MacDonald, more diplomatically, described as 'an unsatisfactory reply'.[31] It was clear that the Opposition would vote with the Labour Party; if MacDonald's amendment were pressed to a division the Government might lose. 'Barnes says yes,' Hardie noted; 'opinion against him.'[32] Next day the debate was resumed. After the Government had given an assurance that the spirit of the Labour Party's amendment would be observed in future, and that the cases MacDonald had raised would be referred to an inter-departmental committee, an officers' meeting was hurriedly called to decide what line to take. It decided to abstain: 'Barnes alone', as Hardie put it, 'wanting to vote for our own party motion.'[33] Thus the House was treated to the curious spectacle of 150 Unionists voting for the Labour Party's amendment, while the mover of the amendment stayed out of the division lobby, and a number of Labour M.P.s, including Henderson and Shackleton, actually voted against.

III

In MacDonald's eyes, the alternative would have been equally curious and more damaging. He was prepared to fight the Government when the Labour Party's vital interests were at stake, perhaps even to bring it down. In December 1909, in the famous Osborne judgment, the House of Lords had upheld an injunction against the Railway Servants restraining the union from spending its funds on political purposes. In effect, the whole basis of Labour Party finance had suddenly become illegal; and the reversal of the Osborne judgment became an important priority of Labour policy. In the summer of 1910, the Labour Party asked the Government for facilities for a Bill drawn up by the Joint Board, which would have restored the previous position. In spite of frequent deputations to Asquith, however, the Government did nothing; and in the September issue of the *Socialist Review*, MacDonald warned that its attitude was 'tantamount to a declaration of war ... It is to stand supinely by whilst Trades Unionism is being imprisoned within such narrow bounds that it cannot meet with any success the attacks that are now being made upon it. This is a new factor in the situation, and it ought to influence the attitude of the Parliamentary Party.' In November he warned that unless the Government changed its mind, the Labour Party might vote against the budget.[34]

Behind the scenes, however, force had been supplemented by diplomacy. One of the most obnoxious features of the Labour Party, in the eyes of many otherwise friendly Liberals, was the so-called 'pledge', originally introduced into the L.R.C. constitution as a result of the squabble with Richard Bell. The 'pledge' bound Labour candidates and M.P.s to 'accept' the constitution, and to 'abide by the decisions of the Parliamentary Party' in carrying out its aims; and in the Osborne judgment, the Law Lords had fastened on this as unconstitutional. In September 1910, however, the Labour Party Executive agreed to recommend that the pledge should be abandoned, and the party constitution amended accordingly;[35] and as Bruce Glasier pointed out when the amendment was debated at the next party conference, it was widely believed that the Executive's decision was designed to propitiate the class enemy. On October 27th, MacDonald noted in his diary:

> Next move to get pledge removed. It never amounted to much, but the recommendation to remove it has put the Liberal and Tory friends of Osborne into a fix. Laughed over the telephone with Elibank about it. Sent memorandum to [Lloyd] George on Osborne after lunch with him and Masterman.[36]

Towards the end of November, Asquith promised that the Government would introduce payment of members and introduce legislation to allow the trade

ence to MacDonald's actions: the policy he followed between 1910 and 1914 followed logically from the theories he had sketched out in *Socialism and Society* as far back as 1905. But, although they did not lead him to adopt a new policy, they may well have fortified his determination to stick to his old one. Socialism, he had argued in *Socialism and Society*, was the heir of Liberalism. It would come not through conflicts or catastrophe but because men were bound to realize sooner or later that the social reforms advocated by the Liberals pointed in its direction. The obvious implication was that the best way to promote socialism was to encourage the Liberals to carry out the social reforms they advocated, and to support them when they did. When the Liberals were sunk in internal dissension, as they had been at the turn of the century, or sat passively in the face of grave social problems, as they had appeared to do in 1907 and 1908, it would make sense for a socialist to attack them. It would make no sense to do so when a Liberal Government was moving towards socialism in the way that Mac-Donald's theories implied that it should. And, by any test that MacDonald could have required, this was happening. The Liberalism of 1910 – the Liberalism of Lloyd George and Winston Churchill, spurred on by the Liberalism of M.P.s like C. F. G. Masterman, journalists like Massingham and social theorists like L. T. Hobhouse – was very different from the Liberalism of 1900. It was not socialist, but it was socialistic. Implicitly, if not explicitly, it stood for an unprecedented extension of state power and communal responsibility; arrayed against it were the vested interests which most socialists, in common with most Radicals, saw as the chief obstacles to social progress. Its enemies were Labour's enemies; its aims, increasingly, were Labour's aims. If MacDonald's arguments were valid it would be a form of treachery for Labour to do anything other than support it.

How far he was prepared to take his own logic is uncertain: probably he did not know himself. After the election of January 1910, he gave an interview to the *Christian Commonwealth*, implying that the Labour Party might be prepared to support the Government in return for concessions, but that an outright coalition between the Liberal and Labour parties would suit neither potential partner.[47] Presumably he said something similar to the editor of the *Leicester Daily Mercury*, who wrote to him on January 28th:

> Thanks for your letter. Reading between the lines the Government are warranted in seeking the co-operation of those upon whom they must rely, and I should hope to see you in the Ministry. But I understand and appreciate the difficulties at present. The time has not yet come, but a common ground of action is surely appearing.[48]

But although it is clear that some of his Liberal supporters in Leicester would have liked him to take a post in the Government, it is not clear whether or not he had been offered one. Still less is it clear whether or not he would have liked to take office if it had been available, and if there had been no reason to fear objections from his own party. What is clear, however, is that he had never abandoned his old dream of a great progressive party, embracing Radicals as well as socialists and trade unionists. As recently as January 1908, he had told the *Daily News* that he expected the 'advanced wing of the Liberals' to break away from the official Liberal Party after the next election, and that he hoped to see a 'fusion ... of all members of Parliament whose policy made for Socialism. It would not matter if this united party disowned the name of Socialism. All he was concerned about was that the policy should be based upon the present principles of the Labour Party.'[49] A radical breakaway was much less likely in 1910 than in 1908, for by 1910 the 'advanced Liberals', whose participation was essential if it were to occur, were making the running inside the Government. But the dream remained; and MacDonald could have been forgiven for coming to the conclusion that it could be realized only if the Labour Party collaborated with the Radicals in the Cabinet. At the 1910 I.L.P. conference, Keir Hardie declared menacingly that the Labour Party had almost 'ceased to count', and warned that it had forgotten that 'they were there primarily not to keep governments in office, or to turn them out, but to organise the working class into a great independent political power to fight for the coming of Socialism.'[50] For MacDonald, keeping the Government in office and fighting for socialism were different sides of the same coin. He wanted the Liberals to stay in power not, as his critics on the left believed, because he was too timid to turn them out, but because he believed that they were moving in the right direction and at the appropriate speed.

Unfortunately for Barnes, however, MacDonald's attitude did not imply a passive conception of the Labour Party's role, or of the role of its parliamentary chairman. MacDonald's political posture has been shrewdly described as one of 'vehement moderation';[51] and both halves of the phrase count equally. He wanted the Labour Party to support the Government, but he also wanted it to give the appearance of vigour and determination. As time went on he became increasingly convinced that Barnes was incapable of walking this delicate tight-rope. 'Barnes's chairmanship a sad failure,' he noted on June 11. 'He has no energy & no grasp of policy. Our action in the House is consequently feeble, and this has a very bad effect outside.'[52] By August, his growing irritation had exploded into print. 'Is it really a failure?', he asked of the Labour Party, in the August issue of the *Socialist Review*. 'We confess that we feel, that on the whole it is.'[53]

It was clear that he was not alone in this feeling. On August 3rd, W. C. Anderson wrote to tell him:

Lie the fault where it may, the country is not getting full value out of the great gifts which your bitterest enemies grudgingly concede you ...

... the party needs you and in the I.L.P. as well as the Labour Party you are very surely coming into your own. It would be a good thing to stimulate the party with helpful criticism; but it would be a bigger thing to seize hold and do what others have failed to do ...

I earnestly hope you will not finally make your mind up about the Chairmanship. It should have been yours before now, and I know something of what happened. But if you stand aside – then who? It is the party that will suffer, and you have given a big slice of your life to the party.[54]

Few men could resist such an appeal. Yet MacDonald was slow to make up his mind. At some point, probably in the autumn or winter of 1910, Barnes wrote to tell him that he did not want the chairmanship and had 'only held the fort'. If MacDonald were 'free to take it', Barnes continued, 'I shd say it is yours any time.'[55] Perhaps in response to this letter and, if not, in response to a similar one, MacDonald wrote in an undated letter to his wife:

> The Barnes message is a difficult one to answer. I am not to take the leadership of an anarchistic party, for I am not to repeat the Rosebery mistake. If Lloyd George's last speech really means the beginning [of] a new policy I am going to help to carry it out. Our best men seem to be very doubtful of the future, & as I can influence things in other ways I am not going to cut myself off from them by becoming the victim of our folks.[56]

In November 1910, the Government's battle over the House of Lords culminated in a second general election. The result was substantially the same as it had been in January. The Irish still held the balance; the Labour Party, now forty-two strong, would still be unable to indulge in the luxury of voting against the Government for fear of bringing it down. The storms of the 1910 Parliament would be unlikely to subside; the chairman of the parliamentary Labour Party would face as daunting a task as before. At first, MacDonald flinched from the prospect. In December he wrote to Snowden to say that he would on no account accept the chairmanship. A few days later, however, he wrote a second time, asking Snowden to spy out the land.[57] Shortly afterwards, in the midst of these vacillations and uncertainties, the unfortunate Barnes suddenly contrived his own undoing. As chairman of the parliamentary party he had to submit a report to the annual conference, which was to meet in the New Year. His first draft contained a bitter attack on his colleagues' 'slackness', 'timidity', and willingness to follow the Government's lead. At this, Henderson – who already seems to have made up his mind that the party needed a new chairman – threw his formidable weight into the scales. On January 2nd, 1911, he wrote to MacDonald complaining angrily that

> the worst blow at the Party comes from its chairman through his Parliamentary Report ...
> I begin to wonder is he is trying to out-distance Grayson[,] McLaughlan [,] the S.D.P. and all the bunch against whom we have been contend-

ing. Of this I am convinced this par will be used with much effect by those named above and also by the Tory Press.

When we remember that his report will be public property before the meeting of the Parliamentary Party it will be said by a section that we refused to re-elect him because he had spoken too plainly. Further it is obvious we cannot re-elect him after this attack. At any rate I cannot support him. I did not do so last year because I was sincerely convinced he lacked those qualities necessary to the position. He has proved a conspicuous failure and now seeks to blame the Party for all the failures and blunders of leadership. It wont do and though he may succeed in bluffing a few extremists he will not escape when in the Party meeting. If nobody else will put the correct position I shall try to do so. This however only increases our difficulty with regard to the chair. I can appreciate your position especially as [? our] opposition to any change is sure to come from Hardie and the I.L.P. members. We must face the difficulty or the Party will be broken. You ought in spite of all the drawbacks to throw yourself into the breach and accept nomination.[58]

Less than a year before, Henderson had been complaining bitterly about MacDonald's attitude to him, and insisting that it should be inquired into by the party Executive. Now he was urging MacDonald to stand for the chairmanship. It is unlikely that he did so out of a sudden access of personal affection, or even out of admiration for MacDonald's character and abilities. He wanted MacDonald as chairman, partly because he wanted to be party secretary himself and believed correctly that he would be a good one, partly because he believed – again correctly – that MacDonald was the only potential candidate capable of reconciling the I.L.P. to the moderate line favoured by the unions. By the same token, it is unlikely that MacDonald had suddenly abandoned his earlier suspicion of Henderson. But personal affection, though a useful aid to political co-operation, is not indispensable to it. MacDonald and Henderson differed in taste, temperament and political background, and it is doubtful if either ever liked the other. Henderson was frequently exasperated by MacDonald's moodiness, unpredictability and unwillingness to communicate; he may also have suspected, not altogether unreasonably, that MacDonald undervalued his talents and took him too much for granted. MacDonald, for his part, found Henderson unimaginative and domineering, and, in later years at any rate, was never quite sure of his support. But although the partnership between them was to have many stormy interludes, and to dissolve in the end amid bitter suspicions and recriminations, it was to be one of the most effective partnerships in British Labour history. To all intents and purposes, it began with Henderson's letter in January 1911.

For MacDonald's long and hesitant journey to the party leadership was now almost over. On January 17th, *The Times* reported that he had decided to offer himself for the Labour Party chairmanship. At about the same time, Barnes was taken ill on the train to Manchester.[59] On the 21st, the *Leicester Pioneer* reported that MacDonald was under strong pressure to accept the chairmanship, but that he would do so only on the understanding that the term of office would be longer than two years. On the 26th, T. D. Benson, the I.L.P. treasurer and one of the leaders of the right wing of the party, wrote to MacDonald to say that there was only one chance that the Labour Party could be

> made into a party and that is for the leadership to fall into the hands of a strong man who can lead. In the Party the strong men are limited as far as I can see to those who have already led and to yourself. Clynes I do not know sufficiently to speak about but he seems very good natured and too cautious. There remains only yourself possible ... If you will not accept it then it is 'God help the Party'. Except Henderson you have no leader. Hardie could hardly be called a Leader. He [was] merely an individual, largely unapproachable, preferring always to plough a lonely furrow, and always wishing to do things off his own bat[.] This in a democratic Party was impossible. It probably split up the Party at its most critical moment, the moment of its birth. If you cannot pull the Party round, no one can. I consider that the attempt is a duty which you cannot refuse to undertake however distasteful it may be to you. I shall be exceedingly disappointed unless you accept.[60]

At about the same time, MacDonald wrote mournfully to Bruce Glasier to say that he saw 'nothing but storms and heartaches ahead', that he could not keep the secretaryship if he became chairman and that if he were to give up the £150 a year which the party paid him as secretary, he would have to make it up in some other way. 'Who will say that I ought to accept the Chairmanship?', he concluded delphically. 'Only one man. And he will simply shrug his shoulders and say: "Who else?" '[61]

The parliamentary party met on February 6th. A letter was read from Barnes, announcing that he did not offer himself for re-election.[62] According to Snowden, a bargain had been struck at the party conference the previous month, whereby MacDonald was to resign the secretaryship in Henderson's favour, in return for becoming chairman.[63] As for the chairmanship, the *Labour Leader* wrote that 'the necessity of having a permanent chief for a fighting force is becoming more and more obvious,' but it is not clear whether this necessity was formally accepted, or even whether it was informally agreed upon.[64] One thing, however, was clear enough. As the *Leicester Pioneer* put it at the end of the week, 'The unanimous election on Monday of Mr Ramsay MacDonald M.P. to be chairman of the Parliamentary Labour party will ... mark a new epoch in the history of the party.'[65]

IV

In the summer of 1910, in the midst of the struggles over the Parliament Bill and the negotiations with the Government over the Osborne judgment, MacDonald noted:

> July 4. My little David's birthday but no little people were calling when I awoke 'Happy Birthday'. Sometimes I feel like a lone dog in the desert howling from pain of heart. Constantly since he died my little boy has been my companion. He comes and sits with me especially on my railway journeys & I feel his little warm hand in mine. That awful morning when I was awakened by the telephone bell, & everything within me shrunk in fear for I knew I was summoned to see him die, comes back often too.[66]

In the summer of 1911, six months after his election to the chairmanship, he suffered an even heavier blow. Margaret had been hit hard by her son's death; it is possible that she never wholly recovered from it. In April 1911, one of her closest friends, Mary Middleton, the secretary of the Women's Labour League and wife of James Middleton, assistant secretary of the Labour Party, died after a long illness. To MacDonald, it seemed in retrospect that the 'will to live' seemed to go out of her. Her work went on: committees, deputations, inquiries, and the care of a growing family. But her resistance had been undermined by years of strain and overwork, and the emotional blows she had suffered had undermined it still further. Towards the end of July she fell ill with blood poisoning;[67] and, as MacDonald put it later:

> On Thursday, the 20th ... she went to Leicester with a member of the Home Office Committee appointed to investigate the management of Industrial Schools; on the morning of Friday she attended a meeting of an Anglo-American Friendship Committee; a little after noon she joined me at the House of Commons with one whom she had desired to meet ever since she had read his pathetic book on the negro, Professor Du Bois; that afternoon we went to the country for a week-end rest. She complained of being stiff, and jokingly showed me the finger carrying her marriage and engagement rings. It was badly swollen and discoloured, and I expressed concern. She laughed away my fears: 'It is only protesting against its burdens!' On Saturday she was so stiff that she could not do her hair, and she was greatly amused by my attempts to help her. On Sunday she had to admit that she was ill and we returned to town. Then she took to bed.[68]

On September 8th, 1911, she died. Part of MacDonald died with her.

For some weeks, he seems to have been in a state of shock. Margaret's body was cremated at Golders Green on September 12th, and the ashes were buried in

Spynie churchyard a few miles from Lossiemouth. The day after the Golders Green service, Bruce Glasier—already MacDonald's closest friend in the inner circle of the I.L.P., and from now on a closer friend still—visited MacDonald at Lincoln's Inn Fields. MacDonald, Glasier wrote later, told him, 'I have sorrowed so much and wept so much that I have no more sorrow or tears left.'[69] Soon afterwards, MacDonald escaped to Lossiemouth; but in the middle of October he had to return briefly to London, for consultations on the Government's Insurance Bill, which was then going through Parliament. He paid a brief visit to the flat at Lincoln's Inn Fields. 'As though the unseen things thought I had not been quite sure,' he wrote in a letter to the Glasiers, 'they howled at me from every nook and corner that she was dead and I was alone.' Since then, he added, 'A horrible reaction has come upon me ... and if work will not give me peace I do not know what I shall do. Oh, if she could only come back and tell me if she knows about us all and cares about us all.'[70]

Condolences poured in, one of the most touching—even at sixty years' distance—from James Middleton at the Labour Party offices:

My Dear Chief,
    As you know, the Emergency Committee of the Party was meeting here just as I got word of your and our loss, and although the news was expected by all of us, none of us could quite realise its truth. The Committee asked me to assure you of their real sympathy with you in your trouble and their high appreciation of Mrs. MacDonald's life work in our Cause. Words are very futile at a time like this and you know so well the spirit of affection and admiration in which she was held by all of us officially connected with the Party. We have some idea of the great blank that will be left in your life—that will be shared very greatly by some of us, you know—and the chief consolation we have and in which we know you will find ease for your heart-ache is that the fruits of her patient, loving service have been gathered by thousands of our working folk. To continue her work more than ever imbued with her spirit of utter selflessness, is the highest way in which we can all pay tribute to her memory and in which you can spend the years that yet remain.
    That you command our kindliest thoughts in this sad hour and our loyal comradeship always may be some little comfort to you.[71]

'We are but two of the many whom she linked so happily together in the movement as a much loved sister keeps the ties of a household gently drawn round all ... ,' wrote Bruce Glasier. 'In the kind letter you wrote me and my sister when my mother died you said that the one great compensation for the loss of dear ones was that it reconciled us to going away ourselves. I remember telling your wife at the time how deeply that thought had touched us all. And now it must be your own chief comfort.'[72]

But MacDonald, as he put it himself, was 'one of those unfortunate people who sorrow alone'; no one, not even the closest friend, could help him much. Partly because of this, and because it was Margaret's dying wish, he wrote a short memoir of her, which was privately printed and circulated to friends. 'I felt myself hearing *her* approval of it,' wrote Katharine Bruce Glasier, 'so much so that I seemed to see her hand on your shoulder as you wrote – & grew foolishly weakly blind with tears for the pain that was there.'[73] The following year, in response to insistent pressure from his friends, MacDonald wrote a longer and fuller biography, which was published in the ordinary way. Both, and especially the memoir, are among the most revealing things he ever wrote. But this public expression of grief, however necessary it may have been psychologically, was not a substitute for the private release of emotion which was now, more than ever, impossible. The memoir ends on a peaceful note:

> I have just returned from a walk she loved to take at nightfall. The vast expanse of the black sky was glittering with stars as when she and I walked together, and she talked of hope like a gem sparkling upon a background of despair; the sea was moaning as it did when she said 'Do not let us speak: let us walk silently, because then we speak most truly'; the weird call of the curlew, flying away into the night, came out of the darkness as it did when I first brought her here, and she shuddered and told me it made her wonder, and wonder, and wonder what was in the heart of the Unknown and the Infinite.[74]

In fact, there was no catharsis; the wound never healed.

Little by little, MacDonald gathered up the threads of his life. Financially, his circumstances were unchanged. The income from Margaret's trust fund – now around £800 a year – was paid to him, partly in respect of the children and partly in respect of himself.[75] A Dutch housekeeper called Miss Byvoets was engaged to look after the children; the household at Lincoln's Inn Fields went on; he plunged more deeply into his work. But at the centre of his life a nagging loneliness remained. In December 1912, Katharine Bruce Glasier wrote:

> I am gathering courage to tell you how over the fire one night we two wives searched our hearts together & fearlessly said to one another that love like ours had no room for one jealous throb. Mary Middleton had spoken to us unfalteringly of her hope that Jim would 'love & live' again in all fulness & I said to Margaret that I knew Bruce's need of the love & sympathy of a true woman so well that were I to go from him my last words would be seek & soon another woman who would 'mother' both him & the bairns for me. And Margaret put her cheek against mine – a very unusual demonstration – you know – & said, I *think* it was – 'And so would I'. – But anyhow I never doubted but we were wholly in sympathy. The feeling that I *have* to tell you this, – almost as if she herself were insisting on it – has been with me for weeks past & I have not dared ... But I am too *sure* of what she

would have wished ... not to have courage to speak out now. I was 12 when my mother died & until my father married again when I was nearly 16 I had no home happiness at all. His grief and loneliness put out the sunshine for us children. And the second wife was tenderly good to us. And Margaret – what of her motherhood? ... It is her will that you *live* – live to carry on the noblest Socialism in the world today – to live gloriously down every mean aspersion of personal ambition & to accomplish the creation of a strong sane Collectivist Party in Britain capable of government in every sense of the word ... She *believed* in your future & she knew your need of sympathy & help. She told me much of your mother. – You know both of us had special reason to love & honour our husbands' mothers & learn from their sorrows & struggles a fiercer morality than any the ordinary world holds. We both *believed* in real marriage: in 'men & women working shoulder to shoulder' – you yourself record that. And here I will stop – proudly holding out both hands to you because I *know* that she who is gone loved & trusted me & showed me glimpses of her innermost soul.[76]

Mrs Bruce Glasier was right. MacDonald did need 'sympathy and help'. Yet the very fact that she was right, it may be, made it impossible for him to take her advice. More than most men, he needed the warmth and security of the home and family he had never had in his own childhood; more than most public figures, he needed the trust and support of others, yet found it hard to give himself away in his relations with them. Margaret had given him what he needed. With her, as with no one else, he was safe. He had repaid her with total devotion. Now she was dead, it was as though the strength of his feeling for her forced him to show over and over again that no one could fill her place. As his son Malcolm remembered years later:

[A]t the time of my mother's death ... my father's grief was absolutely horrifying to see. Her illness and her death had a terrible effect on him of grief; he was distracted; he was in tears a lot of the time when he spoke to us, and, as I say, it was almost frightening to a youngster like myself ... [T]his continued right down the years and over and over again not only during the next years but the next decades one would catch sudden glimpses of his eternal devotion to my mother. For example, on the anniversary – the first anniversary of her death – at the very hour when she died, he asked for all us children to come up to the room where he had been working; and again he was in a state of terrible grief. I may be exaggerating this but if I remember correctly he had his watch out ... on his desk or in his hand and he sat there and he said when the actual moment came of her death, twelve months beforehand, that Mummy had now died and he spoke to us about her, of course in a wonderful way, but with this terrible tear-stained agony of grief ... And always on the anniversary in one way or another he indicated to us, even when he was appallingly busy, in after years, that this was the day of the tragedy ... one got glimpses of this down the ... twenty-five years ... that passed after her death before his own death ... I can remember, for example, some visitor, I think an American, being at lunch with us one day at Chequers or somewhere, and this rather foolish person, utterly well-meaning, said to my father: 'Why have you never married again?' And my father's face just went absolutely still and profoundly serious, and he said: 'My heart is in the grave' ... And one always felt that that was so.[77]

It would be wrong to exaggerate. MacDonald was not broken by his loss. His greatest triumphs and failures were still to come; and in private life, he made warm friendships with a number of women—Lady Margaret Sackville, Mrs Molly Hamilton, Cecily Gordon-Cumming, Lady Londonderry—who gave him some of the emotional support he needed. But these relationships could not fill the gap. Now, and for the rest of his life, he was alone.

CHAPTER 8

Pressure group under pressure

I

THE leader of a new party, like the leader of a new nation, must build his power on personality, not precedents. MacDonald was not a party leader at all in the sense in which Conservatives or Liberals understood the term. His office was still subject to annual election and did not even carry an automatic right to a seat on the party Executive. His followers in the House of Commons could scarcely be considered a party in the normal sense. They did not aspire to govern the country, but to win concessions from those who did; the few who rebelled against the limitations of pressure-group politics rarely put forward positive policies of their own. Trade-union M.P.s owed their first loyalty to their unions and were often away on union business. I.L.P. members were apt to see themselves as independent political guerrillas rather than as members of a disciplined parliamentary force. Yet, in three years, MacDonald extended the power and authority of his office far beyond the limits accepted by his predecessors. He was unanimously re-elected at the beginning of every session. In accordance with his bargain with Henderson he resigned the secretaryship before the 1912 party conference, but the constitution was promptly amended to make it possible for him to go on sitting on the Executive as party treasurer, still as the representative of the conference as a whole and not of any one section. Above all, a subtle change took place in the emotional and symbolic aspects of the chairmanship: in the mood and style of the chairman's relations with ordinary party members, in the tone in which he was referred to on ceremonial occasions, in his role as the party's public representative and embodiment. In 1914, as in 1911, the parliamentary Labour Party was still in practice little more than a trade-union pressure group attached to a mass movement. But, to an extent which few Labour men would have thought possible, or perhaps desirable, in 1906, it was now a pressure group with a leader.

This change, however, was accompanied by growing discord within the party. The years of MacDonald's chairmanship were among the most turbulent in modern British history. Industry was disrupted by great strikes. Militant suffragettes employed increasingly violent forms of direct action. Ulster Protestants threatened armed rebellion. The Liberal Government faced these upheavals with great sang-froid and skill; so far from growing stale in office, it seemed to gain new vitality and boldness. All the same, the Liberal Party was a child of the long peace of the nineteenth century. It took for granted an expanding economy, without irreconcilable conflicts of interest, and it also took for granted a stable political order, in which the wishes of the majority would prevail without appeals to force. The sharp increase in industrial unrest cast doubt on the first of these assumptions; the suffragettes, and still more the Ulstermen, posed a direct challenge to the second. MacDonald and most of his colleagues shared the liberal assumptions which were now called in question. The challenge to the Liberals was also a challenge to them; on the most contentious issues of the time they fought on the Government's side – not because they were pusillanimous or unprincipled, but because they recognized that its enemies were their enemies too.

Although most Labour men found themselves at one with the Liberals, however, a minority did not. A few were actively hostile to Liberalism. Others saw the struggle between the Liberals and their enemies as a pointless and perhaps sinister diversion from the struggle between labour and capital. The gulf between these two attitudes was widened by the new situation ushered in by the 1910 elections, and by the Liberals' success in adapting themselves to it. As we have seen, many ordinary members of the I.L.P. had been bitterly discontented with the performance of the parliamentary party as early as 1906 or 1907. Until 1910, however, their discontent had not been reflected in the parliamentary party itself. All Labour M.P.s had been able to denounce the Government's inactivity during the trade depression of 1908; all Labour M.P.s had been able to welcome the People's Budget and the perspectives it opened up. When the Liberals lost their overall parliamentary majority, this ceased to be true. Those who saw the parliamentary party as an instrument for winning limited and tangible concessions for the 'Labour interest' were now reluctant to risk bringing down a Government which had already done much for their constituents, and which might do more once the struggle with the Lords was out of the way. Those who saw it as a protagonist in the class war, and in the long run as the vehicle for a new society, were anxious to follow a more adventurous course.

As time went on, moreover, the Government did carry through more social reforms and the parliamentary party did win further concessions for the 'Labour interest'. In the process, its leaders drew still closer to the Government, and in doing so they provoked still more hostility from those of their followers who rebelled against the limitations of pressure-group politics. Not for the last time in the party's history, success bred more dissension than failure. The 'Labour Alliance' had been formed to give the organized working class a voice of its own in the House of Commons. By 1914 many of its members were complaining loudly that the voice had nothing to say.

II

The first big milestone on this road was reached in May 1911, when Lloyd George introduced the National Insurance Bill on which he and his officials had been working spasmodically for almost three years. It was a vast and complex measure, but the principles were simple. There was to be an elaborate system of state insurance against sickness, compulsory for all men and women employed under contracts of service, and against unemployment in certain trades. The system was to be administered largely through approved Friendly Societies, though there was to be a special class of Post Office contributors to cover those unable or unwilling to join an Approved Society. There were to be premiums, partly paid by the state, partly by the employer and partly by the employee. Politically, this last provision may have been indispensable. As Beatrice Webb noted sardonically, Lloyd George's first asset was 'the word *insurance*', which to the governing class implied 'the voluntary contributions of the persons benefited – a method of raising revenue which has saved the pockets of all other persons'.[1] Precisely because of this, however, that part of the scheme aroused intense opposition from the Left. Beatrice Webb's Minority Report on the Poor Law had rejected the contributory principle; by an overwhelming majority, the 1911 I.L.P. conference had called for a non-contributory scheme. Fabians and I.L.P.-ers now joined hands in opposition to Lloyd George. The National Insurance Bill, they declared, was a palliative which left the fundamental cause of destitution untouched; it would do nothing for the poorest workers, for they would be unable to meet the conditions of benefit it laid down; it was a misguided and mischievous attempt to cure the 'poverty of the workers' by 'taxing their poverty'.

To MacDonald, these arguments were anathema. Privately he thought the Bill 'very crude'. It was 'amazing', he noted, 'to find how little it had been thought out on the industrial side.'[2] In public, too, his initial response was guarded. The premiums, he declared in the House of Commons on May 4th, were almost certainly too high; the balance as between state, employer and employee was unfair; and the position of the trade unions needed to be safeguarded.[3] On two fundamental points, however, he had no misgivings. Lloyd George's proposals, he argued in the second reading debate, implied that the state had at last accepted a responsibility to protect the wage earner against the accidents of life which 'smashed the road right away in front of him'; as such, they marked one of 'those advances which one finds in public opinion happening periodically about once every century'.[4] As for the contributory principle, this was not only not a drawback; it was a positive advantage. As he put it in the *Socialist Review*:

On the 4th May the Chancellor of the Exchequer introduced a scheme of Industrial Insurance so wide in its scope and so bold in its conception that even to this day we do not feel competent to pronounce on its general effect. Its foundation, however, is quite simple – Insurance. To this, objection has been taken on the ground that great masses of people live under the poverty line and ought not to be asked to contribute to any Insurance scheme, and ... appeals have been made to the gallery and we have been told that the grand result of the proposal is to make the wage-earners pay towards their own sickness and invalidity the enormous sum of £10,000,000 a year ... We shall content ourselves with two comments ... The first is that the German Socialist Trade Unions, after having opposed insurance, are now its doughtiest advocates ... The second observation we make is that without some system of premium payment, the whole scheme would degenerate into a national charity of the most vicious kind, which would adversely affect wages and would not help the Socialist spirit.[5]

Thus the battle was couched not in terms of principle against expediency but in terms of one principle against another; and the longer it lasted, the more heated the combatants became. Towards the end of June, a special conference of trade unions was held to determine the movement's attitude to the Bill; by a comfortable majority, it voted to accept the contributory principle. Meanwhile, the Bill's opponents gathered their forces. On May 26th, Beatrice Webb recorded a visit from George Lansbury to discuss the 'amendment or postponement' of 'Lloyd George's rotten scheme of sickness insurance'.[6] At the end of June, the *Labour Leader* declared that 'So far as Socialism is concerned, the advocates of a non-contributory scheme stand on the firm ground of policy and principle.'[7] In July, the annual meeting of the Fabian Society also decided to oppose the Bill. By now the clash between the socialist and trade-unionist wings of the Labour Alliance had reached the floor of the House of Commons. On July 6th, the Government brought in the Finance Resolution. MacDonald announced that 'nobody in the Committee need have the least doubt but that the Labour Party stands for a contributory scheme so far as this Bill is concerned.'[8] At the end of the debate, Lansbury and Fred Jowett, chairman of the I.L.P. the previous year and an old opponent of MacDonald, acted as tellers for an amendment opposing the contributory principle. It was defeated by 220 to 9, Snowden and Keir Hardie voting for it and the majority of the party voting with the Government. 'If the I.L.P. will stand that,' Snowden wrote in a letter to the *Labour Leader*, 'it will stand anything. If it submits to this it is time to go into voluntary liquidation as a preliminary to affiliating with the National Liberal Federation.'[9]

MacDonald and his supporters were equally indignant. Tom Fox, the representative of the Trade Councils and local Labour Parties on the National Executive, wrote that it would be 'the beginning of the end of the Labour Party if every time there is a difference of opinion we are to blazon forth into newspaper controversy' and urged that the Executive should consider the whole matter.[10] W. C. Robinson, also a member of the National Executive and one of the leaders of the textile workers, hoped that MacDonald would 'conquer these disappointed and dissatisfied demons'.[11] To the issue of the Insurance Bill and its merits had been added the even more high-charged issue of party discipline. 'If a Party is to enjoy the least respect or influence in the House of Commons it must be united ... ', MacDonald wrote menacingly in an editorial in the *Socialist Review*. '[W]e are afraid that members are beginning to abuse the liberty they enjoy in the Party.'[12]

The abuse was easier to identify than to put right. In the summer a great meeting to oppose the Insurance Bill was held at the Memorial Hall, addressed, among others, by Snowden and George Lansbury. Somewhat unconvincingly, MacDonald compared its organizers to the Unionist die-hards who had been engaged at about the same time in a last-ditch fight against the Parliament Bill,[13] but the agitation continued undeterred through the recess. At the end of September, Henderson wrote MacDonald a long letter, complaining about the activities of 'friend Hardie', instancing among other delinquencies Hardie's stand on the Insurance Bill, and urging that 'the Party meeting must take the matter in hand immediately we resume in the Autumn Session.'[14] The party meeting duly took place at the end of October; and the party decided, once again, that the Bill should be supported. Next day, Lansbury and Will Thorne, the gas workers' leader, divided the House against the Government's motion to suspend standing orders, and in December nine Labour M.P.s voted against the third reading. MacDonald had begun his chairmanship with high hopes – looking forward, in his anonymous editorial in the *Socialist Review*, to the possibility that 'Mr. MacDonald can get better work out of his colleagues than they have yet given.'[15] By December he was complaining, with understandable bitterness, that the Labour Party had been prevented from following a consistent policy by 'a kind of irregular guerrilla warfare without plan, which only confused the public'.[16]

His bitterness was due, in part, to the damage which had been done to his authority as chairman. But it was not only due to that. '[W]hilst the Socialist demonstrators were speaking,' he wrote contemptuously of the campaign against the Insurance Bill during the summer, 'the plenipotentiaries of the Labour Party were extracting concessions from the Government.'[17] This was not an idle boast. Before the second reading, MacDonald listed a number of detailed improvements which he wanted to see in the Bill. Instead of the employee paying a weekly contribution of 4d., the employer paying 3d. and the state, 2d., he wrote, each should pay 3d. The provisions for married women should be improved; it should be made 'much clearer than the Bill at present does' that trade unions could be approved as Friendly Societies; finally, the proposals about contributions to be paid by low-paid workers should be 'simplified'.[18] On the first and most far-reaching of these suggestions, the Labour Party staged a gallant fight in committee and was soundly beaten. On the others, the record was remarkably satisfactory. A number of important concessions were made in respect of married women. It was made clear that the unions could act as Friendly Societies without jeopardizing their freedom of action in industrial disputes. Low-paid workers were eventually exempted from contributions. Meanwhile – and, from the Labour Party's point of view, at least as important – the Government honoured its commitment to bring in payment for members of parliament. At the beginning of August, MacDonald told the readers of the *Leicester Pioneer*:

> It would be very dull to explain point by point how we are moulding and improving the Insurance Bill. All I need say at present is that there is more to follow, and that the amendments which are to be accepted on future clauses and schedules will convince our friends once more that a little trust in their party is to be more than amply repaid. It is all very well for a gathering of men who know little about what is going on … to pass what appear to be valiant resolutions, but it is our duty to stick to our work, to fix upon faults, to concentrate our attacks upon them, and to bring up, clause by clause, and day by day, essential amendments. May I also add it is the duty of the men outside to see that they do not weaken our power by their own haste and folly.[19]

The tone was, perhaps, a little self-righteous, but in the circumstances the content was reasonable enough.

III

By the autumn of 1911, then, MacDonald and the Labour Party leadership had obtained a number of modifications in the Insurance Bill, and had been largely instrumental in persuading the Government to introduce payment for members of parliament. In doing so, they had drawn closer to the Government than they had ever been before – so much so that, in mid-October, Elibank sent MacDonald an advance copy of the Government's guillotine motion, with a covering note explaining that he would 'get into great trouble with the House if it were known that I had issued this document'.[20] They had reached this position partly because of the pressures of the parliamentary situation and partly because of their conception of the function of their party – a conception which most of their colleagues had no wish to change. Yet the position in which they found themselves was not altogether satisfactory. If they were to win concessions from the Government, they had to make concessions in return; though they influenced it, their influence was that of an ally, not of a partner. They could modify its policies in detail, but they could not help to determine its underlying strategy.

From the Government's point of view, the position was still less satisfactory. It needed Labour support in the division lobbies, but although it was usually able to obtain that support, it could not count on it. To make matters worse, its tacit alliance with the leaders of the parliamentary Labour Party was not always reflected in the country. At the general election the Labour Party had, on the whole, avoided three-cornered fights, but at by-elections they were more frequent; and now that the Government's parliamentary majority was so precarious, by-elections mattered. From the Government's point of view, the logic of the situation pointed more and more clearly to an outright coalition with the Labour Party.

As we have seen, there had been some speculation along these lines early in 1910. In the summer of 1911, it was renewed. In June a French paper, *La Dépêche*, announced that the Liberals were thinking of setting up a Ministry of Labour, with MacDonald as the minister. Towards the end of July, the editor of the *Sheffield Guardian* sent MacDonald a telegram, asking whether it was true that he was about to take office in the Government.[21] These rumours appear to have been without foundation. By the autumn, however, the situation had become still more favourable to a coalition. MacDonald was now working more closely with the Government than ever before; the Insurance Bill was still a long way from the statute book, and opposition to it seemed to be growing in the country; in November, the Unionists gained a seat from the Government at a by-election in Oldham, in a three-cornered fight. The effect of these factors can be seen in MacDonald's diary:

> 22nd October. Breakfasted with Chancellor of Exchequer. He sounded me on coalition Government: 'not just yet.'

> 13 November. Saw Elibank. Wanted to know privately if coalition were possible at next Election. We shd. like it, he said, but it is question for those who wd. come in. This was in connection with Oldham by-election which that day was being lost to Liberals by three-cornered fight.

> 14. Oldham Election. Excellent result for Labour Candidate. Poll from 1,000 to 2,000 more than expected ...

> 15. Liberals very angry about Oldham. Long interview with Elibank who says Premier very much upset. Specially angry because it is such a good beginning for Bonar Law. Tells me he is to fight 3 of my men ... [22]

MacDonald's reply to this mixture of cajolery and bullying is not known. As we have seen, he had looked forward for years to a progressive alliance between Labour and the Radical wing of the Liberal Party. As recently as May 1911, he had written that the Labour Party and the 'Socialistic Radicals' were 'converging upon Socialist positions', and had prophesied that a merger would take place between them when the Radicals had 'capitulated to the Labour Party in the same way as the Liberal Unionists capitulated to the Conservatives'.[23] The Insurance Bill, it could be argued, was a sign that this capitulation had now occurred. Years later, moreover, Arthur Henderson told the Webbs that in 1910 or 1911 MacDonald had proposed to enter a 'Coalition Cabinet with Lloyd George and Balfour (to oust Asquith)', and had offered Henderson an under-secretaryship which Henderson had refused.[24]

Yet none of this is conclusive. MacDonald had argued in favour of combination, not with the Liberal Party as such, but only with its Radical section. Henderson's story was told ten years after it was alleged to have taken place, and is clearly inaccurate in its details. It is true that Lloyd George had flirted with the idea of a coalition with the Conservatives in 1910, but there is no evidence that his plans had included a place for MacDonald, who was not chairman of the parliamentary Labour Party at the time. There is no evidence that Lloyd George contemplated a coalition with any Conservatives in October or November 1911 – least of all with Balfour, who had just been deposed from the leadership of his party. Nevertheless, it would be foolish to dismiss Henderson's story altogether. What may well have happened is that, when he told his story to the Webbs in 1921, he had conflated the rumours which he must have heard of a Liberal–Conservative coalition in 1910 with Lloyd George's offer to MacDonald in 1911; the 'not just yet' in MacDonald's diary may have been Henderson's opinion rather than his own. In all this morass of speculation, however, two points are clear: no coalition was formed; but the pressures which had made it a possibility continued.

For a while, other pressures seemed to point in the opposite direction. 'I have been working hard for six months re. the Transport Workers upheaval,' wrote Ben Tillett on July 5th, 1911. 'We are now having to deal with the miniature earthquake.'[25] Since 1906 real wages had fallen, largely owing to rising prices. Meanwhile, the strength and militancy of the unions had increased. Since 1907, the number of days lost in industrial disputes had grown considerably, and during the hot summer of 1911, while the negotiations over the Insurance Bill preoccupied Whitehall, rising tension in two major industries reached a crisis at about the same time. In June, there was a series of sporadic strikes by the seamen at various ports. In July, unrest spread to the docks, notably in London and Liverpool. By August, the strike on Merseyside had spread from the dockers to the railwaymen; and from them it spread rapidly to railwaymen in other parts of the country. This is not the place to examine the complex history of the dispute. The fundamental points were that most of the railway companies refused to recognize the unions; and that a strike on this issue had been averted in 1907 by a Conciliation Agreement, setting up a form of compulsory arbitration, accepted by both sides under Government pressure, but nevertheless based on proposals emanating from the employers. Now the men were in revolt against the Conciliation Agreement: by mid-August about 50,000 of them were on strike. It was clear that unless the union leaders took action of some kind, their authority would be undermined. On August 15th, the executives of the railway unions met at Liverpool, and agreed to issue an ultimatum to the employers. The railway companies were given twenty-four hours in which to agree to negotiate the basis of a settlement with the unions. If they refused, there would be a national strike. Once again, recognition was the crux. If the companies agreed to deal with the unions, that in itself would be victory for the men.[26]

At first, the dispute drove a wedge between the Government and the leaders of the parliamentary Labour Party, at a time when the negotiations over the Insurance Bill were drawing them closer together. MacDonald was, of course, bitterly hostile to any suggestion that strike action could, in itself, be an effective substitute for parliamentary action; the syndicalist ideology which some observers saw behind the so-called 'labour unrest' of these years seemed to him foolish and dangerous – a form of 'flamboyant impossibilism', and a 'feeble' form at that.[27] The syndicalist strategy of the general strike, he thought, was almost bound to fail. Syndicalists, he wrote, assumed that in a general strike society would become more and more helpless in the strikers' hands. The opposite was the truth. The longer the strike lasted, the more apt society would be to see the striker as its enemy. Little by little, it would organize itself against him, as in the recent strikes in Sweden where 'Coachmen drove cabs, gentlemen manned ferry-boats, citizen volunteers cleaned the streets … On the day of his first triumph, when he declares his strike, the Syndicalist signs his own death warrant and puts the noose about his own neck.'[28]

In the strike wave of 1911, however, he did not believe that syndicalism was a significant influence. The labour unrest, he argued had been provoked partly by a 'Byzantine display of vulgarity and extravagance' on the part of the plutocracy, and partly by the class bias revealed in the Taff Vale and Osborne judgments.[29] In such a contest, his instinctive sympathies were with the men. In the *Socialist Review* of September 1911, he 'hail[ed] with unalloyed delight the uprising of Labour on the industrial field'.[30] A month later, he pointed out savagely that 'The people who have been weeping with poor children during the strike, kicked them before the strike; the gentle hearts who bled when Liverpool's scavengers ceased to clean the streets were flint when we have been attacking slums … The people represented by *The Times*, the *Daily Telegraph*, the *Liverpool Post* and such like papers have been spewing out a filthy slush of hypocrisy.'[31] He was even more indignant with the activities of Winston Churchill, now home secretary. Churchill had already sent troops and warships to Merseyside, presumably to overawe the dockers. There were riots and accusations of police brutality. '[O]ne way to maintain law and order', MacDonald declared in the House of Commons, 'is not to allow a policeman to break a man's head and then say no inquiry is going to be made for three or four months, while the man who retaliates in hot blood is hauled up before the magistrates next morning.'[32] But the Government seemed unrepentant, and on the day that MacDonald attacked the Liverpool police in the House of Commons, it gave the railway companies an assurance that, in the event of a strike, they could call on the military for help. By October MacDonald was warning that if the military became

a habitual feature in Labour disputes ... two things will happen. The first will be a seditious propaganda amongst the troops themselves and refusals on their part to obey officers; the second will be that every strike here will be accompanied by bloodshed, and the shedding of blood will not be all on one side. An unarmed crowd is not always to face an armed soldiery. If capital is to command the military as the railway directors did ... [w]orkmen must shoot as well as be shot. Let Mr. Churchill sow his tares; then, do not let him suppose he is only to reap wheat.[33]

Little by little, however, events drove the Government and MacDonald closer together. In the course of long and intricate negotiations with representatives of the railway unions' executives, in which MacDonald played a leading part, the Government offered to set up a royal commission to inquire into the working of the 1907 agreement. On the understanding that it would sit, as MacDonald put it, 'practically day by day', and that the companies would pledge themselves to accept its findings even if it were to recommend recognition and the 'complete upsetting of the Agreement of 1907', the unions agreed to call the strike off.[34] The settlement was widely attacked in the Labour movement, where it was seen as a surrender; even Bruce Glasier, normally a strong MacDonaldite in such matters, described it privately as a 'bloody fiasco'.[35] As so often, MacDonald found himself defending a compromise reached with the Liberal Government behind closed doors against criticisms made in the open by his own followers. He did so with considerable skill — pointing out that criticisms had come from a spectrum ranging 'from the *Clarion* to the *Times*, from the *Church Family Newspaper* to the *Licensed Victualler's Gazette*,' alleging that the same papers would have published the same articles no matter what settlement had been arrived at and claiming that, if the unions marshalled their case properly, the commission was bound to find that the 1907 agreement was unworkable.[36] Within a few weeks, however, his chief argument had backfired badly. The commission reported towards the end of October, in terms unacceptable to the unions. At the beginning of November, the union executives decided to reject the commission's recommendations and demanded an immediate meeting with the employers. This the railway companies refused, on the grounds that, as part of the settlement which had been reached in August, the unions had promised to abide by whatever findings the commission might arrive at.

Once again, there was deadlock; once again, it was broken by an initiative from the parliamentary Labour Party. On November 22nd, in one of his best debating speeches, MacDonald moved a resolution declaring that the companies' refusal to meet the representatives of the men was 'contrary to the public

F

interest', and asking the Government to bring the two sides into conference without delay.[37] A modified form of MacDonald's motion was passed without a division, and early in December negotiations between the unions and the companies at last took place. Though the final settlement was a disappointment to them, this was at least a partial victory for the men: and it was a victory which MacDonald and his colleagues in the parliamentary party had done much to win. Yet the victory had paradoxical implications. In the negotiations, MacDonald and his colleagues had been drawn, willy-nilly, into the position of middlemen, standing between the Government and their own constituents in the unions. To their collective role as the representative of the 'Labour interest' had been added another, potentially in conflict with it: that of honest broker between the 'Labour interest' and the 'national interest', as represented by Downing Street. MacDonald's success as an honest broker, moreover, strengthened his tendency to see himself and his party less as the political arm of the organized working class than as one element in a greater national consensus, transcending all sectional interests. 'We are too fond of imagining there are two sides only to a dispute ... ,' he told the House of Commons in February 1912; 'there is the side of capital, there is the side of Labour, and there is the side of the general community; and the general community has no business to allow capital and labour, fighting their battles themselves, to elbow them out of consideration.'[38] His formulation would probably have been echoed by most of the Cabinet: as time went on, the assumptions behind it were to encounter increasing hostility from a section of his own party.

For the industrial unrest of 1911 grew still more intense in 1912. In March, the Miners' Federation called a national strike to secure a minimum wage throughout the industry. Once the strike had begun, MacDonald defended the miners by speech and vote. The minimum wage, he declared, had 'taken its place among the axioms of moral men and women'; as for the charge that the strike was causing hardship to the rest of the community, 'Who has told the public with greater emphasis than members of the Labour movement that a great mass of the wage earners are not more than ten days removed from starvation if the mills stop and the mines are closed?'[39] But although he defended the miners while the strike was in progress, he made no secret of his antipathy to the 'unreasonable section' of the union, whose members he denounced as 'syndicalist Anarchists of the ordinary type, who find in Socialism the greatest obstacle to their absurd economic and political ideas'.[40] In the London dock strike, which broke out at the end of May, he was even more outspoken. The Transport Workers' Federation, which Ben Tillett had formed two years earlier, and which had played a leading part in the strike wave of 1911, tried once again to carry the dockers' battle to the rest of the country. This time, the attempt failed. The Port of London Authority refused to make concessions while the strike was in progress, and in the end the men were forced back to work. Once again, MacDonald defended the strikers in the House of Commons – condemning the employers for breaking their agreements with the union and insisting that the dispute had been prolonged because they wanted to destroy the union altogether.[41] Outside Parliament, however, he was bitterly critical of the dockers' tactics. 'This long series of strikes and tall talk', he wrote angrily at the beginning of June, 'has brought us face to face with the question of compulsory arbitration ... [I]f we are to go about our business in a harum-scarum sort of way, breaking contracts and plunging the whole country into a state of unsettlement ... we cannot retain that liberty of action which we have secured up to now.'[42]

To some extent, no doubt, this was merely the expression of a natural institutional rivalry, exacerbated — as such rivalries are apt to be — by the looming shadow of failure. One reason for MacDonald's irritation with Tillett and the dockers' leaders was that they wanted to call on the parliamentary party for help, without showing any sensitivity to parliamentary opinion; no doubt, one reason why he was anxious to blame their 'harum-scarum tactics' for turning public opinion against them was that he wanted to make sure that the parliamentary party was not held responsible for their defeat. Behind his criticisms, however, there lay a much deeper difference of principle. Implicit in his approach to the dock strike, as in his tactics during the railway strike the year before, was an assumption that the industrial unrest of the period was a temporary breakdown in an essentially stable system, to be put right as soon as possible by men of goodwill. To a large section of the I.L.P., however, and still more to trade-union militants now gaining ground among the miners and transport workers, it was an episode in the class war. And in war honest brokers are suspect.

IV

The class war was not the only one which disturbed the fragile harmony of the parliamentary Labour Party in the summer of 1912, or which widened the existing gulf between MacDonald and the I.L.P. The wave of militancy which swept through the trade-union movement in the years before 1914 was accompanied by an even more spectacular outbreak of militancy on the part of an extreme section of the movement for women's suffrage, and for a while the second was as potent a source of disunity in the Labour movement as the first. The Labour Party was the only party which had formally committed itself to the principle of votes for women. As the campaign of the militant suffragettes gathered force, however, a sharp difference of opinion appeared within the party between the majority who viewed militant tactics with varying degrees of abhorrence and a minority who saw the militants as the innocent victims of Government repression, and militancy itself as the inevitable result of the Government's delaying tactics.

MacDonald had been a supporter of the 'women's movement' since the 1890s. His mature position was outlined at some length in *Socialism and Government* in which he argued that women's suffrage was a necessary part of a socialist programme. If the sole function of the state had still been to protect its citizens from attack, he conceded, the classical objections to female enfranchisement might still be valid. In fact, the state was increasingly assuming the functions of the family. The family was not an exclusively masculine institution, and the socialist state could not be exclusively masculine either:

> It must be created from the same experiences, motives and sentiments, from which the family itself has been built up. In a much more literal sense than the expression is generally supposed to mean, the family is the foundation of the State. In short, it is not merely to do justice to women ... that Socialists should favour women's suffrage. It is because women's experience is different from men's that women should be enfranchised.[43]

Women's suffrage, in other words, was desirable because it would benefit the the state, not because it would benefit women: and it would benefit the state not because women had the same rights as men, but because they performed different duties. This position was by no means identical with that of even the more moderate suffragists of the National Union of Women's Suffrage Societies, but it was sympathetic enough to allow a degree of co-operation between them. During the spring and summer of 1912, MacDonald helped to work out an agreement for joint action in by-elections between the Labour Party and the N.U.W.S.S.; by October, one of the suffragist leaders was able to claim that more than £800 of suffragist money had been spent on Labour candidatures.[44] The suffragettes of the Women's Social and Political Union were a different matter. MacDonald opposed the violent methods they used for the same reason that he opposed violence in industrial or international relations: because in his eyes it was irrational and did more harm than good. 'I have no objection to revolution, if it is necessary,' he exclaimed in a characteristic outburst in the *Leicester Pioneer*, 'but I have the very strongest objection to childishness masquerading as revolution, and all that one can say of these window-breaking expeditions is that they are simply silly and provocative. I wish the working women of the country who really care for the vote ... would come to London and tell these pettifogging middle-class damsels who are going out with little hammers in their muffs that if they do not go home they will get their heads broken.'[45]

His opposition was based on deeper and more intangible reasons as well. In his memoir of Margaret he described her attitude to the suffrage question as follows:

> The woman question was always a very big and a very deep one to her. She regarded womanhood as something elusive which dwelt in a Holy Place where one approached silently and with adoring awe. Therefore the home was to her a temple where only the Levites were to enter ...

Moreover, just as maternity embodied to her all the love, the pathos, and the purity of womanhood, so she could never think of any woman's movement apart from a man's movement. Manhood and womanhood were quite distinct revelations to her, and she never regarded even with toleration those women who appeared to follow upon manly paths. Nor could she bear the anti-man woman.[46]

Whether or not this was true of Margaret, it was undoubtedly true of Mac-Donald, and it provides an important clue to his attitude. The essence of his argument in *Socialism and Government* was that women deserved the vote because they were women: because of the unique role they played in the family. When the suffragettes appeared on the scene, with their window-breaking, hunger-striking and incendiarism, it became somewhat less plausible to argue that the reason for giving women the vote lay in their role as guardians of hearth and home. It was not surprising that MacDonald's opposition to the suffragettes should have hardened as their campaign continued. For their violent methods were, in a sense, merely the outward and visible signs of their revolt against precisely that conception of womanhood which MacDonald shared with many die-hard opponents of women's suffrage: and which, paradoxically enough, he had put forward as the chief reason for enfranchising women.

Others in the Labour Party reacted in a very different way. In 1910 and 1911 the House of Commons had passed the so-called 'Conciliation Bill', which would have given the vote to women householders. In 1912, however, the Conciliation Bill was defeated. Its defeat gave a powerful stimulus to suffragette militancy. Parliamentary methods, it seemed, had failed: only militancy remained. The Government became even more determined to prove that militancy did not pay; and, against that background, George Lansbury was called upon by the Speaker to withdraw from the chamber, after a furious scene in which he accused Asquith of torturing innocent women. MacDonald loathed parliamentary scenes, but he wrote Lansbury a sympathetic letter, which elicited the revealing response, 'yes we are different & I suppose each have our bit of work to do ... it was a relief to get your note as I know how it all hurt you.'[47] The rest of Lansbury's campaign was conducted in a more acrimonious atmosphere. In October, he circulated a memorandum to Labour Party branches and affiliated organizations, calling on all Labour M.P.s to vote against all Government legislation until women were given votes. He was condemned for disloyalty by the National Executive,[48] but this only made matters worse. In November, he resigned his seat at Bow and Bromley, so as to force a by-election which he proposed to fight on the suffrage issue. He refused to pledge himself to accept the Labour whip if he were re-elected, and the National Executive accordingly decided that his candidature should 'not receive either the collective or the individual support of the Labour Party'. But two votes were cast against this application of party discipline, and one of them was Keir Hardie's.[49] When the Executive met the following month, it had before it a letter from Keir Hardie, resigning his seat on it in consequence of his action in supporting Lansbury's candidature.[50] Hardie took his seat again on the new Executive, elected at the party conference in January 1913.[51] But there could be no doubt that, two years after MacDonald's election as chairman, the party was at least as badly divided as it had been under any of his predecessors.

V

'I am being persuaded against my will by the action of the Party itself that it is hopeless to go on,' MacDonald noted lugubriously at the end of July 1912. 'The members see so little ahead & know so little of how to fight that [they] give life to every rumour which disrupts us. My leadership has consisted not in leading the party against an enemy but in shepherding its ranks so that they did not become a disorganised mob.'[52] It would be a mistake to take his grumbles at face value. As we shall see, the rest of his career was to be punctuated by lugubrious notes and diary entries of that sort, and although the black moods were real enough when they came they did not stop him from staying in politics for another quarter of a century. All the same, the note throws a good deal of light on his state of mind ten months after Margaret's death. At some stage in 1912 he struck up a friendship, which was to last for four or five years, with Lady Margaret Sackville – the daughter of Earl De La Warr and a somewhat sentimental poetess, with the slightly precious good looks which were then considered beautiful.[53] She sent him volumes of her poetry and wrote him puzzled letters, in a large, round, immature hand, sympathizing with his concern for social justice yet deploring his attacks on the landed aristocracy.[54] But it is doubtful if her friendship made more than a marginal difference to him. 'I feel the mind of a solitary stag growing upon me,' he told Katharine Bruce Glasier in March 1912. 'My fireside is desolate. I have no close friend in the world to share either the satisfaction of success or the disturbance of defeat. So I get driven in upon myself more and more, and I certainly do not improve.'[55] All the evidence suggests that his loneliness must have been as acute in 1912 as in 1914.

Politically, too the prospects must have seemed bleak. In March 1912, Lloyd George had once again suggested that the Labour Party should join in a coalition Government. According to a note in MacDonald's papers, he had thought that it would be possible 'to give men like Snowden under-secy's'; MacDonald, however, had told him that 'the idea was quite impossible.'[56] Three months later, his overture was followed by another, described by MacDonald as follows:

Monday. June 24. Elibank took me into a private room behind the Speaker's chair. Laying his hands on my shoulders he looked me in the face & said: 'Are you ever unhappy about your position in this House?' I asked what he meant & he replied: 'Are you not wasting your influence? There are few men here who can do better things than you. You are one of our best debaters. The Opposition are really frightened of you. You are not having enough scope. Will you not join the Cabinet? Of course it would be a high office & you would have to put your brains into the common stock. George has had to do it.' I said it was impossible. A proper coalition, he remarked, was impossible as yet. He thought it would come, but in the mean time [*sic*], he thought I might consider joining the government. I replied that it was out of the question for two reasons 1. I was not prepared to support the Govt. through thick and thin. 2. It would do great evil to the Labour Party.[57]

But although he had rejected Elibank's offer, there must have been times when he wondered privately where his existing course was leading him. He was forty-six and at the height of his powers. He had been in Parliament for six years and had overcome his earlier qualms about speaking in the chamber; in the Labour Party, only Snowden equalled him as a parliamentarian. The lure of the dispatch box is one of the strongest forces in British politics. It is unlikely that MacDonald never felt it.

To be sure, he was chairman of the parliamentary Labour Party; and, as such, a significant figure in British politics as well as a commanding figure in the Labour movement. But the chairmanship of the parliamentary Labour Party offered little scope for constructive work, either then or — on any reasonable assumptions about the likely course of British politics — in the future. The notion that the Liberal Party was doomed and that the Labour Party was bound by some inexorable sociological law to replace it as the main anti-Conservative party in Britain would have seemed absurd, not only to most Liberals, but to most Labour men as well. The Labour Party seemed to be stuck in the doldrums, its energies consumed by petty personal bickering and ideological feuds. Partly because of this, MacDonald's chairmanship, which had begun in an atmosphere of almost universal approval, was running into increasing criticism. Even W. C. Anderson, one of his strongest supporters, had written to him in April 1911, warning him that his followers found him 'too stern and intellectually cold', and urging him to try to 'rope some of your men nearer to you by a kind word and, when possible, by a confidential chat about their difficulties and misunderstandings'.[58] All the evidence suggests that such feelings were even more widespread in 1912. There were rumours that he might not stay on as chairman after his second year, and that he might be opposed if he tried to do so.[59] He seems to have feared that Snowden might stand against him; and, at the end of August, Arthur Henderson found it necessary to write him a brisk note, assuring him 'There is not the remotest chance of Snowdens election. You must buck yourself up and go through with it.'[60] To cap it all, his health was showing signs of strain as well. 'The unvarnished truth is that I am worn out,' he confessed in the *Leicester Pioneer* in July. 'An August rest will enable me to work away until Christmas, but will not permit my going on for another year.'[61] In October, his friend and supporter, Paul Campbell, wrote to say how distressed he was 'to learn this morning that your health has given way, & that you have had to lie up ... You have been doing far too much, & I don't believe you have been taking proper care of yourself.'[62]

It must have been with a strong sense of relief that, in December 1912, he sailed again for India – this time as a member of the royal commission on the Indian public services, headed by Lord Islington, which the Government had set up during the summer to investigate the problems of Indianization. The Islington commission spent most of the first four months of 1913 in India, and returned again in the autumn. It came to the conclusion that the proportion of Indians in the higher ranks of the service was too small, and put forward a number of proposals designed to increase it. But the report was not signed until August 1915, and was not published until 1917; by then, the Indian appetite for self-government had grown, and the commission's proposals, which might have seemed quite adventurous three years before, seemed, to most educated Indians, hopelessly inadequate.[63] Though the Islington commission's work for India was soon superseded, it was of great value to MacDonald. His experiences as a member of it provided the foundation for another book on Indian problems; less directly, but more importantly, they also helped to lay the intellectual and emotional foundations of his Indian policies in the early 1930s. Last, but by no means least, the commission gave him a much-needed respite from the tensions of Westminster. By the time he reached Madras, in January 1913, he was able to write home that 'the ailments which troubled me for some time before I left England have gone,'[64] and when he arrived home in May the *Leicester Pioneer* was able to report that he looked 'brown and bronzed and hearty, and physically twice the man he was when he went away'.[65]

He was soon to need all the heartiness he could muster. In June 1913, the Liberal M.P. for Leicester, Crawshay-Williams, applied for the Chiltern Hundreds after being cited as a co-respondent in a divorce case. A by-election in the second seat at Leicester therefore became inevitable. For seven years, the Labour and Liberal Parties had shared the representation of the borough between them. If the Labour Party contested the by-election, the tacit agreement which had made this state of affairs possible might come to an end, and Mac-Donald's seat might be endangered. If it did not, its claims to independence would once again be called in question, and in peculiarly painful and embarrassing circumstances.

On June 13th, the *Leicester Pioneer* reported that 'a meeting of the Labour Party was held last night to decide as to whether or not the two sections of the Capitalist Army should be fought,' but that the meeting had adjourned without taking a decision. On June 15th, however, the executive of the Leicester I.L.P. decided to instruct the I.L.P. delegates to the Labour Party meeting to vote in favour of contesting the seat and to propose Alderman Banton, a leading member of the local I.L.P., as candidate.[66] On the 16th, the Leicester Labour Party voted by 67 to 8 to contest the by-election and unanimously selected Banton as its candidate; and that night A. H. Reynolds, MacDonald's agent, wrote in alarm to MacDonald, 'The B.S.P. said frankly if we did not fight they should. It will need a strong hand to stop it … *You* are the *only* man who can stop it I think.'[67] 'Stopping' it proved to be even more difficult than Reynolds had expected. On June 17th, an emergency sub-committee of the Labour Party National Executive met a deputation from the Leicester party and decided that it was inadvisable to fight; it agreed, however, that Henderson and George Roberts, the Labour chief whip, should go to Leicester to consult the local party.[68] On the 18th, the parliamentary committee of the I.L.P. N.A.C. took a similar decision. In view of the shortage of time, the fact that there was no chance of a victory and the still more disconcerting fact that the Leicester I.L.P. wanted the national party to pay the expenses, the parliamentary committee decided not to sanction an I.L.P. candidature. However, T. D. Benson would visit Leicester on the committee's behalf, and report back.[69]

That night, Henderson, Roberts and Benson duly met the Leicester party. They had a stormy reception. Benson explained the N.A.C.'s decision, concentrating on the financial aspects, and Henderson put the position of the N.E.C. According to the minute book of the Leicester I.L.P.:

> Mr. Henderson spent much time speaking of such things as the 1909 election on the constitutional issue, and Home Rule. He repeatedly stated that we must keep this Government in till next January because of the Trade Union Act, Home Rule, etc. Then he proceeded to quote the figures for the last four Parliamentary elections in Leicester, which showed that the Tories had an average for the four contests of 8,166 votes. The electoral barometer was rising in their favour; he anticipated the Tory would poll at least 9,000 votes on this occasion, and if the Labour Party put a man into the field the result would be that the Tory would get in, a general election would be brought appreciably nearer, and the Labour Party was not ready for a general election.[70]

These arguments were unavailing. The meeting lasted till 11 p.m.; and at the end a resolution in favour of contesting the seat was carried unanimously. 'Mr. Henderson', the N.E.C. minutes record, 'was subjected to many angry interruptions when giving the reasons against a contest from the national standpoint.' Worse still, he reported to the Executive that if there were no Labour candidate 'some of the delegates at the meeting would not only vote Tory but would use all their influence with the rank and file to induce them to do the same.'[71]

This did not shake the N.E.C. On June 19th, T. D. Benson reported back to a special meeting of the I.L.P. council's parliamentary committee. He had been 'greatly impressed by the intensity of feeling' in Leicester, he told them, and believed that considerable local funds would be forthcoming. Accordingly, the parliamentary committee reversed its previous decision, and agreed to sanction Banton's candidature, on condition that the local party would be responsible for all expenses other than the returning officer's fees. This decision was to be forwarded at once to the Labour Party Executive. That same day, however, the Labour Party Executive met once again and stuck to its decision that no Labour candidate should be run.[72]

The result was an acute crisis of confidence in the Leicester Labour movement. The B.S.P. had already threatened to run a candidate if the Labour Party did not do so. It now carried out its threat. E. H. Hartley of Bradford was nominated as the B.S.P. candidate, and on June 21st, Walter Borrett, the secretary of the Leicester I.L.P., wrote agitatedly and unreassuringly to MacDonald:

> It is quite impossible to measure the effect this affair will have upon our local organisations, and equally impossible to gauge the loss of confidence which you, or the National Executive, or us local officers may have sustained.
>
> Feeling certainly ran high at the meetings during the week, and hasty words were spoken, which, in the light of calm reflection, our comrades may realise the folly of ...
>
> The B.S.P. are promoting the candidature of ex-Alderman E. H. Hartley of Bradford, whose adoption meeting took place on Friday evening, the platform including five I.L.P. Councillors, viz., J. W. Murby (President) in the chair, J. K. Kelly, J. S. Salt, W. E. Wilford and N. C. Perkins.
>
> We are threatened with resignations on every hand, so we are getting prepared for a season of trouble. It is very hard on those of us who have been toiling and struggling during the past few months to build up the I.L.P. organisation. Numerically we were never as strong, and everything appeared to indicate the gaining of ground rapidly. I fear it will take a long time to recover from this week's blow. If the B.S.P. secure a large following as a result, our hopes of recovering are the more remote[.][73]

This was bad enough, and worse soon followed. On June 25th, *The Times* reported that George Banton had written to Hartley's agent announcing his support for Hartley. MacDonald had already drafted, but had decided not to send, a letter to the local press, denouncing those in Leicester 'whose passion is misleading them at the present moment into a thoughtless and reckless support' for Hartley, and implying in carefully veiled terms that in certain unnamed circumstances he might be forced to break his connection with the town.[74] He now dispatched a more forthright letter in the same terms to Banton:

> I have not written to you at all about the election because I did not desire to influence you one way or the other as I felt perfectly certain that whatever steps you took would be after full consideration of the whole facts as they presented themselves to you, and on this occasion as on all others I have taken the view that my Leicester friends ought to do what they con-

sider right, irrespective of my position in the borough. I also assumed that you know my views about the election, and as we were both exceedingly busy I have not troubled you with an expression of them in writing. I think, however, after the letter which you have written to Hartley's agent … that I ought to leave no doubt in your mind as to how I regard this election. I consider it to be one of the greatest tests imposed upon the Leicester Movement. You know Hartley and his antecedents, his relations to us in Bradford, his action during the Newcastle bye-election, and the general character of his propaganda in the country … I have been connected with you now for something like fifteen years and whatever may be said you must admit that during all that time I have been perfectly consistent, both as one of the rank and file and latterly as an officer of the Party, in my policy and in the guidance and advice I have given to the Party. Today I stand where I have always stood, and what this bye-election is to answer, so far as I am concerned, is whether the movement in Leicester has a mind and a will of its own. If it has, I stand by it, facing its enemies both on its right and its left and willing to undergo more worry and trouble in keeping it straight. I made up my mind, however, some ten days ago that if the I.L.P. or the Labour Party officially backed Mr. Hartley or anybody else at its bye-election I could not be its candidate when the next appeal to the country comes. I did not communicate this to the Party because I thought it would have been very unfair and would have been undue pressure. I am prepared to take my own burdens upon my own shoulders and make the best of them. Fortunately the action of both the I.L.P. and the Labour Party made it unnecessary for me to pursue these thoughts, but I want to say, in a way that you cannot misunderstand, that if the voting on Friday shows that Mr. Hartley has the support of Labour electors in Leicester, I will regard that as an indication that the hopes I have had of the Party have been false and that without delay you will have to find someone else to fill my shoes.[75]

When polling day came on June 27th, MacDonald's perturbation turned out to have been unnecessary. The Liberal candidate polled more than 10,000 votes to the Conservative's 9,279 and Hartley's 2,580. But by now the electoral behaviour of the citizens of Leicester was almost a minor consideration: wider and more explosive questions were at stake. Two days before polling day, MacDonald, Henderson and Roberts had met a deputation from the Leicester party at the House of Commons. According to a private memorandum he wrote a few days later, MacDonald told them that if the result of the by-election 'showed a want of confidence' in him, he would have 'to consider the whole position'. He was pressed to allow the deputation to convey this statement to a private meeting of the Leicester Labour Party that night: and in the end it was agreed that if the deputation thought it necessary to do so, they were to explain to the party meeting that 'a heavy Hartley vote would have to be regarded as a censure

which Mr. MacDonald could not overlook.' This was all to take place in private;
so far as the Leicester newspaper-reader was concerned, no official communication was to be made by MacDonald to his constituents until after the election.

At this point, however, the tightrope which MacDonald was attempting to
walk was pulled away from under him by a strange display of clumsiness, or
over zealousness, on the part of one of his leading colleagues. Later that day,
George Roberts happened to meet Sir Maurice Levy, the Liberal M.P. for
Loughborough, and told him what had been decided at the meeting with the
deputation from Leicester. Levy telephoned the information to the Liberal
headquarters in Leicester;[76] that evening, Sir Tudor Walters, a Liberal M.P.,
read out at a Liberal election meeting what purported to be an official resolution,
passed by the Labour Party Executive, warning Labour voters in Leicester that
their 'indiscipline' might 'impel Mr. MacDonald to sever his connection' with
the town, and declaring that

> [e]very Labour voter who is concerned to preserve Party discipline and
> understandings and who agrees to the desirability of retaining Mr. Mac-
> Donald in Leicester should give no encouragement to the candidature of
> Mr. Hartley, which is not recognised by the official Labour Party.[77]

The result was an unseemly storm of charges and counter charges. MacDonald
was accused of bringing illegitimate influences to bear on his supporters in
Leicester; he, in turn, accused the Liberals of dishonesty; five I.L.P. branches
threatened to withhold their affiliation fees or to make no contribution to the
party's Special Effort Fund. In the end, the affair was smoothed over. The
Labour Party Executive passed a resolution, drafted by a special sub-committee,
which blamed the Liberals for everything which had gone wrong; and at the
same meeting it accepted Roberts's apologies for his conversation with Levy.[78]
So far as the N.E.C. was concerned, that was the end of the matter.

VI

The wider issues raised by the by-election could not be disposed of so easily.
In a long article in the *Labour Leader* on July 3rd, MacDonald defended the
Executive's refusal to fight, on the grounds that in a two-member constituency
there was no point in contesting the second seat purely for propagandist reasons.
In such a seat, 'the sole justification' for intervening was a 'tolerable certainty'
of victory, and in Leicester this did not exist. A Labour candidature would
merely have made a present of the seat to the Conservatives – and however unsatisfactory the Liberal Party might be from Labour's point of view, the
Conservatives were worse. As he put it on July 17th,

> The attack made upon us is that we are too Liberal. That I deny. But I wish
> to point out that a great many of those who make it are nothing more than

anti-Liberal and the one fault is quite as grave as the other ... [W]hat is the indictment? That Liberal foreign policy is bad. I agree. If it were under the charge of Lord Curzon, would it be as bad, or worse? The Liberals have employed troops during trade disputes, and that merits our strongest opposition, but the clamour at the time from the Conservatives was that they were not using them enough.[79]

Even if it were true that there was no difference between the two capitalist parties, support for the Liberal Government could still be justified. 'Those who held the two great parties in the most supreme contempt', MacDonald told the 1914 party conference, 'were just those who ought to support the Party loyally in the view that they had taken, that it was not worth while undergoing the trouble and expense of a General Election to turn Tweedledum out in order that Tweedledee might reign in his stead.'[80]

These arguments did nothing to dam the flood of criticism and rebellion which was now sweeping through the I.L.P. During the by-election, the *Labour Leader* – now under the editorship of Fenner Brockway, a lifelong opponent of MacDonald – had denounced the National Executive for undermining the enthusiasm of the rank and file, which was now 'pulsating with life' and 'eager to come to grips with the forces of capitalism'. As for the argument that a Conservative victory would have led to the defeat of the Government and the loss of Home Rule,

We protest against a cessation of activities until Home Rule is safe. Are we to forget the Government's attempts to intimidate the railwaymen? Are we to forget the Government's callous betrayal of the London dockworkers? Are we to forget the Government's rejection of a minimum of 21s a week for the railway workers? Are we to forget all the defects of the Insurance Act? Are we to forget the Government's denial of a living wage and the eight-hour day? Are we to forget the Government's broken pledges to the women suffragists? Are we to forget the Government's surrender to the armaments ring? Must we overlook all these things on the alleged grounds that Home Rule may be endangered?[81]

The *Labour Leader* was not alone in its criticisms. Keir Hardie, too, thought that it had been 'a great mistake' not to contest Leicester, and denounced the 'slobbering talk with which the Liberal press was filled on the Monday following the election, about the friendly understanding between the Liberals and the Labour Party'. More ominously still, he drew the moral that the I.L.P. must take greater care to preserve its separate identity. 'We are already heavily overweighted by the Labour Alliance,' he wrote. 'What I want to insist upon is that members of the I.L.P. must not allow its identity to be merged in that of the Labour Party.'[82] At the Labour Party conference in January 1914, the section of the Executive's annual report dealing with the Leicester by-election was carried without a vote. But it was significant that in the debate on it, as in the debate on the Party's parliamentary policy which preceded it, none of the I.L.P. delegates spoke in support of the leadership. Even W. C. Anderson, one of MacDonald's staunchest supporters only three years earlier, argued that 'in the last two or three years the workers' battle had been more strongly fought by industrial methods outside than by political methods inside the House of Commons.' As for MacDonald's argument that there was no point in turning Tweedledum out of office in order to put Tweedledee in,

> If Tweedledum was told that, what was the result? Tweedledum would know what they were going to do. Tweedledum would know that the Labour Party might criticise but would not turn Tweedledum out and Tweedledum might do exactly as it liked.[83]

To MacDonald — as to the great majority of the parliamentary party — the possibility that Tweedledum might do as it like remained far less alarming than the possibility that Tweedledee might replace it. This second possibility was by no means academic: by a curious paradox, moreover, if it came about, a good deal of the responsibility might lie with the Labour Party itself. For Labour's strength and self-confidence had grown considerably since the two elections of 1910. Its membership had increased; its finances were healthier; its organization had improved. It was beginning to appoint full-time agents in a number of constituencies. Above all, it was in a position to field more candidates than before. By May 1914, in addition to its existing seats, it had sanctioned 18 new candidatures. A further 22 candidates had been selected but not sanctioned, and there were another 44 constituencies in which the party's position was described by Head Office as 'Uncertain'.[84] The Labour Party, in other words, was beginning to break out of the confines set by the MacDonald–Gladstone *entente* eleven years before; and the implications for the Liberal Party were as painful as they were obvious.[85] Already the Liberals had lost a number of by-elections as a result of Labour intervention; equally, the Labour Party had lost at least two seats to which it believed itself to be entitled, because the Liberals had refused to acknowledge its claim to them. A general election was due, at the latest, in 1915; if the pattern of the by-elections were repeated then, the Conservatives might win a majority in the House of Commons, not because they had a majority of the electorate behind them but merely because the two progressive parties had been unable to settle their differences.

Such an outcome would have been unwelcome to MacDonald at any time: in the special circumstances of 1914 a Conservative victory would have seemed to him not merely unwelcome but disastrous. For more than a year, British politics had been dominated by a shrill and unrelenting Conservative campaign against the Irish Home Rule Bill; across St George's Channel, the Ulster Volunteers were drilling and were about to arm. No one could tell how seriously Unionist threats of violence were meant, but it seemed clear that the

Opposition hoped to intimidate the Government either into abandoning Home Rule altogether, or at least into holding a general election on the question. A Conservative victory in such an election would be a victory for passion and violence, and a defeat for everything MacDonald stood for in politics. In 1913 the wayward Radical M.P., Josiah Wedgwood, had sounded him out on the chances of a 'firmer alliance between the Government and the Labour Party', and had added that if such an alliance were to be formed 'your chief weapon will have to be a big new policy, to fight for which combination is not only excusable, but necessary.'[86] In 1913, no such 'big new policy' had been in sight. By 1914 it had begun to look as though Ireland might provide a substitute.

On March 3rd, MacDonald received an urgent letter from Lloyd George:[87]

> My dear Ramsay,
> I want to have a serious talk with you about the relations of Liberalism and Labour. If we go on as we have been doing during the last couple of years more especially, both your Party and ours will meet with the worst disaster which has befallen us. A Tory victory now would mean not merely Tariff Reform — that would be bad enough — but it would involve something which is very much worse from the Labour point of view. The repeal of the Parliament Act, the setting up of a strong Second Chamber which would be a permanent barrier to all legislation of a Progressive character.
> If we do not make every effort in our power to avert this catastrophe I am sure not only the present generation, but all future generations will condemn us for our short-sightedness and our lack of courage at the critical moment.
> I have talked the matter over with some very important people in the Government, and I have some suggestions to put to you. Will you turn into my room some time this afternoon?
> Ever sincerely,
>
> D. LLOYD GEORGE

According to a private memorandum found among his papers, MacDonald duly went to Lloyd George's room that afternoon, and was told that Lloyd George wished to communicate 'certain private matters' on the authority of the 'Inner Cabinet'. MacDonald replied that he thought he ought not to discuss such matters except in the presence of a trusted officer of his own, and suggested that another leading Liberal ought also to be present. Accordingly, an appointment was made for 6.30 that evening, when MacDonald was accompanied by Arthur Henderson and Lloyd George by the Liberal chief whip, Illingworth. MacDonald's memorandum continues:

> Mr. George informed us that what he was to say and the negotiations which might follow had the full consent of Mr. Asquith to whom he was to report everything that transpired. He informed us that the Cabinet had now made up its mind as to what it was to offer to Ulster, that there was the very best

reason for believing that the Conservatives would accept nothing, as they were out for trouble and would on no account agree to peace short of a complete withdrawal of the Home Rule Bill. The Inner Cabinet had therefore decided to approach me with a view to making preparations for a conflict in the country which would settle the matter once for all. Three things had to be settled:

1) The question of candidatures. They were prepared to allow us a sub-stantial increase in our membership which was to be secured by a withdrawal of certain Liberal candidates in constituencies that we would be likely to win on a straight fight with the Conservatives. We on our part were then to withdraw our candidates from the other constituencies so far as we possibly could.

2) A programme was to be agreed upon which the Government, if it were a Liberal Government, was to pursue after the Election.

3) If we desired representation in the Cabinet it was to be given to us.

We were informed that the Government expected that when Mr. Asquith made his statement on Monday an indication would be made that the Conservatives would not accept it and that, as the debate went on after the Adjournment the policy of resistance would be developed and the whole Unionist Party committed to it. The final act, according to the Cabinet's information, was to be the rejection of the Army Annual Bill by the House of Lords. The Cabinet had decided that this Bill would be brought forward at an earlier stage this year than is customary in order that the crisis might be forced to a climax. During the following week we were to keep our eyes open and we were informed that any decisions of the Cabinet and any in-formation given to it would be communicated to us without delay. We left Mr. George and Mr. Illingworth, agreeing to meet again on the follow-ing Wednesday unless in the meantime something arose which compelled an earlier meeting.[88]

MacDonald's response is not known. Such evidence as there is suggests, how-ever, that he welcomed Lloyd George's suggestion with enthusiasm. In his column in the *Leicester Pioneer* three days after his interview in Lloyd George's room, he published a virtual paraphrase of the arguments which Lloyd George had put to Henderson and him.[89] Two weeks later, the situation in Ulster was still further inflamed by the so-called Curragh mutiny. In the House of Com-mons, MacDonald denounced the army officers as 'party politicians' acting as a 'standing military committee of the National Union of Conservative Associa-tions'. The Government, he declared, must get the Home Rule Bill on the statute book as soon as possible, 'and then we will take the consequences what-ever they may be.'[90] In the *Leicester Pioneer* two days later he wrote that the situation was 'drifting nearer and nearer to the condition of things which the Long Parliament had to face in Charles I's time'. He would not be surprised, he added, if the Government went to the country on the question; if it did so and lost, 'the clock is back at least a century.'[91] At about the same time, he suggested in a letter to *The Times* that an election should be held as soon as possible after the Home Rule Bill was passed, but before it had come into operation.[92] On April 3rd he declared in the *Leicester Pioneer*, 'When the election comes, one of the issues must be the Tory Army plot and all that it means, so that the fight will be as exhilarating as it was in 1906.'

Meanwhile, at its meeting on March 17th, the National Executive had discussed the chances of an election in 1914 and decided that a full report should be prepared on the party's 'present and prospective constituencies'.[93] There is no record of what was said at the meeting, but two things seem clear. The first is that Lloyd George's offer must at least have been discussed; the second that any proposal of the kind was anathema to Keir Hardie who promptly took steps to kill it. At the I.L.P. conference that Easter, Fenner Brockway—acting on Hardie's instructions[94]—alleged that the 'logical outcome' of MacDonald's policies was an agreement with the Liberals at the next election. 'The statement that there was an agreement had been denied,' Brockway pointed out, 'but in very careful terms.' Brockway's allegations were indignantly denied by MacDonald, who declared delphically that 'there is no approach between the Labour Party and the Liberal Party that means that the Labour Party is going to change its policy by one hair's breadth.' This, of course, was not the point: it was Labour's electoral tactics that were in question, not its policy. In any case, the force of MacDonald's denial was weakened, if not destroyed, by a bombshell dropped later in the debate by Philip Snowden. According to the *Labour Leader*,

> Referring to Mr. MacDonald's denial of a Labour–Liberal alliance, Mr. Snowden asked if it was denied that negotiations had gone on? It was something more than a rumour. At a recent Executive meeting of the Labour Party a definite proposal had been made.
>
> Mr. Keir Hardie intervened to say that no proposal had been made. The matter had been mentioned only.
>
> Mr. Snowden good-humouredly remarked that he would accept Mr. Hardie's account of what had occurred. What Mr. Hardie said was quite sufficient.[95]

By now, however, the prospect of an early election had begun to recede. MacDonald continued to hanker for it. 'They tell us the House of Lords is going to throw out the Army Annual Bill,' he declared towards the end of April. 'I hope they will force us to the country on this issue.'[96] But the House of Lords did not come up to expectations, and neither did the Government. As MacDonald himself conceded, the Curragh incident seemed to have given the Liberals cold feet: by May, the implacable ministerial mood of March had given way to an atmosphere, on the Government's side if not on the Opposition's, of sweetness and light. As the prospect of an early election receded, so, it seemed, did the prospects of a wider agreement between the Government and the Labour Party. In May, Liberal intervention at a by-election in North-East Derbyshire cost the Labour Party a seat. Later in the month, the Labour Party retaliated in kind at a by-election at Ipswich; once again the Conservatives gained a seat on a minority vote. 'Ipswich is the direct result of North-East Derby,' MacDonald commented aggressively on May 29th:

> The Conservatives will ... continue their attempts to get a Parliamentary majority on minority votes, and if the Liberals ask us to prevent that by giving them every seat they want, the Conservatives will succeed, for we will agree to no such proposal. If the Liberals run candidates against us they can do so, and when that policy of stupidity has ended in devastation we will ask them how it pleases them. If that should come we shall begin to build up again with the knowledge that we shall be in a far better position than the Liberals themselves to make good our losses, and that in this country, as on the continent, the fight ... will then be between a great Labour Party and a strong reactionary party, with a small Liberal Party standing between, cut off from every source of inspiration and opportunity of growth.[97]

MacDonald's belligerence may have been less menacing to the Government than it seemed. He may still have been hoping for an agreement with the Liberals, along the lines Lloyd George had suggested in March. Labour's intervention at Ipswich may have been a bargaining tactic, designed to put the Liberals into a suitably accommodating frame of mind in case further negotiations took place; MacDonald's defiant comments after the by-election may have been written with the same end in view. It is equally possible, however, that he had finally abandoned any hope of coming to terms with the Government, and had decided to prepare for war *à outrance* against it. What is certain is that progressive politics in general, and MacDonald's career in particular, had now reached a crossroads. The Labour Party had to choose between moving closer towards the Liberal Party, as Lloyd George had proposed, and moving further away from it, as the militants of the I.L.P. advocated. A closer alliance between the Liberal and Labour parties might provoke further desertions to Conservatism among wealthy Liberals; in the long run it might solidify into the Radical-Labour progressive party, socialistic in deed even if not socialist in name, after which MacDonald had hankered for so long. On the other hand, it might also lead to the secession of the I.L.P. and the destruction of the 'Labour Alliance' which he had done as much as any man to build. The second course might lead to a Conservative victory at the next general election, and almost certainly would lead to widespread Labour losses in the short run; in the long run that might be a small price to pay for the 'great Labour Party', at once the heir and the grave-digger of the Liberal Party, whose coming MacDonald had foretold in his article of May 29th. Each alternative had dangers as well as advantages, and it was impossible to tell which of them MacDonald and his colleagues would choose. Sooner or later, however, the choice would have to be made: if not by design, then by default.

Yet, within a few weeks of the Ipswich by-election, both alternatives disappeared and the choice between them became irrelevant. For, on June 28th, the Archduke Franz-Ferdinand was murdered at Sarajevo. The ponderous machinery of alliance diplomacy slowly came into action. By August 4th, Britain was at war.

CHAPTER 9

Voice of reason

I

On Saturday, August 1st, 1914, MacDonald was staying at Walton Heath with Robert Donald, the editor of the Liberal newspaper, the *Daily Chronicle*. During the day, the Government chief whip, Percy Illingworth, telephoned to ask him to come to London. MacDonald arrived there at 4 p.m.; according to a note he made in his diary some weeks later, he 'found that war was inevitable'. Illingworth said it would be unpopular; according to the same diary entry, MacDonald 'laughed & told him no war was at first unpopular'.[1] On Sunday the 2nd, the British section of the Socialist International held a great demonstration in Trafalgar Square to protest against any steps which the Government might be taking in support of Russia and to demand that Britain should 'rigidly decline to engage in war'. The demonstration was addressed, among others, by Keir Hardie, Arthur Henderson, Will Thorne, George Lansbury and R. B. Cunninghame Graham; MacDonald, who had been summoned to a consultation in Downing Street, was not present. That evening, he dined with Lloyd George, John Simon, C. F. G. Masterman and Sir George Riddell, at Riddell's house. 'Masterman jingo, George ruffled, Simon broken,' he noted afterwards. 'George harped on exposed French coasts & Belgium but I gathered that excuses were being searched for. Walked home through the Park feeling that a great break had come.'[2]

Like most such breaks, it had been preceded by a long period of tension and foreboding. On most questions, as we have seen, MacDonald's position in 1914 was closer to the Government's than it had been in 1906. On foreign policy, it was further away. He had taken a keen interest in foreign politics since the 1890s, and had been a regular attender at the congresses of the Socialist International since his election as secretary of the Labour Representation Committee in 1900. He had a wide range of contacts among foreign socialists, notably among the revisionists in the German Social Democratic party; Eduard Bernstein, the leading theorist of German revisionism, was a frequent correspondent as well as a philosophical mentor. At a deeper level, he was an instinctive internationalist, in a sense true of few of his colleagues. Though he spoke no foreign languages apart from a little French, he liked foreigners and got on well with them; and it is clear from his travel writings that he felt a sense of excitement and liberation when he went abroad. Unlike many of his countrymen, he did not find it shocking or outrageous that foreigners should sometimes question Britain's motives or act in a way that did not conform to Britain's interests. At a deeper level still, he loathed violence and threats of violence. These attitudes were not embodied in a coherent foreign policy; his writings and speeches on foreign affairs consisted mainly of reactions to events, and contained only the sketchiest and most tentative of alternatives to the policy actually followed by the Government. They did, however, give him a vantage-point from which to judge the Government's policy; and, as time went on, his judgments became increasingly hostile.

Like most Radicals and Labour men, he was bitterly opposed to the Government's friendship with Tsarist Russia. In 1908, his opposition to a projected visit to the Tsar on the part of Edward VII earned him a curt rebuke from an anonymous group who signed themselves '*English* working men'. 'We say go back to your own place and learn Manners,' they had written, 'you dirty Scotch dog.'[3] The following year he had been one of the four chairmen at a great demonstration in Trafalgar Square, held to protest against the Tsar's visit to England, and addressed by most of the leading figures in the socialist movement, from Shaw to Hyndman. It was the Government's German policy, however, which aroused his deepest misgivings. For he believed that the key to peace was held by the growing forces of German Social Democracy — the chief enemies of German militarism, and the natural friends of this country. One of the primary aims of British foreign policy, he argued, should be to cultivate their friendship, and to help them in their struggle to democratize Germany. It seemed to him that Sir Edward Grey and the Foreign Office were oblivious of their existence. British foreign policy seemed to be made in a political vacuum; it equated Germany with the German Government, and took no account of German public opinion. As a result, it was ham-fisted and provocative; in the long run this could only alienate Britain's friends in Germany, weaken their influence and strengthen the German Right.

Thus, in the so-called naval scare of 1909, when the Government decided to expand its naval programme, MacDonald pointed out bitterly that the German socialists had 'never voted a brass farthing to enable their Government to build up the German navy. They have always opposed every naval credit. They and we are the nucleus of an effective peace organisation in Europe, and I, for one, cannot desert them.'[4] He took a similar line in the debates in the Labour Party about the possibility of preventing war through a general strike. The party was not officially in favour of the proposal, largely because of trade-union opposition, and the discussion led to a rather unedifying squabble between the I.L.P. representatives on the National Executive, and the trade unionists. Arthur Henderson actually refused to propose the Executive's resolution at a special conference on armaments and the international situation in January 1911, on the grounds that Keir Hardie intended to move an amendment com-

mitting the party to support a general strike in the event of war.[5] In sharp
contrast to his attitude on most domestic questions, MacDonald here aligned
himself with the I.L.P. and against the unions. He conceded 'the almost un-
answerable force in the argument that if the masses of the people cannot prevent
war through their representatives in Parliament, an attempt to get them to
paralyse hostilities will fail'. But that, he argued, was not the point. A commitment to call a general strike if war broke out would be 'a demonstration of
solidarity' with the working class in other countries; its mere existence would
'hamper scaremongers and mischief-makers'.[6]

The Agadir crisis in the summer of 1911 – and still more Lloyd George's
famous Mansion House speech, warning the Germans that if Britain were
treated as if she were of no account, peace would be a 'humiliation' – added to
his anxiety. In November, Bernstein sent him a list of questions about the course
events had taken during the summer in order to provide materials for a speech
which August Bebel, the leader of the German socialists, was to make in the
Reichstag. On November 14th, MacDonald had an interview with Lloyd
George, in order to find out the answers.[7] But Lloyd George's answers did not
satisfy him. The Mansion House speech, he wrote in the *Socialist Review*, had
turned out to be 'a maddening irritant to Germany'. Though it was perhaps
time for a British minister to speak out, Lloyd George's way of doing so had
'smashed up friendship for Britain amongst great masses of the German
people'.[8] In the *Leicester Pioneer* he was gloomier still. The attitude expressed
by Lloyd George in the summer and by Grey in the recent foreign affairs
debate, he wrote in December, 'is to defeat the magnificent efforts being put
forth by the German Social Democrats to establish friendship between Germany
and ourselves; it is to compel Germany to go on building Dreadnoughts; it is
finally to bring those Dreadnoughts into use.'[9]

From then on, he remained deeply suspicious of Lloyd George. When the
Liberal journalist, H. W. Massingham, wrote that Lloyd George was contemplating resignation rather than provide money for the naval programme,
MacDonald commented scornfully that the idea was 'nonsensical'. Whatever
trouble there might be in the Cabinet, he added, 'Mr. Lloyd George will not
resign on anything anti-German. He is anti-German, and the trust which the
reasonable Peace people place in him is altogether misplaced.'[10] And if Lloyd
George seemed untrustworthy, Winston Churchill, who became first lord of
the Admiralty in 1912, seemed far more so. MacDonald had already formed a
low opinion of Churchill, as a result of his behaviour as home secretary during
the 1911 strike wave; Churchill the war-lord alarmed him even more than
Churchill the strike-breaker had done. While Churchill's attitudes were in the
ascendant, he wrote indignantly in July 1912, 'millions upon millions of our
national wealth will be squandered, and whilst there is no public opinion
demanding that Ministers must have some policy other than merely building
more ships than their neighbours, there will be no end to the folly except war.'[11]

By July 1913, he was writing, more acidly, that 'Mr. Churchill is a very dangerous person to put at the head of either of our fighting services. He treats them as hobbies.'[12] In January 1914, the *Leicester Pioneer* reported that Mac-Donald had returned from a visit to India 'in fighting trim', determined to direct all his energies 'to a strenuous opposition to any increase in armaments which may be advocated by Mr Winston Churchill and his Imperialist friends';[13] and, for the next three months, one of the main themes of his parliamentary activities was his struggle against what he described as Churchill's vision 'of an armed world, with navies in every sea and dockyards in every harbour'.[14]

Thus, when war broke out in the end, it did not seem to him, as it seemed to many of his countrymen, either an incomprehensible catastrophe or the result of a deep-laid plot hatched in Berlin. On the contrary, he saw it as the terrible culmination of a long process of provocation and counter-provocation, for which Britain and Germany were equally to blame, the consequence of which he had foreseen only too clearly, and against which he and his comrades on the continent had warned in vain. His actions during the next few weeks must be seen against this background.

II

On Monday, August 3rd, Sir Edward Grey made it clear to the House of Commons that Britain was committed in honour to support the French, and that war with Germany was now almost unavoidable. He was followed by Bonar Law, who pledged full Unionist support for any measures which the Government might find it necessary to take, and by John Redmond who did the same on behalf of the Irish. Then MacDonald rose to state the view of the Labour Party. The line he was to take had already been agreed at a party meeting. It was a difficult and complicated line, but MacDonald was to remain substantially faithful to it for the next four years, and it must therefore be considered with some care. Grey, he began, had delivered a speech, 'the echoes of which will go down to history'; even those who resisted the conclusion could not resist 'the moving character of his appeal'. Nevertheless, Grey was wrong, and the verdict of history would be that he was wrong. If he had been able to show that the country was in danger,

> I do not care what Party he appealed to, or to what class he appealed, we would be with him and behind him. If this is so we will vote him what money he wants. Yes, and we will go further. We will offer him ourselves if the country is in danger. But he has not persuaded me it is. He has not persuaded my Hon. friends who co-operate with me that it is, and I am perfectly certain, when his speech gets into cold print tomorrow, he will not persuade a large section of the country. If the nation's honour were in

danger we would be with him. There has been no crime committed by statesmen of this character without those statesmen appealing to their nation's honour. We fought the Crimean War because of our honour. We rushed to South Africa because of our honour. The Rt. Hon. Gentleman is appealing to us today because of our honour. There is a third point. If the Rt. Hon. Gentleman could come to us and tell us that a small European nationality like Belgium is in danger, and could assure us that he is going to confine the conflict to that question, then we would support him. What is the use of talking about coming to the aid of Belgium, when, as a matter of fact, you are engaging in a whole European war which is not going to leave the map of Europe in the position it is in now. The Rt. Hon. Gentleman said nothing about Russia. We want to know about that. We want to try to find out what is going to happen, when it is all over, to the power of Russia in Europe, and we are not going to go blindly into this conflict without having some sort of a rough idea as to what is going to happen. Finally, so far as France is concerned, we say solemnly and definitely that no such friendship as the Rt. Hon. Gentleman describes between one nation and another could ever justify one of those nations entering into war on behalf of the other. If France is really in danger, if, as a result of this, we are going to have the power, civilisation, and genius of France removed from European history, than let him so say. But it is an absolutely impossible conception which we are talking about to endeavour to justify that which the Rt. Hon. Gentleman has foreshadowed. I not only know, but I feel that the feeling of the House is against us. I have been through this before and 1906 came as part recompense. It will come again. We are going to go through it all. We will go through it all. So far as we are concerned, whatever may happen, whatever may be said about us, whatever attacks may be made upon us, we will take the action that we will take of saying that this country ought to have remained neutral, because in the deepest parts of our hearts we believed that that was right and that alone was consistent with the honour of the country and the traditions of the party that are now in office.[15]

Next day, Britain declared war on Germany. For a while, it seemed that the Labour Party might remain faithful to the position MacDonald had put forward in the House of Commons. On August 5th, the National Executive resolved by 8 votes to 4 that the war was the result of 'Foreign Ministers pursuing diplomatic policies for the purpose of maintaining a balance of power'; and that 'our own national policy of understanding with France and Russia only' was bound to endanger good relations with Germany. The resolution condemned Sir Edward Grey for committing 'the honour of the country to supporting France', and declared that it was the duty of the Labour movement 'to secure peace at the earliest possible moment'.[16] But the National Executive's resolution marked the end of an old road, not the beginning of a new one. Like its counterparts on the continent, the British Labour movement had always been in favour of 'peace'. It had inherited the anti-militaristic attitudes of the nineteenth-century Radicals who were its real intellectual ancestors; at a more superficial level, sections of it had also absorbed something of the Marxist notion that the working classes would be, in some special sense, an obstacle to any conflicts which might be unleashed by their rulers. But these attitudes ran alongside a deeper vein of old-fashioned patriotism; they were easily over-whelmed by the wave of abhorrence and indignation which was let loose in Britain when the Germans invaded Belgium. On August 5th, the parliamentary Labour Party decided to support the Government's request for war credits of £100,000,000. MacDonald promptly resigned the chairmanship. 'I saw it was no use remaining as the Party was divided and nothing but futility could result,' he wrote in his diary. 'The Chairmanship was impossible. The men were not working, were not pulling together, there was enough jealousy to spoil good feeling. The Party was no party in reality. It was sad, but glad to get out of harness.'[17] The 'great break' which he had sensed four days before was already much wider than he could have foreseen.

A week later he widened it still further with a long and passionate article in the *Labour Leader*, analysing the causes of the war. The real cause, he began, lay in the 'policy of the balance of power through alliance'. This policy had divided Europe into two hostile camps. Its progeny was 'suspicion and arma-ments'; its end result was 'war and the smashing up of the very balance which it is designed to maintain'. An *entente* of the sort which Britain had had with France was, moreover, the most dangerous form of alliance. Asquith and Grey had continually assured the House of Commons that Britain had contracted no obligations. Their assurance was 'literally true but substantially untrue ... Had we had a definite alliance with France and Russia the only difference would have been that we and everybody else would have known what we had let ourselves in for, and that might have averted the war.' The dangers in Grey's policy had not ended there. Through the *entente* he had, in effect, committed Britain to go to war if France did so. But if British intervention were to be supported by the British people it would have to be justified; Belgium provided the justification. The British Government knew that, in the event of war between Germany and France, German troops would have to pass through Belgian territory. In itself this did not make it necessary for Britain to declare war on Germany: in similar circumstances in 1870, Gladstone had recognized that in a general conflict formal neutrality might be violated. In fact, Mac-Donald maintained, Germany had offered guarantees of Belgian integrity and independence; these guarantees would have been enough for Gladstone. Indeed if the shoe had been on the other foot, they would have been enough for Grey. If 'France had decided to attack Germany through Belgium', MacDonald wrote, 'Sir Edward Grey would not have objected but would have justified himself by Mr. Gladstone's opinions.' Thus the German invasion of Belgium was not the true cause of the war; it merely gave the British Government a heaven-sent pretext to whip up patriotic emotions in the country:

> It is well known that a nation will not fight except for a cause in which idealism is mingled. The *Daily Mail* supplied the idealism for the South African War by telling lies about the flogging of British women and children; our Government supplied the idealism for this war by telling us that the independence of Belgium had to be vindicated by us. Before it addressed its enquiries to France and Germany upon this point ... it knew that France could reply suitably whilst Germany could not do so. It was a pretty little game in hypocrisy which the magnificent valour of the Belgians will enable the Government to hide up for the time being.

Grey, MacDonald conceded, 'strove to the last to prevent a European war'. But the *entente* had been too much for him. When his failure to keep the peace had at last become obvious to him, 'he worked deliberately to involve us in the war, using Belgium as his chief excuse.'[18]

MacDonald's breach with the official Labour Party was accompanied by a *rapprochement* with the I.L.P. Resolutions of support poured in from I.L.P. branches all over the country. Altrincham thanked him for his 'manly and brave opposition to the policy which has led to the participation of Great Britain in the terrible war now raging'. Batley hoped that he would see his way to remain at the head of the Labour Party, and hoped that he would 'receive the support from them that will enable you and us to effectively hold up the Banner of Peace'. Bush Hill expressed their 'high appreciation' of his speech in the House on August 3rd. Devi, in South Wales, expressed their admiration for his 'noble stand'. Norwich sent him 'hearty congratulations'. Plymouth trusted that 'the whole movement will rally to your support'. The Bradford I.L.P.-er, William Leach, wrote that he had just finished reading MacDonald's article in the *Labour Leader*, and that he supposed 'there'll be no such magnificently lucid nor courageous statement of the case if all the world writes the history of this bloody business ... I have a great satisfaction that I've trusted you throughout when dogs have yapped at your heels. Now you've repaid me a thousand fold.' It was a common reaction, even among those who had done the 'yapping'. 'It has often been my misfortune to differ from what I conceived to be your ideas on Parl. policy,' wrote the general secretary of the Bristol I.L.P. on August 7th, 'but may I say how proud I feel of the action you have taken over the war ... It is an action expressive of your own brave true self.'[19] These attitudes were warmly reciprocated. 'From every a/c the I.L.P. has been given a new spirit,' MacDonald noted enthusiastically towards the end of October, 'the old one of comradeship & confidence.'[20] What this meant was that he was once again one of the comrades: it was not the I.L.P. which had changed, but his attitude to it.

Yet the support of the I.L.P., however heartwarming it might be, would not be enough to change public attitudes. As MacDonald knew better than most, the I.L.P. was still little more than a sect, cut off from the main stream of British politics. In any case, the I.L.P.'s attitude to the war was by no means identical with his. Most leading I.L.P.-ers were straightforward pacifists; for them, MacDonald's arguments about the origins of war did not affect the rights and wrongs of the question, however useful they might be as ammunition. Some of the rank and file were Marxists or near-Marxists, for whom war was the inevitable product of capitalism. They, too, could co-operate with MacDonald; but their fundamental attitudes were opposed to his. Thus, if an effective rallying centre against the war was to be created, the I.L.P. could only be one part of it. Another, and from MacDonald's point of view a more important, part would have to be provided by the handful of anti-war Radicals on the left wing of the Liberal Party who remained true to their old position, in spite of the invasion of Belgium and Lloyd George's support for Grey and Asquith. MacDonald had had good contacts with this section of the Liberal Party for many years; within days of the outbreak of war he had begun to explore the possibilities of common action.

On August 10th, he dined with Philip Morrell, Norman Angell, Charles Trevelyan, E. D. Morel and Arthur Ponsonby. They decided, in MacDonald's words, 'to form a committee to voice our views'.[21] By the end of the month the nucleus of such a committee was in existence; and on August 24th, Mac-Donald wrote a long letter to Morel, arguing that such 'mechanical changes' as the establishment of a parliamentary committee on foreign affairs were not enough to prevent future wars, that public opinion would have to be changed and that a 'private conference of representative men' should be convened at once, so as to prepare for public action when the time was ripe. The committee, he ended, should also make it clear what the Government ought to have said to France:

We ought to have told her quite plainly that whilst our *entente* with her would make us sympathetic even to interference on her behalf in any quarrel into which she might be drawn in her own interest ... we would not in any way consider ourselves bound to interfere if that quarrel came upon her in consequence of her alliance with Russia. The situation then would have been that we might have confined the war first of all to Austria and Serbia, or ... to Germany and Austria on the one hand and Austria and Ser[b]ia on the other. The value of this would be to make it clear (and I think we must do this) to our people that France was involved not because Germany attacked her or because she had any interest whatever in the quarrel but only because she had bound herself to do whatever Russia did. That gave Russia the whip hand in the Triple Entente, and everything else followed.[22]

It is not the least of history's ironies that that was to be one of the axioms of British foreign policy between the wars.

Meanwhile, the relationship between MacDonald and the majority of the Labour Party remained in confusion. There were rumours that he was about to return to the chairmanship; and on August 17th, Arthur Ponsonby wrote to him in alarm:

> I must say I wish you were not going back to your chairmanship. It ties you, & ties you to a heavy log difficult to move. The Labour Party appear to me to be chiefly occupied with questions of organization & internal squabbles. If as the Times foreshadows the war is to be a long business we shall want of [*sic*] a very strong vigorous & alive body or party to be gradually growing all the while. It will be the only issue and to lay the foundations of a new European system will be the only object worth fighting for. You are the man to lead such a party but you ought to be quite free to do it.[23]

It is not clear how far MacDonald was influenced by Ponsonby. It is clear, however, that Henderson must have appealed to him to return to the chairmanship at about the time that Ponsonby's letter was written. It is also clear that MacDonald rejected the appeal in uncompromising terms. On August 24th, he wrote to Henderson:

> The Party must make up its mind what it is to do for the next month or two. Is it to throw itself out of action altogether and allow each individual to drift whither it seems good to him? Or is it to attempt to take up a distinctive position which will in due course be the rallying centre for those who will wish that this war should not have been fought in vain. If it is to do the latter, it must think things out from now onwards, and it must be prepared to co-operate with outside organisations with which it agrees in this respect. It has been suggested to me that it might be possible for the Party to pass some kind of resolution which I could accept and which would not, in view of the statements of my position which I have made, make it impossible for me to continue in the chair ... I do not see how some of those who spoke at the last meeting of the Party could support a vote of confidence and a resolution that I should withdraw my resignation, more particularly as the resolution would have to be sent to the press. I should therefore imagine that the Party will really have to fill my position and let me become one of its rank and file.[24]

The letter for the Party which he enclosed contained a more elaborate statement of his position, and it is worth quoting at some length. He began by referring to the Party's appointment of a deputation to try to persuade him to withdraw his resignation. This, he declared, was impossible. On four big issues – the causes of the war, the need to 'keep these causes before the electors', the need to 'prepare the public mind for a settlement which will be in accordance with the international policy of Labour' and the need to 'formulate our objections to the military and diplomatic policies which have been pursued just as much in this country as on the continent' – he felt it his duty to put his 'energy and influence' at the disposal of any movement which expressed his views. The Labour Party no longer did so:

I never had any doubt as to how the majority of the Party would act on these questions if they were fairly put before it, or as to what the active sections of the Party in the country would say. But in a great time like this when a firm advocacy is required of principles which are infinitely more important than any expediencies ... I cannot bear to speak or act as chairman of the Party when even a minority of the colleagues whose co-operation I have always valued ... find themselves in disagreement with me. This is not the time for public demonstrations, but it is the time for educational work in the press and at private meetings of those upon whose activities the Labour Party has to trust for its enthusiasm and its success at elections, and I cannot take my part in this and be chairman of the Party at the same time after the vote of Thursday week.

Had the Party been united it would have been, as it has been for three years now, a pride and a pleasure for me to have acted as its chairman in carrying out this work. On the 3rd August when I outlined to the Party what I proposed to say after Sir Edward Grey had spoken, there was agreement and after I had spoken there was equal unanimity that I had said in the House of Commons exactly what I had indicated beforehand at the Party meeting. But on the following Thursday when I left the Party to come to its own decision without any expression of opinion from me, it not only took the view that we should vote for the credit of £100,000,000 (I thought we should not oppose it) but that we should not take that last opportunity of reiterating our position in view of the publication of the White Paper. In this silence I could not acquiesce because I felt it not only implied a political attitude which repelled me, but imposed a continued inactivity which I could not promise to observe. I could do nothing in the circumstances except vacate the office of Chairman of the Party. As a private member of the Party I can claim, as others have done on other matters, the right of following my own beliefs without forfeiting my general loyalty to the Party, but this is impossible whilst holding the position of chairman. As the Party is not unanimous and as the issues are vital and enormous in their importance, it would be repulsive to every sentiment of that friendly co-operation I had always tried to follow with colleagues if even a minority felt itself injured and aggrieved by any action which I, whilst chairman, was compelled to take by my inner sense of right and wrong.[25]

Thus, by late August 1914, MacDonald had embarked on joint action with a group of anti-war Radicals who were drifting, with increasing speed, from their old party moorings. He had also refused Henderson's invitation to return to the Labour Party chairmanship, in terms which suggested that he had drifted a long way from his own moorings as well. The structure of left-wing politics in Britain bears the marks of both those steps to this day.

III

MacDonald's position in the first few weeks of the war was based on the assumption that, as he put it in the *Labour Leader* on August 29th, 'it is unthinkable that Germany should win.' For an anxious period in early September, however, it looked as though the unthinkable might have to be thought after all. On September 4th, MacDonald reported to E. D. Morel that he and Norman Angell had both heard that the Germans were expected to be in Paris in a fortnight, that they were then expected to capture Boulogne soon afterwards, and that they would then place big guns on the heights above the town which would command the Channel and effectively close the Port of London.[26] Not all his associates agreed with him. In a letter to Arthur Ponsonby on September 7th, C. P. Trevelyan wrote that he did not share MacDonald's view, and that he believed the Government was spreading the rumour deliberately so as to help its recruiting campaign.[27] But even Trevelyan conceded that MacDonald and Angell might be right; and it is clear that MacDonald, at any rate, believed that the risk of a German victory was great enough to justify a significant change of tactics on his part.

On August 29th, the Labour Party Executive had agreed that the party whips should take part in a recruiting campaign organized by the Government. In the I.L.P., this decision seemed a betrayal of all that the Labour movement stood for. '[W]e refuse to take our stand by militarists and enemies of Labour with whose outlook and aim we are in sharpest conflict, and who will assuredly seize this opportunity to justify the policy leading up to war,' wrote the National Administrative Council in a letter to the branches. 'Now that the country has been drawn into a deadly and desperate war, which may involve in the end our existence as a nation, it is not a matter for speech-making, least of all from those who will not themselves be called upon to face the horrors of the trenches.'[28] These attitudes were undoubtedly shared by MacDonald; moreover, as he had warned Bob Williams, the secretary of the National Transport Workers' Federation, he believed that the recruiting campaign might be the thin end of a wedge leading to compulsory military service.[29] On the other hand, he did not want Britain to be defeated. For a pacifist, this would have been irrelevant. But MacDonald was not a pacifist. For him, the possibility of a British defeat could not be left out of the reckoning. Thus, when he was invited to attend a recruiting meeting presided over by the mayor of Leicester in the second week of September, he refused. But he did so in a letter of such tortuous ambiguity that it must have been unclear to most of those who heard it read out at the recruiting meeting whether their member of Parliament was in favour of the war or not. He was, he wrote,

> very sorry indeed that I cannot be with you on Friday. My opinions regarding the causes of the war are pretty well known, except insofar as they have been misrepresented, but we are in it. It will work itself out now. Might and spirit will win and incalculable political and social consequences will follow upon victory.
>
> Victory must therefore be ours. England is not played out. Her mission is not accomplished. She can, if she would, take the place of esteemed honour among the democracies of the world, and if peace is to come with healing on her wings the democracies of Europe must be her guardians. There should be no doubt about that.
>
> Well, we cannot go back, nor can we turn to the right or to the left. We must go straight through. History, will, in due time, apportion the praise and the blame, but the young men of the country must, for the moment, settle the immediate issue of victory. Let them do it in the spirit of the brave men who have crowned our country with honour in times that have gone. Whoever may be in the wrong, men so inspired will be in the right. The quarrel was not of the people, but the end of it will be the lives and liberties of the people.
>
> Should an opportunity arise to enable me to appeal to the pure love of country — which I know is a precious sentiment in all our hearts, keeping it clear of thought which I believe to be alien to real patriotism — I shall gladly take that opportunity. If need be I shall make it for myself. I wish the serious men of the Trade Union, the Brotherhood and similar movements to face their duty. To such it is enough to say 'England has need of you'; to say it in the right way. They will gather to her aid. They will protect her when the war is over, they will see to it that the policies and conditions that make it will go like the mists of a plague and shadows of a pestilence.[30]

This strange effusion was not received with much pleasure. 'Your name received a very mixed reception when the Mayor read your letter,' MacDonald's agent reported. 'What the public don't seem to understand is that you should not be on the platform at a town's meeting, & yet the Citizen placard next morning all over the town says you asked for recruits.'[31] In the I.L.P., the reaction was even more hostile. At the next N.A.C. meeting MacDonald was criticized for his 'recruiting meeting letter to Leicester' and told that it had given offence and caused trouble in the branches. 'The NAC', he commented sadly in his diary, 'will not face the question of what non-Tolstoyans ought to do.'[32] In the orthodox Labour Party, however, it seemed that MacDonald's apparent endorsement of the war effort, however half-hearted, might be enough to build a bridge between him and the majority. On September 14th, Henderson wrote to say how pleased he was to see MacDonald's letter to the mayor. 'Nothing has given me so much satisfaction for a long time,' he added. 'It enables the movement to see that we are not apart as some imagine.'[33] Henderson's overture was followed by an approach from a more surprising quarter. On October 8th, MacDonald noted:

> Lunched at Montagu's with M. & Lloyd George. Begged me to do nothing to undo my influence which they and certain of their colleagues in the Ministry will want when peace comes ... They agreed Grey's Foreign policy responsible for war. Belgium did not determine Grey's attitude, but if Germany had not invaded Belgium Cabinet wd. have been hopelessly split & Chancellor himself wd. have resigned. M. said Grey stated to him at lunch on 3rd August that had it not been for the invasion of Belgium the majority of the Cabinet wd. probably have declared for neutrality & that in that event he wd. have resigned. The[y] agreed that the permanent heads of the Foreign Office were pro-Russian & that at least two were anti-German. George urged me to speak at once when the House of Commons meets & make my position perfectly clear. The controversies had somewhat obscured it.[34]

Lloyd George's advice was rejected. MacDonald did not speak again in the House of Commons for more than eighteen months; though he took steps to make his position clear, he did so in a way that widened the gulf between himself and the Government. His reconciliation with Henderson was short-lived also. Soon after his lunch with Lloyd George he received a letter from the Labour Party national agent, Arthur Peters, enclosing a proof copy of a manifesto entitled *The British Labour Party and the War*. It asserted that the British Labour movement had always stood for peace, but that the 'German military caste' were 'determined on war if the rest of Europe could not be cowed into submission'. Thus, the parliamentary Labour Party recognized that Britain was 'bound in honour' to 'resist by arms the aggression of Germany'. It was for this reason that the Labour Party had agreed to take an active part in the recruiting campaign, 'organised by the various parliamentary parties'. This policy, the pamphlet concluded, was dictated by a 'fervent desire to save Great Britain and Europe from the evils that would follow the triumph of military despotism'; there would be no peace until 'the power which has pillaged and outraged Belgium and the Belgians, and plunged nearly the whole of Europe into the awful misery, suffering and horror of war' was beaten.[35] These assertions were, of course, incompatible — in content, and even more in tone — with the line which MacDonald had taken in the House of Commons on August 3rd, and, for that matter, with the resolution which the National Executive had passed two days later. If it were really true that 'the German military caste' had been determined on war all along, and if it could be said that Britain had 'exhausted the resources of peaceful diplomacy', MacDonald's criticisms of Grey's foreign policy were groundless, perhaps mischievous. It is not surprising, therefore, that MacDonald should have seen the pamphlet as a cowardly and politically damaging concession to the war fever which the recruiting campaign would in any case intensify. On October 16th, he wrote to Henderson to protest against the manifesto.[36] Parts of Henderson's reply were reassuring; parts, however, were not. It would, Henderson wrote,

> be very much better if some opportunity could be provided for a few of us to have occasionally an informal talk on matters affecting the International as well as the Home position. I am apprehensive that we are dividing ourselves off into small groups which, unless care is exercised, can only have a destructive effect upon the influence of the Labour Party. I have done what I could to follow the line which would leave the Party at the end of the War as strong, if not stronger than we were when hostilities broke out. I only signed the Manifesto after a good deal of thought. I had nothing to do with its drafting, and I was busy in Barnard Castle when the proof was sent forward. It was represented to me by two or three members of the Executive and the Parliamentary Party that a very bad impression had been created in neutral countries and that it was desirable that some statement should be made that might exercise a counteracting influence ... It is not easy at all times to decide what course one should adopt, though you must admit that you and others that are acting with you have thought fit to take an almost exclusive line both in private conference and public agitation. From some of those with whom you have been acting, especially members of the N.A.C., some of us have received no word except that of discouragement and censure from the moment that we decided upon the recruiting campaign. In fact, I consider their treatment, and especially some of the things that have been circulated through the 'Labour Leader', have been nothing less than shameful. It appears to me that it is always right to rush into print if one line is taken, but it is never right not even to attend a recruiting meeting or to make a public reference if it be opposed to the policy which some people have adopted. I again say that much unpleasant feeling might be avoided if some of us who do not see eye to eye on all points but who largely agree on fundamentals, could occasionally come together.[37]

The first part of Henderson's letter was as near to an apology as he could reasonably have been asked to go. The second part was less satisfactory. Taken to its logical conclusion, the argument that criticisms of Grey's foreign policy had had a bad effect on neutral opinion might rule out all opposition to the Government. By the same token, the suggestion that the I.L.P. had done something 'shameful' in acting 'exclusively' might rule out any concerted

G

action by a minority group within the party. In any case, MacDonald did not, in fact, believe that criticisms of the Government were winning support for the enemy in neutral countries. Yet he was as anxious as Henderson to avoid a complete break. On October 20th, he replied to Henderson's letter of the 16th, with a revealing mixture of wariness, cordiality and belligerence:

> I do not believe a bit in all these stories about neutral countries. I am in close touch with various people who are getting, by consent of the censor, newspapers from abroad, and the use that is being made, even in Germany, of these paragraphs is absurdly and maliciously exaggerated here ... Excellently as we are behaving, I am sorry to say that so far as I can make out other nations are showing us even a better example. What I felt about the Manifesto was that if much had been made of it in the press it would have broken the Party hopelessly in two. The N.A.C. was meeting the day that it came out and I was very frightened that something might be done by it by way of reply. In these matters we must go by the majority of the N.A.C. and that majority has not always been very wise ... I deplored the action taken in the 'Leader' regarding your recruiting decisions. As you know I did not agree with the decision, but I do not think the 'Leader' improved matters.[38]

Like Henderson's, however, his cordiality had limits. On October 23rd, he wrote to Henderson again, rejecting an invitation to discuss the party's tactics in the coming session with the officers:

> I think on the whole you had better just have your meeting and appoint your officers in the old way. The Party cannot possibly go on with a temporary Chairman. If it is going to survive at all it must hammer out some distinctive policy ... and carry that policy through. Besides in view of the very clear decision which the majority apparently have now taken up, regarding the causes of the war, it is only right that they should take the most definite steps possible to leave no doubt in the mind of the outsider as to where the Party as a whole stands. That will leave those of us who disagree with the majority all the freer to express our views, because we shall not be constantly feeling that we are encouraging misunderstanding and trading upon connections that appear to be hopelessly severed.[39]

In spite of these rebuffs, Henderson continued to hope against hope that MacDonald would soon return to the chairmanship. On November 18th, MacDonald attended a private meeting of the officers. According to his diary, he 'declined to allow my name to be considered for chairmanship, & further declined to make any promise as to future action. I said everything was so uncertain I did not know. I made up my mind to say nothing during the sittings of Parliament, & to attend but little.'[40] The saga ended on December

10th, at another meeting between MacDonald and the officers, at which, so MacDonald noted afterwards, he

> told them point blank I would not stand for the chairmanship. Henderson first asked me to bind myself to go back after war. I declined. After some explanatory talk it was agreed that Henderson would agree to act on condition that it was known that it was to be temporary. This was confirmed at meeting, Henderson stating that he wished to retain his Secretaryship of the Party and the right of reversion to Chief Whipship. Some did not agree. They are very bitter (only one or two not more than three chief of whom is Roberts who cheated me so badly over the Leicester bye-election & is paying me out for my forebearance with him) & some are jealous (again insignificant). I feel that the breach is widening. They never seemed to be more ineffective than they were today muddling away over their scales of pension & payment to soldiers, but still their instinctive action is so often right.[41]

MacDonald was right in thinking that the breach was widening. If we are to understand the course that their relationship was to take in future, it is important to recognize that Henderson, at any rate, had some grounds for believing that it was MacDonald's fault that this was so.

IV

It is equally important to understand why MacDonald responded to Henderson's overtures in the way that he did. Henderson's motives are clear enough. As so often, his chief aim was to preserve the unity of the Labour Party. He knew that MacDonald was the only man who could keep the socialist and trade-union wings of the alliance together; knowing this, he believed that MacDonald was the best possible leader. Like most successful politicians, Henderson was ambitious, but for power, not for place. His own tenure of the chairmanship had been unhappy and not particularly distinguished; it suited him to control the party machine from behind the scenes, while leaving MacDonald in the limelight as party chairman. His position on the war, moreover, was a good deal closer to MacDonald's than it was to appear later. They differed most over recruiting, but even there the difference between them was not great. Henderson was prepared to take part in recruiting meetings, and MacDonald was not. But Henderson took part in them only with misgivings, while MacDonald's letter to the mayor of Leicester suggested that, although he was unwilling to appear physically on a recruiting platform, he was prepared to give the proceedings a kind of disembodied blessing in absentia. On other issues, their differences were narrower still. MacDonald was no more prepared to see Germany win the war than Henderson was. Henderson had no more enthusiasm for Grey's foreign policy than MacDonald had, and it is unlikely that he was any more anxious to see the Labour Party giving it retrospective endorsement. Henderson was a party man, first and last; and as events were to show, he was prepared to go with the party in almost any circumstances. But, although solid evidence is lacking, the most plausible interpretation of his conduct is that he did not want his more bellicose trade-union colleagues to stampede the party into an unreservedly pro-war position: and that one of his reasons for wanting MacDonald as chairman was that he thought that MacDonald and he together would be able to prevent that from happening.

Then why did MacDonald not accept Henderson's invitation, resume the chairmanship and try, from the chair, to turn the Labour Party into an instrument for the democratic foreign policy and just peace in which he believed? Part of the answer, no doubt, is that he had been so worn down by the strain of leading the party before the war that he could not bear the thought of facing the even heavier strain of leading it through the war. At another level it is clear that he had been hurt, as well as shocked, by the party's decision to vote for war credits: and that he had been, if anything, even more hurt by the line it had taken in the recruiting pamphlet. First it had repudiated the position he had put forward, in its name, on August 3rd; then it had endorsed a totally contrary position. Though he did not say so, there can be little doubt that Henderson's suggestion that he should behave as though nothing had happened must have seemed to him a humiliating one. At another level still, he may have suspected that Henderson was trying to trap him. If he returned to the chairmanship at Henderson's invitation he would do so as Henderson's man, not as his own. Even if he only promised to return to the chairmanship after the war, the promise might be used against him if, on some future occasion, he found himself even further away from the majority position than he was already.

Much more important than any of this, however, was his attitude to war as such. Politically, his position was only a hair's breadth away from Henderson's. Emotionally, the hair's breadth was a yawning chasm. As we have seen, MacDonald was not a pacifist. He did not believe that no war could ever be justified, or that taking human life was always wrong. Though he detested militarism, he had a certain admiration for the military virtues; though he refused to take part in recruiting meetings, he strongly approved of the mood of self-sacrifice and idealism which he detected in many of the recruits who flocked to the colours after the German invasion of Belgium. Yet no pacifist could have hated war more than he did. The fashionable belief that war against Germany could serve the cause of peace and democracy seemed to him a perversion of the truth: and he saw it as a perversion, not just because he believed that Britain was as much to blame for the war as Germany was, but because of his instinctive loathing for war itself. However evil German militarism might be, he wrote in the *Labour Leader* towards the end of August, it would have been better that 'militarism had flourished for another ten years than that we should have sent thousands of men along the path of privation, hate and pain to death, that we should have clouded thousands of happy firesides, that we should have let loose in Europe all the lusts of battle and all the brutalities of war'.[42] War, to him, was a crime: and those who were now supporting a war that need never have been started, in spite of their earlier opposition to the foreign policy which had led to it, were aiding and abetting after the fact. The discovery that his own former followers were among its supporters came as a bitter personal blow. 'I heard last night that Sedden & Bellamy have gone to America to talk to T. Uists there on the justice of the war!', he noted on October 12th. 'At the Government's expense! It is contemptible. What I have been leaning on! No one can believe how relieved I am to be free of it.'[43] That almost despairing sense that his party had proved itself unworthy of the hopes he had placed in it was to become even stronger as the war went on, and it goes a long way towards explaining his attitudes and actions, not only then but later. It was not MacDonald who had changed his ground, after all, but the party. To ask him to return to its leadership while it gave its approval to what seemed to him to be unnecessary bloodshed was to ask him to betray the values which mattered to him most of all.

His attitude had a more hard-headed justification as well. The second reason for his unwillingness to return to the chairmanship while the party supported the war lay in his concern for the character of the peace that would follow. A punitive peace, he believed, would sow the seeds of future wars. Yet it seemed to him that a punitive peace would follow inevitably if the tide of popular opinion continued to flow in the direction it had taken since the war broke out. 'Who is to be the victor?', he asked in the *Labour Leader*. 'Not what is vaguely called "the Allies" ... Far more likely is it that this war is the beginning of a new military despotism in Europe, of new alarms, new hatreds and oppositions, new menaces and alliances; the beginning of a dark epoch, dangerous, not merely to democracy but to civilisation itself.'[44] It followed that an opposition movement was needed to keep alive the still, small voice of reason. The recruits currently flocking to the colours, he pointed out in the Glasgow *Forward* at the beginning of October, hoped 'that this is to be the last of wars'. If their hopes were to be realized, it was necessary to ensure that the kind of diplomacy which had prevailed before the war did not reappear afterwards. All previous wars had been ended by 'military persons and diplomatists whose minds are unresponsive to democratic ideals ... For this reason war follows war.' The only way to ensure that they did not have their way yet again was to create a public opinion which would not tolerate their machinations, and the only way to do that was to keep on criticizing the diplomacy which had made the war inevitable in the first place.[45] The debate over Grey's foreign policy, in other words, was not, as Lloyd George and the Labour Party majority seemed to think, an academic argument, of no practical importance now that the war had begun. It was a debate which had to be won if civilization was to be saved from even bloodier wars in future. And MacDonald believed, not without reason, that the Labour Party majority had now contracted out of it.

He believed too that the opposition movement should have an international dimension as well as a national one, and that the only way to give it an international dimension was to keep alive the Socialist International – the one institution through which the working-class movements of the belligerent countries could communicate. In a long and important letter to an American socialist, dated November 3rd, MacDonald pointed out that the socialist and Labour movements of Europe had tried to build up 'an international Socialist understanding' so close that it would have made war impossible. But their methods had not matched their aims, and they must now learn from their own mistakes:

The German Social Democrats kept themselves far too much aloof from other German movements making in their direction and were thus never able to use their enormous backing in the country to destroy Prussian conservatism and its military organisation. They were too much concerned in far-off events to pay that attention to the immediate political situation which was necessary. Had they done the latter they could have overthrown Prussianism in Prussia and with that would have gone Prussianism in the rest of Germany. Our French comrades, on the other hand, acquiesced too readily in the Russian alliance which was being exploited by the ordinary political parties for ends that were purely militarist and Chauvinist ... We, ourselves, in Great Britain have, I believe, the best record of all. Whilst we were working for peace in a general way we declined to support in any particular the policy and proposals of those making for war. Our feebleness consisted in the fact that Great Britain was asleep in foreign matters ... Our people are indifferent to Foreign Office transactions and are perfectly content to allow their foreign relationships to be discussed and settled in secret by men who are not called upon to explain what they are doing and what they have in mind. The result has been that we never have been able to get up popular interest in foreign policy and when the war broke out the minds of our people were quite unprepared to consider why we were involved, or what the issues of the war were to be ... The intention of the country, however, is quite clear. We have been roused by the German invasion of Belgium and all our old enthusiasm for small States and for the inviolability of treaty obligations has been awakened ... It is a war for liberty and democracy so far as the man in the street is concerned.

Those of us who decline to be swept off our feet, even whilst we pay homage to our national enthusiasm, cannot help welcoming this temper ... Our work at the present moment is to strengthen it and to prevent it from being swamped by the deterioration in thought and purpose which always comes from a protracted war ...

So far as Socialists are concerned, they must continue their efforts to keep the foundations of the International intact so that at the earliest possible moment they may begin to rebuild upon these foundations what the war has destroyed. Above all, they must co-operate to put an end to secret diplomacy and to the handing over of foreign policy to a small handful of men drawn from the aristocratic and plutocratic classes. The one danger which this war has revealed is not that of militarism, because that is secondary, but that of class diplomacy, for upon that all militarism, both German and British rests ... That is what the Socialist Movements of Europe will have to strike at when this war is over. If they succeed, this will be the last of our wars; if they fail it will be but the first of a series of conflicts.[46]

It was, perhaps, an unrealistic vision, but it was not an ignoble one; and MacDonald's struggle to turn it into reality provides one of the major themes of his career for the next eight years. It seemed to him almost self-evident that his vision could not be realized by a party which had allowed itself to be swept away by the emotions which the class diplomatists had deliberately let loose.

The third, and perhaps the most important, reason for MacDonald's cool response to Henderson's overtures was the effect on him of his own participation in the anti-war movement. By the end of the year, the little group which had dined together at Philip Morrell's on August 10th had developed into an organized campaign. Early in September, MacDonald, Charles Trevelyan, Norman Angell and E. D. Morel sent a circular letter to presumptive supporters, asking for volunteers to help campaign for 'parliamentary control over foreign policy', for the opening of 'negotiations with democratic parties and influences on the Continent' when the hostilities ended, and in the meantime for peace terms which would not involve the 'humiliation of the defeated nation or an artificial rearrangement of frontiers'. This was followed shortly afterwards by a second letter, which was sent to the press, and which mentioned the provisional title of the new organization as the 'Union of Democratic Control'. On November 17th, the Union of Democratic Control was formally constituted at an inaugural meeting. Four 'Cardinal points' were adopted. No province was to be transferred from one country to another, without the consent of the population. No treaty or agreement was to be entered into by the British Government without the consent of Parliament. British foreign policy was to aim, not at maintaining a balance of power, but at setting up an international council with machinery for securing an abiding peace. Finally, as part of the peace settlement, Britain was to propose a drastic disarmament agreement between the powers and the general nationalization of armaments industries.[47] Meanwhile, the I.L.P. had also begun to marshal its forces against the war. Inevitably, there was friction between the two movements. On October 16th, for example, MacDonald noted in his diary that at the N.A.C. meeting that day, 'Hardie was objecting to Union of Democratic Control because it took away from energy and cudos [*sic*] of ILP.'[48] On the whole, however, the co-operation between them was close. Twenty I.L.P. branches were represented at the inaugural meeting of the U.D.C., and increasingly the U.D.C. provided the I.L.P. with its foreign policy. More important still, the very fact that both groups were swimming against one of the strongest and fiercest tides of opinion in recent British history created in both an exalted, almost religious, atmo-sphere of dedication and solidarity – the solidarity of persecution.

MacDonald shared this atmosphere, helped to create it, and was in turn sustained by it. To some of the inner circle, in both the I.L.P. and the U.D.C., he remained an enigmatic, even a slightly suspect, figure. Arthur Ponsonby noted in his diary in April 1915 that MacDonald 'gives a general impression to people that he is not to be trusted though no one has yet been able to tell me why or mention one occasion on which he has been false'.[49] A similar impression was made on Leonard Woolf, who came into contact with him later in the war.[50] Thorough-going pacifists in the I.L.P. found it hard to forgive his recruiting letter to the mayor of Leicester; revolutionary Marxists had not forgotten his moderate policies as chairman of the parliamentary party before 1914. But these suspicions were confined to a small circle. To the vast majority of those who opposed the war, whether they did so for religious or political reasons, MacDonald was a hero. He symbolized their hopes, voiced their aspirations and suffered for their principles. His courage confirmed their faith: their support restored him, and drove him on. Inevitably a bond was created between them more akin to the bond between a religious leader and his flock than to the mundane relationships of everyday politics.

One example must suffice. Here is the *Labour Leader*'s report of a great meeting in Briton Ferry in South Wales, held early in 1916, at which Mac-Donald was the main speaker:

> For days we had known that the enemies of freedom were scheming to wreck the enterprise. The tickets had been duplicated, and were it not for a secret sign on the authorised tickets, the hall might have been packed with a crowd of people bent on preventing our case being put. But they were frustrated ...
>
> The wreckers had reached the dynamo the night before, after 10 o'clock, and removed parts of the engine, rendering it impossible to light the hall by electricity. The plumbers had been working all day on Sunday laying on a supply of gas, and fearing that might 'accidentally' give out during the meeting, there were hundreds of candles in the pockets of members scattered about the hall ...
>
> It was exactly 8 o'clock when Mr. MacDonald rose to address the meeting. Over and over again the cheers swelled and rolled over the heads of the handful of opponents sitting at the foot of the gallery. In less than

two minutes, MacDonald was in his stride – and what a stride! He began
quoting a beautiful parable from the book of Ecclesiastes ... It was the story
of a poor wise man who had stood alone in the time of a great crisis and
had saved this city from destruction. The I.L.P., he declared, is to-day the
representative of that wise man ...

... 'Who is entitled to mourn and weep over the sorrows of martyred
Belgium? Not the men who have outraged the people of the Welsh valleys
by huddling them together in houses that were not fit for pigs. The people
who are entitled to mourn and weep today are the people who mourned
with you and wept with you and led you in a holy crusade before the war
began.'

... War was the result of secret undertakings and secret diplomacy without the consent of democracy, and war would again be the harvest of any
understanding in which the voice of the people was not a determining factor. 'Sincerely, seriously, reverently', he said, leading up to a thrilling
peroration, 'I ask you in the name of God to consider the problems in front
of you. The I.L.P. is bending under the force of a blinding storm today, and
our ultimate confusion is the hope of our enemies. But they will not
succeed. We shall go on, and when the fair weather comes again, we shall
confront the world with faces unashamed, and shall say to posterity, "We
await your verdict". And the verdict will be: "Blessed is the peacemaker, for
he shall be called the child of God."'[51]

Men still remember MacDonald's great meeting in Briton Ferry, held by
candlelight after the lighting had been sabotaged. At the time, the impression
MacDonald's audiences made on him must have mattered as much as the
impression he made on his audiences. It was not an impression which made for
good relations with his pro-war colleagues, then or later.

CHAPTER 10

Public enemy

I

At gatherings like the one at Briton Ferry, half-way between a political meeting and a conventicle, held under threat of physical violence, boycotted or misrepresented in the press, MacDonald slowly secured a hold over the imagination and loyalty of the I.L.P. second only to Keir Hardie's in earlier years—a hold which became even stronger after Hardie's death in 1915. There was, however, a price to be paid. The British responded to the war with one of the most remarkable displays of collective courage and self-sacrifice in history, but there was also an uglier side to the mood which produced the great volunteer armies of 1915 and 1916. As early as September 1914, MacDonald had written to E. D. Morel, describing the effects of the 'war spirit' in Lossiemouth:

> As an amusing indication of the state of mind here, I tell you this story. A friend of mine came to see me last Saturday. He was not well known here and a report that he was the German Emperor secretly arrived by aeroplane went round *and was believed*. If someone had only said that he was Morel of the Congo, my house would have been blown up. The Kaiser's wickedness is known, Morel's would have been supplied by the imagination.[1]

That was in Lossiemouth, where he had been known since his birth. Elsewhere, the 'war spirit' had more unpleasant effects. Within a few weeks of the outbreak of the war, MacDonald had become the victim of a newspaper campaign of extraordinary savagery. It began in the staid columns of *The Times*. On October 1st, 1914, *The Times* published a leading article entitled 'Helping the Enemy', in which it wrote that 'no paid agent of Germany had served her better' than MacDonald had done. Accompanying it was a letter in similar vein by Sir Valentine Chirol. No one in the British Isles, Chirol wrote wildly, bore a heavier responsibility than MacDonald did for 'the incredibly fierce hatred of England throughout Germany'. His attacks on Grey's foreign policy had had no effect in Britain. In Germany:

> They were greedily welcomed as affording just the materials that were required for bolstering up the German propaganda, not only in Germany

but throughout neutral countries all over the world ... Is it a mere coincidence that the German Chancellor himself ... invariably bases his denunciations of Great Britain's perfidy on just the same sort of arguments which Mr. MacDonald employs? ...

We may be rightly proud of the tolerance we display towards even the most extreme licence of speech in ordinary times ... Mr. MacDonald's case is a very different one. In time of actual war ... Mr. MacDonald has sought to besmirch the reputation of his country by openly charging with disgraceful duplicity the Ministers who are its chosen representatives, and he has helped the enemy State, ... Such action oversteps the bounds of even the most excessive toleration, and cannot be properly or safely disregarded by the British Government or the British people.

Two days later, the *Spectator* pushed the moral home. 'Is it a right thing that Mr. Ramsay MacDonald should be drawing £400 a year from the British taxpayer,' it asked on October 3rd, 'when so far as we can judge by his correspondence in the Press, the chief work he is doing for the country at the moment is heartening the enemy?' The Government, it concluded, 'should move against him at once'.

The Government could be forgiven for thinking that there was no need to do so when others were so eager to do its work for it. Shortly after the *Times* article, an organized campaign of intimidation was mounted in MacDonald's constituency. On October 13th, Walter Borrett, secretary of the local I.L.P., wrote to warn him that the *Leicester Mail* had suggested that there should be 'organised opposition' at a meeting which MacDonald was due to address the following weekend, and that a certain Captain Pritchard, who was organizing recruiting in the county, had inadvertently told a Labour supporter that 'it had been arranged that MacDonald shall not be heard on Sunday. He is to be "booed down".'[2] In the end, Captain Pritchard got little for his pains. 'Some rowdies beaten up and inflamed for a week by "Leicester Mail", "John Bull" and blackguards in general,' MacDonald noted after the meeting. 'Meeting a great success. Opposition cowed and beaten. I really suspect my peace principles so do I revel in meetings such as this.'[3] Even so, he must have wondered how often it would be necessary to cow such opposition in future.

More distressing than the activities of Captain Pritchard was a bizarre episode which took place two months later. At the end of November, the Liberal M.P., Captain Murray, suggested to MacDonald that he might find an outlet for his organizing abilities in a volunteer ambulance corps which had been set up by Dr Hector Munro and which was then attached to the Belgian army at Furnes, near Dunkirk. MacDonald accepted the suggestion; and, although it is not certain what his role was to be, it is clear that he agreed to go out to Belgium at the beginning of December, to investigate the work of the corps on the spot and to make appropriate recommendations to the committee in London.[4] What happened next is less clear. According to Lord Elton, MacDonald duly crossed to Dunkirk, from where he was driven to his quarters for the night. Next morning he could not be found; and after agitated inquiries it was discovered that, on instructions from the British authorities, he had been placed under arrest – allegedly because his pass was not in order, but in reality because he was considered too dangerous to be allowed within reach of the front. With some difficulty, Munro managed to get him released, but only on condition that he was driven back to Dunkirk, escorted by a Belgian military guard, and placed on a boat for England.[5] Elton's account may not be wholly accurate. A letter in the MacDonald papers from the Belgian minister of war to the Belgian socialist leader, Emile Vandervelde, explaining that MacDonald had arrived in Furnes without the necessary authorization, and regretting his misadventure,[6] suggests that his arrest may have been ordered by the Belgian authorities, not by the British ones. It is clear from his diary, however, that MacDonald believed that the British were to blame.[7] In any case, the episode clearly came as a shock. MacDonald returned to Furnes a few days later, this time with the proper permit, and was taken on a tour of the front by General Seely, next to whom, at one stage, he found himself sitting in a French support trench, while a German trench two hundred yards ahead was cleared by French infantrymen.[8] But, although he wrote his report for the ambulance corps, he took no further part in its activities.[9]

Uglier shocks were in store for him. As the casualty lists lengthened, popular attitudes hardened and the anti-war movement became even more isolated. By the summer of 1915, there were anti-German riots in the East End; U.D.C. pamphlets were being seized by the police; and the offices of the I.L.P. and *Labour Leader* were raided. By 1916, conscientious objectors were being hounded and humiliated. All the leading figures in the I.L.P. and U.D.C. suffered in varying degrees. Morel was imprisoned on a trumped-up charge.[10] Clifford Allen, a brilliant young Cambridge graduate who had been a protégé of MacDonald's before 1914, almost died as a result of the treatment he received as an absolutist conscientious objector.[11] MacDonald's experiences were mild in comparison; but they too hurt badly. The *Morning Post* accused him of deliberately distributing copies of his pamphlets criticizing Grey's foreign policy to the relatives of men killed at the front.[12] In Lossiemouth, old acquaintances sent him postcards addressed to 'Herr Ramsay MacDonald'.[13] When he stayed in Glasgow with his pacifist friend, Hugh Roberton, founder of the Orpheus Choir, a policeman watched in the street outside.[14] On rare occasions his meetings were broken up: men still remember how he stood his ground at I.L.P. meetings while being stoned by the mob.[15] More often, the press reported disturbances where none had taken place, presumably in order to deter proprietors from letting their halls to him; and this policy of denying him a hearing, MacDonald believed, was actively encouraged by the police.[16]

Like many other opponents of the war, he often took refuge at Garsington

Manor, in Oxfordshire, where Lady Ottoline Morrell – the daughter of the Duke of Portland, wife of the anti-war Liberal M.P., Philip Morrell, and mistress of Bertrand Russell – used to hold court at weekends over a glittering, if somewhat precious, assortment of artists and intellectuals, whose leading lights included D. H. Lawrence, Duncan Grant, Aldous Huxley and Lytton Strachey.[17] Garsington's 'god', as Mrs Hamilton put it in her memoirs, was Bertrand Russell; MacDonald was, at most, a minor prophet.[18] Russell thought he had 'much virtue and some sense', but was exasperated by his habit of telling long and boring Scottish stories that never seemed to come to a point.[19] Lady Ottoline enjoyed listening to him read aloud and was particularly moved by his rendering of Walt Whitman's 'Good-bye My Fancy', but she was put off by his histrionic air and found his stories even more exasperating than Russell did.[20] What MacDonald thought of Garsington is not known, but the respite it offered must have been welcome or he would not have continued to go there.

It was only a partial respite, however. Two episodes, in particular, cut deep. The first was the sustained attack on him by Horatio Bottomley's notorious journal, *John Bull*. 'The success of recruiting', wrote *John Bull* in February 1915, 'is almost as painful to the I.L.P. as it is to the Kaiser'; the ringleaders of the 'pro-German Campaign' whose activities it was unmasking were MacDonald and Hardie.[21] Later that month, A. G. Hales discovered that MacDonald had had the temerity to make public his scepticism about the atrocities allegedly committed by German soldiers in Belgium:

Think of it; dear, sweet-faced old dames, trembling on the verge of the grave – dishonoured and then shambled. It puts the scalping knife and tomahawk of the savage on a plane higher than Germany's vaunted civilisation … Girls of tender age … have been ravished. Husbands have been hurled out of homes at the point of a bayonet, that wives might become the prey of uniformed ghouls. Vestals have been shamed in front of older relatives; women in the presence of their children … It is hard to believe that a British Member of Parliament would lower himself to whitewash criminals in uniform, and I hope that Mr. Ramsay MacDonald can step forward and vindicate himself against the charge to which I have referred.[22]

MacDonald, of course, did no such thing; and on June 19th, *John Bull* devoted a long, two-page article to the 'high priests' of 'Damnable Treason'. There were two high priests, it turned out: MacDonald and Hardie. Of the two, MacDonald was evidently the more dangerous. 'We call him Traitor, Coward, Cur,' *John Bull* concluded. 'We demand his trial by Court Martial, his condemnation as an aider and abetter of the King's enemies, and that he be taken to the Tower and shot at dawn.'

This might be dismissed as the pardonable exuberance of a popular paper: and there is no evidence that it disturbed MacDonald's equanimity in any way. The culmination of *John Bull's* campaign, however, was a different matter. This appeared in the issue of September 4th, 1915, in an article headed 'James McDonald Ramsay. Leicester M.P.'s name and origin—can he sit in Parliament?' The article pointed out that

> For months past—ever since the man who calls himself James Ramsay MacDonald, but whose real name is James McDonald Ramsay, has stood aloof from the almost unanimous response of the nation to the call of the King—we have persistently labelled him as a traitor and a coward; and we have called upon Leicester to rid itself of the stigma of having such a 'representative' in Parliament. But, despite all provocation, we have so far confined ourselves to criticising and exposing his words and deeds in the capacity of a public man—of a paid servant of the State. Even when we were recently described by him as having spent most of our time 'on the threshold of the gaol', we simply retorted that if he wished to push us through the door the machinery of the criminal prosecution for libel was available to him. For, whatever our knowledge concerning his antecedents, we felt that even in the case of a traitor, there was a recognised line beyond which journalistic revelation should not travel. So we have remained silent with regard to certain facts which have been in our possession for a long time. First of all, we knew that this man was living under an adopted name — and that he was registered as *James McDonald Ramsay*—and that, therefore, he had obtained admission to the House of Commons in false colours, and was probably liable to heavy penalties to have his election declared void. But to have disclosed this state of things would have imposed upon us a very painful and unsavoury duty. *We should have been compelled to produce the man's birth certificate.* And that would have revealed what today we are justified in revealing—for the reason we will state in a moment. It would have revealed 'James Ramsay Macdonald', M.P. for Leicester, late 'leader' of the Labour Party; late member of a Royal Commission, under the seal of His Majesty; the leading light of the 'Union of Democratic Control' — libeller and slanderer of his country—it would have revealed him *as the illegitimate son of a Scotch servant girl*!

The article was accompanied by a facsimile reproduction of MacDonald's birth certificate, which of course revealed that he had indeed been registered at birth as 'James McDonald Ramsay'. Today, such a revelation would presumably not be worth making. Fifty years ago, however, a stigma was still attached to illegitimacy—particularly, perhaps, among the respectable working class from which the Labour Party derived most of its support. Even so, the correspondence which survives among MacDonald's papers suggests that Bottomley may have miscalculated. Letters poured in, from I.L.P. and Labour Party branches, from individual friends and from complete strangers. John Scurr of the *Herald*, noting that he had 'from time to time criticised your general Labour policy', felt obliged to emphasize his resentment of 'such reptilian methods of controversy as are indulged in by Horatio Bottomley'. The Secretary of the National Union of Police and Prison Officers tendered his 'sincere sympathy with you at the cowardly and outrageous personal attack of Mr. Bottomley'. Fenner Brockway of the *Labour Leader* deplored the 'loathsome attack made upon you in this week's *John Bull*', and apologized for the fact that Bottomley had been able to hang his article on a sentence in an article in the *Labour Leader* by E. D. Morel. The Mid and East Lothian Miners' Association offered their congratulations 'on the great honour that has been bestowed upon you. You ought to be proud that you have been selected as the man to enable "John Bully" to reach the limit of infamy.' The Shepherd's Bush branch of the N.U.R. forwarded a resolution recording their 'high appreciation of Mr. James Ramsay MacDonald, M.P. who has served the working classes honourably and with conspicuous ability for many years', and their belief that it was because of this that he had been singled out 'for all sorts of calumny and abuse'. Katharine Bruce Glasier wrote that her only regret was 'that any Englishman lives capable of such', and added, 'For you – I can't think of anything for the moment but the glowing light of your wife's smile as once I was privileged to see it, into your dear mother's eyes. She was so proud of her. And so was Lossiemouth.' Most remarkable of all, perhaps, was an anonymous letter on writing paper headed with crossed union jacks, which ran as follows:

> For your villainy and treason you ought to be shot and I would gladly do my country service by shooting you. I hate you and your vile opinions – as much as Bottomley does. But the assault he made on you last week was the meanest, rottenest lowdown dog's dirty action that ever disgraced journalism EVER![23]

MacDonald's private reaction, however, makes it clear that Bottomley had drawn blood. On September 12th he noted in his diary:

> On the day when the paper with the attack was published, I was travelling from Lossiemouth to London in the company as far as Edinburgh with the Dowager Countess De La Warr, Lady Margaret Sackville and their maid. Breaking the journey at Aberdeen, I saw the Contents Bill of the paper announcing some amazing revelations about myself and when I rejoined the ladies at the station, I saw the maid had John Bull in her hand. Sitting in the train, I took it from her and read the disgusting article. From Aberdeen to Edinburgh, I spent hours of the most terrible mental pain. Letters of sympathy began to pour in upon me. The first time I had ever seen my registration certificate was when I opened the paper at Aberdeen. Never before did I know that I had been registered under the name of Ramsay, and cannot understand it now. From my earliest years my name has been entered upon lists, like the school register, etc. as MacDonald. My mother must have made a simple blunder or the registrar must have made a clerical error. In any event, the affair is most mysterious.[24]

The second episode occurred almost a year after the *John Bull* attack; and MacDonald's friends all seem to have agreed that it hit him harder than any other experience in the entire war. In August 1915, a group of members of the Moray Golf Club, of which MacDonald was a member, and where he and his sons used to play when he was in Lossiemouth, submitted a motion demanding that MacDonald's name be removed from the roll of members, on the grounds that the character of the club was endangered by his membership. The council refused to take action. After a tart note from MacDonald to the club secretary, pointing out that the council of the golf club had not been elected to make political judgments, but 'to preserve sobriety in the club house, to see that gentlemen do not insult ladies – or Radicals – on the course, and to put appropriate penalties on rabbit scrapes, ditches and people who play too well,' no further developments took place for nearly a year.[25] In August 1916, however, thirty members – most of whom had not signed the previous motion – submitted a new motion, alleging that MacDonald's continued membership had caused several other members to resign; quoting from MacDonald's articles attacking Sir Edward Grey and from German newspapers which had also quoted them; and demanding a special meeting to discuss the question of removing MacDonald's name from the club roll. A month later, the special meeting was held in the Burgh court house in Elgin, with nearly one hundred members present. A London barrister named Noad moved a resolution declaring that MacDonald's conduct had endangered the character and interests of the club, and that he had forfeited his right to membership. In spite of the opposition of the local M.P., the motion was carried by 73 votes to 24.

MacDonald had already consulted the Lord Advocate on the possibility of obtaining a court injunction to prevent the club council from holding the special meeting, and had been told that there was none. Nevertheless, he still seems to have considered going to law – a course from which he was deterred, partly by friends who wisely pointed out that he would be foolish to show publicly how deeply he cared about the whole matter, and partly by the Glasgow pacifist solicitor Rosslyn Mitchell who advised him that although an English court in similar circumstances would be concerned 'to do equity', a Scottish court would only be concerned to ensure that the formalities had been complied with. According to Mitchell, MacDonald would have little chance of success unless he took the case to the House of Lords. MacDonald therefore had to content himself with a pained letter to the club secretary:

> I am in receipt of your letter informing me that the Moray Golf Club has decided to become a political association with the Golf Course attached, and that it has torn up its rules in order that some of its members may give rein to their political prejudice and spite. Unfortunately, for some years, the visit of any prominent Liberal or Radical to the Moray Golf Club has been resented by a certain section which has not concealed its offensiveness

either in the Club House or on the Course. Though I am, therefore, not sorry that the character of a number of members of the Moray Golf Club has been advertised to the world, I cannot help regretting that the Club, of which I was one of the earliest members, should be held up to public ridicule and contempt.[26]

He never played on the Lossiemouth links again.

II

In public, MacDonald preserved a stoic front. Even in private, his guard rarely slipped. After Sir Valentine Chirol's outburst in The Times, for example, he noted sarcastically:

> Furious attack on me in the Times editorial & by Sir Valentine Chirol. I am a bogy. It is really very flattering if I cared for that sort of thing. They apparently think I do, poor dears! They give me big type on the centre page & then tell me I am nobody! They have no humbler conception of me than I have of myself. I am bodily & spiritually tired of all this notoriety & would welcome gratefully a summons to the silences. But the end is not yet & I am doomed to my burdens ...[27]

But the despairing note of the last sentence is more convincing than the brisk good cheer of the other four. In fact, the strain told: more heavily, perhaps, than MacDonald himself realized. The courage which enabled him to defy public opinion through four years of abuse was sustained at great cost: and part of the cost was the strengthening of less attractive characteristics. He had always found it hard to trust others unless he had positive reasons to do so, and equally hard to give himself away psychologically in a manner that might have led others to trust him. The self-reliance which had made it possible for him to make his way to the forefront of British politics in the face of intimidating odds had always been accompanied by a streak of moral and intellectual intolerance. In the conflicts which had surrounded him throughout his political career, he had always been apt to give the impression that his opponents were wicked as well as mistaken, and perhaps treacherous also. These traits were all intensified by his experience during the war. So were the loneliness and isolation which lay behind them.

Thus we find him writing on September 12th, 1915:

> This is the fourth anniversary of the funeral. This year I had had to spend the 8th in a Bristol hotel. The afternoon was strangely like that when she died bright, sunny, peaceful. I was very weary both in mind & spirit & as I sat through the hours of the death agony alone in my room, it was not sorrow that came to me but a sad weariness & a wonder if she was or was not, if she cared, or knew, or what. From time to time, I have been reading

spiritualist literature, automatic writing, etc. but it repels me on the whole. And the war & the conduct of clergymen have all but shattered belief in anything but popularity & irrationality.[28]

'Oh Lord,' he prayed in a note in his diary in January 1916, 'For thy mercy's sake, save us from the cynicism which is the only creed which now seems justified by the facts';[29] and he evidently felt that the prayer was necessary. Five months later he wrote, in an open letter to 'A Conscientious Objector' in the *Labour Leader*, 'A Bishop and a Moderator of one of the Scottish Kirks lead the hoarse crowds which cry to you that if you do not fight you ought to leave the country. The welcome of Barabbas takes many forms and this is one of them.' And he added, in a phrase which revealed more of the author than of those to whom it was addressed, that 'if the hardships you have had to endure lead you to feel that only you are right you will run the risk of being whited Saints or irreconcileable Ishmaels.'[30] For consciousness of the danger of becoming a 'white saint' did not give him immunity from it. 'When I arose on Friday as fraternal delegate the Congress cheered again & again ...,' he noted after the T.U.C. conference in September 1915. 'They know that I have no axe to grind & that I have acted straight and sincerely.'[31] That, too, was a recurrent note.

It was accompanied by a growing contempt for the trade-unionist majority in his own party, most of whom supported the war. The war brought with it an unprecedented extension in the economic power of the working class, and in the political importance of its representatives in Parliament. Between 1914 and 1919, the total affiliated membership of the T.U.C. grew from less than 2,500,000 to more than 4,500,000, and that of the Labour Party from 1,600,000 to more than 3,000,000. Eventually this expansion was to make it possible for Labour to become a major party for the first time. For the present, however, the forces behind it tied Labour's leaders more and more closely to the Government. It was clear that the war could not be won unless the state intervened more directly in the labour market, as well as in other sectors of the economy. But if the state was to intervene successfully in the labour market, it would need the co-operation of the unions; and if it was to obtain the co-operation of the unions, it would need the support of the Labour Party. We have already seen how the parliamentary party, under MacDonald's chairmanship, slowly acquired the position of middleman between unions and Government during the labour unrest of 1911 and 1912. Much the same happened now, but on a greatly extended scale. Gradually, the Labour Party was pulled closer to the Government and, so long as it supported the war, it had no valid reason for resisting. The process itself was not new. Indeed, it was merely an accelerated version of the process which had been in operation before 1914. The difference was that MacDonald was now opposed to it, whereas before 1914 he had been one of its prime movers.

The first big step along this road came in May 1915. Asquith finally decided that the war could not be prosecuted successfully with a purely Liberal Cabinet. The Unionists were brought into the Government; and the Labour Party was invited as well. The parliamentary party rejected the invitation. But the National Executive voted to accept it, by 9 votes to 3; and a joint meeting of the parliamentary party and the Executive did the same by 17 to 11.[32] An attempt to insist on an undertaking that the Government would not introduce any form of conscription was defeated; and Henderson duly joined the Cabinet as president of the Board of Education, with a free hand from his party to make what terms he chose. The first and most obvious result to be expected from the coalition, C. P. Trevelyan predicted in an indignant letter to Arthur Ponsonby, was that 'there will be no effective party in the Cabinet anxious for an early peace.'[33] The second was conscription. MacDonald was equally indignant. The Labour Party, he pointed out in the *Labour Leader* on June 3rd, had always believed that it would lose influence by joining a coalition. If the Liberals had asked it to join the Government so as to resist an Opposition demand for conscription, it might have been justified in accepting the invitation. In fact, the opposite was the case; and the Labour Party would be bound to be implicated in whatever the rest of the Government did. '[A] man may assure us that he is only lighting a fire to warm his hands when he is putting a match to a hay-rick,' he warned, 'and he may do it quite honestly, but the rick will blaze all the same. No party can be in the Cabinet and not of it.'

His warning soon came true. The Labour Party had always been strongly opposed to conscription. Indeed, it had justified its support for the Government's recruiting campaign by the argument that conscription was the only alternative. MacDonald had been sceptical of this argument from the start. Conscription, he had argued, was inevitable without a fundamental change in foreign policy; and the attitudes engendered by a recruiting campaign made such a change harder to bring about. In September, his arguments were given a new boost. Ever since the formation of the coalition in May, sections of the Unionist party and press had been conducting an agitation in favour of compulsory military service. On September 15th, the National Executive met to consider the 'grave' state of affairs which this agitation had created. It decided to summon a special meeting with the Parliamentary Committee of the T.U.C., the parliamentary party and the management committee of the General Federation of Trade Unions to put Labour's opposition to conscription to the Government.[34] At the end of the month, the meeting duly took place. After speeches by Asquith and Kitchener on the gravity of the military situation, a resolution was passed affirming Labour's belief that the army could obtain the men it needed by voluntary methods.[35] 'The leaders of Labour are hopeless,' MacDonald noted afterwards; 'they are facing problems with which they are unfamiliar; they are just pliable putty in other people's hands; and poor dear flattered and innocent things they think they are heroes working for the safety of their country.'[36]

Labour resolutions could not change the situation on the Western Front or dam the conscriptionist tide. In December 1915, the Government finally decided that voluntary recruiting would not produce enough men. On December 30th, the Labour Party National Executive decided that Labour's attitude to the Government's decision could only be settled by a representative conference;[37] and on January 6th, 1916, the conference duly met at the Central Hall, Westminster. The National Executive submitted a resolution reaffirming the vote of the Bristol T.U.C. against conscription, but leaving individual Labour M.P.s to vote on the Government's proposals as they saw fit.[38] This, of course, would allow Henderson and his colleagues in the Government to vote in favour of conscription even if the movement as a whole opposed it. But the N.U.R. submitted an amendment recommending the parliamentary party to oppose the Government's measure in all its stages. Henderson made a passionate speech, announcing that he personally would vote for conscription whatever the conference might do, and that he would be prepared to resign his seat and ask his constituents to endorse his action. He was followed by MacDonald. According to the *Labour Leader*,

> Mr. MacDonald received the ovation of the day. The cheers rose to a crescendo, they fell, then they rose again, they fell, and then they rose a third time. So challenging was the welcome that some of his opponents thought it necessary to ... reply, but it was a pathetic effort ...
>
> Mr. MacDonald emphasised the point made by previous speakers that the principle of Compulsion cannot be restricted to this measure ... Mr. MacDonald argued that the real difference in the Labour movement at the present time centres on the question of military necessity ... The function of our movement ... is to co-ordinate the demand of the military expert with other national demands ... National life is not maintained by soldiers only even in time of war ...
>
> One of Mr. MacDonald's best sentences was: 'You can win the war, and in winning it pay such a price that the nation will have lost ... '

In the end, the N.U.R. amendment was carried by 1,715,000 to 934,000. Delegates leapt to their feet, waving hats and handkerchiefs, and shouting themselves hoarse. In the excitement another resolution was carried without a card vote, demanding the complete withdrawal of the Government's Bill and pledging the Labour movement to support the voluntary system. Then the 'Red Flag' was struck up; and, as the *Labour Leader* put it, the delegates left the hall 'still cheering over their triumph over our "British Prussians" '.[39] Their triumph, however, was short-lived. In the National Executive, the atmosphere was less exalted. After the conference, Henderson made a lengthy statement to the Executive; and after what the minutes refer to as 'considerable discussion', it was resolved by 16 votes to 11 that the Labour Party could no longer remain in the Government.[40] On January 12th, however, a joint meeting of the National

Executive and the parliamentary party was given a number of assurances by the prime minister, and proceeded to reverse its previous decision. By 25 votes to 8, it was resolved that the three Labour ministers should withdraw their resignations, pending the decision of the annual conference in a few days' time.[41] 'Some of my colleagues were born to hew wood and draw water,' MacDonald noted, 'and with a little flattery they can be backed to fulfill [sic] their destiny.'[42] At the end of the month, the conference passed a resolution declaring its opposition to the Government's Military Service Bill, but defeated another resolution pledging the Labour movement to agitate for its repeal. The Labour ministers duly remained in office; and MacDonald noted bitterly:

> The Trade Union leaders hang pretty much together. They are ignorant of the issues, their speeches show a simplicity of mind which confuses one. It is upon this simplicity which is based their determination to do whatever is required of them. They voted again against compulsion but had not the gumption to see that they had to oppose the policies that were making it inevitable. Their feebleness is discouraging. I begin to doubt as to the future of the Party.[43]

His doubts were soon reinforced. In April 1916, the Government decided on a further extension of the Military Service Act. On April 15th, the parliamentary party resolved that it could not agree to any extension with the information then at its disposal;[44] and ten days later Asquith, Kitchener and Bonar Law addressed a joint meeting of the parliamentary party and the National Executive, augmented by representatives of the miners, transport workers, railwaymen and engineers. In spite of the prime minister's efforts, the National Executive decided that a national conference should be summoned.[45] Next day, however, it learned that the T.U.C. Parliamentary Committee and the management committee of the G.F.T.U. had both agreed to support the Government's new proposals. Thereupon the National Executive solemnly decided that it would, after all, be undesirable to summon the special conference for which it had voted the day before.[46] Once again, Labour's walls of Jericho had crumbled at the first blast of a ministerial trumpet. 'In the history of the reaction,' MacDonald wrote a few weeks later, 'this chapter will be headed: "How we succeeded with Labour." '[47]

III

Behind the struggle over conscription, loomed the more important issues of the International and the peace settlement. MacDonald had believed ever since the war broke out that Labour's support for the Government would make it more difficult to keep the International alive, and would therefore damage the prospects of a moderate peace. The more closely the Labour Party identified itself with the war effort, the more his forebodings were borne out. As early as January 1915, Camille Huysmans, the secretary of the International Socialist Bureau, had written to MacDonald suggesting that delegates of the affiliated parties should meet the I.S.B. executive at The Hague to discuss 'the last events'.[48] MacDonald had written to Jim Middleton at the Labour Party headquarters to sound out the possibilities.[49] But there had been no response, and the meeting had not taken place. In the late spring, however, the I.S.B. executive invited the British section to send a deputation to The Hague to explain British Labour's attitude to the war. The invitation was accepted, and MacDonald and Henderson were appointed as the Labour Party's delegates. But when Henderson joined the Cabinet he resigned from the delegation, and at the end of June the National Executive decided that no delegation from the British section of the International should go to The Hague after all.[50] This was bad enough, and worse soon followed. In July, the anti-war German socialists, one of whose leaders was MacDonald's old friend, Eduard Bernstein, issued a manifesto, setting out their peace terms. MacDonald urged the British working-class movement to follow the German example, and for a while it looked as though his advice might be taken. On August 13th, the British section of the I.S.B. agreed to publish an official answer to the German manifesto based on the resolutions which had been carried at a conference of Allied socialist parties earlier in the year.[51] In the middle of September, however, the Labour Party Executive instructed its delegates to the British section of the I.S.B. to oppose the publication of any Labour manifesto on the peace settlement. The delegates did so; and no manifesto was published.[52]

MacDonald continued to campaign for a Labour Party statement of war aims, but against increasing opposition. In March 1916, Huysmans attended a meeting of the National Executive accompanied by Émile Vandervelde, the President of the International. They explained that, although they realized that it was impossible for the International to meet if the Allied parties objected, they believed that the time had come for each national section to consider the problems which would eventually arise when the peace settlement had to be reached. Accordingly, they suggested that the socialist parties of France and Britain should prepare memoranda, setting out their views on the eventual peace settlement. Even this was turned down by the parliamentary party; and MacDonald noted acidly that after the meeting Huysmans had told him that 'it was the most ignorant crowd he had yet met.'[53] In the circumstances, this was a pardonable reaction. For MacDonald believed that the war was now approaching a turning-point, in which the attitude of the Labour movement might be of decisive importance. As he put it in the *Labour Leader* at the beginning of April, there was 'a new feeling in all the belligerent countries'. Thanks to increasing war-weariness, the peoples of Europe were ceasing to put their trust in military operations alone, and were beginning to ask their Governments to define their war aims. In this situation the socialist parties, which were not responsible either for the outbreak of the war or for its continuation, had a unique opportunity to lead public opinion.[54] '[I]t is for you above every organ of civilisation', he wrote grandiloquently in an Open Letter to the International Socialist Bureau in May, 'to prepare the way for reason and reflection by removing the misunderstandings which keep the peoples apart.'[55] As he must have known, the International was in no condition to play such a role, even if it had been willing to do so. But the emotion that led him to define its role in such terms was deeply felt, and his growing indignation with the patriotic wing of his own party cannot be understood unless the force of that emotion is taken into account.

By now, MacDonald's campaign for a Labour Party war-aims statement had merged into a wider U.D.C. campaign – launched under the inspiration of E. D. Morel in the latter part of 1915 – for a Government statement and a negotiated peace. At first, MacDonald had had doubts about the wisdom of campaigning for a negotiated peace in public. 'To announce suddenly that there is a party in favour of negotiation now would only have a hardening effect on public opinion,' he explained to C. R. Buxton in October 1915. 'On the other hand, I think there are a great many people ready to receive a *little* light, and suggestions that negotiation must not be forgotten even in the midst of the fighting will, I think, bear fruit.'[56] He was still fairly cautious in February 1916. 'I am still of opinion that no good can be done by a debate on peace ... ,' he wrote to C. P. Trevelyan on the 10th; and he added, revealingly if not altogether relevantly, that in Leicester a Zeppelin raid had 'played havoc with reasonableness & one of my supporters who keeps a shop has been molested by a company of soldiers on a route march. If we had a meeting here at present it would certainly be broken up.'[57]

By May, he had changed his mind about the value of a 'debate on peace'; in a debate initiated by Arthur Ponsonby he argued that a statement of British war aims would make it impossible for the German Government to 'misuse and misrepresent' Allied statements in its propaganda to its own people. It would also quash the rumour that Britain had made a secret bargain with Russia which would entail the continued subjection of dissatisfied national minorities to foreign rule. An even more important consideration was that

This War ought to end in the destruction of militarism in Europe. How are you going to do it? ... I had a letter ... from a member of the Reichstag some time after the War broke out, a man, who, if there is a pro-English-man within the borders of Germany, deserves that epithet, and in that letter he said: 'Tell your fellow countrymen not to imagine that they are going to help us by military victories to rid ourselves of the shackles of Junkerdom. What they are doing is, they are hammering those shackles much more firmly upon our wrists ... '

... We ourselves must make our own offers. It is not enough for Rt.

Hon. Gentlemen to say that we only want to crush Prussian militarism. Prussian militarism is the magnificent fruit and flower of this poisonous plant upon which there are less perfectly developed fruits and less perfectly developed flowers.[58]

The Government made no move, and nor did the Labour Party. If anything, MacDonald's position in the party continued to weaken. By October 1916, his indignation with the party leadership had gone so far that he was prepared to take part in setting up a new United Socialist Council embracing the I.L.P. and his old enemies in the British Socialist Party, which had by now shed its pro-war right wing, and was well on the way to its eventual destiny as the immediate forerunner of the Communist Party. The new Council agreed at its first meeting that common policy should be prepared 'upon all matters where that is possible', and that demonstrations should be initiated at national and local level. According to the minutes of the first meeting, it also discussed elections to the Labour Party Executive and resolutions at the Labour Party conference.[59] When Edward Pease of the Fabian Society, which had also been invited to join, asked for an assurance that the Council would only act with the consent of the delegates from all the bodies represented on it, MacDonald replied, irrelevantly but significantly:

> I do not know what circumstances may compel me to do, nor do I know what other members of the Council may propose, so that my hands might be forced. I have no desire to raise unnecessarily any questions relating to things that have been done and cannot be undone, but if at any stage either during or after the War, the complete success of the Socialist Movement in this country requires a consideration of the action of the pro-war Socialists, I shall certainly raise the question.[60]

His impatience with the 'pro-war Socialists' was soon to reach even greater heights. At the beginning of December 1916, Asquith was replaced as prime minister by Lloyd George. Lloyd George was the leading champion of the 'knock-out blow'. His elevation was an unmistakable defeat for the forces of moderation in the Government who might have been prepared for a compromise peace, and a victory for the most bellicose sections of the Unionist party. Yet Henderson and a majority of the parliamentary Labour Party—having remained loyal to Asquith until the last moment—seemed content to transfer their allegiance to the new Government. On December 6th, MacDonald noted savagely:

> The crisis has developed & Brutus has killed Caesar. Of course Labour is in. It will not leave its position in a hurry. It is professing simple patriotism again & Mr. Henderson after saying that Asquith was indispensable at a meeting last week told us at a specially summoned meeting of the Labour Party today that he thought he should be allowed to stay in the new

government. It was very much against his inclination etc, etc, in that vein, but – He reminded me of the story of the virgin nuns who kept Satan behind them until someone suggested spiritual service & thereafter kissing & holiness were combined.[61]

His public comments were almost as outspoken. Until now he had been careful not to question the loyalty of the pro-war majority of the party to the fundamental assumptions on which the party was based. However deep his private disgust with their support for the war, he had never suggested that they should be drummed out of the party, or that the anti-war minority should secede from it. Indeed, he had gone out of his way to oppose such suggestions from the more militant elements in the I.L.P., and had insisted that the issues of the war and of party unity should be kept in separate compartments. His restraint was, of course, equalled by Henderson's restraint in refraining from any attempt to remove him from the party treasurership or to carry out a purge of the anti-war section; and in the long run both men could claim much of the credit for the fact that the British Labour Party was not split irrevocably by the war, as most continental socialist parties were. The formation of the Lloyd George coalition, however, put MacDonald's restraint under heavier pressure than ever before. In his column in the Glasgow *Forward* on December 16th, he argued that there was a critical difference between joining the Asquith coalition in 1915 and joining the Lloyd George coalition now. The Asquith coalition, he maintained, had at least been able to claim that it was a national government, standing above party. No such claim could be made for the Lloyd George coalition, if only because the official Liberal Party had refused to join it. In taking office in it, Henderson and his colleagues had called into question the very basis of the Labour Party. 'I have disagreed with the policy of the majority of my colleagues since August, 1914,' MacDonald concluded menacingly, 'but I have never believed that they were abandoning their principles ... The condition today, however, is not quite that. The majority of the Party has now taken a decision which means that under normal conditions it is prepared to ally itself with other [parties], that the policy of independence is no longer the policy of the party.' There is no way of telling how far he was prepared to push his own argument, but no impartial reader could doubt that it pointed in the direction of a split.

IV

'Melancholy is on me,' MacDonald noted in a lugubrious diary entry on Christmas Eve, 1916. 'Sitting with a blank mind with my dead near me is all I can do. The dying year, the hollow mockery of this Christmas time, the destruction of confidence oppress me.'[62] Four days later he noted that he was having 'bad nights', and added: 'How lonely one is. One seems to sit just waiting like a servant at a master's door.'[63] On New Year's Eve he sat up to see the new year in, and noted:

> I cannot go to bed till the New Year comes in, & the Old is at the point of death. It demands an account of my stewardship to take with it — where? Who knows. Maybe into nothingness. What can I say. Work, work! Effort, effort! That is all. I can find nothing in my heart to say to it as it goes except 'May the New Year be better than you'. But the worst of years counts as one against us. Good or bad they are all the same so far as Time goes. My prayer for the New is: 'Keep me at work — the same work — uphill work — fighting the wild beasts of error' — & I would add 'Keep my mind open so that I may see Truth — more Truth.'[64]

In the next few weeks, the 'wild beasts of error' became even wilder than before. In December 1916, President Wilson appealed to the belligerent powers pointing out that their stated war aims were much the same, and suggesting an exchange of views. In January 1917, the Allies replied in uncompromising terms, reaffirming their own innocence and Germany's guilt and demanding, among other things, the dismemberment of the Austro-Hungarian empire. On January 31st, Germany announced that she had decided to embark on unrestricted submarine warfare, and on February 3rd, the United States broke off diplomatic relations with her. Meanwhile, MacDonald suffered more petty pinpricks of the kind to which he had grown so accustomed over the past thirty months. He was harassed by a mysterious Mrs Perring, who claimed to be a Pole working for an independent Poland, but whom MacDonald and Morel both believed to be an *agent provocateur*, employed by the War Office to trap him into indiscretions.[65] Early in January he was interrupted at a meeting in Leicester by a man who accused him of being a traitor, holding up a photograph of a soldier as he did so. 'You are a damned fool,' MacDonald replied, 'if you believe what you are saying.' The local newspapers reported that he had insulted the dead soldier son of one of his constituents by calling him a damned fool.[66] A few days later, a U.D.C. meeting in Walthamstow at which he had been due to speak was broken up by a group of Canadian sergeants, said to have been brought there for the purpose by the *Daily Express*. Next day he noted despairingly:

> Newspaper reports of last night's meeting are as I expected. I was replied to by a soldier — when I had never spoken; I was carried out — when I was never touched ... Oh, the lies, lies & the malice! It is a pity that the papers said nothing about the fine way in which the sergeants bustled women, even when one had a baby in her arms. When I see these men I know what rubbish is our talk about the Huns. The soldier's trade & training are so demoralising that he will do anything once he gets a start.[67]

Yet even now he did not give up hope altogether. Hitherto his position on the war had consisted of a series of negations — courageous negations, but still negations. He had opposed the declaration of war. He had opposed the Government's recruiting campaign. He had opposed the Labour Party's decision to join the coalition. He had opposed conscription. But he had not put forward a clear alternative to the foreign policy which, on his showing at least, had led to the war in the first place, and which had therefore made recruiting and conscription inevitable. In January 1917, however, he published a short study of the foreign-policy questions raised by the war in which he tried to sketch out an alternative. It was entitled *National Defence*; and although it was hastily written, and left many questions unanswered, it throws a great deal of light not only on MacDonald's mood and preoccupations when he wrote it but on the attitudes and assumptions on which his foreign policy was to be based for most of the next fifteen years.

He began by rejecting most of the rival panaceas on offer. Pacifism, he argued in the first chapter, was no guarantee of peace. The British people had not wanted war: and war had engulfed them all the same. 'The pieties of a peace movement which stops at sentiment', he wrote, 'delude the country during peace and are swept away during a war.'[68] But if pacifism was inadequate, its opposite was positively dangerous. In his second chapter, MacDonald turned to the argument developed before 1914 by the French socialist, Jean Jaurès, in favour of a citizen army. In his *L'Armée nouvelle*, Jaurès had argued that a citizen army was inherently defensive and therefore a bulwark against militarism. This, MacDonald replied, had been disproved by what had happened in August 1914. France, Britain and Germany had all leapt to the sword; if anything, it was Britain, where there was no citizen army, which had hesitated most.[69] In any case, Jaurès's implied distinction between a defensive and an offensive war was meaningless. The maxim that attack is the best form of defence, MacDonald wrote, was 'a law in diplomacy'.[70] Threatened countries always measured themselves against potential enemies; a country which believed itself to be threatened did not rest content with arming itself, but sought allies as well. But no alliance could ever be purely defensive; its motives were bound to be mixed. The Triple Alliance had been formed for defensive reasons and had developed into an offensive one, and the Franco-Russian alliance had not been exclusively defensive either. Jaurès had assumed that war was made by the popular will: in reality, the popular will was subordinate to the logic of alliance diplomacy. It was like 'a leaf floating on the current; it must drift with the stream and go whither the rush drives it.'[71]

If a citizen army was no guarantee of peace, neither was an armed league of nations formed to enforce it. By the end of 1916, moderate supporters of the war were becoming increasingly convinced of the necessity of establishing such a league when the war was over. MacDonald viewed the proposal with suspicion, bordering on hostility.[72] At best, it seemed to him that the proposal to set up a league of nations was a diversion from the central issue of disarmament. At worst, it was a hypocritical fig-leaf with which the enemies of peace hoped to cover their nakedness. He acknowledged that an armed league of nations would be an advance on the traditional balance of power. But he denied that it could achieve the aims which its supporters believed that it would achieve, since by definition it was either unnecessary or inadequate. If the assumptions on which its champions based their case were valid, it was possible to take much more drastic steps; if the peoples of the world were sufficiently enlightened to be capable of protecting their interests within such an organization, they were equally capable of ending the conditions which made it worth having.[73]

Next, MacDonald turned to the most popular panacea of all: the notion that peace would be secured by the destruction of Prussian militarism and the forcible democratization of Germany. This notion, he argued, was not merely false, but the reverse of the truth. So far from democracy being a guarantee against militarism, militarism was in fact a guarantee against democracy. 'In its evolution, militarism is grasping the whole life of the nation,' MacDonald wrote, 'everything has to be subordinate to it; within the net it is casting, every activity and service must be caught.'[74] Unless the war ended in a clean break with militarism, conscription would have to become permanent, and permanent conscription would mean the end of democracy. Supporters of conscription, MacDonald pointed out, had been 'quite open in their advocacy of militarism on the ground that it will keep the working classes in their place.' From their own point of view, they had been right. As a matter of fact, British military strength had been undermined by British democracy; if Britain was to be militarily strong in future, it would be necessary to give the military 'increased respect in the country and authority in the State'.[75] Moreover, permanent military conscription would both facilitate, and in a sense necessitate, permanent industrial conscription as well. For, in a militarized state, strikes would threaten national security, and it would be necessary to eliminate the threat by using the armed forces. In 1910, the French railwaymen had gone on strike in a dispute over trade-union recognition. Briand, the prime minister, had 'instantly mobilised the Army and put it to running the trains. Thus Jacques left his engine one night as a Trade Unionist and stepped upon it next morning as a soldier under instructions to defeat himself as a Trade Unionist.' In a nation with a conscript army, such episodes were inevitable: 'A nation of conscripts is a nation of potential strike-breakers.'[76] Thus, a forcibly democratized Germany would sooner or later return to militarism, and as soon as she did so, she would abandon democracy.

But if pacifism, the citizen army, the league of nations and the forcible democratization of Germany were all to be ruled out as inadequate or dangerous, what was left? Clearly, this was the most important question of all. If MacDonald failed to answer it, he would be saying, in effect, that the militarists were right and that war was, after all, a necessary part of the human condition. In fact, he gave two answers: open diplomacy, and disarmament. The true cause of war, he implied, was not national rivalry, but suspicion and secrecy. Remove the secrecy, and the pressure of peace-loving public opinion would do the rest:

No people wants to fight any other people. Public opinion in times of peace is always against war; it becomes warlike only when roused by the bugles of war, blowing from Foreign Offices, Ministries of War, and through newspapers. How are national disputes to be settled by the people before their passions are aroused? ... [T]his is apparently difficult, but in reality the ease with which it can be done is the greatest obstacle to doing it. Foreign affairs in some mysterious way have been withdrawn from the light of the world. They are transacted in rooms with blinds drawn, with back-stairs entrances and secret doors and waiting chambers ... The whole corrupting system should be swept away. It stands like a dirty old slum area, full of vermin and disease, in the middle of a district cleared and improved. It belongs to the kind of evil which exists by leaning on a similar evil which, in turn, exists by leaning upon it. Few seem to see that a kick at any of the supports will bring the whole offensive fabric down.[77]

The same was true of disarmament. '[S]o long as there are armies,' Mac-Donald wrote, 'there will be wars.' To imagine that permanent peace was possible without disarmament was like 'expecting a warm, gentle, nourishing rain when the temperature is below zero'.[78] But how could these precepts be translated into policy? How could a sub-zero temperature be raised to a more accommodating level? How was the vicious circle by which fear produced armaments and armaments produced fear, to be cut through? In effect, Mac-Donald's answer was to act as though it did not exist. The conflicts of interest which had appeared during the war, he implied, could easily be settled if only the peace conference were 'representative of the people'. German militarism could easily be destroyed if only the Allies were prepared to trust the Germans. The obvious danger that, if one nation refused to disarm, others would be forced to follow suit in self-defence, was dismissed as irrelevant:

It is not our business to content ourselves with allowing other people to take the initiative, and to consider ourselves wise in merely countering their moves; we ought to have a clearly mapped-out policy to secure peace, and we ought to pursue it ... [T]his game of following an evil lead is one of life and death to the nations, because it is an endless game. The resort to militarism provides the conditions which make militarism necessary — more militarism and still more militarism, more danger and still more danger. The 'practical' man ... whose mind is satisfied by reflecting that disarmament is at present unpractical is, as usual, not practical at all. He is a passive dreamer ... By an effort of will we must become civilized men. Nothing else will be of any use. We are like a squirrel in a revolving cage; the faster we run, the faster we have to run. One day, the nations will have the courage and the wisdom to step out. The instant they do so, they will find themselves in a peaceful world.[79]

The weaknesses in the argument are obvious enough. The way to disarmament, MacDonald was saying, was to disarm; the way to peace was to behave peacefully — profound truths, at one level, but the truths of a prophet, not of a policy-maker. There was, in fact, a curious parallel between *National Defence* and his earlier writings on socialist theory. Just as his conception of evolutionary socialism had lacked a strategy by which the processes of evolution might be mastered and furthered, so his analysis of power politics lacked a strategy by which a different system of international relations might gradually be put in their place. His solutions, in fact, were not solutions at all. They were elaborate attempts to deny that there was a problem to be solved. The people, it turned out, were pacific after all. They had merely been misled by secret diplomacy and the bugles of war. The way to ensure that they were not similarly misled in future was simply to stop misleading them. But if they had been misled so easily in the past, what reason was there to suppose that it would be more difficult to mislead them on future occasions? And if there were no reason, what reason was there to believe that secret diplomacy and arms races could ever be ended?

Yet these criticisms miss the point. MacDonald was as remote from power as it is possible for a politician of his stature to be. He had no conceivable hope of putting his policies — or, indeed, any other policies — into effect. In these circumstances, there was no point in writing like a policy-maker: a prophet's role was the only one that offered him a chance to influence events. In later years, as we shall see, he tried hard, and at first with some success, to put the principles he had outlined in *National Defence* into practice; later still, he came sadly and reluctantly to recognize that it was not possible to put them into practice in a world which did not accept them. But, when he wrote *National Defence*, he was not trying to put them into practice. He was trying to gain acceptance for them: to change public opinion, so that it might be possible to put them into practice when the killing stopped. In the end public opinion did change, partly because of his efforts. But it changed too late; and it was partly because it changed too late that his attempts to put his principles into practice, when he had the opportunity to do so, did not produce the results for which he had hoped. But the fact that mankind did not make the 'effort of will' needed to step out of the squirrel's cage does not prove that he was wasting his time when he urged it to do so. An equally plausible conclusion is that the world would have been a happier place if he had been listened to.

CHAPTER 11

Defeat

I

WITHIN a few weeks of the publication of *National Defence*, it suddenly began to look as if the 'act of will' for which MacDonald had called might be forthcoming after all. On March 15th, the news of a revolution in Russia reached a half-empty House of Commons; when Bonar Law announced that the news was true there was, MacDonald noted, 'gleeful excitement'.[1] Next day, he noted, with equal satisfaction, that the Russian socialists had 'fought for their hand in great contrast to our own Labour Party', and had joined the provisional government on conditions.[2] On March 29th, he dined with a group of U.D.C.-ers, including Norman Angell, Trevelyan, Ponsonby, Hobson, Morel and the Radical journalists, H. W. Massingham and H. N. Brailsford. They discussed how to make contact with the new Russian government, and decided to send a telegram to the minister of justice, Kerensky. 'The new Russian Government is popular & will not tolerate diplomatists if [the war] can be ended by negotiation,' MacDonald noted hopefully. 'We must strengthen this spirit ... [I]f Russia will keep democratic, she could now end the war very shortly, spread her revolution over Europe, each country being influenced in accord with its own conditions, & open the door for a real international democracy.'[3] On April 3rd, he noted, more succinctly, 'Everybody of my faith immensely invigorated by Revolution.'[4]

They had good reason to be. Mounting casualty lists, rising prices, stories of profiteering, and resentment against the wartime suspension of trade-union rules had already begun to undermine support for the war among the more militant sections of the working class. On the Clyde, in particular, 1916 had seen sporadic industrial unrest, the growth of a powerful shop stewards' movement centred on the Clyde Workers' Committee, and the deportation of many of the shop stewards' leaders.[5] There were similar tendencies in South Wales. The Russian revolution gave a new impetus to this working-class militancy; it also gave new hope to the intellectuals of the U.D.C. The Tsar, after all, had been brought down by the workers of Petrograd. If Russian workers could change the course of history, British workers might do the same. The new Russian ministers were the spiritual cousins of the British I.L.P.-ers and left-wing Liberals. They had been the victims of the Tsarist persecution: now they were in power. The Petrograd Soviet, which provided the driving force behind the new regime, proclaimed itself in favour of a peace without annexation or indemnities. For the British Left, it was a second fall of the Bastille.

MacDonald welcomed the revolution in ecstatic terms, and lost no opportunity of identifying himself and the I.L.P. with it. In his column in *Forward* at the end of March, he ridiculed the suggestion that the revolution would 'aid the war'. The Russian socialists, he pointed out, 'take up the general attitude of our own I.L.P., only they are a little more extreme'. It was the socialists, he added, who had made the revolution; and the socialists who would continue it.[6] On April 14th, he pointed out that the 'Petrograd Workmen's Committee is pacific and controls the Russian Provisional Government.' In the programme of the Petrograd Soviet, he added, 'the I.L.P. finds a new justification and expression of its policy.'[7] At the I.L.P. conference in April, he moved a special resolution welcoming the revolution, and expressing the party's 'whole-hearted admiration for the courage and devotion which have won a victory not only for Russia, but for all Europe'. Thanks to what had happened in Russia, he declared, 'they felt a sort of spring-tide of joy had broken out all over Europe.'[8] 'The reward of generations of suffering and martyrdom has at last been reaped ... ,' he told a cheering meeting in Glasgow at the end of the month. 'It is the Red Flag that floats over the Imperial Palace at Petrograd.'[9] Yet his enthusiasm was tempered by apprehension. The revolution, he believed, was threatened by at least three dangers. The first was that the Western Allies, as he put it in his diary on March 29th, might 'mislead' the new regime and 'get it mixed up in their "fight to a finish" and other perversions'. The second was that the 'extreme pacifist Left' in Russia, led by Lenin, whose arrival in Petrograd MacDonald recorded with alarm at the end of April, might discredit the revolution and play into the hands of the war party.[10] The third was that the extremists might win and make a separate peace with Germany. This, MacDonald believed, would be a disaster. 'The great service which the Russian Revolution could render to Europe', he wrote, would be to bring about 'an understanding between the German Democracy and that of the Allied countries'.[11] A separate peace between Russia and Germany would do the opposite. It would confirm German militarism in power, and make a democratic understanding between the peoples of Europe even harder to achieve than it was already.

Hence his course during the next few weeks. In speeches and articles addressed to the I.L.P. rank and file, he continued to bang the revolutionary drum, with such effect that Lloyd George saw him in retrospect as a potential British Kerensky.[12] After a series of May Day meetings in Leicester, he noted 'Most successful meetings. 7000 in Market Place & no murmur of dissent. Russian revolution has greatly changed minds of many people & has made them breathe the atmosphere & feel the sentiments of Revolution. Our people are more cocky & believe they are winning.'[13] At the beginning of June, he played a major part in the famous Leeds convention, organized by the United Socialist

Council to celebrate the Russian revolution, and discuss its relevance to Britain. Four resolutions were carried, the first welcoming the Russian revolution, the second pledging the conference to work for a peace without annexations or indemnities, the third proclaiming its adherence to civil liberty, and the fourth calling on the organizations represented at the conference to establish councils of Workmen's and Soldiers' Delegates so as to initiate and co-ordinate working-class activity in support of these policies. The convention had been held without the endorsement of the Labour Party Executive, and in defiance of the disapproval of many of its members. In his speech moving the first resolution, MacDonald drew the obvious moral:

> When this war broke out organised Labour in this country lost the initiative. (Hear, hear.) It became a mere echo of the old governing classes' opinions. (Hear, hear.) Now the Russian Revolution has once again given you the chance to take the initiative yourselves. Let us lay down our terms, make our own proclamations, establish our own diplomacy; see to it that we have our own international meetings. Let us say to the Russian democracy, 'In the name of everything you hold sacred in politics, in morality, in good government, and in progress, restrain the anarchy in your midst, find a cause for unity, maintain your Revolution, stand by your liberties, put yourselves at the head of the peoples of Europe.'[14]

British Labour, in other words, should follow the Russian lead, and throw off the pro-war yoke. But there was also a less obvious implication. If the Russians failed to restrain the anarchy in their midst, they might fail to put themselves at the head of the peoples of Europe. The key to peace was held by the Petrograd Soviet, but revolutionary fervour would have to be supplemented by political skill if the key was to be turned. As time went on, MacDonald became increasingly convinced that, in order to ensure that the Russians understood how much they depended on them, direct contact should be made with the moderate revolutionaries like Kerensky, whom he saw as the Russian equivalents of the I.L.P. and in whose hands he believed that the fate of Europe rested. As early as April 4th, he noted that the *émigré* Russian socialist, Soskice, had advised him to go to Russia, and had pointed out that 'The leaders of the revolution knew me & would welcome me.' But he added sardonically, '[O]ur government would no more think of letting me go to Russia than a keeper would think of letting a lion have a constitutional out of his cage.'[15] Later that month the Government sent two pro-war Labour M.P.s, Will Thorne and James O'Grady, on a mission to Petrograd. Presumably they were sent there to persuade the Russians to carry on fighting. MacDonald was contemptuous. The Russian socialists, he pointed out, were 'inspired by intellectuals, who will immediately discover the political poverty of our deputation, with whom they have little in common'.[16] With all their limitations, however, Thorne and O'Grady were on their way to Petrograd; and this made it all the more neces-

H

sary for the anti-war position to be represented there as well, if only as an antidote. Probably about this time, MacDonald accordingly drafted a letter to Kerensky, warning him of the dangers of a separate peace and urging him to put revolutionary Russia at the head of the democratic forces of Europe:

My Dear M. Kerensky,

I do not know if you have received the various messages of congratulation which my colleagues & I have sent to you, but I hope you have. You have cheered us in these dark days & restored in our hearts a faith in democracy & a hope that for the first time in history a peace which will be founded on freedom may follow a war. We follow Petrograd events with difficulty because they are recorded by our newspapers coloured & twisted for our own special purposes & the deputation of workmen which our Government sent will soon be back & will be telling us its own tale which may or may not be reliable. It is of the utmost importance that the Russian revolution should not be exploited by our government or any other of the Allied governments for their own purposes, but that the Russian people should come into direct contact with our people &, taking council together, should in the common emotions & thoughts of free people announce the programmes upon which Europe may be at peace. I hail with gladness the pronouncements of your Provisional Government. If the wisdom behind these pronouncements & statesmanlike policy embodied in them had guided the Governments of the Allies during the past two years, how different the outlook today would have been ...

My own view since the beginning of the war — but I have been in a sad minority which however is steadily increasing in numbers — has been that the chaos now reigning in Europe can be ended only by the people themselves. Mere emotional pacifism is of no use, a separate peace between Russia & Germany would only leave Europe more helpless than it now is in the hands of evil doers. Russia should therefore put itself with its freshly purified soul & its new enthusiasm for liberty at the head of the European democracy & defining a programme of peace & co-operation with other peoples should offer it to Europe. Then the Governments must make peace upon it or declare to mankind that they reject justice ...

We are particularly gratified here with your insistence upon the non-conquest & non-aggression determination of the Russian democracy. But would it not be possible to carry the matter further & state at any rate in general outline a programme of peace which the German democracy, if it be a democracy, could not reject? This should be drafted after consultation with Allies. I do not think that a consultation with German comrades is necessary in the first instance, because, if drawn up as a document of justice & not of revenge, it could be issued in the ordinary way to Europe & the Germans would have to take cognisance of it ...

I cannot end this without expressing once more our profound gratitude to your people & our great admiration for them in this crisis of their national life; & I pray that no evil may divert them from the path of freedom upon which they have set their feet.

I am, dear M. Kerensky, with fraternal salutations to you & my comrades of the revolution, yours,

J. RAMSAY MACDONALD.[17]

On April 25th, the Belgian pro-war socialist, Vandervelde, who was on his way to Russia, asked MacDonald to write him a letter which he could show the Russian socialists, opposing a separate peace. MacDonald noted that he had replied 'that if he wanted my help, he should get me sent to Petrograd. He shrugged his shoulders. As I am very anxious to get my views before the Petrograd leaders, I consented to write.'[18] But his letter made few concessions, and contains the clearest surviving statement of his position at the time:

I now put on paper ... my view of what ... our Russian comrades ought to do at once in view of the great influence which their revolution has had on the European situation ...

1. [I]t is essential that they should act for European democracy as a whole ... [I]f they merely drew out of the war on purely Russian guarantees they would leave all the difficulties ... in which the life of Europe is now plunged, for others to settle.

2. [O]ur Russian comrades should formulate a democratic programme of peace ... which the democracies of all European countries ought to be able to accept ... [T]his pronouncement ought to be made after some consultation and might be issued by our Russian comrades jointly with those of other nations.

3. The declaration should consist of two main sections.
   A. The actual settlement ... [T]he restoration ... of Belgium, the means for settling Balkan nationality problems, the internationalization of the Dardanelles, the unification and independence of Poland, and so on. This should indicate that some of these problems can be solved only by International Commissions whilst others admit of no bargaining. To the first the Balkan difficulties belong; to the second the restoration of Belgium ...
   B. The political conditions under which alone any settlement can be permanent. The chief ... is that the nations of Europe shall be democratic ... and that even where the Governments are nominally democratic, such changes shall be made in administration that international affairs shall be placed ... under democratic authority ...

4. [I]f this greater view of their responsibility is taken by our Russian comrades, their policy must be to lead and inspire the whole of Europe and not merely leave Europe in the lurch. It will be necessary for them

however, to let their present Allies understand ... that Democracy in
Russia is not to be a mere tool in the hands of the Governments, but that
it is placing itself at the head of an international democratic movement
which is to use this war for the establishment of its own ideals and its
own power.

5. When the contents and form of the manifesto are agreed upon, it ought
to be communicated to the German and Austrian people in such a way
that they may definitely understand what our intentions are, and ... take
what steps are necessary to associate themselves with the new movement.[19]

Letters, however, were no substitute for personal contact. As the summer
approached, MacDonald was more and more appalled by the Government's
unimaginative response to the prospects which the revolution had opened up.
'The Russian Revolu. has thrown into a high light the stupidity & lack of
democratic feeling of our Government ... ,' he noted on April 26th. 'Their
blood is up & they will sacrifice everything for a military victory. An unscrupulous gang commands the press & the government is afraid of it. Some ministers
represent the worst type of narrow minded & hypocritical Englishman, the
people with the English twist in their character, whose style has brought upon
their nation for generations the contempt of people who see in a straight line
& in a clear light.'[20] The Labour Party Executive was scarcely any better. At
the Executive meeting on May 9th, the secretary reported that the Dutch
socialists had intended to convene a special meeting of the International at
Stockholm, which had been postponed until June 4th, in order to give the
French socialists time to decide whether they would take part. The Executive
decided that the British Labour Party should not be represented at Stockholm,
that a conference of the Allied socialist parties should be held in London as soon
as possible, and that Henderson, George Roberts and an obscure trade unionist
named Carter should be sent to Russia to persuade the Soviet to send delegates
to it.[21] MacDonald refused nomination to the deputation, and commented
acidly:

Meeting of the Labour Party Executive. The stupidity of some of its
members is painful & today they were particularly trying. They refused to
recognise the Stockholm conference because (a) it was pro-German & (b)
they are bound by the Manchester Labour Party resolution that no International should be held. On my suggestion they decided to send a deputation to Russia, but wished to tie it down so much that only one side could
go. Then they elected two ministers & an unknown Trade Unionist. The
Russian movement will of course scorn them & the British Labour Party
continues to amble about like a feeble old man full of vanity and delusions.
Here are great chances for this child of my heart, & I am doomed to sit &
listen to & witness the most appalling proofs of its imbecility.[22]

The 'stupidity' of the Government and the 'imbecility' of the Labour Party Executive obviously made it all the more essential that MacDonald should go to Petrograd as well; and shortly after the Executive's meeting on May 9th, it began to seem that this might be possible after all. By now, the Russians had given a further twist to the story. The Petrograd Soviet had also decided that an international conference should be held, representing the majority and minority factions in each socialist party, and had invited the minority socialists in France, Germany and Italy to Russia. On May 10th, a joint meeting of the I.L.P. and B.S.P. decided to apply for passports,[23] and MacDonald launched a vigorous campaign to persuade the Government to grant them. On May 12th, he pointed out in *Forward* 'that the I.L.P. leaders have great influence in Petrograd, that their names are the only ones respected and trusted by the Workmen's Council and that the peoples of the warring countries have a right to be allowed to consult with each other'. In the debate on the Consolidated Fund Bill on May 16th, he urged the Government to 'put yourselves into sympathetic relation with the Russians,' and argued that this could best be done by sending a 'representative deputation' to Russia, as the Petrograd Soviet had asked.[24] On the 20th, he noted that the debate in the House of Commons four days earlier was 'having great influence'.[25] On the 24th he heard that the Government had decided to grant him a passport, and that Henderson had left secretly for Russia.[26] On the 29th he had a long interview with Lord Robert Cecil, who asked him why he wanted to go to Petrograd, and confirmed that he would be given a passport. Cecil then reported their conversation to the prime minister as follows:

He said he wished to go there primarily to carry greetings to the Russian Socialists, and to do his best to help them in establishing the Revolution, which he said was very far from secure as yet. He added that he was going to discuss with the Russian Socialists the meeting of an International Committee, and he hoped also to take the opportunity of increasing the democratic movement in Europe.

I told him that I had no objection to any project of that kind, especially as I supposed that Germany would be included.

He said certainly: Germany was the great obstacle to democracy ...

I showed him the recent Note sent to Russia, and asked him how far he agreed with it.

He read it carefully, and said that doubtless he would have to answer questions about the German Colonies and Alsace-Lorraine; but, speaking generally, he entirely agreed with the Note, and thought there was very little difference between his views and those expressed there.

I asked him about a separate peace.

He said that he regarded a separate peace with absolute horror, as it would mean the destruction of everything he cared for in Europe, and he would do his utmost to prevent the Russians taking any such step.

He was also very strong as to the danger of anarchy in Russia.

I said to him that, speaking quite frankly, he was in a position to do a great deal of good, and also a great deal of harm, in Russia.

He was very much pleased at the observation, and assured me that his only object was to do good.[27]

On June 8th, Cecil announced in the House of Commons that MacDonald would be given a passport, on the understanding that he would not be allowed to communicate directly or indirectly with enemy subjects.[28] That night, MacDonald dined at Walton Heath with Lloyd George, who was 'particularly friendly', and who 'spoke of war as one of liberation'. MacDonald replied that 'he might have been reading my speeches.' He was asked to arrange a meeting between Lloyd George and Kerensky, and taken back home in Lloyd George's car.[29] Next day he left London in a crowded train for Aberdeen, accompanied by Fred Jowett and the Fabian, Julius West, who were going to Russia with him. George Roberts, as befitted a minister in the Coalition Government, travelled in a separate compartment.[30]

II

MacDonald and his companions arrived in Aberdeen on the morning of June 10th. On their way to their ship, they were followed by the notorious 'Captain' Tupper of the Seamen's and Firemen's Union. Tupper had been present at the Leeds convention, where he had been shouted down after trying to put an extreme pro-war view. Since then he had appeared in Aberdeen, where he had been holding meetings denouncing MacDonald and the I.L.P. The best source for what followed is MacDonald's diary. In a long entry dated June 13th, he noted:

> Arriving at ship, Tupper pointed me out to some of the crew standing on board & finding that no one was allowed on board till the afternoon, I went back to a hotel & was followed by pickets. Got into communication with the Prime Minister & he asked Roberts to send down official wire with full information. Negotiations with Tupper carried on by Roberts & A. M. Thompson (Dangle) who was going to Stockholm. Tupper agreed to settle if we stated that we regretted he was not better heard at Leeds, & that seamen should be compensated for illegal acts on sea by Germany. We told Roberts that such had always been our views on both points & wrote that. Later on, Tupper informed Roberts that he had called the crew together & they would not agree to anything. We had good reason to believe that it was never put to them in such a way as to commend it. Finally, naval commander called at Hotel & informed us (showing it) that

he had had a message from the Admiralty saying boat must sail & if crew objected to take us we must be prevented from going on board. This was delivered with great glee & vociferously by the little perky man who expressed great contempt for the civil control of the Admiralty, hoped I would get a bullet through my head & so on amusingly. We stayed at the Hotel. — 11th. Remained in Aberdeen waiting the settlement. Could get nothing through till afternoon when Roberts' secretary asked him to return at once. We meanwhile got in touch with Glasgow & heard that Shinwell was offering a crew, that the Executive of the T.C. was to meet, that protest meetings were to be held. Late at night Snowden advised us to return if we saw no advantage in staying at Aberdeen, and we decided to return as the matter ought perhaps to be raised in the H. of C. & the protest movement organised. — The whole incident left me very little moved. The crew had just been worked up & doped with lies about us & what happened at Leeds. It is humiliating just a little, but still more alarming if it indicates a real grip of ignorance & blackguardism.[31]

Complex negotiations followed between MacDonald, the Government and Havelock Wilson, the seamen's leader. But Wilson was obdurate, and the Government was unable or unwilling to coerce him. On this rock, MacDonald's visit to Petrograd foundered. On June 15th, he wrote a long letter to the Petrograd Soviet, setting out the approach he hoped the Russians would urge on the other Allied socialist parties, explaining that he had hoped to convey the greetings of the 'British Socialist Majority' in person, and apologizing for the fact that he had been prevented from doing so by the 'malignant action of one or two officials of the Seamen's Union'. In spite of the seamen, he wrote,

you must not be ungenerous to us, for though it is true that a part of our Labour movement is now the merest echo of what its political masters say, the heart of this country is right ... If you judge us by the newspapers and journals which seem to be most popular here to-day, I fear the only message you get from us is one which rings with political reaction or be[ll]ows with ignorant vulgarity, but do pray remember that the sober minority, always great in numbers, is daily growing, and that you your- self have added to its strength and awakened its activities ...

In addition to expressing our gratitude to you and our joy that your martyred comrades have risen from the dead through your great triumph, I would have consulted with you regarding the help that a free Russia could give to European democracy ... To us the thought of a separate peace, which not only in Germany but in other lands would mean the establish- ment of militarism and the acceptance of imperialist conquest, is alien and offensive. We strive, not so much for the mere ending of the war as for the bringing of peace to Europe, two objects which do not mean the same thing ... You have laid down a fine challenging formula — no annexations and no indemnities. You will probably find that you will have to go further and consider in detail some of the more outstanding problems which the war has compelled Europe to face ... We must survey the national map of Europe and tell the peoples who wish to be free that we know who they are, and that we are prepared to support their claims. You will not be able to bring peace until you have shown how the settlement of Europe can be made without war — surely not a difficult thing if the peoples would speak their own thoughts.

There is also the tremendous problem of the tropics, thrust by the events of this war, especially in Africa, into the forefront of the concerns of European democracy ... How are we to protect the native in the enjoyment of his own life, to save his lands from the exploiter and his peace from the profiteering trader?

Finally there is the question of guarantees for future peace. In the old world which you have done so much to shatter the feeble wisdom of Imperialism chattered about preparing for war in order to maintain peace ... That folly is written on the face of Europe to-day in countless grave yards where the best of our sons sleep, in homes that are a mass of ruins, in fields once fruitful now torn by shot and shell. We have our own guarantee in a great International of the democracies, organised as a Parliament of the world and strong in the Legislatures of every nation ...

... By the destruction of your Tsardom you have opened the way to this new world. You must supply for the meeting of the International, which cannot be long delayed, the basis of the agreement which, will not be that which the victor imposes upon [the] vanquished, and which in consequence would be unjust, but which free men of good will, sobered by the war and enlightened greatly by your magnificent action will mutually accept, mutually respect, and mutually defend.[32]

But, although it was an eloquent letter, it made little difference to the course of events in Russia. For the next six months, MacDonald was condemned to watch impotently while Russian Social Democracy slowly lost control of the revolution, and the hopes he had placed in it ran into the sand. Lenin and the Bolsheviks were steadily gaining ground in the Petrograd Soviet, and the Russian army's morale was steadily crumbling. At the beginning of July, Kerensky launched a new offensive, which had disastrous results. There were demonstrations in Petrograd and armed clashes in the streets, and although the demonstrations were eventually put down it was clear that the moderate revolutionaries were increasingly vulnerable to attacks from the extreme Left. An undated letter to Lord Robert Cecil conveys a vivid impression of MacDonald's reactions:

The news from Russia is not at all good and if we are to be of any assistance to the middle anti-anarchist section every day's delay is a missing of opportunities ... My reading of the position, not only in Russia but else-where, is that it is now getting very critical owing to the sudden inrush of political ideas and methods and expectations; and that has to be handled with quiet firmness but with knowledge and sympathy ... Some of us *representing both minority and majority* should be sent off at once.[33]

But the Government seemed incapable of realizing that its pursuit of a military victory at all costs could only play into Lenin's hands. On July 19th, the German Reichstag carried a resolution in favour of a peace of mutual understanding and reconciliation. On the 23rd, MacDonald noted that he had been urged to move the same resolution in the House of Commons, and that although 'speaking gets more distasteful to me' he had agreed.[34] On July 26th, in the debate on the Consolidated Fund Bill, he duly moved a resolution, noting that the Reichstag had voted against the acquisition of territory by force and calling on the British Government to re-state its own peace terms accordingly. Everyone, he declared, would 'hope and pray that the Gethsemane of suffering through which Russia is now going will soon pass away. We watch from day to day with breathless interest this extraordinary fabric built up in a night, sometimes so tottering and so assailed that we are almost afraid we are wit-nessing its premature end. If that should happen, then it will be the worse for Europe - and not merely for Europe.' The Russians had shown that there was no need for secret diplomacy. The new Russian Government had not been afraid 'to ask its people to say what they thought, and there has been no more valuable ally of the Russian Provisional Government than the Workmen and Soldiers' Council of Petrograd.' They had also shown that new war aims were needed. For the new Russian Government was not a partner in the original Allied war aims; it had declared that it was willing to give up the Tsarist Government's claim to Constantinople, and for that reason alone the Allies should meet together and prepare new aims. Above all, they had shown that it was necessary to encourage

the consultation of Allied peoples. There are two organisations which stand pre-eminently before the world as international organisations. One is Labour and the other is the Church. The God of Christianity is not a village idol or a national idol ... So with us in the Labour movement ... When the people speak and when they know their minds – when the representa-tives of the people have an opportunity of finding out from each other where they stand, and what they want and what they are aiming at, then, Mr. Speaker, my conviction is that the War will be very well over.[35]

MacDonald noted afterwards that the veteran Irish home-ruler, John Dillon, told him that his speech was the greatest he had ever heard delivered from below the gangway.[36] But his resolution received only nineteen votes, and the Government turned a deaf ear to his pleas. By now the United States had declared war on Germany; and it seemed to MacDonald the result had been 'a decided hardening in the dominating opinion of this country'. Government circles, he wrote in a letter to an American embassy official in London, 'consider that we can now prolong the war until America has become an effective partner in it, and that if Russia is crushed and compelled to make peace, the Allies can still refuse all overtures, negotiations, or political approaches of any kind and pursue a programme of a complete military issue'.[37]

This analysis was certainly borne out by the Government's behaviour. In July the Labour Party was officially invited by the Petrograd Soviet to send delegates to a conference of the International at Stockholm. At the end of the month, Henderson came back from Russia, where, as Lloyd George put it, he seemed to have caught 'the revolutionary malaria'.[38] On Henderson's advice, the National Executive decided to summon a special party conference to decide whether or not to send delegates to Stockholm.[39] Henderson, MacDonald and Wardle, acting chairman of the parliamentary Labour Party, then went to Paris to consult with the French socialists, accompanied by two delegates from the Petrograd Soviet. In Paris, agreement was reached on the constitution and procedure of the Stockholm conference.[40] But by now Henderson's colleagues were growing increasingly alarmed at the spectacle of a British minister consorting with notorious pacifists and pro-Germans. In the famous 'doormat' incident of August 1st, they kept him waiting for an hour outside the Cabinet room while they sat in judgment on his conduct in Paris. There could be only one result if Henderson was to retain his self-respect; and it was not long in coming. On August 10th, the special Labour Party conference took place at the Central Hall. After a powerful speech by Henderson in favour of Stockholm, it voted to accept the Russian invitation by 1,846,000 to 550,000. Next day, Henderson resigned from the War Cabinet.

His Labour colleagues in the Government did not resign with him, however, and it soon became clear that a majority of the trade-union leaders still supported the Government. As well as voting in favour of Stockholm, the Central Hall conference had resolved that the Labour Party delegation should not be supplemented by delegations 'from any affiliated or unaffiliated body in this country'. This would have excluded the I.L.P., and was in direct conflict with the terms of the Russian invitation which had made it clear that minorities were to be represented at Stockholm as well as majorities. The conference had accordingly been adjourned for ten days;[41] and, when it met again on August 21st, the Stockholm resolution was carried by only 3,000 votes. A week later, a conference of the Allied socialist parties took place in London. It voted in favour of Stockholm, but failed to agree on a statement of war aims to be put forward there. Its only real decision was to set up a standing committee, which would represent the Allied parties and eventually summon another Allied socialist conference at some time in the future.[42] 'Minorities here were the majorities,' MacDonald noted afterwards, 'were in best heart, knew own minds best, were the virile & confident sections.' The following day he took part in a private conference of the 'minority' socialists, at which there were 'striking statements of belief that England was responsible for unnecessarily continuing the war'.[43] Meanwhile, the British Government had announced that, whatever the Labour Party might decide, no passports would be issued to British delegates to Stockholm; and at the beginning of September the T.U.C. resolved that 'a Conference at Stockholm at the present moment could not be successful.' In effect, the proposal was dead.

A letter from Eduard Bernstein to MacDonald, scribbled on a train journey to Copenhagen, poignantly conveys the significance of its death:

> Dear Friend,
>
> I am on a day's journey in [sic] Kopenhagen and utilize the opportunity of dropping a few lines to an old friend and now 'enemy-friend'. It is greatly to be regretted that the Stockholm conference has not so far come to pass. It could certainly not have brought about peace at once but could, and would in my opinion pave the way for such a peace as every honest democrate [sic] would desire ...
>
> At present the hopes for an early and good peace are still very low. For the governments it is almost impossible to come to an agreement. Help must come from other sources, and who more called to provide it than the socialists? But they can only provide it if acting internationally on an agreed basis. There is at present going on ... an agitation for an international simultaneous general strike ... Seeing what humanity in both senses of the word suffers I am not so opposed to it as I would under other circumstances ... But from what I know of my country, I must in all honesty confess that there are the greatest odds against its feasibility ... [W]ith a most strongly organised military government at the helm ... the whole middle classes, the majority socialists, the big trade unions as opponents, they would have little chance of lasting any length of time ... There is no means of saving the labour of bringing about an understanding of the mass of the socialists in all the countries. Had the Stockholm conference come to pass, we should, I am sure, [have] achieved a good step in this direction. We must go on in the work of pressing public opinion in its favour. Governments must be made [to] understand that they risk worse things if they continue in blocking the conference ...
>
> In writing this all I am driven by the conviction that the time has come where an exchange of views should take place between English and German Socialists ... I hoped to meet you and some of your comrades in Stockholm. Unfortunately, the short-sightedness of foolish politicians has willed it otherwise. Is there no means to meet on less suspicious ground? ... I have followed as much as opportunities allowed your doings in your country and I believe it qualifies you to [sic] the role of a socialist ambas-

sador, a call worth striving for at this time of disgrace and disruption.[44]

But the Governments seemed impervious to the voice of moderation. More than a year of bloodshed and suffering was to pass before MacDonald and his German comrades could meet. By then, the chance of a democratic peace, agreed between the socialist parties of Europe, had been lost. The chance of a democratic Russia had been lost with it.

III

In spite of its failure, the struggle for Stockholm had produced great changes in the Labour Party. Labour ministers still held office. But they did so as the creatures of Lloyd George rather than as the representatives of the organized working class. By however a small majority, and with however many qualifications, the party had pronounced itself in favour of a meeting with the socialist parties of Germany and Austria. The party machine, moreover, was controlled by Henderson; and although many fundamental differences remained, Henderson's position on many of the central issues of Labour diplomacy was now very close to MacDonald's. Both accepted the Russian formula of a peace without annexations or indemnities. Both opposed a separate peace between Russia and Germany. Both wanted a meeting of the International. Both opposed the policy of the knock-out blow. Both distrusted Lloyd George.

Yet the suspicion and bitterness of the last three years could not easily be forgotten, and even if MacDonald and Henderson were ready to let bygones be bygones, their respective followers were not. The very fact that Henderson appeared to have been converted to the policy of MacDonald and the U.D.C. made it all the more necessary for him to defer, wherever possible, to the trade-union leaders whose support he would need if he was to carry that policy into effect, and who still looked upon the I.L.P. as a nest of subversives. By the same token, MacDonald was bound to look warily at overtures from Henderson. The I.L.P. was now his only political base. Without it he would be isolated. Even if he had not shared them, he would have had to pay tender regard to the susceptibilities of his followers there, most of whom regarded the trade-union wing of the party as traitors to international socialism and peace. Thus he noted in his diary on September 9th that he had just returned from a visit to Henderson:

> Bitter with Ll.George. Said some Labour Ministers do not mean to return to Party. Wishes co-operation. Says Ll.G. wants to form new party & some Labour men will join him. His own position however, not yet clear & I did not discuss things very freely with him.[45]

For the rest of the war, to some extent for the rest of their political lives, this was to be the dominant note in their relationship. Tacitly rather than openly, they did manage to co-operate; though Henderson was unable – and perhaps unwilling – to go as far as MacDonald, they did so to such effect that by the autumn of 1918 a united Labour Party was ready to break with the Coalition, and to fight a general election as an independent entity, on a platform almost identical with that of the U.D.C. But their co-operation was uneasy, spasmodic, and punctuated by bursts of sharp mutual hostility.

On September 18th, Henderson wrote guardedly to MacDonald:

> Yours of the 15th to hand which I have read with great interest as my own mind has been running much on the same lines. I am afraid I am not so hopeful as to the result of our next effort though it may be I am too much influenced by our recent failure. What I am clear upon is we cannot risk a second failure. Nor am I convinced that the Belgians and the French majority and certainly I myself would agree with those who refuse to ratify the finding of the Conference of Feb. 14 1915 ... Nor have I any desire to risk another failure owing to such speeches as the one made by Snowden at the close of the first special Conference. If we are to make another attempt, then I agree with your position that we must agree among ourselves and then agree with the French. I am inclined to the view that for the present it would be best if those who constituted themselves into an inter-allied conference of minorities and the Russians at the Fabian Hall should work together in an open way. An exchange of views could eventually take place and possibly the working together and refusing to accept the decision.[46]

Ten days later, the National Executive and the T.U.C. Parliamentary Committee set up a joint sub-committee on the international situation. Among the N.E.C. representatives were Henderson, Sidney Webb and MacDonald.[47] At the end of October, the committee approved a memorandum on the issues of the war, based on a similar memorandum which had been presented to the Special Conference on August 10th.[48] At the end of November, the movement for a negotiated peace was given further impetus by a letter from Lord Lansdowne to the *Daily Telegraph* supporting the idea. On December 12th, the amended Labour memorandum was approved by a joint meeting of the National Executive and the Parliamentary Committee;[49] on December 28th, it was overwhelmingly endorsed by a special conference representing the societies affiliated to the T.U.C. and the Labour Party.[50]

The statement consisted, in essence, of an amalgam of the views which had been developed over the last three years by the Fabian Society on the one hand, and the U.D.C. on the other. It called for the complete democratization of all countries, the limitation of armaments, the abolition of private arms manufacture, the establishment of an International Court and Legislature, self-determination and the holding of plebiscites to decide territorial disputes. Its detailed proposals included the creation of new nation states in the Balkans, a guarantee that the peoples of Poland, Luxembourg and Alsace-Lorraine should decide their own futures, and the restoration of Italia Irredenta to Italy. On the evening of December 28th, a deputation representing the two Labour Executives, and including MacDonald, presented the statement to the prime minister.[51] At 9.15 the next morning, MacDonald had breakfast with him in Downing Street. Later he noted:

> Discussed meeting of International to which he did not show hostility but thought large meeting not best way to proceed. I told him whom I thought essential ... Expressed rather unfriendly views of Curzon & Henderson, & of those who had supported & then hampered the Govt. I handed him the copy of Bernstein's letter to me ... Long discussion on Alsace & Lorraine ... Impression that he was unhappy about prospects, about his own position, that he was looking for a way out. Was most friendly.[52]

Lloyd George was, however, a master at creating impressions: and MacDonald was not the only Labour leader whom he wished to impress. On January 5th, 1918, he made a speech to a conference of trade unions, calling for the sanctity of treaties, the recognition of the right of self-determination and the creation of an international organization to limit the burden of armaments. This was the nearest the British Government had yet come to announcing its war aims; shortly afterwards, President Wilson promulgated his Fourteen Points. At this point, the fragile unity which had been built up between MacDonald and Henderson began to crack. As Henderson saw it, the primary purpose of Labour's new policy was to influence the final peace settlement by bringing pressure to bear on the Allied Governments. From this point of view, the apparent conversion of the British prime minister and the American President was an episode of the greatest importance, to be welcomed for its own sake. MacDonald's attitude was more aggressive. He had no faith in the Allied Governments, and not much more in Labour's ability to influence them. For him, a peace influenced by the Labour movement would be a second best. What he wanted was a peace made by the Labour movement: and made by the Labour movements on both sides, negotiating directly with each other. He welcomed the Labour Party's statement of war aims, not because he believed that it represented the kind of peace settlement which ought eventually to be reached, but because it was the first step towards a confrontation with the socialist parties of Germany and Austria.

At the Labour Party conference in January 1918, he seconded a resolution, moved by Henderson, which welcomed the statements made by Lloyd George and Wilson, pressed the Allied Governments to publish a joint statement of their war aims in the same terms, and called upon the working-class movements of Germany and Austria to formulate theirs.[53] But his speech was much more critical of the Government than Henderson's had been; and when the conference was over he became equally critical of the Labour Party. The delegates, he pointed out in his column in *Forward*, had refused to call upon the Labour ministers to withdraw from the Government; their refusal had made nonsense of the rest of Labour's policy. For the War Aims memorandum had not been published, 'to become the plaything of Governments, but to be the first word in a democratic conference. It was meant not so much for Mr. Lloyd George ... but for the German and Austrian democracy, and if it is not to be misused further steps should be taken to make its purpose clear. If the Labour Party, having made its pronouncement, lapses back into the acquiescence which it has shown since the war broke out, its Memorandum may do more harm than good.'[54]

As in his struggle against the Lib-Labs fifteen years before, the dominating issue for him was Labour's attitude to political power. So long as they stayed in the Government, he believed, the Labour ministers could never be more than hewers of wood and drawers of water. Only by leaving the Coalition could Labour hope to shape events instead of being shaped by them. It might fail to force a change of Government, but only if it spurned Lloyd George's embrace could it expect the socialist parties of Germany and Austria to listen to it; only if they did listen to it could it hope to achieve a peace settlement made in its own image. But these ambitions were too grandiose for the party Executive; even Henderson seemed less willing to assert Labour's independence from the Government than he had been before Lloyd George's speech at the beginning of January. Shortly after the special War Aims conference of December 1917, it was decided that another Allied socialist conference should be summoned as soon as possible;[55] in February a deputation, consisting of Henderson, Webb, MacDonald and four trade unionists, went to Paris to consult with the French socialists.[56] Before leaving, MacDonald asked Henderson for an assurance that, if he went to Paris, 'the ILP view may be put into the common pool as the French minority view will be put.'[57] Henderson replied curtly that these conditions were 'so contrary to the decisions of our recent Joint Meetings' that if MacDonald insisted on them he could no longer be included in the deputation.[58] MacDonald thereupon pointed out that, if the French wanted to make changes in the British memorandum, it was only reasonable that 'the sections which became parties to the agreement ought to be present to ratify (or otherwise) the new one.'[59] To this, Henderson replied that there was no question of 'any new set of proposals being produced'.[60] The correspondence ended with both men sticking pointedly to their original positions, in order, as MacDonald put it, to avoid 'misunderstanding'.[61]

On this somewhat insecure basis, MacDonald went to Paris, where he played an important part in persuading the French to accept the British memorandum. By February 18th, he was back in London, noting:

Our mission completely successful – not so much owing to us but to events. Everyone is seeing that something must now be done & those who months ago were hard of heart until, as they said, Germany was beaten to her knees, now speak & think more cautiously & are willing to try negotiations. Brooded much as I saw this trend of things in Paris of the months of slaughter & increasing ruin spent by those people in making up their minds to come to our views. It is a great triumph for us, though people may not see it. The people never know at whose shrines they are worshipping – Christ or Paul: their Gods are all mixed up & misnamed. – When we arrived [on] the 15th went to the Chamber of Deputies & met Parl: Socialist Party: I spoke to them & got good reception ... 16th ... Conference with the Socialist Inter Allied Representatives, making good progress with the Memorandum on War Aims; 7. Huysmans & I went to the French Minority Socialist Conference – crowded, smoky, stifling, noisy, confused but quiet hearing for us & some little enthusiasm. Dined us afterwards. – Note food appears plentiful in Paris & is in great contrast to what it is in London. But for its emptiness & its mourning, Paris shows no signs of war. – 17th Went to meeting of French Soc: National Council & spoke & afterwards did pilgrimage to Pere La Chaise to where Communists made last stand. In its shaded seclusion it seems to be brooding over what it has seen. If you passed it without knowing its history you would feel: A place for dark & sad deeds.[62]

On February 20th, the Allied socialist conference opened in London. Once again, the main points in the Labour Party's memorandum were adopted. For more than three years, MacDonald had urged the Labour Party to formulate its war aims and to negotiate directly with the German socialists on the basis of that formulation. Now the first stage in his programme had been carried out, and the Labour Party's formula had been endorsed by the French and Italian parties as well. But during the last few weeks, he had lost confidence in the National Executive's ability to move from the first stage to the second stage, and his reaction to the Allied socialist conference was remarkably subdued. 'Unanimity has been reached, but upon a very imperfect basis ... ,' he noted morosely on February 23rd. 'The danger is that it might be regarded as a defeatist document for Germany, & that instead of putting their case in reply the Germans may simply reject it & pull it to pieces as indeed they will find it far too easy to do.'[63]

Developments in Russia added to his anxieties. In November 1917, the Bolsheviks had seized power; and, within twenty-four hours of their doing so, Lenin had announced that the new Government wanted peace negotiations as soon as possible. At the beginning of December, an armistice was signed between Russia and Germany; by the end of December, negotiations for a peace treaty were under way at Brest-Litovsk. As good Marxists, Lenin and Trotsky assumed their revolution would spread to the rest of the capitalist world; Trotsky's tactics at Brest-Litovsk were to play for time until he was rescued by

22 Family group, Lincoln's Inn Fields, around 1907. The children are, left to right: Malcolm, David, Ishbel and Alister

23 At the I.L.P. Conference, Stockton-on-Tees, 1906. MacDonald is at the extreme right of the second row

24 At the House of Commons, 1907

the working-class uprising in the west. But the working classes of the west obstinately refused to rise. No rescue came; and the negotiations at Brest-Litovsk dragged on until March, when the Russians had to sign one of the most punitive peace treaties of modern times.

MacDonald had warned repeatedly that, if the Western Allies continued to insist on a military victory, the moderate socialists would lose control in Russia; and that, if the Bolsheviks came to power and signed a separate peace, it would be a disaster for Europe. But, although he was horrified by Kerensky's fall, he refused to blame Lenin for opening negotiations. It was Britain's fault that 'Russia negotiates alone with Germany', he wrote scornfully at the end of December 1917, 'and we please ourselves by making little Jack Horner moral comments on the duty of the Allies.'[64] 'I would not call myself a Leninite but what does that matter?', he asked at a meeting at Rutherglen at the beginning of January 1918. 'There is this man voicing the position of the Russian democracy, striving to keep liberty in Europe, with a peace programme that is satisfactory to the people. I do not care who he is or what he is, that man should have the support of every Government that honestly means the democracies to win as the result of this war.'[65] Soon afterwards, he was introduced to Maxim Litvinov, the unofficial Bolshevik representative in London, whom he described in his diary as 'a cannon ball which will roll straight ahead & smash the diplomatic china',[66] and whom he saw a number of times in the next few months. On February 12th, after consulting Litvinov,[67] he devoted his speech in the debate on the address to a biting attack on the Government's Russian policy, ending with a plea that it should recognize the new regime. At Brest-Litovsk, he declared,

There was the man Trotsky, representative of a beaten nation, no army behind him, no force at his command, meeting these liveried, uniformed representatives of German militarism ... and in the end striking far more deeply into the heart of Germany than you have done during the last three years, with all your Armies. We stood by supinely, and everyone who understands the situation ... had their hearts broken at the incompetence of our Government to seize the magnificent opportunity which the Brest negotiations gave ...

... Russia in revolution has much to get from us; Russia in revolution has much to give to us, and the alienation of Russia from England and of England from Russia is one of the most disastrous events of the last twelve months. The Government can still retrieve a good deal of that position. The Government can recognise the Russian representative who is over here. By that it does not require to recognise everything that is done in Russia ... But they might recognise that there is a Government in Russia ... and that it will be to the mutual interests of both Russia and this country if that amount of recognition is given.[68]

The Government did nothing of the kind; and by early summer there were signs that its policy was about to take an even more alarming turn. On May 14th, Litvinov told MacDonald that the Japanese were planning to invade Siberia and that the Allies were supporting counter-revolutionary agents. 'I explained that I was not a supporter of everything which the Bolshevik Govt. did & that, indeed, I was not a Bolshevik,' MacDonald noted, 'but I shall support every revolutionary govt. so far as to give it a chance to settle Russia & establish the Revolution.'[69] In June, Kerensky made a dramatic appearance at the Labour Party conference, where he was given a tumultuous reception and delivered a passionate speech in Russian to the assembled delegates. 'I was full of suspicions ... ,' MacDonald noted. 'It's a great advertisement & probably marks some new move e.g. overthrow of Bolshevism, Russia under reaction of a Liberal kind, declaration of war again upon Germany, Allied troops in Siberia.'[70] His suspicions were well founded. By August, British troops were landing at Archangel. MacDonald wrote an angry editorial in the *Socialist Review*, attacking the British governing classes for behaving as their great-grandfathers had done when they insisted on restoring the Bourbons to the throne of France, and praising Lenin for giving Russia a chance to 'settle down' and for saving her from a 'reign of terror'.[71] But his protest had no effect on the Government, while, for its part, the Labour Party Executive decided, with majestic impartiality, that the Allied intervention in Russia should neither be condemned nor approved, but accepted as an accomplished fact.[72]

Meanwhile, his worst forebodings about the ineffectiveness of the Allied socialist conference in February had come true. It was not until July that the Labour Party Executive learned from the Dutch socialist leader, Troelstra, what response the socialist parties of the central powers were likely to make to the Allied socialist memorandum, and even then, the German majority party made it clear that they were reluctant to enter into discussions on the basis of the Allied memorandum, and preferred an alternative which had been drawn up by the neutral parties.[73] In any case, the time for negotiation was passing. The static trench warfare of the Western Front was giving way to a war of movement, and by August the Allies could look forward with some confidence to the complete military victory which MacDonald had always seen as the worst enemy of a just peace. Early in August, Henderson and Bowerman, the secretary of the T.U.C. Parliamentary Committee, asked for passports to Switzerland, where they hoped to discuss the German attitude to the Allied socialist memorandum with Troelstra. The request was refused, and the National Executive passed a resolution deploring the refusal.[74] But the passports were not granted, and the meeting with Troelstra was not held. The International did not meet before the fighting was over, and the final peace settlement justified MacDonald's fears rather than his hopes. Whether his policy would have produced a different result can never be known. What is certain is that he had no evidence to the contrary: and no cause to love the pro-war majority in his own party who had made it impossible for him to put it to the test.

IV

At first sight, MacDonald's sympathy for Bolshevik Russia seems strangely out of character. He had always detested violence, whether it came from the Left or the Right; and for more than thirty years he had seen dogmatic Marxism as a cruel and mischievous irrelevance. It is true that the nature of the Bolshevik regime was not yet clear. MacDonald may well have met Lenin before the war, but he had not followed the intricate factional squabbles of the Russian Social Democratic party, and he probably did not realize how dogmatic Lenin's Marxism was. In any case, his sympathy for the Bolsheviks was based on their foreign policy, not on their actions inside Russia. In 1918, they alone seemed to stand uncompromisingly for the original Soviet formula of a peace without annexations or indemnities. In that, at least, their aims were MacDonald's aims, and his enemies were their enemies. But although all this is true, it is not the full explanation of his attitude. As we have seen more than once, there were two sides to his character. Side by side with the sober gradualist, a romantic rebel ran in uneasy double harness. In the long years of manœuvre and compromise as secretary of the Labour Representation Committee and chairman of the parliamentary Labour Party, the rebel had fallen behind. During the war, he had a second wind. To most of his countrymen, MacDonald had become a figure of malevolent wickedness; even in his own party he was excluded from power. His support came from rebels and outcasts — pacifist intellectuals, renegade aristocrats, insurgent shop stewards. Before the war, he had seen himself as the champion of reformism: farseeing, disdaining the jibes of demagogues and rabble-rousers, moving slowly and imperturbably towards a distant goal. Now he saw himself, in a way that he had not done for thirty years, as a lonely David pitting his sling against the Goliath of authority. 'Before the war, I felt that what was called the "spirit of the rebel" was, to a great extent, a stagey pose,' he confessed revealingly in a booklet called *Socialism after the War*. 'It is now required to save us ... Everything that involves the spirit of man in a material system of advantage, that stifles it in a mechanical machine and in formal order, is loss, unless with it is preserved the rebellious spirit.'[75] In that mood, even Lenin and Trotsky looked for a moment like kindred spirits.

The trade-union leaders who dominated the Labour Party Executive and annual conference looked, on the other hand, not only dangerously insular, but dangerously smug and bureaucratic as well. In 1915, the famous study of political parties made by the former German socialist, Robert Michels, was published in Britain in translation. MacDonald reviewed it for the *Labour*

Leader,[76] and his analysis in *Socialism after the War* was heavily influenced by it. Michels thought that socialist parties were peculiarly vulnerable to an 'iron law of oligarchy', which condemned originally democratic bodies to ossify into bureaucracies, in which the rank and file were manipulated or controlled by their leaders. MacDonald seized on Michels as a stick with which to beat the trade-union leaders whose block votes had kept the Labour Party on its pro-war course. The war, he wrote in a pregnant passage, had brought with it two great dangers – that of 'bourgeois sentiments' capturing 'successful working-class leaders',[77] and that of 'government by an inert mass, inert because only at the official top does real responsibility rest'.[78] Trade unions were organized on military lines, and 'subject to the rules and methods of an army'; a political party could not be organized in the way that trade unions were organized unless, like the German Social Democrats before the war, it too was 'modelled on military experiences'. By the same token, a trade union that joined a political party would have to recognize that it had two quite separate functions to perform. As an industrial organization it had to accept the principle of absolute majority rule; in its political capacity it had to recognize minority rights.[79]

This was more than an academic theory. It had a direct and painful relevance to the changes which were taking place in the internal organization of the Labour Party. In September 1917, less than two months after his resignation from the Cabinet, Henderson had submitted a long memorandum to the National Executive, advocating a wide extension of party membership, the strengthening and development of local parties, the promotion of a larger number of parliamentary candidates and the adoption of a party programme.[80] A sub-committee was appointed to consider the matter; and on October 16th, the proofs of a draft constitution, prepared by the sub-committee, were circulated to the Executive.[81] In January 1918, the new constitution was submitted to the party conference and it was finally adopted at a special conference in February. The result was to turn the loose-knit 'Labour Alliance', created by Hardie and MacDonald, into a national party with a mass membership and a network of local branches. Admittedly, the party was still a federation, the constituent parts of which remained intensely jealous of their own autonomy. But the federation was much more centralized than it had been in the past. The National Executive now had twenty-three members instead of sixteen; of these, five were reserved for representatives of the local Labour parties, and four for the new women's sections which replaced the old Women's Labour League, partly founded by Margaret MacDonald. Thirteen seats were reserved for affiliated organizations, both trade unions and socialist societies. The entire Executive, moreover, was to be elected by the party conference, in which the socialist societies and local parties were overwhelmingly outnumbered by the block votes of the trade unions.[82] The new constitution helped to lay the foundations for Labour's emergence during the next few years as a potential governing party. At the time its most obvious consequence was that the trade unions had become more powerful than ever before, while the I.L.P. had become correspondingly weaker. Local I.L.P. branches would be subject to competition from the new Divisional Labour parties. The separate I.L.P. representation on the National Executive had disappeared. In elections to the Executive as well as in voting on resolutions, the I.L.P. delegates to the annual conference would be overwhelmed by the massed battalions of the trade unions.

MacDonald served on the sub-committee on whose proposals the new constitution was based. But, although he accepted the need for a new constitution, his proposals were radically different from those actually adopted. The constitution which eventually emerged from the National Executive was largely the work of Henderson and Sidney Webb; MacDonald's attitude to it varied from grudging acquiescence to sharp disapproval. To some extent, of course, this was merely because he wished to defend the interests of the I.L.P. But there was more to his objections than that. In the circumstances of 1918, Henderson's constitution was probably the best obtainable. The trade unions were being asked to pay higher affiliation fees; they were hardly likely to do so without a *quid pro quo*. Their old suspicion of the I.L.P. was at its height, and there was a danger that some of them might secede from the Labour Party and set up a trade-union party instead. In giving the unions more power, Henderson and Webb could argue that they were acknowledging a fact of life. Nevertheless, in the structure they created, there was a built-in tension between the trade unions which paid the bills and controlled most of the votes at the annual conference, and the local parties which did the work on election day and regarded themselves as the political élite of the movement. This was the nub of MacDonald's criticism. Like Henderson, and unlike some of the more narrow-minded members of the I.L.P., he believed that the local parties should be strengthened and developed. Unlike Henderson, he also believed that they should be given more power at the centre, and the trade unions less. The kind of party he wanted was more unitary and less federal than the old one: but less oligarchic and more democratic than the new.

Thus he noted in October 1917 that he had drafted a memorandum on a new constitution for the Labour Party, 'strengthening power of Local Parties at annual Conference and on Executive, thus diminishing power of the National Trade Unions, but making Party more responsive to genuine political impulses. The tyranny of the vote of the big T.U.s has become intolerable.'[83] Two days later he noted that Henderson had submitted an alternative memorandum, which was 'Very badly drafted in form & in spirit & grasp just an election agent's document. Certainly not the vision of a new democratic party'.[84] On October 15th, he delivered a powerful attack on the trade-union block vote in his column in *Forward*, complaining that, in the proposals currently under discussion, the local parties would be 'practically wiped out so far as National Policy is concerned'. The same day he went to a meeting of I.L.P. M.P.s at Snowden's house, which decided 'to oppose the election of the Executive by

the whole conference and to continue the attack on the block vote'.[85] Next day
he commented angrily:

> Lab. Party Executive to discuss new Constitution. We were defeated by
> 5 to 4 votes in our attempt to get each section nominating for a separate
> panel also to elect from that panel. But the T.U. representatives wd. have
> nothing of this. They were to control with, & because of, their money. The
> new constitution is only a new coat of paint – pouring new wine into old
> bottles.[86]

One of the 'old bottles' in question was the trade-union block vote. Another,
and from MacDonald's point of view a potentially more objectionable one, was
trade-union control over the selection of parliamentary candidates. ' "Paul may
plant and Apollo water, but God giveth the increase," ' he complained, enig-
matically but indignantly, in his *Forward* column on October 27th. 'The local
Parties may nominate and the political sections wish to elect, but it is the Trade
Union card vote which is to determine who is to get seats.' The evils of trade-
union control over the selection process were, however, easier to offset than
were the evils of the trade-union block vote at the annual conference. It is
doubtful if MacDonald seriously expected the I.L.P. view of the constitution
to prevail, though he fought hard for it, and he had no patience with those
I.L.P.-ers who wanted to break with the Labour Party altogether in protest
against the I.L.P.'s loss of influence.[87] But one reason for his impatience was
that he recognized that, even if they were outvoted at the party conference and
in the elections to the National Executive, the 'active political elements' in the
Labour Party could redress the balance when parliamentary candidates were
selected, provided that they displayed enough energy and determination. Thus
in article after article he urged his readers to ensure that suitable candidates
were selected, and warned them that the job of a member of Parliament was a
specialized one, demanding its own skills and qualifications.[88] As he put it in a
letter to an anonymous correspondent, who must have written to him to
complain about one of these articles,

> Every man has to do his own work and anybody who has been in the
> House of Commons for ten or twelve years and known the sort of work
> that is required by members who are to have control of opinion in the
> House, holds that opinion. When we are dealing with mining legislation
> the men who have been officials of the Miners Federation naturally take the
> lead: when we are dealing with foreign complexities, those men do not
> necessarily take the lead ...
> ... Everyone who has had any knowledge of the Labour Party organisa-
> tion has felt time and time again that men become candidates, who, but for
> the fact that they had Trade Union money behind them, would never have
> been selected. We have had to fight contests which we could have won

had we had candidates given to us who could fight. I have a contest in my mind at the moment where we sent up men all of whom came down saying that the task was hopeless because the candidate was so useless. If we are to have a Labour Party in the House of Commons that is to do the work that a strong Labour Party will have to do ... we shall not have to go ... disheartened by failure in constituencies which ought to be won, and still more disheartened by ineffective work in the House of Commons.[89]

In some constituencies, candidate selection presented an even more ticklish problem. In the next few years, many of the anti-war intellectuals who had belonged to the Liberal Party before the war and who had campaigned with MacDonald for a negotiated peace found their way into the Labour Party — in most cases, by way of the I.L.P. Some of them were to play leading parts in Labour politics; together they helped to transform the Labour Party from a working-class pressure group into a national party, capable of winning and holding power in what was still a highly class-conscious and deferential country. Indeed, it can be argued that this was one of the most important consequences of MacDonald's stand during the war, and one of his most important legacies to the Labour movement. At this stage, however, some anti-war Radicals — and notably the two leading anti-war Radical M.P.s, C. P. Trevelyan and Arthur Ponsonby — were still reluctant to throw in their lot with the Labour Party. Perhaps because he was unduly influenced by Trevelyan and Ponsonby, MacDonald did not himself expect or advocate a great Radical influx into the Labour Party. What he did foresee was the emergence of a group somewhere between the Liberal and Labour parties, analogous, he thought, to the French Radical-Socialists.[90] Thus he noted in December 1917 that he had had lunch with 'one of the many Liberals who have joined the ILP' — adding, somewhat ungratefully, that 'it would have been better had they managed to create a marginal group in touch with Radicalism on the Right & ourselves on the Left.'[91] But, although he did not expect dissident Liberals to join the Labour Party, he was acutely aware of their importance for the future of left-wing politics and anxious that they should not be driven back into the orthodox Liberal fold from which they were now drifting away. 'There are one or two men still nominally Labour members whom no Independent Labour Party branch can be forced to support ... ,' he warned in an outspoken editorial in the *Socialist Review* for January 1918. 'On the other hand, there are some men like Mr. Trevelyan, Mr. Ponsonby, Mr. Richard Lambert whom no Independent Labour Party branch can be forced to oppose ... So long as there is chivalry and loyalty and fine spirit in politics, we shall share our political crust with these men.'

That was easier said than done. At the beginning of February 1918, Ponsonby, who had been repudiated by his local Liberal Association, announced that he intended to fight Dunfermline Burghs as an Independent Democrat. The Fife miners were anxious to contest the seat as well; and, at the end of March, MacDonald went to Dunfermline with Ponsonby to try, as he put it in his diary, to 'persuade my friends not to oppose him'. After two fine meetings, however, he 'came up against the red tape snares set for Labour feet that do not walk for ever on the high roads. Probably there will be further trouble, but what care I? Ponsonby ... is worth twenty of the average candidate who is likely to be brought out against him.'[92] Further trouble duly came, as the following letter from MacDonald to one of the officials of the Scottish miners' union makes clear:

> The question as to whether the Dunfermline Burghs are, or are not, to be fought, does not rest with the Miners, or with me, or with anybody except a properly convened Conference, and in preparation for that Conference, the Miners and I, and anybody else, have a perfect right to advise fighting or refraining from fighting. I have advised refraining from fighting and when the Conference has decided, I shall accept its decision.
>
> The statement ... that I have violated the Constitution, is nothing but an absurdity. Mr. Ponsonby is not a Liberal ... If he is returned, he will act with the Labour Party as he has done for the last three years, and will have a clearer vision of Labour needs and Labour policy than a good few of the Labour men who have been in the House of Commons ...
>
> I ... observe ... reference to disloyalty. That comes rather badly from ... the Scottish Miners Executive, whose last widely advertised action was to back up Mr. Havelock Wilson in preventing a Labour Party deputation going to Petrograd, and it comes with equally bad grace from the Fife Miners who have official responsibility for the action of their representatives at Conference who have done so much to spread resentment and ill-will inside the Labour Party, by moving and carrying by sheer weight of block votes, resolutions which the I.L.P. considers to amount to a breach of faith and of contract.[93]

This was scarcely calculated to soothe the Fife miners. On May 29th, a letter was reported to the National Executive from the Miners' Federation of Great Britain, enclosing an inquiry from the Scottish Mineworkers Association, asking whether MacDonald's appearance on Ponsonby's election platform at Dunfermline did not constitute a breach of the party constitution. After what the N.E.C. minutes describe as 'considerable discussion', it was agreed that MacDonald should make a statement to the Executive the following day. Next day, MacDonald duly made a statement, accepting that 'in view of the attempts that are being made to dis-rupt the Labour Party, and the use that might be made of my action', it had perhaps been inexpedient of him to act as he did. The Executive thereupon accepted his statement, and expressed the opinion 'that his action was at variance with the spirit of the Constitution'.[94] 'This is really a terrible revelation of the mind & spirit of sections of the Labour Party,'

MacDonald confessed in a gloomy letter to Ponsonby, '& makes me unhappy lest the fine ideas of liberty & catholicism we associate with the Party are all humbug. I am sorely tempted to write you a letter for publication, but I suppose that would be bad policy & useless ... I am ashamed of my friends.'[95] In his diary he was less gloomy but equally indignant. 'Lab: Party Exec: censured me for going to Dunfermline ... ,' he noted on May 30th. 'I am rather amused. Henderson gave vent to spleen & his display of vanity & jealousy was crushingly painful.' It was not the least of the humiliations he had suffered since August 1914.

V

The new constitution was soon put to the test. As early as February 1918, the National Executive decided 'to make immediate arrangements' to set up organizations in all constituencies, and to nominate parliamentary candidates wherever the local party wished to do so.[96] By the middle of April, the National Agent was able to report that 115 candidates had been selected, and that a further 131 selections were pending.[97] By the end of July, the National Executive was seriously considering the possibility that a general election might be held during the winter;[98] at the beginning of August, MacDonald warned the readers of *Forward* to expect a ' "low down" fight' in November.[99] At the end of August, Henderson disclosed that 226 Labour candidates were now in the field, and that the figure would reach 300 within a month.[100]

But although it was clear that a general election was not far away, it was far from clear how or under what banner the Labour Party would fight it. Mac-Donald was anxious that it should fight as an independent entity, in opposition to the Coalition, and made it clear that he was willing to face an 'unholy combination against everyone who has thought and acted independently';[101] the Labour ministers and most of the parliamentary party were anxious to be part of any 'unholy combination' which the Government might set up. As late as July 31st, the Labour ministers submitted a memorandum to the National Executive, deploring the party's decision to end the political truce and pointing out that this was inconsistent with repeated conference decisions to support the Coalition. In a discussion with Henderson, Barnes complained that the National Executive had given the impression that it no longer stood for the successful prosecution of the war, and demanded that this impression should be removed.[102] These attitudes did not disappear as victory approached. On October 28th, MacDonald noted:

> Situation for us getting difficult again ... Push continued, Governments delayed diplomacy, papers vociferous and stirred up feeling using atrocities as usual. At first Gen: Election seemed to recede, then (especially from this morning) came clear to front ... House met 15th Oct. and we had con-

ferences with Labour Ministers to try and agree upon election policy.
Failure so far. Barnes impossibilist and others self-satisfied. The conference
was suspended with no agreement when election seemed to be put off.
Also Party Executive tried to get agreement with Lab: Parliamentary
Party on Election statement and two meetings held so badly attended that
nothing could be done.[103]

In November, Parliament was dissolved, and a special Labour Party conference was summoned to formulate the party's election policy. On November
7th, the National Executive met to decide what recommendations to make to
the conference. The parliamentary party wished to remain in the Coalition
until the peace treaty was signed; Clynes put this view to the Executive with
passion and conviction. If Labour fought independently of the Government
and in opposition to Lloyd George, he warned, it would court electoral
disaster. Even Henderson seems to have been shaken. Richards proposed a
resolution, based on a draft originally prepared by Henderson, recommending
the conference to call for the resignation of the Labour ministers when the
peace terms were settled. MacDonald and Maxton, however, proposed an
amendment, calling for the resignation of the Labour ministers when Parliament
was dissolved; in the end, their amendment was carried by 12 votes to 4.[104]
At the special conference a week later, the Executive's recommendation was
accepted by a majority of over a million. When the election came in December,
the Labour Party found itself arrayed in somewhat ragged opposition to Lloyd
George.

For MacDonald, at least, the price was high. Leicester had been divided into
three single-member constituencies. MacDonald was the candidate for Leicester
West. The coalitionist candidate was J. F. Green, formerly a member of the
S.D.F. and now the champion of respectability, patriotism and national unity.
But it soon became clear that Green was not his most formidable opponent.
Nationally, the election of 1918 became a referendum on the character and
patriotism of Lloyd George: in Leicester, it also became a referendum on the
character and patriotism of MacDonald. The record of the opposing candidate
hardly mattered; his own policy and programme mattered even less. The issue,
as defined by all three coalitionist candidates and still more insistently by the
local press, had nothing to do with the peace settlement or post-war reconstruction. The sole question before the electorate, it seemed, was whether or not
MacDonald's opposition to the war and to the foreign policy of Sir Edward
Grey had disqualified him from representing the people of Leicester. Members
of Parliament, wrote the *Leicester Mercury* at the beginning of the campaign,
'offer "an account of their stewardship" on these occasions, and seek renewal of
confidence upon that, as well as on promises as to the future. Mr. MacDonald
will not expect to be relieved of that ordeal ... [A]t the beginning of the war
he misjudged and so misrepresented Sir Edward Grey and the policy of the

Government. In that course he ran counter ... to the interests of the nation, just as it entered upon a tremendous conflict ... [H]ad his advice been followed, and that of the organisations on whose platforms he appeared, there would have been not a peace after victory, but a cessation of hostilities by negotiation. We cannot forget these things.'[105]

Day after day, the local press hammered away at this theme. MacDonald's attempts to divert the argument into other channels, or to counter the accusations of his opponents, only intensified its efforts. When he answered the charges brought against him, he was accused of 'falling into mere vituperation';[106] when he failed to answer them, he was accused of having something to hide. Inevitably, he was forced on to the defensive. 'How they lie about Ramsay MacDonald,' ran the headline of one of his campaign leaflets;[107] but each time the leaflet gained a new reader, the lie concerned gained extra circulation. The effect on MacDonald can easily be imagined. 'I am writing from the stour,' he wrote in his column in *Forward* half-way through the campaign, 'and it is a pretty fine stour here in Leicester.'[108] When the campaign was over he described his reactions at greater length:

> The cars scurry hither and thither. Poverty and debauchery hob nob with affluence and flush. Children showing their skins through their tatters run yelling amidst the rush. Someone breaks the spell by a shake of the hand and fervent wish of good luck, and I am reminded that I am the centre of it all – the object of the offence and the defence. My opponent, a pure Marxian Socialist to whom the I.L.P. was but milk and water, whizzes past embowered in Union Jacks, the trophy of expectant Capitalism, the pride of a strenuous reaction ...
>
> But the haunting memory is of the women – bloodthirsty, cursing their hate, issuing from the courts and alleys crowded with children, reeking with humanity – the sad flotsam and jetsam of wild emotion ...
>
> This is the drama of representative Government enacted in such times as these. Here the reason of the anti-Parliamentarian has it all its own way. One of these friends of mine remarked the other day, 'This is the fetish you worship.' 'The very Gods go mad sometimes,' I replied. But what respect can we pay to decisions which can be worked in this fashion?[109]

Polling day was December 14th. Three days before, Sir Gordon Hewart – solicitor general and coalitionist candidate for Leicester East – devoted his entire speech to an attack on MacDonald's war record. The contest in Leicester, he declared, was 'essentially one and indivisable'. MacDonald had 'put an odious stain and stigma upon the fair name of Leicester'. But it was not an indelible stain. The citizens of Leicester now had their opportunity of wiping it away and 'of meting out to its author his well-merited reward'.[110] Next day, the *Leicester Mercury* took up the charge. 'In the gravest known crisis in our national history,' it wrote, 'Mr. MacDonald took a course as representative of

Leicester at variance with the sentiment of the borough. Elected as its representative, he became its misrepresentative.'[111] On the eve of the poll, it drew the moral. In an editorial entitled 'Tomorrow's Duty', it declared sententiously that Hewart's indictment 'is not answered, the evidence stands in all its convincing strength, and the electors of West Leicester have tomorrow to return the verdict.'[112]

MacDonald had ended his campaign in a mood of fierce exultation. He expected to lose, he noted in his diary, but he thought it quite possible that he would lose by as little as 500 votes. 'We fought in fine style and my meetings were great,' he wrote. 'It was a question of lifting the constituency by argument and fervour, and I all but succeeded I think. I certainly felt inspired by something, and I really held the other side and its candidate in a kind of loathing contempt.' At the beginning of the campaign, he went on, the betting had been 5 to 1 against him; by the end, it was 2 to 1 in his favour.[113] All this must have made the eventual result even harder to bear. When the votes were declared, two weeks after polling day, Green received 20,510 votes to MacDonald's 6,347. At first, MacDonald did not feel the full impact of the blow. 'The end of the old song has come,' he noted with comparative equanimity on December 28th. 'I did not feel my defeat till I got home and felt the disappointment of my children. Their little sad faces made a tightening in my throat and a swelling of something in my eyes.'[114] During the next few days, however, the full significance of what had happened began to sink in. On December 29th he noted:

> How lonely one feels at a time like this. I sit in my room ill & write to keep myself doing some-thing, but there seems to be a log in the way of the free flow of thoughts & words, & they come in trickles. I have become a kind of mythological demon in the minds of people. How reputation makes us up for the stage of life & how grotesque is the clothing & general garb in which — often without our knowledge — we play our parts — thieves as saints, saints as blackguards. Enquiries are made about my intentions. As though one could rub up intentions in an hour after such an experience. I am too much absorbed trying to grasp the mentality of the people who voted. Are we right about man, or have we elevated the species to gratify our own vanity? But no more of it. I am truly sorry that my Parlia: and public work is broken, & that, though there are one or two good men in it, the Labour team is altogether inadequately equipped for the part it ought to play. The degradation of this Parliament is not merely a step down but a precipice. Many condolences begin by congratulating me. That is bad. Whoever is in Parlt. honest men shd. be there to do their duty.[115]

New Year's Eve was lonelier still. In Leicester, he noted, the link with Margaret was unbroken:

She was with the people I met, especially the women; I met her on the streets; there was a ward in the hospital called after her & the cast of her memorial was in the museum. It is gone. She has gone further away from me. The gloom ahead gathers thick ... I have been invited out, but no. I shall keep solitary vigil tonight.[116]

CHAPTER 12

Rebuilding a career

I

TEN days after the news of his election defeat, MacDonald attended a joint meeting of the National Executive and the new parliamentary party. To judge by his diary, the proceedings were as depressing as the surroundings in which they took place:

> The meeting was held in the Central Hall that embodiment of pretentious & tasteless Weslyianism [*sic*]. Brace moved ... that Party should be the official Opposition. Sexton, Adamson, Turner, Gould supported only O'Grady opposing in a rambling & pointless speech ... Then the Executive withdrew & the Party proceeded to elect Adamson & Clynes chairman & vice-chairman ... & four Whips — the Chief a good rough fellow, but very doubtful in that job though the best; one absolutely useless; & two new men. I was struck with the rawness of the men. No generous word for past work; no hesitation regarding their own capacity & this was highlighted by a speech of Webb who offered his 'Parliamentary experience' to them freely — and who means to run them ... [S]ome of the new men may prove equal to the task. The old will not. They will mislead. They have tasted the flesh pots.[1]

His reaction was understandable. He was now fifty-two; and, after twelve years in the House of Commons, his political career appeared to be in ruins. He had just lost his seat by a majority twice as large as his own total vote; the party he had helped to create appeared to be firmly under the control of those who had rejected his leadership in the first great crisis in its history. The anti-war section had all lost their seats; even Henderson had been swept away by the coalitionist tide. The most prominent figure left on the Labour benches was the worthy and inoffensive J. R. Clynes, who had fought to the last to stay in office. Apart from the railwaymen's leader, J. H. Thomas — a shrewd and capable negotiator, whose stand during the war had been more moderate and less bellicose than that of most trade-union secretaries — the rest of the parliamentary party consisted of little more than a handful of novices and a pro-war rump.

Worse still, the essential gradualist values of reason and compromise, which had always been central to MacDonald's political philosophy, seemed to be in universal retreat. The new House of Commons contained 339 coalition Conservatives and 136 coalition Liberals. Opposing them were less than 30 independent Liberals, and 59 Labour men. The way in which the Government had obtained its majority was even more alarming than its size. The election campaign, MacDonald wrote in the *Socialist Review*, had been 'an assassination rather than a battle';[2] and he feared, with good reason, that the success of the assassination would strengthen the anti-parliamentary tendencies already at work in the Labour movement. Reaction in Britain, moreover, confronted chaos in central and eastern Europe. In November 1918, the German empire had collapsed. A republic had been proclaimed, and a socialist Government had taken office. But the extreme Left of the German Labour movement, represented by the revolutionary shop stewards and the so-called Spartacus League, rejected parliamentary government and tried to force the German revolution along the road taken by the Bolsheviks in Russia. In January 1919 they rose in revolt. The Government turned for help to a Free Corps controlled by former officers of the Kaiser's army. The revolt was crushed, and shortly afterwards the Spartacist leaders, Rosa Luxemburg and Karl Liebknecht, were brutally murdered. Two months later, a Soviet republic was proclaimed in Budapest; shortly after that another abortive revolt took place in Bavaria. To MacDonald, watching in impotent distress from Britain, all this was the antithesis of socialism — a sign that the passion and hysteria of the war had infected even its opponents. 'After war the world goes mad,' he wrote in a revealing column in *Forward* towards the end of January:

And our own people go mad. We have our dreams of a better world — calm dreams they ought to be ... But after war these dreams become frenzied ... The furious violence of hate takes possession of them. The ruling classes have drenched Europe in blood. The slaves ... rise to make more blood flow. Then horror creeps over people's minds and fear fills their hearts. The crisis passes, and the old evil order returns ...

Rosa ... was a born revolutionary, a bundle of restless energy. Her face, in which the muscles never seemed to be in repose, was the mirror of a mind always on the attack. I have seen her like a flame of revolt, standing on a table howling and howled at, laughing, laughed at, provoking and provocative ... I can believe that she was 'the man of the revolution' and that Liebknecht was but a lieutenant in her command.

They have both gone down to the grave and to history together, their end ... encompassed in hate, passion and chaos ... [I]t will add to Europe's frenzy; it will make eyes wilder and hearts more passionate ... [3]

Sometimes he was tempted to give way to despair. 'Revolution in Portugal, strikes in Yorkshire & threatened everywhere, football swindling, murder of Seton by Rutherford, murder of Liebknecht & Rosa Luxemburg,' he noted after a weekend in the country spent discussing the problems of the I.L.P.; 'chaos, passion, evil; in other words war and civilization. Is one of any use in the world except thinking & speaking from one's own fireside?'[4] Political isolation went hand in hand with personal loneliness, and, at least for a while, with comparative financial hardship. The loss of his parliamentary salary of £400 a year had been a severe blow – and it was followed in March 1919 by a letter from the trustees of his wife's estate, telling him that they had to reduce their payments to him by £100. 'Prospects look beautiful!', he noted sardonically: 'What an end to comfortable leisure and work done in ease of mind for public ends.'[5]

A far more serious blow was the news that Bruce Glasier had been told by his doctor that he had only a few months to live. 'They go so quickly now,' MacDonald noted. 'We seem to see the trumpeter with his bugle at his lips & our hearts wonder if the blast he is to blow is our own. So one slips gently down into the dark becoming more and more solitary.'[6] Even family festivals had an undertone of melancholy. 'Ishbel's 16th birthday,' he noted on March 2nd. 'Oh, Time, Time why do you go so fast — a moan that will not be understood by the young but be made by the ageing till Time is no more.'[7] Two months later he noted: 'To-day Alister is 21; yesterday he was a toddling babe. So we drive on like mad flies to our graves. We had a happy family gathering, but the two blanks were there. I saw the little boy lying in that mortuary behind the glass.'[8] It was the same emotion that led him to write, in a characteristic diary entry in April 1919:

> Worked all morning at book & finished first complete draft. Freedom came like Spring into my soul & I walked out on the Heath. The wind & the sun were fine. The young people told me I was old. I was alone & my dead came to keep me company. I stood on the top & looked down on London in its grey gauzy misty drapery & wondered how long I should be here.[9]

These entries show only one side of the truth. Like many lonely and introspective people, MacDonald used his diary as a safety valve for emotions which could not be expressed in any other way; it would be a mistake to imagine that the black moods recorded in it reigned without interruption. As time went on, the scars left by the war and the 1918 election slowly began to heal. In many ways the early nineteen-twenties must have been among the happiest and most fruitful periods in MacDonald's life. He was out of Parliament, of course; but the 1918 Parliament was a good one to be out of. His political energies were fully — and in the circumstances more usefully — absorbed in other ways. Between 1919 and 1922, he wrote a number of pamphlets and one fairly substantial work of socialist theory. He was editor of the *Socialist Review*, the theoretical quarterly of the I.L.P., which later became a monthly. He contributed a weekly column to *Forward*, the organ of the Glasgow I.L.P., as well as frequent articles to the *Labour Leader* and the New York *Nation*. He was equally active on the platform; and although his activities cannot be traced in detail, it is clear that a large part of his time must have been spent in the exhausting routine of an itinerant propagandist—travelling to provincial centres by train, speaking at meetings, staying with supporters or at indifferent hotels. At the same time, he played a more active part than any other leading British socialist in the laborious and often exasperating task of rebuilding the International—a task which had the compensation that it enabled him to indulge his passion for foreign travel, but which must have exacted heavy toll in nervous and physical energy.

In any case, politics was only part of his life, and it was probably a less important part than it had been for most of the last fifteen years. Some of his closest friends—like Alec Martin, a buyer at Christie's, or Alexander Grant, another 'Lossie loon', who had made a fortune as a biscuit manufacturer—were not in politics at all. Others—like Hugh Roberton, the founder of the Glasgow Orpheus Choir, or Willie and Martha Leach, the Bradford I.L.P.-ers—were active in the I.L.P.; but even with them his relationship was primarily a non-political one.[10] Financially, his circumstances seem to have improved—partly, perhaps, because of the intervention of an eccentric businessman called Henry Markwald, who admired the stand he had taken during the war, and who seems to have contributed financial support of some kind, at least to the extent of buying insurance policies for him.[11] He was not remotely well-off, but he was able to afford an extensive journey to the Middle East in the early months of 1922, and with Alec Martin's help he began, on a modest scale, to buy occasional pictures and pieces of furniture. He did not buy much, but what he bought showed discrimination and judgment, if of a rather old-fashioned kind.[12] The same was true of his reading. Freedom from day-to-day parliamentary chores gave him the time to read quite widely in politics, sociology and economic history. In these fields he tried, with some success, to understand the ideas of the younger generation even when he did not agree with them. His tastes in literature were more conventional. He admired Thomas Hardy and Conrad, but the new writers who flowered during and after the war do not seem to have interested him, and it is clear from his diary that his favourites were the classics of the eighteenth and early nineteenth centuries—Gibbon, Defoe, Boswell, Addison and Sir Walter Scott.[13]

Next to reading, perhaps even ahead of it, his chief relaxation was walking, preferably in the rough hill country of Wales or Scotland. 'I have been a day & a night in the hills in wild weather,' he wrote to a supporter in South Wales in the summer of 1920. 'It soothes me & being able to tramp over miles of wet heather & to sleep in a bed of wet stuff & get up as fresh as a daisy to see the sun & wash in roaring torrents of icy water makes me feel that there may be some kick left yet.'[14] This was a characteristic note. His columns in *Forward* were full of references to long tramps in the Border Country, or the Lake

I

District, or the Cairngorms; and, although these descriptive writings seem rather mannered and high-flown to a modern reader, they provide a curiously touching picture of MacDonald at his most relaxed and contented — free from the tensions and conflicts of politics, and able to give full vent to the solitary and romantic aspect of his character which was normally submerged beneath the practical man of affairs. Here, for example, is a characteristic description of a tramp in the Cairngorms with some of his children:

There were mists on the mountains and foam on the river, but whoever turns back from these things deserves the fate of Lot's wife. Besides, the heather and the pine woods never smelt sweeter, rain had laid the dust and laden the air with the scents of field and forest; the prospect was like alluring music. In the woods one came upon the cruel, gashing handiwork of man. The Rothiemurchus forest was being turned into deals and cash. It was like an abandoned being sitting by the roadside in dishevelled rags, its trees lying lopped like human arms and legs, its heather torn, its paths in confusion. How a State, now that the science of forestry is so well known, can allow a private individual to desecrate God's earth and waste national wealth, as has been done here, passes comprehension ...

I left the miserable, tortured thing behind me, crossed a mountain stream that welcomed me with greater fuss than I have ever known it to show — an ominous greeting — and went up to the long slopes of the Cairngorms. The fleecy outposts of the dark cloud ahead met us with gentle warning. They thickened and cleared, drove past and swirled round, like happy children at play; but as I looked back the hills and lakes below were being screened by an ever-thickening curtain ...

I lay down that night under shelter of a great granite boulder, which, in times when the poor earth was convulsed with pain, came down like an angel from the heights to minister to the comforts of man. The wind moaned like a wild beast prowling around; I could hear the drip, drip of the rain in the little pools round the stone; the rush of the streams was like a gale in a wood ... At eight o'clock we stretched ourselves out to sleep without a dry square inch of clothing on us and with the brittle stalks of heather, which had mercifully been left by whoever had last taken a night's lodging in this free 'hotel for travellers', pricking us.

And we did sleep — a happy, dreamless sleep. Now and again the bed became too hard, or the heather too sharp, or the wind puffs too cold, but the dark moments of wakefulness only added to the pleasure. No king in his feather bed was happier. We were alone amidst the clouds, the companions of the storm and the rushing waters. We were to have started again at four: we slept till six. Fifteen well-measured miles on the map were before us, and the last train which returned us to civilization and a bankrupt world left at 2.50 ...

Waiting for the train, we surveyed Messrs. Menzies' bookstall, stocked for the enlightenment of the world. We found it was being used for the dissemination of leaflets on 'Direct Action'. We took one, laughed and wept at its rubbish, invested in a Conrad, and so home to supper and bed.[15]

II

In politics, too, the shadow of the war lifted more quickly than MacDonald had expected. Over most of western and central Europe, the decade ushered in by the Spartacist revolt and the murder of Rosa Luxemburg turned out to be the Indian summer of gradualism: the last chance for men of compromise and reason to shape their own societies and the international community in the optimistic image of reformist Social Democracy. In this, Britain mirrored her neighbours. The swollen coalitionist majority of 1918 concealed striking changes in the structure of politics. The Liberal Party was split. Meanwhile, Labour had increased its share of the total vote from under 8 per cent to almost 24 per cent. This advance was the outward and visible sign of a more fundamental change in working-class attitudes. Trade-union membership had doubled during the war, and Labour Party membership had doubled with it. The forces which had brought about this expansion grew more powerful and more explosive when the war ended. By 1920, the total membership of the trade unions affiliated to the T.U.C. had reached 6,500,000, while Labour Party membership had reached over 4,300,000. The militancy of organized labour increased *pari passu* with its numerical strength. A growing number of working men and women had begun to reject an economic order in which they were treated as 'hands', with no voice in the decisions that shaped their lives. Their rejection was no doubt confused, inarticulate and unsystematic; the struggles it inspired were largely rearguard actions in defence of existing positions, not deliberate assaults on the citadels of power. Nevertheless, it did provide inspiration; and in doing so, it provided the central theme of labour politics in the early 'twenties. The number of working days lost in strikes far surpassed the figure reached in the bitterest period of labour unrest before the war. Between 1911 and 1913 it had averaged twenty million days a year. Between the beginning of 1919 and the end of 1921 the average figure was forty million.[16] It is true that the growth of trade-union membership, and the wave of industrial unrest which had accompanied it, both came to an end when the post-war boom ended in 1921. But the boom was soon followed by a severe trade depression and a sharp rise in unemployment. These made militant industrial action more difficult, but they also made a mockery of Lloyd George's promises in the 1918 election, and destroyed his hold on the working-class electorate. The explosion of class consciousness which took place immediately after the war, and the bitterness engendered by the depression which followed it, could hardly fail to have dramatic repercussions on the political system. It was they, rather than the split of 1916, which destroyed the old Liberal Party; and it was they which made it possible for Labour to replace it as the main progressive party in Britain.

In doing so, they also gave MacDonald – the lifelong opponent of a class conception of labour politics – the chance to return to the leadership of the Labour Party. For, as a result of his stand during the war, he had acquired one of the most valuable assets a left-wing leader can possess. He had become a symbol, even a legend. Mrs Lucy Middleton, the wife of MacDonald's old assistant at Labour Party headquarters, Jim Middleton, remembers how at a U.D.C. meeting in London in 1917, where she was sitting in the front row, she suddenly had a sense that a disturbance had taken place at the back of the hall. There was no explanation for it – no interruption, no heckling, no movement by the audience. Yet somehow the atmosphere had changed: the temperature had been raised. Eventually she looked round to see what had happened. The disturbance was that MacDonald had entered the room.[17] Mary Agnes Hamilton, one of his closest and most perceptive friends, made the same point in her memoirs. MacDonald, she wrote, did not need to strike an extreme note in order to evoke extreme emotions. His presence was enough. So, during the war, he had not needed to expound the pacifist creed.

> He made us feel it. He did not denounce the horror of war – he showed it. We were in the awful battle: we heard the dark rush of the wings of the Angel of Death as they fanned the hot tormented faces of the wounded on the field. He told us we were 'the custodians of their sacrifices', and we trembled and exulted. Great speakers – speakers who can seize and play on the nerves of their hearers ... actually need to say far less than mediocre ones do; it is the dull speaker who has to exaggerate, promise, denounce, vilify, tear himself to pieces and his passion to tatters, in order to rouse his audience. Mac did not have to say 'strong' things; he seldom did.[18]

The art of the orator is by nature evanescent, impossible to analyse, and difficult even to describe. Moreover, styles change. What is moving, even inspiring, to one generation may seem flatulent or ridiculous to the next. Yet even now, old newsreel shots of MacDonald in his decline (there are none of him in his prime) convey a faint impression of the power he possessed in these years, and evoke a faint shadow of the emotion he could command. For his power on the platform was now at its height. To some extent, this was due to his oratorical style – richer and more emotional than it had been before 1914, and perhaps in consequence cloudier and less precise. It was also due to the handsome frame and noble features: the flowing locks, the drooping moustache, the fine bones, the lines etched deep on a poetic brow; the liquid gestures and expressive face; the seductive accent and commanding voice. All this helped him to dominate the imagination of the Labour movement, irrespective of his position in its formal hierarchy; beside him, the other leaders seemed prosaic, even commonplace. But there was more to it than appearance or style. During the war, and in the years immediately after it, men went to a MacDonald meeting as an act of defiance. They were swept along, not only by what he said or even by the way he said it, but by the fact that it was said by him. Thus it was possible for him to denounce the class war, and still appeal to the emotions behind it. What he said was as moderate as ever, sometimes almost gratuitously so. Coming from him, it was the equivalent of a call to the barricades.

As a result, he was able to straddle the divisions within the Labour movement more successfully than any other leading Labour politician. He was able to be, at one and the same time, the hammer of the Communist Party and the Third International, and the symbol of the insurgent proletariat of the Clyde: the most effective defender of parliamentary methods in the Labour movement, and the most effective critic of the drab and timorous leadership of the parliamentary Labour Party. At the same time, he was able to straddle the gulf between the Labour movement as a whole and potential Labour voters outside it; and in the long run this was a greater asset still. For the upsurge of militancy which transformed labour politics in the early 'twenties was confined to a minority. Even at the crest of the post-war boom, when total trade-union membership exceeded eight million, most of the working population did not belong to a trade union; and, once the boom subsided, trade-union membership rapidly declined.[19] By the same token, the woollen towns of the West Riding or the mining valleys of South Wales, where an 'old' working class had to defend itself against the contraction of an 'old' staple industry, were in a different world from Birmingham or the south-east. Thus, the Labour Party was compelled to speak to a number of different audiences at once. The organized minority of the working class provided it with its money, its local leadership and its electoral base. But if it was to advance beyond this base, and become a party of government rather than of protest, it would have to appeal to other groups, whose values and attitudes were very different from those of the embattled, class-conscious minority. If it was to enter into its inheritance as the successor of the pre-war Liberal Party, in other words, it would have to construct a new version of the pre-war Liberal coalition. The core would consist of a minority of active trade unionists and socialists. But the coalition would also have to include social groups and individual voters who had been contentedly enrolled in the Liberal coalition only a few years before.

By temperament and conviction, MacDonald was better fitted than any of his potential rivals to become the focal point around which such a coalition could take shape. The ambiguities of his personality and philosophy were assets: the fact that no one knew exactly what class he belonged to, exactly what policies he would introduce, exactly what kind of person he was, made it possible for each section of the coalition to see in him what it wanted to see. His romanticism, his imprecision, his dislike of sharp outlines and his fondness for vague, elusive metaphors, all helped him to blur the differences between his heterogeneous and sometimes incompatible potential followers. Much the same was true of his complex, ambivalent attitude to the 'Establishment' and its conventions. In later years, he was often accused of snobbery. In fact he was not a snob. He was not a social climber, and he did not despise his social inferiors. But there is no doubt that he was fascinated by the idea of the aristocracy, and perhaps also by the idea of himself as the intimate of aristocrats – not, as his enemies alleged, because he wished to desert his own class, but because he liked to picture himself as a man without class, equally at home in cottage or castle: as a man, in Mrs Hamilton's words, who had 'been everywhere, done everything, known everyone'.[20]

In the early 'twenties, this side of his character was less obvious than it later became. No great houses would have been willing to open their doors to a notorious pacifist and presumed seditionist, even if he had been willing to accept their invitations. It was already possible, however, to detect a related trait, which may have been more fundamental and was certainly of longer standing. When one of his daughters was passing through a phase of militant republicanism and refused to stand up when 'God Save the King' was played, MacDonald told her gently that one stood up for 'God Save the King' not out of respect for the monarchy, but out of respect for the society of whose history it was part. This almost Burkeian sense of the role of convention as the invisible thread binding society together was perhaps a logical corollary of his evolutionary theory of society. But it had deeper emotional roots than a social philosophy. Perhaps because of the war, MacDonald had become more conscious than ever of the fragility of any kind of ordered society, more aware of the value of stability and continuity, and more sceptical about human nature in the mass. He was shocked by the irreverence of the bright young intellectuals of the 'twenties, in revolt against the manners and standards of their parents. 'Felt the virtues of the Victorian times so condemned by Mr Strachey,' he noted while reading *Queen Victoria*. 'The simple honesties can always be made a butt by the impish unreliabilities.'[21] When he had finished he was relieved to find Strachey 'enmeshed in Victoria's virtues & the real drama of her last phase. As a good Victorian I shd. like to let myself loose upon him. A psychological study of unusual interest.'[22] It was the same attitude which led him to contemplate writing a biography of John Knox, in whose letters he found '[g]ood sombre clouds of travail & theology';[23] and to note, in a revealing entry in his diary in March 1919, 'Oh the mediocrity of this Parliament. But the people understand these men & so they rule ... In youth one *believes* in democracy; later on, one has to *accept* it ... I read for consolation Gibbon's *Decline & Fall* [and] the minor Prophets ...'[24]

It was a characteristic remark. Yet it did not imply any weakening in MacDonald's emotional commitment to the Labour movement and the class it sought to represent. Shortly before the great miners' strike of 1921, he noted that the middle and upper classes would 'shoot us with even more pleasure than they shot the Germans. For after all, their quarrel with the Germans was with powers in whom they believed – of their own class.'[25] The 'us', and the instinctive class solidarity it implied, were as revealing as his admiration for John Knox or his scepticism about the intelligence of the mass electorate. His respect for tradition included, among other things, respect for his own traditions: for the traditions of the fishermen and farm workers of Morayshire, and their long struggle against aristocratic oppression. During the holidays at Lossiemouth, when his children were young, he used to take them on a ceremonial walk through the property of the local laird – a defiant and deliberate trespass, ritually marked by cutting the barbed wire which was supposed to prevent entry into the laird's land. That, too, was characteristic: and so, to complete the confusion, was the fact that the laird and he later became close friends.[26]

In all this, MacDonald mirrored the contradictions which a successful Labour coalition would have to embrace. It would be a mistake to imagine that the Labour movement of the 'twenties consisted exclusively of dedicated egalitarians, determined to sweep away the elaborate gradations of status and position so characteristic of the British social system, or to abolish the traditional protocol of British public life. The available evidence – fragmentary and anecdotal though it is – suggests that the great majority of the Labour Party was only too anxious to prove itself fit to govern in the traditional way, and only too willing to accept the traditional standards of fitness. When Beatrice Webb set up her Half Circle Club to help the wives of Labour leaders learn how to conduct themselves in society, she found no shortage of recruits; as Philip Snowden later pointed out, most Labour voters were pleased rather than outraged when their newspapers published pictures of their representatives arrayed in all the glory of court dress. Labour men and women were in revolt against an economic system which denied them human dignity, but they wished to make it easier for people like themselves to rise within the status hierarchy, not to overturn it altogether.[27] If this was true of the Labour movement, moreover, it was even more true of the former Liberals whose votes Labour would need if it was ever to form a Government. For many of these, the notion of Labour in power must have carried alarming overtones of upheaval and expropriation. If they were to be persuaded to vote Labour, they would have to be convinced of Labour's respectability. No doubt Clynes or Henderson would have been able to do this as successfully as MacDonald did. Only MacDonald, however, combined respectability with panache.

He also possessed one further asset. Unlike the purists of the Left, he had always recognized that the future of progressive politics in Britain lay in an alliance between organized labour and the Radical wing of the Liberal Party. This had been one of his central objectives as candidate for Southampton, as secretary of the Labour Representation Committee and as chairman of the parliamentary Labour Party; in pursuit of it he had fought more than one battle against his own political colleagues. Unlike some of his rivals on the Right, however, he had also recognized consistently that, if such an alliance was to come into existence, Labour would have to be an equal ally, negotiating from a position of strength. Now, for the first time in his career, there was a possibility that the progressive coalition for which he had hankered since the early 'nineties might come into being under the aegis of the Labour Party. If this happened while he was leader, it would represent, as it would for no other Labour politician, the culmination of the efforts of a quarter of a century.

III

None of this guaranteed his return to the leadership. The odds against him, though not quite as overwhelming as they seemed in January 1919, were nevertheless formidable; and a long and determined struggle was needed to overcome them. It is a mark of MacDonald's toughness and resilience that, within a few weeks of his election defeat, the struggle had begun.

It did so at Berne, in February 1919. The long-awaited conference of the Second International, for which MacDonald had been calling since the outbreak of the war, had at last assembled. The city was swarming with police spies and *agents provocateurs*. MacDonald recognized a female agent whom he suspected of having been used as 'bait' for him by the War Office once before, and reported ungallantly to the readers of *Forward* that she was beginning to look 'thin and scraggy under her make-up'. Later in the proceedings, some documents which had been found in the street were brought to him for inspection. They turned out to be the letters of an agent in British pay, reporting back to his superiors in London and asking for more funds. The British delegates, MacDonald reported, copied them out and returned them with their compliments 'very emphatically expressed' to the British Legation.[28]

These, however, were minor distractions. The conference had two main purposes: to bring the influence of organized labour to bear on the peace conference at Paris, and to reconstruct the International as a bulwark against future wars. MacDonald played a leading part in the pursuit of both these objectives. On the third day, the commission which had been debating the International's attitude to the proposed League of Nations, currently under discussion at Paris, put forward a resolution demanding that it should be organized on the basis of self-determination, disarmament, free trade and the international control of the production and distribution of food and raw materials. MacDonald proposed an amendment, insisting that the governing body should be elected by the Parliaments of the member-states instead of being appointed by their governments. During the war, his attitude to a future League of Nations had been lukewarm — largely on the grounds that it might divert attention from the supreme issue of disarmament. Now he was more enthusiastic. He made it clear that, for him, disarmament still had pride of place; but he was now prepared to concede that a properly constituted League would be an important asset for peace. This, however, made it all the more essential to ensure that it was subject to democratic control:

> The League must have legislative functions. It should determine peace or war, make economic arrangements, decide whether a nation is to be punished or not and settle whether soldiers have to march across frontiers. Are we going to place in the hands of a League of Governments, a League of Cabinets – the power to make peace or war? I am not ... Our League of Nations must be ... a League of Parliaments, a League of Peoples ... Unless that is made clear ... the people will find something very much akin to the Holy Alliance ... dressed up in democratic garb and appealing for confidence in democratic language.[29]

MacDonald's amendment was carried unanimously, and he left Berne with the applause of his comrades ringing in his ears. On its last day the conference set up a permanent commission to carry out its resolutions, and bring pressure to bear on the peace conference at Paris. The permanent commission elected a delegation of nine to present the resolutions to Clemenceau, the president of the peace conference; and a committee of action to follow the proceedings at Paris and intervene whenever possible on behalf of the International. MacDonald was elected to both bodies; and in March he travelled back to Paris for a meeting of the action committee. On his journey to Berne he had found the atmosphere of the peace conference surprisingly hopeful.[30] This time, his impressions were more gloomy. By now, the draft covenant of the League of Nations had been made public. It made a mockery of MacDonald's vision of an international legislature, responsible to democratic electorates. The League it foreshadowed was a League of Governments: and of victorious Governments at that. 'The executive of the League, as it is proposed to be constituted, is but an executive of the present Allies,' MacDonald wrote in an indignant attack on 'the new Holy Alliance' in the *Labour Leader*. 'The neutral nations have not been consulted; the Central Democracies have not been consulted, nor has Russia; and the constitution has been so drafted that even when these come in they are to occupy a position in the League which they will not accept if they have any self-respect.'[31] Perhaps because of this, Paris now seemed 'broken and dirty', and the captured German guns which lay in hundreds in the Place de la Concorde, had come 'to look like the overflow of a store of a dealer in old iron'.[32]

All the same, MacDonald and his colleagues did their best to carry out the mandate they had been given at Berne. The French socialists, MacDonald noted despairingly, were 'savages as regards punctuality',[33] but in spite of unnecessary delays the committee managed to pass a number of resolutions on the League, which it then presented to Lord Robert Cecil. Cecil assured them that Russia and Germany would be admitted to the League as soon as possible, but to MacDonald his manner seemed oddly evasive. His 'line of reply', MacDonald noted suspiciously, was ' "I agree with you but I am overruled by the other states." '[34] Further disappointments were in store. A month later, the permanent commission elected at Berne met at Amsterdam. It reaffirmed the need for a comprehensive League, elected by the Parliaments of the member-states; passed a series of resolutions on the territorial settlement, based on the principle of self-determination; decided that the committee of action should insist on seeing the Council of Four at Paris; and announced that it would oppose any peace settlement that conflicted with President Wilson's Fourteen Points. But in spite of these brave words, MacDonald found the conference disappointing. 'Fault of the International is that it has become too Parliamentary & has no vision ... ,' he noted sourly. 'A body representing the sections in such diverse states of political development & Socialist national parties which differ so much in degrees of power must not be controlled by men who are burdened with responsibility. Parliamentary life dulls the fires of enthusiasm.'[35]

His forebodings were soon justified. At the beginning of May, the draft peace treaty was presented to the German delegation at Paris; at the end of June the final version was signed amid the ominous splendours of Versailles. By the standards of the settlement which the Germans had imposed on the Russians at Brest-Litovsk, or even by the standards of the settlement which the French would have liked to impose on the Germans, it was an enlightened document. But for MacDonald, as for most liberals and Social Democrats, such comparisons were irrelevant. 'We are beholding an act of madness unparalleled in history,' he wrote in the *Labour Leader*. 'Two or three men, baptised with Christian rites, and born and brought up under civilisation, in order to taste the sweet satisfaction of power, are breaking to pieces all the barriers which time has raised between order and chaos.' The economic clauses of the treaty meant that, for years to come, the German worker would be 'an economic slave to other nations'; and since slavery was indivisible, this meant that the British worker would lose his freedom too. The principle of self-determination had been violated. Worst of all, peace had been jeopardized.[36] This 'peace to end peace', moreover, was the inevitable result of the war to end war which had preceded it. President Wilson had been outmanœuvred, and the idealistic supporters of the war had been betrayed. As MacDonald put it in the *Socialist Review*:

President Wilson ... went to Paris sincerely intending to bring away from it ... a League of Nations which would be representative of the people, and would secure peace by removing the causes of war as they arose. The American, however, was no match for the European diplomatists ... M. Clemenceau, the avenger ... has been the supreme power at the Confe-rence ... The Italian Government was frankly out for conquest ... Finally, there is Mr Lloyd George, clever but unanchored, resourceful but without knowledge ... Of all the plenipotentiaries he was the least fitted for his task. He immerses himself in whatever he has in hand; he is a mere spill on whatever current he happens to float. He has been on both sides of every controversy that has divided the Conference ...

Such being the authors, need we be surprised at the proposals? To inflict punishment on Germany, they outrage Europe; millions of Germans, Russians, Jugo-Slavs, Bulgarians, Turks are cut off from their racial kinship; boundaries are drawn without reference to the popular will; areas rich in minerals are attached to foreign states to please the greed of capitalists ...

The Independent Labour Party and the overwhelming majority of British Socialists may be excused if they behold these events with some complacency. For they all belong to the logic of war ... Figs cannot be gathered from thistles. Those who in the name of 'sacred national unity' caught up the emotions which were let loose in August 1914 may reject this treaty, but they sowed the thistles.[37]

In the long run, this argument was to be one of MacDonald's greatest political assets. The 1919 peace settlement was greeted with a chorus of indignation from the liberal intelligentsia. Within a few months, Keynes's famous *Economic Consequences of the Peace*, which reads in places like an expanded, better-written and more acidulous version of MacDonald's criticisms in the *Socialist Review*, appeared on the bookstalls. Before long, the folly and wickedness of Versailles were articles of faith on the Left. Even the Right soon ceased to defend it; and many of those who had taken part in sowing the thistles in August 1914 slowly came to believe that MacDonald had been right in opposing them.

In the short run, however, the asset yielded few dividends. At the beginning of May, the action committee of the International refused to adopt a manifesto drafted by MacDonald, condemning the draft treaty 'in detail & in spirit', and insisted on watering down his criticisms in order to make them more acceptable to the Council of Four. 'The International cannot back up its decisions,' MacDonald noted. 'It is not a power lying through the days, but a thing that comes up now and again.'[38] The reaction of the British Labour Party was equally disappointing. At the party conference in June, MacDonald moved a resolution attacking the 'harsh provisions' of the treaty, demanding the speedy admission of Germany to the League, and calling on the Labour movement to promote a vigorous campaign to win popular support for this policy.[39] The resolution was passed: but in the parliamentary party, at least, vigorous campaigning, indeed vigour of any sort, was conspicuous by its absence. When Lloyd George presented the peace terms to Parliament at the beginning of July, MacDonald was horrified to notice that 'Labour's speech in reply missed every weak point in the Premier's statement.'[40] The final vote at the end of the month horrified him even more. Only one Labour M.P. went through the division lobby against the Government. 'In the whole history of the failures of the Party there is nothing to be compared to this,' MacDonald declared, with justifiable indignation. 'The Party with all it stands for in international politics was completely let down.'[41]

IV

The battle for the peace settlement had been lost. To MacDonald, this made it all the more necessary that the battle for the International should be fought. For four years he had warned that a military victory would lead to a military peace, and that a military peace would sow the seeds of future wars. Everything that had happened since the Armistice seemed to prove him right. Militarism and secret diplomacy had triumphed, as he had said they would, with the results he had foreseen. In these circumstances, the scattered and divided forces of international Social Democracy seemed to represent the last, faint hope of preventing his own prophecies from coming true, and for the next three years the central theme of his political life is to be found in a long, stubborn struggle to bring them together. To a generation for whom the whole concept of international socialism is at most a memory, this struggle may seem at first sight remote and irrelevant – the more so, since it has to be pursued through drab committee minutes and forgotten polemics. Even in MacDonald's own generation, many must have seen it as a distraction from the urgent tasks the Labour movement faced at home. To MacDonald, it was the reverse of irrelevant. The struggle to prevent a new war was the supreme issue of politics, and in that wider struggle the struggle to reconstruct the International had a central place.

It had to be waged on at least three fronts. At the beginning of March 1919, a month after the Berne conference, the foundation congress of the Communist International was held in Moscow. It adopted a manifesto declaring its members to be the sole legitimate heirs of Marx and Engels, and denouncing the parties of the Second International as 'hangmen of the working class'; and it committed itself to the dictatorship of the proletariat and the self-rule of the masses in place of parliamentary government. But the split between the Second and Third Internationals was only one of the obstacles to be overcome if the Second was to be rebuilt. Another was the internal disarray of the Second itself. Two groups were represented at Berne – the pro-war parties, like the British Labour Party, and the majority faction of the German Social Democrats; and the anti-war parties like the I.L.P., the German Independents, the Austrians and the followers of Jean Longuet in the French party. From Moscow's point of view, there was nothing to choose between the two. If anything, 'social pacifists' were more obnoxious to Lenin than 'social chauvinists'. But, to the anti-war parties themselves, the distinction was of crucial importance. They believed, with some justification, that the pro-war parties had betrayed the cause of internationalism and working-class solidarity, to which they themselves had remained faithful in the face of ostracism and persecution; and they could not help remembering that on the over-riding issue of the war, Lenin and they had been on the same side. Thus they were anxious to avoid an irreconcilable split between Moscow and Berne, and hankered after a comprehensive International on the pre-war pattern, representing the entire working-class movement from the Bolsheviks to the British Labour Party. To Lenin and his followers, however, such notions were anathema. The only International they were prepared to join was an International under their own control; and they regarded all other bodies which claimed to speak for the working class with implacable and unrelenting hostility. Thus, working-class politics after the war fell into a strange, triangular pattern. At the base of the triangle, the Communists and the old, pro-war Social Democrats glowered at each other from their respective corners. At the apex were the anti-war parties of the Second International, vainly trying to arrange a reconciliation between the other two — and receiving more abuse than gratitude for their pains.[42]

MacDonald's position in this triangle was at first ambiguous. The scars left by the war had by no means healed. His attitude to the Bolsheviks was still coloured by his admiration for Trotsky's stand at Brest-Litovsk, and for Lenin's courage in forcing through a social revolution in the face of foreign intervention and civil war. The stories of a Red Terror which filled the capitalist press seemed to him a smokescreen, put down by the Allied Governments to conceal their own interference in Russian affairs.[43] All this inclined him to the middle group of socialist parties, which hoped to avoid an outright split between Moscow and Berne. On the other hand, he was a lifelong democrat and a convinced believer in parliamentary methods. Bolshevism in Russia might be inevitable, and should certainly be defended against outside intervention. But the spread of Bolshevism to the rest of Europe was a danger to be averted, not a promise to be welcomed; and the spread of Bolshevik ideas in the Labour movements of the west was at best modish frivolity — 'trying to dance a Russian ballet in kilts,' as he put it in *Forward* — and at worst a serious threat.

Thus, when the Berne conference debated the famous resolution on Democracy and Dictatorship proposed by the Swedish socialist, Hjalmar Branting, which declared that socialism could only develop on the basis of parliamentary democracy and free speech, he sat uncomfortably, though not inelegantly, on the fence. 'Liberty, democracy, freedom,' he declared, 'must be their steady and unchangeable goal.' On the other hand, it would be premature to make a pronouncement at this moment:

Who among them could define Bolshevism? Would they define it in accordance with Lloyd George's speeches, or from the columns of the capitalist press? Or would they define it from the pamphlets that ha[d] been allowed to go into the Entente countries during the war? Speaking for Great Britain, wherever Bolshevist pamphlets were to be found, they were seized by the police ... He appealed to those who did not altogether agree with the resolution, to register their protests, but to do nothing that would split the International. In a month or two, when things might be clearer, he wanted another Conference with their Swiss, Italian and other comrades present when this subject could be discussed at greater length ... At the moment, all that they should do ... was to hold up the flag of Socialism, on the same flagstaff, planted on the same place as before.[44]

MacDonald's fence, however, was soon shot away from under him. The Branting resolution was countered by the so-called Adler–Longuet resolution, put forward by the Austrians and the anti-war section of the French party. This denounced the pro-war parties for making international co-operation more difficult, warned against placing a stigma of any kind on the Soviet regime, and insisted that membership of the International should be open to all socialist parties conscious of their class interests. The Branting resolution was carried, but the Adler–Longuet resolution was supported by most of the neutral parties as well as by its two sponsors. During the spring and summer of 1919, more-over, the attitudes behind the Adler–Longuet resolution gained ground still further. The Bolsheviks were fighting for their lives, against powerful White Russian armies, backed by the Western Allies. In this situation, arguments about the precise nature of the Soviet regime seemed a form of pedantry, and of treacherous pedantry at that. At the end of May, MacDonald visited Italy on behalf of the International, to discuss the policy of the Italian socialists. The mood he found there was becoming increasingly representative of the Labour movement in the rest of Europe. 'The Italian workman', he reported, 'grasps quite definitely that if the present Russian Government goes it is Liberty and Socialism that go — not only in Russia;' as a result 'the demand of "Hands off Russia" ' had become the 'shibboleth test of Socialist rectitude'.[45] A few months later, the Italian socialists decided to affiliate to the Third International.

Similar tendencies were at work in France and Germany. In March 1919, the German Independent Socialists adopted a programme approving the Soviet system and the dictatorship of the proletariat. In August, the permanent com-mission of the International met at Lucerne, to prepare the way for a full conference the following year. Once again, the conference was deeply divided in its attitude to Russia; once again, MacDonald found himself in the un-enviable position of a mediator between two warring camps. Pierre Renaudel, the leader of the French Right, submitted a resolution condemning the peace treaty without mentioning Allied intervention in Russia. This was opposed by the Austrian leader, Fritz Adler, who put forward an alternative resolution denouncing Allied intervention and proclaiming that the International should be based on the uncompromising pursuit of the class struggle. After some complicated diplomacy, in which MacDonald seems to have played a leading part, the conference passed a compromise resolution denouncing Allied intervention without raising more contentious issues. It was clear, however, that the International was seriously endangered by the growing appeal of Moscow, and even more by the growing division between its own right and left wings. As MacDonald reported in a muddled, but revealing, editorial in the *Socialist Review*:

I sat on the Commission where the chief issues were discussed, patiently striving for agreement until, thoroughly worn out in body and in temper by Renaudel's incessant chatter and his utter incapacity to deal with any point without making a tedious rambling speech, I declined to proceed any further and decided to let a prolix statement go to the Conference ... Lucerne lost its chance, and the one clear cut piece of work which it did, the resolution against intervention in Russia ... was completely covered up in a mass of other resolutions ...

... At the moment the contrast between Bolshevism and the Second International appears to be the contrast between deeds and words, and it is impossible to rebut with complete success the arguments adduced in support of this view. But we must not lose grip on realities ... The simple reason is that we have not political power, and I say further that we do not have it because we have never had the patient and intelligent persistence to win it. Some of my friends prefer funicular railways to paths in order to gain mountain tops. There are no funicular railways to Downing Street and to the benches on the right of the Speaker in the House of Commons ... [T]he danger to the Second International is not the Third but sections in itself.[46]

But the funicular railway of the Third International was becoming more and more attractive all the time. In December, the German Independents at last decided to seek affiliation to it; in France, Jean Longuet reported, 'we shall be *absolutely unable* to maintain our party in the 2nd, the only alternative to the third, being to remain outside of both.'[47] Meanwhile, the Belgian socialist party, one of the pillars of the Second, had decided to join a coalition under clerical leadership – thus driving another nail into the Second's coffin and, as MacDonald pointed out indignantly in *Forward*, giving its opponents a new argument to use against it.[48] More ominously still, support for Moscow was gaining ground even in Britain. In December 1919, the Scottish Divisional Council of the I.L.P. voted in favour of affiliating to the Third International; by January 1920, R. C. Wallhead was writing ominously that he felt 'certain that the vote of the Scottish Div upon the 3rd. International is going to influence other divisions to go in the same way. I am attending the Welsh Conf on the 24th. & the Lancs on the 31st. in order to put up a fight but the difficulty will be that upon this question most of the delegates will be instructed.'[49]

V

It was a critical moment in Labour history, and a critical moment in Mac-Donald's career. In Britain, only a few tiny and unrepresentative Marxist sects, with no significant following in the working class and no hope of building a mass party, had so far made overtures to Moscow. The I.L.P. was a very different proposition. In comparison with the Italians or the German Independents, it was a small party. But its membership was booming,[50] its morale was high and it enjoyed influence out of all proportion to its size. If the I.L.P. decided to affiliate to the Third International, there was a distinct possibility that a strong Communist party, able to speak in native accents and to appeal to native traditions, might come into existence on British soil. In the turbulent climate of 1919 and 1920, such a party might make considerable headway. Even if it did not, Moscow would have won a big psychological victory in its struggle for the soul of the international Labour movement.

MacDonald had some sympathy with the attitudes behind the drift towards the Third International. He, too, saw Allied intervention in Russia as a threat, not only to the Russian revolution itself, but to democracy and social progress throughout Europe. He, too, deplored the weakness and timidity of the right-wing Social Democrats who had failed to offer effective resistance to the Allied Governments. But, unlike many I.L.P.-ers, he refused to apply double standards to the use of violence and terror. It was hatred of violence — and still more, perhaps, of the irrationality and fanaticism that go with it — which had inspired his campaign for a compromise peace and his opposition to the strategy of the 'knock-out blow'; he was not prepared to abandon his hatred of violence and terror merely because they were now being employed by people who had been on the same side as he had during the war. Nor was he prepared to deceive himself about the true character of the Bolshevik regime. His initial sympathy for Lenin's internal policy soon wore off. By the summer of 1919 he had come to the conclusion — far more clearly than had most of his supporters on the left of the Labour movement — that the cruelty and fanaticism of the Bolsheviks were not accidental excesses, but the inevitable consequences of the Leninist creed, and from then on he threw himself into a passionate campaign to save the I.L.P. from the Leninist embrace.

It was conducted with considerable subtlety. Communism, he insisted again and again, was 'pre-scientific' and, indeed, 'pre-Marxian'; it could be applied only in countries 'in a pre-capitalist stage of evolution'.[51] In the West, at any rate, flirtations with Communism damaged the Labour movement and strengthened the extreme Right, without even benefiting the Russians. In the recent elections in France, he pointed out in January 1920, the socialists had 'espoused the cause of Soviet Russia' so warmly that they had come near to advocating Bolshevism as an election issue; the result was a 'union of all the forces of reaction and constitutionalism', and a sharp reduction in the number of socialist deputies.[52] The Italians' adherence to the Third International, he argued soon afterwards, 'has not had the slightest effect upon Italy's internal policy nor upon Italy's support for Russia. Indeed, had there been the same proportion of I.L.P. members returned to the House of Commons as there has been Italian Socialists to the Chamber of Deputies, we would have done more for the Russian Revolution than the Italian Socialists have done.'[53] In Germany, he wrote a few months later, the Independent Socialists had 'in a nerveless way swung hither and thither', compromising with the Spartacists and failing to reunite with the majority; it was partly because of this that the elections there had displayed the 'chaos of the German mind' and were likely to intensify the 'chaos of the German state'.[54] For what socialism needed most of all was unity, and support for the Third International could only divide it. Thus, the French supporters of the Third International were committing 'a crime which deserves the support of every sagacious capitalist in Europe',[55] while the Scottish Divisional Council's vote in favour of it was 'a blow to the permanent good of the Socialist cause, and if it were to be repeated by the National Conference at Easter we should be faced with troubles both internal and external which would put those of the war into the shade.'[56]

As we have seen, however, MacDonald's opposition to the Third International was coupled with a deep distrust of the leadership of the Second. Besides, he believed, with some justification, that if the Third International and the discredited, pro-war leaders of the Second were left to fight it out alone, the Third would probably win. From his point of view, it was therefore essential, not merely to fight Communism, but to drive a wedge between Communism and left-wing Social Democracy; and to do that he had not only to win a debating victory against the supporters of the Third International, but to carry at least some of them with him. Hence, his attacks on the philosophy and strategy of the Third International were combined with equally hard-hitting attacks on the atmosphere and style of the Second. In the summer of 1919, he wrote a 30,000-word defence of parliamentary socialism, entitled *Parliament and Revolution*. In many ways, it was the most effective polemic he ever wrote: but one reason for its effectiveness was that it conceded so many of the criticisms of the Second International then current in the Labour movement. The Second International, MacDonald wrote, had allowed itself to be treated with contempt. It had met at Berne and declared itself on the great international issues of the day:

Nothing has happened ... Its Permanent Commission has met in Amsterdam and again in Lucerne. It has repeated its wisdom and the Governments have repeated their rebuffs. Never has a more ample supply of crumbs been thrown from the master's table; never with more insult has Labour

been refused a place at the feast ... No one requires to come and tell me, by
marshalled argument and indignant rhetoric, of the humiliation under
which Labour suffers. It cuts like a thong into one's soul.[57]

On two essential points, however, he made no concessions. The first was the
fundamentally anti-socialist character of the Soviet system itself. Workers'
soviets, MacDonald argued, were less likely than a democratic Parliament to
lead to a socialist commonwealth. Class did not guarantee opinion: in Britain,
it was notorious that a large number of trade unionists voted against Labour
candidates. The real purpose of the Soviet franchise was to give power, not to
the proletariat, but to 'an intellectual minority of the minority'.[58] Worse still,
the system of indirect election – in which only the local soviets were directly
responsible to the people, and in turn elected the sovereign authorities of the
state – was the antithesis of democracy:

> It is a mean conception ... and in the end will result in bureaucracy of a bad
> kind. If it is impossible to get decisions on great questions of national
> importance from the mass of electors, if it is impossible to create the supreme
> political authority directly by popular votes, then let us frankly abandon
> our democratic creed ... We give up the ideal of self-government. As a
> matter of fact that is what the Bolshevist theory leads to. It is in essence and
> spirit a government of the select.[59]

The same was true of the dictatorship of the proletariat. At the height of a
revolution, MacDonald conceded, representative government was impossible.
But, even in a revolution, force and repression should be kept to the minimum,
since they could only make it harder for the revolution to take root. A revolutionary dictatorship might be necessary to 'guide a revolution into democracy',[60]
but it must be a short-lived expedient, not a permanent feature of the landscape.
For Lenin, however, dictatorship was not a short-lived expedient. On the
contrary, he had made it clear that it would have to last throughout the long
period of transition from capitalism to socialism. His was a 'tyranny to end all
tyranny',[61] as dangerous a concept as the militarist's war to end all wars. Faced
with this,

> [T]he Independent Labour Party has to repeat all the political arguments it
> used during the war – arguments that received the crown of fulfilment
> almost as they were being uttered. A revolution made in the spirit and with
> the weapons of the old society cannot be made the occasion of the birth of
> the new world. That principle guided us well in the war; it must guide us
> now. Tyranny, like war, breeds its progeny after its own kind ...
>
> ... Repression increases the difficulties which it was begun to meet and it
> entangles and does not free; repression ... once begun influences the whole
> of the policy of the government as a drop of dye in a glass of water;
> repression multiplies the general difficulties which the 'dictatorship' has to

meet in emerging ... into the democratic phase of the revolution; repression makes a government lose itself in daily details and obscures general intentions; repression transfers policy from the personalities which alone can maintain a 'dictatorship' into the bureaucracies ... which work repression, and so the revolution changes from being a movement of ideas to becoming a series of bloody events; repression finally develops into a complete policy of extermination and destroys that of national conversion ...

... When the policeman and the soldier are called in ... they accept the invitation, not to help ... but to dominate ... But if the soldier is not to be used, the preparation before the Revolution must be one of political propaganda, which creates the new society in the bosom of the old as the butterfly grows in the chrysalis. Unless Society is prepared to adopt the new order before the Revolution, there is no guarantee that it will do so after it.[62]

This was the second point of principle; and because of it there could be no compromise with the Third International. In a parliamentary regime, MacDonald was arguing, Leninism was either doomed or unnecessary. If the society concerned was ripe for socialism, socialists could win power through the ballot box; if it was not, they could not ripen it by force. The notion that a socialist party which had just been defeated in a free election could proceed to win power by a revolution was 'fanciful romance';[63] and the notion that an elected socialist Government would have to use revolutionary methods to overawe its parliamentary opponents was equally fanciful. If it had public opinion behind it, it need not fear parliamentary obstruction; if it did not, it would be as incapable of carrying through a revolution as of managing Parliament. But Lenin refused to accept that circumstances varied from one country to another, and seemed determined to force the entire Labour movement of Europe into the Russian mould. Few of the supporters of the Third International in the I.L.P., MacDonald pointed out in the *Socialist Review*, really believed in the dictatorship of the proletariat or in the necessity of an armed uprising against the bourgeoisie. If they wished to join the Third International, however, they would have to accept these 'credal points' whether they liked them or not.[64] Moscow, he pointed out at the I.L.P. conference in April 1920, had laid down the dictatorship of the proletariat 'not as a Russian expediency, but as a British expediency as well'.[65] If the I.L.P. applied for membership of the Third International, it would in fact be saying, whether it intended to or not, that the time had come to arm the working class and start a violent revolution in Britain.

VI

MacDonald's arguments seem commonplace today. They were far from commonplace fifty years ago. In April 1920, George Lansbury – a lifelong

pacifist, and one of the most humane figures in the history of British socialism —
solemnly assured the readers of the *Daily Herald*, on the strength of a short visit
to Russia, that it was untrue that membership of the Third International would
commit the I.L.P. to violent revolution,[66] and denied that Lenin wanted other
socialist parties to follow the Russian model. Lansbury spoke for most of the
delegates to the I.L.P. conference. In spite of MacDonald's opposition, it
decided by a crushing majority to disaffiliate from the Second International, and
although it shrank from outright affiliation to the Third it also decided to send
a deputation to Moscow to discover the terms on which affiliation could be
obtained. 'What we are really driving at is this,' MacDonald commented
scornfully in *Forward*: 'We hope that Moscow will say for our benefit that it
is not Moscow, that dictatorship is not dictatorship, revolution not revolution,
and that in the Russian turmoil the English language as well as the bourgeoisie
has been upset.'[67]

Undeterred by his mockery, however, the I.L.P. deputation duly departed
— only to return with conditions even more onerous than those he had foreseen. Moscow, it turned out, really was Moscow: revolution really did mean
revolution. Even in Britain, declared the executive of the Third International,
the bourgeoisie could only be defeated by violence. As for the difference between Communism and other forms of socialism, there were no other forms:
there was only Communism. Although this reply killed the notion that the
I.L.P. could find a satisfactory home for itself in the Third International, most
I.L.P.-ers still refused to return to the Second. Accordingly, the party council
put out feelers to the German Independents and the Swiss, and in December
1920 it joined with them in summoning a preliminary conference at Berne, to
discuss the principles on which a comprehensive International could be based.
The conference issued a manifesto denouncing the Second International for its
reformism, and the Third for its dogmatism; and agreed to establish an International Working Union of socialist parties to begin the work of reconstruction. In February 1921, the first conference of the International Working
Union — soon known as the 'two-and-a-half International' — took place in
Vienna; and the split between the right and left wings of Social Democracy
seemed complete.[68]

MacDonald watched these developments with an increasingly sceptical eye.
In July 1920 he visited Berlin for the first time since the war. Germany, he
found, was still reeling from the effects of the Allied blockade. He was particularly shocked by the 'large hungry eyes' of the children in the streets, and the
sight of university students, 'buttoned up to the necks for economy's sake',
eating meals supplied by charity.[69] Only one degree less shocking, however,
was the failure of German socialism. For it seemed that the sole effect of the
revolution had been to strengthen German capitalism — and the chief responsibility for this lay with the socialists, particularly with the Independents. They
had refused to take part in a socialist Government because they could not obtain

all that they asked for; and their refusal had made any sort of socialism impossible. Their position, MacDonald commented ominously, was 'a warning to the I.L.P. to make up its mind where it stands'.[70]

The warning was underlined a few weeks later when he visited the Menshevik Republic of Georgia with a deputation from the Second International. MacDonald loved the East, and he responded enthusiastically to the visual spectacle of mountain peaks 'flashing in eternal snow', and horsemen 'like Greek Gods with fine cut faces', daggers at their waists and flowing sheepskin coats around their shoulders. The journey to Kazbek, in particular, left an indelible impression:

> Just as the pink was fading from the distant snows and the nearer greys and the greens were being submerged in the rising tides of deep blue, two horsemen wheeled into the middle of the road with a shout that was like a war cry, and proceeded ahead of our car in a wild gallop. One carried a red flag on a spear shaft. As we went down, new groups joined, until, about us and behind, there must have been a hundred horsemen, and the valley was filled with riotous shouts and echoes ...
>
> At the villages, there were waiting crowds and triumphal arches bearing in different forms salutations to Socialism and the International. We could just see them as we whizzed through, slackening our speed to let the torrent flow with us. At one place we stopped. The crowd blocked the way, speeches had to be made and ceremonies of welcome performed ... For the first time we could examine our escort, and the first impression was that we had been captured and made prisoners ...
>
> But who can describe the lithe virile riders who sat on their horses as though horse and man were one, who were never still for a moment, whose faces were like glowing pages telling of many battles, wild slaughter and much else that man does when his blood is hot ... The whole surged with ebullient animation, which could not be controlled when an old greybeard rode up to receive us into the fellowship of the mountains and to welcome us as men whose names had gone before them and who came as the ambassadors of the Socialist International to the new mountain State of Georgia.
>
> They danced and they sang before us on the roadway — strange gallant dances, just a little like our own barn dances, but with a barbaric demeanour in them, we clapping our hands in rhythmic time; they fought mimic fights with sword and shield. Higher and higher rose the excitement, the choruses, the shouts. And over all, the moon and snowclad mountains imperturbable, and the fluttering red flag borne on a spear.[71]

He responded even more to the sight of Social Democracy in action. The land had been expropriated from the large landowners; the mines, the forests and the railways had been nationalized; schemes for the democratic control of industry were in preparation. The Georgian socialists, moreover, believed in

democracy and parliamentary methods. Free elections had been held, and
freedom of speech was allowed. To MacDonald, all this was welcome, not only
for its own sake, but as a proof that the ideals of the I.L.P. would work in
practice. 'I never felt prouder of being a member of the Independent Labour
Party,' he concluded rhapsodically. 'I saw what I should like this country to
be—a real community of men and women, dancing and singing in the gaiety
of heart.'[72] This paradise of Social Democracy and political harmony, however,
was already menaced by Bolshevik subversion and the threat of invasion by the
Red Army. Once again, the moral seemed obvious.

Meanwhile, the increasingly moribund Second International had advanced
a stage further towards disintegration. In August 1920, it held a conference at
Geneva. But the socialist parties of France, Italy, Switzerland, Norway and the
United States were not represented; nor, of course, were the German Independents or the I.L.P. All that was left of the International of Bebel and Jaurès
was an anti-Communist rump, dominated by the British Labour Party and the
German Right. If such an organization spoke in the name of the workers of the
world, no one would listen. Accordingly, the conference decided that the headquarters of the Second International should be moved to London, and called
upon the British Labour Party to negotiate on its behalf with the parties which
had refused to send delegates to Geneva. After some hesitation, the Labour
Party Executive agreed; and in November 1920 it invited MacDonald and the
dockers' leader, Harry Gosling, to act as joint secretaries of the International
until the negotiations were completed.

For MacDonald, it must have been an embarrassing invitation. No one had
denounced the Second International more vigorously than he. Indeed, he had
even denounced the suggestion that the Labour Party should try to reconstruct
it. Moreover, the I.L.P. was now outside it, and was actively trying to replace it.
On the other hand, the policy of the I.L.P. and its sister parties on the continent
made sense only on the twin assumptions that the split between Communism
and Social Democracy was due to the Social Democrats as much as to the
Communists, and that it could be healed altogether if only the Social Democrats would make the necessary concessions. To MacDonald, both assumptions
seemed false: and they seemed even more false by the winter of 1920 than they
had seemed in the spring. Doubtfully, and with much heart-searching, he
accepted the Executive's invitation.[73] A month later, he was censured for doing
so by the I.L.P. council.[74] He persuaded it to rescind its decision without much
difficulty; but it was clear that he was running a considerable political risk.

VII

For the next eighteen months, at least, he must have felt that his doubts had
been only too well founded. His policy as secretary was simple. 'There must be

an International apart from the Third,' he wrote in January 1921, 'and it will be a great calamity if that other will be composed only of the political Right.'[75] Once again, his objective was to drive a wedge between the moderate Left and the extreme Left: to isolate Moscow by uniting the rest of the international Labour movement against it. But this was easier said than done. MacDonald's policy was totally at variance with that of the Vienna Union, and the Vienna Union was not prepared to abandon its position without a struggle.

His first act as secretary was to draft a long statement on the International to be sent, in the form of a letter from the British Labour Party, to 'the Socialist and Communist parties of the world'. The letter, MacDonald explained privately to the Dutch socialist leader, Pieter Troelstra, was not a definitive statement of principles. It was merely 'an argument for an attempt to reconstruct the International', and its sole purpose was to bridge the gulf between the parties which still remained in the Second International, and those which had left it.[76] In spite of the sugar around it, however, MacDonald's letter contained a pill which the Vienna Union could not possibly swallow. This was a paragraph insisting that any future International would have to be based on unequivocal support for democratic methods in countries where democracy already existed.[77] This, of course, begged the fundamental question. The Vienna Union wanted a comprehensive International or nothing. It had no interest in collaborating with the Second International unless the Communists could be brought in as well. The fact that the Communists were not prepared to come in only made it all the more determined to stick to its guns.

In the face of this adamantine perseverance, MacDonald's negotiating skills were of no avail. In April 1921, the executive of the Second International held a joint meeting with the Bureau of the Trade Union International at Amsterdam to discuss reparations. This was one of the most burning issues of post-war politics; and one ideally suited to joint action by the Labour movements of Europe. But the Vienna Union, which was also holding a conference at Amsterdam on the reparations issue, refused to take part in any discussion at which representatives of the Second International were present. In the end, MacDonald reported disconsolately, 'we exchanged documents with the Trade Union Bureau alone, over a cup of tea and a cigar (the only remnant that remains of a cheap and democratic Holland).'[78] Two months later, the annual conference of the Labour Party called unanimously for consultations between the executive of the Second International and the Vienna Union. Once again, the Vienna Union refused to take part in discussions with the Second International, and although it was finally persuaded to take part in a conference with the Labour Party Executive instead, it soon became clear that the gulf between them was unbridgeable. The conference took place in the Caxton Hall in October 1921. MacDonald made a gallant attempt to play the honest broker, but his attempt was foiled — partly by the brusque intransigence of Henderson, but even more by the prolix refusal of the Vienna delegates to take part in any international conference without the Communists.[79] As he noted afterwards:

> Vienna people playing to preserve appearances lest they be accused of reformism. Henderson on the other hand bullying & no sense of spirit of negotiations. Tried to smooth difficulties without abandoning our position & got Executive to take that view. The tone of written reply sent by Vienna Executive ... made further negotiations impossible, & when Committee of Lab: Party Executive met at H. of C. in the evening to receive the reply ... it was no use my carrying out my intention to move for a joint meeting in the morning. The Labour Party, we decided[,] should send a reply in writing regretting the decision of Vienna & there the matter ended.[80]

Two months later, however, the situation was transformed by Lenin's famous speech to the ninth Soviet congress in favour of peaceful co-existence with the capitalist world, and by the decision of the Third International to abandon its hostility to any form of joint action with other working-class organizations in favour of a 'united front' with Social Democracy. For the Communists, these decisions represented a tactical retreat, made necessary by the domestic situation in Russia after the civil war; the 'united front' was merely the external corollary of the abandonment of war Communism and the inauguration of the New Economic Policy. Indeed, the executive of the Third International explicitly declared that the point of the united front was to discredit the Social Democratic leaders and win over the rank and file to Communism. Nevertheless, its change of course had a dramatic effect on the Labour movement throughout Europe. In January 1922 the Vienna Union issued a general invitation to an 'international conference of the class-conscious world proletariat'; and at the beginning of April a preliminary conference representing the executives of the three Internationals was held in a crowded, smoke-filled room in the Reichstag building in Berlin, while a snowstorm raged outside.[81] It was the first time since August 1914 that representatives of all the tendencies in the international Labour movement had met under the same roof.

From the point of view of the Second International, the mere fact that the Berlin Conference had taken place at all was, of course, a setback. MacDonald had hoped to unite with Vienna against Moscow. Now it looked as though he might be forced to unite with them both, in order to prevent them from uniting against him. 'I regret that the Vienna Union, now that it has been forced to meet with the Second International, has insisted that the Third should be there as well,' he explained candidly in his column in *Forward*. 'We should have faced our difficulties by stages, and, first of all, united those who were divided without good cause.'[82] In spite of these misgivings, however, he played an active part in the conference and, in the private discussions of the Second International delegates, his position was a good deal more flexible than that of his colleagues. The Second International had only agreed to take part in the preliminary conference on condition that its delegates could raise the questions of the Soviet invasion of Georgia and the treatment of the Social Revolutionary prisoners in Russia. On the first day, the Belgian leader, Émile Vandervelde, insisted that before a united front could be formed the Communists would have to provide evidence of their good faith on these two issues. His answer was an abusive speech from Karl Radek, who demanded a full conference without conditions. Next day, the Second International delegates agreed that unless Radek modified his position, it would be a waste of time to prolong the conference – MacDonald alone urging that even if it broke down, a further attempt should be made to make contact with Vienna.[83] When the conference resumed, he gave the Second International's reply to Radek:

> Georgia had a Socialist Government. The party in Georgia responsible for that Government is affiliated to us; the party in Georgia responsible for that Government is represented here by a delegate sitting at this table. You suppressed it by military force. You hold your position now there to-day by military force. We say: How can we act together until the Government for which we are responsible is re-established – or at any rate until the military occupation which has excluded them from the country is withdrawn and the people of the country have a chance of saying whether they want you or us ... We offer you a proposal: send a commission representative of Socialist tendencies, give them a chance of enquiring and issuing a report ...
>
> ... Vandervelde asked for information ... with reference to prisoners. You hold these men in your prisons, and you are going to try them. Vandervelde asks: 'Will you satisfy the International Socialist movement as to the nature of the trial?' Radek ... tries to stir up our feelings by mentioning the name of Rosa Luxemburg. What did Rosa Luxemburg try to do? She tried to liberate Germany from what she considered to be a tyranny. (*Interruption: You agree?*) I am glad that Radek agrees to that way of stating it. What were those prisoners you hold trying to do? They were trying to liberate Russia from what they considered a tyranny. You say the Government in power here was responsible for Rosa Luxemburg's murder. Why do you go and copy the same thing yourselves? ... Those men are our colleagues ... [C]an you imagine us saying that this is all going to be put in the background ... whilst you hold the lives of our comrades in your hands because they are our comrades? Your strategy is too refined. Your tactics are too clever.[84]

In the end, after long and heated negotiations, agreement was reached on terms very close to those laid down by MacDonald and Vandervelde. The Second International agreed to take part in a general conference, as a first step towards a united front. In return, the Third International promised to abandon

the tactic of infiltrating Social Democratic parties and trade unions as a preliminary to splitting and destroying them; and agreed that all the relevant
documents about the situation in Georgia would be placed before a commission
representing the three Internationals. Radek promised that no death penalty
should be imposed on the Social Revolutionary prisoners, and that Vandervelde
would be given a safe conduct to Moscow to act as their defence counsel.
Finally it was decided to set up a committee of nine, consisting of three representatives from each of the three executives, to continue the work of the
conference. MacDonald was chosen as one of the Second International's representatives on the committee of nine, and left Berlin in euphoric spirits. 'I was
really very glad to meet the delegates of the Third,' he wrote triumphantly, if
implausibly, in *Forward*. 'I disagree with them, and told them in public that
they would have to retreat from their political, as they have from their economic, tactics. I believe they are making up their minds to do this.'[85]

These hopes were soon disappointed. A few days after the Berlin conference
broke up, *Pravda* reported that Lenin had criticized the Communist delegates
for making too many concessions to the 'reactionary bourgeoisie', and in
particular for promising that no death penalty would be imposed on the Social
Revolutionary prisoners. Towards the end of April, the Paris representative of
the Social Revolutionary party wrote in alarm to MacDonald, to tell him that
the Soviet minister of justice had declared that the Berlin agreement would
not prevent the judges concerned from sentencing the prisoners to death.[86]
Meanwhile, Radek had demanded an immediate meeting of the committee of
nine to discuss the forthcoming international conference at Genoa — a serious
matter for the Russians, who feared that the capitalist powers might decide to
take joint action of some kind against them.[87] MacDonald assured Radek that
he, too, wanted the committee to meet as soon as possible,[88] but Otto Wels,
the German leader, feared that excessive haste might play into the hands of the
Vienna Union,[89] and in the end no meeting took place until May 23rd. By then,
the Genoa conference was over; the Russians had made the Rapallo agreement
with Germany; and the chief Communist motive for a united front had disappeared. At the meeting of the nine, MacDonald submitted a memorandum
accusing the Communists of reneging on the undertakings they had given at
Berlin. Radek thereupon withdrew, after denouncing the Second International
as a tool of reaction.[90] The united front had collapsed before it had been
established.

MacDonald had been awaiting this opportunity for eighteen months. At the
end of May, he wrote to Adler, to say that 'in view of the disastrous divisions
in the Socialist ranks kept up by the separation of the Second International and
the Vienna Union, but even more pressingly in view of the terrible state of
Europe, both politically and economically,' the British Labour Party intended
to call a conference in London of all the parties affiliated to the Second International, and hoped that the Vienna Union might 'even now ... consider

whether it is not imperative that a new attempt should be made to bring about co-operation'.[91] In spite of his appeal, the London conference was confined to the Second International. Nothing daunted, it issued yet another invitation to Vienna to take part in a world Labour conference, and by the late summer there were signs that the Vienna Union was beginning to respond. When the Second International executive met at Prague in August 1922, MacDonald was able to write, with justifiable complacency, in his column in *Forward* that the Vienna Union was changing its policy and that there was once more 'a chance of recreating a real International ... The work which I undertook has been finished, the Third International is out, the Vienna Union can no longer obstruct and the time has come to appoint officers for the future rather than for the immediate present ... I give up my office at Prague.'[92] The following May, the Vienna Union and the Second International held a joint international congress in Hamburg. This set up a new 'Labour and Socialist International', which remained in being until the Second World War. MacDonald was unable to be present, but he had the satisfaction of knowing that the struggle which had occupied a big part of his energies since August 1914 had at last been crowned with success. Only time could tell whether his achievement would bear the fruit for which he had hoped.

CHAPTER 13

Woolwich and after

I

THE argument over British Labour's part in the struggle to reconstruct the International was intertwined with an even more complex series of questions. What kind of party was the post-war Labour Party to be? Into what channels was the upsurge of working-class militancy to flow? Was the British Labour movement to remain faithful to its democratic and non-violent traditions? If so, what was the proper relationship between parliamentary action and industrial action – and what was the proper posture for the parliamentary party in the face of the Government's overwhelming majority?

Here, too, MacDonald's position was, at first, ambiguous. In July 1920 he noted in his diary:

> A year without an entry – a busy & victorious year, writing as the Apostles did for the Churches, wandering & preaching as they too did, fighting the Devil, also like them, both in & out of the Churches. The twelve months – silent so far as this diary is concerned, but silent here because they have been anything but silent elsewhere ... have been spent calling on the ILP to be strong & upon the Labour Party to be vigorous & to forget the purple bondage & the flesh pots of Egypt which were its reward for the sorry part it played in the war.[1]

From MacDonald's point of view, a 'vigorous' Labour Party was a precondition of a 'strong' I.L.P.: the blandishments of the Third International could be denounced effectively only if the 'flesh pots of Egypt' were denounced with equal vigour. All his life, he had believed that organized labour could only achieve its aims through Parliament. But he could not forget that while he had been struggling in the wilderness, most of the trade-union leaders and the vast majority of the parliamentary party had enlisted under Lloyd George's banner. Beatrice Webb's diaries make it clear that he was still regarded with uneasy suspicion by the Labour Party leadership; his own diary, that he was only too happy to repay its suspicions with interest. 'Sections of the Labour movement', he noted in January 1919, '[are] now more dead to everything which democracy calls progress than the most snobbish middle class sections;'[2] and he asked himself gloomily whether the trade-union link should be severed altogether.

The Parliamentary Committee of the T.U.C., he exclaimed angrily a few weeks later, had 'neither thought nor vision'; the 'flashpoint' of its members was 'so high that a blazing torch could not set them on fire'.[3] The 'Labour Party leaders', he commented after a conversation with Lord Haldane in July 1920, 'seem unable to hide their jealousy and the walkers on the highway see it.'[4]

Wartime memories were exacerbated by peacetime observation. With one or two exceptions the Labour benches in the 1918 Parliament were bereft of political talent. Again and again, MacDonald found himself groaning in spirit at the incompetence of the leaders and the complacency of the led. To make matters worse, he had good reason to suspect that their incompetence and complacency reflected a much deeper failure of political will. As we have seen, the parliamentary party had resisted leaving the coalition in 1918. When it found itself on the Opposition benches after the election, it seemed strangely uncertain, not only of its tactics, but of its role. Many Labour members visibly hankered for their old client relationship with Lloyd George, and saw themselves, not as a potential governing party, but as a glorified pressure group of the kind they had formed before 1914. In those days, MacDonald had also accepted the limitations of pressure-group politics; and had, indeed, exploited them with considerable skill. In the new circumstances created by the war, he recognized — more clearly and consistently than any other leading Labour politician — that, if it displayed enough audacity and courage, Labour could now aspire to political power in its own right.

Apart from his own attitudes, he could not ignore the attitudes of his supporters in the I.L.P. Between 1918 and 1920, as we have seen, its membership had increased substantially.[5] The young men and women who joined it in such numbers were separated by a vast gulf of mutual incomprehension from the elderly trade-unionists who were supposed to represent their cause in Parliament. They were anxious to build the New Jerusalem, not in ten or twenty years' time, but at once. In default of building it, they wished to fight for it — with passion, and without compromise. The tide which swept them towards the Third International was driven by a variety of forces; but one of the most powerful was undoubtedly an irritation with the ineffectiveness of the parliamentary party, which easily spilled over into impatience with parliamentary action as such, and contributed to a muddled feeling that socialism could be achieved more quickly through the direct use of industrial power than through the laborious processes of the ballot box. Snowden, the party chairman until 1920, sought to provide a 'steadying influence', and fell out of sympathy with the younger men.[6] MacDonald also saw the need for a steadying influence, but he was less rigid than Snowden, and better fitted to bridge the gap between the pre-war and post-war generations. He remembered what it was like to be a young man in a hurry, and he realized that the enthusiasm of the young was a priceless asset for the whole Labour movement. He took care to keep on good terms with younger leaders, like Clifford Allen and Emanuel Shinwell;[7] he was a frequent visitor at Hugh Roberton's house in Glasgow, where the Glasgow I.L.P.-ers gathered;[8] he read the books of the younger intellectuals, like G. D. H. Cole.[9]

Immediately after the 1918 election, he was even prepared to flirt cautiously with the notion of direct action himself. 'We must strike industrially with good effect,' he noted in a gnomic diary entry in April 1919. 'The Parliamentary party cannot back up anything.'[10] The use of the strike weapon for political purposes, he argued in an article on the debate about direct action at the 1919 Labour Party conference, had 'nothing whatever to do with the Constitution'. The only relevant question was whether it would work. Clynes, who had opposed direct action at the conference, was 'the Hobbes of Representative Government' — 'more servile to authority than the Whigs'.[11] Direct action was only illegitimate, he argued in the New York *Nation* a few weeks later, if Parliament was truly representative:

> This Parliament is, however, not representative; therefore for the defence of representative Government, mass democracy is entitled to act, first of all on great issues like the unconstitutional war against the Russian Government, and in the next place to bring down the Government and compel it to go to the country again.[12]

Little by little, however, he began to sound a more cautious note. A small but influential section of opinion, he warned in August 1919, was deliberately trying to provoke organized labour in order to put 'soldiers on the streets';[13] and after the great rail strike of September 1919 he implied that, if organized labour challenged the authority of the Government, it would play into the hands of its enemies.[14] By 1920, his position had become more cautious still. That summer, organized labour did challenge the Government, and with considerable success. In April 1920 the Poles launched a major offensive against the Red Army; in May, the dockers at the East India docks refused to load the *Jolly George* with munitions allegedly destined for Poland. By early August the tide had turned and Soviet troops were threatening Warsaw. There were signs that the British Government wanted to intervene on the Polish side. On August 9th, the Parliamentary Committee of the T.U.C., the Labour Party Executive and the parliamentary party agreed to set up a 'Council of Action' to stop the Government from going to war. A deputation was sent to the prime minister; a conference at the Central Hall unanimously authorized the Council of Action to take any steps it thought necessary; local councils sprang up all over the country. MacDonald applauded these developments from the sidelines,[15] but his applause was tempered by anxiety. Labour had saved the country from war, he insisted in August; but he warned that the Council of Action might give the prime minister 'a chance for another election and another majority. In the imaginations of our people there is an unlimited supply of bogeys. Mr. Lloyd George can extract them as a magician takes rabbits out of a hat.'[16]

His attitude to the 1921 miners' strike was more complex, but as cautious. For a while in April 1921 it looked as though the miners would be supported by the railwaymen and transport workers, and perhaps by a general strike. In an angry diary entry, MacDonald implied that the miners had been provoked by Lloyd George's 'vanity' and stubbornness,[17] but in a guarded article in *Forward* he warned that, although they had justice and common sense on their side, a strike would play into the hands of 'scaremongers' who wished to discredit the Labour Party electorally.[18] The collapse of the Triple Alliance on 'Black Friday', April 15th, filled him with indignation. 'Too depressed & disgusted to go out & see anyone,' he noted. 'This may be even more serious in the end than a lost battle after a strike. Goodness knows, no one wants a strike but this seems a criminal blunder of the most colossal kind.'[19] But this only reinforced his misgivings about direct action. The miners themselves, he wrote at the beginning of May, now saw that a 'fight which had started purely as an industrial one, will have to be settled as a political one.'[20] A week later, he returned to the charge with a sympathetic but gloomy description of the situation in South Wales:

> There is one sin against the law which I have seen committed, but which, I must confess, does my heart good. One evening on the edge of the sand dunes I met a group of miners armed with sturdy walking sticks and apparently out to enjoy nature. But on the sand dunes Brer Rabbit is good ... and my friends had the sticks for fell purposes. The poacher is nature's gentleman ... and it was hard for me to bid them adieu ...
>
> But the sombre background will intrude. The weakness of Labour ... is only too apparent when one goes to the crowded canteens where the children are fed, or when one gets the mother of a family to speak. Then, one understands the folly of those who would use 'direct action' as a remedy for every social and political ill ...
>
> Meanwhile, Capital suffers comparatively little. It suffers no famine and no canteens have to be opened for it. It cancels the rooms it took for a week-end's golfing at Porthcawl, and it dines and golfs at home instead.[21]

MacDonald's attacks on direct action were, however, combined with a steady barrage of criticism, directed against the ineffectiveness and timidity of the parliamentary party, partly because he knew that they would be well received in the I.L.P., but even more because he was genuinely exasperated by the parliamentary party's repeated failures to exploit its position properly. His opposition to direct action was based on the premiss that parliamentary action was a better road to political power. But it was not enough to send Labour candidates to Westminster: they also had to tread that road once they got there. This the parliamentary party seemed incapable of doing. Labour M.P.s, he complained, were lax in their attendance at the House. When they did attend, they often made the wrong points in debate; sometimes they even voted in the wrong lobby. Above all, they had the wrong psychological attitude.[22] Lloyd George and his ministers, MacDonald noted in his diary, 'ought to have been criminals in the dock'.[23] Instead of fighting them 'with the sword of the Lord and of Gideon',[24] the parliamentary party wasted its time in pettifogging detail, and tried to win concessions when it should have been trying to drive the Government from power. As he put it in *Forward* after the 1920 party conference:

> Perhaps the most essential thing said at Scarborough was by Colonel Wedgwood when he urged that the Labour Party should become the Opposition in fact [as well as in name]. This involves a mental change, as well as great Parliamentary activity. Talking about this later on at Scarborough, a member said that Colonel Wedgwood's suggestion could not be adopted because the Government was to produce a very satisfactory Workmen's Compensation Bill! That is just it. We must be opposed in our hearts before we are opposed in our actions. And unless we are opposed in our hearts and let the Government know it ... [t]hey will throw enticing apples at us so that we may lose the race.[25]

II

This barrage of criticism continued throughout the 1918 Parliament. As late as July 1922, MacDonald asked despairingly in his column in *Forward*, 'Where is the Opposition?', and attacked the parliamentary party for wasting its time on the details of the Trade Union Political Funds Bill instead of fighting the Government on the great issues of foreign policy.[26] His criticisms gradually became less violent, however, and the intervals between them grew longer. The bitter memories which provided part of the explanation for them continued to rankle, as they were to do for the rest of his career. The political differences they had reflected slowly narrowed, as the war and the Versailles settlement receded into the background, and the struggle against the Third International and the Communist Party came to the fore. In the summer of 1920, a special committee of the parliamentary party invited MacDonald to advise the party on its tactics in the House of Commons. He accepted, subject to the proviso that he would not act 'in any subordinate position'. In the short run, the invitation probably did more harm than good, for it was withdrawn by a full party meeting after it had been leaked to the press—a blunder which greatly upset MacDonald, who feared that it had injured him in the country, and who refused to be mollified by an apology from the parliamentary party.[27] Even so, the episode was a sign that some of the party leaders, at least, were anxious for a reconciliation.

Before long, MacDonald was offered another olive branch. In January 1921,

Will Crooks — who had been Labour member for Woolwich from 1903 to 1918, and had been returned unopposed for the new constituency of East Woolwich in 1918 — was forced by ill health to resign his seat. At Henderson's suggestion, the National Executive invited MacDonald to stand at the by-election.[28] At first, MacDonald was doubtful. He had already been adopted as prospective candidate for Aberavon, in South Wales. In Aberavon, there was a strong I.L.P. branch and an anti-war tradition. In Woolwich, there was neither. The local council was under Labour control, and the party was well organized. But the biggest employer was the Woolwich Arsenal, and there was a substantial ex-serviceman's vote. On January 31st, MacDonald discussed the position at length with the 'quiet but redoubtable' Councillor Barefoot, the Woolwich agent. Barefoot assured him that, in spite of the personal attacks which would probably be made on him, he had a fighting chance of victory.[29] After a discussion with his committee at Aberavon, he decided to stand. 'Am doubtful,' he noted privately, 'but attracted by risks.'[30]

His doubts were soon justified. On February 8th, he was adopted, 'enthusiastically & unanimously';[31] and the campaign began. His opponent was a Captain Robert Gee — the son of a Leicester frame-maker, who had served in the ranks for twenty-three years before being commissioned, and who had won the Victoria Cross at Cambrai. In his column in *Forward*, MacDonald denied that Gee's military prowess would determine the result. 'The Woolwich ex-serviceman knows', he wrote hopefully at the beginning of the campaign, 'that military decorations are no indication of political wisdom, and that a Parliament of gallant officers will be a Prussian Diet and not a British House of Commons.'[32] At the same time, he did his best to neutralize Gee's decorations by mobilizing an impressive array of ex-soldiers to appear on his platforms, by promising that if he were elected he would press the Government to convert the Woolwich Arsenal to civilian uses, and above all by insisting that the coalition Government had betrayed the dead. As he put it at his first meeting:

> There are responsible men today, men who say that under present circumstances ... the best thing you can do is to prepare the for next war! Then they talk about people who have been traitors. Can you imagine anyone who is more worthy of being called traitor than a man who has betrayed the sentiments of the dead? (Hear, hear.) Can you imagine anyone against whom the finger of scorn and reproach should be pointed more than the man who said to our youths, 'Go out and die', and when the youths went, who says that their aspirations must be forgotten ... ?[33]

By the end of the first week, he was reasonably confident. He could not help being impressed by the size and enthusiasm of his meetings, though he tried not to let them warp his judgment. He also noticed that Labour had the upper hand in Beresford Square — the 'great cockpit of Woolwich controversy' by the Arsenal main gate, where street-corner orators had to shout into megaphones

K

to make themselves heard above the clanging of the trams.[34] It was on the doorsteps, however, that the battle would be won or lost; and on the doorsteps MacDonald was already on the defensive. The constituency was invaded by an army of women canvassers, sent by the Primrose League. MacDonald, they insisted, was an atheist; a revolutionary; a traitor. After the war, he had drunk toasts to the 'European Revolution' and 'Our German Friends'. During it, he had opposed paying pensions to soldiers, and applauded the sinking of hospital ships. He opposed marriage, and approved of women who had children while their husbands were away at the front. He wished to reduce policemen's pay, and to raise the income-tax limit to £5,000 a year so that his own income would be exempt.[35]

Each day, MacDonald answered items from what he called 'the Ananias Daily Bulletin'; but, as he knew from Leicester, it was much harder to scotch scandal than to spread it. As the campaign progressed, moreover, Gee was reinforced. The executive committee of the Communist Party issued a manifesto denouncing MacDonald as an intruder in 'proletarian overalls', who planned to crush 'the revolting masses into submission with the spiked club of the exploiters'.[36] This may have done him more good than harm; but Gee's other ally was more formidable. At first, MacDonald's old enemy, Horatio Bottomley, had announced that since Woolwich was essentially a Labour seat, he would take no part in the election. A week later, however, he declared in John Bull that Gee's selection as the coalitionist candidate had 'revolutionised the situation', and that patriotic citizens would no longer have any excuse 'for sending to the House of Commons a man whose war record will stand for all time as a blasphemy on the fair name of Britain'.[37]

Bottomley's intervention may well have been the decisive factor. Trams passing through Woolwich were covered with placards asking 'A Traitor for Parliament?' At Cannon Street station, there were hoardings with the same message; and at Woolwich station, posters announced 'Ramsay's Terrible Record'.[38] This was more than flesh and blood could stand. A week before polling day, Bottomley was due to speak at Plumstead baths. Two hours before the meeting, a crowd of several thousand had gathered in the street; after the doors were opened, eight thousand people were left outside. Coalition speakers were greeted with jeers and Labour songs. When Bottomley's car drew up, it was welcomed by 'derisive howls and terms of execration' which the Woolwich Gazette described as being unfit for 'the ears of clean-minded people', and surrounded by a crowd of ex-servicemen and unemployed workers. Eventually Bottomley was rescued by a police charge into the crowd, and taken to the police station nearby. When Captain Gee emerged from the baths after the meeting, he was assaulted, so his headquarters alleged next day, by a 'virago of a woman', brandishing a chair leg.[39]

From Gee's point of view, the incident could hardly have been more suitably timed. The assault, he claimed, had affected old war wounds in his head; as a result he had been obliged to spend the whole of the following day in bed. For the rest of the campaign, the press reverberated with stories about specially imported Labour hooligans, and references to Gee's war wounds. Bottomley kept the pot boiling with parliamentary questions about ruffianism at by-elections, and offered a reward of £100 for evidence identifying the organizers of 'the outbreak of hooliganism' at Plumstead. MacDonald announced that a careful investigation had been carried out, which had revealed that the crowd had been good-tempered throughout and that no one had been injured.[40] But there was no denying that Bottomley had been prevented from speaking, or that, for the first time since the campaign began, the coalitionist camp had a genuine grievance.

On the eve of the poll, the Labour Party organized a great march through the constituency, culminating in a mass rally in the main square. According to the *Daily Herald*, twenty thousand people were present; and it commented confidently that 'the demonstration leaves no doubt as to what the result will be.'[41] On polling day, however, Gee was returned with 13,724 votes to MacDonald's 13,041. 'They have polled every non-political vote in East Woolwich,' Mac-Donald declared, with pardonable bitterness,[42] and in his diary he noted 'It was a great & strenuous fight but the filth used was absolutely disgusting. Hope never to go through another such racking hour as when the votes were being counted. I miss my dear dead companion at such times. Lonely, lonely.'[43]

III

'Woolwich is a Coalition gain,' wrote the *Evening Standard*. 'But it is still more a Ramsay MacDonald loss.'[44] This was the general verdict. By common consent, the press agreed that MacDonald's war record was still an insuperable barrier to membership of the House of Commons, and a casual newspaper-reader could have been forgiven for concluding that he had suffered as great a setback as in 1918. In fact, his position in the Labour movement had almost certainly been strengthened. In 1921, he stood for the I.L.P. administrative council, to test opinion in the branches; and although his policy as secretary of the International was radically different from that favoured by most articulate I.L.P.-ers, he was triumphantly elected at the top of the poll, with 471 votes to his nearest rival's 270.[45] No doubt, he would have been elected in any case; but it is hard to believe that Bottomley's attacks had no effect on the size of his lead – while in orthodox trade-union circles, the equally virulent attacks of the Communist Party probably had a similar effect.

Little by little, in fact, he was returning to his old position as the chief mediator between the I.L.P. and the trade-union wing of the movement; and by the summer of 1921, there was no longer any doubt that he was once again firmly established in the inner councils of the party. At the Labour Party conference that June, Clynes, who had succeeded Adamson as chairman of the parliamentary party, was led to believe that there was a possibility that the Government might fall, and that he might be sent for by the King. MacDonald's diary speaks for itself:

> Henderson summoned C, Webb & myself to consult on the subject in the most private way in the most private of rooms at 9.30 pm. Webb was anxious lest we should quarrel over the Premiership & was very voluble lest one of us might begin such a terrible discussion. He talked on nothing necessary in order to keep talking & the other two were rather silent as they were as afraid to say anything as Webb was to hold his tongue. W. assured them however that the King would send for the chairman — though that was not constitutionally necessary, & then jumping back from such dangerous ground, told of the personal difficulties that existed in Ld. John Russell & Palmerston's day. 'Thank goodness', he said, 'there are no such difficulties now. Everyone who counts (with emphasis) will come in.' It was comical. I could not laugh, I could only smile — the difference between the comical & the funny. H. made lists of Cabinet whilst Webb chattered & evidently wished to read them out but in the end folded them up & put them in his pocket.[46]

During the next twelve months, he became one of the most active members of the National Executive. By 1922 he was a member of the National Joint Council, a new body which had been set up to co-ordinate the activities of the Labour Party and T.U.C.; of the Joint International Committee; and of sub-committees of the National Executive on organization, finance, general purposes and elections. He also belonged to the Adjustments Board which dealt with the party's agents on the Executive's behalf.[47]

Yet there was a marked difference between his position in the early 1920s and his position before the war. Then he had been, so to speak, an 'insider' in the party's collective leadership — perhaps the chief insider. Now he was an outsider, suspicious of and sometimes bitterly hostile to, those he saw as being on the inside. As the struggle over the International had shown, his stand on particular questions was often closer to that of the old, pro-war 'right' of the party than to that of the I.L.P. But it was the I.L.P. which provided him with his political base and, more importantly, with his political home: and it was to the I.L.P., rather than to the Labour Party, that he devoted most of his political energies. 'The Labour Party', he confessed gloomily in November 1921 to Arthur Ponsonby, by now an I.L.P.-er himself, 'knocks the heart out of me';[48] the propaganda work needed 'to keep the I.L.P. going vigorously to see that its Socialist idealism will not be swamped in the political opportunism of the Labour Party', he complained to the American socialist, Algernon Lee, 'taxes my strength to the utmost'.[49]

It was a revealing complaint. In 1922, MacDonald's old protégé, Clifford

Allen, now thirty-three years old and perhaps the most talented spokesman of the younger generation of middle-class intellectuals who had joined the I.L.P. during and after the war, was elected as treasurer. Allen's conception of the function and purpose of the I.L.P. was, in many ways, very different from MacDonald's. His election coincided with the adoption of a new party pro-gramme, of which he had been one of the chief architects, and which was deeply influenced by the guild socialist idea of 'workers' control'. In his first year as treasurer, he raised £11,000 in donations from wealthy sympathizers, and caused raised eyebrows among some of the more puritanical members of the party council by insisting that its funds should be invested in capitalist stocks and shares. He forced through a radical transformation of the worthy but unreadable *Labour Leader*, which was rechristened the *New Leader* and put under the editorship of the well-known socialist journalist, H. N. Brailsford, who was paid a salary of £1,000 a year and turned the paper into an intellectual journal of considerable literary distinction.[50] MacDonald's attitude to all this was distinctly mixed. He admired Allen's drive and administrative efficiency, and responded to his formidable charm, but he was sceptical about his activities as a fund-raiser, and at bottom hostile to his conception of the *New Leader*. He disliked the title, and opposed Brailsford's appointment as editor. His own conception of the paper was that it should appeal 'to a type that has intellectual interests of what may be called a gentlemanly, democratic and on the whole, amateur kind'. Its psychology, he wrote, should be that of a 'club running a movement: genial: confident: gallant: attractive'. In practice, this meant that it should be rather like 'the old *Clarion*, the early *Labour Leader*'.[51] This, of course, was exactly what Allen and Brailsford did not want; and although the issue was comparatively unimportant, the difference of opinion was more funda-mental than it appeared. It seems clear that Allen's ultimate aim was to turn the I.L.P. into an intellectual pressure group, capable of generating policies of its own and of campaigning for their adoption by the rest of the Labour move-ment. MacDonald's aim was very different. 'I should like to find a greater emphasis placed upon Socialist propaganda and education,' he wrote in a characteristic criticism of the draft constitution which the N.A.C. submitted for consideration by the party in November 1920, 'and fewer traces of barren theorising and provisional architecture.'[52] In politics, as in religion, he shied away from doctrinal precision; and the last thing he wanted was to be tied down to detailed policies. Like Allen, he wanted to preserve and strengthen the I.L.P. But the I.L.P. he wanted to strengthen was the old, familiar I.L.P. of Hardie and Bruce Glasier, just as the *New Leader* he wanted was really the old *Labour Leader* with a more modern typeface.

Much the same is true of his most substantial literary production in these years. Before 1914, he had made a gallant attempt to work out a gradualist ideology which could bridge the gulf between the socialist aspirations of the I.L.P. and the more prosaic ambitions of the trade unions, and thus provide a theoretical justification for his own strategy as secretary of the Labour Representation Committee. Since then, the political landscape had been transformed; and he evidently felt the need to revise his pre-war theories to fit the altered circumstances of the 1920s. The result was a 90,000-word treatise entitled *Socialism: Critical and Constructive*, which first appeared in 1921, and was republished in 1924 and 1929. The organic metaphor was used more sparingly than in the past, and the evolutionary argument was not deployed at such length. More space was devoted to the moral case against capitalism, and there was more discussion of the steps which a socialist Government might take to reach its goal. More significantly still, MacDonald conceded explicitly that, before the war, signs of 'slackness' had appeared in the socialist movement, whose leaders had 'become so completely absorbed in politics, that they appeared to consider that political action alone was the worker's means of improvement, and the political state the only means of expressing the democratic will'.[53] In reality, state socialism was a provisional concept only, suitable for an earlier stage in socialist history.[54] Thanks to the syndicalists and the guild socialists, it was now clear that 'Industrial transformation cannot be made by legislative action or Civil Service interference alone; it must also take place within the workshops themselves by labour having to shoulder increasing management responsibility.'[55] Though the political state would always have to be supreme, since it alone represented the interests of the whole community, 'workshop control' was the next stage on the road to socialism.

But although there were important differences between *Socialism: Critical and Constructive* and MacDonald's earlier theoretical writings, the similarities were more important still. Like Tawney in the *Acquisitive Society*, he brought two charges against capitalism — that a society based on the acquisitive instinct was fundamentally immoral, and that, because of its immorality, it was torn by social tensions which it could not resolve. Under capitalism, the mass of ordinary workers were

> literally driven to the factories by the whip of starvation. This whip will be wielded under any form of Society, for what is consumed must first of all be produced. But it seems clear that the production which a community requires cannot be procured by forced labour. When labour becomes educated until it acquires self-respect and self-knowledge, and when men combine to look after their own economic interest, work done under the whip of physical necessity must deteriorate both in quantity and quality and must increase in repulsiveness ...
>
> This is a major failure of Capitalism. It cannot provide a motive to work when men have gone beyond the state of passive obedience.[56]

Under capitalism, then, capital and labour were irreconcilable and conflict between them was endemic; that was one of the main reasons why socialism was necessary and why, in the long run, it was also inevitable. But this did not mean that labour was always right or that the conflict between labour and capital was positively desirable. All too often, workers in revolt against capitalist oppression behaved like 'a people passionate in their triumph after military victory', and copied the worst trait of their erstwhile oppressors. Socialists did not want to put labour into power merely to pursue 'grouped working class interests'; they wanted to infuse 'into both sides the creative desire to get beyond present divisions and reach a state in which all service will be done for communal ends'. For socialism moved men 'by education and moral idealism ... it takes no part in a purely horizontal tug of war between the working and the capitalist class, but is a Plutonic force beneath both heaving them upwards.'[57] The language was different from that of twenty years before. The argument was the same.

IV

Perhaps, MacDonald wrote gloomily to Arthur Ponsonby in June 1922, there was

> nothing very much for either of us to do except to cherish our memories, bring up our children & launch them upon the world to carry on our voyaging. Everything depends on the next election. Without old colleagues our separate success will be poor, & every day I am made aware of the fact that some people do not want us &, if we are thrust upon them by the votes of the electors, they will give us only a cold welcome. The election is like a mirage. For the moment it does not appear on the horizon at all. But I do not think that it is far away. Parliament shows signs of extreme age & I hear that Ll.G. is worn & weary ... I do hope that your prospects are good, but if I get in you must promise to take no oaths, if you are still out, that you will give up the fight. Five or six of us can even yet do good work, but one or two cannot. The Labour Party will be considerably increased in numbers, & I know that the Cabinet is on paper — made by Clynes, Webb & Henderson. It will be waste paper ... But there is a fine spirit abroad if we had the time and the strength to attend to it. Unfortunately, I fear that my bronchitis has come to stay, & if it becomes bad with the change of the year then I am out. This is anticipating trouble, however, & Providence is full of resources.[58]

Providence turned out to have even more resources than he had expected. Four-and-a-half months after his letter to Ponsonby, the Conservatives revolted against Lloyd George's handling of the Chanak crisis and voted by a large majority to leave the coalition. Lloyd George resigned and Bonar Law became prime minister. On October 26th, Parliament was dissolved and a general election campaign began.

MacDonald was well placed to meet the challenge. After his defeat at Woolwich, he had returned to Aberavon – a scattered county division in mid-Glamorgan, stretching from the seaside resort of Porthcawl and the coastal towns of Port Talbot and Briton Ferry, up the narrow Afan Valley to the wilds of Glyncorrwg. The electorate was overwhelmingly working-class, divided fairly equally between miners and the steel and tin-plate workers of the coast. The agent was Ivor Thomas, a member of the I.L.P. administrative council since the beginning of the war, and one of MacDonald's most devoted friends and admirers. Thomas had built a large and efficient electoral machine, based primarily on the 1,000-strong I.L.P. branch at Briton Ferry. In May 1921, he had held a series of what he called 'representative meetings' in most of the polling districts in the constituency, and carried out a careful scrutiny of the electoral register. The results had convinced him that MacDonald could win the seat even then, and it was clear that by the autumn of 1922 the tide was running much more strongly in MacDonald's favour than it had been eighteen months earlier.[59]

On paper, the odds against him were far from negligible. In 1918, Wales had been a Lloyd George fief; and Aberavon had conformed to the general pattern. The election had been won by a National Liberal war hero, Major Edwards, with a majority of 6,000. But Edwards's majority was an unreliable guide to the opinions of his constituents, even at the time it was recorded. His Labour opponent in 1918 was the ebullient and reckless Bob Williams of the Transport Workers' Federation – a revolutionary Marxist and militant atheist, who was greeted at the polling stations he visited on election day by crowds of children booing and shouting 'the man who don't love Jesus!'[60] A more tactful Labour candidate might have improved on Williams's performance, even in the hysterical atmosphere of 1918; and since then political attitudes in South Wales had undergone a sharp change. Lloyd George's prestige had collapsed, in South Wales as elsewhere. The export market for South Wales coal had shrunk, and the miners had had to fight a bitter rearguard action to defend the gains they had made in the boom conditions that prevailed during and imme-diately after the war. Their pride and solidarity, which had once been a barrier to the spread of socialism, now spurred it on; old ties of religion and nationality began to seem less important than the ties of class. At the beginning of August 1922, Emrys Hughes, a young I.L.P. propagandist and former conscientious objector who was to make his mark in Labour politics later, published an article on the situation in South Wales in the New Leader. It could 'safely be prophesied', he wrote, 'that there will be a clean sweep of the Coalition in the South Welsh mining constituencies;' MacDonald, he added, 'should win Aberavon'.[61]

For MacDonald's exalted oratory and air of brooding mystery were ideally suited to South Wales in the early nineteen-twenties. Some of the younger men, like the 25-year-old Aneurin Bevan, who had returned from the Labour

College in London to his native Tredegar in 1921, and had been elected to the district council there a few months later, had already rejected the romantic socialism of the early I.L.P. in favour of a harder, more class-conscious creed. Among the older generation, however, the pull of the chapel was still strong; and socialism appealed less as an economic analysis or political programme than as a kind of secularized nonconformity. The same, of course, was true of MacDonald himself: and in the little mining communities of the Afan Valley, in particular, he established a rapport with his followers more reminiscent of a religious revival than of an ordinary election campaign. 'Is the Christian, the moral, state never to be anything but a dream?' he asked in the *Afan Sentinel*, the monthly broadsheet of the Aberavon Divisional Labour Party. 'No, my Labour friends, through the darkness of the days we must keep our faith and continue striving to the light.'[62] In cold print, the phrases strike no sparks, but it does not need much imagination to visualize the impact which similar phrases must have had on an audience used to the *hwyl* of the Welsh non-conformist pulpit, and for whom the metaphor of light and darkness still symbolized a profound emotional experience. At Aberavon, Emrys Hughes prophesied when the campaign began, the contest would be 'more than an election campaign, it will be a great crusade for Socialism and Internationalism, for clean politics, for high ideals.'[63] The hyperbole was characteristic: to most of MacDonald's supporters it was not hyperbole at all. As one of them put it years later, MacDonald's effect on his audiences was 'magic': it was as though he was 'a second Messiah coming amongst them'.[64]

Even in South Wales, however, exalted oratory could not win an election by itself. In Aberavon, it was buttressed by careful planning. Before the campaign began, MacDonald had lectured at most of the local chapels on non-political subjects, such as John Knox, or his visit to Palestine. The division was covered by a network of polling district committees, each with its own secretary. A cheap edition of MacDonald's biography of his wife was widely sold, as was a pamphlet life of MacDonald himself. Long before the election, the redoubtable Minnie Pallister, then a young and pretty schoolteacher in Brynmawr, and in Thomas's opinion the best woman speaker in the Labour Party, began to organize the women's vote — to such effect that MacDonald's canvass returns suggested that he had polled as well among women voters as among men. After the women, Minnie Pallister turned her attention to the children; and when the campaign began, the Labour Party's election song, sung to the tune of 'Men of Harlech', seemed ubiquitous:

> Ramsay, Ramsay, shout it;
> Don't be shy about it;
> Labour's day is sure to come —
> We cannot do without it.[65]

The campaign opened with a maladroit attempt by the local Conservatives

to persuade Edwards to withdraw, on the grounds that the only way to keep
MacDonald out was to form an anti-Labour alliance. Edwards was said to be
lax in his attendance at Westminster and a poor constituency member, but he
was not prepared to give up his seat without a fight; and he turned the invitation
down. Instead of supporting him as the lesser evil, however, the Conservatives
decided to run a candidate of their own, and with a great fanfare of publicity
adopted a local employer and former mayor of Port Talbot named Byass.
Byass, declared the *Western Mail*, was 'not keen on political ambitions'. He had
come forward only because he realized 'that a crisis has been reached in the
nation's history when public duty is more important than political ambitions,
and that every means must be taken to prevent the seat going to the Labour
Party'. His patriotism was sure to be rewarded: the more so since 'moderate
men' were looking forward to 'a period of rest from the class war that Mr.
Ramsay MacDonald preaches with ever-increasing bitterness'.[66] But, although
the *Western Mail*'s readers were left in no doubt about MacDonald's iniquity,
they were not given much chance to read what he had said. The fullest newspaper account of a speech by MacDonald in the 1922 election is to be found in
the *Llais Llafur* — an old organ of the I.L.P., published in the mining village of
Ystalefera, where MacDonald spoke in support of William Jenkins, the candidate for Neath. The report is worth quoting at length, not only because of the
impression it gives of what it felt like to be present at a meeting of MacDonald's
in the early 1920s, but because MacDonald's speech was devoted to the chief
plank in Labour's election platform, the capital levy. This was presented by the
Liberal and Conservative parties as a flagrant example of class hatred and a
dangerous attack on private property. Like most Labour candidates, Mac-
Donald presented it primarily as a method of reducing income tax, though with
the strong implication that it would also stop rising prices and solve the unemployment problem. According to the *Llais* reporter,

> Quite a little time elapsed before Mr. MacDonald could commence to
> speak because of the sustained applause which greeted him. He opened his
> remarks by expressing the hope that things were going as well in Neath as
> they were in the Aberavon division. (Applause.) In Aberavon they were
> improving day by day, the only exception being his voice. (Laughter.) ...
>   Touching the Capital Levy, he said ... [t]he nation owed its money-
> lenders eight thousand million pounds, and in order to pay the interest had
> to find by taxation 350 million pounds, so that by Thursday night the
> nation would have found a million pounds for the owners of that debt ...
> So long as this enormous debt was to be borne by the people, so long
> would the £ be worth only 15s. or 17s. in purchasing power ...
>   No one but a fool would say it was confiscation of wealth ... To-day in
> round numbers there were 42 million people in this country. There were
> only 250,000 people who had more wealth than £5,000, and the capital

levy would only be taken from people with over £5,000. Those levied would be 250,000; 42 million people would not be touched at all ...

Labour had a good programme, but they had something better, too — they had a glorious cause and magnificent principles. What was the great difference that divided them from other parties? It was Labour's conception of human qualities. (Applause.) ... The Labour movement came from the heart of the people; the Labour movement came glowing with idealism; with spiritual power, making an appeal to them to rise up, to look up; to strike, not in hate, but in love; to reconstruct, not to destroy; to claim those human qualities for the divine destiny of government, and to that he called them and made an appeal to them to send Alderman Jenkins to represent them in the House of Commons. (Prolonged applause.)[67]

On November 13th, the *Western Mail* reported that Byass was 'drawing to his side the moderate men of all parties who know his sterling worth', and that he would make Aberavon 'a big surprise' to the Liberals and socialists. Two days later, MacDonald was returned at the head of the poll, with 14,318 votes to Byass's 11,111 and Edwards's 5,328. His election, commented the *New Leader*, was 'enough in itself to transform our position in the House. We have once more a voice which must be heard.'[68]

V

The Conservatives had 347 seats in the new House of Commons, a majority of 88 over the other three parties combined. The Independent Liberals had 60 and the National Liberals 57. For the first time, Labour, with 142 seats, was unmistakably the second party in the state. The new parliamentary Labour Party, moreover, was a very different body from the old one. In 1918, 48 Labour M.P.s had been sponsored by trade unions, and only three by the I.L.P. Now about 100 members belonged to the I.L.P., while 32 had actually been sponsored by it, as against 85 who had been sponsored by trade unions. The change in class background was equally significant. In 1918, no Labour M.P.s had been to public schools, and only one to a university. Now there were 21 university graduates, and 9 public-school men. In 1918, only two of the non-trade-union Labour members had followed professional occupations before their election. Now the figure was 26. In the country, the Labour Party was still an overwhelmingly working-class organization. In Parliament, it could present itself for the first time as the movement of opinion rather than of class which MacDonald had always hoped it would become.[69]

In doing so, it could also present itself for the first time as a potential governing party. In 1918, it had contained only a handful of serious politicians; and, although Henderson had subsequently been returned at a by-election, the number had not greatly increased before the general election. Now, most of the established figures who had lost their seats after the war were back, together with a dazzling array of newcomers. Snowden, who was now at the height of his powers as a parliamentarian, with a deadly command of sarcastic invective and an equally deadly lucidity of argument, had also returned from the wilderness – a lonely and ultimately tragic figure, impossible to work with but equally impossible to ignore. Two other veterans who had returned to Westminster were Fred Jowett, one of the architects of the Bradford I.L.P., and that extraordinary bundle of passion, sentimentality, egoism and selflessness, George Lansbury. These were joined by an equally impressive collection of former Liberal M.P.s, who had graduated to membership of the Labour Party through the U.D.C. and I.L.P. Two of them belonged to the landed class which had provided most of the rulers of Britain since 1688. Arthur Ponsonby, now the Labour member for the Brightside division of Sheffield, was the son of Queen Victoria's private secretary, and the grandson of Lord Grey of the Reform Bill. After Eton and Balliol, he had served in the Foreign Office, before entering the House of Commons as Liberal member for Stirling Burghs. Sir Charles Trevelyan, member for Central Newcastle and the owner of great estates in the north-east, was the son of Sir George Trevelyan, the biographer and nephew of Macaulay. Like Ponsonby, he was a founder member of the U.D.C.; unlike him, he had held junior office in the Liberal Government. The brothers Noel and Charles Roden Buxton, were less well known; but they, too, had sat in the House of Commons as Liberals, and had made names for themselves before the war as experts on foreign affairs and critics of the Government's foreign policy.

Among the new members, Sidney Webb, Patrick Hastings, the fashionable barrister, and E. D. Morel, the organizing genius of the U.D.C., had all made varied but considerable reputations outside. Greater parliamentary reputations were to be made in the years ahead by MacDonald's protégé and admirer, Herbert Morrison, a shrewd and perky cockney who was already beginning to build the political machine which was to give his party control of London for nearly thirty years; by the self-effacing Old Haileyburian, Gallipoli veteran and former Mayor of Stepney, Clement Attlee; and by the canny Glaswegian trade-union organizer and propagandist, Emanuel Shinwell. Reputations of a more flamboyant kind were also to be made by some of the other Clydeside members – notably by the cadaverous former schoolteacher, James Maxton, whose stirring oratory belied his lazy good nature and lack of administrative drive; by the former engineer, David Kirkwood; and, above all, perhaps, by the rotund and formidable John Wheatley, a self-made Roman Catholic businessman, and probably the ablest leader the left wing of the parliamentary Labour Party has ever had.

There was a price to be paid for this array of talent. Parties of the left are almost always less homogeneous, socially and intellectually, than parties of the right. This had been true of the Liberals before 1914; it was far more true of the Labour Party now. To a degree which is difficult to appreciate, but essential to understand, the Labour Party of the early nineteen-twenties was still, in structure, a loose federation of local bodies and special interests rather than a unitary organization with a single purpose: and in membership, a haphazard collection of individualists rather than a disciplined political regiment of the kind that confronted it incredulously from the Government benches. Inside and outside the House of Commons, the 'movement' was full of fissures — fissures between the trade unions and the I.L.P., between the I.L.P. and the Divisional Labour parties, between different unions and different sections of the same union, between 'intellectuals' and manual workers, between pacifists who had been in prison during the war and patriots who had spoken from recruiting platforms, between 'Right' and 'Left', between respectability and revolt. The ballast of the party was provided by the trade unions. It was their votes which controlled the party conference, their money which financed the machine, and their nominees who gave the party managers that steady, reliable *bloc* of support without which no party can function. But the unions did not form a homogeneous body themselves. They were all intensely jealous of their autonomy; the big unions, in particular, were mostly controlled by powerful and dominating men who had risen to the top, not by the genteel arts of the professional man, but in ruthless struggles on the waterfront, in the pit yard or on the factory floor. On occasion, if the stakes were high enough, they were prepared to co-operate with each other; but their co-operation was wary, suspicious and apt to break down at the slightest strain. If this was true of the trade-union wing of the party, it was still more true of the rest of it. Despite the smattering of middle- and upper-class newcomers (and most of these were in temperament rebels or outcasts, dogmatic, prickly, and often inclined to self-righteousness), most Labour members of parliament had reached Westminster after years of hoarse-voiced oratory at street-corners and in obscure halls. They were dedicated, occasionally even saintly: but they were not emollient. 'High explosive, handle carefully,' proclaimed an illuminated button on the coat of one of the new Clydeside M.P.s when he and his colleagues set off for London.[70] It could have been worn as appropriately by half the parliamentary party.

The new party's first task was to elect its officers for the coming session, and in view of the importance of this episode in MacDonald's career it is necessary to discuss it at some length. In normal circumstances, Clynes, as the sitting chairman, might have expected to be re-elected without a contest. But the circumstances were not normal. The new party was twice as large as the old one, and there was widespread agreement among the new members that they needed a more vigorous chairman than Clynes if the party was to make a better showing in the new Parliament than it had done before the election. The Clydesiders had already discussed the situation informally before reaching London. With a revealing parochialism and lack of political realism, Maxton apparently thought that it would be possible to replace Clynes with Wheatley, who was unknown south of the Border and had never sat in Parliament before. Despite some opposition, however, the consensus was in favour of MacDonald, as it was in the I.L.P. as a whole. At a private meeting of the I.L.P. members before the main party meeting, Shinwell proposed that MacDonald should be supported. Not surprisingly, his proposal was carried; although Snowden and Maxton both spoke against it, it is unlikely that the opposition of one notoriously embittered member of the old guard and one new member can have carried much weight.[71] Meanwhile, some moves seem to have been made in the opposite direction, though the evidence for these is much more scanty. MacDonald certainly believed that the 'machine' was against him, and noted in his diary that it had made 'calculations & preparations' to keep him out.[72] On the day of the election, Lansbury's *Daily Herald* made what must have been a crude, last-minute attempt to persuade his backers to withdraw. 'Only one thing need be said about today's elections of leaders for the Labour Party in Parliament.' it wrote excitedly: 'They must be unanimous. Any contest, any pressure of opposing claims, would not only give the enemy cause to exult; it might lead to an unfortunate fissure in the Party itself.'[73]

MacDonald's own activities are not known. According to Snowden, he canvassed actively for support, particularly among the new Scottish members.[74] This is unlikely, since he obviously had no need to do so; and it is much more probable, both because it would have been better tactics and because it is more in keeping with his character, that he stayed aloof from any canvassing that may have taken place. In any case, there was scarcely any time for canvassing, since the election was held only six days after polling day. What does seem clear, however, is that MacDonald expected to lose, and that his activities were directed less to capturing the party leadership than to establishing a position from which he would be able to challenge it in future. His election to the chairmanship, he noted in his diary afterwards, had taken place 'most unexpectedly'.[75] In his weekly column in *Forward*, he even suggested that he might not sit on the Labour front bench at all. '[T]he second bench below the gangway on the Opposition side will have such attractions to me that I do not think I shall be able to pass it,' he wrote: 'From it, we fought our great fight against the rest of the House in the mad years of war.'[76] This, of course, was written for publication. It cannot have been designed to influence the election, however, since it did not appear until the election was over, and it is much more likely that it genuinely expressed what was in MacDonald's mind when he wrote it. The same applies to the thinly veiled menace of the rest of the article:

> The failure of the Party in the last Parliament was that it never was an Opposition and was never led as an Opposition. It never impressed itself upon the country as an alternative Government with an alternative national

policy, and it won its great series of bye-elections mainly by votes which the Coalition had thrown away ...

Before this is published, the question of the Front Opposition bench may be settled. There are only two advantages in the Front Bench. The first is that you can put your feet up on the table, and the second that you have a box of nice convenient height whereon to lay your notes ... The importance of its possession lies in the fact that it is a symbol of authority ...

When the Liberal Party almost disappeared in 1918, the Labour Party lost its chance of occupying the whole Bench ... If the Labour Party is to conduct the work of an Opposition, it must have the facilities and recognition of an Opposition.[77]

This last point was more significant than most of the readers of *Forward* could have realized. Clynes opened the fateful party meeting on November 21st by reporting what he had done to combat the Speaker's proposal that the Labour Party should share the Opposition front bench with the Liberals, and apparently made it clear that he had done little. At the beginning of the meeting, MacDonald had sat tense and silent, but when Clynes finished he made what Shinwell described as 'a fiery speech of protest', and after this his spirits seemed to revive.[78] The meeting then proceeded to elect the officers for the coming session. A proposal by MacDonald's supporters that the election should be by secret ballot was turned down, and as the *Manchester Guardian* reporter put it, 'the I.L.P. members found themselves compelled to vote openly for Mr. MacDonald and against Mr. Clynes.'[79] In the end, Clynes received 56 votes to MacDonald's 61. MacDonald's election was then put to the meeting as a substantive proposition, and carried unanimously, Clynes's reactions were understandably mixed. With characteristic generosity, he deputized for MacDonald at an I.L.P. meeting that evening, and declared that the whole party was determined to support the new leader. At the same time, he issued a press statement complaining about the activities of the new members who had decided in favour of a change before the party meeting took place, and stressing, somewhat pointedly, that this was the seventh occasion on which the party had changed its chairman.[80]

The official statement issued by the Labour Party after the election gave a more accurate indication of its significance. MacDonald, it declared in a pregnant phrase, had been elected 'Chairman or Leader'. The *New Leader*'s comment was the most prescient of all. 'No man has more respect than our newly-chosen leader for the forms and spirit of democracy,' it wrote. 'But character will tell. By his ability to give, in initiative, in speech, in tactics, a powerful expression to the will and ideals of the whole party, Mr. MacDonald will infallibly become the symbol, and personification which we have hitherto lacked.'[81]

VI

In the six months which had passed since his election to the party leadership, MacDonald noted in a diary entry in May 1923:

> Various small attempts have been made to undermine me but so long as I go pretty well they will not succeed. My difficulty is to interpret myself to three or four good fellows who have no sense of Parliamentary methods & who expect Front Benchers to live in a perpetual state of fighting exaltation & be noisy. I go on exactly opposite lines & [the] Party as a whole steadily improves. The work is prodigiously heavy but I flourish under it. I am lonely though. All my people are dead. The victory has come when there is no one to cheer.[82]

The conflict he hinted at went much deeper than he implied. The 'three or four good fellows' to whom he found it difficult to interpret himself were the Clydesiders, notably Maxton and Wheatley. But he was wrong in thinking that they had 'no sense of Parliamentary methods'. Maxton and Wheatley, in particular, both developed into skilled and effective parliamentarians, and Wheatley had great administrative gifts in addition. What divided them from MacDonald was not any lack of parliamentary expertise on their part, but a profound difference of opinion about the nature and purpose of parliamentary activity. For the Clydesiders, and no doubt for most of the ordinary party members in their constituencies, the function of a Labour member of Parliament was to articulate, as powerfully as possible, the grievances and aspirations of the class he was there to represent. Parliament was the soap-box writ large; suggestions that the techniques of the soap-box might be out of place in it were signs of timidity, if not of treachery. Debates in the House of Commons were skirmishes in the class war; and the war had to be fought outside the chamber as well as inside. Casual social intercourse with members of the older parties was suspected; friendship was impossible. The Clydesiders would have indignantly rejected the accusation that they were opposed to parliamentary methods or in favour of violent revolution. All the same, their conception of parliamentary methods was incompatible with the pursuit of power by democratic means within a parliamentary regime. For them, the purpose of parliamentary activity was not power, but propaganda: and the propaganda was aimed, not at the uncommitted voter whose support Labour would need if it was to increase its 142 seats to 300, but at the militant, class-conscious minority who voted Labour already. Their conception might have had something to be said for it, particularly in the turbulent conditions of the nineteen-twenties, if it had formed part of a coherent revolutionary strategy. But the Clydesiders were not revolutionaries: they were agitators. Maxton's biographer describes more than once how the chamber filled when Maxton rose to his feet.[83] This was not surprising. The Conservatives and Liberals who flooded in to hear him knew that he would provide a splendid oratorical performance. They also knew that his performance would present no threat to them.

At a deeper level, no doubt, the same was true of MacDonald's performances. Indeed, there is a sense in which MacDonald and the Clydesiders were the mirror images of each other — parliamentary utopianism reflecting agitational utopianism, and *vice versa*. MacDonald had no clearer idea than the Clydesiders had of the strategy which would have to be adopted by a socialist Government determined to maintain its principles while still administering a predominantly capitalist society. But although he had no strategy for using power, he had an extremely clear strategy for gaining it. As he saw it, Labour now had two central objectives. In 1918, it had emerged as the strongest opposition party largely by default. Even in 1922, its position was weaker than it looked at first sight. It was true that it had more seats than both wings of the Liberal Party put together, that most of the Lloyd George Liberals owed their seats to Conservative support, and that Lloyd George himself did not appear to favour a reunion with the Independent Liberals. But although all this was true in December 1922, there was no guarantee that it would remain true for ever. It was still possible that the Liberal split might be healed; and if the Liberal split were healed, the Liberals, with the dynamic figure of Lloyd George at their head, might yet regain their old position as the main anti-Conservative party in Britain. MacDonald knew only too well from his experiences before the war that British politics have a built-in bias in favour of the two-party system; and that if the Liberals did heal their differences and recapture their old position as the main progressive party, all hope of a Labour Government would once again recede into the distant future. On the other hand, he also knew that if the Labour Party could retain its lead over the Liberals for long enough to establish itself as the only plausible alternative to the Conservatives, then the built-in bias of the system would work to its advantage. These, then, were his two objectives. The first was to ensure, if possible, that politics revolved around a struggle between the Conservative and Labour Parties, in which the Liberals could be dismissed as irrelevant. The second was to ensure that the Labour Party presented itself as an alternative government, capable of winning and holding power, not in some remote classless society, but in Britain in the 1920s. In British conditions, he wrote in June, 'we shall always tend to return to two great Parties, and that is the position to-day. The two parties fighting for supremacy are our own and the Tory Party of reaction.'[84] What he asserted as fact was, in reality, aspiration.

Hence the dispute at the beginning of the session over the allocation of seats on the Opposition front bench. Hence too the constant bickering between MacDonald and the Clydesiders about the party's attitude to the conventions of parliamentary debate. If MacDonald's strategy was to succeed, the Labour

Party would have to demonstrate its competence as a potential government; and the only way it could do this while it was in opposition was by proving that it was as capable as the older parties of working the parliamentary machine. Noisy demonstrations of socialist fervour were a waste of time; attempts to bring the machine to a halt were positively dangerous. As he put it in an outspoken article in the *Socialist Review*, commenting on the turbulent behaviour of some of his followers which had scandalized outside observers and old parliamentary hands in the first weeks of the session:

> If the Party fails in Parliament, it fails in the country, and the dream of a Labour Government will vanish for a generation. Hitherto nothing has happened to justify in the remotest degree such prophecies, but the reason for them is that the Party has created a few 'scenes' and indulges rather freely in interruptions ...
>
> ... A genuinely spontaneous outburst ... will always be condoned, and may even have its uses, but for a Party or any section of it to get into the frame of mind which is always issuing in violent action is fatal ... A Party with the reputation of an old London Vestry will never be allowed to form a Government in this country ...
>
> ... If [this] were the result of the egotism of men ... who have no conception of the restraints necessarily imposed upon a body of 600 Members, then indeed the prospects of the Party would be black. Two or three such men could undo in a few minutes all the work done by others in as many years, and the position of no leader would be tolerable. He would have to save his Party and his cause by denouncing his followers ... [85]

His warning was disregarded. In April 1923, the Labour Party forced a division on the motion that 'Mr. Speaker do now leave the Chair', as a protest against the Government's unsympathetic reply to a debate on its treatment of ex-servicemen in the civil service. Next day, in protest against the Government's handling of the situation, it refused to take part in a division on a motion that the House should resolve itself into a Committee of Supply; and a number of Labour members stood in their places, singing the 'Red Flag'. The following month, Walton Newbold, the eccentric Communist member for Motherwell, refused the Deputy-Chairman's request to leave the chamber; and, when approached by the Sergeant-at-Arms, replied with the shout, 'I am here in the name of the Communist International!' In the end, he was suspended, but in the division nearly ninety Labour members voted against his suspension, even though the front bench abstained. The climax came towards the end of June, when Maxton, Wheatley, Campbell Stephen and George Buchanan were all suspended, after having denounced Sir Frederick Banbury, the Conservative member for the City of London, as a 'murderer'. The storm had begun with an outburst of genuine passion from Maxton; and in a sympathetic intervention from the Opposition front bench, MacDonald had done his best to find a form of words which would allow him an honourable withdrawal. But Maxton had rejected the olive branch; and MacDonald, who had turned pale with anger, had been forced to listen while Maxton's three colleagues deliberately repeated his offence in cold blood, and in an atmosphere of increasing hostility.[86] Once again, the front bench abstained in the divisions on the four suspensions; but, even so, nearly half the parliamentary Labour Party voted against. The episode was a clear challenge, not only to MacDonald's parliamentary strategy, but to his authority as party leader; and at the beginning of July, a special party meeting was held in Caxton Hall to consider the matter. MacDonald made a fifteen-minute speech, urging better teamwork and pointing out that if the Labour Party damaged the parliamentary machine while it was in opposition, it would pay for its folly when it came to power.[87] Maxton and his colleagues, however, refused to apologize; and MacDonald's attempts to negotiate with them were unsuccessful.

In the end, their suspension was lifted without an apology on their part, and after a further scene, in which they were prevented by the police from entering the precincts of the Palace of Westminster to take their seats before the House had finished debating the prime minister's motion to reinstate them. In his speech on the prime minister's motion, MacDonald managed to preserve an appropriately relaxed and conciliatory tone.[88] Between the lines of his editorial in the *Socialist Review* a few weeks later, however, he betrayed rather more of the irritation he must have felt. At the beginning of the session, he wrote, the older parties had expected that they could push the Labour Party into the background. By firm handling, their attempts to do so had been foiled; now the party's position has been established. On big affairs it was now 'the Tory Government and the Labour Opposition'. This method had been attacked as a surrender, but in reality it was only the lazy and incompetent who trusted to 'slap-dash' methods instead. And social transformation required services 'which the slap-dash person can talk about, can hamper, but cannot give'.[89]

VII

'Tory Government and Labour Opposition': this was MacDonald's aim in a nutshell. It had an obvious corollary: Tory prime minister and Labour alternative prime minister. For success would depend, in large measure, on MacDonald's personal success as leader of the Opposition. As the *New Leader* had foreseen, he had become the symbol and personification of the whole party; if he faltered, the party would falter. In the British system of government, the leader of the Opposition always has a difficult role to play. Unlike the incumbent prime minister, he cannot make news. To some extent, at least, he can hardly avoid dancing to the prime minister's tune. When he has not held office himself, his difficulties are greater; when his party has not held office either, they are greater still. This, of course, was precisely the position in which MacDonald now found himself. It was as if, in our own day, the leader of the Liberal Party suddenly found himself sitting behind the Opposition dispatch box. The only equivalent in modern British history is the position in which Disraeli found himself in 1846; and Disraeli's position was not quite analogous to MacDonald's, since the leader of his party was in the House of Lords and had held Cabinet office not long before.

Nevertheless, MacDonald had two important assets. The first was that the great figures of the recent past were all, for various reasons, discredited or irrelevant. Asquith was a spent force. Lloyd George's reputation was tarnished by the honours scandal and the Black and Tans. Churchill had never recovered from the Dardanelles adventure. F. E. Smith had passed on to the mausoleum of the House of Lords, and was now the Earl of Birkenhead. Carson was a judge. Grey was for all practical purposes out of politics. The result of the election, like the Conservative rebellion which had precipitated it, showed that the British people wanted new faces. Apart from Bonar Law and Baldwin, his chancellor of the exchequer, the Cabinet was almost as unknown as the Labour front bench. Impatience with the old faces, whose owners had blundered into war and mismanaged peace, was even greater on the left than on the right. Few could appeal to it with greater justification than MacDonald.

His chances of doing so were greatly enhanced by the fact that in 1923 political attention was concentrated, to a remarkable extent, on foreign affairs. Lloyd George had been brought down in the end by the threat of war with Turkey. No sooner was that crisis over than another developed in central Europe. At the end of December 1922, the Reparation Commission declared Germany in default of deliveries of timber. At the beginning of January 1923, a conference of Allied prime ministers rejected Bonar Law's proposal of a four-year moratorium on Germany's reparations payments. On January 9th, the Reparation Commission declared Germany in default of deliveries of coal. Two days later, French and Belgian troops began the occupation of the Ruhr. The result was a catastrophic fall in the value of the German Mark, the ruin of the German middle class, and a prolonged campaign of passive resistance in the occupied areas. For the rest of the year, the British foreign secretary, Lord Curzon, made intermittent but unsuccessful attempts to mediate between Germany and France, to the accompaniment of growing indignation in left-wing circles with the rapacity and intransigence of the French.

Foreign crises usually strengthen the Government of the day. This one brought greater benefits to the Opposition. MacDonald knew more about foreign affairs than Bonar Law or Baldwin, and spoke on them with greater authority. Curzon's aims were not, in fact, very different from the Labour Party's; but they were pursued without much appearance of conviction, and it was easy to claim that the Government was following half-heartedly where Labour led. Above all, the crisis itself seemed to make nonsense of the assumptions on which British foreign policy had been based for almost twenty years. It shattered the *entente*, vindicated Labour's opposition to the Versailles settlement, and even suggested that MacDonald might have been right during the war. In doing so, it discredited not merely the Government but both wings of the Liberal Party as well.

Accordingly, most of MacDonald's speeches and writings as Leader of the Opposition were devoted to the crisis in the Ruhr, and the underlying issue of reparations; and, although it is not necessary to follow his argument in detail as it developed over the next few months, the broad outlines of his position are of considerable interest. It rested on three main pillars. The first was a straightforward appeal to economic self-interest. British trade, MacDonald argued in his first speech on the subject in December 1922, had been badly damaged by the fall of the Mark. That, however, was the result of the weakness of successive German Governments, for which the Allies were to blame, and of the economic dislocation of central Europe, caused by the reparations imposed on Germany at Versailles.[90] This argument was linked with a more subtle appeal to national pride. Britain, MacDonald claimed, was consistently outvoted on the Rhineland Commission and the Reparation Commission, and her rights under the peace treaty were flouted. Yet the Government did nothing: and, by doing nothing, encouraged Europe to drift towards another war.[91] This was the third pillar and, emotionally at least, it was probably the strongest. As MacDonald put it in the House of Commons in March 1923:

> [T]he French are saying things of us, and we are saying things of them – the fault is on both sides – they are thinking things of us, and we are thinking things of them, that are bound to end in hostile organisation, either armies, submarines, air services, alliances, *blocs* – I do not care how ... Surely it is our duty to see that the dragon's teeth of words and thoughts that are now being sown, and that are bound to give us a harvest of armed men, shall be raked up ... The baffling and the maddening thought is this, that we are paralysed.[92]

The only solution was the old U.D.C. formula of open diplomacy. The House of Commons, MacDonald suggested, should set up a select committee on the occupation of the Ruhr and the wider problems of reparations and European security, and then invite the French and Belgian Parliaments to set up similar committees to exchange views and information with its own. This proposal was, of course, turned down by the Government, as MacDonald must have foreseen. Foiled in the House of Commons, he turned to his own version of direct action. At the end of March, a conference of socialist deputies from France, Belgium, Italy and Britain was held, on the initiative of the British Labour Party, in the French chamber of deputies. Léon Blum was in the chair. It is clear from the hastily jotted notes which MacDonald made at the time, however, that he, rather than Blum, played the most active part in the discussion;[93] and, although nothing came of it, he was able to point out, with some justification, that the Opposition had done more than the Government to solve the problem.

At the end of April, Curzon at last took the initiative, and invited the Germans to make a firm offer; and when the Germans announced at the beginning of June that they would accept the decisions of an impartial body of experts, MacDonald was quick to claim the credit for the Labour Party.[94] By now, Bonar Law had resigned and Baldwin had become prime minister; and when Poincaré's refusal to budge made a further British initiative necessary, it fell to Baldwin to tell the House of Commons that the Government was determined that the problem should not be evaded in a series of friendly exchanges between the Allies, and that the situation must not be allowed to 'sink into irretrievable ruin'. This was strong language. MacDonald replied with an assurance that the prime minister could go on holiday knowing that 'the great mass of opinion in the House of Commons is behind him'; and then launched into an ingenious piece of debating, designed to show, without saying so in so many words, that the Government was in fact carrying out Labour Party policy; that this proved that the Labour Party had been right all along; and that the Government's change of heart logically implied still further moves in Labour's direction.[95]

VIII

The honeymoon between the two front benches proved shortlived. During the recess, the Government's policy was abruptly reversed. On his return home from his customary summer holiday at Aix-les-Bains, Baldwin stopped briefly in Paris for a meeting with Poincaré. After their meeting, a communiqué was issued to the effect that the two prime ministers had discovered that there were no differences of principle between them. The policy of neutrality between France and Germany was now a dead letter. Four days later, the German Government abandoned passive resistance, and resumed deliveries of reparations in kind. Poincaré had won: and with British support.

This was not the only change in Government policy. In a speech to the National Unionist Association in Plymouth towards the end of October, Baldwin suddenly and inexplicably announced that although he would honour Bonar Law's pledge not to introduce protective tariffs in the lifetime of the existing Parliament, he had come to the conclusion that he could not fight unemployment effectively without protecting the home market. Parliament met on November 13th with the shadow of a dissolution hanging over it; and on the 15th, in a packed and noisy House, MacDonald moved a motion censuring the Government for its failure to deal with the needs of the unemployed or pursue a satisfactory foreign policy. To all intents and purposes, his speech was the first shot in his election campaign; and, although he began with a vigorous attack on the Government's record on unemployment, it is worthy of note that he reserved his heaviest fire for its handling of foreign affairs. Trade and peace, he argued, were indivisible; the unemployment problem at home could not be solved until central Europe had been pacified and the reparations issue resolved. All over Europe, people were 'begging and praying that we may put into active operation the old liberal spirit and sentiment that they have associated with our country in the past. I know perfectly well that whoever touches foreign affairs to-day with a new policy must be a man of infinite patience, and behind him must be a body that is willing to wait for results. Yes, but they have got to begin.'[96]

Next day, Parliament was dissolved, and MacDonald's strategy as leader of the Opposition was put to the test in one of the strangest election campaigns in British history. As Richard Lyman has pointed out, two quite separate struggles were superimposed on each other.[97] The first was the struggle between the Conservative and Liberal Parties over the historic issue of free trade, a struggle in which the Liberal and Labour Parties were allies. The second was the struggle between the Labour and Liberal Parties over which of them was to emerge as the strongest progressive party in Britain; and in this they were deadly enemies. It was the second struggle which presented the real challenge to MacDonald. In spite of *The Times*'s comment, in its review of the year, that 'Mr Ramsay MacDonald has led his party with success and he has risen to big occasions in a big way,'[98] he must have approached it with some trepidation. The Liberal Party was now reunited. On the issue which had provoked the election it could claim, with some justification, to be a more credible anti-Conservative force than the Labour Party. The last time a general election had been fought on the issue of free trade was in 1906; and it was far from inconceivable that working-class voters who had since deserted to the Labour Party might return to their old allegiance when they heard the old tunes. MacDonald had only had a year to establish himself as the alternative prime minister. In the middle of the campaign an anonymous article in the *New Leader* described him as being 'head and shoulders above his competitors' in 'knowledge, tact, ability and judgement', and gave particular praise to his 'kindliness and geniality' in dealing with his followers.[99] But there was no way of knowing whether the electorate would agree.

Such anxieties as he may have felt cannot have lasted for long. His campaign began with a motor tour from London to South Wales, by way of Gloucester, Bristol, the Forest of Dean, Newport and Cardiff. At Gloucester, he addressed what *The Times* described as a 'crowded meeting'; at Bristol he had an audience of 4,000. At Lydney, in the Forest of Dean, he addressed 1,000 miners and agricultural workers on the fallacies of protection; and in the industrial areas of South Wales, his progress, according to a later account by an eye-witness, was that of a 'Messiah'.[100] In Newport, his car was towed nearly a mile through the streets, and he and the local candidate were carried shoulder-high.[101] By the time he reached his own constituency, the *New Leader* wrote, it was clear that

> here was no mere manifestation of party spirit, no ordinary expression of loyalty to a party leader. In a major degree the demonstration reflected partly that uprising of the soul of a movement, of which MacDonald spoke so eloquently during the tour, and partly the enthusiasm and affection that MacDonald's own personality and single-minded intensity of purpose have created during the stern testing time of the past eight years ...
>
> The last stage of the journey was along moonlit roads to the constituency. The Cowbridge meeting was inspiring, and Kenfig Hill gave the first indication of what the final rally was likely to be. The people turned out *en masse* and pulled the car for a mile in a procession headed by a brass band. The Port Talbot welcome began at Taibach, a mile and a half from the centre of the town. The crowd bore down on the car like an avalanche. What mattered it that the windows were smashed? — the eager men whose arms went through could not help themselves in the impetuous rush of the hundreds who pressed round the car ...
>
> It took the car nearly two hours to travel a mile. That speaks for itself. The long procession, with a flaming torch held aloft at its head, filled the roadway solidly. At the end came the car, with a great horseshoe of flowers held on the bonnet ... Finally, in the open space in the town came the climax. It is enough for us to know that rarely, if ever, in the English political history has such a scene been witnessed ... [W]ho could be a pessimist after it?[102]

Polling was on December 6th. In Aberavon, MacDonald was returned in a straight fight with Byass by a majority of 3,512. Nationally, the Conservatives lost 115,000 votes as compared with 1922, while the Liberal and Labour Parties gained 180,000 and 120,000 votes respectively. Thanks to the quirks of the electoral system, however, the change in seats was much more striking. The Conservative Party now had 259 seats in the House of Commons, the Labour Party 191 and the Liberals 159. Neither the Labour nor the Liberal Party had won, but it was clear that the Conservatives had lost — and in an election called by them on an issue of their own choice. MacDonald returned to London on December 8th to find that the evening papers were prophesying that Baldwin would resign after the weekend and advise the King to send for him. 'Ah! were she here, to help me,' he noted. 'Why are they both dead — my mother and she?'[103]

CHAPTER 14

Prime minister

I

THE evening-paper headlines turned out to be premature. A group of Conservative malcontents, headed by Lord Birkenhead, tried to use the prospect of a Labour Government as an excuse for removing Baldwin from the leadership of the Conservative Party. They failed; but Baldwin had to abandon his original intention of resigning straight away, and decided to stay in office until the new Parliament met.[1] In the next few days there was much wild talk about the dangers of allowing Labour to take office, and many wild schemes were designed to avert them. The *English Review* thought that the 'sun of England seems menaced by final eclipse'. Winston Churchill, who had just been defeated as Liberal candidate for Leicester, West, declared that a Labour Government would be a 'national misfortune such as has usually befallen a great state only on the morrow of defeat in war'. *The Times* advocated a coalition between Liberals and Conservatives. Lord Balfour thought it was Asquith's duty to keep Baldwin in power, Lord Long that the Conservatives should offer their support to Asquith. In some quarters it was suggested that the best solution would be to set up a government of 'national trustees', headed by McKenna, who had deserted politics for banking and had not sat in Parliament since 1918.[2]

Consternation in the more excitable sections of the older parties was mirrored by a revealing mixture of awe, incredulity and apprehension in the Labour movement. Over the weekend, when it still seemed possible that Baldwin would resign in the next few days, Sydney Arnold and Lees Smith advised MacDonald not to take office, on the grounds that a Labour Government would be bound to fail and that the party would then be 'overwhelmed'.[3] The Clapham I.L.P., H. N. Brailsford reported, held a discussion on the pros and cons of taking office, in which 'every single speech was against'.[4] Little by little, however, MacDonald and his closest colleagues became convinced that if they were given the opportunity to form a Government it would be folly to turn it down. On December 9th, as well as talking to Arnold and Lees Smith, MacDonald discussed the situation with J. A. Hobson and J. H. Thomas. Hobson, he noted later, advised him to 'risk it', and to appeal to the nation with a policy of 'European settlement, improved unemployed [*sic*] schemes, housing, co-ordinate pensions &c, Committees on Agriculture [and] National Debt'. 'Not sure', MacDonald wrote, 'if party wd. give confidence to do this moderate work, but think it would.' Thomas's view, he noted, was the 'same as is forming in my own mind'.[5] On December 10th, the party leaders decided to jump the fence if it were presented to them. As MacDonald put it in his diary:

> Massingham telephoned result of sounding McKenna, as I had asked, re. action in City. Reply favourable: bankers now regard themselves as semi-officials & would not countenance panic. Would be fair ... [S]aw Haldane who indicated willingness to accept Lord Chancellorship (I had thought of Sankey) & talked over difficulties. Thought Lords not very difficult; Services more difficult. Wd. think points over & see me at dinner on Sunday. Met Clynes, Thomas, Henderson, Snowden & Webb at Webb's. All agreed that we shd. take office ... Discussed Foreign Policy, Unemployment & Budget. Unanimous that moderation & honesty were our safety. Agreed to stand together. H. evidently very sore at being out. Spoke of what he wd. sacrifice if he attended to the country & was not in & asked for a safe seat.[6]

In the next two days, the position was considered, in turn, by the Labour Party National Executive, by a joint meeting of the National Executive and the T.U.C. General Council, and by the executive of the parliamentary Labour Party. At each of these meetings, MacDonald pointed out that if the Labour Party were to refuse office after defeating the Government with the aid of the Liberals, and if Asquith were then to form a Government instead, the Liberals would sit on the Government benches. The Opposition front bench, and most of the other Opposition benches as well, would be occupied by the Conservatives. The Labour Party would be relegated to the position of a group, and would probably sit below the gangway on the Liberal side of the House. When the Liberals were defeated, as they would be in due course, it would be they, and not the Labour Party, who would take the Opposition front bench. By refusing office, Labour would lose all the parliamentary advantages it had gained by becoming the official Opposition in 1922; its position in the country might be put back by a decade.[7] These arguments proved conclusive. On December 12th the National Executive resolved that 'should the necessity for forming a Labour Government arise, the Parliamentary Party should at once accept full responsibility for the Government of the country without compromising itself with any form of coalition.'[8] 'One against taking office,' MacDonald noted, 'but he voted for to make unanimity.'[9] On December 13th the joint meeting of the National Executive and General Council followed suit; and in the afternoon the parliamentary Labour Party executive did the same. On December 18th, Asquith made it clear, in a speech to the parliamentary Liberal Party, that the Liberals would not keep the Conservatives in office or join in any combination to keep Labour out. If a Labour Government were ever to be tried, he declared, 'it could hardly be tried under safer conditions.' Whoever might be in office, 'it is we, if we really understand our business who really control the situation.'[10] To all intents and purposes, a Labour Government was now certain.

Its composition remained highly uncertain; and it is still far from clear how some of MacDonald's decisions were reached. He spent the Christmas holidays at Lossiemouth, where he received a good deal of advice, both solicited and unsolicited, about his appointments. But although there is some evidence about the pressures which were brought to bear on him and about the way in which he responded to them, it is tantalizingly incomplete. What does seem clear, however, is that it was taken for granted that MacDonald would be prime minister and that he would enjoy as much freedom in appointing the rest of the Government as his predecessors had done. Like them, he had to pay attention to the opinions of his colleagues and followers; like them, he was obliged to make some appointments which he had not at first wished to make. Among his papers is a handwritten list of the ministerial offices he had to fill, with a corresponding list of names beside them;[11] it is clear from this that in most cases he had to change his mind at least once, and in some cases a number of times, before the final appointments were made. But although his freedom of action was limited by the requirements of the political situation, by the preferences of his colleagues and by the reactions, actual or expected, of the parliamentary party, no one challenged his right to make his own appointments or suggested that the conventions which had been followed by Conservative and Liberal prime ministers in the past might not be appropriate for him. As Sidney Webb put it later, 'The sudden responsibility of so sudden and unexpected an assumption of office gave the Party a shock which sobered even the wildest of shouters.'[12] The fact that its sobriety would substantially increase the power of the party leader, and bind the party still more closely to the system it claimed to want to change, appears to have gone unnoticed.

The hardest post to fill was that of foreign secretary. The reparations crisis, which had provided one of the central themes of Labour's propaganda for the past twelve months, had just entered a new phase; it was clear that foreign policy would be at least as important politically as it had been in 1923. It was therefore essential that the new foreign secretary should be a politician of the front rank, capable of getting his own way in the Cabinet and with his own following in the party. By the same token, however, it was equally important that he should be able to work harmoniously with MacDonald, who would be bound to take a close interest in foreign affairs himself. Only Snowden, Henderson and J. H. Thomas unquestionably possessed the first of these attributes. Only Thomas possessed the second as well; and it seems clear that Thomas was MacDonald's first choice. But the news leaked out and provoked great indignation in the I.L.P., where it was felt that since Labour's foreign policy was largely derived from the I.L.P., only a member of the I.L.P. could be trusted to carry it out. There is some evidence that a group of I.L.P. members of parliament wrote a joint letter to MacDonald, protesting against Thomas's appointment,[13] and on December 11th, Arthur Ponsonby wrote separately to urge him to take the Foreign Office himself. Labour was unlikely to stay in office for longer than a few months, Ponsonby pointed out, and for such a short period it would be perfectly possible for the prime minister to be foreign secretary as well. 'The incredible seems about to happen –,' he wrote. 'We are actually to be allowed by an extraordinary combination of circumstances to have control of the F.O. and to begin to carry out some of the things we have been urging and preaching for years. To give this job to J.T. is simply to chuck the opportunity away.'[14] Ponsonby's arguments went home; when he began to draw up his list, MacDonald had already decided to be his own foreign secretary.

The House of Lords also presented considerable difficulties. One of Mac-Donald's main aims in taking office was to prove that Labour could form a competent Government, without turning to the Liberals for help. To do so, it would be necessary to demonstrate competence in the Lords as well as in the Commons; and in the Lords Labour was almost unrepresented. One obvious solution was to give office to a number of non-party dignitaries who were either members of the House of Lords already, or suitable for elevation to it. Mac-Donald had already made approaches to Sir John Sankey, a judge of the King's bench, who had served as chairman of the 1919 Coal Industry Commission, and to Lord Haldane, who had served as Asquith's lord chancellor for four years and had since drifted far enough away from the Liberal Party to be regarded as non-partisan. At first, MacDonald hoped to have his cake and eat it, by giving the Woolsack to Sankey and some other office to Haldane. Towards the end of December, he offered Haldane a choice between the Admiralty, the India Office and the Board of Education. Haldane replied cryptically that the situation was 'delicate', that management of the Lords would be 'very delicate' and that MacDonald had better come to his house at Cloan and discuss matters there. At Cloan, it was finally agreed that Haldane was to be lord chancellor after all, and that he would also act as chairman of the Committee of Imperial Defence. Sankey got nothing.[15]

Having landed his biggest fish, MacDonald now began to net some smaller ones. Early in January, Sidney Olivier, who had been one of MacDonald's boarders in Fellowship House in the early 1890s and afterwards had a distinguished career in the Colonial Office, wrote that since he was not 'under the popular journalistic and middle-class illusion that ministers are as a rule men of more than average intelligence', he would be willing to take office and, if necessary, to go to the Lords as well. He preferred the Colonial Office, he wrote in a second letter, but added gracefully that he was 'prepared as a veteran of the movement to be used up anywhere'.[16] In the end, he became secretary of state for India. Another eminent recruit was Lord Parmoor, a distinguished lawyer and former Conservative M.P., who had been elevated to the peerage by Asquith and had joined the Labour Party after the war. He became lord president of the council, with special responsibility for the League of Nations. Last, but by no means least, was Lord Chelmsford, a former viceroy of India and a lifelong Conservative, whom Haldane recruited – much to the recruit's surprise[17] – as first lord of the Admiralty. The claims of respectability, at any rate, were satisfied with considerable shrewdness and skill.

The claims of party service and political weight were harder to satisfy. Of MacDonald's leading colleagues, only Snowden presented no problems. He was universally regarded as an authority on finance. His obstinacy and dogmatism only made him more formidable as an enemy. His appointment as chancellor of the exchequer appears to have been taken for granted, not only by himself, but by everyone else as well. As deputy leader, Clynes would also have to be given a senior post. He was appointed as lord privy seal and leader of the House; and to judge by MacDonald's list, he was considered for no other offices. Sidney Webb was a comparative newcomer to Parliament and a bad performer at the dispatch box, but he was one of the leading intellectuals in the party and was thought to possess great knowledge of administration. He was offered, and accepted, the Ministry of Labour at an early stage in the proceedings, and was moved at the last moment to the Board of Trade, for which the first choice had been Arthur Greenwood, because MacDonald decided that the Ministry of Labour ranked too low in the departmental hierarchy. Thomas was more difficult to accommodate. He was general secretary of an important union, a member of the T.U.C. General Council, an adroit negotiator and a persuasive debater. After he had been ruled out as foreign secretary, however, he was considered and rejected for both the Home Office and the Admiralty, and eventually had to be content with a somewhat incongruous resting place as colonial secretary.

Arthur Henderson was more difficult still; and since MacDonald's treatment of Henderson caused great ill-feeling, both then and later, it must be examined with some care. In normal circumstances, Henderson's claim to high office would have been incontestable. He had been a Cabinet minister under Asquith and Lloyd George. He had been chairman of the parliamentary Labour Party during the war, as well as for a short period before it. He had been secretary of the party for twelve years, and in the previous Parliament he had been the Opposition chief whip. On the other hand, he had lost his seat in the general election. No doubt, another seat could be found for him in time, but time might be in short supply. In these circumstances, it was not unreasonable to argue that he would be better employed in supervising the party machine, which would soon be called upon fight another election, than in running a department. According to Mrs Hamilton, Henderson at first accepted this argument himself, but was persuaded by his family and friends that it would be 'unthinkable' for him not to take office.[18] As we have seen, however, MacDonald's diary suggests that, when the party leaders met on December 10th, Henderson had already made up his mind that he did not want to 'attend to the country' and that he wanted to return to Parliament as soon as possible.

The rest of the story is equally obscure. According to Sidney Webb, Henderson was not consulted by MacDonald until 'the last few days', and was then offered the wildly inappropriate post of chairman of ways and means.[19] According to Mrs Hamilton, MacDonald sent Henderson two lists from Lossiemouth, one of which designated him as chairman of ways and means, while the other did not mention him at all.[20] The MacDonald papers, however, throw a different light on the transaction. It is clear from MacDonald's provisional list of offices that Henderson was in fact his first choice as colonial secretary, and that he also considered him for the War Office and the Ministry of Health. It is also clear that he asked Henderson for advice about the chairmanship and deputy-chairmanship of ways and means, and that he hoped for a time that he would be able to persuade him not to take office himself. On December 18th, Henderson sent MacDonald a long list of suitable chairmen, and on the 20th he followed it with a plaintive query:

> The Newcastle East Labour Party has made an enquiry as to my future intentions, and desire to know whether I intend to again become their candidate or to seek to return to the House by means of a by-election. My own feeling is to at once inform them that I do not intend to become their candidate, and this view is shared by the Council of my Trade Union. If you care to give me your view, I shall esteem it a favour.[21]

MacDonald replied two days later:

> As regards Newcastle East: You cannot, of course, wait for that if you are to take upon your shoulders one of the Ministries. I have been going very carefully into this since I came up and I have to admit that we are terribly short of men. There is no use our blinking the fact. We shall have to put into some of the offices men who are not only untried, but whose capacity to face the permanent officials is very doubtful ... I have tried a list of Ministers without you, and with you as Chairman of Ways and Means, and I must admit that it enormously increases my difficulties. The only reason why I would ever think of a list without is that I am terribly impressed with the importance of Eccleston Square. I may be wrong, but, for the life of me, I cannot see this Parliament lasting any time. Asquith's speech is really a very nasty speech, made very cunningly by a man who cares absolutely nothing about principle and who, therefore, can talk without revealing the least passion. It is perfectly evident that we will not get a Dissolution if we ask for it. Although I have seen the importance of getting hold of that card, I have always had doubts about it, and Asquith's speech has been delivered for the purpose of warning the King not to give me the pledge ... We ought, therefore, to have some smart and very much

alive man at Eccleston Square driving with his own energy the whole machinery of the country, getting candidates fixed up and arranging for organisation and propaganda ... My opinion is that if Eccleston Square could be set agoing [*sic*], you ought to come into the House of Commons without delay and, therefore, that you should tell Newcastle East that you must hold yourself free for a Bye-Election.[22]

It is clear, then, that the charges brought against MacDonald by Sidney Webb and Mrs Hamilton were misplaced. He did not send Henderson a list designating him as chairman of ways and means and another leaving him out altogether. He told him that he had drawn up such lists, explained why and went on to explain why he had rejected them. So far from failing to consult him, he told him, with remarkable frankness, how his mind was moving. No doubt he was foolish to imagine that Henderson would be content to stay out of office and supervise the party machine, but for the reasons he gave in his letter the idea had, in fact, a great deal to be said for it. The party machine did not work well in the next election, and it is not at all inconceivable that if Henderson had done what MacDonald wanted him to do it would have worked better. In any case, the real significance of the whole episode lies in the fact that Henderson got what he wanted. He became home secretary; within a few weeks he had been returned at a by-election for Burnley; and he kept his job as party secretary as well. It was a revealing indication of the limits within which the new prime minister had to work.

Early in January, MacDonald returned to London from Lossiemouth. Parliament met on January 8th, and that evening MacDonald addressed a great demonstration at the Albert Hall. With characteristic skill, he managed at one and the same time to tap the vein of emotional, utopian socialism which played such a large part in the Labour movement, and yet to make it clear that the Labour Party would take office in a severely pragmatic spirit. He wanted a Labour Government, he declared,

> so that the life of the nation may be carried on. Nineteen-twenty-four is not the last in God's programme of creation. My friends, we will be dead and gone and forgotten and generation after generation will come, and there will still be the search for the Holy Grail by knights like Keir Hardie. The shield of love and the spear of justice will still be in the hands of good and upright men and women, and the ideal of a great future will still be in front of our people. I see no end, thank God, to these things ... I see my own skyline, but I am convinced that when my children or children's children get there there will be another skyline, another horizon, another dawning, another glorious beckoning from heaven itself.[23]

On January 15th came the King's speech, announcing a full legislative programme. On January 17th, Clynes moved an amendment to the address in the name of the Labour Party. On the 13th, MacDonald had noted in his diary that Cabinet-making looked 'as if it is to be the most horrible job of my life. Am beginning to suspect human nature.' By the 19th his depression had become more acute. 'C. making worse than I thought,' he wrote. 'All but two or three disappointed ... One after another behave as though I insulted them in offering them anything but a Cabinet place. To-day a wild letter had come from the wife of one who refused subordinate office which will give me a sleepless night. I feel like an executioner, I knock so many ambitious heads into my basket.'[24] Little by little, however, the process was completed. January 21st was the culminating day. As MacDonald described it later:

> Consultation with Thomas, Henderson, Clynes, Snowden, Spoor. Produced my proposals for Ministers and under Secys, etc., List generally approved after explanations of why & wherefore. Wheatley finally fixed. Necessary to bring Clyde in. Will he play straight ... Hurried dinner with Leach's party; Speech at 9.47. Govt. defeated & so I am to be P.M. The load will be heavy & I am so much alone.[25]

On January 22nd, Baldwin left office. At midday, MacDonald went to the palace to be sworn of the privy council. The King complained about the singing of the 'Red Flag' and the 'Marseillaise' at the Labour Party meeting in the Albert Hall a few days before. MacDonald told him that if he had tried to stop it, there would have been a riot, and that it had required all his influence to prevent his followers from singing the 'Red Flag' in the House of Commons itself on the night the Baldwin Government fell. They had 'got into the way of singing this song', he explained, and it was 'by degrees that he hopes to break down this habit'.[26] In the afternoon he returned to kiss hands as prime minister. Later he noted privately:

> My dear Ishbel is splendid. The little maid is sedate as a judge and reminds me every day of her mother. 10.30 Party meeting. Watched the disappointed ones and charity came into my heart. H. raised his special grievance, but his complaint published in the Sunday Express has only added to the completeness of his downfall ... Had to go to Buckingham Palace & meeting had to be adjourned – 12. sworn member of the Privy Council, & afterwards had 55 minutes with the King. He explained as House met today, better not to swear me in as First Lord of the Treasury until it rose. He talked so steadily that I could hardly thank him. Most friendly. Referred to Lansbury's King Charles speech & Albert Hall songs. I pointed out that if there had been any counter demonstration effect would have been serious & very uncomfortable to both of us. He agreed. Fixed appointment after the adjount. of the House. 2.45 House met. One or two ineffective speeches. I took no part & declined to be drawn – 4.30 Returned to King & 'kissed hands'. Another long talk. Referred to Russia. Hoped I would do nothing to compel him to shake hands with the murderers of his relatives.

King plays the game straight, though I feel he is apprehensive. It wd. be a miracle were he not.[27]

The new Cabinet held its first meeting the following day. Thomas either came in smoking, or started to smoke when the meeting began. Other ministers followed suit, and so the new administration established its first precedent. Haldane began the proceedings with a lesson in ministerial etiquette. Mac-Donald, he explained, must always be addressed as 'prime minister'; other ministers could be referred to either by their surnames or by their titles.[28] MacDonald then urged his colleagues to 'make every effort to secure punctuality'. It was agreed that a committee on unemployment and housing should be set up under the chairmanship of Sidney Webb, and that a committee on agricultural policy should be chaired by Noel Buxton. Finally, the home secretary gave his colleagues a report on the supply of milk, food and coal in the event of a railway strike. It was agreed that he should keep the Cabinet informed of future developments; that there should be no proclamation of emergency powers without Cabinet approval; and that if the home secretary thought that the position was becoming serious he should consult the prime minister, who would then decide whether to summon the Cabinet to an emergency meeting.[29] 'Without fuss, the firing of guns, the flying of new flags, the Labour Govt. has come in,' MacDonald noted later. 'At noon there was a Privy Council at Buck. Pal; the seals were handed to us — and there we were Ministers of State. At 4 we held our first Cabinet. A wonderful country. Now for burdens & worries.'[30]

II

'Interviews galore,' MacDonald noted ebulliently, ten days after taking office, '& I laugh at myself as panjandrum & wonder if it is a stage play. By heavens, though, it is not.'[31] Five years before, it had looked as though his career was in ruins. Less than three years before, his defeat in the Woolwich by-election had appeared to rule out all hope of his return to Parliament. Now he was prime minister, at the head of the first Labour Government in history. His stand during the war had been vindicated; forty years of agitation and propaganda had earned him a reward which would have seemed wildly improbable as recently as twelve months earlier. Years later, Clynes recalled in his memoirs how he had marvelled at 'the strange turn in Fortune's wheel which had brought MacDonald the starveling clerk, Thomas the engine driver, Henderson the foundry labourer and Clynes the mill-hand' to receive the seals of office from the King, amid the gold and crimson of Buckingham Palace.[32] MacDonald had travelled further than Clynes, and had taken more hard knocks on the way. He would not have been human if he had not felt at least an occasional twinge of excitement and triumph.

Yet the twinges were far from frequent. Like most successful politicians

L

MacDonald had an ample share of personal ambition: without it, he would never have been able to struggle through the storms of the preceding ten years, or fight his way to prominence in the first place. But his ambition went hand in hand with a much more complex mixture of shyness, fastidiousness and self-consciousness, which was apt to make the fruits of ambition seem shadowy and unreal, and the effort needed to gather them distasteful and even repellent. He wanted success; but he wanted it on his own terms. When it came, his first instinct was to shrink back and wonder whether it was worth having. There are no traces in his letters or diary of Disraeli's delight at reaching the top of the greasy pole; the closer office approached, the more he was racked by loneliness and self-doubt. 'Times of sad reflections & gloomy thoughts,' he wrote when he got back to London from his Christmas holiday in Lossiemouth, two weeks before he kissed hands as prime minister. 'The people of my heart are dead; their faces on my walls; they do not share with me. Had much difficulty in returning. How vain is honour now.'[33] Ten days later, just before the Conservatives left office, he noted that the palace authorities had been in touch with him about the procedure to be followed when he became prime minister. 'Queer unreal feeling about it all,' he wrote. 'Sometimes feel should like to run away home to Lossie to return to reality & flee from these unreal dreams. I am a Socialist because I prize above all things the simple life & here I am in this, encountering it on the way to Socialism ... So I swing between my two beings & go on.'[34] When his mother's younger sister, a nanny in Sussex, came to see him a few days after his arrival in Downing Street, he noted mournfully:

> Aunt Bella came. To see her was worth everything else. She is as proud as punch—in a dignified way. 'Eh. Never did we think this was to come'. That was all. We are a great lot & hide our hearts well. Had there been others to share with Aunt Bella, who is the last, it would have been good. But these rewards come when one is nearly the last survivor. The great feasts have few sitting at the head of the table.[35]

During the next few weeks, his self-confidence returned and his mood became less despondent. At the beginning of February, he wrote that he was beginning to see 'how officials dominate Ministers. Details are overwhelming & Ministers have no time to work out policy with officials as servants; they are immersed in pressing business with officials as masters.' But he added cheerfully, 'I think I have good men. Curzon apparently treated them badly and the F.O. was on the edge of broken health & revolution. Gentlemanly treatment will do much.'[36] At the beginning of March he asked himself, 'Can we be more than a hope mingled with a warning? I shall be content with that.' But he also recorded the more hopeful conclusion that 'I now see that we are to last.'[37] By the end of April he was writing, still more hopefully, that the country was 'taking us splendidly'.[38]

Yet it is doubtful if he enjoyed power in the way that most successful politicians do. As we have seen, the business of forming a Government had been deeply distasteful to him. His responsibilities for ecclesiastical patronage were more distasteful still. He received so many requests for preferment in the Church, he told Lord Chelmsford disgustedly, that he had to have a special secretary 'to deal with the letters which come like snowdrifts';[39] and in his diary he complained that the pressure on him to make political appointments 'has been most troublesome. Why I, a Presbyterian, should be bothered with Bishops, I know not. A self-respecting Church would not allow me to interfere.'[40] Chequers, with its visual beauty and romantic associations, was a constant source of delight, but Downing Street was another matter. Life at No. 10 was the reverse of sybaritic. MacDonald's salary as prime minister was £5,000 a year, but it would cease as soon as he left office, and there was no knowing when that would be. Since he received no entertainment allowance, and had to pay out of his own pocket for such items of household equipment as linen and china, he felt he had to economize. The family groceries were bought, as before, from the Co-op and delivered to Downing Street in a Co-op van; to save coal, the family ate their meals not in their private quarters but in the sparsely furnished official banqueting-rooms which were centrally heated at the Government's expense.[41]

MacDonald, moreover, was constitutionally incapable of delegating matters of detail to subordinates. According to one story, which may or may not have been apocryphal, he was once discovered looking up the times of trains for one of his secretaries; and this trait, together with a related element of what one of the civil servants in his private office later described as his 'Highland suspiciousness',[42] also helped to make his life as prime minister more onerous than it need have been. When he first came into office, he insisted that all letters that arrived for him at Downing Street should be sent to him unopened for his personal attention[43] and, although he soon realized that the practice was not feasible, it seems clear that he never brought himself to make full use of the well-tried official machine which was now at his disposal.

He wisely retained the Cabinet secretariat, which had been created during the war and survived under the post-war coalition, and which had greatly increased the prime minister's ability to control and co-ordinate the work of the Government. Its head, Maurice Hankey, had cannily paid him a visit in his house in Howitt Road just after the election, while the Conservatives were still in office, and was rewarded for his shrewdness by becoming, if anything, more influential under the new Government than he had been under the old one.[44] Hankey's assistant, Tom Jones, had been unusually close to Baldwin and, initially at least, MacDonald regarded him with an understandable lack of enthusiasm. But although this coloured Jones's impressions of the new Government,[45] there is no evidence that it damaged the work of the secretariat in any way. In the private office at No. 10, however, MacDonald was at first reluctant to give his full confidence to the officials whom he had inherited from the previous regime. Miss Rose Rosenberg, his dark and vivacious private secretary, was installed in an office leading out of the Cabinet room, and it was to her rather than to his official secretaries that he entrusted his most confidential papers. They were stored in a tall, japan-tinned cupboard, to which she and MacDonald had the only keys, and she was given firm instructions to show them to no one without his permission.[46] There can be little doubt that all this impeded the smooth working of the office. In his diary, MacDonald confessed that his working day stretched 'from 7 am to 1 am, with occasional extras',[47] and although he added defiantly that he enjoyed it, it is clear that he worked too hard, slept too little and worried too much. To some extent, at least, it was his own fault.

His constituency party at Aberavon added to the strain. It was by no means a safe seat, and he was expected to pay as much attention to it as before, even though he was now prime minister and foreign secretary as well as its member of parliament. He was expected to lobby on behalf of Port Talbot as the venue for the National Eisteddfod, to subscribe on a distressing scale to local charities and to persuade the Great Western Railway to arrange for trains travelling between Port Talbot and Tonmawr to stop at Efail Fach.[48] Above all, he was expected to show himself to his constituents. In February, his agent, Joe Brown, sent Rose Rosenberg the details of the arrangements he had made for MacDonald's next visit. 'Monday afternoon two meetings on at the same time,' Brown wrote. 'The New Theatre and the Grand Hall, and in the evening attend the annual meeting of the divisional Labour Party. On Tuesday afternoon at Briton Ferry, in the evening at Glyncorrwg and Abergwynfi. I know every district will be asking for him at the E.C. meeting.'[49] In the end, the visit had to be cancelled because it clashed with budget day. The cancellation, Brown reported, produced an 'unpleasant feeling' at the annual meeting, when 'quite a number expressed their disappointment stating that the valley people had spent a very large amount of money in preparing for the visit, several resolutions were passed all appertaining to the same'. Rose replied, as emolliently as she could, that it was essential for the prime minister to be present in the House when the budget was introduced, and pointed out that MacDonald's responsibilities were, after all, heavier than those of any other member.[50] Such constitutional niceties cut little ice in Aberavon. In May, Brown wrote again, enclosing a complaint from the secretary of the Glyncorrwg Labour Party about MacDonald's failure to appear in the valley, and adding pointedly that he had received several other letters 'of the same nature'.[51]

Complaints about MacDonald's non-appearance paled into insignificance beside the flood of correspondence which arrived at Downing Street during the summer about the magistrates' bench. On May 11th, Brown wrote to ask that his own name should be included in the list of suitable nominees which he had sent to the prime minister. '[I]f the Prime Minister thinks I am worthy of this honour,' he wrote, 'then I can state that no choice would have been more popular with all sections of the community.' Rose replied that MacDonald had not forgotten and that Brown's name had been included.[52] Other claims presented greater problems. In May and June a complex, three-cornered correspondence took place between Rose, Joe Brown and the secretary of the Kenfig Hill Labour Party, who complained bitterly that although Kenfig Hill was a community of 8,000 people, with only one J.P., and that one a Conservative, Brown had ignored it when he drew up his list. Rose managed to parry these assaults with the argument that if too many Labour names were submitted, none at all might be appointed.[53] At the end of June a new hazard appeared. Brown wrote in alarm to say that he had been told that when MacDonald next visited the constituency he would be approached on behalf of unsuitable candidates for the bench, whose characters were 'not very clean' and whose appointment would 'bring you to ill-repute'. The only safe course, Brown insisted, was to stick to the original list, which consisted of 'men of very high standing', who had proved themselves to be 'worthy members of the Party'.[54] In the end, however, Brown's efforts were unavailing. He did not become a magistrate after all, and he had to be content with an assurance from Rose that MacDonald was 'very disappointed with the result', coupled with a warning that 'once the selection Committee had decided what it has to do, political interference must stop, and the Prime Minister is therefore afraid that the matter must remain where it is for the present.'[55]

MacDonald's eldest daughter Ishbel acted as his hostess at No. 10, and her support was a great solace. 'How happy I am with her,' MacDonald wrote on her twenty-first birthday. 'Daily she grows more like her mother. Neither of us like the social side, but she shows how it can be done without vanity or vulgarity of swollen head. I see my ideals of democratic dignity carried out.'[56] But Ishbel could not fill the gap left by her mother's death. 'Felt the presence of them all, especially the two of them,' MacDonald noted after helping to open a baby clinic which had been set up as a memorial to his wife and Mary Middleton. 'I wonder if they know & are happy & do their friends know they are happy. It is an odd thing to have a dead man as a Premier to look after a living world.'[57]

III

A few days after the new Government was formed, Arthur Ponsonby, who had started life as a professional diplomat and was now MacDonald's parliamentary secretary at the Foreign Office, noted in his diary that he was already going to the Foreign Office 'as if I had never ceased going there these last 22 years'. The cries of alarm which the prospect of a Labour Government had provoked in respectable circles rapidly subsided; the mixture of awe and apprehension which it had provoked in the Labour movement evaporated along with them. The new ministers soon settled in to their responsibilities; MacDonald proved to be a skilful chairman of the Cabinet, with a shrewd sense of when to allow a discussion to run on and when to draw it to a close with his own summary of the sense of the meeting. Haldane, who had served as a Cabinet minister under Campbell-Bannerman and Asquith, noticed that MacDonald had always read his papers and described him as 'an excellent President'.[58] Sidney Webb, by no means an uncritical admirer in the past, wrote later that MacDonald's 'behaviour in Cabinet was perfect. He was never discourteous, never overbearing, never unduly dogmatic, patient to everyone, watchful to give everyone a chance to speak.'[59] His public performances appear to have been equally well received. At the beginning of March, Ponsonby wrote that the Government's growing prestige was 'derived almost entirely from MacDonald's powers and personality, which are most remarkable'.[60] Six weeks later he commented, 'J.R.M. is thoroughly settled in the saddle. He continues to be an outstanding figure and both in the House and outside he is winning great praise.'[61]

It was not a comfortable saddle. Unemployment among insured workers had not fallen below 10 per cent since the collapse of the post-war boom nearly three years before. This had given extra force to Labour's claim that the ills of capitalism were incurable and that the workers by hand and brain could receive their due only in a new social order; in so doing, it had helped to put Mac-Donald and his colleagues into office. Now they would be expected, if not to solve the problem, then at least to indicate what kind of solution they would have introduced if they had been given a majority. But this was easier said than done. Britain's economic problems were the symptoms of a deep-seated and long-drawn-out crisis of maladaptation, of the British economy's inability to adjust itself to changing world conditions, of the inertia and complacency of those who owned and managed the old staple industries which faced competition from newer rivals, of the unwillingness of a once dominant society to abandon attitudes and assumptions dating from the days of its supremacy. The Labour Party was in revolt against that society; but it had been shaped by it all the same. Its leaders had mostly grown to maturity in the 1880s or 1890s; it was as difficult for them as it was for their countrymen to recognize that the world which they had taken for granted as young men no longer existed. Their ideology was a cry of protest against the injustices of that world: it provided little guidance for the world in which they found themselves now. They hated poverty, and wished to relieve it; they believed in socialism, and hoped to introduce it. But apart from the capital levy, which was of dubious relevance to the problem of unemployment and idle resources, they had no distinctive economic or fiscal policies of their own.

Problems of policy were compounded by a more fundamental problem of political strategy. The previous two months had shown that there were still many middle-class voters — and, no doubt, many working-class voters as well — to whom the whole notion of a Labour Government seemed somehow shocking and unnatural. If the Labour Party was to establish itself unmistakably as the main anti-Conservative party in Britain, at least some of these voters would have to be won over. Office provided a golden opportunity to allay the fears and prejudices which had so far held them back. Yet if the new Government courted them with too much enthusiasm, it would disappoint, and perhaps alienate, some of its most energetic supporters. Many Labour men had not wanted the party to take office at all, for fear that it might be captured or contaminated by the system which it would be called upon to administer. Most of these had been persuaded to abandon outright opposition, but many still looked askance at the whole enterprise and waited uneasily for the first sign of cowardice or treachery. Others believed that office should be used deliberately to step up the class war, and urged the Government to ride for a fall by introducing socialist legislation which the older parties would then join together to reject. Neither group would derive much satisfaction from a minority Government which appeared to be content with the role of caretaker or apprentice.

It was against this background that Parliament reassembled on February 12th, after a short recess to allow the new ministers time to prepare their programme. The galleries were filled to capacity, and the gangways on the floor of the House were crowded with members who could not find seats. After questions, MacDonald rose to deliver a dignified and forceful exposition of the Government's policy, lasting for nearly two hours and deftly designed to present himself and his colleagues as the sober and responsible, yet at the same time sturdy and independent, custodians of the nation's welfare. No prime minister, he pointed out, had addressed the House in comparable circumstances. For the time being, no party had a majority; that would necessitate changes in some 'House of Commons habits'. In the past, Oppositions had practised 'all sorts of ingenuities' to turn Governments out after a snap vote. This Government had no intention of being forced out in such a way. It would go out if it were defeated in a vote of confidence, but it would introduce its business 'accepting the responsibilities of a minority and claiming the privileges that attach to those responsibilities'. It intended, first of all, to carry on the administration of the country. In addition, it would set up an authoritative committee to examine the whole question of the national debt, do its best to revive trade and employment, make the administration of unemployment benefit more humane and 'get right into the heart' of the housing problem. Above all,

The Government will concern itself with what it considers to be great national and international interests, which it will present to this House from its own standpoint. Coalitions are detestable, are dishonest ... Therefore ... we shall bring before this House proposals to deal with great national and international problems, and we are not afraid of what fate we may meet in the process. If we wind up this week ... we shall have made our mark upon the history of these islands ...

... [A]t this time of irrational timorousness, when pessimism and optimism are striving for mastery — I appeal to everybody, I appeal to the House, to go out ... not for tranquillity, but for security and confidence based on goodwill, and to be just and worthy of respect. In that spirit, the Labour Party propose to act.[62]

'Security and confidence based on goodwill', 'to be just and worthy of respect' — the slogans were unexciting, but excitement was the last thing MacDonald wanted to create. As we have seen, his most compelling argument for forming a Government in the first place had been a defensive one: that if Labour shrank from the challenge it would jeopardize the gains it had made since the war and risk losing its position as a major party. His policy in office followed the logic which had persuaded him to take it. As he saw it, he and his colleagues were there not to defy or even to subvert the established order but to infiltrate it — to prove that they, too, could carry on the King's government if they were given the chance, and in doing so, to consolidate their lead over the Liberal Party. To do this, they had to trump the Liberals' cards. They had to show that the jibes of the Liberal press were without foundation, that working men could hold the highest offices of state with dignity and authority, that although they might lack experience they were neither wild nor incompetent, that MacDonald, rather than Asquith or Lloyd George, was now the true custodian of the Liberal tradition of ordered progress through the ballot box. Above all, they had to show that a Labour Government was part of the normal scheme of things; and to do that, they had to behave, in defiance of the facts, as though they believed so themselves.

Half a century later, these aims seem modest, even pusillanimous. There is no evidence that they seemed so to MacDonald's Cabinet. His strategy was not imposed by prime-ministerial authority on unwilling colleagues; it was dictated by the nature of the Labour Party and by the circumstances in which it found itself. His critics could complain, with some justification, that he had condemned his Government to fight on its opponents' ground. But no other ground was available. The alternative of riding for a fall was incompatible not only with his political philosophy and emotional attitudes but with the philosophy and attitudes of most of his followers. It was based on a catastrophic view of social progress, which most Labour men rejected; its purpose would have been to fan the flames of a class war, which only a minority of the Labour Party was seriously anxious to fight. In any case, there was no guarantee that the King would grant a dissolution to a minority Government which had been defeated after introducing legislation which it knew the House of Commons would not accept. Even if he did, the Labour Party might well lose ground in an election in which the Conservative and Liberal parties would, by definition, have joined forces against it. Yet if riding for a fall were ruled out, some variant of MacDonald's strategy was all that remained. If it failed, the party would, at any rate, be no worse off. If it succeeded, Labour might break through the web of custom and deference which had so far confined it to its existing working-class base. To succeed, the new ministers would have to bend over backwards to demonstrate their respectability; but that was the price they paid for belonging to a working-class party which aspired to govern a class-divided and hier-archical society. That, or something like it, was the logic of MacDonald's speech on February 12th. In one form or another, it was to seem equally convincing to his successors in 1945 and 1964.

Sometimes he behaved even more circumspectly than his own logic dictated. One of the first problems that confronted the new Government was the question of court dress – trivial in itself, but of considerable significance as a symbol. By tradition, Cabinet ministers wore a special uniform to attend the court. George V attached great importance to ceremonial, and he was anxious that his new ministers should follow the custom. Even before the Government took office, his private secretary, Lord Stamfordham, wrote to the Labour chief whip, Ben Spoor, to say that the necessary uniform could be obtained for £30 from 'Messrs. Moss Bros'.[63] Early in February, the question came before the Cabinet. It was decided that in future negotiations with Stamfordham, the prime minister should try to arrange that ministers attending levees should be allowed to do so in black evening dress and knee breeches, that a panel of ministers who already possessed or were willing to acquire the necessary uniform should be set up, that the ministers who were required to attend the King at court should be drawn from this panel, and that ministers who did not possess a uniform should be excused from attending functions at which it was obligatory.[64]

This compromise provoked angry criticism in the more Cromwellian sec-tions of the Labour Party, where it was seen as a surrender to the class enemy; even Mrs Hamilton, who later wrote a skilful defence of MacDonald's under-lying strategy as prime minister, pointed out that it would have been perfectly possible for the Government to have 'asked for the allowance of the Party's peculiar point of view in relation to ceremonial and the social hierarchy'.[65] MacDonald's diary makes it clear that his own attitude was based at least as much on his fondness for colourful ceremonial and on the affection and respect which he felt for the King, as on a political calculation that it would be unwise to offend him. 'If the poor spirits that are disturbed by pageantry only felt the spirit of ceremony,' he wrote at the beginning of March, 'how much richer they would be & how much more powerful as the pioneers of a new world.'[66] On May 12th, he noted:

Have been at Victoria again to receive crowned heads, & I suppose the anti-gold lace people will be at me again. They are a dull-witted lot. A wily friend who is always at me not to do substantial work but to employ cuts & appearances constantly uses such people as his best argument that Socialism is not really an intellectual system but one of clap-trap. To the mind of many if I give sixpence a day from public funds to everybody who asked for it, I would be a Socialist. These braids & uniforms are but part of an official pageantry & as my conscience is not on my back, a gold coat means nothing to me but a form of dress to be worn or rejected as a hat would be in relation to the rest of one's clothes. Nor do I care a fig for the argument that it is part of a pageantry of class, or royalty or flunkeyism. If royalty had given the Labour Government the cold shoulder, we should have returned the call. It has not. It has been considerate, cordially correct, human & friendly. The King has never seen me as a Minister without making me feel that he was also seeing me as a friend. I record a remark I made to one of the Left incorruptibles who asked why I had been at the Palace: 'Because its allurements are so great that I cannot trust you to go' ... The stay at Windsor – 26, 27 April – was a revelation in spirit. The kindly homeliness was that of a cottage & sat well in gilt halls. It was the natural blending of the two that was such a welcome experience. 'Sycophancy' growls the incorruptibles [sic]: 'Not at all. The dignity & authority of human quali-ties.'[67]

At other times, he was prepared to break with tradition. Two days after the Labour Government came into office, General Sir Borlass Childs wrote from Scotland Yard to the private office at No. 10, enclosing, 'in accordance with custom,' a copy of his weekly report on revolutionary movements in Great Britain and asking whether the prime minister wished the practice to be con-tinued. MacDonald's private secretary replied on January 30th:

I asked the Prime Minister about the continued circulation of your paper. His view, after reading it was that little of the news contained in it was likely to be unfamiliar to members of the Government or, indeed, to any-one who reads the 'Workers' Weekly' and similar papers, so that in its present scope, he doubts whether it would provide very edifying or interest-ing reading to members of the Cabinet.

He thought, however, that it might be made at once attractive and indeed entertaining if its survey were extended to cover not only com-munistic activities but also other political activities of an extreme tendency. For instance a little knowledge in regard to the Fascist movement in this country and its main apostles ... or possibly some information as to the source of the 'Morning Post' funds might give an exhilarating flavour to the document and by enlarging its scope convert it into a complete and finished work of art.

Perhaps you would consider the continued circulation of the document in the light of this proposition?[68]

General Childs was not amused. He wrote back stiffly to say that he had never thought it right to investigate movements which wished to achieve their aims peacefully, that he already possessed 'a very complete knowledge' of the Fascists and that he was not aware that the *Morning Post* had ever advocated revolution. If the prime minister wished him to extend his operations, he added, he would doubtless receive instructions.[69] General Childs won his battle. The weekly report remained in circulation, and the vision of a police investigation into the finances of the *Morning Post* remained unrealized.[70]

IV

General Childs was not alone in his obduracy. All the available evidence suggests that the home departments accepted, and in some cases even welcomed, their new masters — in part, no doubt, because no important changes of policy were made. The service departments, and particularly the Admiralty, were harder nuts to crack. The first big battle took place in March, over a proposed new naval base at Singapore. The proposal had been approved in principle by Lloyd George's Cabinet in 1921, and confirmed by the Imperial Conference in 1923. In February 1924, however, the new Cabinet appointed a committee to re-examine it, and also to inquire into the naval building programme. The Admiralty got the building programme it wanted. It fared less well over Singapore. At the first meeting of the committee at the end of February, Armiral Beatty, the first sea lord, made a long and impassioned statement on the historical, strategic, economic and diplomatic aspects of the question, designed to prove that trade to the value of £890 million a year would be imperilled, and Britain's position in the far east destroyed, if the base were not built.[71] The second meeting at the beginning of March, however, resolved itself into a prolonged duel between Beatty and MacDonald. MacDonald acknowledged that the Foreign Office favoured the base, but declared that '[s]peaking purely as a non-party Secretary of State for Foreign Affairs', his own view was that unless the proposal were shelved, there would be no hope of reaching an international agreement on disarmament. The official record of the discussion that followed provides a vivid illustration of the problems faced by an insecure civilian government in conflict with determined military advisers:

> Lord Beatty ... pointed out that by a previous Cabinet decision all question of the possibility of war with the United States of America had been ruled out. If a base was not provided at Singapore the possibility of successfully carrying on a war with Japan in the Pacific was also out of the question. Consequently there remained only the possibility of a war with the Mediterranean powers. If the two former conditions were accepted our present naval forces could be very largely reduced and yet be equal to the French and Italian fleets. He considered that it was of no use keeping a great fleet

in being which was unable to exercise its function ... [T]he Admiralty wished for the provision of only a very small sum during the next twelve months. This would be expended on preliminary work, borings etc. ... and every twelve months' delay in commencing these borings put off the date on which the British Empire would no longer be dependent on the good-will of other powers in the Pacific ... If the Government's decision was against the policy of a base at Singapore he considered that it would be better to carry out that policy *in toto* and scrap at least half the British Navy ...

Mr Ramsay MacDonald ... pointed out that it was not a question of scrapping the Navy ... If we commenced Singapore now he considered that it would make any chance of success on the lines of limitation of armaments very remote. Once Singapore was commenced circumstances would inevitably continue to build up a military situation in the East until we reached a state similar to that in the North Sea in 1914. If we found we were unable to reach agreement to limit armaments he considered that the case for Singapore had been made out ...

Lord Beatty stated that when it was considered what we had at stake — the British Empire, millions of money — the cost of building a base at Singapore did not seem a very large insurance. He urged that the work should be commenced at once in order to reduce the length of time during which this country was in the position of having to exist in the Pacific on sufferance of another power.

Mr Ramsay MacDonald said that the word 'sufferance' was only comparative. On paper it might be argued that we had at stake the British Empire and the millions of trade involved; in practice he did not consider that this was so.

Mr Walsh enquired if war broke out in the East in the next twelve months, what could we do?

Lord Beatty replied that the whole of our Eastern trade East of Aden would go. India would be open to attack and our Ports of Trincomali, Colombo, Rangoon, etc., would fall ... He assured the Committee that the great responsibility which rested on him whilst our fleet was powerless to act in Eastern waters was very heavy indeed. He would do anything in his power to shorten the period during which our fleet could not be considered capable of carrying out its traditional duties in the Pacific ... [72]

In the end, Beatty lost. The committee decided that 'in the light of the new atmosphere the prime minister was trying to create in regard to foreign policy' the base should not be proceeded with, and that no further expenditure should be incurred on it. But this was by no means the end of the matter. A long struggle took place over the precise form of words in which the decision should be made public, and the Admiralty fought a vigorous rearguard action to limit the extent of its defeat. Journalists were briefed about the alleged value of British trade and shipping in eastern waters.[73] Chelmsford tried unsuccessfully to persuade his colleagues to spend an additional £15,000 on preliminary work at Singapore, on the grounds that if this were not done, the full value of the expenditure already incurred would not 'be available in the event of the work being resumed at some future date'.[74] Under pressure from the Admiralty, the Cabinet agreed that the statement in which its decision was to be announced should include a phrase making it clear that the naval staff had taken a contrary view – thus undermining one of the central pillars of the doctrine of ministerial responsibility.[75] On March 18th, MacDonald duly told the House of Commons that, although arguments in support of the base had been urged upon the Government 'from the point of view of naval defence,' it had decided not to proceed with the plan.[76] He was entitled to congratulate himself on his victory, but he must have wondered how often he could afford to challenge such a formidable antagonist.

His next battle with the service departments took place on superficially more favourable terrain, but this time his tactics were more circumspect and the outcome was less successful. In the summer of 1924, the proposal to build a Channel tunnel – which had been mooted at intervals since the 1880s, and invariably turned down on strategic grounds – was revived by an all-party committee, supported by over four hundred M.P.s. MacDonald was in favour of the idea, but as he put it to a deputation from the Channel Tunnel Committee at the end of June, he was anxious to take the question 'right out of party politics'.[77] Accordingly, he summoned a special meeting of the Committee of Imperial Defence to re-examine the question, which all living former prime ministers were invited to attend. The committee met on July 1st, after a heavy barrage from the services, ably assisted by Hankey. The chiefs of staff committee reported that the tunnel would lead to the disappearance of the cross-channel steamer service, thus inflicting great damage on the navy, and impede the growth of cross-channel air services, thus damaging the R.A.F. Worse still, it might create a feeling of insecurity in the country and lead to a public demand for an undesirable concentration of forces near the tunnel entrance. Hankey circulated a paper prepared by the Home Ports Defence Committee in 1920, warning of the dangers of surprise attack, a memorandum by Lord Balfour, arguing sagely that the tunnel might put an end to Britain's position as an island power, and a paper of his own, pointing out that Sir Garnett Wolsely in the 1880s and Sir Henry Wilson in the 1920s had both argued that if the tunnel were built Britain would become a continental power and would therefore be obliged to maintain forces on a continental scale.[78] When the committee met on July 1st, the tunnel was attacked, in turn, by Beatty, Sir Hugh Trenchard, Balfour, Asquith, Lloyd George, Baldwin and even Sidney Webb.[79] MacDonald had no alternative but to give in. On July 7th, he made a statement in the House of Commons, announcing that the Committee of Imperial Defence had decided unanimously against the proposal.[80] With understandable chagrin he noted privately:

> Presided over meeting of Committee of Imperial Defence with ex-Premiers present on subject of Channel Tunnel. Amazed at military mind. It has got itself and the country as well in a rut where neither fresh air nor new ideas blow. Like old woman who seals doors & windows to keep her from shivering. My burdens are so heavy & so many that I cannot take up the Tunnel at present, but it must be taken up. Meeting most unsatisfactory.[81]

V

MacDonald's battles with the service departments were fought out behind closed doors. The Government's first big public test came in the middle of February when the Transport and General Workers' Union called a national dock strike, and the Cabinet made it clear that it was willing, if necessary, to proclaim a state of emergency under the 1920 Emergency Powers Act. Behind the scenes, it made ready to activate the machinery which the coalition Government had created to deal with such situations. A supply and transport committee was set up and it was decided that Josiah Wedgwood, the chancellor of the duchy, should be ready to act as chief civil commissioner. Privately, Wedgwood warned the union that the Government was prepared to use troops to keep essential supplies moving.[82] At the same time, however, the dispute was referred to a court of inquiry, which found in favour of the men. The strike ended in a victory for the dockers, and without an open conflict between the union and the Government.

A more serious test of the same kind followed a month later. Once again, the dispute began with the Transport and General Workers, but this time other unions were brought in as well. On March 21st, the London tram workers went on strike. A court of inquiry found that a wage increase was justified, but that the employers could not afford to pay it unless the Government introduced legislation to co-ordinate London's fragmented public transport services. On March 26th, Ernest Bevin, the Transport and General Workers' truculent and formidable general secretary, announced that the railway unions had agreed to bring the London underground to a halt in two days' time. MacDonald told the Cabinet that he had already written a personal letter to Bevin, warning him that any extension of the strike was 'bound to bring in the Government', and it was decided that he should repeat the warning when he saw Bevin that afternoon. Bevin was not impressed. The union, he pointed out in his reply to MacDonald's letter, had submitted its claim to the employers before it was known that a Labour Government was likely; there was therefore no need for MacDonald to accept any responsibility for its actions. A joint committee of the T.U.C. General Council and the Labour Party National Executive passed a resolution deploring any resort to the Emergency Powers Act and urging the Government to take over London's public transport, and to pay the men higher wages with the aid of a subsidy.[83] The Government, it seemed, had either to sit back and watch while the population of London walked to work, or engage in a head-on collision with the unions and the party.

According to Sidney Webb, the Cabinet's answer was unanimous.[84] On March 27th, it approved a draft proclamation of emergency. It was decided that alternative transport should be provided for Government employees, hospital patients and similar categories; that the Government should 'offer adequate protection to any omnibus, tube or tram services that found themselves able to run'; that special constables should be recruited to provide protection; and that the Admiralty should at once begin preparations for using naval ratings in the power stations. The Supply and Transport Committee's proposal that the minister of transport should provide a char-à-banc service for the general public should not be announced.[85] At ten o'clock that evening, MacDonald told the House of Commons that a state of emergency had been proclaimed, but made it clear that negotiations were continuing, that the Government still hoped that it could avoid putting the powers that were now available to it into operation, and that as an interim solution it intended to introduce an admittedly unsatisfactory Bill to reorganize London traffic which it had inherited from its predecessors.[86] On this somewhat shaky basis the dispute was settled next day. The London Traffic Bill received its second reading with Conservative support, though in the teeth of vigorous opposition from a group of London Labour members led by Herbert Morrison, and the union and employers agreed on a compromise settlement of the wage claim.

VI

Public-opinion polls had not then been invented, and the fluctuations in the Government's popularity cannot be measured precisely. On the whole, however, the available evidence suggests that its stock rose fairly steadily. In March, Ponsonby wrote that the Government 'is accepted and there is no serious animosity in any quarter'.[87] In April he commented that, although it had 'yielded unnecessarily to the gigantic pressures of authority and tradition', its moderation was gaining it 'great support from the middle opinion of the country'.[88] By-election results pointed in the same direction. In March, Henderson was returned at Burnley with a majority of 7,000 over the Conservatives, against a Labour majority of only 2,000 in the general election three months before. In part, the improvement may have been due to the absence of a Liberal candidate in the by-election, but even so, the result could hardly fail to give great comfort to the Government.

In Parliament, things went less smoothly. In March, a number of I.L.P.

members voted against the Government on the service estimates, and *Forward* declared angrily that 'Comrade Chelmsford and Lord Beatty and Admiral Tyrrwhit are in a position to dictate the policy of the Labour Government.' In the same month, forty-five Labour M.P.s abstained from voting on the Government's Trade Facilities Bill, which was carried with Conservative and Liberal support.[89] 'The rank and file', Ponsonby wrote, 'still behave like an Opposition. They rightly complain of our weakness, but they have no mercy and seldom do any of them give us any support.'[90] MacDonald was still more upset. 'My great concern at present is the failure of our backbenchers to respond to the new conditions,' he wrote at the beginning of March. 'Some of the disappointed ones maintain a feud & are as hostile as though they were not of us.'[91] More serious still from a parliamentary point of view, the Government failed to establish harmonious relations with the Liberals, on whose votes it depended to stay in office. As a result, it lacked the two most powerful weapons which are normally at the disposal of all British Governments: control of the parliamentary timetable, and an automatic majority for Government business. Ministers were condemned to live from hand to mouth, with no way of knowing whether they would survive from one week to the next, or what storms they would have to encounter if they did.

To some extent, this was due to personal factors. MacDonald had never had a high opinion of Asquith and he would have been superhuman if he had not felt some irritation at the patronizing tone which Asquith habitually adopted towards him and his ministers. His opinion of Lloyd George was even lower. Like most people on the left he had been shocked by the cynical and unprincipled style of the post-war coalition, and he could neither forget nor forgive the part which Lloyd George had played during the war and at the peace conference. Again and again, his diary reveals the depth of his animosity to the two rival Liberals. 'The Liberals get meaner & meaner,' he noted two weeks after Parliament had resumed, '& we respect the Conservatives more & more.'[92] The struggle for the Liberal leadership, he noted at the beginning of the summer, 'is really being badly conducted as such quarrels by small men usually are. None of the claimants attend the H. of C. very regularly, but when they do they plume themselves vulgarly (interrupt, cock their heads in the air, smile with superior airs—and have a good Liberal press next morning).'[93] Although Asquith was head and shoulders above the other Liberals, he wrote, 'I have never hit it off with him. His behaviour to C.B. was too much the natural way of the man.'[94] As for Lloyd George, he noted during the summer that he had thought of making a speech on the recent degradation of honours, and had rejected it as being too dangerous. 'I discussed this with the King at Windsor,' he wrote. ' "That was that Welshman", he once remarked. The credit of that cheapjack is justly low.'[95]

Yet the relationship between the Liberal and Labour Parties in the 1924 Parliament cannot be explained primarily in personal terms. By far the most important factor was the electoral rivalry between them. They could not both be the major progressive party in Britain at the same time; so long as they were in competition for the position, there could be no lasting agreement between them. Liberals, then and since, complained that the Government treated them as 'patient oxen', who were expected to help in pulling Labour's chariot through the division lobbies, only to be slaughtered when their work was done. There was some truth in the complaint; but the alternative to slaughtering the Liberals would have been to slaughter the Labour Party. By the same token, Liberals could not be expected to work with unmixed enthusiasm for the survival of a Government, the chief motive of which was to replace them as soon as possible. In the absence of an agreement, relations between the two parties could hardly fail to deteriorate. The Liberals dared not turn the Government out, for fear of losing ground at a general election. But if they were to justify their existence as a separate party, they had to differentiate themselves from it; and to do so, they had to engage in continual petty skirmishes, designed to wound but not to kill. These tactics provoked increasing resentment on the Labour benches, where they were seen as a final proof of the iniquity of all capitalist parties and of the disingenuousness of the Liberals' claim to be a party of the left.

At the end of February, Wheatley scored a personal triumph in a censure debate on his decision to rescind the notorious 'Poplar Order'. 'Mr Wheatley's speech was a masterpiece,' MacDonald reported in his letter to the King. 'Quiet and fluent in its delivery, clear in its exposition of facts, logical and precise in its marshalling of arguments, vigorous in defence, humorous and decisive in attack.'[96] This was followed by reasonably calm weather for a month, until a big storm blew up at the end of March. Early in the session, a Labour backbencher, Benjamin Gardner, had introduced a Private Member's Bill dealing with the growing problem of evictions. Thanks to Liberal support, it had been given a second reading, but Wheatley had given it no encouragement and it had made little progress in committee. David Kirkwood had then intervened with a bitter personal attack on MacDonald, and in order to placate the Left Wheatley decided to bring in a Government Bill.[97] On March 25th, he circulated a memorandum on evictions under the Rent Restrictions Act, arguing that the recent increase in the number of evictions was due partly to increasing unemployment, and to consequent non-payment of rent. This aspect of the problem, he proposed, should be dealt with by prohibiting evictions in cases where the non-payment of rent was due to unemployment, unless the landlord could satisfy the court that greater hardship would be caused by refusing to grant an order for possession than by granting it.[98]

As Beatrice Webb later pointed out, the proposal was an administrative folly — inequitable as between one landlord and another, and likely to encourage all landlords to discriminate against tenants who seemed likely to become unemployed.[99] At the Cabinet meeting on March 26th, however, it was agreed that legislation on the lines of Wheatley's memorandum should be introduced. On March 27th, a draft Bill was sent to the Cabinet office by the Ministry of Health, and on March 28th this was considered by the Home Affairs Committee. The Committee agreed to recommend the Cabinet to authorize the introduction of the Bill 'forthwith'. It was placed on the agenda for the Cabinet meeting on April 2nd, but owing to the pressure of other business the relevant item was not reached. However, the Bill had already been printed and circulated; and that afternoon it came up for its second reading debate.[100] Asquith made it clear that although the Liberals agreed with the objects of the Bill, they could not support it in its existing form;[101] and that the Government would therefore be defeated if they persisted with it. Despite a passionate speech by Maxton, urging the Government to face defeat and go to the country on the issue, Clynes held a hurried conference in his room with a few ministers he could find.[102] At eight o'clock, he intervened in the debate to announce that the Government would withdraw the offending clause and substitute a new one, throwing on to public funds the cost of maintaining a distressed tenant in his home.[103]

Clynes's statement provoked an uproar. In reply to a question from the indefatigable Pringle, the Speaker announced that a new clause on the lines promised by Clynes could not be inserted within the existing Bill, and that a Money Resolution would be necessary. After a quarter of an hour of tumult, however, Pringle proceeded to talk the Bill out; and for a while the Government was saved. More humiliation soon followed. Immediately before the House rose for the weekend on April 5th, Clynes made a statement announcing that the Government now proposed to throw the burden on the local authorities. This led to a new explosion. Kirkwood savagely attacked the Government as 'jellyfish' who had betrayed their pledges; and the unfortunate Clynes then proceeded to turn yet another somersault, promising that although the cost of maintaining distressed tenants would be borne by the local authorities in the first instance, the Government were prepared to consider 'recouping the local authorities from State funds'.[104] This suggestion was promptly condemned in a memorandum by the relevant officials from the Treasury, Scottish Office and Ministry of Health, on the grounds that it was undesirable to 'embark on a system of Government subsidy in aid of rent which would be most likely to have the most serious financial and economic consequences'. They advised that, if it were thought unavoidable to announce some financial concession to the local authorities, the Government should make it clear 'that experience must first be gained of the actual effect of the new proposals, and that the Government is entitled in this connection to take into account the effect of their unemployment proposals'. Any promise on these lines, they went on, should be limited to 'necessitous areas'. Above all, it was essential 'that the problem should not be definitely linked up with the question of rent, which is only one of the factors to be taken into account in connection with Poor Law Relief, but that it should be treated on a general basis'.[105]

The House reassembled on April 7th in a confused and febrile state. Confusion soon grew still more confounded. Since Pringle had talked the debate out the previous Wednesday, he held the floor; and after he finished, MacDonald rose from the Government front bench to explain the new position. He had originally intended to reserve his intervention to a later stage; as he later confessed disarmingly to the King, 'it might have been better perhaps if he had acted on his original intention.'[106] He began by explaining that the Government's position had not changed. In his speech in the original second reading debate, Wheatley had acknowledged that the burden of protecting unemployed tenants should be borne by the whole community, not merely by their landlords. That was still the Government's position. They proposed to amend clause 1 of the Bill to make it illegal to issue an eviction order until the tenant had had a reasonable opportunity to apply to the local poor law authority for relief and until the authority had had an opportunity to consider the application. In essence, this was what they had always wanted; it was not the Government that was being inconsistent, but the Opposition. His attempt to take the offensive misfired badly. *Hansard* records the central passages of the rest of the speech as follows:

Judging by the Official Report, promptings have come, again and again, that this Bill can only be accepted if the Government withdraw Clause 1 and substitute another with State assistance provided for after putting on the Order Paper a Money Resolution. [Interruption]. If that is not the situation, what is the situation? [Hon Members: 'Yes, what is the situation?']

If that is not the situation, if the suggestion was not that State funds should be used, then why the pressure for the Money Resolution? ... The situation therefore is perfectly clear. [Laughter] ...

... The Government put forward this Bill, limited in accordance with their aim and intention in introducing it, that no unemployed man or his family shall be evicted without first of all every step possible being taken to keep him in his house, and in doing that the burden shall not be placed upon the owner of the house, but shall be placed upon public funds. Owing to the technical use of the term 'Public funds', I dare say some misunderstanding arose about the Money Resolution, but the position right through from the very beginning has been that this was to be a public charge.

Mr. Austen Chamberlain: I am really trying my best to understand upon what public fund it is proposed to make this charge.

The Prime Minister: No order shall be issued until a tenant has had a reasonable opportunity to apply to the Poor Law authority for relief, and that authority has had an opportunity of considering any such application.

Mr. Chamberlain: That does not answer the question.

The Prime Minister: I think it does ... [107]

After this, it was scarcely surprising that the Government was defeated by

221 to 212. Next day, MacDonald announced that the rejection of Wheatley's Bill had made it impossible to introduce another Bill on similar lines during that session, and that the Government therefore proposed to support a Private Member's Bill on the same subject which had been introduced earlier in the session by Sir John Simon.[108] So far as evictions and rent restrictions were concerned, that was the end of the matter.

VII

In a wider sense, it was far from being so. The whole affair had revealed a dangerous lack of administrative and political cohesion. Even before the Government's defeat on April 7th, Hankey had carried out an investigation into the background, which showed that at the meeting of the Home Affairs Committee which had approved the draft Bill, only three ministers had been present—the chairman, Lord Haldane; Josiah Wedgwood; and Wheatley himself. Wheatley's memorandum on the subject had not been received at the Cabinet office until the afternoon of March 25th, even though the Cabinet was due to consider it the following day. 'The moral', Hankey wrote, 'appears to be, firstly, that the habit which has recently grown up of raising questions at the Cabinet without sufficient notice and without giving members time properly to consider the papers and have them examined in their departments, should be strongly discouraged; secondly, that the Cabinet should insist on the regular attendance of ministers at the Committee of Home Affairs; and thirdly that recommendations of the Committee of Home Affairs should not be acted on until approved by the Cabinet.'[109] Shortly afterwards, Sir Patrick Hastings submitted a memorandum on similar lines, complaining that the law officers were not being properly consulted, alleging that he had not even seen the Government's proposed amendment to the Rent and Mortgage Interest Restriction Bill until the day of the debate, and suggesting that in future all important Bills should be shown to the law officers before they were printed.[110]

On April 15th, the Cabinet duly decided that ministers who wanted to submit proposals to the Cabinet involving legislation should arrange that the law officers should be notified as soon as possible, and that questions were to be put on the Cabinet agenda only if the ministers concerned had circulated a memorandum at least five days before the Cabinet meeting, unless the prime minister gave express permission to the contrary.[111] But these changes were only part of the solution. The political weaknesses revealed by the rent restrictions fiasco were more serious than the administrative ones. It had been caused partly by Wheatley's unwillingness to resist his old friends from the Clyde, and partly by a general lack of co-ordination within the Government, for which MacDonald was ultimately responsible. A fortnight before the crisis, Beatrice Webb noted in her diary that the parliamentary party was 'drifting', that Clynes was incompetent, that the chief whip was weakened by recurrent bouts of malaria, and that the 'dull-headed miners' in the whips' office did not earn their salaries of £1,000 a year. '[R]elations between the leading ministers on the Treasury bench', she wrote, 'either do not exist or are far from cordial.' Henderson, who was still in charge of the party machine, found MacDonald unapproachable; Clynes, who was in charge of the Government's business in the House, found the same. 'No. 10 and no. 11 see no more of each other', Henderson told her, 'than if they slept and ate a hundred miles apart.'[112] MacDonald, she added in another diary two weeks later, 'remains the "mystery man" to all his colleagues – who know little of his thinkings and doings'.[113]

These judgments cannot be accepted uncritically. Beatrice Webb was a good hater, and her feud with MacDonald went back for more than twenty years. Yet there was an element of truth in her criticisms. Since his wife's death, MacDonald had made his decisions in solitude – proceeding, particularly in crisis situations, by intuition rather than by analysis. He had always been elusive and secretive; in spite of his skill as a negotiator, consultation did not come naturally to him. These traits were reinforced by the legacies of the past. Snowden, the only leading member of the Cabinet who had been on MacDonald's side during the war, had been a savage critic of his leadership before 1914 and had opposed the I.L.P.'s decision to nominate him as leader in 1922. Clynes, Henderson and Webb had all belonged to the pro-war wing of the party, which he had fought, with considerable bitterness on both sides, for almost eight years; they, too, had opposed his return to the leadership. Perhaps for this reason, Thomas was the only leading figure in the Cabinet to whom MacDonald was at all close; and Thomas, though a host in himself, was not a substitute for a team of ministers, working together.

Deep-seated personal characteristics and the scars of old battles could not be wished out of existence; complaints about MacDonald's aloofness, unapproachability and autocratic tendencies continued to be made. Nevertheless, the rent restrictions crisis led to an important change in procedure. Towards the end of April, MacDonald noted in his diary that his chief difficulty was the 'co-ordinating & guidance work of the Premiership', and recorded a demand by a group of discontented ministers to discuss their grievances with him.[114] Perhaps as a result of their initiative, he began soon afterwards to hold regular lunches on Mondays for what Beatrice Webb called the 'Fathers of the Labour Movement' – Henderson, Clynes, Thomas, Snowden, her husband and the chief whip.[115] The lunches were informal, and no record of the agenda or proceedings survives. According to Beatrice Webb, those present discussed the business before the House during the coming week, but it is not clear whether wider questions of policy were discussed as well. The results are hard to assess. The group presumably acted as a kind of inner Cabinet, but the effect of its deliberations on the real Cabinet is uncertain. What is clear, however, is that the Government's cohesion improved; that there were no more parliamentary fiascos and a number of parliamentary successes; and that by the end of the summer, the Government's standing had risen appreciably.

At the end of April, Snowden was universally applauded in the Labour and Liberal parties for an adroit and popular budget, which cut indirect taxes by £29 million and direct taxes by £14 million, and which its author proudly described as 'the greatest step ever taken towards the Radical idea of the free breakfast table'. Soon afterwards, the Labour Party gained a seat from the Conservatives in a by-election at West Toxteth, and increased its vote by 3,000. At about the same time, the Conservatives held Kelvingrove with an increased majority, but at the expense of the Liberals, whose vote fell from 4,600 to 1,300. Meanwhile, MacDonald's foreign policy was beginning to bear fruit, and there were signs that the Labour Party might gain the credit for solving the reparations crisis. The only big fly in the Government's ointment was the stubborn impermeability of the unemployment figures, though even here it could point to a significant reduction since the previous summer, and it was on these that the opposition parties and the Government's critics in the Labour Party all concentrated their fire.

On May 17th, the I.L.P. administrative council resolved that MacDonald should be asked to 'bring to the notice of the Government the immediate improvement that would accrue by the establishment of a 48 hour week for all workers and an all-round increase in wages'.[116] At the end of May, the Conservatives put down a motion to reduce the minister of labour's salary. MacDonald made it clear that the Government would go to the country if it were carried, and in his winding-up speech on May 29th, he made a vigorous counterattack on his predecessors, coupling it with a touching description of the difficulties in the Government's path and a glowing account of its ambitions:

On 16th October 1923, the then Minister of Labour ... made this statement ... that £50,000,000 was to be spent immediately upon a winter programme ... [I]n November 1923 [he] said ... 'It amounts, in round figures, on a very conservative estimate, to about £100,000,000' ... We came effectively into office not before the beginning of February. What did we find? Great machinery at work that was going to absorb before the end of the winter £100,000,000? Not at all! The bills have been paid at the end of March — £250,000 ...

... [I]f we are really going to cheapen our electrical supply, as Switzerland, Norway and Sweden have been able to cheapen theirs, by the use of water power, Scotland and Wales are pre-eminently the place where the exploration should take place. But this must all be worked out ... As soon as the Commissioners ... produce a scheme, they have to hold a local enquiry. All the expense and paraphernalia of that has to be gone through, and so on and so on; and because we are baffled in that way ... the Conservative Party produce an Amendment to reduce my right hon. Friend's salary by £100 because in four months, he has not produced that legislation, put it into operation and produced its results ...

Then there is the question of afforestation. I believe in afforestation. Whilst the planting is going on it gives employment. When the growth starts and the first pruning begins it is a great work for the country. But there is one condition. You cannot get London unemployed people to go up to Perthshire to plant trees. Afforestation, if it is to be any good at all, must be associated with a well-considered scheme of land settlement ... Again you come up against this problem of how the State may have ... to acquire control over the land which at the moment it has not got ...

... It may be that Kelvingrove has its attractions and West Toxteth has its terrors. Never mind! Let them go into the Lobby tonight ... I can assure you I shall do my best to meet you on every platform throughout the country.[117]

It turned out to be Kelvingrove that had the terrors. The Liberals had threatened to vote with the Conservatives, but they had second thoughts during the debate and in the end the Government survived. But MacDonald's description of the delights of electrification and afforestation had given a better impression of his aspirations than of his Government's achievements. As we have seen, one of the Cabinet's first decisions had been to set up a committee on housing and unemployment, chaired by Sidney Webb. This had split up into two sub-committees, one on housing, chaired by Wheatley, and the other on unemployment, chaired by Shaw. Wheatley rarely summoned his sub-committee, and worked out his highly successful housing policy in virtual isolation from his colleagues. The unemployment sub-committee met frequently and submitted regular reports to the Cabinet, but the results were far from spectacular. Most of its members were heavily burdened by departmental administration. According to Webb, the local authorities which would be called upon to give effect to its decisions were in any case 'plunged up to the hilt' in relief works which had been set on foot between 1921 and 1923. Above all, it soon became clear that unemployment was heavily concentrated in shipbuilding, engineering and cotton textiles; and it seemed equally clear to the sub-committee that these industries could not recover without a revival in world trade. As they put it in their first report to the Cabinet, the most hopeful solution lay 'in the re-establishment of normal peaceful conditions throughout the world' – a solution which even the most zealous committee of domestic ministers could hardly be expected to bring about.[118]

After some weeks, a more adventurous note was sounded; and, in the middle of April, the Cabinet decided that the unemployment committee should pay special attention to the possibilities of electrification on the railways.[119] Nothing was done, however, and by the summer it was clear that new administrative machinery was needed. The day after MacDonald's speech in the censure debate, the Cabinet accordingly replaced the old unemployment committee with a new, and much more powerful, unemployment policy committee, chaired by Snowden and including Haldane, Henderson, Webb, Shaw and Gosling. The new committee was asked to examine the policy set out in MacDonald's speech and to report on the administrative and legislative changes which would be needed to stimulate electrical production, construct arterial roads and develop afforestation.[120] Perhaps because MacDonald's speech had created a new sense of urgency, perhaps because Snowden, as chairman, was committed to success and therefore needed to carry the Treasury with him, it was much more effective than its predecessor had been. On July 9th, the Cabinet approved a complex set of proposals on electrical development.[121] On July 30th, Snowden told the House of Commons that the Government was planning to standardize electrical frequencies, to construct a national grid with the aid of exchequer grants, to subsidize electrical development in rural areas and to set up a committee to examine the feasibility of the Severn Barrage.[122] On August 5th, Gosling was instructed to prepare legislation for the autumn session.[123] Meanwhile, the Cabinet had agreed to a proposal of MacDonald's, originally put forward in the report of the Haldane committee on the machinery of Government four years before, to set up a permanent committee on economic questions, modelled on the Committee of Imperial Defence.[124]

The significance of this spurt of energy should not be exaggerated. The Government had responded to political pressure: it had not suddenly abandoned the assumptions of its collective lifetime. Like its supporters, it still worshipped the old free-trade shrines; like its supporters, it had not yet begun to recognize the real nature of the problem it faced. With strong leadership, MacDonald's new committee might develop into a valuable administrative counterweight to the Treasury. At the lowest, it might strengthen the prime minister vis-à-vis the chancellor. But its members and advisers would share the assumptions on which the Treasury's policy was based. By the same token, there could be little doubt that if the new initiatives which Snowden had announced on July 30th were to conflict with the claims of a balanced budget, then the balanced budget would win. But it is doubtful if many Labour M.P.s worried over such considerations as they dispersed for the summer recess. What mattered to them was that the Government had survived for six months; that it had scored a number of successes and made only one serious blunder; and that it now appeared to be grappling with the country's most pressing problem at least as successfully as, and a good deal more energetically than, its predecessors had done. MacDonald had not become prime minister to devise a new economic policy, but to prove that Labour could form a presentable Government and to drive the Liberals out of the middle ground of politics. By the summer of 1924 he seemed to be succeeding. Government and prime minister alike were riding high.

CHAPTER 15

Foreign triumphs

I

SOBER competence at home was accompanied later in the summer by a much more spectacular success in foreign affairs. For most of 1923, European politics had been dominated by the reparations crisis, and in particular by the French occupation of the Ruhr. The German economy had been disrupted; the fragile Weimar republic had been placed under terrible strain; militant German nationalism had been gratuitously strengthened. At the end of November, however, while British election platforms were resounding to the comforting slogans of protection and free trade, a break came in the clouds. The Reparation Commission adopted a watered-down version of a proposal originally made by the American secretary of state, and decided to set up two expert committees to examine Germany's economic position and to discover how to reconcile her resources with her obligations under the peace settlement. The first committee, which was to find out how to stabilize the Germany currency and balance the German budget, met under the chairmanship of the American, General Dawes, a week before the Labour Government took office in London. The second committee, chaired by Reginald McKenna, which was to investigate the alleged flight of German capital abroad, met the following week.[1] For fifteen years, MacDonald had denounced the foreign policy which had led to the First World War and the Versailles settlement; as leader of the Opposition, one of his strongest cards had been the apparent breakdown of that policy and the growing public demand for an alternative. Now it seemed that he might be given an opportunity to show that he could succeed where his predecessors had failed. In personal terms alone, it was one of the greatest challenges of his life.

And not only in personal terms. MacDonald has often been criticized for devoting too much of his attention to the mysteries of foreign policy and too little to the urgent domestic problems of unemployment and economic stagnation. As we have seen, the implied conflict between domestic and international priorities did not then appear to exist. To MacDonald and, for that matter, to the rest of the Cabinet, it seemed obvious that Britain's domestic problems were the product of a much wider international crisis, which could only be solved by international agreement. When the unemployment sub-committee of the Cabinet reported that the most hopeful solution lay in a return to normal conditions throughout the world, they were expressing what most of them regarded as a truism. After all, unemployment was concentrated in the export industries; British exports could hardly be expected to recover without a recovery in British export markets. It was not fatalism or apathy which led the Government to seek a revival at home through a return to peace and economic stability in central Europe. It was the belief, most powerfully expressed by Keynes in *The Economic Consequences of the Peace*, and common to most people on the left, that the victors could not prosper while the vanquished starved — a belief which events since the peace settlement had steadily borne out. In retrospect, it can be argued that this belief was mistaken and that it would have been possible even then to promote economic recovery in Britain while insulating the British economy from the international system of which it was a part. By the end of the decade, such ideas were beginning to be discussed seriously in political circles. In 1924, however, the discussion had not begun. The Conservatives had just fought a general election on the ticket of protective tariffs, but it would be an anachronism to equate Baldwin's protectionism in 1923 with the economic nationalism of the 1930s. In any case, protectionism in any form was still anathema to the British Left as well as to a majority of the British electorate. On the left it seemed self-evident that prosperity was indivisible, that the key to Britain's economic recovery lay in recovery in the rest of the world, and that the precondition of recovery in the rest of the world was an end to the economic dislocation of the strongest industrial country of the European continent. Even now, it is far from certain that the Left was wrong.

Even in narrowly electoral terms, moreover, Labour's claim to be a party of Government rested, to a larger extent than has sometimes been realized, on its claim to possess a superior grasp of foreign affairs. The sight of a Labour foreign secretary grappling successfully with problems which had baffled a Curzon or a Balfour would do more to disprove the charge that a working-class party was unfit to govern than would any conceivable action which minority Government could take at home. Failure would confirm snobbish middle-class voters and deferential working-class ones in their suspicion that only the gentleman's party could be trusted to speak for Britain on the world stage. At a deeper level, the Labour Party had become the residuary legatee of the dissenting tradition in foreign policy which went back to Gladstone, and before that to Cobden and Charles James Fox. With Asquith and Lloyd George both discredited, the one by 1914 and the other by 1919, it was now MacDonald who spoke for those who believed in right as against might as the arbiter of international relations, in discussion and compromise as against force and threats of force. If he failed as foreign secretary, he would discredit not merely himself but all those who had warned of the drift to war before 1914 and who had risked ostracism and vilification in pursuit of a compromise peace. If he succeeded, he would help to vindicate a whole political philosophy and attitude to life.

In any case, MacDonald himself believed, with some justice, that the most dangerous threat to the values he believed in was to be found abroad rather than at home. Unemployment and economic stagnation were serious problems; the threat of another war, which would plunge Europe into another outburst of collective hysteria and barbarism, was incomparably more serious. Without an equitable solution of the reparations crisis, the vicious circle of competitive national hatred which had been in existence ever since the peace settlement seemed bound to continue; if it continued, another war seemed only a matter of time. Since 1914, MacDonald had seen the prevention of another war as the greatest single object of his political life. In the end, of course, his efforts failed and his worst forebodings came true. But it would be perverse to conclude that his efforts were not worth making or that they deserved a lower priority than he gave them.

II

The challenge presented by the reparations crisis was partly diplomatic and partly political. Behind it lay the still more complex and sensitive questions of European security and of the balance of power between France and Germany. The lesson of the First World War was that, in a conflict between France and Germany, France would be overwhelmed. At the peace conference, she had demanded the creation of a neutral zone on the right bank of the Rhine and the establishment of an autonomous state or group of states on the left bank. This had been turned down by the United States and Britain on the grounds that it would violate Wilson's Fourteen Points. Instead, they had promised to guarantee France against a new German attack at some time in the future. But the American Senate had refused to ratify the Frano-American guarantee, and the British had then reneged on their part of the bargain as well. To some extent, the gap had been filled by alliances between France and Germany's neighbours in eastern Europe. From the French point of view, however, these were not enough. In 1921 they had made an abortive attempt to conclude a pact with Britain, and in 1922 the project had been extensively discussed by Lloyd George and Briand, and later by Lloyd George and Poincaré. These talks, however, had foundered on one central difficulty. What the French wanted was a British guarantee to guard against the danger that a future revanchist Germany might try to isolate her by attacking her allies in eastern Europe. This the British refused to give. They were grudgingly prepared to guarantee France against a direct attack from Germany of the kind which had occurred in 1914. They were not prepared to bind themselves to go to war as a result of events in eastern Europe which did not appear to threaten their own security. By the end of 1922 therefore the French still had no guarantee, no autonomous Rhineland and no safeguard against a German invasion fifteen or twenty years later.

Reparations offered them a new route to their old destination. In 1921

Germany's total liability had been fixed at the enormous sum of £6,600 millions. If the Germans paid, they would be bled white. If they did not, French troops could occupy an even larger area of Germany and, under the cover of military occupation, the Rhineland might be detached after all. The French occupation of the Ruhr and their promotion of a separatist movement in the Rhineland suggested that this was exactly what Poincaré was trying to do. By early 1924, as a Foreign Office official reported at the beginning of February, the French were in control of the whole of the Rhineland apart from the British zone. The railways were administered by a Franco-Belgian company; a uniform customs barrier had been erected around the area; the French were proposing to introduce a new tariff with no relation to the German tariff; attempts were being made to establish a new currency. '[T]he occupation of the Rhineland', he summed up, 'was intended to be purely military and purely temporary. It bids fair to become political, economic and permanent.'[2]

If the French were to be prised out of the Ruhr, however, it was pointless, even self-defeating, to quarrel with them, for that could only strengthen the sense of insecurity which had sent them there in the first place. The reparations problem could be solved only by agreement; since the French would have to be parties to any agreement as well as the British and German, it was necessary to pay some regard to their interests. But although this seems self-evident in the cool of hindsight, it was by no means self-evident at the time. The British had grown rather ashamed of the bellicose orgies of 1919. The Germans now appeared as the under-dogs of Europe, and the French as the bullying top-dogs. The fears and suspicions of the continent seemed shadowy and unreal — products of overheated imaginations, not bitter experiences. The notion that Germans might hate Frenchmen and want to be revenged on them, or that Poles and Czechs might hate Germans and fear their domination, was incomprehensible to most people in this country. If they had understood it, it would merely have confirmed them in their determination to avoid continental entanglements. For their mood was more isolationist than it had been since the death of Queen Victoria. Now that the German fleet was no longer in existence, their own safety seemed assured; all that they asked of the continent was that it should put its own house in order as quickly as possible.

These feelings were amply reflected in Whitehall. They lay behind the attitude of the service departments to such problems as the Singapore base and the Channel tunnel, and they also played a part in departmental arguments over the reparations question. Although the problem was at bottom political, it was superficially economic, and the Treasury was as closely concerned in it as was the Foreign Office. Understandably enough, the Treasury saw it primarily as a matter of international credit and finance, in which the return of economic sanity was blocked by the greed and stupidity of France. The same was true, though for different reasons, of MacDonald's political followers. The Labour movement had forgotten its support for the wartime coalition and the knock-out blow. It had embraced the once heretical doctrines of the U.D.C. with all the fervour of a convert; it was now more MacDonaldite than MacDonald was himself. France had come to occupy a position in left-wing demonology akin to the position which Germany was to occupy thirty years later. Suggestions that the French might have genuine grievances and legitimate interests, and that concessions might have to be made to them if the problem were to be solved, provoked uneasy apprehension. They smacked of power politics: and it was well known that power politics was wicked.

Thus, MacDonald's freedom of action was limited. If he made too few concessions to the French, no agreement would be reached; if he made too many, he would outrage his followers and perhaps split his Cabinet. In any case, he shared many of his countrymen's attitudes, though he had reached them by a different path. He was not an isolationist by instinct, and at this stage, at least, he did not believe that Britain could turn her back on the continent. He was, however, a lifelong opponent of military pacts and alliance diplomacy. He was no more prepared than was anyone else in British politics to offer the French what they really wanted: a firm military guarantee, which would be brought automatically into operation the moment Germany tried to upset the peace settlement. That path had led to 1914, and the whole point of his foreign policy was to avoid treading it. Somehow or other, the French would have to be persuaded that the fears which had led them to take it were groundless. 'France must have another chance,' he noted in his diary shortly after taking office. 'I offer co-operation but she must be reasonable & cease her policy of selfish vanity. That is my first job. Armaments & such problems that are really consequences must wait. The "weather" must be improved.'[3]

That was his policy — and his problem — in a nutshell. For the French did not believe in the possibility of better weather: what they wanted was a more reliable raincoat. The main theme of British policy for the next eight months is to be found in MacDonald's attempt to bridge the gap between the French desire for security and the British belief that they did not need it.

III

Until the expert committees reported, there was little he could do beyond laying the foundations for initiatives later on. On January 26th, in one of his first acts as foreign secretary, he broke with diplomatic precedent by writing a personal letter to Poincaré, expressing his regret that there were so many outstanding differences between Britain and France and his confidence that they could be resolved by 'the strenuous action of goodwill'.[4] Two days later Poincaré sent a gracious reply; and MacDonald explained to the Cabinet that he was 'acting on the principle that the Government wished to maintain entirely friendly relations and believed that the French Government would co-operate, but that this did not mean that they had no policy of their own'.[5] On February 21st, he wrote a second and slightly more outspoken personal letter to Poincaré, in which he set out the British view of the problem and did his best to blur the differences between the two countries by a display of mellifluous sympathy. He began by recognizing the French need for security and acknowledging that the collapse of the Anglo-American guarantee had given them some justification for seeking 'more tangible safeguards'. But, he went on, Britain had legitimate interests too. Her 'economic existence' was endangered by the dislocation of her European markets and the 'economic chaos' in Germany. As a result, the British people were coming to believe that France was determined to 'ruin Germany and dominate the Continent'. These beliefs could not be removed by another 'wearisome round of controversy' on detailed questions. What was needed was a broad agreement on 'the main principles which inspire us', and joint action by France and Britain, 'undertaken with full sympathy for their respective requirements and with wise regard for the interests of the world at large'. He was, he ended, 'fully prepared' for the co-operation this implied.[6]

MacDonald's letter had deliberately begged most of the difficult questions. No doubt because of this, Poincaré's reply was mildly encouraging. He insisted that he, too, was anxious for a better understanding between Britain and France, and wrote that 'the whole of Europe, the whole of humanity' would pay for its absence.[7] This was followed by an even more encouraging letter from Lord Crewe, the British Ambassador in Paris. The recent fall in the value of the franc, he reported, had had a 'chastening influence' on the Quai D'Orsay, and a growing number of Frenchmen now wished to see a change in policy towards Germany.[8] Distinctly less encouraging, however, was a sharp reminder of the political risks involved in the whole operation, which came at about the same time. Towards the end of February, Henderson declared at a by-election meeting in Burnley that revision of the Versailles settlement was 'very much overdue' – a stock-in-trade of Labour Party rhetoric, but a red rag to the French. Lloyd George promptly put down a private notice question asking whether Henderson's statement represented Government policy, and MacDonald was forced to steer an obviously unhappy, and inevitably rather evasive, course between repudiating his own home secretary and destroying any hope of reaching an agreement with Poincaré.[9] Even so, he remained optimistic and in good spirits. 'I get more confident', he noted in his diary, 'that M. Poincaré & I can agree. I hear the Experts will present a unanimous & satisfactory report. Then the chance will come. I may have trouble with some of our own people but not with the country; with Liberal petty pinpricks but not the H. of C.'[10]

His optimism was soon put to the test. On April 9th, the experts' reports were published. The report that mattered was the one produced by the first committee, chaired by General Dawes; the members of the committee who mattered were the British bankers, Kindersley and Stamp. The report contained a mass of detailed technical proposals, but the fundamental principles were simple.

Germany, said the Dawes committee, could not meet her obligations unless her currency was stabilized and her budget balanced. This could not be done unless her economic unity was restored. The military aspects of the question were outside the committee's terms of reference; nevertheless, the report explicitly emphasized that if foreign troops remained in Germany they must not 'impede the free exercise of economic activities'. Next, it proposed a complicated procedure by which Germany's annual reparations payments would gradually increase as economic stability returned and economic growth resumed. In the first year, the total payment would be only £50 million, rising to £125 million by the fifth year. Finally, it emphasized that no reparations at all could be paid in the first year without a foreign loan of £40 million.[11]

From the British point of view, it was an ideal solution. In time, Britain might actually receive some reparations payments. Much more important, she could look forward to an economic revival in central Europe which might lead to a revival of her own export trade. The report, wrote Otto Niemeyer, 'establishes especially on the more vital points a great many of the principles which British opinion has been maintaining';[12] Sir John Bradbury, the British representative on the Reparation Commission, recommended that it should be 'unhesitatingly welcom[ed][13] by His Majesty's Government. For that very reason, however, it was a blow to the French. It did not condemn the French occupation of the Ruhr in so many words, but it certainly did so implicitly; and it made it clear that French policy – not only in the Ruhr but in the Rhineland as well – would have to be changed fundamentally before reparations payments could be resumed. Worse still from the French point of view, the central premise of the report was that future French Governments should not be allowed to disrupt Germany's economic life in the way the Poincaré Government had done in 1923. It had skated over the delicate question of how the plan was to be enforced in the event of a German default, but it had explicitly declared that no sanctions should be applied except in the case of a 'flagrant failure' on the part of the Germans to carry out their obligations. If such a failure occurred, the creditor governments should act 'with the consciousness of joint trusteeship'. The implications were clear – no more Rhinelands, no more Ruhrs and no more opportunities to treat reparations as the key to French security.

If the French were to accept all this, a great diplomatic struggle would have to be waged; and it was this which absorbed the lion's share of MacDonald's energy for the next four months. His strategy contained three main elements. The first was an attempt to isolate the French by creating a united front of the other allies, and in particular by detaching the Belgians from them. The second was an attempt to frighten them with a vague but menacing cloud of warnings about the effect which continued intransigence would have on Britain. The third was an attempt to reassure them, by making it clear that their faces would be saved if only they did as the British wanted. The underlying policy was not very different from Curzon's and was closely in line with Foreign Office thinking. The style, with its blend of lofty Highland sentiment and dogged Lowland sense, was MacDonald's own.

On April 10th, the British ambassadors in Paris, Brussels, Rome, Berlin, Washington and Tokyo were instructed to inform the governments to which they were accredited that Britain was prepared to accept the experts' report in its entirety, provided that the other countries concerned did the same.[14] Next day, the Reparation Commission approved the report as a 'practical basis for the rapid solution of the Reparation problem'.[15] On April 16th, the Germans announced that they, too, were prepared to co-operate in putting the plan into effect.[16] The struggle to win over the French could now begin in earnest.

On April 16th, the British ambassadors in Paris and Brussels were instructed to protest against the French and Belgian violation of the Rhineland agreement and to warn that if it continued the British Government would be obliged to express its disagreement 'definitely and openly'.[17] Next day, MacDonald told the Belgian ambassador in London that if the Dawes report were not accepted, he would not 'take up the mainly passive attitude' which had contented his predecessors. If Poincaré agreed to evacuate the Ruhr, he declared, Britain would be only too happy to 'save his face and enable him to inform the French public that he had got his conditions'. But he also made it clear that he wanted no elaborate arrangements to impose sanctions on Germany in the event of another default. 'We ought to tell Germany', he explained, 'that we accepted her word, that we had made no provisions whatever for sanctions, because we wished to place upon her, in the most solemn way, an obligation to fulfil her bargain.'[18] As he put it in a public speech shortly afterwards, 'Let us say to Germany, "We have no preparations to meet any default on your part. If after this solemn obligation you do default then we and our Allies will be closer than ever and will wait for the event." '[19]

Poincaré could hardly be expected to regard high-sounding declarations of this sort as a satisfactory substitute for the presence of French troops in the heart of industrial Germany. On April 24th, the Belgians announced that they, too, were prepared to accept the Dawes report in full, but, on April 25th, the French declared grudgingly that although it was undoubtedly a competent and realistic document, it contained nothing more than 'indications'. The Reparation Commission would have to interpret it; then the Governments concerned would have to decide what to do about it. Meanwhile, it was clear that since it had imposed obligations on Germany as well as on the Allies, it could not come into effect until the German Government had made the legal and administrative changes which would be necessary to enable Germany to carry out her part of the plan.[20] Soon afterwards, Poincaré told Lord Crewe that it would be essential for the Allied Governments to agree on the sanctions they would impose if Germany defaulted, and explained that the sanction he had in mind was another occupation of the Ruhr.[21] At the beginning of May, the Belgian prime minister and foreign minister visited MacDonald at Chequers. They reported that Poincaré was so suspicious of Germany that he would insist on keeping a skeleton force in the Ruhr, and retaining enough control over the local railways to protect his troops. More ominously still, they also reported that he was determined to obtain a firm commitment from MacDonald that if Germany defaulted, a range of sanctions, perhaps including a British blockade of Germany, would come into operation automatically. If he failed, he would probably refuse to co-operate in putting the plan into effect.[22]

A firm commitment was, of course, exactly what MacDonald was determined to avoid. British public opinion, he told the Belgians, would never agree; in any case, he could not commit a future Parliament. A blockade was out of the question. It would not work unless the Americans, the dominions and the neutrals joined in; and they would be most unlikely to do so. A prior agreement of the kind Poincaré wanted was, in fact, impractical. 'Schemes could not be made like automatic chocolate machines which delivered the goods when anyone put a penny in the slot.' No one could foresee the circumstances in which a future German default would take place, and it would be absurd to agree what to do about it long before it occurred. As for Poincaré's threat to block the report if he did not get his way, that was playing with fire:

> For Great Britain it would be necessary in that case to begin by challenging the whole legality of the Ruhr occupation ... It was the last thing that he desired to do, because it could lead to nothing but a continuance, if not aggravation, of the chaotic situation in Europe. It would also be certain to increase enormously the danger of a close rapprochement between Germany and Russia. The French said they were very nervous, and, perhaps, rightly so, as to the danger threatening them from a thoroughly recovered and strengthened Germany ... With the help of Russian man-power, Russian resources, and other forms of assistance, Germany would become so powerful that whatever precautions France might take, there was the risk of great catastrophe.[23]

The Belgians were evidently impressed. But the point of the exercise was to impress the French; and that was more difficult. Elections were due in France on May 11th, and MacDonald feared that if Poincaré lost by a narrow margin he would be stronger in opposition than in office. In the circumstances, there was only one course to follow. 'My policy', he noted, 'is not to assume any change & act as though there were no elections & no doubts.'[24] On May 9th, Poincaré was invited to follow the Belgians to Chequers; and the stage was set for a confrontation between the new diplomacy and the old.

M

IV

It would have been a revealing encounter. In the end, however, it did not take place. The Bloc National lost the elections; Poincaré resigned; the well-meaning Edouard Herriot, Radical mayor of Lyons, took his place. At first, the change seemed a mixed blessing from the British point of view. Herriot, as Mac-Donald's advisers repeatedly warned, was a poor negotiator and a weak man. He seemed to have no clear idea of what he wanted to achieve, or of the sticking-point he was determined to hold; under pressure, he was apt to promise more than he could deliver. But, although MacDonald found him exasperating to deal with, his arrival in office was a turning-point. Like all Frenchmen, he feared Germany and wished to guard against a revival of German power. Unlike Poincaré, however, he did not believe that France could do this by herself. He wanted British friendship, and he was prepared, however reluctantly, to pay for it. Above all, he belonged to the same world as MacDonald. He, too, was a moderate who believed in discussion and compromise; he, too, wished to turn his back on the harsh methods of Versailles. In a muddled way, he did his best to defend the negotiating position which Poincaré had bequeathed to him. But his defence was irresolute and unconvincing, for in his heart of hearts he did not accept the premises on which it was based.

When Poincaré fell, Herriot was invited to Chequers instead. He arrived in London on June 20th, and on June 21st and 22nd he and MacDonald discussed the situation at length in the soothing surroundings of a country-house week-end. Their talks revolved around four main topics: the evacuation of the Ruhr, the hardy perennial of sanctions, the sensitive question of whether the experts' recommendations should be put into effect by Allied *fiat* or by a negotiated agreement between the Allies and Germany, and the still more sensitive question of French security. On all but the first, MacDonald got substantially what he wanted, though at the cost of one significant concession.

Despite MacDonald's warning that he had discussed the problem with American bankers, who had told him that it would be impossible to raise the necessary foreign loan unless France withdrew most of her forces from the Ruhr, Herriot insisted that evacuation could not even begin until the Germans had started to operate the sections of the Dawes report which applied to them, and that he would have to retain control of at least some of the Rhineland railways in order to protect his troops. After this, however, the talks went more smoothly. Herriot conceded that there was no need to decide in advance on the sanctions to be imposed in the event of a German default, and announced that he would be satisfied with a British declaration that if Germany did default, she would be faced by united action on the part of the Allies, even if it was not clear what form that action would take. He insisted that he did not wish to impose a settlement on Germany, and accepted the British view that the final agreement would have to be arrived at by negotiation between Germany and the Allies. He pointed out that he would be accused of capitulation if he moved too fast, but suggested that the Allies should first agree among themselves and that a second conference should then be held, at which the Germans would be represented as well.

On the central question of European security, progress was more difficult. In 1923, the Assembly of the League of Nations had accepted a draft treaty of mutual assistance, designed to outlaw 'aggressive war', and based essentially on the French attitude to the problem. Signatories to the treaty were to bind themselves in advance to come to the assistance of any other signatory which became the victim of aggression, and to accept the ruling of the League Council as to who the victim was. Smaller defence pacts might be made between parties to the treaty; and it was laid down that the signatories' commitment to provide military assistance to the victims of aggression would be limited to states in the same region. Although the draft treaty was based to some extent on proposals originally put forward by Lord Robert Cecil, it was viewed with great hostility in Whitehall. The Admiralty pointed out that it would impose a virtually unlimited commitment on Great Britain, since the regional limitation could not apply to a world-wide empire, and concluded that if the British Government signed, it would be necessary to increase Britain's naval forces substantially. The dominion governments were equally hostile, and at the beginning of April the Committee of Imperial Defence recommended the Government to turn it down. From the French point of view, however, the draft treaty was an ideal solution; and when the problems of sanction and negotiations with Germany had been dealt with, Herriot asked pointedly what Britain's attitude would be. The Foreign Office record of the rest of the discussion is worth quoting at length:

Mr. MacDONALD: ... Before undertaking an engagement I must assure myself of the support of all the Dominions. I am anxious to warn you loyally and to be frank with you. There may be a difficulty. Another difficulty is that, just as M. Herriot may say that M. Poincaré is not dead, I for my part have to count with Mr Lloyd George ... As for the treaty of mutual guarantee, I must not hide from you that all my experts of the navy, army, air force and Foreign Office are opposed to it ... I can assure you besides, confidentially, that Sweden, Denmark and Holland are equally hostile to it ... To save the situation I suggest that France, Belgium and Great Britain first of all proceed to an examination of the situation together; if we begin by the treaty of mutual guarantee, that will bind our hands and prejudice the question when the United States calls a disarmament question. For my part I see a great advantage in broadening the question ...

M. HERRIOT: I understand the situation in which Mr MacDonald finds himself, but since we are speaking as good friends, I must explain to him the situation of France ... My country has a dagger pointed at its breast, within an inch of its heart. Common efforts, sacrifices, deaths in the war, all that will have been useless if Germany can once more have recourse to violence ... France cannot count only on an international conference, and the United States are a long way off ... Can we not try to find a formula of guarantee against a danger of such a sort that it would render the Dawes Report useless. I speak to you here from the bottom of my heart, and I assure you that I cannot give up the security of France, who could not face a new war.

Mr. MacDONALD: ... I shall do all that lies in my power to avoid a new war, for I am certain that in that case it would not be only France but all European civilization which would be crushed ... I do not wish to take an easy way which offers itself to me to join in an offer to France of a military guarantee of security. I should only be deceiving you; none of the Dominions would support me, a reactionary Government would replace mine, and finally France would only have a false security ...

M. HERRIOT: ... I ask permission to continue the conversation on this point, because it is the subject which touches my heart most, and which imposes upon me the greatest of duties.

Mr. MacDONALD: This is what I think: we are going today to settle the questions raised by the Dawes Report; but in doing so we are only taking the first step in the conclusion of a long series of agreements. When we have got the Dawes Report out of the way, I am quite ready to go to Paris to pay you a visit and spend a couple of days talking to you on the question of debts and security and so on ... The general perspective which opens before my eyes is that of a new method of settling questions between allies; that of a friendship and a constant collaboration ... We must assure our well-being, but we will work also to resolve the great moral problems of the peace of the world. Let us therefore settle first the question of the Dawes Report; then we will go on to that of inter-Allied debts, then to the problem of security, and we will try to remove from Europe the risks of war which threaten it ...

M. HERRIOT: I think Mr MacDonald warmly for what he has just said. In effect, the most important result of our interview is a sort of moral pact of continuous co-operation between us for the good of our two nations and in the general interests of the whole world. I will do all that is possible and even the impossible to respond to his appeal ... [25]

In retrospect, the language may seem inflated: at the time, the hopes behind it were real.

So, however, were the obstacles in their way. During the next few weeks, Herriot's pact of continuous co-operation came under heavy strain. When the

Chequers talks were over, the Foreign Office sent out invitations to an inter-Allied conference in London on July 16th — making it clear that in the British view the Reparation Commission should no longer be empowered to declare Germany in default, and thus implying that the Versailles settlement would be superseded if the Dawes report came into effect. As a contribution to public enlightenment, this was admirable; as a step towards a diplomatic solution, it was less satisfactory. There was an outcry in the French chamber, where Herriot was accused of surrendering vital national interests under British pressure. He sent an urgent appeal to MacDonald to rescue him, and on July 8th and 9th a second round of talks took place, this time in Paris.[26] Once again, Herriot painted an eloquent picture of French weakness in the face of a future resurgent Germany; once again, he tried to persuade the British to redress the balance with a guarantee of French security; once again he was fobbed off with the promise of further consultations and discussions, accompanied by protestations of understanding and sympathy. (With France, MacDonald declared in the most revealing phrase of the entire exchange, Britain wanted 'the closest of alliances, that which is not written on paper'.)[27] After this inauspicious start, however, the discussion turned to the forthcoming inter-Allied conference and here MacDonald made a number of concessions.

After prolonged bargaining, agreement was reached on a joint Anglo-French memorandum, defining the agenda for the conference and suggesting the broad outlines of an agreement. It contained four central clauses, all of which were to become the subjects of minute and passionate textual exegesis in the next six weeks. In deference to the French, the memorandum declared firmly that the Reparation Commission must not be weakened — a major victory for Herriot, since one of the chief objects of British policy had been to do precisely that. In deference to the British and American bankers, however, it also acknowledged that the putative subscribers to the £40 million loan would need some security for their investment. This was to be provided in one of two ways. The two Governments promised that they would do their best to ensure the enlargement of the Reparation Commission, by the addition of an American member, thus making it more impartial as between France and Germany. If this proved impossible, they would recommend that if there was a division of opinion on the Commission about an alleged German default, it should 'call in' the agent general for reparation payments, who was to be an American citizen. The second of the four main clauses was less complicated, but equally controversial. It was agreed that if the Reparation Commission ruled that Germany had committed 'an important wilful default', the Governments concerned would confer among themselves on how to operate 'such measures as they shall agree to take in order to protect themselves'. Next, the memorandum suggested that the plan for restoring German economic unity, once the Reparation Commission had ruled that the Dawes report was in operation, should be settled at the inter-Allied conference. Finally, it proposed that a special body should be set up to advise the recipients of German reparations on how to put them to proper use.[28]

Like most compromises, the memorandum was full of loop-holes. The role of the Reparation Commission was still obscure. It was not clear how far the Versailles settlement would have to be amended. Nothing had been said about the evacuation of the Ruhr, or about Germany's position in the negotiations leading up to the final settlement. Above all, the fundamental conflict between the demands of French security and German prosperity remained unresolved. A few days after his return from Paris, MacDonald received an anguished memorandum from the German ambassador in London, complaining that too many concessions had been made to the French and warning that as a result the German Government would now find it difficult to carry through the legal changes which the Dawes committee had proposed. The political dangers were almost as great as the diplomatic ones. Before leaving for Paris, MacDonald had received an official warning from the executive of the parliamentary Labour Party, pointing out that many of its members had 'consistently opposed the policy of reparations' and making it clear that they felt 'certain doubts' about the whole Dawes scheme.[29] When he got back, opposition grew more vocal. E. D. Morel denounced the Government for trying to 'square the circle' and 'make the violation of economic truths compatible with economic truths'; George Hardie declared that if a vote were taken, he would have 'the greatest possible pleasure in voting against the Government'.[30]

There was one great compensation on the other side of the account. At last the prologue was over. After six months' waiting, the play could begin.

V

The first session of the inter-Allied conference opened at 11 a.m. on July 16th, in MacDonald's room in the Foreign Office. MacDonald began the proceedings with a firm though graceful speech. He welcomed the representatives 'of nations that fought by our side whilst the war was raging, and that now share with us the responsibility of bringing peace and security to Europe,' but then declared uncompromisingly that the policy they had so far followed had not only failed to yield the expected reparations, but had led 'to an unsettlement in the minds of the peoples concerned, a growth of aggressive militarism, and a strengthening of a fear which overshadowed all sense of security'. That state of affairs could be ended only by taking the Dawes report as a whole, as its authors had recommended. They must eschew the 'fatal habit of connecting one question with another', and 'go step by step, isolating each question as far as possible and solving it before going on to the next'. Above all, they must recognize that agreement would have to be based on 'the intelligent and moral assent of the nations'.[31]

After this, the conference settled down to work, taking the Paris memorandum as its basis. It decided to set up three committees: one to deal with the politically explosive questions of the role of the Reparation Commission, the procedure for declaring a German default and the security to be given to the subscribers to the loan; a second to settle the plan by which German economic unity was to be restored; and a third to examine the more technical question of how reparation payments could be put to the best use. The first committee was to be chaired by Philip Snowden, the second by J. H. Thomas and the third by the banker, Sir Robert Kindersley. 'One thing gives me confidence,' Mac-Donald noted afterwards. 'Everyone assumes that an agreement must be reached. We are all most friendly & I have got business through in an hour which would have taken a day in previous Conferences.'[32]

At first, his optimism seemed justified. By July 30th, he told the Cabinet, the second committee had produced 'an extraordinarily satisfactory report'; and it looked as though a compromise would be achieved even on the one outstanding question of the Rhineland railways. He was equally hopeful about the evacuation of the Ruhr. Since the British Government had steadily refused to recognize the Franco-Belgian occupation, it could hardly enter into public negotiations about ending it. Behind the scenes, however, he had told Herriot and Theunis that since their Government had entered the Ruhr for economic reasons, it would be illogical for them to stay there once the Dawes report had been put into effect and the economic problems had been solved. Herriot and Theunis, he reported, had replied by raising the question of inter-Allied debts, but he had refused to 'mix up these questions', and had insisted that the question of the Ruhr should be discussed 'in its historical aspects'. Despite these skirmishes, however, the chances of a settlement were high. The German Government was believed to be willing for the Ruhr to be evacuated in stages, and it looked as though an agreement could be reached on those lines.[33]

The first committee was more dilatory, largely owing to the perverse behaviour of its chairman; but even there progress was slowly made. Snowden opened the proceedings on the afternoon of July 16th by declaring that the committee should not regard itself as being bound by the Paris memorandum, which had merely laid down the agenda. It could make any proposals it liked, provided they fell within the scope of the memorandum, whether they were actually mentioned in it or not. Having done his best to annoy the French by undermining the procedural basis of the conference, he then proceeded to inflame them by implying that the security which the memorandum had provided for the subscribers to the £40m loan would probably turn out to be inadequate. Not surprisingly, the French delegation violently objected to whittling away the concessions they had received from MacDonald only a week before; and for the rest of the session no progress was made.[34] During the next few days, however, the gulf between the British and French positions was slowly bridged; and on July 19th the committee agreed on the recommendations it would put before the full conference. It was decided that the service of the loan would be given absolute priority over any sanctions which might have to be imposed after a German default, and that no sanctions would be imposed at all unless the Reparation Commission had consulted both the agent general for reparation payments and a representative of the foreign bondholders before a default was declared.[35]

It was not enough; and for a while there was deadlock. At a meeting between the governor of the Bank of England, the American banker, Lamont, and the finance ministers present at the conference, the bankers declared that the proposed safeguards would not guarantee the success of the loan in the London and New York money markets. After prolonged and anguished negotiations, however, the committee agreed to shelve the problem by suggesting that if further assurances were needed to guarantee the loan, they should be arrived at by direct negotiation between the Germans, the bankers and the Reparation Commission. Thanks to a concession from the French, a compromise was also reached on the procedure for declaring a default. The committee agreed that if any member of the Reparation Commission disagreed with the majority in believing that a default had occurred, he would have the right to appeal to arbitration. On August 2nd, the plenary session of the conference met again. After more hard bargaining, it accepted the reports of its three working committees, and agreed that a formal invitation should be sent to the Germans to negotiate a settlement based on them.[36] MacDonald noted afterwards, 'We have agreed and great is the relief. Now for the Germans. They bring a delegation of about 40. Asses! If clumsiness is of the devil, the Germans are supreme as his tools.'[37]

The Germans were only one of his problems. Another was his chancellor of the exchequer. Snowden's assets were lucidity, obstinacy and confidence in his own judgment; tolerance and generosity of spirit were less conspicuous. He could marshal a complex argument with remorseless clarity, and puncture an opponent's evasions with a kind of steely contempt. But his mind was like the headlights of a car, which light up the road immediately ahead at the cost of plunging the surrounding countryside into greater darkness than before; and his temperament was as rigid as his intellect. Like most politicians, he liked popularity. But he was unwilling, or perhaps unable, to court it. If other people agreed with him, well and good. If not, they were fools, and perhaps knaves as well. In either case, it was his duty to expose them; if they were foreigners into the bargain, it was his duty to expose them even more unmistakably. Like MacDonald, Snowden had opposed the war and had spent four years out of Parliament for his pains. But he had opposed it as a pacifist little-Englander, a latter-day Bright or Cobden, not as a socialist internationalist. He had shown no interest in what happened to Europe after the war: what mattered was that Britain should play no part in it. It was the same with reparations. The French were wrong, and it was necessary to say so. Anything else was humbug: the fact that the humbug was supported by MacDonald only made it more suspect.

During the previous two weeks, Snowden's patience had worn steadily thinner. By the beginning of August, it was close to breaking-point.

He was fortified in his suspicions by the Treasury and the bankers. The exact relationship between these two groups is far from clear. Sometimes the Treasury acted as the spokesman for the bankers: sometimes the bankers behaved like agents of the Treasury. But whatever the relationship between them, the two together constituted, for all practical purposes, an independent power with a separate policy of its own. It was a power of formidable weight. There could be no settlement without the loan, and no loan without the bankers. If the Treasury as the voice of the bankers, or the bankers as the voice of the Treasury, said that certain conditions were essential for the loan, a mere prime minister or foreign secretary could hardly challenge them. Already, the bankers and the Treasury between them had secured substantial modifications in the position which MacDonald and Herriot had agreed upon in Paris, and had pushed the French so hard that the conference had come near to breaking down. It soon became clear that their appetite had grown with feeding. On August 6th, a Treasury official (or perhaps Snowden himself) warned MacDonald that the French would have to make further concessions if a settlement was to be worth having:

> The main difficulties have not yet been faced at all. Meantime, the public
> ... are led to believe that all is going well and that an agreement is in sight.
> The very existence of this atmosphere (diffused all over the world) makes it
> all the more difficult to get the only kind of agreement likely to yield
> practical results. How could France yield in such an atmosphere, even if she
> wished to do so? Are we not wilfully deceiving her by suppressing the
> Bankers' views? These views are bound to come out in the end, together
> with the fact that we know them. What will the world say if ultimately we
> reach agreement (on assumptions we know to be incorrect) and then the
> money cannot be raised? I can imagine no more ignominious position for
> H.M.G. to occupy, and nothing more fatal to the moral influence of this
> country. There will be plenty of critics at home to point this out, even
> within your own Parliamentary party ...
>
> It must be remembered that the Bankers ... *are playing the British Govern-
> ment's game.* They are demanding precisely the conditions which every
> Britisher knows in his heart ought to be given, and supporting (eg. on
> sanctions and the Ruhr occupation) the publicly-expressed views of succes-
> sive British Governments. Why should H.M.G. run away from its own
> shadow?[38]

Snowden, at any rate, was determined not to do so. The first plenary session of the international conference took place on August 5th. The atmosphere, MacDonald wrote later, was 'freezing'; and when the Germans were intro-duced, Herriot 'looked as though he were having a tooth drawn'.[39] The real work of the conference began next day, with a long legalistic wrangle over the proposed new procedure for declaring a German default. The inter-Allied conference had accepted the recommendation of the Dawes committee that sanctions should only be imposed in the case of a 'flagrant' failure on the part of the Germans to carry out their obligations. What, the Germans demanded, did 'flagrant' mean? The French insisted that this would have to be decided by the Reparation Commission, or if the Commission would not agree, then by arbitration; and in this they were supported by MacDonald. The Germans, however, insisted that there must be prior agreement as to the meaning of 'flagrant' before the Germans could accept the Allied proposals. The foreign affairs committee of the Reichstag, Stresemann declared, had already questioned him about the meaning of 'flagrant'; he would face great opposition if he could not explain it when he returned home. In his most cutting style, Snowden supported the Germans against his own prime minister. 'Flagrant', he pointed out, was a new word which had not been used in the peace treaty. In any case, what was the objection to defining it? 'Surely there could be no difference of opinion among the delegates present that the meaning of "flagrant default" was wilful large-scale default. If they were all in agreement, then why not say so?'[40]

This was only the beginning. The problem of 'flagrant' was solved the following day, when the Germans accepted the interpretation which MacDonald had suggested in the House of Commons two days earlier.[41] A new problem arose next day over the £40m loan. The Germans insisted that they must have an assurance that the loan would materialize before they accepted their new obligations, and demanded that the conference should make direct contact with the bankers. The time to make contact with the bankers, MacDonald replied, was after a political agreement had been reached; and the French delegate, Clementel, added that he had recently discussed the position with three important American bankers, who had agreed 'in begging the Governments not to mix them up in discussions of a political order'. This led to another acrimonious exchange between MacDonald and Snowden. The opinion of 'anonymous United States bankers', Snowden declared icily, could not be allowed to pass. His information was 'entirely opposite'; and he added for good measure that if the bankers rejected their solution, it would mean the collapse of the Dawes scheme and 'financial and economic chaos'.[42]

On August 8th, there was another bitter argument over the relations between the German Government and the proposed transfer committee, which was to supervise the payment of German reparations to the recipients. It had been agreed at the inter-Allied conference that if the transfer committee and the Germans disagreed, the decision should rest with an arbitrator. This, said the Germans, would derogate from German sovereignty in financial and economic matters — while Herriot insisted that if arbitration were abandoned here, it would undermine the entire inter-Allied agreement. Once again, Snowden supported the Germans in characteristically intransigent language. Arbitration between the German Government and the transfer committee, he declared, would be a 'menace to British industrial interests', and give foreigners 'complete control over Germany's industrial concerns'. It involved a fundamental departure from the Dawes report, which everyone had agreed to accept as a whole. By now, MacDonald was also beginning to lose patience. Unless faster progress was made the following week, he warned, the conference might have to be adjourned,[43] and he noted later that

S. has been terribly clumsy today & has negotiated like a drill sergeant giving orders. H[erriot] was furious & protested against one of us openly opposing in a hostile way the findings of the Inter Allied Conference. It is not so much the case that S. has, but the spiteful kind of way in which he states it. He makes a calm consideration impossible & gives me a great problem in diplomatic handling.[44]

The intransigence of the British chancellor was fully equalled by that of the French minister of war, General Nollet. Like Snowden, Nollet appeared to have an independent policy; and he was as suspicious of Herriot as Snowden was of MacDonald. As before, the formal proceedings of the conference were only the tip of the iceberg. The negotiations over the evacuation of the Ruhr still took place in private meetings behind the scenes, and Nollet's role in these mirrored Snowden's in the negotiations over the loan. By the end of July, it had become clear that the solution would lie in evacuation by stages, but the timetable was still uncertain. On August 5th, MacDonald reported to the Cabinet that the French were now offering evacuation over a period of two years, and that in his view this was far too long.[45] Next day, he had a private discussion with Nollet, whom he described as a 'strange, excitable, small-minded man, with a face that reveals him';[46] and on the evening of August 7th he held a meeting at Downing Street, with Herriot, Theunis, Hymans and the interpreter, Camerlynk. It was an eventful occasion. As he described it in his diary:

Maps were out & Herriot was beginning to unburden himself. The door opened & Berry announced that the French Minister of War had come. I caught a glimpse of him through the door. He had followed Berry upstairs, evidently determined to force his way in. Poor Herriot was in despair; Theunis flung up his arms; a bomb had burst ... He entered pale, stiff, bristling, looking defiantly over us, shouting by his demeanour: 'You conspirators!' ... Then began an hour & a half of the most excited & consternating wrangle. To reason with Nollet is impossible: he just goes off. I disconcerted him with my calm. 'You cannot break the Treaty for your convenience': 'You feel like a great soldier, my dear General, we like honest men of affairs' & such like, said with a genial smile. This made him pull himself up every now & again, & I got that hard mouth to smile

sicklily & those flashing eyes to soften. But only for a minute. The machine
of unreason & passion went off again ... Theunis sat in the corner of the
couch by me, looking queerly across but almost dumb, Hymans in a chair
beyond smoking a cigar, Herriot in a high chair in front of me by the fire
looking distressed & dumbfounded but saying little ... Camerlynk sitting
at the table by Herriot, confused & distressed, translating bits here & bits
there when I asked to know what was being poured out. My F.O. boxes
were piled up on my desk & at eleven I brought the Conference to a close.
When I had finished some work, I went down stairs & Berry rushed along
the passage to meet me. 'Quiet', he whispered & pointing to the Cabinet
room said, 'They are in there still fighting & I have sent for refreshments'.
I slipped upstairs & went to bed.[47]

Eventually, Herriot decided to return to Paris to consult his Cabinet. In the
hope of strengthening his hand, MacDonald sent him and Theunis a sharply
worded letter, pointing out that the Dawes plan could not be carried out unless
the Ruhr was evacuated, and protesting in vigorous terms against Nollet's argument that the French were justified in staying in the Ruhr to protect themselves
against future aggression on the part of Germany.[48] For a while, it seemed that
this had done the trick. When the conference resumed on August 11th, progress
was fairly rapid; and at the meeting of the Allied prime ministers in the morning, Herriot reported that his Cabinet had agreed to cut the evacuation period
to a year.[49] Next day, however, tempers rose once again. Arbitration between
the Germans and the transfer committee, Herriot insisted, had been agreed by
the inter-Allied conference, and could not be abandoned now. The Germans
insisted that in interpreting the Dawes report to German public opinion they
had always laid great stress on its recognition of Germany's right to control her
own economic destiny. On the other hand, they were anxious for an agreement; and they therefore proposed the setting up of a special committee, to
examine the principles on which arbitration could be based. This was seized on
by MacDonald; but Herriot stuck to his guns. At this Snowden waded in on
the German side, but in a fashion which was much more royalist than the King.
He had 'every sympathy with Herriot's proposals', he declared in his most
sarcastic manner, 'and expressed the hope that he would be equally enthusiastic
when the occasion arose of applying the same principles to other questions. His
view was that arbitration, unless it were most strictly limited in its incidence,
impaired German sovereignty.' After more haggling and bad temper, Mac-
Donald finally managed to get agreement to the proposal that a committee
should be set up to consider the matter, so for the moment the issue was
shelved.[50] The effects of Snowden's behaviour did not appear till the following
day. No formal negotiations took place, but what MacDonald later referred to
as the 'side-shows' were more harassing than before. At 3 a.m. on the morning
of August 14th, he noted in his diary:

Marx, Stresemann & Luther saw me at 2.30 & reported that Herriot was in a bad state of mind ... & that they had come near to deadlock. H. offered evacuation at the end of a maximum period of a year but wd. not say when it began to run or under what conditions the maximum would be shortened ... I sent for Theunis at once. He was a bit worried but thought some agreement might be come to during the afternoon ... Then Herriot was announced ... I scented trouble. Something happened as the result of his interviews with that scoundrel Loucheur. He is also much cut up about Snowden whom he has come to regard as a mere mischief-maker ... They returned to their conference with the Germans & I went to see the Chancellor. Found him with Sir O. Niemeyer. He began by producing a letter to the French Finance Minister which would have smashed the Conference to smithereens & proposed that it should be sent not by the Treasury but by the Government ... I declined to send the reply & directed that it be sent to me as a memorandum. The Chancellor had a pile of Conference points which he wished to raise. I referred to the bad effect of his interpositions ... yesterday when he enraged the French ... With cynical glee he informed me that unless the French went out of the Ruhr at once the bankers told him there would be no loan. I pointed out that we had not to represent bankers but make the best political agreement we could ... He seemed to revel in the idea of giving trouble & the fine crisis that would follow upon breakdown. — When I returned to my room I found Herriot & Hymans sad & excited waiting in the small drawing room. No agreement had been reached. H. was in a particularly distracted condition, voluble & gesticulating. On saying that I had just left the Chancellor, he burst out 'If Snowden tomorrow speaks against me & my country I shall with my delegation leave the Conference. Snowden is my enemy & the enemy of my country.'[51]

That evening, MacDonald and Hankey went together to *Saint Joan*, in a box presented by Sybil Thorndike. They spent a harassing evening. 'Telephone messages were coming in all the time,' MacDonald noted. 'Evidently much excitement among the French & Germans. Whilst Joan was being condemned, I agree to see Stresemann at midnight.' Stresemann 'poured out his soul', and told him that a twelve-month occupation of the Ruhr would make the position impossible.[52] MacDonald went to bed at 3 a.m., having rearranged the programme for the following day, and written as follows to Snowden:

I have had the most terrible evening — a furious, wounded Herriot, telephone messages sent to a theatre, Stresemann at midnight. Your remarks yesterday have played havoc & the whole French delegation has been mischief-making the livelong day ... I cannot persuade Herriot that your remark about his position on arbitration was anything but a personal attack on his honour ... The effect has ... made Herriot close up like an oyster, and unless he is in a better frame tomorrow, I fear the Conference may fail.

After I saw you, Theunis & Herriot came up here, & Theunis assured me that Morgan told him on Saturday that he would wait for the political agreement & then see what could be done. It is a mistake for us to urge the bankers' view ... We should make the best political agreement we can now & see its effect. I am seeing the Premiers to-morrow [this] morning & shall try to restore the spirit of last Monday. If I fail, I fear the worst.[53]

Next morning, the Allied prime ministers agreed to a proposal of Herriot's that the twelve-month period for the occupation should run from the day when the final agreement was signed.[54] MacDonald and the American ambassador then saw the Germans, and communicated the terms of Herriot's offer to them. The Germans asked for evacuation in stages, the first stage to begin as soon as possible, and said that they would need time to consider their reply. In the afternoon, they saw MacDonald again, and told him that they could say nothing until Saturday, since Dr Luther was flying to Berlin to consult his Government. MacDonald urged them to consult it by telegram, and eventually they agreed. Meanwhile, he had been pressing Herriot to agree to the immediate evacuation of part of the Ruhr, suggesting the Dortmund district as a possibility. In the end, Herriot agreed, subject to the consent of the French Chamber and on condition that no announcement was made until the final agreement had been reached.[55] When MacDonald was going to bed that night, a letter arrived from Snowden, threatening resignation.[56] But despite the political dangers involved it was clear that, in diplomatic terms at least, the end was in sight. On August 15th MacDonald noted:

> Newspapers encouraging on the evacuation proposal. Sent for Kindersley & arranged Hankey should see McKenna. Occurred to me that if the French would agree to 'progressive' evacuation it might be easier for the British public to swallow the year's occupation of the Ruhr. Belgian, American, Japanese & Italian representatives agreed. French came late. Herriot sulky & apparently very tired. On my proposing 'progressive' Herriot flared up, shouted, gesticulated, threatened to resign, lifted up his papers & went to the door. A painful & humiliating scene ... In the midst was called to preside over the Empire delegation. Snowden absurdly mischievous. Raised every imagineable petty fogging point, the underlying one being that we could trust the French in nothing. Gave him all the rope he took & in the end everyone was against him ... 5.45 Germans called & informed me that Berlin reply was virtual acceptance ... Thanked me for my help & expressed regret that something had got into press indicating otherwise. Hoped to get away to-morrow but late in the evening was told they were still haggling & had adjourned.[57]

The last session of the conference took place on August 16th, when the final protocol was signed, together with a series of subsidiary agreements. Altogether, there were four agreements. The first of them, between Germany and the Reparation Commission, had already been signed on August 9th, and laid down the arrangements for carrying out the sections of the Dawes report which applied exclusively to Germany. The second and third agreements were between Germany and the Allies. The second laid down the procedure for interpreting the first, and for settling disputes which might arise out of it; and also laid down the arrangements for carrying out the sections of the report which applied to the Allies as well as to Germany. The third contained the plan for restoring Germany's economic and fiscal unity. The fourth, which was confined to the Allies, set out the procedure for imposing sanctions in the event of a German default. In essentials, the Dawes plan was now agreed; the skeleton produced by the experts had been clothed in political flesh. Only time would tell whether the solution would work, but there could be no doubt that the outlook for stability and peace in central Europe was brighter than it had been since the war.[58] In an attractive farewell speech, MacDonald thanked 'the colleagues, from Premiers to typists', who had worked to make the conference a success, and declared, with pardonable pride:

We are now offering the first really negotiated agreement since the war ... This agreement may be regarded as the first Peace Treaty, because we have signed it with a feeling that we have turned our backs on the terrible years of war and war mentality ...

... We have a long way to go before we reach the goal of European peace and security. The all-important thing to-day is that we should be sure we are on the right road. I think that in our deliberations here we have found it, and, however prolonged or brief may be the rule of each of us – mere straws in the puffs of popular favour – we have every reason to be proud that it has been our good fortune to take part in this historical Conference, which is now about to end so successfully.[59]

It was the high point of his Government – perhaps of his career.

VI

One last thread remained to be tied. In his talks with Herriot, MacDonald had promised to discuss the question of disarmament and mutual security again when the Dawes report was out of the way, and he had also committed himself to make a joint appearance with Herriot at the League of Nations Assembly in September, when the replies to the draft treaty of mutual assistance were to be considered. As the time approached to honour his commitment, the prospect of another exhausting bout of personal diplomacy became more and more unwelcome, and the difficulties seemed more and more formidable. In an irritable letter to Parmoor, written at the height of the London conference, MacDonald complained that he could not 'go through the summer without a good break' and warned that it might not be possible for him to make the journey to Geneva after all.[60] At about the same time, he explained to Sir Ellis Hume-Williams that he did not think 'the psychology of Europe at the moment is good enough for a real advance in the direction of disarmament', and that, although he was 'anything but passive', he had come to the conclusion that the most he could do for the time being was to keep his hands free 'to take advantage of any change that may take place in the general orientation of international policy'.[61] In spite of his misgivings, he arrived in Geneva on September 3rd, but the atmosphere he found there did nothing to reassure him. As he put it later in his diary:

> The newspapers had been announcing that I was to make a great pro-nouncement – & I had nothing prepared. The friends of the League appealed to me to say something that would revive them, otherwise the League was dead. I talked the situation over with some old friends, went home to my hotel, & put down a few points. Herriot suggested a consultation but I thought that wd. be a mistake. It was a time for candid declarations & plain speaking ... On the whole, the delegates made a chilling impression on me. I may have done them wrong, but I felt their craft & cynicism ... I was terribly disappointed again with the French. Herriot is admirable. But somehow, a French delegation as a whole always strikes me badly. It works but it conspires; it makes great speeches with wide ideas, & fusses about the most vain & self-seeking matters. The *Frenchman* is too promi-nent.[62]

His speech on September 4th was a resounding success. It was the first time a British prime minister had addressed the Assembly; as Mrs Swanwick put it, he had arrived, with the reputation of a 'Superman who is to get Europe out of the mess'.[63] The speech itself seemed to point to a new era of co-operation and harmony, in which the fears and suspicions of the last ten years would be laid to rest. He began by repeating the British objections to the draft treaty of mutual assistance, which had already been set out in the Government's reply to the league secretariat. Britain, he declared, did not believe that security could be achieved through a military alliance. A military alliance within an agreement for security was 'like a grain of mustard seed. Small to begin with, it ... will grow and grow until at last the tree produced from it will over-shadow the heavens.' But this did not mean that nothing could be done. In the first place, Germany should be admitted to the league. Secondly, it was neces-sary to tackle the 'problem of national security in relation to national arma-ments'. It was an illusion to think that this could be done by 'putting certain phrases upon paper', in the hope of creating an enforceable obligation. What was needed was a system of arbitration to remove grievances and unmask would-be aggressors, an early but well-prepared disarmament conference and, above all, a steady extension of the influence and authority of the league:

25 MacDonald with Margaret and (left to right) Malcolm, Ishbel, David and Alister, around 1908

26 Golf at Lossiemouth, with Malcolm and Alister, 1909

27 Off to Copenhagen for the International Socialist Congress, 1910. MacDonald with Margaret and W. C. Robinson

28 Labour M.P.s in the House of Commons, 1910

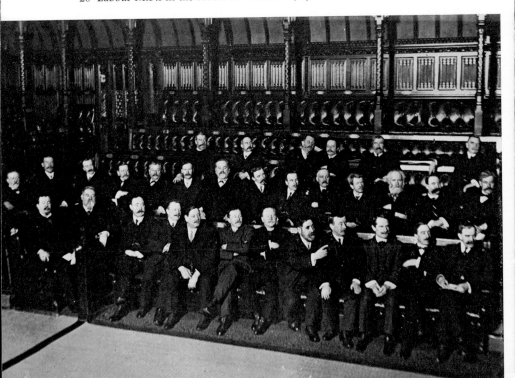

29 Labour on the march: MacDonald with Arthur Henderson. November, 1910

30 Margaret MacDonald with colleagues

31 MacDonald, Margaret and Joan with Andrew Fisher (the first Labour prime minister of Australia) and Mrs Fisher, around 1911

32 At the Labour Party National Executive, 1912. *Seated:* R. J. Wilson, Keir Hardie, MacDonald, Ben Turner, W. C. Robinson, Tom Fox, George Roberts. *Standing:* Jim Middleton, A. Peters, J. Hodge, Arthur Henderson, E. R. Pease, J. J. Stephenson

The one method by which we can secure ... an accurate attribution of responsibility for aggression is arbitration ... A system of arbitration is a system of watching the clouds ... of warning when a cloud, just the size of a man's hand, appears above the horizon, and the taking of steps at once, not of a military kind but of a rational and judicial kind, to charm it out of existence. The test is, Are you willing to arbitrate? The test is, Are you willing to explain? The test is, Will you come before us and tell us what you propose to do? The test is, Will you expose your commitments? Are you afraid of the world? Are you afraid of daylight, a lover of darkness and timorous lest the world should know what is in your mind? Such is the test, the only test ...

... Supposing that this Assembly was here and now to convene an International Conference for the reduction of armaments. What would happen? Absolute failure. Why? Because the preparations for it have not been adequately made ...

... If we had the beginnings of arbitration ... what a substantial step forward that would be! ... [I]f the large nations and the small represented here to-day would only ... create the right commission, and inspire it with the determination that we had in London that no obstacle should baulk us, the success of that commission would be assured within a year, and the League of Nations would be able to summon the nations to a conference and then, by careful handling ... obtain a successful issue ...

... A machinery of defence is easy to create, but beware lest in creating it you destroy the chances of peace. The League of Nations has to advance the interests of peace. The world has to be habituated to our existence; the world has to be habituated to our influence; we have to instil into the world confidence in the order and the rectitude of law, and then nations ... can pursue their destinies with a feeling of perfect security, none daring to make them afraid.[64]

MacDonald sat down to loud applause. One eye-witness reported that his 'predominant impulse was to sing', and that he had refrained from doing so only because 'Onward Christian Soldiers' seemed inappropriate in such a pacific gathering;[65] the New Statesman wrote that, if the prime minister kept a diary, 'he might fairly write in it of his visit to Geneva, "I came, I saw, I conquered".'[66] The sequel was less satisfactory. On September 5th, it was Herriot's turn to address the Assembly. Just before he spoke, he received information from Paris that the German Government intended to repudiate the so-called 'war guilt' clause of the peace treaty, on which all reparation claims were ultimately based, and which the German chancellor had recently attacked in a statement to the Reichstag.[67] In these circumstances, it was not surprising that Herriot should have struck a different note from MacDonald's. He echoed MacDonald's call for arbitration, but he emphasized that arbitration was not enough. The French, he declared, 'regard these three terms – arbitration, security and disarmament – as inseparable'; and he warned that arbitration without security might become 'a snare for peaceful nations'. As for Germany's entry to the league: 'In our League, there must be neither exceptions nor privilege; respect for treaties and pledges must be the common law.'[68]

The best source for what followed is MacDonald's diary:

At 11 that night Mr Wickham Steed came to my room & told me that the situation was serious & that disintegrating forces had apparently won with the French leading & that I ought to do something to retrieve the situation. A speech by Ld Parmoor had upset everybody & given the mischief makers a handle. I decided to do two things at once – one of them I intended to settle the next day. Draft a resolution for the Assembly embodying the points of my speech (except German inclusion which had been jeopardised by the German statement about war guilt) & see Benes at once & ask him what he was doing. I went down with Mr Steed to his (B's) room below mine & sent him off to see the French delegation having informed him what I proposed to do, & he agreeing to support me. Sat up late & rose early & drafted resolution which Benes took to French & later returned & told me that they agreed with it but were to propose some verbal alterations. Later the amended resolution was handed to me & I accepted the changes for none had any substance. Still later, the French asked for four amendments of substance, one of which altered the Covenant of the League on a technical point. I refused three & accepted one on conditions which I put in writing & to which the French agreed. They finally wished the resolution to be known as the Anglo-French resolution & not 'the MacDonald resolution' & that the President of the Assembly should read it & not I! I moved, Herriot seconded & then we went home.[69]

The Anglo-French resolution called for a disarmament conference as soon as possible. Meanwhile, the relevant committees of the League were to examine the obligations contained in the covenant, 'in relation to the guarantees of security which a resort to arbitration and a reduction of armaments may require'; to consider possible amendments to the articles dealing with the settlement of disputes; and to see whether the so-called 'optional clause' of the statute of the permanent court of justice could be made more precise. The resolution was adopted on September 6th. After another three-and-a-half weeks of detailed negotiations, an agreement of twenty-one clauses, designed to prevent aggressive war and known as the Geneva Protocol, was put to the Assembly. On October 2nd, the Assembly unanimously recommended it to the Governments concerned. In his speech moving the Anglo-French resolution, MacDonald had declared, to loud applause, that although Herriot and he started off on the opposite sides of the road, they would continue their journey

'arm in arm'. Now the journey was over. It only remained to be seen whether
they would both be satisfied with the destination.

The Protocol provided for an elaborate system of arbitration, as MacDonald
had suggested; but, as Herriot had insisted, arbitration was to be backed by
force. States which refused to submit to arbitration when they were required
to do so by the League council, or which refused to carry out the arbitrators'
decisions, were to be regarded as aggressors; at the discretion of the council,
aggression might be punished by the range of sanctions provided for in article
16 of the covenant. A disarmament conference was to be held in June 1925;
the Protocol would come into force when that conference reached agreement.
Thus France was to be lured into disarmament by the promise of British participation in a system of collective security; Britain was to be lured into a system
of collective security by the promise of French disarmament.[70]

It was an adroit, indeed a brilliant compromise between Herriot and Mac-
Donald — between the French fear that they might be left alone with resurgent
Germany, and the old U.D.C. doctrine that military pacts led to war. It was
not, or not in the same sense, a compromise between France and Britain. For
France, British participation in a system of collective security was a vital
interest, for which it was worth paying a high price. For Britain, French disarmament was a political luxury — passionately desired by some, but a matter of
comparative indifference to others. Those who gave a high priority to the
pacification of Europe, and who believed that the road to peace lay through
disarmament, saw the Protocol as a great step forward. Those whose chief
priority was to keep out of European quarrels, or who objected on pacifist
grounds to any form of collective security which might involve Britain in war,
viewed it in a much more hostile light.

A warning shot was fired as early as July. At the meeting of the Committee
of Imperial Defence on July 28th, Admiral Beatty pointed out that the reply
sent to the League secretariat on the question of the treaty of mutual assistance
differed from the draft reply which had been approved by the Admiralty, and
now contained a suggestion that further powers might be granted to the international court. The Admiralty, he declared, 'were inclined to be anxious',
since this might be taken to imply that, in future, reference to the court might
become compulsory. Haldane replied soothingly that there was 'no cause for
anxiety', since he had recently written a memorandum arguing that it would
be impossible for Britain to strengthen the court in this way.[71] On September
27th, Chelmsford circulated a memorandum to his colleagues, complaining
that the provision by which signatories to the Protocol were to undertake to
safeguard the sea communications of an attacked or threatened state would
place the Royal Navy in a 'false situation', since it might have to take part in
naval actions without a declaration of war.[72] On September 29th, the proceedings at Geneva were discussed by the Cabinet. According to the minutes,
'some apprehension' was felt in case Britain might be committed, by the sig-

natures of the British representatives at Geneva, to protocols which 'the Cabinet and the Government departments had had no opportunity to examine'. It was decided that MacDonald should send a telegram to Parmoor, insisting that the Assembly's decisions must take the form of recommendations, and instructing him to make it clear that he could not commit his Government to accept them.[73]

Yet this was little more than preliminary skirmishing. It reveals little about the strength or composition of the forces on either side, and it would be a mistake to draw firm conclusions from it. The service departments were clearly opposed to the Protocol. So was the ubiquitous Hankey. Haldane and Chelmsford were opposed. So, presumably, were the other service ministers; so, probably, were Snowden and Wedgwood. The dominion Governments were hostile: Thomas, as the minister responsible for relations with the dominions, might well have shared their hostility. On the other hand, Henderson and Parmoor, who had conducted the detailed negotiations after MacDonald's return from Geneva, were strongly in favour. MacDonald's position is not known. He was instinctively sceptical of the value of legalistic formulae in international politics; security would be achieved by improving the 'weather', not by specifying, in minute and implausible detail, the steps to be taken in the event of a storm. From this point of view, the Protocol was almost as objectionable as the treaty of mutual assistance had been. On the other hand, he also believed that disarmament was the key to peace. There could be no disarmament without the French; as he knew better than most, there was no hope of persuading the French to disarm unless they were given something in return. The Protocol was a small price to pay for a disarmament agreement. The sanctions it envisaged were already provided for in the covenant; as MacDonald himself put it later, they were little more than a 'harmless drug to soothe nerves'. The Protocol had emerged directly from the Anglo-French resolution of September 6th, which MacDonald had moved and for the terms of which, as we have seen, he was largely responsible. Although there can be no certainty the high probability is that, when the battle over the Protocol began in earnest, MacDonald would have fought in its support.

By the beginning of October, however, arguments about the pros and cons of the Protocol had begun to seem remote and academic. On September 29th, Parmoor wrote MacDonald a long and detailed letter from Geneva, rebutting the Admiralty's fears about the possible dangers to the Royal Navy. At the top of Parmoor's letter is a hasty scrawl in MacDonald's handwriting: 'Reply saying that next week we may be defeated. J.R.M. 2/10/24.'[74] The last phase of the Government had begun.

CHAPTER 16

Domestic setbacks

I

By September 1924, MacDonald had been carrying the double burden of No. 10 and the Foreign Office for over seven months. He had spent most of July and the first two weeks of August in a gruelling round of negotiation, conciliation, argument and persuasion, drawing heavily on his reserves of patience, charm and good humour. It had been a virtuoso performance, but it had exacted a heavy toll in nervous energy. By the end, he had begun to show signs of stress. On August 15th, he noted that he had slept badly and got up 'worried'.[1] On August 18th, one of his private secretaries reported to the Palace that the 'strain upon the Prime Minister during the last few weeks has been terrible', and that he had left for Lossiemouth feeling 'very tired'.[2] But Lossiemouth had failed to work its usual magic. 'Every day dispatches & papers came & the sun forgot to shine,' MacDonald noted disconsolately. 'It was one of the worst summers I remember. Not once did I lie out in my whins & sun myself.'[3] After two disappointing weeks in Scotland, he had plunged unrefreshed into another exhausting round of negotiations in Geneva; and when he stopped to receive the freedom of Dundee on his way back to Lossiemouth a few days later, people were struck by his 'extreme fatigue and pallor'.[4] It was a bad start for the six weeks that were to follow.

Soon after he had entered office, his old friend, Alexander Grant, whose father had worked as a guard on the Highland railway with MacDonald's uncle, had lent him a Daimler car and £40,000 in securities. It was a complicated transaction, but although the details are obscure, the outlines are clear enough. On February 4th, MacDonald wrote to his solicitor, W. H. Thompson, to say that an unnamed wealthy friend of his 'wishes to give me the loan of £40,000 for the time being, so that I may not require, whilst absorbed in public duties, to worry about income'. His friend, MacDonald continued, 'proposes that I should invest the money in safe securities and take the income but that, in the event of my death, or before if I care, the capital will be the possession of his son, not as a gift from me but simply owing to the termination of the loan'.[5] Next day he wrote to Grant, enclosing a 'recommendation made by one of our very best stockbrokers', and asking when it would be possible for Grant to deliver the car.[6] On February 8th, Grant wrote back to say that he could arrange 'for you to have £30,000 5% Preference Shares in McVitie & Price', and to suggest that so far as the other £10,000 was concerned, MacDonald should 'buy the best home Trust securities that your friend recommends'. 'If there are any other ways in which I can help you,' Grant concluded, 'will you please let me know, because I will do it as willingly as any brother man ever had.'[7]

Meanwhile, complications had arisen at MacDonald's end. On February 9th, Thompson wrote to him to suggest that the £40,000 should be invested either in MacDonald's own name or in the name of 'one or two trustees'. Whoever held the securities should execute a deed of trust to pay the interest to Mac-Donald, and on MacDonald's death to pay the capital 'to the son of your friend'.[8] MacDonald did not like this suggestion, however, and on February 11th he wrote back to Thompson:

> I do not think the Trustees' idea will do. I think the best way to handle it is to put a declaration, which will be attached to my Will, if that is legally possible. Failing that, would it be possible to have joint ownership of the script, so that in the event of my death the remaining person would own them? The trouble there, of course, would be that supposing he dies before me, the money might become my absolute property — but you could provide against that, could you not?[9]

It is not clear which course, if either, was followed, but it is clear that the transaction was completed the following month, when Rose Rosenberg wrote to the McVitie & Price offices in Birmingham to acknowledge the receipt of the share certificates. It is also clear that, if MacDonald had adopted his solicitor's suggestion that the money should be paid to him by trustees, he would have been saved a good deal of embarrassment later.

In April 1924, Grant was recommended for a baronetcy, in recognition of his many philanthropic activities, and in particular of his donation of the Advocates' Library to Scotland. On April 18th, he wrote to thank MacDonald for recommending him:

> I have your very kind letter, a letter I will always preserve for its kindness, telling me you are proposing to put my name forward for a Baronetcy and I am simply writing to thank you, and to hope I shall always be worthy of your recommendation and I will not be disappointed if you are unable to carry this through.
>
> Regarding the Advocates Library I have always felt it was the duty of everyone, who wanted to build up a big business, to have larger ideas in the giving away, as well as in the taking in. I am a great believer in the 'passing on' habit.
>
> I remember when I was a young man of receiving help from a friend and when I asked how I could repay him his answer was 'pass it on' and for

many years now I have tried to cultivate this habit and get far more pleasure than if I spent it on myself. My wants are few. There are many words I would like to write but I am not a good hand at writing a long letter and they will need to wait until we meet but I can assure you I am getting more satisfaction out of your success than if it were myself.[10]

In the next honours list, he duly became Sir Alexander Grant. It was an act of remarkable folly, which could only have sprung from a remarkable mixture of unworldliness and arrogance. It is clear that Grant's public services were worthy of recognition; it is also clear that neither he nor MacDonald saw any connection between the baronetcy and the £40,000. But this was 1924, only a short time after the honours scandals which had done so much damage to Lloyd George, and one cannot help being astonished at MacDonald's failure to recognize the risk he was running.

He was to learn soon enough. On September 11th, the *Daily Mail* published a report by its city editor, revealing that MacDonald had acquired 30,000 £1 shares in McVitie & Price the previous March, thus becoming the second largest individual shareholder. That evening, MacDonald told the press that the capital did not belong to him and that he owned the shares only 'technically'; Grant, he added, had been awarded his baronetcy for his public services. On September 13th, *The Times*, *Daily Mail* and *Daily Express* all carried as their lead stories a report from the Lossiemouth correspondent of the Central News, who wrote that MacDonald was 'deeply vexed over the reports which had been circulated about these shares, more on account of his friend than of himself'. MacDonald, the Central News correspondent continued, had told him that he had talked to Grant soon after becoming prime minister, that Grant had offered to give him a car, that MacDonald had replied that he would have to be content with hiring one since he would leave office as poor as he had been when he entered it, that Grant had then offered to endow the car and that the shares had been transferred to him for that purpose. On September 15th, Grant wrote to MacDonald:

> I have your letter from Lossiemouth and what you feared was to take place has come like a flash of lightning ...
>
> My great regret was the fear that you would suffer through something that I, who would almost lay down my life to be of assistance to you, had been the cause of, but I do not think that any right-thinking people will allow themselves to be side-tracked by this ...
>
> Cheer up, it is only the opinion of good people that matters and that guides public opinion, however loud the others may be.[11]

At the end of the year, MacDonald returned the shares and the car to Grant. On December 4th, Grant wrote, 'Regarding the last conversation we had in London about your shares in McVitie and Price, I enclose the Transfer and should be obliged if you would sign it and return it to me at Moray House.'[12] On December 17th, MacDonald wrote, 'The month is now wearing through and I am off on Monday. I suppose if I ask my chauffeur to take the car to Moray House some time next week you will be able to take it over.'[13] But by then, the damage had been done.

Its nature and extent can only be guessed at, but the guess is not a difficult one to make. No doubt, Labour men and women exaggerated the effect of the disclosure on public opinion: then, as now, politicians were apt to overestimate public interest in their doings. But this does not mean that it had no effect at all. As Mrs Hamilton put it later, 'a trickle of talk was set going and kept going'; as she also pointed out, the trickle gained extra force from the way in which MacDonald handled the affair. No doubt, she was deceiving herself when she wrote that '[e]veryone would have been delighted'[14] if he had made the whole story public in March, but there can be little doubt that his obvious confusion and embarrassment in September helped to create an atmosphere in which hostile rumours could flourish. For, as we have seen, the explanation he gave the Central News correspondent was incomplete and unconvincing. Even in those days, the cost of maintaining a Daimler car and of paying the chauffeur's wages was less than the income from £30,000 in 5% preference shares, and many newspaper readers must have realized this. In fact, of course, Grant had lent him £40,000, not £30,000; and there is no suggestion in the MacDonald papers that he did so solely to pay for the upkeep of the car. It is much more likely that the loan was designed, not only to cover the running costs of the car, but also to supplement MacDonald's salary — which was barely adequate to cover his expenses as prime minister. But there was nothing discreditable in this; and MacDonald would have done himself much more good than harm if he had explained the circumstances in full. A less reticent man in similar circumstances might have taken that course; for him it was out of the question. Not for the first or the last time in his life, his shyness and self-consciousness looked suspiciously like evasiveness.

At the lowest, all this gave Conservative and Liberal hecklers a useful weapon, and put Labour supporters on the defensive. In a long, breathless and, in the circumstances, less than tactful letter of commiseration to MacDonald, Katherine Bruce Glasier wrote that 'poor old Baronet Grant's motor car misery ... is flung in our teeth at every village green meeting just now'; and although she added consolingly that 'the crowd *feel* how we love & trust you & that carries you forward better than a Daimler,'[15] it is doubtful if the salve did much to heal the wound. For although there is no direct evidence of MacDonald's reaction to the publicity, there can be no doubt that he must have been deeply hurt by it. He was painfully scrupulous in money matters; although he disliked the honours system, and rejoiced on the rare occasions when someone who had been recommended for an honour turned it down on grounds of principle, he had been deeply shocked by the honours scandals of the post-war coalition and was, if anything, excessively anxious to make sure that his own honours lists were beyond criticism. In the McVitie & Price affair he had behaved with extraordinary imprudence, but the imprudence was, at bottom, a proof of innocence: if he had wished to cover his tracks to hide what he believed to be a corrupt action he would have taken his solicitor's advice and arranged for the share capital to be transferred to trustees. Now he was being accused of behaving like a second Lloyd George, and the fact that the accusation was being made *sotto voce* and by insinuation rather than openly and directly, can only have made it more painful. On September 22nd, Jim Middleton wrote:

> I am very sorry indeed to hear from Ben Spoor how depressed you have been feeling. It is not surprising considering all the happenings of the last few weeks, and you certainly have not had the sort of break that would do you much good. When this was supplemented by the news, per wireless last night, that you had caught a chill on your way down from Lossiemouth, it made it all the easier to realise what a burden you are really bearing.[16]

It would be wrong to suggest that the McVitie & Price affair was a major burden, but it undoubtedly made the other burdens harder to bear. And the other burdens were steadily mounting in weight.

II

By now, MacDonald was back in London, having arrived in Downing Street 'longing for a rest'.[17] Instead, he was faced with two long conversations with Zaghlul Pasha, the Egyptian nationalist leader who had become prime minister of Egypt at the same time that the Labour Government took office in Britain; and with an agitated series of comings and goings over the boundary dispute between Ulster and the Irish Free State. During the parliamentary recess, moreover, the second big foreign-policy question of 1924 had come to a head, and it was beginning to look as though the Government's survival might be in doubt.

One of MacDonald's first actions as foreign secretary had been to recognize the Soviet Union. In February, he had told the House of Commons that negotiations to settle the outstanding differences between the Soviet Union and Britain would begin as soon as possible.[18] They eventually began in April, but although MacDonald took the chair at the first meeting with the Soviet delegation, he played little part in the negotiations thereafter and left his parliamentary secretary, Arthur Ponsonby, in charge. The negotiations that followed revolved around two main issues—the possibility of concluding a commercial treaty to encourage Anglo-Soviet trade, and the position of British bondholders whose claims on the pre-revolutionary Russian Government had been repudiated by the Bolsheviks. It soon became clear that the Soviet price for an agreement was a British loan; and by Whitsun, Ponsonby was writing privately that without a loan, 'the whole thing must break down. I have given them a fortnight to explore in the City but from what I hear the prospects are far from reassuring. My last card will be a Government guarantee but I doubt if I can carry this.' MacDonald, he added, 'accepts all I ask and is ready to back me, but when it comes to my asking for a Government guarantee (if it does reach that point) I doubt if I shall carry him.'[19]

Ponsonby's fears were disproved six weeks later. In July, he circulated a memorandum to the Cabinet, explaining that 'substantial agreement' was in sight, provided the Government guaranteed a loan of £30 million. The Russians, he wrote, had promised to spend two-thirds of the money in Britain; if the Government guaranteed the loan, they would yield on the remaining points still in dispute. Without a guarantee the negotiations would break down. Ponsonby's paper was discussed by the Cabinet on July 30th. In the teeth of strong opposition from Snowden, MacDonald managed to persuade his colleagues that if the Russians accepted the British position on the claims of the bondholders, the Government would recommend Parliament to guarantee the loan.[20] But the battle was not yet over. Negotiations were resumed on August 4th, and, after a nineteen-hour session, broke down in the early morning of August 5th, over the precise wording of the article dealing with compensation for nationalized property. Ponsonby's diary contains a vivid picture of the sequel:

The news [of the breakdown] was published and as I expected our M.P.s were in a state of fury ... [Some] M.P.s met me at the House on Tuesday afternoon. Purcell, Chairman of the T.U. conference, very hostile to me, Wallhead, Morel, Mills etc. I told them the case. In time everybody there met Rakovsky and others of the Russian delegation. They brought me a formula from him ... I had a hectic meeting with my colleagues at my room at the Foreign Office. The Russian formula would not do. We devised another and sent Gregory with it to Rakovsky. He could not accept it and drafted another. Sir S. Chapman in the meanwhile drafted yet another on quite different lines. I examined all of them, took Chapman's in my pocket, tore over to Downing Street, by a miracle met Snowden in the lobby, got him in a waiting room with a Treasury expert. A moment of hesitation, but he accepted it. Tore upstairs, found J.R.M. discussing holidays with Ishbel and know him well enough to be sure that he must not be interrupted, mutter, an apple tart almost stuck in my throat, but I was rewarded for not bursting in. He turned to me, I explained the position, got his consent to the new formula and munching pie-crust ran down to the House and made up my mind on the way to use the M.P.s and not the officials. I gave Purcell and Morel the new formula and asked them to go at once to Rakovsky ... Back at the Foreign Office ... [t]he telephone rang. Rakovsky accepted the formula. A plenary session was immediately arranged, the final formulations gone through, and for an interrupted hour in my room I had to try and fix my mind on what I was to say in the House.[21]

There were two treaties, not one – a fairly straightforward commercial treaty, and a wider general treaty. The general treaty provided for further negotiations between the bondholders and the Soviet Government. If the results of these negotiations were approved by the holders of not less than half the total capital value of the bonds in question, and if the other outstanding claims between the two Governments were settled, a third treaty would be concluded. When that treaty was signed, the British Government would guarantee a loan.[22]

The general treaty, in other words, was not a real treaty at all. It was a diplomatic signpost, pointing vaguely in the direction of a treaty, which might or might not be signed at some stage in the future. Even so, it provoked fierce opposition. The Conservatives insisted that the Government should not sign it until it had been debated by the House of Commons; and in the end, the Government agreed to let it lie on the table for twenty-one parliamentary days between signature and ratification, thus ensuring that it would not be ratified until after the summer recess. But, although MacDonald refused to give way on the question of signing the treaty, his statement explaining the Government's decision was the reverse of robust. 'If my signature is attached to this treaty,' he declared, 'I shall not be labouring under the foolish delusion that the House of Commons has sanctioned it;' and he went on to enunciate the novel doctrine that the Government's signature on a treaty implied nothing more than a willingness 'that that agreement should be put before the House of Commons for rejection or acceptance'.[23]

During the recess, his attitude stiffened. On August 13th, he wrote to Ponsonby to ask him to send the text of the treaty to Lossiemouth so that he could study it in detail. 'We shall have a fight to get it through,' he wrote, 'but we shall face the House of Commons in a fighting spirit and defy them to turn it down. The great thing is – keep your fighting spirit up and no surrender.'[24] By September his blood was up. It had been clear ever since the treaty was signed that it would be opposed by the Conservatives, and during the recess it became increasingly likely that they would be joined by a significant section of the Liberal Party as well. By the end of August, Simon, Runciman and Lloyd George were all joined in opposition. On September 3rd, the Liberal Party publication department announced the publication of a pamphlet called 'A Sham Treaty'. On September 8th, the Daily Chronicle began a series of articles on the theme 'In Darkest Russia'. Two days later, Lloyd George delivered a sustained attack on the treaties, calling on the Liberal Party to challenge the Government, and declaring that if they failed to do so, they would 'forfeit the respect and confidence of the nation'.[25]

Little by little, Asquith was stampeded. On September 22nd, he published a letter in *The Times*, associating himself with the protests made by his colleagues and describing the treaties as 'crude experiments in nursery diplomacy'. In another passage, he appeared to be trying to leave the door open for a compromise, by which the Liberals would not vote to reject the treaties after all, but only to amend them. He may have hoped that these tactics would give him the best of both worlds—enabling him to retain his hold on the Liberal Party, where opposition to the Government's Russian policy was rapidly gaining ground, without defeating the Government and forcing a general election. If so, the manœuvre backfired. There is some evidence that the Cabinet discussed a possible deal with the Liberals,[26] but it is clear that MacDonald was violently opposed to anything of the kind. 'The attack on the Russian Treaties looks less & less honest as one considers it,' MacDonald wrote on September 26th. 'I am inclined to give the Liberals an election on it if they force it. I have no intention of deserting a post of difficulty but the conditions of office perhaps bribe me to take this chance of ending the present regime.'[27] Next day, he made a long speech at Derby, leaving open the possibility of a compromise on the details of the loan, but making it clear that there could be no compromise on the principle of a guarantee and that the Government would be prepared to fight an election on the issue:

> We shall take no words from the House of Commons or party leaders like 'I am in favour of trade with Russia and peace with Russia, but I am not going to accept these treaties' ... An agreement with Russia on these lines, embodied in our two draft Treaties ... is now an essential part of the Labour Party's policy, and if the House of Commons will not allow it, the House of Commons had better censure us. (Loud Cheers).[28]

'The Liberal attitude is mean and unscrupulous,' he noted afterwards, 'the tactics of pettyfogging & disgruntled partisans—a combination of vanity & sulks—not a pleasant judgement to write but a true one. A contemptible coterie with a lazy old man at their head whom I have always tried to respect but have failed.'[29] At a meeting of the parliamentary Liberal Party four days later, Asquith condemned the guarantee, and a motion was passed, attacking the loan in such sweeping terms that compromise seemed impossible.[30] If the Liberals stuck to their guns, the Government's fall could only be a matter of time.

III

Meanwhile, a more dangerous storm had begun to gather in a different quarter. Its origins lay in a series of blunders and equivocations two months earlier. On July 25th, an article had appeared in the *Workers' Weekly*, the official organ of the Communist Party, calling on soldiers in the British Army 'to let it be known that neither in the class war nor in a military war, will you turn your guns on your fellow workers'. On July 30th, the director of public prosecutions brought the article to the notice of the attorney general, Sir Patrick Hastings. Hastings was a brilliant advocate, but a novice in Labour politics; he appears to have given no thought to the effect which a prosecution might have on the Labour movement. He decided that the article was an incitement to mutiny, and he instructed the director of public prosecutions to bring such proceedings under the Incitement to Mutiny Act as he thought fit. The following Saturday, a warrant was granted for the arrest of the editor, John Campbell. The news was reported in the press; and on August 6th, Hastings had to answer questions about it in the House of Commons. There were angry protests from the Labour benches. Maxton asked whether the prime minister had read the article and whether he was aware that the point of view expressed in it was shared by a large number of Labour members; Buchanan pointed out that the article expressed 'the views and findings of Labour party conferences'; Scurr and Lansbury threatened to raise the matter in the debate on the Appropriation Bill. After questions, Hastings saw Maxton and some of his colleagues in his room at the House. They told him that Campbell was only the acting editor, and that he had an excellent war record; it can be assumed that they also told him that if he persisted with the prosecution, he would incur bitter hostility from the left wing of his own party.[31]

What happened next is less clear. MacDonald had not been consulted formally about the case, and had learned about it by accident from Ammon, the parliamentary secretary to the Admiralty. Ammon told him that the War Office and the Air Ministry had both agreed to the prosecution, and that the Admiralty had been asked for its views. Ammon himself was opposed to the prosecution, and had written a minute to that effect; MacDonald told him to add that the prime minister must be informed before any action was taken.[32] According to a letter which he wrote to Lord Stamfordham on August 22nd, however, MacDonald heard nothing more until the news of Campbell's arrest appeared in the press. When he saw it, he was 'furious', and, as he put it to Lord Stamfordham,

> I sent for the Attorney General and the Public Prosecutor and gave them a bit of my mind ... They replied that the whole matter could be dropped. I told them that, as they had begun, they had to go through with it. Later on I was informed that the editor was prepared to write a letter which would amount to an apology for what he had done. I agreed that, if he did that, the matter might be dropped.[33]

Hastings's account is slightly different. According to him, it was his conversation with Maxton which made him think that a prosecution might, after all, be ill-advised. He had made his reputation as a defence counsel, and he asked himself how he would conduct the defence if some other attorney general singled out for prosecution as a dangerous Communist a man 'who had had both his feet almost blown off in the war, who had fought through the war from beginning to end, and who had been decorated for exceptional gallantry'. After talking to Maxton, he therefore sent for the director of public prosecutions. The director was away, but the assistant director, Sir Guy Stephenson, came instead; and it was from him that Hastings learned that Maxton's story was true. The conversation between Hastings and Stephenson took place in MacDonald's room at the House of Commons, but at first MacDonald was not present. When he came in, he made it clear, according to Hastings, that he thought the prosecution 'ill-advised from the beginning'.[34]

At six o'clock that evening, the question came before the Cabinet. Hankey was away, and his deputy, Tom Jones, acted as secretary instead. Jones's notes of the remarkably muddled and incoherent discussion which followed were filed with the Cabinet minutes and have since been published; although they are not as clear as they might be, they make it possible to reconstruct at least the broad outlines of what must have taken place. The proceedings began with an unseemly bout of mutual recrimination, summarized in Jones's notes as follows:

> Prime Minister: First I heard in House of Commons, Ammon said he'd had a minute from Admiralty. War Office agreed. Air agreed and Admiralty asked for views. He minuted against it. But I said 'It will not be begun until I know'. You add 'P.M. must be informed before action taken'. In papers I read it — done.
>
> Snowden: Had been done then.
>
> P.M.: I sent for Assistant Director Public Prosecution. I asked him to take files on which he acted. Hastings said he did not authorise action. He was asked and said article criminal. Gave legal view. Assistant Director saw me — he produced Minute: S. of S. agrees to go on with prosecution.
>
> Henderson: No. We agreed to transfer letters we'd received to the Director of Public Prosecutions ... Nothing about prosecution. I asked A-G if he'd authorised proceedings. He agreed with you. He is under A-G not under me.
>
> P.M.: I misread Minute also.
>
> Henderson: My Secretary has known for a week that I was opposed to prosecution.

After more crying over spilt milk, Hastings came in. He accepted full responsibility for what had happened, and made it clear that he still thought that proceedings should be taken. He also told the Cabinet, however, that Campbell had only taken on the editorship temporarily, while the editor was on holiday, and that this would provide a 'possible way out' if the Cabinet wished to drop the case. Jones's notes continue:

> Prime Minister: Settled that no one else will be arrested — I'd rather go through once started than show white feather. If you stop prosecution you

will be asked all round what going to do. Editor is known — why not arrest him.

Walsh: Worst article I've ever read. One paragraph atrocious. I thought it would come before Cabinet. It would be peculiarly weak action if we abandoned prosecution having regard to all the circumstances ...

Prime Minister: If put to me I should not have sanctioned it. I know the men and the game. Now in press and House of Commons. Answer given.

J. H. Thomas: Don't withdraw now in view of House of Commons ...

Attorney-General: No debate tonight or tomorrow. Man arrested prepared to write letter to say he was only few days.

J. H. Thomas: Real fight will start two months hence.

Attorney-General: I'll accept his letter — reply being we had to take cognisance reluctantly.

Henderson: More questions tomorrow.

Attorney-General: Steps have been taken. Nothing to add.

(Attorney-General authorised).[35]

These unhappy proceedings were then summarized by Jones in an official minute. Like most Cabinet minutes in this period, it was fairly brief, and did not name the participants in the discussion or give a full account of the arguments which had been put forward. The attorney general, said the minute, told the Cabinet that 'inasmuch as it transpired that the person charged was only acting temporarily as editor and was prepared to write a letter to that effect steps could be taken not to press the prosecution in the circumstances against this particular offender, if the Cabinet so desired.' The Cabinet, it concluded, agreed:

(a) That no public prosecution of a political character should be undertaken without the prior sanction of the Cabinet being obtained:

(b) That in the particular case under review the course indicated by the Attorney-General should be adopted.[36]

Four points emerge, with varying degrees of clarity, from all this bickering and confusion. In the first place, it is clear that MacDonald was seriously at fault in failing to make his views known to Hastings as soon as he heard that a prosecution was contemplated, and in relying instead on a casual verbal instruction to a junior minister. He was preoccupied with the London conference, and was working under heavy strain. But although his behaviour was understandable, and in the circumstances perhaps even excusable, the consequences were damaging in the extreme, not only to him but to the Government and party of which he was the head; and his unwillingness to accept his share of the responsibility for them was, to say the least, unedifying.

The second point is more complicated. There could be no doubt that Hastings was entitled to consult the Cabinet, and, having done so, to decide that the prosecution should be withdrawn. But, although Hastings was entitled to withdraw the prosecution, the Cabinet was not entitled to instruct him to do so. In fact, as Jones's notes make clear, the Cabinet did not instruct him. The suggestion that the prosecution should be withdrawn came from Hastings, not from the Cabinet; and the meeting ended with Hastings informing the Cabinet of the steps he intended to take. But, although this is clear from Jones's notes, it is not at all clear from the minute which he wrote the following day. On the contrary, the minute, by lumping the conclusion on the Campbell case together with the conclusion on the general issue of prosecutions of a political character, suggests, if anything, that the Cabinet had taken the decision on both and had illegitimately given the attorney general instructions on a matter over which it had no proper jurisdiction.

The third point is more speculative. At first, MacDonald argued vigorously that the prosecution should be continued. At the end of the meeting, he appears to have supported, or at least to have acquiesced in, the decision to drop it. Why did he change his mind? His own answer is contained in his letter to Lord Stamfordham of August 22nd. As we have seen, he told Lord Stamfordham that he had at first insisted that Hastings should 'go through with' the prosecution; that he had subsequently been told that the editor was prepared to write a letter 'which would amount to an apology for what he had done'; and that he had then agreed that 'if he did that, the matter might be dropped'. It is true that Jones's notes do not mention an apology. They and the minute based on them do, however, make it clear that Hastings told the Cabinet that Campbell was prepared to write a letter explaining that he had been acting as editor for only a short time. Such a letter, even if Campbell himself did not intend it to be an apology, could no doubt be treated by a hard-pressed Government as 'amounting to an apology' – thus allowing faces to be saved all round. On the whole, then, it seems likely that MacDonald told Lord Stamfordham the truth. At first, he had argued against dropping the prosecution, because he did not want to be accused of running away from the Clydesiders. When he was told that Campbell was willing to write a letter which could be treated, however implausibly, as an apology, he changed his mind, because he saw that this would make it possible for the Government to retreat without appearing to do so.

The fourth point follows from the third. If this interpretation is right, what mattered to MacDonald was Campbell's letter, not his war record or even the temporary character of his editorship. But the minute which Jones drafted after the Cabinet meeting did not make this clear. It said that the Cabinet were told that Campbell was prepared to write a letter. It did not suggest that the most important member of the Cabinet had agreed that the prosecution should be dropped only because he expected the letter to be written, or that the Cabinet's decision was to be implemented only after the letter had arrived. For the most part, the minute faithfully reflected the notes on which it was based; perhaps for that reason, it has been widely assumed that its accuracy must be beyond dispute. On the question of Campbell's letter, however, there is a discrepancy between the notes and the minute. According to the notes, Hastings told the Cabinet, 'I'll accept his letter — reply being that we had to take cognisance reluctantly.' He was then 'authorised' — presumably to take the steps he had just outlined, among them, accepting and replying to the letter. The minute, on the other hand, merely says that the Cabinet agreed that 'the course indicated by the Attorney-General should be adopted,' without making it clear that that course included not only withdrawing the prosecution but accepting and replying to the letter as well. The discrepancy was not large, and it is not particularly surprising that Jones did not spot it. He was a civil servant, not a politician; he could hardly be blamed for failing to appreciate the full political significance of the letter — particularly if, as is quite possible, none of the ministers present at the Cabinet meeting wished to spell it out. The fact remains that, on the evidence of his notes, his minute did not do full justice to the discussion, and may well have given a misleading impression of the decision.

Further blunders followed. Next morning, Hastings saw the director and assistant director of public prosecutions and told them that he had decided not to proceed with the prosecution.[37] He appears to have said nothing about a letter from Campbell. Meanwhile, Jones finished drafting his minute and sent it to Hankey. MacDonald was presiding over a meeting of the heads of delegations at the London conference, and was later called out to intervene in a debate on the Russian treaty, which was taking place on the adjournment motion. At some stage during the morning, Hankey showed him Jones's minute for his approval. It is not clear whether he had time to read it; if he had, it is unlikely that he read it with close attention. At all events, he made no changes in it. At 3.20 that afternoon, copies of the draft minutes were circulated in the usual way to members of the Cabinet, accompanied by the usual note asking for corrections to be sent to the secretary.[38] But at five o'clock the House rose for the summer recess.[39] Many ministers must already have left for their holidays; others must have been about to leave. No corrections were sent in, and the minute was left as it stood.

On August 13th, the prosecution was duly withdrawn, even though Campbell's letter had not arrived. In a phrase which was to be quoted a great deal in the next few weeks, the Treasury counsel, Travers Humphreys, told the magistrates that it had 'been represented' that the article had not been designed to seduce servicemen from their allegiance, but merely to oppose the use of troops in industrial disputes.[40] He did not say where the representation had come from; and the obvious inference was that it had come from the Government. To make matters worse, the Communist Party proclaimed impenitently that they regretted the abandonment of the prosecution, and announced that they would have called MacDonald and other ministers as witnesses for the defence, if the case had come to trial.[41] In the climate created by the mounting agitation over the Russian treaties, all this made it seem that the Government

N

had something to hide. *The Times* asked pointedly who had made the representation referred to in Travers Humphreys's statement.[42] On September 20th, it reported that Sir Kingsley Wood was tabling a question to Hastings, to ask why the charges against Campbell had been dropped, and to MacDonald, to ask whether he had sanctioned the withdrawal of the prosecution and whether he had received any intimation that he would be required to give evidence at the hearing. On September 24th, Sir John Simon joined the hunt, with a speech drawing attention to the form of Humphreys's statement and implying that the Government had acted improperly.[43]

It was far from certain that the hunt would end in a kill; but there could be little doubt that the quarry would need more agility than it had displayed in the last two months if it was to escape unharmed.

IV

There is no direct evidence about MacDonald's reaction when he learned of Sir Kingsley Wood's questions, but it is not difficult to imagine what he must have felt. He was still smarting from the McVitie & Price affair, which can be assumed to have made him even more sensitive than usual to personal criticisms and innuendoes. Now his good faith was coming under attack again, and in an even more damaging way. This time, moreover, he had some reason to feel that he was being asked to pay for the mistakes of others. It was Hastings, not he, who had authorized the prosecution in the first place and who had then suggested that it might be withdrawn. It was Hastings who had told the Cabinet that Campbell was willing to write a letter, and who had then failed to make sure that the letter would arrive before instructing the director of public prosecutions to withdraw the charges against him. If the letter had arrived, as MacDonald had been told it would, Humphreys would have been able to produce it in court and would not have needed to talk vaguely about 'representations' having been made. The article in *The Times* might never have been written, and Sir Kingsley Wood's questions might never have been tabled. It was true that MacDonald had been given an opportunity to correct Jones's minute, and that he had failed to take it. But Hankey had shown it to him in the worst possible circumstances, when he was heavily occupied with more pressing business. MacDonald had always been apt to succumb to a mood of injured innocence when he was under attack, and to hit out blindly at his critics, without giving adequate thought to the consequences. On this occasion, these traits must have been reinforced by a nagging, and not altogether unjustified, suspicion that he was being cast as the scapegoat for Hastings and Jones, and by a strong feeling of resentment against the unfairness of fate.

On September 22nd, he asked Hankey to show him the minute of the Cabinet's discussion of the *Workers' Weekly* case, and queried the accuracy of the final conclusion. There is no record of what he said but, in view of his letter to Lord Stamfordham a month before, it seems probable that he must have pointed out that the minute said nothing about Campbell's letter. No doubt, he also pointed out that the minute wrongly gave the impression that Hastings had been instructed to withdraw the prosecution, and failed to make it clear that the suggestion had come from Hastings himself. Hankey said nothing to Jones about MacDonald's query, and apparently took no steps to have the minute checked.[44] On September 27th, MacDonald spoke at Derby, and then left for Chequers, 'with a heavy load of cold & a splitting headache'.[45] On the 28th, he returned to Downing Street, and noted afterwards that he was 'Chilled & wretched'.[46] On the 29th, he had another long conversation with Zaghlul. On the 30th, Parliament reassembled to debate the Government's Irish Free State Bill, which embodied the results of the negotiations which had taken place during the summer over the Ulster boundary dispute.

Before the debate began, Hastings and MacDonald had to answer Sir Kingsley Wood's private notice questions. Hastings was asked why the charges against Campbell had been withdrawn, and whether he had received any representations on the matter. In a long and adroitly phrased answer, he said that he had decided to direct the director of public prosecutions not to offer evidence against Campbell, because inquiry had revealed that his character and degree of responsibility were such that a prosecution might fail. As for the second part of Wood's question, he said that he had 'received no representation of the sort suggested in the question, or of any kind whatsoever, relating to the matter, from the defendant or from any person whatsoever'. Apart from the solicitor general, he added, 'no member of His Majesty's Government suggested or even knew of the proposal until I myself informed them of it.' Not surprisingly, Hasting's answer provoked a long string of hostile supplementaries; and in the end Baldwin asked whether the prime minister would grant a day to debate the matter when the House resumed at the end of October. MacDonald replied that he was not content to wait until then, and that if the other party leaders agreed he would prefer a debate the following week.[47]

Then Sir Kingsley Wood put his second private notice question, this time addressed to the prime minister – 'whether any directions were given by him, or with his sanction, to the Director of Public Prosecutions to withdraw the proceedings against Mr Campbell, the editor of the "Workers' Weekly", and whether he received any intimation that he would be personally required to give evidence on behalf of the defendant at the hearing?' Hastings had just managed to skate over some remarkably thin ice. MacDonald crashed through. His answer sent a 'shiver' down Tom Jones's spine, and was later described by Hankey as a 'bloody lie'.[48] It ran as follows:

I was not consulted regarding either the institution or the subsequent with-drawal of these proceedings. The first notice of the procesution which came to my knowledge was in the Press. I never advised its withdrawal, but left the whole matter to the discretion of the Law Officers, where that discretion properly rests. I never received any intimation, not even a hint, that I should be asked to give evidence. That also came to my attention when the falsehood appeared in the Press.[49]

So far, the affair had been an embarrassment. MacDonald's reply turned it into a crisis. He claimed later that he had been so incensed by the wording of Sir Kingsley Wood's question, and in particular by its implied suggestion that he had caused the charges against Campbell to be withdrawn because he was unwilling to appear in the witness box, that he had assumed that the question was solely concerned with that aspect of the matter and had therefore failed to realize that the first sentence of his reply was misleading. This claim may well have contained an element of truth. For what it is worth, MacDonald's diary entry for September 30th suggests that he was badly rattled by the whole affair, and in a mood to hit back first and think afterwards. 'Political advantage was mainly in Tory & Liberal minds & they coursed that hare like hounds,' he wrote bitterly. 'There was also personal enmity. The petty & sneaky spite of Sir John Simon & the personal triumph that beamed from Sir Douglas Hogg were humiliating to behold.'[50] In any event, it is hard to believe that his answer could have been carefully calculated, though the text appears to have been prepared beforehand, if only because calculation would have shown that he had much less to lose by telling the truth than by being caught out in an attempt to mislead the House. For, although the Government's behaviour had been inept, it had not been unconstitutional. No one could seriously argue that the attorney general had no right to withdraw a prosecution in the light of new evidence or to consult the prime minister and Cabinet over a case which, by definition, involved the security of the state. If MacDonald had admitted that Hastings had consulted him, and had insisted firmly that he had every right to do so, he would have suffered nothing more than a few minutes' embarrassment at the dispatch box. As things were, he got the worst of all worlds. His answer was both untrue and unconvincing as well; a good many people were in a position to know that it was untrue. On the most favourable construction, it was an appalling blunder; and there can be no doubt that it has left a bad blot on MacDonald's reputation.

At first, there was little public criticism of his performance. On October 1st, *The Times* published a leader attacking the attorney general, but it said nothing about MacDonald. The *Manchester Guardian* took a similar view. Its first leader was headed 'Unsatisfactory'; but it, too, was directed against Hastings, not against MacDonald. In the next few days, however, the situation changed. On October 1st, the Conservatives put down a motion censuring the Government for its handling of the Campbell case; as we have seen, the Liberals put down a motion rejecting the Russian treaties.

MacDonald reacted with glee. In his diary he noted:

I am living in rare air tonight; the end is definitely in sight, & by a blunder of the Liberals my path has been cleared. The Tories are to censure us & it is expected that the Liberals will vote with them. Had the fall come upon the Attorney alone, & had his mistake been kept isolated from other issues, a dissolution would have been an awkward thing to ask for & an equally awkward thing to have justified to the country. Mr Asquith's blunder in giving notice of a resolution to reject the Russian Treaty gives a general political significance to the vote of censure & brings the whole political forces into the battle. So I am unburdened tonight ... [51]

His glee was shortlived. On October 2nd, the Liberals put down an amendment to the Conservative motion of censure, calling for the establishment of a select committee to inquire into the matter. During the day, Macmillan, the Scottish Lord Advocate, saw MacDonald and told him that his reply to Sir Kingsley Wood was inaccurate.[52] Presumably in a rather desperate effort to defend himself in case the inquiry took place, MacDonald instructed Hankey to file a statement with the Cabinet minutes, recording that the prime minister had questioned the accuracy of the minute on the *Workers' Weekly* ten days before. Meanwhile, Tom Jones learned that the accuracy of his minute was being questioned, and showed the rough notes on which he had based it to Hankey and Rupert Howorth. They read them through, but failed to notice that there was, in fact, a discrepancy between them and the minute, and according to Jones 'agreed that, on the evidence before them, the Minute was, if anything, an under-statement'.[53] In his diary MacDonald noted:

The papers are full of the coming election. No one has any doubt now that it is coming ... Friend remarked I was happy & lively & wished to know why: 'Because I see the end'. But in the afternoon it changed. The Lord Advocate came & pointed out to me that my reply to Kingsley Wood on the Communist prosecution was inaccurate & to my horror I found it was. I had concentrated my thought on personal allegations in which this man is always revelling, & took him to charge me with personal interference in withdrawing prosecution. [O]n that I said I had never been consulted & that in cold print implies I was never spoken to on the subject. The House is generous however & will acquit me of misleading it as it knows I never intended. It never rains but it pours & with this blunder of mine came a reminder of a most imperfect & misleading Cabinet minute which by its wording seems to give the lie to everything we have said. The minute is quite wrong & I drew attention to its errors some time ago. Now Sir Maurice Hankey tells me that I saw it at the time but confesses he put it before on the 7th Aug: whilst I was presiding over the London Conference (I have looked back in this diary & the conditions are described). Again &

again I have told colleagues that I shall not be responsible for opinions expressed or decisions taken if they ask for them under such circumstances, & as 'everybody' went off on the 6th or 7th I doubt if Ministers read the minutes to check them. So the day was worrying. Then in the evening I saw the Liberal amendment to the welcome vote of censure. The draft of pettifogging attorneys with the gentlemanly & honourable sense of an Italian assassin. No minority government is to be safe especially before an election. The majority may order a disclosure of papers to a Select Committee upon which the Government must be in a minority & cannot decently be represented by any Minister. The report is inevitable. And all this worry over petty tactics when the load of public work is of itself too heavy to bear. Oh, if the public only knew.[54]

From then on, the crisis slowly gathered momentum. On October 3rd, *The Times* reported that there was a growing feeling that MacDonald would ask for a dissolution if he were beaten on the Liberal amendment. The *Manchester Guardian*, however, was anxious to avoid an election. On October 3rd, it wrote that the Campbell affair was 'a pretty bad failure, but it is not exactly a deadly one, and to force the Government to resign because of the lapse of the Attorney-General would be indefensible unless on the ground that it ought in some case to be got rid of.' On October 4th, it reported that some ministers were prepared to accept a select committee, even though MacDonald was not, and that the Liberals were unwilling to vote for the Conservative censure motion. Over the weekend, MacDonald made a belligerent speech, declaring that the only select committee whose judgment he would accept was the twenty million electors of Great Britain;[55] and on October 6th, *The Times* reported that Labour members objected even more strongly to the Liberal amendment than to the Conservative motion. Even the *Manchester Guardian* appeared to accept that an election was now inevitable.

Yet the outcome was still in doubt. At the Cabinet meeting on October 6th, it was decided that the censure motion and the Liberal amendment should both be treated as motions of censure, and that if either were carried, MacDonald should ask for a dissolution. With Hastings dissenting, the Cabinet also decided that the Government should not offer a less partisan form of inquiry, by a royal commission, by the judicial committee of the Privy Council or by a judge. At the same time, however, it decided that on the first motion to be put from the chair — that 'the words proposed to be left out stand part' — its supporters should either be asked to vote 'aye' or to abstain.[56] If this manœuvre succeeded, the Liberal amendment would then have been defeated, and only the Conservative motion of censure would remain. Since the Liberals were also opposed to the censure motion, they would presumably vote with the Government against it; and it, too, would be defeated. The Labour Party, in other words, would first vote with the Conservatives to defeat the Liberals and then with the Liberals to defeat the Conservatives. During the day, it was discovered that copies of the minute of August 6th had been widely distributed in some departments, and MacDonald appears to have suspected that the Opposition might have got hold of it.[57] When he came to write his diary entry, however, his mood was surprisingly optimistic:

A bad distracting week. Information given to me about leakages of Cabinet minutes and disloyalty & carelessness in Departments. The atmosphere clears, however, in spite of intrigues. Sir John Simon's head is put with Sir Douglas Hogg's. They are considering what will happen if we vote with the Tories or abstain in the first Division, how the second can then be manipulated & so on, & they are not happy. The moves are not exhausted yet & for the moment I am an interested spectator. 'How the country is governed' — my next book. I am told that Ll. G. is now working hard for his own hand. He wanted us to fall on the Russian Treaty & deliberately wished that the Liberal Party wd. be split so as to secure his own ascendancy in the small group that would then fall heir to the name. When the crisis was hastened he supported the vote of censure policy for the same reason. He hoped Asquith will go. This I got from journalists in touch with his friends & on Liberal papers. His reputation is as low as it can be.[58]

The debate came on October 8th. After questions, MacDonald made a tortured and unhappy personal statement, apologizing for his misleading answer to Sir Kingsley Wood. He began by quoting the last part of the question, which referred to the possibility that he might have been required to give evidence at the hearing, and then went on:

The form and the suggestion of the question concentrated the whole of my mind upon myself and upon my own personal and separate part in this affair. I have been accused in certain papers of having known that I was going to be summoned, and with that knowledge, and because of that knowledge, of personally interfering. I have felt that very warmly. It was absolutely untrue. The accusation was one of those things that made one feel most resentful, and in concentrating my ideas about a personal approach, on account of personal reasons, I used an expression which, when my attention was drawn to it two days afterwards, I had to admit went a little further than I ought to have gone, because it implied not merely that I, as a person, was either approached by the Attorney-General or approached the Attorney-General for personal reasons — a thing I had repudiated hotly — but it also implied that I had no cognisance of what was going on. I am very sorry. I did not mean to imply that. It was simply the concentration of my personal resentment at that gross imputation which made me for a moment forget that officially, and in conjunction with colleagues, the matter was talked about when no personal considerations were in our minds at all. If I have misled any hon. Members, I apologise for having done so.[59]

After some angry exchanges with Austen Chamberlain, Sir Kingsley Wood and Sir John Simon, in which MacDonald added nothing of substance to what he had just said, the debate began. It was opened by Sir Robert Horne, who moved the Conservative censure motion in a somewhat sententious speech, accusing the Government of interfering improperly in a decision which should have been left to the attorney general. He was followed by Hastings. Once again, Hastings skated with great skill over some thin ice—notably in his treatment of his meeting with MacDonald during the afternoon of August 6th, and still more in his treatment of the Cabinet meeting which followed it. On the constitutional issue, however, he hit back with great force; and demonstrated that the law officers had frequently consulted the Cabinet about prosecutions in which political considerations were involved. Sir John Simon then moved the Liberal amendment. He turned the attack away from Hastings and on to MacDonald, and declared that if the Government preferred a general election to an inquiry, it 'would be in the position of a man who is asked to produce a document from his desk but prefers to burn down his house'. MacDonald then made a lame and unconvincing speech, in which he revealed that he had wanted the prosecution to continue and insisted that, although the Cabinet had discussed the matter, the decision itself had been left to Hastings. If either the censure motion or the amendment were carried, he concluded, the Government would go to the country.

MacDonald was followed by Asquith, who chided the prime minister for preaching the Government's funeral oration before the patient was dead, and offered that, if necessary, the places which the Liberals would expect to be allotted on the select committee could go to Labour members instead. His speech went down well. The *Manchester Guardian* reported, 'Almost every one of his delightful sentences filled the Chamber with laughter,'[60] and it seems clear that he was going as far as he could to find a way out of the trap which his followers had set for themselves the week before. But he did not go far enough. At 8.45 the Cabinet met in the prime minister's room at the House and discussed the situation as it had developed so far. After half an hour's discussion, they decided that they should continue to oppose both the Conservative motion and the Liberal amendment, and that when Thomas wound up, he should 'be friendly, dignified, firm, fair, but that he should make it perfectly clear that, so long as the Vote of Censure and the Liberal Amendment remained on the Order Paper, there could be no question of discussing any form of Inquiry.' Yet the possibility of a last-minute reprieve had still not disappeared altogether. The Cabinet also decided that 'if he thought fit the Colonial Secretary should be authorised to renew the offer, already made by the Attorney-General, to give any further information that might be required, including, if so desired, political information,' and – still more significantly – that the advice to be given to their supporters on the first motion should not be decided until the last possible moment.[61]

The Government's fate was not sealed until Baldwin spoke towards the end of the debate, and announced that the Conservatives would vote for the Liberal amendment and against their own motion. After a vigorous and combative speech by Thomas, and a short intervention by Lt-Commander Kenworthy, the fatal question – 'That the words proposed to be left out stand part of the question' – was finally put by the chair. The Labour Party voted in the 'aye' lobby – in other words rejecting the Liberal amendment – and the Conservatives voted with the Liberals in the 'no' lobby. The final result was Ayes 198, Noes 359; and when the amended motion calling for a select committee was put, it was carried by 364 to 198. At 11.30 the Cabinet met in the prime minister's room, and 'took note of the Prime Minister's intention to see the King at 10 a.m. on the following morning', in order to ask for a dissolution.[62] That night MacDonald noted:

11.50 p.m. So the chapter ends after a great day when at the close we stood higher in the House of Commons than ever & when men going into the lobbies to defeat a Government showed no hilarity but looked rather as though they were marching to their own destruction. We had knocked them all over the ring & they were ashamed of themselves. The Attorney-General's vindication of himself pulverised the opposition. I have never known such a transformation in Parliament ... As the day went on members got more miserable. Tories as well as Liberals were trying to find a way out, but the Leaders were out for destruction. For the Tories Hogg wound up & having pledged himself to speak for ten minutes, he went on for half-an-hour ... Cheering crowds waited outside but I escaped with a handful to Downing Street & am now going to bed. Alister & Ishbel came in with me to say goodnight. I am getting to like this room & leaving it touches me. This is the first time I have looked tenderly at it.[63]

At ten o'clock next morning he went to the Palace. After a conversation with Stamfordham he spoke to the King. According to his diary,

The King was most cordial & interview at times almost touching as we assured each other that we had done the best we could for each other. I did not have to ask for the dissolution. He had been prepared & he talked as though I had asked for it. He regretted the reason & hoped we might have found it possible to remain, but understood if we had accepted this defeat or even avoided it, we should only be worried for a few weeks more & than have to go. I told him I regarded this as one of the moves in a game which made our position for further fighting intolerable. He remarked that no other Party could form a Government that could last. He would protect

himself by sending me a memorandum saying that he granted the election
with great reluctance, and hinted that I might say so. I warned him that
that would bring him into politics, but that I should receive a memorandum
if written for historical purposes and perhaps send him one in turn. Then
we talked about a variety of things from the Red Flag, the Marseillaise and
other revolutionary songs, the 1886 Trafalgar Square riots, Cunningham
Graham [sic], Ireland, Grey's remarks about an Irish Republic. He remarked:
'You have found me an ordinary man, haven't you?' ... To the House of
Commons at 2.45. When I announced an immediate dissolution blank
dismay settled upon the benches opposite and below the gangway. They
must have known it before, but to hear it announced seemed to be disconcerting. Still as T.P. said on his way back from the House of Lords, Sir
Wilfred Lawson once remarked: 'It is easy to go to the country but not so
easy to come back from it.' At 4 went to wind up the Conference. Wonderful inspiration, glorious singing, sang 'Auld Lang Syne' like a religious
exercise. Then returned to the House of Commons and the end. As
Baldwin walked up to the Lords he too seemed depressed. 'You have done
at least one big thing,' he said – 'The London Conference.' And to-night I
go into a new world, and the dead come to me and in companionship I
have spent an hour with them.[64]

V

The election campaign which followed was dominated by the twin issues of
the Campbell case and the Russian treaties, which soon merged into the single
issue of the Bolshevik menace. From the first, it was one of the most virulent
campaigns in British history. *The Times* said of Labour's proposal to set up a
national system of electricity-generating stations that 'some such project was
dear to Lenin'; the Conservative candidate for the Abbey division of Westminster declared bluntly that a 'vote for the Socialists is a vote for the Communists'. Conservative posters depicted Russian bogy-men, in rags and fur hats,
leering down at the British voting public. Next to a British workman saying,
'I need work', was a Russian saying, 'I wantski £40,000,000.' Conservative
leaflets warned parents to be on their guard against 'plausible men and women
who invite their children to join Sunday Schools and join clubs' – such activities
were a cover, enabling children to be 'baptised into the Communistic faith',
given practice in 'mimic warfare' and taught 'the principles of street-fighting'.
Women were warned that Communism destroyed marriage; that Communist
spies might be disguised as health visitors; that if the Communists came to
power, their children would be taken from them and made the property of
the state.[65]
In the face of all this, Labour's chief answer was MacDonald. His campaign

centred around two great speaking tours, involving continuous oratory and continuous physical and emotional strain. The support provided by party headquarters was hopelessly inadequate. For seven days he was not even accompanied by a secretary. 'The smooth working of such a plan', Mrs Hamilton wrote later, 'required the science of a skilled man, always a stage ahead, to plan and handle the press and other arrangements. No such person was there.'[66] The fundamental assumption on which the tour was based was even more fatally misconceived. According to Mrs Hamilton, MacDonald was constitutionally incapable of delivering five-minute whistle-stop speeches; he had to make a major address or nothing. He made this clear at the start. But the party headquarters did not appreciate the corollary that the tour should be arranged as a series of mass meetings at a few key places. Instead, it became a series of whistle stops, with a major speech at each stop.

MacDonald left Euston at ten o'clock in the morning on Monday, October 13th, having spent Sunday quietly celebrating his fifty-eighth birthday. He addressed a large crowd at the station, another at Rugby, a meeting of over two thousand people at Crewe, and a mass meeting at Glasgow that evening. According to one observer, the enthusiasm was 'far beyond anything in Gladstone's Midlothian campaign'; in a celebrated phrase, P. J. Dollan, the Glasgow I.L.P. leader, described MacDonald as 'the Gladstone of Labour'.[67] But, as Mrs Hamilton pointed out, enthusiasm 'is thrilling, but also fatiguing'. MacDonald's speech at Glasgow on the first night of the campaign she wrote, raised his audience to 'white heat'. But she added that signs of fatigue were already present — notably the 'forcing of voice and gesture and the restless moving about the platform', which made the speech a bitter disappointment to those who heard it over the radio.[68]

MacDonald left Glasgow at nine o'clock the following morning. By lunchtime had had spoken at Bishopriggs, Kirkintilloch, Kilsyth, Stirling, Alloa, Bannockburn, Lachert, Falkirk and Linlithglow. At 1.30 he addressed an audience of three thousand in the Waverley Market in Edinburgh; the press commented that 'he managed to make his voice heard'. From Edinburgh he drove to Portobello, Musselburgh and Dalkeith, addressing large crowds at each place. At 4.30 he spoke in the Lauder Town Hall. By six o'clock he was at Jedburgh; by nine o'clock in the evening, having been delayed for an hour by thick fog, he was speaking to an audience of four thousand in Newcastle town hall, while another twelve thousand stood outside in the fog, listening to him over the loudspeaker. Next morning he started at Gateshead, and before arriving at Durham at 9.40 he had already spoken there and at Chester-le-Street. He spoke at Durham, Ferryhill and Darlington on the way to Ripon; and at Ripon and Harrogate on the way to a meeting of six thousand at the Corn Exchange in Leeds. From Leeds he went to Dewsbury, Batley and Cleckheaton; and from Cleckheaton he was driven to Huddersfield, where he addressed an audience of twenty thousand and had tea with the Snowdens. From Huddersfield, he went to Oldham, where, in Mrs Hamilton's words, he spoke to a crowd 'immeasurable in the darkness'; and after a day which would have taxed the energies of a champion athlete, he arrived at the Belle Vue Gardens in Manchester, where he spoke to yet another 'huge crowd' for an hour and a half.

On October 16th, he travelled across the Potteries and the Black Country to Birmingham, speaking on the way at Macclesfield, Hanley, Wolverhampton, Wednesbury, and West Bromwich, as well as at Birmingham itself, where he addressed a crowd of fifteen thousand. On October 17th, he motored 130 miles from Birmingham to Aberavon, speaking at Worcester and Gloucester, before arriving at Newport where he said 'a few words' to 'vast crowds'. At Cardiff, his voice failed; but after lunch, he was able to say another few words, before being driven to Barry where he addressed a great meeting at the Theatre Royal. From Barry, he was driven through large crowds to Bridgend, and from there to Kenfig Hill, where he confessed that he was 'absolutely tired, physically and mentally'.[69] A huge crowd surged about his car, and a group of Labour ex-servicemen, who had planned to escort him, were swallowed up in the throng. *The Times* reported:

> Mr MacDonald arrived in his constituency at about 7 o'clock to-night, and made a slow progress, lasting more than an hour, to his hotel here through crowds of onlookers, who cheered and swarmed on the footboards of his car. Rockets and fireworks heralded his approach, and at Port Talbot the crowd was so thick that the formal reception which had been planned was impossible. [U]ltimately, the Prime Minister's motor car was brought to a standstill in the main street, and he did the last quarter of a mile from the square to the Walnut Tree Hotel only by climbing into an omnibus, which forced a passage through the crowd.
>
> Motor coaches had brought parties of young people, many of them women, from the valleys which lie back from the coast ... Others trudged in from remote districts to swell the crowds ... [70]

What kept twelve thousand people standing in the fog outside Newcastle town hall, and brought coachloads of young miners and their womenfolk to the main square of Port Talbot? What hopes did they bring with them, and how far were their hopes fulfilled? Questions like these cannot be answered with any precision; perhaps they cannot be answered at all. Yet they hold the key to a chapter of British history. If we are to understand the rise of the Labour Party and the part MacDonald played in it, we must picture the dense crowd outside the Walnut Tree Hotel, gradually working itself up to a pitch of anticipation and excitement: the sudden appearance of the car: the momentary glimpse of the romantic figure in the distance; the 'scenes of frantic delight' when he appeared at his window to say that 'Aberavon had helped to make the history of the Labour movement.'[71] Scenes like these were a testimony to

MacDonald's hold over his followers. They were also a testimony to something deeper and more enduring. Before 1924, Labour's place in British politics had been uncertain. Its success in 1922 could be dismissed as the fortuitous result of the split between Asquith and Lloyd George. It had formed a Government in 1924 by permission of the Liberals, after an election in which its distinctive claim to power had been partially submerged by the old issue of protection and free trade. Now the Liberals had turned against it; and, on the surface at least, the split between Asquith and Lloyd George was over. Labour was fighting for the first time on its own record in office: and on the claim that working men could sit in the seats of the mighty. MacDonald had first staked that claim as the candidate for Dover in the early 'nineties. It was not the least of his achievement that he had now become its most challenging symbol.

VI

By now, he was in a state of near exhaustion. Since midsummer he had faced a succession of calls on his energies, each more demanding than the last – the talks with Herriot, the London conference, the League Assembly, the McVitie & Price affair, the Campbell case and the first week of the election. But it was too late to change plans: he was trapped by the momentum of the campaign. After a weekend in his constituency, he was driven to Leicester. Next day, he spoke at Sheffield in the morning, travelled to Gloucester in the afternoon and, in the evening, made a detour to Bristol, for no better reason than that Winston Churchill had spoken there the day before. Then he went north to Bassetlaw, where his son Malcolm was a candidate.[72] By October 23rd, he was back in Aberavon, where, *The Times* reported, 'a hoarse Prime Minister, tiring obviously and becoming less eloquent, is finding it more difficult to carry his crowds to the heights which they climbed unaided in the early days of enthusiasm'.[73] During the first week of the campaign, he had concentrated almost entirely on the Campbell case and the Russian treaties. Now he began to realize that this had played into his opponents' hands. On October 22nd, he ignored the Bolshevik issue and concentrated on the reductions which the Labour Government had made in taxation.[74] The change came too late. On the morning of Saturday the 25th, Philip Snowden was woken by J. H. Thomas, who had been staying the night with him after speaking for him in Colne Valley the day before. 'Get up, you lazy devil!', shouted Thomas, hammering at his door. 'We're bunkered.'[75]

'Civil War Plot by Socialists', announced a banner headline in the *Daily Mail*, on October 25th. 'Moscow Order to our Reds. Great Plot Disclosed Yesterday.' 'A secret letter of instruction from Moscow to the British Communist Party,' it reported, had come into the possession of the *Daily Mail*, which had sent copies to the other London papers. It was signed by Zinoviev, the President of the Communist International, and addressed to A. MacManus, the British representative on the Comintern Executive. The letter was dated September 15th, and, the *Daily Mail* alleged, had been delivered to MacDonald and Henderson 'some weeks ago'. On October 22nd, the Foreign Office had decided to make it public, together with a protest which the British Government had sent to the Bolshevik *chargé d'affaires* in London.

The text of the Zinoviev letter has been published more than once, and there is no need to quote it in detail here. It began by warning that the 'fierce campaign raised by the British bourgeoisie' against ratifying the Russian treaties proved that reactionary circles in Britain were opposed to 'consolidating the ties between the two countries', and then called on the British proletariat to 'show the greatest possible energy in the further struggle for ratification'. It was imperative that the section of the Labour Party which sympathized with the treaty should bring increased pressure to bear on the Government, for a settlement of relations between the two countries would 'assist in the revolutionizing of the international and British proletariat' and at the same time 'make it possible for us to extend and develop the ideas of Leninism in England and the Colonies'. This was not all. Work in the British army was weak, in the navy not much better. Accordingly, the British Communist Party was instructed to set up cells in all military units, and also in munitions factories and military store depots. The 'military sections of the British Communist Party', the letter continued, suffered from 'a lack of specialists, the future directors of the British Red Army'; MacManus and his colleagues should therefore contemplate the formation of such a group, which would become 'in the event of an outbreak of active strife, the brain of the military organisation of the Party'.

The British protest was signed by J. D. Gregory, of the Northern Department of the Foreign Office. It had originally been drafted in the Foreign Office, on MacDonald's instructions, and had then been substantially re-written by MacDonald himself, in intervals snatched from the election campaign. In the second paragraph it described the letter as a 'direct interference from the outside in British domestic affairs'. In the third it declared that there could be no doubt of the intimate connection between the Communist International and the Soviet Government, and added menacingly that no Government could tolerate 'an arrangement with a foreign Government by which the latter is in formal diplomatic relations of a correct kind with it, whilst at the same time a propagandist body organically connected with that foreign Government encourages and even orders subjects of the former to plot and plan revolutions for its overthrow'. The Soviet Government, it pointed out in the fourth paragraph, had undertaken not to support bodies which aimed at spreading discontent or fomenting rebellion in any part of the British Empire; and in the fifth it concluded:

His Majesty's Government meant that these undertakings shall be carried

out both in the letter and in the spirit, and it cannot accept the contention
that whilst the Soviet Government undertakes obligations a political body,
as powerful as itself, is to be allowed to conduct a propaganda and support
it with money, which is in direct violation of the official agreement.

The Soviet Government either has or has not the power to make such
agreements. If it has the power it is its duty to carry them out ... If it has
not this power, and if responsibilities which belong to the State in other
countries are in Russia in the keeping of private and irresponsible bodies, the
Soviet Government ought not to make agreements which it knows it
cannot carry out.[76]

As Mrs Hamilton pointed out later, the fifth paragraph of the British protest
was so much milder in tone than the third as to be virtually inconsistent with
it. The third took it for granted that the Comintern was under the control of
the Soviet Government; the fifth merely asserted that it might be. The fifth
contained no hint that relations might have to be broken off; the third implied
that they would. Mrs Hamilton's conclusion was that the fifth paragraph had
been written by MacDonald, and that he had intended it to supersede the third,
which had been written in the Foreign Office.[77] She may well have been right.
But subtle nuances of this sort were hardly likely to be grasped in the middle
of a violent election campaign, which was now approaching its climax. What
mattered to the press, and no doubt to the public, was that the Government
had apparently accepted the letter's authenticity, and that it had made a protest
only when it had been forced to do so by the threat of publication. The effect
on the Labour Party, and still more on MacDonald, was little short of catastrophic. When the election campaign was over, he recorded his impressions
of the incident in his diary; and since his part in the affair was of central importance, the entry must be quoted at length:

The story of what I suspect to be a forgery is as follows: Amongst the
papers I dealt with before leaving my Manchester host's house on the
morning of the 16th was the copy of a letter purporting to have been sent
by Zinovief [sic] to the British Communists. I did not treat it as a proved
document but as I was on the outlook for such documents & meant to deal
with them firmly, I asked that care shd. be taken to ascertain if it was
genuine, & that in the meantime a draft of a dispatch might be made to
Rakovsky. I said that the dispatch would have to carry conviction & that it
should be drafted with a view to being published. I was in the storm of an
election & it never crossed my mind that this letter had any special part to
play in the fight. Diplomatically, it was being handled with energy &
precision, circulated to the Service Depts. concerned & sent to Scotland
Yard. The trial draft waited for me at Aberavon as I had gone to Bassetlaw
to help Malcolm, Bristol etc. I found it on my return to the hotel on the
23rd, substantially rewrote it, was not satisfied with it, but being pressed to

go to meetings then waiting me, I decided to send it up for copying & to make sure it wd. come back, did not initial it. This reached London on the 24th. In my absence, the anti-Russian mentality of Sir Eyre Crowe was uncontrolled. He was apparently hot. He had no intention of being disloyal, indeed quite the opposite, but his own mind destroyed his discretion and blinded him to the obvious care he should have exercised. I favoured publication; he decided that I meant at once and before Rakovsky replied. I asked for care in establishing authenticity; he was satisfied and that was enough. Still, nothing untoward would have happened had not the *Daily Mail* and other agencies including Conservative leaders had the letter and were preparing a political bomb from it. When Sir Eyre Crowe and Mr. Gregory were actually considering the moment when the dispatch should be published, they were informed that the *Daily Mail* was to publish next morning and without further consideration they decided to send off the dispatch at once and give it out for publication that night. Though I was on the telephone they never consulted me; [here MacDonald added a footnote; 'I have found that the decision was reached about noon and the dispatch did not go to Rakovsky till 4 or 5 and I was on the end of the telephone all the time and never heard from the office.'] & I was dumbfounded to be asked by a pressman attending one of my meetings that evening if I had authorised publication. I had two other meetings to take before returning to my hotel & it was late before I got back. I asked for information & was told that Sir E. Crowe assumed I wished for publication at once & referred to my initialled draft. But I had purposely refrained from initialling it so that I might see it again. Then a second telegram from Sir E. Crowe came correcting the statement that I had initialled it. I repeated my request for information & was told that it would be sent by a messenger. It came late that evening (Sat. 25th) & meanwhile I had to speak at Swansea and could say nothing.[78]

MacDonald's silence made things even worse. The *Manchester Guardian* wondered whether his 'attitude of unruffled aloofness' was to be regarded as 'affectation or prudence, or simply [as] the assertion of a lofty rectitude'. Before committing himself to the 'severe and uncompromising chastisement of Mr Zinovieff' contained in the British protest, it pointed out, he must have 'at least believed himself to be in possession of all the needful information as to the authenticity of the document and as to the responsibility of the Moscow Government in regard to it'; his silence now was therefore difficult to explain.[79] The *Daily Mail* did not find it difficult at all. The Zinoviev letter, it wrote on October 27th, was 'an act of such treachery and bad faith that everyone would have expected our Socialist Ministers immediately to reply by expelling every Bolshevik in Britain'. MacDonald's silence was a proof that he was planning to deceive the British people; it was on a par with his behaviour during the

McVitie & Price affair and the Campbell case. These assertions were given extra force by the obvious disarray of the Labour Party. Left without a lead, Labour leaders reacted in a bewildering variety of ways. Clynes declared that the letter, 'if authentic, would imperil any arrangement with Russia'. Thomas boasted, 'If it is not a fake, then it shows that the British Government immediately pulled up the Russians.' Josiah Wedgwood responded similarly, as did Snowden. Sir Charles Trevelyan, on the other hand, described the letter as 'the usual white lie from Russia'; Ponsonby thought it 'not unlikely' that the letter was a forgery; Hastings, more cautiously, that it 'might' be one. Stephen Walsh declared gallantly that it did not matter whether it was a forgery or not.[80]

It was thus against a confused and unhappy background that MacDonald finally gave his explanation at Cardiff in the afternoon of October 27th; and it was hardly surprising that his attempt to clarify the situation succeeded in making it even more confused and unhappy than it was before. He began by declaring that the election had started 'in one mare's nest – the Campbell case' and that it was 'likely to finish in another mare's nest – the great Russian Red Plot'. The newspapers, he pointed out, were 'full of it, and yet in every paragraph and in every column they confess they know nothing about it.' This was 'the great chance for Tory propagandists – to talk about a big stunt of which they know nothing.' Then he turned to a detailed recital of the facts, concluding with the events of the last few days:

> On the 21st the draft – the trial draft – was sent to me at Aberavon ... I did not receive it until the 23rd. On the morning of the 24th I looked at the draft. I altered it, and sent it back in an altered form, expecting it to come back to me again with proofs of authenticity, but that night it was published. (Cries of 'Shame').
>
> I make no complaints ... The Foreign Office and every official in it know my views about propaganda ... On account of my known determination to stand firm by agreements and to treat them as Holy Writ when my signature has been attached to them, they assumed that they were carrying out my wishes in taking immediate steps to publish the whole affair. They honestly believed that the document was authentic, and upon that belief they acted.
>
> If they acted too precipitately, what is the accusation against us? Why don't these newspapers say we are in too great haste? Ah, that won't catch votes against us ... Therefore, they have to put up the story that we shilly-shally ... [O]nly nine days have elapsed from the first registering of the letter and the publication of the dispatch last Friday. (Cheers) ...
>
> But that is not the whole story ... It came to my knowledge on Saturday ... that a certain London morning newspaper ... had a copy of this Zinovieff letter and was going to spring it upon us ...

... [H]ow did it come to have a copy of that letter? ... I am also informed that the Conservative Headquarters had been spreading abroad for some days that ... a mine was going to be sprung under our feet, and that the name of Zinovieff was to be associated with mine. Another Guy Fawkes (laughter) — a new Gunpowder Plot ...

... [T]he letter might have originated anywhere. The staff of the Foreign Office up to the end of the week thought it was authentic ... I have not seen the evidence yet. All I say is this, that it is a most suspicious circumstance that a certain newspaper and the headquarters of the Conservative Association seem to have had copies of it at the same time as the Foreign Office, and if that is true how can I ... avoid the suspicion — I will not say the conclusion — that the whole thing is a political plot? (Loud cheers) ... [81]

In the circumstances, it is hard to see what else MacDonald could have said. It is now known that his suspicions about the letter's authenticity were justified. It had been concocted by a group of White Russian *emigrés*, and foisted on the Foreign Office with the connivance of at least some members of the Conservative Central Office and of the Intelligence services.[82] But although this is known now, it was not known then. MacDonald could hardly state his suspicions as facts, when a mistake would have had such obviously damaging consequences. On the other hand, it would have been equally foolish to avoid mentioning them altogether, since it was they which explained his failure to send a protest at once. Much the same applies to his references to the Foreign Office. He went out of his way to defend his officials for having acted as they did; it is hard to see how he could have gone further without giving a totally misleading account of what had happened. It was, after all, the Foreign Office's fault that he had had to keep silent on Saturday. His silence had done enough damage already; if he refused to explain it, the damage would be even greater. The only explanation available was the truth. But, although it is clear that he had no alternative but to take the line which he took, it is equally clear that that line was another nail in his coffin. As he put in it his diary:

On Monday I was told that Mr. Gregory was coming down to see me, but he came after my Cardiff meeting at 3. There I used dates sent me in a secret memorandum showing how promptly the Foreign Office and myself had handled the document[.] As it had become a political stunt and was being mixed with the Russian Treaty I had to make it clear that no proofs of authenticity had been furnished to me and that the dispatch had gone without my final sanction. Thereupon the scoundrels of the press accused me of violating the honour (or something) of the Civil Service, and the personal vendetta which had been carried on throughout the election increased in fury.[83]

This was an understatement. 'Mr Ramsay MacDonald made disclosures regarding the Zinovieff letter which are a staggering blow to himself and his party,' wrote the *Daily Express* on October 28th. 'He declares that the Foreign Office honestly believe the letter to be authentic. Yet he talks of a "mare's nest" and "another Guy Fawkes plot" giving the impression that his own opinion differs widely from that of subordinates whom he is bound to support.' Mac-Donald's method, declared the *Daily Mail*, was 'to hint and insinuate. In order to shuffle out of his responsibilities he was not ashamed to throw doubt on the good faith of the officials of his own Department.'[84] Never in modern experience, wrote *The Times*, had a minister of the Crown 'descended so low as to expose the Civil Service, which has no power publicly to defend itself, to attacks on policy for which the Minister alone is constitutionally responsible'.[85] The *Manchester Guardian* pointed out, less pompously but perhaps more damagingly, that MacDonald could not have the best of both worlds. If the letter was a hoax, as he seemed to think, his Department had made an 'egregious blunder'; if it was genuine, he could not accuse his enemies of 'having fabricated a plot'.[86]

Polling day was on Wednesday, October 29th; and it soon became clear that the Conservatives had won one of their most decisive victories in modern times. They gained 155 seats, and returned to power with 413 members in the House of Commons. Labour lost 40 seats, and now held 151. The Liberals lost 118 seats and returned a mere 40. As always, the result in votes was less dramatic, but even so it was dramatic enough. The Conservative vote in Great Britain went up by 2 million, from 5·3 million to 7·4 million. The Labour vote also went up, from 4·4 million to 5·4 million. The Liberal vote went down from 4·3 million to just under 3 million. In Aberavon, MacDonald held his seat with a reduced majority – 2,000 as against 3,500 in 1923 – once again a straight fight, but on this occasion against a Liberal and not against a Conservative.

On October 30th, he returned to London. One of his first acts was to see Sir Eyre Crowe, who was ill in bed. According to MacDonald's diary, Crowe was 'heartbroken, but his loyalty & sincerity were undoubted. When I asked him if it occurred to him that he should have warned me & let me know before he took such a big decision of a political kind, he said he did not. He had heard of the D.M. affair at noon; he issued the dispatch to the papers at 6 p.m.; it never entered his mind to let me know.'[87] Next morning, the Cabinet met to inspect the wreckage. According to Jones, who took the minutes, MacDonald came in looking pale and serious and 'as if not certain what his reception was going to be'. A long, and evidently rather acrimonious discussion took place, in which Haldane and Snowden strongly defended the Foreign Office, while Parmoor, Trevelyan, Thomas and Wedgwood demanded an inquiry into the role of the secret service. MacDonald said that when he was told of the publication of the letter by a *Daily News* reporter in South Wales, he 'felt like a man sewn in a sack and thrown into the sea', but he resisted the suggestion that Crowe and Gregory had deliberately tried to damage the Labour Party and went out of his way to defend Crowe's good faith. In the end, the Cabinet decided to appoint a committee, consisting of MacDonald, Parmoor, Haldane and Henderson, to examine the letter's authenticity. On MacDonald's insistence it was agreed that there should be no inquiry into the conduct of the Civil Service and no mention of that aspect of the matter in the minutes.[88]

The Cabinet committee spent most of Monday, November 3rd, examining Scotland Yard, the War Office and Sir Eyre Crowe. According to MacDonald's diary, the War Office thought the letter was probably a forgery, but had no proof one way or the other. Scotland Yard 'thought so little about it that it put it on its file & took no action'. Crowe alone had taken it seriously.[89] On November 4th, the Cabinet met for the last time. Copies of the committee's report were handed around, and it was agreed that a communiqué should be issued saying that on the evidence before it the committee had been unable to come to any conclusion about the authenticity of the letter, since no Government department had seen the original. After this, the Cabinet agreed that MacDonald should place its resignation forthwith in the hands of the King. On Haldane's motion, it also agreed to record its 'warm appreciation of the invariable kindness and courtesy with which the Prime Minister had presided over their Meetings and conducted the business of the Cabinet'.[90] At 5.30 that afternoon, MacDonald saw the King to hand in his resignation. Next day he noted:

> Papers seem fairly quiet at our outgoing. Touch of the heavy father in them and impressions of how they really hate us whilst trying to subdue their hate. They have escaped from terrors, are not a little unhappy, & are anxious lest we should return. All that is bottled up in their demeanour. How difficult it is to resist being infected by their class psychology & to frankly range oneself against them armed with their own weapons of class antagonism. Their wild anger against anyone who joins us from their own ranks, & their fear of anyone who remains independent of their rewards & allurements, control their action. And yet if democracy & Socialism is [*sic*] to be positive & constructive, it must fight to resist this reaction of feeling in itself. If it is not better than they, it may be revolutionary & riotous, but creative – never.[91]

As soon as he could, he escaped from London on a walking tour in the West Country. 'If friends fail,' he wrote revealingly in a long article in *Forward*, 'the hill road never does. When you are up it never blames; it has no grievances if not put in a Cabinet and its ruts are not made in reverence; when you are down it does not attribute its misfortunes to you.'[92] But even the 'gauzy mist' and 'white frost' of the downs could not wholly restore his equanimity. He came back to London at the end of November. At a party at a friend's house, he met a woman who claimed that she had foretold his coming premiership a year before by palmistry. As he put it later in his diary, 'Ask[ed] as to the future now, she took my hand, hardly looked at it & let it go. "When I came into the room", she said, "I wondered who in it was to suffer a great disaster. It is you!" She would say no more.'[93]

CHAPTER 17

Portrait of a sexagenarian

I

MacDonald's spirits had not recovered when the new Parliament assembled at the beginning of December. 'Seemed as though I had never left the place & it repelled me,' he wrote miserably on his first day back at Westminster. 'Am still nervously worn out & stupid. Nothing comes easy.'[1] Defeat is never pleasant; in MacDonald's case, pride, sensitivity and a vivid imagination gave it an added sting. But, although he can be forgiven for flinching inwardly at the knowledge that he would have to face a swollen Conservative majority crowing in triumph from the Government benches, to say nothing of the even more painful knowledge that he would also have to face his own disappointed and resentful followers in the lobbies, it was an unfortunate mood in which to begin the struggle that lay ahead.

He had been leader of the Labour Party for a little more than two years. For the first twenty-one months, he had been astonishingly successful. Thanks partly to his generalship in opposition, his raw and turbulent followers had built on their success in the 1922 election to such effect that they had found themselves in office only fourteen months later. In office, they had proved that a working-class party could govern the country at least as competently as could its rivals; MacDonald himself had won a personal triumph for his part in solving the outstanding international crisis of the day. Then his feet had slipped: and he had brought the whole party down with him. No doubt, the disaster was not as great as it seemed. The real significance of the 1924 election lay in the crushing defeat of the Liberal Party, and for that even a large Conservative majority was a small price to pay. But, although this is clear in retrospect, it was not so clear at the time. At the time, what mattered was that sixty-four Labour members of parliament had lost their seats, that Labour candidates all over the country had been put on the defensive in a humiliating and sometimes alarming fashion, that no lead had come from MacDonald until it was too late, and that when he had at last broken his silence he had made things worse than they were before. The mood of a political party after an election defeat is rarely generous, and the mood of the Labour Party in November and December 1924 was less generous than those of most defeated parties. Labour had gained seats in three successive general elections, and it had come dangerously near to assuming that the process would continue almost automatically. Now its hopes had been dashed, and it had returned to the position it had occupied two years before. Labour politicians would not have been human if they had not been tempted to look for a scapegoat.

The obvious scapegoat was MacDonald. In a speech in Canada, Ethel Snowden declared openly that MacDonald was responsible for Labour's defeat.[2] Her husband was more vindictive and only slightly more discreet. In a letter to Shinwell, Snowden wrote that Labour's opportunities had been 'wantonly thrown away by the most incompetent leadership which ever brought a government to disaster'.[3] According to Mrs Hamilton, he also urged Henderson to stand for the leadership against MacDonald and, although Mrs Hamilton does not say this, it must be presumed that he offered Henderson his support if he did so.[4] Ernest Bevin, a good hater all his life, and already one of the leading figures in the trade-union movement, had not forgiven MacDonald for his handling of the dock and tramway strikes; according to his biographer, he, too, was anxious for a change of leader.[5] Similar, and rather louder, mutterings came from the left wing of the party, notably from George Lansbury, who wrote to Clifford Allen suggesting a 'pow-wow' on the leadership.[6] Towards the end of November, Beatrice Webb noted in her diary that there was great bitterness against MacDonald among the Clydesiders, and that MacDonald himself feared that Wheatley might stand against him.[7]

In the end, the talk fizzled out. Apart from Snowden and Bevin, MacDonald's most embittered critics were on the left: that in itself helped to ensure him the grudging support of his old enemies on the right. Besides, respect for majority decisions and loyalty to the elected leadership have always had a high place in the ethic of the Labour movement, particularly in the trade unions. Trade-union M.P.s, who had voted for Clynes in 1922 for no better reason than that he was the incumbent leader, would now support MacDonald for the same reason. Henderson, Clynes and Webb appear to have discussed the possibility of a change, but, according to Beatrice Webb, they decided that 'rot' would set in if the party got into the habit of changing its leaders whenever they offended the Left.[8] According to Mrs Hamilton, Henderson in any case thought that MacDonald was the best available leader and that his critics did not represent feeling in the party.[9]

He may have made a less altruistic calculation as well. Henderson was one of the greatest party managers in Labour history. Although he was sometimes slow to make up his mind, he could display unshakeable persistence and determination once he had done so, as Lloyd George had learned to his cost in 1917. But he was also capable of behaving in a pompous, prickly and self-important fashion when he felt ill-at-ease, and in I.L.P. circles, in particular, he was regarded as an unimaginative disciplinarian. Despite the retrospective halo which he was to acquire as a result of his actions in 1931, his standing in the parliamentary party before then did not reflect his position in the party machine,

and was not as high as some subsequent writers have assumed. In the elections
to the parliamentary committee which were held at the beginning of the new
Parliament, he came tenth out of twelve successful candidates, with only 38
votes as compared with Snowden's 62 — scarcely a creditable performance for
a potential leader.[10] Clynes was the same uninspiring figure whom MacDonald
had beaten in 1922. Webb was by no stretch of the imagination a possible leader.
The strongest potential candidate from the old pro-war right wing of the party
was, in fact, J. H. Thomas — the general secretary of an important union as well
as an effective parliamentary debater, who won 53 votes in the parliamentary
committee election. But Thomas would have been more objectionable to
MacDonald's critics than MacDonald was himself. Much the same was true of
Snowden. Next to MacDonald, he had been the most successful minister in the
1924 Government, and he had more support in the parliamentary party than
had any other potential challenger. But no one would kill MacDonald to make
Snowden king.

By the beginning of December, Snowden's overtures to Henderson had
been rebuffed and it was clear that the right wing of the party would rally
behind MacDonald. For a while it remained unclear whether a challenger
would emerge from the Left. But the strongest potential left-wing candidate
was Wheatley and, as Beatrice Webb put it cynically, Wheatley did not 'mean
to be too previous'.[11] When the parliamentary party met on December 3rd to
elect its officers for the new session, MacDonald was the only candidate for
leader. But the meeting was a stormy one, and the motion to re-elect him was
not carried without opposition. As he described it in his diary:

> The Left wing were out for my blood & had not the sense to restrain itself
> [sic]. Some members do no work but much talking & wish to turn floor of
> House into a sort of national street corner soap box. They are encouraged
> by our press which is in bad hands & we must fight them. The difficulties
> of the Party are within more than without, & though I write 'the Left Wing',
> the inspiration really comes from those who were disappointed that I did
> not put them in the Ministry. Five voted against me & I expected more.
> The party is still disturbed about the Zinovieff letter, & think they can get
> something out of an enquiry. A few thought that no chairman ought to be
> elected till the enquiry had been held & one or two of these abstained.
> To begin with at any rate the Party is to call for deft handling. Of course
> some one gave a report to the press & some of my friends outside are
> convinced that I shall have to leave the Party & that there will be a split.[12]

II

As so often with MacDonald, the clouds ahead seemed even blacker than they
were. He was still badly shaken by the events of the last three months, and it

would be wrong to accept his forebodings at their face value. But it would be equally wrong to dismiss them altogether. The mutterings against his leadership were only the tip of a much more menacing iceberg. Even in the parliamentary party, the elections to the parliamentary committee showed a marked swing to the left and a marked hostility to ex-ministers. In the Labour movement outside Parliament, the situation was more threatening still. Before the election, criticisms of the leadership had been stifled by loyalty and pride. Now the attacks of the Left seemed justified by events. What, after all, had Labour achieved in ten months of office? Labour ministers had kow-towed to royalty and threatened trade unionists with emergency powers. The interests of the working class had not been greatly advanced and socialism was as distant as ever. Even MacDonald's success in foreign affairs left a sour taste in many mouths. No doubt, the reparations crisis had been solved. But reparations were still going to be paid, the Versailles settlement was still in force and the reign of peace and justice was no nearer.

In the trade unions, feelings like these encouraged a new revulsion against the compromises and evasions of parliamentary politics. The pendulum of working-class opinion had begun to swing back towards direct action even before the election. Modest economic recovery and a slight fall in the level of unemployment had given the unions a chance to win back some of the ground they had lost after the collapse of the post-war boom. The result was a wave of wage claims, and although fewer working days were lost in strikes in 1924 than in 1923, the number of stoppages was greater and union membership went up. At the same time, the balance of power in the T.U.C. General Council shifted to the left, partly because moderate leaders like Thomas, Margaret Bondfield and Harry Gosling, the dockers' leader, resigned their positions when they were appointed as ministers. After the election, the pendulum swung further still. Political action, it seemed to many, led only to failure and humiliation: in future, the workers must rely on their own industrial right arms. These attitudes were given extra impetus by the so-called minority movement,[13] which had been launched under Communist inspiration at the end of 1923 and the beginning of 1924, but it would be a mistake to imagine that they were called into existence by the Communist Party or that only Communists shared them. They were voiced as powerfully by Ernest Bevin as by A. J. Cook, the passionate and reckless South Wales miner and Communist sympathizer who had become general secretary of the Miners Federation in January 1924, and for the next eighteen months they were to be one of the main influences on trade-union behaviour, among Communists and non-Communists alike.

As such, they posed a direct and unmistakable threat to MacDonald's whole strategy. As we have seen, his over-riding aim as party leader was to consolidate Labour's position as the main progressive party in Britain. To do this, he had to win and hold the support of former Liberals who did not share Labour's ideology or commitment to working-class interests, but who might be per-

suaded to vote for it on the grounds that it was the only alternative to the
Conservative Party; to do that, he had to prove that Labour was as capable of
working the parliamentary system as the Liberals were, and as committed to
the assumptions on which it was based. If the trade unions put their faith in
direct action this would no longer be possible. Even today, the trade unions are
the sheet anchor of the Labour Party. In the 1920s they were much more than
that. Most divisional Labour parties consisted, in practice, of the most politically
active trade unionists in the constituency concerned; the annual conference of
the Labour Party was little more than a replica of the annual conference of the
T.U.C., with different times on the agenda. If the unions challenged the
traditional assumptions of parliamentary politics, the Labour Party would be
under enormous pressure to follow them; and if the Labour Party followed
them, everything which MacDonald had achieved since 1922 would be in
danger.

This is not to say that MacDonald's strategy was right, or even that it was the
only strategy which could have been adopted by a non-revolutionary labour
movement. Political success could only be had at a price. It could be argued
that the price was too high, and that a sustained and deliberate attempt to
promote social change by means of industrial action would have brought
greater benefits to the working class than any parliamentary strategy could
bring. But, although this could be argued as an academic proposition, few argued
it at the time. The unions were swept towards direct action by a mood, not by
an argument. They had no clear idea of what they wanted to achieve or of how
far they were prepared to go, and still less of what they would do if their action
brought them into conflict with the state. Even Bevin, the most far-sighted
and resolute of their leaders, had no coherent strategy of industrial action, and
most of his colleagues on the General Council had not even begun to think in
strategic terms. Even if they had, it would have been no consolation to
MacDonald. Throughout his career, he had believed that the working class
could only make lasting gains through the ballot box. A coherent and systematic attempt to use industrial action as an alternative would have been an even
greater threat to him than the muddled and unsystematic attempt which in fact
confronted him.

Much the same was true of the developments which took place at the same
time in the I.L.P. The situation here was even more confused than it was in
the trade-union wing of the movement. Personal differences overlapped with
political ones; arguments over policy merged imperceptibly into a struggle for
power. If we are to understand MacDonald's behaviour during the next few
years, however, we must pick our way through the confusion. The I.L.P. still
played a much more important part in labour politics than its membership of
less than 60,000 might suggest. The decline of the Fabian Society had left it as
the only independent source of new policies in the Labour Party. At the same
time, it was still a political machine in its own right, capable of returning a small

but significant bloc of members to the House of Commons. MacDonald himself still attended the Labour Party conference as an I.L.P. delegate and was nominated as party treasurer by the I.L.P. council. At a deeper level, he still liked to think of himself as a member of the I.L.P. first and of the Labour Party second. Like most elderly men, he looked back on his early years through a haze of nostalgia. The bitter arguments which had in fact divided the I.L.P. of Hardie and Bruce Glasier were smoothed over in recollection. What stood out was the memory of a band of comrades, preaching the gospel in fellowship. Attacks from the I.L.P. hurt more than attacks from any other quarter, and called forth correspondingly indignant replies, not because they were more dangerous but because they conflicted with this idealized picture of what the party had once been and still ought to be.

Attacks from the I.L.P. had been frequent enough before the election, and they were to become much more frequent after it. Clifford Allen, the party chairman, had done his best to transform it from a primarily propagandist body into a policy-making one, but he had aroused great resentment in the process. To the Clydesiders, in particular, and to their allies like Fenner Brockway, the party secretary, and John Paton, the assistant secretary, Allen's tactics seemed too subtle, his manner too bourgeois and his loyalty to MacDonald too pronounced. They had no objection to the policies produced by the so-called 'commissions of inquiry' which he persuaded the I.L.P. to set up after the 1924 party conference. Indeed, they were happy to appropriate them on their own. But apart from Wheatley, most of them took little interest in policy. The task of the I.L.P. was to fight the class war: policy was of value only in so far as it could be used as a weapon in the struggle. Conflict with the class enemy was not merely unavoidable, it was positively desirable. There was no hope of achieving socialism without it, and the best way to speed up the transition from capitalism was to provoke it. Like the trade unionists who swung towards direct action, the Clydesiders had few clear ideas about how far they were prepared to go, or about what they would do if the conflict they talked about took place. But in the aftermath of the 1924 election, clear ideas counted for less than enthusiasm and indignation. The Clydesiders had plenty of these; and their influence in the I.L.P. steadily increased. Here, too, the threat to MacDonald was direct and unmistakable.

III

It was a forbidding prospect. In the winter of 1924 MacDonald was fifty-eight — six years older and less resilient than he had been when he had lost his seat at Leicester after the war — and if we are to understand his response to the challenge from the Left, the approach of old age must be taken into account. He still possessed great reserves of energy and endurance. A few years before he had been able to boast that he could outwalk Gladstone at the same age;[14] and he could still tramp for miles across the hills without ill effects. In 1925, at the age of fifty-nine, he was taken for his first flight in an aeroplane and promptly became, as he put it in his letter of thanks to Sir Hugh Trenchard, who had arranged the flight, 'a keen convert to your ways of getting about'.[15] As we shall see, he could still inspire great audiences and play a dominating part in complex international negotiations. But the effort was becoming more burdensome, and the cost greater. There are frequent references to rheumatism, bronchitis and other ailments in MacDonald's letters and papers; and in the spring of 1927 he contracted a mysterious throat infection during a visit to the United States, and almost died. He had to go into hospital in Philadelphia towards the end of April, and was not allowed home until the end of May. When he got back, The Times reported that he was given an enthusiastic welcome by his followers in the House of Commons, but that he had to lean heavily on his stick and was obviously a tired man.[16] On his doctor's orders, he spent June in Lossiemouth. He went back to London at the beginning of July but as late as July 25th he wrote that for the last four weeks he had only been, 'nibbling at Parliamentary work'.[17] Altogether he was out of harness for the best part of five months.

His secretary, Rose Rosenberg, did her best to protect him. 'I have seen him, after a big effort at a meeting, almost broken up,' she wrote in April 1926, 'and I sometimes wonder if the Movement realises the tax that it is placing on him. If the Labour Party in the country wish to keep him it must remember that he is only a human being and is just flesh and blood.'[18] But the problem was more complicated than that. To enthusiastic party workers in the constituencies, Parliament was apt to seem remote and rather unreal: the job of a Labour M.P., and a fortiori of the party leader, was to make converts at the grass roots, not to waste his time on the rigmarole of the Palace of Westminster. MacDonald was one of his party's chief electoral assets: a hard-pressed organizer with a conference to arrange or a by-election to fight could hardly be expected to remember that the asset might wear out with excessive use. In any case, the Labour Party lacked the resources to treat its leader as flesh and blood; the 'tax' it imposed on MacDonald was imposed partly by inexperience and over-enthusiasm, but most of all by poverty and bad organization. In March 1927, to take an example at random, he was sent by the party headquarters to Ormskirk. When he got into the train, as he complained in an indignant letter to G. R. Shepherd afterwards, he was presented with a circular which had been sent out from Eccleston Square, informing the local parties that he would address two meetings in the evening:

Not a word about this had been said to me. You will remember that I was presented in exactly the same way with a statement for which I was not at all responsible and at the time knew nothing about, that you agreed I should address the Conference in the afternoon. Under protest I accepted this and added to my absence the whole of the morning. The grand result was that I had to make three speeches instead of one and of one of the three I had heard nothing until I was actually on the way. My day's performance had to run into two-and-a-half hours' speaking. I arrived at 3 o'clock from that hour until 7 o'clock never had a moment's rest, but was kept pestered by people who wanted meetings, who were grumbling about Head Office neglect of their interests; even at tea they came and bothered me and when I got into a little side room which had not even a comfortable chair in it, I was still invaded ...

In addition to this, there was not a scrap of literature in the place, no reports, no leaflets, and absolutely nothing for the people to take away with them. Very rarely in my long experience have I come across a Conference so badly organised. We did our best in the circumstances, but really something more must be done to make these gatherings businesslike and get them to produce fuller results than a mere propaganda speech or two can yield.[19]

It was the same story in his own constituency. The Aberavon party was chronically short of money, and the machine which Ivor Thomas had built up before the 1922 election often seemed to be on the verge of disintegration. In November 1925, the agent, Joe Brown, reported that only eight of the twenty-eight miners' lodges in the Division had paid their affiliation fees and that the party had only £17 in the bank.[20] In 1926, none of the lodges in the Division could afford to pay their fees, and by March 1927 the balance in hand at the end of the financial year stood at £7. 4s. 1d. The party had no office, and Brown had to work at home.[21] Most of his time appears to have been spent in a desperate search for the funds to pay his own salary and, even so, it was often in arrears. In 1927, he decided to resign and take up a post as a publican;[22] although he changed his mind later, it seemed clear that he could not be relied upon to remain as agent for long. Meanwhile, there were rumours that the Conservatives and Liberals were spending large sums in the district, and that the miners' support for the Labour Party was waning as a result of apathy and Communist propaganda. To make matters worse, there were constant complaints that MacDonald spent too little time in the constituency, and when he did appear there the programmes Brown arranged for him were far too demanding. Constant appeals for financial help were more embarrassing still. In 1924 MacDonald had spent £350 out of his own pocket on his election expenses. He still subscribed £20 a year to the party, but it was not enough and he was continually being asked for more.[23] 'I must get down between the New Year and the sitting of Parliament again,' he conceded in a letter to his agent in December 1926. 'I never get clear of work, however, and coming down so often is becoming a most terrible problem. I think you will have to get hold either of a millionaire or of someone who does not have to look after a family and pay heavy bills!'[24]

This was a constant refrain. MacDonald earned no salary as leader of the Opposition, and his salary as a member of parliament was still only £400 a year. His children were growing up; and, although evidence is lacking, it seems clear that the income from Margaret's trust fund was less than it had been before the war. With some difficulty he persuaded the party Executive to pay him an allowance of up to £800 a year to cover the secretarial expenses he incurred as party leader, but it is clear from his papers that this was barely adequate for his needs. In the twelve months ending at the beginning of November 1925, he paid out £720. 11s. 5d. Petty cash expenses, he pointed out in a plaintive letter to the financial sub-committee of the Executive, had been kept down 'to the very bone'; and this had only been made possible 'by my paying out of my own pocket monies which other Parties pay out of Party funds, and by not entering a somewhat heavy expenditure on telegrams against this income'.[25]

To make ends meet, he had to rely on the drudgery of freelance journalism. While Parliament was sitting, Monday to Thursday would be spent at Westminster. Friday and most of Saturday would be spent on propaganda meetings in the country. Sunday would be spent earning a living – and a far from princely living at that. For in spite of occasional windfalls, like a visit to the Sahara desert for *Answers*, MacDonald's literary earnings were not at all large, particularly for a former prime minister. One of the most attractive features of his character was a strong streak of innocence in money matters. He found it 'a perfect nightmare' to complete his income-tax return – not only because of the time it took, but because 'as a matter of fact these things are not in one's line'.[26] His personal affairs were in a state of confusion, and he consistently failed to exploit his name and reputation at their full market value. He turned down an offer of £50,000 for his memoirs, on the grounds that there was 'nothing I shrink from more than making public personal impressions of people';[27] and although he sometimes earned fairly generous fees – £50 from *Answers* and an offer of 60 guineas from *John Bull* are among the most generous for 1925[28] – much of his journalism was hardly rewarded at all. The New York *Nation* paid him only a little more than £5 an article. In the autumn of 1925 he resumed his weekly column for *Forward*, but although this was of considerable use to him as a politician, it did nothing for his pocket.

The strain was heavier than any but his closest intimates realized. 'So far as finance is concerned,' he wrote in May, 1925, 'my ship is scraping bottom.'[29] 'I simply cannot get my work done and, trying to do too much, means that it is done badly,' he confessed to a friend a few months later.[30] 'Nobody knows better than I do how the tired horse wants help up the bank,' he wrote in reply to an invitation to speak for Sidney Webb in Seaham Harbour, 'and nobody knows more painfully than I do that another old tired horse is not the best creature to give him the pull.'[31] 'You imagine that we have got nothing to do except come on platforms and talk—no House of Commons work that requires preparation, no work required for bread and cheese, no rest and no recreation,' he snapped in response to a request to help with the party's rural campaign in Berkhampstead. 'If Capitalism was so inconsiderate of the flesh and blood it employs as some of our Labour people, our society would have been wiped out of existence long ago.'[32]

Worse than the strain itself was the consciousness of what it cost. 'This terrible weariness of brain that is upon me is like the malignant ill will of the devil,'[33] he noted in a diary entry in June 1926. 'Friends will send invitations & thank goodness they do,' he noted a month later, 'but some lame excuse from me for not going is a bad way of showing my pleasure at having been invited.'[34] It was the same story the following year. 'To keep up with the business of the House of Commons & *to think about it* & work at it; to speak in the country & even faintly satisfy the exacting demands of the Party; to write every weekend enough to keep the house going—it is impossible almost & means incessant drudgery with no rest, no gaiety, no lilt in life ... ,' he noted in April 1927, shortly before his visit to the United States. 'I am like a man wading in a river with the water up to his neck & not knowing but that the next step will take him out of his depth.'[35] That was written just before his illness, but the situation was no better after his recovery, and by January 1928 his mood was, if anything, more despairing still:

How tired I am. My brain is fagged, work is difficult, & there is a darkness on the face of the land. I am ashamed of some speeches I have made, but what can I do? I have no time to prepare anything. It looks as though it will be harder to make my necessary income this year. I wonder how this problem of an income for political Labour leaders with no, or small, independent means is to be solved. No one seems to understand it. To be the paid servant of the State is objectionable; to begin making an income on Friday afternoon & going hard at it till Sunday night, taking meetings in the interval, is too wearing for human flesh & blood. On the other hand, to live on £400 a year is impossible. If it killed one in a clean, efficient business-like way why should one object, but it cripples & tortures first by lowering the quality of work done & then by pushing one into long months of slowly ebbing vitality & mental paralysis.[36]

IV

From time to time there was a break in the clouds. Towards the end of the war, he and his family had moved from Lincoln's Inn Fields to Howitt Road near Belsize Park tube station. In 1925, a legacy from his friend, Henry Markwald, made it possible for him to move from Howitt Road to Upper Frognal Lodge, a spacious and attractive old house in Hampstead. The legacy also enabled him to indulge his passion for foreign travel.[37] In December 1924, he had a month's holiday in Jamaica.[38] The following winter he took his daughter Sheila to Ceylon.[39] His visit to the Sahara took place in October 1926, and occupied the best part of a month. In the spring of 1927, he visited the United States; and in the summer of 1928 he spent several weeks in Canada.[40] The Sahara, in particular, appealed profoundly to his love of solitude, and perhaps also to the fatalistic element in him, which jostled uneasily with his admiration for the puritan virtues of effort and hard work. As he described it in a talk for the B.B.C. after his return:

> There is nothing to do here but to open your heart and let the breeze of feeling pass gently over it. The life of the world of busy, quarrelling, aspiring men comes but faintly in that breeze like an astringent smell ... You give no direction from your bare foot on the neck of the camel; you just go on. Sooner or later an oasis comes. You ride down to its clear springs and, under the shade of the date palms you pass along the white bottom of the courses that flow like chalk streams at home ... In some cool, palm-bowered place you have your meal, and they bring you fruits with herb tinctured tea or coffee, and perhaps you watch them make fire by rubbing sticks and light your tobacco from the smouldering dust ...
>
> ... [T]he Sahara ... is the loose remains of rocks of a late age that could not hold together against the fierce sirocco, the dying sun and the torrential rain ... How the torrents come down, it is difficult to imagine. One day we experienced it ... We were driving from Tozeur to El Mamma. The hills to the north were under a black pall of sky ... Thunder rumbled like heavy artillery, but no showers fell on us. Our way was rough and over a sandy and stony waste, crossed occasionally by shallow dry depressions, evidently made by water. Suddenly we came upon a furiously rushing torrent, mad like a crowd of fanatics seeking a victim. We tried to cross it; the water at once rose to the top of our wheels; mercifully, we came up against a boulder and stuck. A foot or two further and we should have been overwhelmed ... Some half a dozen times during the remainder of that day we had to go through similar torrents. In some places the beds were deeply cut, an enormous quantity of fine mud was brought down and one of the streams had transported from the hills huge fields of snow and hail that lay on both sides of the course as much as two feet deep. In due course, the sun and wind will play upon this bulky debris. Thus the desert shifts, obliterates its path and is renewed.[41]

He developed a keen interest in broadcasting, and corresponded briefly, but revealingly, with Sir John Reith, the managing director of the B.B.C., about the need to develop a form of popular entertainment which would close the 'gulf between your jazz on the one hand, and your high-brow stuff on the

other'. What was needed, he wrote, was 'delightfully simple, melodious singing'. It was a waste of time to aim at 'great muscial effects', which the medium
could not in fact achieve.[42] Reith replied that good artists were hard to come
by, and that they were apt to be either 'too amateurish or too professional';[43]
and MacDonald then sent him a much longer letter, amplifying his earlier
criticisms:

> You will never broadcast a great stage scene. Take, for instance, the 'Out
> damned spot' scene in Macbeth. The words are wonderful, and the tone in
> which a great actress would convey them would also be wonderful, but
> you will never get the scene from those two wonders because there are all
> sorts of other things that enter into the total effect. In devising the art of
> radio drama you have to work as it were on two dimensions: The actual
> dramatic value of the words and the tone of voice. Can you ever devise a
> drama with such limitations? Are you not confined to the realm of reading
> and the realm of jokes? ...
>
> My suggestion to you is that you should study the development of the
> simpler entertainments, basing it upon the folk mind. Make no mistake
> about it, the old-fashioned concert that we used to have with simple but
> sincere singing touching with great variety the chords which are available
> in the simplest human mind, is your best foundation ... If you consider I
> think, wherein lies the success of the more religious part of your broad-
> casting ... you will come to the conclusion that it is not because people are
> religious, but because they are tremendously pleased to have certain very
> fundamental feelings appealed to. I cannot work this out, it would take too
> much of my time and yours, but I think your safe road lies upon the
> evolution of this.[44]

An even more characteristic example of MacDonald's concern for what would
now be called the 'quality of life' was his interest in the preservation of old
buildings and the protection of the countryside. 'The newest block of flats in
Park Lane ought to be blown up,' he wrote in a typical outburst in February
1928. 'But what are we to do? Men of wealth have no idea of how to spend it
except for their own vulgar decoration, and Parties that pretend to guard our
finer traditions are busy selling them in the market place.'[45] An appeal to him
to act as a patron for a 'Come to Scotland' movement earned the disconcerting
reply that 'the mere tourist, up to now at any rate, is disgusting and disquieting.
Where you have a huge town like London or Paris he is lost, and the advantages
of his presence completely overshadows any disadvantages, but send him out
into the country, turn him out on our roads, get him to invade our finer spots,
and he spoils everything he touches and completely destroys the spirit of our
land.'[46] In a long letter to one of the organizers of a countryside and footpaths
preservation conference, he exclaimed angrily:

> [E]very day that goes past some offensive bungalow or some abomination

O

of a building scheme, or some horror of a wayside pump station, or some blatant vulgarity of an advertisement destroys not only the immediate spot where it is placed but the whole sweep of the countryside ... Something really must be done to stop it and nothing can be done until public opinion is shocked by the atrocities ... Up to now, though we have been unable to cross a fence or wander off the wayside without undergoing the penalties of ... 'trespassers will be prosecuted', nobody has been able to deprive us of the beauty of the scene. Now they have found out how to do that, and the lover of the countryside finds himself wandering about it like a bereaved soul.[47]

Meanwhile, he spent an increasing proportion of his time in art galleries and sale rooms, and his private correspondence was full of references to pictures, old furniture and rare books. 'What a wonderful production it is!' he wrote in a letter to Alec Martin, who had sent him a copy of the Holford catalogue. 'I want about half of the pictures, especially the Cuyp of Doidrecht, but I suppose I must want on until it and I get to heaven.'[48] The tone was characteristic – as were the pleasure he got from his appointment as a trustee of the National Gallery in 1928, the energy he spent in private negotiations to acquire Orchadson's 'Voltaire' for the Scottish National Gallery with the help of Sir Alexander Grant, the effort he devoted to amassing a collection of early socialist writings and the minute attention to detail which he displayed in a long correspondence with J. D. Morgan of Rhiwbina about the specifications of an antique Welsh dresser which he wanted to buy for his house in Hampstead.[49] To judge by his diary, he got the same kind of satisfaction from his sittings for a bust by Epstein:

> Dirty & dishevelled surroundings. Studio on first floor of dwelling house 23 Guildford St. Walls dusty colour; windows black paint; floor originally stained on margins but grey with dry clay dust; lower parts of walls spattered with clay splashes; sofa of worst type upholstered in carpet material in plush sort of cheap stuff blocking fireplace; place strewn with clay pails, stands, tables; some beautiful work amidst it all – Chinese priests or priest-king, Egyptian heads, pottery: the playground of disorder. Epstein quivering with energy; eye & movement sharp & quick. Jumps round you with his eye on you all the time like a prize fighter or duellist; up on a box to survey the top of your head, down on his toes & sitting on his heels to examine your chin; rubbing clay between his palms all the time, & daubing it on with energetic smacks.[50]

'Parlt. again,' MacDonald noted at the beginning of the new session in November 1928. 'I felt as though my ticket-of-leave had been exhausted & I had returned to a public institution inhabited by snivelling inmates.'[51] For many politicians, the gossip and bustle of the lobbies are the breath of life; the chamber of the House of Commons, or perhaps the Cabinet room at No. 10 Downing

Street, is the centre of the universe. For others, the tensions and conflicts of politics are made bearable only by the possibility of escape; a life outside politics is a precondition of political activity and, still more, of political success. MacDonald belonged emphatically to the second category. He was incurably addicted to politics, and could not have flourished without them. But he hated them too, and needed periodically to escape from them. As he grew older, his need to escape grew more acute; and if he had been cut off from his non-political interests and friendships, he could not have played a leading part in politics for long.

In some ways, this was a political asset. Many Labour men and women had been inspired as much by a revulsion from the ugliness and materialism of late nineteenth-century industrial society as by a hatred of poverty and injustice. It was partly because he spoke to and for this strand in British socialism, the strand which produced the I.L.P. Arts Guild of the middle 'twenties and which looked back to Walter Crane and William Morris, that MacDonald was able to capture the imagination of the Labour movement in a way that a narrowly political leader would have found it hard to do. By the same token, it was partly because his life so obviously had a non-political dimension – because he could so easily be pictured 'sitting and dreaming by his fireside or wandering with a knapsack on the moors alone with Nature,' as the German socialist, Egon Wertheimer, put it – [52] that he could appeal more successfully than any other Labour politician to a wider public outside the Labour Party. Yet his non-political activities were not all equally acceptable to his colleagues and followers. There were good socialist precedents for communing with nature in unspoilt scenery. Wasting time in sale rooms and consorting with connoisseurs of old furniture was another matter. In a characteristic diary entry after the 1926 T.U.C. conference at Bournemouth, where she had a long and evidently somewhat painful talk with MacDonald, Beatrice Webb wrote:

[W]hat interested me was J.R.M.'s conversation. He was particularly gracious to us; came to our table and took us into his private sitting-room. But he was evidently absorbed in the social prestige of his ex-premiership enhanced by a romantic personality. Immaculately groomed and perfectly tailored – too deliberately so for artistic effect – it made him look commonplace – he went out of his way to tell me that he was going on to stay with Mrs Biddulph near Cirencester – 'The Hon. Mrs Biddulph', he added, and then described her as a patron of good English craftmanship in furniture. Once again he spoke of the difficulty of getting old pieces of furniture – 'the Americans are buying it up' – and described his adventures with this dealer or that. 'Then I am going to stay at' – I forget the place – with the Princess Hartsfelt (?). She was a Cunningham you know. Do you know her? A remarkable woman'. After that visit, I gathered, he was going on a motor trip in North Africa with Noel and Charles Buxton and then to

London for the session, with the Labour Party conference intervening. I was always trying to bring him back to politics – but without result ... Of course so long as he does his duty in public speaking and in attendance in Parliament, his social relations are his own concern ... But MacDonald is not working at his job; he is not thinking about it; he is not associating with those whom he has and would have to guide and from whom he could get enlightenment. His thoughts and his emotions are concentrated on his agreeable relations with the men and women – especially the women – of the enemy's camp ... he is becoming impatient with the troublesomeness of the working class.[53]

Beatrice Webb had sharp eyes as well as a vivid pen, and her picture undoubtedly bore some resemblance to the original. But it was a hostile caricature, not a rounded portrait. One side of MacDonald's complex and contradictory personality was drawn in acid; the rest was left out. If we are to discover the truth, it is necessary to dig deeper. For MacDonald, even more than most people, was not all of a piece. As a Scot, and a Highlander at that, he did not fit neatly into a predetermined slot in the English class structure; socially, he was an exotic, in the way that a Canadian or an American might be. His journey from the sea town of Lossiemouth to the world of Liberal politicians and journalists in which he had begun to move as an unknown young man in the early 'nineties had been long and difficult enough. It would have been much longer if he had been born in a working-class district in Leeds or London. Like many Scots – and, for that matter, like many Irishmen and Welshmen as well – he almost certainly derived a certain sneaking satisfaction from the thought that he could move at will up and down the English social scale, and storm the heights of London society. In spite of his protestations to the contrary, he enjoyed going to dinner parties and receptions at great houses, just as he had enjoyed wearing court dress and taking part in the ceremonial at Buckingham Palace. As he put it himself just before becoming prime minister, he 'swung between two beings'. His craving for solitude and peace went hand in hand with a love of colour and excitement. He liked circuses, and enjoyed being driven at high speeds in a powerful car; he got the same kind of pleasure from the glitter of a tiara at the top of a famous staircase.

Yet all this was, at bottom, a sign, not of snobbery but of an odd, and even rather touching, mixture of insecurity and naïveté – the naïveté of a child at its first party. MacDonald was a complicated man, but he was not a sophisticated one. In spite of his love of books and pictures, he was not an intellectual; and he had none of the intellectual's self-awareness and capacity for self-concealment. Like many Celts, he had a tendency to tell people what he thought they wanted to hear, and this sometimes led him into deviousness. At the same time, he was strangely lacking in guile. His vanity was an open vanity; the enjoyment he got from the occasional forays into high society which he was now able to make as a former prime minister was equally so. His tastes were unpretentious—Harry Lauder, the Orpheus Choir, Scott, Stevenson, Turner, the 'simple and sincere singing' for which he had asked in his letter to Reith—and his way of life was unpretentious too. He spent little on himself and got no enjoyment from fine wine or food; his favourite meal appears to have been a stolid Scots high tea.[54] Harold Nicolson, whose eye for the nuances of behaviour was as sharp as Beatrice Webb's, and whose judgment was less clouded by the memory of ancient feuds, got to know MacDonald during the second Labour Government. Nicolson's impression of an encounter, just after a division in the House of Commons in January 1931, deserves to be set alongside Beatrice Webb's impression of her conversations at the Bournemouth T.U.C. While walking across St Stephen's Yard, Nicolson wrote,

> I observe a small figure in front of me with collar turned up. He turns to see who is behind him and I see it is Ramsay MacDonald ... We walk across to Downing Street ... We reach the door of No. 10. He knocks. The porter opens and stands to attention. Ramsay asks him, 'Is Berry in?' 'No, sir, he has gone'. 'Is Ishbel in?' (not 'Miss Ishbel'). 'Yes, sir'. 'Would you ask her to bring two glasses to my room?' We then go upstairs. The room has an unlived-in appearance. Turners over the fireplace. Ishbel is there. He asks her to get us a syphon. Says she can't find any whisky. Ramsay says it is in the drawer of his table. He finds it. 'What about some champagne?', he says, 'to celebrate the victory?' I say I will not have champagne. Malcolm comes in. 'A cigarette?' I say I will. 'Malcolm, we have got cigarettes, haven't we—in that Egyptian box?' Malcolm goes to search for the Egyptian box. Then there are no matches.
> ... Ramsay ... sees me out. Nothing will convince me that he is not a fundamentally simple man. Under all his affectation and vanity there is a core of real simplicity.[55]

Of course, MacDonald had friends in what Beatrice Webb called the 'enemy camp'; so did Beatrice Webb. But although one or two of his friends were rich, notably Sir Alexander Grant, few of them were smart; apart from Grant, the friends he cared for most were neither. At a dinner at Buckingham Palace during the 1924 Government he had been placed next to the famous Conservative hostess, the Marchioness of Londonderry. Each had begun the evening with a prejudice against the other—Lady Londonderry, because of MacDonald's 'pacifism' during the war and MacDonald, because of Lady Londonderry's politics.[56] But Lady Londonderry was a Highlander too, descended, on her mother's side, from the Mackenzies who had been out in the 'Forty-five. To their mutual surprise she and MacDonald had discovered a strong common interest in Gaelic myth and folklore and had greatly enjoyed each other's company. Next day, MacDonald had been warned that Lady Londonderry was a 'dangerous woman': undeterred, or perhaps intrigued, by the warning, he had invited the Londonderrys to stay at Chequers, and a few years later, when he was once again leader of the Opposition, he scandalized Hugh Dalton by revealing that he had been invited to an eve-of-session reception at Londonderry House.[57] But, although his friendship with Lady Londonderry was to play an important part in his life in the 1930s, it had hardly begun in the period under discussion here. In any case, there is no evidence that MacDonald's non-political friendships made any difference to his behaviour. His philosophy and strategy as leader of the Labour Party in the 1920s were remarkably close, given the changes which had taken place in the meantime, to his philosophy and strategy as secretary of the Labour Representation Committee nearly thirty years before: his greatest fault was not that he abandoned his principles as he grew older, but that he stuck too rigidly to the doctrines and assumptions of his youth, and failed to adapt them to changing circumstances. At a different and much deeper level, no doubt, he could fairly have been accused of failing to live the socialism he preached. But that charge could have been brought as fairly against most of his colleagues and most of his critics. It proves not that MacDonald was an insincere man, but that socialism is a hard creed.

The evidence is confused, highly coloured by the varying prejudices of its authors and correspondingly difficult to interpret. All the same, the picture that emerges from it is not that of an empty social climber, jettisoning the beliefs and associations of a lifetime to win the goodwill of a few society ladies. It is of a lonely and overworked old man, whose wife was dead and whose children were growing up, who sometimes preferred frivolous gossip to serious political discussion, and who occasionally enjoyed a wistful flirtation across a dinner table. For MacDonald's personal life was as bleak and solitary as it had ever been. Like Disraeli, he got on better with women than with men — partly, no doubt, because they sensed his inner loneliness and need for reassurance. He enjoyed feminine gossip about people and clothes, and he would discuss the right shade of colour for a dress with the same care and attention to detail that he gave to furnishing his house.[58] Even in old age, he was strikingly good-looking, and many women must have found him attractive. But none of his women friends could fill the emotional gap which had been left by his wife's death; and in the period under discussion here, none of them came remotely near to doing so.

For a time in the early 'twenties, his children had thought that he might marry Mrs Hamilton — the daughter of a Scottish university professor and a graduate of Newnham College, Cambridge, who later became a Labour member of parliament and the biographer of Arthur Henderson. In old age, she was an amusing talker with a shrewd insight into people; as a young woman, to judge by her photographs, she was handsome rather than pretty, with fine eyes and a determined chin. Who Mr Hamilton was is not clear. He had left her soon after they were married; according to one story, she was unable to divorce him because he could not be traced. She had met MacDonald once before the war and had not been impressed by him, but she had fallen under his spell after she joined the anti-war movement.[59] For a while, they used to read aloud together, and in the 'twenties she sometimes did research for him and helped him with his speeches. She published two character studies of him under the pen-name 'Iconoclast', one in 1923 and the other in 1925.[60] The tone of the first certainly suggests that her attachment to him was emotional as well as political; it is also possible, though this is a great deal more speculative, that she wanted more from their relationship than he was willing to give. She kept no papers and although he kept a number of photographs of her, none of her letters has survived among his. Her later memories, though sympathetic and perceptive, were coloured by the pain of their disagreement in 1931, and the nature of their relationship can only be guessed at now. In any event, her second study was a good deal cooler in tone than the first; and it is clear that, after 1924, she ceased to be a 'devotee', as she put it in her memoirs, and became a 'loyal but critical follower'.[61] How close she came to taking Margaret's place will never be known. What is certain is that no one did.

As always, his children were a great consolation. 'One of the happinesses restored to me at 9 How: Rd,' he noted in December 1924, not long after the general election, 'is our Sunday readings together. Then the family becomes a cosy group. How I missed that at Downing St.' But he added rather sadly, 'My fifteen months' granddaughter came & I thought of Sheila at her age. Time flies & the apparently long road proves to be so short.'[62] His eldest son Alister had got married in 1922 and had become the father of MacDonald's first grand-child in 1923. Malcolm had come down from Oxford in 1924, but although he and Ishbel still lived at home, as they were to do for many years, they both had their own lives to lead. Joan, the fourth surviving child, left for medical school in 1927 and Sheila, the baby of the family, went up to Somer-ville College, Oxford, in 1929. The formidable Miss Byvoets still ran the household with devoted, if somewhat Spartan efficiency, but the family circle must have been less closely knit than it had been in Lincoln's Inn Fields, or even in the early days at Howitt Road.

Even more than in earlier years, MacDonald found his thoughts turning to the past. 'These ranks of the dead grow,' he noted after his sister-in-law's death in 1928, '& I live more & more with them — not at all good for a Parliamentary gentleman.'[63] 'A Christmas will be the last —,' he noted after his Christmas holiday a few months later, 'how commonplace & how complete as a statement of human affairs. As usual I lived much with the days & the people who are gone.'[64] Occasionally, he dabbled in spiritualism, but it is doubtful if it gave him much comfort. In March 1925, one H. Denis Bradley, who was evidently an expert in these matters, wrote to tell him that he had 'brought over from America George Valiantine, who is certainly the greatest voice medium in the world,' and to invite him to take part in an 'experience' at his house. At the end of November, Bradley wrote again, enclosing a copy of his book *The*

Wisdom of the Gods, and drawing MacDonald's attention to page 402, where 'you will find a brief account of the one experience you had with me'.[65] MacDonald's reply suggests wistful interest rather than enthusiastic conviction. He thanked Bradley for the book, and continued:

> I am going to take it away with me as for the next fortnight I shall find reading impossible on account of very heavy work. I should really take much interest in the subject, but the hours fly and there I am drudging all the time.
>
> I wish I could see you oftener but our paths never seem to cross.[66]

Such comfort as he got cannot have gone very deep. 'I see the impediments which my life puts upon me,' MacDonald noted in April 1929. 'Someone to share the duties would have meant that they would have been done & that smoothly. How often I think of the dead. Oh, had she been here these last years. I wonder if they know.'[67]

V

Loneliness, worry and overwork are bad recipes for a relaxed and easy-going approach to life, and there can be no doubt that they aggravated the touchiness and apparent aloofness which had so often marred MacDonald's relations with his colleagues. He had never been a cheerful Anglo-Saxon extrovert. He was a black and moody Celt, with a Celt's long memory and a Celt's capacity to cherish his grievances. Beneath the urbane and polished former prime minister whom the outside world loathed or admired according to taste, it was still possible to detect the lonely young Scot of forty years before, fiercely determined to make his way in the jungle of the big city and ready to bristle at the first hint of a snub. 'They can say what they like,' he noted bitterly in the summer of 1926 when he turned down an honorary degree at Cambridge on the grounds that it had been opposed by certain members of the university Senate, 'but those of us connected with Labour are still *sudras* in the eyes of "good society".'[68] That nagging sense of being a sudra among brahmins, an outsider among insiders, had not disappeared with age and success; and in some respects the traits associated with it became even more pronounced than they had been in his youth.

He was still inordinately reserved for a politician, and inordinately sensitive to criticism. Like many men who have had to fight their way to the top, and who have acquired scars in the process, he was also inordinately suspicious of the actions and motives of critics — real or imaginary. The wounds left by the war and its aftermath were still unhealed, and the treatment he had received from the pre-war leaders of the party while he had been struggling in the wilderness still rankled. As late as 1930, he explained in a letter to a friend that he had stood against Clynes in 1922 not because he wanted the job but only because 'I believed that he & his colleagues had behaved badly to me & because I wanted to avenge the cause of the righteous.'[69] His correspondence is full of dark hints from his supporters about mysterious plots, cabals and machinations on the part of his enemies, and although solid evidence is often lacking it seems clear that he paid far more attention to them than he should have done. He had always hated being attacked, but as a young man he had been ready to fight back, and had usually given as good as he got. Even now, he could rout his enemies when he had to, but as he grew older an increasingly weary and intolerant note appeared in his replies.

Like many shy men, moreover, he got on best with people who could unobtrusively penetrate his defences while at the same time respecting them; and, as Mrs Hamilton pointed out, there were few people who could do this in the parliamentary Labour Party. In parties of the left, the relationship between the leader and his followers is often an awkward one. In theory, all are equal. In practice, everyone knows that the leader is much more equal than the rest. The contrast can easily introduce an element of tension into the relationship; and when the party concerned is as new to power, as suspicious of the whole notion of leadership, and as full of angular individualists as the Labour Party was fifty years ago, the tension is likely to be more acute than it would be otherwise. In MacDonald's case, the result was a sad, but all too comprehensible, vicious circle. Partly because of his shyness and partly because of their own awkwardness, few of his colleagues felt comfortable with him. Because the relationship was uneasy, he was inclined to look for more congenial company outside politics. That, in turn, made his colleagues even more uneasy with him and the relationship between them became more awkward still.

Of course, there were exceptions. J. H. Thomas, Mrs Hamilton wrote, 'could get through any guard, thanks to his blessed unawareness of it';[70] and it was not an accident that, in spite of their differences of temperament and taste, Thomas was the only leading member of the parliamentary party with whom MacDonald was on anything like intimate terms. Lord Thomson, the charming and easy-going man of the world and former military attaché, became a close friend as well as colleague. But these were exceptions that helped to prove the rule. In March 1924, Sidney Webb was invited to tea with MacDonald at his room in the House. When he arrived, he discovered that the entire parliamentary party was being invited to similar functions in twos and threes, and that he was expected to wait for the other members of his group while MacDonald transacted business with a secretary.[71] During the summer, Fenner Brockway went to see MacDonald with a resolution passed by the I.L.P. parliamentary group, and was greeted with the famous remark, 'Well, Brockway, what commands have you brought me today?'[72] After the Russian treaty was signed, Arthur Ponsonby dined with MacDonald, and noted, 'not one word of relief, pleasure, commiseration or sympathy did he give me on the whole weary and unspeakably difficult business.'[73] Shortly afterwards, he got a letter of thanks, and noted more philosophically that MacDonald 'is an extraordinary mixture. He is inconsiderate and impersonal rather in the same way as C.B. was. I think it must be the Scottish temperament.'[74] Even Mrs Hamilton described the 'chill' of going into MacDonald's room and of being 'looked at, if looked at at all, as though not there'.[75]

His relations with socialist academics and intellectuals were, for the most part, equally uncomfortable. He recognized that they were essential to the kind of party he wanted to lead — not only because of the skills they could offer it, but because their presence would help to transform it from a class party into a national one. He tried to find a parliamentary constituency for John Strachey,[76] encouraged G. D. H. Cole in his parliamentary ambitions,[77] took advice from Harold Laski[78] and asked R. H. Tawney to come with him on his campaign tour in the 1929 election as a speech-writer.[79] But, although he realized that intellectuals like these had an indispensable contribution to make to the Labour Party, he did not feel at ease with them or they with him. They were not 'homely' — one of his favourite and most revealing words for people he liked. They were too hard, too clever, too self-confident; the knowledge of history and literature, which he had acquired by a painful process of self-education in the Guildhall Library, they took for granted. To cover up his uneasiness he was apt to behave in a way which they found artificial and insincere. Moreover, he lacked the inner security to admit his own ignorance of fields in which they could claim to be experts; as Mrs Hamilton put it in a deadly phrase, he would talk 'science with scientists, music with musicians, medicine with doctors, Buddhism with Indians'.[80] In some cases, class probably created a further unacknowledged barrier. Academic recruits to the Labour Party knew where they were with Bevin or Henderson, who fitted the middle-class stereotype of a Labour leader. MacDonald did not fit that stereotype, but he had not been to Oxford or Cambridge either. All too often, communication was impeded by a gulf of uneasiness and embarrassment, of the kind nicely conveyed by Margaret Cole's description of a visit which she and her husband paid to Chequers during MacDonald's second Government:

> MacDonald performed in his best style — several parts in the course of one afternoon. He was obviously delighted with Chequers, with its buildings, its plenishings, and its importance, and his first role was that of an inheritor of broad acres, deeply sensitive to the traditions of the countryside. But he was also (for a few minutes only) the Son of the People, not born to all this glory but called to it by Fate in order that he might create beauty for all the other sons of the people who had not been so called; later, he was for quite a long time the Lonely Leader grappling with problems which none but he could understand and burdened with inferior colleagues not one of whom really appreciated him or inspired his confidence or could

be trusted to carry out policy ... All this for an audience consisting of two MacDonald girls who looked as though they had heard it all before, and a pair of sceptics.[81]

All this was a handicap in a party leader. In Parliament and the party head-quarters, Wertheimer wrote, MacDonald moved 'in a personal vacuum that is almost painful to behold'; and his colleagues complained incessantly about his 'inaccessibility', his 'schoolmasterish condescension', his 'hypersensitiveness' and his 'vanity'.[82] In many ways, these criticisms were unfair. MacDonald was not the only touchy and suspicious member of the Labour Party; the charges which his critics brought against him could often have been brought, with equal justice, against them. The fact remains that his touchiness and suspiciousness help to account, to mention only the most flagrant examples, for his foolish decision to exclude Lansbury from his Cabinet in 1924, for his infinitely more foolish attempt to exclude Henderson and for a number of bitter quarrels with Snowden and Bevin. More generally, they also help to account for the steady deterioration in his relations with the I.L.P., which had once provided him with his main political base, and for his failure to establish satisfactory personal relations with more than a small minority of the right-wing Labour politicians and trade-union leaders, on whose support he increasingly came to depend. The Labour Party of the 'twenties, with its loose organization and heteroge-neous membership, was closer in spirit to a feudal kingdom than to a modern nation state: and one of the chief attributes of a good feudal king was his ability to win and hold the confidence of his barons. MacDonald could often dominate the barons of the Labour Party, but after the war, at any rate, he never quite won their confidence. Part of the reason was that he did not try hard enough to do so.

Yet the walls of reticence and reserve which deterred approaches even from people who knew him well were not erected deliberately, and the garrison behind them was only too anxious for besiegers to break in. MacDonald lacked the gift of ready intimacy, but he needed intimates all the same. As Ponsonby noticed, he found it hard to say kind things, but he made up for that by doing kind deeds — where possible by stealth. Rose Rosenberg was devoted to him; the servants in Downing Street thought him an unusually considerate and charming employer; Compton Mackenzie found him 'a loveable person-ality' and was struck, above all, by 'a kindness in him'. James Margach, who frequently interviewed him while he was staying at Lossiemouth, thought him remarkably approachable and 'free and easy'.[83] He was capable of treating admirers like Clifford Allen and even Mrs Hamilton with brusque insensitivity, and of hurting them quite deeply in doing so. He was equally capable of lavish-ing time and energy which he could not afford on choosing the right birthday presents for his family and friends, on secretly drumming up financial help for his old supporter, Minnie Pallister, when she was ill,[84] or on finding the best

available medical advice for his flamboyant and lazy parliamentary private
secretary, McNeill Weir.[85]

VI

Minnie Pallister and McNeill Weir were friends, but in the late 'twenties one
of the chief beneficiaries of this side of MacDonald's character was a stranger
—the once notorious Oscar Slater. The Slater case had been a *cause célèbre*
before the First World War, and became so again for a few months in 1927
and 1928. MacDonald took care to keep himself out of the limelight, but played
an active part behind the scenes; although the story cannot be told in detail
here, it deserves more than a passing mention. Slater was a German Jew who
had been found guilty of murdering an elderly spinster named Miss Gilchrist
in her flat in Glasgow in December 1908. He had been tried in 1909, and
convicted by a majority verdict of nine to six. The death sentence had been
commuted to one of life imprisonment; when MacDonald became interested in
the case Slater had been a prisoner in Peterhead gaol for over eighteen years.
Arthur Conan Doyle had become convinced of Slater's innocence before the
war. Thanks to him, an inquiry had been held into the case in 1914, but the
commissioner who had conducted the inquiry had upheld the original verdict.
The agitation was reopened in 1927, when William Park published a book
about the case called *The Truth About Oscar Slater*, in which he showed that
the prosecution's evidence had been flimsy in the extreme, and accused the
police of suppressing evidence which would have told in Slater's favour at the
inquiry. Conan Doyle evidently sent to MacDonald a copy of Park's book
during the summer of 1927. Characteristically, MacDonald decided that it
would be 'undesirable' for a former prime minister to take a part in the public
agitation which followed. Equally characteristically, he devoted himself to
highly effective, but largely thankless, lobbying in private.[86]

In September, he sent Park's book to H. P. Macmillan, his Lord Advocate
in 1924. He explained that he could not help feeling that 'there has been an
extraordinary miscarriage of justice as regards this man', and asked for Macmillan's views. Macmillan replied that the case had been 'an uncomfortable one
all along', and that there might be something to be said for remitting the rest
of Slater's sentence. MacDonald wrote back there was more at stake than
Slater's personal fate, and pointed out that 'if Park's book is really true it does
leave a very nasty cloud hanging over the security that we feel in the working
of our criminal law.'[87] Meanwhile, he had also written to Sir John Gilmour,
the secretary of state for Scotland, asking him whether he was happy with the
case, and urging him to take steps to put matters right if he were not. Gilmour
replied that Park's book 'appears to raise no new points', but that he had sent it,
together with other material relating to the case, to the solicitor general, who

would bring a fresh mind to the problem.[88] By now, Macmillan had finished Park's book, and on September 23rd he wrote back to MacDonald, 'Like yourself, I have an unpleasant feeling that there has been a miscarriage of justice & I do not think the verdict was right.' However, he went on, Slater was not the 'innocent martyr' Park had painted; although he should now be released, there was no need for a further inquiry.[89] This was not enough for MacDonald, who replied:

A very disturbing new piece of evidence has just been placed, in great confidence, in my hands and, as you are not only a valued adviser but an ex-Lord Advocate, I do not think that I am committing any breach of confidence if, also in confidence, I tell what it is.

When Lieut. Trench found himself 'bullied and derided by the 1914 Commissioner (I am quoting from a communication) and realised that he was a ruined man' in his fury he tore or cut a page from the police archives and this was found among his papers by his widow after his death ... [I]t practically proves that the police were pursuing a right clue and suddenly dropped it and went on another tack ...

I have just heard from Gilmour ... He tells me that the matter has been put before the Solicitor General for consideration and report. What the report will be I know not, but unless it is favourable to Slater as a man accused of murder, it will be wrong. I do not venture to advise you at all but I do venture to put a question to you: is it in any way consistent with your position for you to find a means of letting the Solicitor General know that your view is as you have expressed it in the first paragraph of your letter? I am really terribly distressed about this case and blame myself very much for having taken no interest in it earlier. I do not care ... who Slater is or what his life has been, but that a man should have been sentenced to death in a Scottish Court, not only for a murder which he did not commit, but upon evidence which was palpably inadequate, and that after the event enquiry after enquiry failed to bring out the truth, is a terribly shocking thing.[90]

By late October, it seemed clear that the Scottish Office were prepared to release Slater, while still resisting any suggestion that the case should be reopened or that a new inquiry was needed. Meanwhile another piece of evidence had come to light. Helen Lambie, one of the chief prosecution witnesses at Slater's trial, told a reporter that she had been bullied by the police into giving false evidence. On October 24th, MacDonald wrote to warn Conan Doyle that the authorities were likely to take the attitude that once Slater had been released, no further action would be needed.[91] He also wrote a long letter to Gilmour, in which menace and supplication were skilfully blended, in roughly equal proportions:

You will now have seen that to all intents and purposes the Slater case ha[s] ended and I again venture to address you, purely in a personal capacity, and appeal to you to make the ending both handsome and generous.

Since I have taken the matter up I have had placed in my possession some most unpleasant evidence which involves the police and the person who apparently committed the crime. I am not one of those who desire a great Parliamentary debate on the matter, but it is bound to come, unless in the meantime the Scottish Office has satisfied those of us who I believe to be reasonable ...

... The Scottish legal authorities and the police strove for his conviction by influencing witnesses and with-holding evidence, and that is the point you will now have to meet and which, I venture with respect to submit to you, must influence your decision as to how you are to wind up the matter.

I almost shudder at the thought of a Parliamentary debate on the subject and I hope you will be able to avoid it, not by trying to refuse opportunities, which you cannot do successfully, but by enabling some of us who have now gone into the question to range ourselves alongside of you.[92]

In his reply, Gilmour asked stiffly why MacDonald should assume that the case was over, but added that he was anxious to examine any new evidence that bore on it and that he had 'invited a correspondent who had referred to a document in his possession ... to make it available to me and I need not say that if evidence has been communicated to you I am anxious to receive it.' MacDonald wrote back next day to say that he could guess what the document was, that had been shown to him in confidence, but that he was prepared, if necessary, to 'make enquiries as to whether it is not possible to give you the information'. His own view, he added was that 'the Lambie statement is conclusive and, as the document in question involves other parties it would be very advisable, I think, to keep it out of your dossier.' After getting permission from Conan Doyle he wrote to Gilmour again on October 31st, to say that he was 'now empowered to show you a copy of the page which was torn from the Police archives by Trench when he was smarting under the injustice of his treatment and when, faced with what he considered to be a lying conspiracy against him, he felt he was justified in possessing himself of material which would protect his own honour'. At the beginning of November, Gilmour wrote asking to see MacDonald at the House of Commons. They met on November 8th, and on November 9th, MacDonald wrote to Gilmour that the more he thought about their conversation 'the more convinced am I that in the interests of everybody and everything concerned you should have an enquiry which I would advise you to announce at the same time as you tell of Slater's release.'[93]

On November 10th, Gilmour announced, in reply to a parliamentary question, that Slater was to be released;[94] and on November 15th, Slater duly left prison.[95] On November 15th, Gilmour told the House of Commons that, if the Opposition were prepared to co-operate, he would introduce a single-clause bill to make it possible for Slater to appeal under the Court of Criminal Appeal (Scotland) Act of 1926.[96] The appeal was heard by the High Court of Justiciary in Edinburgh in the summer of 1928; and on July 20th Slater's conviction was set aside. Conan Doyle wrote immediately to thank MacDonald for what he had done, and on July 23rd, MacDonald replied:

Thank you so much for your letters. You must be tremendously pleased with the result of the Slater case, but how sad it is that poor Park is dying, and yet how well that he should have lived to see his work crowned with success.

One of the great mysteries of life to me is that people whom I know very well and who in their ordinary personal relations are enlightened and just, have a very different nature which they show every now and again when something makes them leave their natural selves and become official or formal or representative.[97]

That was not a charge which could fairly have been brought against him.

CHAPTER 18

Under fire

I

For some months after the 1924 election, there was an uneasy truce in industry while the unions waited to see what the new Government would do, and the Government wisely did nothing. MacDonald's critics in the parliamentary party were less quiescent. At the beginning of February 1925, Beatrice Webb noted, not altogether disconsolately, that the Clydesiders were 'very cold and go straightforward with their "pure socialism" policy, without paying the remotest attention to anything J.R.M. or other front-bench members say'.[1] Soon afterwards, the I.L.P. head office sent out a whip to members of the I.L.P. parliamentary group, instructing them to vote against the London Electricity Bill – thus implying that they owed their primary allegiance to the I.L.P. rather than to the Labour Party.[2] Meanwhile, David Kirkwood had put down a motion criticizing a foreign tour by the Prince of Wales, which had been arranged by the Labour Government.[3] By the end of the month, MacDonald was complaining privately that 'for a generation yet, leading the Labour Party will mean endless work. The team spirit is so rudimentary, however great the heart may be.'[4] A few days later he warned his Glasgow supporter, George Kerr, 'As regards one or two of the men here, things will soon reach a crisis as it is impossible to go on as they have been for some little time.'[5]

Soon afterwards, he was involved in a more serious controversy. In February 1925, the Labour Party's international advisory committee drew up an elaborate memorandum, advocating far-reaching changes in the Foreign Office. In the next Labour Government, they argued, the foreign secretary's 'principal Private Secretary' should be an experienced member of the Labour Party. The parliamentary secretary should rank above the permanent secretary. A new department, headed by a minister of Cabinet rank, should be set up to deal with League of Nations affairs. Last, but by no means least, the next Labour Government should be prepared 'to change the Heads of Diplomatic Missions if necessary on grounds of policy'. These changes were made necessary, the advisory committee argued, by the 'profound distrust of the personnel of the Foreign Office entertained by the Labour Party', by the 'absence of anyone in high positions of the Foreign Office or Diplomatic Services, who even remotely understands the mentality of labour' and by the lack of anyone, apart from the

foreign secretary, who could provide a link between the Foreign Office and the party.[6]

The advisory committee had put its finger on an enduring problem, which applied to other departments as well as to the Foreign Office and which, in one form or another, has perplexed the Labour movement ever since. MacDonald's reaction is therefore of great interest. At the beginning of March, he sent a fairly temperate reply to party headquarters, arguing that it was untrue that no one in a high position in the Foreign Office understood the mentality of the Labour Party, and that if it were true, temporary expedients of the sort proposed would do more harm than good. At the end of the month, he wrote a much more outspoken letter to Henderson, which is worth quoting at length:

I have received a copy of a Memorandum on Foreign Office Secretaries which is coming from the International Advisory Committee to the Executive of the Party ... [L]est I should not be present I am writing this letter because I feel very strongly on the matter and hope that my views will be placed before the Executive ...

On their merits the proposals amount to this:

That whenever a Government changes, the key position in Departments shall be seized by the Party in power, and political appointments made to override Civil Service officials. In essence this is the American system of the spoils to the victor with a vengeance, and is a complete reversal of all our ideas regarding the Civil Service ... If the Labour Party were to give its intimation to the Civil Service that it had no confidence in its impartiality and that it would on assuming office put outsiders into controlling positions ... we would raise such a hornet's nest inside the Service that, so far from promoting efficient and loyal service, we would destroy both ... A Civil Service upon its honour may work; but a Civil Service told quite frankly that we have no confidence in it would never work at all ...

... Who is to appoint this heaven-sent Private Secretary ...? Is it to be the Party or is it the Minister? Supposing I were to go in again and say that I found Mr Selby invaluable ... and re-appointed him to his old post? ... Or supposing I appointed as my Private Secretary a member of the Party who was not a high-flyer but in whose judgement I had great confidence? Would that be carrying out the intention of this document? If this appointment is left to the Foreign Secretary himself, it is as likely as not to give no results whatever ... If, on the other hand, the appointment was log-rolled by the Party Press or Party Committee, — let us be perfectly honest with each other, — would the Private Secretary really be expected to be an unofficial Secretary of State who is as much a watch-dog placed upon the Secretary himself as upon the Foreign Office staff?

... I think that the proposal made by the International Advisory Committee is both subversive in its principle and impracticable as a business proposition ... [I]f ever the remote possibility happened of my again being Foreign Secretary, I should not dream of pursuing the policy intimated in the Memorandum.[7]

In the end, MacDonald won. No doubt in deference to him, the international advisory committee's original proposals were watered down. A new memorandum was put forward, suggesting that under a Labour Government, the foreign secretary's private office should be reorganized under two private secretaries — an 'official' one, provided by the office, to take charge of communication between the foreign secretary and the department, and a 'political' one, who should be a member of the Labour Party, to maintain contact between the foreign secretary and all persons or organizations outside the department.[8] In the event, even the revised version was ignored. Henderson in 1929 and, for that matter, his successors after 1945 and 1964, all followed the MacDonald line. In this, as in so much else, it turned out that MacDonald represented his party better than his critics did.

In spite of the Clydesiders and the international advisory committee, the beginning of the Easter recess found him in a comparatively benign mood. In March, he had made a powerful speech attacking Austen Chamberlain, the new foreign secretary, for abandoning the Geneva Protocol;[9] and he had also finished the negotiations to buy his Hampstead house. Just before leaving for the annual conference of the I.L.P. he noted:

> The group whisperings in the Party have gone on, but there has been a great improvement which, however, owing to the implacable enmity of one or two, I regard only as a truce. Owing to a speech or two I made on Foreign Affairs ... towards the end of this part of the session, the Party pulled better together. Our press has served us worse than ever ... Nothing done inside the Party, on its executive or its own meetings, has been kept private & the Press has periodically announced splits, rows & what not. It has been a patience racking time, but the irritating elements have really been insignificant & have cut poor figures in the open. The great consolation is that all parties are & have been alike, & all leaders have had the same troubles. These things are not reflected in the Party outside which keeps as sound as a bell. When out speaking as at Swindon & Lincoln, the crowds have been magnificent & the hearty enthusiasm moving. Meanwhile I prepare for the days of my rest. I have fallen in love with a house, away from the world with the sun shining upon it & a garden of peaceful retirement ... I am just leaving for a meeting at Worcester & the I.L.P. conference at Gloucester. The Agenda of the latter has some of the usual criticisms of those who live in phrases and intentions, & also of those whose sense of duty & rectitude is satisfied by showing the 'head anes' how much better things would have been done if the critics had been in power. But whatever trouble they may give us they are not the [whole]

Agenda which is full of excellent matter showing how well the I.L.P. is facing the real problems for which Socialists have to find a solution.[10]

This mood did not last for long. At the conference, the Yorkshire divisional council moved an anodyne resolution congratulating the 1924 Government on its record at home and abroad. In an organization which had provided not merely the prime minister and foreign secretary in the Government concerned, but also the chancellor of the exchequer and a number of other Cabinet ministers, such as resolution might have been expected to pass without difficulty. In fact, it was savagely opposed by George Buchanan and Campbell Stephen, both of whom made bitter personal attacks on MacDonald. Stephen, at least, drew blood. Years later, John Paton recalled in his memoirs how he had taken a message to MacDonald in the middle of Stephen's speech, and how MacDonald had turned to him, his face flushed, his eyes alight with fury and his knuckles white as he gripped the table in front of him, and had spat out in a hoarse whisper, 'That damned little swine – Campbell Stephen!'[11] In the end, after a curiously apologetic speech by MacDonald, pointing out that governing the country was 'quite different from getting resolutions through the I.L.P. conference', the Yorkshire council's resolution was carried by 398 votes to 139.[12] On paper, it was a comfortable majority: what mattered for the future was the ominous size of the vote against.

Most of the omens that came MacDonald's way in the next few weeks were equally unpropitious. At the end of April, Ben Spoor, the chief whip, who was already a sick man and who was organizing a big dinner in MacDonald's honour, wrote gloomily from the 'wilds of Dartmoor' that 'much hangs on it. We must in the interests of the "Movement" smash this unholy Henderson, Snowden and Wheatley effort to disrupt.'[13] MacDonald replied equally gloomily:

> There is a great deal of mischief about. People do not seem to be able to settle down and contribute, without thought of personal advantage, what they can to a common cause, and the power of the whisper and the private comment is really wonderful. [M]onths and months of this continued nagging and back-biting may have an effect and produce suspicion and doubt to an uncomfortable extent. Our great weakness in combating that is that our press is just as nagging and sulky as it possibly can be. If it would play up and think more of the Party than of any individual we could snap our fingers at the activities of certain people.[14]

The iniquity of the socialist press had been one of MacDonald's chief preoccupations since before the election, and for some months he had devoted an inordinate amount of time and energy to a project to acquire a controlling interest in the *New Statesman* for a consortium of supporters, in the hope that this would provide a platform for what he described rather vaguely as 'a very fine band of young fellows down from Oxford'.[15] In spite of his efforts, however, the project hung fire. Meanwhile, he was subjected to a furious onslaught from C. P. Trevelyan, who attacked him at the foreign affairs committee of the parliamentary party for his subservience to the permanent officials of the Foreign Office, and resurrected the international advisory committee's proposal that the next Labour foreign secretary should be obliged to appoint an experienced party member as his private secretary.[16] Most embarrassing of all, he was involved in a trivial but nevertheless embarrassing dispute with Josiah Wedgwood, which still further embittered his relations with his critics in the party.

The dispute began with a letter to MacDonald from a Bulgarian socialist deputy, named Grigor Vasileff, complaining about the attacks which had been made on the Bulgarian regime by a group of three visiting Labour M.P.s, one of whom was Wedgwood. The three M.P.s, Vasileff claimed, had arrived in Sofia in April, without telling the Government or getting in touch with the socialist party. While they were there a bomb had exploded in Sofia cathedral, killing 200 people. When they left the country, the Labour M.P.s had accused the Bulgarian Government of operating a White Terror. The truth, Vasileff went on, was that the Bulgarian Government – a coalition between the socialists and the Democratic Entente – had long enjoyed 'the special attention of the Governors of Moscow'. In 1923 the Communists had tried, and failed, to provoke a revolution. In 1924 they had turned to terrorist tactics, culminating in the outrage in Sofia cathedral. Vasileff concluded by emphasizing his respect for the British Labour Party, and asked, in a tone of sorrow rather than of anger, whether the three M.P.s were its accredited representatives.[17]

Foolishly, though perhaps understandably, MacDonald failed to consult Wedgwood or the other members of the group. Instead he replied guardedly:

I am much obliged by your letter ... commenting upon the statements made by two (not three – the third was not a Member) British Members of Parliament regarding events following the explosion of a bomb in the Sofia Cathedral. No one is responsible for these statements except the Members themselves. They were not appointed by the Labour Party but happened to be in Bulgaria privately. They have made no official report to any Labour organisation so far as I know – certainly none has come through my hands. It is impossible at this distance to pass any judgement upon what they had said. Our newspapers were full of statements, all of which were no doubt exaggerated. I generally question all Moscow politics; the Labour Party had shown again and again its unshakeable opposition to Bolshevism. It knows perfectly well that if Moscow or any of its agents in the European nations were able to create a revolution, it would have no scruples whether it would do it by bombing people in churches or cutting their throats in their beds ... At the same time they are no doubt the subject of forgeries, police plots and suchlike, so that as regards any special event we have to be very careful and critical lest we are being deceived.[18]

The results were disconcerting. At the beginning of June, the secretary of the Partick branch of the I.L.P. wrote indignantly to MacDonald, protesting against his action in 'writing to the Bulgarian press informing them that the three British officials who happened to be there at the time of the outrage were not an *official* delegation', and pointing out severely that as 'head of our movement' he ought to have known that 'Com. Maxton M.P. and others were doing their utmost to have the wholesale massacre, which was going on in that country, stopped.'[19]

This was more than MacDonald could bear. For seven months he had watched his party plunge widly in a direction which he believed to be disastrous. He had been subjected to bitter attacks from the Left, and had had little support from the Right. His normal sensitivity to criticism had been exacerbated by incessant overwork and a growing sense of political isolation; and he was suffering from arthritis into the bargain. It was hardly surprising that his nerves should have been on edge. He replied to the Partick I.L.P. with what must be one of the most astonishing outbursts ever addressed by a party leader to a group of ostensible followers:

I overlook what to the Partick Branch must evidently be a slight inaccuracy – that I wrote to the Bulgarian Press, as I did nothing of the kind. A letter to the effect quoted in your letter was sent by me, however, to an accredited official of the Bulgarian Socialist movement. What does the Partick branch mean by passing such a resolution? Perhaps it would mind its own business and regard Socialism not as the creed of a lot of blethering easie-oosie asses who are prepared to pass any resolution without knowing its meaning and on any subject without understanding it, but as something which requires rectitude of thought and consideration of action ...

I really would advise your Branch not to interfere in matters that it knows nothing about, and to refrain from passing resolutions which show not only their inability to state the facts, but their equally great inability to come to any respectable conclusions from them.[20]

The secretary of the Partick I.L.P. replied icily that his members regretted their inaccuracy in stating that MacDonald's letter had been sent to the Bulgarian press, and accepted his assurance that it had in fact been sent to an official of the socialist movement. They still felt, however, that it should not have been sent at all. They also felt that the tone of his letter to them was uncalled for, and 'contrary to their conception of Socialism'. They were therefore sending it to the socialist press, 'so that the "blethering easie-oosie asses" may know your opinion of them'.[21] It was duly published, and caused a minor sensation. The secretary of the Enfield Labour Party wrote to thank MacDonald 'for your letter to Partick I.L.P. I hope the whole movement will take it to heart, and stop the braying.'[22] Beatrice Webb, on the other hand, noted hopefully that this 'amazingly indiscreet letter of J.R.M. reveals a state of mind and manner inconsistent with the leadership of the Parliamentary Labour Party'.[23] It was not the first time in MacDonald's career that a storm in a teacup had revealed an alarming propensity to sea-sickness — on his part, and on the part of his critics.

II

By now, the industrial truce had ended too. In April 1925, the Government had returned to the gold standard at the pre-war parity. British export prices were substantially increased, and British exporters had to cut their costs or risk losing their markets. In labour-intensive industries, the obvious solution was to reduce wages. But, as Keynes pointed out, the old 'theory of the economic Juggernaut', according to which wage levels were fixed by the laws of the market, had been challenged since the war by a rival conception of economic society, which implied that they ought to be determined by some standard of equity or reasonableness. This second conception was, of course, one of the central pillars of Labour's creed. It had helped to inspire the upsurge of working-class militancy of the early 'twenties; it linked the day-to-day haggling of the labour market with the vision of a new society; and it ensured that wage reductions would be fought, not only on grounds of self-interest, but in the name of solidarity and social justice.

The conflict between these two conceptions was particularly fierce in the mining industry, where it was given extra bitterness by the pressures of industrial decline. Profits and export sales had fallen dramatically even before the return to gold, and the owners were determined to prevent them from disappearing altogether. By April 1925, over 60 per cent of the collieries in the country were working at a loss; between January and July over 500 had to close. It was clear that the only alternative to wage reductions was some form of Government intervention and subsidy. But Government intervention was anathema to the owners, who saw it as the thin end of a wedge which could only lead to nationalization. At the end of June, the mining association gave notice that the existing wages agreement would come to an end on July 31st, and proposed a new agreement involving the abandonment of the guaranteed minimum wage, a substantial increase in profits and a sharp fall in wages.[24]

The miners were as determined as the owners. Once, they had been among the aristocrats of labour; they still had the self-respect and group loyalty of an élite. They were prepared to fight rather than accept a further reduction in earnings which had already fallen in money terms to a little more than half what they had been four years before. The owners' terms were rejected, and the miners' leaders made it clear that they would not negotiate until the terms had been withdrawn. In similar circumstances in 1921, the alliance between the miners, railwaymen and transport workers had broken down, and on 'Black Friday' the miners had been left to fight alone. Partly because they still felt a little shamefaced about their behaviour then, and partly because they believed that the miners' wages were the first line of defence for the working class as a whole, the leaders of the other big unions made it clear that on this occasion they, too, were prepared to fight. The T.U.C. General Council placed itself unreservedly at the disposal of the Miners' Federation; plans were made to 'black' the movement of coal by road, rail or sea; and it was clear that if the lockout took effect, British industry would be brought to a halt. For months, the Government had insisted that the mining industry must settle its problems by itself, and that there could be no question of a subsidy. Now its nerve cracked. On July 31st, Baldwin announced that the owners' notices had been withdrawn, that yet another royal commission would inquire into the industry, and that it would be given financial assistance until May 1st, 1926. 'Black Friday' had been wiped out by 'Red Friday'.

As the member for a mining constituency, MacDonald was well aware of the hardships of the lower-paid miners. Like most people who studied the problem, he was convinced that wage reductions offered no real solution. Like everyone else in the Labour movement, he believed that the only permanent answer was nationalization, and that extensive Government intervention was indispensable. But although he welcomed the Government's decision on the merits of the case, he could not help recognizing that its surrender had enormously strengthened the forces he most feared in Labour politics. Again and again, Labour members of Parliament had pressed the Government to intervene. Again and again, they had been rebuffed. Now Baldwin had conceded to force what he had refused to argument. Political action had failed, and industrial action had won a painless victory. To make matters worse, it was clear that the victory could only provide a temporary breathing-space. The royal commission could hardly be expected to discover a new solution to the problems of the mining industry. When the subsidy ran out, both sides would be back where they were before. The Government had climbed down, not because it had suddenly recognized the justice of the miners' case, but because it believed that they had public opinion on their side, and to some extent because it feared that it would be unable to maintain essential services if the other unions supported them. It could not afford to climb down a second time.

For fifteen years, MacDonald had argued that if the unions tried to coerce the state, the state would win. Nothing had happened to alter his opinion. It was still as true as it always had been that the only alternative to parliamentary socialism was revolutionary socialism, and that in a democracy, revolutionary socialism was a disastrous cul-de-sac. It must have seemed to him essential that the euphoria of Red Friday should be dissipated as soon as possible. In the House of Commons, he took a cautious line – attacking the Government for failing to intervene earlier, accepting the need for a subsidy and paying tribute to the 'unanimity and harmony' which had been displayed by the unions. Even in the House of Commons, however, he warned that the line between trade-union mobilization for legitimate industrial self-defence and trade-union mobilization for presumably illegitimate political purposes was 'extraordinarily thin'.[25] Outside the House, he was much more outspoken. In a lecture to an I.L.P. summer school at Easton Lodge at the beginning of August, he argued that the real reason for the miners' victory was that they had been supported by the general public. As for the Government's surrender:

> It has handed over the appearance of victory to the very forces that sane, well-considered, thoroughly well examined Socialism feels to be probably its greatest enemy.
>
> The Tory Government, in … the methods it adopted to bring this temporary settlement into being, has sided with the wildest Boshevik, if not in words, certainly in fact and in substance.[26]

In the short run, at least, MacDonald's attempt to rally the opponents of direct action probably did him more harm than good. Henderson visited the Webbs in August. According to Beatrice, he was 'full of the decline in Mac-Donald's influence', and attributed part of it to the Easton Lodge speech. He prophesied that the thirty Labour M.P.s who had made up their minds to turn MacDonald out of the leadership would succeed, and said that he would himself support Snowden as leader, and that the Clydesiders and the I.L.P. would do the same.[27] In the whispering gallery of Westminster – particularly at the end of the summer, when nerves are frayed and tempers short – the most trivial and insubstantial rumours carry over long distances. Soon after Henderson's visit to the Webbs, the indefatigable Ben Spoor wrote to warn MacDonald, 'Wheatley is dangerous, but remember that there are others too, equally un-resting.'[28] A few days later, he reported an even more bizarre discovery:

> The Wheatley–Cook combination pursues its ineffective way – perhaps its a good thing this unholy alliance has been formed. Quite frankly, I'm much more afraid of J.H.T. whose ambition has no limit & whose success has 'spoilt' him. I can see he is being 'boosted' very much in the Press (he is a past-master in Publicity & has many satellites). Moreover he quite expects to be the next P.M. & told me as much before Christmas last. For real tragi-comedy commend me to the Trade Union element in the Labour Party. But don't worry – Socialism is too big to be 'nobbled' by opportunists. And you've got far more than 'half a dozen of men active in loyalty to the Party & socialism'. Mac: believe me, you'll sweep the country in the next fight.[29]

Thomas, too, was on guard. In the middle of August he wrote reassuringly 'I am at the desk watching things pretty closely. I am convinced that we are going to have a hard battle ... However, so far as railwaymen are concerned I am quite happy and will take some shifting.'[30]

Gossip of this sort flourishes in all parties at all times; in normal circumstances, it is a mistake to attach much significance to it. In the summer of 1925, however, the circumstances were not normal. The Labour movement was in turmoil; the party was deeply divided, not only over tactics but over the most fundamental questions of strategy and philosophy. It is clear that MacDonald had enemies in the parliamentary party and that, thanks to Ben Spoor (and, no doubt, to others as well), he was only too well aware of this himself. In retrospect, there can be little doubt that at least some of his tactical aberrations were due to the tension and sense of insecurity which this awareness inspired. Even at the time there could be no doubt that the intrigue and backbiting in the parliamentary party would get worse unless the movement outside Parliament could be rallied to the leadership.

For the moment, it was the trade unions that mattered most and here the prognosis was gloomy in the extreme. When the T.U.C. assembled at Scarborough, Thomas's forebodings about a 'hard battle' turned out to be only too well founded. Alonzo Swales, the chairman, called for a 'militant and progressive policy', and described the Soviet Union as a 'workers' republic rising, Phoenix-like, from the ashes of the most despotic regime in History'. An avowedly revolutionary motion, calling on the T.U.C. to organize for the overthrow of capitalism, was passed by a majority of two-to-one. The Congress also passed resolutions condemning the Dawes plan, which had enabled MacDonald to win his triumph at the reparations conference, and supporting the General Council's attempts to bring the Soviet trade unions into a single trade-union international. It was true that a contrary current could be detected under the surface. J. H. Thomas and Margaret Bondfield returned to the General Council, and a motion to increase the General Council's powers in the event of a strike was remitted to it for consideration.[31] But this combination of brave words and cautious deeds was potentially the most dangerous that could have been devised, and from MacDonald's point of view it was the reverse of reassuring. It was hardly surprising that when he gave a party for some of his colleagues, in the middle of September, he looked ill and depressed and that even Thomas seemed less bouncy than usual.

It was clear that the Labour Party conference at Liverpool would see a critical, and possibly decisive, trial of strength. If it followed the lead given by the T.U.C., the party's electoral prospects, which had already suffered great damage, might be destroyed altogether. Henderson's prophecy that MacDonald would be turned out of the leadership might come true. Even if it did not, his authority would be hopelessly undermined. MacDonald, at least, had no doubt of what was at stake. In a rare appeal to Snowden, he wrote:

I have been so busy that I have not been able to look through the Agenda
of the Liverpool Conference until yesterday, and I am rather surprised that
it is such a pernicious document. I do not think that we will go down in
any of the important divisions, but the Communists will have to be
fought with the gloves off. I do hope you are going up to Liverpool. It
is one of those occasions when I think everything ought to be put on one
side in order that there should be no doubt about the result ... [32]

III

Liverpool was a triumph for the leadership. On the first day of the conference,
Willie Gallacher, later a Communist member of Parliament, who was present
as delegate from the Paisley Labour Party, moved the reference back of the
section of the Executive's report urging that trade unions should not appoint
members of the Communist Party as delegates to local Labour Parties or to the
Labour Party conference. His motion was defeated by the crushing majority
of 2,870,000 to 321,000, and the substantive Executive resolution banning
Communists as trade-union delegates was carried by 2,692,000 to 480,000.
Even more satisfying from MacDonald's point of view was the fate of a resolution moved by Ernest Bevin, committing the Labour Party not to take office
again unless it had a majority in the House of Commons. In his speech opening
the debate Bevin did his best to avoid personalities, but that could not alter the
fact that his resolution was a thinly-veiled attack on MacDonald's decision to
enter office and on his conduct as prime minister. As such, it gave MacDonald
a welcome opportunity to hit back at his critics, and he did so in a speech which
reveals more than any sociological analysis could about the mixture of pride
and deference in the Labour movement of those years:

> He did not like anyone saying that, with great searching of heart when
> the division bell rang, he had to decide whether he would stand by the
> Labour Government or stand by his class ... [T]hey had had many Govern-
> ments since Walpole started as Prime Minister. They had had many
> Governments that were good, many bad, and many indifferent; but when
> they and he were dead, and when their children were dead, and when a
> more remote succession of generations read of the twentieth century, he
> did not think it was flattering the Labour Government or flattering the
> Party if he said they would then be loud in their praise when they read
> that in the year 1924 the men from the pits, the men from the factories and
> the men from the fields, coming into office with a minority, and for the
> first time ... accomplished as Labour Ministers a work that would be
> enshrined in the records of the British people.

Bevin's reply was muddled, vituperative and ineffective. He began by saying that MacDonald's speech reminded him of 'the old Leicester arrangement over again', and when he was shouted down, repeated angrily that he had 'never forgotten the tactics with Gordon Hewitt and the Liberals before the war'. This caused an uproar, and the chairman made the bizarre ruling that it was not in order to refer to events which had occurred before the war. To the accompaniment of further interruptions, Bevin then explained that he was the last man in the world to hit anyone below the belt, since he had his reputation for fairness to keep up, but that since MacDonald had made an offensive remark about him, he was entitled to reply. Finally he launched into a rambling attack on the evasiveness and dishonesty of the politicians, coupled with the cryptic, but faintly menacing, assertion that 'whatever was done on the political side, on the industrial side they were going on with their organisation, uniting their forces and developing Trade Union consciousness, which would find expression on the political field.' In spite of the transport workers' block vote, his motion was lost by the decisive margin of 2,587,000 to 512,000.[33]

MacDonald had ample cause to congratulate himself. 'The spirit of the Conference was that of earlier times ... ,' he wrote in a euphoric article in *Forward*. 'I returned to a desk heaped with letters from people who had been wondering whether the Movement they helped to create was being disintegrated, and who saw in Liverpool a renewal of youth.'[34] His Glasgow supporter, George Kerr, reported that 'everywhere and everybody in Glasgow who are interested in sanity and sanctity are tremendously bucked up with your great work and influence at Liverpool – you saved the Labour Party in the country.'[35] The Welsh Labour M.P., William Jenkins, who lived in MacDonald's constituency, wrote that he was 'delighted with your stand at *Liverpool. it* has enhanced your previously good reputation, *Aberavon Division is highly pleased.*'[36] Even Beatrice Webb noted that MacDonald had 'done brilliantly' and 'reasserted his dominance'.[37]

When the House resumed after the summer recess, it was clear that in the parliamentary party, at least, he was firmly in the saddle again. Nothing more was heard of the thirty M.P.s who had decided to oust him from the leadership, and the tide of gossip and demoralization, which had seemed likely to swamp him in the previous sessions, appeared to have subsided. His morale improved, and his speeches were noticeably better than they had been before the recess. In November, he delivered a rousing attack on the Government's failure to deal satisfactorily with unemployment.[38] At the beginning of December, he consolidated his position with an even more effective onslaught on its decision to prosecute twelve leading members of the Communist Party, who had been arrested following a police raid on the party headquarters. This was one of the Government's worst lapses during this period, and MacDonald's indignation was deeply felt:

Upon what grounds did the trial rest? Hon. Members must remember that it was preceded by a general search. It was none of your old-fashioned, stilted pieces of constitutional rectitude, when the search took place for a specific thing, and, if that specific thing was not found, nothing else was disturbed. No; that is an old habit, an old prejudice of British constitutionalism which the modern Tory party has torn up like a scrap of paper. They went into offices and they took everything from love-letters to death-sentences — everything they could lay their hands on; furniture and chairs I believe, certainly documents and books of all kinds ...

... [A]s regards the documents and books, they were really ... subversive nonsense — but so is Toryism; and should ever the day of calamity come, I will take the same attitude towards hon. Members opposite as I take now, because, if we once give away the great, precious foundation of our liberty, you and I ... are deprived of the right to stand in our open places ... and say, 'This is what we believe'. Let that go, and you are face to face with nothing between reaction on the one hand and revolution on the other ...

... [R]ight to the marrow of my bones, I object to the proceedings which the Government have taken. I think it is a political trial, inspired by political motives. Old ladies must be frightened in order that young Tories may be elected.[39]

The fount of power in Britain is the House of Commons, and the fount of power in the House of Commons is the dispatch box. However odd and irrational it may seem, a party leader's standing with his followers depends, in the last resort, on his capacity to hold his own debate. After a good speech, his reputation soars; after a bad one, it plummets. With MacDonald, who never felt quite at home in the post-war House of Commons, and who was in any case unusually sensitive to atmosphere, the process was cumulative. He needed the encouraging roar of cheers behind him to make good speeches; and the better his speeches became, the louder the roar was likely to be. The improvement in his parliamentary performances which can be detected after the recess must have been due, in part, to the improvement in his morale which followed the Liverpool conference — and it in turn must have strengthened the swing towards him which Liverpool had begun.

So did the tactical follies of his enemies. Early in December, Lansbury and Wedgwood proposed a motion at the party meeting, instructing the chief whip to organize the party into relays of thirty in order to hold up all Government business 'save such as may be considered by the party as tending to reduce unemployment'. Ben Spoor reported that the 'overwhelming majority' of those present opposed the proposal, and it was killed by the appointment of a sub-committee to inquire into the best way of improving the opportunities available to backbenchers.[40] The elections to the parliamentary committee were equally satisfactory to the leadership. Lansbury, Wheatley, Kirkwood and Maxton announced that they would refuse to stand. Henderson persuaded the first three to change their minds, and only Maxton persisted in his decision. The result was a striking victory for the Right. Wheatley was defeated and Sidney Webb, who had won only 23 votes the year before, regained his seat.[41]

IV

Outside Parliament, the position was less satisfactory. The Royal Commission which Baldwin had promised began its work, under the chairmanship of Sir Herbert Samuel. At the same time, the Government prepared for a second round with the unions. Behind the scenes, an elaborate organization was set up to ensure that law and order would be maintained, and essential supplies transported, if a general strike took place. Sir John Anderson, the permanent secretary to the Home Office, was put in charge, and England and Wales were divided into ten areas, each under a minister who would act as a civil commissioner if the need arose. Anderson's machinery was for use, not show. It was kept secret, and was therefore of no value as a deterrent – though MacDonald and his leading colleagues, who had faced a somewhat similar situation on a much smaller scale in 1924, must have had some idea of what was going on.

Secret plans, however, were supplemented by a more public threat. At the beginning of September, it was announced that a private body called the Organisation for the Maintenance of Supplies had been set up with official blessing to recruit volunteers, and Joynson-Hicks, the home secretary, declared that it was a 'patriotic act' to join it. Meanwhile, the *Daily Herald* asked whether the workers should take up arms, and Wheatley wrote that he wanted to see '10 million men who are prepared to fight rather than see Britain made a land of coolies'.[42] Even Bevin, who had no sympathy with the revolutionary flourishes of the Clydesiders and the Minority Movement, grossly overestimated the benefits which direct action could produce and underestimated the risks involved in a second collision with the state.[43] To MacDonald, the prospects seemed doubly alarming. He knew the trade unions well enough to realize that, in spite of the excited talk at Scarborough, there was no danger that the T.U.C. would deliberately precipitate a revolution, but it seemed to him that there was a very real danger that it might allow itself to be swept into a conflict from which only reactionaries or revolutionaries could gain. The formation of the O.M.S., he warned in *Forward*, proved once more that

> If anyone thinks that there can be a general strike that does not as a reaction draw society together in self-defence, he is living in a fool's paradise ... If anyone believes that a Government can stand by whilst the life of a community is being paralysed pending the settlement of the dispute, he had better use his imagination to get a grip of the condition that would soon develop ... Those who want to bring organised Labour into revolutionary

conflict with all the resources of Governments and Society are quite right in trying to create a general national strike. That is why ... the Home Secretary and his backers join with the Communists in believing that we had better assume that there is to be a fight, have it out and be done with it.[44]

His warning was ignored. The trade-union leaders were the prisoners of their own success. Having won the first round, they could hardly draw back from the second before it had begun. They had no desire to engage in a 'revolutionary conflict' with the Government, and bent over backwards to avoid making plans for one. They were equally unwilling to prepare themselves or their members for a retreat. In any case, they had no room for retreat. If the miners were right in the summer, they were right in the autumn. If wage cuts had to be resisted in the summer, they would have to be resisted in the spring. Thus, the General Council could neither move forward nor back. It marked time, hoping against hope that Samuel would succeed where his predecessors had failed, that a formula would be discovered which the Government and the miners could both accept, and that the problem would somehow go away.

While the T.U.C. waited, the I.L.P. took another stride to the left. In September, Clifford Allen tried to persuade the N.A.C. to invite MacDonald to resume the editorship of the Socialist Review. After a long and exhausting argument, he was forced to drop the suggestion. Instead, it was agreed that MacDonald should be asked to write the monthly editorial notes, and that Allen should become editor himself. A few days later, Maxton, who was acting as the I.L.P. representative on the standing orders committee of the Labour Party conference, agreed to incorporate an official I.L.P. resolution on land nationalization into a composite resolution which opposed compensation. In doing so, he committed the I.L.P. to a view which he passionately held himself, but which Allen as passionately opposed, and which had been rejected by the I.L.P. annual conference. This was the last straw for Allen, who resigned from the chairmanship on the grounds of ill-health.[45] His physical weariness, he explained to MacDonald, was due to the months of 'unintelligent bickering' which had come to a head in the 'series of disgusting events concerned with the Liverpool Conference and the Socialist Review'. As a result, he had come to the conclusion that it was 'useless going on with these people, unless a new group of loyal and reasonably intelligent colleagues can be found'.[46] For all practical purposes, the Clydesiders and their allies now dominated the N.A.C.

Meanwhile, MacDonald's relations with them had been still further embittered by a somewhat foolhardy foray on his part into the depths of Glasgow municipal politics. A few days after the Liverpool conference, Maxton told a packed meeting at the St Andrews' Hall that he still believed that Communists should be allowed into the Labour Party. Soon afterwards, MacDonald's friend, George Kerr, the sitting councillor for the Springburn ward, was defeated by 74 votes to 73 at a ward selection conference to choose the Labour candidate for the forthcoming municipal elections. The men's section of the Springburn Labour Party, Kerr reported in a long letter to MacDonald, were represented by 10 delegates, all of them members of the Communist Party. In the women's section, the normal membership of between 25 and 35 was inflated to 90 at the meeting when it decided how to cast its vote: its delegation of 10 also voted for the Communist candidate. Similar tactics were employed to swell the membership and voting strength of some of the trade-union branches. 'The Springburn I.L.P. meets tomorrow, Sunday,' Kerr wrote. 'I am going to urge them to put me up as their candidate and I will fight.'[47]

MacDonald replied, promising to do 'anything I could to help' and urging him to allow no time to be wasted:

> This matter will have to be fought out.
> Glasgow is becoming the laughing stock and at the same time the fear of our movement. If Maxton continues his present policy I shall come definitely out against him. We cannot allow the good results of Liverpool to be frittered away by people who put up no fight there and who prefer to continue to do mischief from the platform when our backs are turned.[48]

He also sent Kerr's letter to J. H. Thomas, explained that it 'shows one of the most outrageous moves that has ever taken place inside our Party', and added that he was prepared to write a letter supporting Kerr if Kerr asked for one.[49] Kerr duly fought, but lost to his Moderate opponent by 2,198 votes to 2,860. Payne, the Communist who had supplanted him as the official Labour candidate, won 1,401. 'I am not only Ex-Baillie and Ex-Councillor,' Kerr wrote sadly after the election, 'but in addition I am extinguished.' The result would have been very different, he continued, but for the behaviour of the local M.P., George Hardie. In his desire to 'get on the right side of the SHOUTERS', Kerr wrote, Hardie 'rushed on to the platform of the Communist Party Candidate, in the guise of the official Labour Party Candidate, addressed two meetings on his behalf and was the only speaker who did so who was not a member of the Communist Party of Great Britain, and he also sent a letter regretting his inability to attend a final rally on the eve of the poll.' The Communists naturally made full use of Hardie's support, and circulated bills with the slogan:

> George Hardie, M.P., is supporting Payne,
> Follow his example and do the same.

The only M.P. who spoke for Kerr was Neil McLean. Kerr's canvass returns had indicated that he was winning easily, but Hardie created such confusion among Labour voters that they stayed at home on polling day. The moral, Kerr concluded, was that:

> My fight and work will have been in vain unless the challenge is taken up by the National Executive of the Labour Party. It is their obvious duty to

the Labour Movement in Glasgow and throughout the Country to make the fullest possible inquiry into the reason why the Springburn Branch of the I.L.P. and George Kerr were fight[ing] a Candidate supported by the Springburn D.L.P. and the Glasgow Trades and Labour Council and I personally appeal to you to use all your influence to see that such an inquiry is held and that whoever is appointed to do the investigations does it thoroughly and in Glasgow.

Unless the Glasgow Trades and Labour Council and the local D.L. Parties in Glasgow are compelled to give effect to the Liverpool Conference decisions then you might as well have held your tongue and the Conference not been held.[50]

MacDonald promptly wrote to Egerton Wake, the Labour Party National Agent, urging him to make inquiries. 'If we let this sort of thing pass,' he wrote, 'it is only encouraging the wreckers, and we shall not have such a good chance of challenging them as this contest provides.'[51] For good measure, he also published a pointed attack on 'the spiteful and the wirepuller, the hidden hand and the plot' in an article in Forward, and declared roundly that the circumstances under which Kerr lost his seat were 'a disgrace to Glasgow Socialism'.[52] His intervention was not conspicuously successful. Egerton Wake replied fatalistically that Glasgow was a 'nest of intrigue', and although he did not say it in so many words, his tone strongly suggested that he thought it was a waste of time to try to improve the situation.[53] The affair was discussed by the National Executive in December, and referred to the organization sub-committee.[54] The organization sub-committee took no action, however, though in June 1926 the Springburn divisional party was disaffiliated after all, on the grounds that it had refused to operate the Liverpool Conference decisions on the affiliation of Communists.[55]

Meanwhile a Glasgow I.L.P.-er named Kelly had written to MacDonald to complain that the position was more complicated than he had implied in Forward. The truth, said Kelly, was that there had been two selection conferences, not one. Payne had been selected at the first, but a second had been called owing to allegations of irregularities. At the second, Payne and Kerr had both been asked whether they would abide by the result. Payne had said that he would, but Kerr had only said that he would be 'in the hands of the I.L.P.'[56] To this MacDonald replied unrepentantly, and with more than a hint of self-righteousness:

I confess to you quite candidly I was moved very deeply by old friendship for Kerr ... I was told in August by some of our leading men in Glasgow that a dead set was to be made at him when he came up for re-nomination, and that it was part and parcel of certain things that were going on in the city which, if not stopped, were going to smash up our movement altogether. I could not believe it but as time went on I saw that it was maturing ... I really felt that in Kerr's case a stand had to be taken and I admit that in doing so it seemed as though I were flying in the face of Conference decisions. Although I am constantly fighting against men who do that sort of thing habitually, I have never objected to those who did it on very rare occasions and under circumstances which seemed to justify such action. If we did not do that we should invite more factions to come in and boss us ... I still think that the action of the Selection Conference ... ought not have been passed without challenge, and the vote that Kerr got is at any rate a part justification for what was done.[57]

On that note, the affair petered out, leaving a residue of bad blood behind it. Although it would be wrong to exaggerate its significance, it must have confirmed the Clydesiders in their belief that MacDonald preferred fighting the Communists to fighting the class war. It certainly confirmed MacDonald in his belief that the Clydesiders and their friends were wrecking the Labour Party, destroying its chances of winning an election, and giving aid and comfort to its enemies.

The breach widened still further in the first few months of 1926. On February 16th, Brockway sent MacDonald the minutes of a joint meeting of the Consultative Committee of the N.A.C. and a special committee of the I.L.P. parliamentary group which had been set up to consider the group's future. It had been decided that the parliamentary group should appoint a committee of seven, including the three N.A.C. members of parliament, to consider the business of the parliamentary Labour Party 'with a view to bringing suggestions before the Party and making proposals on the business coming before it'. The committee was to appoint a convener, meet weekly and invite the General Secretary to attend its meetings. MacDonald pointed out in his reply to Brockway that if this meant anything it meant that the I.L.P. had decided to 'set up a rival and concurrent authority' to that of the parliamentary party; and he warned that it would 'not endear the Members to their other colleagues in the House of Commons'.[58] By the middle of March he was writing to a supporter in Bothwell that

The I.L.P. ... is a terrible problem. The way in which it at present is being handled is making it a mere tool of the Communists, who ... will simply make ducks and drakes of a Party getting its tactics from rather incompetent people. The result will be that the I.L.P. will come into serious conflict with the Labour Party and the Labour Party will bring to bear upon it the massed votes of the Trade Union movement. The grip that the I.L.P. has upon the larger movement will then be loosened, and there will be the end of the chapter ... [59]

P

V

Early in March 1926, the Samuel Commission reported; and the fears MacDonald had expressed in the autumn rapidly came true. In many ways, the report was favourable to the miners. It turned down an increase in hours, declared that national wage agreements should continue and recommended extensive reorganization of the industry—including improvements in working conditions, pit amalgamations to eliminate unprofitable collieries and the nationalization of mining royalties. But this was the sugar on the pill. Before the benefits of reorganization could be felt, the Commission insisted, wages would have to come down. The miners were being asked to pay now for future benefits which might never materialize. They refused to budge.

So did the owners. They made it clear that they wanted, not only wage reductions, but the abandonment of national agreements as well. By the middle of April, negotiations between the two sides had broken down, and the owners had posted notices terminating existing contracts on April 30th. The collision, against which MacDonald had warned six months before, was now only a matter of time. On April 29th, after several days of prodding by the Government, the owners reluctantly agreed that national agreements should continue, but only at the price of an increase in hours from seven to eight. The miners' slogan was 'Not a penny off the pay, not a minute on the day.' An increase in hours was as obnoxious to them as a cut in wages. This time, however, they did budge—though only fractionally. They rejected the owners' new proposals, but they made it clear that they would be willing to take part in further negotiations on how to implement the Samuel Report (thus implying that wages were not entirely sacrosanct), provided they had a firm guarantee that reductions would be accompanied by reorganization. For a while, it seemed possible that the deadlock might be broken. On Saturday, May 1st, the trade-union executives who had assembled in the Memorial Hall two days before voted by an overwhelming majority to hand over their autonomy to the General Council, and agreed that notices should go out for a national strike to begin at 11.59 p.m. on Monday, May 3rd. With evident relief, the miners' executive saw this as a sign that the die had been cast, and disappeared to their districts. The General Council, however, was still determined to reach a settlement if it could. Over the weekend, its representatives spent several weary, but not wholly unproductive, hours in further talks with ministers: and it was not until just after midnight on Sunday that the Government broke the negotiations off, on the grounds that the compositors at the *Daily Mail* had refused to set an allegedly inflammatory editorial entitled: 'For King and Country'.[60]

For MacDonald, it must have been a black moment. He had fought the idea of a general strike since its reappearance in labour politics before the war, and he had fought the attitudes behind it since his twenties. In the weeks leading up to the crisis, his role had inevitably been both limited and frustrating. Towards the end of March, he had quarrelled bitterly with Cook, who had announced patronizingly and inaccurately at a public meeting that MacDonald and the Labour Party had pledged themselves to follow the miners' lead on the conduct of the dispute,[61] but in public he had felt obliged to support the union. The true lesson of the Samuel Report, he insisted, was that public opinion should rise up in 'moral indignation' to demand nationalization of the business; whatever recommendations it might contain, it proved that wage reductions would never put the industry on an efficient footing.[62] At the end of April, he and Henderson took part in some of the discussions between the Government and the T.U.C. negotiating committee, and were present at the executives' conference at the Memorial Hall. At the famous meeting on May 1st, which authorized the dispatch of strike notices, he made what Walter Citrine, the T.U.C. general secretary, later described as a 'glorious speech'.[63] But he had no influence on policy, and his public support for the miners was accompanied by growing private anxiety. On May 2nd, as the last, faint hope of a settlement ebbed away, he noted in his diary:

Wonderfully serious & spiritually united Conference sat for two days in Memorial Hall ... Miners' plea that they were defending general standard of life of workers has united T.U.'s with them, and as the real problem of breakdown of mining industry has been dealt with in propaganda minds & by stunt phrases, we are up against the hard face of impossibility as miners cannot budge from 'not a shilling & not a minute' formula. The Government has woefully mismanaged the whole business ... But the T.Us have been equally blameworthy: 1. Miners' impossible formula. 2. Allowing themselves to fall into general strike psychology. General strike declared & at the meeting of T.U. General Council yesterday evident no forethought. No definite idea of what they are to consider as satisfactory to enable them to finish & go back to work. Position wonderfully like 1914. Strike cannot settle purely economic problem of bankruptcy of industry. Were it to be 'won' industry remains bankrupt. Employers in the various trades may not remain passive, but may raise own trade matters. Will strike continue to help section after section? At T.U. Gen: Council Meetings men like Bevin, Thomas etc. saw this and were plainly trying to avoid it. Question raised: How far could they pledge miners to accept a readjustment of wages. But alas, miners' executive gone home & Cook who alone is in town declined responsibility of answering for them. Rightly! It really looks tonight as though there was [sic] to be a General Strike to save Mr. Cook's face. Important man! ... The election of this fool as miners' secretary looks as though it would be the most calamitous thing that ever happened to the T.U. movement. The chief criminal, however, is the Government.[64]

Now Baldwin and his colleagues had left the T.U.C. with no honourable way out. MacDonald appears to have decided to swallow his own misgivings and to concentrate on keeping his followers together. On Monday May 3rd, Bevin, Pugh and the miners' leaders, Smith, Cook and Richardson, agreed on a compromise formula to be put to the Government. It was turned down by the miners' executive, but accepted by the General Council; and Bevin still hoped that it would provide the basis for a deal which would make it possible for the strike notices to be withdrawn. He gave a copy of the formula to Frederick Leggett of the Ministry of Labour, and another to MacDonald, who was to speak in the House that evening. The Government were told that MacDonald would probably refer to Bevin's formula in his speech, in order to find out the Government's attitude.[65] MacDonald, however, said nothing about it and confined himself to a vague offer that the Labour Party would be prepared to help in 'further explorations'. Most of his speech, moreover, was devoted to a powerful defence of the miners' position, and although he ended with an appeal to the Government to make a last effort to avoid disaster, the passage on the central problem of miners' wages was not at all conciliatory:

> The miner says 'I must defend my standard of life'. Whether he defends it by complicated methods of calculating his wages or not, is no matter; there is no complicated calculation required for the money he gets at the end of the week. There is no complicated calculation in the little group of pay-sheets which I have showing these wages — £1 8s 9d., £2 0s 9d., £2 11s 2d., £2 1s 3d., £1 5s 5d., and £1 5s 5d. If ... these figures were your incomes — there is not a single one of you that would be very pliable if the proposition was made to reduce those wages, and if the proposition was made to you to reduce much higher wages, you would be very careful that you did not entertain the proposition without careful investigation first of all.[66]

Later that evening, he and Henderson made a personal approach to Baldwin and Churchill, when they may have been more conciliatory.[67] If so, it served no purpose. At midnight, the strike notices took effect, and when he got back to Hampstead from Westminster MacDonald noted despondently, 'Just home by tube for last time — for how long?'[68]

VI

The answer came all too soon. Working men and women responded to their leaders' call with great loyalty and unselfishness, but it soon became clear that their leaders did not know what to do next. Like nuclear weapons in our own day, the general strike turned out to be too destructive for anything short of total war. Ministers insisted that the strike was unconstitutional, and the T.U.C. insisted with equal vehemence that it was not. This semantic fog obscured the real problem. Only the miners were in dispute with their own employers. Whatever the T.U.C. might say, the rest of the trade-union movement was striking against the Government. If the Government gave way, it would tacitly acknowledge that it was no longer the supreme authority in the state. The T.U.C. faced the same problem in reverse. The economy had now been paralysed, and could not be paralysed all over again. On the other hand, essential services were maintained and essential supplies got through. If the T.U.C. tried to disrupt them, it might provoke the Government into using force and would certainly encourage Conservative diehards to press for punitive measures against trade unionism. If it did not, the Government would sooner or later win. On May 7th, the General Council began to look for an escape route; and on May 8th, MacDonald noted:

11. T.U.C. General Council. Negotiating Committee reported conference with nameless gentleman who is Herbert Samuel ... 3. Took Henderson to Miners' headquarters in Russell Square & discussed situation with H. Smith & Cook. Found them unimaginative but reasonable. Verbally admit this not only miners' strike, but yet all action is based upon miners' mentality ... They will accept temporary readjustment in wages provided base & subsistence not lowered. Every such conversation shows with greater force the criminality of the Government in its handling of the Situation ... 6.20 Returned General Council. Negotiating Committee reported interview with Samuel (mentioning his name for the first time) ... S. told how, a fortnight before he had offered to return & help in the negotiations but his services were declined by the Government. He made certain proposals as a basis of agreement and the Negotiating Committee thought they might be effective. But S. then told them that he had seen the P.M. & that the P.M. had said he could hold neither direct nor indirect negotiations with anyone whilst general strike lasted.[69]

Samuel and the T.U.C. negotiating committee spent the next three days searching for a formula combining wage reductions with reorganization, which the miners and the Government could both accept. Inevitably, they failed. With good reason, the miners distrusted the Government and the coal owners so deeply that no conceivable formula could satisfy them. They stuck to their guns, and refused to discuss wage reductions in any form. Baldwin also stuck to his guns and refused to negotiate until the strike was called off. Meanwhile, the fragile unity of the first days of the strike rapidly broke down. The miners suspected that the negotiating committee was planning to betray them. The other union leaders suspected that the miners were trying to drag them into a full-scale war which they did not want to fight. On May 11th, in an atmosphere of recrimination, muddle and mistrust, the General Council decided to end the strike, on the vague understanding that the memorandum which the negotiating committee had agreed with Samuel would somehow provide the basis for a settlement. The miners fought on.

MacDonald's role in these events was as peripheral as it had been before the strike began. He protested to the B.B.C. about the biased nature of its broadcasts, but his request to be allowed to broadcast himself was turned down.[70] He spoke in the House of Commons debate on the emergency powers proclamation, and made a rather muddled appeal to the House as a whole to 'supplement goodwill and common sense and see whether we cannot settle it'.[71] Through Baldwin's parliamentary private secretary, Captain Herbert, he did what he could to persuade the Government not to break off all communication with Samuel and the negotiating committee.[72] For the most part, however, he was a spectator, albeit in a ringside seat. He was present at the meetings of the General Council, but he had no say in its decisions, and he was forced to watch impotently from the sidelines as it slithered towards defeat. Yet his reactions are of great interest, both for the light they throw on the crisis itself, and for the light they throw on his actions afterwards.

As one would expect, he agreed with the General Council's decision to make peace and shared its growing exasperation with the miners. It seemed as obvious to him as it did to Bevin and the negotiating committee, and as it had appeared to do to the miners' leaders themselves for a fleeting moment on the eve of the strike, that there could be no settlement without some reduction in wages at some time. But, although he was exasperated with the miners' refusal to 'face the objective facts', as he put it in his dairy, he recognized that another reason for their stubbornness was that they did not trust the Government or the coal owners. To him, the real moral of the split between the General Council and the miners was not that the miners were being pig-headed, but that a general strike was bound to fail; the right solution to it was not just to end the general strike but to 'clear decks of everything except miners' claims', and provide them with financial assistance while they fought the lockout. Above all, he was more apprehensive about the consequences of the General Council's final decision than those who took it could allow themselves to be.[73] The T.U.C., he noted on May 10th, 'have little appreciation yet of the difficulties they have to surmount in declaring the strike off and returning to work',[74] and in a long diary entry on May 11th he noted:

> This was evidently the final day. The G.C. saw that there was no end to the road on which it was travelling. The negotiating Committee returned to Sir H. Samuel, amended & expanded yesterday's draft, returned to Ecc. Square & the General Council decided to accept it & call the strike off. This took the day. At 8 p.m. the Miners' Executive came & a joint sitting was held. Pugh opened in a firm speech in which he said: 'This may be the

last time we sit together'. It was not tactful however & put up the miners' backs. Herbert Smith believed that the document had been imposed by somebody upon the G.C., that they had been sold. Pugh's reply unfortunately was awkward & had I not known what had happened it would have increased my suspicions. The scene was tense & sometimes the silent instants in speeches were painful. After expressing ill will for the document H. Smith said 'In that spirit we shall retire & consider the answer we shall give to you'. It was after 11 before this ended & they retired. Smith had been brutal in his contempt and opposition. He was offended that no Miners' representative had been present that day in the final discussions with Samuel; he treated as nothing apparently the help the others had given to the miners; he put the backs of the G.C. up. When the miners went angry speeches upon their 'stupidity', ingratitude, and &c., were made, & not a friend had they. The G.C. was absolutely unanimous & angry & determined. We waited long & the miners returned at 12.45 with a rude rejection. Smith also said that as they had not been consulted in the latter stages of the negotiation they might not consider themselves bound by their promise to continue to act with the T.U.C. what ever its decision may be ... Then came furious speeches on T.U.C. standing together to a man, consideration of some points for tomorrow, a final decision to call the General Strike off, and the making of an appointment with the P.M. for noon. Departed at 1.40 a.m. & thus ended one of the most lamentable adventures in crowd self leadership of our labour history. There will be a mess & I am sure the men will not understand their leaders. The return to work will be dangerous, the Churchill gang will shout & yell, provocation will be rampant, our troubles may be beginning ... The Samuel document may not be worth the paper it is written upon, but it has enabled the G.C. to face the inevitable. My task now is to protect the political party from the same crowd rush of emotion which has brought the G.C. to this sorry pass.[75]

On May 12th, the strike was called off. That afternoon Baldwin was wildly cheered in the House of Commons. 'He made his announcement like a hypocritical party leader ... ,' MacDonald noted indignantly. 'What is the value of the Samuel document? That troubles me.'[76] Next day the situation seemed still worse. In the morning, MacDonald went to Eccleston Square and found the General Council in session. 'Reports show utter confusion,' he noted later. 'Employers imposing impossible conditions of work. Provocation everywhere on street and newspapers wicked. Surrender described as unconditional and rioting possible.' Later that day there was a party meeting. '[D]ismayed and unhappy,' MacDonald noted. 'Urged them to refuse rigidly to take responsibility for anything, but to use H. of C. to get settlement.'[77]

That afternoon he spoke to a packed House, his object being, as he put it in his diary, to 'get Baldwin to say some more pieties about peace and to make it plain unions not beaten. Thus employers may be influenced.' He began by appealing to Baldwin's better instincts, and then switched to a less conciliatory note:

> The Prime Minister spoke yesterday. There is, unfortunately a great contrast between what he said yesterday and what is in the 'British Gazette' this morning. I think it is a great pity that that should be so, a profound pity. It is not helpful, it is only provocative, and I am rising to ask whether a change cannot take place ...
>
> ... Threats are the last thing I should think of, but let there be no mistake about this, if there is any attempt to smash up trade unionism, if any section of the country or any foolish person in the country thinks that after the events of last week and yesterday he can scrape the faces of trade unionists in the dust he is very much mistaken. We want no guerilla warfare to begin ... We want no resentment left behind. But if that is going to be avoided, it has got to be avoided by treating men as independent, self-respecting working men, who are not going to crawl back ... with the yoke of absolute subordination riveted to their necks.[78]

MacDonald's speech, coupled with representations from the General Council the night before, may have had some effect. Baldwin declared that he would not countenance any attempt to force down wages or to attack trade unions as such.[79] Next day, MacDonald was more optimistic. 'P.M.'s statement to House showed great improvement,' he noted. 'The Unions are getting out of this all right.' With affectionate malice he added, 'Thomas rang me & spoke through tears. He had been photographed with the railway managers & feels that the old happy world has returned.'[80]

CHAPTER 19

Regaining the initiative

I

AFTER two months as a spectator of events beyond his control, and eighteen months in which he had had to swim against the dominant current in labour politics, MacDonald now had an opportunity to take the offensive. For nine terrible days, the union leaders had found themselves staring over the edge of a precipice which they had never seriously intended to reach. They had retreated as soon as they could. Having retreated, they began to march down the hill up which they had marched during the previous two years. Direct action and the class war fell out of favour: class collaboration took their place. In 1927, only a few more than one million working days were lost in strikes, as against nearly eight million in 1925. By 1928, some of the most influential union leaders in the country, with Bevin in the van, were engaged in the so-called Mond–Turner talks with leading employers, in an attempt to find mutually agreed solutions to the problems of industrial reconstruction and foreign competition. The change of climate did not come all at once, but it was clear within a few weeks of the strike that the chief threat to MacDonald's political strategy had disappeared. For the first time since the general election, there was a possibility that the working-class pendulum might swing back to politics and that the political wing of the movement might regain the electoral support which the cry of Bolshevism had lost it in 1924.

Yet it was far from easy for MacDonald to translate these possibilities into facts. The failure of the strike had created dangers for the parliamentary party as well as opportunities. The first and most obvious was that the unions might be so crippled by victimization and hostile legislation that they would have no energies to spare for politics. The second was that ordinary trade unionists might be so demoralized by their leaders' surrender that they would sink back into apathy or bitterness. A third and more subtle danger, of which the Mond–Turner talks were an example, was that the unions might swing back, not to political action of the kind MacDonald wanted, but to business unionism on the American pattern and to a new version of the Lib-Lab attitudes which he had fought so often in the past. A fourth was that the movement might tear itself to pieces in mutual recrimination. Thus, MacDonald had to walk delicately if he was to take advantage of the opportunity that faced him. He had to do what little he could to protect the unions and their members from the consequence of their defeat. He had to keep the movement together, and avoid encouraging a futile search for scapegoats. At the same time, he had to show that, although industrial action had failed, parliamentary action could still succeed. Above all, he had to appeal to the uncommitted voters whose support Labour would need if it was to dislodge the Government from power.

It was a complex and difficult role, and it would be a mistake to suggest that MacDonald played it with complete success. Privately, as he told George Kerr a few days after the strike, he was 'very sick of things', and convinced that the 'hot air merchants as you call them will have to be kept in their places in future'.[1] In public he was more discreet. He was careful not to attack the trade-union leaders, and bent over backwards to praise the loyalty and courage of ordinary trade unionists. But even in public, a wounding note of 'I told you so' sometimes crept into his comments. In an article in Forward, he described the general strike as a 'glowing point in the history of British Labour', but added pointedly that it was now clear that industrial action could be used for political purposes only 'with arms in our hands'.[2] In the Socialist Review, he urged a 'thorough reconsideration of trade-union tactics', and argued that the blame for the failure of the strike lay with those who had 'induced the workers to blunder into it'.[3] The result was another quarrel with Bevin, who was even more sensitive to criticism than MacDonald was himself, and who regarded the trade-union movement as a closed preserve which mere politicians were not allowed to enter. At the beginning of June, Bevin wrote a long letter to Arthur Henderson, announcing that he could not continue to support the Labour Party so long as 'Mr J. R. MacDonald as its leader continues his present policy in relation to the industrial side', and demanding that the matter be placed before the National Executive. According to Bevin's biographer, Henderson brought the two men together and tried to patch the quarrel up.[4] The results were disappointing. On June 10th, MacDonald noted cryptically in his diary that Bevin was 'trying to come to the fore', and on the 22nd that the chief trouble with the General Council was 'the vain Mr Bevin'.[5] On June 23rd, he recorded a still more depressing development:

> Henderson came to my room to tell me someone had told him I had talked to Thomas in an unfriendly way about him—had blamed him for conspiring with Bevin against me ... How far we have to go; how well I understand why the Israelites took forty years to go from Egypt to Canaan.[6]

Yet, in spite of occasional failure of tact and errors of judgment, MacDonald succeeded where success mattered most. Under his leadership, the 'dismayed and unhappy' Labour Party of May 1926 recovered its unity and momentum; little by little, one of the strongest Conservative Governments of the century was forced on to the defensive. For most of the summer and autumn, politics were dominated by the long, hard and lonely struggle of the miners. It rapidly became clear that the owners would be satisfied with nothing short of unconditional surrender. If necessary, they were prepared to starve the miners out, even at the cost of great damage to themselves and greater damage to their industry. They demanded not one pound of flesh, but three—lower wages, longer hours and the abandonment of national agreements as well. Against this, the miners' only weapons were their own powers of endurance and their loyalty to each other and to their leaders. As they saw it, they had been abandoned by the other unions and betrayed by the General Council. Their response was not unlike the response of the British people as a whole to the fall of France in 1940: 'Very well, alone.' They tightened their belts, and waited.

At first, the Government tried to discover a compromise solution, based on the Samuel memorandum. It failed, for the same reason that Samuel had failed. The miners were not prepared to accept present reductions as the price of future reorganization, even if the reorganization were guaranteed. The owners were equally unwilling to accept reorganization without a struggle which a Government committed to the principle of private ownership could hardly wage. Rebuffed by the miners, the Government slowly drifted closer to the owners, even though the owners had rebuffed them too. Baldwin resisted the owners' pressure for a while, but in June he finally agreed to bring in legislation allowing them to reimpose the eight-hour day. It was a fatal concession. Until then, he had appeared to the general public as a man of peace, standing above class conflict. Now it seemed that the Government had ranged itself alongside the owners, in a final attempt to force the miners to their knees. For the first time for nearly two years, the Conservatives could be presented as the party of class war, and Labour as the party of reason and moderation.

MacDonald was outraged by what he saw as a surrender to the die-hards in the Cabinet. For him, it was 1916 or 1917 all over again. The chance of a compromise peace had been thrown away: Baldwin was trying to smash the miners as Lloyd George had tried to smash the Germans. Before the introduction of the eight-hour Bill he had been, as he put it in his diary, 'appalled at the way the miners' case is being handled and the unnecessary suffering entailed on the miners and the nation by the sheer incompetence of the leaders'. At some risk to himself, he had persuaded the respected miners' M.P., Vernon Hartshorn, to try to hammer out a compromise settlement with Cook.[7] Now he noted angrily that Baldwin's statement announcing that the eight-hour Bill was to be introduced was 'despair. It showed Govt. abandoning the position of negotiator and coming down against men. What little hope I had in the Hartshorn–Cook negotiations has gone.'[8] '[W]e have been wondering what Baldwin's position is,' he noted savagely a few days later. 'It is still generally assumed that he is honest and that he tries to be the fairminded humane man of easy-going goodwill. If this be so, his weakness is pathetic.'[9] The Government, he wrote in Forward, had abandoned 'every pretence of working for the nation

as a whole, of holding an even balance between rival interests, and of maintaining the position of an arbiter'; its policy was 'the knock-out blow and peace
by surrender'.[10] The eight-hours Bill, he declared in the second reading debate
at the end of June, was 'purely an owners' bill ... This is not peace; this is a
sword.'[11]

As MacDonald knew only too well, however, the Labour Party could not
defeat the Bill; and it could not even reverse it later without the support of a
wider public. Like all party leaders, he had to speak to two different audiences
at once – to the angry and passionate Labour backbenchers behind him, and
to uncommitted voters who had no particular allegiance to the miners, but
who might be shocked by the callous way in which the Government was
treating them. As the lockout dragged on, and the suffering in mining districts
grew worse, it began to look as though he had a receptive audience. Labour
candidates did better at by-elections than they had done since the general
election. In mid-July, a deputation of Church leaders tried unsuccessfully to
persuade Baldwin to renew the subsidy, so that the men could go back to work
on the old conditions while a compromise was hammered out. These were
straws in the wind, and when MacDonald replied to Baldwin in yet another
coal debate at the end of the month, it must have been with the welcome
sensation that public opinion was at last moving to his side:

> The Prime Minister ... finished by saying – how easy it is for any of us to
> say it – why cannot the two sides negotiate? Why? Very largely owing to
> the right hon. Gentleman himself ...
> ... The Government has had offer after offer and opportunity after
> opportunity given to it to make peace ... Again and again, the Prime
> Minister has said, here and outside, that he wishes for peace, and from the
> beginning of the struggle to this moment he has never lifted his little
> finger ... He has first of all handed over a weapon to the owners. He has
> equipped them with knuckle dusters. Then he comes up this afternoon,
> in the thirteenth week of this deplorable struggle, having armed one side,
> and says to both sides, 'Why not negotiate?'[12]

So far, ministers had been able to point in their own defence to the intransigence of the miners. In the middle of August, however, a special conference of
the Miners' Federation resolved by a narrow majority to empower the executive
to open negotiations with the owners and the Government. But the talks
between the miners and the owners broke down almost before they had
begun. The owners had the scent of victory in their nostrils. They were determined to smash the Federation and they refused even to negotiate on a national
basis. It was even clearer than it had been before that the two sides could not
resolve their differences on their own, and that the Government would have
to act if a settlement was to be reached. It was also clear that the miners were
facing not merely defeat, but a humiliating disaster in which their union might

be destroyed. MacDonald had already tried to intervene once before, and had been frustrated by the eight-hour Bill. He now decided to try again.

On August 30th, at what he described in his diary as a 'disappointing meeting' between the miners' executive and the executive of the parliamentary party, he urged the miners' leaders to ask their delegate conference for authority to negotiate on all the issues in the dispute. Next day, the House debated the Government's motion renewing its emergency powers. Before the debate, MacDonald had a brief conversation with Churchill, who was leading for the Government in Baldwin's absence. According to his diary, he 'urged him to be reasonable and told him if he were I could get final negotiations opened'.[13] In his speech a few minutes later he attacked the Government for taking the owners' side on wages and hours, but ended with a conciliatory passage urging it to 'go back to its old wisdom' and make another attempt to bring the two sides together.[14] Churchill's reply was equally conciliatory, and next day MacDonald persuaded the miners' executive to authorize him to try to reach an agreement with the Government about the basis on which negotiations could take place. Somewhat incongruously, he then paid a visit to Christie's sale room, and from there he telephoned Churchill to arrange a meeting. They agreed that he should motor down to Churchill's home at Chartwell that afternoon, and after he arrived they spent some hours in informal negotiations broken by dinner and what MacDonald described in his diary as a 'pleasant dinner talk on superstition & ghost topics'.[15] According to a note in the Churchill papers,

Mr MacDonald explained that the object of his visit was to see if he could develop the situation along the lines of the invitation in Mr Churchill's speech in the House of Commons ... He did not come as the authorised agent of the miners. No-one knew and no-one would know that he had come ... If, however, he was to undertake the task of trying to persuade the Delegate Conference to make 'real proposals', he thought that it was only right that he should have some private assurance as to what the Government would regard as proposals of such a nature as to require them to fulfil their promise to call a conference. Would some general undertaking to discuss wages and hours be sufficient? He did not suggest that proposals that ruled out any discussion of hours could be expected to be treated as 'real proposals'. As to district variations he saw no difficulty. He would not disclose the fact that he had the authority of the Government for saying that the formula agreed upon would be acceptable, but would consider himself at liberty to say that he had good reason to believe that that was so.

Mr Churchill said that this was a request which it was quite impossible for the Government to refuse ... But it must be understood that all the Government could commit themselves to if the formula was accepted by the men was to invite the owners and men to a tripartite conference. It was quite likely that the owners ... might refuse to come, or, if they did come, might take a line that would make progress impossible. If they put themselves in the wrong in this way, the Government would make no secret of their opinion that they were in the wrong, but the powers of actual coercion that the Government possessed were very limited.

Mr MacDonald said ... he was quite content with that.[16]

In the end, Churchill and MacDonald agreed on a formula by which the miners would declare that they were prepared to negotiate on wages and hours, that they stood for national agreements 'in accordance with the established custom of the Federation', but that they recognized the need for district variations.[17] In spite of the concession on district variations, the vital principle of national negotiations had been preserved, and Churchill, at any rate, was morally committed to it. MacDonald left Chartwell after midnight and arrived home at two o'clock in the morning, well pleased with his day's work.[18]

Next day, the miners' delegate conference authorized the executive to 'submit proposals for the setting up of a National Agreement for the Mining Industry'.[19] MacDonald gave Smith and Cook a copy of the formula he had agreed with Churchill and agreed to meet the miners' leaders at noon the following day, after the executive had had time to consider it. On September 3rd, as he noted later, he met the executive again:

> Long discussion on a resolution they had passed. Awkwardly worded & did not express meaning of Executive. Pointed that out with knowledge of what was in their minds, & telephoned Churchill to come up at once & arranged meeting at Abe Bailey's house at 3 p.m. ... Saw Churchill. Began by pouring out his difficulties. Asked him if he stood by our Wednesday night/Thursday morning agreement. Said he did. We discussed the Miners' resolution which I showed him & explained it. He went to see colleagues & I returned to Russell Square ... 3.30 rang me up and asked me to take the four miners' officials to Abe Baileys to see him. Executive agreed providing meeting was informal & no part of ultimate negotiations with owners. Met him with Tom Jones at 6 & he produced a new formula based on our conversation. One verbal alteration was made & one provision about district agreements struck out on my suggestion & by keeping them severely to business agreement was reached within half an hour (Oh for a rope for the man who starts irrelevant talk without knowing what he is doing). Returned to Executive which had been adjourned till 7. Began business at 7.15. Explanations. At 7.30 agreement on the amended formula, letter dispatched to the Government and a hearty vote of thanks to myself. Went home for a bite, took Ishbel to a theatre & thus ended a day when I changed the whole strategic position of the miners. They have now the ball at their feet instead of it being at the owners'. Will they kick it for sure? I have given them their chance, & can go with my mind

relieved to Bournemouth tomorrow. Now that this stage is reached the past mishandling by the Government is more apparent than ever ... Perhaps I ought to have stepped in earlier but without an understanding with the Government such as I got on Wednesday night I could do nothing. It is also clear that the Eight Hours Act is the main obstacle to peace.[20]

In the final formula, the miners recognized the need for a reduction in labour costs. But there was no mention of district variations and it was made clear that the negotiations were to be 'for a new national agreement'.[21] As MacDonald pointed out in *Forward*, the miners could 'now hope anew. A national agreement can be preserved; the crushing defeat that was planned for them, which would have left them broken and disheartened for a short time and revengeful for a long time, will not happen.'[22]

It was a false dawn. The owners refused to negotiate nationally, and after much procrastination and confusion the Cabinet eventually decided not to coerce them. At the end of September, Baldwin told the House of Commons that he and his colleagues had 'got pretty well to the end of our powers for mediation', and made it clear that, for all practical purposes, the Government's only policy was to wait until the miners were beaten. MacDonald commented savagely:

Some weeks from now, it may be some months from now in some places ... the usual pilgrimage of miners down into the pits will be resumed, shepherded by despair and starvation. The owners will then call upon the Prime Minister and thank him for the great assistance that he has been to them, and they will review, I suppose, the stream of workmen coming and going – workmen whose risks of life and limb they have increased, whose poverty they have intensified, and whose sullenness they have darkened; and they will depart their ways, after their mutual congratulations, knowing that ... the result of their work has been to increase the hate and banish the hopes of peace and the feeling of goodwill from the minds of our people.[23]

By the end of the year, this prophecy had come true. The miners were forced back to work on the owners' terms; and the British working-class movement suffered one of the most terrible defeats of its history. The economic cost was incalculable. Export markets were lost; unemployment in the industry went up; the miners' standard of living went down. The cost in dignity and self-respect was even heavier. In some places, the union was almost broken. Everywhere, men were victimized and blacklisted. In mining districts, the scar has lingered to this day.

II

The moral seemed plain. The Miners' Federation was the strongest trade union in the country, yet it had suffered a humiliating defeat. It had been defeated not because its cause was bad or because its members were irresolute but because the Government of the day had supported the employers. It had always been clear that the Federation's ultimate aim of public ownership could be reached only through the ballot box. Now it seemed that it could not even defend its members' living standards unless a friendly Government was in power. Within a few months of the miners' defeat, the Government proceeded to teach a similar, though milder, lesson to the rest of the trade-union movement. In 1927, in the teeth of bitter opposition from the parliamentary Labour Party, it carried the Trade Disputes and Trade Union Act, which made general and sympathetic strikes illegal, substituted 'contracting-in' for 'contracting-out' and forbade established civil servants to join unions that were affiliated to the T.U.C. No doubt the damage to trade unionism was symbolic rather than real, but that did not make the lesson any less effective. By the summer of 1927, it seemed clear to most union leaders that they needed the Labour Party as much as the Labour Party needed them.

MacDonald welcomed the unions' change of mood from the sidelines but, after his brush with Bevin in the summer of 1926, he did his best to avoid sensitive toes, and took care not to interfere in trade-union affairs. In January 1927, he had another quarrel with A. J. Cook, who accused him of trying to discredit the miners and demanded to be told in writing why he had said, in a speech in the House, that the Federation was 'broken' and what he had meant by referring to 'Mr Cooke's incompetence'.[24] MacDonald replied contemptuously:

> Your extract about the Federation was incomplete and misleading. Hansard gives quite accurately what I said on that subject, including that the Federation would be built up and that its power would return to it.
>
> The extract regarding yourself is perfectly accurate. In all my experience of Trade Union leadership ... I have never known one so incompetent as yourself. I have no objection, however, to your sending this correspondence to the Press.[25]

In spite of his feelings about Cook, his behaviour towards Cook's union was scrupulously correct. Early in 1927, George Spencer, a Nottinghamshire miners' M.P. of moderate views, had the Labour whip withdrawn from him after he had been repudiated by the county miners' association and the Broxtowe Labour Party for forming a breakaway union. MacDonald had considerable sympathy for Spencer, and no love for Spencer's opponents. In a letter to Frank Lee, another Nottinghamshire Labour M.P., who had urged him to try to prevent a final breach between Spencer and the Labour Party, MacDonald wrote that it was 'very hard that men who had served us faithfully, building up the Party for a great many years, should be turned out because some person or movement has come along which has brought destruction near to us'.[26] But although he claimed that he had done all he could to keep Spencer in the party, his attempts to do so do not seem to have been at all energetic; and when a former Labour M.P. named T. S. B. Williams wrote to him to protest against Spencer's expulsion, he replied coldly that Spencer had 'forfeited the confidence of his Labour electors and his organised supporters', and made it clear that he was not prepared to take any further action on Spencer's behalf.[27]

His relations with the other unions followed a similar, though less stormy, pattern. In December 1926, George Hicks, the chairman of the T.U.C. for the year 1926–7, sent him the text of a speech he intended to make, calling for the establishment of a 'People's Congress', representing all sections of the Labour movement, to prepare a programme for an attack on poverty. MacDonald replied sympathetically, but non-commitally, that he had 'long felt the need for more cohesion in our movement', but that what was needed was an informal arrangement to 'rub knees oftener', not a new organization.[28] The tone of distant cordiality was symptomatic. MacDonald had always recognized that the Labour Party needed the unions, but he had always resisted the idea that it should be solely, or even mainly, a trade-union party; and although his tactics during the miners' strike must have been designed, at least in part, to encourage the unions to turn back to politics, he made no effort to court them. In an article in *Forward* just before the 1926 Labour Party conference, he commented approvingly that there was universal agreement among the delegates that 'the genius of destruction has brought the whole Trade Union movement "up against it". There is really nothing for it but to rally the political forces, strengthen them and prepare for victory. Such is the talk amongst Trade Unionists.'[29] Four months later, when the T.U.C. held a long-awaited conference of executives to consider the lessons of the general strike, he wrote pointedly, 'The result was never doubted by anyone who had the least glimmering of the facts. It is easy to keep up a show of the heroic when the fellow you are firing at is twenty miles off; when sword klinks on sword, the hero has to be more cautious.'[30] Apart from a few scattered comments of this sort, however, he was content to let the facts speak for themselves.

His patience was rewarded. Twenty-six years before, he had helped to persuade the unions that the remedy for the Taff Vale judgment lay in political action through the Labour Representation Committee; in doing so, he had begun the process by which the fragile 'Labour Alliance' of 1900 had developed into an effective electoral machine. Slowly, the same thing happened again. In July 1927, Bevin invited him to deliver a fraternal greetings from the Labour Party at the biennial Transport and General Workers' conference in Swansea.[31] By September 1927, he was able to write that the T.U.C. conference at Edinburgh was 'one of the best that has ever been held'.[32] The Labour Party conference a month later saw even more striking evidence of the unions' new attitude. MacDonald moved the Executive's resolution, reaffirming the Labour Party's commitment to nationalization of the mines. The experience of the last two years, he declared, had taught him:

> The mining industry was the most significant example they had of the absolute folly of private enterprise ... He was in the negotiations prior to the dispute. He saw the representatives of the Government and he was in close touch with them. The result had been that his mind was far narrower now than it was two years ago. He was compelled to admit – against what he liked, against what he had hoped – that there was a bitterness, a steel hand still behind the velvet glove ... He wanted to say to his miner friends, 'If you and we are spared together, we have got a big fight yet. You have been through it. God knows you have been through it, but you have not yet come to the end of it. Now we are going to stand shoulder to shoulder, and the fight is not only going to be against the owners ... '

The resolution was seconded by the dour, indomitable Herbert Smith. MacDonald's speech, he urged, should be printed and distributed to the public at large. 'Some of them', he added, 'had lived long enough to know that whenever Mr MacDonald put his hand to a thing it was to uplift the general ideas of the community and make the world a better place to live in.'[33]

III

Smith's tribute would have been echoed well beyond the hall where it was paid. By now, the humiliation of 1924 had been forgotten. Direct action was dead: in the parliamentary party, the mutterings against MacDonald's leadership had almost subsided. At the annual conferences of 1927 and 1928, he dominated his party as no leader has dominated it since.

Yet his position was not quite as strong as it looked. While the trade unions slowly swung back to gradualism and parliamentary action, the I.L.P. continued to move, raggedly but unmistakably, in the opposite direction. In April 1926, Maxton was elected as chairman; though he and Brockway did not get their way without opposition, they and their allies controlled the N.A.C. and increasingly determined the party's official line. Clifford Allen ceased to count, and his conception of the I.L.P. as a policy-making pressure group, in close and friendly touch with the leader of the Labour Party, was abandoned. For Maxton and Brockway, the I.L.P. was not primarily a policy-making body: it was the vanguard of a potentially revolutionary working class. There was no point in trying to convert MacDonald: it was necessary to fight him and to destroy his influence. Of course, Maxton and Brockway did not speak for the whole I.L.P. Some of MacDonald's supporters, like Shinwell, William Leach and Tom Johnston, still had great influence in it. Most I.L.P. members of parliament supported him. So did the Glasgow *Forward*, which Johnston edited and for which MacDonald still wrote a regular column. Outside Parliament, however, his supporters were in a minority; and as time went on, the minority grew weaker. The gulf between MacDonald and the N.A.C., which had been wide enough before Maxton's election, steadily widened; by 1929, his old political base had to be regarded, for all practical purposes, as hostile territory.

At one level, its hostility hardly mattered. The I.L.P. had no big battalions to deploy at the Labour Party conference: in that curiously deferential forum, its attacks on the leadership were beaten off with little difficulty. In the parliamentary party, they may have done MacDonald more good than harm. Then, as now, the trade-union ethic of group solidarity was an effective barrier to dangerous thought, and majority loyalties were more likely to be reinforced than undermined by the spectacle of a a dissident minority within the ranks. But, as MacDonald knew from his own experience, political strength cannot be measured solely in conference votes or applause at a party meeting. During the war, he had often been in a minority in the Labour Party, yet he had become leader of the party for a second time only four years after the war had ended. One reason was that he had been sustained emotionally and protected politically by the I.L.P. As Aneurin Bevan and Hugh Gaitskell were both to discover in different ways a generation later, the dedicated loyalty of a minority can be much more valuable to its leader than the size of the minority would suggest. From 1914 to 1922, the I.L.P. had given MacDonald the kind of loyalty which the Bevanites were to give to Bevan in the 1950s, and which Gaitskell was to receive from the Campaign for Democratic Socialism in the early 'sixties. Its revolt against him in the late 'twenties was a bitter personal blow. It was also a political setback, of greater importance than has sometimes been realized.

It had a wider significance as well. Partly because it was a personal blow, MacDonald took it extremely seriously himself and did all he could to combat it. In doing so, he dug himself more and more deeply into the ideological position which he had occupied at the beginning. Like all politicians, MacDonald sometimes changed his mind and did not always practise what he preached. But this was not because he thought preaching unimportant. Doctrine mattered to him as much as it had mattered to his Free Kirk grandmother. When he was confronted with a doctrine which he believed to be false, his instinctive reaction was to try to refute it; and he assumed, with touching, though no doubt exasperating, innocence, that the best way to refute it was to preach his own doctrine even more loudly than before. These traits gave his conflict with the Maxton–Brockway leadership of the I.L.P. an acerbity which a more tactful leader might have managed to avoid. They also gave it an ideological resonance which was not fully apparent at the time. For the issues at stake included not only the hardy perennial of parliamentary socialism as against the class war but the causes of and remedies for mass unemployment and, at a deeper level, the relationship between socialist values and what would now be called economic growth. MacDonald's doctrine is of enduring interest as a contribution to a debate which still continues today. It also throws a vivid, and in some ways an unexpected, light on his attitude to the problems which were to destroy his second Government.

Ironically enough, much of the ammunition for the N.A.C.'s attacks on MacDonald was supplied by one of Clifford Allen's 'commissions of inquiry' – the famous commission on the 'living wage'. The chairman was MacDonald's old associate, J. A. Hobson. The other members were H. N. Brailsford, the editor of the *New Leader*, E. F. Wise, a former wartime civil servant who was later to become a Labour M.P., and Arthur Creech-Jones, a research officer of the Transport and General Workers' Union, who ended his career as Attlee's colonial secretary. Their report was published in September 1926. It advocated a system of family allowances, to be paid for by taxation; the nationalization of the Bank of England, to secure state control of credit and monetary policy; and Government bulk purchase of foodstuffs and raw materials. But these were only the trimmings. The core of the report was a proposal to introduce a national minimum wage and to set up an Industrial Commission to reorganize the industries unable or unwilling to pay it. The resources needed to finance higher wages, the report emphasized, could not come from taxation. They would come instead from the increased production which higher wages would themselves call forth. For higher wages would lead to higher consumption; and the 'pressure of higher consumption', as Hobson called it, would force industry to produce more wealth and employ extra labour. With one blow, the 'living wage' would solve the unemployment problem and raise working-class living standards to a tolerable level.[34]

The 'living wage' report was a milestone in the history of the British left. In spite of oversimplifications and gaps in the argument, it pointed the way to the managed welfare capitalism which was to transform most of the western world after 1945: in approach, if not in detail, it offered the Labour movement at least the basis of a reformist alternative, both to revolutionary Marxism and to its existing unhappy mixture of utopian aspiration and fiscal orthodoxy. Before the commission had finished its work, however, the concept of the 'living wage' had acquired political overtones, which were, at bottom, incompatible with the economic assumptions on which the report was based. As Hobson saw it, the point of the 'living wage' was to eliminate the 'underconsumption' which he had always regarded as the root cause of unemployment. Once that had been done, the system would operate in the old way (though with the help of new machinery), and obey the old laws. Implicitly, if not explicitly, the report's economic proposals were based on the premiss that capitalism could be made to work: that the extra resources which were needed to raise the standard of living of the wage-earner could, and would, be produced by the normal processes of capitalist economics once the capitalists knew that there was a market for their products.

The most enthusiastic advocates of the 'living wage', however, were the left wing of the I.L.P.; and the left wing of the I.L.P. did not want to make capitalism work. In any case, they did not believe that it was possible to do so. Capitalism, Maxton declared in August 1925, was now on the verge of collapse, and could no longer be 'saved by repairs and patchwork'.[35] For him and his allies, the point of the 'living wage' campaign was not to squeeze concessions out of a bankrupt system, but to force a conflict in which the system would be destroyed. John Paton spoke for many when he wrote in his memoirs that his attitude to the 'living wage' proposals was one of 'enthusiastic acceptance. I did not greatly concern myself as to whether they were 'practical' or not. I looked upon them ... as first-class points of attack on Capitalism, and was certain that if we could only force a Labour Government to attempt their application, the real struggle for power and supremacy would be precipitated.'[36]

The campaign for a 'living wage' programme was launched in earnest in Brailsford's *New Leader* in January 1926, with the slogan 'Socialism in Our Day'. The object of the campaign, it wrote, was to 'challenge the deadening idea that Socialism can only be estabished by slow gradualism over generations of time'. The Bradford *Pioneer* put it more simply. The 'living wage' programme, it wrote, was 'An Alternative to Gradualism'. At the I.L.P. annual conference three months later, the N.A.C. put forward a composite resolution entitled 'Socialism in Our Time', embodying the interim proposals of the 'living wage' commission, together with the conclusions of other policy committees. The resolution called for a national 'living wage'; for the nationalization of the banks, the railways, the mines, the land, electricity generation, and the importation of food and raw materials; and for the payment, 'out of direct taxation, of supplements to working-class incomes, varying with the number of persons in each household'. It had become clear, the preamble declared, that 'the old order is breaking down' and that a resolute socialist policy was needed to 'carry us rapidly through the period of transition from the old to the new civilisation'.[37]

MacDonald was no stranger to the theory of 'under-consumption', on which the 'living wage' proposals were based, and which had provided much of the inspiration for his speeches on the I.L.P.'s 'right to work' Bill twenty years before. His knowledge of economics was superficial, and he was too cautious a man to defy established opinion in a field in which he had no claim to expertise. Snowden was still the Labour Party's chief financial spokesman in the House of Commons, and MacDonald would have needed a good deal of persuasion to challenge Snowden's bleak certainties head-on. Yet his own approach was quite different from Snowden's. Where Snowden regarded any departure from strict free-trade orthodoxy as mischievous folly, MacDonald still had a good deal of sympathy for Hobsonian economics and welcomed new thinking

on such matters as the gold standard and the control of credit. To Sir Oswald
Mosley, who had already become one of the Labour Party's leading exponents
of expansionist economics, he described Keynes's famous pamphlet attacking
the return to gold, *The Economic Consequences of Mr Churchill*, as a 'smart piece
of work';[38] to Mosley's lieutenant, John Strachey, he wrote vaguely, but
benignly, 'I am sure you are right in the value that you put upon the question
of money and credit.'[39] When Sir Otto Niemeyer asked him to sign a message
congratulating the National Savings Committee on its tenth anniversary and,
among others things, paying tribute to the social importance of saving,
MacDonald replied:

> It is a pretty tall order to ask me to sign a message couched in the language
> of the one which has been drafted ... Consider, for instance, your fifth
> paragraph, and how it would be read by an intelligent working man who
> accepts, say J. A. Hobson's political economy ... [T]he smug spirit and
> self-satisfied talk of the whole thing ... can quite likely be objected to not
> only by the man in the street, but also by the better educated sections of
> the Party which I represent.[40]

But although he did not object to the economic assumptions of the 'living
wage' report, he could hardly fail to object to the political assumptions behind
the campaign for 'Socialism in Our Time'. Socialism was, by definition, a plant
of slow growth; and it would grow out of the success of capitalism, not out
of its failure. Attempts to force the pace could end only in disaster. He had
preached these views since the turn of the century; and nothing had happened
since to make him change his mind. What the *New Leader* denounced as a
'deadening idea' had been the central premiss of his political philosophy for
thirty years. In the *Socialist Review* for March 1926, he condemned the 'Socialism
in Our Time' proposals, on the grounds that they would be like 'millstones'
around the parliamentary party's neck. In *Forward* he declared, in language
which might have been taken straight from his writings twenty-five years
before, 'The real distinction between the evolutionist and the revolutionist is
that the former believes that Socialist growth is to come from the vigorous
activities of society forcing new forms of life, whilst the latter uses the unhealthy
and dead parts ... These policies may be good or bad in themselves, but they
will have to be decided on their merits. They are not Socialism.'[41] In spite of
his opposition, however, the I.L.P. conference in April 1926 adopted the
'Socialism in Our Time' resolution as its official policy. The new leadership of
the I.L.P., MacDonald commented privately, was 'cheapening the whole
movement and misleading it with superficial stuff'.[42] To an invitation from
John Paton to speak at a conference on the new policy, he replied curtly, 'I can
speak at no conference to popularise absolutely meaningless phrases and to
mislead the whole of our Socialist movement.'[43]

Privately, he insisted that his quarrel was with the N.A.C., not with Hobso-

nian economics or even with the 'living wage' commission. In a long letter to
Margaret Bondfield at the end of March 1926, he explained that he distinguished
between the 'resolutions and manifestoes' issued by the I.L.P. head office, and
'research work' undertaken by party members who had given up a 'good deal
of time to the subject'. The former had 'no more weight than the opinions of
any other group of people interested in political tactics or points of view'. The
latter deserved the 'most careful consideration by everyone interested in the
progress of Socialism'.[44] In October, Hobson sent him a copy of the 'living
wage' report, with a remarkable covering letter, which made it clear that he
shared many of MacDonald's doubts about the whole enterprise. Hobson
explained, rather defensively:

> I was asked as an economist, not as a politician, to join the small Com-
> mittee which drew it up, and am not concerned with the use which may
> be made of it in the Labour Party or the Country ... In the Committee at
> an early stage I found some disposition to utilise the minimum wage in a
> way that seemed to me dangerous. Its present form is not I think at all
> open to such criticisms. How far all its proposals are financially practicable
> I do not feel sure, but in this country it is necessary to formulate fairly
> drastic proposals in order to get *anything* done.[45]

MacDonald replied sympathetically:

> I am exceedingly obliged to you for your letter about the pamphlet on the
> living wage. I have glanced through it and it is as I expected an admirable
> economic document which requires the most careful consideration by
> everyone who has responsibility for policy. I did not believe for a moment
> that you were supporting the use that is being made of it by Brailsford.
> The politics that have become associated with it are really deplorable.
> I do not know what has possessed our friend; the only word I can use
> regarding his recent outburst is that he has become cranky.[46]

But by now, the economic theory of the 'living wage' hardly mattered. What
mattered was 'Socialism in Our Time'; and it mattered less as a programme
than as a weapon in a struggle for power.

IV

The details of the struggle need not concern us. The summer of 1926 was taken
up by a long and dreary squabble between MacDonald and Fenner Brockway
about MacDonald's status as a member of the I.L.P. delegation to the Labour
Party conference. Unwisely, as it turned out, MacDonald fired the first shot
by explaining that he would be placed in an 'equivocal position' if he had to
oppose I.L.P. resolutions while serving as an I.L.P. delegate, and by trying to

get the N.A.C. to agree that he should serve on the delegation as a representative
of the 'large section' of I.L.P. opinion which agreed with him in opposing the
N.A.C.'s policies. Not surprisingly, the N.A.C. refused to do anything of the
kind. MacDonald, they insisted, was constitutionally entitled to serve on the
delegation, since he was the I.L.P.'s nominee as treasurer of the Labour Party.
It was up to him to decide whether or not to take advantage of this entitlement,
and it was on this rather unhappy basis that MacDonald attended the conference in the end.[47]

The next big skirmish took place at the Labour Party conference at Margate.
This time, the honours went to MacDonald. The I.L.P.'s resolution on the
living wage was so altered in the process of compositing that the Executive
was able to accept it. As proposed by Brailsford, it merely declared in general
terms that it was necessary to increase the 'purchasing power of the masses',
and requested the National Executive, if possible in co-operation with the
T.U.C. General Council, to appoint a commission of inquiry to consider what
methods should be adopted to establish the principle of the living income, and
what part the socialization of key services should play in the necessary industrial
reorganization. It contained no criticism of the 1924 Government and no
commitment to bind the next Labour Government. In his reply, MacDonald
assured the delegates, in tones of sweet reasonableness, that the Executive was
'never afraid of inquiry'; was, in fact, conducting a number of inquiries already;
and was quite happy to appoint yet another committee of inquiry if the conference wished. His own opinion, he added ominously, was that 'not much
good would be done by it.' The debate ended with John Wheatley vainly
trying to speak amid loud cries of 'Vote'. A motion to suspend standing orders
so that Wheatley could address the conference was lost by 1,629,000 to 654,000;
and Brailsford's resolution was then carried.[48] The committee of inquiry was
duly appointed, though only after a long delay; and after more delays, decided
that, since it would take several years to cover the whole field, it should restrict
itself to the more manageable question of family allowances.[49] When the
general election came in 1929, it had still not completed its work.

The N.A.C. had had its revenge long before then. In February 1927, Mac-
Donald gave up writing his monthly 'Outlook' for the *Socialist Review*, on the
grounds that he no longer felt that the I.L.P. was 'a good Socialist body, working in a disinterested way for the propagation of Socialist opinion'.[50] In March,
partly, perhaps, in retaliation, the N.A.C. at last decided that he should no
longer be nominated as the I.L.P.'s candidate for the treasurership of the
Labour Party. The decision was announced in a strangely apologetic fashion.
The N.A.C. issued a statement in the *New Leader*, explaining that they did not
wish to cause MacDonald any embarrassment, and that they wanted him to
remain as treasurer, even though they themselves were no longer prepared to
nominate him; Maxton pointed out that the I.L.P. delegation to the Labour
Party conference could still vote for him, and claimed that twenty-nine other

affiliated organizations would be prepared to nominate him instead.[51] Apologetic or not, however, the decision hurt MacDonald a great deal – the more so, since the N.A.C. had also decided that he should not be invited to address the demonstration on the eve of the I.L.P. annual conference, which was to be held that year in Leicester. He wrote an indignant letter to John Paton, pointing out that the N.A.C.'s official explanation of the decision did not mention their refusal to ask him to speak 'in a place which has pre-eminently been my own field of work'.[52] In *Forward*, he confessed that the many letters he had received 'from old comrades in arms ... touch my heart'.[53] To Arthur Salter, who had organized a letter of support for him, which was signed by sixty I.L.P. members of Parliament, he wrote:

> In addition to the document which you have already signed ... I am receiving letters from friends in the country and branches of the Party. All this touches me very keenly ... I am most grateful to you and your friends and will ever cherish the memory of what you have done.[54]

Yet in spite of this slap in the face, MacDonald did not leave the I.L.P. altogether, as Snowden did in 1927. He played no part in its organization, stayed away from the annual conference, cancelled his subscription to the *New Leader* and refused even to send it a goodwill message at Christmas time. But he still intervened assiduously in the party's affairs; he still devoted the lion's share of his columns in *Forward* to the developments that took place in it; above all, he still hankered visibly after a return to his old relationship with it. As late as 1929, he was to be found urging Shinwell to stand against Maxton for the chairmanship,[55] receiving reports from William Leach about the state of feeling in the Bradford branch,[56] and explaining to the Leicester branch, which had nominated him as its delegate to the I.L.P. conference at Easter, that he would 'like very much to go', but felt that under the circumstances it was best for him to 'keep out'.[57] In October 1926, he had explained to Clifford Allen:

> Taking the Party as a whole ... it is the most inspiring thing of our time but, unfortunately, right at its centre is a seething nucleus of pettifogging egotisms which every now and then almost makes life unbearable ... I am particularly disturbed about the I.L.P. Wherever I go I find wonder and irritation at its methods. I still believe it would be a real calamity to our movement if it were abandoned, and yet if it cannot do better than it is now doing I think I shall have to give it up. I understand that there is to be an attempt to get a better N.A.C. elected next year, and for that I shall wait.[58]

He was still waiting three years later, but he still could not bring himself to break the ties of thirty-five years.

V

One reason was simply that ties which have been in existence for thirty-five years are in any case hard to break. Another was that the I.L.P. still had great influence on opinion in the Labour Party. No Labour leader who wished to retain his hold on the loyalty of ordinary party members could simply ignore the campaign for 'Socialism in Our Time'. If he opposed it, he had to explain why and convince his followers that he was right. But there was more to MacDonald's attitude than this. Soon after the 1925 I.L.P. conference he told Walton Newbold, who had left the Communist Party to become a passionate MacDonaldite, 'I can understand a conscious revolutionist although I profoundly disagree with him, but I neither agree with nor understand those who run a policy which can only result in revolution at the same time that they have condemned revolutionary methods.'[59] This, MacDonald insisted again and again, was exactly what the Maxton–Brockway leadership of the I.L.P. were doing. Their campaign only made sense on the assumption that Britain was ripe for revolution, an assumption which the general strike had just disproved. They were making the same mistake as the German general staff, which had tried to get to Paris through Belgium—'undoubtedly, on paper, the shortest route'.[60] No doubt they did not realize this themselves, but that only made their campaign more dangerous. For it was only too easy to create 'for propaganda purposes ... a situation from which there is no evolutionary way'.[61] That road could lead only to disaster. Even the Bolsheviks had discovered that socialism was still two generations away. If a British Labour Government tried to emulate them, they would sooner or later 'have to suppress freedom and publication, probably increase their staff of prison warders, and annex some remote island, not to exploit it but to people it with exiles'.[62]

If revolution were ruled out, only persuasion remained. The incentive to engage in socialist propaganda, MacDonald wrote in April 1927, was that 'if we can get people to think and act socialistically, Socialism is at our doors, and many of our practical problems will disappear, because they are problems not of things themselves, but in the minds of the public.'[63] Or, as he put it in a diary entry in June 1926, 'The mentality that by attack from outside the walls of Capitalism are to fall is also spreading, contrary to the proper I.L.P. conception that changes in form follow changes in internal—eg. intellectual & moral—desires.'[64] That was what he meant when he told Clifford Allen that the disappearance of the I.L.P. would be a 'calamity to our movement'. For the Labour Party—immersed, as it was, in a day-to-day struggle for power—could never 'get people to think socialistically' or achieve the 'internal' changes without which socialism would be impossible. That could be done only by a disinterested body of propagandists, solely concerned to preach the gospel.

That was the proper role for the I.L.P., and if the I.L.P. refused to play it, no one else would play it instead.

He returned to this theme again and again. The I.L.P., he wrote in January 1928, had denegerated into another 'Labour political party and is obscuring its Socialism as much as the Labour Party itself does'.[65] This was damaging, not only to the I.L.P., but to socialism as well. For socialism could be achieved only if people were persuaded to think socialistically, and they could be persuaded only by a specialized body, remote from the day-to-day struggle for power. The social and economic changes of the last ten years had made such a body more necessary, not less – partly because many old ideas were now out of date, and partly because Labour's political success had tied the Labour Party more closely to the values and assumptions of the society around it. As he put it in a long and unusually relaxed *Forward* column in August 1928:

Our pre-war armoury has many muzzle-loading guns in it and should be thoroughly examined and brought up to date. This can only be done by a body charged with the job ...

Moreover, in the day-to-day conflict between ... evolving Capitalism and its victims, the Socialist vision is apt to be obscured in dust ... A political party cannot be the best guardian of Socialist thought and criticism because it is bound in the very nature of things to deal with daily problems and to see these problems out of proportion to the remote whole ...

... When a Socialist Party becomes responsible for either Opposition or Government, it runs the risk of identifying the success of Socialism with the expediences in the art of patching and puttying, which it is part of its duty to study and practise ...

... It is because the I.L.P. is becoming more and more a mere political party ... that Socialists are becoming increasingly doubtful of its utility. When it comes to be a question of politics, of methods ... the I.L.P. is much less likely to be right than is the National or Parliamentary Executive of the Labour Party. When it is a question of the propaganda of Socialism, the I.L.P. ... is much more likely to be energetic and clear visioned than any political headquarters ...

... As a wing of a political party, the I.L.P. will sink into insignificance ... [A]s the maker of social opinion, it has a function to perform in which it has no rival, and in which it will have nothing but support and goodwill.[66]

Not only did the Maxton–Brockway leadership play the wrong role, they preached the wrong gospel. Capitalism, MacDonald warned in September 1927, had 'made us far more than we imagine. It has given us notions of value that are wrong ... and it itself, being so grossly materialistic and having given economic resources such an important place in life, has misled us when we search for remedies against it.' The result was that socialism was in 'danger of being nothing but a guerilla fight with Capitalism'.[67] The N.A.C. was engaged in precisely such a guerrilla fight. Instead of challenging the materialistic values of the society around them, they had implicitly accepted them. Their programme was, at bottom, un-socialist, if not anti-socialist, for it was based on the essentially capitalist assumption that the object of social action is material enrichment rather than an improvement in the quality of life. Under capitalism, he wrote in December 1928,

> The poor strive to get what they want so sorely; the rich are afraid that they may lose what they have. And there is no resting on one's oars. One must go on accumulating whether one has £1,000 or £1,000,000. One must make higher and higher demands for wages and more and more provision for public aid lest personal efforts should fail. There is no satisfaction in this sleepless urge, and therefore there is no end to it. The generations will come and go, but the last will still be pursuing and still be in fear. It is the fear that I emphasise – the fear ever brooding over the insecurity of material possession – the struggle on a purely material plane for something that in its nature is purely ephemeral and passing – the destruction of all values of being and living by reason of the tragic pressure to possess things.
>   That is why ... Socialist politics must always be subordinate to Socialist ideals of life. That is why I am sometimes nervous about some tendencies in the Labour Movement to-day ... Socialism is in danger of being shut in amongst shoddy jerry built politics; and Movements like the I.L.P. are being led into muddy bogs.[68]

The I.L.P.'s real task was to challenge the acquisitive instinct, and to campaign, not for higher wages or even for the relief of poverty and unemployment, but for an alternative conception of man and society. That could be done only if it returned to the values of the pioneers. As he put it in a long, and rather touching, article in *Forward*, written during his convalescence in Lossiemouth in the summer of 1927, when he was 'exiled' from Westminster and condemned to spend his time wandering about the whins, playing golf and sitting by his fireside, reading Addison and Scott:

> [T]here is a chapter in our Socialist faith that fits ... into these hours. It is that which considers the artistic and spiritual life of man. That chapter is not read so often as it used to be ... The struggle for life on the economic plane is so severe, the problem of filling cupboards and clothing backs so pressing, that it seems indecent to spend time and thoughts on other things. Why spend a pound or a minute on beauty and culture when there are a million unemployed and goodness knows how many underfed and improperly housed? Let us brush aside the interests of endowed leisure until we have it ...
>   ... [T]hat has not been the position of the I.L.P., and because it was not its position, it drew round it one of the finest bands of propagandists who

ever preached a gospel ... Their attack upon Capitalism was not only because the present distribution of wealth was unjust, but because the present quality of life was inhuman ...

... They might have talked the 'iron law of wages' and 'the class war' till the grave closed over them and would have left nothing behind but a few disillusioned men sore and bruised by kicking against the pricks. They talked economic justice made kinetic by reason of human idealism ... and they left behind a great movement.

... The hardness of life during and after the war, coupled with our success in the political field, may have brought us into shallow waters and made us think too much of the rocks and channels that immediately beset us, and not enough of the voyage ... But we shall weary even in salvage work if we forget the peace of the heaven we seek ... and if we forget the temper in which we must do our navigating.[69]

It is not difficult to spot flaws in the argument. MacDonald's distinction between the Labour Party's role as a political party, and the I.L.P.'s role as a 'maker of social opinion', was artificial in conception and would almost certainly have proved unworkable in practice. Socialism could not be preached *in vacuo*, as a set of abstract principles: the I.L.P. could hardly make social opinion if it were debarred from expressing its views on the day-to-day problems in which society was interested. Much the same is true of his charge that the N.A.C. had abandoned the non-materialistic values of the pioneers. No doubt, it was true that the pioneers had looked forward to a better quality of life as well as to a more equitable distribution of wealth, but it was equally true that most of them had seen the second as a necessary condition of the first. But if it was right to try to improve the condition of the unemployed through the 'right to work' Bill, why was it wrong to try to eliminate unemployment through 'Socialism in Our Time'? If 'Socialism in Our Time' was to be ruled out, on the grounds that its assumptions were materialistic and un-Socialist, what policies were to be adopted instead? Did MacDonald's rejection of materialism rule out all attempts to solve the problem of poverty and unemployment before the socialist society of the future had actually arrived? If so, was socialism anything more than a purely ethical doctrine, without political significance? If not, what solutions should socialists put forward?

MacDonald never gave a satisfactory answer to these questions. In private, as we have seen, he had at first drawn a distinction between the politics of 'Socialism in Our Time' and the economics of the 'living wage'. He never explicitly attacked the latter head-on. Intentionally or not, however, his criticisms of the N.A.C.'s 'guerilla fight with Capitalism', and his denunciations of their surrender to the values of the society around them, applied even more to their economics than to their politics. If 'Socialism in Our Time' was materialistic and un-socialist, so was the 'living wage'. So too was the Hobsonian theory on which the 'living wage' report was based; and so, presumably, was any attempt to increase consumption and reduce unemployment by Hobsonian methods. By a curious irony, in fact, MacDonald's arguments against the N.A.C. cut the ground from under his own feet. Probably without fully realizing it himself, he had rejected not merely the detailed proposals of the 'living wage' report but the whole approach: and with it, the most promising gradualist solution to the greatest social evil of the day.

All the same, he had put his finger on a real dilemma, to which there was no easy answer. Socialists wished to create a better society, with better values. In order to do so, they had to win power in society as it was. Since their potential supporters had, after all, been shaped by that society, they were under constant pressure to water down their own values and adapt themselves to the values which they had set out to replace; and if they resisted the pressure, their values might never be realized at all. Those who believed that the 'victims of evolving capitalism' were, by definition, the agents of social progress could dismiss this dilemma as trivial or imaginary. All that was needed to create a better society was to destroy capitalism; all that was needed to destroy capitalism was to wage the class war as vigorously as possible. But MacDonald had never believed that; and, to put it at its lowest, it would be difficult to argue that history has proved him wrong. Revolution has not, in practice, provided an escape from the dilemma he posed. In one form or another, it has faced nearly all socialist parties, revolutionary as well as reformist; and the social and political changes of the last forty years have made it more acute. Chief among these changes, moreover, has been the Keynesian revolution in economic management, of which the 'living wage' report was one of the precursors. But although Keynesian techniques have raised living standards in a way which would have seemed almost inconceivable a generation ago, it would be hard to argue that the vision of the socialist pioneers has been brought any nearer. Ten or fifteen years ago, MacDonald's warning that the quality of life might be sacrificed in the pursuit of material prosperity, and that socialists might lose sight of their non-material objectives in the struggle for votes, could be dismissed as a piece of sentimental obscurantism. It cannot be dismissed so easily today.

CHAPTER 20

Labour and the nation

I

WHEN the coal strike ended in late 1926, the 1924 Parliament had almost reached its halfway mark. The next election was due, at the latest, in November 1929; and for most of 1927 and 1928 politics was dominated by its approach. It was a perplexing period for the politicians who lived through it, and it is equally perplexing for the historian. Under the combined prodding of Neville Chamberlain at the Ministry of Health and Winston Churchill at the Treasury, the Government carried through a number of reforms – notably a sweeping change in the structure and finance of local government. But although its policies were in many ways more progressive than they had been in its first two years of office, its style was out of keeping with the mood of the time, and public opinion continued to drift away from it. The Trade Disputes Act probably did it more harm than good with uncommitted voters, who no longer had cause to fear the unions, while a maladroit attempt to reform and strengthen the House of Lords was widely attacked as a device to undo the Parliament Act and had to be abandoned after John Buchan led a backbench revolt against it. The ham-fisted conduct of the home secretary, Joynson-Hicks, alienated liberal-minded people, and the rupture of relations with the Soviet Union after a police raid on the Arcos Trading Company probably did the same. By-election results suggested that when the election at last took place, the Government's majority would be sharply reduced and might be eliminated altogether.

They did not, however, suggest that Labour would be the only, or even the chief, beneficiary. In October 1926, Asquith resigned as leader of the Liberal Party. He was replaced by Lloyd George – still, at sixty-three, the most formidable, and potentially the most creative, figure in British politics. In 1924 it had looked as though the Liberal Party was dead in all but name. With Lloyd George's reputation, Lloyd George's money and Lloyd George's restless talents at its disposal, the corpse began to walk. The Liberal Party machine was overhauled by Sir Herbert Samuel and its thinking was brought up to date by an impressive array of working parties and study groups. Meanwhile, Liberal candidates did disconcertingly well at by-elections, often at Labour's expense; and it became increasingly clear that the Labour Party would have a hard fight on its hands if the Liberals were to be kept unmistakably in the third place.

In public, and to some extent even in private, MacDonald pooh-poohed all talk of a Liberal revival. When the Liberals did well at a by-election, he would write an article proving that the result meant nothing. When they did badly, he would announce that the electorate had seen through them. The Liberals, he wrote, were nothing but the 'kept Left' of the Conservative party; their by-election campaigns were managed by a 'touring show'; their famous 'yellow book' of 1928, which put forward an ambitious programme of Government intervention in the economy, was no more relevant to the country's real problems than were 'the contents of Johanna Southcott's box'.[1] Lloyd George, he told Beneš in November 1928, was 'a strange, ineffective figure now, and somehow or other fails to impress himself upon us'.[2] But this pose was belied by the frequency with which it had to be adopted. If MacDonald had felt as confident as he sounded, he would not have needed to say so. In fact, as he knew well, the Liberals now presented a more serious threat to his whole strategy than they had done since his election as party leader.

One of Labour's most powerful arguments was that there was no real difference between the two 'capitalist' parties: that the historic conflict between them had become a sham, and that the only conflict that mattered was the conflict between capitalism and socialism. That argument had never been wholly convincing, but before Asquith's retirement it had generally appeared to fit the facts. Though individual Liberals sometimes took a radical line, there was no coherent Liberal position on the issues which had emerged since 1918, and the Liberal Party could easily be portrayed as the bankrupt survivor of a vanished epoch. Lloyd George made nonsense of this portrait: and in doing so, he threatened to make equal nonsense of the argument behind it. The policies produced under his inspiration might or might not be workable, but they were unquestionably relevant to the needs of the time; though they were not 'socialist', they were at least as radical as anything produced by the Labour Party. For the first time since the war, it could plausibly be argued that the choice between capitalism and socialism was a false one: that there was a middle way after all, and that the Liberals knew how to find it.

The consequences seemed certain to be unpalatable from Labour's point of view. The Liberals had no chance of making serious inroads into Labour's working-class base—as MacDonald told his old friend Jean Longuet, the French socialist, in January 1928, 'our people come up all right when a General Election is on'[3]— but they might well prevent the Labour Party from breaking out of it. With the help of Lloyd George's 'ill-gotten gains', MacDonald complained to Lady Courteney in October 1928, the Liberals were insisting on running 500 candidates—half of them 'in absolutely hopeless constituencies with no chance of effecting any issue except the defeat of the Labour candidate'.[4] The Liberal candidates in these constituencies could not conceivably do well

JAMES McDONALD RAMSAY.

LEICESTER M.P.'S NAME AND ORIGIN——CAN HE SIT IN PARLIAMENT?

For months past—ever since the man who calls himself James Ramsay Macdonald, but whose real name is James McDonald Ramsay, has stood aloof from the almost unanimous response of the nation to the call of the King—we have persistently labelled him as a traitor and a coward ; and we have called upon Leicester to rid itself of the stigma of having such a " representative " in Parliament. But, despite all provocation, we have so far confined ourselves to criticising and exposing his words and deeds in the capacity of a public man—of a paid servant of the State. Even when we were recently described by him as having spent most of our time " on the threshold of the gaol," we simply retorted that if he wished to push us through the door, the machinery of a criminal prosecution for libel was available to him. For, whatever may have been our knowledge concerning his antecedents, we felt that even in the case of a traitor there was a recognised line beyond which journalistic revelation should not travel. And so we remained silent in regard to certain facts which have been in our possession for a long time. First of all, we knew that this man was living under an adopted name— that he was registered as *James McDonald Ramsay*— and that, therefore, he had obtained admission to the House of Commons in false colours, and was probably liable to heavy penalties and to have his election declared void. But to have disclosed this state of things would have imposed upon us a very painful and unsavoury duty. *We should have been compelled to reproduce the man's Birth Certificate.* And that would have revealed what to-day we are justified in revealing— for the reason we will state in a moment. It would have revealed " James Ramsay Macdonald," M.P. for Leicester, late " leader " of the Labour Party ; late member of a Royal Commission, under the seal of his Majesty ; the leading light of the " Union of Democratic Control "—libeller and slanderer of his country—it would have revealed him *as the illegitimate son of a Scotch servant girl !* No fault of his, it is true ; and even although he was playing the *rôle* of pro-German, and was otherwise acting as a traitor to the King, we would have been the last to lift the veil behind which he has sheltered himself for years.

OUR JUSTIFICATION.

But when we have had to submit to all kinds of cowardly innuendoes about our own parentage ; and when we find them focussed in Ramsay's organ, the *Labour Leader*, we are entitled to speak out ; just as the British Army is justified in giving the Huns a taste of their own medicine. Well, in the *Labour Leader* dated August 19th, great prominence is given to an attack upon the names and presumed nationality of certain newspaper editors ; and after giving various particulars concerning them, the writer comes to ourselves, and says " *John Bull*, editor Mr. Horatio Bottomley, *birthplace and parentage unknown*." Of course these " unknown " particulars could easily have been ascertained by a search at Somerset House, where a copy of our Birth Certificate could have been obtained on payment of the usual small fee. But the wicked insinuation is obvious—and, therefore, we no longer feel any compunction about reproducing the subjoined copy of Ramsay's Birth Certificate, which we have obtained from the Registrar of the district in which he was born.

No wonder the Moray Golf Club, of which **he is a** member, requests him to resign ; notwithstanding that, out of his hard earned, or inherited, money he is now said to have built himself an excellent residence at Lossiemouth (shouldn't the first syllable of the name be spelt differently ?). Surely Leicester will not be behind Moray ?

Let us repeat that we derive no sort of pleasure or satisfaction from the publication of these facts. It is entirely contrary to our temperament to rake over the dunghill of personal scandal—but when a man is openly posing as the enemy of his country ; is sitting in Parliament under an assumed name, and replies to the criticisms of a public journalist by cowardly and wicked innuendoes, we are surely entitled to draw attention to any circumstances likely to afford light upon his character. Perhaps, indirectly, we have explained the mystery of how it comes about that a member of the British Parliament, drawing a substantial salary for his supposed services, is capable of defying public sentiment in the hour of his country's trial.

What says Leicester now ?

What says the country, which is paying this man £400 a year to vilify and discredit it ?

And—what says Ramsay ?

OFFICIAL COPY OF BIRTH CERTIFICATE OF *James McDonald Ramsay*—now known as James Ramsay Macdonald !

No.	When and Where Born.	Name, if any.	Sex.	Name, Surname, and Rank or Profession of Father. Name, and Maiden Surname of Mother. Date and Place of Marriage.	Signature and Qualification of Informant, and Residence, if out of the House in which the Birth occurred.	When and Where Registered, and Signature of Registrar.
	EXTRACT OF AN ENTRY IN A REGISTER OF BIRTHS, of 17° & 18° VICTORIA,			kept in the undermentioned PARISH or DISTRICT, in terms Cap. 80, §§ 56 & 58.		
131	James McDonald Ramsay Illegitimate	1866 October Twelfth 11h. 30m. P.M. LOSSIEMOUTH	M	Anne Ramsay Domestic Servant	(Signed) Anne Ramsay Mother	1866 November 2nd at Lossiemouth (Signed) Al. Wiseman Registrar

33 *John Bull* article with facsimile of MacDonald's birth certificate, September, 1915

34 A peaceful moment in 1914

35 Tug-o'-war at a Labour summer school, Easton Lodge, 1923

36 Electioneering in Aberavon

37 White heather for luck, 1923 general election

38 With Malcolm at Lossiemouth, December, 1923

39 Arriving at No. 10 for Labour's first Cabinet meeting, January, 1924

40 The first Labour Cabinet, 1924. *Back row:* Webb, Wheatley, F. W. Jowett. *Middle row:* C. P. Trevelyan, Stephen Walsh, Lord Thomson, Chelmsford, Olivier, Noel Buxton, Josiah Wedgwood, Vernon Hartshorn, Tom Shaw. *Front row:* Adamson, Parmoor, Snowden, Haldane, MacDonald, Clynes, Thomas, Henderson

enough for the Liberals themselves to form a Government, but it was quite conceivable that they might do well enough to prevent the Labour Party from forming one. If they did so, they would give the Conservatives another five years of power. More alarming still, they might go on to recapture their old position as the main anti-Conservative party. Labour had held office only once, in highly unusual circumstances, for less than twelve months; it had been a major party for less than ten years. If it did not form a Government after the next election, there could be no certainty that it would ever form one again.

To MacDonald the conclusion seemed obvious, and although he rarely spelled it out, it can be inferred without much difficulty from his actions. The election result would be determined, not by class-conscious trade unionists or committed socialists, who had voted Labour even in 1924, but by the undecided voters who had been frightened into the Conservative camp at the last election and were now beginning to desert it. These voters were timid creatures. At heart, they were moderately progressive. They had rallied to the Government during the general strike, but they had no wish to see the miners crushed or the permanent Conservative majority in the House of Lords given extra power. Properly handled, they could be persuaded to vote Labour, particularly if they could be convinced that it was a waste of time to vote Liberal, but they would run for cover again if the Labour Party gave the Conservatives an excuse to unleash another red scare. As MacDonald put it in July 1927, after the Liberals had cut the Conservative majority at Westbury from 1,700 to 200:

> We have convinced the country that great changes must be made. But the country hesitates. It does not like new ideas even when its reason has to accept them. When it begins to trust to its reason someone or other appears on our platform or papers in war feathers, gives a grand Buffalo Bill whoop, and back flee the converts to shelter.[5]

If the Liberal challenge was to be beaten off, it was necessary to prevent Lloyd George from recapturing the moral and ideological initiative which the Liberals had lost to the Labour Party during and after the war. To do that, it was necessary to smother the 'Buffalo Bill whoops' of the I.L.P., and to produce an alternative which would enlist the allegiance of ordinary Labour Party members and at the same time appeal to middle opinion in the country.

The analysis was no doubt unsophisticated, and the conclusion unheroic. Electorally, at least, the strategy based on them was to be one of the most successful in the Labour Party's history.

II

As in somewhat similar circumstances in 1923, one of MacDonald's chief assets was his role as leader of the Opposition and alternative prime minister,

Q

and the way in which he exploited this asset is of great interest. Like all leaders of the Opposition, he spoke on a wide variety of subjects. Increasingly, however, he concentrated on foreign affairs, where his Government had scored its greatest success, where the contrast between Lloyd George's record and his own was in his favour and where the Government made a number of blunders which might have been calculated to alienate the section of public opinion which he most needed to capture.

In January 1927 the British concession at Hangkow was attacked by a rioting mob. At the end of the month, the Government announced that British troops were being sent to Shanghai to protect the international settlement there from a similar incident. This resort to gunboat diplomacy caused great indignation in left-wing circles. In February 1927, in the debate on the address, MacDonald attacked the foreign secretary on the grounds that he had united both factions in the Chinese civil war against Britain, and that in doing so he had made negotiations more difficult.[6] It was a vigorous and effective debating speech but in a private letter to Miles Lampson, the British minister at Peking, MacDonald made it clear that his opposition to the Government was a good deal less whole-hearted than it had sounded on the floor of the House:

> I have really been trying my best to help you and the Foreign Office in the terribly difficult problem you have to face in China. You may have seen that I have had to disagree with the sending of troops to Shanghai. Up to that I had no word of disagreement to say with what was being done, and was getting my political friends into whole-hearted agreement with me. In the end I was hoping to bring them right out in full support of the Government's action, and by communicating our views to the Canton Government, try to counterbalance some of the very subversive information that must be working upon it ...
>
> ... If you find it necessary to prompt any of the Press, I give you the fullest liberty to repeat as often as you like that I am not in favour of scuttling, and that I am profoundly convinced that if either the North or the South of China would trust to the goodwill of the British Government, they would have no cause in the end to regret it. News gets out that is garbled and pernicious. Whatever you see, however, please read and judge with the knowledge of this last sentence.[7]

Lampson replied effusively at the end of March:

> I think we all realise how much we owe to you in our present difficulties out here. I am sorry that you could not rally to the despatch of troops to China, for after Hangkow it seemed to me quite inevitable. What happened at Hangkow was bad enough, but if anything of the sort had happened at Shanghai it would have been perfectly appalling ...
>
> I have no doubt that in letting the Canton Government know your

views you did a great national service, for undoubtedly there are influences at work there which are not out for settlement with us on any terms less than the total deprivation of the foreigner of all his rights in China ...

In closing may I say this—the whole British Community out here realises how helpful you have been and what they owe to you. I have heard comment on it on every side, and not only the British Community, but my foreign colleagues as well.[8]

On Shanghai, MacDonald spoke with his tongue in his cheek. On the central questions of security and disarmament, which came to the fore again in the summer and autumn, it was a different matter. In 1925 he had welcomed the Locarno Pact on the grounds that it had removed the remaining obstacles to the Protocol, and hence to disarmament. In 1927 events took a turn for the worse. It seemed clear that the British had little chance of persuading the French to disarm on land unless they themselves were prepared to disarm at sea. Here, the main problem lay outside Europe, in the three-cornered naval rivalry between the United States, Britain and Japan. In 1922 a disarmament agreement had been signed at Washington, covering capital ships. In other categories, however, the naval powers continued to build against each other, and the competition between them seemed, if anything, to be accelerating. In 1927 President Coolidge invited the signatories of the Washington treaty to another conference, to reach agreement on cruisers and auxiliaries. The French and Italians refused to come, but the British and Japanese accepted the invitation, and the conference duly began at Geneva at the end of June. It soon became clear, however, that the British and American positions were hopelessly far apart, and that neither side was prepared to make concessions to bridge the gap. At the beginning of August, the conference broke up, to the accompaniment of a shrill chorus of recrimination from both sides of the Atlantic.

MacDonald was careful not to join the chorus, and made it clear that he thought both Governments equally to blame. The Americans, he wrote, flaunted their wealth 'like a plutocratic schoolboy with too much pocket money'; the British, on the other hand, refused to admit that 'the world is changing'.[9] During the autumn, however, his attacks on British policy became much sharper. At the League of Nations Assembly in September, Sir Austen Chamberlain declared that Britain's imperial responsibilities made it impossible for her to accept new commitments over and above those she had entered into at Locarno, and bluntly refused a Dutch invitation to reopen consideration of the Protocol. 'Geneva has revived the protocol as I knew it would have to do as soon as it would be convinced of the futility of considering armaments apart from security,' MacDonald noted in a diary entry on September 14th. 'Sir Austen Chamberlain's speech is a model in [sic] how policy ought not to be stated or conducted.'[10] He also wrote a letter to the *Manchester Guardian*, denouncing Chamberlain's speech as a 'disaster, not to the ideas of the Protocol but to the British Empire itself', and advocating the setting up of a League of Nations commission to re-examine the 1924 draft so as to make it acceptable 'as a practical pledge of security and safety'.[11] In a covering letter to C. P. Scott, the editor, he wrote:

> One of the Ministers of a foreign State called upon me last night. He did so because he felt so terribly distressed about the position of our country as left by Sir Austen Chamberlain on Saturday, and he told me that several of his colleagues in the Diplomatic Service were privately discussing matters in the same nervous way that he was. Unfortunately, it looks as though this question is going to be thrust into the whirlpool of party politics, because we shall certainly have a great deal to say about it in the autumn and winter campaign. I have been approached already from two rather important quarters asking me if a continental move was made for the revival of the Protocol, whether I could give my countenance to it, because the reputation of the Labour Government is still the biggest asset which our country has, in popular continental opinion. I have not yet given a reply but I am rather inclined to agree, although I know what can be said against it.[12]

MacDonald's initiative was not an unmixed success. On September 16th, Snowden published a long letter in the *Manchester Guardian*, violently attacking what he described as 'uncritical supporters of the Protocol', and describing the text as 'a mass of contradictions'. The reason it had been greeted with enthusiasm in many continental countries, he wrote scornfully, was that they had little or nothing to contribute and a great deal to gain from British adhesion. 'Oh, how one's own colleagues go out of their way to put difficulties in the path,' MacDonald noted privately. 'The letter at this moment serves no purpose except to do mischief—an oar put in at back-water to stop the pace of the boat ... The only consolation one has is in reading the biographies of dead politicians.'[13] Another consolation occurred to him in the next few days. On September 20th, he noted:

> Have had a letter which indicates that Snowden has been acting in conjunction with Ll.G. ... An ex-Minister asked me if I proposed to bring Snowden's conduct before Party or Executive. Why should I? It is this fault which has kept him out of the lead. He has destroyed himself & I am sorry.[14]

In his *Forward* column four days later, he returned to the charge with a new argument, aimed more directly at the Labour movement. 'Europe is afraid to reopen the books of Peace ... ,' he wrote. 'No one can say what devil may escape from their opened clasps.' Only the Protocol could create the sense of security without which a revision of the peace settlement was impossible. On the 26th, he wrote a slightly disingenuous letter to Snowden, explaining that he did not want to start a controversy on the matter, but that he had 'always understood that the Party had agreed to the Protocol idea and that it was known to all of us that the document that came from Geneva in 1924 was but a first draft to be very carefully scrutinised and to be fitted into circumstances by further negotiation'.[15] He expressed more of his true feelings in a letter to Tom Johnston on September 27th:

Let there be no mistake about my intention. I had started and planned the article before I read Snowden's letter but, having read it, I finished the article in such a way that it covered the ground he did.

I think his intervention was most unfair and was just one of those incidents which are constantly happening when we get a chance of planting a good smack on the jaw of the other fellow — someone comes in and destroys the effect of the blow. We never seem to be able to get a clean smack at anybody or anything and I am getting rather sick at it. Did we ever have a better chance of using once more our foreign policy as a well-shod battering ram to smash the Government? If our papers and propagandists had been worth anything they would have gone like furies to seize the opportunities ...

All my reports from Geneva — and I have had them from Americans and other foreigners, as well as from our own friends, both officially and unofficially — are to the effect that we have been vindicated in a most extraordinary way; that the 1924 Assembly lived as though it were held only yesterday; that everybody was talking about it and that our position was used as a tremendous encouragement to the smaller nationalities to revolt against the big ones, to force the pace and give new life to the League.[16]

He had plenty of 'clean smacks' at the Government's foreign policy in the next eighteen months, however, and as time went on they became increasingly effective. Soon after the House reassembled for the new session, he moved a censure motion, deploring the Government's unwillingness to accept the principle of arbitration or to promote a security system guaranteed by the League. The naval conference, he declared, had failed because the Government had used 'war methods rather than peace methods'. In reality, the problem of security was psychological rather than military. What was needed was to inculcate 'habits of arbitration and disarmament'; and this could be done only if the fears that impeded them were allayed by a security system on the lines of the Protocol. As these habits took root, however, the danger of war would recede; and as the danger of war receded, the danger that sanctions might have to be put into effect would recede too. Thus, although the risks involved in setting up a new security system might be 'as black and big as you like on paper', the real risk would be 'practically nil'.[17]

In an age of armed peace, which has lasted for almost a quarter of a century, and in which it is taken for granted that the way to avoid war is prepare for it, MacDonald's argument may seem naïve, even disingenuous. He was asking his countrymen to sign what was in fact a blank cheque, on the grounds that it was made out for only a small sum and that it would never be presented for payment. Would it not have been better to face the truth that there is no certain way of avoiding war, and that the real argument for collective security is not that there are no risks attached to it but that the risks of isolation are even greater? But although this seemed clear in the 'forties and 'fifties it did not seem so clear in the 'twenties. Men may or may not learn from history, but they can hardly be expected to learn from history that has not yet happened. MacDonald was trying to avoid a repetition of 1914, not of 1939; and the lesson of 1914 appeared to be that arms would sooner or later be used, and that the only way to avoid war was to disarm. Since it was clear that there could be no disarmament without the French, and that the French would not disarm without a security system, a security system of some sort was necessary as well. For MacDonald, however, the object of the whole exercise was not security but disarmament — or rather security through disarmament. The last thing he wanted to do was to create an armed pact to deter war, on the lines of NATO or the Warsaw Pact. He wanted to create a climate in which men would decide that deterrents were no longer necessary.

He took a similar line on the Franco–American proposals for a pact to renounce war. In the autumn of 1927, the French proposed a bilateral pact between themselves and the United States. At the end of December, F. B. Kellogg, the American secretary of state, proposed a multilateral pact instead. Kellogg's note, MacDonald conceded, was nothing more than a declaration, but at least it pointed in the right direction; British policy, by contrast, was one of 'senseless impotence'.[18] At the same time he made it clear that, for him, the real value of such a pact would lie in the psychological effect which it would have on its signatories, not in the detailed provisions, and that the real value of the Kellogg note was that it could be used to prise the Americans out of their isolation. The expression 'outlawry of war', he told Professor Shotwell, one of the leading American exponents of the idea, in April 1928, was 'one of those slogan expressions which convey an aspiration rather than a definite proposal ... If America is to help us to secure peace it must take some responsibility and I believe, when we get down to actual problems, it will do so.'[19] It would be easy to show that Kellogg's proposals were impractical, he argued in a foreign affairs debate in May, but the Government should nevertheless sign without reservations — partly because a pact renouncing war would at any rate make it impossible for the signatories to use the threat of war as an instrument of diplomacy, and even more because America would not be able to stand aloof if a country which had signed the pact suffered aggression as a result.[20]

Britain eventually signed the Kellogg Pact, along with fourteen other countries, in August 1928. In the meantime, however, the Government had denied itself most of the benefits which its signature might otherwise have brought it by a bizarre diplomatic *démarche*, which came to be known as the Anglo–French naval compromise. By this compromise Britain agreed to accept the French view that trained reserves should not be included when calculating the size of land forces for disarmament purposes. At the same time, both Governments agreed to put forward a joint plan for naval disarmament, which had been carefully tailored to suit their own requirements, but which took no account of the interests of the United States. Anglo-American relations, which had been badly damaged by the failure of the naval conference the year before, deteriorated still further; and the plan was promptly condemned by the United States and, for good measure, by the Italians as well. At the Labour Party conference in October, MacDonald moved an emergency resolution condemning the Government, and warned the delegates to remember what had happened between 1906 and 1913, when honest men could deny that Britain had made any binding agreement with the French:

> In 1914 ... they had to implement, not their agreements, they had to implement their winks and their smiles and their little nudges and their indefinite walkings-out — (laughter) — because they had changed, and changed insensibly, until they became stronger than were the Italian bonds to the Triple Alliance. They should read what took place at Geneva since 1924, the stories of the breakdowns here and there, the stories of the delays in the correspondence that preceded our Government's definite reply to the Kellogg Pact; they should read the Anglo–French understanding that had just been revealed and try to understand what was the meaning of it. And what would they find? They would find that the history of 1906–1914 was rewriting itself.[21]

He banged this drum again and again in the next six months. After the conference, he left for a short visit to central Europe, accompanied by the Mosleys. He made a fervent call for disarmament in an address to the Reichstag in Berlin, and reported afterwards to Philip Noel-Baker that his speech 'had exactly the effect that I wanted — a soothing effect in Germany and a curseworthy effect on "Pertinax" '. Lacy Cynthia's dress, he added, with more enthusiasm than tact, 'would have aroused the envy of your wife'.[22] In other respects, his impressions were less cheerful. All over Europe, he wrote in *Forward* at the end of October, affairs were falling 'back into the ruts along which they moved prior to the war in 1914 ... After all these years since the war, our Government has not yet caught a glimmering of what a continental policy is.'[23] The Government, he declared in the debate on the address in November, would never get disarmament so long as it continued to 'babble so much about security'.[24] The white paper giving the terms of the Anglo–French agreement, he wrote a few days later, was 'the most ominous document on our foreign policy published since the war'; Baldwin's speech about it at the Lord Mayor's banquet was 'the sort of thing that used to be said before 1914 by Lord Grey and others'.[25] Even the French, he wrote hopefully after a visit to Paris in December, now wished to see a change of government in London, since they recognized that the Conservatives were forcing Germany 'into the old, deep ruts of a diplomacy which rejects the methods of peace'.[26]

It was Anglo–American relations, however, that concerned MacDonald most. He was quite prepared to criticize the Americans. In a letter to Paul Warburg, the American banker, in January 1928, he wrote bluntly that 'the only country that stands in the way of the restoration of what I might call a natural economic system in Europe, is the United States.'[27] 'It is no use hiding the facts and always flattering America,' he wrote in November to another American correspondent, who had written to him in defence of the Monroe Doctrine. 'What America means by self-defence entitles every other nation on earth to put its own convenient meaning on the same phrase.'[28] Britain, he told Sir Michael Sadler, had 'not improved the position by being too appealing to America in some of our approaches, because we have given America to understand that it is so essential that we cannot do without it: that is a profound mistake'.[29] But these were the criticisms of a sympathizer. MacDonald had known America since the 1890s, and had many American friends. More important still, he felt at home there – particularly, perhaps, in the parts of America which upper-class Englishmen were apt to regard as alien or barbaric. Most important of all, like many British radicals of his class and generation, he saw America as a symbol of hope – as the land of democracy and social equality, where his values had been realized more fully than in his own country. As he put it in an article for the New York *Forward* during the 1927 naval conference:

There are no two peoples in [*sic*] the face of the earth that ought to be on terms of more friendly co-operation than America & ourselves. All that is required is candour & some trouble to understand each other objectively. I am told that the part of America which is most antagonistic to us is the West & Middle West. As a matter of fact, no other part of America should be more friendly to the struggles & aspirations of the plain man who is the life & soul of our democracy ...

With so many reactionary governments in power, it would be foolish for anyone to treat lightly the unsettled state of the world. Dictatorships, whether of the Right or Left, are always a danger to peace. But the naval programmes of both America & Britain are excessive ... We ought to leave this sort of thing to the twin governments of Italy & Russia. Our two nations have better things to do.[30]

Sentimental considerations apart, it seemed clear that if Anglo–American relations continued to deteriorate, the result would be a naval race between

Britain and the United States, which could only strengthen American isolationism and damage the prospects of disarmament. A Bill authorizing the construction of fifteen cruisers and one aircraft-carrier had been sent from the House of Representatives to the Senate in the spring of 1928. The Senate had decided to postpone it until the following session, and in his message to Congress in December, Coolidge urged that it should be passed without delay. Meanwhile, the Democratic candidate for the presidency, Al Smith, had been crushingly defeated by Herbert Hoover. Most of MacDonald's American friends were deeply depressed by the result. The New York *Nation*, Oscar Garrison Villard told him, had refused to advise its readers how to vote, but in the end 'Hoover's dreadful speeches drove me into coming out personally for Smith.' Anglo-American relations, he continued, seemed likely to become even worse:

> Everyone in Washington says that the Fifteen-Cruiser Bill will go through with a rush 'just to give the Britishers what's coming to them' ... There can be no doubt whatever that Baldwin's blunder in the matter of the Franco-British Alliance has done infinite harm ... People here have the feeling that Baldwin, Bridgeman and Churchill were caught ... cheating at cards as it were, and the fact that they have now dropped their cards on the floor in no wise satisfies people here. I read with profoundest gratitude what you have said on this subject and continue to pray you may again and soon be in a position to direct British foreign policy along intelligent as well as humanitarian lines.[31]

MacDonald evidently shared Villard's fears. After the elections he sent Smith a private note expressing 'the admiration which fills me for the extraordinary fight you put up for the Presidency', and urging him to 'stick to public life where you have been of such signal service to your people.'[32] Early in 1929, he published an article on Anglo-American relations in the New York *Nation*. The Anglo-French naval agreement, he wrote, was not 'directed against the United States. It was simply stupid.' It would be highly improper for him to comment on the American cruiser programme, he added; he would only 'say that the execution of that program will be a great blow to the nation from whom the Kellogg Pact originated'.[33] In February, however, the so-called cruiser Bill was passed by the Senate, and signed by the President. Its passage, Villard wrote in a letter to MacDonald on February 13th, 'has been a complete disaster for those of our point of view; we have been routed and we might as well face it, for there is no sense in self-deception. The jingo elements are in the saddle and are to be reckoned with.'[34] By April, MacDonald was writing despondently to Colonel House:

> The relations between our two countries are bad, and there is no use shutting our eyes to the fact. The conversations I hear, both with Americans

and English people, are neither helpful nor hopeful, and it is the duty of all of us to exert some supreme effort to change the mentality of both. I should be so happy if I could help in any way in doing this.[35]

It was not long before his wish was granted.

III

For most of 1927 and 1928, MacDonald acted as Labour's main spokesman on foreign affairs. He also played a leading and perhaps decisive part in a prolonged, though largely hidden, struggle to determine the shape of the party's domestic programme. By the summer of 1927, it had become clear that the party would need a platform on which to fight the next election. A sub-committee of the National Executive, of which MacDonald and Henderson were both members, drew up a draft programme, which was then submitted to the executive of the parliamentary party. The parliamentary party, however, passed a resolution urging the National Executive not to publish it — according to Dalton because it was 'much too long and awfully dully written'. On Henderson's suggestion it was then agreed that a resolution should be put before the next annual conference, instructing the National Executive to prepare a programme of 'legislation and administrative action' for a Labour Government.[36] At the Blackpool conference in October 1927, MacDonald moved the Executive resolution in a remarkably ambivalent speech, which must have left many delegates wondering whether he agreed with the proposal or not:

> He was one of those who regarded authorised programmes with a good deal of suspicion. They had some experience of such programmes, and probably nothing did more to begin the process of killing the Liberal Party than the Newcastle Programme ... But that was only true when a political Party was dealing with surface issues ... The Labour Party's programme was not a flashy, superficial programme. It was a programme dealing with great fundamental issues that would remain fundamental issues until society had got the intelligence and will to face them successfully ... There was another thing they wanted to do ... Authorised programmes might have a certain number of inconveniences, but unauthorised programmes had many more inconveniences ... Therefore, part of his reason ... was that when this programme was issued it would be a programme of the Party position ... What they were asking the Executive to do was ... to consider all the resolutions that had been carried at their Conferences from time to time, to co-ordinate them and put them into a system, not for the purpose of stating what the Labour

Government was going to do in its first year of office, but for the purpose of providing a plan which a Labour Government ... would work at ...

The resolution was seconded by George Lansbury. After Bevin had delivered a vehement attack on the 'living wage' and Shinwell had delivered a vehement attack on Bevin, it was carried without opposition.[37]

'Another birthday with a distinctly autumnal feeling about it ...,' MacDonald noted benignly on October 12th. 'Blackpool has made it easy to be old. How fine our movement is.'[38] The sequel was less comforting. At some stage in 1925, he had appointed a committee, consisting of Willy Graham and Lord Arnold, to examine the party's financial policy. They had co-opted a number of other members, and had eventually recommended the party to abandon the capital levy and replace it with a special surtax on unearned incomes. The proposal was put to Snowden, who raised no objection. Shortly afterwards, MacDonald wrote to Graham, proposing that the finance committee should now be amalgamated with the committee on banking and currency and that Lees Smith, one of the co-opted members of the finance committee, should serve as chairman.[39] At the party conference, Lees Smith moved an Executive resolution calling for a surtax on unearned incomes of more than £500 a year. The surtax, Lees Smith made clear, would be paid by the same people who would otherwise have been subject to the capital levy, and would raise more than the levy would raise. The resolution was carried;[40] and the proposal was promptly condemned by the Liberal weekly, the *Nation*. Snowden, who was in an even more prickly mood than usual after his quarrel with MacDonald over the Protocol, thereupon withdrew his support. On October 14th, he wrote indignantly to MacDonald:

I am expressing the feelings of all my colleagues who have talked with me on this subject. We are all feeling that somehow — it is difficult to explain — we cannot get inside you. You seem to be protected by some impenetrable barrier. I called it aloofness in my last letter. It was not so in the old days of the NAC ...

Perhaps I may explain what I mean by referring to an incident. You said in a speech at the Conference that you had appointed a Committee consisting of Arnold and Lees Smith to consider the nationalisation of banking and the question of credit. This is news to me ... I do not know if Graham was consulted, but I should have thought the ex-Chancellor would at least have been consulted. Do not think for a moment that I am nursing any grievance. I am not. I am always glad to be relieved of work others are ready to do.

But this Committee has got the party into an awful mess. Either through culpable ignorance, or through some grievous misunderstanding, the basis of the scheme is all wrong. The criticisms of the NATION are incontrovertible ... I gave my support to the scheme on the definite assurance of

Lees Smith that the Inland Revenue had certified the estimate of the yield. It now turns out that they never did anything of the sort ... [Y]ou may take it from me that the financial basis of the scheme has been blown sky high by the first wind brought against it. Lees Smith has based his case on the statement that it was to be a tax on *individuals* with over £500 a year unearned income. He now admits that it will involve the taxation of company reserves, the great reservoir of capital savings. Even then on a liberal estimate he is over £20 millions out in his reckoning.

We cannot defend the scheme, and I shall make no attempt to do so. But I have some reason to be indignant at the way we have been misled. The party will have to get out of it as best it can.[41]

Next day, MacDonald sent for Arnold and Lees Smith and discussed the matter with them. He also wrote a surprisingly conciliatory reply to Snowden, which reveals a great deal about his relations with his most formidable colleague, and even more about the difficulty of making policy in a loose-knit, heterogeneous and inadequately staffed party of the left:

What you say about the sur-tax is disturbing. You were at the meeting that finally settled it, I was told ... and until I got your letter this morning I thought you were wholeheartedly supporting the report. I wish you had let us know before Blackpool ...

You are quite wrong about the appointment of the Committee. It has been in existence since 1925 & you were consulted about it. Indeed, I proposed to you that you should go on it or a Rating one. You chose the latter & are on with Wedgwood & agreed that Graham & Arnold should be the nucleus of the former ... As to the reference to the same Committee in continuation of its work on the question of Banking, were you not present at the Executive meeting at which this was done in July? ... Are you quite sure that I did not mention it to you apart from the discussion at the Executive? I certainly had it on a note of things to be done & have an impression that I did see you, but it was in those bad days in July when I was little in the House. I have a fairly distinct recollection of a talk with you at the table when there was a third person present on my left. Though I am willing to believe anything about July, I am less willing than usual to believe that I did not speak to you on this because Graham asked me to be sure to do it. If I did not do it, I am truly grieved.

When I heard of the *Nation* attack on the scheme I had both Arnold & Lees Smith to see me & impressed them with the seriousness of the attack ... Arnold has gone into it again with Treasury officials, & he assures me that everything is quite sound ...

The mistake you have made about the instance you give showing 'aloofness' does not remove the substance, which however is no matter of aloofness at all but of overburdening work ... Nor does it effect [sic] me alone.

I try to get at others with no great success. The problem is how to be leisurely in the midst of rushing machinery. You speak of NAC days. Molehills since then have become mountains & thickets forests, but there is no other change so far as I am concerned.[42]

Snowden's opposition to the surtax leaked out, and caused great embarrassment to the Labour Party. In spite, or perhaps because, of Snowden, however, MacDonald went out of his way to nail his own colours to the surtax mast. In a vigorous article in *Forward*, he conceded that the surtax had so far had a bad press and that the 'usual stage properties about thrift and the usual woebegotten actors who by privation and their own labour have saved £10,000 have appeared once more,' but he also declared confidently that public opinion would change as soon as it was realized that the national debt was being used as an excuse for curtailing the social services.[43] In private he was less confident. 'These moments through which we are now living are more critical than any since the 1924 election,' he explained to Tom Johnston on October 28th. 'We have now to begin our final spurt for the coming election and if we start with stroke rowing one pace, the next man another, and the third man catching crabs every time he puts his blade in the water, all I can say is, God help us!'[44] On November 3rd, he wrote to Johnston again:

The action of Snowden and the failure of our papers to stamp on it immediately by saying that Snowden was consulted and that he did agree to the memorandum, has undoubtedly given us a bit of a knock back and I deliberately went to my constituency ... to shove the Surtax ... without in any way committing myself to the amount it would yield – right back in the forefront of our programme. Our candidates have been writing up in a state of confusion and panic, but now things are settling down. After the decisions at Blackpool, we could no more revise our decisions on the Surtax than fly to the moon.[45]

Meanwhile, the Labour Party's policy-making machinery slowly ground on. At the end of October, the National Executive appointed a sub-committee to prepare a draft programme in accordance with the conference decision. MacDonald, Henderson and Lansbury served on it *ex officio*. The other members were Herbert Morrison, Sir Charles Trevelyan, Ellen Wilkinson, F. O. Roberts, the railwaymen's leader, C. T. Cramp and the party's most glittering rising star, Sir Oswald Mosley.[46] The star turned out to shed a disconcerting light. Mosley was now thirty-one. He belonged to an old landed family, and had been elected to Parliament in 1918 as a Conservative coalitionist. He had joined the Labour Party in 1924. In 1926 he had substantially increased the Labour majority in a by-election for Smethwick, and at the party conference which had just finished he had replaced Hugh Dalton on the National Executive. He was rich, handsome, clever and personally magnetic: he was also restlessly ambitious, sublimely self-confident and savagely contemptuous of those with whom he did not agree.

Mosley was one of MacDonald's favourites among the younger generation of Labour politicians. He visited MacDonald in Lossiemouth, travelled with him on the continent and wrote him letters addressed to 'My dear Chief'. These civilities did not affect his behaviour on the committee. In his so-called 'Birmingham proposals' two years before, Mosley had put forward an expansionist economic programme, based on assumptions akin to those of the 'living wage' report, but derived from Keynes rather than from Hobson. He now decided to use his position on the programme committee to push the Labour Party down the Birmingham road. Early in November, he sent MacDonald a long and rather breathless memorandum, urging the Labour Party to carry out a revision of monetary policy on the lines advocated by Keynes and McKenna; to introduce children's allowances; and to offer an extra £1 a week pension to people who were still at work over the age of sixty-five, on condition that they were willing to retire. He also advocated a tax on luxuries, an embargo on the export of capital, bulk purchase of foodstuffs and raw materials, the establishment of an Economic Council and the appointment of a commission, with members like Keynes, McKenna and Stamp, to examine the banking system. Such a commission, Mosley concluded hopefully, would almost certainly report in favour of a change in monetary policy. If the Bank of England proved recalcitrant, powers should immediately be taken to override it. With the help of judicious pressure it would then be possible to bring about a trade revival.[47]

MacDonald's response to these proposals is not known. They were less radical than the 'living wage' report, which he had carefully refrained from attacking; and many of them found their way into the programme in the end, though sometimes in a diluted form. But whatever MacDonald may have thought about the substance of Mosley's memorandum, he and Mosley differed fundamentally over the politics of the exercise. Mosley wanted a precise and unambiguous programme of action for the next Labour Government. MacDonald wanted a generalized statement of the party's philosophy and aims, carfully avoiding firm commitments and designed to appeal to middle opinion. As he put it in a diary entry in January 1928:

> I have been pondering over Labour Party affairs. Obviously someone who would put the trumpet more frequently to his lips would be a better leader, but would that be good for the Party? I do not think it would. Quiet cautious leadership is what I think is wanted. There are plenty [of] inflammatory influences in the Party to keep it hot, but for the work it ought to do confidence goes further than programmes.[48]

Mosley's attempt to force a reluctant MacDonald to play the trumpet were foiled in the next two months. Three documents were submitted to the sub-committee – a long one by MacDonald, and shorter ones by Mosley and Ellen Wilkinson. The sub-committee asked the Executive for instructions; and at the end of February, the Executive resolved that MacDonald should be asked to complete the longer document.[49] The next skirmish took place at the end of March. A draft was circulated, but MacDonald explained that it was not yet 'definite': that he had written an earlier draft, which had then been redrafted by R. H. Tawney; and that Will Henderson, Arthur Henderson and he were now at work on Tawney's redraft. He asked to be allowed to go on working on it, and Roberts loyally moved that the matter should be deferred so that he could do so. Mosley moved that the draft should be considered immediately, but his amendment was defeated – though only by the narrow margin of 8 votes to 10.[50] After that, it was plain sailing. The amended draft was finally agreed at the end of June. The policies came from a variety of sources. The style was unmistakably Tawney's: the conception as unmistakably Mac-Donald's.

It was a formidable combination. In October, the draft programme was presented to the party conference at Birmingham under the reassuring title, *Labour and the Nation*. It consisted in essence of a high-minded, if sometimes prosy, statement of the moral case for gradualist socialism, heavily flavoured with the scientific optimism of the day. With great skill, the Labour Party was portrayed as a movement of all classes, ranged against a small minority of property owners, and socialism as the creed, not only of the working class, but of all 'practical men and women' who wished to apply 'the resources of science to bring within the reach of all the conditions of a dignified and civilised existence'. 'Without haste, but without rest,' land, coal, power, transport and life insurance would be transferred to public ownership. Taxation would be 'scientifically adjusted' to the ability to pay; arms expenditure would be cut down; and the social services would be extended. The ultimate goal was a 'Socialist Commonwealth', based on the conviction that co-operation was 'the law of life'.

On the harsh questions of unemployment and economic policy, the programme was less satisfactory. Most of the ideas which had been canvassed in progressive circles since the last election made at least a fleeting appearance. Control over the Bank of England would be vested in a public corporation. A system of bulk purchase would be set up for imported grain and meat. An inquiry would be held into financial methods and credit policy. A national economic committee would be established on the lines of the Committee of Imperial Defence. 'Sound' schemes for providing work would be promoted by an employment and development board. Waste and inefficiency in industry would be attacked. Most radical of all, industrial recovery would be assisted through a 'direct increase of purchasing power in the hands of the workers'. But there was no strategy, no set of priorities and, above all, no suggestion that the claims of economic recovery might conflict with the demands of fiscal orthodoxy or free trade. With a brave flourish, *Labour and the Nation* denounced the 'placid assumption that, in the twentieth century, the recurrence of involuntary idleness is still to be regarded, like tempests and earthquakes, as an act of God'. It then proceeded to demonstrate that, in practice, its authors had no other assumption to put in its place.

Yet it is doubtful if many party members noticed the omission. A general election was in the offing, and the tide seemed to be flowing in their direction. They had no wish to quarrel or recriminate. In any case, the hesitations and confusions of *Labour and the Nation* reflected a deeper confusion, which was common to most of the Labour movement. Labour men were anxious to improve the condition of the unemployed, and to do what they could to reduce unemployment. At the same time, they took it for granted that unemployment was caused by capitalism, and could be cured only by socialism. Most wished to break with the economic orthodoxies of the past, but only a tiny handful believed that it was possible to do so while the means of production were privately owned: the question that divided the party was not how best to promote recovery within the existing system, but how fast to replace the system with a better one. On that question, MacDonald's critics played into his hands. Just as he talked gradualism, but lacked a strategy for the transition period he presupposed, so they talked class war, but lacked a strategy for the crisis they appeared to welcome. Thus demands for an expansionist monetary policy quickly turned into demands for the nationalization of the banks, and demands for nationalization of the banks turned into demands for a revolutionary confrontation, for which no one was prepared and in which only a minority wished to be engaged.

The conference debate on *Labour and the Nation* lasted for three days. It was a triumph for the Executive, and most of all a triumph for MacDonald. He introduced and wound up the 'second reading' debate on the first day, and also dealt with most of the detailed amendments later in the week. On the first day, Maxton attacked the programme on the grounds that socialism could no longer be approached by a 'long, slow process of gradualistic, peaceful, Parliamentary change'. Capitalism was in a state of crisis, and the only way in which a Labour Government could redeem its pledges was to introduce public ownership 'at tremendous speed'. Wheatley declared that, even when the programme had been implemented, socialism would be as far away as ever, and ended with the cry, 'let your slogan be: "Socialism is the only remedy."' But after MacDonald had asked pointedly in his winding-up speech whether its critics were parliamentary democrats or not, the programme was adopted without a vote, and an attempt by John Paton to refer back certain passages so that the party could commit itself to the 'living wage' instead was defeated by 2,780,000 to 143,000. The debate on financial policy later in the week saw an even more striking victory for the platform. Snowden, who introduced it, declared bluntly that currency questions could be settled only by international agreement, that inflation was as bad as deflation, that a Labour Government might have to increase taxation to restore the nation's finances to a state of 'stability and soundness', and that if unemployment were suddenly reduced by manipulating the credit system, the country would pay a 'terrible price'. Apart from a speech by E. F. Wise, who argued that it was not enough to nationalize the Bank of England without nationalizing the joint stock banks as well, this was received without a squeak. After Dalton had supported Snowden's views on the gold standard, and Pethick-Lawrence had denounced 'monkeying' with the currency, the financial sections were unanimously approved.[51]

After the conference MacDonald commented in *Forward* with pardonable complacency that the message of Birmingham was 'He conquers who believes he can – and we have that belief.'[52] To judge by their votes, the delegates agreed.

IV

In one important respect, MacDonald was now in a much better position to lead his party to conquest than he had been in 1923 or 1924. As we have seen, his constituency at Aberavon had been a source of anxiety to him for some years, and it is clear from his correspondence that his anxieties became more acute as time went on. In February 1928 one of his staunchest supporters there reported, in response to an inquiry from Rose Rosenberg, that there was a great deal of apathy in the constituency, that Joe Brown, the agent, was still looking for another job, and that many of the miners, whose votes would determine the result, would abstain when the election came.[53] At about the same time, a plaintive letter from MacDonald to Joe Brown, asking for a report on the constituency, earned a testy reply that 'if I neglected the Division, as a good many other Agents do, then perhaps, I should be a little appreciated'; and although Brown ended his report with the defiant conclusion that 'we have nothing whatever, to fear, from any political Party,'[54] he produced little evidence to justify his confidence. Six weeks later, another local supporter wrote to urge MacDonald to 'show your presence among us' more often, and warned him that unless he did so, the Liberal candidate, who was 'actively "warming" himself into the people', would win the seat.[55]

In the meantime, however, Sidney Webb had decided not to stand again at Seaham Harbour, the Durham mining constituency which he had represented since 1922 and where his majority at the last election had been 10,624. At the end of March, MacDonald wrote to warn Joe Brown that he was under great pressure to 'take the Seaham Harbour Division. They offer me a constituency which I need not visit more than once a year and where, at a General Election, three or four speeches at the outside would be all they would ask of me ... They guarantee that no subscriptions will be asked for and that the whole organisation is maintained from local sources.'[56] These were powerful inducements. In April, MacDonald refused an invitation from the Blackhall Colliery Labour Party to nominate him as prospective candidate for Seaham, on the grounds that his friends in Aberavon 'stood by me in bad times and I wish to show them my gratitude',[57] but his scruples were gradually overborne. In May, the executive of the parliamentary party decided unanimously that he should go to Seaham if he could, and on May 28th, Beatrice Webb noted that Henderson and her husband were 'conspiring to hand over the safe and cheap seat of Seaham Harbour to our leader'.[58] In spite of the opposition of the Seaham party secretary, George Bloomfield, who was said to have parliamentary ambitions himself and who had already written to the National Executive to protest against the proposal that MacDonald might become the candidate,[59] the Seaham party unanimously decided to invite MacDonald to succeed Webb, on condition that the Aberavon party agreed to release him. After a meeting with Henderson, the Aberavon executive decided to recommend their party to do so; and at a special conference on July 14th, the Aberavon party voted reluctantly by 100 to 24 to accept the recommendation.[60] In Aberavon, the bitterness created by MacDonald's departure is still remembered.

It was a sad end to the chapter which had begun with such enthusiasm in 1922, and it seems clear that MacDonald felt rather shamefaced about the break. He was invited to attend the special conference on July 14th, but excused himself on the grounds that he had an engagement to speak at Smethwick which he could not break.[61] On July 18th, he wrote a curiously stiff and defensive letter to the chairman of the Aberavon party, Joe Branch, which is worth quoting at length:

I have now heard that the Conference last Saturday decided to release me from Aberavon. I do not know if any of you understand how very sorry I am at what has happened, but believe me, nothing that I have done has given me more regret than this.

You will remember that from time to time I have warned you that the existing condition of things could not go on. The almost unceasing demands for money and time have broken my back and I have had to face the inevitable fact that I cannot possibly add constituency cares to the ordinary troubles and responsibilities of Party leadership. During the last twelve months I have been very greatly disturbed by the financial outlook of the constituency. I put in both from my own pocket and those of my friends sums of money which cannot be repeated, in the hope that difficulties would be tided over and that adequate financial provisions would be made for the smooth working of the Party. I see no hope of that, and you are faced with the necessity of having somebody who can do far more than I can in that respect ...

Over against all that I have had to place the leaving of what I consider to be a perfectly safe seat if the organisation is properly handled and work is put in, and all the elements kept in co-operation and in life. Even above that is the grief at leaving the finest and most delightful set of people that ever a Member of Parliament could wish to represent. That indeed is the greatest pain that I have.

I believe that some of my friends think I ought not to have left, but whether we agree or disagree about that I have tried to find every sort of excuse and justification for continuing to bear the burdens, and only when impossibility met me at every turn have I decided to go.[62]

His regrets must, however, have been powerfully assuaged by an exchange of correspondence with Bloomfield in October. On October 22nd, he wrote to Bloomfield to confirm:

(1) That in going to the constituency I pay all my own out-of-pocket hire of necessary cars and also hotel bills.
(2) That I am not to be responsible for any of the expenses of the local party or the organisation.
(3) That I am to be responsible for none of the expenses of the election.
(4) That I am not to be expected to subscribe to local charities, sports, or any of the score of things that in my present constituency I have to support.[63]

Bloomfield replied reassuringly on October 23rd, that these were the conditions which had prevailed with Webb.[64] On October 26th, he wrote still more reassuringly: 'if you will pardon my reference to it, I would by far prefer having you at either the Reistag [sic] or Vienna or Timbuctoo to give the death-knell to Wholesale murder, than speaking in Seaham Division. We ought to be able to do our work here and allow you to do yours in larger issues.'[65]

V

The general election was now only a few months away. As in 1923, Labour had to fight on two fronts; as in 1923, the Liberals were, in many ways, a more dangerous enemy than the Conservatives. On November 6th, MacDonald noted that the by-election results showed only that the Government would be defeated, not that an independent Labour Government would succeed it. 'If the three party system is to remain,' he wrote gloomily, 'it is obvious that the question of coalitions in some shape or form has to be faced. Our immediate duty is to place every obstacle we can in the way of the survival of the three party system.'[66] Despite occasional misgivings, however, he was optimistic enough to speculate about the form which the next Labour Government might take. On November 7th, he noted that he had been 'cogitating' about whether or not to be his own foreign secretary again. 'We need a P.M. who will drive policy and keep the reins of every office in his hands ... ,' he wrote. 'But if that is done & the office of the P.M. is transformed, can both offices be held by one man? That is more doubtful.'[67] Three months later, his doubts had been resolved. On January 30th, 1929 he noted:

> My friends get more & more confident that there is to be a Labour Government & the bye-elections justify such confidence. If that is to happen must find a Foreign Secretary, for this time I must develop the work of the P.M. so as to co-ordinate the State policy of the various departments ... I want to create a real advisory committee for the P.M., a body that will work out schemes, watch developments, conduct investigations & generally, keep the machinery of Government running steadily. Our conception of the functions of Government means a new position for the P.M. & I must work at that. Unemployment will also require much attention from the P.M.[68]

During the next few weeks, however, it became clear that the result of the election was not yet a foregone conclusion. The Conservatives were fairly quiescent, but the Liberals were buzzing ominously with activity. On January 31st, R. H. Tawney wrote to warn Arthur Henderson:

> An acquaintance who is well-informed as to the intentions of the Liberals writes to me that they propose to make a big plan of public works the centre of their election programme. The idea is to create employment until the total unemployment is brought down to half a million.
>
> If the Labour Election Programme is to be any use it *must have something concrete and definite* about unemployment. The pages on that subject in Labour and the Nation are ... not up to the mark ... [W]hat is required is a definite statement that (a) A Labour Government will initiate productive work on a larger scale, and will raise a loan for the purpose. (b) that it will maintain from national funds all men not absorbed in such work ...
>
> This matter ought to occupy a prominent place in the Election Manifesto. Do get the Leader to authorise a bold statement.

Tawney's letter was sent to MacDonald by Arthur Greenwood, accompanied by a covering note: 'Middleton passed this to me today. It happens to be in line with what is being done. But I thought you ought to see it.'[69] Greenwood's assurances turned out to be widly overconfident. At a dinner for Liberal candidates on March 1st, Lloyd George announced that the Liberal Party had prepared a series of public-works projects, which could be put in hand the moment a Liberal Government came to power, and which would reduce unemployment to 'normal proportions' in a year. The projects were set out in a pamphlet with the alluring title, *We Can Conquer Unemployment*: 350,000 men were to be employed on road-building, 60,000 on housing, 60,000 on telephone development and 62,000 on electrical development. The cost would be £250 million, and the money would be raised by loan. Since the increase in tax revenue and the fall in unemployment expenditure would compensate for the cost of servicing the loan, there would be no burden on the exchequer. In the next three months, Keynes and his protégé, Hubert Henderson, published a pamphlet in support; Lloyd George addressed a series of great meetings up and down the country; and the Government was provoked into issuing a special white paper, proving that the plan was unworkable. In Trevor Wilson's words, it was the 'Indian summer of the old Liberal Party';[70] and, as sometimes happens with Indian summers, it was at least as spectacular as anything that had happened during the real one.

There is no evidence about MacDonald's private opinion of *We Can Conquer Unemployment*. He was temperamentally hostile to grandiose schemes of this sort, suspicious of the whole idea that unemployment could be cured by public works and even more suspicious of anything that emanated from Lloyd George. On the other hand, the Liberal plan did not emanate solely from Lloyd George. Its progenitors also included less suspect figures, like Keynes, Walter Layton and Seebohm Rowntree; and, apart from the loan, most of the ideas it contained could also be found, though only in embryo and without any precision, in *Labour and the Nation*. MacDonald would never have committed himself to figures and a timetable in the way that Lloyd George did, but that was a difference of style rather than of principle. It is difficult to believe that he would ever have supported the Liberal proposals with any enthusiasm, but if they had been presented to him by a group of dispassionate experts, as a contribution to public enlightenment, he might at least have considered them sympathetically. But they were not presented to him as anything of the kind. *We Can Conquer Unemployment* was not a dispassionate contribution to public enlightenment. It was the opening shot in an election campaign: and one of its chief targets was Labour's claim to be the main party of the left. MacDonald's response, like the Labour Party's, has to be seen in this context.

In a breathless and unconvincing reply to Lloyd George, written by G. D. H. Cole and entitled *How to Conquer Unemployment*, the Labour Party deployed four main arguments. Lloyd George's proposals, it declared, had been 'stolen' from the Labour Party. Financially, they were unsound, for it was well known that loans had to be paid for. Furthermore, Lloyd George could not be trusted to carry them out. In any case, unemployment could not be cured by 'palliatives', but only by a 'lasting restoration of industry', which only the Labour Party was equipped to carry out. MacDonald's response was simpler, and almost certainly more effective. In a letter to Oscar Garrison Villard on March 18th, he wrote cheerfully:

The Lloyd George unemployment stunt has fallen pretty flat. A high dignitary in the Church, who is favourably inclined to us, wrote in a letter which I saw the other day that 'certain rash statements' made by Lloyd George the other day at a Luncheon when he launched his project, was doing him a great deal of harm amongst people who were quite determined not to vote Conservative but were a little bit doubtful about voting for us. The curious thing is that he has appealed to our Communists more than [to] anybody else, but my own impression is that before many weeks are over the whole thing will have died down and the Liberal Party will have to fight as though no such pronouncement had ever been made.[71]

His optimism cannot be taken at its face value, but it contains an important clue to his tactics. Lloyd George was trying to rewrite the agenda of politics to suit himself. If he could force the other parties to fight on his ground, he would have won a major victory before the battle had started. To answer his arguments point by point would be to play into his hands. The most damaging reply to him was to refuse to take him seriously—to treat his campaign as an ordinary electioneering stunt, and to focus attention, not on its contents, but on its authorship. With one or two exceptions, this is what MacDonald did. Lloyd George, he wrote patronizingly, had 'gleaned a few stalks' from Labour's field. His programme was a 'gambler's throw of exactly the same character as the issue of coupons in 1918 and the high-falutin programme of hangings, last pennies, the land for heroes and what not'.[72] He was like an ageing showman, vainly trying to attract a crowd into his tent at a village fair:

The fat woman ... is painted on canvas behind him, the brass band with its chief instruments the trombone and the big drum has introduced him, and he has gone through his patter and his tumbling. The lady has smiled from the pay box, the minor members of the troups are inside ready to begin, but no one has mounted the steps and paid the admission fee.
... The fact is that the crowd has recognised an old performer at familiar tricks and are having no more of him. They had heard his patter before and knew it by heart. There was a time when the trombone, blaring tunes about a land fit for heroes ... filled the booth, but they are gone never to return. The mood of the crowd to-day is not that of the trombone ... It is that of an assize, and the old performer is to be one of those who are to stand in the dock.[73]

However undistinguished intellectually, it was a highly effective argument politically—not least because it contained an obvious element of truth. MacDonald employed it again and again in the next ten weeks. Parliament was dissolved at the beginning of May, and on May 9th, he noted 'Off to the fight. Not so optimistic as my friends. The difficulties—press, money, Society—are great, but we are to do well & I shall not spare myself.'[74] In comparison with its predecessors, the campaign that followed was a sedate affair. There were no scares and little excitement. Baldwin fought on the slogan 'Safety First';

Lloyd George tried to turn the election into a referendum on the Liberal unemployment plan; MacDonald appealed in general terms to the country's desire for a change, but treated unemployment as one issue among several and made no firm promises.

At the Manchester Free Trade Hall on May 24th, he delivered a brisk attack on Lloyd George's record, and returned to the well-worn, but still telling, argument that the Liberals were trying to steal Labour's clothes.[75] In a broadcast appeal to the electors on May 28th, he denounced the idea that unemployment could be cured by 'patchwork' and declared that Labour's solution was 'not a programme of relief works upon which the capital spent will be mainly lost to the country. It is a programme designed to add to the wealth and efficiency of the nation, to give a spur to industry and to open the way to markets.' A vote for the Liberals, he concluded, would be a vote for a minority Government, dependent on parliamentary compromises and without real responsibility for its actions.[76] For the most part, however, he concentrated on other issues — the defects of the Government's 'safeguarding' policy, the need for a body to co-ordinate the economic activities of the state, the responsibility for the general strike and, above all, the danger of a drift to war. The last was probably his strongest card, and no one who heard this broadcast on May 28th could doubt that it was the one about which he cared the most. What, he asked, had happened to British foreign policy since 1924?

> Failure to come to an understanding with America; failure to be of assistance to the Committee of the League of Nations preparing for a disarmament conference; a military agreement with France which would have been a serious setback to disarmament ...
>
> ... [I]f we lose our chance now ... that chance will not return either to us or to our children. The memories of the last War will grow dim. The world will get back into the old rut, familiar professions and piety about peace will again soothe us to sleep, and the various countries will once more base their security upon military preparation. So they will all, in the end, find themselves drifting hopelessly upon those currents that make for war ... And remember what the next war is to be like. The old lines which divide combatants from non-combatants, the weak and the diseased from the strong and the robust, men from women and children, will all be obliterated and civilization itself assailed, and from sea and sky will be brought a heap of ruins.[77]

By now, the campaign was almost over, and although MacDonald was horrified by the slapdash organization in his own constituency at Seaham,[78] his morale was high. His speaking tour had been arranged much more efficiently than in 1924. In April, he had written to Tawney to ask whether he would join him during the campaign and act as a 'companion who would read the newspapers before breakfast and then discuss with me the lines for my speeches during the day'.[79] Tawney had not joined him until May 20th, but even before Tawney's arrival he had been accompanied by two secretaries as well as by Lord Arnold. Perhaps because of this, perhaps because of the fine weather and perhaps because of his reception, his spirits had improved steadily as his tour went on. On May 18th, he had reported to the readers of *Forward* that Labour had 'begun well. We carry into the election the swing and heart of the bye-elections.' A week later he had rhapsodized over the 'Elysian' scenery of the Highlands, 'where the half-moon shone from a clear sky and the morning sun rose over hills which the eagles searched for their morning meal'.[80] In his final column, presumably written during the last week of the campaign, and published on June 1st, he remembered the 'fine hill and moorland air', described the 'great audiences' which had listened to him and wondered what they meant.

By the time his column was published, he knew at least part of the answer. Polling day was on May 30th. In Seaham, MacDonald was returned with a majority of 28,794. In the country as a whole, the Conservatives won 8,664,000 votes, the Labour Party 8,360,000 and the Liberals 5,300,000. But the bias of the system worked in Labour's favour, and in the House of Commons the Labour Party had 287 seats, the Conservatives 261 and the Liberals 59. Labour had gained over 130 seats, and for the first time in history it was the strongest party in the state. Egon Wertheimer had written not long before:

> After the inglorious fall of his Government, accompanied as it was by a whole series of *faux pas*, Ramsay MacDonald's future, crowed the wise-acres of London, was not worth a single cent. Yet he sits more firmly in the saddle than ever. His leadership was never less disputed than at the present moment. For this his ability to compromise and reconcile is beyond doubt responsible in part. The true reason, however, is to be sought outside the immediately political. In the imagination and consciousness of thousands his position is beyond party politics ... [I]n the slums of the manu-facturing towns and in the hovels of the countryside he has become a legendary being – the personification of all that thousands of downtrodden men and women hope and dream and desire. Like Lenin ... he is the focus of the mute hopes of a whole class.[81]

Wertheimer's judgment would have been echoed by most of Mac-Donald's followers.

CHAPTER 21

Second innings

MacDonald went back to London from his constituency on May 31st. A great crowd was waiting at Darlington station to see him off. Green and white – Labour's colours in the north-east – seemed to be everywhere, waving from the crowd and waving back from the train. At each stop on the way south, more crowds gathered on the platform, cheering and calling for a speech.[1] When the train arrived at King's Cross at 11 p.m., 12,000 people were waiting outside the station, 'cheering like mad'. According to one observer, MacDonald was 'literally swept off his feet'. Someone tried to lift him shoulder-high. He began to speak, but could get no further than 'I am very grateful, but–.'[2] Then the crowd closed in on him, and he was swept along to a waiting car.

Next day, he saw Clynes, Snowden, Thomas and Henderson at his house in Hampstead; and the five agreed together that Labour should take office for a second time. The Foreign Office, MacDonald noted, would be a 'difficulty. Henderson told me some weeks ago he would not return to H.O. but would put in plea for F.O.'[3] On June 2nd, he issued a slightly querulous statement, warning that it was up to the other two parties to decide whether or not there was to be another election in the next two years, and declaring that he would 'stand no "monkeying"'.[4] For the time being, at least, no monkeying occurred. On June 4th, Baldwin resigned. During the day, he met MacDonald in the Athenaeum and promised, as MacDonald put it in his diary, not to ' "worry" me in office. Would fight & would come back but would give fair play.' MacDonald also noted, however, that he had seen Thomas and Henderson with less agreeable results. 'Row over F.O. & had to threaten would take it myself,' he wrote. 'Proposed Thomas for F.O. & Henderson for unemployment. Not satisfactory but must work material.'[5] On June 5th, he saw the King at Windsor, and kissed hands. Afterwards, he noted 'Communicated to four colleagues further proposals for ministry. Same row & then settled.'[6]

The 'row' over the Foreign Office was more serious than MacDonald's diary implies, and there can be little doubt that it left ugly scars behind it. In April, MacDonald had discussed possible Cabinet appointments with Snowden, Thomas and Henderson. According to his diary, they told him

'I could not take the F.O. this time. H. wants it! Has told me he will not go back to the H.O. I insisted that whatever consultations I might have *I* was to be responsible for the appointment of Ministers.'[7] No further discussion appears to have taken place until after the election. On June 4th, as we have seen, MacDonald suggested that Thomas should become foreign secretary and that Henderson should take charge of the Government's unemployment policy. According to Snowden, whose autobiography is the best source for what followed, Henderson then 'became very angry, and threatened to refuse to have anything to do with the new Government'. Thomas refused to take the Dominions Office again, and MacDonald ended the discussion by saying that he would take the Foreign Office himself for two years, as well as being prime minister. That evening, Henderson told Snowden that he was planning to write to MacDonald, to say that he would not serve at all if MacDonald insisted on being his own foreign secretary. Next day, however, Thomas announced that he was willing to take the Dominions Office after all. Henderson shook him by the hand, said 'That leaves me the Foreign Office,' and left for another meeting. Thomas complained that Henderson had tricked him; insisted that he had agreed to take the Dominions Office only because he thought MacDonald was taking the Foreign Office; and, for a while, he too threatened not to serve. According to Snowden, the dispute was not resolved until the following day, when Thomas finally agreed to take the unemployment port-folio which Henderson had rejected two days before.[8]

Snowden's account contains one obvious, though trivial, inaccuracy. Thomas had been colonial secretary in 1924, not dominions secretary, so there could be no question of his taking the Dominions Office 'again'. It is also inconsistent with MacDonald's diary. According to MacDonald's diary, the row was 'settled' on June 5th; according to Snowden, it did not end until June 6th. According to a minute of Lord Stamfordham's, moreover, MacDonald said on June 4th, that he had 'offered to give up the Prime Ministership and go to the Foreign Office himself, but this was not agreeable to the Party'.[9] This, of course, is inconsistent with Snowden's story that MacDonald had suggested that he should take the Foreign Office, not instead of, but as well as, being prime minister. But Stamfordham's version, though not inconceivable, is highly improbable and has not been corroborated; the most likely explanation for it is that it was based on a misunderstanding. Though Snowden's story may be inaccurate in detail, there is no reason to doubt its main outlines. It is clear from MacDonald's diary that he had originally wanted Thomas to go to the Foreign Office and Henderson to take charge of unemployment. From his point of view, Thomas, whom he liked and trusted, would have been a much better choice as foreign secretary than would Henderson, with whom he got on badly and found it difficult to work. Yet, in the end, Thomas took charge of unemployment and Henderson became foreign secretary. Something must have happened to change MacDonald's mind. It is unlikely that he changed it willingly, and much more probable that he was bullied into doing so by Henderson's theat not to serve.

Few men like being bullied. The first and most obvious consequence of the dispute was that relations between MacDonald and Henderson became even worse than they had been before. Each had a new grievance against the other — Henderson, because MacDonald had tried to keep him out of the office on which he had set his heart; MacDonald, because Henderson had forced his hand. Each allowed the grievance to rankle, and each watched suspiciously for further acts of aggression in future. Each found what he was looking for. MacDonald took charge of the central problem of Anglo–American relations himself, and he could not resist interfering in other areas of foreign policy as well. Henderson resented the interference, grumbled loudly to his friends and, towards the end of the Government's period in office, rebelled outright on an issue of central importance. MacDonald, who was in any case prone to suspect others of conspiring against him, became more and more convinced that Henderson was not to be trusted, and less and less willing to listen to what he said.

The row also had another consequence, which was to prove even more significant for the future. As foreign secretary, Henderson was the only minister with an undoubted place in the front rank of Labour politics who had no departmental responsibility for economic policy. It turned out to be one of the luckiest escapes in recent British history.

II

As in 1924, MacDonald hated the business of forming a Government, and filled his diary with gloomy reflections on his colleagues' importunities. 'I have broken hearts — ,' he noted on June 7th, 'one man all but fainted when I told him he could not get what he expected. Most painful days in one's life. Not good experience for maintenance of respect for mankind.'[10] 'Personal worries fray my nerves more than the election — ,' he confessed on June 8th, 'indeed, I should much rather fight half a dozen elections than make one Cabinet.'[11] By June 9th, the strain was beginning to tell. 'Very bad night,' he noted, 'sleep is not kind to me & I have almost constant pain in my head. I must go to Lossiemouth. Too incompetent to work & went with Arnold in his car to see Aunt Bella.'[12] By June 10th, however, the job was almost done, and MacDonald was able to write:

Finished the making of Ministries except a few minor posts which can wait. I felt like Christian with his load off. Now for aftermath. I have disappointed some good men & offended others. It has been like one of those dreaded nightmares where one meets a malign fate & can do no right.[13]

Yet by any objective test, the fate that met him in 1929 was less malign than it had been in 1924. Once the dispute over the Foreign Office had been settled, only one serious difficulty remained. This was the question of what to do with the Left. In 1924, Wheatley had acted, in effect, as the Clydesiders' representative in the Cabinet. He had been universally applauded for his debating skill and administrative competence. Since then, however, the battle over 'Socialism in our Time' had been fought and MacDonald's relations with the Clydesiders had soured; though Wheatley had never identified himself completely with Maxton and Brockway, he had been just as opposed to MacDonald. Moreover, his reputation had been damaged and his self-confidence shaken by an unsuccessful libel action, and by May 1929, Egon Wertheimer could write that he had become 'politically almost insignificant'.[14] MacDonald was determined not to give Wheatley office again, and had told Snowden, Thomas and Henderson so before the election. Henderson had demurred, but the other two had agreed;[15] and on this, MacDonald got his way. To compensate for Wheatley's exclusion, Lansbury – who had been kept out of office in 1924 – was brought into the Cabinet as first commissioner of works, and given the daunting task of helping Thomas in his attempts to grapple with unemployment.

The other posts were filled more easily. In spite of his behaviour over the Protocol and the surtax, Snowden returned to the Treasury – apparently with no qualms on MacDonald's part, and with no recorded opposition from his colleagues. Of the other leading members of the 1924 Cabinet, Clynes became home secretary, and Sidney Webb, now elevated to the peerage as Lord Passfield, colonial and dominions secretary. Haldane had died in 1928; Sankey, whom Haldane had pushed out in 1924, became lord chancellor at last. Parmoor, at the advanced age of 77, returned to his old position as lord president of the council, with special responsibility for the League of Nations. More refreshing appointments were made lower down the list. Wedgwood Benn, a member of a famous Liberal family who had been a Liberal M.P. for twenty-one years and had joined the Labour Party only two years before, became secretary of state for India. The Admiralty went to A. V. Alexander, a weighty figure in the co-operative movement, who had started life as a stoker in the Royal Navy and who was soon to become a stalwart champion of the Admiralty Board. Willy Graham, a devoted Snowdenite, staunch free-trader and lucid debater, who had won his spurs as financial secretary to the Treasury in 1924, became president of the Board of Trade. Margaret Bondfield, a pillar of the women's Labour movement and a member of the T.U.C. General Council, who had begun her career as a salesgirl in Brighton, became minister of labour and the first woman to hold Cabinet office.

It was a competent, if unadventurous, Cabinet. In the less exalted posts outside it there was a good deal of talent waiting for promotion. Christopher Addison, once a minister in the Lloyd George Coalition, fought hard for a ministry but had to be content with the parliamentary secretaryship to the Ministry of Agriculture and the promise of elevation when Noel Buxton, the minister, moved elsewhere.[16] Shinwell, one of MacDonald's chief allies in his struggle against the Maxton–Brockway leadership of the I.L.P., received a meagre reward as financial secretary to the War Office. Hugh Dalton, an admirer and protégé of Henderson's, followed his patron to the Foreign Office where he became parliamentary secretary. Herbert Morrison, who had proved his effectiveness as a backbench critic of the Government in 1924, was given an opportunity to prove his administrative capacity as minister of Transport. A more spectacular, though more intimidating, opportunity was given to Mosley, who became chancellor of the Duchy of Lancaster. Like Lansbury, he was designated as one of Thomas's assistants, but unlike Lansbury, he had no departmental responsibilities to distract him; and, although the exact relationship between Thomas and his ministerial assistants is far from clear, it seems reasonable to suppose that Mosley was intended to act as Thomas's first lieutenant, while Lansbury was supposed to act as a high-level, but part-time, adviser. They were joined by Tom Johnston, the editor of *Forward* and another effective backbench critic of the 1924 Government, who was also supposed to assist Thomas and became parliamentary secretary at the Scottish Office.

III

As soon as he could, MacDonald escaped to Lossiemouth. Much to his disgust, a bonfire was lit in his honour and he was hauled in triumph through the town, but in spite of these distractions he was able to enjoy ten days of peace and quiet before flying back to London on June 20th.[17] He spent the following weekend at Chequers, and on June 23rd, noted that

> it seemed but yesterday since I was last there. Two memorial panes have been added to the windows of the long gallery & these alone mark change & time & event. I had my familiar walks & visited my friendly places. They seemed a little dishevelled like a woman whom one has not seen for some time & upon whose person carelessness has been stamped. Speaking of this to the housekeeper I gathered from what she said that even in this the feeble hand of Toryism is seen. Sitting under the trees I read a boy's book & was refreshed & a character study of myself. I was vain & I do not know what! This concentration of mine & shyness — what virtues but what stumbling blocks.[18]

The defensive tone of the last sentence was characteristic, but so, for the moment at least, was the peaceful, slightly elegiac, tone of the earlier ones. In 1924, MacDonald had been a squatter, in constant danger of eviction. Now, he was a tenant with a lease. His mood when he returned to office was noticeably more relaxed, more equable and more self-confident than it had been when he entered it for the first time. His diary records no sudden spasms of trepidation and self-doubt and, for that matter, no moments of triumphant exultation: for the first few months after the 1929 election, the tone is generally matter-of-fact, and though it is sometimes possible to detect an under-current of tension, the current is usually a long way beneath the surface.

As in 1924, Rose Rosenberg was brought into the private office at No. 10, and, as in 1924, she acted not only as MacDonald's personal secretary but as a channel of information to and from the parliamentary party and the press. Another political appointee was Herbert Usher, an Oxford graduate and former Labour candidate, whose role is harder to pin down, but whose presence in the private office suggests that MacDonald felt it necessary to supplement his official staff with advisers who possessed a background in Labour politics. But he made no more attempts to open all his own mail, and though the evidence is scanty it seems clear the the 'Highland suspiciousness' which had occasionally marred his relations with officials in 1924 had become less obtrusive. In 1924, Hankey's deputy, Tom Jones, had been a suspect figure to MacDonald, thanks to his earlier activities as one of Baldwin's confidants and speech-writers. Jones's relations with Baldwin had been equally close between 1924 and 1929, but this time MacDonald made full use of him, even to the extent of sending confidential information to Baldwin through him. Robert Vansittart, who had been seconded from the Foreign Office to serve as one of Baldwin's private secretaries, expected to leave No. 10 after the election, and warned MacDonald that, if he were kept on, the Labour Party might object. MacDonald brushed aside the warning, and told him 'My need is for somebody who will say No to me and I think you will.'[19] Vansittart stayed at No. 10 until 1930, when he went back to the Foreign Office as permanent secretary. He wrote in his memoirs years later: 'from James Ramsay MacDonald I got so much trust and affection that saying No was not easy.'

In a way, Vansittart's tribute was double-edged, though unintentionally so. MacDonald had mellowed in the five years since he had last been in office, but he had aged as well. He was more easily deflected by opposition and more apt to take 'No' for an answer; what he really needed was someone to say 'Yes'. He was more prepared to listen to new ideas than his critics have realized and, as we shall see, he did more than most prime ministers to widen the range of advice on which he could draw. But, without fully realizing it himself, he had become more set in his attitudes, more fatalistic about the role of Government and more sceptical about the possibilities open to it. In foreign affairs, he still took it for granted that he could achieve dramatic results if he tried, and struggled hard to do so. He struggled in home affairs too, but he assumed instinctively that no dramatic results were possible and was easily convinced that those who thought otherwise were fools or charlatans. The approach of old age had more straightforward consequence as well. He still drove himself hard – getting up at seven o'clock for a walk around St James's Park before breakfast, sitting long hours at his desk and ploughing methodically through

great quantities of paper. But although he still possessed a formidable capacity
for work, he paid a heavier price and did so more quickly. He tired more
easily, had to escape more often to Lossiemouth, found the return journey to
London more irksome, became more depressed when things went badly and
took longer to recover.

Yet it would be a mistake to suggest that his powers were failing, and a
greater mistake to suggest that contemporaries were conscious of any failure.
In this, as in so much else about MacDonald, hindsight is even more dangerous
than it usually is. In the early 'thirties, his powers did begin to fail, though more
slowly than has often been supposed; and impressions of earlier stages of his
career have often been confused by impressions drawn from the 'thirties. In
the summer of 1929, he was still a tough and resourceful politician and, at the
same time, a figure of commanding authority, abroad as well as at home. No
doubt, he was less vigorous and less flexible at sixty-three than he had been at
fifty-eight, but there was nothing surprising about that. He was still a skilful and
patient chairman of the Cabinet; he still dominated his party, in Parliament
and in the country; he still held his own, and often more than held his own, in
the House of Commons; he was still capable of playing the leading role in a
great international conference, and of holding the threads of a complex set of
negotiations in his hands. To Egon Wertheimer, he seemed 'beyond question
the outstanding figure of International Socialism'.[20] A profile in the New York
Times compared him to Danton, thought his foreign policy 'more spirited'
than Palmerston's and noticed that, within a week of the election, Baldwin,
Lloyd George, Chamberlain and Churchill had all discovered that 'it was
MacDonald on whom the spotlight had been switched.'[21] Even Beatrice Webb
conceded that he was 'the only possible leader at present'.[22] He was to remain
so for some time to come.

IV

MacDonald was still a profoundly lonely man, but his loneliness was no
longer as acute as it had been for most of the last five years. Much to the disgust
of Beatrice Webb, who described it in her diary as 'almost ... a public scandal',[23]
his previously rather distant friendship with Lady Londonderry gradually
became closer, and by the summer of 1930 his letters to her were no longer
being addressed to 'My Dear Lady Londonderry' but to 'My Dear Ladye';
they were signed 'Hamish', the Gaelic form of James. She stayed with him at
Chequers and he visited her and her husband at Loch Choire in the Highlands,
as well as making frequent appearances at Londonderry House. Occasionally
he wrote her rather plaintive poems full of Celtic twilight; in return she gave
him a collection of medieval Latin love lyrics and – more prosaically – a roll of
Rogart tweed.[24] They did not pretend to see eye to eye about politics. 'How wrong

you are about Socialism,' MacDonald expostulated early in 1931. 'Shall I throw one of my poor books at your head? I shall not because I don't want to convert you. You would be a Left Winger & do nothing but give me trouble.'[25] But their friendship flourished all the same. By December 1930, MacDonald was writing that he would 'always think of you as "my dear Ladye" remote but intimate, with ermine on your shoulders but a wild forget-me-not in your hand ... That is what I mean when I send you my love for the Christmas & the New Year. Think of me as the shepherd going home in the dark blowing softly on his pipe because he sees a light in "a window in the castle high".'[26] By May 1931, he was assuring her, more simply, 'I, too, according to many of your friends, was a traitor & spy during the war, but you know I was not; whilst you, according to many of my friends, are a horrid & bad woman, & I know you are a dear good creature.'[27]

But, although their friendship had set some tongues wagging as early as 1930, it mattered much more to MacDonald after the formation of the National Government than before, and it really belongs to a later chapter in his life. At this stage, Lady Londonderry almost certainly took second place to Cecily Gordon-Cumming, the daughter of the once-notorious Colonel Sir William Gordon-Cumming, the laird of Gordonstoun, who had been ostracized by London society after bringing an unsuccessful suit for slander following an allegation that he had cheated at baccarat at a house party in the late 1880s. She was a pretty and vivacious girl in her early twenties, a year or two younger than Ishbel, and although their friendship developed fairly slowly, it is clear that MacDonald became deeply attached to her. They met on a cross-channel steamer, probably in 1928; but when the general election came in 1929, they were not yet on first-name terms. A few days after the election, MacDonald wrote to 'Dear Miss Gordon-Cumming' to thank her for her congratulations.[28] In July, he wrote from Chequers, 'where you must come some day', to invite her to Lossiemouth 'for golf & gossip. I get dull for want of gossip.'[29] By the end of the month, he was writing to 'My Dear Cecily (You cannot have it all your own way)', to say that he would be 'glad to play at Spey Bay on Friday, God & work allowing'.[30] From then until his death in 1937 he addressed a stream of letters and postcards to 'My Dear Cecily' or, more often, to 'My Dear C'; and until she married in the summer of 1931, she probably played a more important part in his life than she herself realized.

It is a difficult relationship for a stranger to capture at a distance of more than forty years — not remotely a love affair, yet carrying an emotional charge of which one of the parties preferred to remain unaware. MacDonald read aloud to her, mostly from Hazlitt and the classics of the nineteenth century; she stayed at Chequers and walked for miles with him in the Buckinghamshire countryside where he had once walked with Margaret; they gossiped together about people and clothes; he tried to educate her and gave her improving books; sometimes he held her hand under the rug while they rode together in the back of his car.[31]

41 With Joan at Chequers, outdoors, February, 1924

42 With Joan at Chequers, indoors, February, 1924

43 Golf at Spey Bay, with Ishbel and Malcolm, August, 1924

44 Snowden arriving at No. 10 for a Cabinet meeting, September, 1924

45 Moscow demonstration, November, 1924. The placard depicts the destruction of MacDonald – 'the king-lackey and betrayer of the workers'

46 Lunch at Prague with Masaryk (facing camera, centre) and Beneš (back to camera

47 'Focus for the mute hopes of a whole class' – MacDonald in the mid-1920s

Once she sent him a present of gulls' eggs, and he thanked her gravely for 'the eggs of gulls *alias* plovers, or plovers *alias* gulls. They are good with a Blairs flavour.' Once she knitted him some stockings, and he wrote to thank her for 'a piece of beautiful work. They *are* just on the tight side especially over the instep but I think they will stretch by wear. Were you here I would kiss your hand for them.'[32]

She was never in love with him, but conceded years later that he might have been 'in a small, far-away way ... slightly in love with me'. But he never said so, was never 'tiresome' and never 'pounced'.[33] His letters to her were affectionate, allusive and brief—often only a few lines, rarely more than a page or so, hinting wistfully at things that could not be said and feelings that could not be admitted. 'My Dear C,' he wrote in March 1930. 'Verily I long for Spey Bay, but it cannot be—like some other things.'[34] 'What a fine time I had in Morayshire,' he wrote a few weeks later, '& flew down as though somebody were waiting for me at Hendon.'[35] After she had stayed for a weekend at Chequers, he wrote:

My Dear C

Thank you, kissing your hand, for the bread & butter note. It was good to have you. Oh, the dull weight of things does get on to my poor temperamental mind & I am like a bird in a cage trying to sing & can just chirp at intervals. But be careful of yourself. Don't overdo your quacks, don't fall in love with old men—and a few other things, including: keep up your spirits & don't do anything to depress them. All of which is good advice from a greybeard beginning to be a philosopher & lecturer on the ways of living. My thumb is all right again, but it wants to know why its fate was so hard. Why did Fate cho[o]se it for misfortune?

You must come again & study the graceful figure of Hygiea, her pose & her draperies.*

Always

JR.

*and, as you say, give me 'a glimpse of the lighter side of existence'—just a glimpse.[36]

In another letter, probably written at about the same time, he grumbled plaintively, 'Saturday & Sunday were indeed wonderful days but those who would cherish me if there were no one else available, were all out with their best boys & I was left like a pelican in the wilderness, an owl in the desert. So I stuck to work, played croquet against myself, & such like.' But he was not often as outspoken as that. Sometimes, he gave her fatherly advice. 'Don't talk or think of a wasted life,' he wrote in a letter wishing her 'many happy returns of yesterday', in May 1930. 'None of us looking back are happy, for how many precious hours have we wasted; but looking forward we can see how to be more economical. And after all what more can we do.' Often, he

R

used his letters to her as a safety valve. 'It is good to be here … ,' he wrote in a
letter from Lossiemouth, in December 1929. 'But the world is a perfect devil
with all its whims & tempers, spines & jealousies & I often long for the Pacific
Island.' 'Next week I return to the bogs in which I live,' he wrote in September
1930, '& must just try & splash a bit in them & find out if there be any bottom
to the slush.' On the whole, however, he did his best to be light-hearted.
'Your news about yourself is scanty but what there is is bad,' he wrote in July
1930. 'I want to hear good news of your best boy & you give me bad news of
your nose. So like the world.' Towards the end of October he wrote:

> My Dear C.
> You are still twenty and I am about the same. I dearly love those shows
> & would walk miles to see a lady in a flaxen wig & plush robes ride into a
> village at the head of a circus …
> This is sad about your finger. I shall wear the stockings with all the more
> reverence as they have been dyed by your blood. Poor dear!
> Ever
>
> R.[37]

That letter probably catches the flavour of their relationship as well as any.
In 1931, she got married. MacDonald heard the news in April, and wrote
from Lossiemouth to congratulate her:

> My Dear
> I greet you in spirit in your own little house. May it be a bower of
> happiness to you. When I am lonely and ninety you will perhaps put a low
> comfortable chair at your fire side & allow me to chatter, with long
> drawn-out monotony, on old times whilst you darn & knit and be polite
> but deaf.
> So it is coming off. Good luck to you. This morning I sat by my fire here
> after a bracing walk through the cold winds of the harbour and read some
> things from Johnson's *Rambler* about Juno & Hymen & wayward women.
> Then a letter from Flour Millers bidding me to a feast; then an autograph
> affection from George V all in his own hand, then an interview with a fish
> wiffie, then a line from my best grandmother, then yours. Thus the
> morning & my post. And it rains on my window & a train rattles south,
> & the gutters gurgle with running water from my roof, and the day goes,
> and I send everybody to perdition & am mightily impelled to go there
> myself. What a day yesterday was in the air. I sang songs to the winds &
> the clouds & the mists, admired the handsome fur boots I was wearing &
> was as vain as a peacock. A great day.
> Now I must remember that you are a sedate missus with a 'hoose o' yer
> ain', a bourgeois, dignified & solemn, one of the county in spite of being
> called O'Brien. Bless you to bless 'his nain sel' ' & be as happy as a laverock.

We'll kiss no more, By sea or shore, Ahint a door; For noo she's mairrit,
Happy & pairit, Her auld jos maun bear it ...
    A hearty welcome to both of you to the fair land of Moray.
    Ever

                                                        R.[38]

After the wedding, he wrote again to ask what her husband's name was and
whether she wanted a present. 'I was hoping to see you at lunch today (Tuesday),' he added, a little forlornly. 'But my dear, blessings & always blessings.'[39]

                                    V

By then, the shadows were closing in, but in the summer of 1929 the Government's prospects seemed bright. The Conservatives had been hit hard at the
election, and were unlikely to want another in the near future. In spite of all
their efforts, the Liberals had increased their representation by only nineteen
seats. Though their total vote had gone up, their share of the vote in the seats
contested by a Liberal candidate was lower than it had been in 1924; they too
would think twice before forcing the Government out. The new Parliament
was unlikely to last for anything like a full term, but MacDonald and his
colleagues could reasonably look forward to a honeymoon period of several
months in which to prepare for another election at a time of their own choice.
They seemed well placed to take advantage of it. Trade seemed to be reviving
a little. Unemployment was slightly lower than it had been twelve months
before, and exports were still rising. Abroad, the omens were still more favourable. The Young committee on reparations had completed its labours in May,
and there were good reasons to hope that a permanent solution was at last in
sight. Most encouraging of all, there were signs that the new administration in
Washington did not wish to carry out the threat implicit in the cruiser Bill,
the passage of which had so alarmed MacDonald and his American friends,
and that it might after all prove possible to reach an agreement on naval disarmament with the Americans and in doing so to pave the way for a wider agreement with the other naval powers, and perhaps for land disarmament as well.
    MacDonald's actions during the next few months must be seen against this
background. Before the election, he had decided privately that, if he became
prime minister again, he would leave foreign policy to someone else while he
concentrated on unemployment and on co-ordinating the work of the departments.[40] Now he changed his mind. The King's speech on July 2nd gave pride
of place to foreign affairs. It was made clear that the Government intended to
sign the so-called 'optional clause' of the statute of the international court and
to resume diplomatic relations with the Soviet Union. More ambitiously, the
speech also looked forward to a settlement of the reparations question, pointed

out that this would make it possible to begin the evacuation of the Rhineland and announced that conversations on naval disarmament had begun with the American ambassador, in the hope that they would lead to 'an early reduction of armaments throughout the world'. The domestic proposals were prosaic in comparison. There were to be inquiries into the cotton and steel industries, the licensing laws and the law governing parliamentary elections, but apart from a vague promise to remedy the situation created by the 1927 Trade Disputes Act and to reorganize the coal industry, there was little mention of positive action.[41]

MacDonald's speech in the debate on the address echoed these priorities. Understandably enough in the head of a minority Government, he began with a conciliatory passage, in which he promised to consult 'responsible leaders of other parties' about the allocation of parliamentary time and wondered whether it might be possible for the House to 'consider ourselves more as a Council of State and less as arrayed regiments facing each other in battle'. Then he turned to the Government's policy. The Government, he declared, existed to deal with two 'dominating concerns' – unemployment and peace. Unemployment could be reduced only by sound policies to stimulate trade; peace could be secured only by reaching a better understanding with the United States. The first, he made clear, was a matter for Thomas; though he did not say so explicitly, he made it equally clear that his own efforts would be concentrated on the second.[42]

As always, he played his cards close to his chest, rarely consulting his colleagues and never spelling his strategy out. But, although there is no direct evidence, it is not difficult to guess how his decision was arrived at. We know now that the improvement in employment which took place in the summer of 1929 was a false dawn, and that the forces which were about to produce the worst trade depression in history were already at work. MacDonald and his colleagues did not know this. They knew that unemployment was too high and that they would be expected to bring it down, but as they had repeatedly said in the general election, they did not believe that it could be brought down quickly; they had no way of telling that they would soon be faced with the much more alarming problem of how to prevent it from rising. As they saw it, unemployment was a problem for the long term. What they needed was a dramatic success in the short term, which would make it possible for them to go to the country with a reasonable prospect of winning an absolute majority. As the *New York Times* pointed out, there could hardly be a better overture to an election campaign than an agreement on naval disarmament with the United States, followed by a successful international conference.[43]

As the *New York Times* also recognized, however, it would be wrong to suggest that MacDonald's decision to concentrate on naval disarmament and Anglo–American relations was based primarily on electoral considerations. As he had warned in his election broadcast, he believed that the world was drifting towards another war, in which civilization might be destroyed; with some justification, he also believed that the drift could not be halted unless Britain and the United States ended their naval rivalry. For fifteen years he had argued that peace could be secured only by disarmament, and that disarmament could be achieved only by cutting through the vicious circle of fear and suspicion which had prevented it in the past. As in 1924, he now had an opportunity to practise what he had preached. He has sometimes been criticized, if only by implication, for neglecting domestic problems in order to seize that opportunity; few of his critics have recognized that it would have been a betrayal of his deepest convictions to let it slip.

VI

As in 1924, the situation MacDonald faced when he came into office was more promising than it looked at first sight, but in some ways it was even more difficult than it had been in 1924 to make sure that the promise was fulfilled. In 1924, he had had to act as the arbitrator between France and Germany; though Britain had had much to gain from a settlement, her own security had not been at stake. This time, the question at issue went to the heart of Britain's position as a great power — perhaps of her national survival. A foolish reparations agreement might have cost Britain money and jeopardized the peace of Europe: a mistake over naval disarmament might make it impossible for her to defend herself. Partly for this reason, MacDonald's freedom of action was more limited than it had been five years before. Even then, he had had to take account of the attitudes of the Treasury as well as of the needs of the Germans and the fears of the French. Now he had to reckon with the Admiralty: and the Admiralty had more weight over naval disarmament than the Treasury had had over reparations. Whatever constitutional textbooks might say, MacDonald had to carry the Admiralty with him; to some extent, at least, he had to treat it less as an instrument of Government policy than as an independent power with a negotiating position of its own.

The problems of substance were formidable too. Naval rivalry between Britain and the United States was a legacy of the war, when the U.S. Navy Board had recommended that the American navy should ultimately be made equal to the most powerful foreign navy. Since then, the demand for 'parity' with Britain had been one of the central pillars of American naval policy. The Washington treaty had given the Americans parity in capital ships. Parity in cruisers was more elusive. There were two categories of cruiser — the 10,000-ton cruiser, armed with eight-inch guns, and a small cruiser, of around 5–6,000 tons, armed with six-inch guns. The British, with their worldwide empire, needed a large fleet of cruisers to protect their communications, but they could not afford a large fleet of big ones. The Americans, with fewer bases, needed cruisers that could cruise for long distances; they concentrated on the first category and virtually ignored the second. The results were paradoxical. In tonnage, the British cruiser fleet was much larger than the American, and if tonnage was to be equated with strength, parity would entail British reductions, or American increases, or both. But the British refused to make this equation. An eight-inch cruiser, they claimed, could sink a six-inch cruiser before coming within the latter's range. Tonnage, they insisted, was only one element of strength among many; and they strenuously resisted American demands for parity on a tonnage basis. This was the rock on which the 1927 Geneva conference had foundered. The British had demanded 15 eight-inch and 55 six-inch cruisers; the Americans had demanded 25 or 30 eight-inch ones. The gulf had been too wide to bridge, and Anglo-American relations had deteriorated steadily ever since.[44]

A deeper gulf of attitude and perspective loomed through the fog of technicalities. The United States was a rising power; Britain, a declining one. The Americans had no cause to fear for their own security; the British had. For the Americans parity was a symbolic assertion, not a military necessity; they wanted parity with Britain, not because they feared her or intended to fight her, but for its own sake. For the British, parity was a real problem, not a symbolic one; in certain circumstances, it might even be a matter of life and death. They were happy enough to give parity to the Americans – 'heaped up and flowing over', as MacDonald put it in a characteristic phrase – but they could not afford to do so in such a way as to jeopardize their superiority over the other naval powers. As MacDonald pointed out again and again, Britain did not build against the United States but against the rest of the world; and no one who had lived through the war could doubt that circumstances might arise in which her survival would depend on having done so. But the Americans did not only want parity. They also wanted arms reductions; and the combination of parity and reduction threatened to disturb Britain's existing relationship, not only with the United States, but with Japan and even with France and Italy. And though war between Britain and the United States was unthinkable, it was not at all unthinkable that Japan might menace Britain's interests in the Pacific or that France and Italy might combine against her in the Mediterranean.

There were more hopeful factors to balance against the difficulties. Ships cost money, and neither side really wished to pay the costs of a naval race. At a deeper level, neither side really wished to fight the other. Their relations were clouded by suspicion and jealousy, but the hatreds and fears which impeded disarmament on the mainland of Europe were absent. In spite of MacDonald's disappointment at Al Smith's defeat, Hoover's arrival at the White House turned out to be a hopeful factor too. Before his inauguration, he let it be known that he was willing to engage in conversations with Baldwin; in his inaugural address, he appealed for cuts in military spending and emphasized that he wished to reduce armaments and not merely to limit them. On April 22nd, Hugh Gibson, the American delegate at the League of Nations preparatory commission on disarmament, broke new ground with a suggestion that naval strength might be measured in such a way as to take account of factors other than tonnage—notably, age and gun calibre.[45] Though it soon became clear that Gibson had promised more than he could deliver, for there was no scientific formula by which tonnage could be equated numerically with age and gun calibre, this speech began a new chapter. The Americans still demanded parity, but they had at last recognized publicly that if they were to obtain it, it would have to be defined in a way that took account of Britain's needs as well as of their own.

It was not, however, an easy chapter to write. MacDonald came into office at the beginning of June, six weeks after Gibson's speech. On June 14th, General Dawes, the new American ambassador to Britain, arrived in Southampton. Two days later, MacDonald met him at Forres, near Lossiemouth. According to MacDonald's diary, the meeting was a 'great success'; Dawes, he noted amiably, was a 'cordial & earnest man, spare, thin, in navy stripe & odd looking pipe'.[46] They agreed that naval disarmament should be isolated from the more contentious questions of belligerent rights and the freedom of the seas, and that MacDonald should visit Washington when an agreement had been reached. At a second meeting on June 25th, they agreed that a five-power naval conference should be held, either in Washington or in London, provided that Britain and the United States had first reached 'substantial agreement' on the best way to compare cruisers in different categories.[47] At the end of June, the British formally accepted the principle of parity, and in early July, MacDonald told Dawes that he had decided to slow down two of the cruisers in the 1928-9 building programme; it would have a 'fine effect', he added pointedly, if Hoover did the same.[48] The British decision was announced on July 24th; Hoover responded by announcing that preparations for the construction of two American cruisers would be slowed down as well. On July 25th, Esmé Howard, the British ambassador in Washington, reported that the two announcements had made a 'great impression' and that Hoover had said that he would welcome a visit from MacDonald, provided that a preliminary agreement had been reached on questions of principle.

Hoover's proviso was more onerous than it sounded. The Americans alleged that Britain's cruiser fleet, built, building and projected, totalled 402,000 tons, and that she had altogether 24 large cruisers—14 in being, 7 under construction and 3 authorized. The British indignantly denied that they had anything of the kind. Britain's fleet of large cruisers, the Admiralty insisted, came to 22, built and building, not to 24. Four of them were 'Hawkins'-class cruisers, which had been laid down in 1916 and could not be equated with modern eight-inch cruisers. These ought to be included in the six-inch category instead. 'Hawkins'-class cruisers, the Americans replied, carried seven-and-a-half-inch guns and had come into service between 1918 and 1925: American naval experts did not understand how MacDonald and his advisers could place such vessels in the six-inch class. Still fiercer arguments took place over the relationship between the main categories themselves. An eight-inch cruiser, MacDonald wrote in a moment of abandon, was worth 'almost an infinity of smaller craft and guns'. Not so, replied the Americans: a six-inch shell could penetrate the armour of an eight-inch cruiser, while a six-inch gun could be fired more rapidly than could an eight-inch gun. That was an academic argument, the British answered patronizingly; their own view was not based on theory but on the experience of battle.[49]

So the negotiations dragged on. They must have been among the most frustrating in MacDonald's career. He excelled at face-to-face encounters, when he could bring his charm and magnetism to bear on his opposite number and get around awkward corners by blurring the differences at stake. Now he had to fight with different weapons. He soon established a warm relationship with Dawes, and by mid-July was sending Mrs Dawes a copy of his biography of Margaret.[50] But Dawes was a messenger-boy, not a plenipotentiary; he had no power to settle, and on at least one occasion the State Department repudiated him. The negotiations themselves were conducted at one remove, and sometimes at two. MacDonald would write to Dawes, and Dawes would then convey the contents of his letter to Washington. The State Department would then send a reply to Dawes, and Dawes would send the text of the State Department's telegram to MacDonald. To make matters worse, it was not always clear whether the State Department's telegram expressed the view of Harry Stimson, the secretary of state, of Hoover, or of the Navy Board, and there were times when the three seemed to be speaking with different voices. MacDonald did his best to strike a personal note, even to the extent of beginning one of his letters to Dawes by telling him that it was being written 'early in the morning when only the birds are up and even they are sleepy'.[51] Though the result sometimes lacked precision, he managed to convey an impression of warmth and urgency which must have done a great deal to dissipate earlier American suspicions of British policy. But it all took time: and with a minority Government in office, time was in short supply.

Little by little, however, the two sides edged closer together. The first big hurdle was the size of the British cruiser fleet. At the 1927 Geneva conference, Britain had demanded 70 cruisers altogether. After the election, the Admiralty agreed that MacDonald should ask for 60. Privately, MacDonald believed that even this figure was too high, but the first sea lord, Sir Charles Madden, had made it clear that he would not accept a lower one without an assurance that the Japanese, French and Italians would make reductions as well. Thus MacDonald had to walk warily. At a meeting with Dawes on July 29th, he suggested that Britain should have 15 eight-inch cruisers, and 45 six-inch.[52] Next day, he wrote to Alexander, suggesting that 'if we could get a good agreement with the Five Powers, we could bring our cruiser requirements nearer to 50 than 60.'[53] For some days, he fought on two fronts – asking for more cruisers than he thought he needed when he dealt with the Americans, and behind the scenes doing his best to whittle the Admiralty's figure down. The State Department rejected his proposals of July 29th, on the grounds that they would entail an increase in Britain's existing cruiser fleet of 52. MacDonald replied firmly that he had to take account of other naval powers as well as of the United States and that if he failed to do so, 'my existence as Prime Minister would soon be ended'.[54] Soon afterwards, however, he persuaded Madden to agree, in the guarded language of a Cabinet minute, 'that if the European situation was so improved as to give reasonable security for ten or twelve years, with a chance of further improvement, he was willing to come down to a strength of fifty cruisers'.[55] Armed with this concession, MacDonald then wrote again to Dawes to say that, if the Americans were willing to wait until 1936 before reaching parity, Britain would be content with 50 cruisers after all.[56]

His offer was accepted on August 15th. But although the first big hurdle had now been jumped, a bigger one remained. Even after MacDonald's concession, Stimson wrote, Britain would have a cruiser fleet of 330,000 tons in 1936. If the Americans were to reach parity, they would have to stick to their existing programme of 23 eight-inch cruisers. This would give them a cruiser fleet of 300,000 tons, and it would probably be possible to agree on a formula to close the gap of 30,000.[57] Stimson's proposal seemed as outrageous to the British as the British claim to 60 cruisers had seemed to the Americans. It had just been agreed that Britain was to have 15 eight-inch cruisers. In asking for 23, Stimson was demanding a lead of eight. In doing so, moreover, he was dangerously close to offering the Japanese a lead of one. The Washington treaty had laid it down that, in capital ships, the ratio between the American, British and Japanese fleets should stand at 5:5:3. But the Japanese were now demanding a ratio of 5:5:3½. If the Americans had 23 eight-inch cruisers, this ratio would give the Japanese 16, and Japan would then have more eight-inch cruisers in the Pacific than Britain had altogether. The most the British could accept, MacDonald insisted, was a Japanese fleet of 12 eight-inch cruisers, and an American fleet of 18.[58] Beyond that, they could not go.

For a while, it looked as though the gap would prove too wide to bridge. 'Wordy dispatch in bag from America,' MacDonald noted on August 17th. 'It insists upon treating us as a potential enemy & is disappointed when we do not do everything it tells us.'[59] As late as September 11th, he noted gloomily:

American negotiations hang, the real truth being that our circumstances are so different that it is almost impossible to co-ordinate our needs. The desire to do valiantly struggles along, every obstacle making it more determined. Ambassador cables that I ought to go to Washington agreement or no agreement, but that in latter case President will not *invite* me: between devil & deep sea. What a solitary life this is. I live in this room all alone like a clerk in his office with a day long procession of secretaries

& others with bunches of papers in their hands demanding judgement. At odd moments of leisure I am reading Carlyle & wondering what those who are no longer here are doing & thinking—if at all. Looking at old photographs the other day. They seemed to be terribly alive & yet would not hold communion. The riddle of the Sphinx is that she symbolises the dead ... [60]

Eventually, however, the 'desire to do valiantly' prevailed. On August 30th, MacDonald offered to scrap the 'Hawkins' class prematurely in order to simplify the problem of categorization. There was no response.[61] On September 9th, he suggested that the Americans might equip five large cruisers with six-inch guns, and implied that if they did so he would then be willing for them to have 23 large cruisers altogether.[62] At this, they nibbled. On September 11th, they announced that the Navy Board were now asking for only 21 eight-inch cruisers. This, they pointed out, meant that the difference between the two sides had been narrowed down to the question of whether three out of the 21 American 10,000-ton cruisers were to be armed with six-inch or eight-inch guns. This question, they suggested, could be settled by mutual compromise. Though they thought that the differences between the Admiralty and the Navy Board could not be resolved before the five-power conference. Hoover now wished MacDonald to visit the United States.[63] With that, MacDonald had to be content. 'There are shadowy entities behind me,' he wrote appealingly, in his last letter to Dawes. 'A spirit photograph would show you unaccompanied, but round me would be the ghosts of the other nations.'[64] The ghosts were still haunting him when he and Ishbel set sail on the *Berengaria* on September 28th.

VII

He left Downing Street with mixed feelings. Before leaving he noted apprehensively:

I go today. There is autumn outside, a snap in the air, yellowing leaves & a misty atmosphere ... The American programme planned by generous & enthusiastic hosts has no attractions for me. Rather, I shrink from it. I am lonely & my heart is in results only. I pray I may be equal to the nervous strain & that accuracy and responsiveness of touch, which is true diplomacy, may be mine. My friends smile & are happy in their adieux, but I am in no way 'lifted up'. There will surely be an aftermath when our failure to make good *all* our promises before Christmas comes.[65]

After a while, the black mood lifted. When MacDonald appeared at Waterloo station, a group of workers climbed on to the taxis, and struck up the 'Red Flag'; later, they switched to 'For He's a Jolly Good Fellow.'[66] 'Great crowds to see me off with friends close by me ... ,' MacDonald noted. 'Without having any idea of planning something big, something big has happened.'[67]

The 'something' was bigger than he could have realized. It was the first time a British prime minister had visited the United States: MacDonald in 1929 was the precursor of Churchill after 1940 and of a long line of prime ministers after 1945. He came, moreover, in pursuit of an agreement which was intended to confirm the end of Britain's supremacy at sea. His visit was a milestone in British foreign policy: it was an even greater milestone in America's hesitant emergence as a world power.

He arrived in New York on October 4th. An editorial in that morning's *New York Times* described him as 'unpretentious, unspoiled, with dignity fitting his position, yet with the simple dignity of one who knows how fleeting is fame and by what aid of good fortune men arrive at eminence'.[68] After a nineteen-gun salute in New York harbour and a ticker-tape parade along Broadway, Mayor Walker presented him with the freedom of the city; in Washington, where he arrived that afternoon, the cheers and applause of the crowd outside Union Station were said to have drowned the booming of the artillery. He spent most of October 5th in Washington, and in the evening he and Ishbel were taken to Hoover's camp on the banks of the Rapidan river in the Blue Ridge mountains, where they spent the night and the following day. According to the *New York Times* 'a small mountain of personal letters and telegrams' arrived at the British embassy. One letter described MacDonald as a 'saint'; a telegram from a man and his wife 'stated simply that they both loved him for his personality and accomplishments'. At Rapidan, a headline promised, 'President and Premier will make history in silent retreat.'

In fact, the talks at Rapidan settled nothing. Though the Americans had agreed several months before that the question of belligerent rights at sea should not be mixed up with naval disarmament, Hoover insisted on raising it. At first, MacDonald agreed that the official communiqué on the talks should include a commitment to examine the question later, and should make it clear that Hoover wished to declare food-ships free from interference in time of war. The result was a howl of fury in London, ably orchestrated by Hankey, who sent MacDonald three telegrams of protest—one from himself, one from Snowden, who was acting as prime minister in MacDonald's absence, and one from the chiefs of staff committee.[69] At this, MacDonald gave way and, with some difficulty, managed to persuade his hosts that the communiqué should say nothing about belligerent rights after all.[70] The talks were only a little more productive on disarmament. At first, Hoover insisted that all further concessions would have to come from the British, but in the end he agreed to meet Britain half-way, provided that Britain made further reductions as well. It had already been agreed that the British Government should issue formal invitations to a five-power conference to be held in London in the third week in January; and this was done on October 7th. The only firm decision taken at Rapidan, however, was that discussions should continue on how best to close the remaining gap.

Any disappointment MacDonald may have felt must have been outweighed by the events of the next few days. The pastor of Rutgers presbyterian church prayed for him; the pastor of the West End presbyterian church described the Rapidan talks as 'unparalleled in the history of Christian civilisation'; and the former dean of the Cathedral of St John the Divine compared him to Grotius and Henri IV. Dr Poling described his visit as 'primarily a spiritual adventure', and William Green, the president of the American Federation of Labor, opened its annual convention by declaring that MacDonald's was a 'holy mission'. On October 7th, MacDonald addressed the Senate. 'In words obviously unstudied, without giving a thought apparently to the literary finish of what he had to say, he made a deep impression by the genuine emotion which he first felt in his own soul, and was then able to convey to his audience ... ,' wrote the *New York Times*. 'If this be not lofty oratory, it is something finer and grander.' On October 10th, he left Washington for New York — visiting Philadelphia *en route*, and entertaining the doctors and nurses who had looked after him two years before. On October 11th, he received a group of New York socialists, led by Norman Thomas; spoke at a lunch given by the St Andrew's Society, the St George's Society, the St David's Society and the English Speaking Union; attended a reception given by the Foreign Policy Association where he made another speech; and finally spoke at a dinner given by the New York Council on Foreign Relations. On October 13th, he left New York for Canada, with the plaudits of the *New York Times* editorial writer ringing in his ears:

> The British Prime Minister leaves New York today for Canada, with every token and testimony that his American visit has been an overpowering success. Though he modestly puts away the personal aspect of it, it has been a distinct triumph for Ramsay MacDonald, the man. His bearing has been perfect ... His eloquence has been that of elevation of mind and nobility of purpose. On divers strings he has sounded the one clear note of a passion to secure established peace on earth through every reasonable and honorable means. Such speaking as his, coming to a climax as it did in his magnificent address on Friday night, has seldom been heard in any country, from the lips of a citizen of another.

After a strenuous two weeks in Canada, MacDonald sailed for England on October 27th. He arrived at Liverpool on November 1st, and on November 3rd noted privately 'the unity & fairness of it all have enabled me to do my very best. Ishbel was splendid & did inestimable service by her demeanour & her representation of young England to America.'[71] On November 5th he reported on his visit to the House of Commons. 'No Ambassador', he declared, 'could have received a warmer welcome; no government or people could have opened their doors, their minds or their hearts wider to a guest.' Baldwin and

Lloyd George both followed him, and they both went out of their way to pay tribute to his success. MacDonald had acted throughout 'as the Prime Minister of the United Kingdom and not as a party leader', Baldwin declared. 'We all owe him a great debt of gratitude.' Lloyd George admitted that he had had doubts about the wisdom of visiting the United States before the five-power conference took place, and that he now realized that he had been wrong. MacDonald's visit, he declared, had been a 'real triumph'.[72] Even the ranks of Tuscany joined in the cheering. Beatrice Webb described MacDonald's tour as a 'feat of endurance and triumph in political activities'.[73] Dalton wrote that the prime minister had 'made for himself an eternal niche in the temple of history'.[74]

VIII

In August, Snowden had delighted the press and public by his acidulous defence of British interests at an international conference on reparations which had taken place at The Hague; in September, he had returned home with a satisfactory agreement in his pocket and had received a hero's welcome. Now Snowden's triumph had been capped by MacDonald's. Meanwhile, the Government had signed the optional clause and had reached agreement with the Soviet Union on the steps by which diplomatic relations were to be resumed. But although the foreign policy set out in the King's speech had been remarkably successful, the supreme prize of a disarmament agreement remained to be won. Thanks largely to MacDonald, Anglo-American relations were better than they had been for some time: perhaps than they had ever been. But although an Anglo-American understanding was a necessary condition of a five-power agreement, it was far from being a sufficient condition; and if a five-power agreement were not reached, the Anglo-American understanding might collapse in ruins. The logic which had impelled MacDonald to concentrate on Anglo-American relations in the first place thus impelled him, with equal force, to keep his hand to the plough until the five-power conference was over.

For two months, he devoted himself to domestic problems, but towards the end of January 1930, the five-power conference at last assembled in London. It was a distinguished gathering. The French delegation was led by the prime minister, André Tardieu, and also included the formidable figure of Aristide Briand, 'veteran of a hundred conferences' as Harold Nicolson described him,[75] and now the foreign minister. Stimson led the American delegation and Mussolini's foreign minister, Dino Grandi, the Italian. The Japanese delegation was headed by a former prime minister, Reijiro Wakatsuki; Britain was represented by MacDonald, Henderson, Alexander and Wedgwood Benn. On January 21st, while the streets outside were blanketed by fog, the first plenary session of the conference was opened by George V amid the Victorian glories of the Royal Gallery of the House of Lords;[76] subsequent meetings were held in St James's

Palace. Following precedent, MacDonald was chosen as chairman. After expressing his thanks for the honour, he defined the objectives of the conference in a speech which, to the initiated at least, must have given an ominous foretaste of the conflicts that were to come. The Kellogg Pact, he declared, was:

> a mighty moral bulwark against war — and we must never underestimate the effectiveness of moral bulwarks with no bayonet nor bludgeon behind them. The entry of the United States into the Permanent Court of International Justice, the growing confidence in the court, and the increase in the number of nations who have signed the Optional Clause mark definite and, I believe, irrevocable steps in the displacement of military power by judicial process in the settlement of international disputes. Public servants like us will fail in our duty if we do not diminish military power in proportion to the increase of political security ...
> ... I dare affirm that, in the naval programme of the leading naval powers, there is a margin between real security needs and actual or projected strength, and the world expects this Conference to eliminate that margin.[77]

'Moral bulwarks with no bayonet nor bludgeon behind them': the language could have been taken from U.D.C. manifesto of fifteen years before. As MacDonald knew better than most, however, it begged the really awkward questions. By now, the gap between Britain and the United States had almost been closed. For some time, the Americans had advocated what was picturesquely described as a 'holiday' in battleship construction until 1936. Their suggestion was violently resisted by the British Admiralty, on the grounds that it would disorganize the yards; and in his talks with Hoover, MacDonald had stuck to the Admiralty brief. He had done the same at the first meeting of the Cabinet committee to decide Britain's tactics at the conference. Soon afterwards, however, he had received an angry letter from Snowden, denouncing the Admiralty for trying to stampede the Government and warning that, if it succeeded, the Labour Party would be driven into revolt. At this, MacDonald had changed his mind; and before the conference began, the British had adopted the American position.[78] Early in February, the Americans responded by adopting the British position on eight-inch cruisers, and decided that they could make do with 18 to Britain's 15 after all. Soon afterwards, a compromise was reached on the total tonnage of the American cruiser fleet, and by February 27th, MacDonald was able to note 'Stimson & Reed discussed the Anglo-American position & complete agreement was reached subject to Admiralty comments.'[79] In spite of some muttering from Madden, the British delegation accepted the agreement next day.[80]

The Japanese presented a more formidable problem. Socially, they had great merit. 'Dinner & reception at Japanese Embassy last night,' MacDonald noted enthusiastically on January 17th. 'Talked not of ships but of old houses. Delightful persons.'[81] His enthusiasm waned when they turned from old houses to naval ratios. They made it clear at an early stage in the proceedings that they would no longer accept the so-called 'Rolls Royce : Rolls Royce : Ford' ratios of the Washington treaty, which had allowed them 60 per cent of the British and American strengths in capital ships. Instead, they demanded 70 per cent of the American strength in eight-inch cruisers and, for good measure, insisted that they should also be allowed to keep their existing submarine fleet of 78,000 tons, built and building. In doing so, they threatened not only to block a wider agreement but to undermine the Anglo-American agreement as well. For the Anglo-American agreement was based on the premiss that Japan would be content with 12 eight-inch cruisers to the Americans' 18. A 70 per cent ratio would entitle her to 12.6; and if 12.6 were interpreted to mean 13, Australia and New Zealand might insist on a larger British fleet, and the whole elaborate structure on which MacDonald had laboured for so long might come crashing down.

It was the French, however, who presented the most formidable problem of all; and if we are to understand MacDonald's activities during the next three months or, for that matter, his role in international politics during the next five years, the differences between the French and British positions at the conference must be examined with some care. The Washington treaty had given France and Italy parity in capital ships. Understandably enough, the Italians demanded parity in auxiliaries as well. But, as the French pointed out *ad nauseam*, France had interests in the Channel and the North Sea as well as in the Mediterranean, whereas Italy had interests only in the Mediterranean. Thus, parity between France and Italy would give the Italians superiority in the Mediterranean and, among other things, enable them to cut the French lifeline with North Africa. With Mussolini in power, this was not an academic consideration. The French navy was larger than the Italian; and so long as France had to depend on her own efforts for her security in the Mediterranean, she was determined to keep it so. Towards the end of December, the French sent an obscurely worded note to London, advocating a Mediterranean pact of non-aggression and mutual guarantee;[82] and before the conference had started, it was clear that they would do all they could to link the naval negotiations with the pact, and to resist cuts in their building programme until their security in the Mediterranean had been guaranteed in other ways.

Yet the Mediterranean pact was a means to an end, rather than an end in itself. The French meant what they said when they talked about the threat from Italy, but it is hard to believe that they meant all that they said, and clear that their real reason for wanting guarantees lay deeper. From their point of view, Europe had become a steadily more uncomfortable place since the early 'twenties. In 1924, they had been cajoled out of the Ruhr; in 1925, they had watched the burial of the Geneva Protocol. The Protocol had been replaced by the Locarno Pact, but the pact had been carefully designed not to provide guarantees against German aggression in eastern Europe, and did not apply to the Mediterranean either. The Locarno Pact had been followed by the Kellogg Pact, but the Kellogg Pact provided no machinery for enforcement. Meanwhile, Germany had been admitted to the League of Nations; German reparation payments had been cut; and the German economy had been revived with the help of lavish American loans. In relative power, France had lost ground; and she had gained only high-sounding declarations in exchange. Now it looked as though the same thing might happen again. The Anglo-French naval compromise had been torn up, and the new British Government had just spent six months working out an agreement with the United States, which offered no obvious advantages to France, yet to which she was expected to accommodate herself. Now, as always, what the French really wanted was to find some way of binding Britain to the continent; the fact that Britain seemed increasingly reluctant to be bound only made them more anxious to find it. They arrived in London in the suspicious and resentful mood of a jilted lover, seeking in verbal assurances a substitute for a change of heart.

A change of heart was exactly what the British were not prepared to make. France was the strongest military power on the continent. She had created a chain of alliances on Germany's eastern frontier; the vaults of the Bank of France were stuffed with gold. In these circumstances, it was hard to argue that she was seriously threatened by Germany or Italy; to many people in Britain it seemed that, if anything, the boot was on the other foot. The British were willing to reaffirm the commitments they had already made. They were not willing to make new ones; above all, they were not willing to make commitments which might one day oblige them to fight in a French quarrel which was no concern of theirs. That was why Britain had refused to guarantee Germany's eastern neighbours in the past: the same motives determined British policy now. These attitudes were held, with varying degrees of intensity, by most British politicians, by most of Whitehall and almost certainly by most of the British electorate. In MacDonald's case, they were reinforced by another set of attitudes, deriving from a different source but pointing in the same direction. In 1924, he had played a central part in the negotiations that led to the Geneva Protocol; in 1927, he had gone out of his way to revive the Protocol as a political issue. On both occasions, he had shown some sympathy with the French demand for extra guarantees and had apparently accepted their argument that disarmament and security must go hand in hand. By a curious paradox, however, the attitudes which had led him to show some sympathy for French demands in 1924 now led him to view them with acute and growing suspicion. For more than twenty years, he had believed that alliances led to war, and that peace could not be secured by the threat of force, but only by allaying the fears and suspicions that led men to resort to it. For him, the point of the Protocol was that it was not an alliance: that it involved no new commitments: that, in his own words, it was merely a 'harmless drug to soothe nerves'. This time, however, he gradually came to believe that the French wanted not a harmless sedative but a dangerous narcotic; with some justification, he also came to believe that they were trying to blackmail him into prescribing it.

IX

The Japanese problem was solved comparatively easily, though only after long and exasperating delays. At first Stimson and his colleagues insisted that the old Washington treaty ratio gave Japan all she needed for self-defence. Eventually, however, they offered to delay the completion of three American eight-inch cruisers until 1935, on condition that the Japanese stuck at twelve and cut their proposed submarine tonnage by a third. This gave Japan the cruiser tonnage she wanted for most of the period covered by the treaty; in submarines, she would have parity. At first, Wakatsuki stalled, but in the middle of March, the Japanese delegation at last decided to accept the American offer; and at the beginning of April, the Japanese Government followed suit.[83] The French and Italians were more obdurate. Grandi made it clear that, whatever figures Tardieu and Briand put forward, he would demand the same. The French were equally intransigent. Parity with Italy, they insisted, was out of the question: if the British were not prepared to give them a security guarantee, their only possible course was to maintain their existing lead over Italy by building more than the Italians could build. To MacDonald, however, the French demand for guarantees seemed either unnecessary or sinister. They claimed to fear that, in certain circumstances, Britain might refuse to obey a decision of the League Council to apply military, as opposed to economic sanctions, against an aggressor; they would cut their programmes, they implied, only if Britain undertook to follow the Council's recommendations in the event of aggression in the Mediterranean. But, as MacDonald pointed out again and again, the Council could not take a decision to apply sanctions unless Britain voted for it. It was inconceivable that a future British Government would refuse to operate the sanctions for which the British representative on the Council had just voted: if Britain did not wish to operate sanctions, she would instruct her representative to veto the decision to apply them. If the French meant what they said, they were asking the British to promise that they would keep past British promises. To put it at its lowest, this was an odd request. If Britain could be trusted to keep her word, there was no need for her to say so: if she could not, new British commitments would be as valueless as the old. The obvious conclusion, MacDonald decided, was that the French did not mean what they said, and that their real purpose was to drag Britain into a military alliance of the kind he had opposed for thirty years.

Thus, the negotiations between Britain and France rapidly became a dialogue of the deaf. Tardieu and Briand put forward a wildly inflated programme, painted a harrowing picture of the dangers that would threaten France if they reduced it, and hinted broadly that the question could be settled only if it were approached 'from the political angle'. MacDonald ignored their hints and employed all his resources of eloquence and moral earnestness to persuade them that arms gave only a false security, that the dangers against which they wished to protect themselves were imaginary and that it was their duty to run risks for peace. From time to time, both sides made approaches to Grandi — who hovered ineffectually but inflexibly in the wings — only to discover yet again that Italy would accept any figure, provided that it gave her parity.[84] It is hardly surprising that progress should have been slow, or that tempers should have become short. Before the negotiations began, MacDonald congratulated himself on his good relations with the French, and noted 'Tardieu working with me. Without arrangement or negotiation we are together.'[85] Before they ended, he had come to the conclusion that Tardieu and Briand were not to be trusted, that the French were deliberately trying to wreck the conference and that France was trying to drag Britain into a private quarrel with Italy. No doubt, Tardieu and Briand felt as harshly about him.

The process began on February 12th, when, after long delays, the French at last announced that by 1936 they planned to have 10 eight-inch cruisers, almost 100,000 tons of submarines and around 450,000 tons of auxiliaries altogether.[86] 'France becomes the peace problem of Europe,' MacDonald noted indignantly. 'Mentality is purely militarist.'[87] By February 16th, he had become even more gloomy:

> A weekend of black depression was mine. The spirit of grey loneliness was upon me except for those who had passed away. I really lived in Spynie, but could not make out if those who were there knew the things of this world. On Saturday night I was the most solitary man in the world. I am overworked & the French position blind as it seems to be to the only way we can pursue towards peace was discouraging. Whilst willing to discuss security & understanding relating to it, I am determined not to drift into the position in which Grey found himself. That gives France a free hand in determining European policy with Great Britain a bound follower ... That will mean alliances & war, & I shall prevent it so long as I am in office.[88]

On February 17th, the French Government fell because of a financial crisis. Tardieu and Briand had to go back to Paris, and although they both remained in office, neither returned to London until March. When the negotiations were resumed, MacDonald spent another ten days in a forlorn attempt to bring the French figures down without giving concessions in return. His ingenuity was in vain. When he tried to persuade Tardieu to produce new figures, based on a hypothetical Italian programme of 400,000 tons, Tardieu tried to inveigle him into promising that, if it turned out that the Italians would not accept 400,000 tons after all, Britain would then endorse the French programme of February 12th; Grandi refused to make any concessions whatever; and MacDonald's suspicions of the French were still further inflamed by a report that their minister of marine had told one of the Japanese delegates that the Americans were trying to cheat Japan over submarines, and had urged the Japanese not to join in a tripartite agreement with Britain and the United States.[89] By March 20th, he was noting 'I begin to feel the Conference may not be saved. I can get Italy to fit itself in, but France will do nothing which amounts to anything. France is taking steps to enable it to fight Italy. War is the central fact of its mind.'[90]

For more than a month, he had tried to talk the French into reducing their programme. Slowly, and with evident reluctance, he now acknowledged that exhortation had failed. On March 19th, Briand went back to Paris. MacDonald dined with him before he left and told him that, although he was not prepared to join a military alliance or to add to Britain's military commitments, he was willing to co-operate in strengthening the peace-keeping machinery of the League.[91] During the next few days, a good deal of agitated discussion took place among the British and American delegations about what concessions to make. In a dramatic, though considerably less than fulsome declaration, Stimson promised that, if the French demand for security were met by others, the Americans would consider taking part in a consultative pact. MacDonald declared that, although he could not give an undertaking 'which would result, independently of the merits of the dispute, in the British Fleet being drawn in', he was prepared to reaffirm a commitment contained in an annex to the Locarno agreement, under which Britain was 'bound to co-operate loyally and effectively in support of the Covenant'.[92] On March 25th, Briand agreed to come back to London, and on March 27th, he and Henderson agreed that their officials should try to work out a formula which both sides could accept.

It was a doomed enterprise. The results were put before the British delegation on March 30th. MacDonald must have felt that his worst forebodings had been justified. The Foreign Office had produced a draft committing the signatories to comply with the recommendations of the League Council if the covenant were violated, to support a series of amendments which had recently been put forward to widen the scope of the covenant and to consult together if the amendments did not come into effect. In addition, the French wanted to insert a paragraph declaring that, unless the League Council decided otherwise, a state which went to war in breach of the Kellogg Pact should *ipso facto* be considered to have broken the covenant, and that sanctions should immediately be applied against it. As the Foreign Office pointed out, this went further than any existing British commitment. Under the covenant, sanctions could be enforced only if the covenant itself had been violated: under the French proposal, they would be enforced in the event of a breach of the more sweeping Kellogg Pact. Whereas the covenant covered all the member-states of the League, the French proposal covered only the powers represented at the naval conference; thus Britain was being asked to assume obligations which most member-states of the League did not share. Henderson made it clear that the French had at no stage been given any reason to believe that a proposal of this kind would be accepted, and the French draft paragraph was rejected out of hand.[93]

For all practical purposes, that was the end of the five-power conference. Shortly afterwards, the Japanese Government decided to take its delegation's advice, and accept the American offer – thus ensuring that the conference could not be written off as a failure even if the negotiations with France broke down, and so removing one of the strongest cards from the French hand. 'Practically given up Five Power Agreement ... ,' MacDonald noted on April 6th. 'France has striven hard to chain us & has only succeeded in making me suspect that we are being manœuvred into a trap.'[94] On the 7th, the Cabinet had two meetings to discuss a revised Foreign Office draft, which had now been put to Briand on the understanding that it had not yet received Cabinet approval. This followed the same lines as the draft which had been discussed by the British delegation on March 30th, but with the objectionable French paragraph removed. Even so, it went too far for the Cabinet, which insisted that it should be made clear that the British representative on the League Council should not have to agree to any recommendation for military sanctions until Parliament had been consulted.[95] It need not have bothered. Even the unrevised British formula, Briand reported, had been received with 'a certain amount of disappointment' in Paris.[96] It soon became clear that there was no hope of persuading the French that the revised formula was an adequate *quid pro quo* for a cut in their programme, and that the French figures could not be brought down unless the Italians could be persuaded at the eleventh hour to abandon their claim to parity. But the Italians would not budge either; and on April 10th, a joint meeting of the British, French and Italian delegations decided that there was no longer any point in pursuing a five-power agreement, that the conference should endorse the three-power agreement instead, and that it should then adjourn, on the understanding that negotiations between Britain, France and Italy were to continue.[97]

The final session of the conference was held on April 22nd, when the treaty was signed. Part I provided for a 'holiday' in battleship construction from 1931 to 1936. Part II laid down a number of restrictions on submarine building. Part III contained the three-power agreement between the British, Americans and Japanese, and also included an escape clause allowing them to build more if their national security were threatened by the building of any other power. Part IV imposed restrictions on submarine warfare. Part V provided that the treaty should remain in force until December 1936. Parts I, II, IV and V covered all five participants at the conference; part III covered only the three powers concerned. In a graceful speech before the signing ceremony, MacDonald declared:

The Conference has done a great work. We have secured a Three-Power Agreement on building programmes—no mean or unimportant achievement. This, with other points embodied in the Treaty, has repeatedly defied solution ...

... We have stopped the replacement of battleships and reduced their numbers. We have limited the tonnage of auxiliary craft. We have shown how the equipment, the building and the replacement of fleets can be brought within the realm of international order. We have proved how, when the world likes, the menace of arms can be removed by treaties regulating their development. True, the work has been but partially done, but all great advances of this kind must be in stages, and we have gone much further than has as yet been possible ... We must just go on strengthening the new mentality of peace and applying it, step by step, in further and further reductions.[98]

His hopes were not realized, but his verdict has stood the test of time. The London naval treaty was a limited achievement, no doubt, but it was a real one; the Anglo-American understanding which preceded it and made it possible was a greater achievement still. The Government had gone only a small part of the way towards the 'early reduction in armaments throughout the world' to which it had looked forward in the King's speech, but it had gone further than any Government before and at least as far as any Government since. No doubt, it could have gone further still if MacDonald had been prepared to give the French a firm guarantee. But, although MacDonald's suspicions of the French seem perverse forty years later, there can be no doubt that most of his countrymen shared them: the Government was much more likely to be attacked for giving the French too much than for giving them too little. Given the state of British public opinion at the time, the three-power treaty represented the most that any Government could have achieved. If it had been signed in normal circumstances, it would have been one of the most triumphant moments in MacDonald's career.

By April 1930, however, circumstances were no longer normal. The day after the signature, MacDonald noted: 'Wanted so much to get to Lossiemouth to stretch my mind & body but weather too cloudy & thick to fly so have to remain here. Ran down in rain to Brighton & shivered.' His shivers ushered in one of the most dismal summers of his career.

CHAPTER 22

Slump

I

'WERE it not for industrial condition government looks as if it would live for ever,' MacDonald noted apprehensively in September 1929, 'but the *were* is a big one.'[1] His apprehensions were well founded. The trade revival which accompanied Labour's return to office lasted for nearly six months. As late as November 1929, 100,000 fewer people were unemployed than in November 1928. Then the tide turned. Industrial production in the United States had already started to decline; the Wall Street crash in October and November gave a strong further push to a downward spiral of falling output, dwindling investment and rising unemployment. The flow of American lending, which had sustained the fragile prosperity of central Europe, had already begun to dry up; soon the German economy was dragged down too. Meanwhile, world commodity prices collapsed, and the primary producing countries had to cut back their imports of manufactured goods. By the early months of 1930, the worst trade depression of the century was unmistakably under way, and the familiar British problem of structural unemployment in the old staple industries was compounded by the effects of a worldwide crisis. In January 1930, 1,533,000 people were out of work, as against 1,433,000 in January 1929. By March 1930, the figure was 1,731,000. By June it was 1,946,000 and by December, 2,725,000. By June 1931, two years after MacDonald's triumphant appearance before the crowds at King's Cross station, it had reached 2,735,000.[2]

These figures spelt suffering and degradation for the unemployed and their families and gnawing fear for millions of others who thought that they might become unemployed. For the Labour Party, which had consistently proclaimed that unemployment was the inevitable consequence of the social order which it alone was committed to transform, and which now found itself presiding over the worst increase in unemployment in living memory, they spelt failure, bitterness and a sense of guilt, all the more corroding for being unadmitted. For MacDonald, whose strategy and philosophy had been triumphantly vindicated by the election results a few months before, and who now found himself leading his party and country into a deepening morass from which he could find no escape, they spelt a kind of baffled anguish, verging on despair.

In outline, at least, it is a familiar story. Yet a great effort of imagination is needed to see it through the eyes of those who took part in it. In the 'economic blizzard', as MacDonald called it, old landmarks were obliterated and old assumptions overturned. Looking back, it is hard to remember what the assumptions were or where the landmarks used to be. Before it began, governments were still struggling painfully to rebuild the economic order which had been undermined by the war: before it ended they were beginning, often unwillingly, to lay the foundations of the order we know today. One of its chief legacies, moreover, was a revolution in economic thought as profound as any in the history of ideas. As much as Copernicus or Darwin, Keynes transformed the way men looked at the world: so completely that it is hard to remember that they once looked at it differently, and harder still to remember that the Keynesian system did not spring fully armed from the brow of its creator, but had to be hammered out over a period of years by a process of trial and error. For, like most revolutions, the Keynesian revolution was a messier affair than it seems in retrospect. The classical system, which Keynes replaced, possessed great intellectual power as well as the weight of tradition and authority. Its defenders had effective weapons to deploy and, to contemporaries, at least, it did not always seem that Keynes could match them. In any case, economists did not fall neatly into two camps, one 'Keynesian' and the other 'pre-Keynesian'. Under the pressure of events, many began to question the doctrines in which they had been brought up. Few answered in a wholly consistent way.

What is true of the world of ideas is more obviously true of the world of policy and decision. With hindsight it is tempting to picture the politics of these years as a Manichaean struggle between the forces of light, which wished to break with the economic orthodoxy of the day, and the forces of darkness, which wished to cling to it. The truth is more complex. In the first place, arguments between the orthodox and the unorthodox were not always as one-sided as has sometimes been supposed. Orthodoxy had some able champions: its enemies sometimes put their case in a jejune and unconvincing way. More important still, orthodoxy and unorthodoxy overlapped, not only in the middle of the spectrum, but at both ends. In all parties, there were politicians who borrowed from Keynes. Not all who did so grasped the full significance of Keynes's teaching. Like early Christian converts blending old tribal rituals with the doctrines of the Church, many politicians used Keynesian arguments at one moment and reverted to classical arguments at the next. Advocates of increased spending on public works proceeded to advocate cuts in Government expenditure; apparent 'economic conservatives', who opposed a big public-works programme, were sometimes more iconoclastic about the traditional dogmas of free trade than were apparent 'economic radicals', who wished to mop up unemployment by increasing home demand. The old distinctions between Left and Right grew so blurred as to be almost meaningless, but no new distinction took their place. Politicians of all parties found themselves in unknown territory, groping for the way ahead. Attempts to impose a clear pattern on their gropings confuse more than they explain.[3]

All this applies with special force to MacDonald and his colleagues. They were socialists, committed to the eventual abolition of the capitalist system. They were also members of the Labour movement, committed to the defence of working-class living standards. But these commitments, however deeply felt, offered scant guidance to ministers grappling with an economic crisis. British socialism was an ethical doctrine rather than an economic one. It had been inspired by a revolt against the inhumanity and injustice of late nineteenth-century capitalism, but it offered no theoretical alternative to late nineteenth-century economics. Socialists assumed that poverty and unemployment would disappear if the means of production were taken into public ownership. They had given little thought to the way in which a publicly owned economy would function or to the part which public ownership might play in helping to combat poverty and unemployment in an economy, most of which remained in private hands. Still less had they foreseen the possibility that a privately owned economy might collapse about their ears, or worked out distinctively socialist methods of stopping poverty and unemployment from getting worse. Labour's commitment to the working class was an equally uncertain guide. It was easy enough to agree that the Government had a special duty to protect the living standards of its working-class constituents. But the working class was not a homogeneous block with a single set of interests. It was a collection of groups, whose interests often seemed to be in conflict. Farm workers in East Anglia would gain if cereal prices were stabilized: workers elsewhere would lose if the price of bread went up. Miners would gain from quota arrangements to maintain the price of coal: workers in other industries would lose from higher fuel costs. The unemployed would gain if tariffs on imported goods made it possible to pursue expansionist policies at home: those in work would lose if tariffs led to higher prices and so reduced real wages. Again and again, ministers were confronted with an apparent choice between the interests of one group of workers and the interests of the rest, and although it seems clear in retrospect that many of these dilemmas were false, it is important to realize that they seemed real and painful at the time.

Thus, the Government had no chart to steer by. It swung about from one emergency to the next, now facing in one direction and now in another, arguing fiercely about which course to take. But although the results often conformed to the dictates of economic orthodoxy, it would be an oversimplification to conclude that they always did so. As we have seen, Labour had fought the election on a negative ticket. It had denounced the Liberal proposal of a big public-works programme financed by Government borrowing as a costly palliative, which could only postpone a thorough cure; it had also denounced the Conservative policy of 'safeguarding'. In *Labour and the Nation*, it had assembled a miscellaneous hodge-podge of proposals, including 'sound' schemes for providing employment, an attack on waste and inefficiency in industry, an inquiry into the financial system and the establishment of an economic committee on the lines of the committee of imperial defence. This hazy collection of prohibitions and aspirations provided the framework within which the Government's policy evolved. Protection had been ruled out; so had 'unsound' public works, paid for by a loan. Instead, ministers relied on *ad hoc* attempts to shame or cajole the ailing staple industries, where most of the 'abnormal' unemployment of the time was concentrated, into making themselves more efficient. These attempts were buttressed by a new system of consultation and intelligence, and coupled with a search for public-works projects which could be justified by the existing criteria and financed in the existing way; the prospect of a more expansionist monetary policy, following an inquiry into the financial system, hovered tantalizingly in the background.

If radicalism is equated with Keynesianism, it was not a remotely radical policy. But it was not a strictly orthodox policy either. Though it contained no hint of modern methods of demand management, it looked forward to the more detailed kinds of economic intervention which became fashionable in the 1960s and 1970s: Thomas, as lord privy seal, was in many ways the unacknowledged predecessor of George Brown, as secretary for economic affairs, and of Anthony Wedgwood Benn, as secretary for industry. Like theirs, his activities were based on the premiss that private enterprise could not solve its problems for itself; like them, he sought neither traditional socialism nor traditional capitalism, but a partnership between the private sector and the state. Unlike his modern successors, he had no sanctions to make his interventions bite: he could give advice, but he could neither threaten nor reward. All the same, his approach was, at bottom, incompatible with the old classical assumptions that the market should be left to its own devices and that attempts to interfere with it would do more harm than good. The real tragedy of MacDonald's second Government was not that its underlying approach was too orthodox, but that after its first six months in office that approach ceased to be relevant: that while Thomas struggled laboriously to drain the old pool of structural unemployment, the economy was engulfed in a raging torrent of new unemployment, against which piecemeal interventions could offer no protection, and in its response to which the Cabinet was hopelessly divided.

II

At first, all seemed to go well. A co-ordinating committee of permanent secretaries was set up under Thomas's chairmanship, and he was also given the assistance of a small secretariat, headed by Sir Horace Wilson. The activities of the unemployment grants committee, which had been sharply reduced under the previous Government, were extended in scope and scale. The Ministry of

Transport was encouraged to expand the road programme, and embarked on a long struggle to squeeze the money out of the Treasury. In his favourite role as the 'Director-General of British Industry', Thomas spent several weeks in Canada trying to foster British exports and travelled up and down the country, exhorting industrialists to introduce schemes of 'rationalization', designed to cut costs and improve competitiveness, particularly in the export trades.[4] After what he later described as 'long and delicate negotiations' with Montagu Norman, he was able to announce triumphantly that the money to underwrite soundly based schemes of this sort would be forthcoming from the City. As a result, he boasted, his office became the link between industry and the 'financial machine' — interviewing industrialists, discussing their problems, putting them in touch with sources of finance and promoting mergers.[5] Meanwhile, the inquiries into the cotton and steel industries promised in the King's speech duly began; and an authoritative committee, chaired by Lord Macmillan, and including Keynes, Bevin and McKenna among its members, was appointed to examine the working of the banking and financial systems and to make recommendations 'calculated ... to promote the development of commerce and the employment of labour'.[6]

MacDonald watched these developments with a benign, but distant, eye. When the Government was formed, he spent some time helping to set up the administrative machine which was put at Thomas's disposal, but for the next five months he was too deeply immersed in foreign affairs to have much energy to spare for the economy. In spite of his foreign preoccupations, however, he still seems to have hankered vaguely after a change in monetary policy. Towards the end of July, Oliver Baldwin, the Opposition leader's son, who had just been elected as a Labour M.P., wrote to him to urge the Government to abandon the gold standard, or at least to increase the money supply by raising the price of gold. MacDonald's reply was non-committal, but surprisingly sympathetic. Baldwin's suggestion, he wrote, was 'receiving very active consideration, but I am sure you will understand that there are all sorts of delicacies involved in actually getting the hare out on to the field.'[7] In a letter to Snowden shortly afterwards he made the characteristically oblique comment that

> After I saw you yesterday afternoon, Stamp looked in and we had a long talk about trade in general, the Bank of England, Currency problems and the Reparations Conference ... I think it would be worth your while having a talk with him some time about his views of how the gold standard should be worked. He takes a somewhat mid-way view between what I imagine [are] the rather hard rigidities of Norman and the more risky ideas of McKenna.[8]

Equally characteristically, however, Snowden does not seem to have replied, and MacDonald made no further attempt to influence the Government's economic policies until his return from Canada at the beginning of November.

His next initiative was more robust. As we have seen, the 1924 Government had decided to set up a committee on economic questions on the lines proposed by the Haldane commission a few years before. The Government fell before anything was done, and the Conservatives then set up a more anaemic body, with some of the same functions, called the committee of civil research. Meanwhile, the notion of an 'economic general staff' appeared in a number of left-wing manifestoes, including *Labour and the Nation*, and was also taken up by the Liberals. For MacDonald, with his orderly temperament and touching faith in human reason, it had great attractions. He believed in getting up early, answering his letters promptly and reading his papers thoroughly; by the same token, it seemed obvious to him that the way to solve a difficult problem was to set up a committee to marshal the facts, study them and come to a conclusion. Just as he believed that war could be avoided by arbitration and conciliation, so he took it for granted that economic conflicts could be resolved if the interests concerned could be persuaded to thrash out their differences around a table, in the light of an objective examination of the evidence; perhaps because of his early scientific training, he was apt to forget that economic problems are not always analogous to scientific ones, and to assume that once a problem had been studied in sufficient depth, enlightenment would automatically follow. At a more mundane but equally important level, it seems clear that he was reluctant to give Snowden undisputed control over the Government's economic policies, and anxious to provide himself with an independent source of economic advice, which could act as a counterweight to the Treasury. As soon as his American visit was over, he took steps to revive the 1924 Government's committee, in a more ambitious form.

Preliminary soundings were made in November, and in December MacDonald held a series of lunches at No. 10 to discuss the project. They were impressive gatherings. The economists present included Keynes, Hobson, G. D. H. Cole and Walter Layton; the businessmen included Lord Weir, the engineering magnate, Sir Andrew Duncan, the steel master, and Sir Kenneth Stewart, the director of the Manchester chamber of commerce. Walter Citrine, the general secretary of the T.U.C., represented organized labour; Thomas represented himself. At one lunch, the Treasury's watchdog was the permanent secretary, Sir Warren Fisher; at the next one, it was Snowden.[9] Consensus proved elusive. Stewart launched a vigorous attack on trade-union restrictive practices, and was stoutly backed by Thomas; Citrine made it clear that the unions had no intention of giving them up without a *quid pro quo*; Lord Weir hinted darkly that business confidence could be restored only if the Government abandoned its legislative programme. The proposed body's scope and functions were more controversial still. It was generally agreed that there was a place in Whitehall for an expert staff to encourage research, assemble information and study difficult problems. The Treasury, supported by Thomas and Lord Weir, wanted to stop there; MacDonald also wanted a wider body, representing the

Government and both sides of industry, whose conclusions would be carried out by the interest groups involved, and whose existence would keep policy on an even keel. As he put it in an endearing cry from the heart during an exchange with Lord Weir:

In 1929 one section or interest is predominant, and brings pressure to bear on the Cabinet. In 1930 there will be another interest predominant. Hence inconsistencies and mess and no man can possibly stop it. You can have a body thinking, but it must think on actualities which cover the whole of the problem. Otherwise you will wiggle waggle from one side to another … You cannot isolate the Council as merely a thinking body. If it meets on Monday it must be ready for action to be taken on Tuesday. Such action may have to be taken through the F.B.I., or through the Cabinet or through Ministers. It must be something positive instead of the negative interference with which we have been cursed.[10]

In the end, he had to lower his sights. The new body was set up in January 1930. It was called the economic advisory council; and, as its name implied, it had no executive functions. All the same, it was a remarkable innovation. It had fifteen full members — including Keynes, Cole and Tawney; a weighty phalanx of businessmen; and Bevin and Citrine, as representatives of the unions. Attached to these was a small staff of economists and officials, headed by Tom Jones as secretary and Keynes's old associate, Hubert Henderson, as assistant secretary.

The council's impact on policy, though far from negligible, was intermittent and uncertain. On some questions, reports from its sub-committees had considerable influence, but on the central problems of how to deal with unemployment and promote recovery, it was no more united than were the politicians whom it was called upon to advise. Yet it would be a mistake to dismiss it as an ineffective talking-shop. In the history of British economic policy, it deserves little more than a footnote; in the history of British government, it deserves much more. First as assistant secretary and, after Jones's retirement, as joint secretary, Hubert Henderson acted, among other things, as MacDonald's personal economic adviser. Though he followed the Treasury line more often than might have been expected in an old supporter of Lloyd George's, he did not follow it slavishly or totally, and on some questions he undoubtedly reinforced MacDonald's own opposition to it. In any case, Henderson's real significance lay less in what he said or did than in the fact that he existed: that for the first time in British history, the prime minister had an economic adviser, working within the Government machine yet independently of the Treasury. Much the same applies to the council itself. In some ways it looked forward to the N.E.D.C. of the early 'sixties; in others to the D.E.A. of a few years later. No doubt, it produced fewer results than its author expected, but in the circumstances this was almost inevitable. Though the business interests represented on it welcomed *ad hoc* Government interventions when it suited them to do so, they did not recognize the corollary that the economic order which had sustained Britain's industrial greatness in the nineteenth century had broken down. Yet without the support of the businessmen, the economists and trade unionists on the council could do little. The fact remains that MacDonald was the only prime minister between the wars who made a serious attempt to adapt the creaking administrative structure he had inherited to the needs of the modern world.

III

He got little thanks for doing so. The Government's stock had fallen badly since his triumphant return from Canada three months before. In November 1929, Margaret Bondfield introduced a maladroit Bill, liberalizing the conditions for obtaining unemployment benefit, in a way which was known to be unsatisfactory to the T.U.C. She provoked a storm of indignation on the Labour benches, and after bitter protests from trade-union M.P.s, she had to withdraw the offending clause and substitute the more liberal formula which the unions had wanted in the first place – thus contriving to make the Government appear mean, incompetent and pusillanimous all at once.[11]

There is no evidence that MacDonald opposed the decision to change the formula, but it is clear from his papers that he was deeply disturbed by the rebellion and even more disturbed by the results. At the beginning of December, he noted privately: 'Disgruntled revolt against Unemployment Bill. We have a group of members who work with us when it pleases them. Some are fools who cannot relate the desirable to the possible; some are troubled by consistency to statements made as though time was no element in building up; some are moved by the sole fact that they are *ex* Ministers, some are afraid that they may be attacked in their constituencies – none have a deep & instructed sense of loyalty.'[12] When the Bill obtained its third reading he was even more gloomy:

> Last night the Unemployment Bill went through. I have no heart for these doles. The last Government administered with such feeble inefficiency & with so little care to impress people with the justice of the limitations it placed upon the system of 'doles' that the inevitable reaction had to be met. Perhaps we may have gone too far. Now, we must be rigid, for to establish people in incomes which represent no effort to get or to do work is the very antithesis of Socialism. The State as Lady Bountiful may be a fatal extension of Toryism but is not the beginning of Socialism.[13]

By now, a more serious storm had blown up. Early in December, the Government published its long-awaited Bill to reorganize the coal industry. It was an intricate and carefully balanced measure, which had been hammered out after long negotiations with both sides of the industry; though it satisfied neither, it probably represented the best obtainable compromise between them. Miners' hours were to be reduced from eight to seven-and-a-half; exports were to be subsidized by national and district levies; production was to be limited by quotas.[14] In striking contrast to the Government's policies for other industries, no attempt was made to cut costs or promote rationalization. It was a producers' Bill, not an economist's: still less a consumer's. In the circumstances, it is hard to see what else the Government could have done. Nationalization was ruled out by its lack of a majority; short of nationalization, the miners' claim to lower hours could be met only if concessions were made to the owners. Forced rationalization would have led to closures and redundancies, and would have been fiercely resisted by owners and men alike. But arguments of this sort cut little ice with the Government's opponents. The Bill, Winston Churchill declared, was a 'dear coal Bill', which had been foisted on the country by the use of the miners' power in the Labour Party.[15]

Churchill could be discounted; the Liberals could not. Apart from a few sporadic forays by Lloyd George, they had so far caused the Government little difficulty. Partly because they were tired of being taken for granted, partly because Lloyd George and Samuel both believed that the industry's problems could be solved only by forcing amalgamations and rationalization on it from above, they now decided to flex their muscles. On December 2nd, MacDonald noted that he had taken part in a conference on the coal Bill with Lloyd George, Samuel and Sir John Simon. 'Lloyd George led & Samuel echoed,' he wrote, 'Simon remaining more detached. Opposed marketing, proposed amalgamation of pits ... Agreed to consider & instructed Graham to continue discussions with Samuel.'[16] Graham's efforts produced no results. On December 5th, MacDonald noted:

> Liberal leaders conferred on coal — Lloyd George, Simon, Samuel, Graham, Thomas, Henderson, Turner & myself. They would look at nothing but compulsory amalgamation. They admitted it would take at least two years to complete & that it made no contribution to immediate economic difficulties. We informed them that so soon as this Bill was off the hands of the Department we should proceed with an amalgamation Bill & introduce it next session. They would not accept that & we told them we could go no further. They quite evidently did not mean to agree & came to break off ... Samuel was evidently under Lloyd George & Simon was silent with an air of sympathy & doom.[17]

A week later, he noted that the Liberals had decided to put down an amendment to the second reading of the Bill, and added that, if it were carried 'of course we go out. An election cannot follow & some Government must be formed from this Parliament. It would really be a relief. This office has no attraction for me.'[18]

The second reading debate followed two weeks later. In the first day's debate on December 17th, Graham denied that the Bill would subsidize uneconomic pits, and Samuel made a lucid, if somewhat academic, speech, arguing that it would impede reorganization and amalgamation.[19] On December 19th, Lloyd George attacked it root and branch as an 'incredibly bad Bill', which combined 'the worst features of Socialism and individualism without the redeeming features of either'. Churchill, who wound up for the Conservatives, made an adroit speech, flattering the Liberals and denouncing the Government for 'erecting a nation-wide monopoly trust to be set up by Act of Parliament'. MacDonald wound up for the Government, and made it clear that it would be prepared to accept amendments designed to strengthen the Bill once it had reached its committee stage.[20] The Bill then received its second reading by 281 votes to 273. Two Liberals voted with the Government; six ostentatiously abstained.[21] Afterwards, MacDonald's pent-up feelings flooded out in a savage diary entry:

> Lloyd George & Winston Churchill had laid their heads together & did their best to defeat us ... Lloyd George is like Samson shorn of his locks & bent on destruction. We had two consultations on the Bill when it was apparent that he meant to come to no agreement ... He made a speech not only hostile but bitter, & included a personal attack upon the Minister of Mines. He deliberately made it impossible for me to answer his questions for had I done so it would have made us an object of jeering & would have destroyed our influence with our independence & respect. It was a challenge not an enquiry ... I decided at once to take the risks & let him do his worst. The Labour members were splendid. The Parliamentary problems of keeping going a Minority Government are baffling. Winston Churchill conspires against his leader & with Lloyd George ... They are two of the most sinister politicians in our public life today. The former is a soldier of fortune, the latter one of those men who are never happy unless they are the leading figures or are pulling down others. An examination of the latter's war record would be one of the most unpleasant bits of history ever written. His energy is supposed to have saved the country during the war & into the material knock-out blow part of the business he reigned supreme. The nation is now paying for the lack of every quality of statesmanship in those critical months. He made us victorious by bringing us to ruin & his policy whilst imposing great hardships on the vanquished made their future prosperity assured. He degraded our public life & its honours; he was a friend who never felt friendship, a colleague who was ever disloyal; he never used a partner but for his own ends & sacrificed everyone who ever trusted him.[22]

His chagrin was understandable. The Liberals had not broken the Government, but they had undoubtedly damaged it; and it was clear that they were well placed to damage it again. For the Government to drop the Bill would be to admit that it held office only on sufferance. If it persisted, it would face the possibility of defeat and the virtual certainty of a debilitating series of snap votes, late nights, narrow escapes and petty humiliations. The obvious solution was to amend the Bill in the way that the Liberals had suggested in the debate on the second reading. Yet even that was easier said than done, since the Liberals' objections went to the heart of the tacit compromise between miners and owners on which the whole shaky edifice was based. In any case, the Liberals were out for bigger game than amendments to the coal Bill. The Government had promised in the King's speech to hold an inquiry into the law governing parliamentary elections. In a delphic passage in his speech in the debate on the address, MacDonald had reaffirmed his own long-standing opposition to any form of proportional representation, but in reply to an interjection from Lloyd George he had implied that the question would nevertheless be examined when the inquiry took place.[23] After long delays, a three-party conference was set up in December, under the chairmanship of Lord Ullswater; and before the House returned from the Christmas recess at the end of January 1930, Lloyd George made a speech at the National Liberal club, hinting as clearly as it was possible to do without actually saying so that he intended to use the coal Bill as a lever to prise electoral reform out of the Ullswater conference.[24]

From MacDonald's point of view, this was an even more distasteful prospect than continuous harassment from the Liberal Party: perhaps even than a defeat and a general election. He had opposed proportional representation even in the days when the Labour Party might have had something to gain from it: he saw no reason to abate his opposition now that it had a great deal to lose. Since 1922, one of the main objects of his political life had been the destruction of the Liberal Party; the 1929 election results suggested that, in spite of all the obstacles, he was well on the way to achieving it. Once introduced, proportional representation would be there to stay; it would perpetutate the Liberal Party as a serious force in British politics, not just for a Parliament or two, but for the indefinite future. No doubt, the Liberals would give the Government some security of tenure in exchange, but even that was a poisoned chalice. The sole issue on which the Liberal Party was united was free trade; and MacDonald was already coming to suspect that complete free trade might be incompatible with economic recovery. In any case, Lloyd George was not in secure control of his flock, and might fail to deliver what he had promised. At a deeper level still, MacDonald had now come to see Lloyd George as an unprincipled adventurer, who would do or say anything to get back to power, and whose return to it would be a disaster to the country; though he did not admit it, there can be little doubt that he also saw him as his own chief rival for the leadership of the British Left, and as a potential cuckoo in any nest into which he might be allowed to climb. Like all politicians tough enough to reach the top, MacDonald was prepared to come to terms with people whom he distrusted and disliked when he was convinced that it was necessary. In the case of Lloyd George, he was to need a good deal of convincing.

Just before Christmas, the Cabinet decided that, in spite of its narrow majority in the second reading debate, the coal Bill should be proceeded with; that Graham should draw up amendments to take account of the points made in the debate; and that he should have a free hand in negotiations with the opposition parties.[25] Early in the new year, the Liberals announced that they did not wish to wreck the Bill, but intended to press for its improvement. At the beginning of February, however, the gulf between the Government and the Liberals was still unbridged; and, with evident reluctance, MacDonald agreed to discuss the situation with Lloyd George. The results were not encouraging. On February 3rd, he noted:

> Ll. G. came & talked with Thomas, Snowden, Henderson & myself about an agreement to keep us in office for from two to three years. Turned upon whether we would give him a bargain on Electoral Reform ... He is fighting for his life & asks us to give it to him. In the two years, he will take to himself our good record & leave for us our bad. The bargain proposed really amounts to this: we get two years of office from the Liberals & give them in return a permanent corner on our political stage.[26]

Next day, he amplified his misgivings in a powerful memorandum, full of political horse-sense, presumably written for his senior colleagues:

> I am a little disturbed about the possible development of the conversation we had with Mr Lloyd George yesterday. In general terms, I am in favour of some agreement, but I am not in favour of making it definite in details or committing it to writing. We should apply the conditions which, without hampering either Party, were observed after the second election of 1910, when we held a balance and kept the Liberal Government in.
>
> If we go further than that, we shall have to face the following difficulties: —
>
> 1. Neither an agreement nor an understanding can be kept private, and will have reactions on the spirit of the Party, both inside and outside the House of Commons.
>
> 2. Its details will be almost impossible to fix, and once we admit that we are definitely in the hands of the Liberals and cannot in any way appeal for consideration at the hands of the Conservatives, the attempt to fix details from week to week will put us more and more in a position subordinate to the Liberals.
>
> 3. It will strengthen Mr Lloyd George's grip upon his own Party and will increase his authority in the country.
>
> 4. It will hamper us at bye-elections and generally in carrying on in the country an offensive against the Liberals.

S

5. It will commit us to a Government Electoral Reform measure, and in the present temper of our Party no such measure could be introduced in an agreed form. It would lead to an abandonment of any expectation we may have [of] returning to a two-Party system.

6. Up to the present we have kept the initiative in our hands, however troublesome some of the situations which have arisen and will arise, may be. If, as I see it, we will have to face a conflict with the House of Lords sooner or later, that will put the Liberals very much in our hands and we should lose whatever advantage that will give us.

7. We should, therefore, delay the conversations and endeavour to go on week by week negotiating on troubles as they arise. That undoubtedly leaves our tenure of office somewhat uncertain, but the price we shall have to pay for a two years' security will be so high that we cannot pay it.[27]

For the time being, MacDonald's arguments prevailed. The Government agreed to a Liberal request that consideration of part I of the Bill, containing the quota provisions, to which the Liberals were most strongly opposed, should be deferred until the end of the committee stage, but it made no concessions on electoral reform. The next trial of strength came when part I was debated at the end of the month. On February 20th, Lloyd George warned MacDonald that the Liberals were determined to vote against the quota and, according to MacDonald's diary, 'begged' the Government not to stick to it.[28] The Cabinet called his bluff; and on February 27th, a Liberal amendment deleting the quota provisions from the Bill was defeated by 280 votes to 271 — four Liberals having voted with the Government and eight having abstained.[29] Before the debate, MacDonald had noted that the Cabinet had voted to 'let Lloyd George do his worst. I think it will break him.'[30] It looked as though he had been proved right.

During the next three weeks, however, there occurred one of those odd and, in retrospect, barely explicable shifts of mood which make parliamentary government the despair of the tidy-minded. Perhaps because of some deep calculation of which no evidence now survives, more probably because their resistance had been worn down by the strains of the last two months, MacDonald's senior colleagues suddenly decided that, although they had successfully beaten off two Liberal challenges, they could not bear to face a third. On March 20th, the House was due to debate a clause providing for district minimum prices. The Liberals were in principle opposed to it, and a number of Liberal M.P.s had put their names down to a Conservative amendment to delete it. In similar circumstances a month before, ministers had decided to stand and fight. This time, they got cold feet. On March 18th, MacDonald noted:

Conference of Snowden, Clynes, Thomas & self discussed relations with Liberals in view of Coal Bill debate & division on Thursday & decided with only myself unwilling to tell Liberals we would introduce an electoral reform bill if we remain in office. The Liberals then decided not to vote against us on Thursday on the ground that the naval conference had reached a critical stage! The decision may perpetuate the Liberal Party but on the other hand it may lead to its painless extinction & absorption.[31]

The Liberals duly abstained; and the Government won a majority of forty-five. Yet even now the saga was far from over. MacDonald and his colleagues had promised to introduce an electoral reform Bill. Nothing appears to have been said about the form which such a Bill should take. The Liberal representatives on the Ullswater conference put forward a complicated scheme to establish two different varieties of proportional representation in different parts of the country. In some areas, there would be multi-member constituencies, in which M.P.s would be elected by the single transferable vote; in others there would be single-member constituencies and the alternative vote.[32] From Labour's point of view, the alternative vote had something to be said for it. An analysis carried out by Transport House suggested that if the alternative vote had obtained in the 1929 election, Labour's representation would have been increased by around fifteen seats and the Liberals' by over forty, while the Conservatives' representation would have fallen drastically.[33] The Liberal plan was a different matter. As we have seen, MacDonald had agreed to the deal over the coal Bill only because he had been outvoted by his senior colleagues. It is clear that his opinions were unchanged; though the evidence is fragmentary, it seems equally clear that he now decided to reopen the subject, using the Liberal proposals at the Ullswater conference as his excuse. In an undated memorandum, headed 'Very personal & confidential', and presumably written in April or May 1930, he urged:

The Party problems which have arisen out of the Ullswater Committee ought to be faced by us, keeping as a background a general survey of our political position.

I. From the birth of the Party until now we have held rigidly to the position that we were standing on our own legs and that has been inculcated as a cardinal principle from John o' Groats to Land's End. It has become part of the very nature of the Party, and in any way to modify it would bring confusion into the minds of great masses of our followers, including the most active of them, and would undoubtedly strengthen the so-called Left Wing.

II. What is the Parliamentary position which it would create? Assuming that there were no trouble about the Business we bring before the House of Commons ... we might secure another two years of office. Would we ... be able to strengthen our appeal to the country at the end of that period? This certainly will not happen unless we can do two big things:

(i) Improve our hold on agricultural constituencies;

(ii) Straighten out the industrial situation, particularly as regards unemployment.

I have given a great deal of attention to the first, and at the moment I am completely baffled ... We might, however, do something which would secure confidence amongst that class of the electorate, but up to the present I do not see how even that can be done unless we are to be pliable in the economic and political principles which we apply to agriculture ...

As to the second point, I am doubtful if we can do anything of a very dramatic character. Our industry is undergoing a very disturbing revolution, the effects of which will not have spent themselves within two years, and I see no hope of great statistical results from the mere expenditure of public money either in doles or in relief employment.

III. The proposals themselves ought to be carefully scrutinised. If we are to agree to Proportional Representation in the industrial areas, an examination of figures convinces me that we shall lose seats of consequence, and the proposal made regarding the more rural and residential areas would not compensate for the losses. In operation, the scheme proposed by the Liberals would secure for them the very maximum possible representation, and for us the minimum of our electoral strength. It is difficult to say without a very close examination what its effect would be upon the Conservatives, but I am inclined to think that it would solidify their representation in the House of Commons, and present it to us as a very solid wall, and give them a chance of remaining the strongest of the three Parties even when they have not an absolute majority.

IV. Supposing we agreed to support the scheme, we should have to get it through the Party, both in Parliament and at the Annual Conference. This we could not possibly do without being quite candid as to our reasons. We cannot say that we are supporting it because it will be an advantage to the Party so far as representation in the House of Commons is concerned; we should have to use arguments which will admit that we have given up hope of creating two parties, one of which would be ourselves, and that we have fallen back upon the assumption that a progressive majority in Parliament would always have to be found by a combination which would either frankly be a Coalition with a sharing of offices, or a Government such as we have at the present moment depending upon the support of the Liberals.[34]

The rest of the story is obscure. Presumably at about the same time that MacDonald's memorandum was written, Lord Arnold suggested that the Labour and Liberal members of the Ullswater conference should submit a joint resolution, advocating the alternative vote, the virtual abolition of university representation, the abolition of the business vote and the stricter limitations on election expenditure.[35] This did not go far enough for the Liberals. On May 19th Lloyd George and MacDonald discussed the situation, and according to MacDonald's diary, Lloyd George

> Told me could not get his party to accept alternative vote: would only have Proportional Representation. I said we would not accept P.R., but would offer alternative vote as a compromise. He said that the Ullswater Confer: would then end in nothing, & the Government would be defeated speedily. We discussed the serious condition of the country & the effect of a Tory Government. Both of us had electoral meetings tomorrow & we agreed to report results to each other.[36]

Next day, however, the Labour Party National Executive met to consult the party's representatives on the Ullswater conference. Lord Arnold made it clear in his opening statement that some of them favoured the alternative vote, but in the end the Executive decided by eleven votes to six that they should be instructed to oppose it.[37] For the time being, at least, that was the end of the matter; and in July the conference broke up with no achievements to its credit.

It was widely assumed at the time that MacDonald had been overruled by the National Executive. According to one story, he made an eloquent plea for the alternative vote, but lost the battle after Henderson had pointed out that the party was opposed to it.[38] Though there can be no certainty, this seems highly implausible. As we have seen, it is clear from his diary and papers that MacDonald was bitterly opposed to a pact with the Liberal Party, both on grounds of policy and on grounds of political expediency, not only in February but later as well. Though the Executive minutes throw little light on the discussion, they make it clear that the meeting was summoned specially at MacDonald's request. Constitutionally, at any rate, there was no reason to summon it. The Labour representatives on the Ullswater conference did not sit as delegates from the National Executive; if they were responsible to anyone, they were responsible to the Cabinet or to the parliamentary party. MacDonald was the last person to consult the National Executive when he had no compelling need to do so; and although he cannot have been certain, he must have had a shrewd idea of what the Executive's attitude was likely to be. In March, his colleagues had decided to make a deal with the Liberals against his wishes. So far from the Executive overruling him, the high probability is that he consulted it deliberately, knowing that it was likely to support him against his colleagues, and make it impossible for them to prevail again.

IV

Such satisfaction as he may have felt at escaping from the Liberal embrace cannot have lasted for long. His negotiations with Lloyd George had taken place against the background of mounting unemployment and growing dissension among the ministers responsible for dealing with it. As early as December 12th, he had noted:

> Visit from Mosley on behalf of Lansbury & Johnston & himself, saying impossible to work with Thomas, & threatening resignation. Probably impossible to work with them, but I fear that T. has handled them badly. Both sides seem to hold each other in something like contempt & neither know[s] how to work [with] the other.[39]

This warning shot was followed by a more formidable explosion. On January 23rd, Mosley sent MacDonald a copy of a long memorandum on the economic situation, on which he had been at work for well over a month, and which has gone down to history as the 'Mosley Memorandum'. It made three main assertions – that the machinery of government should be drastically overhauled, that unemployment could be radically reduced by a public-works programme on the lines advocated by Keynes and the Liberal Party, and that long-term economic reconstruction required 'a mobilisation of national resources on a larger scale than has yet been contemplated'. The existing administrative structure, Mosley argued, was hopelessly inadequate. What was needed was a new department, under the direct control of the prime minister, consisting of an executive committee of ministers and a secretariat of civil servants, assisted by a permanent staff of economists and an advisory council of outside experts. The problems of substance, he went on, had to be looked at under two quite separate headings, which had so far been muddled up. First, there was the long-term problem of economic reconstruction, which could be solved only by systematic Government planning, designed to create new industries as well as to revitalize old ones. Second, there was the immediate problem of unemployment. This could be solved by making road-building a national responsibility, by raising a loan of £200 million and spending it on roads and other public works over the next three years, by raising the school-leaving age and by introducing earlier retirement pensions. Whatever their faults, Mosley concluded flamboyantly, his proposals 'at least represent a coherent and comprehensive conception of national policy ... It is for those who object to show either that present policy is effective for its purpose, or to present a reasoned alternative which offers a greater prospect of success.'[40]

It was a young man's memorandum – brash, perhaps lacking in a sense of administrative practicality, yet with an intellectual vitality and panache that still sparkle through its pages forty years later. MacDonald's response was much less hostile than might have been expected. Whatever private doubts he may have had about large-scale public works as a solution to unemployment, he liked Mosley, admired his energy and wished to keep him in the Government. In an undated note, entitled 'Re Memorandum on Unemployment', which was presumably intended to be a first draft of a reply to Mosley, he wrote irritably but open-mindedly:

I. Machinery Proposals:

There are two points in this section of the memorandum

  (i) that the Prime Minister should preside and be virtually the head of the organisation; and

  (ii) that the organisation should have authority and should work.

As regards (i) this was very carefully considered and found to be impossible.

As regards (ii), the decision as regards machinery amounted to this: that a Minister with whom at first two and, later on, three others were associated was given full powers to organise a machine. The head of the Civil Service was put at his disposal, departments were to be examined in order that they might be co-ordinated in their work as regards unemployment, a free hand was given as to the selection of staff, and the powers asked for in the memorandum were in fact given to the Minister and the body set up. The Prime Minister was to be in the background, but it was clearly understood that any powers or facilities required which he could provide were to be at the disposal of the unemployment body ...

For some reason or other, the provisions made have not worked and there has been a lack of co-operation.

II. Economic Advisory Council:

Parts of the machinery section of the memorandum covered ground which has been the subject of prolonged consideration and negotiation between the Civil Service, leading business men, economists and so on. These are now in an advanced state of preparation ... The proposal put up in the memorandum is, however, much too complicated for a beginning. It is, however, being worked out and appointments will be made at once.

I could refer to other proposals regarding machinery ... but it would only be to reinforce my case that, as regards that part of it, it contains nothing new and that what apparently has happened is that the machinery has not worked as I hoped it would have done ...

III. Programmes:

Before work had actually begun and whilst the Government was still in process of formation, an agreement was come to that policy should be in two sections — first, the section of immediate relief so as to try and bring down the unemployment figures; and, secondly, the reconditioning of industry. Up to now we certainly have not succeeded in doing the former. Week after week thousands of people have been turned out, not because our industry is diminishing but because our labour efficiency is being increased ... It is a terrible situation to face. But the failure is not owing to a mixing up of the two lines of policy, whatever the explanation may be.

I have had a talk with the Minister of Transport and he is as firm as ever upon (1) the utter impossibility of a purely national responsibility for the building of roads of a certain class, and also upon (2) the comparatively

small effect that could be had by the application of this policy as regards
the numbers on the unemployed register ... This is surely a case where
pros and *cons* can be hammered out on the committees & in the Departments concerned, and everybody is so anxious to reduce unemployment
figures that if any promising plan can be devised, it will be supported. It is
impossible for me without going into the arguments on both sides and
weighing them up, to say I side with one or the other ...

I really have not the time at the moment to write a long or closely
examined reply to the memorandum, but this note indicates the lines upon
which it would proceed. I am terribly disappointed by the way that
opportunities have been used. The best machine in the world would be
nonproductive unless there was some harmony in its working. I shall see
the Lord Privy Seal and find from him what are the reactions [to] your
memorandum which you tell me you have sent to him.[41]

MacDonald's evident hope that the explosion could somehow be contained,
and that further investigation would somehow produce a solution equally
acceptable to all concerned, was doomed to disappointment. Though he
displayed surprising patience during the next three months, Mosley wanted
action, not investigation – and still less compromise. He wished to save his
country and believed, not wholly without cause, that he had found the way to
its salvation; no doubt, he also believed that his countrymen would be eager to
follow him along that path if they had the chance. If the Cabinet wished
to adopt his plan, well and good; if not, he would rather fight than talk. The
Treasury and the Ministry of Transport were equally intransigent on the other
side – the Ministry of Transport, because it believed that the road proposals
were unworkable, the Treasury, because it believed that a vast development loan
spelt national bankruptcy. On February 3rd, the Cabinet had a rambling and
inconclusive discussion about the memorandum, and eventually referred it to a
committee consisting of Snowden, Shaw, Greenwood and Margaret
Bondfield.[42] After interminable delays, the committee reported back to the
Cabinet on May 1st, and the stage was set for one of the most remarkable
struggles in recent British history.

As was to be expected, the Snowden committee condemned the memorandum
root and branch. Mosley's administrative proposals, the committee claimed
'cut at the root of the individual responsibilities of Ministers, the special responsibility of the Chancellor of the Exchequer in the sphere of finance, and the
collective responsibility of the Cabinet to Parliament'. They could be reconciled
with the principles of parliamentary government only if the proposed new
department were confined to an advisory role, which could be better discharged
by the economic advisory council. Mosley's distinction between long-term and
short-term problems indicated a 'confusion of mind'; his suggestion that the
Government should itself plan the process of long-term reconstruction would

mean departing from the principle that risk capital should be raised on the market. His short-term proposals were attacked from three quite separate standpoints. To over-ride the local authorities as he had proposed, the committee wrote, would mean replacing Britain's democratic system of local government with a 'bureaucratic system on the continental model'. The road proposals took no account of the inevitable delay between approving a programme and putting men to work. During the summer, the Government had sanctioned two road improvement programmes, to the total value of £37 million. So far, only £27 million worth of schemes had been approved; by February, only 1,620 men had been given jobs. The same thing would happen to Mosley's programmes; and in the short term, at least, they would therefore do nothing to bring the unemployment figures down. In any case, the supply of investment capital was limited. If resources were frittered away on unnecessary roads, they could not also be devoted to improving the competitive power of British industry; by the same token, a Government loan of the kind Mosley wanted would disrupt the capital market, force up interest rates and destroy confidence.[43] Though the Snowden committee did not say so in so many words, the implication was clear. State action to reduce unemployment was inherently suspect, and the Government's existing policies were already pressing against the margin of safety. To go further would be to plunge the country into ruin.

The Snowden report found MacDonald in a mood of despairing agnosticism. Before leaving for Lossimouth for the Christmas recess, in December 1929, he had noted, 'Unemployment is baffling us. The simple fact is that our population is too great for our trade ... I sit in my room in Downing Street alone & in silence. The cup has been put to my lips – & it is empty.'[44] By February 1930, he was asking himself:

Is the sun of my country sinking? The prospect is indeed cloudy & seriously threatening at points. The structure of the Empire is threatened & industrial England leaned much upon that. The war & the wild promises made to win it drew a line across our history. Our war politicians were like men who break up their homes in order to warm their hands at a blaze ... The spirit of nationality as encouraged by the war is selfishness. It insists upon wearing the badge & adopting the manners of the newly created, & still not very sure, independent. China, Egypt, India & the Dominions as well as the new European nations show this. The multiplication of Tariff walls is a serious blow to our industry. In addition we are backward in methods & the financier has played havoc with sound business. We have to adjust ourselves & meanwhile the flood of unemployment flows & rises & baffles everybody. At Chequers one can almost see it & hear its swish in the figures I have been studying.[45]

Since then, the swish had become even more ominous. Between February and April 1930, unemployment went up by 170,000, against the seasonal trend; in a by-election in February, the Labour majority in Sheffield, Brightside, fell from 10,349 to 2,931. There were mutterings of discontent in the parliamentary party, and louder mutterings in the T.U.C. It was clear that something had to be done: but to MacDonald, at least, all the solutions on offer seemed equally unpromising. He was appalled by what he described in his diary as 'Snowden's hard dogmatism expressed in words & tones as hard as the ideas',[46] yet the notion that prosperity could be miraculously restored by borrowing money to spend it on public works seemed glib and unconvincing. 'All this humbug of curing unemployment by Exchequer grants', he complained wildly but revealingly to Walton Newbold at the beginning of June, 'is one of the most superficial and ill considered proposals that has ever been foisted upon the Party. There is no more Socialism in it than there was in the cup of tea that I had at breakfast this morning.'[47]

Apart from public works, however, no alternative to Treasury dogma seemed to be in sight. A committee of the economic advisory council, which had been set up under Keynes's chairmanship to work out heads of inquiry, had got itself bogged down in ideological disagreements between the businessmen and the economists; though Hubert Henderson, who by now had started work as the council's assistant secretary, was willing enough to engage in an academic discussion of possible remedial measures, his only firm suggestion was that the depression would probably cure itself in a year or so by bringing about a fall in interest rates.[48] By the end of April, moreover, MacDonald had spent the best part of three months in the bickering and intrigue of the naval conference. At the beginning of March, he had noted that he was 'getting tired & feel it right to the centre of my being. Had a bad lapse of memory today. Must do my best to keep it dark, but how can I rest?'[49] By May he must have been even more tired.

Yet, in spite of fatigue and nervous strain, his actions after the Snowden committee reported showed a good deal of his old skill. On May 8th, the Cabinet decided that the Snowden report should be referred to a committee of the ministers most closely associated with the Government's unemployment policies; that this committee should 'pay special attention to the importance of pushing on rapidly with schemes already approved for the relief of unemployment'; and that it should be presided over by MacDonald.[50] Though the Cabinet minutes give no indication of the line MacDonald took in the discussion, it is hard to believe that these decisions could have been taken against his will. Yet, by any standards, they represented a sharp slap in the face for Snowden. Snowden's committee had taken three months to complete its report, and although its proceedings had been remarkably dilatory, it could reasonably be assumed to have mastered the subject. Yet instead of being adopted, its findings had now been referred to another committee, chaired by the prime minister and with terms of reference that made it clear that the Cabinet was dissatisfied with the existing policies, which the Snowden committee had endorsed. It would be a mistake to suggest that MacDonald was prepared to over-ride or repudiate Snowden, and a greater one to suggest that he had an alternative policy of his own. All the same, there can be little doubt that, if only to avoid political embarrassment, he was anxious to find a more hopeful approach than that contained in the Snowden committee's blank negations.

By now, however, Mosley had lost patience. On May 13th, the new committee had a rather inconclusive discussion with Thomas's three associates, at which MacDonald made much of the discovery that only £10 million of the £95 million which had been made available for public works had so far been used, while Mosley insisted that the local authorities would have to be 'short circuited' and that an adequate road programme could be financed only by loan.[51] The next meeting took place on May 19th, but before it began, so MacDonald noted later,

> Mosley came to see me ... had to see me urgently: informed me he was to resign. I reasoned with him & got him to hold his decision over till we had further conversations. Went down to Cabinet Room late for meeting. Soon in difficulties. Mosley would get away from practical work into speculative experiments. Very bad impression. Thomas light, inconsistent but pushful & resourceful; others overwhelmed & Mosley on the verge of being offensively vain in himself.[52]

As before, the discussion centred on the delays involved in putting road programmes into effect. Morrison insisted that they were inevitable. After the money to build a road had been voted, plans had to be drawn up, plant moved, physical difficulties got around and local residents and property-owners bought out. Mosley replied that a Napoleon could spend £200 million in three years if he wanted to, quoted the authority of Keynes against the Treasury and declared yet again that the only solution was a loan. As before, the meeting ended in deadlock.[53]

At lunch-time next day, Mosley resigned. At yet another meeting that afternoon, MacDonald tried to dissuade him, and pointed out that the Cabinet had not, in fact, adopted the Snowden report. Mosley insisted that the only way to stop him resigning was to accept his memorandum: 'It was a case of Snowden v. Mosley and plainly Mosley must go.'[54] Afterwards, MacDonald noted bitterly:

> Mosley handed me his resignation in a letter with a note of graceless pompousness. My friend's most scandal spreading enemies would delight if they saw both letters. The Secy: to the Parlty. Party said to me 'Some people get things too easily & they are ruined'. Test of a man's personality is his behaviour in disagreement. In every test he failed ... So the Government staggers on.[55]

V

The Government was now facing a serious, though still containable, crisis. At a party meeting on May 21st, Mosley was persuaded to postpone a motion censuring the leadership until the following day. Next morning, the Cabinet discussed the situation at length, and a careful reading of the minutes makes it clear that the meeting must have seen something approaching a revolt. A number of suggestions were made – including the provision of old-age pensions at sixty, the raising of the school-leaving age, an expansion in the road programme, the formation of an emergency council of ministers meeting several times a week, a conference of local authorities and Government acquisition of emergency powers.[56] At the party meeting that evening, Mosley made an eloquent speech expounding his memorandum, and MacDonald a vague and unconvincing one in reply; Thomas declared that it was the 'most humilitaing day of his life'. The debate was wound up by Henderson, who appealed to Mosley to withdraw his motion so that his proposals could be discussed in detail at later meetings. Mosley asked whether it could be postponed. When his request was turned down by the meeting, he insisted on putting his motion to the vote and was beaten by 210 to 29.[57] Afterwards, MacDonald noted:

> Heavy day finishing with Party meeting on Mosley. His behaviour crushes one's value of friendship. Dramatic moment when chance of withdrawing his resolution came & he bargained & was smart, and vanity overstepped itself & he missed everything ... 29 votes against us & over 200 for is all right when the whipping & converting are taken into account. Shortly before the vote a henchman went up to Mosley: M. How many have we? H. 50. M. Go on then. Thomas becomes more & more a wreck.[58]

Thanks to Mosley's tactical misjudgment the party meeting had passed off less damagingly for the Government than it might have done. But it was easier to win the vote at a party meeting upstairs than to win the argument on the floor of the House. On May 28th, the Conservatives moved a motion of censure on the Government's unemployment policy. In a lame and faintly apologetic speech, MacDonald declared that the rise in unemployment was caused by factors outside the Government's control, explained that many worthwhile schemes had been delayed by administrative and legal complications at the local level, announced that the Government intended to summon a conference of local authorities to try to speed things up and appealed to the other parties for co-operation. Mosley then delivered one of the most powerful resignation speeches of recent times, repeating the arguments he had used in his memorandum and, for the first time, calling explicitly for measures to 'insulate' the British economy from 'the electric shocks of present world conditions'; the Government's present policies, he declared contemptuously, were providing work for only about 80,000 people a year.[59]

Before the debate, MacDonald had feared that the Government might be defeated, but in the end only five Labour members abstained and it survived with a majority of 29. Victories in the division lobbies, however, could not still the doubts of backbench Labour members. At the beginning of May, Labour had lost West Fulham to the Conservatives; on May 27th, the Conservatives had increased their majority in Central Nottingham from 2,998 to 7,023. On May 30th MacDonald noted: 'The Party showing signs of panic owing to the Nottingham bye-election, and as happens in all crowds which have not a coherent psychology every man pursues self-preservation & spreads the panic ... Mosley is hard at work capturing the party. His supporters are buzzing in the lobby and signing petitions & talking about others — one asking Thomas to resign.' [60] It was clear that speedy action was needed if Mosley's challenge was to be repulsed.

MacDonald turned first to that well-worn standby of the beleaguered prime minister, the ministerial reshuffle. 'Up from week-end at Chequers of mist within & without', he noted on June 1st. 'Reconstructing Cabinet and fitting variously whittled pegs into variously bored holes.'[61] The results of his labours were announced on June 5th. The main victim was Thomas, who ceased to be lord privy seal and was shunted into the Dominions Office, which he had refused a year before. Passfield, who had held the combined portfolio of colonial and dominions secretary, now had to make do with the Colonial Office alone. Thomas's post as lord privy seal was taken by Vernon Hartshorn, who had served as one of the Labour representatives on the Simon Commission and had not been available for office when the Government was formed. Mosley's successor as chancellor of the Duchy was the other Labour member of the Simon Commission, Clement Attlee. Noel Buxton resigned as minister of agriculture and was succeeded by Christopher Addison. These changes of personnel were accompanied by a more dramatic change in structure. A panel of ministers was set up to develop the Government's unemployment policy with MacDonald as chairman and Hartshorn as his deputy; under Hartshorn there was to be a secretariat of civil servants, headed by the formidable, if somewhat unsparkling, figure of Sir John Anderson.[62]

The changes were not equally welcome to all concerned. At the Cabinet meeting on May 22nd, Thomas had fought hard against being thrown to the wolves. On June 15th, he returned to the charge, with a long memorandum to MacDonald, listing his activities in the sphere of rationalization. Accompanying it was a letter, pleading that he should be allowed to continue them:

> [T]he economic position is, as you so rightly said, a world one and no temporary schemes, so far as spending Government money is concerned, can cure it: it is the bigger policy that must be faced. In that connection

the Governor saw me yesterday—he has been away and knew nothing about the changes, but naturally was very apprehensive, inasmuch that he made it perfectly clear that for the first time, the City, at the request of the Government through me, came definitely to the help of industry, and although our own people do not understand the significance of that, I want to emphasise that it is well understood in business circles ... The Governor very naturally raised the question as to what is now to be the position. Certain contacts have been made, daily negotiations take place and the firms and Banks now look upon it as the right thing to seek our advice ...

... [T]he Governor ... has made it perfectly clear that he was most anxious that this side of it should not be interfered with.[63]

Though he has rarely received much credit for it, MacDonald believed in standing by his friends. It is clear from his diary that he thought that Thomas had become the scapegoat for the Government's misfortunes, and that he felt guilty about replacing him. When he came to London after the Whitsun recess, he noted sadly that Thomas was in 'a bad way' and had become 'too easy a prey to criticism which is neither just nor generous; speeches have deteriorated. Had to change things and yet not let him down ... Hope that in happier conditions he will recover his equilibrium.'[64] At some stage after receiving Thomas's letter, he decided to allow affection and loyalty to override administrative neatness. Before the end of the month, Thomas had received the consolation prize of continued responsibility for rationalization.

CHAPTER 23

Looking for a policy

I

WHEN the reshuffle was over, MacDonald flew to Lossiemouth for the Whitsun recess. For a week, he was able to enjoy the whins and broom of Morayshire, think solemn thoughts in the churchyard at Spynie and relax with old friends. Half-way through he received the freedom of nearby Inverness – an honour of which he was particularly proud.[1] He came back to London in the middle of June, and for a week or two he seems to have been in reasonably good spirits. He watched cricket in 'wonderful weather' at Lords, had a 'happy lunch' with the Londonderrys and found time to buy pictures for Malcolm and Joan at Christie's.[2] By mid-July, however, the effects of his holiday were wearing off. On July 15th, he noted: 'Yesterday a baffling day with unemployment. To find work defies everyone ... During the night I dreamt of the worries & have got up tired out.'[3] Two days later he confessed: 'Last night one of the worst speeches in House I ever made. Said what I did not want to say & did not say what I wanted. Very annoyed but was worn out & my head would not work.'[4] On July 21st, he noted: 'The prospect of the country weighs upon me ... If more bottom falls out, there will be none left.'[5] Even Lossiemouth brought scant relief. 'I cannot see any daylight through the forest of unemployment ... ,' he noted on August 23rd. 'All kinds of evil possibilities are as real to me as though I was in them, & my head won't work. No one will know what horrors I have to endure. How long can it last?'[6]

The strain and tension that lay behind such entries mounted as time went on. The four months ushered in by the ministerial and administrative changes of early June were among the most critical in recent British history: they were also among the most critical in MacDonald's career. By moving Thomas and taking charge of unemployment policy himself, he had managed to quell the disaffection which Mosley's resignation had brought to a head. But he had staked his reputation on his ability to succeed where Thomas had failed; and, in doing so, he had used up the Government's chief alibi. Yet in themselves the changes had settled nothing. At most, MacDonald had bought time. Everything depended on the way the time was used.

Should the Government after all embark on a big public-works programme, financed by loan? If not, what should it do instead? Was there a halfway house,

somewhere between the Mosley memorandum on the one hand and the
Snowden report on the other? How could the Government's existing public-
works expenditure be made more effective, and the delays in implementing its
decisions be cut down? Were there any other escape routes, apart from public
works; and, if so, where did they lead? These questions of policy, hard enough
to answer in themselves, were complicated by a cruder, but equally insistent,
question of political tactics. From late March until late May, the Liberals had
kept the Government in office in the expectation of electoral reform. Then the
Labour Party Executive had turned it down. Should the Government make a
new attempt to come to terms with the Liberals, and, if so, on what basis? Or
should it go back to the position which had obtained at the beginning of the
year, when it had had no security of tenure but had nevertheless managed to
call the Liberals' bluff whenever they had threatened to withdraw their support?
These questions had been skated over in the muddle and acrimony preceding
Mosley's resignation. Now they would have to be answered. Though no one
could have foreseen it in the summer of 1930, the answers were to determine
the shape of the Government's economic policy for the next twelve months.
There is a strong case for saying that, in doing so, they were also to determine
the shape of British politics for the next ten years.

MacDonald's part in finding the answers has often been misunderstood.
Psychologically and intellectually, he was ill-prepared for the storm he now
had to ride. If he stood for anything in politics, he stood for orderly progress,
for cautious adaptation, for the slow processes of persuasion and compromise.
His lifelong belief that socialism would be built on the success of capitalism
rather than on its failure was a matter of instinct and temperament as well as of
conviction, reflecting an attitude to life which had become more and more
ingrained as he grew older. He knew, of course, that progress might be interrupted, that persuasion might fail, that catastrophe was possible: he had seen
that during the war. But the notion that catastrophe might speed up the rate of
progress, that a crisis might create opportunities to be seized as well as dangers
to be avoided, was profoundly alien to him. In a diary entry in August 1930, he
wrote, 'The whole economic scheme is breaking down for the very reasons
foreshadowed by Socialists'; and in speeches to the party faithful he said the
same thing in more elegant language. In reality, his socialism had had no place
for a breakdown: its central premiss was that breakdowns would not occur.

All this made it difficult for him to grasp the nature of the crisis which had
engulfed him, and still more difficult to realize that he could tackle it best by
turning his back on assumptions which he and most of his colleagues shared
with most of their generation. It was common sense that money could be spent
only if it was there: that capital should be invested only on projects that offered
a return: that loans could be raised only when there was a good prospect of
paying them back. The suggestion that common sense should now be stood
on its head – not in calm weather, when experiments might be justified, but

in the middle of a raging hurricane, when all the risks were magnified –
smacked, not only of frivolity, but of sharp practice. In these circumstances
even his virtues – his stubborn courage in adversity, his unwillingness to trim
his sails to avoid unpopularity, his distaste for glib slogans and easy panaceas –
turned into disadvantages. A less scrupulous or more reckless prime minister
might have been more willing to change course when things went wrong and
to gamble on untried ideas, in the way that Roosevelt was to do so brilliantly
in the United States. MacDonald's instinct was to keep his head down and plod
on in mournful rectitude.

Yet it is misleading to depict him, in the way that many historians have done,
as a utopian sentimentalist incapable of coming to grips with everyday realities,
or even as the helpless prisoner of Treasury orthodoxy. As we have seen more
than once, his approach to politics was in many ways surprisingly doctrinaire,
but in economics he was, above all, a pragmatist. It was not an accident that he
had borrowed from Hobson in his speeches on the 'right to work' Bill before
the war, that he had praised the economics of the 'living wage' report, or, for
that matter, that his economic adviser was a protégé of Keynes and a part-
author of the Liberals' unemployment policy. The elegant symmetry of classical
economic theory had never appealed to him in the way that it obviously had to
Snowden. He was instinctively suspicious of any neat and all-embracing
theory, whether orthodox or unorthodox. He was profoundly sceptical about
the public-works solution advocated by Mosley and Lloyd George, not least
because of the sweeping claims they made for it, but he was at least as sceptical
of the dogmatic negatives of his chancellor; though he followed the Treasury
line on some issues, he was anxious to break with it on others. What mattered
to him was to find a solution that seemed likely to work irrespective of its
theoretical or ideological pedigree. He could see as well as Mosley could that
the Government's existing policies did not work, and during the summer and
early autumn most of his energies were devoted to the search for an alternative.
As we shall see, his real undoing was not that he did not find one, but that,
having found it, he lacked the strength, and perhaps also the energy and will,
to push it through a hostile Cabinet.

II

For the time being, at least, the easiest question to answer was how to deal with
the Liberals. Here, the Government's weakness was a source of strength. Like a
cantankerous valetudinarian threatening his dependants with the prospect of his
own demise, MacDonald could blackmail the Liberals into keeping him in office
by holding out the prospect of a general election in which they would almost
certainly suffer even more disastrously than would the Labour Party. In effect,
that was the course which he had advocated in his two memoranda earlier in

the year. With one modification, that was the course which the Government followed now.

The modification was more apparent than real. In his speech on May 28th, MacDonald had appealed for co-operation from both the opposition parties. On June 3rd, Hankey had lunch with Lloyd George, who told him that he had decided to accept the prime minister's invitation to co-operate, on condition that he saw all the papers and had access to the officials; Lloyd George, Hankey noticed, was 'full of tactics' and would be in a 'strong position to launch out on his own' if his terms were met.[7] Next day, the Cabinet approved a letter from MacDonald to Lloyd George, inviting him to confer regularly with a committee of ministers appointed for the purpose, and promising that if he did so the conferences would be attended by the relevant officials and that he would receive papers 'giving all the information you require on the subjects upon which we shall confer'. Presumably to assuage backbench fears that it was contemplating an outright coalition with the Liberals, the Cabinet also decided that, if Lloyd George agreed, a similar letter should be sent to Baldwin.[8] Since MacDonald had already made it clear that the Conservative nostrum of safeguarding was ruled out, no one can have expected Baldwin to agree; and on June 20th, he turned the offer down. Lloyd George accepted; and on June 26th, the first of a series of two-party conferences was held at No. 10.

They were not fruitful occasions. MacDonald distrusted Lloyd George and Lloyd George despised MacDonald, or at least pretended to; both knew that, although their short-term interests coincided, their long-term interests were as far apart as ever. Before the conferences were properly under way, moreover, relations between the two parties were soured by a lighthearted parliamentary frolic, of the kind beloved of Opposition whips, which made MacDonald even more suspicious of the Liberals than he had been before. On July 9th, the Liberals moved an amendment to the finance Bill, to provide that company profits used for re-equipment should be exempted from income tax. Snowden refused to accept it, and announced that the Government would treat it as a question of confidence. Lloyd George insisted that he did not wish to defeat the Government, but also insisted on pressing the amendment to a division. Many Conservative members were away, and the Government did not appear to be in danger. When the division bells rang, however, a flood of extra Conservatives, who had been concealed in hiding places in and around the Palace of Westminster, suddenly appeared in the lobby. Though the Government scraped through with a majority of three, it did so only because a number of Liberals rebelled against their leader and abstained.[9]

Understandably enough, MacDonald assumed that Lloyd George had planned the whole escapade in collaboration with the Conservative whips, and noted indignantly:

Very narrow squeak; saved by 3 votes. Should have been glad had it been otherwise & the House been faced by our defeat. Liberals swearing at Ll.G. for deceiving them. He assured them there was no crisis whilst he was plotting with the Tory Front Bench. He is the most consummate cheat & wirepuller of the time. The scene in the lobby after the division was animated but the centre of the lively group was blanched faced Liberals trying to restrain their anger & pouring out their wrath on the head of their leader. Tomorrow he will be coming to me in the demeanour of a co-operating ally! I shall receive him suavely & smoothly as though he were a gentleman of honour, but I doubt if he will notice the satire.[10]

MacDonald's suspicions may have been unfounded. It is conceivable, though scarcely probable, that Lloyd George had told the truth when he said that he did not want to defeat the Government, and that he had intended only to demonstrate that the Liberals were not to be taken for granted. But even if he had not planned to defeat the Government on a question of confidence, he had made it clear that he was prepared to run the risk of doing so. Though the two-party conferences limped on into August, the Government could no longer be under any illusion that Lloyd George would regard them as a satisfactory *quid pro quo* for guaranteed Liberal support in the division lobbies. There is no evidence that the episode led MacDonald to abandon his earlier objections to a deal with the Liberals, but he must have been uneasily aware that the pressures which had pushed his colleagues into wanting one five months earlier were as formidable as they had been before.

For the next few months, however, it was the policy questions that concerned him most. By now, the unemployment panel had started work, and the Ministry of Transport had found a formidable ally in its running fight with the Treasury, in the shape of the prime minister. At the end of May, MacDonald wrote to Snowden asking him to give immediate attention to Morrison's request for extra expenditure on trunk roads; in spite of strong resistance from his officials, Snowden agreed on June 5th, that the trunk road programme should be increased from £13.5 million to £21 million.[11] On June 17th, the conference of local authorities foreshadowed in MacDonald's speech on May 28th was held at the Guildhall. In his opening speech, MacDonald blamed the 'slow and cumberous' machinery of many local authorities for the delay in putting men to work; in reply, the local authority representatives blamed the proliferation of Government departments and the inadequacy of Government grants.[12] The upshot was a series of measures designed to liberalize the conditions on which grants were made available to local authorities, to give bigger grants in areas of high unemployment and to speed up the process of compulsory purchase.

The results were far from negligible. At the end of February 1930, the total value of all approved public-works projects stood at £70 million. By the end of June, the figure was £110 million, and by the end of September, nearly £140 million. On June 30th, the projects which were actually in operation were valued at £44 million; six months later that figure had increased to £86 million.[13] During the summer, Hartshorn's office estimated that by the time Parliament reassembled in November, the total number employed directly and indirectly as a result of the Government's expenditure on public works would be about 150,000.[14]

By the standards of the past, these were impressive figures. Set against the needs of the present, they were pitifully small. On June 24th, MacDonald noted: 'Unemployment is baffling us for [the] moment. Up 110,000 in a fortnight. Nothing can dam the flow at present.'[15] In July the number on the register went above the two-million mark for the first time in history; by September, it was over 2,200,000.[16] Yet it seemed increasingly clear to the ministers and officials concerned that the existing criteria of economic need left little scope for spending more. As Sir John Anderson put it on July 30th:

> My colleagues on the Secretariat and I ... have been at work for just over seven weeks ... In the result certain facts stand out with almost embarrassing clearness ...
>
> The hard core of the problem is represented by the unemployment in the depressed areas and here there is clearly a need for constructive work; but there is no escaping the conclusion that a fundamental attack on this part of the problem is out of the question so long as it is overlaid by the unemployment due to general world conditions ... You cannot drain a bog while the surrounding country is still under water.
>
> Apart from the special remedies for which the depressed areas call, we have been considering very fully ... what has been the standby of all Governments confronted with a great unemployment problem — the artificial provision of employment. Our investigations have convinced us that we are now nearing the limit of works which will conform to any reasonable standard of economic utility or development. Here and there further lines of development can be found but the total cost of such works still waiting to be done cannot be more than a few millions and their employment value is relatively insignificant ...
>
> ... As I see it the position of the Government may be likened to that of the captain and officers of a great ship which has run aground on a falling tide; no human endeavour will get the ship afloat until in the course of nature the tide again begins to flow ... [T]he task of those in command during the period of waiting is to see that the ship does not suffer permanent damage, to maintain the spirit of the passengers and crew and to do whatever lies in their power to ensure that the earliest and fullest advantage shall be taken of the returning tide.[17]

Hartshorn's view was much the same, though, as we shall see, the conclusions he drew from it were less fatalistic. So far as public works were concerned, he wrote on August 18th, 'I confess that, before I had an opportunity of investigating matters for myself I thought that a great deal more could be done ... After fully examining the position, I am satisfied that not much more is possible.'[18]

Meanwhile, another attempt by MacDonald to intervene in the sphere of monetary policy had proved abortive. In late June or early July, Sir Frederick Leith-Ross of the Treasury sent him a memorandum on the possibilities of Government action to halt the fall in world prices, in which he argued that a large part of the responsibility for the depression lay with the dear-money policies of the French and the Americans. The disease could be cured, Leith-Ross argued, only by an international policy of cheap money and a worldwide expansion of credit, brought about by lowering the central banks' gold reserve ratios. Though interest rates were now falling, it was far from clear that all the authorities concerned were equally convinced of the need for them to do so; so far, no steps had been taken to reduce central bank reserve ratios. 'This being the position,' Leith-Ross concluded, 'it is obvious that remedial action cannot be undertaken by any one Government or country, but is essentially a matter requiring international co-operation'. However, he went on, the central banks were now beginning to co-operate, and in these circumstances Government intervention might do more harm than good.

MacDonald was less defeatist. In the margin of Leith-Ross's memorandum he scribbled: 'Can Treasury do anything in conjunction with B. of Eng.'; and on July 14th, he wrote to Snowden:

> I have read ... Leith-Ross's Memorandum on the possibilities of Government action in regard to the recent fall in world prices, and think it is a very valuable one.
>
> I note his view that remedial action is essentially a matter requiring international co-operation, and that it is difficult to exert pressure from this country. Though he points to directions in which the outlook is hopeful, progress seems likely to be very slow. No doubt you are considering these questions, and I should be very glad if you would look particularly at the possibility of speeding up the developments from which the Memorandum sees the best hope for the future.

The results were disappointing. Presumably on Snowden's instructions, Leith-Ross sent MacDonald a second memorandum, proving that nothing could be done after all. 'I do not think that the Government can do anything effective to speed up international action with a view to influencing the level of world prices,' he wrote. 'The only immediate action that rests with them related to the Report of the Gold Delegation of the League of Nations ... But any attempt on the part of the Governments to get decisions on questions of credit policy formulated by the League would almost certainly result in a deadlock and do harm rather than good.' Even on the technical question of whether cheaper money would in fact help to solve the problem, he beat an undignified retreat. Economists, he pointed out sagely, differed strongly, both in their diagnoses and in their suggested remedies:

> In this country the Cambridge group of economists are convinced that the trouble is due almost entirely to monetary causes and their view is supported on the Continent by Professor Cassel. But many economists in this country would not accept this view ... while on the Continent and in America it is regarded as quite unfounded. Moreover, the economists who hold this view have at different times adopted so many inconsistent positions and are ready on occasion to advocate remedies so desperate ... that no banker in the world would go to them for practical guidance.
>
> So far as there is any common ground on the subject, it is that the monetary factor is an important but a subsidiary cause of the present troubles ... On this view the fall of prices is to be ascribed to the large changes of technology and of taste which have developed during and since the war ... In these circumstances any expansion of credit would only have gone to promote still more surplus production or to foster stock exchange speculation and would not have affected to any large extent the demand for prime commodities.[19]

Even the central banks, it seemed, could do nothing to help: as for the unemployed, they would presumably have to wait for jobs until tastes changed or technological progress reversed itself.

III

If Anderson and Hartshorn were right in thinking that the existing criteria of 'economic utility' would not justify much more spending on public works, one obvious conclusion was to change the criteria, and to raise a development loan in the way that Mosley had advocated in his memorandum and that Lloyd George and the Liberals had advocated in *We Can Conquer Unemployment*. This solution had, of course, been vehemently, indeed violently, rejected by the Snowden committee. But the Snowden report had never been endorsed by the Cabinet; and since it had appeared, Mosley had resigned, the two-party conferences had begun and the unemployment figures had risen even more alarmingly than before. MacDonald had not shown much enthusiasm for the Snowden report at the beginning of May: in spite of his own scepticism about a big public-works programme, he was not prepared to treat it as the last word on the subject at the end of June.

The Treasury's position was unchanged. In a memorandum commenting on Mosley's resignation speech of May 28th, it explained that it was not opposed to a 'reasonable volume' of public-works expenditure, but once again denounced the view that 'abnormal schemes of public expenditure can be financed without affecting other capital requirements.' In theory, it conceded, Government investment might speed up the circulation of money, and so stimulate employment. But no such policy could succeed without the co-operation of the investing public, and in present circumstances an attempt to float a large Government loan would be more likely to produce greater 'business despondency and depression'. The familiar confidence argument was buttressed by what might be called the 'real wages' argument. Fifty years ago, wrote the authors of the Treasury paper, the remedy for depression was simple: 'Reduce your wages, pay your workmen less for the same amount of labour, for the same quantity of goods produced. You can then reduce the price of your goods, recapture your markets and keep your men in employment.' Today, that remedy was no longer available, and those who believed that real wages were too high had to achieve their ends by more covert means. This was what Mosley's policy would mean in practice:

> Its object must surely be a rise in the price level to be secured by the vast outpouring of a flood of money. That is commonly called inflation. Vast Government loans are to be raised – at what rate of interest you will – and the proceeds are to be poured at breakneck speed into the hands of quarry owners, of road contractors and of the proprietors of the businesses ... which supply the goods the Government will need ... There is no doubt that the plan can make prices rise. There is no doubt that it would in the process reduce real wages. There is not the smallest prospect that it will restore the industrial equilibrium.[20]

By July, the Treasury had discovered a more recondite objection. State borrowing, Donald Fergusson argued in a paper circulated to the unemployment panel, was perfectly legitimate when the project on which the money was spent was capable of yielding a money return sufficient to cover the interest and sinking fund. In other cases, it was inherently unsound. Borrowing for projects which did not yield an adequate money return would mean throwing the burden on posterity, 'notwithstanding that posterity must either shoulder or pass on to a still later generation the cost of the similar equipment it requires'. That was why the cost of road building had so far been met out of the annual revenue of the fund. To meet it by borrowing would mean departing from the 'sound principles which now govern national finance'.[21]

The Treasury's warning did not achieve its purpose. A week after receiving Fergusson's paper, MacDonald sent Sir John Anderson a copy of the Mosley memorandum, with covering note asking him to 'Examine the proposals made here and see what is in them.'[22] Meanwhile, Lloyd George was using the two-party conferences to press for a big road programme, and in July and August the ground covered by the Snowden committee was traversed all over again by the unemployment panel and secretariat. It soon became clear, however, that the Treasury was not the only departmental opponent of a big public-works programme. The Ministry of Transport was equally opposed, and its objections, though less sophisticated intellectually, were much harder to meet.

At one of the two-party conferences at the beginning of August, Sir Henry Maybury, the Ministry of Transport's consulting engineer, was asked to report on the feasibility of 'largely increasing the number of men engaged in roadworks during the coming winter'. His conclusions were pessimistic in the extreme. Even if the Government decided to embark on 'works of great magnitude lying outside the range of the usual activities of local authorities', and to set up a new centralized apparatus to build them, Maybury wrote, it would be unable to find more than £20 million worth of useful projects. Even if exceptional powers were taken, he went on, it was technically impossible to spend more than 20 per cent of the total value of any road programme in the first year. Maybury assumed that for every million pounds of expenditure, 2,000 men would be employed directly and another 2,000 indirectly. Thus, on the most favourable assumptions, a £20 million programme would create only 16,000 extra jobs in the first year.[23]

These figures were hotly disputed by the Liberals. At the next two-party meeting, Lloyd George described Maybury's report as 'impotent', and declared stoutly that the Liberal Party's proposals were based on 'the highest expert advice available'; if Maybury's conclusions represented the Government's final view, he added menacingly, there was no basis for further meetings.[24] Another bout of discussion followed, this time between the Liberals' technical adviser, Guy Humphreys, and the engineers at the Ministry of Transport. On August 25th, Herbert Morrison summarized the results as follows. The Liberals, he wrote, had proposed spending £145 million on roads in a two-year period. The programmes suggested by Humphreys, on which this figure had been based, closely resembled those planned by the Ministry of Transport itself. The difference between the Liberals and the ministry concerned timing, not programmes; and, on examination, it had turned out that Humphreys's report provided no basis for the Liberals' claim that £145 million could be spent in two years. Moreover, Humphreys had not made a sufficient allowance for the expansion which had since taken place in the ministry's own programme; so far as trunk roads were concerned, the ministry had prepared a map for Lloyd George showing that 'nearly the entire length' of the roads which Humphreys had selected had now been provided for. The Liberals' estimates on ring roads were equally vulnerable. They had proposed spending £20 million on ring roads in two years. But ring roads entailed extensive demolitions of property and presented formidable engineering difficulties as well; they were notoriously difficult to build quickly. Altogether, Morrison concluded,

Mr. Humphreys said that the time estimate in the pamphlet was based on the hypothesis of a virtual dictatorship under which no regard would be paid to the protests or views of individuals, public bodies or even statutory undertakings. Even so nowhere in his report does he commit himself to a two years' period of execution except in regard to rural roads ...

An analysis of the figures ... shows that the average expenditure in the first eighteen months of ... five earlier programmes averaged between 20% and 25%. The original 1924/25 programme (over £8 millions) showed only 2% expended in the first ten months and 17% in the following year. The supplementary programme (£5½ millions) showed 15% in the first year.[25]

It is conceivable that if the Ministry of Transport had accepted the Liberals' calculations, MacDonald might have been willing to fight Snowden head-on — though it is hard to imagine him doing so without a good deal of trepidation and uncertainty. The combination of the Treasury and the Ministry of Transport was irresistible. During the next few weeks, there was a good deal of agitated discussion among ministers and officials about the need to speed up the Government's existing road programmes, but no one appears to have challenged Maybury's estimate of what could be done in future. Even the Liberals were more impressed by it than they were willing to admit. They denounced the Government for lack of drive and continued to demand a development loan. But, in the revised programme which they published in October, they gave first place to a reduction in industrial costs and a cut in Government spending; public works, they emphasized, were not a substitute for these. Next came a bizarre plan to settle 100,000 families on the land; the loan came third.[26] Road-building still figured in their programme, but it did so as one item in an odd mixture of expenditure and economy, not as the chief hope of the unemployed.

To MacDonald and most of his colleagues, it seemed clear that Morrison and Maybury had won the argument. On September 22nd, MacDonald advised Hartshorn to 'keep in almost hourly touch with the Liberals now. You see that their game is as we have beaten them on programmes, to fall back upon "drive".'[27] A few days later, he told the Cabinet that Lloyd George's 'figures had been shown to be wrong, and his statements to be at variance with the views of his experts'.[28] He was preaching to the converted. It was not until the end of September that the Cabinet explicitly decided that nothing more could be done through public works,[29] but for all practical purposes the question had been settled when Maybury reported in the middle of August. Orthodoxy had prevailed: but it owed its victory to the road engineers of the Ministry of Transport, not to the mandarins of the Treasury.

Few would now dispute that the question was settled in the wrong way or that the Ministry of Transport could have found more roads to build if it had wanted to look for them; though Morrison was probably right in his estimate of what could be spent in the first year, big road expenditures in the second and third years would have been of great value. But although it is clear in retrospect that Maybury should have been overruled, it is hard to believe that any Government at the time would have been prepared to overrule him. As the revised Liberal programme showed, no leading politician, with the possible exception of Mosley, had yet grasped the central point of the doctrine which Keynes was now beginning to hammer out – that what influences the level of unemployment is the effect of Government spending on demand, not the intrinsic value of the projects on which Government money is spent. No one realized that a depression could be ended as effectively by paying men to be idle as by paying them to work: by the same token, no one was prepared to advocate that men should be paid to do work for which there seemed to be no economic justification. The Government's retreat before the massed battalions of the Ministry of Transport was one sign of this doctrinal vacuum: another was the Liberals' perverse combination of more public works and less Government spending. In these circumstances, any Government wishing to provide employment through public works would have had to fight on Maybury's ground: and in any battle fought on Maybury's ground, Maybury would have been likely to win. No doubt he found it easier to convince MacDonald, who was instinctively suspicious of the public-works solution, than he would have found it to convince Lloyd George. But although a Lloyd George Government would probably have squeezed more jobs out of the Ministry of Transport than MacDonald's Government did, it is doubtful if it would have squeezed enough to make much difference to the problem.

IV

By late August, MacDonald's attempt to hasten the leisurely processes of central bank co-operation had been frustrated, and a big expansion in public works had been turned down. To a growing minority in the Cabinet, it seemed clear that only one solution was left. As Hartshorn pointed out in a long memorandum summarizing the conclusions he had reached after two-and-a-half months as lord privy seal, no conceivable measures of rationalization could restore Britain's traditional staple industries to their old position. Since it was now clear that little more could be done through public works, the only realistic solution to the country's economic problems was to develop production for the home market at the expense of imports. That, in turn, raised a fundamental question of policy, which only the Cabinet could answer. '[I]f present fiscal conditions are unfavourable to the expansion of certain established industries or the establishment of new ones,' Hartshorn asked heretically, 'ought we not to be prepared to consider a modification of our fiscal policy?'[30]

MacDonald had little doubt about the answer. As early as January 1930, Tom Jones had overheard him tell Thomas, 'The day is coming when we may have to give up orthodox free trade as we inherited it from our fathers.'[31] In July, he shocked Snowden by remarking casually during a debate in the House that the best way for Labour to win the next election would be to campaign for a three-point programme, consisting of no reductions in the social services, a 'forward' policy on unemployment and a 10 per cent revenue tariff.[32] At about the same time, he noted in his diary, 'I should not be surprised if *our* next appeal to the country were on: Maintenance of Social Services, and taxation of imports.'[33] In a longer entry in mid-August he mused anxiously:

> The trade of the world has come near to collapse and nothing we can do will stop the increase in unemployment. Promises made under different conditions cannot be fulfilled until the conditions return and meanwhile we are challenged to do something spectacular. Schemes of a panic or 'war' character are put up but we have to consider whether in appearing to relieve the present abnormal registers we shall not of a certainty make industrial conditions worse ... Protection in some form or other must be discussed. The Budget alone will compel us to do something it appears. But it will divide the Cabinet – even more than the Party.[34]

His fears were well founded. Pressure to protect the home market had grown steadily ever since the depression had first made itself felt at the beginning of the year. Part of it came from the industries in which a high level of unemployment seemed directly due to foreign competition – notably from agriculture, and from iron and steel. Part came from ministers whose responsibilities made them specially responsive to the needs of such industries – notably from the two ministers of agriculture, Buxton and Addison, and from Thomas. Part came from the Conservative Party, where a combination of world depression and a campaign by Lords Beaverbrook and Rothermere had woken the sleeping dogs of tariff reform and prodded Baldwin into rediscovering his protectionist past. An intellectually more formidable voice was that of Keynes, a lifelong free-trader, who first announced his conversion to protection in his evidence to the Macmillan committee in February, and who proceeded to fight for it in his capacity as chairman of the economists' committee of the economic advisory council.[35] A more influential one, at least in Whitehall, was Hubert Henderson's. Henderson was another old free-trader, but at the end of May he worked out an ingenious scheme by which the proceeds of a 10 per cent revenue tariff would be used to set up an 'Industrial Reconstruction Fund', to be spent on capital investment and on helping to meet the deficit on unemployment insurance. No 'competent economist', Henderson wrote provocatively, 'would dispute that, under such conditions as now obtain, the effect of a 10% tariff on imports would be beneficial to employment'.[36] His paper was circulated to the Cabinet and put on the agenda for a meeting at the beginning of June. It was never discussed, but, as Tom Jones put it in his diary, 'Henderson's bombshell ... must have been in everybody's mind.'[37]

The pressures were formidable, but the resistance to them was formidable too. For more than a generation, free trade had been an article of faith to most people on the left—not a convenience to be applied or discarded as circumstances changed, but the economic expressions of the libertarian and internationalist political creed which most Labour men, as well as most Liberals, had taken for granted all their lives. Among ministers, its high priest was Snowden, who saw any attempt to depart from it as a symptom of moral flabbiness as well as of mental inadequacy, and who made it clear on several occasions that he was prepared to die in the last ditch for his beliefs. Snowden's chief acolyte—later to become a notable apostate—was Willy Graham, whose position as president of the Board of Trade gave him an influence on fiscal policy second only to Snowden's own. As foreign secretary, Henderson played a smaller part in the argument, but on at least one critical occasion he too threw his weight behind the free-trade camp. Lesser devotees included the ageing but not yet negligible peers, Parmoor and Passfield. The parliamentary party's position was unclear. Traditionally, the Labour movement had seen tariffs— above all tariffs on food—as evil devices to lower working-class living standards. On the other hand, if Labour M.P.s could be convinced that protection was the alternative to unemployment, most of them would probably opt for protection. The Liberals' position was more straightforward. Free trade for them was what the Thirty-Nine Articles were for the Church of England: though individual Liberals might have doubts, the Liberal Party could not abandon it without destroying the chief justification for its existence as an organized body. Lloyd George was widely believed to have an open mind on free trade, and might well have introduced tariffs himself if he had been in power. But Lloyd George was not in power. He was the leader of a weak and increasing fissiparous party in opposition; and whether they liked it or not, the one proposition about which most of his followers could agree was that free trade was good and protection bad. They were condemned to go on doing so whether they accepted the proposition or not.

Thus, the battle lines over protection cut bewilderingly across the battle lines over public works. In retrospect, there can be little doubt that a policy of home development was incompatible with free trade, as Keynes had recognized in his evidence to the Macmillan committee in February and as Mosley had recognized in his resignation speech. With the rest of the world strenuously deflating (most of it behind tariff walls), Britain could not have followed an expansionist policy at home without taking steps to restrict imports. If she had tried to do so, much of the increased demand would have leaked out into imports and the policy would soon have run into a balance-of-payments crisis of the kind which successive British Governments were to face after 1945. The British economy, in the words of an authoritative recent study, was 'locked into' a collapsing world economy:[38] so long as Britain stuck to free trade, she had no way of breaking the lock. It would be wrong to suggest that the protectionist camp consisted wholly, or even mainly, of sophisticated expansionists who argued their case in these terms. Many protectionists were concerned only with the narrow interests of their own firm or industry; most were at least as orthodox in their other economic views as were most free-traders. The fact remains that free trade went hand in hand with deflation, while protection was the logical corollary of a policy of home development. Yet the Liberals, who were among the strongest advocates of a policy of home development, were also among the strongest opponents of protection.

In these circumstances, MacDonald had a difficult hand to play. How far he was influenced by the wider economic arguments for protection is not clear, but there can be no doubt that he became increasingly convinced that there could be no escape from the depression without it – if only because it appeared to offer the only way of balancing the budget without increasing direct taxation, and so undermining business confidence still further. At the same time, however, he wanted to keep his Cabinet together and his party in power and believed – with stronger justification than has sometimes been realized – that he could not afford a head-on clash with Snowden and an outright breach with the Liberal Party unless he could carry most of his colleagues with him. His often puzzling and sometimes perverse behaviour as the argument developed must be seen in this context.

V

His first big test came over agriculture. Opposition to taxes on food lay at the heart of the free-trade faith, yet there was no industry where the effects of free trade were more damaging to those engaged in it than they were in agriculture. Cereal growers were particularly hard hit, and by February 1930, the Ministry of Agriculture was already campaigning to establish a marketing board for the home wheat crop, coupled with quotas on imports. These proposals came before the Cabinet on February 11th; and after a long discussion the Cabinet decided that 'no proposal that involved either a crude subsidy or protective tariffs should be considered.' It also decided, however, that a committee including a number of officials and representatives of outside interests should be set up to examine agricultural policy in the light of the ministry's proposals, and that the terms of reference should be drawn up by MacDonald.[39]

The committee was duly set up, and spent the best part of six weeks on its deliberations. Meanwhile, MacDonald decided to intervene more actively. He had already written one memorandum advocating action of an unspecified sort to protect British cereal growers from 'bounty fed' produce from abroad.[40] On February 24th, he followed this with a more far-reaching minute, advocating a complicated mixture of duties and subsidies. Arable agriculture, he wrote, was in 'a most precarious position', and it was impossible for the Government to 'stand by doing nothing'. So far, Labour's policy had centred around the establishment of marketing boards, but this would involve legislation for which there was no time in the current session. Hence, he concluded,

> This idea has come into my mind. Could we in the Budget impose a registration fee on imported grain — wheat, barley, oats — and spend the proceeds up to a named figure to keep prices of home production up to a 'cost of production' level? ... Is it possible under existing treaties? What sum would be required? Could it be raised without increasing costs to [the] consumer to any appreciable extent? Upon what basis should the losses to the home farmer be paid?
> If anything is to be done to influence this year's agriculture, it must be done at once.[41]

The outcome gave an illuminating indication of the weight of the forces involved. On February 25th, a conference of ministers and officials met under MacDonald's chairmanship at No. 10. MacDonald opened the proceedings by referring to his minute of the day before, and said that he had received a note from Snowden saying that he could not accept the suggestion of a registration fee. Buxton welcomed MacDonald's proposal, and pointed out that 3,000 agricultural workers were unemployed in Norfolk alone; to guarantee prices of 50s. a quarter for wheat, 40s. for barley and 30s. for oats would cost only £13 millions. Sir Warren Fisher, who was present as the Treasury's representative, then intervened with a passionate statement of the free-trade case, which could not have been bettered by Snowden himself. A subsidy was out of the question, Fisher declared, while the registration fee was 'just as much open to objection as a tax on food'. At this, MacDonald produced a new proposal by which farmers would receive a disguised subsidy, equivalent to the cost to the exchequer of extending unemployment insurance to agricultural workers. This provoked even more opposition from Fisher than the registration fee had done. A state payment of this kind, Fisher declared, 'could not be disguised as an insurance scheme, and it would have to be regarded as a subsidy ... The sum provided would be devoted to supporting production, whereas insurance is always regarded as a tax on industry, not as a subvention to it. Other industries would complain that they were being taxed to provide this subvention.' The meeting ended with Fisher half-heartedly agreeing that MacDonald's proposal should be examined, and warning ominously of the probable size of next year's budget deficit.[42]

Nothing more was heard of the registration fee or of a Government subsidy. But although the Treasury was strong enough to block MacDonald's attempt to solve the problems of the cereal growers, it was not strong enough to make the problems disappear. At the beginning of March, a great crowd of between 20,000 and 35,000 farmers and farm workers gathered on Parker's Piece in Cambridge to demand 'immediate attention to the plight of the ploughland'.

The meeting, wrote W. B. Taylor, one of the agricultural group of Labour M.P.s, was 'a Portent which, in my judgement as a *countryman*, cannot be overlooked by Parliament'.[43] It was now clear, Buxton wrote on March 3rd, that the Government would have to make some response to Baldwin's new policy of guaranteeing the price of wheat; the 'best method available of a spectacular character' was to set up an import board, empowered to buy up the entire supply, whether it had been produced at home or abroad.[44] Shortly afterwards, Hubert Henderson circulated a paper arguing that agriculture was facing an emergency and that emergency solutions were needed. The best solution, he suggested, was to compel millers to buy a certain quota of their wheat from British farmers and to guarantee the price of home-grown wheat at whatever level was considered appropriate.[45]

A long and bitter struggle followed. At the end of March, the agricultural policy committee at last reported – in favour of a system of co-operative marketing, but against import boards or a quota. The Cabinet duly decided that a marketing Bill should be drafted as soon as possible, but in spite of its committee's recommendations it also decided that Buxton and Snowden should consult 'with a view to the production of a scheme for a statutory quota of home-grown wheat which should not involve any appreciable charge on public funds'.[46] By the end of April, the Ministry of Agriculture had produced a draft white paper advocating a quota, Thomas had written to Buxton giving it his support, and Buxton's parliamentary secretary, Addison, had reported that although he had been opposed to the quota at first he was now 'quite certain (1) that it could be worked, (2) that it will give material help'.[47] Meanwhile, the free-traders had rallied their forces too. Adamson, the Scottish secretary, attacked the quota on the grounds that Scottish consumers would have to pay higher prices 'solely to ensure an increased return to English farmers'.[48] Snowden circulated a characteristically lucid and utterly negative memorandum, pointing out that the whole object of the quota was to raise prices, that higher prices meant lower real wages and that the proposal was based 'on the same assumption which underlies the proposals made from other quarters for currency inflation or for fiscal protection'.[49] In a covering letter to MacDonald he warned:

> It seems to me that we are in grave danger of involving ourselves in a policy of raising prices to the consumer all round: first Coal, next Cereals and then Agricultural Produce generally. If our real object is to raise prices and so reduce wages we had better adopt wholeheartedly the inflation policy of McKenna or Keynes or the whole-hog protection policy of Baldwin. Personally I am in favour of a policy which will protect the consumer, maintain real wages and compel our industries to make themselves efficient by exposing them to the cold blast of reality.[50]

It is unlikely that Snowden's classical pieties evoked much enthusiasm from MacDonald. Partly, perhaps, because of his own peasant background, and partly because of his long-standing friendship with Joe Duncan, the secretary of the Scottish Farm Servants' Union, he had taken a close interest in agriculture for many years, and had long ago come to the conclusion that its problems could not be solved without state aid. An undated note in his papers, evidently written during the spring or summer of 1930, makes it clear that although he saw practical difficulties in the quota, he supported the principle behind it. All industrial countries, he pointed out, were now taking steps to protect arable farmers from the collapse of world prices — by tariffs, by bounties, by other forms of financial aid or by marketing schemes. Though it was true that more efficient organization would help farmers a great deal in the long run, there was a danger that, in the meantime, the acreage under cultivation would be reduced 'very substantially'. The Cabinet had to decide whether or not it wished to retain arable farming, not just as a 'convenience', but as 'an essential part of ... national life'; and if it answered in the affirmative, it would have to recognize that 'its answer means money & that it should take a firm stand upon that in its declarations.' The money could be provided directly or indirectly; and since direct provision was not favoured (presumably a reference to the registration fee), indirect provision would have to be made instead. The quota was merely one of a number of possible forms of indirect aid. The vital point was to accept the principle that the Government should 'secure ... the maintenance of the national minimum requirement in arable cultivation'.[51]

Perhaps because he had burned his fingers over the registration fee, however, or perhaps because he was preoccupied with Mosley's revolt and its repercussions, MacDonald did little to translate his heresies into action. In the excitements of the spring and early summer, ministers had little time to spare for agriculture; and when Buxton left office, no decisions had been made. Meanwhile, the plight of the cereal growers had become worse, and demands for action had grown louder. In June, Attlee, Mosley's successor as chancellor of the Duchy, was asked to investigate the problem. He reported that unless the Government set up an import board or established a quota, 'a very serious situation will arise, worse than that over the Mosley memorandum': Snowden's argument against the quota, he added drily, 'is of course fatal to any project whereby a special position is given to any branch of British industry. It applies equally against the Beet Sugar Subsidy, the Coal Bill and most Socialist proposals.'[52] Buxton's successor, Addison, fought vigorously for an early decision in favour of import boards, so that the Government would have firm proposals to put to the imperial conference which was to meet in October.[53] MacDonald, however, lay low; and although he may have supported Addison in Cabinet, he appears to have taken no further initiatives himself. Perhaps because of this, Addison's efforts were of no avail. Faced with the choice between higher unemployment and higher prices, the Cabinet prevaricated. At the end of July, it decided that no decision could be taken on import boards until the imperial conference policy had studied the question, that the quota was open to serious objection, that the whole subject required further deliberation and that the discussion should be adjourned until the autumn.[54] On August 1st, Snowden made a statement in the House promising that the Government would bring in a marketing Bill and that, once the imperial conference was over, it would take 'whatever practicable steps can be devised to put cereal growing in this country on an economic foundation'.[55] With that, the farming community and its allies in the Cabinet had to be content.

VI

The free-traders' victory over import boards and the wheat quota was followed by a more far-reaching victory over the Government's whole strategy for foreign trade. At the heart of its economic policies when it first came into office lay a deep-seated belief that exports held the key to prosperity, and that the unemployment figures could be brought down only if exports could be increased. Rationalization was seen primarily as a method of increasing exports; another method was the so-called 'tariff truce'. At the League of Nations Assembly in September 1929, Graham proposed an international agreement prohibiting increases in tariffs for a two-year period, during which phased reductions should be planned in tariff levels. In February 1930, eleven countries, of which Britain was one, signed a convention at Geneva by which they committed themselves not to increase their tariffs until April 1931. The convention had to be ratified by November 1930; and in June, Graham began a vigorous campaign to push ratification through the Cabinet.

At first, he met strong resistance. As he pointed out himself, ratification would rule out both Hubert Henderson's proposed revenue tariff and the 'various forms of agricultural protection' which had been proposed since the beginning of the year;[56] though he did not say so, it would also rule out any other significant change in the Government's economic policy. The Cabinet's instinctive response in such situations was to delay matters, and in June it decided that ratification should be postponed.[57] At the beginning of August, Graham made another attempt. In a thin Cabinet, with only seven ministers present, he argued that the reasons which had led the Government to delay ratification in the past no longer held good, since 'he gathered that no-one proposed now to put on a tariff in connection with Agriculture or anything else'; if the Cabinet were unwilling to ratify straight away, he urged that when he went to Geneva again in September he should be allowed to announce that Britain intended to ratify before the time limit had expired. This time, the protectionist group in the Cabinet made most of the running. Ratification, it was pointed out, would make it impossible to introduce even a revenue tariff, and would therefore have a 'further depressing effect on industry'. The other signatories had shown no willingness to make reductions; instead of ratifying,

T

Graham should insist that negotiations for tariff reductions should begin at once, so that Britain could see whether the other countries concerned were prepared to act in the spirit of the convention. The last suggestion gave the Cabinet the way out for which it was looking. In his summing up, MacDonald declared stoutly that most of those present opposed ratification until the results of the negotiations could be forecast, and instructed Graham to 'work out his policy at Geneva on the assumption that this was the policy of the Cabinet'. If Graham thought that the policy needed reconsideration before he left for Geneva he was to get in touch with the prime minister.[58]

Once again, the free-traders rallied their forces with great skill; and, once again, MacDonald shrank from fighting them in the open. The next meeting of the Cabinet took place at the beginning of September. MacDonald had spent most of August in Lossiemouth, but on the 26th he flew to London for urgent meetings with Addison and Lloyd George. Instead of staying in London for the Cabinet meeting, however, he flew back to Lossiemouth on August 29th.[59]

There is some evidence that before leaving London, he told Graham that he thought the Cabinet should stick to its previous decision;[60] from Lossiemouth, he wrote to Thomas, urging him to 'see to it that the full significance of ratification, before we know what is really going on at Geneva, will be thoroughly considered'.[61] An absent MacDonald, however, was no match for a present Snowden. When the meeting began, Graham explained that he had come to the conclusion that Britain's position at Geneva would be undermined if she refused to ratify. He was supported by Parmoor, on the grounds that a failure to ratify would be a reversal of policy, and also by Arthur Henderson who declared sententiously, 'In his view it would be necessary on an early opportunity to make an announcement that the Government had no intention of changing the traditional Free Trade policy of the Labour Party.' Thomas did his best to carry out MacDonald's instructions—pointing out that almost every commercial and trading interest in the country opposed ratification, that many European countries had already increased their tariffs, that ratification would tie the Government's hands at the imperial conference which was due to start in only a few weeks' time, and that, by ratifying, 'the Government would, in effect, declare that the only source of revenue from which prospective deficits could be met would be direct taxation.' Snowden, who was acting as prime minister in MacDonald's absence, then wound up the proceedings with a passionate declaration of faith. Failure to ratify, he declared, would 'mean complete surrender to the Protectionist Party'. As for the argument that the Government should keep its hands free so as to be able to introduce import duties in the next Budget, he wished to make it clear as chancellor of the exchequer that 'such a proposal, so far as he was concerned, was out of the question.' In his view, he declared, 'the national honour of the country was at stake.'[62]

The combination of Snowden, Henderson and Graham was too much for Thomas. After Snowden had finished, the Cabinet voted by eight to two in favour of ratification — the minutes making it clear, presumably on Thomas's insistence, that the decision had been taken only 'by a majority'.[63] Next day Graham reported to MacDonald:

Two members, Adamson and Thomson, did not vote, the former merely, I think, because a question which he raised regarding agriculture had been put too late (several members having intimated that they must go), but otherwise he was in favour of ratification and I think that that is also Thomson's attitude ...

... Only Thomas and Hartshorn favoured the view of 8th August. Since I saw you I have gone through the papers very carefully ... Believe me there is not the slightest prejudice to our position at the coming Imperial Conference, unless we intend to abandon the free trade policy of the movement, which I cannot believe is seriously contemplated. And again as regards anything that might be proposed in the next Budget we shall be able to test the preliminary stages of the negotiations on specific groups of commodities when we could, if necessary, give notice to withdraw ...

I know that this subject has given you anxiety, which I regret in the midst of the great pressure under which you work; but I trust you will accept this assurance that our position is not prejudiced in any way, and we shall do our best, however difficult the circumstances, to contribute to any downward movement of European tariffs which may be possible.[64]

On September 4th, Snowden wrote soothingly, 'I am sure we have done the right thing. We shall show good faith and still remain free if the other countries do not play the game.' Even more soothingly, he added, 'I think there are slight signs of an improvement in trade. Cotton mills and steel works are re-opening.'[65]

MacDonald cannot have been much consoled. As Snowden and Graham both pointed out, the Government's hands were not tied for ever. The truce was due to expire in April, and protection would then become possible once again. The fact remained that it had been ruled out for at least eight months: and that, in ruling it out, the Cabinet had effectively condemned itself to face the winter without changing its existing policies. Its decision also had a wider — and, from MacDonald's point of view, a still more ominous — significance. His reasons for hurrying back to Lossiemouth instead of waiting for the Cabinet meeting are unknown. Perhaps he trembled at the thought of provoking Snowden's wrath: perhaps he thought he would find it easier to coax his colleagues into protection if he did not expose his hand too fully, and decided that the best way to avoid exposing it was to stay away: perhaps he guessed that the free-traders would win, and did not wish to risk humiliation at their hands: perhaps he merely wished to continue his interrupted and much-needed holiday. Whatever his reasons, however, his colleagues had now voted heavily in favour of free trade: of the senior members of the Cabinet, only Thomas, by now a battered and discredited figure, had declared against it, while Henderson and Snowden had joined forces in its defence. There is no way of telling whether a firmer lead by MacDonald would have produced a different result: it may be that the forces on the other side were, in any case, too strong to beat. All that can be said with certainty is that he had failed to give a firm lead, and that he had also failed to make his views prevail. In retrospect, it can be argued that these were among the most fatal failures of his career. Even then, it must have been clear that he had suffered a damaging defeat.

VII

Meanwhile, ominous cracks were beginning to appear in the fragile parliamentary ice on which he had so far contrived to skate. As we have seen, he had strongly opposed the suggestion of a pact with the Liberals when Lloyd George had first made it earlier in the year. During the summer, he had tried to fob them off with the two-party conferences; and although they had made it clear in return that they were prepared to vote against the Government if they thought fit, no disaster had occurred. Since then, the two-party conferences had fizzled out; the unemployment figures had continued to go up; and the Government's popularity had continued to fall. From John Buchan, MacDonald received reports that Lloyd George had been putting out feelers for a National Government;[66] in political circles, dark rumours were beginning to circulate about a possible agreement between the Liberals and the Conservatives. There were signs of increasing restiveness in the T.U.C.;[67] and there could be little doubt that in the next session the Government would be under strong pressure to make a reality of its promise to amend the 1927 Trade Disputes Act. But repeal could not be carried on Labour votes alone, and if the Liberals were to be persuaded to let it through they would have to be given something in exchange. MacDonald's personal opinion of Lloyd George was as low as ever – the depression, he noted caustically during his holiday in Lossiemouth, was 'a war harvest, & much of it was sown by Mr Lloyd George as a war & peace minister' – [68] but in the circumstances that faced him now, he could not allow personal likes and dislikes to determine his conduct. Slowly and reluctantly he began to edge his way towards an agreement of the kind he had almost certainly helped to reject six months before.

The first move came from Lloyd George. On September 10th, Addison reported to MacDonald that the well-known social reformer, Seebohm Rowntree, had given him 'what was clearly intended to be a message from Lloyd George to the effect that Lloyd George was anxious to arrive at an understanding with us as to unemployment and the agricultural programme, and if we could agree, was prepared to back it, and if need be, to secure special procedures for forcing it through Parliament'. Rowntree, Addison added, had stressed that Lloyd George believed that 'unless we can do something to save the situation, the whole lot of us – Liberals and Labour alike – will be swept away by a great Protectionist wave.'[69] MacDonald had no faith in Lloyd George's unemployment policy, but on agriculture he probably saw him as a potential ally. He responded to Addison's message with alacrity, and on September 12th wrote to Lloyd George:

> Would it not be advisable for us to have an informal exchange of opinions upon Agriculture? Nobody can appreciate better than you how impossible it is for me to master the thousand-and-one details involved in this pressing subject. I want to cut knots, take reasonable risks, and get something done without delay; but I find that, as regards every proposal made, there are networks of criticism and objection, and I want to end that stage, however necessary it may be to protect us against very serious blunders.
>
> I understand that you now have information upon the various points included in the statement made by the Chancellor ... to the House of Commons on the day that it adjourned, and I should like to find out how far we can co-operate in carrying through that programme. It does not cover the whole field which I have in mind, but our programme of next Session is going to be of a most formidable length, and some items, which are very pressing upon us, are perhaps not likely to get your whole-hearted support. I should like, however, to get an agreement about these agricultural proposals, and, if it is possible, perhaps extend them ... Whoever is in office during the next six months is to have one of the stiffest bits of country to go over that a Government has ever had to face, except during the worst days of the War. Until we have reached the bottom of the trade depression, and can see what is the precise nature of the problem which the unemployment figures present to us, I really do not think we can do much to build things up, except as regards Agriculture, and, undoubtedly, a very heavy Party attack is to be made upon us in consequence. Should that attack be successful, the mind of the country is such that we cannot prevent a real nationalist protectionist Government being returned for a full period of Parliamentary life; but I think that an agricultural programme might just provide the time necessary to enable the country to do a little more thinking, and to come to steadier conclusions.[70]

Lloyd George's reply cannot have been altogether welcome. From his point of view, MacDonald's offer had considerable drawbacks. He was being asked to keep an increasingly unpopular Government in office in order to carry through an agricultural programme of distinctly modest dimensions, and had been offered nothing in return. If the Government's popularity revived, he could be thrown aside; if it continued to decline, he would be dragged down with it. On the other hand, he needed MacDonald as much as MacDonald needed him; without the Liberals, the Government could not stay in office, but without the Government, the Liberals could not get electoral reform. He replied to MacDonald's invitation in menacing, though not wholly unfriendly, terms:

> My colleagues and I are ready at any time to resume discussions. But I might suggest that at this stage it would tend to advance matters more rapidly and effectively if you and I could have a heart-to-heart talk on the position as a whole – with or without a colleague. That we have not had since you took office. Hence many misunderstandings which might have been averted.
>
> You refer to measures in contemplation by the Government which might not appeal to my friends and myself. We do not want to be brought up against measures of this kind without some preliminary effort at an arrangement. Another Coal Bill struggle would bring this Parliament to an end. The Tories this time will bring up every man; they dare not do otherwise with all the criticisms that are directed from within their ranks against their slackness in attack. The support of the Liberal Party can alone save the Government, and that support must come from the party as a whole – the votes of a few would not avail if the others went the other way. I write frankly because I want to avoid the possibility of accidents which a candid talk might avoid. The Parliamentary position can only be assured by a frank understanding. If you contemplate legislative proposals not agreeable to Liberal sentiment there must be some give and take. You will forgive me for pointing out that so far there has been none. We have no desire to put in a Protectionist Government, but it is no use stumbling along for another year or two, and finding out at the end of it that we have only postponed disaster, and in doing so aggravated it for you and our-selves ... If a General Election were impending, the Tories would soon make up their differences and the country in its despair will clutch at any change. I trust you are not misled by those who see signs of returning prosperity. Everything points to the worst winter we have ever had. Unless something is attempted on a bold scale, there will be a parliamentary revolt.[71]

Next day, MacDonald replied vaguely that he agreed with Lloyd George's comments on the general situation and that he had talked the matter over with the heads of certain departments where 'They wait for somebody whom you say waits for them, and I am waiting for both'. He and Snowden, he suggested, should meet Lloyd George, either alone or with a colleague.[72] On the same day, he wrote to Snowden to say that he had now had a reply from Lloyd George and that he did not wish to talk to him alone.[73] The meeting took place on September 19th; MacDonald was accompanied by Snowden and Lloyd George by the Marquess of Lothian.

On September 25th, MacDonald made a long report to the Cabinet. His report and the discussion which followed were evidently considered to be too sensitive to be minuted in the ordinary way, but Hankey made a manuscript record which was filed in the Cabinet office. The conversation, MacDonald reported, had concentrated on public works and roads. On trunk roads, Lloyd George had nothing more to say; a minor point concerning country roads and the strengthening of bridges had since been examined by the Ministry of Transport, and had turned out to be of no significance. Lloyd George's only remaining argument was that the Government lacked 'drive'. However, MacDonald went on,

Behind all this was the background of the political situation. The Prime Minister had found an opportunity to discuss the question with Sir Herbert Samuel, who thought the Government ought to be kept in office for two years longer, and that this might be arranged on terms. In this respect Sir Herbert Samuel's mind was on the same lines as Mr. Lloyd George's. They said in effect 'our support is bringing us no credit, rather the contrary. If we are going to have a fight, we had better have it now. If we are going to keep you in office we must have an understanding covering wider ground than at present'. The points on which such an understanding were desired were the following:

1 – The provisions of the Trades' Union Bill. There appeared to be an understanding on this matter by an interchange of views.

2 – Electoral Reform. If the Government could not agree on some reform based on proportional representation or the alternative vote, the Liberal leaders did not see how they could continue support.

At this point the Prime Minister gave his colleagues, under the strictest confidence, information indicating that Mr. Lloyd George believed that he could come to terms with the Conservative party in the matter of electoral reform, adding that he had reason to know that some members of that party were strongly opposed to such an understanding ... He impressed on his colleagues that, unless they could come to some agreement in regard to electoral reform and some arrangements for closer contact with the Liberals, the Government could encounter the utmost difficulty in maintaining a parliamentary majority.

Snowden made it clear that he agreed with MacDonald; and after a discussion in which great emphasis was laid on 'the inopportuneness of a General Election from the point of view of the Government', the Cabinet decided – apparently without dissentients – that Lloyd George should be told that the Government was prepared to consider the alternative vote, and that if an agreement were reached it would try to persuade the National Executive and party conference to accept it.[74]

VIII

Cracks in the parliamentary ice were accompanied by equally alarming cracks in the ice outside. At the beginning of October, the Labour Party conference assembled at Llandudno. For MacDonald, it was an emotional ordeal even more than a political one. The conference opened the day after the loss of the airship R.101, which had crashed near Beauvais at the beginning of a trial flight to India. Out of 54 passengers and crew, 46 had been killed almost immediately; two more died soon afterwards. Among those killed was Lord Thomson, the secretary of state for air and probably MacDonald's closest friend in politics. It was an appalling blow. As MacDonald described it in his diary on the day of the disaster,

> A little after 6 a.m. to-day my bedside telephone rang. The R 101 was wrecked & Thomson was not amongst the living! As though by the pressing of a button confusion & gloom & sorrow came upon the world – was the world. So when I bade him goodbye on Friday & looked down upon him descending the stairs at No 10, that was to be the last glimpse of my friend, gallant, gay & loyal. No one was like him & there will be none ... Why did I allow him to go? He was so dead certain that there could be no mishap ... This is indeed a great national calamity, & today, I distracted in the midst of it, can but grieve ... Am trying to get out of Llandudno for I cannot face it but I hear it is impossible.[75]

He had to address the conference two days later. Looking 'drawn and haggard', he confessed that if he had listened to his feelings alone he would not have been there. Then he paid a tribute to the dead. Today, the language may seem strained, but MacDonald, like many of his listeners, belonged to a generation which was accustomed to the public display of grief; and there can be little doubt that his own emotion communicated itself to his audience. His 'old friends, the Miners', he began, faced death as an 'ever-present companion' while they earned their daily bread: the crew of the R.101 had been driven to face it by 'that great quality ... that has driven our forebears over seas never hitherto ploughed by keel of ship, over lands never hitherto marked by the path of human feet, and at last we are in the air, and we shall conquer the air as we have conquered the desert and conquered the sea.' Next, he mentioned his personal grief. In Lord Thomson, the air force had lost a great servant: 'Those of us who are human in our hearts and have got all the weaknesses of human hearts ... have lost a companion like unto ourselves, whose place will never be filled.' Then he thanked the French Government and people for their courtesy and consideration, ending his thanks with a phrase which must have evoked many poignant memories in the hall: 'France knows how to stand by the side of the mourner.'[76]

After this, he paused; straightened himself up; and having created an atmosphere in which criticism must have seemed almost tantamount to blasphemy, he launched into a passionate and uncompromising defence of the Government and its record — [77] pointing out that the depression was caused by international forces and that the solutions would have to be international also, arguing that it was impossible to spend more on public works than the Government was spending, promising further action over land settlement and ending with the ringing declaration:

> So, my friends, we are not on trial; it is the system under which we live. It has broken down, not only in this little island, it has broken down in Europe, in Asia, in America; it has broken down everywhere, as it was bound to break down. And the cure, the new path, the new idea is organisation — organisation which will protect life, not property ... I appeal to you, my friends, to-day, with all that is going on outside — I appeal to you to go back on to your Socialist faith. Do not mix that up with pettifogging patching, either of a Poor Law kind or of Relief Work kind. Construction, ideas, architecture, building line upon line, stone upon stone, storey upon storey; it will not be your happiness, it will certainly not be mine, to see that fabric finished. It will not be your happiness, and it will certainly not be mine, to see that every stone laid in sincerity has been well laid. But I think it will be your happiness, as it is mine, to go on convinced that the great foundations are being well laid ... and that by skilled craftsmen, confident in each other's goodwill and sincerity, the temple will rise and rise and rise until at last it is complete, and the genius of humanity will find within it an appropriate resting place.[78]

Politically, as well as rhetorically, it was a *tour de force*. No doubt the *Manchester Guardian* was right in saying that MacDonald had 'touched the heart' of the conference instead of convincing its mind.[79] All the same, he had shown that he was still able to touch its heart in a way that no one else could do. As McNeill Weir put it years later, 'The tumultuous applause that followed the great peroration showed that MacDonald had retained his power as a spellbinder ... He had completely turned the tables on his opponents.'[80] After the cheering had subsided, Maxton moved what amounted to a vote of censure on the Government. He spent some minutes paying tribute to MacDonald's 'very great speech', and went out of his way to make it clear that he intended no personal criticism of the leadership; for his pains, his resolution was defeated by 1,800,000 to 330,000.[81] For MacDonald, it was a painful triumph, but nevertheless a real one. That afternoon, he hurried back to London; and late that night he went to Victoria station to greet the bodies of the victims of the crash. Next day he noted, 'Llandudno. Heartening reception: splendid conference sound as a bell. — Home in 6 hours 20 minutes driving. Went to pay respects to dead airmen. Bowed with grief. Impressive scene. Train arrived 1.20 a.m. Rain, crowds. Bed 3 a.m. So sad.'[82]

The rest of the conference was less heartening. Loyalty to the unemployed tugged against loyalty to the leadership: disappointment with the Government's performance against vicarious pride in its existence. Though Maxton's attack on the Government was beaten off without difficulty, a subtler resolution calling on the Executive to examine the proposals contained in the Mosley memorandum and to report on them to all affiliated organizations received more than 1,000,000 votes and was defeated only by the comparatively narrow margin of 200,000. Later in the week, when the spell of MacDonald's oratory had worn off, Thomas lost his seat on the National Executive, while Mosley was triumphantly re-elected to the constituency section, with more than 1,300,000 votes.[83]

MacDonald had spent the best part of four months in the search for an alternative economic policy. In every direction he had found a blank wall. Now he had to lead an obviously troubled and unhappy party into what promised to be one of the most critical sessions of its history. His summer had been cheerless enough. Everything suggested that his winter would be worse.

CHAPTER 24

Marking time

I

AFTER the funeral service for the victims of the R.101 disaster at the beginning of October 1930, MacDonald noted that he was 'very tired & numb & unable to work except under pressure.'[1] During the next few weeks, his spirits sank still further. 'I am tired & wonder more & more if it is possible to go on,' he noted on October 19th. 'Flesh & nerves can hardly stand it.'[2] Sometimes there were compensations. On October 20th he noted, 'Londonderry House. Hostess charming as ever.'[3] But this was only a momentary gleam of light in a darkening sky. By now the long-awaited imperial conference had assembled in London. In part, it was concerned with the legal and constitutional relationship between the British and dominion parliaments; in part, with the far more explosive question of imperial economic co-operation. The constitutional questions were settled without much difficulty, and need not concern us here. The economic ones provoked a long and bitter struggle in the Cabinet, in which it became clear that the free-trade majority was as strongly entrenched as ever.

At an early stage in the proceedings, the Canadian prime minister, R. B. Bennett, called for a system of reciprocal imperial preference, coupled with higher tariffs on non-Empire goods. This provoked Snowden into a display of intransigence, brutal even by his standards. After a meeting of the dominion prime ministers the following day, MacDonald noted:

> Snowden opened out in a hard mischievous speech provocative in tone & in phrasing. At times the Premiers gasped with anger mingled with surprise. During the discussion I tried to get negotiation believing we could show that their proposals amounted to very little advantage to us on the balance & that by examining the facts we might come to good conclusions on other lines. But the Chancellor would have none of it. He was out for a debate on tariffs & to tear protectionists to tatters. He told Mr B. that Canada ought to cultivate economic relations with the United States as it could not help itself. B's face flushed ... He also (without seeing that he was telling them not to buy dear goods from us or consider standards of life or anything but price) told Mr Bennett that he welcomed dumping from

Russia or anywhere else & as regards everything ... One of the [Canadians] said he would give the Chancellor $5,000 to go and make that speech in Canada for his party interests, but would pay the same amount to keep him at home in the interests of goodwill between Canada & ourselves.[4]

This was only a rehearsal for what was to follow. In the end, the Cabinet decided that although no new taxes should be imposed on imported foodstuffs or raw materials, preferences should continue to be given to Empire products where duties were already in existence. When the time came to translate this decision into action, Snowden suddenly decided that, although there was no possibility of removing the duties, it would be unconstitutional to make an announcement to that effect and told the Cabinet that he would resign rather than make it.[5] After a stormy meeting with MacDonald, Henderson, Graham and Thomas, he was prevailed upon to change his mind, but although he made the declaration in the end he took rapid steps to destroy the effect by making it clear that it had no binding force. Meanwhile, the Cabinet had turned down a proposal made by Graham and Thomas to establish a quota in the British market for dominion wheat;[6] and although it was eventually agreed that the proposal should be re-examined at the next imperial conference, it must have been plain that the concession had been made with great reluctance. When the conference ended on November 14th, no one can have been under any illusion that the balance of forces in the Cabinet had changed. In a wistful diary entry in mid-October, MacDonald noted that he had been lying in bed 'thinking of a Revenue Tariff put on now to balance Budget'.[7] By mid-November, he must have realized that, for the moment at least, such thoughts were academic.

By mid-November, moreover, he had more distressing thoughts to occupy him. Parliament had resumed on October 28th. The King's speech set out an ambitious programme for a minority Government – including the promotion of land settlement, the raising of the school-leaving age, electoral reform, the reform of trade-union law and the setting-up of a Royal Commission on unemployment insurance –[8] but it was savagely attacked from all sides for failing to deal with the central problem of unemployment. Lloyd George denounced the Government for failing to deal with the abuses in the insurance system straightaway and, in a biting passage, declared that MacDonald was 'too busy to do his job'. Mosley denounced the strategy behind the tariff truce, and declared revealingly, 'If we wait until the sweet small voice of the President of the Board of Trade at Geneva has drowned the strains of "Giovinezza" in every Fascist capital, we shall have to wait for a very long time.' Maxton denounced the Government for abandoning its principles to please the Liberals, and demanded to know whether MacDonald and Snowden still believed in public ownership. Fred Jowett moved an amendment criticizing the Government's failure to put forward proposals for the 'Socialist reorganisation of industry, agriculture, banking and the import and export trades';[9] though it was defeated by 156 votes to 11, many Labour backbenchers must privately have agreed with it. Finally, the Conservatives put down an amendment regretting the absence of measures to 'check the continued growth of unemployment'. It said nothing about protection, and MacDonald evidently feared that it might attract Liberal support. 'Walls close in,' he noted on November 2nd. 'Debate this week is serious (a) as to possible issue and (b) that it takes place. I cannot go on with worried & divided attention.'[10]

In the end, the debate was marked by a strange air of unreality. The Liberals did not want a general election any more than the Labour Party did: even the Conservatives may not have wanted one as much as they pretended. Chamberlain, who moved the Conservative amendment, devoted most of his speech to the case for protecting the home market, thus giving the Liberals an ideal excuse for refusing to vote with him. Lloyd George, who spoke again on the last day of the debate, began by declaring that free trade and protection were both 'beside the mark', but then announced that although he agreed with the Conservatives' strictures on the Government he would not vote for their amendment since Chamberlain had made it clear that it was a protectionist one. The Government, he argued at length, was wrong to claim that its failures were due to Liberal obstruction: on the contrary, the Liberals had pressed unsuccessfully for more vigorous action. Nevertheless, he now intended to save the Government again, in the hope that Liberal pressure might be more effective in the future than it had been in the past.[11]

On this somewhat tenuous basis, the Government was reprieved. In the whole debate, only two Labour backbenchers had come to the aid of their own front bench; though the Government's critics were hopelessly divided among themselves, no one could pretend that their criticisms had been answered. Yet after MacDonald had wound up the debate with one of the unhappiest and least convincing speeches of his life, the Conservative amendment was defeated by 250 votes to 281.[12] 'Continuous & fatuous interruptions made it impossible for me to develop my argument,' he noted peevishly. 'Speaking after 10 is becoming impossible. Some are drunk & some are such asses that they can listen to nothing.'[13]

II

Parliamentary performance is not always an accurate index of ministerial competence, but on this occasion there could be little doubt that the Government's feebleness in debate was a symptom of a deeper malaise. In the five months since Mosley's resignation, the Cabinet had rejected all the economic policies available to it. Thorough-going deflation on classical lines would have entailed drastic cuts in public spending and provoked furious protests from the Labour Party; though it might have been favoured in the innermost recesses

of the Treasury, ministers had not seriously considered it. Snowden preached
the deflationary orthodoxy of his youth with what was later described as
'ghoulish enthusiasm',[14] but his colleagues had not allowed him to practise it;
and his sermons were belied by the increases in public-works expenditure which
had been squeezed out of him since the Government took office, to say nothing
of the deficit in the unemployment insurance fund which had grown steadily
since the depression began. But although ministers shied away from full-scale
orthodoxy, they had refused to adopt an alternative. The public-works solution
advocated by Mosley and Lloyd George had been vetoed by the Ministry of
Transport even more effectively than by the Treasury; in the struggles over
agriculture and the tariff truce, protection had been vetoed as well. Yet the
Government's original policy of rationalization was manifestly irrelevant to a
world in depression: monetary changes were in abeyance until the Macmillan
committee reported: the Treasury's hope that the central banks would stimulate
a trade revival by agreeing to bring down interest rates was an aspiration rather
than a policy. Meanwhile, the unemployment figures rose remorselessly; the
strain on the insurance fund and the exchequer grew heavier; and the prospect
of a yawning budget deficit, followed by yet more damage to confidence and
employment, drew nearer.

Understandably enough, it seemed to many that the country was slithering
towards a crisis with which a weak and divided minority Government could not
deal. From there, it was a short step to concluding that none of the established
parties could deal with it and that the only way out was to break with the existing party system altogether. On the left, this mood was reflected in the I.L.P.'s
increasing willingness to defy the official Labour whip: on the right, in the
widespread hostility to Baldwin's leadership among younger Conservative
backbenchers. Another symptom of the same mood was a steady trickle of
gossip and speculation, mostly on the fringes rather than in the centre of the
political world, about the need for a non-party government, which in some
unspecified way would save the nation. Lloyd George had talked in these
terms as early as the summer holidays. In the autumn, the theme was taken up
by others. Mosley tried unsuccessfully to persuade his Labour supporters to
make common cause with dissident Conservatives and Liberals, so as to create a
national consensus about the need for emergency action.[15] In a series of doom-
laden editorials, J. L. Garvin, the ageing but still formidable editor of the
Observer, campaigned for the speedy replacement of the Labour Government
by a National Government which would 'hold office for an emergency period'
and include 'the foremost statesmen of the three parties'. Similar ideas were
canvassed more discreetly by MacDonald's old friend, Lord Mottistone,
formerly Colonel Seely, the secretary of state for war at the time of the Curragh
incident; by Henry Mond, the son of the Liberal politician and creator of I.C.I.,
Sir Alfred Mond; by Sir Arthur Balfour, the steel magnate; and by the ubiquitous Sir Abe Bailey, the Transvaal mine owner.[16]

In spite of their eminence in their own spheres, however, none of these could deliver votes at Westminster. Almost by definition, most of those who could had scant enthusiasm for the project. The Conservatives had every reason to expect a victory at the next election and no reason to burden themselves with the responsibilities of Government before then. Labour men could hardly be expected to give unmixed approval to a suggestion the underlying premiss of which was that their continuance in office would be a national disaster. The only politician of weight who gave a clear welcome to the notion was the inveterate rogue elephant, Lloyd George; and support from him was scarcely calculated to recommend it to the solid Conservative party wheelhorses without whom it could not become a reality. It was somehow symptomatic that Garvin could produce no more plausible a candidate for the headship of his proposed Government than the Marquess of Reading—a former viceroy of India and lord chief justice, and before that a distinguished attorney general who had managed to emerge unscathed from his involvement in the Marconi affair, but hardly a figure to inspire the nation or to rally opinion in the House of Commons. As R. J. Skidelsky has put it, 'the only national combinations formed in the autumn of 1930 were those scribbled on the backs of menus at select dinner parties'.[17] Whatever their effects on the digestive systems of those concerned, neither parties nor menus had any discernible effect on the course of British politics.

All the same, the talk about a National Government in 1930 was the first faint harbinger of the crisis that led to a National Government in 1931; and MacDonald's reaction to it is therefore of great interest. As so often, the evidence is fragmentary, confused and even contradictory. When John Buchan reported that Lloyd George had been advocating a National Government, MacDonald replied vaguely:

> I have heard that your guest has been talking in that way. I have done everything I possibly can to make such a thing possible, if there is any desire for it. I think that an election within the next two years will be a very bad thing for the country, and I shall be no party to forcing it, if others will come to any reasonable agreement to prevent it. You are as much aware as I am, however, of the entangling difficulties of such an attempt. Still, I shall not stand in its way, and would be very glad to go into the background, if that would make it easy. My recent experience of your guest, however, is anything but fortunate, and I would far rather deal with some of your friends.[18]

By October, his mood had changed. On October 1st, Sir Arthur Balfour sent him a long and gloomy letter, arguing that the economic situation was rapidly deteriorating and that 'some form of Coalition Government' was essential to avert a crisis.[19] This time, MacDonald's reply was much cooler. What alarmed him most about the economic situation, he wrote brusquely on October 2nd, was 'the incapacity of so many of the leading business men whom we come across'; as for a Coalition,

> I am afraid that in the circumstances a Three Party Government, or as you call it a National Government, is out of the question. Remedies proposed by each are so contrary; but what we ought to have is a Government secure in office for three years so that it will have the time required to develop a policy, and study results. If you say that that will give a bad Government too much shelter, I reply that the present system gives a good Government neither shelter nor peace of mind to do its work.[20]

In November, his mood changed again. On October 29th, he noted that he had been to a dinner at the Athenaeum given by 'Jack Seely'; that the purpose had been 'to discuss national crisis & national coopn. of Parties'; and that those present had included his son Malcolm, Lloyd George, Churchill, Reading and Sir Robert Horne.[21] He made no record of what was said or of how far he agreed with it, but in the next few days his entries became more expansive. On November 6th the Conservatives won a by-election at Shipley with a majority of more than 1,600, overturning a Labour majority of more than 5,000. On the 8th, the News Chronicle published a dramatic front-page story, headed: 'Cabinet Split over L.G. Loan. Snowden Must Bend or Go.' MacDonald, it reported, had been faced with a 'powerful, and it would seem, irresistible' demand for the resignation of Snowden, Alexander and Wedgwood Benn, on the grounds that they had opposed import boards and a development loan. If MacDonald resisted the demand, he would be 'in the greatest peril'. In the inner circles of the Labour Party, the News Chronicle added, 'Some think he will himself give up office to Mr Arthur Henderson.' The Daily Express carried a milder version of the same story; and it, too, went out of its way to add that suggestions had been made that MacDonald might 'give place as head of the Government to Mr Arthur Henderson'. Next day, it was the Observer's turn to stir the pot. It reported that MacDonald had denied the News Chronicle story and implied that he had been justified in doing so, but added that there was strong feeling against Snowden among rank-and-file members of the Labour Party and that some Labour backbenchers were talking of replacing MacDonald with Henderson. For good measure, it also published a passionate editorial calling for a National Government, on the grounds that Snowden's intransigence on the fiscal question had made it impossible for the Labour Government to solve the country's problems.

MacDonald had been in politics long enough to know that reports of this sort rarely appear in the newspapers by accident. As long ago as July 22nd he had noted, 'Saw paragraphs issued by members of L.P. publicity staff saying I am to resign & that intellectuals of Party want Henderson. So the old games of Byzantine times go on.'[22] Even a less suspicious man might have seen the stories in the *News Chronicle* and the *Daily Express* as evidence that equally Byzantine games were being played now. On November 9th he noted:

> A canard published yesterday in the *News Chron.* & *Express* that the Cabinet was split & that I had difficulties with Snowden, who must 'bend or go', has raised in a more virulent form the project of a national government. The canard I am told was given by some one from our back benches who is a mouthpiece of our Mozley [*sic*] — Henderson cave. Lady Londonderry & the Duke of Sutherland were down at Chequers today & she talked about it. No doubt Ministers are unwilling to face unpleasant facts & I cannot get them to act unpleasantly & my work with these Conferences prevents my taking charge of details of Depts. I have warned them against Royal Commissions for Unemployment & begged them to produce something on their own responsibility, but the responsible ones & the Cabinet as a whole have been, & are, against me. Now we come to a dead wall & I must act. The proposal is that the Government somehow (events will show) should resign, that there should be no election (no one except a group of Tory partisans wants it & it would not be good for the country) but a Cabinet formed from all parties. From one quarter I am urged to remain Prime Minister, but others think that none of the leaders should take that office. Lady L. says she thinks I should go to the F.O., 'departyise' it & remain after the next change. My own feeling is to go out altogether, give a pledge that I shall not hamper the govt., but be free to express views of my own which party responsibility renders impossible (difficult role but possible) & offer to do anything for the Govt. which it wishes but out of office. This I fear would break the Party but it has broken itself. Even if the present clouds were to roll by (the most they can do, however, is not to break) the position of the Government is steadily becoming worse. With blunders like Palestine & feebleness like the Unemployed borrowing Bill, I can do nothing. Then, the secret plots of those who are enviously unhappy undermine the whole structure, & I am certainly not going to waste my time fighting against a 'MacD. must go' movement. It does not exist at the moment, but it may appear as the attack on the Govt. from within & without deploys.[23]

By the following weekend, his suspicions of Henderson had become still more acute. The Sunday papers, he noted on November 16th,

> make it plainer that the plots are against me as well as Snowden & they are right. Henderson wants the job. Snowden told me on Thursday that a member of the Consultative Committee had asked him if he would agree to Henderson succeeding me. To the surprise of the enquirer S. said 'No'. On Friday I lunched with Barrie, Baldwin being present. When I was chaffing Baldwin about his internal troubles he told me that a Labour

Member had asked him how he got rid of Lloyd George & whether a leader could be dispensed with without bringing down a Government! We enjoyed the prospect of our mutual deaths.[24]

A more outspoken conversation followed two weeks later, when Baldwin came to see him to discuss the succession to the viceroyalty of India when the existing incumbent, Lord Irwin, left office. It is clear from his diary that MacDonald had been pressed to become viceroy himself, and in the course of their discussion Baldwin 'casually & gingerly' mentioned this possibility, making clear that the Conservatives would welcome it. According to his diary, MacDonald then 'raised the possibility of a change of govt. without an election. He thought I meant putting him in office & was favourable but I corrected him & explained that I meant a national govt. He said protection made that impossible & I agreed. I further said that if such a step were taken the parties would have to go into the melting pot & the present grouping would not be maintained.'[25] Next day, MacDonald dined at Lord Reading's with a miscellaneous group, including Churchill, Horne and Gwilym Lloyd George. According to MacDonald's diary Churchill said, 'If all we have said were taken down only Horne would be kept in his party,' and added, 'Ramsay, you have had devilishly bad luck, but I say no one could have done better. That cheer is *sotto voce*.'[26] So far as MacDonald was concerned, Churchill's cheer brought the episode to an end. He remained acutely suspicious of Henderson and became even more gloomy about the state of the Labour Party, but there is no reason to believe that he thought seriously about taking part in a National Government until the question was revived in very different circumstances nine months later.

The evidence is confused enough: its significance, still more so. It is not clear what MacDonald said at the dinner parties mentioned in his diary; why the tone of his letter to Sir Arthur Balfour differed so sharply from the tone of his letter to John Buchan; why he agreed so readily when Baldwin told him that protection made a National Government impossible; or whether he was right in thinking that a 'Mosley–Henderson cave' was plotting against him. Still less is it clear whether he wanted a National Government at all or, if so, what kind of National Government he envisaged. When he wrote in his diary that 'we come to a dead wall & I must act', was he expressing a settled intention, or reflecting a momentary spasm of irritation? When he sounded Baldwin out on the possibility of a National Government did he hope for a favourable reply, or did he hope to scotch the idea, realizing that Baldwin would turn it down? If he did want a National Government, however fleetingly, did he see it as an equivalent of the wartime coalitions, with at least the bulk of the Labour Party joining in? Or did he see it as a way of escaping from the Labour Party altogether into a new and more congenial political home?

None of these questions can be answered with any certainty: the evidence quoted above could be used, with equal plausibility, to support any of a wide range of interpretations. All the same, some points are clear enough, and others can be guessed at. It is clear that MacDonald had been profoundly exasperated by the frustration of the summer and early autumn. It is clear that there were mutterings against his leadership, of unknown strength. It is clear too that on the central question of domestic policy his views were closer to the Conservatives' than those of the free-trade majority in his own Cabinet. Since the summer, he had believed that a revenue tariff was needed to balance the budget, but after the battles of September and October he cannot have had much hope of getting a revenue tariff through. Yet, if tariffs were ruled out, a damaging budget deficit could be averted only by almost equally damaging increases in taxation, or by cuts in expenditure which would be deeply unpopular in the Labour Party. A National Government might provide a way out of this dilemma; from MacDonald's point of view, that in itself must have been a strong argument in its favour. On the other hand, there was no point in having a National Government unless it had security of tenure; and in practice, this meant that it would have to be supported by both the big parties. In spite of his irritable diary entries, it is almost inconceivable that MacDonald would have been prepared to join a National Government without Labour Party support at a time when there was no immediate crisis to force his hand: as we shall see, even in the crisis conditions of 1931 he was profoundly reluctant to form a National Government which he expected his party to oppose and hesitated a great deal before doing so. Quite apart from old ties of sentiment and loyalty, which meant as much to him as they did to most of his colleagues, he was experienced enough to know that if he joined a coalition without a following of his own he would be putting his head into a political noose. And he was also experienced enough to know that a National Government supported by both big parties was a remote prospect in time of peace.

The most convincing interpretation of his behaviour is therefore as follows. He was attracted by the idea of a National Government, but as a vague and uncertain option for the future, not as a settled policy for the present. In some moods, he blew hot; in others, cold. Even when he blew hot, he did so, not because he had any immediate intention of taking the option up but because he thought it possible that he might want to take it up at a later stage. So he wrote encouragingly to Buchan and discouragingly to Balfour; so, he took part in Lord Mottistone's dinner party at the Athenaeum. Then came the press reports of splits in the Cabinet and backbench speculations about a change in the leadership. There is no way of telling whether these reports had in fact been planted by friends of Henderson's, but they bore all the marks of having been planted by someone. Even if they were not planted, they made it even clearer than it was already that MacDonald's leadership was running into fire and that Henderson, as the only senior minister who could not be blamed for the Government's economic failures, had become a potential rallying-point for backbench malcontents. It would have been out of character for Henderson to seek such a position deliberately, and there is no evidence that he did so. Yet he had been highly critical of MacDonald's leadership in the past, and had taken it as an affront when MacDonald tried to appoint Thomas as foreign secretary; though it is unlikely that he encouraged MacDonald's critics, it would be surprising if he had not sometimes let it be known that his own enthusiasm for MacDonald was less than total. Parliamentary life being what it is, one can be fairly sure that, if he did, there would have been plenty of gossipmongers on hand, eager to carry back the news. The same applies to the rumours which were then current about an approach which Mosley was alleged to have made to Henderson in the foreign secretary's room in the House of Commons, in which Henderson had been urged to lead a revolt against MacDonald in order to seize the prime ministership for himself.

MacDonald was a suspicious man at the best of times. After the pounding he had received in the debate on the address and the humiliation of the Shipley by-election, to say nothing of the setbacks of the previous five months, his nerves were more than usually on edge. Probably wrongly, but not altogether incomprehensibly, he jumped to the conclusion that he was faced with an organized 'cave' on the back benches which might try to remove him from the leadership; after another week of brooding he also came to the conclusion that Henderson, whether or not he belonged to the 'cave', actively wanted his job. His gingerly overture to Baldwin followed—not because he had made up his mind in favour of a National Government, but because the rumours of a possible revolt against him in the Labour Party had at last brought him to the point of putting his toe in the water. What he would have done if Baldwin had replied favourably can never be known. Assuming that his diary gives an accurate account of their conversation, all that can be said with certainty is that when Baldwin produced a remarkably flimsy objection, he beat a hasty retreat.

After 1931, when the angry and bewildered Labour Party had to construct an explanation for the catastrophe which had engulfed it, many Labour men and women came to believe that MacDonald had deliberately engineered the fall of the Labour Government, and some also came to believe that he had been planning to do so for months, if not for years. In spite of appearances to the contrary, his behaviour in November and December 1930 lends little support to such a view. He emerges not as a cold-blooded conspirator pursuing a predetermined aim but as a prisoner of circumstances beyond his control, searching despairingly for a way of escape. His diary entries show that he had toyed with joining a National Government well before he formed one: they do not show that he had planned to form one, still less that his actions nine months later conformed to such a plan. It was an ominous episode, for him and for his party. But its significance lies less in his desultory and unconsummated flirtation with the idea of a National Government than in the light it throws on his deteriorating relationship with his chief potential challenger, on the atmosphere of suspicion and intrigue which had grown up among his followers and on his growing jumpiness and sense of isolation as the political and psychological pressures bearing down on him increased in weight.

III

For a few weeks after the *News Chronicle* story, he was able to take at least spasmodic refuge from these pressures in the intricate cross-currents of Indian nationalism. In 1927, the Conservatives had appointed a statutory commission, headed by Sir John Simon, to examine the working of the 1919 Government of India Act. In 1929, the viceroy, Lord Irwin, made a formal declaration reaffirming that Britain intended to give India dominion status, and MacDonald announced that the whole question would be examined by a round table conference representing all shades of Indian and British opinion. When the Simon Report eventually appeared in the summer of 1930, however, it was already out of date. At the end of 1929, the Indian National Congress came out for complete independence. In March 1930, Gandhi launched a great campaign of civil disobedience with his famous march to take salt illegally from the sea; and in May he was arrested, in an atmosphere of growing disorder. It was clear that India could not be governed peacefully unless another attempt was made to meet the nationalists half-way: it was also clear that the Simon Report, which did not even mention dominion status, provided no basis for doing so.[27] Though Congress refused to participate, the Government stuck to its decision to hold a round-table conference; and on November 12th, it was opened in London by the King–Emperor, George V. MacDonald presided over most of the plenary sessions. He also chaired the key sub-committee on minority representation; and from mid-November 1930 to mid-January 1931 most of his time and energy were absorbed by the baffling problem of how to reconcile India's communal differences with the twin objectives of Indian unity and eventual Indian self-government.

Like everyone else who tried to square this circle, he was forced to admit failure in the end. On December 14th he noted, 'Yesterday a Moslem–Hindu gathering at Chequers showed worst side of Indian politics ... India was not considered. It was communalism & proportions of reserved seats.'[28] By December 18th, he had become even gloomier. 'Hindu–Moslem not coming together,' he noted. 'They have no mutual confidence & Hindu too nimble for Mosl: brethren. Hindu can appear to be reasonable because he has the pull.' The Moslem leader, Jinnah, he added, 'assured me that the conference must fail.'[29] In the new year, Moslem assurances became more menacing. 'Busy day with interviews, most important being Mohammedans headed by Aga Khan with Shafi & Jinnah,' MacDonald noted on January 13th. 'Practically threatened civil war if their claims for security were not admitted. They would not trust

Hindus, nor really cooperate with them on terms of confidence. They begged me to settle now — in their favour of course.'[30] The Sikhs were equally intransigent. 'Great tussle at St. James Palace over Hindu–Moslem question,' MacDonald noted on January 14th. 'Brought it to verge of settlement in Punjab but Sikhs stood out against the pressure of every section on 1. Opposition to 50% of the seats going to Moslems 2. Refusal to accept any proportion under 20% for themselves.'[31]

Eventually, the sub-committee produced an anodyne report, acknowledging that it was 'particularly desirable' that the major communities should reach agreement, but confessing lamely that no such agreement had, in fact, been reached. Yet the conference was an important milestone, in British history even more than in Indian. To the surprise of many, the representatives of the princely states agreed to join an eventual all-India federation. Subject to a reservation by the Moslems, who made it clear that they would accept no constitution unless they were given adequate safeguards, the conference adopted a report from a sub-committee chaired by Lord Sankey, laying down the principles on which a federal constitution should be based.[32] Above all, it made it possible for the two front benches in the House of Commons to draw even closer together.

At the final plenary session on January 19th, MacDonald announced that the Government wished to transfer responsibility for Indian affairs to provincial Governments responsible to provincial legislatures and to a central executive responsible to a federal legislature. Meanwhile, the conference was to be adjourned so that Indian opinion could be consulted further. A few days later, Gandhi and his leading colleagues were released unconditionally and the ban on the Congress Working Committee was lifted. The day after Gandhi's release, the whole subject was debated at Westminster. MacDonald opened with a powerful speech, pleading for continued co-operation from the other parties and arguing that the only alternative to concessions was 'Repression and nothing but repression ... the repression of the masses of the people'. Halfway through, Churchill launched a savage attack on the Government's policy as wanton, reckless and incontinent. At the end, Baldwin repudiated him, welcomed the vision of a 'United States of India' in glowing terms and pledged himself to support the search for an agreed solution, in or out of office.[33] 'Winston was distracted ... ,' MacDonald noted triumphantly. 'Baldwin's throw-over of Winston was complete.'[34]

He was entitled to his triumph. It was not the first time that Baldwin had taken risks for the sake of the Government's Indian policy. In October 1929, when Lloyd George had savagely attacked the Irwin declaration, Baldwin had been careful to phrase his own attack in the gentlest possible terms and had gone out of his way to endorse the principle embodied in it.[35] The Conservatives had listened to him in silence, and at the end of his speech he had been cheered by the Government's supporters rather than by his own. In the summer of 1930, when many Conservatives, led by Austen Chamberlain, had wanted to stand pat on the Simon report, Baldwin had given MacDonald a private pledge that he would not support them.[36] Now he had thrown down an unmistakable challenge to Churchill and the right wing of his party, at a time when his leadership was already under attack. But although the emerging bipartisan consensus on India owed much to Baldwin, and even more to Irwin, it also owed a great deal to MacDonald. In Opposition he had caused great indignation among the Left by agreeing that Labour should participate in the Simon Commission, and had appointed Hartshorn and Attlee as the Labour representatives. In government, he and Wedgwood Benn had been careful not to move faster than the Conservatives could be persuaded to move and had once again encountered fierce criticism from the I.L.P. In retrospect, it can be seen that Baldwin's speech of January 26th pointed the way to the Government of India Act of 1935, and so to eventual Indian independence in 1947 and to Britain's steady withdrawal from empire in the 1950s and 1960s. Even then, MacDonald could legitimately regard it as a vindication, not only of his Indian policy, but of his whole approach to politics. In early 1931, such a vindication must have been doubly precious.

IV

Even while the round-table conference was in session, it is doubtful if the constitution of the Punjab was as potent a source of anxiety for MacDonald as was the constitution of the United Kingdom. As we have seen, the Cabinet had decided towards the end of September that it would try to make a deal with the Liberals over electoral reform, and then recommend it to the National Executive and party conference. A long and rocky road had to be traversed, however, before the deal was made. Partly because he could not afford to give right-wing Liberals the impression that he had made up his mind to support the Government whatever it might do, and partly because he passionately believed that bolder action was needed to stop the depression from getting worse, Lloyd George had continued to attack ministers for their feebleness, while boasting, rather incongruously, that pressure from the Liberals would force them to mend their ways. From MacDonald's point of view, the boasts were more galling than the attacks, and in his speech to the Labour Party conference at the beginning of October he had accused the Liberals of 'run[ning] to the newspapers' after his meetings with them, and of failing to observe 'gentlemanly conduct'.[37] This had called forth a pained rebuttal from Lloyd George, and for a while, negotiations between the two parties hung fire while their leaders exchanged indignant letters accusing each other of bad faith.[38]

The imperial conference was probably a bigger stumbling-block. Perhaps because he did not want to strengthen the free-traders in the Cabinet at a time when there was a chance that they might be forced on to the defensive,

MacDonald held the Liberals at arm's length until the conference was over. On October 20th, he noted that he had had an 'amiable' talk with Lloyd George and that he had told him the contents of the King's speech.[39] Amiable or not, however, the talk brought the Liberals no nearer their goal. At Lloyd George's request, the King's speech contained a commitment to electoral reform.[40] But the nature of the reform was left unspecified; and in his speech in the debate on the address, MacDonald skirted around the subject, leaving it uncertain whether the Government intended to change the electoral system or merely to carry through minor reforms in electoral law.[41] As late as November 17th, the Cabinet formally decided that it had not yet made up its mind on the subject.[42]

By then, however, the imperial conference had dispersed, and it had become clear that the free-trade citadel was still unbreached. On November 18th, MacDonald noted cryptically, 'Ll.G., Samuel, Henderson & myself discussed co-operation to give Government security. One of the counters being Alternative Vote';[43] and on December 1st, his private secretary wrote to Clynes, asking him to prepare a memorandum on electoral reform as soon as possible, since the question might soon become 'urgent'.[44] Yet even now he had to be pushed. On December 5th, he wrote irritably to Henderson:

> When I went down to the House yesterday just a few minutes before going in to answer Questions, I found that I was expected to announce that the Electoral Reform Bill should be introduced before Christmas. If we are not very careful we are going to get into a very bad fix on this matter. To introduce important Bills in dummy is not at all a good plan, and we cannot yet say how the Party in the House or the Executive will react.[45]

Henderson was unmoved. As we have seen, the Liberals had made it clear from the start that they were unhappy about the Government's proclaimed intention of repealing the 1927 Trades Disputes Act. Henderson's reply to MacDonald suggests that they had proceeded to make it clear that they would not allow repeal through unless they were given the alternative vote in exchange and that Henderson, with his usual sensitivity to trade-union opinion, thought it necessary to buy them off. He was sorry that MacDonald should have found himself in such a position, Henderson wrote brusquely,

> but I thought the matter had been explained at the Cabinet that as a result of the conversation to which you invited the Chancellor and myself that [sic] it had been suggested after you left that something should be done on this question and also on the Trades Disputes Bill. I fully agree about the difficulty, but having regard to the circumstances in which we are working and very definite promises made at the two interviews with the Trades Union Council and in connection with the committee presided over by the

Lord Chancellor on the Trades Disputes Bill, I don't see there was any alternative but to proceed to introduce the Bill.

With regard to Electoral Reform: as you are aware this is included in the King's Speech and at no Party meeting has any exception been taken to its inclusion, and the Chancellor and myself could not very well do other than agree with the suggestion that the Bill should be introduced in dummy form before the House rose for Christmas. Now that notice has been given, I feel that the Bill should be prepared for submission to the Cabinet at an early date to include the Alternative Vote and all points submitted to the Ullswater Committee by the Labour Representatives.[46]

That was the end of the matter. On December 17th, the National Executive considered the question for a second time. After receiving an assurance from Henderson that the Government had made no pact with the Liberals, it voted by 16 to 3 for a resolution supporting the inclusion of the alternative vote in the coming electoral reform Bill. Next day, a joint meeting of the Executive and the parliamentary party carried a similar resolution by 133 votes to 20.[47] After almost a year of blandishments and threats, Lloyd George had been given what he wanted. By an odd but not altogether inappropriate historical irony, it was Henderson, his old minister of wartime days, who had done most to ensure that he got it.

The deal brought only temporary comfort to the Government. At the end of January 1931, the Trades Disputes Bill was given its second reading by 277 votes to 250. The Liberals abstained; only a handful voted against. At the beginning of February, the electoral reform Bill was carried by a majority of 65.[48] But by now a more serious crisis was looming up. During the previous twelve months, the unemployment insurance fund had run further and further into debt. By June 1930, £44 million of its £50 million borrowing authority had been exhausted. At the beginning of August, legislation had been passed to increase its borrowing powers to £60 million. By the end of November, the increase had been used up. Another borrowing Bill was passed, raising the limit to £70 million. It was assumed that the extra £10 million would last until the end of March 1931, but it was clear by the beginning of February that it would run out a month earlier than expected. This was only the beginning of the story. There were three kinds of unemployment pay, not one. There were insurance benefits, paid out by the fund to those who had paid in thirty contributions in the previous two years. There was so-called 'transitional benefit', paid by the exchequer to those who were not entitled to insurance benefits, but who had paid either eight contributions in the previous two years or thirty since entering the scheme. Lastly, there was public assistance. The deficit in the fund was due to the increase in the numbers drawing insurance benefits. But the numbers receiving transitional benefits had risen much more sharply; and so had the cost to the exchequer. Early in 1930, the Treasury had estimated that transitional benefit would cost £10½ million in the course of the year. In fact, it had cost £22 million. By January 1931, it was estimated that the cost in the coming year would be £30 million.[49]

So far, ministers had managed to fend off the mounting parliamentary pressure for economy with a series of delaying actions. In the summer, they had secured parliamentary approval for the first increase in the fund's borrowing powers by setting up a three-party committee to examine the exchequer cost of un-employment. At the same time, they had set up a sub-committee of the economic advisory council, chaired by G. D. H. Cole, to examine the abuses in the system. In October, they had promised to set up a Royal Commission. In November, they had persuaded the Liberals to let through the second increase in borrowing powers by promising that the Royal Commission would issue interim reports and speed up its consideration of transitional benefit. But, although each delay-ing action had won them a breathing space, each breathing space had made it more difficult for them to go on doing nothing. The three-party committee had got nowhere. But, in spite of the political sympathies of its chairman, the Cole committee had declared uncompromisingly that the existing system imposed an 'unjustifiable burden' on the exchequer, and had made two highly restrictive recommendations — that deficits in the fund should be met by cutting benefits or increasing contributions rather than by borrowing, and that those claiming transitional benefit should be subjected to a means test.[50] The Royal Commission had not yet reported, but in setting it up ministers had strengthened, and in a sense legitimized, the arguments of the opposition parties, and had still further curtailed their own freedom of manœuvre.

By the new year, it looked as though they had run out of expedients. At the beginning of January 1931, Snowden circulated an apocalyptic paper to the Cabinet warning that the budget deficit for 1930–31 was now expected to be £40 million, and that unless policies were changed the deficit for 1931–2 might be as much as £70 million. Britain, he went on, could not afford 'any sort' of deficit. Not only would it damage business confidence at home, but it would also imperil foreign confidence in sterling. Already, there were signs that funds were trickling away from London. Yet a flight from the pound would be 'fraught with the most disastrous consequences'. It was therefore imperative to take steps to prevent it. Increases in taxation would make matters even worse; the only solution was to cut expenditure, above all on unemployment. Transi-tional benefit, Snowden concluded inexorably, was the main cause of the budgetary crisis. Unless 'stern measures' were taken to lift the burden from the exchequer, the economic stability of the country would be in danger.[51]

On protection, MacDonald and Snowden were in opposing camps. On economy, they found themselves in uneasy and incomplete agreement. Like many of his generation, MacDonald had an odd and, to a modern eye, a slightly unattractive streak of social hardness in his make-up — the hardness of Drainie parish in the 1870s: the hardness also of a social worker in the 1890s, afraid that well-meant but ill-considered acts of philanthropy might demoralize those they were supposed to help. He would take endless trouble to help an individual person in distress: faced with collective distress, he was apt to react with a strange mixture of socialist fundamentalism and Victorian individualism. Emotionally, if not intellectually, the notion that men should be paid to be idle went against the grain. If there was no work to be had, there was obviously no alternative. But it was still a palliative; and there was still a danger that it might make it more difficult for those concerned to stand on their own feet. It would be wrong to suggest that these attitudes determined his line in the Cabinet's struggles over economy, but they were undoubtedly there in the background. Partly because of them, he was apt to pay more attention than he should have done to the wild stories that circulated in respectable circles about work-shy idlers drawing 'doles' to which they were not entitled. They may have made him marginally more receptive than he would have been in any case to the arguments of those like Keynes and G. D. H. Cole who believed that the existing insurance system impeded economic recovery. They undoubtedly helped to sharpen his irritation with his colleagues' response to Snowden's paper.

Though he still believed that the budget could not be balanced satisfactorily without a tariff, he no longer thought — as he seems to have done in the summer — that tariffs would solve the problem by themselves. In any case, a majority of the Cabinet had shown on a number of occasions that it would not budge from free-trade orthodoxy. But if protection was ruled out, it seemed clear that the only alternative to economy was an increase in direct taxation; and, as MacDonald knew well, not only the business community, but Keynes and the other members of the economists' committee of the economic advisory council, all believed that an increase in direct taxation would have a disastrous effect on confidence, and therefore on employment. With all his occasional vagueness, MacDonald was a logical man; and he had been driven near to distraction by the Cabinet's persistent refusal to face the implications of its own decisions. If his colleagues wanted free trade, they could have it: but if so, they must accept the budgetary corollary. At the end of December, he wrote to Snowden, promising 'I shall back you in any proposal you make to reduce expenditure ... I am sure a bold policy will reveal general support.'[52] On January 12th, he noted, 'Discussed political & financial condition with Snowden & strongly urged no increase in taxation but firm reduction in expenditure.'[53] Two days later, the Cabinet considered Snowden's paper. Afterwards, MacDonald noted, 'Cabinet discussed the very serious financial outlook. I would both economise & put on duties.'[54] But there is no evidence that he argued the case for duties, either privately or in the Cabinet; and it seems clear that, for the moment at least, he had decided to concentrate on the first half of his policy and let the second half wait.

The prime minister and chancellor of the exchequer made a formidable coalition. This time, it was not formidable enough to have its way. On January 14th, the Cabinet decided that the situation described in Snowden's paper was indeed 'very serious': and that Snowden should consider it further, in collaboration with Graham and Alexander.[55] The next round came on Feburary 5th. Margaret Bondfield submitted a scheme, drawn up after consultation with Snowden and MacDonald, for emergency legislation to cut benefit rates by 2s. a week and to restrict the benefit rights of married women, seasonal workers and short-time workers. She estimated the saving to the exchequer at £6 million a year and the saving on borrowing at £17½ million. If transitional benefit were not renewed, she added darkly, the saving to the exchequer would be £13 million.[56] Even the decorous formulations of the Cabinet secretariat make it clear that her proposals provoked a bitter struggle. It was pointed out that the Cabinet had agreed that no changes should be made until the Royal Commission had reported, and that the Royal Commission had not started work until mid-December. It was also pointed out, in the words of the Cabinet minutes, that 'if the proposals now under consideration were adopted without corresponding financial sacrifices elsewhere, the burden would fall exclusively on the unemployed ... It was suggested that this was hardly consistent with the spirit of the general policy of the Government, so frequently announced, of "work or maintenance".' In the end, it was decided that Margaret Bondfield's scheme could not be considered in isolation; that the committee appointed on January 14th should continue its deliberations; that, in the meantime, Margaret Bondfield should prepare yet another borrowing Bill, this time for £20 million; and that transitional benefit, which was due to expire in April, should be extended until October.[57]

There was another battle a few days later. On February 11th, MacDonald told the Cabinet that he had heard informally that the Royal Commission would not report until June or even July. As Hankey had pointed out to him the day before,[58] this meant that if no changes were to be made while the Commission was sitting, it would be necessary to wait until the summer recess to draft the legislation which would be needed when transitional benefit expired in the autumn. Though the minutes do not say so, it seems clear that MacDonald fought hard to persuade the Cabinet to decide its policy on transitional benefit before the report was ready. If so, he failed. The most it would do was to instruct him to ask the chairman of the Commission to produce an interim report on transitional benefit not later than the middle of May.[59] 'Cabinet again weak on Unemployment payments & the new extension Bills required,' he noted angrily. 'Henderson visionless & bullying at his worst. We must not break at this moment, however, but I shall not go on much further.'[60]

Meanwhile, the Liberals had given a further twist to the screw. As we have seen, the revised Liberal programme of October 1930 had put economy first and national development third. Since then, development had fallen further into the background, while economy had been given still more prominence. Early in February, the Conservatives tabled a motion censuring the Government for its 'policy of continuous addition to the public expenditure'. Soon afterwards, the Liberals tabled an amendment calling for an independent committee to advise the chancellor of the exchequer on how best to carry out 'all possible and legitimate reductions in the national expenditure consistent with the efficiency of the services', and on February 9th, MacDonald wrote to Snowden:

> I have been looking through the business for the week, and I note an Amendment to the National Economy Resolution for Wednesday in the name of Lloyd George ... What is your feeling about this? It may get us into a Parliamentary difficulty, if it is carried right through. The Speaker will first of all put that the words after 'House' stand part of the question. Against that both the Liberals and ourselves will presumably unite. Then he will proceed to put that the words proposed be there inserted. We might arrange that some of our Members who also have Amendments to the Resolution should get up and talk the Resolution out, and the chances are that the Liberals will not be nimble enough to move the closure immediately they see someone up to continue the Debate. If they should do this, however, and get it, we should be in a somewhat awkward fix and might even be defeated.[61]

Nimble or not, the Liberals soon made it clear that they were not to be put off by exercises in parliamentary gamesmanship. On February 11th, Margaret Bondfield saw the Liberal chief whip, Sir Archibald Sinclair, and told him that the Government proposed to bring in legislation to raise the fund's borrowing powers by another £20 million and to extend transitional benefit for six months. Sinclair, she reported, 'said that he would have some difficulty with his people, but it would help if the Chancellor of the Exchequer accepted the Liberal motion of economy'.[62] The Cabinet decided that Snowden should make it clear that the Government had no objection to the Liberal amendment, and that 'the financial situation might involve sacrifices in which everyone might have to bear a share'.[63] The debate began that afternoon. After some preliminary debating points about the extravagance of his predecessors, Snowden launched into a spine-chilling warning about the disasters that would follow if foreigners came to suspect that Britain's budgetary position was unsound, and called on the nation to unite to put its financial house in order.[64] He finished amid Opposition cheers, while Labour members sat in sullen and bewildered silence; and at the end of the debate, the Liberal amendment was carried by 468 to 21 — the Conservatives and Liberals voting with the Government in favour, while a small group of Labour dissidents voted against, and a larger group of Labour members abstained. A month later, the committee of inquiry which the Liberals had demanded was set up under the chairmanship of Sir George May, the former secretary of the Prudential Assurance Company.

The Cabinet had bought itself another breathing-space. This time, the price was even higher than it knew.

V

Snowden's speech in the economy debate was the smokescreen for a retreat, not the signal for an advance. He and MacDonald had been beaten in the Cabinet; Labour reactions during the debate and at a party meeting afterwards made it clear that they had no hope of calling in the parliamentary party to redress the balance. At the end of the month, Snowden had to go into hospital for a prostate operation. He was out of action for several weeks, and while he was away a strange calm fell on Treasury chambers. There were no more warnings of approaching bankruptcy, and no more attacks on transitional benefit or the insurance fund; in Whitehall, at least, it was clear that significant cuts in expenditure had now been ruled out, and the focus of battle shifted away from economy and back to protection.

At the end of October 1930, the economists' committee of the economic advisory council, chaired by Keynes, had produced an authoritative report on the causes of and remedies for the depression. It made three main recommendations. First, business confidence should be revived, by reforming the unemployment insurance system and by balancing the budget without increasing direct taxes. Secondly, home investment should be increased, partly by public works and partly by curtailing British investment overseas. Thirdly, a temporary revenue tariff should be introduced, perhaps coupled with bounties on exports.[65] The economists' report was submitted to the Cabinet in November, and referred to a Cabinet committee chaired by Snowden.[66] It was then lost to sight for four months. In March 1931, however, it surfaced again—this time at the economic advisory council. Before the tariff sections of the report were considered, Keynes sent MacDonald the proof copy of an article he was about to publish in the *New Statesman*, arguing the expansionist case for import duties. He urged in a remarkable covering letter:

> Speaking not as a member of the E.A.C., I feel that there are a thousand reasons for wishing the present Govt. to remain in office. But for this a crisis of financial confidence, *which we are very near*, must be avoided at all costs. Also there can be no policy of the left worth the name, unless the Budget is not merely balanced somehow but by some bold stroke shows a margin. There is no way of securing all this except by a Revenue Tariff; and the overwhelming mass both of instructed and of general public opinion knows that is so.[67]

Keynes's letter found MacDonald in a curiously limp and passive mood, as though the buffeting of the last ten months had drained him of emotional energy. In a long diary entry a few days before he had noted glumly:

Ishbel celebrates her birthday which is tomorrow. What a comfort she is. But do I hamper her as I do Malcolm? Is she sacrificing herself for me? That so often happens. Gloom is upon me, & the virgin purity of a snow-clad world adds to my depression. Is it worth while? The industrial situation baffles us. We make no headway with it, & conditions get worse. A mere mechanical reorganisation is full of dangers. It crushes whilst it economises, & the human position created is ominous. I am not happy about our own work. It is too much of the onlooker, oppressed by circumstances. Have we not too many stiff & inflexible minds? What is to happen with the Budget? The mischief of the Mosley move is that influences which ought to fructify inside are taken outside & a planned advance becomes a warring chaos. I am so overwhelmed in detail that I cannot plan policy. And what is most paralysing is the mind of the Party itself. If I leave it, or split it, what remains? New companions, new creating etc. On that my mind too is stiff. I am old. My friends are dead. I feel solitary. A 'national government' is attractive. The nation needs Parliamentary cooperation, but who will join it? Not the Labour Party ... Three good days this week at Bournemouth with Grant & Greig. Still sleepless. Just enough to make me know how tired my head is & I now suffer from the reaction.[68]

In this state of weary uncertainty, the thought of another pitched battle on the fiscal question must have been even more daunting than before, while the risks involved in it must have seemed even more alarming. So he procrastinated, encouraging the protectionists when he could, but doing as little as possible to upset the free-traders. On March 9th, he replied despairingly to Keynes that the position was 'getting very critical and the illness of the Chancellor has enormously increased my difficulties. It will be a fortnight or three weeks before I can see him to exchange views'.[69] Later that day he noted, still more despairingly, 'Told that Treasury people say it is now impossible to impose revenue duties as machinery cannot be organised. Some members of the Cabinet will say they have been sold.'[70] In spite of his apprehensions, however, he does not appear to have questioned the Treasury's judgment or to have taken any steps to discover whether the difficulties it had discovered could be overcome. At the economic advisory council on March 12th, Keynes repeated the arguments he had used in his letter to MacDonald, and made it clear that the revenue tariff was the 'essential link' in the economists' proposals. For his part, MacDonald declared firmly that the case for free trade had 'completely gone'.[71] But it was not until March 20th that he wrote to Snowden to ask for a meeting;[72] and not until March 29th that the meeting took place.

By then, it was beginning to look as though the Government had entered calmer waters. From January, 1930 until February, 1931, the unemployment figures had risen inexorably, month by month. In March 1931, they fell; and although it is clear in retrospect that this did not invalidate Keynes's argument, it must have seemed to MacDonald that a chink of light had appeared in the clouds. The Government's political prospects seemed brighter too. Like shipwrecked passengers in an open boat, Labour M.P.s assumed instinctively that their only hope of survival was to huddle together against the storm: when a few hardy souls jumped overboard, the rest clung to each other even more tightly than before. At the end of February, Mosley and his closest followers resigned from the Labour Party; shortly afterwards, Trevelyan resigned from the Cabinet. By an odd but not altogether unpredictable quirk of group psychology, these blows stiffened the morale of the loyalist majority. On March 3rd, Trevelyan explained his resignation at a party meeting, and launched a bitter attack on MacDonald. He was heard in what MacDonald described in his diary as 'silent resentment' and when he sat down received no cheers.[73] Soon afterwards, Will Thorne, the old Social Democrat, founder of the gasworkers' union and the member for Plaistow since 1918, wrote encouragingly that he and many of his trade-union colleagues thought Trevelyan's resignation 'particularly mean'.[74] W. B. Taylor, the member for South-West Norfolk, wrote even more encouragingly: 'Listening to you yesterday, at the Party meeting, following the wail of the retiring Minister, revealed the "bigness" of your view ... It may be thought intrusive, but when letters of resignation arrive, why not one more, to express the intense confidence some of us feel in your leadership.'[75] 'Don't be driven from office by resignations and "Mosleyism",' wrote Ben Turner, the veteran trade-unionst and M.P. for Batley, a few days later. 'The Cotton and Wool trades are lifting. India is excellent. Disarmament questions are progressing, and our folks will get the dislikes against them removed.'[76]

Relations with the Liberals improved as well. At the beginning of February, MacDonald and Lloyd George had dined together in a private room in the House of Commons, ostensibly to discuss the round-table conference, but in fact to discuss the respective positions of their two parties. Afterwards, MacDonald noted, 'Ll.G. expanded on unemployment in manner of sunrises on Welsh mountains. Something shd. be done in his spirit, however, though to do what he wants would ruin the country.'[77] This rather grudging private admission was followed by more public gestures. On February 12th, the day after the economy debate, the Government accepted a Liberal motion calling for a programme of national development and for loans to finance it. In his opening speech, Samuel made it clear that the Liberals no longer demanded a big development loan on the lines suggested in their 1929 election programme and that they would be content with a series of small loans, tied to particular projects. In return, MacDonald explicitly repudiated his old formulation by which public works were referred to pejoratively as 'relief works', implying that they added nothing to the country's long-term economic strength;[78] and after the debate Hartshorn arranged a series of consultations between the Liberals and

48 MacDonald, Henderson and Ben Tillett leaving Eccleston Square at the end of the General Strike

49 With the Mosleys, Vienna, October, 1928

50 Lady Londonderry

51 Bathing party 1930s. Lord Hailsham is immediately behind MacDonald with Lady
Londonderry in the background.

52 Princess Bibesco

53 Clifford Allen

54 Mary Agnes ('Molly')
   Hamilton

55 E. D. Morel

56 Cecily Gordon-
   Cumming

57 John Wheatley

58 Ishbel MacDonald

the departmental ministers concerned with telephone development and rural housing. A few weeks later, Hartshorn died unexpectedly after a short illness, but the consultations were continued under the new lord privy seal, Tom Johnston. By the beginning of April, there were three joint committees in existence, dealing respectively with telephones, town planning and the housing of farm labourers.[79]

Much the same happened on the floor of the House. At the end of February, the Conservatives and Liberals joined forces to carry a Liberal amendment to the Trades Disputes Bill, designed to ensure that general strikes remained illegal, but drafted in terms even more unwelcome to the unions than those of the 1927 Act. The Government was forced to withdraw the Bill, but in spite of a good deal of angry muttering among trade-union M.P.s, it went ahead with electoral reform. Another upset came in March, when the Government was defeated after a number of Liberals had rebelled against their leaders and voted with the Conservatives against the abolition of university seats. But the rebellion had a paradoxical result. On March 18th, MacDonald noted:

6 pm. George, Samuel, Archie Sinclair came to my room & met Thomas, Henderson & myself. Results of Govt. defeat on Monday. At Liberal meeting this afternoon, Ll.G. gave notice that [he] would raise the question of dissentients at a meeting on Tuesday and ask the Party to support the Govt. ... Conditions which were to be quite satisfactory to us were to be put in the resolution which I am to see on Monday. Ll. G. seemed thoroughly 'up' against the disturbers of his peace & repeated that they were bought by Tory pledges that they could fight without opposition.[80]

On March 20th, MacDonald wrote to Lloyd George to suggest that 'it might be profitable and helpful if the little conversation which six of us had the other day might become a weekly event ... [A] weekly talk would enable me to see how things are going generally from your point of view and would enable me to concentrate my attention upon the various points of weakness.'[81] Three days later, the Liberal Party meeting followed the Lloyd George line and voted by 33 to 17 in favour of continued support for the Government.[82]

Thus, by the end of March, MacDonald could have been forgiven for thinking that he had more time to play with than he had had for months. Meanwhile, Snowden's illness had given him a strong incentive to postpone a final decision on the Government's fiscal policy yet again. It was clear that Snowden would resist a revenue tariff with all the ferocity he could muster. So long as he was chancellor, a change was almost inconceivable; yet, if he were forced to resign against his will, the political consequences might be disastrous and the effects on confidence still more so. Whatever Lloyd George's private views about protection, the Liberals could hardly continue to support the Government if Snowden resigned from it on the free-trade ticket; and although a revenue tariff could no doubt be carried with Conservative votes, the Con-

U

servatives would be unlikely to go on supporting the Government once the change was made. MacDonald had faced this dilemma in one form or another for nearly a year and, rightly or wrongly, he had decided not to take the risk of trying to resolve it. Now there were signs that it might be about to disappear. On March 12th, Beatrice Webb noted that Snowden had told her husband that he did not want to fight another election, and that he would be willing to leave the Treasury in the summer and to go to the Lords as colonial secretary.[83] There is no evidence that MacDonald knew of this, but it is clear from his diary that rumours of a possible vacancy at the Treasury had begun to circulate in political circles, and that he had begun to sound out his colleagues about a possible Cabinet reshuffle.[84] Though there is no direct evidence, it seems equally clear that he decided that, in these circumstances, his best course was to keep the fiscal question in the background until Snowden's intention were clear.

Two days before his visit to Snowden, he received a minatory letter from Mrs Snowden, warning that although her husband was well enough to receive visitors, it was essential to say nothing 'that will either cloud his spirits or irritate his nervous system. His policy is well known; his Budget will be ready in due time.'[85] MacDonald obeyed her instructions, and left Snowden's bedside little wiser than he had arrived. As he described it in his diary afterwards, 'Today went down to see Chancellor. Uncanny impish aspect, like that of a being of a thousand years looking very young for his age. Did not press him on his Budget but got from him that no tea duty.'[86] Two days later he reported to the Cabinet that he had seen Snowden over the weekend, and that Snowden had told him that he hoped to make his Budget statement at the end of April. The Cabinet decided that he should write again to Snowden to ask whether, in view of the political situation, Snowden would be willing to give his colleagues earlier notice than usual of what the Budget would contain. MacDonald duly wrote, only to receive the disarming reply from Snowden: 'I do not think there is anything in the situation which calls for any variation in the universal practice of withholding information about the Budget until near the date of its introduction ... There will be two features in it – not new or additional taxes – which it is most vital should not become known before the opening and past experience has shown that a premature Cabinet disclosure is as good as a full page advertisement in the Daily Mail.'[87]

With that, the Cabinet had to be content. Snowden made his Budget statement on April 27th, unencumbered by consultations or instructions of any sort. There were no significant changes in economic policy; and the deficit which had loomed so large in January was conjured away by a series of accounting devices.

VI

The interlocking problems of economic policy, relations with the Liberals and a future Cabinet reshuffle were no easier to settle after Easter than they had been before. In spite of his tactful behaviour at Snowden's bedside, MacDonald continued surreptitiously to prepare the ground for a revenue tariff once the Treasury became vacant. At a meeting of the economic advisory council on April 16th, he implied that he now wanted, not merely a temporary tariff on the lines recommended in the economists' report, but a permanent one, leading to a 'radical change in the whole economic system of the country'. A month later, he asked the trade survey committee of the Cabinet for memoranda on the steps that would have to be taken if it were decided to terminate Britain's existing commercial treaties, and on the extent to which the other signatories would be 'able or likely' to retaliate.[88] While Snowden remained at the Treasury, however, these opening moves could not be followed up; and it became increasingly clear that Snowden's future could not be settled in isolation from the future of the rest of the Cabinet.

Here, the biggest stumbling-block was Henderson. After Easter, he told MacDonald that he did not intend to fight Burnley again, and asked to go to the Lords, while staying on as foreign secretary. In other circumstances, MacDonald might have been happy enough to see Henderson disappear to the other place, but he was understandably reluctant to lose his two chief lieutenants from the Commons at the same moment. 'I asked if he thought who was to do H. of C. work if S. & he both went,' he noted caustically; 'he thought that would go all right.'[89] Soon afterwards, he had to face a still more annoying development. In May, the League Council unanimously invited Henderson to preside over the disarmament conference which was due the following year. It was a deserved tribute to his work as foreign secretary, and indirectly, at least, to the Government's foreign policy, but it made MacDonald's task even more awkward than it had been before, and it is understandable – though, no doubt, unedifying – that his reaction should have been considerably less than enthusiastic. 'Henderson without consulting any one of us had accepted "in principle" (wily man) the presidency of the Disarmament Conference,' he noted angrily on May 19th.[90] Next day, he carried the story a stage further in a still more revealing entry:

As I expected, Henderson runs the press & makes it impossible for Cabinet to consider the matter or to veto it. Cabinet today refused to sanction but asked me to inform him that we left decision with him ... Later on in day H. telephoned saying he would like Cabinet to congratulate him & to approve of his decision. Scratch meeting of ministers much amused feeling that we could not afford to say what we felt decided to say what we did not feel so that no obstacle should be placed in the way of success. I regard this as serious for us here. H's absence will be considerable & that will put more work on others; one responsible for F.O. must be chosen (he thinks that I can take it); new leader – Minister – for the Conference Brit. delegation must be provided, & so on. – The Government gets into a steel net work of difficulties which are woven mainly from circumstances & the material at its disposal.[91]

Agriculture was a more familiar source of strain. As we have seen, Snowden had made a statement just before the 1930 summer recess, promising that as soon as the results of the imperial conference were available, steps would be taken to put cereal growing on an economic foundation. Nothing was done until December, when MacDonald persuaded the Cabinet to set up a committee to work out the Government's policy.[92] In March 1931, however, the committee produced a majority report in favour of a wheat quota, while a minority opposed it on the grounds that it would destroy 'the main case against food taxes'. The Cabinet characteristically decided that no action could be taken until Snowden had recovered;[93] and the next few weeks were taken up with a series of ranging shots as the two factions began to manœuvre for position. The Daily Herald published an article in favour of a wheat quota, apparently based on information leaked from the Ministry of Agriculture; Snowden protested angrily about the leak and warned that he was more than ever convinced that the quota would mean 'suicide'; the aged Parmoor declared that he 'could not at the present moment, and under the present circumstances, do other than support the Chancellor of the Exchequer'.[94] Faced with these contrary winds, MacDonald tacked even more bewilderingly than before — at one moment telling Snowden that, although he agreed with the principle behind the quota, he had no confidence in any of the proposed methods of carrying it out;[95] at the next, urging Addison to lobby Lloyd George, so that, if the Cabinet decided in favour of the quota, the Liberals would support it as well.[96] But his tacking brought the Government no nearer to port. On April 15th, the Cabinet devoted two long meetings to a debate on the quota, only to decide once again that no agreement could be reached and that Addison should be asked to see whether he could work out a satisfactory alternative.[97] Three weeks later, Addison reported that it was impossible to work out an alternative 'within the limits of the Government's policy'.[98] Once again, there was a long battle: once again, it ended in deadlock.

MacDonald had returned to London after the Easter recess in fairly cheerful spirits. Now he sank back into his earlier mood of frustration and despair. 'A day with the gloom upon me,' he noted on April 20th.[99] 'Despair of being able to do anything that requires time for working out comes upon me when I meet some of my friends ... ,' he noted after a meeting with the miners' group of M.P.s at the end of the month. 'We can go on suffering but not fighting on a plan'.[100] The biannual torment of the honours list added to his depression. 'Honours again rising over the horizon,' he noted at about the same time, '& I am deluged with applications of the nature of begging letters ... Twice a year the "moonstruck" steal out of their places & come to me in their nude reality.'[101] Occasionally, he even toyed with the idea of leaving office and retiring to the back benches. 'I have now to consider some reconstruction of the Cabinet & am so overworked that I ought to reconstruct myself out of it,' he noted towards the end of May.[102] In a letter to Jim Middleton a few days later he burst out:

Thank you for your letter. I offered you the honour to show, in a way which P.M.s only can do, how much I admire you & the work you have done. At the same time, I am not surprised that you declined it & only wish that the same spirit was in the Party. Men whose names would surprise you, clamour for a badge & a title, & one has just written me one of the most offensive letters I have ever received, because I told him I could not include him in my list. Another only thinks of the love he bears for his wife! It is disgusting & makes me more & more of a cynic. I am glad however that I refused everything offered to me whilst still in opposition, that the solitary thing I have I could not avoid & yet take office, & that what is now said to me is that they would give me this or that, but that I know I would not accept it. Some of the badges mean much that is good & really decorate appropriate chests. I feel that way sometimes about the Knight of the Thistle which I could now get at any moment, but I shake my head, though that may properly be the pardonable pride of every Scotsman provided he has earned it. Still, you may never weep for my backsliding in that respect.

My great darkness is that I sometimes fear lest the work itself may not last. The Trade Union guidance is not Socialist and our young men are not very conspicuous in their Parliamentary efficiency. But I suppose every one of an old gang thought that in his later days. I really want to get out & would do so without much delay if I saw where the stream was to flow in & fill up vacancies. It is easy to slip into public life, but the most difficult thing in this world is to slip out. I want to do some work before I go which is impossible so long as I am P.M. or even leading the Opposition. Besides, I am not at all sure but that the Party would be better of a change. Old age may be the reason why the Cabinet is so divided in policy & stiff necks may bring us down. After two years of heavy drudgery I am more tired in body & mind than anybody knows, & some of the distasteful things happening in the Party add to my weariness of spirit.[103]

VII

After Whitsun, his spirits revived; and he made another attempt to bring matters to a head. Perhaps because he calculated that once Snowden had gone to the Lords the question could be reopened in more favourable circumstances, perhaps because his doubts about the proposed machinery had been reinforced, or perhaps because he had come to the conclusion that this would be the easiest way to produce a decision, he now abandoned his old position of benevolent neutrality on the wheat quota and came down against it. On June 4th, he told a special Cabinet meeting that it was now clear that this quota could not be carried on Liberal and Labour votes alone; and the Cabinet accordingly decided that in these circumstances it could not be adopted 'as the main feature of the Government's cereal policy'.[104] On June 11th, he turned to the reshuffle and discussed the situation with Thomas, Clynes, Snowden and Henderson. Here, he was less successful. Once again, Henderson said he wanted to go to the Lords; once again, MacDonald tried to persuade him to change his mind; once again, Henderson resisted his blandishments. As MacDonald put it in his diary afterwards:

> Henderson said he wanted to go if asked to serve the Party in that way! I pressed objections including the manning of Front Bench in Commons & the inevitable loss of the Burnley seat. He pressed hard. Said would not fight Burnley again though he said he might if the General Election is precipitated [soon]. Then put irrelevant arguments re. obligations to Union &c — Snowden also said he has fought his last fight. Snowden *is* out. I remarked that I should soon be left alone to fight as I had no intention to go up.[105]

At this point, his cogitations were interrupted by a new crisis. The most controversial feature of Snowden's budget was a proposal to levy a tax of 1*d*. in the pound on the capital value of every unit of land in the country, starting in the financial year 1933-4, and to prepare the way by valuing all landed property. However irrelevant economically, the land-tax clauses of the 1931 finance Bill were politically explosive — evoking memories of the People's Budget and of the old Radical cries of the nineteenth century, and raising, albeit in a more traditional form, the spectre, only recently laid, of a tax on capital. They were savagely denounced by the Conservatives, but at first they were warmly welcomed by Lloyd George. By the beginning of June, however, the Liberals had cold feet. The central principle of Snowden's proposal was that it should apply to landed property as such, whether developed or undeveloped. This meant that the owners of premises on which income tax was paid under Schedule A would be taxed twice over on the same property. Though this had been implicit in the proposal from the first, the Liberals suddenly decided that it was a monstrous injustice, and put down an amendment to exempt land already subject to income tax from the new tax.[106]

At first, the Cabinet decided to stand firm. On June 9th, MacDonald noted, 'Decided not to yield to Liberal Land Tax amendment [and] so run the risk of defeat. Feeling spreads among colleagues that the present Parliamentary position cannot last & that Tories ought not to be allowed to enjoy luxury of opposition through the dark days till dawn.'[107] But it was one thing for the Cabinet to run the risk of defeat: another for Labour backbenchers in marginal seats to do so. On June 10th, MacDonald noted, 'Sounded some of our men on a crisis. They do not like it.'[108] On June 12th, he wrote a long letter to Snowden, urging him to compromise, on the grounds that the 'great bulk' of the parliamentary Labour Party were not prepared to risk defeat for the sake of a tax which would not be levied for two more years.[109] By June 14th, it was beginning to look as though the Government would escape after all. Sir Stafford Cripps, who had recently joined the Government as solicitor general, suggested a compromise by which the Government would stick to the principle of a single tax on the capital value of all land, while graduating it on developed land according to the degree of development. 'Ll.G. called & we went to Sir H. S's where he, Cripps & Clem Davies were working at the matter,' MacDonald noted sardonically. 'Harmonious. Parliamentary situation, however, had to be considered. What to do with their printed amendt.? They suggested that they should move our proposal! They were very frightened.'[110]

The climax came on June 15th. At eleven in the morning, MacDonald had a meeting with Snowden, who had just arrived from the country, and found him 'unwillingly amenable to a new proposal put up by Cripps, but disturbed that the Liberals might accept it'.[111] At 11.30, Snowden, Thomas, Henderson, Clynes, Graham and MacDonald discussed the situation. 'Very agreeable,' MacDonald noted, 'but I had a feeling that there was thunder in the air or an earthquake in the bowels of things.'[112] The earthquake soon erupted. At twelve Lloyd George arrived, accompanied by Samuel, Sinclair, MacLean and Clement Davies. According to MacDonald's diary,

Chancellor's first words to Ll.G: 'Well, you have been thinking things over. What have you to say?' Shortly we agreed to the principle of the Cripps proposal, Chancellor getting increasingly at cross purposes & provocative. Joint Committee appointed by complete consent to fill in certain required figures … Then followed discussion on how amendments agreed upon should be put on paper & moved. LL.G. wished Liberals to initiate & when that objected to he lost his temper & walked out of the room (mem. the T.U. Bill negotiations). No one took any notice. Then Henderson bullied Samuel & the episode was closed by his saying he did not say what he had said. Adjourned till afternoon & Joint Committee set to work. (Reported later it could not agree) … Liberals came in as in the morning & proposed Cripps' proposal altered only as regards tax on fully developed sites … Chancellor silent coldly & critically examined whispering with Graham & Cripps. Would say nothing. Meeting adjourned. We continued. Chan. got report that he would get only £400,000 from 8,000,000 hereditaments. Rejected & offered no alternative. Would not be bullied by Ll.G., surrender to Liberals &c, &c. We pointed out surrender by & not to Liberals. No effect. Liberal Party meeting waiting for our decision meanwhile adjourned. We adjourned for a meal & resumed at

8.15 pm ... We went on with Chancellor. Would listen to nothing. All consequences put before him, the rest of us being unanimous. Deadlock. Called members of Cabinet & 14 present. All unanimous though Graham took a seat on the fence & his uncertain mind wiggled like a compass needle. Chan. refused to cooperate with the decision in favour of agreeing to principle [sic] Liberal (originally in substance our own to which he had agreed in the morning) offer. When pressed, rose & said he would not cooperate. Asked for ten minutes to consider. We sat discussing for 50 minutes. No message. 11 pm. by then & went on to bench to announce decisions on clause 19. I saw him in interval & put full issues & consequences before him. 'I do not care about the money. I shall not be humiliated by Liberals'. Mind has ossified on that irrelevancy. Just as I was moving him, Hudson prompted by the Treasury secretaries, who had played a most subversive part playing on Chan.'s obstinacy, came in fussy state & said 'Revolt amongst M.P.s against surrender to Liberals'. That settled it. I was furious. Returned to waiting Cabinet & said 'hopeless for the moment'. Graham sitting with Chan. on bench. I sent for him to ask what game he was playing. Came & said Chancellor was stuck on bench. We gave him a few lashes. Said Cha. wished the matter adjourned till ... morning. Decided Cabinet meet at 10 a.m. to have Chan. decision. Meanwhile Liberals held adjourned meeting & decided to put what was virtually our amendment on the paper. Day ended thus at 11.30 p.m. — Took sleeping pills.[113]

MacDonald woke before five and got up at six. Either just before going to bed, or just after getting up, he made one more appeal to Snowden, this time by letter:

I am making one last appeal to you to help us to avoid a great disaster. If we bring defeat upon ourselves tonight, we face a foregone conclusion of an electoral debacle. The Party is in no way prepared to fight, and in places like Lancashire our candidates will simply be mown down without a chance. If you resign, I must try and gain time for a rally before the inevitable end, and was ever such a task put upon anyone? You know the internal position and I need not put it upon paper. The patched up Ministry could not last long and yet I cannot throw the people who have supported us for two years cruelly to destruction without an attempt to gain a better position upon which to fight. In the later divisions yesterday, the feelings of our Members were the same as those of your Cabinet colleagues and they were trying to whistle to dispel their apprehensions.

   The position *did* change yesterday when we secured a full valuation and a land tax which is to be levied on all site values, together with a scheme of a sliding scale upon every item of which we agree excepting one ... Yesterday's negotiations made a fight impossible. We won ... That ... makes it impossible to us to strike at the Liberals. *We on the inside may have our feelings about them, but our knowledge and experience in this respect cannot be communicated to the public or be effective weapons for a public fight.* The people will simply not understand us and will put us down as thin-skinned incompetents and squabblers who at a time like this put sensitive personal feeling before everything else ...

And there is the other consideration. Are you justified in finishing all our other work at this stage and for this reason? Is not this a case where one has to submit to what one does not like — rightly or wrongly — because one has to bear burdens and serve in teams and give something to great causes? ...

I am really too disturbed to put what is in my mind as effectively as it ought to be put. But the mere fact that I write this as a last prayer not to doom to defeat — and even more — the Party and that crowd of friends who sit with us in the Commons, will I hope find you not unresponsive. I can do no more, and must leave it with you. Do not destroy — as far as it can be destroyed — the work of our life-time by scattering our flock and leaving it torn, and disgusted with its leaders and itself. Our lives have been made hard by the many obstacles we have met; do not let it be said that in the end one silly little one came which broke us and that the men who saw the birth of the Labour Party assisted at its death.[114]

MacDonald's appeal turned the scales. When the Cabinet met later that morning, Snowden announced that, following a letter he had received from the prime minister, he felt that 'he could no longer persist in his refusal to fall in with the views of his colleagues in regard to the Liberal amendment.' After some procedural discussion as to whether the Liberal amendment would be in order, the Cabinet decided that if it were allowed to stand Snowden should accept it in substance, and that if it turned out not to be in order he should make it clear that the Government would bring in a new clause based on it.[115] After the meeting MacDonald noted sardonically, 'Cabinet met at 10 a.m. Chancellor opened with a statement that he had letter this morning from me which he could not resist & yielded. Thus the crisis ends. Still there was a postcript & it was touched with ridicule. When the Liberal amendment came up, it was ruled out of order! ... Later in the evening I heard that dinners had been arranged & almost excursions run like Lourdes pilgrimages, & every seat in the House taken to see the end of the Bull fight & the death of the Bull.'[116]

Once the crisis was over, MacDonald could turn back to the reshuffle. The difficulties were formidable. Passfield and Parmoor were both old and tired, and wanted to retire as soon as possible. Henderson still fought hard to go to the Lords, even though MacDonald believed that this would endanger Labour's position in the Commons. As we have seen more than once, MacDonald hated exercising his powers of patronage, and found the business of appointing and replacing ministers even more distasteful than that of weeding out an honours list. He had recognized that a reshuffle was necessary as early as March 15th, but the task still remained to be carried out when the House rose at the end of July. Little by little, however, he inched his way towards a decision; and although it is doubtful if he had made up his mind by the beginning of the recess, the direction in which he was moving seems clear enough. In a much-quoted letter to Passfield on July 14th, he wrote, 'As you know, I am in a most awful difficulty about the House of Lords ... We have not the material in our Party that we ought to have. The solution will have to come, I am afraid, by moves which will surprise all of you.'[117] At the end of the month, Lloyd George dictated a memorandum to his secretary, Frances Stevenson, recording a conversation with MacDonald in which MacDonald had said that the Labour Party 'would like an alliance. They would be prepared to drop some of their present Ministers ... Ramsay would be Prime Minister, Lloyd George would be Leader [of the House] at the Foreign Office or the Treasury.'[118]

The evidence should not be pushed too far. The 'moves which will surprise all of you' may have had nothing to do with the Liberals; the overture recorded in Lloyd George's memorandum may have been a tentative attempt to explore the ground rather than a firm statement of intent. If MacDonald had taken a definite decision to bring Lloyd George into his Cabinet it is surprising that there is no record of it in his diary or papers. Even if he had made up his mind, it does not follow that he would have been able to carry his colleagues with him; and without the support of his senior colleagues, at least, he would have had to drop the idea.

All the same, it is reasonable to assume that he wanted a coalition if he could get one: that Lloyd George wanted one as well: and that both believed that they were more likely than not to have their way. Relations between the Liberal and Labour Parties had improved out of all recognition in the last few months, and there were no longer any serious policy differences between them. Through the joint committees established by Hartshorn and Johnston, Liberal 'experts' were becoming more and more deeply enmeshed in the Government machine: for all practical purposes, the policies that emanated from Johnston's office were now indistinguishable from Lloyd George's. The 'little talks' which MacDonald had suggested at the end of March had continued too; and the tone of his diary entries suggests that his personal relations with Lloyd George were better than at any time since the outbreak of the war. A coalition would prevent a repetition of the land-tax crisis and give the Government security of tenure for up to three more years: it would also give the Liberals a badly needed taste of office. Though purists on both sides might object, both parties had much more to gain than they had to lose; and in such circumstances, the objections would be unlikely to prevail.

Even without the added security of a coalition, there was some reason to hope that Labour's third year of office would turn out more successfully than had its second. Whatever happened to Henderson, Snowden's elevation was only a matter of time; and once Snowden had left the Treasury, the biggest a single obstacle to revenue tariff would be out of the way. The prospects for a change in monetary policy had brightened too. In July, the Macmillan committee at last reported – in favour, among other things, of a managed currency, designed deliberately to raise the price level and to break the deflationary spiral of the last few years. As we have seen, MacDonald had tried more than once to nudge the Treasury in this direction, each time without success; and three weeks before the Macmillan report appeared, he had written a long letter to Montagu Norman, complaining about the speeches made by the Bank of England's economic adviser, Professor Sprague, who thought that monetary policy was powerless to alleviate the depression and that wages would have to follow commodity prices down. Sprague's views, MacDonald wrote, amounted

to a policy of despair. There is no national or world dictator who can say that to-morrow all wages, prices in shops, etc. must be reduced by 10 or 20 per cent. Every reduction involves tension and many of them will only take place after bitter resistance. Moreover the experience of the last 10 years teaches us that downward adjustments of this kind do not take place equitably and universally. Some wages and costs – as in the exporting trades – fall steeply. Other wages and costs, many payments, such as rents, interest on Government loans and industrial debentures, either do not fall at all but actually rise both nominally and really, or if they do come down it is only after the passing of years. Is it surprising therefore that there is a growing feeling amongst all classes that as the value of money in terms of goods does both change and fluctuate, efforts should be made to reduce the relative value of money rather than that of all goods?[119]

Now these heresies had received the *imprimatur* of one of the most impressive committees of inquiry in British history; and although this did not mean that it would be easy to carry them out, the chances of doing so looked more promising than at any time before.

Whether MacDonald made these calculations is unknown, but it would be surprising if some such thoughts had not occurred to him as the recess approached. As late as mid-July he could look towards the future, if not with total confidence, then at least with a certain guarded optimism.

CHAPTER 25

Crisis

I

MUFFLED echoes of the crisis which was to make a mockery of MacDonald's hopes reached Chequers as early as June 6th, when the German chancellor and foreign minister, Heinrich Brüning and Julius Curtius, arrived for weekend talks. They had a doleful tale to tell. Following the failure of the great Austrian bank, the Kreditanstalt, three weeks before, Germany's already tottering credit had been undermined still further by panic withdrawals of foreign funds. The Germans believed that they had no hope of restoring confidence while they had to carry the burden of reparations. Under the Young plan, they had the right to suspend certain reparation payments if their foreign exchange position warranted it. Now Brüning warned that although they would continue to pay reparations for as long as possible, suspension would have to come by November at the latest.[1]

MacDonald listened sympathetically. 'Bruning looks like a wise doctor & supports impression by demeanour, voice & spectacles,' he noted when the talks were over. 'Curtius looks efficient & alert. Most friendly time. They [are] in [a] severe fix & I wonder how Germany has come through so many crises.'[2] It was a revealing comment: as much because of what it failed to say as because of what it said. Like most people on the left, MacDonald had always believed that the reparations clauses of the Versailles settlement were foolish as well as wicked – ruinous not only to the Germans but to everyone else as well. In 1924 he had won a personal triumph for his part in whittling down Germany's obligations. Now he decided that the time was ripe for more ambitious steps in the same direction; and after Brüning and Curtius had left he wrote a personal letter to Henry Stimson, the American secretary of state, urging that Britain and the United States should do all they could to rescue Germany from her plight.[3] But, although he realized that the German crisis was serious and believed that it was in Britain's interests to help to end it, he did not realize how acute it had become. Still less did he realize that Britain's credit was now so shaky that a crash in Central Europe might drag her down as well.

He learned quickly enough. On June 20th, President Hoover made his famous proposal for a year's moratorium on all reparations payments and inter-governmental debts. MacDonald heard the news with delight. 'I am very happy to have been in it & indeed to have started it by my letter to Stimson ... ,' he noted enthusiastically. 'These things I dreamt of when in the U.S. in 1929 but hardly thought would happen. A suspension ought to mean that we shall not make the mistake of resuming.'[4] His delight was short-lived. In Paris, Hoover's proposal was seen as a sinister device to protect American investments in central Europe at the expense of France. With a characteristic mixture of ingenuity and short-sightedness, the French insisted on a modification to the moratorium, by which Germany would continue to pay reparations but would then receive the money back in the form of a loan. In the two weeks of haggling that followed, the drain of funds from Germany became a flood. When the French and Americans at last reached agreement in the early hours of July 7th, Germany's reserves were almost exhausted and her top-heavy banking system was on the verge of collpase. On July 13th, cash payments were suspended: on the 15th, exchange controls were imposed by emergency decree.[5] As early as July 1st, MacDonald and his Cabinet colleagues had been warned that the German crisis might have 'serious repercussions' on Britain.[6] Now the warning came true. On July 15th, the Bank of England suffered heavy losses. By August 1st, a quarter of its reserves had gone.[7]

MacDonald watched these developments with a mixture of despair and rage. 'France has been playing its usual small minded & selfish game over the Hoover proposals ... ,' he noted on July 5th. 'To do a good thing for its own sake is not in accordance with French official nature. So Germany cracks whilst France bargains.'[8] By July 11th, he had become even more indignant. 'The behaviour of the French has been inconceivably atrocious ... ,' he noted. 'We have put a virago into authority in Europe. Another war is inevitable if an independent nation in Europe is to exist.'[9] In the next few days the virago became even more domineering. In return for the German visit to Chequers, MacDonald and Henderson arranged to visit Berlin on July 18th. On the 14th, Henderson went to Paris to discuss the situation with the French. On the 15th, MacDonald received a message from the British ambassador in Washington to say that the Americans would support Britain in calling an urgent conference in London, preferably that week, with the limited object of ending the immediate crisis in Germany. After the Cabinet had agreed that such a conference would succeed only if the French were willing to co-operate, MacDonald telephoned Henderson to suggest that their visit to Berlin should be postponed, and to tell him that his colleagues wanted him to find out whether the French were prepared to help in preventing an 'economic collapse' in Germany.[10]

An intricate diplomatic fencing match followed, in which MacDonald's already strained relations with his foreign secretary came close to breaking-point. The French were willing to offer substantial long-term credits to Germany — but only on harsh terms, and only if the Germans were willing to give up their attempts to revise the peace settlement. The Germans were now so desperate that it looked as though they might be induced to accept the French terms.

For MacDonald, who had always believed that the peace settlement needed revision, and who had now come to believe that France was trying to use her financial strength to dominate the rest of Europe, this was an alarming prospect. From his point of view it was essential to prevent the French from squeezing political concessions out of Germany: and equally essential to prevent bilateral negotiations between France and Germany, in which the Germans would have no protection against French dictation. Henderson had other ideas. In 1924 he had campaigned for revision himself, and had caused MacDonald great embarrassment in doing so. Since then, his attitudes had changed. He was anxious to persuade the French to offer financial help to Germany, but he was equally anxious to persuade the Germans to offer political concessions to France; though he conveyed the substance of MacDonald's message to the French, he did so with scant enthusiasm. When the French told him that it would be foolish to hold a conference without proper preparation and that the Germans would have to make concessions before they could expect to receive help, he readily agreed. He then suggested that he and MacDonald should go to Berlin to find out what concessions the Germans were willing to make. When the French accepted his suggestion, he sent a remarkably disingenuous telegram to MacDonald, concealing his own part in the discussion, implying that it was the French who had insisted that the Berlin visit should go ahead, and giving the impression that they might decide to take part in a conference after all, once the results of the visit were known.[11]

MacDonald had no way of knowing that Henderson had defied the Cabinet's instructions and had carefully refrained from pushing the idea of a conference. He assumed that the French had turned down the suggestion, in order to spin things out while Germany plunged towards ruin and the pound began to go the way of the mark. 'Day of French worries,' he noted later. 'Draughts on gold; governor distraught & says moratorium may be necessary. French delaying, talking, killing time whilst London bleeds as did Berlin.'[12] The text of his reply to Henderson has disappeared, but it seems clear that he insisted that the pressure on the Bank of England was now so heavy that an immediate conference was essential to save sterling, and that another attempt must be made to persuade the French to attend. This time, Henderson did as he was told and, with some difficulty, induced the French to come to a conference in London on July 21st. But they still refused to come to London until the Germans had come to Paris; and in the end it was agreed that Henderson should go alone to Berlin the following day in order to persuade the Germans to do this.[13] In the meantime, however, MacDonald had decided that the conference should be held on the 20th and not on the 21st; that invitations should be issued forthwith; and that he and Henderson should go to Berlin after all, and bring the German ministers back to London with them. When Henderson telephoned Downing Street some time after midnight and reported his agreement with the French, MacDonald replied firmly, according to his diary, 'that my arrangements would have to be kept'.[14]

MacDonald went to sleep believing that he had outmanœuvred the French and imposed his authority on Henderson. He woke up to discover that the French had outmanœuvred him and that Henderson had revolted. After his conversation with MacDonald in the early hours of July 16th, Henderson telephoned the French prime minister, Pierre Laval, and told him that the date of the international conference had been changed from the 21st to the 20th. Laval agreed to the change, but declared that the Germans would still have to come to Paris first. Henderson then sent for the German ambassador in Paris, told him that the Berlin visit on which MacDonald had just insisted had been cancelled and added that it was 'vital' for the German ministers to come to Paris as soon as possible.[15] When he discovered what had happened, MacDonald noted indignantly:

A day of confusion. Henderson's vanity has overcome him. He is working to keep everybody 'off the grass' except himself. Telephones to Paris & Berlin reveal that he has cancelled the Berlin visit without consulting me or the Germans. He has assured me that the Germans have agreed whilst our Ambassador at Berlin says direct from Bruning that they have not & German Ambassador has called to tell me that Bruning is in consternation & that cancellation will do harm. Henderson says proposal to cancel was made by German Ambassador in Paris; Bruning says it was made to Ambassador by Henderson. The Govt. has been doing everything it could to prevent Germans going to Paris & having an ultimatum presented by French. Henderson has thwarted us.[16]

But by then it was too late. The news of the cancellation had appeared in the German papers, and MacDonald had no alternative but to accept defeat. The fact that he had to accept it at the hands of the one member of the Cabinet who had a serious chance of supplanting him as party leader cannot have made it more palatable.

The sequel was equally disagreeable. On July 18th, the German ministers duly arrived in Paris, only to find that the French terms for a loan included a German commitment to accept the terms of the peace settlement for ten years. This was a commitment which no German government could possibly have given; and the Paris meeting broke up without reaching agreement.[17] On July 20th, the international conference on which MacDonald had pinned his hopes opened under his chairmanship in London. It too was a dismal failure. It had been a condition of holding the conference that the reparations question should not be raised, and when Snowden made a characteristically tactless attempt to raise it, MacDonald felt it necessary to disavow him. As for a long-term loan to Germany, Britain had lost so much gold and foreign exchange in the last few days that she was in no condition either to take part in such an operation herself or to put effective pressure on the French to offer a loan on terms which the Germans could accept. In the end, the conference managed to agree only that non-governmental foreign credits to Germany should be held at their existing level, and that the short-term credits which the other central banks had recently advanced to the Reichsbank should be renewed when they ran out. Even this was achieved only after hard bargaining; and although it kept Germany on her feet, it did nothing to improve her long-term prospects or to check the world-wide confidence crisis, of which the German crisis had been merely the most obvious local symptom.[18]

On July 22nd MacDonald noted:

Agreement Germany needs help but French never heartily in & act as freezing mixture. They are solely responsible for the failure of the Hoover Plan & the present position ... Again & again be it said: France is the enemy; we shall pay with all our honour for that war ... All day, France blocked & poured cold water. They want long term loan with slave conditions. I tried to get them to take their share in the short credits & shame them out of it. But they were obstinate as brass ... The meeting of Finance Ministers finished report & we end to-morrow. Will Germany be helped by the little we have been able to do?[19]

When the conference ended on the 23rd, Britain's problems were already beginning to loom larger than Germany's. 'Run on Bank of England,' MacDonald noted. '£5,000,000 exported ... Spoke to Snowden urging him to study Budgetary situation & to Graham instructing him to go into immediate trade prospects & watch German dumping.'[20] How far he blamed Henderson is not clear, but it is hard to believe that he can have exonerated him completely.

II

As MacDonald's diary entry implied, the real loser from the conference was Britain. Foreign holders of sterling, who had been forced to withdraw funds from London when their German assets were frozen, were still unable to withdraw their money from Germany. British banks which had lent to Germany were in the same position. As the flow of funds from London continued, what had begun as a liquidity crisis gradually turned into a confidence crisis; like all confidence crises, it fed on itself. If the conference had produced some bold new plan for solving the world's liquidity problems, the crisis might have been halted before it was too late. Once the international financial community realized that the conference had produced nothing, confidence in sterling ebbed still further. On July 23rd, the last day of the conference, bank rate was raised to $3\frac{1}{2}$ per cent. On the 24th, Snowden was warned by his officials that 'the gold exodus is unprecedented ... Unless we take such steps as are open to us to rectify the situation, there is a real danger of our being driven off the gold standard.' On the 26th, the Bank of England obtained a credit of £50 million, half of it from the Bank of France and half from the Federal Reserve Bank of New York. On the 30th, bank rate was raised again – this time to 4½ per cent.[21] Meanwhile, the May committee, which had been appointed nearly five months before, following the Government's surrender to the Liberals at the time of the economy debate in February, had completed its report. It forecast a huge budget deficit of £120 million and recommended sweeping economies in Government expenditure – including a cut of nearly £67 million in expenditure on the unemployed, and totalling £97 million altogether.[22] Its report was presented to the Cabinet on July 30th; and a committee consisting of MacDonald, Snowden, Henderson, Thomas and Graham was appointed to consider it.[23] As the political world dispersed for the summer recess next day, the report was published – accompanied by no statement of Government policy, and by no attempt to mitigate the damage it was likely to do to confidence. 'House rose with feeling that it is not for long,' MacDonald noted. 'As international bankers we are in a precarious position.'[24] It was perhaps the greatest understatement of his career.

His forebodings did not prevent him from showing an interest in an aspect of Labour politics with which he has not often been associated. On August 2nd, Captain Bennett, Labour M.P. for Cardiff Central, wrote to tell him that he had received a letter from Attlee and G. D. H. Cole, urging him to support the setting up of a proposed 'new Fabian Research Bureau', and mentioning MacDonald as one of its other supporters. In view of the fact that the Labour Party itself conducted a good deal of research, Bennett wrote, was there any need for a new body of this kind?[25] On August 8th, MacDonald replied that he too doubted the value of endless committees of inquiry, but that he had discussed the proposed new Fabian committee with Cole, and had decided to support it because of the assurances which Cole had given him about its purpose:

The Socialist Movement in this country is going to rack and ruin, because it is being controlled by people who are nothing more than critics of the Government, inspired by the idea that all you have to do is to hand out largesse to the community. All sense of principle, of communal organisation, and of service given with one's whole heart to the community, has gone and we are in danger of drifting into a Poor Law frame of mind. Cole told me that he wishes to stop that, and to produce documents relating to existing conditions which were inspired by Socialist ideas throughout. If anyone can do that, they shall certainly have my blessing, whether they are critics of the Government or otherwise. No one is more sensible than I am that a Government, which has been more overwhelmed than any of its predecessors by day to day problems, ought to receive guidance from the outside. The only condition I stipulate is that its proposals should be practical and realistic and not merely fireside theorising. I therefore said to Cole that I would not consider his action in any hostile frame of mind, but would look forward to his results with great expectation, as I was fully aware of how helpful they might be.[26]

By now, however, he had little time to spare for socialist theory. When the House rose on July 31st, he left for Lossiemouth, and from there he wrote to Keynes to ask for his views on the May report. On August 5th, Keynes replied that his views on the subject were not fit for publication, or even for circulation to the economic advisory council, but that he welcomed MacDonald's invitation to let him know his reactions privately. The committee's recommendations, Keynes continued, clearly represented 'an effort to make the existing deflation effective by bringing incomes down to the level of prices'; if adopted in isolation, they would result in 'a most gross perversion of social justice'. His own advice was that the existing deflation should not be made effective — partly because it would entail a substantial increase in unemployment, partly because the necessary cut in money incomes would not be tolerated by those who would have to submit to it, partly because he knew of no way to ensure that bondholders would suffer an equivalent cut, but above all because

it is now nearly *certain* that we shall go off the existing gold parity at no distant date. Whatever may have been the case some time ago, it is now too late to avoid this. We can put off the date for a time, if we are so foolish as to borrow in terms of francs and dollars and so allow a proportion of what are now sterling liabilities to be converted into franc and dollar liabilities ... But when doubts as to the prospects of a currency, such as now exist about sterling, have come into existence, the game is up ...

I suggest that you should consult a Comee. consisting of all living ex-Chancellors of the Exchequer whether [*sic*] they believe that deflation *à outrance* is possible and are in favour of attempting it, or whether we should not at once suspend gold convertibility and then take collective thought as to the next step.

We might, I think, try to convert disaster into success ... I should seek forthwith to win the hegemony of a new Currency Union by inviting all Empire countries to join us in adhering to a new currency unit ... I should further have it in mind to invite ... all South America, Asia, Central Europe, Italy and Spain ...

The new currency unit might be a gold unit obtained by devaluing existing units by not less than 25 per cent. It is *vital* that the change should not be smaller than this, and preferably greater ...

Having thus put exchange difficulties behind us, we should then proceed to organise activity and prosperity at home and abroad along the boldest possible lines.[27]

Keynes's untidy scrawl contained at least the germ of an alternative, not merely to the May report, but to the crumbling halfway house between deflation and expansion in which the Government had been locked for the past fifteen months. If his advice had been followed, the world might have been spared much unnecessary suffering; an outward-looking Britain, rather than an inward-looking United States, might have been the first great power to pioneer the techniques of the New Deal. We shall never know whether his vision of a new and expansionist currency block could have been realized, but there can be no doubt in retrospect that the risks entailed by its pursuit would have been much smaller than those entailed by a forlorn attempt to save a parity which was by now past salvation.

But, although this seems obvious today, it was far from obvious in August 1931. Just as generals prepare for the last war, bankers and finance ministers try to avert the last economic crisis. Even after eighteen months of the worst depression in history, men were haunted by the memory of the great central European inflations of the early 1920s. Once it was freed from the disciplines of the gold standard, what was to stop a government debauching its currency in the way that the German Government had debauched its currency in 1923? If Keynes had his way and sterling were devalued, what guarantee was there that the process would stop at 25 per cent? Why not 50 per cent, or 100 per cent, or even 500 per cent? At a more sophisticated level, the gold standard could be defended on expansionist grounds as well. Whatever might be true of agricultural France or self-sufficient America, Britain's prosperity was bound up with the prosperity of the rest of the world. The depression could be halted in Britain only if it were halted in the rest of the world: it could be halted in the rest of the world only if Britain gave the lead. If Britain abandoned the gold standard, she would no longer be in a position to give such a lead; and she might provoke a wave of retaliatory measures which would dislocate world trade and harm her more than it harmed anyone else. Earlier in the summer, Bevin and Thomas Allen had signed a minority addendum to the Macmillan report suggesting, in guarded language, that devaluation was preferable to deflation.[28] At that time, Keynes had been in favour of sticking to the gold standard and against devaluation. Now he had changed his mind. It is not altogether surprising that others should have failed to jump when he jumped.

In his letter to MacDonald, Keynes wrote hopefully that, even in the city, 'far more people than you might expect' would support a policy of the kind he had outlined. As we shall see, the messages that came to MacDonald from the city were very different. As we shall also see, no one in the Cabinet disputed the need to save the parity; though there is no direct evidence, it is unlikely that many did so in the parliamentary Labour Party. Hubert Henderson, who was almost as critical of the May report as Keynes had been, and who shared Keynes's belief that confidence in sterling was rapidly evaporating, drew almost exactly the opposite conclusions from those which Keynes had drawn. The May report's criterion of what counted as a balanced budget, he wrote in a memorandum to MacDonald on August 7th, went 'far beyond what would have been

regarded as the requirements of prudence in the heyday of orthodox finance';
confidence factors apart, its recommendations would do more harm than good.
Yet, in the circumstances that now obtained, none of this was relevant:

> An important Treasury Committee has proclaimed in effect to the world:
> 'The British Budget is hopelessly unbalanced. It has got into a thoroughly
> unsound position as the result of the inherently profligate tendencies of our
> competitive party politics. If our politicians have the courage to make
> drastic and unpopular retrenchments, it is not too late to put our house in
> order. But if they lack this courage, it is all up with us'. This picture may be
> fair or unfair. In my opinion ... it is largely unfair. But if after this has been
> said so authoritatively ... nothing, or nothing substantial, is done along the
> lines indicated by the Committee, the conclusion will be widely drawn that
> sterling is doomed ... The ill consequences of an abandonment of the gold
> standard can no doubt be exaggerated; but they would be formidable and
> enduring; and I cannot think that the time has yet been reached when we
> should reconcile ourselves to so serious a step ...
>
> Unless, therefore, we are ready to abandon forthwith to attempt to main-
> tain sterling at parity, I conclude that the situation calls imperatively for
> retrenchments amounting to a substantial proportion of the savings indi-
> cated by the May Committee.[29]

In the Bank of England matters were seen in a less academic fashion. Between
August 4th and August 11th, it used up £11 million of its own reserves and
nearly £10 million of its borrowed reserves to defend the parity.[30] As early as
July 30th, the joint committee of the British Bankers' Association and the
Accepting Houses Committee had written to MacDonald and Snowden, warning that a 'progressive deterioration' in the budgetary position and in the
balance of payments now threatened a 'depreciation of the currency with all its
consequent evils'; and that unless urgent steps were taken to balance the budget
and improve the trade balance, the credits which had just been obtained from
Paris and New York would 'simply "go down the drain" '.[31] On August 6th,
the chairmen of the London clearing banks wrote to MacDonald, supporting
the pleas made by the joint committee and warning that, in spite of the
foreign credits arranged by the Bank of England, confidence had not been
restored.[32] On the 7th, Sir Ernest Harvey, the deputy governor of the Bank of
England, who was in charge of the Bank while Norman was away ill, wrote to
Snowden to say that in the last four weeks the Bank had lost more than £60
million in gold and foreign exchange; that it now had almost no foreign exchange left, apart from the credits it had received from Paris and New York;
and that 'If the flood does not abate we cannot maintain ourselves long.' The
only solution was a 'rapid readjustment of the budgetary position'; already the
time available to carry out such a readjustment might be 'much shorter than
recently seemed likely'.[33] Snowden sent Harvey's letter to MacDonald in the

overnight pouch to Lossiemouth, and accompanied it with an equally alarming covering letter of his own:

The action of the three Central Banks in arranging the £50 m. credit has not had the desired effect and the Bank is still losing gold and foreign exchange very heavily. At the present rate the point of exhaustion will come very soon with disastrous consequences. The panic of two days ago was due to a passing misunderstanding but the root causes remain. You will note in the Deputy Governor's letter that the Treasury Advisory Committee of the Bank (consisting of the most experienced bankers and financiers) attribute that root cause to the belief of foreigners that our budgetary position is unsound and until that is remedied, or until there is evidence that we are taking drastic steps to set it right this uneasiness abroad will continue ... Whatever real foundation there may be for this impression abroad there can be no doubt about its reality and it is up to us to take immediate action to remove it as far as possible. I doubt if we can wait until the date we have fixed for the meeting of the Cabinet Economy Committee on the 25th. The collapse is almost certain to come before then if we delay ...

I have been thinking seriously and constantly about the whole situation these last few days, and the more I think the more I am convinced of the terrible gravity of it ... Three millions of unemployed is certain in the near future and four millions next year is not out of the question. We are getting very near exhausting our borrowing powers for unemployment, and the only course will be to try to raise money for the unemployed grants by a Public Loan for the purpose which, I am sure would be a failure, and in that event would be an admission of national bankruptcy.

Would it be possible to get the Committee together as soon as possible? We cannot allow matters to drift into utter chaos, and we are perilously near that.[34]

Thus, by August 8th, MacDonald had been presented with two sharply conflicting diagnoses and two diametrically opposing remedies. On one side was Keynes: on the other, the feverish cohorts of the City and the Treasury, followed, rather less feverishly, by Hubert Henderson. Keynes believed that the parity was doomed and that it was a waste of time to defend it. Henderson believed that it could be saved and was still worth fighting for. Harvey and the bankers were so convinced of its necessity that they did not even discuss the possibility of abandoning it. Keynes wanted to suspend gold convertibility and to devalue by 25 per cent, as a preliminary to 'organising prosperity' at home and abroad. The others wanted to restore foreign confidence in sterling by balancing the budget and carrying out big cuts in Government expenditure. So far, MacDonald had contrived to follow a middle way between the harsh orthodoxies of the past and the still untried doctrines of the future. Now he had reached a crossroads where he had to choose between them.

There is no evidence about the way in which he saw his dilemma, but it is not difficult to guess what his reactions must have been. He was a profoundly cautious man. He was also a brave and patriotic one, with an almost masochistic sense of duty. Like most prime ministers, he saw himself as the ultimate custodian of the nation's interests. If his Government allowed Britain's credit to crash in the way that Germany's had done only three weeks before, his colleagues would be able to shelter behind him. The responsibility would be his, morally as well as politically. Seven months before, he had been convinced that cuts in expenditure were needed to avoid a crisis: now that the crisis had come, it must have appeared to him as a dreadful confirmation of the common-sense assumption that unbalanced budgets would sooner or later lead to bankruptcy. Forty years later, it is easy to see that Keynes's solution was, in fact, more prudent as well as pleasanter than the alternative. To MacDonald it probably seemed both rash and cowardly—rash because it appeared to carry the risk of a complete collapse of the currency of the kind which had just occurred in Germany; cowardly, because it offered yet another escape from the hard realities which had been evaded so often in the past. How and when MacDonald's decision was taken is uncertain: perhaps, like many momentous decisions, it was not taken consciously at all, but was slipped into little by little as events drove on. But, whether consciously taken or not, the consequences became clear all too soon. Keynes's advice was rejected; within a few days, the Government's future had been staked on a defence of the parity. It was the most tragic, as well as the most disastrous, mistake of MacDonald's life.

III

Few questioned his decision at the time. On August 7th, when Snowden's letter was written, MacDonald was staying at Rogart, a village in the depths of Sutherland, where he had been discussing war debts and disarmament with Stimson, who happened to be there on holiday.[35] On the 8th he went back to Lossiemouth, where he found Snowden's message waiting for him. As he described it later in his diary:

> Telephoned wd. leave on Monday or before if necessary. Later, told Monday wd. do & Chan: see me on Tuesday.—Met Chancellor 11.20 a.m. & found gloomier prospect than ever. Deputy Gov: & Sir Peacock came at our request 12.40, adjourned for lunch, I having fixed up to see Mr. McKenna, met again at 3 p.m. & sat till 4.30. Their position was: The credit of dollars & francs being badly run on & have not established confidence; Bank considering how much more it is justified in using or whether it is hopeless to try & keep £; situation got beyond them & only Govt. can act. We pressed them to say what they meant. Reply: the failure to balance Budget is forfeiting confidence in sterling; something shd. be done at once to prove that

Budget is to be balanced. A renewed declaration not enough but at same time full details not required. H. of C. might meet. I pointed out how damaging that might be unless simultaneously with summoning it the Govt. announced its programme. They said something wd. have to be done within a few days – a fortnight at the outside. They wished to see representatives of the Opposition & we said they ought. Sir Peacock thought that some small point about floating debt might be dealt with & have a good psychological effect; also Import Tax for Revenue; also some saving though not exactly on my lines. – Then discussed with Chancellor and decided to call Cab: Sub. Comm: for tomorrow afternoon & next day; work at details maybe separately during week-end; return Monday & come to conclusions; see representatives of other parties – but precise course to be determined at Cab: Sub:[36]

The economy committee duly met on August 12th, and again on the 13th. It was then adjourned until Monday the 17th, and met again on the 18th. No minutes were taken, and no contemporaneous record of its proceedings survives. But although some of the details are obscure, there is not much doubt about what took place. Presumably at the first meeting, Snowden gave his colleagues a Treasury estimate which suggested that on current policies the budget deficit would be £170 million, and not £120 million, as the May committee had forecast.[37] According to his diary, MacDonald 'proposed "the 1924 standards" as a basis for working out a scheme of economy & value of money eg. cuts in unempt. pay and reductions in fixed income by taxation'.[38] Meanwhile, he had told the press that the Government was 'of one mind' in its determination to balance the budget.[39] Thus, it must have been clear from the first that Mac-Donald and Snowden, at least, wished to end the crisis by eliminating the budget deficit rather than by devaluation. Though there were to be fierce disagreements later about the way in which it was to be achieved, this fundamental objective does not appear to have been discussed, much less opposed.

To judge by MacDonald's diary, the first disagreements appeared at the third meeting on August 17th. As he noted later:

Travelled overnight: arrived 7.30 a.m. & after breakfast went to work. Chancellor has found week-end all too brief for preparations & I found a letter from him saying he would not be able to meet Liberals & Tories tomorrow as arranged, so I sent messages to Chamberlain, Samuel & Maclean accordingly. When letters & papers dealt with slept a little over 'John Knox' – a very smart but prejudiced book with little critical judgement on the mystery of personality – not an easy matter as regards simple & ordinary men but one requiring some genius in understanding as regards those of great power & at the helm of life. – At last 4 o'clock & the meeting of the Cabinet Sub Committee on Economy … When we began Henderson at once showed his hand. He wanted the whole scheme. I pointed out that we had met to make it. He objected to the sacrifices being on one side – his reason alleged being that we were to discuss savings first. I said that first or last we should have to discuss them. Then he launched out into eloquence on the inadequacy of the unempd. grants & what we had all said for 30 yrs. We pointed out that this was a special crisis & we hoped temporary: that if the income was not there, there could not be the expenditure. He could not reply but lapsed into sulky silence for a time & we went on with business. It was a bitter day & grievous is our just complaint against Providence. We dispersed at 10 o'clock having ticked down expenditure provisionally by £87,000,000 per annum.[40]

Next day there were more disagreements. 'Long discussion from 10.30–1 & 2.30–6, reducing our salaries & imposing new taxes,' MacDonald noted. 'I am disappointed & disheartened. Discussed a revenue tax, 4 in favour & the Chancellor against.'[41]

A fuller account can be constructed with the help of other sources. The Treasury's records make it clear that Snowden wanted to raise approximately £90 million from increased taxation and to cut expenditure by £99 million. £67 million was to come from unemployment insurance, £12 million from education and the rest from the armed services, roads and a variety of smaller programmes. The £67 million cut in unemployment insurance expenditure was to come from three main sources – a 20 per cent cut in the standard rate of benefit, to yield nearly £15 million; an increase in contributions, to yield £10 million; and a cut in the exchequer cost of transitional benefit, to yield £23 million.[42] According to a memorandum by Graham, written after the fall of the Government, Henderson urged that taxation should be considered before economy so as to make sure that the cuts were as small as possible. When this course was rejected, he and Graham insisted that 'they were merely engaged in a preliminary examination; after that examination there would be a report to the Cabinet, not necessarily with specific recommendations.' They also objected to the proposed cut in unemployment benefit, which was eventually deleted. According to Graham, the revenue tariff was voted on twice, and not once, as implied in MacDonald's diary. First, the committee rejected it by four votes to one. Then it decided, also by four to one, that it was preferable to a cut in unemployment benefit. On taxation, Graham added, Snowden explained in general terms that £67 million would have to come from direct taxation, including 'further differentiation against unearned income'.[43]

The committee's report was presented to the Cabinet on August 19th. With one big exception, it conformed fairly closely to the Treasury's original proposals. Taxation was now to yield £89 million as against £90 million, and economies £78·5 million as against £99 million. The cut in education expenditure had been slightly reduced, and the cut in defence expenditure increased. The only significant change was that unemployment insurance was to be cut by

£43·5 million, instead of by £67 million. The rate of benefit was to remain unaltered. £10 million was to come from increased contributions, £3 million from so-called 'anomalies', £8 million from reducing the benefit period to 26 weeks, £20 million from transitional benefit and £2·5 million from an item entitled 'premium'.[44] According to a note in MacDonald's papers by R. B. Howorth, who was acting as Cabinet secretary in Hankey's absence on holiday, the cut in transitional benefit was to be achieved by transferring £20 million of the total cost of transitional benefit from the exchequer to the poor law authorities – thus adding to the burden on the rates and throwing at least some of those receiving transitional benefit on to public assistance. The 'premium' – which had been 'most vigorously pressed by Mr. Henderson' – was a flat deduction of 1s. a week from all unemployment benefits, and amounted to a small cut in benefit under another name.[45]

The report's status was soon to be the subject of fierce controversy. As we have seen, Graham claimed later that he and Henderson had insisted that they would take part only in a 'preliminary examination'; Henderson, he wrote, had made it clear from the first that he could be committed to nothing until he had seen 'the complete picture'. Henderson made the same claim, in almost the same words. Their claims were strongly disputed by Howorth. The committee's report, he pointed out in a memorandum to MacDonald, had been approved unanimously; in a detailed commentary on the speech in which Henderson's claim was made, he added, 'No record can be traced of Mr. Henderson's statement that he would reserve his decision until he saw the complete picture. No such reservation is recorded in connection with the list of economies first proposed by the Cabinet Committee, and he was present at every meeting of that Committee.'[46] The Cabinet records tell the same story – or, rather, non-story. The Cabinet paper containing the committee's report consists merely of a list of figures and says nothing about reservations on the part of those who produced it. The Cabinet minutes for the meeting at which the report was discussed say that a memorandum was circulated 'containing suggestions for balancing the Budget, prepared by the Cabinet Committee, under the Chairmanship of the Prime Minister'; they too say nothing about reservations. The summary of conclusions at the end of the minutes says that some members of the Cabinet 'intimated that their acceptance of the proposed economies was conditional on effect being given ... to the proposals concerning direct taxation';[47] Henderson may have been one of these. Even if he was, this does not imply that he was still waiting for the 'complete picture', but that he already possessed it and wanted to make sure that there was no departure from it.

In fact, the 'picture' contained in the committee's report was as complete as anyone could expect it to be. A member of the committee which had drawn it up could reasonably insist that he could not be committed to any individual item unless the other items were carried out as well. He could hardly insist that he needed further information before deciding whether or not he agreed with it, since all the relevant information was available to him already. In a strictly constitutional sense, no doubt, the report did not bind its authors in the way that Cabinet decisions are held to bind the members of a government. As Graham's memorandum and the Cabinet minutes both make clear, the committee did not make decisions or even recommendations, but only 'suggestions'. The fact remains that it sat for many hours and produced a unanimous report at the end. Whatever private reservations Henderson may have had, he did not vote against the report; he did not even insist that his reservations should be recorded in the minutes. In these circumstances, his colleagues on the committee were entitled to assume that, even if he did not agree with it, he was at any rate willing to accept it and stand by it.

Yet it would be a mistake to conclude that Henderson's claim was altogether groundless. He was by no means the plaster saint that later Labour mythology made him out to be, but he was not the man to break his word once he had given it. He knew nothing of economics or finance, and lacked the intellectual self-confidence to question the Treasury's underlying strategy or to put forward an alternative strategy of his own. But although he allowed the report to go through, it is quite conceivable that he may have made a verbal reservation of some sort, no doubt in fairly ambiguous terms, which meant one thing to him and another to his colleagues. In any case, it seems clear that whatever the other members of the committee may have thought, he did not regard the report as binding and did not believe that he was morally committed to it. Not for the first or the last time in political history, muddle and confusion at an early stage of a crisis were to provide an ideal breeding ground for suspicion and bitterness later.

The Cabinet began its consideration of the economy committee's report at 11 a.m. on August 19th, and sat until 10.30 p.m., with only brief intervals. According to the minutes, MacDonald, Snowden and other unnamed members of the committee 'explained the grave character of the financial position, the reasons for immediate action and the various measures, designed to secure budgetary equilibrium, which in the view of the Committee must be taken forthwith if public confidence at home and abroad is to be re-established'. Once again, this fundamental objective was not questioned. Conclusion 1 of the minutes explicitly states that the Cabinet adopted the committee's conclusion 'that the Budget must be balanced by the application of a common sacrifice and effort'. The committee's proposals for increasing taxation were also accepted, as were most of the departmental economies.[48] In other respects, the proceedings were less harmonious. Most of the day was taken up in discussing a revenue tariff, though whether as an addition to the economy committee's package or as an alternative to part of it is not clear. In the end, five of those present said that they would support a tariff on all imports and ten that they would support one on manufactured goods only.[49] But, presumably because the minority included Snowden, whose resignation at this point could be expected to deal a disastrous blow to foreign confidence, it was agreed that the discussion should be adjourned until the 21st. An even fiercer battle took place over unemployment insurance. The economy committee's decision to maintain the standard rate of benefit was endorsed, but its proposals for saving £20 million on transitional benefit were turned down, on the grounds that they would inflict too heavy a burden on the local authorities. After a long argument, it was agreed that a sub-committee should be set up under Margaret Bondfield to see whether the same amount of money could be saved by spending the proceeds of the 'premium' on transitional benefit, together with the proceeds of a further increase of 2d. a week on employees' insurance contributions.[50]

As so often, the Cabinet had ducked the two most difficult problems. Yet when the meeting broke up, it still made sense to hope that an agreed solution could be reached by the end of the week, and that it could then be carried through Parliament. Twenty-four hours later, it was clear that such hopes had been built on sand. At 10 a.m. on August 20th, MacDonald and Snowden met Chamberlain, Hoare, Samuel and MacLean and told them the size of the projected deficit and the broad outlines of the Government's proposals. Chamberlain and Hoare declared that the proposed savings in unemployment insurance were hopelessly inadequate; all four opposition leaders insisted, as Snowden put it at the Cabinet meeting that evening, 'that they could not possibly contemplate the imposition of new taxation of the order of £100 million'. During the afternoon, MacDonald had another meeting with Chamberlain, who insisted that there was no hope of restoring confidence unless the economy programme were increased by around £30 million. Even more ominous was the outcome of a similar meeting between Graham and Samuel. In the past, the Liberals had usually come to the Government's rescue at moments of crisis. Now Samuel made it clear that they too demanded 'drastic action' on unemployment insurance, including a cut in benefit.[51]

The next few hours brought still gloomier tidings. The Cabinet met again at 8.30. After Snowden, MacDonald and Graham had reported on their various meetings with the opposition leaders, and Henderson had reported on a meeting he had had with the parliamentary Labour Party consultative committee, Margaret Bondfield announced the results of her committee's investigations. The 'premium', she reported, had turned out to be impractical; an additional 2d. a week on employees' contributions would yield only £4 million; another £5 million could be saved by making transitional benefit subject to a means test. This, she added, left another £19 million to be found in other ways. Her report provoked a violent outburst from Snowden, who pointed out that her committee had been appointed to save £20 million and had made a net saving of £4 million. As a result, the exchequer was to be saved a total of only £52 million, leaving a gap of £118 million to be filled by taxation. After a brief and unhappy discussion, in which no decisions were taken, the meeting was then adjourned until the following morning.[52]

There followed the most critical confrontation of the week. At three o'clock that afternoon, the economy committee had taken part in a joint meeting with the T.U.C. General Council and the Labour Party Executive. The National Executive had decided to leave matters with the Government, but the General Council was less tractable. It insisted on another meeting, and appointed a deputation to put its views to the Cabinet; and when the Cabinet dispersed at 9.30, the economy committee stayed behind to meet the T.U.C deputation. The T.U.C.'s opening barrage was fired by Citrine. The T.U.C., he declared uncompromisingly, could not 'acquiesce in new burdens on the unemployed'. Nor could it acquiesce in reducing the pay of teachers and policemen. Instead, it suggested that fixed-interest securities should be subject to a special tax, that an attempt should be made to reduce the burden of war debt and that the sinking fund should be suspended. As for a revenue tariff, the General Council had discussed the question, but had come to the conclusion that it was a matter of policy which only the annual congress could decide. Citrine was followed by Bevin, who made many of the same points in rougher language, and who ended by emphasizing that the General Council felt 'that the Government's proposals meant a continuance of the deflation policy, and to that the Council were opposed'. In reply, Snowden declared, as uncompromisingly, 'that if sterling went the whole international financial structure would collapse, and there would be no comparison between the present depression and the chaos and ruin that would face us'. After Bevin had denied this, and Snowden had insisted that Bevin was wrong, the meeting broke up without even a flicker of agreement.[53] The economy committee stayed behind to discuss the position, but to scant effect. The T.U.C. deputation, MacDonald noted later,

included Hayday, Citrine, Bevin, Pugh, Walkden M.P. Their statement was that they were not to support the policy indicated by us in the afternoon, that we could balance the Budget by taxing the rentier, suspending the Sinking Fund (all) & such like, but no economies. Chancellor replied & I observed that all I had to say was that their observations did not touch our problem arising out of immediate financial necessity. They withdrew. It was practically a declaration of war. I was very tired & snatched a few minutes' rest whilst Henderson once more told us what he had proposed days ago & how everything had been initiated by him – except the things opposed by the T.U.C. people. He surrendered. He proposed to balance the Budget with insignificant economies, keeping the Unemployed assistance what it is now (except perhaps £5 mill: of combing & the £3 m. gained already by anomalies), suspending Sinking Funds (which he stated many times was his proposal made days ago admitting that he was only now aware that some were statutory) & putting on a revenue tariff. How tired of it all one feels. We had a rather pointless discussion without concentration on the one point of any importance: 'Are we to go on?' Henderson

never showed his vanity & ignorance more painfully. I told them to go to
bed & we rose at 11 p.m. I was depressed & saw nothing but a great humiliation to us all. The T.U.C. undoubtedly voice the feeling of the mass of
workers. They do not know & their minds are rigid & think of superficial
appearances & so grasping at the shadow lose the bone.[54]

IV

So far, MacDonald had been grappling with a financial crisis. Now he faced a
political crisis as well; and for the next four days these two crises reacted on, and
exacerbated, each other. The opposition leaders had made it clear that the
Government's proposals would be turned down unless bigger cuts were made
in unemployment insurance than those proposed by the economy committee.
The Cabinet had rejected the economy committee's proposals for cutting transitional benefit. Margaret Bondfield's committee had discovered that there was
no more palatable way of cutting unemployment expenditure by the same
amount. The T.U.C. had shown that it would oppose any cuts, not merely in
unemployment insurance, but in any of the social services. Henderson had retreated from the totals which he had accepted, however grudgingly, two days
before. Meanwhile, the reserves had continued to pour away. On August 11th,
Harvey and Peacock had told MacDonald and Snowden that something would
have to be done within a fortnight if the parity was to be held. Ten days of the
fortnight had gone; and no decision was in sight. In his memorandum to Mac-
Donald earlier in the month, Hubert Henderson had conceded that the dangers
involved in leaving the gold standard could be exaggerated. Before long, he was
writing that the choice did not lie between holding the parity and devaluing
by 10 or even 20 per cent, but between staying on gold and letting loose 'a real
dégringolade', which would lead to a 'complete collapse of the currency, after the
manner of the mark and the rouble', unless it were halted by far harsher cuts
than any so far contemplated.[55] Henderson was a cautious man, not given to
exaggeration and by no means wedded to Treasury orthodoxy. If the threat of
a *dégringolade* had come to seem real and immediate to him, it must have seemed
far more so to others. In that shadow, fears which had been acute enough to
start with began to verge on panic; as the tension rose, tempers frayed and
suspicions multiplied. The bankers' demands for action became more insistent,
and the resistance to them more stubborn and resentful; the differences in the
Cabinet hardened into deadlock; the longer the deadlock lasted, the closer the
shadow of a *dégringolade* approached.
 All this creates great difficulties for the historian. As their divisions deepened,
the tired and angry men who faced each other across the Cabinet table must
have found it harder and harder to remember from one day to the next exactly
what they had decided and exactly what arguments had been advanced; when

the dust had settled, memories were already beginning to be distorted by hind-sight and wishful thinking. Yet, if we are to understand the way in which the crisis developed, and still more the way in which it was resolved, we must see it as the protagonists saw it at the time, and not as they afterwards wished or imagined that they had seen it. The most important point to grasp is that the political crisis which had now been superimposed on the financial crisis had been provoked by a protest against the consequences of the economy committee's decision to hold the parity, not by a challenge to the decision itself. In his addendum to the Macmillan report in July, Bevin had suggested that even a unilateral devaluation would be better than continued deflation. Probably under his influence, the General Council followed his example in September. At the crucial meeting between the T.U.C. deputation and the economy committee, however, his position was much less clear-cut. He denied that 'chaos and ruin' would follow if Britain were forced off gold. He did not suggest that the parity should be allowed to go, or deny that measures of some sort should be taken to hold it. Bevin and Citrine were expansionists by instinct, and it is clear that they felt in their bones that the Government's strategy was economically mistaken as well as socially unjust. But although they and their colleagues on the General Council were soon to hammer out a more promising alternative strategy, they had not done so when they arrived at Downing Street in the evening of August 20th.

What is true of the arguments between the economy committee and the T.U.C. is more obviously true of the arguments in the Cabinet. On August 19th, it had implicitly endorsed the economy committee's recommendation that confidence in sterling should be restored, and had decided explicitly that the budget should be balanced. In all the disputes that followed, that decision went unchallenged. There were fierce arguments about the size and nature of the economies needed to eliminate the deficit, but there is no evidence that any member of the Cabinet denied that it should be eliminated somehow. Yet, as Hubert Henderson had pointed out,[56] the sole argument for balancing the budget was that there was no other way to restore confidence in sterling. The object of the exercise was to reassure the foreign holders of sterling who were withdraw-ing their money from London: to carry it out in a way that failed to reassure them would be a waste of time. Already, the joint committee of the accepting houses and the British Bankers' Association had told MacDonald and Snowden that confidence could not be restored without big cuts in Government expendi-ture. Before long, Sir Ernest Harvey made it clear that he agreed.[57] In giving this advice, Harvey and the other bankers were, of course, expressing their own political prejudices: to that extent, later charges that the Government had been faced with a 'bankers' ramp' contained an element of truth. But the 'ramp' was not a conscious one. The bankers' prejudices were shared by the other central banks and by the rest of the international financial community as well: if Harvey wanted to know how foreign sterling holders would react to the Government's proposals, his own instinctive reactions provided an ideal litmus paper. The choice did not lie between taking the Bank of England's advice and balancing the budget in some less obnoxious way. It lay between taking the Bank's advice and abandoning the gold standard. And although most Labour people later came to believe that the gold standard could have been abandoned after all, no member of the Cabinet said so at the time.

Thus the Government was trapped. At the beginning of the week, the economy committee had agreed that expenditure had to be cut by £80 million. Then the savings on transitional benefit were struck out by the Cabinet. The total savings now stood at less than £60 million, and the savings on unemployment insurance at around £20 million. It soon became clear that these figures were too small to satisfy the Bank of England or, *a fortiori*, the foreign sterling holders; and that they could be increased significantly only if a large part of the rejected cut in expenditure on unemployment insurance were replaced. Margaret Bondfield, the departmental minister concerned, was strongly opposed to the economy committee's original suggestion that the exchequer cost of transitional benefit should be cut by £20 million, on the grounds that it would mean transferring the able-bodied uninsured unemployed to the poor law.[58] She was, however, prepared to accept a cut in the rate of unemployment benefit proper as a lesser evil; and it was on this that the pressure for economy now concentrated.

In practice, then, the choice lay between abandoning the parity and cutting unemployment benefit. No member of the Cabinet wished to abandon the parity: in logic, no member of the Cabinet could oppose cutting unemployment benefit. Yet that conclusion struck savagely at the deepests instinct of the Labour movement. For most Labour men and women, the unemployed were not candidates for charity but victims of injustice; the traditional slogan of 'work or maintenance' was the expression, not merely of humanitarian sentiment, but of class solidarity reflected in a social philosophy. Hence the legislation liberalizing the conditions for obtaining unemployment benefit, which the Government had introduced in its first few months of office. Hence the Cabinet's long rearguard action against the opposition parties' clamour for economies. And hence the mingled sense of guilt and outrage which many ministers must have felt when they were told that the crisis could be ended only by cutting expenditure on unemployment insurance. The unemployed had been victimized already by being thrown out of work: to victimize them all over again, in order to find a way out of a crisis which was none of their making, would be to make a mockery of everything the Labour Party stood for.

As the meeting with the T.U.C. had shown, it would also cause harsh dissensions in the party and impose unprecedented strains on the links between the party and the unions. For Henderson, in particular, this was probably the decisive consideration. Henderson was, by instinct, a man of the majority – a minister in the wartime coalition when the consensus of trade-union opinion was in favour of the fight to the finish, and an opponent of Lloyd George's when it swung behind a compromise peace; a Lib-Lab in ideology before the war, and one of the architects of Labour's commitment to public ownership in 1918. Policy and ideology were secondary concerns for him: what mattered was to keep the 'movement' together. Though he had opposed the Treasury's original proposal to cut unemployment benefit by 20 per cent, he had accepted the savage £20 million cut in transitional benefit and had not only accepted, but had pressed vigorously for, the 'premium'. Not only then, but later, he agreed that confidence in sterling should be restored and that the budget had to be balanced to restore it. There is no evidence that he shared Bevin's scepticism about the dangers of a forced devaluation; to judge by his public utterances, at least, he was as anxious to defend the gold standard as were Snowden and MacDonald. But once the T.U.C. had spoken, these considerations hardly counted. As he saw it, the question at stake now was how to save the 'movement', not how to end the crisis. The T.U.C. had made it clear that if the Cabinet took the Bank of England's advice and returned to the economy committee's totals, the 'movement' might be smashed. For Henderson, only one conclusion was possible. Rather than do what the bankers wanted, Labour should hand over responsibility to the Conservatives and Liberals and leave office as a united party. Though the details of the Cabinet's discussions are not known, it seems clear that at the meetings on August 19th and 20th Henderson had either sided with MacDonald and Snowden or kept silent. Now he swung into opposition to them; and the group of ministers who had opposed the economy committee's proposals from the start[59] found themselves with a leader as well as with a cause.

MacDonald's initial reaction to the meeting with the T.U.C. did not differ from Henderson's as much as might have been expected. As we have seen, the first question that occurred to him after the meeting was 'Are we to go on?' But what Henderson saw as a moral imperative was, for MacDonald, a fleeting temptation. Like Henderson, he had spent his life in the Labour Party: like Henderson, he knew that it could not last for long without trade-union money and trade-union votes. But his conception of the party and of its proper relationship with the unions was sharply opposed to Henderson's. For Henderson, the party and the unions were different limbs of the same body: for MacDonald, they were partners, whose aims might overlap but by no means coincided. The unions represented a series of sectional interest-groups; the party represented – or sought to represent – the nation as a whole. The party's voters and the unions' members might come from the same class; to a large extent, they might be the same people. That was irrelevant, for the party represented them as citizens, not as members of a class. All his life, MacDonald had fought against a class view of politics, and for the primacy of political action as against industrial; for him, the logical corollary was that the party must be prepared, when necessary, to subordinate the sectional claims of the unions to its own conception of the national interest. It was under that banner that he had fought

59 Ticker-tape parade in New York, October, 1929

60 Lord Sankey and A. V. Alexander demonstrating Labour's respectability

61 The second Labour Government at ease, 1929. *Left to right:* Graham, MacDonald, Adamson, Wedgwood Benn, Lansbury, Greenwood, Alexander, Snowden, Noel Buxton, Parmoor, Shaw, Clynes, Thomas

62 Birthday treat – with Winston Churchill in New York, October, 1929

63 Broadcasting from No. 10

64 With Margaret Bondfield, the first woman Cabinet minister, in the garden of No. 10

Richard Bell and the Lib-Labs when the party was in its infancy. He had fought the same battle during the war, when the unions, as he saw it, had betrayed the cause of internationalism and peace to gather the crumbs from the coalition's table. It seemed to him that he now had to fight it again. The nation was hastening towards the worst financial crisis in its history, and the unions were trying to make it impossible for the party to avert disaster. If it had been necessary to resist them in the past, it was even more necessary now. For the party was now in Government, and a Government that flinched from doing what it believed to be necessary for fear of offending the sectional interests closest to it would have betrayed its charge. A Labour Government that did so would also have destroyed the party's claim to be considered as a governing party in future.

It is doubtful if the gulf between MacDonald and Henderson could have been bridged if they had liked and trusted each other. In fact, their relations had deteriorated steadily ever since they had taken office. During Henderson's visit to Paris, new salt had been poured into old wounds; now they viewed each other through an acrid fog of incomprehension and mistrust, in which differences of attitude looked like symptoms of delinquency and shifts of opinion like acts of treachery. To Henderson, MacDonald's unwillingness to abandon a policy which seemed bound to split the Labour Party must have appeared arrogant, disloyal and, in the deepest sense, frivolous. To MacDonald, Henderson's change of front after the meeting with the T.U.C. appeared cowardly, hypocritical and opportunistic — the product of a deep-seated inability to stand up to be counted in an unpopular cause and, still more, of an ill-concealed ambition to seize the party leadership. In attack, MacDonald often vacillated, but when he believed that others were attacking him his instinct was to dig in and fight it out. So it was now. He believed with growing desperation that only sweeping cuts in expenditure could save the country from bankruptcy, and would in any case have fought hard to push his policies through. He fought all the harder because he thought that the unions were trying to dictate to him, and that his chief rival in the Cabinet was trying to stab him in the back.

Immediately after the meeting with the T.U.C., he had been half-prepared to throw in his hand. By the morning of August 21st, however, he had recovered his nerve. 'Not a bad night and woke in fighting mood,' he noted grimly. 'If we yield now to the T.U.C. we shall never be able to call our bodies or souls or intelligences our own.'[60] At 10 a.m. the Cabinet met to discuss the previous night's meeting with the General Council. MacDonald announced that he had met Harvey earlier that morning, and that Harvey had told him that it was necessary, not merely to balance the budget, but to balance it by means of 'very substantial economies' — covering half the estimated deficit and including big cuts in the cost of unemployment insurance. Since swift action might have to be taken at any moment, it was imperative for the Government to remain in office; accordingly, the Cabinet should proceed with its programme and include in it 'sufficient economies to restore public confidence'. After a long

AI

argument, the Cabinet decided to reject the T.U.C.'s representations and to review its list of economies with the aim of 'bringing them into conformity with the conditions laid down by the Prime Minister'. But although MacDonald had won the first round, it soon became clear that he had little chance of winning the match. The question that mattered was how to increase the savings on unemployment insurance from a figure around £22 million to one closer to the economy committee's £43·5 million. Three possibilities were suggested, though by whom is not clear — a cut of 5 per cent in unemployment benefit, to yield about £6 million; a cut of 10 per cent, to yield £12·5; and a cut of 11½ per cent, to correspond with the fall in the cost of living since the Government had taken office and to yield £15 million. There was no support for the 11½ per cent cut, while the 5 per cent cut was rejected on the grounds that the yield was so small that it was not worth making. On the 10 per cent, however, the Cabinet was equally divided:[61] and, as MacDonald put it in his diary, he and Snowden 'told them that their proposals were now impossible but that we should consult the reps. of the Bank of England & of the other two political parties'.[62]

The critical decision had now been taken, yet with the forlorn tenacity that sometimes afflicts a deadlocked committee, the Cabinet continued to plod laboriously through the list of economies which had emerged from its previous meetings — making minor changes here and there, and in the end producing a total of £56 million.[63] The next few hours must have been among the most harrowing of the week. MacDonald and Snowden presented the new total to Harvey and Peacock at 4.15. As might have been expected, Harvey and Peacock said that it was inadequate, and that it would probably make the position worse rather than better. More alarmingly, they also said that if the drain went on at the existing rate, the reserves would last for only four more days; that it was essential to obtain substantial credits from New York and Paris; and that unless the Cabinet raised its bid they could 'make no change in the present situation.'[64]

The next arrivals at Downing Street were the opposition leaders, Chamberlain, Hoare, Samuel and Maclean. The day before, they had been led to believe that the Cabinet intended to make economies of £78 million, and to cut unemployment insurance by £48 million. Now they were told that the total had been reduced to £56 million and the cuts in unemployment insurance to £22 million. They asked whether this was the Government's last word and were told that it was. Then they asked what would happen if the measures failed to restore confidence. Snowden replied, 'the deluge'. It is hardly surprising that the opposition leaders should have been taken aback. They asked if they could consult together in private, and retired to MacDonald's room upstairs. After a brief interval, they returned together and announced that the Government's proposals were 'wholly unsatisfactory' and that they would join forces to defeat them as soon as Parliament reassembled. They also urged that Parliament should be summoned as soon as possible and warned that if the crisis occurred before then 'the sole responsibility must rest with the Government.' Finally, they suggested that the King should be consulted and they asked if they could discuss the position with their colleagues and return later that evening.[65]

At 6.15 MacDonald gave a report of the meeting to the few Cabinet ministers who could still be found, after which it was agreed that a full Cabinet should be held next morning.[66] At 9.30, he and Snowden met the opposition leaders again. Chamberlain declared that if these were indeed the Government's final proposals, the two opposition parties would 'turn them out immediately the House met'; that the crash would come before then; that it was MacDonald's duty to avoid the crash; and that the Conservatives would 'give him any support in our power for that purpose, either with his present or in a reconstructed government'. Samuel followed in similar terms, adding that it would be dangerous to delay a solution even for the weekend. MacDonald's response was far from clear. According to Chamberlain, he 'began by drawing a touching picture of his own position', and then said that he would remain as prime minister and 'invite his colleagues to support him, and tell those who would not that they might go when they liked'. According to Hoare, he 'implied ... that he was ready to break with the dissidents and carry on as best he could', but made it clear that he felt the task would be beyond him.[67] MacDonald's diary suggests that it was Chamberlain and Samuel who made the running, and that he said little in reply. Chamberlain, he noted,

> reported colleagues supported what I had been told earlier, & would oppose proposals; wished House called at once when both parties would oppose. Warned me of immediate crisis & begged if we could not agree together that I see the King at once & report & advise. Wished to add if I wished to form a govt. with their cooperation they were willing to serve under me. Sir H. Samuel concurred. I told them I should take all they said into account & wd. see them together after the Cabinet to-morrow. — Liberals at my request returned & I put the position to them in a more intimate way. They said Ll. G. associates himself with what they said & thinks I should ask King to see leaders of other Parties.[68]

V

The bankers' warnings and the opposition leaders' offers had carried the crisis into its final stage. It was no longer a question of restoring the confidence of unknown foreign holders of sterling within an undefined period of time, but of obtaining specified credits from specified sources within a matter of hours. If the credits were not obtained, sterling would crash; if the Cabinet refused to cut unemployment benefit, no credits would be forthcoming; if it stayed in office without obtaining the credits, the crash would be its responsibility. Before MacDonald's meeting with Harvey and Peacock on Friday afternoon, it had decided to stick at a £56 million economy programme, and to present that programme to Parliament when the House was recalled. That decision no longer made sense, for the House could not possibly be recalled before the reserves had run out. If a crash was to be avoided, the Government had either to make more cuts immediately or to leave office immediately. And it was now clear for the first time that if it left office it would be up to MacDonald to decide whether it would be followed by a Conservative–Liberal coalition or by a National Government under his leadership.

For more than a generation, Labour men and women were to take it for granted, not only that MacDonald had betrayed the Labour Party in forming a National Government, but that he had been indecently eager to betray it. No such eagerness can be detected in his behaviour during the critical weekend of August 21st–23rd. Chamberlain and Samuel made their offer on Friday night. So far from accepting it, MacDonald spent most of Saturday and Sunday in a long-drawn-out attempt to persuade his colleagues to stay in office and make the extra economies themselves. When the Cabinet met at 9.30 in the morning of Saturday August 22nd, he reported the conversation he had had the day before with Harvey and Peacock and the opposition leaders, and urged the Cabinet to authorize him to tell them that the Government was now prepared to add another £20 million to the economy programme – 'to be made up as to £12½ millions by a 10 per cent reduction in Unemployment benefit, and as to £7½ millions in other ways'. The Cabinet refused; and Snowden and Thomas asked that their dissent should be recorded in the minutes. After another appeal from MacDonald, however, it was agreed that, on the strict understanding that they were to make no firm commitments, MacDonald and Snowden should find out whether the opposition leaders would, in fact, be satisfied if the economy programme were increased by £20 million, supposing that the Government were prepared to increase it.[69]

From MacDonald's point of view, this characteristically convoluted decision was a step forward, if a small one. During the next few hours he used all his diplomatic skill to inveigle his colleagues into making further steps in the same direction. When the Cabinet met again at 2.30, he reported that he had now sounded out the opposition leaders on their attitude to the possible addition of another £20 million to the economy programme; that the opposition leaders had replied that the question should be put to the financial authorities who would have to raise the proposed loan in Paris and New York; that they had given the impression that if the financial authorities were satisfied, they would be satisfied too; and that he had accordingly asked Harvey to come to Downing Street at three o'clock. The Cabinet, MacDonald urged, should now authorize him to ask Harvey the same question that he had put to the opposition leaders, and should also give Harvey permission to discuss it in confidence with the Federal Reserve Bank in New York. After some muttering, the Cabinet agreed; and after Harvey had undertaken to get in immediate touch with New York, it decided that if the Federal Reserve Bank gave a favourable reply, MacDonald should see the opposition leaders again. It also decided that its next meeting should take place at 7.0 p.m. on Sunday, when MacDonald would report on the bankers' reply and when, if necessary, a final decision would be taken on whether to make the extra economies or not.[70]

Thus, by the afternoon of August 22nd, MacDonald had managed to prise open the door which had been slammed shut on the 21st: having decided against a cut in unemployment benefit only a little more than twenty-four hours before, the Cabinet now found itself poised to decide the matter all over again in twenty-four hours' time. More encouragement arrived at Downing Street during the evening. At seven o'clock Harvey telephoned to say, as one of the secretaries in the private office recorded later, that 'if the three parties back the scheme they might get away with it.' At ten o'clock he telephoned again, to say that the request for a loan had to be addressed to the Government's American bankers, J. P. Morgan & Co., and not to the Federal Reserve Bank; that he would not have the final answer until the following day; but that he was 'not unhopeful'.[71] But although MacDonald's hopes may also have flickered a little, it is unlikely that they rose far. That evening the King left Balmoral for London by the overnight train. MacDonald saw him at Buckingham Palace at 10.30 a.m. on Sunday the 23rd, and told him about the request which had been put to New York. Even if the Americans were prepared to offer credits on the basis of a £76 million economy programme, MacDonald warned, it was possible that Henderson, Graham and other Cabinet ministers would resign rather than accept the necessary cut in unemployment benefit. If they did so, the Government's resignation would be inevitable.[72]

According to Sir Harold Nicolson, the King then decided that the correct constitutional course was to consult the leaders of the Conservative and Liberal Parties. Baldwin had come back from his holiday at Aix-les-Bains the night before, but could not be found until after lunch. Samuel, however, arrived at Buckingham Palace shortly after noon. Samuel told the King that it would be best if the Labour Government carried out the necessary economies itself, but that if that turned out to be impossible, the 'best alternative' would be a National Government, representing all three parties, preferably with Mac-Donald as prime minister. When Baldwin arrived at three o'clock that afternoon, the King asked him whether he would be prepared to serve in a National Government under MacDonald. Baldwin said that he would, and added that if MacDonald insisted on resigning he would also be prepared to form a Government himself, provided he could count on Liberal support.[73]

Nicolson's account, which was based on a note made by the King's private secretary, Sir Clive Wigram, suggests that it was not until he had talked to Samuel that the King decided that a National Government would be the best solution. MacDonald's diary gives a different impression. At some stage after his visit to the Palace MacDonald noted:

Saw King today at 10.30 a.m. Great crowd & cordial reception. King most friendly & expressed thanks & confidence. I then reported situation & at end I told him that after to-night I might be of no further use, & should resign with the whole Cabinet. He asked if I would advise him to send for Henderson. I said 'No', which he said relieved him. I advised him in the meanwhile to send for the leaders of the other two parties & have them report [the] position from their points of view. He said he would & would advise them strongly to support me. I explained my hopeless Parlty. position if there were any number of resignations. He said that he believed I was the only person who could carry the country through. I said that did I share his belief I should not contemplate what I do, but that I did not share it. He expressed horror at an election. I said there would be no election till the crisis was well over & then that so far as I could see, & on the assumption of resignations, no man could avoid it then. He again expressed thanks & sorrow ... Henderson & others (Alexander, Lees Smith, Johnston &c) met after Cabinet yesterday and decided to resign on 10% cut. They will be in good tactical position as Opposition if the crisis is avoided. Am preparing a statement too if I resign to give to the press at once. I commit political suicide to save the crisis. If there is no other way I shall do it as cheerfully as an ancient Jap. Indeed, this morning of sunny weather, my spirits have returned & my heavy weariness has gone. The 'mistress of Upp: Frog: Lodge' has returned and is making love to me. How few people understand the unattractiveness of this place & this office to me. And, curiously enough, were it not so I could not have done what I have.[74]

This makes it clear that, even before his discussion with Samuel, the King was anxious that if the Labour Government resigned, MacDonald should stay in office with Conservative and Liberal support; though it does not say in so many words that he urged MacDonald to form a National Government in such circumstances, it is difficult to see what else he could have meant. More important still, it also makes it clear that MacDonald was reluctant to do anything of the kind and preferred to 'commit political suicide to save the crisis'.

A note made at the time by MacDonald's daughter Sheila gives the same impression. It is dated 'Saturday August 23rd', and describes a conversation at No. 10. Saturday was, in fact, August 22nd; and it seems clear from internal evidence that it must have been on Sunday that the conversation took place. The most important passages in the note are as follows:

Present — Prime Minister
    J. H. Thomas
    Sheila MacDonald ...
Cabinet meeting —
    Definite split — Cabinet v JRM & J.H.T. No grappling with [illegible].
    Cannot face up to difficulties — shirk responsibility. All this sentimentality

about workers is trash. Unemployed must sacrifice too.
Criticism esp of 'a certain person' (Henderson)
   Lees Smith
   Alexander
   Snowden.
'A certain person' playing for leadership of party himself. Thinks Daddy
far too selfish, [illegible] and individual.
Just a chance for agreement if America agrees to 10% employment [*sic*]
reduction – that is if Bk. of Eng. will be able to borrow money. Constvs.
will support Govt. on this condition. Three possibilities for Daddy –
   1) Resign along with Cabinet & lead Oppost. but oppost. wld. be insincere
as he wants drastic economy – moreover, hostile following.
   2) P.M. of coalition govt. (this is what King wants). Wld. have to face
whole antagonism of Labour movt. Seeming desertion of principle & playing for office. Lose hold of party – this what 'a certain person' wants.
   3) Resign leadership – be independent member below gangway. Both
PM & J.H.T. incline to support this view. Must make statement to country
– carry unemployment reduction & resign as not complete agreement. No
cowardice no playing for office. Adherence to principles ...[75]

MacDonald's son, Malcolm, who was on holiday in Lossiemouth at the time,
but who spoke to his father on the telephone every day during the crisis, formed
the same impression of MacDonald's intentions as did Sheila. On August 22nd,
he noted that his father had telephoned at lunchtime and that 'He feels pretty
certain that he will resign either tonight or tomorrow.' On the 23rd, MacDonald
telephoned Malcolm again and afterwards Malcolm noted:

J.R.M. on telephone at breakfast time ... Says he managed to persuade the
Cabinet to let him go ahead sounding the Opposition leaders and the
bankers on the proposals which he advocated. His colleagues, I gather, did
not commit themselves to accept the proposals even if the Opposition
leaders and bankers were fairly friendly to them (though the communiqué
says the Cabinet have been putting the finishing touches to a plan 'which,
it is believed, will meet the situation ... ') but agreed to consider the situation when the PM reported back to them. This he will do at seven o'clock
this evening. After the Cabinet meeting yesterday afternoon he saw the
Opposition leaders. They thought the plan did not go far enough. The
P.M. said that was all they would get from him. They agreed not to oppose
it. He saw the representative (or representatives?) of the Bank of England.
He (or they?) said it did not go as far as he could have wished, but it might
be enough. Was it sufficient for the raising of a loan? the P.M. asked. The
reply was that it might be, but that soundings would have to be made first.
These soundings are to be made, and the representative of the Bank
promised to let the P.M. know the result as early as possible. Already last

night the P.M. had heard that the position was hopeful, but final information was to come today, before the Cabinet meeting. So there is a chance that the P.M.'s plan may prove satisfactory from the financial and sufficiently so from the political Opposition's point of view. But he has grave doubts whether, even so, at the Cabinet it will be accepted. Many of the Ministers are scared by the proposal for a 10% reduction in unemployment benefits. Inside the Cabinet Henderson has formed a 'cave'; he is apparently opposed to cuts in benefits, and wants to institute an enquiry into the constitution of the banks, to 'fiddle whilst Rome burns'. But Henderson is playing a political game, and it is impossible to tell what his attitude at tonight's meeting will be. Snowden is awfully tired, and his worst qualities of stiffness and rigidity are coming out. He approves the plan (no doubt a great deal of it is his own concoction), but, as often, he is its own worst champion. Thomas is distracted, almost off his head. Graham is extremely uncertain, wavering, frightened of the 10% cut in unemployment benefits, and, the P.M. thinks, will probably end up on Henderson's side. The P.M. is disgusted with the behaviour of many of his colleagues; they lack grasp of the situation and guts to face it. Tonight the P.M. will put up another fight. The decision will be taken tonight or tomorrow; and is in doubt. The P.M. thinks he may be in a minority, or else have a slight majority. He will carry on if he can. But it is more likely that the situation will be such that he has no alternative but to resign.

If he wins in the Cabinet the immediate crisis is over. But there is then of course the Party to face. There would be a tremendous fight there. But the P.M.'s view is that the situation is so serious that, if necessary, he must commit his own political suicide in order to pull the country through the immediate financial crisis.

If he is beaten in the Cabinet, the Government will resign and the Tories come in. Shortly afterwards there would be an Election. The Labour Party would in the meantime doubtless have carried a motion of censure on him and those who agreed with him, and would fight drastically on the 'claptrap programme' of Henderson and his friends.[76]

Since the end of July, MacDonald had been swept along by events like a swimmer caught in a treacherous tide. He had had no time to think out what course to follow, or even what destination to aim for. All his energies had gone into coping with new developments as they occurred, and each new development had made it harder for him to see ahead. Sheila's note, Malcolm's note and his own diary entry throw much-needed light on his state of mind as the crisis moved towards its climax, but they record a mood, not a decision; in any case no decision in the circumstances could have been more than provisional. All the same, the mood deserves close attention. It is clear that by the afternoon of August 23rd, MacDonald expected Henderson and Henderson's supporters in the Cabinet to resign rather than accept a 10 per cent cut in unemployment benefit, and assumed that if they did so they would be supported by the rest of the Labour movement. It is clear too that the three choices which he saw ahead of him were all profoundly uninviting. If he continued to lead the Labour Party in opposition, he would have to attack measures which he believed to be essential in the national interest. If he formed a National Government, he would provoke the united hostility of his old followers. If he left office, resigned the Labour leadership and made it clear that he supported cuts in unemployment benefit, he would become an increasingly isolated figure, with diminishing influence on events. Finally it is clear that, of these three choices, he still preferred the last. He had toyed with the idea of forming a National Government ten months before, when it had been little more than a dinner-table fantasy. Now that it had become a practical possibility he shied away from it. During the last few months he had often been exasperated by the Labour Party, and on the central question of cuts in Government expenditure he had become more and more alienated from it. Yet he still saw it as his political home; though he thought it would be 'suicide' to support a reduction in unemployment benefit from the Labour benches, he felt instinctively that it was better to commit suicide inside it than to risk exclusion from it.

There is no way of telling exactly when and why he changed his mind. What is certain is that if he had stuck to his instincts for another twenty-four hours, his next six years would have been a good deal happier than they were.

VI

At 7.0 p.m., the Cabinet met once again. MacDonald announced that the reply from New York was expected later that evening. After what must have been a highly frustrating discussion of the parliamentary situation, the meeting was adjourned at 7.45 and for over an hour ministers walked and talked in the garden of No. 10. At 9.10 the meeting was resumed.[77] MacDonald read out the telegram which had been addressed to him by Harrison of the Federal Reserve Bank. It was a cautious, not to say cagey document, which must have come as a bitter disappointment to its recipient. A public loan, Harrison wired, could not be raised at the moment. The most that could be offered was a short-term credit of between $100 million and $150 million. Even that could not be guaranteed until the following day, and would be forthcoming only if the French were prepared to offer a similar amount. Finally, the Federal Reserve Bank wished to know if it was right in assuming that the Government's programme would have the 'sincere approval and support of the Bank of England and the City generally': its ability to help, Harrison concluded woundingly, would depend on the public's response to the Government's measures, particularly in Britain.[78]

Then began the final battle for the soul of the 1929 Government. After he had finished reading Harrison's message, MacDonald told the Cabinet that the Bank of England had sounded out 'certain important and influential financial interests in the City of London', all of which would support the £76 million programme, and added that Harvey thought that, if the necessary legislation were passed quickly, the credits mentioned in Harrison's telegram would suffice. After Snowden had announced that he was satisfied with the technical aspects of Harrison's offer, MacDonald threw all his energies into a last desperate effort to win the Cabinet over. Even the dry prose of the Cabinet secretariat conveys at least a hint of the emotion he must have felt:

> The Prime Minister informed the Cabinet that a situation had now been faced of a peculiarly difficult character because, if the Labour Party was not prepared to join with the Conservatives and Liberal Parties in accepting the proposals as a whole, the condition mentioned in Mr Harrison's message regarding a national agreement, would not be fulfilled ...
>
> The country was suffering from a lack of confidence abroad. There was, as yet, no panic at home, but the Prime Minister warned the Cabinet of the calamitous nature of the consequences which would immediately and inevitably follow from a financial panic and a flight from the pound. No one could be blind to the very great political difficulties in which the giving effect to the proposals as a whole would involve the Government. But, when the immediate crisis was over and before Parliament met, it would be possible to give the Labour Party [a] full explanation of the circumstances which had rendered it necessary for the Government to formulate such a drastic scheme ... The only alternative was a reduction not of 10 per cent, but of at least 20 per cent, and he could not believe that the Labour Party would reject the proposals when they knew the true facts of the position: he was confident, indeed, that a majority of that Party would accept them. A scheme which inflicted reductions and burdens in almost every other direction, but made no appreciable cut in Unemployment Insurance benefit, would alienate much support and lose the Party their moral prestige which was one of their greatest assets. In conclusion, the Prime Minister said that it must be admitted that the proposals as a whole represented the negation of everything that the Labour Party stood for, and yet he was absolutely satisfied that it was necessary in the national interest to implement them if the country was to be secured. He then pointed out that, if on this question there were any important resignations, the Government as a whole must resign.

Each member of the Cabinet then gave his opinion on the 10 per cent cut in unemployment benefit. Eleven were in favour and nine against. But although a majority of the Cabinet supported the cut, it was clear that some of the dissidents would resign rather than accept it, and that the Government could not continue. MacDonald announced that he intended to see the King at once, and that he would advise him to hold a conference between Baldwin, Samuel and himself the following morning. The Cabinet agreed, and authorized him to inform the King that all members of the Cabinet had placed their resignation in the prime minister's hands.[79] He left Downing Street at 10.10 — telling Harvey, whom he passed on the way out, 'I'm off to the Palace to throw in my hand.'[80]

The next thirteen hours were the most critical in MacDonald's career, and among the most critical in recent British history. Before the Cabinet meeting, he had expected to leave office with his colleagues, and to support a cut in unemployment benefit from the Opposition benches. Though the evidence is scanty and inconclusive, there is some reason to believe that it was after his next meeting with the King that second thoughts began to creep in. When he arrived at the Palace — looking 'scared and unbalanced', as Wigram put it later — he told the King that he had no alternative but to tender the Cabinet's resignation. According to Wigram, the King 'impressed upon the Prime Minister that he was the only man to lead the country through the crisis and hoped that he would reconsider the situation'. MacDonald asked whether the King would confer with Baldwin, Samuel and himself next morning, and the King agreed.[81] At 10.40 he returned to his waiting colleagues, reported that he had told the King that it was impossible for them to continue in office as a united Cabinet and said that Baldwin, Samuel and he would discuss the position with the King at 10 a.m. next day. The Cabinet decided that he should be authorized to tell the opposition leaders about Harrison's telegram, and that it should meet again at noon.[82]

After the Cabinet had dispersed, MacDonald saw Baldwin, Chamberlain and Samuel. He explained that although the necessary credits could be arranged, the Cabinet was split; and, according to Chamberlain, whose diary is the main source for this meeting, he added, 'For himself he would help us to get these proposals through, though it meant his death warrant, but it would be of no use for him to join a Government. He would be a ridiculous figure unable to command support and would bring odium on us as well as himself.' Chamberlain then tried to persuade him either to form or to join a National Government, pointing out that although he would have little support in the House he would have a great deal in the country, and that his membership of such a Government would carry great weight abroad. Chamberlain was supported by Samuel; Baldwin sat silent. In the end, Baldwin and Chamberlain both left Downing Street under the impression that Chamberlain's advocacy had failed, and that MacDonald still intended to resign and support the new Government from the Opposition benches.[83] MacDonald's diary, however, suggests that by now his intentions were less firm than the opposition leaders supposed. In a cryptic entry obviously written after his second meeting with the King, he noted, 'Cabinet ... decided to resign but to meet at 12 tomorrow to see if any new situation would arise as result of interview with the King with Baldwin & H.

Samuel at 10 a.m. tomorrow.'[84] Though this was a reasonably accurate summary of the Cabinet's decision, it seems unlikely that he would have used that form of words if he had been convinced that no 'new situation' was possible. And the only 'new situation' which was still on the cards was one form or another of a National Government.

On the whole, then it seems probable that when MacDonald went to bed on August 23rd, he was no longer certain that he would leave office next day and was beginning to toy with the notion that he might take the King's advice after all. He had still not made up his mind the following morning. On August 24th, Malcolm noted:

> J.R.M. rang up Ishbel at breakfast time. The Cabinet meeting last night lasted until after midnight. The P.M. got a majority in the Cabinet to agree with his proposals, but Henderson, Graham and Alexander led a strong opposition. Despite the P.M.'s majority a decision to go ahead with his plan would have involved seven or eight resignations, so that it was obviously impossible for the Government to carry on. Resignation of the Cabinet was inevitable.
>
> The King has implored J.R.M. to form a National Government. Baldwin and Samuel are both willing to serve under him. This Government would last about five weeks, to tide over the crisis. It would be the end, in his own opinion, of J.R.M.'s political career. (Though personally I think he would come back after two or three years, though never again to the Premiership. This is an awful decision for the P.M. to make. To break so with the Labour Party would be painful in the extreme. Yet J.R.M. knows what the country needs and wants in this crisis, and it is a question whether it is not his duty to form a Government representative of all three parties to tide over a few weeks, till the danger of financial crash is past — and damn the consequences to himself after that).[85]

In the next few hours MacDonald's uncertainties were resolved. At ten o'clock he and the other two party leaders were received by the King. MacDonald said that he had the Cabinet's resignation in his pocket, but the King replied that he trusted that there was no question of the prime minister's resignation. He hoped that the prime minister 'would help in the formation of a National Government, which the King was sure would be supported by the Conservatives and the Liberals. The King assured the Prime Minister that, remaining at his post, his position and reputation would be much more enhanced than if he surrendered the Government of the country at such a crisis.' The King's appeal turned the scales. By 10.35 it had been agreed that Baldwin and Samuel would serve under MacDonald in a National Government 'until an emergency bill or bills had been passed by Parliament, which would restore once more British credit and the confidence of foreigners'. After that, the King would grant a dissolution, and although the National Government would remain in being during the election, each party would fight the election on its own lines. The King then withdrew, to leave the party leaders to settle the terms of a communiqué to the press. He returned at 11.45, to find that they had agreed on a seven-point memorandum, apparently drawn up by Samuel. A National Government was to be formed to deal with the financial emergency. It would not be a coalition in the ordinary sense, but a co-operation of individuals. When the emergency had ended, the parties would return to their ordinary positions. The economies and new taxes would be based on those agreed by the Labour Government. The election which might follow when the Government's work was finished would not be fought by the Government, but by the parties. Pending legislation which was generally accepted by the different parties, and which was necessary for special departmental or other reasons, might be put through. The Cabinet would be reduced to a minimum.[86]

MacDonald then returned to Downing Street, taking a copy of this memorandum with him. At noon, the Labour Cabinet met for the last time. MacDonald announced that the King would invite certain individuals, as individuals, to take on the burden of carrying on the Government; that he had not failed to present the case against his taking part in such a Government; but that 'in view of the gravity of the situation he had felt that there was no other course open to him than to assist in the formation of a National Government on a comprehensive basis for the purpose of meeting the present emergency.'[87] According to Passfield, 'He announced this very well, with great feeling, saying that he knew the cost, but could not refuse the King's request, that he would doubtless be denounced and ostracised, but could do no other. We uttered polite things, but accepted silently the accomplished fact.'[88] The Cabinet agreed that MacDonald should place the Government's resignation in the King's hands that afternoon and, on the motion of Lord Sankey, decided to record 'their warm appreciation of the great kindness, consideration and courtesy invariably shown by the Prime Minister when presiding over their meetings'.[89] It was a strange end to the journey which had begun at the Memorial Hall in Faringdon Street nearly thirty-two years before.

CHAPTER 26

Split

I

By August 24th, MacDonald had spent nearly two weeks under intense and mounting strain. For days, he must have been torn by conflicting emotions — burning resentment towards his opponents in the Cabinet pulling against loyalty to the party in which he had spent his life; fear of political and personal isolation against fear of national bankruptcy and a gnawing sense that it was his responsibility to avert it. It is doubtful if he could have given a clear account of his state of mind when he agreed to form a National Government, either at the time or later. He was like a hesitant diver who had at last made up his mind to plunge. While his feet were leaving the diving board he was in no condition to analyse his feelings; by the time he had reached the water, he could no longer remember what they were. Partly because of this, there is no direct evidence about his motives and expectations at the critical moment. His diary and letters throw a great deal of light on his fluctuating moods after the new Government took office. They reveal little about his hopes or fears between the end of the Cabinet meeting on Sunday night and his arrival at Buckingham Palace on Monday morning: and still less about his reactions between the beginning of the Buckingham Palace meeting and his return to Downing Street at midday. As we have seen, it is clear that he had originally expected to leave office with his colleagues. It is also clear that he changed his mind in the end. Now, as then, his reasons for changing it are matters for speculation.

If the speculation is to produce results, we must try to picture the Labour Government's last twenty-four hours through his eyes. At lunch-time on Sunday, he and Thomas had agreed that if he formed a National Government he would 'face the whole antagonism of the Labour movement'; they had also agreed that he should go into opposition instead. Then came Sunday's Cabinet and the final battle over unemployment benefit. Though these cast no doubt on the calculation which he and Thomas had made earlier, they may well have made it seem irrelevant. MacDonald was a proud man, who hated being beaten. He had always been reluctant to throw his own authority into the scales when he thought that a majority of the Cabinet would be against him, but on the economy programme he had seen no alternative. For three days he had fought with desperate ingenuity to push his policy through; the longer the struggle had lasted, the more committed he had become. In the end, he had been more successful than he could have hoped. On Friday, the Cabinet had been evenly divided; on Sunday, it voted in favour of the 10 per cent cut by 11 to 9. But the victory which had been won at such heavy cost in emotional wear and tear turned out to be illusory. In spite of his warning that the Cabinet would have to stand or fall together, the minority made it clear that they would resign rather than carry out the decision for which the majority had just voted. At one level, MacDonald had expected this: he had told the King as much only that morning. But it was one thing to anticipate defeat in cold blood: another to experience it in hot. He had been angry enough with Henderson and Henderson's allies before the Cabinet assembled. By the time it broke up, he must have been seething with indignation. If this was what the Labour movement was like, why bother to avoid its antagonism? If he supported a cut in unemployment benefit from the Labour benches, as he had intended to do earlier, the fact that he had left office would not save him from accusations of disloyalty. Why not give his accusers something to accuse him for?

In the next few hours, more positive influences came into play. After the Cabinet had voted, MacDonald left for his second audience with the King. Soon afterwards, he had his late-night meeting with Baldwin, Samuel and Chamberlain. Once again, the King told him that he alone could lead the country through the crisis; Chamberlain added the telling new argument that his name would carry great weight abroad. Next morning came the climactic three-party conference at the Palace. For the third time, the King urged him to stay on as prime minister, this time in language that suggested that resignation would be tantamount to desertion. It is clear from his diary that MacDonald attached great value to the King's good opinion; it seems equally clear that he attached greater value to it now than ever before. Most people need someone to talk to at moments of crisis and uncertainty; it is notorious that a man under intense nervous and emotional strain is apt to lean heavily on the first rock he can find. MacDonald had no wife and no close confidant either. In this emotional desert, the King's gruff exhortations had a special resonance. They were couched, moreover, in terms to which MacDonald was specially likely to respond. Patriotism; duty; self-respect – the values of Sandringham and Balmoral were also the values of the Drainie school. Some commentators have suggested that it tickled MacDonald's vanity to be told that he was the only man who could save the country. Perhaps it did. Few men reach No. 10 without a bump of vanity, and MacDonald had a large one. But the implied suggestion that he would be running away from a post of danger if he resigned – and that other people would know that he had run away – was almost certainly far more persuasive.

Most persuasive of all, however, was the logic in which he had been imprisoned ever since his first, fatal decision to hold the parity. Once he had agreed that confidence in sterling had to be restored, he had been caught on an acceler-

ating moving staircase from which it became more and more difficult to jump.
The decision to balance the budget; the decision to defy the T.U.C.; the
decision to fight for a cut in unemployment benefit; the decision to apply for
credits to New York; the private half-decision to support cuts in unemployment
benefit from the Opposition benches if the Labour Party left office — each stage
had followed from the last, and had made the next seem almost inescapable.
But the staircase had not stopped because the Labour Cabinet had decided to
resign. The American loan still hung in the balance; the danger of a crash still
loomed ahead. The King and the opposition leaders all insisted that a National
Government would be in a stronger position to avert it than would a
Conservative–Liberal coalition or a Conservative Government with Liberal
support. They might be wrong: but suppose they were right? All along, Mac-
Donald had acted on two assumptions — that a forced devaluation would be a
disaster for the country, and that his over-riding duty was to do all he could to
prevent it, even at the cost of splitting his own party. If it had been right to act
on these assumptions in the earlier stages of the crisis, how could it be right to
act on contrary assumptions at the last moment? Not only the King, but his
own previous actions, told him that if sterling could be saved only by forming
a National Government, then he had no choice but to form one.

So, for a confused jumble of reasons, his resistance collapsed. Some of the
reasons may have been petty, but the chief reason was not. MacDonald acted as
he did because he believed that it was his duty to do so. Now that the dust has
settled, it is hard to see what other decision he could have taken. Today, few
would deny that he was wrong in thinking that the parity could be held, and as
wrong in thinking that disaster would follow if it were abandoned. At the time,
few denied that he was right: and the few did not include his opponents in the
outgoing Cabinet. As we have seen, the argument about the economy programme was not about the need to hold the parity. It was about the nature and
responsibilities of the Labour Party and, at a deeper level, about the nature and
responsibilities of political leadership. The same is true of MacDonald's private
argument about what to do once the Labour Government had fallen. The case
against forming a National Government was, in essence, the same as the case
against cutting unemployment benefit. It was based on the premiss that a
Labour politician's chief function is to represent the organized working class,
and that a party leader's chief duty is to keep his followers together. That view
— a modern version of the view which Disraeli once expounded in his philippics
against Peel — has a great deal to be said for it; and it was both intolerant and
unimaginative of MacDonald to assume that his colleagues who held it differed
with him for base reasons. But they were at least as intolerant towards him. For
he did not hold their view, and never had. In spite of later charges to the contrary, he was deeply attached to the Labour Party; and, as we shall see, he never
recovered from the emotional wounds inflicted by his separation from it. But
he had always believed that party loyalty could conflict with higher national

or international loyalties, and that it should come second if it did. That was why he had gone against his party in 1914: as he saw it, 1931 was 1914 all over again. He has often been accused of betraying his party, but if he had acted differently he would have betrayed his whole approach to politics. He and his party both paid a heavy price for his decision, and there can be little doubt in retrospect that the price was not worth paying. But it was his economics that were at fault, not his motives – his tragedy, not that he deserted to the enemy, but that he fought with characteristic courage in a battle that turned out to be unnecessary: and that in doing so he came near to wrecking the achievements of a lifetime.

II

He did not, however, fight with his customary skill; and if his generalship had been more adroit, the battle might have been less damaging – not only to him, but to the Labour Party as well. On any rational calculation, it was in his interests to win as much support from the Labour Party as he could. But although he wanted it, he made only fitful and half-hearted attempts to get it. Before taking his decision, he has assumed that if he formed a National Government, the Labour movement would turn against him. Now he shrank from facing the attacks he had anticipated; and, in shrinking, gave his enemies in the party new grounds on which to attack him.

Yet later Labour suggestions that he was glad to break with the party and no longer cared what it thought of him do not fit the facts. Nor, for that matter, do suggestions that his main concern was to prevent it from splitting, and that his actions were consciously and deliberately directed to that end. The only clear conclusions that emerge from his behaviour immediately after the Buckingham Palace conference are that he had no plan for the future, and that he was in no condition to make one. All his energies had gone into deciding whether or not to form a National Government; he had given little thought to the problems he would face if he decided in favour. After the struggles of the last few days, more-over – above all, perhaps, after the long inner struggle of the last few hours – he had no reserves of energy to tap. It is clear that the thought of more nerve-racking struggles and exhausting confrontations was more than usually abhor-rent to him; it is clear too that he felt acutely isolated and was even more sensitive to criticism than usual. But although these two threads run through nearly everything he did, it would be misleading to force his actions into a con-sistent pattern. In some moods, he dreamed vaguely of launching a great propa-ganda campaign to win the movement back to a purer and less materialistic socialism; more often, he believed that his political career was over. Sometimes, he tried indirectly to encourage potential supporters to follow him and, on at least one occasion, he made an ingenious attempt to spike the guns of a potential opponent. At other times, he sat back in melancholy dignity, giving his friends the impression that it would not make much difference, either to him or to events, whether they followed him or not. More than once, he insisted that he did not want promising young men to sacrifice themselves by taking office under him; privately, he was bitterly hurt when they took his advice. He was still much tougher and more resilient than has sometimes been realized, and within ten days or so he had recovered his nerve and was beginning to look ahead. But if we are to understand what happened in the new Government's first week, when the Labour Party's attitude to it was still uncertain, we must recognize that he was too bruised and exhausted either to formulate a coherent strategy or to follow it once he had done so.

As we have seen, the last meeting of the Labour Cabinet took place immediately after the Buckingham Palace conference. The only reliable accounts of what took place are those contained in the minutes and in a letter which Passfield wrote to his wife immediately afterwards.[1] Subsequent accounts are all heavily distorted by hindsight and throw more light on the attitudes of the Labour Party in the 1930s and 1940s than on what happened in August 1931. It is clear that MacDonald explained what he had decided to do and why – in Passfield's phrase, 'very well, with great feeling' – and that his decision was not discussed at any length. It is not clear whether he asked openly for support or gave any indication of his future attitude to the Labour Party. The probability, however, is that he did neither. Charges that he appeared 'jaunty' or unconcerned, or that he did not appear to regret the break-up of the Government, square so badly with his diary and letters and for that matter with Passfield's letter and the minutes that they can safely be disregarded. On the other hand, it is not at all impossible that he seemed distant, brusque and high-handed. A few hours before, the Cabinet had decided to resign. Now it was told that its leader was about to form a coalition with its opponents. There is no evidence that he apologized for his failure to consult it, that he expressed any wish to return to the Labour Party afterwards or that he made any declaration of continued loyalty to the movement. Even if he had, it is doubtful if he would have made much difference to the minority which had opposed him over the cut in benefit. He might, however, have made a great deal of difference to the subsequent behaviour of the majority. The most damaging charge that was to be brought against him later was not that he had cut unemployment benefit or even that he had formed a National Government, but that he had deliberately and cold-bloodedly plotted its formation. To put it at its lowest, his behaviour at the last meeting of the outgoing Cabinet did little to prevent such charges from being made.

When the meeting was over, he asked Snowden, Thomas and Sankey to stay behind, and invited them to join the new Government.[2] All three agreed, thus ensuring that it would at least get off the ground. Then came another puzzling episode. At 2.30 he met the outgoing junior ministers. According to Dalton, whose diary is the best source for this meeting, MacDonald told them that he was committing political suicide and would not ask any of them to do the same, but then added, 'But ... perhaps some of us *would* be willing to travel the same road with him. The best plan will be for him to write to us individually and enquire.'[3] At 4.10 he went back to the Palace, formally tendered the old Government's resignation and accepted the King's commission to form a new one. That night he noted:

The culminating day – 10: King, Bal: Sam: Decided only Nat: Govt: wd. do to meet the crisis & on urgent request of all, I consented to continue as P.M. under safeguards written on sheet which I have given to Ishbel. 12 Cabinet: Consternation when I reported but in meanwhile news of terrible run on Bank. It was plain that I should be left almost alone with Snowden, Thomas, Sankey. 'Finis' is being written. They chose the easy path of irresponsibility & leave the burdens to others. Henderson I knew, but as regards some others, I have once more experienced weak human nature. 2.30 Minor Ministers &c. Of course they were not to take the hard side. Their superiors had decided otherwise & whoever reduced unempt. pay whatever the necessity was doomed. The good fellows just bowed to what would be a popular cry; the intellectuals talked of their theories of banking & currency. So they went. The Chancellor was getting pessimistic as the desertions went on & I tried to cheer him up, but indeed it was a dreary matter. Still, we were right. – 3 pm. Samuel & Baldwin – 4.10 King & formally resigned & kissed hands on accepting to form a Govt. This is a lonely job.[4]

In the next few days, it became lonelier still. Most of August 25th was spent in conferences with Baldwin and Samuel, and by the late afternoon the new Cabinet was complete. Like MacDonald, Snowden, Thomas and Sankey all kept their old jobs. Baldwin became lord president of the council; Sir Samuel Hoare, secretary of state for India; Neville Chamberlain, minister of health; and Sir Philip Cunliffe-Lister, the remaining Conservative, president of the Board of Trade. The Liberals only had two places, both of them plums – Samuel going to the Home Office and Lord Reading to the Foreign Office. Meanwhile, MacDonald had found time to send out a letter to all the junior ministers in the last Government, and a similar letter to all Labour backbenchers. In both letters, he argued that the alternative to a 10 per cent cut in benefit would have been a financial crisis, leading, as he put it in the letter to the junior ministers, to 'the most dire results for the mass of the working class'. More significantly, he also argued in both letters that if he had not formed a National Government, Labour would have been swept out of office in ignominy and that, as a result of what he had done, it now had a chance to recover its position when things returned to normal – thus implying that his loyalties were still with the party and that he planned to defend his decision, not only on national grounds, but on party grounds as well.[5]

He had also found time to engage in a more subtle manœuvre. At some time during the day, his private secretary, C. P. Duff, minuted:

On the Prime Minister's instructions I went to see Mr. Henderson at the Foreign Office this morning. I told him that the P.M. was contemplating [a] Resignation Honours List; & would Mr. Henderson press him to give effect to the suggestions which had been made before, that Mr. Henderson should be given a Peerage? Mr Henderson said that the situation had now changed. A hard fight lay before the Labour Party, the more so as some of their erstwhile leaders had parted from them for the time being. He himself had served with the Party for over 40 years: for over 20 years he had been their Secretary: it was due to the Party that he occupied in public life the position which he did. At such a vital time in the fortunes of the Party it would need all the assistance it could get: responsible guidance within it would also be more needed than ever: & his going to the House of Lords might impair the help & guidance which he could give them by remaining as he was. Also, Mrs. Henderson was away, & he would want to ask her: how soon did the P.M. want a reply? (I said tomorrow would do.) ... In a general conversation in which I said that we stood at the parting of the ways, Mr Henderson said that we must not take this too seriously. At the time of the war when Mr MacDonald left the Party he (Henderson) had kept it together & it was ready to receive Mr MacDonald back again. He was parting with the P.M. now in no spirit of anger or resentment; and as regards myself as I said goodbye, he observed 'I could never quarrel with anyone whose wife came from Newcastle'![6]

MacDonald's attempt to remove his old rival from the scene did not succeed. On the 26th, Duff reported that Henderson had telephoned to say that he had now talked to his wife and that 'both of them are of opinion that, with the reduction of the present strength of the Party & the need, as he had explained to me yesterday, for him to exercise a restraining influence within it (!) he would prefer that you should not "for the present" pursue the suggestion which I made to him in your name yesterday.'[7]

Other initiatives were equally unsuccessful. If the new Government was to justify its title, it was important to make sure that it contained a fair quota of Labour members. The Cabinet had four Labour ministers out of ten — as high a proportion as anyone could expect. Outside the Cabinet it was a different story. On August 25th, MacDonald wrote morosely to Margaret Bondfield, who had written to express her admiration for his decision to form the National Government:

I am afraid that the experience of the past nine or ten days must be taken as a final proof that until there is some new spirit in the Labour Movement a

Labour Government will run away from two things: —
(1) The orders of the T.U.C. and
(2) An awkward crisis ...
... I am trying to involve very few of my friends in the new Government because so far as I can see it means their political death, and if we are to have a small Cabinet the available offices are very few. The troublesome thing is that having been deserted by practically all our minor members of the Ministry, I cannot find my proportion of those offices: but it really does not matter ... In everything except finance matters they must simply mark time and keep the machine going. I hope it will not last very long.[8]

One of the outgoing Labour ministers who refused office was Shinwell, who turned down a telephoned invitation to remain at the Mines Department.[9] A later one was Lord Snell, who refused to stay on as parliamentary secretary for India, on the grounds that he was sixty-six, 'very nervously exhausted' and would hate people to say that one of his first acts on becoming a peer had been to desert the movement.[10] A later one still was Sir Stafford Cripps, who wrote on August 28th that he admired 'the courage and conviction which have led you and the other Labour Ministers associated with you to take the action which you have taken', that he hoped that the rift in the party would soon be ended, but that he disagreed with the new Government's policy and was therefore unable to accept MacDonald's invitation to continue as solicitor general.[11] In a slightly different category was Herbert Morrison — no longer a 'minor' minister, since he had been promoted to the Cabinet a few months before. He was an old MacDonaldite and had voted in favour of the 10 per cent cut. He had admired MacDonald's conduct during the battles in the Cabinet, and it seems clear that he agreed with the decision to form a National Government. But although MacDonald almost certainly wanted Morrison to follow him, he could not bring himself to ask; when Morrison asked for his advice, he put the arguments against joining. After much dithering, Morrison too went with the party.[12] In the end, there was only a handful of Labour ministers outside the Cabinet — Lord Amulree, the secretary of state for air; Jowitt, the attorney general; Craigie Aitchison, the Scottish Lord Advocate; MacDonald's son, Malcolm, who became under-secretary at the Dominions Office; and Sir George Gillett, the old secretary for overseas trade who became parliamentary secretary for Transport. It is scarcely surprising that when the new ministers were sworn in on August 26th, MacDonald should have noted, 'Strange eerie feeling glancing round ... My worst fears re desertion of Party realised. We are like marooned sailors on a dreary island.'[13]

Meanwhile, Labour opposition to the new Government had gathered momentum. In the afternoon of August 24th, what Dalton described in his diary as a 'council of war' was held in Henderson's room in Transport House. Among those present were Henderson himself, Lansbury, Bevin, Citrine and

Stanley Hirst, the chairman of the party. The trade unionists, Dalton noted, were 'full of fight' — Bevin declaring, 'This is like the General Strike. I'm prepared to put everything in.'[14] Stevenson of the *Daily Herald* was summoned, and persuaded to make next day's editorial more hostile to MacDonald than he had intended.[15] Later, Citrine issued a statement announcing that a joint meeting of the consultative committee of the parliamentary party, the National Executive and the T.U.C. General Council would be held on the 26th, and adding pointedly that the trade unions would consider that the ministers who had resigned rather than cut unemployment benefit 'have acted as Labour Ministers would be expected to act by the Labour Movement'.[16] On the 25th, the *Daily Herald* praised MacDonald for his sincerity, but attacked his decision to form a National Government as a 'surrender to the City'.[17] During the day, invitations were sent out to a special meeting of the parliamentary party on Friday the 28th. On the 26th, the joint meeting of the three Labour committees unanimously decided that the new Government should be 'vigorously opposed in Parliament and by the Movement throughout the country', and agreed that a manifesto should be issued as soon as possible.[18] On the 27th, the manifesto was published. It denounced not merely the cut in unemployment benefit but all the economies agreed upon by the outgoing Cabinet, and put forward an alternative policy, consisting of the suggestions which the T.U.C. deputation had put to the economy committee nearly a week before, together with a new proposal to 'mobilise' the country's foreign investments.[19]

The tide was running fast. Yet when MacDonald was given an opportunity to do what he could to stem it, he shrank back. He was still a Labour member of parliament; as such, he received an invitation to the party meeting on the 28th. Though it was dated August 25th, it did not arrive at Downing Street until a late post on the 26th, and was not seen by MacDonald until 11 a.m. on the 27th.[20] Before seeing it, he had written to the secretary of the parliamentary Labour Party, to say that he had heard that a party meeting had been summoned for Friday and that if he had known earlier he would have tried to arrange his programme so as to make it possible for him to attend. However, he went on, this was no longer possible:

> The work of the last three weeks has been rather heavy, and the Cabinet must meet on Monday. I hope to get all the machinery properly started ... by 7 o'clock tonight, when I shall go up to Scotland to have a brief two days' pause in work. If I were now to wait until Friday it would mean that I would not get out of London at all.
>
> I have, however, written to each member of the Party, marking the letter personal, so that nothing would be published as I did not want any controversy nor widening of divisions. But the usual thing happened. One or other of our members betrays confidence on every occasion, and the newspaper which gets first information about private Party meetings was

the first to get this letter. Therefore even had it been possible for me to attend the Party Meeting I would have been quite unable to have said anything in detail as to the financial condition which met me about three weeks ago and which steadily deteriorated until a state of great national jeopardy had arisen. I see by the papers ... that various things are to happen regarding myself. When, after very prolonged consideration that I had to take the step which I have taken, I was under no delusion as to what it might mean. I shall therefore be cheerfully prepared to accept any decision to which the Party may come.

When the invitation arrived, he added a postscript: 'This morning a letter with the notice of the meeting came. It was dated 25th inst & must have been delayed in the post or in delivery to me.'[21] But, although the invitation had now arrived, he did not change his plans. That evening, he left for Lossiemouth by the overnight train.[22] When the parliamentary party assembled on Friday afternoon, MacDonald was not there.

III

Would it have made any difference if he had gone? With only a handful of dissentients, the parliamentary party endorsed the resolution passed by the joint meeting on the 26th and the manifesto issued on the 27th. Henderson was elected as leader, again with only a handful of dissentients, with Clynes and Graham as his deputies. Years later, George Strauss, who had been P.P.S. to Herbert Morrison while Labour was in office, thought that nothing MacDonald could have said would have altered the party's attitude; that he would have been savagely attacked if he had come to the meeting; and that, from his own point of view, he was wise to stay away.[23] Later Labour tradition supports Strauss's verdict. Most of the biographies and memoirs of Labour leaders who stayed with the party suggest that the Labour movement rallied instinctively and unanimously to the banner raised by the T.U.C. and the National Executive, and that once a National Government had been formed, it was a foregone conclusion that the vast majority of the Labour Party would go into opposition.

Yet that evidence cannot be accepted at its face value. Memoirs and biographies published after 1931 may reflect the attitudes of the period when they were written: contemporary evidence is nothing like so clear-cut. It is clear that Bevin and Citrine were determined to swing the party behind the policy which the General Council had adopted the week before, and that they succeeded in doing so. It would be foolish to assume that all the hands which went up in support of that policy were raised with enthusiasm. The T.U.C. line was, after all, sharply opposed, not only to the £76 million economy programme which had been accepted by a majority of the Labour Cabinet, but even to the £56 million programme which had been accepted by the minority as well. Some, at least, of the outgoing ministers may have felt uneasy at changing their tune so quickly. As we have seen, Morrison had been torn by conflicting loyalties and uncertain whether to join the new Government. Margaret Bondfield had written to express her admiration for MacDonald's decision to form it. Other former ministers may have had similar feelings. Though the party meeting voted overwhelmingly to go into opposition, it seems clear that Sankey and Malcolm MacDonald, both of whom declared their support for MacDonald, were given a sympathetic hearing. A few days after the meeting, Ben Tillett wrote:

> Malcolm was vivid, and I am sure most of us felt for him. It has gladdened my heart to realise that there is some chivalry left in our movement as well as gratitude.
>
> You, too, would have had a kindly reception had [you] met us, for Sankey was received with great feeling, as well as admiration for his straightforward speech.
>
> Some of the 'squealers' were there, who have cursed us to the cheers of the Tories.
>
> Now they want to be heroes & martyrs, but I spoke strongly against that outrage. Indeed I feel that all of us would have felt tribulation of spirit in deciding what to do.
>
> The clowning of your critics has a wretched form of comedy in its bletherings. But it [is] tragedy for the movement, when hysteria takes the place of sane judgement. I am sure your good work will live, and that shy corner of your brave soul will give you sanctuary.
>
> God love you and yours, always.[24]

It is hard to believe that Tillett can have been entirely unrepresentative of the movement he had helped to create.

No doubt, the parliamentary party would have passed the resolution it did even if MacDonald had come to the meeting. But he might have swung some votes; he would almost certainly have influenced emotions and attitudes. One of the soundest rules of politics is that it is better to be present than to stay away: better to confront hostility in the open than to allow it to build up unanswered. Perhaps because he calculated that he would do more harm than good by going, more probably because he could not bear the thought of what was likely to happen when he arrived, MacDonald flouted that rule.[25] There can be little doubt that he paid heavily for doing so. Many Labour M.P.s must have been in a state of anguish and confusion — instinctively suspicious of the new Government and hostile to its policy, yet unwilling to think badly of men who had given their lives to the movement. If MacDonald had come to the meeting, some of these M.P.s might have been convinced by what he said; more would have applauded his courage in coming. As things were, potential supporters in the party were left high and dry, while opponents were given a new argument to use against him. When Parliament reassembled ten days later, Henderson's bitterest taunt was that, throughout the crisis, MacDonald had never 'look[ed] into the faces of those who had made it possible for him to be Prime Minister'.[26] It was MacDonald's fault that he could say so.

Yet even after the party meeting, there was more personal sympathy for him in the Labour Party than has sometimes been realized. In the next few days, replies arrived to the letters he had sent out on August 25th. J. Allen Parkinson wrote that, although he disagreed with MacDonald, he would always believe 'your decision was the result of conscience'. John Arnott wrote that his place was with the Opposition, but 'My faith in your devotion to our cause has never wavered.' Archie Gossling wrote, 'To have you as my Chief has been my greatest glory. You will always command my reverence & love.' Charles Ammon wrote that he believed 'in your sincerity absolutely'. Attlee wrote: 'while I have no doubt that the action which you have taken has been dictated solely in [sic] the endeavour to serve the country, I personally must take my stand with those members of the Cabinet who disagree with the course adopted'. Jack Lawson wrote hopefully, 'though the political tides seem to carry us in different directions, I trust it is but for the moment'; William Leach, more sadly, 'I trust you will allow me to continue to count myself your friend – very troubled and very anxious.' Ben Riley prayed 'that you may be successful in your efforts, that the severance for [sic] the Party may be of short duration and that the rank and file of the Parliamentary Labour Party may appreciate a great occasion and shew magnanimity and an enlightened broadmindedness'. W. B. Taylor wrote that he knew that 'only the highest & purest motives will guide you.' Ben Turner expressed the hope that 'it will be possible, sometime when the crisis is definitely over, for you to return to your activities in connection with the Labour Movement.' James Welsh wrote that MacDonald had made 'a great mistake', but invited him to stay with him, 'where you'll find a homely welcome & unimpaired faith in your integrity'. Herbert Dunnico hoped that MacDonald's separation from the party would be temporary, and added, 'I should not unduly fret over what has happened. Position is but another name for Pillory, sometimes they pelt you with flowers and sometimes with rotten eggs, but you are still in the pillory.'[27]

Similar letters arrived from old Labour stalwarts outside Parliament. Two days after the National Government was formed, MacDonald's old election agent from Aberavon days, Ivor Thomas, wrote, 'The wolves will be snarling, you will be abused, misrepresented and misunderstood. But we who know you, who fought with you, we understand. May God's blessing rest with you, and comfort you in your days of seeming darkness.' Next day, Jim Middleton wrote, 'On the merits of the situation ... I feel strongly and instinctively unconvinced. As to your own stand – one simply witnesses it with the awe which the heroic is bound to command mingled with almost the deepest sadness I have ever known.' A few days later, Hugh Roberton wrote, 'I should have written earlier but I was not sitting on the fence. I only wish to say here and now that Helen and I are very much with you in these troubled times ... I wish you to know that we trust you absolutely.' Soon afterwards, Canon Donaldson, with whom MacDonald had stayed when he was member for Leicester, wrote, 'I do not see what else you could have rightly done, & I share the feelings of many others that of all possible decisions & courses you chose "the better part".' In an undated letter, three old socialists from Rhiwbina, Edward Lewis, Fred Stibbs and MacDonald's old friend, J. D. Morgan, wrote, 'Whilst we may not agree with certain actions of the new Government, may we assure you that you have a very warm place in our hearts, and never for a moment have we doubted that whatever action you may have taken, has been taken with ... deep sincerity of purpose.' In a covering note, Morgan added, 'I feel I ought to express my gratitude for the fullness which has come to my life thro' my association with you.'[28]

Other letters were more painful; and some provoked revealing replies from MacDonald. To William Lunn, who wrote that he could never agree to cut the benefits of those who had a proper insurance qualification, he snapped back, 'I risked the financial stability of the country for two days longer than I ought to have done, trying to keep a Labour Government in office ... [Y]ou are in a safety hole which my immediate colleagues and I have dug for you, and you are not grateful.'[29] To Gordon MacDonald, who implied that the dangers of leaving the gold standard had been exaggerated, he declared, 'If a man standing at a crack in a river wall, sees great volumes of water flowing through and says to his colleagues, "you have to wet your feet and perhaps go up to the neck in order to stop that breach", and his colleagues say, "you are exaggerating", well, I shall be that man rather than those colleagues ... I shall go, and some of you will remain, and a very hard verdict is to be pronounced against you.'[30] Saddest of all was an exchange with Mrs Hamilton, who wrote on August 28th:

Dear Prime Minister,

I only got home this morning from Austria: had I arrived sooner I should have tried to ring up or call. This is an agonising situation to a great many of us: it is so to me. But greatly as I admire your courage, & ready as I am to believe your gesture may have saved us all, I could not, as I thought the whole situation out on my long journey home, find it possible to support this Government or believe in its policy. It is a very hard decision to make; & this afternoon's party meeting does not make it agreeable to act on —but, there it is. I felt I must write this line to express the deep regret I feel about this, temporary severance between you and the party.[31]

MacDonald replied on September 1st to 'My dear Mrs Hamilton', in tones which do much to explain why the severance turned out not to be temporary after all:

Whether you believe it or not, I have saved you, whatever the cost may be to me, but you are all quietly going on drafting manifestoes, talking about opposing cuts in unemployment pay and so on, because I faced the facts a week ago and damned the consequences ... If I had agreed to stay in, defied the bankers and a perfect torrent of credit that had been leaving the country day by day, you would all have been overwhelmed and the day you met Parliament you would have been swept out of existence ... Still I have always said that the rank and file have not always the same duty as the leaders, and I am willing to apply that now. I dare say you know, however, that for some time I have been very disturbed by the drift in the mind of the Party. I am afraid I am not a machine-made politician, and never will be, and it is far better for me to drop out before it will be impossible for me to make a decent living whilst out of public life.

... Do not lose touch, especially with Malcolm. He has been as brave as a lion, and you have no idea how he regards you. When we all get settled down again at Upper Frognal Lodge, come and see us.[32]

Another painful exchange took place between MacDonald and his agent at Seaham, William Coxon. On August 25th, MacDonald wrote to Coxon, 'Do not believe what is being published in the papers ... It is the war again. I know the pressure which will be brought to bear upon my friends in Seaham, but tell them that I place myself unreservedly in their hands.'[33] On the 30th, Coxon replied that he had put MacDonald's letter before the Seaham party executive the day before; and that the executive had passed a resolution, to put to a full delegate meeting in September, abiding by the National Executive's decision to oppose the new Government and asking MacDonald to resign his seat.[34] On September 1st, MacDonald replied angrily that he still wanted to place himself in the hands of the Seaham party, but that he was not prepared to resign his seat in circumstances which involved 'desertion of a duty'.[35]

With understandable asperity, Coxon replied that MacDonald had at first said that he would place himself in the party's hands and was now saying something different. The Seaham party, he continued, agreed with the National Labour Party and the Durham Miners' Association, and it was only reasonable that it should try to put its opinion into effect. 'I will not dwell upon the mistrust associated with the names of your Conservative colleagues in the Cabinet ...,' he concluded bitterly. 'You state it is the war over again, that is true, more demands for the workers.'[36] MacDonald was unable to let the argument drop; and on September 5th, he wrote to Coxon again, denying that there was any contradiction between his first and second letters:

No man of sense would imagine, if an engine driver says he puts himself in his hands, that that meant ... he would stop in the middle of the journey ... and cause smashes in consequence. The only weakness in my letter was that I assumed, apparently without justification, that the Seaham Executive would at any rate consider the matter before it came to a decision. It never occurred to me that without any knowledge of what you were doing you

would say ditto to somebody else who had said something before you ...
... If there are Conservatives and Liberals in the Cabinet the blame is upon
those who ... resigned the task to others, and relieved of responsibility
formed itself [*sic*] into what was called 'a patriotic Opposition' to measures
practically every one of which it indicated its willingness to subscribe.[37]

By now, however, it was clear that by no means all the Seaham party members
were as hostile as Coxon. On September 1st, George Bloomfield, the previous
agent, wrote, 'I am not prepared to condemn or ostracise JRM till I get to know
fully the case ... I wish you all good speed in what as yet I believe to be an
honest and honourable attempt to do the right thing.'[38] On the same day,
William Grant, the Easington medical officer of health and one of MacDonald's
closest friends in the constituency, wrote, 'I had a visit from Coxon last night
and was disgusted ... The executive consisted of 16 and was ruled by one or two
who are after promotion.' Next day, he reported that the 'opposition to the
Executive is growing very rapidly'. On September 6th, he wrote that he had
been at the Seaham party demonstration at Hartlepool the day before and that
'The first mention of your name brought the cry of "Good Old Ramsay" and
then thunderous applause.' By the 9th, he was writing, 'It is almost certain that
the recommendation of the Executive will be turned down on Saturday ... The
feeling of the man in the street has always been with you but it is growing by
leaps and bounds.'[39]

Grant's forecast turned out to be over-optimistic. The delegate conference on
September 12th voted overwhelmingly in favour of the executive's recommendation that the Seaham party should support the policy of the national party.
On the recommendation that MacDonald should be asked to resign his seat,
however, the meeting was almost evenly divided – 40 voting in favour and 39
against.[40] On September 13th, Grant wrote reassuringly that many of the delegates would have voted differently if they had not been mandated in advance,
and added, 'Have no misgiving, this seat is yours as long as you wish to retain
it.'[41] Soon afterwards, Coxon sent MacDonald a copy of the resolution passed
at the delegate meeting. The voting on MacDonald's resignation, he conceded,
had been almost even; but he added menacingly, 'The conference gave every
indication that it was determined to be true to the Labour Party.'[42] Somewhat
peevishly, MacDonald replied:

> The vote which you report is no guidance to me or to anyone else as to the
> desires of the Seaham Party. I therefore propose to let the matter rest where
> it is for the moment. The action of the new Government has already averted
> the immediate crisis ... and so we have time to understand things a little bit
> better, to use our own intelligences ... and to give proof to the country that
> Labour Parties will never consent to be degraded to the position of un-
> thinking cogs in a big Party machine.[43]

There, for the moment, the matter did rest. But if we are to understand the events of the next few weeks, one further letter which MacDonald received from his constituency deserves to be quoted. It is undated, and tells its own story:

15, *Austin Street,*
Easington Colliery

Dear Sir,

It is with the greatest regret I read of the Seaham Party's attitude to you. We are just a few of the Easington Miners wives who wish to extend our sympathy to you. We know you have done your utmost for us, and you still have and will have our loyal support no matter what the Seaham Labour Party may say. I expect you will know we have hard times as some times for a five-day week wages it does not amount to a full week's dole. We wish you every success in your new task and trust there is better times ahead both for you and us. May we subscribe ourselves,

Your staunch admirers,

Constance Clough
Alice Davidson
Ethel Ward
Elizabeth Daniel
Margaret Logan
Bertha Griffiths
Meggie Taylor
Jane Stubbs
Sally Sloper[44]

IV

MacDonald flew back from Lossiemouth to London on August 31st. On September 1st he noted bitterly:

The desertion of colleagues & the flight of the Lab: Govt. having grievous effect ... [W]hat a destruction of all we have done. Had the Govt. done its duty there would have been little interruption in that work. They ran away & left everything unprotected. If this is the best Labour can do, then it is not fit to govern except in the calmest of good weather. Not only do I lose my seat; but I lose my confidence.[45]

That note was to be heard a good deal in the next few weeks. The cruellest wars are civil wars, and the ugliest quarrels, quarrels within a family. Like most party splits, the breach which had opened between MacDonald and the Labour Party the week before had something in common with both. Each side had legitimate grievances against the other; each was forced in self-defence to question the other's good faith; before long, the split, which few had consciously sought in the beginning, had become too wide to close. Though many Labour people sympathized with MacDonald, many saw his conduct as an outrage. It was bad enough to sacrifice the unemployed; to do so in concert with the class enemy was infinitely worse. These emotions would have been latent in the party in any event; though the new party leadership did not at first appeal to them directly, the posture it took up once the split had taken place was bound to sharpen them. To justify its decision to go into opposition, the party was forced to portray the new Government as the tool of high finance, which Labour ministers had no business to join. Not only did it adopt the T.U.C. policy which the outgoing Labour Cabinet had rejected; increasingly, it suggested that the whole crisis had been a trick, deliberately designed to smash the Labour movement. For a while, most Labour speakers went out of their way not to attack MacDonald personally; many paid generous tributes to the work he had done for the movement in the past.[46] That did not alter the fact that their propaganda cast him, if only by implication, as the agent of a capitalist conspiracy to do down the working class. He, in turn, was forced to defend himself; the best defence to hand was that his colleagues had deserted their posts at a time of national danger, and left him with no alternative but to collaborate with his opponents. Besides, he believed it; and he believed it with growing strength and bitterness as time went on. Though he had expected the Labour Party to oppose the Government, its opposition still hurt when he encountered it. In any case, he can hardly have expected it to swing as far into opposition as it did. As its opposition hardened, his indignation mounted; and the more indignant he became, the more he began to feel that it was his duty, as well as his interest, to answer back.

His feeling was reinforced by the discovery that he had more support in the party than he had foreseen. On September 2nd he noted, 'Feel a change in my favour in rank & file of Party whose branches have rushed to excommunicate;'[47] little by little, he began to wonder whether it might, after all, be possible to appeal over the heads of the new leadership to ordinary party members and voters. When J. H. Sutcliffe, the prospective Labour candidate for Liverpool, Fairfield, wrote that he supported MacDonald and intended to resign his candidature, MacDonald urged him to 'insist upon meeting the Local Party, putting the facts before it and compelling it to face them ... Our friends ought to conduct a campaign of educational propaganda wherever they have influence – not for the purpose of splitting the Party but of saving it.'[48] Soon afterwards, an old Elgin socialist named Murdo Mackenzie wrote that several members of the Moray and Nairn Labour Party hoped that MacDonald would be willing to seek nomination as the Labour candidate there. MacDonald turned down the invitation, on the grounds that he wanted to show Labour Party members in industrial seats that it was impossible for a consistent socialist to support an Opposition which would 'bring back the financial crisis we have had to face, reduce real incomes at a rapid rate [and] lower the standard of living of the very poorest of our people more than they would that of the wealthiest classes'.[49] At about the same time, Craigie Aitchison reported that he had just spent two days in Scotland where he had found 'a considerable body of Labour opinion which is not in sympathy with the official Labour view'.[50] 'I hope that you will not let our case by default in Edinburgh,' MacDonald replied belligerently. 'My letters show a tremendously strong backing in the Party from one end of the country to the other, and that feeling must be rallied ... The issue is — can Democratic leaders lead in a crisis, can they face up to the temporary unpopularity of telling Democracy the truth, weld it into an effective instrument, and not leave it a mere drifting crowd ... ?'[51]

At the same time, it was becoming clear that the financial crisis had not ended after all. Immediately after the National Government took office, confidence in sterling recovered; and by August 28th, the Bank of England was able to announce that it had obtained credits totalling £80 million from New York and Paris. On September 3rd, however, Harvey told the new Cabinet that withdrawals of foreign exchange were 'still larger than the Bank cared to see'. Foreign confidence, he implied glumly, could be restored only if the Government's measures were supported at home. Suggestions that the Government would remain in office for only a short time, Peacock added pointedly, had been 'rather disturbing'.[52] Soon afterwards, Major Church, one of MacDonald's supporters in the parliamentary Labour Party, reported that he had had a long talk with the Bank of England's economic adviser, Professor Sprague, who had told him that all but one of his colleagues at the Bank thought that the best way to restore British credit would be 'an announcement by you ... that the new Government will remain in office until they have formulated plans for the rehabilitation of British industry and the restoration of a favourable trade balance'.[53]

Ten days before, MacDonald had assumed that the Government would last for only a short time, and that his own political career would end with it. Now he began to have second thoughts. In a long and more than usually oblique letter to Baldwin on September 5th, he hinted that the Government could not risk leaving office in the near future in case the Labour Party won the election, and that it should agree on a long-term programme, probably including protection. Provided financial stability could be assured, he began doubtfully, he would not stand in the way of a dissolution. However,

the present Opposition ... has undoubtedly some rather detestable but nevertheless electorally effective cries, and it must be dealt with very seriously. I have not left my Party and have no intention of doing so, but if it were to have a majority or could even form a Government after the next Election, the country would again be faced with a financial crisis which would then in all probability break upon it and ruin it ...

The present Government will last so long as it deals only with the matters immediately before us. Can we draw a line between this time of crisis and a normal condition which is to follow? I do not see any such line. Undoubtedly it would be for the benefit of the country if we stayed on a little time after the immediate trouble is over ... But even the day to day work of administration is to bring us into disagreements with each other, and the late Government had ... many schemes in hand – especially as regards foreign matters which were only beginning or had only advanced to a certain stage – which any period of uncertainty and lack of union in the Government would destroy ...

Behind all this, moreover, there is the question of the re-establishment of trade which is the only real cure for our present ills. Upon how to do this, I am afraid we cannot agree. Personally I am not so far removed from your point of view as are some of my colleagues, but I place a much smaller value upon what can result from your proposals, than I think you do. As a matter of fact, when I was in Berlin, I had a talk with Dr Bruning on this subject and had I had the leisure ... I should have been working with him on some plan ... The same is true of War Debts and Reparations, negotiations regarding which I have opened purely personally with Mr Stimson and, through him, President Hoover ... That is the outlook as I see it, and I think we ought to work together to set the stage in such a way that subsequent movements will come upon plan and not by accident.[54]

'The same problems are exercising my mind,' Baldwin replied unhelpfully on September 7th. 'Maybe we shall have an opportunity later in the week of a quiet talk in which we can turn out what is in our minds and discuss the pros and cons dispassionately.'[55]

While Baldwin waited for an opportunity to turn out his mind, the breach between MacDonald and the Labour Party grew wider. On September 8th, Parliament reassembled for one of the stormiest sessions in recent history, MacDonald moved a motion that the House resolve itself into a committee of Ways and Means, which was treated as a vote of confidence in the new Government. According to his diary, he had suffered 'tortures' in preparing for the debate;[56] perhaps because of this, his speech was one of the most powerful he had made for some time. As so often in the last few days, the nub of his argument was that he and his colleagues had faced 'something like a typhoon', to which long-term solutions, however desirable they might be in themselves, had been irrelevant. It had become clear that the only way to escape the typhoon was to borrow abroad; to obtain a loan it had been necessary to give assurances to the lenders. Some might say that such methods of raising money were humiliating, even unconstitutional; in fact, 'that is precisely what has happened for generations in every public, private or State loan that has been raised in the money markets of the world.' The alternative would not have been a planned and modest reduction in the gold content of sterling, but a collapse of the kind which had taken place in Vienna and Berlin: 'One day it would have been 20s. and the next day 10s. and it would have tumbled without control.' If the House met that day with the pound worth twenty shillings and unemployment benefit paid in good coinage, he ended defiantly, it was because the new Government had given the nation a breathing space. It consisted of 'men belonging to all parties who believe that until this emergency is over party strife should not appear'; when the time came for it to surrender the seals of office, it would take its place 'among the things ... which will never be forgotten, I believe, in the history of this country'.[57]

It was a fighting speech; and, as fighting speeches are apt to do, it provoked a fighting response. 'Every now and then a belligerent note was struck out of the Opposition which surprised many people by its fierceness,' wrote the *Manchester Guardian*; MacDonald, it added, had 'hardly ever mentioned the word "Bank" but the Opposition benches boiled over in wrath'.[58] Henderson, who followed MacDonald, also made a fighting speech – implying that even the £56 million economy programme put to the opposition leaders by the previous Cabinet had only been accepted provisionally; declaring that he would have left politics sooner than cut unemployment benefit; and ending with a ringing assertion of class loyalty: 'The Prime Minister appealed to the country. We appeal to that part of the country that we have tried to represent, and I hope that we will appeal on high, strong Socialist grounds.'[59] In the end, the Government won by 309 votes to 249. But only twelve Labour M.P.s voted in the Government lobby, while another five abstained.[60] On September 10th, Snowden introduced his emergency budget – also to the accompaniment of vociferous interruptions. On the 11th, MacDonald moved the second reading of the National Economy Bill, enacting the new Government's expenditure cuts. They totalled £70 million. The cut in unemployment benefit accounted for almost £13 million; with some variations, the rest of the package was the old £56 million programme, which had been accepted by the whole of the previous Cabinet. Perhaps because of this, tempers on the Labour benches rose higher than before. MacDonald was heckled even more fiercely than he had been on the 8th; Clynes, who led for the Opposition, came close to denying that the Labour Cabinet had accepted any of the cuts contained in the Bill and argued that in any case its members were free to oppose them now; Tom Johnston, who wound up, declared that the House was faced with the spectacle, 'not of a National Government but of a Wall Street Government'.[61]

The effect of all this on MacDonald can easily be imagined. Physically, as well as emotionally, the last five weeks had taken a heavy toll. The day after the confidence debate, he seems to have had a mild seizure of some sort, noting mysteriously, 'Morning of collapse, suddenly going as mist with the sun'.[62] The debate on the economy Bill had a similar effect. 'Not well,' he noted on September 13th. 'My body warns me to behave better.'[63] It is hardly surprising that the attacks from the Labour benches should have drawn blood. On September 9th,

BI

he invited all the Labour members who had abstained or voted with him the day before to his room in the House. For more than an hour he described the arguments in the Cabinet before the Labour Government fell and tried to show how unfair Henderson had been in the debate. 'I felt very sorry for him,' George Strauss noted afterwards. 'He looked worn and pathetically unhappy ... "If I die soon," he said, "I'll die from a broken heart." '[64] In his own diary, MacDonald was less pathetic and more outspoken. On September 8th he exclaimed angrily, 'groups of Labour members behaving badly. How could one ever free from this ill-assorted body join it again.'[65] By the 11th he had become even more indignant. 'Opposition getting out of hand & becoming like old East End vestry in its calibre,' he noted savagely. 'Labour has a scraggy tail.'[66]

V

Yet, even now, the split was not complete; and, in spite of bitter diary entries, MacDonald was still reluctant that it should become so. On August 28th, Baldwin's decision to join the National Government had been unanimously endorsed by a meeting of Conservative peers, M.P.s and parliamentary candidates. It gradually became clear, however, that the Conservatives were not as united in their support of the Government as they seemed. Some suspected that their leaders had sold the protectionist pass; more feared that they might lose their chance of winning a majority at the next election. Even before the House met, sections of the Conservative Party had begun to press for an early election; in the confidence debate on September 8th, Churchill and Amery both made it clear that their enthusiasm for the Government was a good deal less than it might have been, and argued that the country's problems could be solved only by a protectionist Government with a popular mandate behind it.[67] 'Tories not heartily in the cooperation,' MacDonald noted indignantly. 'Winston mischievous speech ... Tories in the crowd from the inside are even worse than from the outside.'[68] During the next few days, Churchill's mischief was repeated by others; and by September 13th, MacDonald was noting gloomily, 'Today discussed election with Editor of Times at Chequers. Both felt early election undesirable but inevitable.'[69]

In the circumstances, gloom was justified. So far, MacDonald had done his best to avoid an irrevocable choice between his new colleagues and his old. In spite of his mounting private indignation with it, he had not left the Labour Party himself and had encouraged his supporters not to leave it either. Though he had defended himself against Labour attacks, his answers had been surprisingly restrained; apart from one or two lapses, the bitterness he felt was confined to his correspondence and kept out of his speeches. He had urged Baldwin to agree to a long-term programme, but the programme he had suggested was one which the Labour Party would have found it difficult to oppose. It would be misleading to suggest that he hoped consciously to return to it, still more that he planned to do so. As before, the evidence suggests that he had no plans at all, and swung about from one mood to another. All the same, it seems clear that the possibility lurked at the back of his mind and that he shrank, more by instinct than deliberation, from anything that would rule it out. In an election, however, such prevarications would be impossible. He would either have to campaign against the Labour Party or appear to endorse its criticisms of what he had done. If he campaigned, he would do so as the ally of the Conservative Party and would find it hard not to end as its prisoner. As he reflected in another diary entry, on September 15th, 'Samuel discussing election time & situation after it. They press me to lead in the fight. But what is to happen after? Quite clear that our position must be defended by me, but how can I remain as P.M. or even as subordinate Minister with colleagues with whom I do not agree?'[70]

These musings were interrupted by a more alarming development. The withdrawals of gold and foreign exchange, about which Harvey had warned the Cabinet on September 3rd, had continued intermittently ever since. Though their chief causes were the world-wide shortage of liquidity and Britain's growing trade deficit, there can be little doubt that they had been encouraged by the talk of an early election. They were encouraged even more by the co-called Invergordon mutiny on September 15th, when units of the Atlantic fleet refused to muster, in protest against the Government's pay cuts. On September 16th, the Bank of England lost £5 million; on the 17th, £10 million; and on the 18th, nearly £18 million.[71] On September 17th, a Cabinet committee chaired by MacDonald agreed that the Government had three courses open to it—to stay in office and announce that it would pass whatever measures were necessary to put the trade balance right, to obtain more foreign credits or to leave the gold standard. It also agreed, however, that the first course was unlikely to succeed, since the necessary legislation would take a long time to carry through. If Britain was to stay on gold, the only course left was to seek further credits.[72]

On the 18th, approaches were made to New York and Paris. This time, they got nowhere. During the afternoon, MacDonald left Downing Street for a weekend at Chequers. When he arrived, he was summoned back for an urgent meeting with Harvey, Peacock and a number of senior Treasury officials. Harvey made it clear that there was now no alternative but to go off gold, and it was agreed that this should be done over the weekend. 'Did a more solemn conference ever meet in Downing St.? ... ,' MacDonald asked himself in an appropriately funereal diary entry afterwards. 'We considered effects, steps to be taken, people to be enlisted to help & so on, & when we could do no more, we walked away silently & solemnly.'[73] Next day, the Bank formally asked to be relieved of its obligations under the 1925 Gold Standard Act; and on Sunday, September 20th, the Cabinet agreed that the necessary legislation should be passed the following day. During the evening, MacDonald saw Henderson at

Downing Street and told him about the change of programme. Henderson, he noted, was 'Pompous & aloof at first but chastened afterwards & said was willing to co-operate in getting business through.'[74] On September 21st, the Gold Standard (Amendment) Bill passed through all its stages. Henderson made a conciliatory speech, advising the Labour Party not to oppose it.[75] In spite of his advice, 112 Labour M.P.s voted against the second reading.[76]

Britain's departure from the gold standard was a watershed for the world as well as for Britain. The old nineteenth-century order, which so many international gatherings had tried to revive, was now past resuscitation; little by little, Governments of all colours began to stumble towards a new order of managed currencies and managed economies. It was also a watershed for MacDonald. The strongest arguments against an early election had been that it might damage confidence in sterling at a time when the parity was in danger. Now that the parity had gone, the confidence argument could be used the other way. It was no longer a question of defending a fixed rate which might go at any moment, but of preventing a steady decline over a period. In these circumstances, it could be argued that it was better to get the election over quickly than to face months of uncertainty with a Government that lacked a stable majority in the House of Commons. At a deeper level, moreover, the balance of power in the Cabinet had shifted. Hitherto, the Conservatives had been tied to MacDonald at least as firmly as he had been tied to them. Without them, his Government would have fallen; but that, in itself, had made it impossible for them to leave it. They had agreed to serve under him in the first place on the grounds that only a National Government could save the country. They could hardly resign and risk precipitating the disaster which they had taken office to prevent; and so long as the threat of disaster remained, it was almost as hard for them to challenge MacDonald's judgment of what was needed to avert it. Once the Government had been forced off gold, however, they recovered their freedom of action. The disaster had now happened, and it was no longer necessary to sacrifice everything to avoid it. Most Conservatives still believed that the country would be better off with a National Government than without one. They also believed, with good reason, that the country wanted a National Government with MacDonald at the head of it, and that their electoral prospects would be enhanced if they were thought to want one too. But they no longer saw it as a matter of life and death. If they were forced to choose between a National Government and an election, they would probably choose an election — both because they thought they would win it, and because they believed that the country's problems could be solved only after an election had given them a mandate for the historic Conservative policy of tariff reform. Within a few days of the decision to leave the gold standard, Conservative demands for an election were even louder than they had been before; by the weekend, the choice which MacDonald had tried to avoid since the Government was formed was staring him in the face.

At first, he played for time. For most of the night of September 21st, he was
kept awake by a violent headache. Next morning, he broke down; and during
the afternoon of the 22nd he was bundled off to rest with an old friend in
Sandwich Bay.[77] From there, he wrote a long letter to Baldwin, arguing that
before deciding whether or not to hold an election the Government should
decide on its monetary and trade policies and take the lead in an attempt to re-
adjust the international financial system; hinting that it would take a long time
to read such an agreement, since reluctant converts to a tariff would now be
able to argue that devaluation had made it unnecessary; and adding pointedly
that most of his friends outside politics would regard an election in current
circumstances as 'a heartless piece of political craft'.[78] Soon afterwards, news
arrived from Rose Rosenberg which must have made him even more reluctant
to pre-empt the future than he had been before. At a meeting of the parliamentary Labour Party that morning, she reported on September 22nd, Henderson had been violently attacked for his conciliatory speech on the Gold Standard
Bill. He had lost his temper and demanded a special meeting to decide whether
or not he was to continue as leader.[79] Next day she continued the story in
another letter:

I had a long talk with Malone. At the resumed meeting yesterday – not of
a full Party meeting however but of the Executive of the Parliamentary
Labour Party – Henderson offered to resign, but he was prevailed upon not
to do so. Arthur Greenwood told Malone this fact later in the day.

Malone felt that Henderson was in a very worried condition all yesterday;
he also gathered that Henderson would be prepared to come to terms with
you to make the Government a National Government with substantial
Labour support, and to avoid a General Election. Several Labour Party
Members would do that as well. Malone says that now that the Gold
Standard Bill makes the pound of less value, the $1\frac{1}{2}\%$ whereby you conten-
ded the unemployed man was better off than he was two years ago, did not
operate, and we could without appearing to give way make some concessions to the Unemployed ... If you did this, the gesture would immediately
bring to your side the best elements of the Labour Party – including
Henderson – leaving people like Wise, Buchanan, Stephen, and the I.L.P.
crowd as the official Opposition. People like Will Thorne would agree to
come over on such terms.

The quarrelling and bad feeling that exists [sic] inside the Labour Party
at the present time is worse than it has ever been – Henderson is having
considerably more trouble already than you have ever had with your
Labour Party backbenchers.

If we go to the country now, Malone is certain that the Labour Party
will lose one hundred seats at least, and that in the process of fighting much
bad feeling will have been stirred up which will leave a bad odour behind ...

Malone is working with Dunnico to see how much support he can bring to you from [the] L.P. benches, and will keep me informed from time to time.[80]

By now, however, time was running out. MacDonald went back to London on September 25th. 'General Election agitation contrary to my expectations increased,' he noted indignantly. 'No doubt engineered from Tory headquarters for the purpose of getting a majority for Tariff Reform ... Doubtful if election can now be avoided, but I must explore the situation at Chequers. In any event, no Tory tool for me.'[81] His explorations took him down a circuitous path. A few days before, Samuel had written a Cabinet paper opposing an early election and warning that the Liberals would not join the Conservatives on a protectionist platform. On September 26th, MacDonald countered with a paper arguing that the agitation for an election had now lasted so long that it was politically impossible for the Government to avoid one, and that the real problem was to decide how the election should be fought. A party fight, of the kind that would take place if the Government were opposed by the Liberal Party as well as by the Labour Party, would not be in the national interest. Instead, 'A National appeal must be made by those who have formed the National Government.' In practice, this meant that the Government should ask for a mandate to deal with problems as they arose—making it clear that it would introduce a tariff if it thought it necessary to do so.[82]

He had not yet burned his boats, however; and on the 27th he wrote again to Baldwin, warning that he had met 'great difficulties regarding an early election', and that 'Two or three of my closest friends in the Ministry tell me that they will not fight if an election takes place with nothing but cuts passed and no steps taken to deal with rising prices, and the difficulties beginning to show in consequence of the fall in the £ ... The idea that it is now only a Conservative Party move has increased like a flood.'[83] On the 28th he dithered again. Wigram reported to the King that MacDonald 'does not like the idea of smashing up the Labour Party at the head of a Conservative association. He does not know how to run with the hare and hunt with the hounds. He has hopes of sitting tight now and attracting a following of [sic] the Labour Party.'[84] When a feeler came from the Labour Party that evening, however, his response was not enthusiastic. As he put it in his diary:

> Malone & Dunnico came & urged me to return or make some junction eg. by asking Henderson to reconsider his position & offering him inducements to join us. Thomas told me they had talked to Henderson first. I was not forthcoming, said I was hoping to end Parlt. life very soon, reflected sadly on the Party as I see it now. Was ill & went home to bed at 9 p.m.[85]

Malone and Dunnico had come too late. Though MacDonald had not yet heard the news, the Labour Party National Executive had decided earlier that day that all members and supporters of the National Government should 'automatically and immediately' cease to be members of the Labour Party.[86] In the circumstances, its decision was understandable, perhaps inevitable. The Labour movement had been built on the trade-union ethic of loyalty to majority decisions. MacDonald had defied that ethic; to many Labour activists, he was now a kind of political blackleg, who deserved to be treated accordingly. MacDonald himself can be forgiven for seeing things in a different light. His life had been bound up with the Labour movement for more than forty-five years. Without him, the weak and loose-knit Labour Representation Committee of 1900 might never have become a force to be reckoned with, and the Labour Party might never have become the main anti-Conservative party in the state. Now he had been contemptuously ejected from it, as though these services had never been. Not only had the Executive struck at him in the present: by implication, at least, it had denied his past.[87] It would be wrong to assume that he would have decided against an election if he had not been expelled. In a letter to the veteran Liberal leader, Lord Grey, on September 30th, he explained that an election had become necessary to stop the 'ominous flutterings' which were taking place in the exchange rate; and in a letter to Lloyd George on the same day, he made the same point.[88] That argument would have had force whether he had been expelled or not, and it might have convinced him in any case. All the same, there can be no doubt that his expulsion had made it much easier for him to contemplate an election than it had been before. 'Necessity of election gets clearer ... ,' he noted on September 29th. 'News about that the Lab: Party executive has expelled us all. The Tooley St. Tailors never die.'[89] Long and complex negotiations were needed before the Cabinet found an election platform on which it could agree. But MacDonald no longer dragged his feet.

VI

The negotiations centred around two questions. In the foreground was the complex, but nevertheless soluble, problem of how to reconcile the increasingly strident Conservative faith in protection with the traditional Liberal gospel of free trade. Behind that lay the inherently insoluble problem of how to ensure that the Conservatives would not use the majority which they seemed likely to win in an election to dominate or humiliate their allies. From MacDonald's point of view, the first problem mattered only because the second was linked to it. Once, he had been a lukewarm free-trader. Now he was, if anything, a lukewarm protectionist. But although he did not see the fiscal question as a matter of principle, his colleagues did; and because they did, he was obliged to behave as though he did too. Samuel and the section of the Liberal Party for which he spoke were passionately and dogmatically committed to free trade. Many Conservatives, headed by Neville Chamberlain, were as passionately committed to protection. Others believed that the time was ripe for it, and that the Conservative Party would gain by pressing for it. The gap between these two positions was widened by personal antipathy and, still more, by political calculation. Samuel was deeply unpopular in the Conservative Party. Besides, the Conservatives could see that if he were replaced by the more amenable Simon they would find it easier to have their way – not only then but in future. They fought for a protectionist platform, not only because they wanted it for its own sake, but because they wanted to force Samuel to resign. By the same token, however, MacDonald was forced to resist them. It was politically advantageous for him to show that the Government was not under Conservative control. It was also emotionally essential. He came to Samuel's defence, not because he agreed with him, but because he could use Samuel's presence in the Cabinet to prove – to himself as well as to others – that the National Government was not a Conservative Government in disguise.

The struggle began on September 29th, when Chamberlain gave MacDonald a draft election statement, calling for a free hand, and adding, 'In particular, we ask for power to control imports, whether by prohibition, tariffs or other measures.'[90] MacDonald accepted this formula himself, but Samuel rejected it. This was what Chamberlain wanted; he told Amery that 'MacDonald is the key, and that it is essential to get him and to keep out Samuel.'[91] The key, however, refused to turn. By the evening of October 1st, no agreement had been reached. Instead of forcing Samuel to choose between resignation and surrender, MacDonald suggested that Chamberlain's draft should be watered down, by deleting the words 'In particular' from the beginning of the sentence, and by changing the words 'other measures' to 'such other measures as may be necessary'. To the Conservatives' horror, Samuel accepted the new formula; but after some excited comings and goings in the lobbies, the other Liberal ministers insisted that they needed more time to consider it. The Cabinet at last broke up at 11.30 p.m., having decided that if the Liberals had not agreed to the new formula by 2.30 the following afternoon, it would be assumed that they had rejected it.[92]

Next day, MacDonald went to Seaham, to address a delegate meeting of the constituency Labour Party. He woke in the small hours, and at 4.30 in the morning wrote a long and remarkably frank letter to Baldwin, asking,

Who is the 'we' seeking power? The united Cabinet or a majority? The new House will be Conservative ... because in present exigencies it must be so. Neither the Liberals nor us can put enough candidates in the field to give us the security of adequate numbers ... Must we then be able to show national unity only by becoming parties to an election which in fact means that if we say we are not ruling tariffs out, we are consenting to their being introduced whether we like it or not? That is the dilemma. It is caused not by the wording of a statement but by the unknown action of those in favour of tariffs. Will they use a majority we have helped to give them irrespective of us? ...

... It is too much to ask us to do that without some guarantee that we are not to appear after the election as the biggest boobies of our time.

The guarantee should be ... that without common agreement we should not apply the tariffs method to control imports until we have finished the currency part of our work, eg. stabilised the £ in particular ... or, if we cannot agree on the use of the power we ask for, we should agree that the Conservative majority, should such there be, must not be used against us until a period of at least eighteen months has elapsed since the Election. For us to have to resign before the New Year and leave a Conservative majority in power for five years would cover us with such ridicule that I cannot agree to run the risk ... Do the Conservatives expect us to accept a formula which if the appeal to the country is successful leaves them at liberty within a week to disagree with us, turn us out and proceed to rule without us? If they don't, what security can they give us.[93]

Baldwin's response is not known. A year later he told Tom Jones, 'I told Ramsay when the National Government was formed that if they [i.e. the Conservatives] tried to hound him unfairly, I would go with him. They could boot me too.'[94] In fact, it is unlikely that MacDonald asked for such a pledge when the National Government was formed. At that stage he did not expect to stay in office for more than a few weeks, and had no reason to fear Conservative 'hounding'. Though it is far from certain, it is much more probable that Baldwin's pledge was given in response to MacDonald's letter of October 2nd. In any case, MacDonald had now made it clear that he was unwilling to be used as a Conservative stalking-horse and that, for the time being, at least, he had linked his fortunes with the Samuelites'.

When the Cabinet met that afternoon, Samuel reported that the Liberals would not accept the amended Conservative draft, and put forward an alternative which he must have known the Conservatives would not accept. After two-and-a-half hours of profitless semantics, the meeting broke up;[95] and when MacDonald got back from Seaham next morning he discovered that the two sides were as far apart as ever. For a while he was tempted to throw in his hand — telling the King that he was beginning to feel that he had failed and had 'better clear out'. The King replied sternly that it was his duty to find a solution, and that even if he resigned, his resignation would not be accepted.[96] With these admonitions ringing in his ears, MacDonald retired for a weekend at Chequers to ponder the situation. He put the results to the Cabinet in the evening of October 5th. Since no agreement had been reached, he announced, the Government now had to choose one of three possible courses — to break up into its constituent parts, to stay in office without an election or to 'go to the country on the general policy on which the Cabinet was unanimous, leaving discretion to the various Parties to deal with control of imports and tariffs on their own lines'.[97] For a long time it looked as though the Government would break up; and at one stage Baldwin began what Sankey described in his diary as a 'valedictory speech'[98]. At the last moment, however, it was decided that the third course should be adopted after all.

It was a defeat for the Conservatives and a victory for MacDonald, but it brought him little joy. After the meeting he noted:

> To-night I ended the cackle. It is impossible to go on now without an election. I tried it on at the Cabinet & Thomas in a thoughtless outburst played into the hands of the Tories & encouraged them to offer resignation instead of examination. I believe Chamberlain scribbled a note to Thomas suggesting resignation. I knew it was useless & impossible. So we are to dissolve. The election will present many difficulties, especially Tariff propaganda & definitions. How sad I feel at the thought of fighting with Tories & Liberals! How I despise the men who ran away. And how hard it is to have to appear to have deserted myself.[99]

He was equally miserable when Parliament was dissolved on October 7th. According to his diary,

> I saw Snowden after it was over walking (crawling) down the corridor to the Ladies' Gallery—his last. He was unmoved apparently. It is all too terrible, but what else could have been done? The people I care for most in my heart suspect me & are confused. Will the old relations & affections return? I shall try, but the machine Labour men will stand in the way.[100]

VII

His forebodings soon came true. Six weeks before, he had promised that when the election came there would be no coupons and no pacts. Now he was about to lead an anti-Labour alliance into battle – to campaign for the defeat of Labour candidates and for the victory of Conservatives and Liberals. A politician who breaks with his party at Westminster can be received back into the fold without much difficulty; the unforgivable sin is to fight against it on the hustings. So it was with MacDonald. When he had formed the National Government, some Labour people had agreed with him; many had sympathized even though they disagreed. Few sympathized now. In the offices of the London Labour Party, Herbert Morrison turned MacDonald's picture to the wall;[101] in miners' cottages in Aberavon, men and women who had once followed him as a 'Messiah' did the same.[102]

During the campaign, tempers rose even further. The election was fought in the shadow of the worst financial crisis in living memory. The gold standard had gone, and nearly 3,000,000 people were out of work. In a sense which has not been true in any election since, the electorate was frightened – not in some vague and generalized way, but directly and personally. In an election fought against this background, the Labour Party would have been at a disadvantage in any event; and the Government managed to make its disadvantage even greater. MacDonald issued a curiously nebulous manifesto, asking for the authority to 'consider every proposal likely to help'. It was endorsed by Baldwin and Samuel, who also issued manifestoes of their own. The Conservatives campaigned for protection; the official Liberals, for free trade. Almost inevitably, therefore, policies played little part in the Government's appeal. Like virtue, it was presented as its own reward. It asked for support, not on the grounds that it had new solutions to the country's problems, but on the grounds that it existed: and that its existence had saved the country once and would go on saving it in future. Such an appeal was bound to seem outrageously unfair to the Labour candidates who had to answer it. Later research has not confirmed the charge, which was to be heard a great deal when the election was over, that the Government's campaign was exceptionally virulent or mendacious.[103] The fact remains that the implicit premiss on which its case was based was that the Labour Party had, in some subtle sense, ceased to be a part of the nation and that a Labour vote was a vote against the country. In many ways, it was reminiscent of the Coalition Government's case in 1918. The difference was that, where the Coalition claimed that it had saved the nation from the Kaiser, the National Government claimed that it had saved it from the Labour Party.

What was even more galling from Labour's point of view was that it was MacDonald who gave this case its force. He was not only the author and head of the National Government; as L. S. Amery put it later, he was also the 'embodiment of the national conception'.[104] In the words of his election posters in Seaham he was 'The captain who stuck to the ship'. The mere fact that he was still on the bridge threw an aura of self-sacrifice over his new crew, and could be used as an argument against the crew which had abandoned him. It was a powerful card, and once the campaign had begun, MacDonald played it with great skill. Unlike Snowden, he did not make the mistake of attacking his old followers directly or of repudiating policies which he had advocated in the past. In his opening broadcast, he did not mention the Labour Party at all, and concentrated on the need for national unity to stabilize sterling and stop prices from rising.[105] In his final broadcast on the 24th, in which he replied to a broadcast by Henderson the week before, he was more belligerent. But, even now, his tone was one of sorrow rather than of anger. Labour's programme, he declared, was 'the old programme of ordinary party fights' – reasonable enough in normal times, but out of keeping with 'a time of special distress which calls for the co-operation of all parties'. For the moment, the issues were graver:

My watchword to you all is: Until these days are over, stand by the interests of the nation. No party can work out its policy on crumbling and shifting economic foundations. Let us see to it now that what we do will place our credit and our reputation on a basis which will be unassailable for many a long year to come, and no class of the community is more interested in this than the man with the scanty weekly wage and his wife, the marvellous chancellor of his exchequer.[106]

After the broadcast Sir William Rothenstein wrote, 'I never heard any words so sincere, so moving or so passionately disinterested as yrs. last night'. His wife was even more enthusiastic. 'I want to thank you with all my heart for that wonderful speech of yours we have just heard,' she wrote. 'It was so profoundly moving in its utter sincerity that it hurt & tears were in the eyes of all who were listening to you.'[107] The Rothensteins spoke for many. In the eyes of the Labour Party, that was perhaps MacDonald's greatest crime.

Much the same was true of his constituency at Seaham. It had been a Labour seat since 1922. Sidney Webb's majority had varied between 10,000 and 12,000; and, as we have seen, MacDonald's majority in 1929 had been more than 28,000. It was dominated by coal-mining and had no middle class to speak of. MacDonald's fate would depend on his ability to persuade highly-unionized. working-class Labour voters to vote across class lines and to ignore the appeals of all the representative bodies in the Labour movement. He had no roots in the constituency and had represented it for only two years. The Labour candidate — his old agent, Coxon — was a local man. In most places, Labour was on the defensive; in Seaham, it assumed that it would win. When Parliament was dissolved, the *Daily Herald* forecast that MacDonald would be defeated, and would then take refuge either in a safe Conservative seat or in the House of Lords.[108] Hannen Swaffer, who spent most of the election covering Mac-Donald's campaign, reported when he arrived that he had found no support for MacDonald, while Labour was 'united and more determined than ever'.[109] After speaking in the division, Dalton wrote privately of MacDonald, 'It seems impossible that *he* can win.'[110] Harold Laski was equally confident. 'I have no sort of doubt,' he assured the readers of the *Daily Herald* on the 17th, 'that Seaham will give Coxon a staggering majority.'

MacDonald arrived in the constituency on the 12th. According to Swaffer, he looked 'tired and grey and ill and nervous'.[111] That evening he addressed a crowd of more than a thousand at the Hippodrome Theatre, in Easington Colliery. He was greeted with cheers, mingled with boos and catcalls, but during the evening the opposition faded. 'Never has Mr MacDonald been heard to give a more impassioned speech in the Division,' reported the *Durham County Advertiser*. 'He carried the audience with him to the end and his voice was often drowned in applause.'[112] He had four main themes — the danger of inflation, the need to prove to the outside world that 'they can trust this country to guard its honour', the Labour Party's refusal to 'say hard things to you in honesty, rather than ... smooth things to you in order to keep their popularity', and his own record as a Labour pioneer. When he had taken on the secretaryship of the Labour Representation Committee, he declared in a bitter but telling passage, he had begged better-known Labour leaders to join it: 'And they all said, "It is no good, nothing is going to be done." ' Now, 'those of us who have followed what we consider to be right ... are subjected to the taunts and adverse votes of those men whom we made.' As for the National Government,

> I know a lot of you shook your heads over that National Government. If I might whisper in your ears—I may have shaken my own ...
> I quite understand why my colleagues did not join the National Government. I have not a word to say against them for that ...
> ... But what I do not understand is this: Why, when they went, they did not stand up to what they had done before they went. If I had gone—as I might have gone—I should have stood up in the House of Commons and said, 'Yes, we did that; yes, we did the other thing ... [W]e don't trust you in your general policy, but we will offer no factious opposition to your balancing your Budget'. That was what I expected them to do and they have not done it.[113]

Not all his meetings passed off as peacefully. On the 15th, he was refused a hearing at Shotton, and was only just able to deliver his speech at Thornley. At Hordern, on the 16th, he was howled down.[114] When Ernest Stanford, a former Labour candidate for Worthing, arrived in the constituency to help MacDonald, he was told by the booking clerk in the railway station that 'it was asking too much of any working man to come out openly for MacDonald. Indeed, if he himself did so he would be victimised by his fellow workers and his neighbours.'[115] Then came an episode which was to cause a good deal of head-shaking later, but which seems venial enough in the context of a bitter election campaign. From the start, one of MacDonald's main arguments had been that a demonstration of national unity was needed to stop the pound from sinking further. In his opening meeting, he had reminded the audience that during the great German inflation of the early 'twenties 'you would have found that pantechnicon vans had to come to bring the wages in paper at the end of the week.'[116] Now he decided to make the point more vividly. When he handed in his nomination papers, *The Times* reported on the 17th, he jokingly offered the returning officer, in lieu of his deposit, 60,000 German marks—representing a week's wages in Germany during the slump of the mark. When he spoke a second time at Shotton on the 19th, he used the same gambit. 'Dealing with the results of inflation,' *The Times* reported, 'he showed his audience a German note for 50,000,000 marks, nominally worth £250,000, but which during the German financial collapse could be bought for 2d.' Whether because of this, or because his supporters had now acquired a loudspeaker which made it possible for the chairman to shout hecklers down,[117] the *Durham County Advertiser* commented that this time he was 'cheered to the echo'.

As late as the end of the week, there was a good deal of despondency in the MacDonald camp, but by the following week there were signs that the tide might be on the turn. MacDonald spent the 26th in a tour of the constituency, starting at 10.30 in the morning and finishing at 11.30 at night. A surprising number of MacDonald window bills, *The Times* reporter noticed, had suddenly appeared in places where none had been seen earlier in the campaign.[118] When MacDonald left his eve-of-the-poll meeting in Seaham Harbour, the audience burst into 'Will ye no come back again.' 'I shall always remember the enthusiasm ... ,' Stanford wrote later, 'and the ringing and challenging tone of Mac-Donald's declaration of faith: "Labour I am and Labour I shall remain." '[119] Polling day was on the 27th, and in Seaham the votes were counted on the 28th. By the morning it was clear from the overnight results that the Government had won a crushing victory, but the tension was too much for MacDonald and he left for London before the count.

In his absence, he was declared elected, with 28,978 votes to Coxon's 23,027 — a majority of nearly 6,000. Over the country as a whole, the results were even more astonishing. The Government parties polled 14,500,000 votes to Labour's 6,600,000. In the new House of Commons, the Labour Party had only 46 members; the I.L.P. 6; and the Lloyd George Liberals 4. The Labour front bench was almost annihilated: of former Cabinet ministers who had gone into opposition when the National Government was formed, only Lansbury kept his seat. MacDonald's National Labour group had 13 members; the Samuelite Liberals 33; the Simonites 35; and the Conservatives 471. With 556 supporters altogether, the Government had a majority of 500. The Labour vote had gone down by 1,500,000; in seats, it was no stronger than it had been in 1918.

CHAPTER 27

'Nae my ain hoose'

I

'BACK from election yesterday by air,' MacDonald noted bitterly on October 29th. 'It has turned out all too well. How tragically the Labour Party has been let down ... The Conser: Head Office pretended to do what it never did & indeed played a shady game. It saw its advantage & took it, & unfortunately the size of the victory has weakened me. Once again I record that no honest man should trust in too gentlemanly a way the Conservative wirepullers.'[1]

He was to return to these themes again and again – not only for the next few weeks, but for the next few years. At Seaham, he had won what *The Economist* justly described as a 'personal triumph';[2] in the country as a whole, his Government's victory had surpassed even the Coalition's in 1918. Though his personal following in the new House of Commons was tiny, everyone knew that he had made an enormous contribution to the result. The election had been fought largely on his actions in August, and whatever else the outcome showed, there could be no doubt that he was backed by an overwhelming majority of the electorate; however unpopular he might be in the Labour Party, his authority and prestige, at Westminster and in the country, both seemed impregnable. Yet few victories can have brought less satisfaction to the victor. Before the election, he had been afraid that the campaign would cut him off irrevocably from the Labour movement and make him a prisoner of the Conservative Party. Now it seemed clear that his worst fears had come true; and he reacted with a kind of tormented indignation, which is painful to encounter even at forty years' distance and which must have been immeasurably more painful to experience.

Not all his apprehensions were justified. He was much more successful in fending off Conservative office-seekers than has sometimes been realized; and in spite of their huge majority in the House of Commons, the Conservatives received only eleven Cabinet posts out of twenty. In spite of his success in whittling down their claims to office, however, MacDonald could not help but view the massed Conservative battalions on the benches behind him with a mixture of alarm and distaste. During the campaign, he had been engaged in a number of petty disputes with the Conservative head office about the unwillingness of certain Conservative associations to withdraw their candidates in constituencies where a Liberal or National Labour candidate had a claim to the seat.[3] In retrospect, it seems clear that, except in a few places, the Conservatives displayed as much restraint as they could reasonably have been expected to do. But the exceptions included Preston, where Jowitt, the National Labour attorney general, had to withdraw in the face of Conservative opposition, and also included the Combined English Universities, where he eventually stood and was defeated. In these circumstances, it is not surprising that MacDonald should have felt aggrieved; and when the new Parliament assembled, his sense of grievance was renewed. 'What strange lands I have been pushed into!', he noted on November 10th. 'The first reaction is an increase in my anti-Tory instinct ... The oppression of my companionship crushes out every other feeling.'[4] By the end of the month he was confessing:

> Get no inspiration from H. of C.; feel completely out of harmony with it; point of view & interests of colleagues not mine. I am pulled up by the roots & even what I believe in, in these new conditions, seems dead ... I am worn out & feel more & more isolated. Better retire & get some vigour for work in the country to rally Labour round a policy of Socialism. Close acquaintance with the Tories does not improve one's respect for nor interest in them.[5]

It was his old companions, however, not his new ones, who provoked his bitterest complaints. His eve-of-poll declaration at Seaham Harbour – 'Labour I am and Labour I shall remain' – had been more than platform rhetoric. He still felt instinctively that he was part of the Labour movement, and the knowledge that most of its active members now saw him as a renegade was unbearably painful to him; because he felt part of the movement, he could not shrug that knowledge off. If he had been the cold and calculating class traitor which his enemies in the Labour Party imagined him to be, he might not have cared what they thought of him. Their attacks hurt partly because they were misplaced.

They hurt even more because he saw them as symptoms of betrayal. In retrospect, there can be little doubt that the policy which the T.U.C. adopted after the Labour Government fell offered a better solution to the country's problems than did the policy agreed upon by the outgoing Labour Cabinet. Former Labour ministers who turned their backs on the economies which they had accepted in office, and followed the T.U.C. line instead, were abandoning a doomed policy in favour of a policy which at least pointed the way to the Keynesian techniques of the future. Understandably enough, MacDonald saw their conduct in a harsher light. It seemed to him that they had first run away from their commitments and had then proceeded to cover him with the odium which they should have had the courage to face themselves. As so often, moreover, his sensitivity to criticism was heightened by his tendency to define his position in doctrinal terms. A more opportunistic politician might have been content to defend his actions during the crisis on the grounds of national necessity. MacDonald felt obliged to defend them on grounds of socialist principle as well: and the more violently he was attacked for betraying his convictions, the stronger that feeling became.

In some moods, he longed for a reconciliation with the Labour Party; in others such longings were overwhelmed by a flood of resentment and bitterness. In a letter to J. M. Boltz, the defeated Labour candidate for Bridgwater, who had written to him just after the election to ask why he had 'smashed up' the Labour movement and gone over to its enemies, he rehearsed his familiar reasons for forming the National Government and insisted that if the Labour Party had behaved with 'discretion' after going into opposition he would not have gone to the country at all. However, he went on,

a very important fact arose. Without any consultation with us, or indeed any warning, the Executive meeting of the Labour Party decided that those of us who were sticking to the national problems were to be expelled, and the decision was conveyed to us by a letter, bearing the signature of a sub-ordinate, which he had not even taken the trouble to sign, but was affixed by a rubber stamp initialled by some greater subordinate. Thus the election was forced upon us ...

You were led as lambs to the slaughter, and there you are now in scores ... and it is not only the Party as a whole, but admirable men like yourself for whom I have the greatest affection and whom I would still help with the most profound heartiness, who have suffered.

Is the situation now going to be faced simply by spitefulness and bitter-ness of both heart and mind? Or are we to face it all together and still rescue the Party and the Movement? So far as I am concerned I have changed neither opinion nor principle. I regard my colleagues and myself as being deserted by men who ought to have had proof through a long series of years that the one thing we care for in public life is the Labour Movement, and that if we had been followed the Labour Movement at this moment would have been in a position of strength which it has never hitherto enjoyed ...

I know it may be hard for you ... to see the force of what I am writing to you, but when some little time has elapsed and a complete survey is made of the whole situation, our position will be vindicated and instead of our being regarded as the authors of your troubles it will be seen that we were the only people who strove to avoid the calamity that has fallen upon you. The Labour Movement must be built up again, but that can only be done when the whole facts are considered.

If ever you are in London I should like to see you.[6]

In a letter to Ben Tillett early in November, he covered much the same ground, but in a more aggressive fashion:

I am very glad to have your letter and reciprocate all the friendly and generous feelings in it. I also share your regrets that the Party for which we have done so much was so misguided, and listened to such bad advice as to bring it to this doleful state ...

The miscalculations were two-fold. They did not appreciate how the nation expects that a Government faced with a serious national condition should deal courageously with that condition and not hide it ...

The second miscalculation was [about] how men and women re-act to appeals which take them out of themselves ... The assumption of my late colleagues was that they would re-act as selfish individuals, and that the unemployed especially would hear but one appeal, and that to their pocket. Hard times and long and widespread unemployment lure politicians into that moral trap. This miscalculation, however, was a serious one for the majority of the Labour Party to make, because the Party's pioneers and its own original spirit protested against it ... Nemesis came swift and crashing, and the blows fell heaviest in precisely those districts where the materialist arguments based on poverty were strongest. On the morning after the polls, the Labour paper asked its readers to expect great victories when the votes of the North East Coast and the mining areas were counted. These districts as a matter of fact, recorded the most astounding Labour failures.

... For the moment an acrid bitterness prevails which blinds men to their own mistakes, makes them persist in their own faults and commits them to conduct which is matched only by the worst early Victorian employers. I am sure this will pass and then the Party will be in a frame of mind which will make a survey of these past weeks a necessary and profitable undertaking ... From contributing to that, if I see fit, I decline to allow anyone to exclude me or those who have been acting with me. In any event my colleagues & myself have saved the reputation of the Labour Movement from an unqualified condemnation from the judgement seat of history.[7]

In the next few weeks, he became more aggressive still. At the beginning of November, he replied to William Diack, an old socialist who had sent him a 'word of cheer' during the election campaign: 'The blatant and ignorant passion which has been drawn out by the failure of the Party to face its responsibilities ... is most discouraging for the future. It looks as though all our work has gone into the creation of a petty and passionate class movement whose ideal of Socialism is not much more than public subsidies.'[8] 'The outlook is not at all good,' he complained to the Archbishop of York soon afterwards, 'and the behaviour of the majority of the Labour Party has been most disastrous. I cannot let it go, but up to now see no clear way of saving it ... It has lost its idealism and vision, and has become little more than an attachment to trade union executives.'[9] By December he was writing to Martin Haddow, 'I am afraid that the year is to bring me neither peace nor prosperity, and the worst of it all is what seems to me to be the betrayal by the Labour movement ... of its fundamental socialism and its abandonment of everything except public assistance.'[10] A few days later a National Labour supporter named C. J. Titler reported that he had just had a private conversation with Herbert Morrison, who had thought that he was an emissary from MacDonald and had been 'extremely sympathetic'. A discreet approach should be made to Morrison, Titler suggested, with a view to finding out what could be done to keep the door open for MacDonald's return to the Labour Party.[11] MacDonald snapped back belligerently:

> The paragraphs that have been appearing in the newspapers especially in the 'Daily Herald', that I am trying to go back to the Labour Party, and have appointed emissaries to make soundings, are rather embarrassing and untrue ... You now tell me that you have seen Morrison who assumed that you had come from me. It is very necessary to disabuse him of any such idea. If I were clear of my immediate burdens I should show them that in spite of their excommunications I am a member of the Labour movement, and would defy them and all their caucuses to turn me out of it. But what I should do would be to try to get the movement back to its proper position, and rescue it from being a glorified board of guardians.[12]

II

It was one thing to write grandly about rescuing the Labour movement: another to mount an effective rescue operation. Before the election, a group of MacDonald's Labour followers, headed by his P.P.S., Frank Markham, and Lord De La Warr, one of the few hereditary peers in the Labour Party, had hastily thrown together a National Labour committee to run candidates who would fight under MacDonald's banner. Around £20,000 had been collected, mostly from wealthy friends of MacDonald's: twenty-one seats had been contested; and, as we have seen, thirteen National Labour candidates had been returned. Once the election was over, however, the committee's role and purpose were obscure. In a long and shrewdly-argued memorandum, written in December 1931, MacDonald's private secretary, Herbert Usher, formulated three questions which MacDonald would have to answer before deciding what the committee's future was to be. Did he want to form a new political party? Did he expect to return to the main body of the Labour Party? Or did he envisage the continuation of the National Government for a 'considerable time', and the possible emergence from it of 'a powerful party of the centre'? An attempt to form a new party, Usher wrote, would encounter 'obvious difficulties'. It would be difficult to put forward a distinctive National Labour policy, different from that of the Government's Conservative and Liberal supporters, yet carrying no threat to the Government's unity. In any case, the National Labour group in the House of Commons did not want a new party. Its opinions ranged from 'those of Malcolm — very strongly rooted in Labour thought and tradition — to views very difficult to distinguish from those of your moderate Conservative supporters'; most of its members depended, not only on Conservative votes, but on the support of their local Conservative association as well. As for Mac-Donald's return to the Labour Party, this was unlikely: even if the party's bitterness towards him died down, the existing leadership would find it easy to retain control so long as it kept in step with the more powerful trade-union leaders. That left only the possible emergence of a centre party. This, Usher concluded despairingly, 'is what the mass of the public really wants, but whether our political organisations would ever permit the public to get it is another matter'.[13]

Usher had defined the questions. He had not provided the answers: and it gradually became clear that no one else could provide them either. In January 1932, MacDonald's Leicester friend, Harry Peach, another old socialist who had joined the National Labour group, wrote to say that there was still a great deal of goodwill for him in Labour circles in Leicester, and urged him to 'give some lead' to bring the best elements in the Labour Party together again.[14] MacDonald replied with a revealing mixture of gloom and uncertainty:

> I have been working away at this, but so many important things are still uncertain that the time has not come for saying anything very final. One thing is clear, that, after a somewhat prolonged if quiet struggle within the Party between those of us who are Socialists and make Socialism the found-ation of our political work and those who wish the whole Movement to be dominated by Trade Union officials and the General Council of the Trades Union Congress in particular, the latter have won ...
>
> That is the position today, but is it possible to look at the future system-atically so as to give the lines of the reconstruction that will have to be made? Up to now, I confess I cannot see it ... There is a tremendous opportunity for a movement of reconstruction, and one or two of the younger Tories with whom I have come into close personal contact during the last month or two, are very keen about it ... The tragedy is, however, that one or two men who completely share my opinion, thinking – before the Election – that their seats were safe and that the machine was all-powerful ... decided to hang on to the [Labour] Party. They now find themselves not only aground, politically, but committed to the Labour Party policy. They cannot change their public position and declarations with any appearance of consistency – in fact, if they do not keep hostile they will cut a ridiculous figure. So they are imprisoned in their own mistakes ...
>
> I therefore do not see that the time has come for any big pronouncement on my part. This is a moment for concentration of thought and energy on immediate problems.[15]

These were cogent arguments – and, as so often with cogent arguments for doing nothing, they lost none of their cogency as time went on. The appropriate form for a possible movement of reconstruction remained obscure; old MacDonaldites who had stayed in the Labour Party became more committed to it, not less; MacDonald's thoughts and energies continued to be concentrated on immediate problems, as any prime minister's are bound to be. The National Labour committee remained in existence. It acquired a constitution, an organization of sorts, one or two moderately distinguished members and a rather pallid monthly *News Letter* – edited, at first, by Clifford Allen, who had thrown in his lot with MacDonald when the National Government was formed and who became a National Labour peer in January 1932, and later by Godfrey Elton, Malcolm's old tutor and Labour candidate for Thornbury in 1929, who followed Allen to the House of Lords in 1934. But it had no distinctive policies, no identifiable grass-roots support and, apart from personal loyalty to Mac-Donald, no obvious *raison d'être*. MacDonald constantly lamented its ineffectiveness, tried occasionally to prod it into improving its propaganda, engaged in more than one exasperated wrangle with Conservative central office on behalf of its claim to a fair proportion of by-election candidatures, and dreamed wistfully, as he put it at a National Labour Executive meeting in October 1933, of turning it into a new movement which would 'set this country working, moving and living and expanding for the next half-century'.[16] But he had no time, no energy and perhaps, at bottom, no real wish to turn the dream into a reality. The National Labour committee gave him a much-needed refuge from complete political isolation, but it was a makeshift shelter, not a permanent home.

III

As time went on, his need for a political home became more acute. As we shall see, his relations with his Conservative and Liberal colleagues, though rarely at all close, were, for the most part, reasonably harmonious; only on a few peripheral issues did he argue a distinctively 'Labour' case, at odds with theirs. On the fiscal question, which provided a big bone of contention for the best part of a year, he sided with the Conservatives and Simonite Liberals against Snowden and the Samuelite Liberals; after the free-traders left the Government in September 1932, the Cabinet's internal divisions, though sometimes quite deep, almost always cut across party lines. Yet in spite of all this, MacDonald never lost the sense that he had strayed into foreign territory, where the natives did not really understand him, nor he them. 'Of course the real trouble of [*sic*] my present position is the difference between my own point of view and that of most of my colleagues,' he mused in December 1932. 'That keeps me on a constant strain as to important details.'[17] 'The Tory local *bosses* are an odd lot of colonels & sycophants repulsively vulgar,' he noted in October 1933. '*Note*: I say "bosses", but the Tory hanger-on of whom there are legion is also of the same type.'[18] A few weeks later he complained, 'The more one knows the Tory

Party as a crowd the less one likes it.'[19] It was the same story nine months later. As he put it in July 1934,

> I am really out at elbows with my political circumstances & as the country gets upon its feet again I feel less and less harmony with my political position. My heart is elsewhere. Why? Just because 'This is nae my ain hoose, I ken by the biggin' o' 't'. Colleagues loyal & all that, but I am a Socialist, detached from old colleagues by a crisis in national existence, & alienated from them by their conduct since they got control of the Party.[20]

Few of the old colleagues concerned would, however, have recognized the description. In his letter to Tillett after the election, MacDonald had looked forward to a time when the Labour Party's 'acrid bitterness' against him would evaporate. No such time arrived. Labour politicians had explained the 1931 financial crisis in conspiratorial terms even before the election. After their defeat, many of them began to explain the political crisis which had followed it in the same way. Vague memories of the gossip of late 1930, garbled impressions of the negotiations between MacDonald, Snowden and the opposition leaders before the Labour Government fell, and more immediate memories of MacDonald's brusque and shamefaced behaviour after the Buckingham Palace conference, all seemed in retrospect to point to the same conclusion – that MacDonald had decided to form the National Government months before, and had then engineered or taken advantage of the financial crisis to carry out his decision. MacDonald, Beatrice Webb noted immediately after the election, was 'at once author, producer and chief actor of this amazing political drama'. A few months later, her husband, who had voted in favour of the £76 million economy programme when Labour was in office, made almost the same point in almost the same language, but in an even more definite form. The sixty-three days between the fall of the Labour Government and the National Government's victory at the election, he wrote in the *Political Quarterly*, formed 'a single drama, in all its development foreseen in advance ... only by the statesman who was at once its author, producer and principal actor'.[21] Passfield was probably the first to formulate what Reginald Bassett has called the 'plot theory' in such unqualified terms. He was by no means the last.

Hand in hand with the plot theory went what might be called the seduction theory. As we have seen, criticisms of MacDonald's failings had been rife in some sections of the Labour Party for years. Hitherto, they had been confined to a fairly narrow circle. Now they spilled out into the open. Old enemies rushed forward to testify to his defects; old supporters kept silent, or joined in the chorus of denunciation. His touchiness, suspiciousness, frequent brusqueness, apparent aloofness and undoubted liking for glittering social occasions were endlessly dissected; his kindness, fundamental simplicity and aching loneliness were forgotten or misinterpreted. Little by little, the MacDonald of flesh and blood faded from the party's collective memory. In his place appeared a two-

dimensional monster of vanity, snobbery and social cowardice, whose systematic flattery by the upper class adequately explained both his own behaviour and
his party's downfall. The real moral of the crisis, Passfield implied in his
Political Quarterly article, was that the British governing class had become more
adept at using 'the weapon of seduction'. 'It took some time to make Disraeli the
beloved of duchesses ... ,' he wrote coyly. 'On more recent cases, it is needless
to dwell.' In a long article in *Harper's* a few months later, Harold Laski wrote
that the 'essential cause' of what happened in 1931 lay in

> the relation of Mr. MacDonald's peculiar temperament to the special en-
> vironment of British politics. Timid, indecisive, vain of applause, he shrank
> from the price of unpopularity among a society he had growingly come to
> esteem. Its own self-confidence nourished his lack of it. Its own faith in its
> standards give him standards he could not otherwise attain ... His immedi-
> ate value was seen. He was cultivated with a skill by those who had shunned
> him which lessened the earlier distance he had once deplored. When the
> moment of crisis came, he found that the bridge he had thought a barrier
> of separation was, in fact, the highroad to the safety for which he yearned.
> Henceforth, he could live at ease in Zion ... The ribbon is in his coat; and
> he will not live to read the verdict of history.[22]

Where Passfield and Laski led, many followed.

It is easy to see why. The Labour Party had looked up to MacDonald as it has
looked up to no leader since. It had just suffered a crushing and humiliating
defeat at his hands. It is not surprising that it should have felt betrayed; and not
much more surprising that it should have jumped to the conclusion that the
betrayal must have been planned long before. The plot theory appealed to a
tendency, deeply embedded in human nature, to assume that nothing ever
happens by accident and that one's misfortunes are due to a conspiracy on the
part of one's enemies; the seduction theory, to the vein of social prurience which
is to be found in many parties of the left. Besides, they were based on half-
truths, not inventions. Though MacDonald had not planned the formation of
the National Government in advance, he had toyed with the notion of forming
one: though his attitudes and beliefs had not been observably affected by the
experience, he had enjoyed moving in circles which were socially suspect to the
more censorious members of the Labour Party. As time went on, moreover, the
sequel to the crisis blotted out the prelude. Though the National Government's
economic policies were in many ways more radical than the Labour Government's had been, its social policies were bleak, mean-spirited and inhumane –
while its foreign and defence policies, which were to be criticized later on the
grounds that they took too little account of the risk of war, seemed at the time,
to most people on the left, to be dangerously militaristic. As we shall see,
MacDonald was never the helpless prisoner of the Conservative Party that he
has sometimes been depicted, but he looked increasingly like one to his old

followers on the Labour benches. The longer he stayed on as prime minister, the stronger that impression became; and the easier it was to believe that he must have acted in bad faith when he had formed the Government in the first place. In these circumstances, it is not surprising that the grudges and suspicions which had been confined to a minority of the Labour Party before 1931, should have been seized upon by the rest of the party as well. Labour people were too bruised and shaken to probe their record in office or to analyse their failure to return to it. It was easier, less divisive and, above all, less painful to find a scapegoat; and MacDonald was increasingly well placed to fill the role.

This was no consolation to MacDonald. Sometimes he tried to knock the criticisms back. 'Shown Webbs [sic] article in Political Quarterly,' he noted in January 1932. 'Interesting point is that I alone am blamed & reason for my downfall is flattery. Whole Webbs diplomacy has consisted in flattery & so they have come to see no other influence in life. Article itself is contemptible, but for some time evidence that Webb has been going "gagga".'[23] 'I was so glad to get old Jim's letter,' he wrote to Tillett a few months later.

> Tell him when you are writing to him, that it warmed my heart; and you can add that if I were not a Christian, I would endorse all that he says about some of my late colleagues. I know I was bad enough to get at, because when I lost five minutes I had to make them up before I went to bed. But some of these other people, with their mighty airs, used to give me the sniggers. When they tried to sit down on a chair they seemed to have some Buckingham Palace model in front of them.'[24]

Yet it is doubtful if such ripostes can have brought much relief. Years later, Sidney Campion, who covered the 1931 Parliament from the press gallery, wrote that the way in which MacDonald's old followers used to attack him on the floor of the House was 'stupid, childish, brutish, reducing the House of Commons to the level of a drunken brawl in a backyard slum. The hounds were straining at the leash to kill ... There were occasions when I was so upset, that I set off at about midnight to walk to my Wimbledon home and be solaced by the star-filled sky.'[25] There are no direct references to such attacks in MacDonald's diary or letters, perhaps because he found them too painful to record, but it seems clear that they upset him as much as they did Campion. 'It is a pitiable spectacle ... to see Members of the Front Opposition Bench get up one after another and pour out miserable personal stuff,' he wrote in a letter to his Rhiwbina friend, J. D. Morgan, in November 1931, 'and the men who have bothered me most for office or distinctions of one kind or another are the worst.'[26] 'Newspapers get worse and worse, especially the rage of a Daily Herald in publishing with profusion of thick type and bold streamers anything which creates a sensation & vents their spleen,' he noted in March 1932. 'Labour Opposition follows same course ... What colleagues I have had.'[27] After his return from an international conference in Switzerland a few months later he noted more simply, 'the dogs bark, bite & irritate'.[28] By the end of the year he was complaining to Clifford Allen, 'Nothing do I feel more than the utter and almost contemptible breakdown of our old colleagues. Every time I hear them in the House of Commons shame fills me and despair that the working classes in this country are in such hands.'[29]

More painful than attacks from across the floor of the House of Commons was the rupture of personal relationships that accompanied it. A few Labour people remained on friendly terms with him. The most notable was Jim Middleton, whose loyalty to and compassion for him were as unshakeable as they had always been. Another was James Welsh, a Lanarkshire miner who had been M.P. for Coatbridge from 1922 to 1931, with whom he stayed occasionally and corresponded frequently, and who hoped against hope that he would return to lead the Labour Party, so that 'the Bevans and the others would find where they stood'.[30] A third was Ben Tillett, now a wizened and rather pathetic figure, full of resentment about the Transport and General Workers' ingratitude in refusing to let him keep his office in the union beyond the age of seventy.[31] He and MacDonald corresponded regularly – two lonely old men, keeping each other company. 'This week, has advanced the spleen and uncomradely ingratitude of those, whom, I have worked for,' Tillett wrote in a characteristic exchange in early 1932. 'Don't worry about this doleful note, but the fact of losing the little prerogatives of service; is, a great blow to my pride ... But, you are to go through more fires ... You are the real, "Daniel in the Lions' den"; good luck to you for the daring and the Will to fight, and live, and do; for the brave old Country.'[32] 'I think you have been used simply abominably,' MacDonald replied consolingly. 'If the capitalists used your men in the same way that your comrades have used you what an indictment we [would] put up against them.'[33] A few weeks later Tillett wrote back, 'I wish you all the wisdom of Solomon, and even more than he ever possessed; for you are to be the Solomon, responsible above any man I know, in ruling the world ... May the good Lord give Health and Wisdom, and great Courage, moved by your love of Mankind.'[34] A cascade of such assurances arrived on MacDonald's desk during the next few years, all written with the same oddly touching extravagance, and all spattered with the same profusion of commas, semicolons and capital letters. If they are touching to read now, there can be little doubt that they touched MacDonald even more.

Minnie Pallister, too, refused to allow political differences to stand in the way of personal friendship. In an undated letter, evidently written at some time in 1932 and addressed in the old way to 'Dear Chief', she assured him, 'It would be an impertinence for me to attempt to discuss anything now, when I am so out of everything, but I *understand very well*, that nothing on earth would make you do anything which you felt to be wrong, or prevent you from doing what you felt to be right.'[35] Once the shock of 1931 had worn off, Mrs Hamilton repented of her earlier coldness and took a similar line. Six months after the election, Rose Rosenberg reported that she had just had a note from her, and that:

> To my great delight she said that since she had been in America she had had
> an opportunity of seeing things in another perspective. Although she said
> she had not changed politically, she felt very keenly that it would be absurd
> to allow the friendship of almost a life-time — such as yours and hers — to be
> interfered with by political differences. And so, she said, if you were willing
> to see her, she would be ever so glad to see you again.[36]

As the tone of Rose's letter makes clear, however, Minnie Pallister and Mrs
Hamilton were in a small minority. Three weeks after the election, Snowden
took his seat in the House of Lords. 'Benches, spaces, galleries full — fuller than
attendants have seen,' MacDonald noted afterwards. 'Labour benches empty —
one other manifestation of the pettyness of the creatures.'[37] A similar experience
occurred next day. 'Dinner to me,' he noted, 'fine welcome & good company
but saw only one Labour friend in the 700. How small are the pebbles of which
the Party has been formed!'[38] Experiences like these were to become all too
common in the next few years. A sad exchange in late 1932, between Rose
Rosenberg and J. D. Morgan, tells its own story. On November 9th, Morgan
wrote that William Blackwood had spoken recently at the Cardiff Business
Club, where he had made 'some happy and touching references' to MacDonald.
'How are you keeping?', Morgan ended. 'We often think and talk about you.'[39]
On the 14th Rose replied that MacDonald had asked her to thank Morgan for
his letter, and then continued:

> I hope you will not mind what I am going to say, but you are no doubt
> aware that the division in the Labour Party has given rise to malicious
> stories, and some people who appeared to be the Prime Minister's best
> friends before are freely mentioned as being most active. I heard from
> Wales that both you and Ivor have been pretty bad, and that has made all
> of us here a little bit reticent as we none of us want to thrust ourselves in
> where feelings have changed. I hope you do not mind my reporting this to
> you, because if it is untrue a contradiction would be very helpful.[40]

Morgan's response reveals a great deal about the atmosphere in Labour
circles in these years. On the 22nd he wrote back defensively:

> I received your letter and am bound to say that I was not only distressed,
> but, greatly surprised at its contents.
> ... Whatever criticism I may have made has been political & not personal,
> as a matter of fact among my many friends I have been accused of being
> lukewarm in my resentment to the P.M., after all my wife & I cannot help
> holding him in great affection ...
> Ivor's position is somewhat different, his wife seems to be very bitter &
> I can therefore understand somewhat his position.[41]

If MacDonald's friends had to apologize for displaying insufficient resentment towards him, it is not difficult to guess how the rest of the party must have behaved.

Outwardly, MacDonald maintained a belligerent, even aggressive front. In a letter to Jack Bromley, the railway clerks' leader, in November 1933, he covered the old ground yet again, with all his old pugnacity:

> You have been good enough to write a candid letter — as you call it — and I will be equally candid with you.
>
> The action which you and those who agreed with you, took in 1931 was one of the biggest pieces of betrayal and stupidity that I have ever known or read of on the part of any body of men who professed ordinary political intelligence and any capacity to lead a movement. You were just a lot of cowards who, although you had to confess in your hearts that duty compelled you to face a difficult situation, thought you would keep in an easy job of pandering to a crowd of victims. Had you had the honesty and courage to tell the people you professed to serve that they would have to go through hard times to get to a foundation, you could have kept in office ... and you could have been in command when the revival came. You sneaked away and you deserted both your principles and your people. The leaders of the retreat, whom you now stick up on pinnacles of clay, knew that something had to be done, asked me to interview the leaders of the Liberal and Tory parties to save their faces, and then turned tail. As soon as they were free of their responsibilities they tried to persuade you all (and God knows they had a sorry lot of sheep to persuade) that they had not committed themselves to what, as a matter of fact, they had ...
>
> I cannot help, in spite of all this, having a sneaking regard for you on account of old days, but I would strongly advise you to give up any attempt to bounce yourself out of your responsibilities and to try by whistling to keep your courage up ... to imagine that you are playing anything but an unworthy part at the present moment.[42]

He struck a somewhat similar note a few days later, in a letter to an American friend, Mrs Glendower Evans:

> It is pitiable to see how our Labour movement has become degraded by market-place claptrap, materialism masquerading under the banners of brotherly love, capitalist enmity transplanted into Labour hearts, and the very worst characteristics of old partisan politics being adopted by the caucus which holds possession of the Labour Party at the present moment. One is still proud and happy that there are a few honest I.L.P.'ers, like Maxton, left. There has always been a fundamental difference between Maxton and myself in how Socialism was to come about. I am an evolutionist ... He is a revolutionist, who has never been able to see a transition time. Yesterday

he spoke in the House of Commons and in gentle and genial humour exposed the time-servers and pseudo-intellectuals of the Labour Opposition.[43]

Beneath the surface, his reactions to his old followers' enmity were much more complicated. It is clear that he was deeply hurt by it; it is clear too that the wound never healed. 'What an awful mentality these people are displaying!', he exclaimed in a letter to Clifford Allen in January 1932. 'Just fancy any body of responsible men in their senses going and taking up time announcing that everybody is corrupt except themselves...Nothing shows more plainly the material with which we have had to work.'[44] Eighteen months later he noted, as bitterly, 'Have just read a brave defence of me written by Malcolm. I wish I did not detest and despise so much the antics & dishonesties & spite of my late Labour colleagues.'[45]

As time went on, however, his indignation with the Labour Party became increasingly weary and resigned, while the simple fact of separation from it became even harder to bear. It was the 'machine' that had turned the party against him, he told himself; ordinary, decent party members might listen to his message again, if only he could cut loose from his responsibilities and give them an opportunity to hear it. 'The bitter spitefulness of some of our friends is appalling ... ,' he wrote to Ben Tillett in March 1933. 'If there is any strength and energy left in us when these dreadful times have been got through, we must spend ours in recreating a socialism inspired by the old.'[46] A few weeks later, J. Richardson, a Yorkshire miners' agent, wrote to him to say how sorry he was that 'our Daily Herald never does the fair & right to you.'[47] MacDonald replied with a slightly pathetic mixture of warmth, self-pity and defensiveness:

I am so glad to hear from you. I know there are a great many like you in our Movement who are not at all happy by [sic] the surrender of our Party to superficialities and their senseless abandonment of Socialism for a queer mixture of sentimentality and Poplarism. Our regret must be all the more disturbing that they need never have resigned if they had faced one or two very stern and decisive facts ... If in some directions things have gone badly and have developed on lines which we do not altogether like, the major part of the blame is with themselves [sic] for runing away ...

I cannot put out of my mind a very serious concern for the future of the Movement. It is no longer guided by the Socialism which created it, but by a combination of influences the greatest of which is undoubtedly mere unblushing and reckless vote catching ... Meantime, I am so absorbed in day to day work that I can pay no attention at all [to] the Movement in the country. How I should like to return to that and try and bring the Party back to its old principles and political conceptions, but the years pass and the terrible state in which the world is almost defies all our good offices ... However, your letter is a very welcome one, and I send you my best thanks for it together with my heartiest good wishes to you and your family.[48]

Nine months later, he noted:

> Had Citrine to lunch & afterwards had a talk on *Daily Herald* and its stunts & falsehoods, & the future of the Labour Party of [*sic*] which he was pessimistic especially as to leadership. Told him I was much disheartened both by the poor petty spirit of the Party in the House and its incompetence. I should not return but I was not to lose interest nor cease to be active in propagating in my own way the principles & spirit of the original movement which was 'as far removed from Poplarism as the present party is drowned in it'.[49]

But the vision of a great campaign to rally the Labour movement collapsed whenever it came in contact with reality. After speaking at a by-election in September 1933, he noted that the meeting 'took much out of me. First of what I hope to be a series, but can I stand them? I am oppressed by the feeling that I am not with my own people & that those who should be with me are against me.'[50] 'Preparing speeches but heart not in it,' he noted four months later. 'The poor & spiteful attitude of Labour discourages hope in the Party where in principle my heart is ... I know full well that the leaven is good & sound & worthy of devotion, but when will it leaven the lump?'[51]

Sometimes, he wondered whether he had done the right thing after all in 1931. Once he told Harold Nicolson, 'Any man in my position at the time, knowing all that I did, would have acted as I acted. However, I sometimes wish that someone else had been in my position at the time.'[52] In the privacy of his diary, he was even less sure of himself. 'The desolation of loneliness is terrible,' he noted in December 1932. 'Was I wise? Perhaps not, but it seemed as though anything else was impossible.'[53] He was still torturing himself with the same doubts eighteen months later. 'Wondering whether by sticking to the Labour majority & protecting the Party from the leadership of the poor specimens who now hold it a greater service to the workers would have been done,' he noted in May 1934. 'But at what an awful price of [*sic*] dishonesty ... Some way of saving the movement & the Socialism it embodied will surely be found.'[54]

IV

In spite of his political isolation, MacDonald's personal life was not as unmitigatedly bleak as some of his gloomier diary entries might suggest. In September 1932, his daughter Joan was married to Dr Mackinnon. The wedding gave MacDonald great pleasure – 'what I liked best', he noted afterwards, 'was the great gusto of guests who had not met for years. What a lot of nice people we knew thirty years ago.'[55] The sequel gave him even more. The Mackinnons' first child – christened Margaret Isabel, after the two grandmothers – was born in 1933. MacDonald saw his granddaughter for the first time in late September, and approved strongly. She was, he noted, 'a placid little dear thing & with an unusual amount of comeliness.'[56] By January 1934, her attractions had become even more remarkable. 'Joan very happy,' MacDonald noted after another visit to Leeds, towards the end of the month, 'and Margaret sweetest little thing in creation.'[57] In May he saw her again—noting enthusiastically, 'Margaret is delightful & blows cobwebs away.'[58]

Two adult friendships also helped to blunt the edge of his loneliness. One was with a Rumanian princess, Marthe Bibesco—the dark-eyed, soulful-looking wife of a Rumanian diplomat and an old friend of MacDonald's friend, Lord Thomson, who had met her while he was serving as the British military attaché in Bucharest during the war, when she was still in her teens. She had met MacDonald during the second Labour Government, while she was having tea with Thomson on the terrace of the House of Lords. By a strange coincidence, she had read MacDonald's life of Margaret the night before and had been greatly moved by it; when they were introduced, she told him so. Not long afterwards, she visited MacDonald at Chequers, and when Thomson was killed they met again. MacDonald suggested that they should write to each other 'when the spirit moved them' and she agreed. From then until his death he wrote to her almost every week[59]—wistful, sometimes faintly flirtatious letters, a little reminiscent of the letters he had written to Cecily Gordon-Cumming before her marriage, but wearier and less light-hearted in tone. He teased her about her cat, her love of foreign travel and her Chanel scents, insisted gravely on the moral superiority of his presbyterianism over her Catholicism and signed his letters with a drawing of three swans, as a tribute to three swans that swam in a lake beside her home in Rumania. As their friendship became closer, he also appealed more straightforwardly to her sympathy and treated her as a kind of epistolatory shoulder on which to cry.

'Now do not steal behind by back by assuming so cooly [sic] that there is more scruple in your religion than in mine ... ,' he wrote in a characteristic letter towards the end of February 1932. 'When you have to look after yourself you are much more careful than when Ben is looking after you. When he purrs your way into bliss, you walk without concern—but I shall say no more but leave the rest to Jennie, who when she fell into a bucket of water with one foot remarked that it was as careless in its behaviour as a Roman.'[60] Late March found him in a more melancholy mood. After thanking her for a 'pathetic' account of Briand's funeral, he went on:

The anemones were full of Palestinian memories. Put them on my coffin when the time comes. What courage & sturdiness are in their beauty! They are no pale bloodless things. They are the life which sins without regret or absolution. They believe in a *living* God who has given us his essential elements, who is not to sit on a judgement seat, but who is to walk with us when assigning us our portion in a garden in the cool of the day, & however censorious is to greet us as 'Friend'. Thus you see, I continue in my faith as a pagan Presbyterian who could take the anemone as his symbol.[61]

In mid-November he was more cheerful, complaining

Jason, Christopher Columbus, Captain Cook — none of the great wanderers, not even John Mandeville or Marco Polo — wandered so much as you — or told such stories. One day I shall hear of you from the Pole or a Planet. How can I write to you? It is like casting one's bread on the waters in the vain hope of finding it after many days. In Pliny or some other observant naturalist I believe it is recorded: 'Lady Swans are great wanderers and cannot be relied upon' ...

... But how on earth could you think of me drawing you as a goose! It was a swan — a flying one — a soaring one with J. and R. and M. on your back. Your altitude! Methinks you want either to pick a quarrel or compel me to flatter you. Just look at it again. Did ever more graceful thing cleave the air at the tip of my pen? Note the noble neck! Look at the lovely leg! Behold the beautiful breast! Gaze at the graceful garter! (I am so sorry but every G. I can think of is rather improper. If you find one more flattering to the Abbe put it in and rub out the other.)[62]

By 1935 the tone had changed. 'Read that mournful chapter in Ecclesiastics to know how the voice is hushed here in the land, and the yap of the dog and the murmured miaow of the puss are alike now,' he wrote sadly just after leaving Downing Street. 'When I get some rest & sleep I have no doubt but that I shall be much fitter again, but meantime I am traversing weary country.' 'What a change!!', he added in a postscript. 'Your long looked for letter waited me, and the clouds scudded across the sky. I was no longer without friends, no longer solitary in a dreary world.'[63] A few days later he wrote again:

These are depressing days and the only elevated influences come from your letters. You encourage one to stand up and face things. You lift up clouds and show that hidden behind them, when one gets the courage to look, are bright patches and a shining face ... Only the other day when I felt the mountain of life was too hard to get up, I heard you call out like a trumpet blast: 'Excelsior'. Without your encouragement I felt lost and faint. I found refreshing shade to pursue and end the journey. So from my mood of despair I pull up and lay my offering on your lap.[64]

The second friendship was more controversial. As we have seen, MacDonald had got to know Lady Londonderry as far back as 1924, when they had found themselves sitting next to each other at Buckingham Palace, and during the second Labour Government their relationship had become much closer. After his breach with the Labour Party it became closer still and, thanks in part to the streak of Celtic flamboyance which must have been one of her attractions, it provoked even more gossip in political circles than it had done earlier. For although Lady Londonderry was now a grandmother in her early fifties, she was a woman around whom legends gathered – without, one cannot help suspecting, much discouragement from her. As a girl, she had shocked her relatives by riding Highland ponies astride and sneaking out to play polo in the early mornings; later, she had shocked them even more by campaigning for votes for women. On a visit to Japan before the war, when skirts were worn long, she had had one of her legs tattooed with the figure of a snake. During the war, she had helped to found the Women's Volunteer Reserve, later the Women's Legion, and had been the first woman to be decorated with the military D.B.E. She had also founded a society called the ark, most of whose members were engaged on war work of one sort of another, which used to meet at Londonderry House on Wednesday evenings. Each member took the name of a creature – Churchill was 'Winston the Warlock' and Balfour, 'Arthur the Albatross' – while Lady Londonderry herself was 'Circe', who turned men into beasts. The ark survived the war – in the 1930s its members included John Buchan, James Barrie and Sir John Lavery, as well as a large number of politicians and diplomats – providing an excuse for supposedly intimate, but nevertheless much discussed, parties at Londonderry House, whose lavishness lost nothing in the telling. In a different mood, she threw herself into the part of political hostess, with an extravagance and panache that belonged to an earlier age and that many in the more self-conscious age in which she actually lived found ostentatious and distasteful. Magnificent receptions were held at Londonderry House, at which she would stand, glittering with diamonds, receiving her guests at the top of a huge staircase, and which provoked the sardonic comment from Birkenhead that Londonderry was 'catering his way into the Cabinet'. But politicians were not the only beneficiaries of her hospitality. She also delighted in the role of patron of art and literature, and gave frequent parties for writers, painters and musicians, showing particular favour to those of Celtic origin. In these years, two frequent guests were the playwright, Sean O'Casey, and the Irish poet, James Stephens; and it is worthy of note that O'Casey remembered her later with great affection as a 'charming woman', whose Gaelic enthusiasms enabled her to escape the rascality of politics.[65]

In 'Circe's' ark, MacDonald was 'Hamish the Hart'; when National Government receptions were held at Londonderry House, he stood beside her at the top of the staircase; at her literary parties, he was often to be seen huddled in a corner with the O'Caseys and Stephens, listening to Stephens's stories. But there was more to their friendship than this. Only a few of her letters to him have survived, but they make it clear that she gave him a good deal of moral and emotional support at a time when he badly needed them – telling him about specialists who might help with his eye trouble, congratulating him on his speeches and commiserating with him when he was attacked. After he telephoned her with the news of the Lausanne agreement in July 1932, she wrote:

Your telephone message gave me *such* joy – not only for the greatest event, but on account of the success of your vy dear self ... My whole heart goes out to you in joy and admiration at the manner in which you have pulled it off – Bless you – all my love is yours ...

... To hear it, in your own dear words – was wonderful, I still feel breathless – I always knew you were a great man – so I am not surprised – but I am doubly proud and pleased – All my love dearest H.

from CIRCE[66]

On his sixty-seventh birthday, fifteen months later, she was less effusive but equally sympathetic:

My dearest H –

This is a belated letter to send you all good greetings for your birthday – May we see many of them together ...

... I hope disarmament goes as well as you wish ... We live in horrible times – but I would not change them, since you are you – but what a strange fate that has thrown you up against the World [to] be the bulwark which you are – You the most human and understanding of men – are yet by force of evil Junkers the upholder of Britain's might – Sometimes I wonder if the Powers aloft – are not laughing at all our efforts – Let us hurry to the Western Isles and live there. They are the only sensible people alive I verily believe and they appreciate the just values of what really matters and what does not –

Well dearest H – Take care of your vy nice self – and may we meet sooner than either of us expect[s] is the wish of your most devoted

C[67]

In a letter dated simply '25th June' she was more emotional:

My dearest H.

I feel so distressed about you and so is Charley* – What really is the matter – I do wish I could help – My heart is with you – We can't get on without you – you do realize that, don't you? and you will have, and have all our prayers and thoughts – and lots and lots of love and all good wishes – you dearest dear brave creature – We must please meet soon – All love again from

C.[68]

The emotion was not all on one side. At first, the initiative seems to have been taken by Lady Londonderry rather than by MacDonald. She invited him to join her ark, and he accepted; she asked him to call her 'Circe', and he responded by writing to 'My Dear Ladye'. He was obviously attached to her, but one cannot help suspecting that there was an element of play-acting in the attach-

---

*I.e. Lord Londonderry.

CI

ment. She was a fairy princess, remote in her 'castle high', rather than a real person; their relationship was a diversion from the cares of state, but it is doubtful if MacDonald's emotions were deeply engaged in it. After the political and emotional shocks of August and September 1931, however, its character changed. MacDonald was now desperately lonely – deserted, as he saw it, by his old associates and seething with a kind of exasperated contempt for his new ones. He needed sympathy and affection as never before. If Cecily Gordon-Cumming had still been unmarried, it is conceivable that he might have turned to her, though it is doubtful if a girl in her mid-twenties could have given him what he wanted. Lady Londonderry filled the gap, and it is clear from his letters that he became more and more dependent on her.

'I am old and lonely in the evening grey,' he wrote in one characteristic letter in late November or early December, 1931. 'You do not know how helpful you are, however, to yours ever Hamish.'[69] 'Have you any idea of how good is a little corner in which you have put cushions for me & let me share?', he asked two or three weeks later. 'That is so, however. It is my Isle of Avilon where falls not rainbow nor snow, nor ever wind blows loudly. That I shall enter in 1931 in red & gold. I look forward with many forebodings to 1932, but whatever happens those letters of red & gold will remain as a refuge in memory for me ... My dear, my love.'[70] A few days later he wrote again:

> Dearest Friend o' Mine,
> The best Christmas gift that anyone in these islands got came to me when you told me that when you prayed in church in the morning and thought only of what belonged to the goodness & beauty of the heart & soul you would ask blessings for me. I press your hand to my heart ... I stood by you in church wrapped in the bliss which is the heart of the eternal. Bless you, my dear.[71]

It seems clear that for a while, at least, he was, in most senses of the words, in love with her. In a 'bread and butter letter' in March 1932, he wrote:

> I have been away for a day or two – you will never guess where – & when I left, had not finished my conversation. So the letter has to be a queer mixture of gratitude & regret. I have to tell my hostess how she mothered me, & try & tell her how I loved it. One evening she rubbed a startled nerve & soothed it by the magic of her hand & I could hardly bear her going away, I felt so miserable & deserted ...
> Then, when I said 'good bye', she asked me not to write at all but just telephone. Ah! those moderns who live in a mechanical world & come to regard the engines of motor cars as the wings of angels bringing us to heaven, & the quiverings of telephones as the means of conveying affection. How can I convey by telephone the happy delusion that for three days I seemed to be living an old existence, that my hostess & I had known each

other from the beginning when there was only the Word & nothing but
the Word, & would know each other until the Word resumed its empire,
that with her I wandered in rich autumn pastures where gentle winds blew
& the air was benign?[72]

By late May he was more outspoken. In a letter addressed to 'My Dearest
of Dear Persons' he wrote, 'I have hesitated as to the fate of the enclosed scrap
written after you left for the Court, and meant to be sent in to you, but with-
held on further consideration ... "She knows it all", said the Shy Spirit, "so why
embarrass her with such confessions?" Then, the Shy Spirit won, but now,
holding it over the flames, the Bold Spirit wrestled with the Shy one & persuaded me to send it to you to turn to ashes.'[73] The 'scrap', enclosed in a separate
envelope, reads:

My Dear
    You were very beautiful, and I loved you. The dress, dazzling in brilliance
& glorious in colour and line, was you, & my dear, you were the dress. I
just touch its hem, & pray for your eternal happiness wondering at the
same time what generous hearted archangel ever patted me on the back
& arranged that amongst the many great rewards that this poor unwelcome
stranger to this world was to receive was that he would be permitted before
he returned to his dust to feel devotion to *you*.[74]

'My trouble with you,' he wrote a few days later, 'is that you make me so happy
that I *will* be dainty with you, will pull your leg, will approach you as a devoué.
And you say: "Tiresome creature, why this inferiority complex?" Why because
I am a devotee ... So don't be silly as well as delightful & don't apply democracy
to love.' In a postscript he added:

Here comes another message from you. Bless you for what you say. Would
that we could walk tonight along the sands. We perhaps would not talk
much for the Firth & the hills beyond might do all the speaking. We would
do the listening & the feeling & just be happy together. Of course those who
are bearing heavy burdens, or who work admist gloom or discouragement,
or who have to draw heavily upon nervous & spiritual energy, or who work
by faith or by visions, should have the frankest friendship with the right
kind of the other half. The tragedy of the misfit is heartbreaking and ir-
reperable but the bliss & the power of heaven-chosen mating cannot be told.
Perhaps I have made a mistake in taking memory as the constant companion, but who can say with assurance? The (what I might call) mechan-
ism of mating is so delicate & apt to get out of order that no one can assume
the ideal. But — well, need I say more than [sic] tell you that all you have said
in this letter is true & that with heart & soul I believe it. I leave it to shine &
sing in the realm of feeling. Bless you always.[75]

That note could not be sustained for long. By October 1932, he was asking, more sadly, 'who am I? A man from the sea & of the mist. The day is sure to come when I shall again be of the sea and the mist, & you will continue to reign at your fireside & amongst your own people. "I once knew him", you will say & maybe sigh. And that will be all.'[76] 'My very dearest,' he wrote three months later, 'Your letter just received just fills my heart with joyful affection. But why did Providence wait till youth had gone & the bleak winds had come ... ?'[77] In 1933 the winds were bleaker still, and the note of self-pity in MacDonald's letters became more obtrusive. 'I want a word or only just a look before you go ... ,' he exclaimed towards the end of March. 'What an ass I am to want petting. Burn this & I shall confess that I do, for the world is horrid.'[78] In September, his tone was even more lugubrious. 'How I miss you, dearest of all friends & most desired of all companions ... ,' he wrote on the 26th. 'I have headaches, pains in my bones, a temperature, silent rooms & not a soul about.'[79] As he was the first to recognize, however, the 'petting' he got was still of enormous importance to him. 'What a difference it makes having a friend who knows & sympathises & helps,' he noted in January 1933.[80] 'Packing again for L'mouth ... ,' he noted towards the end of July. 'A friend has been very helpful & but for that I wonder whether I could have gone on.'[81] Though these entries do not mention Lady Londonderry by name, there can be no doubt that they refer to her. It is a sad epitaph in some ways, for MacDonald would have been much better off if he had not gone on as long as he did. But it is not an unattractive one. MacDonald's friendship with Lady Londonderry did great damage to his reputation at the time and, in some quarters at least, it has dogged his memory ever since. It is pleasant to record that it brought him at least some happiness, at a time when he got little from anywhere else. And, for that, she deserves the credit.

Yet she only made his loneliness more bearable; she did not overcome it. In September 1931, a spiritualist medium, Mrs Grace Cooke, wrote to tell him that she had received 'a clear message from your wife in spiritlife' and that:

> She seemed a very lovely woman to me, and she asked me to let you know that she was very proud of your fine response to the influence of the spiritual powers which work [sic] trying to work through you, for the help and progress of humanity. She wanted me to say that she had been with you through the great strain, she wanted you to know that you were not alone, she knew all, and was your constant helper. She was standing by you, and she had had a great deal to do with your decision ... She is with you through everything, and is so proud of your splendid work ...
>
> If I am guilty of any breach of etiqutte in writing you this, I ask your forgiveness, but I honour and respect you, not as the Prime Minister of England, but as a worthy soul, and a noble man, a true servant of God.[82]

Mrs Cooke's letter was dated September 10th. According to the account in her autobiography, she received a reply a few days later, written in MacDonald's own hand, and dated September 13th. In it, MacDonald wrote that although he knew little about such things, he was open-minded and prepared to believe; in any case, he was glad to receive any message that made him feel the presence of the dead and was grateful to those who afforded him the experience. This exchange, Mrs Cooke remembered later, was the first of a long series, stretching over several years. Each time Margaret sent a message, she wrote, it would be 'received and acknowledged kindly – one might almost add gratefully'; and although she did not quote directly from any of MacDonald's letters to her, either in her memoirs or in conversation, her account has the ring of truth.[83] 'Heavy week-end of work,' MacDonald noted on one occasion in the summer of 1933. 'I wandered over Lossie roads holding the hand of my little boy in his dark blue jersey. Very saddening.'[84] The memory of his bereavements had been part of MacDonald's life for more than twenty years. There is no reason to believe that it was any weaker in the 1930s than it had been before.

V

The 'desolation of loneliness' was made still more desolate by failing health and, as time went on, by the consciousness of failing powers. In October 1931, MacDonald was sixty-five; when he left Downing Street in 1935 he was nearly sixty-nine. Signs of ageing had been apparent ever since his illness in America in 1927. Even before the crisis in August 1931, two years of minority government and eighteen months of mounting unemployment had left their mark. As we have seen, he had suffered a slight collapse soon after the National Government was formed and a more serious one after the traumatic weekend when it was decided that the gold standard would have to be abandoned. Then came the exhausting and time-consuming negotiations over the Government's election platform, followed, immediately afterwards, by a much more exhausting election campaign. When the campaign was over, the tension snapped. On November 1st, he noted, 'Worn out & work impossible ... But really head would not work. So depressing.'[85] On the 15th he complained again, 'Working so slowly.'[86]

In January 1932, it was discovered that he was suffering from glaucoma and at the beginning of February he had to have an operation to relieve the pressure on his left eye. The operation, performed by Stewart Duke-Elder, later the *doyen* of British eye surgeons, was successful; but MacDonald's recovery was far from rapid. He spent the best part of two weeks in a nursing home in Park Lane – his recuperation interrupted by ugly echoes of the crisis then raging in the Far East, resulting from the Japanese attack on a Chinese suburb of Shanghai. On February 16th, a communiqué was issued stating ominously that the operation had had a 'very satisfactory' result, but that 'In order to maintain this good result ... it is essential for him to have at least three weeks' complete rest. It has been urged upon the Prime Minister that his sight requires greater care in the future than it has been receiving.'[87] He spent the next three weeks in a hotel at Newquay in Cornwall, with, as he put it in a letter to Princess Bibesco, 'Atlantic rollers beating on both sides'.[88] But although his morale improved, it is clear that his underlying condition still gave grounds for concern. On February 28th, his doctor, Sir Thomas Horder, wrote him a long letter warning that his health would not be safeguarded merely by prescribing the right medicines, and that 'your serenity and your moral strength ... are likely to suffer if you are greatly strained: even *you* must give a little if the burden is not endurable.'[89] When he returned to London in mid-March, the warning was repeated in another communiqué, making it clear once again that although the condition of MacDonald's eye continued to be satisfactory, it had been impressed upon him 'that in order to maintain this satisfactory condition, he must exercise more care and put less strain upon his sight than has been his practice in the past'.[90]

This was easier said than done. Like many shy men, MacDonald was, by nature, a reader rather than a listener; without a regular diet of minutes and memoranda, he pined. In a diary entry at the end of March, he grumbled revealingly, 'Limitation of reading owing to eyes annoying & embarrassing'.[91] Though Horder wrote soon afterwards to congratulate him on 'becoming a model patient',[92] it is hard to believe that he carried out Duke-Elder's instructions as fully as he should have done. In February, the long-awaited disarmament conference had opened at Geneva. MacDonald was technically the head of the British delegation but he had had to miss the opening session because of his operation; when the conference resumed in mid-April after the Easter adjournment, he insisted on going. By now, however, his right eye was giving trouble; and before he left, Horder and Duke-Elder had to issue yet another communiqué, announcing that in normal circumstances he would have been advised to rest for several weeks and that he was being allowed to go to Geneva only 'on condition that he is subjected to as little strain as possible, and that three consecutive hours of every day are given up to complete relaxation'.[93] In a diary entry afterwards, he insisted plaintively that he had tried to obey his doctors and had spent two or three hours every afternoon motoring or playing golf.[94] If so, it was to no avail. By the end of the month, his eye was failing; and on May 1st, he was forced to return to London and to leave a delicate and perhaps critical set of negotiations in mid-air. On May 2nd, Duke-Elder told him that his right eye would have to be operated on as well.[95] The operation was carried out successfully three days later, but, as before, MacDonald took a long time to recover. As late as May 27th, he was writing from Lossiemouth to his Aunt Bella, 'These operations ... take a lot out of you, & you do not always know it until you try to do some work. I have a staff of three up here & manage to get through a good deal though sometimes under difficulties. The doctors gaily say that I will be quite over it all in six months & that if the worst comes I shall not be blind until about fifteen years & by that time I shall be able to afford it.'[96] He was not back in full circulation until June 1st.

For a while, his eyes gave no more trouble, but by now he was ageing more rapidly than before, and in less obvious ways his health was still far from satisfactory. In September, Horder had to urge him to take plenty of rest on a forthcoming visit to Scotland; by October, he needed a tonic for 'brain fag'.[97] In November, Horder issued a statement to the press announcing that the prime minister had to 'conserve his energies for the heavy work of the coming session', and that in consequence he would be unable to accept evening engagements outside Parliament.[98] On December 1st, MacDonald made another visit to Geneva, in a desperate attempt to save the disarmament conference from breaking down. After ten days of intense though ultimately successful negotiations, he returned to London in a state of exhaustion. On the 17th he had to leave for Lossiemouth; on the 26th he confessed to Walter Elliott, 'My trouble is not a cold or anything like that, but just a complete breakdown from top to toe, inside and out, like the wonderful one horse choice.'[99] Next day he noted:

I left Geneva as depressed as though I had got no agreement & a cold caught in travelling made matters worse. I arrived in London able to do nothing with my head and so physically tired that I could hardly walk. If people only knew! After a week in London I had to throw in my hand and came away, & gave Ll.G. the chance to make a spiteful personal attack ... Lossie has taken much longer than usual to work its charm. A mile walk knocked me up some days after I had arrived, but the weather changed & the short cold sunny day has got into my blood & bones, & I climb back. This has been a nasty business, however. The depression has been one of the blackest & has affected everything ... The strain is at last telling on me, & I am feeling as though [in the] last few weeks I have crossed the frontiers of age. I walk as an old man, & my head works like an old man's. — The evenings & mornings here, so calm & beautiful make one think with resignation of Fate, good or ill, the Universe being the universal in which we are but items, limiting our freedom & determining the great things of life & death, success or failure, which are to happen. — How long can I go on? There are limits to an endless strain with daily tugs and jars and jolts, turning from one crisis to another, one worry to another. Were things normal, it would be wise for me to rest now. But if I did, what would happen? Opinion seems to regard me as the linchpin. If I went, would all go? Who wd. be P.M. The Govt. wd. be Consvtve. Could Mr. Chamberlain run it? As yet, he could not. What wd. happen to my own friends who have staked so much — my son for instance who of all can best look after himself after his recent successes! I must think of them. It looks as though I were tied for the time.[100]

So he stayed on – partly out of loyalty to his followers, partly out of a sense of duty to the country, partly because he had succumbed to that most insidious of all prime ministerial temptations, the illusion of indispensability. At a deeper and less conscious level, moreover, these pressures were almost certainly reinforced by others. If Margaret had lived, he might have been anxious to retire while he could still enjoy retirement; as things were, office provided an escape from loneliness. His political isolation probably played a part as well. It would be wrong to suggest that he felt guilty about his actions in 1931, but it is clear from his diary that he felt pangs of doubt. It is hard to resist the conclusion that his stubborn refusal to listen to the promptings of his own body and leave office before his health had been ruined must have sprung, in part, from an inner compulsion to quell such doubts. It was as though he had to convince himself, over and over again, that he had, after all, been right to form the National Government in the first place and as right to fight the election at the head of it; that he could still shape events, in spite of the huge Conservative majority which he had helped to bring into being: that, in spite of Labour's attacks on him, the 'verities' were safe in his hands. If he had managed to cap his successes at the reparations conference in 1924 and the naval conference in 1930 with some great stroke of pacificatory diplomacy, he might have been happy to leave Downing Street in the knowledge that he had achieved something worth while. But although he tried hard enough, at a long succession of conferences and face-to-face meetings, the times were against him. The right moment for retirement never came: the ties that had seemed too strong to break in December 1932 seemed as strong for nearly two-and-a-half years more.

He paid a heavy price for their strength. The insomnia which had plagued him for years, particularly at moments of crisis, grew even worse. 'Weary night sleepless and worried,' he noted in a characteristic diary entry after his return to London from Lossiemouth in January 1933. 'The problems of unemployment were [a] nightmare.'[101] A few weeks later he noted, 'At night my mind [is] like a pool which seeks to be quiet but which is stirred by springs at the bottom. Then a book like [the] Bedside Book soothes by putting old familiar pieces into [my] mind & the springs stop disturbing & quiet shades of memory creep up & over & I sleep.'[102] But the Bedside Book was not as effective as it might have been. By January 1934, he was complaining, 'My insomnia persists & Horder insists that I must take aids. I abhor them, but I must do something. For the first time I am being mastered by being unable to throw off my work.'[103] His depressions became more frequent too. 'Cannot shut eyes to fact that am unusually depressed and no wish to talk,' he noted when a friend arrived at Lossiemouth at the beginning of his summer holiday in 1933. 'Decidedly older and of diminished vigour.'[104] 'Time gone fast, and last days clouded by very nasty depression,' he noted only three weeks later. 'I surely cannot be well or I have got old suddenly.'[105] Occasionally, he suffered more alarming symptoms. At one stage in the early months of 1933 he was seen looking nervously over his shoulder in the middle of a speech in the House of Commons; later, he explained that he had thought that a man in the gallery was about to shoot at him.[106] Something similar may have occurred in the middle of a speech he made at the disarmament conference in Geneva at about the same time. 'At one moment,' wrote Major-General Temperley a few years later, 'I saw him reel backwards and start exhorting the audience to "be men, not mannequins", becoming completely irrelevant. He said afterwards that, for a half-minute, he had completely lost consciousness and did not know what he was saying.'[107]

To judge by his photographs, MacDonald at sixty-five, though obviously worn and tired, had still had the erect bearing and more than a vestige of the flamboyant good looks of his earlier years. When he left Downing Street in the end, he looked an exhausted old man, years older than his real age, peering uncertainly into the camera as though not quite sure what was happening. The same deterioration showed in his speeches. He had always been a prolix speaker, relying for his effects on dramatic gestures, lofty flights of language and long, elaborate periods in which subordinate clauses were piled remorselessly on top of one another. It was a powerful style, but it was also a dangerous one. It needed a speaker in full command of himself and his audience to use it effectively; used ineffectively, it could easily topple over into absurdity. Increasingly, this happened to MacDonald. The dramatic gestures began to seem forced and histrionic; the lofty flights of language disappeared more and more frequently into clouds of mixed metaphors; the elaborate periods lost their way in confusion and anticlimax.

Occasionally, the results were comic, as when he declared, in reply to an intervention by Lloyd George in February 1933, 'He thinks that he is the only impatient man in this House to get things done. I will beat him 50 per cent, any day he likes ... No doubt he has a hawk-like desire for action, without bridle and without saddle, across the Atlantic.'[108] More often, they were merely embarrassing. In the debate on the address in November 1932, for example, he gave this explanation of the Government's reasons for wanting an international economic conference as soon as possible:

The world cannot afford to wait. One is appalled sometimes when one reads articles as though the world is going at the rate of five miles an hour. [An HON. MEMBER: 'It is going quicker than that.'] It is, and the Hon. Member will find it on this side, not on that. The reason is that the politicians, the direct representatives of this Government, that Government and the other Government, brought face to face, will much more quickly find an accommodation, a way out, and will be so minded knowing the larger issues outside, knowing the tremendous importance of getting an agreement—the direct representatives of the Government meeting the direct representatives of other Governments will much more quickly and much

better, as a piece of workmanship, find the accommodation which will lead
to a great world agreement.[109]

Four months later, he described the situation at the disarmament conference as
follows:

Facing that conference and its sub-committees, finding the tremendous
differences that separate delegations from delegations and nation from
nation, and getting conclusions, is going to be no immediately accomplished job. We have to build long bridges over the differences that separate
one from another. But in going along we have to remember that there
must be frequent transformations from the expert study of detail to the
production of practical plans in order to meet this very obvious difficulty,
that when the conference absorbs itself for the time being in detail, then
the various nations, asked to give up this or to agree to that, quite naturally
say, 'But to what plan am I working? I cannot agree to give this unless I
know the complete system into which my sacrifice, as I imagine it to be, is
to be set. Is it to be all sacrifice, or am I going to receive compensations
which I can value as at any rate some measure of return for the sacrifices I
make?'[110]

That was at least comprehensible, if slow-moving. When he reported to the
House on a visit he made to Washington at the end of April 1933, he was
equally diffuse, but less intelligible:

There is a third point, or a third section of interest; it is more than a point.
The stabilisation of the relative value of currency must be attempted by
agreement. I doubt if anyone who has not gone through my experience of
the last two or three weeks can appreciate the danger of unstable international values not only to trade – I take it that the Committee are fully
acquainted with that – but to political relationships. When I was still at sea
– [Laughter.] – Hon. Members laugh; I think it is a very valuable point
which I have conceded – the United States went off gold.[111]

More and more he dreaded the prospect of appearing at the dispatch box.
The night before making a speech, he would lie awake worrying; after a bad
performance, he would torture himself with the memory. 'Fit but with feeling
of coming flop ... ,' he noted apprehensively two days before making the
second of the three speeches quoted above. 'Would I were a Winston Churchill
so that I might express adequately my disgust with myself.'[112] Next day he was
even more apprehensive. 'Trying to get something clear into my head for the
H. of C. tomorrow,' he noted. 'Cannot be done. Like man flying in mist: can
fly all right but cannot see the course ... To-morrow there will be another
"vague" speech impossible to follow &c. and as usual with these attacks of head
& eyes no sleep tonight.'[113] On the day of the speech, he ended the story with
an even sadder entry: 'Thoroughly bad speech. Could not get my way at all.

The Creator might have devised more humane means for punishing me for over-drive & reckless use of body.'[114] The same thing happened when he reported on his Washington visit a few weeks later. 'Spoke Tuesday in House,' he noted. 'Out of sympathy with it & can do nothing when expounding. No speech of any virtue can be made facing the poor crowd as I know them & with men behind who do not share my fundamental beliefs.'[115] But speeches outside the House were no easier. 'Very stupid today … ,' he noted helplessly at the beginning of October 1933. 'Bad appearance at the St. Barts. dinner. These things are crushing.'[116] By January 1934 he was confessing, 'I am a little depressed about my own tired head … To speak now is a great effort & in the ground to be covered and the development of the argument I get more & more confused. One or two failures on the platform will settle me. I remember Joseph Chamberlain's last failures in speech making & do not mean to repeat them.'[117]

Sometimes, he managed to recapture some of his old authority. At the end of October 1933, he delivered a two-hour speech at Crawley. According to one eye-witness, some of his sentences were 'long and involved and their meaning was not immediately clear',[118] but on balance he was entitled to feel reasonably happy with his performance. His speech in the debate on the address when Parliament resumed in November, though long-winded, was noticeably better than his speech in the same debate a year before.[119] At the end of February 1934, he wound up an adjournment debate initiated by the Clydeside M.P., George Buchanan; according to a report from Rose Rosenberg, Maxton told a group of Conservative M.P.s who had been praising MacDonald's performance that 'he greatly admired the way that you had handled the situation'.[120] But these were only temporary oscillations on a downward curve. After Buchanan's adjournment debate MacDonald noted, 'I had to go through tortures to reply. How I am rent by having to speak now.'[121] By the middle of March he was noting, 'Machine run down: stupid in mind & can do no work & sick in body. Whatever be the cost it seems I must have a rest to get straightened up.'[122] Before long, his eyes started to trouble him again; and in June 1934, Duke-Elder reported that they had undergone a 'retrograde movement' during the previous three months, resulting from the strain involved in reading official papers. Horder and Duke-Elder agreed that, although his general health was satisfactory, he needed three months' freedom from close work and that he could best obtain it abroad.[123] He took their advice and left London at the beginning of July — first for Scotland, and then for Canada and Newfoundland. But it is clear that he was less optimistic than they were. 'I am more troubled by my overworked brain than my overworked eyes … ,' he noted anxiously after Duke-Elder's examination. 'I sleep for but a short time and yet [sic] do not reach the land of unforced vitality before the day is done.'[124] He turned out to be a better diagnostician than his doctors were. Within a few days of his return to London at the beginning of October he was grumbling, 'very tired & stupid … head a mere log, no memory, no energy, yawning all day'.[125] In the next few months, that note was to be heard even more frequently than before.

The extent and speed of MacDonald's decline should not be exaggerated. As we shall see, the deterioration which showed in his speeches as early as the autumn of 1932 was much less apparent in his chairmanship of the Cabinet and in his performances at Cabinet committees – at any rate, until his departure for Canada in the summer of 1934. Once the fiscal question was out of the way, he intervened only intermittently in home affairs, often to scant effect, but on the foreign-policy questions, which took up more and more of the Government's time as the international sky grew darker, his influence was usually considerable and often decisive; though it would be absurd to depict him as a strong prime minister, it would be equally wide of the mark to suggest that he was nothing more than a figurehead, who played no part in shaping the Government's policies. Yet, when all is said, there can be no doubt that he stayed on as prime minister for at least two and perhaps three years more than he should have done: and that, in doing so, he condemned himself not only to much private anguish but to repeated public humiliation. When he left Downing Street at last, his reputation was in ruins; and for more than a generation, the memory was to cast a backward shadow over all that he had done before. Political careers often end cruelly. In recent British history, at least, few have ended more cruelly than MacDonald's.

Note

It has been suggested that one reason for MacDonald's physical and mental decline in the 1930s was that he was being blackmailed by a well-known cocotte, with whom he had had an affair during his visits to central Europe in the 1920s, and to whom he had written compromising letters.[126] I find this suggestion unconvincing. It is reasonable to assume that his decline was partly psychological in origin – though it is important to remember that a great deal of the strain from which he was suffering must have been due directly or indirectly to his eye trouble – but it seems to me that the psychological element can be accounted for quite easily by his rupture with the Labour Party and the 'desolation of loneliness' which followed it, and by the slow collapse of his hopes for peace and disarmament. It is also necessary to remember that he was sixty-five in 1931 and nearly sixty-nine when he left Downing Street in 1935; and that some people age more quickly than others. MacDonald in this period was a lonely, disappointed and profoundly unhappy old man. For much of the time he was in pain and for some of it he was unable to see properly. In these circumstances, it is not necessary to assume blackmail in order to explain why his powers slowly failed.

The blackmail story does, however, deserve examination: and it can be dealt with more conveniently here than in the narrative above. There are a number of different and in some ways overlapping versions. One is that the woman concerned was paid off with money from 'Secret Service funds', at some stage during the National Government, and that the letters were then destroyed. Another is that J. H. Thomas was sent to Paris to pay her off with Labour Party money, at some stage during the second Labour Government, and that he lost the money. A third is that she appeared in London during the second Labour Government, tried unsuccessfully to obtain money in exchange for the letters but was frightened off by the threat that the Secret Service would take action of some sort against her. I have tried to establish the truth, but have found it impossible to do so. The alleged sources for the story that the blackmailer was paid off with 'Secret Service funds' are all dead, and the accounts of her alleged activities during the second Labour Government contain too many inconsistencies to inspire confidence. The MacDonald papers throw no light on the matter either. In an entry in his notebook on August 14th, 1930, while he was on holiday in Lossiemouth, MacDonald wrote, à propos of the unemployment problem, 'It is, with private concerns, so unsettling that I have no peace here & must seek it in London.'[127] But there is no way of telling what these 'private concerns' were, and no evidence that they were in any way connected with blackmail. One of the correspondence files[128] makes it clear that in 1935 MacDonald's solicitors did go to some trouble to recover certain allegedly forged letters, purporting to have been written by MacDonald during the First World War and to have contained evidence of pro-German sympathies, from Lady Houston, the proprietor of the extreme right-wing *Saturday Review*. It is conceivable that later stories about recovering letters from a blackmailer may have had their origin here. There is, however, no solid evidence. All that can be said with certainty is that rumours about an alleged blackmail were in circulation in the 1930s, and that according to some of them Secret Service money was used to pay the blackmailer off. But gossip about sex in high places flourishes at all times, and – perhaps sadly – is not always well founded; when sex is mixed with blackmail and vaguely clandestine activities by the Secret Service the result is likely to find a readier market still.

My own view is that it is quite conceivable that MacDonald had an affair during one of his visits to central Europe in the 1920s and that it is equally conceivable that if he did have such an affair he would have written letters to the woman concerned which could afterwards have been used against him. As to whether he was blackmailed or not, it seems to me that the only possible verdict is 'not proven'. The suggestion that the blackmailer was paid out of Secret Service funds seem to me highly implausible. There is no way of disproving it: if such payments were made, it is hardly likely that they would have been recorded in an identifiable way. All the same, I find it hard to believe that a reasonably hard-headed agency would be naïve enough to pay over money to a blackmailer in the way alleged. In any event, it would, I believe, have been wholly out of character for MacDonald himself to have authorized – and still more out of character for him to have ordered – public money to be used in this way.

CHAPTER 28

Crumbling coalition

I

IN November 1931, the misery and humiliation of MacDonald's last years in Downing Street were still some way off. Though he showed signs of wear and tear at close quarters, he still seemed fully equal to the demands of his office; as we have seen, his reputation among ordinary voters was almost certainly at its height. Yet, as he recognized with a kind of despairing clarity himself, his triumph in the election, in confirming that reputation, had also made it more difficult for him to maintain it — at any rate, in the quarter where he most needed to do so. Before the dissolution, the Conservatives, though easily the strongest of the Government parties, had not been strong enough to over-ride the others. As they had discovered in the arguments over the Government's election plat-form, they had not been able to get their way when MacDonald joined the Samuelites in resisting them. These power relationships had been transformed by the election. The Conservatives could now govern perfectly well by themselves and everyone knew it. Even if they did not use their parliamentary supremacy to coerce or humiliate their allies, the fact that they possessed it robbed the Government's claim to a special, non-party status of much of its earlier force. In doing so, it posed a double challenge to MacDonald. As we have seen he had told himself again and again before the election that he would never allow him-self to become a 'Tory tool': for him, the Government's non-party status was an emotional lifeline, to which he clung with increasing desperation the more flimsy it appeared. It was also a political lifeline. The electorate had applauded him for putting country before party, not for exchanging one party for another. Many Liberal and Labour voters, in particular, must have swallowed their distrust of the Conservatives and voted the National ticket largely because MacDonald had convinced them that the country needed a non-party Govern-ment and that he could be trusted to provide it. Voters like these now formed his only significant constituency. If they came to believe that the Government's National label was fraudulent and that it had really been a Conservative Government all along, he, not the Conservatives, would be the target for their anger. If they withdrew their support, he would depend even more heavily on the Conservatives than he did already. That, in turn, would undermine his authority and damage his reputation even more.

His first big test came in the horse-trading over Government appointments that followed the election. He met it more successfully than has sometimes been realized. More than 80 per cent of the Government backbenchers were Conservatives; in the Cabinet, as we have seen, they had only 11 places out of 20. By contrast, 4 went to the minuscule National Labour group, 3 to the Samuelite Liberals and 2 to the Simonites. Not only was MacDonald still prime minister, but Sankey stayed on as lord chancellor and Thomas as dominions secretary; Snowden, who had not stood again in the election and was therefore no longer eligible for the Treasury, went to the Lords as lord privy seal. Samuel was still home secretary, while Simon replaced Reading at the Foreign Office. Walter Runciman, the other Simonite member of the Cabinet, went to the Board of Trade. Of the other senior ministers, Baldwin stayed on as lord president — second in the Cabinet hierarchy, but with no department behind him — while Neville Chamberlain became chancellor of the exchequer.

Only the last of these appointments represented a defeat for MacDonald, and it may not have been as big a defeat as it appears to have been at first sight. On November 1st, he noted, 'Saw Baldwin yesterday at Chequers and gave him figures to which I might try to approach in distribution of offices. Found afterwards a little too generous.'[1] On the 3rd he wrote to Baldwin to say that he had sounded out two of his colleagues about the distribution of posts and that

> They both re-acted very strongly against the method of which you approve, and confirm the feeling I have that the country will regard it with grave misgiving and wonder. The simplest arrangement would undoubtedly be the first I thought of — that Mr. Chamberlain should remain where he is and somebody with leanings on the whole to the other side should take the Exchequer, as Cunliffe-Lister is so good at the Board of Trade. If Mr. Chamberlain goes to the Exchequer there must be a change at the Board of Trade. Then Cunliffe-Lister might become a Secretary of State, say for the Colonies ... In that event, either Reading or Simon — preferably the latter, would go to the Foreign Office, but of course the drawback of that is that the figures are not good for you. The trouble is not unwillingness to give you a very generous share, as I showed you on Saturday, but that unfortunately the men cannot be produced, and I shall be very much blamed indeed by the country if I cannot show that there is a really National touch in the Government with a meaning more comprehensive than that merely the three Parties are represented on it.[2]

This, however, was asking for a great deal — for so much, in fact, that it is hard to believe that MacDonald seriously expected to get it. Stripped of the trimmings, his proposal was that Chamberlain, the leading apostle of tariff reform in British politics, should be fobbed off with the Ministry of Health, while the Treasury went to a free-trader. It was not for this that the Conservatives had just won an overwhelming majority in the House of Commons, and it is not surprising that Baldwin should have dug in his toes. To put it at its lowest, MacDonald's defeat over the Treasury in 1931 was no more serious a sign of weakness than his defeat over the Foreign Office had been in 1929. In other respects, he was entitled to congratulate himself. Though the Conservatives held all three service ministries, these were posts of little political weight when the Government was formed. Of the great civilian departments of state, they held only one. Chamberlain at the Treasury was balanced by Runciman at the Board of Trade; though Runciman turned out to be at most a milk-and-water free-trader, it is worthy of note that he was Snowden's candidate for the post.[3] At MacDonald's insistence, and to Baldwin's apparent regret, the hard-line protectionist, Leo Amery, was kept out of office altogether.[4] Lord Hailsham, who coveted the Woolsack, had to be content with the War Office. The secretary for air was Lord Londonderry – a Conservative, no doubt, but MacDonald's man, whom Baldwin would probably not have appointed. When the list was complete, Baldwin told Amery that the 'dominant fact in the situation' was that he had only been able to make recommendations and had accepted that 'it was MacDonald who was forming his Cabinet.'[5] All the available evidence suggests that Baldwin was telling the truth.

In the end, however, the Government would be judged, not by its membership, but by its policies – and still more, perhaps, by the way in which its policies were presented. Here, the challenge to MacDonald was much more formidable. Then, as now, the Conservatives instinctively saw themselves as the one truly national party. To them it seemed self-evident, not merely that Conservative policies were in the national interest, but that all honest men knew that Conservative policies were in the national interest. They could see that in order to give the Government the 'really National touch' for which MacDonald had asked in his letter to Baldwin it might be necessary to cut down the number of Conservatives in the Cabinet. To many of them it seemed almost self-contradictory to suggest that it might sometimes be inappropriate for a National Government to adopt Conservative policies. Of course, there were some issues on which the Conservatives had no distinctive policies; on others, there was no significant opposition in the Cabinet to the views of the Conservative minister concerned. These caused no problems. Foreign policy, which fell into the first category, was settled outside the Cabinet by MacDonald, Simon and the service ministers. Though the service ministers sometimes differed with MacDonald and Simon, they did so as the spokesmen for their departments rather than as Conservative politicians; in any case, they did not offer a serious challenge to MacDonald, whose control of foreign policy, at least on the most important questions, was almost as complete in this period as it had been in 1924. By the same token, budgetary policy, which fell into the second category, was settled by Chamberlain, in an isolation even more glorious than Snowden's in the previous Government. On other issues, however – notably on India and on the fiscal question – it was a different story. On each of these, the Conservatives' position differed significantly from the positions of at least some of their colleagues, and on both there were fierce battles in the Cabinet. Even on these, the Conservatives did not always prevail. On India, as we shall see, MacDonald pushed through an important modification of policy in the teeth of strong opposition from the secretary of state, Sir Samuel Hoare. But he did so only after a hard struggle, while his attempt to persuade the Conservatives to modify their policy on the fiscal question was an abject failure.[6]

Even during the Labour Government, when his authority as prime minister had been buttressed by his position as party leader, MacDonald had been reluctant to take a strong line when he suspected that a majority of the Cabinet would be against him. He was even more reluctant to pick fights with his Conservative colleagues now. It is clear from his diary and papers that he was uneasy about Sir Henry Betterton's policies as minister of labour – notably over public works and over the administration of unemployment relief – and that he suspected that the Treasury, under Chamberlain, was now insisting on too much economy in public expenditure.[7] But although he tried to persuade Betterton to make the administration of unemployment relief more humane and to adopt a more active public-works policy, his attempts to do so were fitful and half-hearted and were soon abandoned. His behaviour towards Chamberlain was even more circumspect. In a Cabinet paper a few weeks after the election, he argued that although it had been necessary to make sweeping economies during the summer, they had in some cases reduced efficiency and well-being; the time had come to review their effects and to make 'adjustments'.[8] His paper was discussed at two consecutive Cabinet meetings early in December[9] and then, for all practical purposes, forgotten. Chamberlain proceeded on his way as though it had never been written, and MacDonald made no further attempts to disturb him. Meanwhile, he concentrated more and more on foreign affairs – partly because he was understandably dubious about Simon's ability to handle them, partly because a number of critical foreign-policy questions came to a head, but partly, one cannot help suspecting, because it was on foreign policy that his influence could be exerted with least unpleasantness and to most effect. At the same time, he had to undergo two eye operations and two prolonged periods of convalescence. The net result was that, in the nine months from the beginning of November 1931 to the end of July 1932, he was out of the country at international conferences for the best part of five weeks and either in hospital or recuperating from an operation for the best part of ten – a total of fifteen weeks altogether. When he was available he presided over the Cabinet with his old efficiency and courtesy. Simon apart, however, he left his departmental ministers to their own devices and made no real attempt to control or co-ordinate the work of the Government.

On the whole, he seems to have got on reasonably well with his colleagues, but only Thomas, Runciman and Londonderry were more than business associates. To judge by his diary, he actively disliked Samuel, while Simon's silky urbanity[10] grated on him as much as it did on other people. Chamberlain, he viewed with a kind of distant respect, tinged with apprehension. His relations with Baldwin are more difficult to fathom. Baldwin had admired MacDonald's conduct in 1931 and behaved towards him thereafter with scrupulous correctness. At one level, MacDonald realized this; and, as time went on, he trusted Baldwin more and more. At another level, however, he could not help resenting his own dependence on the Conservative Party, and it was almost inevitable that that resentment should sometimes have spilled over into resentment with Baldwin. Though they had a good deal in common politically, moreoever, they were poles apart in temperament, and it is doubtful if either really understood the other. MacDonald was a worrier, for ever wanting to know where he stood and what the future held in store. Baldwin was a ruminant, who hated crossing bridges before he came to them and who believed in letting sleeping dogs lie. From time to time, MacDonald would write anxiously to Baldwin, analysing the problems ahead of them and asking for Baldwin's opinions about them; Baldwin would reply, when he replied at all, with vague assurances of goodwill, which might mean anything or nothing and which must have left MacDonald as uneasy as he had been before. They co-operated well enough from day to day, but they never managed to work out a common strategy; though MacDonald might have liked to, it is doubtful if they even tried. Thus the Government always had a slightly makeshift air about it. It had a huge majority in Parliament, a solid basis of popular support and, in spite of later charges to the contrary, a number of able ministers. But now that the crisis which had brought it into being was over, it lacked a common purpose. As events were to show, it also lacked the internal cohesion to develop one.

II

MacDonald's first big struggle with the Conservatives in the Cabinet came over India. As we have seen, the first round-table conference had broken up in January 1931, in an atmosphere of vague goodwill. In September, it was followed by a second conference – this time with Congress participation and with Gandhi as one of the delegates. For some weeks, however, little progress was made; and by early November it seemed clear that the conference was approaching a crisis. The Moslems were as suspicious of the Hindus as they had been the year before: the Hindus as unwilling to make concessions to the Moslems. Latent British suspicions that India might not be ready for self-government were reinforced, as were latent Indian suspicions that Britain might try to return to the old imperial policy of 'divide and rule'. The British election results had made matters even worse. Many Indians feared that the huge Conservative majority on the back benches might push the Government to the right, and their fears made them even more prickly than they would have been in any event; the more prickly they became, the more apt they were to behave in a way that fortified suspicions on the British side. For, although only a minority of Conservative backbenchers supported the die-hard opponents of Indian self-government, few Conservative ministers showed much understanding of Indian susceptibilities. Even Hoare, the secretary of state, who had already established good personal relations with Gandhi, persistently underestimated the Indians' lack of confidence in British goodwill. On November 8th, the Congress working committee cabled Gandhi to tell him that his presence in London was no longer necessary and that he was wanted at home. He stayed all the same; but there could be no doubt that the Congress party's patience – and, with it, the chance of a peaceful settlement in India – was waning fast.[11]

So far, MacDonald had played only a marginal role in the conference. When the end of the election campaign gave him an opportunity to pick up the threads, however, he rapidly came to the conclusion that, as he put it later in a letter to the viceroy, Lord Willingdon, 'a ruinous policy was being pursued.'[12] Yet it was surprisingly difficult to push through a change of course. On November 11th, MacDonald and Sankey dined with the Indian Liberal leaders, M. R. Jayakar and Sir Tej Bahadur Sapru. They agreed to what MacDonald described rather optimistically in his diary as 'a good plan for settling India',[13] by which the work of drafting a federal constitution would be started around May 1932, while legislation granting autonomy to the provinces would be passed around July – thus meeting the Indian fear that if provincial autonomy preceded self-government at the centre, self-government at the centre might be indefinitely postponed. Next day, Hoare agreed to the plan, and the Cabinet committee on the conference decided to recommend it to the Cabinet.[14] On November 13th, however, the Cabinet watered it down almost beyond recognition – sticking to the notion of a two-stage advance to self-government, with provincial autonomy coming first and self-government at the centre later, but insisting that the commitment to federal self-government should be phrased in a way that would make it possible to withdraw it if the Indians failed to settle the communal problem themselves.[15]

This was a bad blow for MacDonald, and it was soon followed by others. On November 19th, he was pressed by what he described privately as a 'heated' delegation of Conservative peers and M.P.s to give an assurance that the Government would make no declaration of policy to the conference until Parliament had debated it. 'Ld. Lloyd was one and was as usual loquacious & light,' MacDonald noted apprehensively. 'Storms ahead'.[16] Next day, the Cabinet returned once again to the question of provincial autonomy, and decided to bring in a Bill introducing it during the current parliamentary session. Afterwards MacDonald noted indignantly that his colleagues had 'turned down my advice that provincial autonomy was not enough. I stood alone.'[17]

In the next few days, however, he found allies. On November 25th, a letter appeared in the British press, signed by fifteen of the Indian delegates to the conference, denouncing the 'repeated attempts by members of the dominant political party in Parliament ... to bring the proceedings of the Conference to an immediate end', and insisting that 'no political party of any standing in India will in the slightest degree favour the introduction of provincial autonomy as the first instalment with a mere promise of establishing responsibility on a federal basis in the future.' Gandhi, who had not signed the letter, told the Federal Structure committee of the conference that he had now come to the conclusion that the Government did not intend to grant the kind of provincial autonomy that Congress could accept and that he therefore saw 'no tangible result coming out of the conference'. At this, the Cabinet drew back – deciding on November 27th that, in view of Indian hostility, it would not proceed with the provincial autonomy Bill after all.[18] From MacDonald's point of view, this was a step forward. But although his line on provincial autonomy had now been vindicated, more struggles lay ahead. The final session of the conference was held on December 1st. MacDonald's speech winding it up was printed as a white paper, and had to be approved beforehand by the Cabinet. The India Office prepared a draft, which was then amended by MacDonald; and shortly before the Cabinet meeting, Hoare sent him an agitated note, to say that he was 'disquieted' about his amendments.[19] MacDonald was disquieted too. As he described it in his diary in the early hours of December 1st:

> Weekend broken. Went Chequers early Friday to work at statement to India Conference[.] India Office did not send it though promised it ... London presiding over Round Table Conference. Further evidence how India Office was working blindly putting up backs, miscalculating value of this section & that. Miracle is this ends with one friend remaining. Sunday worked at statement which in reference to Prov: autonomy & continuing Conference seemed designed to please a Tory committee & quite oblivious that our problem was the R.T.C. Harrassed & head giving pain & working slowly and badly ... Monday (yesterday) another long day presiding over R.T.C. from 10.30 in my room; 9.15 Cabinet till 11.30 pm. Hoare at it again without any consideration of the human problem. I shudder as to what may happen but if this is over with any success there will be a breathing space.

In the end, MacDonald prevailed – though, according to Sankey, 'he & I had to fight hard to get our way'.[20] In spite of Hoare's misgivings, MacDonald's draft was accepted and his speech at the final session, in which he re-emphasized the Government's commitment to an all-India federation and made it clear that it changed its mind over provincial autonomy, was frequently interrupted by cheers. When MacDonald had finished, Gandhi moved a vote of thanks, congratulating him on driving the conference 'with pitilessness worthy of a Scotsman'.[21] A few days later, MacDonald wrote cheerfully to Willingdon, 'The Round Table Conference has ended far better than seemed to be possible a fortnight ago ... The delegates are going back in pretty good spirit and with something to fight for in their possession.'[22]

In the circumstances, this was not an unfair summary. Though no one could claim that the conference had made much progress, MacDonald's intervention had at any rate prevented it from making things worse; to the extent that it could be described as a success, it seems clear that he deserved most of the credit. Looked at as an episode in British politics, however, its significance lay less in the extent of MacDonald's achievement than in the struggle which he had been forced to wage to achieve anything at all.

III

By now he had to face a more serious crisis. As we have seen, the Conservatives had fought hard to commit the Government to tariff reform before the election. They had failed in that, but they had fought on a tariff-reform platform themselves. They were committed up to the hilt to a policy which most of them in any case saw as the nation's only road to solvency. In these circumstances, there could be no real doubt that tariffs would be introduced sooner or later – if not by the National Government, then by an exclusively Conservative one. But Snowden and the Samuelite Liberals were still committed, emotionally as well as politically, to free trade. They might conceivably be cajoled into accepting tariffs on a more or less temporary basis and for purely pragmatic reasons, but they had no intention of renouncing the free-trade faith which they had preached all their political lives. Thus MacDonald had a peculiarly awkward course to steer. In themselves, tariffs held no terror for him. What did hold terrors for him was the prospect of a split in the Cabinet in which the Government's 'National' label might be ripped off; though he had no qualms about protection himself, he was anxious to find some way of sugaring the pill, so that it could be eased down sensitive free-trade gullets with as little unpleasantness as possible.

At first, it looked as though the pill would be swallowed without much protest. Five days after the Cabinet appointments were announced, Chamberlain warned his colleagues that imports were increasing alarmingly and that the already unhealthy trade balance was rapidly deteriorating.[23] MacDonald asked Chamberlain and Runciman to consult together. Two days later, they presented a joint paper to the Cabinet, showing that the level of imports was abnormally high and suggesting that the Government should take powers to levy duties on abnormal imports if it saw fit. Though Samuel and Maclean objected, the rest of the Cabinet agreed;[24] within a few days, Parliament had passed an Abnormal Importations Act, giving the Board of Trade power to impose duties of up to 100 per cent on a wide range of goods. Shortly afterwards, Sir John Gilmour, the minister of agriculture, circulated two papers to the Cabinet – one asking for permission to announce that a wheat quota would be introduced before the next harvest, and the other advocating protection for certain horticultural products. In spite of a growl of protest from Snowden, both proposals were accepted.[25] At the end of November, Gilmour duly committed the Government to a wheat quota; by early December, the Horticultural Imports Bill had received its third reading.

By now, however, the free-traders were beginning to take fright. On December 2nd, Snowden wrote to MacDonald, to say that he could not 'go on sacrificing beliefs and principles bit by bit until there are none left' and that there were other members of the Cabinet who felt as he did.[26] On the 3rd, MacDonald wrote to Baldwin, warning that there was

> growing disturbance in the minds of several members of the Cabinet about our fiscal policy. I myself am getting unhappy about it. Our recent discussions on duties have been put forward quite openly as protection, not as means of balancing trade; and the Bill which is now before us imposing duties on fruits and fancy agricultural imports is a very clear case in point ...
>
> I am also alarmed at a statement, alleged to have been made by Lord Stonehaven and published in the News Chronicle this morning, that 'we have a National Government with a mandate to carry out Tory policy'. I do not want to show any rift in the lute, but Lord Stonehaven is the executive head of the Conservative Organisation and his words cannot be treated lightly. If he is right, then some of us have grossly misled millions of electors and we cannot possibly remain under that imputation ...
>
> We have all been so distracted by day to day troubles that we have never had a chance of surveying the whole situation and hammering out a policy regarding it, but have had to live from agitation to agitation. Before the Cabinet disperses we shall have to examine the situation as a whole. Appearances at the moment are not at all encouraging.[27]

MacDonald's admonitions evidently struck home. In a speech at Aberdeen next day, Baldwin reminded his followers that the Government's victory in the election had been a National and not a party one, explained that the problems raised by the trade deficit were being examined with an open mind and warned that results could not be expected at once.[28] In other respects, MacDonald was less successful. The fiscal question, he argued in a Cabinet paper at the beginning of December, should be approached, not in the spirit of the nineteenth-century theorists of protection, who had dealt with conditions that no longer existed, but in terms of 'the peculiar conditions of the world to-day'. Solutions were needed to such urgent problems as 'the balance of our own trade, Empire mutual co-operation in relation to our political and economic relations to the rest of the world, development of resources that have been neglected, or that, in relation to outside competition, may or may not be below the line, or just on the margin, of productive use'; to find them it would be necessary to carry out a thorough study of the 'national, imperial and international problems and aims of British industry'.[29] Though he did not spell them out in so many words, the implications were clear. The fiscal question should be seen as a practical problem, not as an ideological one. It should be settled, not by appealing to old theories but by examining new facts; such an examination would show that the problem was far more complicated than either traditional protectionists or traditional free-traders supposed. As he put it in another paper, written in early January 1932, and probably intended as an aide-mémoire for his own use:

> It seems to me to be clear ... that in view of the wholesale upset in the free-play of normal economic actions and reactions on trade, it is impossible to proceed upon the familiar assumptions upon which were based the emaculate [sic] policy of the open market ...
>
> ... The economic effects of the war, supplemented by the political nationalism which was fostered by it [sic] being developed into economic nationalism as well, have set this country in a world different in all its econ-omic features from that of the greater part of [the] last century. And, as the economic policy of the country must be devised to meet its world relation-ships, so it is necessary for us to re-study our setting in order to discover how to meet the new circumstances ...
>
> ... [O]ne of the special features of our problem is how to get over the transition time between the old industrial England and the new. I have recently seen all sorts of people from fishermen to iron and steel magnates, who are asking for Protection. One and all have somewhere hidden in their minds the assumption that by tariff action on the part of the Government they can be allowed to go on in old ways and upon old assumptions. So far as that is their motive, it amounts to an expectation that by enabling them to fix prices or to compete on a market of limited supply, they need not face the problems with which new economic conditions confront them. I think the Cabinet will agree that it must not encourage this state of mind to continue ...
>
> ... [W]e must be very careful in how we pursue the idea of protecting the British producer. It must not be *any* producer, but an efficient producer.[30]

The old theories turned out to have more life left in them than MacDonald had acknowledged. On December 11th, the Cabinet set up a committee to investigate the trade balance, chaired by Chamberlain and with Samuel, Simon, Thomas, Snowden, Cunliffe-Lister, Hilton Young, Runciman and Gilmour as its other members. So far, MacDonald's approach had been followed, but his evident hope that the question could be defused by treating it as one of fact rather than of principle was rapidly disappointed. The committee launched no great investigation of the kind envisaged in his paper. Between December 16th, 1931 and January 18th, 1932 it met only five times; its report was dated January 19th.[31] In these circumstances, it was hardly surprising that its conclusions should have had a strong flavour of the *a priori*. It assumed that retained imports would have to be reduced by £52 million a year and concluded that the way to do this was to impose a general tariff of 10 per cent, coupled with a variable surtax on non-essential goods, which would serve at one and the same time as a protective tariff, as a bargaining counter in international negotiations and as a means of providing higher rates of imperial preference. The free-traders' response was equally predictable. Snowden submitted a memorandum of dissent, denying that an adverse trade balance had been proved to exist and arguing that tariffs would increase costs and reduce competitiveness. Samuel submitted a separate memorandum, suggesting a system of temporary safeguarding duties for industries willing to rationalize, but denouncing the general tariff on classic free-trade grounds and complaining bitterly about the committee's failure to consult outside experts.[32]

Battle was joined at the Cabinet meeting on January 21st. Maclean and Sinclair backed Snowden and Samuel in rejecting the report. Simon and Runciman accepted it, as did Thomas and Sankey. Londonderry declared that he was neither a protectionist nor a free-trader, but that he wanted to bring tariff barriers down; if the committee's proposals resulted in a general lowering of tariffs 'it would be all for the good'. The other Conservatives all gave blanket approval to the report—Eyres Monsell declaring menacingly that, if the Government did nothing, 'the House of Commons would take matters into their own hands.' After a long and occasionally impassioned debate, which had to be resumed in the afternoon after a lunch-time adjournment, Baldwin clinched the protectionists' argument with a brutal though mildly phrased appeal to the facts of parliamentary power. The arguments for and against tariffs, he declared, had been familiar to his colleagues for thirty years and he would therefore say nothing about them; instead, he would confine himself to certain observations, made 'as the leader of the largest political party in the House of Commons'. The election had been fought as a tariff election: the Cabinet would not survive if it did nothing. He had never liked coalitions, but he believed that that National Government was a national necessity: if it fell, he would regret its collapse 'as keenly as that of a Conservative Government'.

After this, MacDonald announced that although he acknowledged the force of Samuel's objections to a flat-rate tariff, he did not believe that the committee's proposals would raise the cost of living, protect inefficiency or damage future attempts to reduce tariffs elsewhere; in consequence, he was prepared to accept them. But Samuel, Snowden, Maclean and Sinclair all refused to budge; and MacDonald then adjourned the meeting until next morning, with the warning that 'all present would have to face what would be the result of the break-up of the National Government.'[33] Later he noted morosely:

Cabinet discussion on Balance of Trade memorandum and at end of afternoon sitting, hopeless deadlock. Snowden, Samuel, Maclean & Sinclair intimated resignation. Not quite prepared for this as though I knew that there had not been complete agreement, I had been led to understand that the minority would not go so far as to resign & end this Govt. 8.30 Saw them at Snowden's (72 Carlisle Mansions). Put their responsibility for the Nat: Gov:, for the result of election; the issues national & internation[al], the position in which I was left. No avail. They admitted everything, but would not budge. Maclean & Sinclair simple political minds; Samuel pettifogging on some doubtful figures of no real importance: Snowden just as stiff necked & unaccommodating as ever he has been. What a situation. Sorry for Thomas who came in to No. 10 at 10.45 p.m. in a bad state.[34]

While MacDonald was vainly trying to persuade the free-traders to think again, however, the protectionists were beginning to have second thoughts of their own. Before the election, many Conservatives had hoped to force the Samuelites out of office. Now, many looked forward to a merger between themselves and the Liberals, and realized that if they were to achieve one they would have to keep the Samuelites in. At a meeting in the evening of January 21, Conservative ministers agreed that at next day's Cabinet the arch-protectionist, Lord Hailsham, should suggest that although the Government should adopt the committee's proposal, the free-trade ministers should be allowed to speak and vote against them while still holding their offices.[35] When the Cabinet met in the morning of the 22nd, MacDonald warned once again that the break-up of the Government would have 'deplorable' consequences. Once again, Samuel refused to budge. Hailsham then intervened with the proposal that 'in the exceptional circumstances of the day some relaxation might be made of the ordinary Cabinet rule of collective responsibility'; and after a short adjournment to allow the free-traders to consider it, Hailsham's offer was accepted.[36] By lunch-time, the crisis was over. 'Solution found,' MacDonald noted, with understandable asperity. 'Free to vote & speak against Tariffs. Put that proposal to the four last night & they rejected it. Will be difficult to work & the usual pundits will declare that it is violating constitution &c &c. Off to Chequers, relieved, a feeling of melancholy tiredness upon me.'[37]

Melancholy and tiredness were both justified. The Government had survived its first serious crisis. But MacDonald's attempt to bridge the gulf between protectionists and the free-traders had failed: and it failed because neither side had been willing to listen to him.

IV

In spite of the problems it had created for the future, the Cabinet's agreement to differ over tariffs had at least kept the Government afloat, and any misgivings which MacDonald may have felt about the behaviour of the crew were soon overshadowed by more pressing worries. On January 28th, a Japanese force from the international settlement at Shanghai marched into the Chinese suburb of Chapei – provoking violent indignation in Britain and the United States, and giving a menacing new twist to the crisis which had begun when Japan had seized control of Manchuria four months before. So far, the Cabinet had paid only scant and intermittent attention to developments in the Far East, and had done little more than endorse the line already laid down in the Foreign Office. With Chapei in flames and a full-scale war between China and Japan at least on the cards, such passivity was no longer feasible; and for the next few weeks, the ministers concerned struggled unavailingly to reconcile their abhorrence of the Japanese action and their reluctance to condone aggression with their knowledge of Britain's weakness and their belief that she could not afford to take part in military or even economic action against Japan.

From MacDonald's point of view, the dilemma could not have been posed at a worse time. On January 25th, he had noted apprehensively that his eye was 'not in good form'.[38] His first eye operation followed on February 3rd; and, as we have seen, he was not back at his desk until the middle of March.[39] Even so, he played a more active part in the Government's search for a far eastern policy than has sometimes been realized. In spite of his fears about his eyesight, he presided over the *ad hoc* committee of ministers which took the key decisions in the few days immediately after the attack on Chapei. Though his role dwindled after his operation, his colleagues still took care to consult him before any important moves were made, and on one critical occasion the now formally constituted far eastern committee of the Cabinet actually met in his nursing-home room.[40]

It cannot be said that he added to his reputation. One of the central questions facing British policy-makers during the Shanghai crisis was whether or not to agree to an American proposal that the two Governments should make a joint protest against Japan's violation of the nine-power treaty guaranteeing China's territorial integrity. In the end, the American proposal was turned down and the joint protest was never made. Instead, Britain promoted a resolution at the League of Nations, insisting that the Sino-Japanese conflict should not be settled by force, but couched in such inoffensive terms that the Japanese did not feel called upon to vote against it and were content to abstain. The British alternative had much to be said for it. The Admiralty had made it clear that Britain was in no condition to go to war with Japan, and, for all their moral indignation, there could be little doubt that the Americans had no intention of going to war either. The difference between them was that the Americans wanted to make a strong protest and the British a weak one. Given that no one was willing to back words with deeds, it could be argued that weak words were more appropriate than strong ones. But although Britain's policy can be defended, its execution cannot. Simon and MacDonald shared their colleagues' unwillingness to take part in a joint *démarche* with the Americans, but they could not bring themselves to tell the Americans so. Instead of making it clear from the start how far they were prepared to go, they dithered and prevaricated, raising expectations which they then had to disappoint. And although Simon was the worst offender, MacDonald was guilty as well. At one moment, he gave the Americans to understand that Britain would do as they wanted. Two days later he approved (or perhaps even initiated) the alternative of a resolution at the League of Nations. At the beginning of March he urged Baldwin to make sure that the British delegation at Geneva moved closer to the Americans; when he saw Stimson in April he explained that he had been in a nursing home when the Cabinet decided to reject the American proposal and had known nothing about it. He was recovering from a serious operation, was able to read only with difficulty and for much of the time was probably in pain. Even so, it was a feeble performance.

But it was also a revealing one; and, if we are to understand his behaviour during the much fiercer storms of the next few years, we must try to understand the reasons for its feebleness. His operation provides part of the explanation, but there is a deeper explanation as well. It is easy to stride forward when the objective is clear and the path towards it familiar. It is more difficult when the objective is covered in mist and the path has suddenly sunk into a bog. That is what happened to MacDonald during the Shanghai crisis. For years he had insisted that arms gave only a false security, that the surest guarantee against aggression was the force of world opinion, that Governments should stop worrying about the risks of war and start running risks for peace. Now these doctrines had been called in question. At the London naval conference, Britain and the United States had run risks for peace. Their reward was a flagrant act of war on the part of the Japanese. World opinion, in the shape of the League of Nations, had called on Japan to withdraw her troops from Manchuria. Japan had taken no notice, and had spread the fighting to Shanghai. Britain was powerless to stop her; and she was powerless because she had failed to maintain her armed forces at the necessary level. It must have been a black moment for MacDonald, and it is not surprising that he should have floundered. There can be no doubt that he was appalled at the Japanese action. In a painful scrawl in his diary, written a few days before his operation when it must have been difficult for him to write at all, he noted indignantly, 'Japan's wicked behaviour at Shanghai'.[41] But he could not make up his mind how to respond to her wickedness. To go to war with her was unthinkable, but it was equally unthinkable to do nothing. A strong protest might lead to war, or at least to a choice between war and a humiliating retreat. A weak protest might encourage the Japanese. The Foreign Office was against taking part in a *démarche* with the Americans, and he was persuaded intellectually by the Foreign Office argument. But the American line struck an emotional chord in him which the Foreign Office did not touch. He prevaricated partly because he was ill and inclined to take the line of least resistance, partly because he valued his friendship with the Americans and did not want to upset them, but most of all because he half-suspected that they might be right and the Foreign Office wrong.

He faced the same dilemma in a different form when the long-awaited but ill-starred disarmament conference opened at Geneva on February 2nd. In happier times, such a conference might have given him an opportunity to vindicate the creed which had been called in question at Shanghai, but by 1932 it was too late. In Germany, Brüning's Government was on its last legs, in desperate need of a diplomatic victory to throw back at the Nazis and the Nationalists. But Germany could win a diplomatic victory only if France allowed her to: and the rise of the Nazis had made the French even more suspicious of Germany than they had been in the past, and even less willing to make concessions to her. It was essential for Brüning to escape from the subordination which had been imposed on Germany at Versailles—either by persuading the wartime Allies to disarm down to Germany's level, or by persuading them to allow Germany to rearm up to a higher level. But the French insisted more vehemently than ever that there could be no disarmament without a watertight security arrangement. When the conference opened, they proposed an elaborate scheme for an international police force controlled by the League of Nations. Germany replied with a sweeping disarmament plan, in effect applying the disarmament clauses of the peace treaty to the victor powers, and a strong speech by Brüning, insisting that German disarmament must now be followed by general disarmament, based on the principle of equal rights for all.[42] In the next few months, many red herrings were to be dragged across the trail and much ingenuity was to be expended in pursuing them. But the quarry that mattered was an agreement between France and Germany, and the longer the conference lasted the more elusive it became.

It is doubtful if such an agreement was possible at all. It is as certain as a hypothetical proposition ever can be that the deadlock could have been broken only if Britain had moved closer to the French position on security than any British Government had moved since the war. But the National Government was no more prepared to do this in 1932 than the Labour Government had been in 1930. Now, more than ever, most people in Britain saw France, not Germany, as the chief threat to peace and harmony in Europe. The German economy was in ruins; the French had suffered less from the depression than the British had. Germany was still disarmed; France was the strongest military power on the continent. In the crisis months of 1931, the Germans had been begging for help; France had turned a deaf ear to her pleas, and had then done her best to ruin the British as well. Six weeks before the disarmament conference opened, the Cabinet decided that it would not give new guarantes to France 'under which, in conceivable circumstances, British forces might be engaged in a war on the Continent of Europe'; less flamboyantly, but as firmly, it also decided that the notion of an international force did not 'commend itself to the Cabinet'.[43] If these decisions had been submitted to a popular referendum, they would have been overwhelmingly approved.

It would be wrong to suggest that MacDonald was responsible for the

Cabinet's policy, but there can be no doubt that he agreed with it. The French, he complained again and again, were tricky, selfish and unscrupulous; they were out to dominate Europe and keep Germany underfoot. It was impossible to trust them, dangerous to make concessions to them and essential to keep up one's guard while negotiating with them. The French position on reparations, he noted after a tussle with Laval in January, showed a 'small, selfish mind at work'.[44] 'I do my best to have confidence in French,' he noted in April, after a meeting with Laval's successor as prime minister, André Tardieu, 'but am always defeated ... The diplomacy of France is an ever active influence for evil in Europe.'[45] Even in the days of the Geneva Protocol, he had refused to give guarantees to France until he had made sure that they would be 'black and big' only on paper; since then his attitude to her had been soured by the wrangling at the naval conference and the battle that followed the Hoover moratorium. Six weeks after the French produced their plan for an international force, he told the Cabinet's disarmament committee that the fundamental difference between Britain and France lay in

> the fact that in our view the League was an instrument created for handling situations on a conciliation basis and that the League should create a moral force strong enough to over-ride attempts to obtain satisfaction by resort to arms. France on the other hand, held the view that there could be no security without armaments; that is to say, that there could be no security unless there was an armed man by your side to ensure it.[46]

He was not a pacifist, and, as the next few years were to show, his faith in moral force had limits. But he had not reached the limits yet. He had opposed the French view for twenty years. He could no more have abandoned his opposition to it than he could have committed British troops to a war in the defence of China.

On the other hand, he also believed that disarmament was the key to peace; and although he hated having to admit it, he was slowly forced to recognize that there would be no disarmament unless the French were given a *quid pro quo* of some kind. As we have seen, he was too ill to take his place at the head of the British delegation until the conference resumed after the Easter adjournment. When he arrived in Geneva towards the end of April, he plunged into a long and exhausting round of informal discussions, in the hope of finding a way to bridge the gap between France and Germany without making concessions to France. For a brief moment, it looked as though he might succeed. Privately, Brüning made it clear that he would be satisfied with a modest expansion in the *Reichswehr* and 'samples' of the weapons which had been forbidden to Germany at Versailles.[47] On April 29th, MacDonald felt able to tell the British delegation that there were 'indications' that if the disarmament clauses of the Versailles settlement were done away with, Germany might be prepared to forgo full equality of status and accept figures to which the French might be willing to agree.⁴⁸ But the moment soon passed. Tardieu had gone down with laryngitis and was unable, or perhaps unwilling, to come back to Geneva to carry on the negotiations. Meanwhile, MacDonald's eye trouble was getting worse; and on May 1st he was forced back to London and his second operation. When he reached home, the optimism which he had displayed at the delegation meeting was already beginning to fade. In a long and rather sanctimonious diary entry summarizing his impressions of Geneva he noted:

1. Stimson & American delegates: worked closely with them ... Hearty cooperators. 2. French: always felt uncomfortable with them; they never seemed straight; & certainly pursued crooked diplomacy & worked behind our backs. They had tools. Least international of any delegation & pursued own interests all the time. Their method was: 'make it worth our while' ... How foolish it is to be crooked & dishonest. Tardieu embodies both qualities. — 3. German: So hammered that they dreaded no consequences: nothing could be worse than the present, so they stood stiff on demands. eg. freedom from Part V of the Treaty of Versailles, no further Reparation payments. Dr Bruning still placid & ready to face his tasks however hard. Von Bulow less friendly in manner, very reserved, precise, able, stiff behind face like a mask with a cherub mouth. 4. Benes, Hyman still friendly & really anxious to cooperate but first still suspected of being under French control. 5. Business in a bad way: not controlled or directed & nothing of any importance done. Henderson a very sick man & delegates I spoke to agreed not equal to his task. 6. *Press* 150 to 200 with nothing to do but to fill columns & had to manufacture interesting stuff & circulate rumours of good publicity value. 7. Geneva itself becoming a city of international intrigue. One or two British like Mrs. Barton devoted to League cause, others permanent representatives of Govts., experts in manipulation.⁴⁹

Little by little, he came to the conclusion that he would have to try a new tack. Early in May, while he was painfully beginning to recuperate from his operation, the French elections produced a marked swing to the left. Tardieu resigned; and it seemed clear that his only possible successor as prime minister was Herriot, MacDonald's old sparring partner of 1924. Meanwhile, the reparations question, which had been simmering in the background since the struggle over the Hoover moratorium the previous summer, began to come to the boil again, as the Governments concerned prepared for another reparations conference, this time at Lausanne. MacDonald had a number of reasons for wanting the conference to succeed. He was unhappy about the way the Government was going, suspicious of the Conservatives, ill-at-ease with the Liberals and anxious about his own position and reputation; though it would be wrong to suggest that he was consciously hoping or planning to resign, there can be no doubt that he toyed with the idea of doing so. But, like most elderly politicians toying with such ideas, he wanted to go out on an upswing and not on a downswing. If

Lausanne went well, he could leave office in a blaze of glory, as the man who had finally healed the worst of the scars of Versailles. At another level, he knew that reparations and disarmament went hand in hand. Failure at Lausanne would still further inflame the fears and suspicions which had produced deadlock at Geneva; if the reparations question could somehow be solved to the satisfaction of all concerned, the prospects for disarmament might be improved as well. Developments in Germany gave him an additional reason. At the end of May, Brüning was forced out of office and replaced as chancellor by von Papen; though MacDonald was slow to appreciate the full significance of Brüning's fall, he could see that it made Europe even more unstable and an agreement on reparations even more desirable. But the French could prevent a reparations agreement as easily as they could prevent an agreement on disarmament and after Geneva it seemed clear that they would do so unless some concessions were made to their point of view. If Tardieu had still been in power, MacDonald might have felt that there was no point in trying to come to terms with them, but Herriot was a different proposition. In 1924, he had got what he wanted out of Herriot at little cost to himself. Before the conference opened, he decided to use his 1924 tactics again. On May 31st, he wrote to Simon:

> From this distance Bruning's resignation is very disquieting, although I cannot imagine any German Government which will not be reasonable at the present time. It is all very well to make high-falutin' speeches with a dummy pistol in your hands, but when you have not only got the real pistol but also the responsibility of leadership in a battle, nature makes your feet cold and grace keeps your head cool. It will mean, however, that we must lead in Europe for some time, and begin with it at Lausanne.
>
> ... If we possibly can we must work with France, and I say that with great emphasis. In order to do it, we must give away no essentials, but we must be prepared to modify within very strict limits. We must therefore have our own scheme, and it will have to be a very comprehensive one. Europe wants a psychological as well as a political and Treasury lead, and we shall have to give it. I believe that, in order to do this it is absolutely essential that there should be a British Chairman at Lausanne. We cannot afford to be presided over by any of those pettifogging wirepullers who will be buzzing behind our backs all day, and who will spring all sorts of things upon us from the Chair, without proper warning. It is going to be a most uncomfortable and arduous job, and may well wreck whoever does it – for the time being – but it has got to be done ...[50]

V

The conference opened at the Beau Rivage hotel in Lausanne on June 16th, and ended on July 9th. It was a star-studded occasion. The British delegation was headed by MacDonald and also included Chamberlain, Simon and Runciman. France was represented by Herriot and by Germain-Martin, the finance minister, as well as by an impressive phalanx of lesser ministers and officials; von Papen, who led the German delegation, was flanked by his foreign minister, von Neurath, and by his finance minister, Count Schwerin von Krosigk. Among the lesser luminaries were the Italian foreign minister and the Belgian prime minister. For MacDonald, it was also a gruelling occasion. As he had hoped, the other delegations agreed that he should take the chair; though his diplomatic footwork was not as nimble as it had been in 1924, or even in 1930, he took full advantage of his position to push the conference in the direction he wanted it to follow. But he paid a heavier price than ever before. His eyes troubled him a good deal, and Londonderry, who came over from Geneva to visit him, noticed that he often had to protect them with his hands and found it difficult to read.[51] Before the conference had even begun, he looked to Hankey 'like a man with jaundice'.[52] Before it had ended, he was prostrated with exhaustion.[53]

For a while, he stuck firmly to the British policy of the 'clean slate' – insisting that the only rational solution was to cancel reparations altogether and that attempts to scale down Germany's obligations to match her ability to pay would merely provoke endless squabbles among her creditors. With equal firmness, the French replied that if reparations were cancelled the Germans would be placed in a privileged position when the depression lifted, and that cancellation would set a precedent for other countries wishing to renege on their treaty obligations. After much sterile wrangling, however, the French dropped the idea of establishing an index of German prosperity. In return, MacDonald made it clear that he would no longer insist on complete cancellation if the French would accept a lump-sum payment instead of annual payments. He also persuaded Herriot to talk directly to the Germans, and by the weekend of June 25th–26th, it was beginning to look as though an agreement between France and Germany might be reached without much difficulty. Herriot and von Papen both went home for the weekend to consult their colleagues, and before leaving von Papen gave an interview to the French newspaper, Le Matin, declaring that he would be the first to acknowledge that if reparations were cancelled, France would have a right to compensation.[54]

At this point, however, the atmosphere suddenly changed. Von Papen's interview provoked a furious outcry in Germany, and he returned to Geneva a different man. On June 27th, MacDonald noted sadly, 'Franco-German talks very bad ... Both French & Germans back at beginning & delivering speeches of 2 hours'.[55] Next day he was sadder still. As he put it in his notebook:

When found Franco-German position last night determined not to allow them peace to forge arms to-day, so called them to meet Brit: delegation, & whole day spent in discussions. Von Papen fussy, emotional, unintelligent, confused, took wrong points, raised wrong issues, could not keep to

65 Lord Thomson (in civilian clothes) with Wing-Commander E. R. C. Nanson

66 The R.101 crash

67 The first National Government, August, 1931. *Seated, left to right:* Snowden, Baldwin, MacDonald, Samuel, Sankey. *Standing, left to right:* Cunliffe-Lister, J. H. Thomas, Reading, Neville Chamberlain, Hoare

68 MacDonald on his way to the House of Commons for the debate on the economy programme, September, 1931

69 MacDonald and Ishbel arriving at Heston from Seaham, October, 1931

70 Family picnic, 1934. Left to right: Alastair Mackinnon, Joan, Malcolm, Iona
Mackinnon, MacDonald, Ishbel

71 Leaving for Buckingham Palace to tender his resignation as prime minister, June, 1935

72 'You have found me an ordinary man, haven't you?' King George V in old age

business. The record of meeting very damaging to Germans. For first time French & us together. Towards end Chamb asked Herriot what would suit him regarding moral & political security, and H. not answering directly, we veered against the French again. If the stakes were not so heavy and I were not in it, I should enjoy the kaleidoscopic changes. Very much struck by the fact that in reality both Germans & French think only of themselves in all this & of politics more than of economics & trade which are the deepest rock foundations of politics. Most tiring day.[56]

On the 30th, the kaleidoscope changed again. After a 'day of slogging' MacDonald noted gloomily:

Germans plainly making for disagreement. Finance Minister inclined to agree & cooperate, but Von Bulow who sits behind him and at the end of every speech bends over & whispers orders to him is his master. They wear masks. No sign of what is within moves their faces. The Minister sits like a Buddist [sic] with eyes downcast & with little movements of his body: Von Bulow looks out from smallish eyes, blue, innocent but the innocence of the Sphinx. His look is from a barred mind. He knows, but he keeps himself in purdah. A man of plots and hard vengeance. He looks bending over the Minister like Satan tempting a monk in an old print. – The records of today very interesting. Looks like the end with the Germans refusing to cooperate, & I may have to devise a policy without them.[57]

By the following day, he was

Beginning to doubt if Germany really wants to settle. It has been humiliated & has a bitter cup in store for the victors if it has a chance to make them drink. The personality of Von Papen & the general attitude of the delegation have shaken my belief that Germany was prepared to cooperate.[58]

The climax began on July 5th. By now, the British had given up the 'clean slate', and the French had accepted the lump-sum payment. After much hard bargaining it had been agreed that the lump sum should be paid into a fund for European reconstruction – thus meeting the German demand that it should not appear to be another reparation payment. But the size of the sum was more difficult to settle. The French had insisted that Germany should pay seven milliard marks (i.e. 7,000 million). The Germans had offered two milliards. At a joint meeting of the creditor powers, it had been agreed that they should be asked for four. Four milliards, the Germans had replied, would bring down the Government and put Hitler in power.[59] MacDonald had already made one change of policy when he dropped the 'clean slate'. Now he decided on a much more far-reaching change. At a meeting with the French delegation, he offered Herriot a consultative pact of the powers represented at the conference and promised that, if such a pact were signed, Britain would give no definite reply

DI

to any future German requests for changes in the peace treaty without first discussing the matter with France.[60] Herriot was obviously attracted by the idea; and, having sweetened the French, MacDonald turned to the Germans. Without saying so in so many words, he implied that if they raised their bid the conference might agree to a political declaration, formally abrogating the hated war-guilt clause of the peace treaty.[61]

It was a neat package. The Germans would have the war-guilt clause abrogated in exchange for making a larger payment; the French would have the consultative pact and a private understanding with Britain in exchange for letting the war-guilt clause disappear. But MacDonald had not reckoned with the Germans. With a remarkable mixture of greed and insensitivity, they asked for a much more sweeping political declaration than the one MacDonald had outlined to them, and in exchange offered to raise their bid by only 600 million marks — from 2 milliards to 2·6.[62] When MacDonald put the German offer to the French, Herriot exploded with rage. According to MacDonald's note book:

This morning Germans had come with a modified offer recorded in minutes & in the afternoon the road had been cleared for a French interview. Two main papers were put before them & a report of the day's conversations with the Germans. As I proceeded with the report I felt a strange change in the atmosphere. Herriot shrugged shoulders; Germain-Martin did the same and raised eyebrows & expanded palms as well. When I finished the storm of emotion burst. Honour, buying German agreement to pay 'compensation' by selling French women & children (!) & so on flashed like fireworks & rumbled like heavy artillery. Herriot would never trust Germans & so on, & there was more than a suspicion that they believed that we had negotiated with the Germans behind French backs. It was the repetition of a scene of 1924 for although Herriot did not actually get up & go to the door today, he put his papers in his pouch, snapped its lock & prepared to go. The trouble arose because the Germans had proposed certain wording for a declaration on war guilt & disarmament & because these two subjects had been referred to in a draft of a resolution which we had proposed shd be considered a basis for one we should discuss with the French & prepare for the Plenary Conference. To the mention of such things the French were opposed with indignation and emotion. They would never think of political conditions. The fact is that Herriot & Von Papen had discussed a political agreement & H himself reported the conversation to me & showed me a draft he had accepted. Von Papen had discussed a war guilt clause with a French delegate here & the latter had drafted a formula which Von P had accepted in principle. I had frequently referred in conversations some recorded to the desirability of facing now some of these political questions & not only was no objection taken [to] that view but this very morning the French had received from us with warmth a document proposing a political agreement with them. The French had not only gone back but were evidently going to accuse us of sharp practice. The Conference seems hopeless now. There is confusion, bewilderment, temper, and that most fatal of all impediments to good understanding & wise decisions – emotion which gushes as from an oil-well.[63]

In spite of his forebodings, MacDonald managed to staunch the flow next day, and after two more days of intense and wearing negotiations agreement was reached on July 8th. In response to an inquiry from Herriot, MacDonald gave the French an assurance that the British offer of a consultative pact and an understanding with France still stood, and it was decided that an appropriate formula should be worked out when the conference was over. After some unmerciful bullying by MacDonald and Chamberlain, the Germans then agreed to pay 3 milliards into the fund for European reconstruction instead of 2·6. In return, they were given a political declaration which made it clear in so many words that reparations were now at an end, but which said nothing about war guilt or disarmament.[64] The final act of the conference was approved a few hours later, and signed on July 9th. From MacDonald's point of view, it was a great victory. He had denounced reparations when the peace settlement was signed, and had looked forward to their disappearance ever since. Now the hopes of thirteen years had been realized. He had had to pay a price, of course; but in the circumstances, the price seemed well worth paying. The consultative pact entailed no new commitments, and the understanding with France would mean only what future British Governments chose to make it mean. As in 1924, in fact, he had persuaded the French to sacrifice important material claims, and had given only kind words in exchange; as in 1924, he had managed, in doing so, to resolve an ugly international crisis in as fair and sensible a fashion as anyone could reasonably have expected. When the signing ceremony was over, he went for a drive in the mountains. Afterwards he noted, with almost audible relief, 'Tired & pained but it was a new world. The desires of years had been fulfilled & I do not mind much what is to come.'[65] He was entitled to feel relieved.

He was equally cheerful when he came home. 'Beautiful day of peace & sun & a crowd at Victoria,' he noted euphorically on July 10th. 'It was a full-flying end. The King & Queen in the garden at the Palace. C. in her mansion, and the curtain falls.'[66] His morale was still further improved by a letter from the American banker, Thomas Lamont, who wrote to congratulate him on 'a most extraordinary victory for world stability'.[67] Even more encouraging was a letter from Keynes, who sent his 'congratulations on your having secured all that was possible' and then went on, with his usual indefatigable optimism:

It is a long time since June 1919 when I resigned from the British Delegation in Paris in an enraged and tormented state of mind. The waste over the intervening years has been prodigious. But it is a comfortable feeling that

at last it is cleaned up. For whatever America may do, this is necessarily the
end so far as Germany is concerned.

The preliminary impediments having been cleared out of the way, it is
now worth while to try to persuade the world to take strong doses of tonic
to recover its economic health.[68]

'You have indeed been vindicated again and again for what you did in 1919,'
MacDonald replied. 'I am a little bit knocked up, but hope to go ahead with
further developments.'[69]

His euphoria did not last for long. It soon became clear that 1932 was not 1924
after all. In the English-speaking world, the Lausanne agreement was seen as a
victory for economic rationality and common sense. In Germany, it was attacked
as a shameful betrayal, not only by the Nazis and the Nationalists, but even by
the Centre and the Right. The news of the Anglo-French understanding on
which MacDonald and Herriot had agreed at Lausanne, the terms of which
were made public on July 13th, was another blow to German pride. An even
more telling blow was delivered at the disarmament conference on July 20th,
when Simon produced a resolution summarizing its work and laying down
guidelines for the next session, but making no mention of equality of rights. On
July 22nd, the Germans announced that unless the conference explicitly recognized their right to equality of status, they would take no further part in it.
When the Simon resolution was put to the vote the following day, Germany and
the Soviet Union voted against.[70]

VI

The German threat could hardly have been made at a more inconvenient time.
The divisions in the Cabinet which had been papered over by the agreement
to differ at the end of January had soon opened up again. Samuel and Snowden
had not only spoken and voted against the Government's tariff legislation, but
had done so with a passionate inflexibility which had made it even more difficult
for either side to compromise in the future than it had been in the past. A more
sordid squabble had followed in June, after the sudden death of the Samuelite
president of the Board of Education, Sir Donald Maclean. Understandably
enough, the Samuelites insisted that Maclean's post should go to another
Samuelite.[71] At first, MacDonald tried to satisfy them. It was 'of the utmost
importance that we should not allow the Government to justify to any degree
the reputation of being party Conservative', he wrote to Baldwin from Lausanne;
the best solution would be to appoint either Lothian or Isaac Foot.[72] But the
Government chief whip, the redoubtable David Margesson, warned that if a
Liberal were appointed there would be a 'real row' in the Conservative party,[73]
and in the end Maclean was succeeded by Lord Irwin, the recently retired
viceroy – not a 'party Conservative' in the narrowest sense, perhaps, but a
former Conservative minister all the same. From Samuel's point of view, the

sequel was even more galling. He accepted Irwin's appointment with surprisingly good grace, but asked that in return MacDonald should give a 'semi-official statement' to the press, making it clear that the next Cabinet vacancy would be filled by a free-trade Liberal.[74] MacDonald replied tetchily, if predictably, that such an announcement would be 'most undesirable'; though he added vaguely that the 'Party arrangements within the National group' would have to be 'straightened out one way or another',[75] it is doubtful if these reflections gave much consolation to Samuel or any consolation at all to Samuel's office-hungry followers.

The squabble was still rumbling on in the background when the imperial economic conference, which had originally been fixed for the autumn of 1931, opened at Ottawa on July 21st. The British delegation was headed by Baldwin, and also included Chamberlain, Hailsham, Gilmour and J. H. Thomas. The sole free-trader was Runciman, whose free-trade convictions by now looked distinctly battered. Before the negotiations were even under way, Samuel fired a warning shot. Ottawa, he wrote in an ominous letter to MacDonald on July 26th, might have a 'considerable bearing' on the whole question of Cabinet appointments and party arrangements; for himself, he had always felt 'a good deal of anxiety as to the possible effect of the negotiations there upon the continuance of the existing political combination'.[76] If Samuel's letter was designed to influence the negotiations, it did not achieve its purpose. The British delegates arrived in Ottawa in a curiously innocent mood, hoping vaguely for great things but with no clear idea of how to achieve them. They left having agreed to introduce tariffs on non-Empire wheat and butter, to impose quotas on non-Empire meat and to raise such duties as were already paid on other non-Empire foodstuffs. In return the dominions were to increase the preferences they gave to Britain – a concession of scant practical value since it was to be achieved not by lowering the exorbitant tariffs they imposed on British goods but by raising to a still higher level the tariffs they imposed on goods from the rest of the world. For the free-traders, these agreements were the last straw. On August 23rd, Snowden and Samuel exchanged letters egging each other on to resignation.[77] On the 27th, Samuel warned the Cabinet that he and his friends could commit themselves to nothing until they had had time to consider the question.[78] On the 29th, Snowden wrote a characteristically brutal letter to MacDonald, accusing him of complacency in the face of the troubles ahead of him, warning that the free-trade ministers would not acquiesce in the Ottawa agreements and declaring that if they did so 'they would be justly objects of contempt and derision'.[79] The crisis which had been postponed so often in the last ten months had arrived at last.

Few crises can have been less welcome to MacDonald. There can be no doubt that he loathed the prospect of staying on as prime minister if the free-traders left. Though his relations with Baldwin were still amicable enough, he had been growing more and more indignant with the Conservative central office and more and more resentful of the Conservatives' predominance in the Government. Irwin's appointment had been a defeat for him as well as for the Samuelites, and he had had to put up with other humiliations as well. After the election, he had tried hard to persuade the Conservatives to find a seat for Jowitt.[80] In spite of all his efforts, no seat had been forthcoming; and in the end Jowitt had left the Government. During the summer a similar battle had been fought over a by-election at Wednesbury. The local National Labour committee wanted to fight the seat and had a candidate ready, but the Conservatives refused to withdraw. MacDonald retaliated by refusing to send the Conservative candidate a letter of support. When his P.P.S., Ralph Glyn, asked Rose Rosenberg to ask him if he would send a telegram instead, MacDonald told her to reply that it was 'quite impossible' for him to send a message of any kind and that 'for some time, the P.M. has been disturbed by the way in which Conservative Associations have been using the present condition ... to advance their own organisation and get a grip upon constituencies where, in the ordinary course of things, they were pretty well "down and out".'[81] By the end of July, he was writing to De La Warr that the time had come for the National Labour group to 'make up our minds what we are to do and what is to be our [relation] to the other Parties. We cannot go on as we are.'[82] More remarkably still, he wrote at the same time to Snowden:

The action of the Conservatives both as to governmental policy but also, and up to now mainly, as to electioneering, is facing us with the problem of our own future in a definite form. I have changed none of my fundamental guiding views and there is no chance of my changing them ... We must face the platform again for, except by us, there can be no effective defence of our views of a national government. The propaganda which is going on in Scotland, as shown by the reports of meetings in the press, is nothing but the most ordinary Tory stuff. The Opposition is attacked by Tories, the Labour Government is condemned in exactly the same way as the present Labour Opposition. The case is: Had the country not returned Labour in 1929 there would have been none of these troubles. When the national government is mentioned, a Tory government is implied. In short, the plain issues being put to the country are, Toryism versus the Labour Opposition. Disaster is ahead of that ...

Think over this. You are in a very independent position and could say what would be inexpedient for me to say just yet. Could you not on some neutral platform or pulpit deliver a good old fashioned address on Socialism with special application to the Opposition policy, but positive as well showing where you still stand. I have been thinking of doing something like that myself, but you could do it better. I might follow it up. I have taken on a special meeting of the Post-War Brotherhood at Southampton in the later part of the year with the idea of doing something like this.[83]

But it was one thing to assert his independence of the Conservatives: another to break with them over the Ottawa agreements and in doing so to bring the Government down. MacDonald had no great enthusiasm for the agreements himself, but he viewed them as a sceptical pragmatist, not as an outraged ideologue. He did not see the fiscal question as an issue of principle in any case, and the suggestion that the Ottawa agreement somehow infringed free-trade principles more seriously than the tariff legislation had done in February seemed to him absurd. If he brought the Government down over Ottawa, he would be bringing it down over a quibble – and over a quibble in which he did not, in fact, believe.

He would be bringing it down, moreover, at a time of growing international danger. At the end of July, he had still been hoping for what he described in a letter to Harold Picton as a 'big democratic reaction in Germany'.[84] By the end of August, his hopes were fading. On August 24th, he minuted that he had been 'considering the delicate situation in which Germany is in relation to the work we are doing for the establishment of European confidence, and have been greatly impressed by the possibility of a German move which might upset it all'.[85] His fears were borne out five days later, when the German foreign minister handed the French ambassador in Berlin a note announcing that Germany would boycott the forthcoming meeting of the bureau of the disarmament conference unless her demand for equality of status were met. Agitated consultations followed as the French prepared their reply, and on September 9th, MacDonald minuted presciently that if the French and Germans were left to settle the question by themselves 'They will drift further and further apart and no agreement will be possible ... I can see the most dire consequences from this stupid action on the part of Germany, and I do not see anybody except ourselves who can stave them off'.[86] In his diary he was equally prescient and more gloomy. 'Simon, Tyrell, Van came to consult on German situation ... ,' he noted. 'This looks serious. Militarism is raising its head in Germany again.'[87] With that spectre in the background, resignation over Ottawa must have seemed irresponsible as well as hypocritical.

He was also influenced by a more painful consideration. On August 31st, he replied to Snowden's warning letter of the 29th. He had, he wrote mildly,

been under no delusions but doubted very much if you would agree to Ottawa. Indeed I am still waiting for further information & do not yet know what I can do. Overshadowing everything is the national & international position, & I am trying to place in relation to that the Ottawa problems both economic & political ...

... I want to consider what political situation is to be left if there are political changes. Eg. Are we to leave the Tories in power alone? Dont overlook that we have a heavy responsibility for the last election & the present distribution of political power.[88]

On September 8th, he visited Snowden in Snowden's flat in Carlisle Mansions, where the two discussed the position for eighty minutes. Next day MacDonald noted:

> He had not read the Ottawa agreements as they were handed to him only as I sat there, but said that he could not remain in office. The Tories had let us down: they could respect other people's opinions: they could not work in a mixed team: they were IT: they were destroying our work & steadily insinuating their views everywhere: he pitied those who had come with us & had isolated themselves. I did not argue with him or press him. He had too much truth on his side, though I should look at the landscape from a different angle. The overwhelming victory & the overwhelming proportion of Tories were unexpected & weakened us National Labourists: we have a great responsibility to the country & to our supporters & we shd. not merely retire; we shd. not think of surrender until our work is done or until we have done all we can: There are some things in the Ottawa agreements which are bad & I doubt if it on the whole amounts to much & it is an unpleasant extension in a permanent form of temporary taxes on food: still, I think we cannot leave the Govt. & take no responsibility for the next chapter ...[89]

It would be absurd to depict MacDonald as a figure of superhuman nobility, motivated solely by impersonal considerations. It can safely be assumed that, like all politicians in such situations, he was also inflenced by vanity, self-importance and a straightforward desire to hang on to power. But there can be little doubt that what influenced him most of all was a nagging sense that he was responsible for giving the Conservatives their majority, and that it was therefore up to him to make sure that they did not abuse it.

He was still unwilling to let the free-traders go without a fight. On September 10th, Samuel told him that he and the other free-trade Liberals had now decided to resign. MacDonald wrote back a few hours later urging them to change their minds. Britain's standing in the world, he wrote, depended on the National Government staying in office: 'Destroy the political structure of today, and every strength we possess is put in jeopardy.' 'At present I am protected against reflections which would rob me of my influence,' he added self-pityingly. 'As the head of a party government, I should have no such protection. I should be regarded as a limpet in office.'[90] On the 12th he wrote to Runciman, urging him to get in touch with Samuel and stake a claim to take part in the Liberals' private discussions.[91] On the 14th he wrote again to Samuel, to say that he still hoped that he would 'take the view which I more and more strongly urge upon you that, without making any new affirmation about "freedom to differ" ... you can state that this is not the moment to break up the National Government but that as soon as the whole picture is filled in at the end of the International Economic

Conference you and your friends will be free to survey the whole position and act accordingly'.[92] He also made a final forlorn plea to Snowden:

> I meant to write to you and report progress but, what with Police cuts, the German claims and other things, I have really had very little chance. There is nothing new. I am seeing the Liberals to-day. The more I think of the international situation which will arise on the break-up of this Government, the more disquieted am I. I have been making discreet enquiries as to what a transformation of the present Government into a purely Party one would mean, and everybody says it is quite unthinkable. It would be all the worse if our Labour ranks were broken. Do you not think that you could tide over the present difficulty by making a statement that it is imperative that the National Government should hold together until the International Economic Conference and, that when that is over, you will survey the situation and feel yourself perfectly free to come to a decision?
>
> Goodness knows, I should be only too glad if I could see my way to get out of it, but in all honour I cannot. I dread an application of another shortsighted economy programme, but if all the resignations which are threatened take place, we shall have no power to prevent it.[93]

It was a lost cause. Snowden replied uncompromisingly that if any concessions were to be made, it was the Conservatives who should make them.[94] Samuel suggested that no action should be taken on the agreements until the world economic conference was over—a way out which proved unacceptable to the Conservatives and which even MacDonald dismissed, not unreasonably, as 'impracticable'.[95] In a last-minute attempt to soften the Liberals, MacDonald wrote to Samuel on September 21st, to say that the French ambassador had just called at the Foreign Office and had said that if the free-traders went, they would weaken Britain's influence in Europe 'at a most inopportune moment'.[96] This cut no more ice than his previous letters had done; and by the 23rd he had reconciled himself to the inevitable. 'Cabinet remaking ... ,' he noted. 'Geoff: Dawson to discuss Liberal Ministers. Thought it might be better they shd. go. Found confidence in Nat. Gvt. wherever he went this year.'[97]

On September 28th, the Cabinet met for the last time in its existing form, in an atmosphere of strained cordiality, strongly tinged with humbug. Baldwin declared piously that he understood the Liberals' difficulties, but that he 'felt that it would be premature to think out the re-alignment of Parties before next year: in fact, they had "signed on for the voyage".' Samuel replied that he too regretted that the combination was likely to come to an end, but that although the electorate had returned the Government in the belief that it would adopt a common policy, 'on fiscal matters there had been no common policy. All the sacrifices had come from the free traders'. Snowden insisted that he had 'a feeling of genuine respect for his colleagues', but revealed that his position in the Government had been growing more and more irksome to him for some time.

MacDonald then declared that he too had considered resigning, but that he had 'found it impossible to square a sense of duty with any form of withdrawal'. However, Samuel's resignation had changed the whole nature of the Government: if his colleagues still wanted him to continue as prime minister, they would have to say so.[98] After lunch, the meeting was resumed, this time without the free-traders. MacDonald opened the proceedings by saying that he wanted to consult his colleagues on the new position. In particular, would the Government still be justified in calling itself a National Government? Runciman declared loyally that it would and that he was strongly of the opinion that MacDonald should remain as prime minister. Baldwin insisted, in another of the nautical metaphors beloved of British politicians in moments of crisis, that the 'Prime Minister ... had taken command of the ship for a definite purpose and must see it through'. After this, MacDonald announced that he was 'willing to continue ... He would do his best to finish this business'. After a committee had been set up to prepare the legislation needed to carry the agreements into law, the meeting ended.[99]

When it was all over, MacDonald noted:

> Cabinet. Series of addresses of admonition & regret, except that by Samuel which was a civil service paper of a case ... Snowden looked unusually unkempt & unshaven as though growing a moustache or beard, cold, repelling, vindictive. I am disheartened. My colleagues are splendid & the vote they passed & the things said were most encouraging, but 'this nae my ain hoose'. I have had doubts as to whether I should stay, but only owing to my own personal feelings. It is a lonely job, but of what I *ought* to do I never doubted.[100]

In some way, the price was even heavier than it had been the year before.

CHAPTER 29

Ebb tide

I

At one level, the free-traders' resignations made less difference to the Government than might have been expected. MacDonald managed the ministerial reshuffle that followed with considerable skill. Samuel's place at the Home Office was taken by Gilmour, and Gilmour's at the Ministry of Agriculture by Walter Elliott. A Simonite Liberal, Sir Geoffrey Collins, followed Sir Archibald Sinclair as Scottish secretary. Baldwin succeeded Snowden as lord privy seal, but without giving up his previous office as lord president. Though the Conservatives had improved their position a little, they were still much less strong in the Cabinet than on the back benches. In the old Cabinet they had had eleven places out of twenty; now they had thirteen out of nineteen. The National Labour group was still widely over-represented, though its representation had fallen from four to three. The Simonites had increased theirs by one. So far as the past affiliations of its members were concerned, the Government's National label was still precariously in place.

Yet, as MacDonald realized only too clearly, this was only part of the story, and not the most important part. The Samuelites were, no doubt, weak and ineffective, with little support in the country and with few distinctive policies apart from free trade. But they were a recognizable political party and, as such, recognizably independent of the Conservatives, in a sense in which the Simonites and MacDonald's National Labour followers were not. Some of them, including Samuel himself, had won their seats against Conservative opposition. More important still, they had a machine, a tradition, a sense of identity and organized loyalties on which to draw. However difficult it might be for outsiders to tell what they stood for, they themselves had no doubt that they stood for something. None of this was true of the Simonites and, as we have seen, it was not true of the National Labour group either. Before the Samuelites resigned, the Government had been a genuine coalition, albeit a hopelessly unbalanced one. Now it was a Conservative Government which happened to have a non-Conservative at its head and a number of other non-Conservatives attached to it. It had never really deserved its title: a Government which was opposed by the second largest party in the state and against which six-and-a-half million votes had been cast in the election could be considered as 'National' only in a distinctly eccentric sense. But while the Samuelites held office its claims had, at least, been endorsed by two political parties out of three. Now two parties out of three denied them.

To the Conservatives, who saw nothing incongruous in the spectacle of a Conservative Government wearing a National label, the change meant little. After the resignations, Chamberlain wrote complacently that they would hasten the 'move towards that fused Party under a National name which I regard as certain to come'.[1] Most of his Conservative colleagues probably shared his complacency even if they did not share his hopes. For MacDonald, who had staked his reputation on the proposition that the National Government would not be a Conservative Government in disguise, it was a different matter. In the early stages of the crisis, while Baldwin was still on holiday in Switzerland, MacDonald had written him a despairing letter, pointing out that if the free-traders went the Government would no longer be a National one, and that would entail 'a return to pure party fighting ... The leader of the House of Commons under such conditions should be a party man & so should the Prime Minister.'[2] Baldwin had stuffed the letter into his pocket and gone off for his morning's walk; later he had sent MacDonald a reply full of warm goodwill, but almost devoid of practical content.[3] Now MacDonald's worst fears had come true. The free-traders had resigned: and the Government had become, for all practical purposes, a party one. Faced with the choice between staying in office in such circumstances and bringing the Government down on what he regarded as a trivial issue, he had chosen to stay in office. He had made his choice with his eyes open. But that did not make the consequences any easier to bear.

To judge by his diary, at least, he emerged from the crisis in surprisingly good spirits. 'Fireworks in evening Crystal Palace,' he noted defiantly the day after the free-traders resigned. 'Sure to be poor jokes to-morrow, but I enjoyed myself and Thomas was in great form.'[4] That mood did not last for long. As on so many similar occasions in the last three years, he hurried off to recuperate in Lossiemouth as soon as the crisis was over; when he came back to London he was already beginning to quail at the prospect ahead of him. 'Things do not go too well,' he confessed in another diary entry, immediately after his return. 'The silence of the Clyde was an accusation amidst the silence of the hills. I shall again urge the Cabinet to do something. They are good fellows; not much bustling energy; not our make-up & point of view.'[5] In the next few months that note recurred with monotonous frequency. 'Our National Labour position is not good,' he complained to his P.P.S., Ralph Glyn, towards the end of December. 'We have not enough in our ranks to take much part in House of Commons work ... There are therefore two of us in the very curious position of being amongst the leaders of a Party to which we do not belong and made responsible for a policy which we cannot control ... '[6] Early in January 1933, he wrote miserably to J. H. Thomas, 'I want very much to have a talk with you about the position in which we find ourselves. I am not at all happy about it, but a way out is hard to find.'[7] By the end of the month he was noting:

> Difficult to keep from depression ... Unemployment work terribly slow and yet cannot be rushed, & I cannot be personally in charge of everything at home & abroad. Treasury not helpful & Health worse. No vision of general situation & only concern to keep Govt. out of practically everything. Deserted by Labour & Liberal parties, National Govt. inevitably tends to fundamental Toryism.[8]

As before, however, he shrank from challenging his Conservative colleagues head-on. It is clear that he was still deeply unhappy about the administration of the means test, both because he realized that it was losing the Government votes and because he feared that it would damage the family life of those affected by it,[9] but he made only a few casual and spasmodic attempts to make the system more humane. He was equally unhappy about the change of machinery which Chamberlain forced through the Cabinet in 1933, and which was carried into law by the Unemployment Act of 1934. Chamberlain's scheme abolished the distinction between transitional benefit and the poor law and set up a new body called the Unemployment Assistance Board to administer relief to all the able-bodied unemployed who were not covered by unemployment insurance – thus superseding the local authorities in this field. It was bitterly opposed by Betterton, on the grounds that it 'applied Poor Law methods, through a Poor Law Commission, in Poor Law language' to what was, in reality, an industrial problem.[10] It is clear from his diary that MacDonald agreed with Betterton. Chamberlain's proposals, he noted after one of the many Cabinet meetings on the subject, were 'Full of pitfalls & the scheme produced savours too much of Poor Law. Will cause great revolt.'[11] His fears were well founded. In many areas, the Unemployment Assistance Board scales were even harsher than those enforced by the old public assistance committees and, when they were promulgated, the protests were so fierce that the Government had to issue a standstill order. But MacDonald was no more prepared to fight Chamberlain now than he had been to fight Snowden in the old days, and in spite of his misgivings he made no attempt to stop Chamberlain's scheme from going through.

He was equally hesitant over economic policy. As we have seen, he had been uneasy about the Treasury's attitude to Government spending and public works for some time, and the dramatic change in American policy, that followed Roosevelt's inauguration as President in March 1933, added to his uneasiness. MacDonald listened on the radio to Roosevelt's inaugural address and noted afterwards that it was 'manly & firm', though 'plainly the address of a fine man who had never been in office'.[12] A few weeks later he visited Washington to discuss Britain's war debt and the forthcoming world economic conference. During his visit, his enthusiasm for Roosevelt mounted, and before he left he was noting wistfully, 'Personally the Pres: gets more attractive. What a fine

colleague he would be ... He is overstrong in a type of free inexperience but
fresh & suggestive & free mind in which we are perhaps overweak.'[13] As he
watched the New Deal take shape on the other side of the Atlantic he became
even more irritated with the stale minds that reigned in Whitehall; and although
he insisted that he did not want to follow the American example, he tried to
use it as a goad to prod his colleagues into more adventurous paths. 'The circus
which the American President has attached to the work of reconstruction is
undoubtedly going to have a very awkward reaction on us here, and people
will demand demonstrations of our activity ... ,' he warned Betterton at the
beginning of August 1933. 'I certainly do not want to pursue a Washington
policy, but everyone concerned ought to be told plainly that that will have to
happen, and they will have to bear the consequences, unless their brains are
fruitful enough to enable us to reach the same end by a better way.'[14] If the
Government was to win the next election, he argued in a long memorandum
for Baldwin later that summer,

> Our domestic programme will require to be infused with a bold energy
> which will not only produce results — as we are doing — but which will
> appear to the public to be alive. The Roosevelt policy in the U.S., whatever
> may be said of it, has whetted the appetite of the world for spectacular
> effects, and whilst its advertisements are fresh, the masses will ask for show
> as well as deeds ... The programme, whatever it may be, must have an
> atmosphere and demeanour of vision and energy. The Government has
> done its work successfully as the cautious administrator and guardian. It
> must now be the leader of an advancing army with some definite objectives
> worth fighting for.[15]

Yet such interventions were conspicuous for their rarity. In many ways, the
Government's economic record was better than its critics realized. The unemployed were treated with a pettifogging inhumanity, the legacy of which has
embittered industrial relations to this day, and the old industrial areas in Scotland, South Wales and the north of England continued to stagnate. But, in the
country as a whole, recovery was by international standards comparatively
rapid. How far this was due to the Government and how far to economic forces
beyond its control is a matter for debate; what is clear is that it broke more
decisively with the orthodoxies of the past than any previous peacetime Government had done. The gold standard had gone, and the constraints it had imposed
had gone with it. The external value of sterling was manipulated through the
Exchange Equalization Account; at home, interest rates were deliberately
pushed down. As under the Labour Government, but if anything with more
enthusiasm, a wide variety of instruments was used to maintain markets and
prop up employment in declining industries. Even the dogma of the balanced
budget, which the Government had proclaimed with such fervour when it first
took office, was more honoured in the breach than in the observance. Its econ-

omic policies were drably presented and timorously pursued, but, with all their faults, they looked forward to the managed economy of the mid-twentieth century rather than back to the self-regulating order of the nineteenth. As we have seen, the same had been true of the Labour Government's policies; indeed, the continuity between the two Governments was much greater than most Labour people would have been willing to admit. But under the Labour Government, MacDonald had himself intervened incessantly over a whole range of economic questions. Now he watched from the sidelines. It is clear from his papers that he played an important, perhaps even a decisive, part in persuading the Treasury to provide a Government loan to finance the construction of the new Cunarder which eventually became the *Queen Mary*.[16] Otherwise, he contented himself with occasional calls for a bolder policy and made no sustained attempt to translate them into action.

One reason was his declining health – a factor which must be borne constantly in mind if we are to understand the politics of this period. Another was his continuing concentration on foreign affairs. He had made two long visits to Geneva and Lausanne in the spring and summer of 1932. December 1932 saw him in Geneva again, this time for ten days. He spent another ten days there in March 1933 and then went on to Rome. His visit to Washington followed in April, and took up another two-and-a-half weeks. In June and July, he spent several weeks presiding over the abortive world economic conference; though it met in London it left him little time to spare for other concerns. Throughout this period, he also chaired the disarmament committee of the Cabinet, which had originally been set up to work out the Government's policy at the disarmament conference, but which steadily extended its scope until it dealt with most of the central problems of foreign policy and eventually with rearmament policy as well; as the international climate deteriorated, this took up more and more of his time and more and more of his waning energies.

Yet his declining health and concentration on foreign policy provide only part of the explanation for his failure to press his views on other matters. Another reason is that, as time went on, the power relationships within the Cabinet changed to his disadvantage. Memories of the last election faded and attention began to be concentrated on the next. Conservative M.P.s in marginal seats forgot that they might not have reached the House of Commons at all but for MacDonald's success in appealing to non-Conservative voters in 1931; instead, they began to ask themselves, increasingly loudly and increasingly sceptically, what use he would be to them when they had to face the electorate again. In 1933 and 1934, there were big swings against the Government in by-elections, and although it would be wrong to suggest that MacDonald's colleagues blamed him for the defeats, there can be no doubt that his authority over them suffered as a result. Meanwhile, the Government's cautious but steady advance towards Indian self-government provoked a revolt among Conservative 'die-hards', led with remarkable panache and an even more remarkable lack of judgment by Winston Churchill. Though it was directed as much against Baldwin and Hoare as against MacDonald, who played only a minor part in Indian affairs once the round-table conference had dispersed, and though only a minority of Conservative backbenchers joined it, it made the Conservative party more restive and, in doing so, added to MacDonald's sense of insecurity. So did two humiliating defeats in Cabinet — one in 1933 and one in 1934 — both of them on issues which mattered a great deal to him, but which were of only marginal importance to the Government as a whole. In these circumstances, it is not surprising that he should have been unwilling to risk further humiliation by provoking battles which he had no need to fight.

MacDonald's authority dwindled slowly and irregularly; it did not suddenly vanish. On foreign affairs, he remained the single most influential member of the Cabinet, at least until the spring or early summer of 1934. As late as April, 1935, when the decline in his powers had gone much further, he led the British delegation to the ill-fated Stresa conference, apparently without provoking any misgivings among his colleagues. Anthony Eden, in this period the parliamentary under-secretary at the Foreign Office, wrote in his memoirs years later that when he listened to MacDonald talk on international topics in Cabinet, 'I was conscious at times of the touch of the master';[17] it is hard to believe that the Government's foreign policy would have followed the course it did unless other Conservative ministers had had the same experience. Even in other fields, the position was more complicated than it appeared at first sight. Like all modern prime ministers, MacDonald had the right to request the sovereign to dissolve Parliament and bring about a general election; as will appear later, he made it clear to Baldwin on at least one occasion that he would use it rather than allow a purely Conservative Government to take office.[18] Thus, the commonly held notion that the Conservatives could have got rid of him at any moment is wide of the mark; he went when he made up his mind to go. By the same token, it would be misleading to depict Baldwin, or, for that matter, any other subordinate minister, as the real head of the Government, with MacDonald as his mouthpiece. Baldwin deputized for MacDonald when MacDonald was away, but, as David Wrench has put it, 'Baldwin's role was to be the Government's chief public relations officer, his speciality, pouring oil on troubled waters'.[19] He did not aspire to be a substitute prime minister, and, in any case, he left policy initiatives to others. The most forceful member of the Cabinet on policy matters was not Baldwin but Chamberlain, who still reigned supreme over his own department, and whose probing finger could increasingly be detected in other pies as well. But although Chamberlain might have acted as a substitute prime minister if he had been in Baldwin's position, he could not do so from his own. He was an energetic and ambitious minister, whose influence on many issues extended beyond the boundaries of his own department, but it would be a mistake to see him as anything more than that.

Yet when all the qualifications have been made, the fact remains that Mac-

Donald's authority did dwindle: and that his reputation, and perhaps also his self-respect, dwindled with it. More than once, he told himself that he would have to resign unless things changed; when they failed to change there was always some new reason for staying on. Superficially, his relations with his colleagues followed the same pattern as before — mutual if slightly uncomprehending trust with Baldwin, distant respect for Chamberlain, growing irritation with Simon. As time went on, however, they increasingly came to see him as an incubus rather than as an asset, while he became increasingly prone to blame them, or at least their followers, for his growing unhappiness and sense of frustration. The Government worked well enough. On foreign policy, the disarmament committee provided a kind of collective leadership; even at home, an informal committee of six, consisting of MacDonald and Thomas from the National Labour group, Simon and Runciman from the National Liberals and Baldwin and Chamberlain from the Conservatives, gave it a certain measure of cohesion. Though it was far from being the best Government of modern British history, it was certainly not the worst. But it was not a happy ship. The captain was the unhappiest of all.

II

MacDonald's first big defeat after the free-traders' resignations came on the complex, tedious but revealing question of the taxation of co-operative societies, which came to the boil early in 1933 when the Raeburn committee, which had been set up to inquire into the problem in 1932, produced its report. Though the technicalities of the question are of little interest, the episode provides a vivid illustration of the way the Government worked, and it therefore deserves more than a passing mention. Hitherto co-operative societies had been exempt from income tax on their trading profits and also on their income from investments. The co-operatives argued that, since a man cannot make a profit out of himself, mutual trading was inherently incapable of giving rise to a taxable profit; hence, they concluded, it would be inequitable to tax them on the profits they made from trading with their own members. The Raeburn committee, however, came to the conclusion that co-operative societies were no longer mutual bodies in this sense, and that it would be unfair to other retail traders if their exemptions continued. Accordingly, it recommended that, in future, co-operative societies should be subject to income tax in respect of all trading profits, and that the 'divi' should be treated as a trade expense. The yield, it estimated, would be around £1,200,000 a year.[20]

To Chamberlain, with his tidy mind and dislike for fuzzy compromises, it seemed clear that the committee's recommendations should be carried out. The yield was irrelevant; so were the objections of the co-operative societies. What mattered was the principle. Besides, Conservative backbenchers had pressed him to tax the co-operative societies before the last budget, and it had been at Mac-

Donald's request that he had set up the committee instead. Having set it up, how could he ignore what it said? MacDonald saw things in a different light. In 1931, when the rest of the Labour movement had treated him as a traitor, he had had a certain amount of support from the co-operative societies; to throw that support away for the sake of £1,000,000 in revenue and some fiscal hairsplitting seemed to him absurd. Moreover, he had given a pledge during the election campaign that he would not remain a member of the Government if it taxed the co-operative societies. Though he insisted vehemently that the pledge had been confined to the 'divi' and had nothing to do with trading profits, he knew only too well that if the Raeburn committee's proposals were put into effect his enemies in the Labour movement would be given a new and highly effective stick with which to beat him. When the report came out at the end of January 1933, he noted morosely, 'Another drift away from moorings. I shall oppose in Cabinet. Bonds to Govt. straining.'[21] Two weeks later, Chamberlain made it clear to the Cabinet that he wanted to carry out the recommendations, and the Cabinet set up a committee, consisting of Chamberlain, Thomas and Hailsham, to consider the matter. 'Chancellor so short sighted that he is willing to sacrifice Coop: support for £1000000 which is by no means sure ...,' MacDonald noted. 'This will probably decide me in my mind not to stand again.'[22]

Private forebodings were accompanied by obvious public embarrassment. On March 6th, R. C. Morrison wrote to warn him that if the Government carried out the Raeburn committee's proposals every hoarding in the country would be covered with placards: 'The Premier's Pledge. Asked during his General Election campaign whether the "National" Government would tax Co-operative Societies, Mr Ramsay MacDonald replied: "No so long as I am a member of the National Government." '[23] On the 8th, MacDonald replied wildly – and with a notable lack of persuasiveness – that what was being said about his pledge was the 'sheerest humbug', that the sole concern of the co-operatives at the election had been to protect the 'divi' and that 'I pity the poor victims of a campaign which is more dishonourable and contemptible than the worst kind of partisan propaganda that has afflicted our national life.'[24] Contemptible or not, however, the campaign was highly effective. A special co-operative congress was held to denounce the Raeburn report. Co-operative societies all over the country wrote to MacDonald to protest against the proposals, their letters filling two thick files in his papers.[25] A. V. Alexander declared at a public meeting that Mrs Lightfoot, the Seaham voter whose question during the election had elicited MacDonald's 'pledge', had written, 'I can assure you that my question was not on dividend: it was on any taxation whatsoever. I had always intended to remind him of it when he came back to this constituency, but he has not come back up to the present.'[26]

Behind the scenes, MacDonald did his best to induce second thoughts in the Treasury. On this occasion, he pleaded in a letter to Chamberlain on March 27th, political considerations were more weighty than usual:

There is a propaganda fund of £18,000 in existence to deal with this matter alone, and there is to be a demonstration in London, representing the Movement from John o' Groats to Lands' End ... I am also informed that a number of Members who habitually support us will dis-associate themselves from the taxation proposals ... To the deputations which are to arrive in London to present petitions and to address meetings have been elected some of our most faithful supporters. For instance, that from Bassetlaw is to be headed by my son's Chairman ...

... Is it worth while? It would be very easy to say to the deputation when you see it — and I hope you can do it before the demonstration — that no decision has been come to. In any event I think we ought to have a full Cabinet discussion on the subject before final positions are taken up.[27]

His pleading had little effect. Chamberlain replied uncompromisingly that, having set up the committee of inquiry,

I should be put in an impossible position if I had to say after all [that] I had decided in view of the political consequences to abandon all idea of carrying the Committee's proposals into effect.

I fully recognise your personal difficulties over this matter ... Nevertheless, I submit the following considerations which I think also might be taken into account.

... What we have to consider when taking stock of political considerations is the effect on the general election. For this purpose we must consider how far it is possible for the leaders of this agitation to maintain over a series of years the indignation of the rank and file on a matter which is in fact not going to touch their pockets at all ...

... My own conclusion is that if we have sufficient firmness to stand up to the agitation for a month or two it will die down and little more will be heard of it.[28]

After two long Cabinet meetings on April 5th, however, Chamberlain agreed to examine the matter with his department to see, as the minutes put it, 'if he could find some basis for settlement'.[29] On the 7th, he reported that, following his examination, he had decided to discuss the report with the co-operatives to see whether a compromise was possible. If it was not, he would propose to carry out the committee's proposals after all.[30] 'Chancellor wishes he had not touched it,' MacDonald noted, with evident relief. 'He never hoped to get money out of it but thought he wd. get a settlement; raised a hornet's nest.'[31] His sense of relief did not last for long. On the 24th, when MacDonald was away in Washington, Chamberlain told the Cabinet that he did not think that there was the least prospect that the co-operative societies would make an offer worth considering. He asked for authority to tell them that he intended to carry through an enabling resolution, covering the whole of the Raeburn report, to become operative when it became part of the Finance Bill. On the assumption that no agreement had been reached in time for the Finance Bill, he would include provisions based on the Raeburn report in the Finance Bill itself. If no agreement had been reached by the committee stage of the Finance Bill, he would come back to the Cabinet for a fresh decision. Chamberlain was supported by Thomas and the Cabinet duly gave him the authority for which he had asked.[32] When MacDonald came back from Washington, the battle was virtually over. On May 5th, Chamberlain told the Cabinet that, as he had expected, it had proved impossible to reach agreement. Three possibilities remained – to do nothing, to devise a new tax to be imposed on co-operative societies instead of income tax or to implement the Raeburn report. Chamberlain made it clear that he was not prepared to devise a new tax or to do nothing; and, after pointing out that the decision would probably cost them their seats, Thomas and MacDonald both agreed that the Raeburn report would have to be carried out. The whole Cabinet, Baldwin declared piously, 'would respect and admire the attitude these members had taken up ... [H]e and his friends could promise their warm support to the Prime Minister up to the end of the present Parliament.'[33] Less piously, MacDonald noted later, 'The Coop: tax is daily seen to be a short-sighted and muddled affair ... I blame myself for not accepting the resignation of the Chancellor. His attitude has been disappointing: willing to sacrifice us all.'[34]

So, it seemed, were some of the chancellor's followers. No sooner had the battle over co-operative taxation ended than MacDonald was confronted with an even more embarrassing challenge on another issue. On May 24th, he reported to the Cabinet that he had just received a letter, with which over 250 M.P.s had associated themselves, asking for a free vote on an amendment to the Finance Bill in the name of Sir George Courthorpe, designed to repeal the land tax clauses of Snowden's last Finance Act.[35] The Courthorpe amendment was directed against a symbol, not against a reality. The land tax clauses had never been operated, and were not likely to be while the National Government was in office. But for MacDonald it was a symbol of great importance. The land tax clauses had been enacted by his Government; if they were repealed now, Labour charges of apostasy would be given a further boost and the extent of Conservative predominance in the National Government would be underlined yet again. If the amendment were carried, he warned, 'he and the Labour Party section of the Cabinet would be placed in an impossible position, particularly as the amendment followed so soon on the decision on the taxation on cooperatives.' This time, his plea was listened to. The Cabinet decided that Baldwin and Chamberlain should see the offending M.P.s and, as the minutes put it, 'bring home to them the importance of maintaining the National Government in office and consequently of avoiding raising questions ... calculated to exercise a disintegrating effect'.[36] After the meeting, Courthorpe and his associates unanimously decided to withdraw the amendment – though expressing the hope that MacDonald would see his way to repealing the clauses in a year's time.[37]

It was a partial victory for MacDonald, but only a partial one; and, as he was the first to realize, it had not solved the underlying problem. 'The Land Taxes affair I regard as very serious ... ,' he wrote in a gloomy and somewhat cryptic letter from Lossiemouth to Ralph Glyn. 'It raises issues of fundamental significance which I am to try and think over whilst up here.'[38] When Usher reported that the National Labour M.P.s who had been present at Baldwin's meeting with the Courthorpe group had all been pleased with the way Baldwin had handled the affair, he replied irritably that Thomas felt 'that we are drifting more and more into a condition of being dominated by one Party and that that will grow ... In that respect he finds me sympathetic, irrespective of what happened at the meeting.'[39] Presumably in an attempt to enlist the Palace on his side, he complained to Clive Wigram, the King's private secretary:

> I really long more and more for a rest as, with the best will in the world, this cannot go on very much longer ... The trouble is the condition of the Tory Party. Whilst it never ceases to assume that it is the Government, and compels me to be vigilant every day regarding the trend of policy, it nevertheless is honeycombed with caves against its Leaders and Front Bench, and these caves are well equipped with a press and with money. I quite agree that a termination of the National Government now could not only be a national, but an international, disaster, but an equally great disaster would be if the Government lost caste and failed to have moral influence and respect. The times, either from the point of view of political tactics or of Governmental problems, are far from happy. Do not bother the King with this, but I think it only my duty to warn you of the trend of affairs.[40]

Two more examples of the same trend followed later in the summer. Sir Arthur Steel-Maitland, the Conservative M.P. for Tamworth, put down a motion for the Conservative Party conference calling for a reform and strengthening of the House of Lords; though nothing came of it in fact, MacDonald's papers show that it caused him a good deal of anxiety.[41] The Clay Cross by-election that August made him more anxious still. The Labour candidate was Arthur Henderson; perhaps for that reason Conservative central office was particularly eager that MacDonald should send the Conservative candidate the message of support which he normally sent to Government candidates at by-elections. MacDonald seems to have had misgivings at first, but in the end he agreed to do so. When the Conservative candidate's election address arrived in London, however, it turned out to contain a number of attacks on 'the Socialists', and praised, in particular, the Government's achievement in 'bringing order out of the chaos' created by the previous Labour Government. The officials at central office agreed that in these circumstances MacDonald could no longer be expected to send a message.[42] MacDonald, however, decided to intervene after all – but in support of the Government rather than in support of its Conservative standard-bearer. He sent a carefully-worded message, which made no mention of either candidate, and called on the electors of Clay Cross, to 'stand by the National Government', 'maintain political co-operation ... *within a national combination*' and 'show restraint in party spirit'.[43] Afterwards, he noted:

> Thinking much of political situation. Conservatives almost bound to break away. Bye-election at Clay Cross shows tendency. Candidate at first fervently national; was to refer to nothing else in his address, certainly no attack on Labour Government such as lost Wakefield. I was to write a letter to him & Malcolm was to support at meetings. When his address arrived it was accompanied by first rate Tory balderdash on the work of the Labour Government. On enquiring at Tory headquarters & Whips in London was told they were astonished at change in what had happened as they had agreed with candidate & understood that I could not write & Malcolm could not speak. I wrote a National Government letter however & am sending it to the press lest the candidate does not use it. We must know where we stand.[44]

III

That was easier said than done. It is clear from MacDonald's papers that his memorandum for Baldwin, to which reference was made earlier in this chapter, must have been written at about the same time as his diary entry about the Clay Cross by-election. Since the memorandum and its fate throw a great deal of light, both on MacDonald's mood when he wrote it and on the way the Government worked in late 1933 and early 1934, the story must be told in some detail. The memordandum began[45] pointing out that the Government would soon have to prepare for the next election. If that election were fought by the existing 'national combination', MacDonald went on, the Government would be reasonably sure of staying in office. But if that was to happen, the Conservatives would have to show more self-discipline than they were showing currently:

> There would require to be recognition of differences within a unity of immediate policy and action. I see no reason why the necessary co-operation could not be arranged, though I recognise its weaknesses and drawbacks for every party concerned ...
> Supposing, however, as may well be the case, that the Conservative Party, especially its local organisations ... will only accept a minimum of further co-operation ... That would mean that the Party would, before the election virtually withdraw from the National Government, and that the Liberal and Labour supporters would either have to agree to absorption or

launch out independently ... This is a point which, in fairness to all concerned, ought to be settled without delay ... The platforms which local Conservative Associations are now giving to recalcitrant Conservatives to attack in particular the non-Conservative members of the Government is already becoming awkward, and in relation to the coming election, will have to be dealt with pretty soon ... The really important issue to which all this leads and which gathers up all the issues within itself is, who is to lead at the next election? Who is to form a Government if the election ends successfully?

Further Note.

(a) I have been approached by certain prominent and wealthy men ordinarily associated with the Conservative Party asking what my intentions are and offering help in promoting them, and several Trade Union officials and influential men connected with the Labour Party have come to me with similar requests ... There is therefore the nucleus of a new party or combination.

(b) Some of the bye-elections ... have been disquieting ... Wakefield and Clay Cross have been the best cases in point. According to my information the former seat was lost by being fought on ordinary Conservative lines. Hundreds of favourable Labour votes were alienated and a very effective National Labour support was thrown away gratuitously ... If this were to be common at a general election the national result will be doubtful. A purely Conservative appeal will not win.

The question is: Will Conservatives who are National candidates fight on a national programme and make a national, more than a party, appeal?

The argument was convoluted, but the message so far was clear enough. If the Conservatives continued to behave as they had done at Clay Cross, they would make it impossible for the National Government to continue. If the National Government broke down, MacDonald would not be as friendless as the Conservatives might think; if the election were fought on party lines, moreover, the Conservatives might well lose. Thus the Conservatives needed MacDonald as much as he needed them.

At the end of the memorandum, after a passage on the Government's programme which need not be quoted here, he returned to the charge with an even more convoluted argument:

I joined not a Coalition but a National Government to meet the emergency of the time, but the position has steadily changed ... the chief consequence of the change being to emphasise the importance of party both in the guidance of the Government and the fighting of elections ... But,

(a) The present Parliament has not a party mandate and considering the part I played in the election I feel a responsibility not to hand over the administration to a purely party guidance, indeed should a party vote end the life of this Government I should feel it my bounden duty to end the life of the Parliament and compel any new Government to seek a vote of confidence from the country before it begins to govern as a party administration ...

... I must apparently adapt myself to a situation which is transitional and drifting on to an election which, as events decide, is to be a party fight or a national policy appeal. To prepare for that election I am willing a little later on ... to give up the Premiership but to remain in the Government as a Minister without portfolio (and without salary) as it would never do for me to retire at once or long before the election, nor, on the other hand, to remain Prime Minister up to the election.

... There is an alternative possible if a national appeal were to be made without a Conservative split. I might fight Seaham again with the chance of being defeated. I should then give all assistance I could at the election and, if defeated myself, would retire. But I begin to doubt if this is possible. I believe that there is a growing feeling in the Conservative Party against a Government so dependent on Conservative backing having me at its head. This is quite natural and I have no grievance and no wonder ... Without not only the consent of immediate colleagues who know how we have worked together, but of the whole combination, I could not continue. Who thinks for a moment that that consent could be granted? I certainly do not expect it.

... The thought underlying this memorandum is that I should make preparations for a gradual withdrawal, which would not only be from the House of Commons but from Parliament altogether.

Here the message was not so clear. The threat to dissolve Parliament rather than allow a purely Conservative Government to take office was unambiguous, but the drift of the concluding paragraphs must have been a good deal harder to follow. Was MacDonald saying that he wanted to give up the prime minister-ship, or that he wanted to keep it? Was he hoping that the Conservatives would give him an honourable discharge from an office which was becoming intoler-able to him, or was he hoping to bring them to heel by the threat of resigna-tion? Was the final sentence, hinting that he might leave politics altogether, a frank expression of his state of mind, or was it a calculated manœuvre, designed to shame or frighten the Conservatives into giving him renewed pledges of loyalty? Or was it, perhaps, a mixture of both?

These questions cannot be answered with any certainty: indeed, MacDonald would probably have been hard put to it to answer them himself. It is clear that he felt his authority and credibility slipping away from him, that he was desper-ately anxious to halt the process and that the prospect of staying in office if things went on as before was deeply distasteful to him. It is unlikely, however, that he had any but the vaguest idea of the changes he wanted to see, and less likely still that he had made up his mind what to do if the Conservatives refused to make any. His memorandum was a cry for help, not a plan of campaign. As such, it was a failure. He gave it to Baldwin at the end of September. There was no response; and by the middle of October he was noting exasperatedly, 'Discussed with Mr Baldwin the future alignment of parties with reference to position at election. Was not forthcoming.'[46] Towards the end of November he tried again. On the 23rd, Rothermere's *Daily Mail* and its stablemate the *Evening News* both published bitter attacks on the non-Conservative members of the Cabinet, arguing that on the evidence of the by-elections, the Conservatives would do better to fight on their own. According to his diary, MacDonald

> At once ... spoke to Mr Baldwin and said that he must discuss the memorandum I sent him. I said the text of the articles was true but that the reason behind it was that the fights were being conducted as Tory Party fights, and that our supporters were alienated almost as soon as they began. This could not go on ... By the evening unfortunately I had a telegram from Rothermere regretting what his papers had published, & the opportunity I intended to take to straighten out the position & give notice that I would begin a process of withdrawing was lost.[47]

Once lost, it did not come again. At the end of April 1934, seven months after he had first given his memorandum to Baldwin, MacDonald sent a copy to Chamberlain with a plaintive covering letter explaining, 'I have repeatedly asked for an examination of it, but, as a matter of fact, have not even had an acknowledgement ... I need not say that I am getting more and more disturbed about the outlook, and that I feel today even more strongly than I felt in August that two or three of us must understand each other and come to an agreement about political alignment for the election as quickly as we can.'[48] Chamberlain was brisker than Baldwin, but no more forthcoming. He replied the same day that he would be 'ready for a talk whenever the time comes', but that 'it would not be possible until some of the present urgent matters give us a little more leisure.'[49] To judge by MacDonald's papers, that was that. There is no evidence that his memorandum was ever discussed; if it was, the discussion had no result.

Meanwhile, the frustrations which had led him to write it in the first place were becoming more acute. In December 1933, he had a distressing tussle with Baldwin over the honours list, noting on the 13th:

> This entry is specially private but in my own interest I must make the record. – Baldwin came into the Cabinet room in the morning, sat down & straight away asked what I had against Julian Cahn. I said he was one of those Honours hunters whom I detested, that his friends & agents had beset me for a long time for a baronetcy for him, that he was not a commendable person, that he had put money into 'Everyman' stating it was in my interests – in short just the man whom I should not dream of honouring. I had

let it be known that do what he might no recommendation for an honour to him would be put up by me. B. replied that I must yield & when I asked why he said that Maundy Gregory's papers & Maundy Gregory's presence here would stir up such a filthy sewer as would poison public life; that many innocent persons had become indirectly involved; that all parties were involved (I corrected him at once & said: 'No[t] ours.' He smiled & said that unfortunately friends of mine were. I replied that if they were I knew nothing about it. Then I remembered that Clynes & Henderson were mentioned at an earlier stage); that people like Winston Churchill, Austen Chamberlain, Birkenhead were involved; that Greogry had been used by Ll.G. & Bonar Law; that the subscription lists for the rebuilding of St. George's Chapel Windsor were involved; and several other things. Gregory, as indeed I know, was a blackguard who netted innocent people who did nothing that was irregular or bad, but whose associations with those who had enshrouded them in a cloud. The dunghill had to be cleared away without delay and £30,000 were required to do it. So I *had* to give the Honour. I pointed out that if I did so the many people who knew of Cahn's baits to me would say at once that he had made one tempting enough and I had taken it, & that in order to do what he wanted I should have to accept odium & be quite unable to explain it away. I asked him to consider the matter for a day & see me again.[50]

Next day, Baldwin relented; and it was agreed that the question of Cahn's honour should be postponed until the next list, in May. In spite of this reprieve, however, MacDonald's morale continued to sink and his indigation with the Conservatives continued to mount. 'Have been considering [whether] I should go on ... ,' he noted at the beginning of January 1934. '[T]he Tories ... imagine that they are the only people with national views—that the Tories are the nation.'[51] He was still 'considering' six weeks later. 'Were it possible, my best policy would be to withdraw from the Government,' he noted on February 18th, 'but ... my colleagues in the Cabinet will not hear of it.'[52] It was the same story in March. 'I have given some serious thought this week end to my own position ... ,' he noted on the 11th. 'I am not happy on [*sic*] prospects. Party points of view come in & cannot be kept out; most of the joint propaganda & elections like the L.C.C. have been pure Tory concerns.'[53]

In April and May he was given a more serious cause for complaint. On April 7th, Baldwin wrote to warn him that his agricultural members were still demanding the repeal of the land-tax clauses, and that although he had 'succeeded in holding my people' the year before, he would be unable to do so again.[54] MacDonald replied firmly next day that no one had received more consideration from the Government than had the agricultural interest, and that 'If the Snowden remnant is removed from the Statute Book ... what support we can give later on to a united appeal will be further weakened. In my opinion it will be a political blunder, and whilst I am certain to lose by it, I really think you are equally certain to gain nothing you have not got.'[55] Baldwin did not reply, and MacDonald may have assumed that his letter had done the trick. If so, he was soon disabused. As he put it in his diary on May 6th:

> To-morrow the Land Tax Clauses (Snowden's) are being considered. S.B. wrote to me about them; I replied at once pointing out our difficulties & not another word from B., but N.C. told me S.B. had shown him my letter. On Friday I was told by the Chief Whip that something would have to be done by Tuesday & that I have asked the six to confer. I am being pushed into a position where I shall lose my reputation with good reliable position because to keep the Government together I have to give free rein to Tory views.[56]

The sequel was even more distressing. On the 11th MacDonald noted:

> The Tories have at last forced our hands on the Land Taxes. I proposed to fight but much to my surprise J.H.T. opposed any resistance on the grounds that if the thing was to be done it had better be done now. I was left alone & had to content myself by putting in my protest. The position is serious not as regards merits but as regards the purpose & mind of the Government. It is the working of a coalition dominated by the strongest party dominated in turn by its sections & not of a national Government dominated by considerations of unity & continued preservation of its parts. I cannot & shall not vote for the Finance Bill as I cannot support the influences & the policy which have secured this change. If they once establish themselves it is the end of the National combination.[57]

Soon afterwards, he had to face the question of Cahn's honour again. This time, he seems to have given in without a fight. On May 19th, he noted bitterly, 'Mr B ... involves me in a scandal of honour by forcing me to give an honour because a man has paid £30,000 to get Tory headquarters & some Tories living and dead out of a mess.'[58] In June, Cahn became a baronet.

IV

As painful as – perhaps more painful than – the decline in MacDonald's authority as prime minister was the slow erosion of the assumptions underlying his foreign policy. As we have seen, he had stayed in office when the free-traders resigned in September 1932 partly because he foresaw 'dire consequences' from the crisis over Germany's withdrawal from the disarmament conference and believed that only a strong lead from Britain could avert them. For the next three months, most of his energies were thrown into a long-drawn-out struggle to bring the Germans back. In the teeth of fierce opposition from the service ministers, he and Simon persuaded the Cabinet to agree that, if Germany promised not to disturb the peace, her claim to equal status should be conceded; that the disarmament clauses of the peace treaty should be replaced by a convention applying to the victor powers as well; and that, in principle, no arms should be denied to Germany which were allowed to others.[59] The Germans accepted the British proposals as a basis for discussion, and at the beginning of December MacDonald went to Geneva for talks with the Germans, French, Italians and Americans. After ten days of semantic disputation, the Germans agreed to return to the conference on terms which the French were willing to accept — MacDonald noting triumphantly, 'So another successful International Conference ended. Luck is bound to desert me some day.'[60] But his triumph paid few dividends. By now, Germany's endemic political crisis had entered a new stage. At the beginning of December, von Papen was replaced as Chancellor by von Schleicher. Two months later, at the end of January 1933, von Schleicher was replaced by Hitler.

This is not the place for a detailed discussion of Britain's response to the Nazi revolution, but a few broad generalizations must be attempted if MacDonald's response is to be seen in the proper perspective. The first is that it is a fallacy to imagine that the British were, in any important sense, deceived about Hitler's motives and intentions, or that they were unable to recognize the true nature of the threat he posed. The second is that it was precisely because they did recognize the true nature of the threat that they could not make up their minds how to meet it. No one who read the dispatches from Sir Horace Rumbold, the British ambassador in Berlin when Hitler came to power, or from his successor, Sir Eric Phipps, could doubt the barbarity and aggressiveness of the Nazi regime; in any case, there was no need to read secret dispatches, since the facts were clearly set out in the newspapers. But it was one thing to know what was going on in Germany: another to decide what to do about it. In retrospect, it is clear that there was no point in negotiating with Hitler. His demands were limitless, and as soon as one demand was satisfied another took its place; in striking contrast to the Soviet leaders, then and later, he was quite prepared to make agreements which he had no intention of keeping. Even at the time, the ministers and officials who dealt with him were at least half-aware that the normal rules of diplomacy did not apply to him. But most of them found the implications of that discovery too horrible to contemplate. For if diplomacy was impossible, only two courses remained. One was to give in to Hitler; the other was to fight him. And for civilized men, who had been brought up on the liberal values which Hitler was trampling underfoot and who had come to believe that foreign, as well as home, policy should be conducted in accordance with those values, surrender and preventive war were equally unthinkable.

In one form or another this dilemma confronted all the civil servants and politicians who tried to influence British foreign policy in these years. It was least acute for old-fashioned Conservatives, who had never really accepted the ethos of liberal internationalism which had inspired the post-war revulsion against power politics. Hailsham and Londonderry, for example, saw Hitler as a new and more disagreeable version of the Kaiser: as a threat to British interests, which Britain should meet by turning her back on the sentimentalists at Geneva and building up her defences. For those who accepted the liberal ethos, however, and even for the much larger number who had been influenced by it without fully accepting it – and there were plenty of these in the Government as well as in the opposition parties – the dilemma was much more painful. They detested Nazism, but they could not suppress an uneasy awareness that the Nazis might never have come to power if Germany had been treated less harshly in 1919. Though they did not trust Hitler or want to make concessions to him, they had no firm ground on which to resist him. When he denounced the inequities of the peace treaty and insisted that Germany should be given parity with the wartime allies, they had no satisfactory reply. By the same token, they were not prepared to allow the disarmament conference to collapse or to rely on force as the guarantee of their security. Reliance on force, they believed, bred war: to abandon disarmament was to admit that war had become inevitable. Though some of them gradually became convinced that it was necessary to rearm, they could not bring themselves to make such an admission. Yet, to avoid making it, they had to negotiate with Hitler – and, in negotiating with him, to pretend that he could be trusted after all.

The dilemma was specially painful for MacDonald, and his response to it was specially complex. Like his colleagues, he was appalled by the brutality and fanaticism of the Nazis and saw the Nazi revolution as a threat, both to Britain and to Europe; unlike some of them, he also saw the threat in ideological terms and recognized from an early stage that Hitler's Germany was not a new version of the Kaiser's Germany, but a phenomenon of a quite different and much uglier kind, to which past experience afforded no parallel. 'I shall not see peace again in my lifetime,' he told his son Malcolm when he heard that Hitler had taken office. 'I hope you will see it in yours.'[61] When the news of the Reichstag fire reached London he noted, with a somewhat heavy-handed irony, that it would lead to 'The development of brutal dictatorship in Germany ... Thus nation after nation contributes its mite to the peace & confidence of the world.'[62] By the beginning of March 1933, only a little more than a month after Hitler had become chancellor, he was beginning to fear 'the dissolution of Europe through a Germany ruled by tyranny'.[63] When Germany withdrew from the disarmament conference and the League of Nations six months later, he noted that any hope of a return to the old pattern of international relations was a 'thin shadow. Fascism in national affairs must ... give rise to a new international technique.'[64] In the past, he added later in the same diary entry, international relations had been controlled by reason, at any rate in peacetime. Now, 'will is to control the peace & the techniques of diplomacy have to be changed.' A few weeks later, he had a long talk with the British military attaché in Berlin, who was 'Much

taken with Hitlerism'. 'I begin to be repulsed by the very grounds on which
Hitler is praised – ,' MacDonald noted revealingly, 'the organiser of the Servile
State, slavery being willingly accepted because the herd mind as a discipline has
taken the place of individual characteristics.'[65] The Polish–German pact of
January 1934, which Germany presented as a proof of her pacific intentions,
brought him no reassurance. Hitler's strategy, he noted, was one of 'temporary
peace arrangements [combined] with effective nationalist aggressive propaganda. In ten years Germany will be the only European country that will respond with alacrity to a call to arms.'[66] He was even more alarmed by the
Dolfuss *putsch* in Austria in February 1934. 'News from Vienna fills me with
foreboding,' he noted when the news arrived. 'Some of the best of men, the
leaders of Austrian Socialism, are being shot down because they will not accept
the Dolfuss tyranny. The Fascist tyranny sweeps over Europe ... Once again
Force stands out amidst the ruins an ugly brute beast.'[67]

But although he could see that Hitler presented a new kind of threat and that
a new kind of diplomacy was needed to counter it, he was no more able than
were his colleagues to work out what that new kind of diplomacy should be.
Understandably enough, he became more and more exasperated with the endless calls for disarmament with which the Government was assailed during 1933,
and which seemed to win increasing support from the well-intentioned and
high-minded as the prospects for disarmament grew worse. 'The pure sentimentalists are upon police bombing with all their lack of thought & objectivity
& blackguard me,' he noted irritably at the beginning of June. 'The right wing
militarist & left wing pacifist are equally determined to make a good bloody
war inevitable and soon.'[68] By the autumn, irritation had turned to alarm.
'German propaganda wilyness & slimness makes [*sic*] me increasingly suspicious
of what Germans really mean to do,' he noted on October 20th, '& there is so
much of the flabby piety of pacifism which has nothing to do with conviction
here that war would be easy for Germany & militarism would be again on the
ascendant in Europe.'[69] By early 1934, he had become even more alarmed. In
February, his old I.L.P. friend, Helen Roberton, wrote to urge him to make a
public speech in favour of disarmament. He replied with a kind of weary
sadness:

My time & thoughts especially during the last month or two have been
absorbed in work ... For the time being my concern is with foreign Governments. It takes two to make a quarrel but ten to make peace. I am trying to
deal with the ten & it looks as though I shall be beaten. My heart gets more
sore against those who refused to face facts which they admitted & deserted
the battle which had to be fought if we were to keep the field & control
events. I cannot conceal from *you* my deep concern that things have become
so baffling. As regard the elements which we have to control abroad our
worst enemies are in our own household. Your Quaker frends [*sic*] thoughts

are Godly but our experience of the last two years show them to make war inevitable. It is not God but the Devil who is in charge of the international situation & those who are working for God in it are poor servants if all they do is to worship God & neglect their duty to circumvent the Devil. On the day of Judgement those whose worship has never stained their white trousers will be condemned to eternal fires whilst those who have thought more of their duty than of their trousers *may* have a chance of Heaven because in their lifetime they have searched for the will of God in Hell itself. This is a poor letter in haste but such is my mood entering what may well be a Waterloo.[70]

Yet, as that letter itself implies, his quarrel with the godly in white trousers did not extend to their values, or even to all of their assumptions. For him, as for them, force was an 'ugly brute beast', no matter who used it, and even when he had become convinced intellectually that force might have to be answered by force, his emotions rebelled against the idea. In a draft letter to Londonderry in October 1934 — more than eighteen months after Hitler had come to power — he complained bitterly that an article in *The Times* on the latest type of bomber had applauded the Government for 'building the very least acceptable means of brutal offence and calling it defence';[71] and although his ostensible reason for writing was that such articles would create a 'very serious revulsion of feeling' among the general public, there can be no doubt that he shared in that revulsion himself. Partly because of this, moreover, he still clung to the old U.D.C. doctrine that to rely on force was to ensure that, in the end, force would be used. Though he expected little from the disarmament conference — noting as early as March 1933 that, with Hitler in power in Germany, it could be nothing more than a 'debating society ... knocking its head, without admitting it, constantly against reality'—[72] he spent enormous amounts of time and energy trying to keep it alive, sometimes in the face of strong opposition from his colleagues; and even when it had become clear that his efforts had failed, he continued to behave as though the corpse could somehow be resuscitated. Even when it was clear that there was no longer any hope for disarmament, the prospect of a large-scale rearmament programme filled him with alarm. So did the prospect of new or more precise military commitments — partly because of his old suspicion of the French, who were the chief advocates of an extension in Britain's commitments, but even more because of his deep-seated belief that true security and military alliances were inherently incompatible. Thus, he found himself in an intellectual and emotional *impasse* — an exhausted old man, searching despairingly for a way to meet the Nazi threat without doing violence to the assumptions of a lifetime, and subject to savage criticisms from his old followers for betraying the values which he was trying vainly to uphold in the face of political disappointment and physical decline.

V

He began the search at the beginning of March 1933, only a little more than a month after Hitler's arrival in office. In December 1932, the Germans had agreed to return to the disarmament conference, and in January 1933, they had carried out their promise. During the next two months, however, no progress was made; and, by late February, the British delegates at Geneva had become convinced that a dramatic new initiative was needed to save the conference from collapse. On March 2nd, Eden, who had been handling the day-to-day negotiations when Simon was away, arrived in London with the message that the conference was doomed unless Britain produced a comprehensive draft convention, complete with figures, in the next few days. He lunched with MacDonald and Simon at the Athenaeum, and in the evening reported to a special meeting of the Cabinet disarmament committee under MacDonald's chairmanship.[73] According to the minutes, Eden warned that the conference was tottering towards failure, and that if it failed Germany would take the opportunity to rearm. If the conference was to be saved, someone would have to put forward definite proposals; the only country in a position to do this was Britain. A sharp tussle then took place between MacDonald and Hailsham — MacDonald suggesting that it was necessary to persuade 'the big nations at Geneva to rally round in a final effort to save the Conference', and that a plan might be needed in order to do this, while Hailsham objected that the plan prepared by Eden was a 'very formidable document' which the War Office would need three days to evaluate, and that it would be 'very dangerous' to produce it in case it was not accepted.[74] Afterwards MacDonald noted apprehensively:

> Terrible day of anxiety ... Simon for day or two with no implication of great urgency has indicated that things were sticking at Geneva and with other pressing things in hand ... the Disarmt. Conference had been ranged amongst the ordinary troubles. Now, it was presented as being on its death bed ... With this, the reports of the American financial situation were coming in & distracting my mind. They were so like the events of August 1931 while the reports of German policy at Geneva and of the intentions of the German Govt. sent secretly from Berlin were so like important events & movements in the summer of 1914 [75]

Next day, he persuaded the disarmament committee to agree that he and Simon should go out to Geneva in the next few days.[76] On March 5th, after he had declared that 'He would like to have a plan in his pocket to produce if conditions seemed favourable ... but he felt that any idea of attempting to produce a plan before he arrived would be doomed to failure,' he also persuaded it that he should have a free hand when he got there.[77] But, although he had managed

73 Lansbury and Attlee on their way to Henderson's funeral, October, 1935

74 'Shinwell elected' — Seaham Harbour, 1935

75 Leaving for the Council of State at Windsor during King George V's last illness

76 With Ishbel at King George V's funeral

7 Leaving the privy council office to attend Edward VIII's accession council, 1936

78 MacDonald's last public engagement. With the Duke of Gloucester after planting a tree at Woodford Bridge, October, 1937

to circumvent the War Office, he was soon to face more formidable adversaries. On March 9th, he arrived in Paris for preliminary talks with the French, to find what he described in his notebook as an 'atmosphere tense with diplomacy'.[78] The press appeared to have been briefed to expect some great new agreement between the two countries, and the British ambassador, whom he saw soon after his arrival, warned that France was disturbed both by Hitler and by Mussolini. To MacDonald, it looked as though the French were hoping that Britain would save them from the results of their own folly. 'I reflect upon the responsibility of France for all this,' he noted suspiciously after the British ambassador had told him about the French Government's fears. 'Its mishandling of its relations with Germany & of its own satellite states could not have been worse, and its treatment of Italy has been shortsighted ... We must not trust France unduly.'[79] When he saw Daladier and Paul-Boncour, the French prime minister and foreign minister, next day, his suspicions were confirmed. They recited a long list of German treaty violations, and asked for a 'manifestation of Franco-British solidarity' to stop Hitler's 'race to ruin'. MacDonald replied evasively that 'they must avoid arousing too great expectations of the results of their visit'; and when the French tried to insert a phrase into the final communiqué, to the effect that the two Governments had agreed to prevent rearmament as well as to promote disarmament, he and Simon refused, on the grounds that such a phrase 'might be misinterpreted as implying some sort of military agreement with France'.[80] 'We stood firm ... & are free,' MacDonald noted after the talks were over. 'The situation is, however, developing very badly.'[81]

The situation at Geneva was no more encouraging than it had been at Paris. On March 13th, after two days of depressing conversations, MacDonald reported to the King that the conference was on the verge of breaking down, and that

> I am convinced that a simple adjournment will be the end, and will be followed by a rearmament of Germany. At the same time the Conference cannot go on talking in public, every speech increasing the difficulty of an accommodation. The British Delegation is therefore considering whether it should not make a general declaration, including what agreement has been come to in the meantime, and proposals regarding armaments, which will be of the nature of compromises that if every country would accept would weaken the relative position of none, and then the Conference could adjourn leaving some representatives to study the plan and report some time after Easter. If in the meantime, the condition of Europe gets worse, everyone will be agreed that no good can be done by going on talking. If, however, it gets better ... an agreement could be patched up for the next five or six years. Meanwhile the Foreign Office could be busy and could agree among themselves how best to face the immediate dangers, the great

EI

objective being to secure that Germany will not tear up the Arms Clauses of the Treaty of Versailles of her own free will.[82]

He unveiled the British plan at a session of the general commission of the conference three days later. For those with long memories, it must have been a painful occasion. MacDonald, who had dominated so many international conferences in more hopeful times, was plainly in decline — a tired and failing old man, straining for rhetorical effects which he could no longer achieve, and in places unable to hold the thread of what he was trying to say.[*] His cause was in decline as well. As he had made clear in his letter to the King, the British plan was a stop-gap, designed, not to achieve disarmament, but to prop up a conference which everyone knew to be disintegrating. As such, it did not even have the united support of MacDonald's own colleagues. At a Cabinet meeting in London the day before MacDonald spoke, a number of ministers had objected to the whole idea of putting forward a draft convention, on the grounds that it would give Germany a pretext for leaving the conference and for putting the blame on Britain. At two successive Cabinet meetings, Hailsham had successfully opposed telegraphed suggestions from MacDonald and Simon, asking for authority to strengthen the proposed controls on tanks; and although the draft as finally presented did not go as far on tanks as MacDonald and Simon had wanted, there can be little doubt that it went too far for Hailsham.[83] Yet, in spite of all this, it looked for a while as though MacDonald had done the trick. When he had finished his speech, Daladier gave the British plan a warm welcome, as did the representatives of Germany, Italy and the United States. 'Days of work & nights of worrying surveys of the day,' MacDonald noted afterwards, 'but it is now over & I have done what I could. I dreaded the speech & as is now usual my head & eyes were pained ... In the end, Daladier, Gibson, German & Italian praised & feeling as Christian without his load I walked back to the hotel.'[84]

   He did not remain free of his load for long. Before he had had time to recover from the strain of Geneva, he hurried on to Rome, where he had been invited by Mussolini. The Italians had prepared the draft of a four-power pact, to be signed by themselves, the British, the Germans and the French, promising Germany equality of rights even if the disarmament conference failed. At first, MacDonald was moderately enthusiastic — noting that although the Italian plan would need 'careful preparation' it was 'Good in idea'[85] — and from Rome he went to Paris to sound out the French. His journeys were in vain. The French made it clear that they would not accept the Italian plan in anything like its original form; and before long MacDonald had come to the conclusion that the French were right. A four-power pact of sorts was eventually signed at the beginning of June, but it was a purely consultative arrangement which said nothing about treaty revision or equality of rights, and which bore little re-

---

[*] It was during this speech that he momentarily lost consciousness, and suddenly began to exhort his audience to be 'men and not mannequins'. See above p. 697.

semblance to the proposal which Mussolini had made in March. Meanwhile the effect of MacDonald's appearance at Geneva had worn off, and the disarmament conference was once again on the verge of collapse. At the end of June, it adjourned for three months, and in mid-October, Germany announced that the refusal of the heavily armed powers to grant her equality of rights had compelled her to leave the conference forthwith, while a simultaneous announcement in Berlin gave notice of her withdrawal from the League of Nations as well. Hitler then held a referendum in which his foreign policy was approved by 95 per cent of the German electorate; and in November he made it clear that Germany would return to the disarmament conference only if she were allowed a conscript army of 300,000 men and given a number of other concessions in addition. As MacDonald had told the King in his letter from Geneva in March, the real object of the British disarmament plan had been to buy time so as to find some way of preventing Germany from 'tear[ing] up the Arms Clauses of the Treaty of Versailles of her own free will'. Now the time had run out; and it was clear that a new policy was needed.

For MacDonald, it was a bitter blow; and it is hard to resist the conclusion that the rapid deterioration of his health during the next six months must have been due, in part, to the emotional conflicts which the search for a new policy brought with it. After a period of confusion and disarray, the ministers concerned reached a rough consensus on two central propositions. It was agreed that German rearmament could not be prevented by force; that at least some German rearmament was therefore inevitable; that it could be limited only with Hitler's agreement; and that since limited German rearmament was preferable to unlimited German rearmament, it was better to try to save the disarmament conference and reach an agreement with Hitler than to consign it to oblivion and leave Hitler to his own devices. It was also agreed, however, that Britain's defences had been run down too far, and that at least a measure of British rearmament was needed to build them up. To this end, a mixed committee of officials and servicemen was established, generally known as the D.R.C. (short for Defence Requirements sub-committee of the Committee of Imperial Defence) to prepare the broad outlines of a comprehensive rearmament programme to fit Britain's capabilities to her commitments. Its chairman was Hankey, and its other members, Fisher from the Treasury, Vansittart from the Foreign Office and the three chiefs of staff.[86] Within this consensus, however, there were sharp differences of emphasis. The service ministers wanted to give top priority to British rearmament; they were sceptical of the possibility of an agreement with Hitler, loath to accept new commitments and even more loath to accept restrictions on Britain's right to repair the deficiencies which the D.R.C. was busily uncovering. Simon – an old liberal in foreign and defence questions, who had resigned from Asquith's Government in 1916 in protest against its decision to introduce conscription – was appalled at the prospect of an arms race between Britain and Germany and wanted to make another effort to save the disarmament conference and reach agreement with Hitler; he recognized, however, that the disarmament conference could not be saved without France and, although he dithered hopelessly in Cabinet and gave his colleagues no clear lead, he was privately convinced that France should be given a new security guarantee. MacDonald was as unwilling as Simon was to embark on an arms race with Germany, but he was equally unwilling to draw closer to France; through nine months of declining health and crumbling authority, he kept hoping against hope that it might be possible to find a third course.

At first, he seems to have thought that it lay in direct contact between himself and Hitler. The day after Germany withdrew from the disarmament conference he noted indignantly that Hitler 'talks smooth words of peace but his actions & mentality make for war & these alone count in the developt. of policy'.[87] A few sentences later, however, he added more philosophically that Hitler was 'an interesting problem which we must understand in all its bearings & meanings if we are to steer wisely through this mess'. During the next few weeks, that thought became a minor obsession. At the beginning of November, the disarmament committee decided – almost certainly on MacDonald's initiative – that Simon should make 'extremely tentative soundings' as to the possibility of a meeting of heads of Government in London.[88] At the Lord Mayor's banquet two days later, MacDonald had a private talk with the German ambassador, Hoesch. According to Hoesch, MacDonald said that he wanted to re-establish international contact and that 'the thought had come to him that a visit from the Reich Chancellor to London might perhaps be a good way ... he was sure that the Reich Chancellor would receive a most friendly reception in England.'[89] Soon afterwards, MacDonald noted that he and Baldwin had arranged 'to meet someone who would bring us privately in touch with Nazi ministers & leading men of influence in Berlin';[90] and at the end of the month, he, Baldwin and Simon had a private meeting with Ribbentrop who was then in London as an unofficial emissary from Hitler.

The meeting was not a success. Ribbentrop, MacDonald noted afterwards, was

A pleasantly spoken man with those clear grey eyes which may be innocent, or hard, or lit with hate, but a mild voice which wins but never disarms suspicion ... Can see no guile in Hitler, no sense of the rights, feelings, nor position of other nations, does not understand why we should not behave as Hitler asks, go to Berlin to meet his convenience & so on. To try him, I said casually: 'A German Minister might come here to consult us?' He at once became slow & hesitant. German opinion would not allow of it! That was a good corner of the curtain lifted. However matters may develop, we must be careful with this new Germany whose mind as yet is of a spoiled child who insists upon having its own way.[91]

How far MacDonald was influenced by Ribbentrop's rebuff is impossible to tell, but, to judge by his papers at least, he made no more attempts to establish direct contact with Berlin. By now, moreover, Hitler's terms for returning to the disarmament conference had become known; and a few days after MacDonald's meeting with Ribbentrop, the disarmament committee discussed a paper by Hankey analysing their implications. If Hitler got what he wanted, Hankey concluded, he would have 'a formidable navy, army and air force, amounting to a substantial instalment of the rearmament of Germany'. Germany would still be unable to fight a war on two fronts, but she would be strong enough to rectify her eastern frontiers at the expense of Poland and Czechoslovakia.[92] Long negotiations followed and many diplomatic notes were exchanged – between Britain and Germany, Germany and France, France and Britain – but the longer the process went on, the more obvious it became that the French could not possibly agree to any proposals which would satisfy Hitler and that Hitler was in any case determined to rearm on a scale which menaced Britain as well as France.

Little by little, MacDonald was forced to question the assumptions which had governed his foreign policy for thirty years. Early in 1934, in an anguished memorandum presumably written for his senior colleagues, he acknowledged that Britain had

> gone further in disarmament than any other country in the world. The United States have made great professions but if you look at what they have done and especially at what they are now doing, they have acted in very contrary ways from their declarations. Japan is putting itself in the position to fight a war in the Far East ... Russia is undoubtedly the most heavily armed nation in Europe ... We have diminished our Fleet very substantially, both in men and material, and our Air Force is the fifth in Europe ... No-one thinks of following our example. Disarmament by example has completely broken down and we alone are not in a position to lift effectively a little finger to protect ourselves in the event of trouble ...
>
> For the moment we are continuing the policy which has been mine from the beginning. But I am only too well aware that at any moment it may be changed, not because this or any other Government wants it, but because it is forced upon us by the refusal of other nations to keep down their arms ... The outlook is most depressing. Mankind seems to be bent upon its own ruin.[93]

Yet, as the final sentence of his memorandum shows, he could only bring himself to question his assumptions, not to abandon them altogether. He had conceded that rearmament might become necessary before long: he had not conceded that it was necessary already. When the air estimates were published towards the end of February 1934, he noted morosely, 'Londonderry's White Paper had to be amended by me as it envisaged a competition in air armaments. This tendency grows.'[94] After the debate on the naval estimates a fortnight later he noted, as morosely, 'Yesterday on the Navy vote the militarists poked out their heads. We are already back to 1912.'[95] More remarkably, he made the same point in a letter to Sir Norman Angell on the same day. 'I am not comfortable about the way things are going as regards Peace,' he wrote. 'We had a debate in the House of Commons yesterday on naval affairs, which recalled the sort of thing said in 1911–1912 ... and I should like to have your views about the outlook.'[96]

Meanwhile, the D.R.C. had completed the report on which it had been working since November 1933. It advocated expenditures which in those days seemed enormous. A five-year programme was needed for all three services, it argued, to meet both an immediate threat from Japan and a longer-term threat from Germany — described by the authors as 'the ultimate potential enemy'. The R.A.F., it urged, should be given an extra 441 aircraft in 40 squadrons. The army needed an expeditionary force of one cavalry and four infantry divisions, capable of taking the field within a month; the total cost was estimated at £40 million. The naval building programme should be increased by around £3 million a year, and should provide for the construction of one capital ship a year from 1937 onwards. The total cost of the whole programme would be £71 million, leaving another £11 million worth of deficiencies to be put right after the five-year period was over.[97] A fortnight after the report was circulated, the French rejected a British disarmament plan, designed to find a compromise between the French and German positions which had been put forward at the end of January. Ten days after that the Germans published their military budget for the coming year, making it clear that they planned to double their expenditure on the army and to treble it on the air force.

The four months between the beginning of March, when the D.R.C. report was circulated, and the beginning of July, when he left for Canada, must have been among the most painful of MacDonald's life. He was becoming increasingly conscious of his loss of physical and mental vitality; he was humiliated over the land tax and the honour given to Julian Cahn; however reluctantly, he was forced to admit that disarmament was dead and that the only question worth asking about British rearmament was how extensive it was to be. In a paper for the disarmament committee at the beginning of April, he made a last, forlorn attempt to persuade his colleagues that, even if disarmament was no longer feasible, it was still possible to avoid both a military alliance and an arms race by linking security to a form of arms control. Britain, he wrote,

agrees in principle with the contention that disarmament without security will not establish peace.

It considers that security in the end rests upon (a) confidence and good will amongst nations and/or (b) mutual defence ... against a state which threatens war.

Our general foreign policy is aimed at securing (a), but (b) presents serious difficulties.

To guarantee France is impossible. It would involve us in serious risks; owing to the unstable positions of French Governments and policy it is impossible to foresee what, as a matter of fact, we are guaranteeing; the opinion of the country would revolt against such a guarantee ...

... The Government cannot give undertakings solely on the assumption that they may prevent breaches or aggressions. That is like guaranteeing an overdraft at a bank which a wise man never does unless he is prepared to pay up ...

It would be easier to guarantee an international agreement essential to world peace and act upon a breach of that agreement, than to guarantee a country in whose hands would remain the right to declare that its security was violated.

How can a body be selected with the power to declare a threat of [sic] world peace? How can the threat be defined? There would require to be (a) an international agreement upon arms permitted and (b) a Body of Control ...

The specific operating act would be the armament of any state beyond the sanctioned limit to such an extent as to make it clear that it was threatening the peace of the world.

Such a decision would involve two processes: (1) a report from the Committe of Control to the Council of the League which would come to a decision on the report; (2) a meeting of the guaranteeing group to consider the decision of the Council.[98]

Nothing came of it. The committee went through the negative paragraphs at the beginning of MacDonald's paper and approved them with only a few modifications, but before it reached the positive paragraphs at the end it was diverted on to a new tack by a long struggle between Chamberlain and the chiefs of staff over a proposal of Chamberlain's for an international force based on the principle of 'limited liability'. On May 8th, it approved a report for the Cabinet, in which it declared, with the even-handed impartiality characteristic of a committee which cannot make up its mind, that the difficulties in Chamberlain's scheme were 'very great', that on the other hand they might not be insuperable and that, for the moment, Britain should put forward no proposals on security at all. MacDonald's proposal was not even mentioned.[99]

By now, he had almost ceased to take part in the argument. In April, 1934, Churchill had carried his campaign against the Government's Indian policy to a new height of absurdity by alleging that Hoare had tried to rig the evidence to the select committee which had been set up to examine the question, and that, in doing so, he had committed a breach of privilege. The committee of privileges had had to consider Churchill's allegation; and for some weeks MacDonald was absent from the disarmament committee on the plea that the committee of privileges left him to time no spare. It was a thin excuse, in view of the relative importance of the two committees; and one cannot help suspecting that his real reason for not attending the disarmament committee was that he was now so out of sympathy with it that he could no longer bear to do so. When he returned to it in June, the Foreign Office put in a proposal for a British guarantee to Belgium. MacDonald fought it hard in committee, and noted afterwards that he was 'Not happy about it. Several colleagues talked in such a way as though they had learned nothing from the processes by which the late war came.'[100] In spite of his opposition, however, the Cabinet agreed on June 27th, that the defence of Belgium was a vital British interest and that that fact should be placed on record at an early opportunity.[101]

Meanwhile, the disarmament committee had begun to go through the D.R.C. report; and on June 20th, Chamberlain put in a powerfully argued paper to it, advocating a cheaper programme involving a drastic cut in Britain's commitments in the far east. The disarmament committee had its first discussion on Chamberlain's paper two days before the Cabinet took its decision on the guarantee to Belgium. MacDonald opposed Chamberlain's strategic priorities, but supported him strongly on the need to cut the programme advocated by the D.R.C. According to the minutes,

> He was in entire agreement with the Chancellor of the Exchequer from the financial point of view ... The whole question had to be considered in the light of the national income and the commitments which would have to be faced ... The Service Departments must understand that it was not possible to contemplate the bill in full which the General Staff put forward. It was the duty of the General Staff to inform the Cabinet as to the maximum risk and it was the Cabinet's duty to reduce the expenditure involved in accordance with the political situation; and it was the duty of the Chancellor and the Treasury to incur no expenditure which could not reasonably or even possibly be met.[102]

In his diary he was more outspoken. 'All these military moves,' he noted, 'make me think that I was in one government which was so sympathetic with the unemployed & then in another which was so anxious about defence that both came to the same bankrupt end.'[103]

For nearly eighteen months, most of his energies had been devoted to a doomed struggle to uphold the values of liberal internationalism in an increasingly hostile world. Now he had come to the end of the road, physically as well as politically. His consultation with Horder and Duke-Elder, at which they had told him that his eyes needed three months rest from close work, had taken place a week before his intervention at the disarmament committee. Two days later, he left London for Lossiemouth. Twelve days after that he sailed for Canada.

CHAPTER 30

Return to Spynie

I

MacDonald and Sheila arrived in Canada on July 19th, and spent the next two-and-a-half months travelling in a leisurely fashion in Quebec, Nova Scotia, Newfoundland and Labrador. It was a peaceful holiday, and it is clear from his notebook that MacDonald enjoyed it a great deal. At Petersfield, he was presented with a spray of heather from a bush which had been planted by the first settlers from the Highlands; the town council, he noted approvingly, 'consists of so many Macs ... that it was like reviewing the clans before the battle of Culloden'.[1] Soon afterwards, he was revelling in the 'sunlit water and entrances of silver' at Conception Bay in Newfoundland; not long after that he noted enthusiastically that he had caught two cod off the coast of Labrador and had visited an Eskimo village.[2] But the peace was not as complete as it should have been. Though he read no official papers, he could not stop himself from brooding on the political situation which he had left behind; perhaps because of this, the holiday did not do him as much good as his doctors had hoped.

'Still pursuing thoughts of future ... ,' he noted two weeks after his arrival. 'A new party does not seem possible because the Labour element would not be strong enough ... I feel myself less and less at home with the Conservatives.'[3] 'Walking up before b'fast to the top of the hill & sat down overlooking bay,' he noted on the first morning of his Labrador visit. 'Again the spirit of the frozen north. Perhaps it was that that led into contemplation of the political future. Evidently no place for men of independent thinking.'[4] When he got back to Newfoundland a few days later he noted, 'Not very well, tired in body & mind owing no doubt to a bad night. Have begun to have nightmares into which politicians & my work enter.'[5] At the end of September he sailed for Liverpool —noting apprehensively that his head was 'still clogged & dull'.[6] Halfway through the voyage, he mused:

It is three months since I left London for Lossiemouth, & in three days I am back. Have been thinking a good deal [about] what I shall do on my return ... I should like to retire; my road is not a Tory one. If anything were proposed like the Co-op tax & the Land relief, that would settle the question, but the general policy may be away from mine & that I cannot agree to any

further, & if there be a strong clamour for any line of action amongst the
Tories, I can do no more than keep it up till an election & then retire ... I
never expected we could do more than keep the country going, & that
done, we can do little more in conjunction with the Tory Party. The problem is now this: I can not help the present Opposition leaders into power;
they would muddle Labour into more distress: I cannot join in reviving
Toryism. A new Socialist influence has to be created & that means propaganda. I am disappointed with the work that our paid officials (Nat: Lab:)
have done: we have laid our hands on no smart man & our chances of keeping & expanding our grip on Labour & Socialist opinion have gone except
by personal propaganda. That is what has to be considered with Thomas &
one or two others. It is most desirable to have another national appeal at a
general election, but how can it be done is the question. An element not
quite certain yet is my own fitness. Last night my memory went badly. I
could remember nothing for some time like my dog's name, certain incidents of my holiday when I got on board this boat & such trifling things.
I certainly have much to do when I return in surveying possibilities.[7]

It soon became clear that he was in no condition to survey them. When he
got back to London his headaches and insomnia returned, and his eyesight
started to deteriorate again. His diary for October and November 1934 is full
of confessions of 'stupidity', 'tiredness' and lapses of memory, and it seems clear
that his performance in Cabinet was beginning to deteriorate as well. At about
this time, Baldwin's close friend and confidant, J. C. C. Davidson, went to see
Baldwin in his room in the House of Commons and was shaken to find Mac-
Donald lying on the couch, apparently in a state of collapse; years later he recalled that, although Baldwin had insisted that MacDonald was still valuable in
Cabinet, 'I knew that his rambling incoherence frequently shocked those who
heard him.'[8] As usual, MacDonald spent Christmas in Lossiemouth, where
the 'old surroundings, the old tongue & the old ways of living',[9] as he described
them in a touching diary entry on the day he arrived, brought a sharp improvement in his morale. But the effect soon wore off. Early in January 1935, he noted
glumly, 'Lunched at I.C.I. and talked of business & political prospects. Begged
me to go away for another holiday rather than give in to sleeplessness and
headaches. The real trouble is not pain but inability to work smartly as before,
to see a whole case or position.'[10] By the end of the month he was noting, as
glumly, that he had discussed the state of his health with Horder, and that Horder
'thinks [I] should not let my brain tiredness go too far'.[11]

The pattern continued in February and March. Towards the end of February,
Hankey noted that MacDonald was now 'really too tired to continue'.[12] At
about the same time, MacDonald came to the end of the thick manuscript
volume in which he had made most of his diary entries during the last twenty-
five years. In a rather self-conscious valedictory entry he noted:

Have had another bad day of headaches & eye strain & work has been slow and not at all good. Have not been able to read in full two speeches which I ought ...

And so this volume ends ... I end rather worn out & the worse for wear; my head slowing up & sometimes hardly working at all; my eyes permanently injured & sometimes specially troublesome, causing just a little foreboding; my days of Office & the political position of the Government, especially of the Tory Party, encouraging me to hope that 'Freedom's (not far) ahead. The allurements of the end become more enticing: Upper Frognal Lodge, the Hillocks, Spynie.[13]

Four days later he caught a bad cold and had to miss the Cabinet. He spent the morning lying on his couch, but insisted on carrying out a speaking engagement in Doncaster in the evening — noting afterwards that his eyes had been so 'muzzy' that he had not been able to read his notes and had had to throw them away.[14] The result was another missed Cabinet, another bout of illness and another two weeks out of action.

II

The Government's fortunes were sagging too. It was still doing badly in by-elections; and the outcry over the unemployment assistance board's relief scales in January 1935 suggested that it was likely to go on doing badly in future. More ominously still from its point of view, its supporters' morale and cohesion were threatened by two damaging flank attacks — one from its Left and the other from its Right. In December 1934, Lloyd George launched another great campaign for a loan-financed programme of national development, on the lines suggested in his 1929 election manifesto. Though he had fewer troops than he had had in 1929, he had, if anything, even stronger arguments. With free trade and the gold standard both abandoned, the chief obstacle to a British new deal had disappeared: with Roosevelt's New Deal actually in operation across the Atlantic the objection that such a policy was impracticable had lost much of its earlier force. Though the worst of the depression was over, unemployment still stood at more than two million; in these circumstances, it was even harder to argue that no new policies were needed. In narrowly electoral terms, no doubt, Lloyd George was in no position to damage the Government. Intellectually, he had challenged it at its most vulnerable point: and in a way which was calculated to win at least *sotto voce* support from the younger and more adventurous Government backbenchers, many of whom were themselves chafing at the dead hand of the Treasury. The challenge from the Right was cruder but if anything more embarrassing. In January 1935, Churchill's son Randolph stood as an Independent Conservative in a by-election at Liverpool, Wavertree, on the ticket of higher arms expenditure and opposition to the Government's

Indian policy. He won more than ten thousand votes; the official Conservative was defeated; and the Labour Party gained the seat. The Conservative party managers had been grappling with the die-hard revolt in the House of Commons for more than two years. Now they faced the infinitely more alarming spectre of a split in the constituencies.

Even if MacDonald's powers had been at their height, he would have been hard put to it to avoid being blamed for the Government's continuing unpopularity, at any rate in the Conservative Party; even if the Government had been doing well, his manifest decline would sooner or later have provoked demands for a change at No. 10., at any rate among those with no personal stake in his staying there. As things were, discontent with him and discontent with the Government fed on each other. Increasingly, Conservatives came to feel that the Government could not recapture the ground which it had lost while MacDonald remained at its head; even those Conservatives who did not share that feeling gradually came to feel that if he stayed on as prime minister much longer, the unity of the Conservative Party would be fatally endangered. Yet it would be wrong to suggest that he was forced out of the prime ministership against his will, or even that there was a concerted Conservative attempt to get rid of him. No such attempt was possible without Baldwin; and, as we have seen, Baldwin had promised MacDonald that the Conservatives would serve under him until the end of the Parliament. Besides, Baldwin was himself old and tired, and was toying with the idea of resigning the Conservative leadership in favour of Neville Chamberlain. Though he was prepared, perhaps even anxious, to become prime minister again, he was not prepared to fight for it, and still less prepared to break his word in order to do so. This is not to say that MacDonald's decision to give up the prime ministership was entirely unconstrained. He knew that a growing number of Conservatives wanted him to go; but for their pressure he might well have stayed on longer than he did. All the same, he made little effort to resist them; and although he complained bitterly about their disloyalty and ingratitude, he was at least half-aware that they were right in thinking that he was no longer able to carry on. Few prime ministers have left office with total equanimity, and MacDonald was not among them. But, as we shall see, it seems fairly clear that the decisive pushes towards his departure were self-administered.

They came after a long period of confusion and acrimony which had begun with the opening of Lloyd George's campaign for a national development plan in December 1934. For a while, there was a good deal of talk in political circles about the possibility that Lloyd George might be invited to join the Government, and it is clear from his diary that MacDonald was at least half-attracted by the idea. Though he was as suspicious of Lloyd George's motives and behaviour as he had always been, he could not help realizing that Lloyd George's energy and reputation would give the Government a badly needed electoral boost; though there is no direct evidence, it is reasonable to assume that he also realized that, if Lloyd George served under him, he could no longer be accused of presiding over a Conservative Government in disguise. 'The Sunday papers make much of Ll.G.'s "come back",' he noted with predictable sourness on December 16th. 'I do not expect that he has a single new idea or proposal.'[15] Later in the same entry, however, he added, much less predictably, 'Hearing of this birth I thought it might give an opportunity to reshuffle the Cabinet & approached colleagues none of whom would have it. They would serve neither under nor with him.' At the beginning of January 1935, Baldwin told him that he had agreed to see Lloyd George. 'I hope something may come of it,' MacDonald noted. 'Ll.G. has had a rest & ought to be fresh; I am tired & the pace of my work is slackening. So I would aid quite gladly a new combination, and now that Ll.G. has worked off so much spleen & has admired such a good display of his own fireworks he might be amenable.'[16] Though he added, somewhat confusingly, that he would not 'risk the experiment', the tone of the rest of the entry strongly suggests that he still saw some advantages in it.

Chamberlain, however, saw no advantages at all; and made it clear that he would refuse to serve in any Government of which Lloyd George was a member.[17] By the end of January, the idea was dead – MacDonald noting that he and Baldwin had had another discussion about Lloyd George, and that they 'Agreed his "trumpet blast" would die down if let alone. Not a new note in it.'[18] Instead, the Cabinet decided to set up a new committee under MacDonald's chairmanship, to be called the General Purposes Committee and to 'discuss matters which did not belong only to one Government Department'.[19] In essence, this was merely a formal version of the informal committee of six which had acted as a kind of inner Cabinet since the Government was formed, though with the addition of one or two younger members on an *ad hoc* basis; and MacDonald's proposal to establish it was strongly resisted by a group of younger ministers, headed by Cunliffe-Lister. After much debate, however, the proposal was unanimously adopted; and at their first meeting the members of the new committee decided that the first subject to be investigated should be Finance in relation to public works'.[20] For all practical purposes, the challenge from the Left had been smothered.

It was the challenge from the Right, however, which concerned MacDonald most. His irritation with the Conservatives had been growing for some time; and in the aftermath of Wavertree it reached new heights. In a long diary entry on January 27th he noted gloomily:

Discussed the political situation with Malcolm; told him the difficulties with which the National Govt. was meeting & the growing determination of sections of the Tory Party to dominate the Government and their constant statement of the issue to be between the Government & Socialism ... This is losing all non Tory support except that of a few old Liberals & making defeat as certain as it can well be ... Found Malcolm in agreement & so advised him to study the future &, with one or two confidential friends, examine the position very carefully. Both of us felt the folly of some of the young Tories [who] plan for trying to keep their seats by yielding to a propaganda like that indulged in by the opposition. We need to set up our own positive ideas and to advance them for both our own protection & the guidance of the country. The strength of the Government is being thrown away ... By appealing to an anti-Socialist vote we are limiting our appeal & raising an issue which will not fight ... This of course raises important issues for myself personally. How long can I remain at the head of a Government whose appeal to the country is anti-Socialism. It does not only mean defeat for the Government but moral embarrassment for myself. I am willing to go some way in view of the necessity to keep the Government together for the sake of the country ... but there comes a point beyond which I must decline to go. I have steered the country past the Charybdis of unprincipled bribery through doles & public charity which are to ruin those who get them & wreck the nation, but my hand is not to remain at the wheel if officers & crew are bent upon smashing us up upon the Scylla of opposition to a principle which offers a guiding inspiration for this generation.[21]

By early February he had become even more gloomy. On the 10th he noted:

Wavertree ... apparently is to end with no official reprobation of the revolters. Rather, it looks today as if they were to be allowed to act as advisers to their Party & dictate the kind of National Government they are to serve & the terms of their service. — Further, whilst the combination has always been loyally served in the Cabinet it has not been so in their speeches, so that the Conservative Party has never been taught that they owe any allegiance to the non-Conservative elements — certainly not to the P.M. So, under the conditions existing for the moment, my Liberal colleagues & myself are but individuals left to bear personally the burdens of disappointments with the Government & especially the fury of the workers. They put up candidates who fight as National on a pure Conservative platform & when we can do nothing in consequence to help them win as they have alienated all our supporters, we are held up as not only useless but encumbrances ... Again & again I have asked my colleagues who represent the three parties to consider the position with reference to the future & can get them to do nothing except admit the position & wait. I am beginning to feel that nothing will be of any use except my own resignation. Something more will have to happen before I desert the country in that way, but that something will happen if they do not stop this drift ... Saw Baldwin & talked situation. Told him that I was dissatisfied with the defence of Govt. as a united whole & drew his attention to the fact that it was Cons. defence of Conser: No colleague ever replied to attacks on me. I was being left to the wolves. He admitted it. I told him I thought it time to change that if the union was to last. I was prepared to do my part & make my contribution as rich as I could but there must be more unity in the country. He referred to the unity in the Cabinet. I agreed but said a united Cabinet required a union in the country manifested & not almost discouraged on platforms. He said he was getting tired and lethargic & would perhaps give up after the India Bill. But he could see no one to succeed. He was disappointed with both Elliot [sic] & Stanley. I said that I was much inclined to draw out too but the best way was to take office without portfolio & remain during an inter-regnum during which election might be fought. We could then make the way smooth for the new men and then leave them to themselves. I said I was sorry to leave Malcolm in the air with no attachments. He said that M. must be in a reconstructed Cabinet. He had a letter from Ld Salisbury blaming him for letting down the Tory Party & begging him to think before he carried his work of destruction further (that the gist not the words). He was a little troubled. It was quite evident by his reticences as well as by his occasional words that the Cons. Party felt neither gentlemanly nor political obligations to us. This conversation may be the parting of the ways. It has made it clear that the Party is to care only for its own fortunes & Mr B. is able to do nothing. His lack of response and his refraining from promising to do anything or to show any active reaction to statements with which he agreed were very marked.[22]

In the next few days, the pace warmed up. On February 11th, MacDonald saw Simon and Runciman, and told them what he had told Baldwin the night before. According to his diary, 'They agreed as to outlook and will have thought matters over for tomorrow's meeting of the six.'[23] The 'six' met at 10.30 the following morning. Afterwards MacDonald noted:

I put the straight question as to whether I as P.M. was hampering Tory re-union. The answer was not with the proviso that it was too soon as yet to decide what might be the position on anything when the question of recon-struction actually arose ... Definite statement from Baldwin & Neville [that] they were not in favour of a Party Government either by reconstruc-tion nor by change before the General Election ... That curiously attractive creature [—] asked interview & begged me to consider Baldwin's difficult position. Only barely can he hold his party & indeed may fail. Could I not magnanimously let him be P.M. and strengthen his hand? I was getting worn out obviously: I had had a gruelling time. I ought not to commit the errors of Ll.G. & hold on until the virtue had gone out of me. That would make a fine ending to my life. John Buchan evidently holds similar views ... Everybody reports a violent ferment in the Tory Party; & the leaders are evidently confused & have been taken unawares. There is a strong rally to Baldwin & I find an increasing move towards me to help him by letting him head the Government: This, if some younger men are brought into the Cabinet is a way to freshen up policy & would provide a good dignified ending for me of which neither I nor my children could be ashamed. I should have done my work.[24]

On the 13th he had another discussion with Simon and Runciman. They both told him that they would serve under Baldwin if he served as well, and, as he put it in his diary, 'that it might become necessary to save the National Government by making the Tories feel that they were not subordinate to their political opponents'.[25]

The die was cast in the next few weeks. On March 12th MacDonald noted, 'Still in bed ... Thomas rung up [sic] rather winged & thick in words saying he had just discussed the 'whole situation' with Neville, had told him certain things I had [told] T. in confidence & had informed him of the plans I was turning over in my mind for the future!!'[26] Two days later he had a telephone call from Horder, who told him that he had just breakfasted with Baldwin, and that Baldwin 'knew what was in my mind to do & was quite evidently pleased'; Thomas, Horder added, 'is going about like a wind in the corn spreading [the] news that I am finished, that he has the whole matter in hand; that he is the master of all the ceremonies'.[27] On the 21st, MacDonald spoke to Baldwin himself, noting afterwards that Baldwin

as usual was bafflingly unhelpful. I asked him to assume that I might have to give up the Premiership this year but on no account before the Jubilee ceremonies & not before the India Bill was on the Statute Book. He put two questions: Would I have any grievance if he did not carry out the desire he once expressed to go with me & not remain in office after me? Would I remain in the Govt.? Apparently he had discussed the matter & at once accepted the assumption with no request for an examination of the position as I expected, so I had to appear to doubt if he could keep the national combination, or at any rate indicate difficulties. I understood the position of the Tory Party, its splits, its desire to have the leadership &c. &c. but I was of opinion that the Tory Party alone could not hold the country (I think some Tory leaders are beginning to feel that Labour is so badly led that they can). Could he, if P.M. unite his Party? Would the result of a more united Tory Party be a higher aggregate vote at the election? We had to take care of that. He spoke of Ll.G. saying if he came in the Tory Party would split again. He evidently had Winston also in his mind. As to his own ideas he would not go beyond detached musings which were of no help in surveying the pros & cons. I must now put specific questions to him on what he would propose to do: indicate the Cabinet changes he would make, the proposal he would make to me as to my work, very particularly the manifesto for the election. He said that 95% of the Tory Party would vote for a National Government. He had evidently talked things over with N. Chamb. I also said the King must be consulted.[28]

As late as the beginning of April, MacDonald complained to the Chief Whip that the Conservatives were trying to use him for their own ends, and warned that he would 'see what they proposed before I decided what I shd. do'.[29] But by then it was too late to draw back. The arrangements for Baldwin's succession were not completed until well into May, but it is clear that the critical decision had been taken by the end of March. It is only slightly less clear that the ball had been set rolling on February 10th when MacDonald told Baldwin that he was thinking of giving up, and that its momentum became irresistible when he discussed his intentions with Thomas, at some stage between early February and early March.

III

The early months of 1935 saw an equally critical decision in another sphere; and, for MacDonald at least, it must have been a profoundly painful one. In 1934, as we have seen, he had slowly come to accept that some British rearmament was necessary; but, as we have also seen, he had backed Chamberlain in his attempt to scale down the programme advocated by the D.R.C. His departure for Canada had coincided with the beginning of a long battle over the D.R.C. report; and in his absence his colleagues had sharply reduced the D.R.C. totals, though without changing the D.R.C.'s strategic priorities in the way that Chamberlain had advocated. Within a few weeks of his return, however, the question was reopened. Tension in Europe continued to rise, and evidence of German rearmament continued to accumulate. By the end of November it seemed clear to the Cabinet that, as the minutes put it, 'In a very short time Germany would possess an army of 300,000 men, as against an army of 100,000 men allowed her by the Treaty of Versailles. There was reason to believe that in a year's time she would have as large an air force as the United Kingdom.'[30] A Cabinet committee was set up under MacDonald's chairmanship to assemble the facts and figures relating to German rearmament, and to make recommendations as to the Government's policy; when the committee reported, it was agreed, in the teeth of strong opposition from Chamberlain, that the expansion of the air force should be slightly accelerated.[31] From MacDonald's point of view it was a sour apple, but he had no doubt that it had to be bitten. 'The outlook with Nazi murders, Nazi education, Nazi horrors of mind & ambitions & Nazi character is depressing,' he noted gloomily on November 21st, 'and whatever may be the immediate consequences it should not be allowed to drift.'[32] By the following day he had become even more gloomy. 'C.I.D. interesting discussions on defence problems ... ,' he noted. 'The militarists are getting too much on top, but up till now defence is so neglected that the time for pulling in has not come.'[33]

'Pulling in' seemed even less feasible in 1935 than it had seemed in 1934. In January, a plebiscite in the Saar recorded an overwhelming majority in favour of its return to Germany. The Saar vote, MacDonald noted, 'brings war nearer ... If there were pooled security now, it would be a serious question as to whether Europe would not now tell Germany that if it did not join in the councils of Europe its refusal would be taken as a *casus belli*.'[34] While he was still in that mood, Hankey wrote to him suggesting that the officials who had drafted the D.R.C. report the year before should prepare a draft of a possible white paper on the Government's defence policy, for publication and debate in late February or early March.[35] MacDonald agreed; and the white paper was eventually published on March 4th. Though the draft prepared by Hankey and his fellow officials had been toned down by the Cabinet, it was still an outspoken document—making it clear that Germany was to blame for the worsening international climate, that Britain could no longer rely on the existing international political machinery for her security, that there were serious deficiencies in her defences and that these deficiencies could be put right only by additional expenditure.[36]

The results were unfortunate. There was a furious outcry from the Labour and Liberal Parties, much of it directed against MacDonald, whose initials had been printed at the end of the paper and who was therefore regarded as its author. Hitler caught a diplomatic cold, and a visit which Simon had been planning to make to Berlin had to be postponed. The Government's nerve, never very strong in foreign-policy questions, weakened again. On March 4th, MacDonald noted:

White Paper on Defence appeared today & as I expected provided such chances for a stunt & hysterical scare that these things happened. The Herald and News Chronicle were specially possessed. When I got to the H. of C. I found unfortunately ... that it appeared over my initials as well as announced a date for the debate—the 11th—before the House knew.— Most annoying blunders. It is rather odd that I cannot be protected by the usual watchful eyes & knowledge against such mistakes. Every stunter announced it as an armaments document, marking the beginning of a new policy on behalf of H.M.G. whereas its lines have been indicated for months & I wrote in the *News Letter* of the 20 December an article on the exact lines of the paper.[37]

It was an understandable reaction, no doubt, for the 'stunters' were appealing to a doctrine which MacDonald had himself expounded for most of his political life, and that must have made their criticisms even more painful than they would have been in any case. But it was also a dangerous one. The whole point of the white paper was to persuade the British people that it was necessary to spend more money on defence. If it was not an 'armaments document, marking the beginning of a new policy', it was a waste of time: if it was, MacDonald's defensiveness boded ill for the success of the operation.

By the following day his mood had become more robust. Once again his diary tells the story:

> The partisan press has been most mischievous about the white paper, without scruple or decency they have beaten their tocsins of false alarms & I have been fixed on as the chief of culprits because by accident my initials, put on to indicate that the document I last saw was the authentic copy to be put in order, were printed. In the afternoon it became known that Hitler had a bad cold and at once the cold was said to be diplomatic, as no doubt 9-10ths of it was ... I am of opinion that Hitler will cool down like a sensible man and that Simon will go to Berlin. If that does not happen we must tell the true reason to our people. This policy of treacle in view of the psychology of Germany at the moment is not only futile and feeble, but is just the one to make Germany believe that ... to get all it wants it requires only to deceive Gt. Britain, break its bonds with threats & trust to the unintelligent love of peace professed & indeed believed in by a lot of easy minded people in this country.[38]

Robust moods were not, however, followed by robust acts. On March 16th, Hitler announced that conscription was to be reintroduced in Germany and that the peacetime strength of the German army was to be thirty-six divisions. This was a clear breach of the peace treaty; and the French sent an urgent message to London, suggesting that the League of Nations should call a conference of interested powers and urging that Simon's visit to Berlin should be postponed. It is clear from his diary that MacDonald recognized Hitler's challenge to the peace settlement for what it was. The Germans, he noted angrily on the day of the announcement, 'have been working to this point for a long time and the excuses upon which they seize ... only shows [sic] their deceit. It may be as well that they have at last unmasked themselves for at any rate we now know what we have to face.'[39] The French request, however, found him coldly unsympathetic. France, he noted on the 17th, was still 'pursuing that futile policy of not agreeing to anything but talking as though Versailles existed in fact as well as on paper'; and he added, with every appearance of enthusiasm, that Baldwin, Simon, Eden, Hankey, Vansittart and he had unanimously agreed that Simon's visit should not be cancelled.[40]

As so often in the next few years, the net result was that Britain spoke with two conflicting voices; as so often, she pleased her enemies and alienated her friends; as so often, she gained only abuse for her pains. On March 18th, a note was sent to Berlin, protesting against the conscription announcement. In the same note, however, the Germans were asked whether they still wanted Simon to come; and, at the Cabinet's insistence, they were also assured that Britain wanted to replace the peace treaty with a freely negotiated agreement.[41] Not surprisingly, they answered that they wanted the Simon visit to proceed; and on the 24th, Simon duly arrived in Berlin, where he was treated to a long list of further demands and told that Germany had reached air parity with Britain. It would be wrong to blame MacDonald for the Government's vacillations: his colleagues, and still more his opponents, floundered at least as badly as he did. But it could hardly be claimed that he had given them a positive lead. Under the pressure of events he had abandoned the liberal foreign-policy assumptions to which he had clung for so long; in principle, at any rate, he now accepted the notion that Hitler's Germany could be dealt with only on the basis of older and harsher assumptions, which he had always rejected in the past. But he was too ill, too tired and, above all, too unsure of his bearings in the illiberal world in which he now had to operate to translate that theoretical acceptance into a coherent policy. When others led, as Hankey had done over the white paper, he was prepared to follow. When no lead came from elsewhere, he was content to mirror the prevailing Cabinet consensus. And, given the opportunity, the Cabinet almost always tried to have its cake and eat it.

Much the same is true of his approach to, and role during, the negotiations that followed Simon's return. Before Simon left for Berlin, it had been agreed that a conference between the British, French and Italians should be held at Stresa, in northern Italy, to discuss what to do about the latest German moves. The initiative had come from Mussolini, and MacDonald, who scented a return to the alliance diplomacy of pre-war days, had little enthusiasm for it. 'The fact is too much is being made of Stresa,' he noted irritably at the beginning of April; 'it is only a continuation of the other talks & the important event is the L. of N. Council at Geneva;' Mussolini, he added revealingly, was approaching it 'in a purely military spirit. We get forced steadily back into the deep ruts which [in] 1911–14 led us straight into war.'[42] It is clear from his diary that he was under strong pressure from Simon's swelling band of critics to lead the British delegation himself, but at first he resisted it. At the last moment, however, Eden, who was to have accompanied Simon, was ordered to bed for a month. At this, MacDonald decided that he would have to go after all – noting apprehensively that he ran 'great risks of being unequal to the task & of making a failure'.[43]

His fears were soon borne out. The conference opened on April 11th and ended on the 14th, but although it did not last for long the strain of even three days of high-level diplomacy was now too heavy for him. He found it difficult to read his papers, and often rambled badly in discussion; on one occasion, the interpreter could make no sense of what he had said and had to be told to invent a speech for him. Vansittart had to keep him away from the press, and even supplied him with collar studs.[44] Yet it is doubtful if the decline in his powers made much difference to the outcome. Before he left London, the Cabinet decided that if the French or Italians asked for Britain's conversations with Germany to be broken off the request should be refused, and that the British delegation should reaffirm Britain's commitments under the Locarno treaty but give no undertakings as to how those commitments were to be carried out[45] — in other words, that Britain should make it clear to her potential allies that she would not join them in a united front against Germany and should proclaim, in general terms, that she intended to keep her promises to them, while refusing, in any particular case, to say what her promises meant. This was MacDonald's brief, and he stuck to it with monotonous rigidity. His chief aim, he noted at the beginning of the proceedings, was to persuade France and Italy 'to agree that the German action should not stop all further negotiations ... This may cost us something but they will get as little from me as is necessary — and even that will be limited.'[46] That was still his position at the end. The conference wound up on a high note, deploring Germany's repudiation of the peace treaty and declaring that the three powers concerned would act together to oppose any future repudiations which might endanger the peace.[47] Thanks largely to MacDonald's refusal to budge from his negotiating position, however, these declarations had no practical content. The Stresa front, as it was to be called, was broken before it was established. But although MacDonald might have been more willing to budge if he had been younger and fitter, it is hard to conceive of any circumstances in which he, or any other British minister at the time, would have budged enough to give the agreement teeth. What doomed it was not MacDonald's lack of diplomatic agility but the entire Government's unwillingness to realize that it had to choose between allowing Hitler to dominate Europe and accepting new, and potentially risky, continental commitments. MacDonald shared that unwillingness and deserves a share of the blame for the consequences. The same can be said of the vast majority of his countrymen.

On a narrower but equally important question connected with the conference, he was more directly culpable. At the end of 1934, fighting had broken out on the ill-defined border between Abyssinia and Italian Somaliland. Mussolini had been hoping to invade Abyssinia for some time, and seized on the opportunity to demand compensation. The Abyssinians refused; and in February 1935, Italy began to mobilize. It is clear from his diary that MacDonald was well aware of what was happening. 'Italian attack on Abyssinia becomes more & more a wolf and the lamb tale,' he noted indignantly on February 21st. 'It is an irredeemable tale of calculated aggression with a plentiful adornment of assumed innocence and lies.'[48] Before he left for Stresa, Eden urged him to raise the Abyssinian question with Mussolini and said the same thing to Simon. At the conference, however, neither MacDonald nor Simon said anything whatever about it.[49] There is no way of telling whether Mussolini would have taken any notice of them if they had; what is certain is that they had an opportunity to warn him, and failed to take it. MacDonald's papers throw no light on the matter, and the Cabinet papers are equally unhelpful. It may be that he originally intended to take Eden's advice, and then quailed at the prospect of a difficult encounter with Mussolini. It may be that Vansittart, who was anxious to keep Mussolini sweet as an ally against Hitler and whose memoirs are somewhat coy on the subject,[50] persuaded him to say nothing. It may be that he decided that there was no point in saying anything; it may be that, in the press of other business, he forgot. But, whatever the reason, it was a bad lapse.

IV

MacDonald arrived back in London on April 15th in a state of exhaustion. On the 16th he noted that he was 'Not well & depressed', and on the 17th that he was: 'Still not at all well & am hoping much good from holiday.'[51] His hopes were disappointed. He spent Easter on the Sussex coast, where he caught another bad cold and had to spend another two days in bed. When he returned to London again on the 23rd he was 'feeling wretched and went to bed at once'.[52] He was back in harness on the 24th, however, and by the 26th was noting 'Considering arrangements for resignation of the Premiership; a mingling of sadness with relief.'[53] On the 27th he wrote to Baldwin, pointing out that 'In spite of the numerous engagements which we have to keep, we must find time for an exchange of views on Cabinet reconstruction and, indeed, on the future of the National Government ... We should meet some time during the coming week as decisions on some points are becoming urgent.'[54] Baldwin agreed, but the meeting brought MacDonald little joy. 'Had talk with Baldwin about our future plans, reconstruction &c,' he noted disgustedly on the 30th, 'but found him most unhelpful. Gave him memos on what I thought shd. be done & I must follow it up by pressure. He thought that Oliver Stanley, Simon & Londonderry would have to be moved or go, but he expressed no ideas worth considering. He said I could suit my own desires as to the office I might fill.'[55]

In the next few days his anxieties were swamped by the pomp and circumstance of George V's silver jubilee. On May 6th, he noted enthusiastically, 'Day of Jubilee rejoicing. Drive to St Pauls through unbroken cheering ... Truly a day glowing with emotion.'[56] On the 8th he was still more enthusiastic, noting happily:

> Reception of Diplomatic corps; was Minister in attendance. Great dignity; fine homage ... Followed by reception of Dominion Premiers the most touching & homely triumph of ceremony & loyal homage ever held. Ireland was out & the gap lay like a shadow of smallness over a ceremony of bigness & graciousness. The King's reply was a perfect expression of sovereign affection & solicitude. When he came to references & reminiscences personal to himself & the Queen his voice broke & tears stood in her eyes. Everyone deeply moved. Here the Empire was a great family, the gathering a family reunion, the King a paternal head. We all went away feeling that we had taken part in something very much like a Holy Communion.

Moved in House that the H. of C. present address to-morrow. Quiet, hearty acquiescence. This Jubilee is having a miraculous effect on the public mind & on the King himself. He is finding confidence & is showing the Prince of Wales' aptitude for saying the right popular thing & feeling the popular mind. But with it all he retains the demeanour and the status of a King & does not step down to get on a lower level.[57]

Next day, the King and Queen received addresses from both Houses of Parliament in Westminster Hall. 'How well everything is going & how deftly the King fills his role,' MacDonald noted. 'Glittering State Banquet & the 24 pipers made a fine show. King asked me to go out upon the Balcony with him & the Dominion Premiers were also present. Vast cheering crowd.'[58]

Once the ceremonies were over, the horse-trading over the change of Government began again. On May 12th MacDonald noted suspiciously, 'Press full of jubilee ceremonies with indications that the stage is being cleared and the real play is the bailing & trial of the Government. That Baldwin is coming in is being taken for granted as is also a strengthening of the Tory element.'[59] During the day, Horder visited him at his house in Hampstead. According to MacDonald's diary, Horder told him that, although his resignation was not essential on health grounds alone, he undoubtedly needed a rest.[60] Next day, MacDonald discussed the distribution of offices in the new Government with Baldwin, noting afterwards that Baldwin 'thought Simon should take a sinecure, look after defence & be Deputy leader H. of C. Hailsham the Woolsack, Oliver Stanley Board of Education, Kingsley Wood Health ... Thomas he was in doubts about, Stanhope War.'[61] On the 14th, he had a similar discussion with Simon, and on the 15th a more distressing one with Thomas, who had suddenly discovered that Baldwin was not as trustworthy as he had thought and feared that the Conservatives were using the change for their own ends. More congenial was a discussion with the King on the 16th. According to MacDonald's diary, the King

Told me [he] knew I had to go & was kind and friendly. Said he had to consent but wished to impose a condition, that I should remain in Cabinet as Lord President so that he might often see me. Knew [I] would not take peerage, but would I accept Thistle. Said it was an Honour which every good Scotsman coveted, but it entailed my becoming a 'Sir' & begged ... to decline assuring him that I would value the offer as I would value the ribbon itself. Said he feared I would not let him show his esteem for myself personally & for the service I had given to him & the country. His words were those of a close personal friend. We talked of the Jubilee & I spoke of his speeches. He blamed me in good humour for having been the cause of his ever speaking into a microphone & said he was still very nervous. I said that only those who were nervous could do so well as he had done. Assured me he understood my desire to take no titles & said if he were one of the new rich the last thing he would do would be to run after a peerage. He did not see that Governor Generals need to be made peers & could not understand John Buchan. He gave me a book 'The King's Book' signed by the Queen & himself. He laughed & remarked there was probably never such a friendly interview between King & Prime Minister.[62]

As the climax drew nearer, however, MacDonald's composure began to crack. On May 23rd, he noted apprehensively that Usher had given him a 'Gloomy report on Seaham & the effect of change in Cabinet. The Tory frame of mind is one of party elation.'[63] On the 27th he had another talk with Thomas, who was even more gloomy than Usher had been. Thomas, MacDonald noted, 'Thinks now it has been a Tory wangle forgetting that he communicated to Tories my private communication to him that I might have to have a rest, and thus started the resignation expectations'.[64] On the 28th, five National Labour members, led by J. A. Lovat Fraser M.P. for Lichfield, wrote to him to say that if he left Downing Street, the result would be 'a serious loss of Labour support in the constituencies & a corresponding weakening of the national character of the Government'.[65] On the same day MacDonald noted:

Horrible night of sleeplessness and worry mostly about shadows. Not at all well this morning ... 4. Committee of 6 leaders to discuss my resignation. Little ungracious. Agreed Baldwin shd. succeed I remaining in Government provided it was to remain really National, test being distribution of offices & common policy for an election. Date of change left to B., S. & myself. We met at once and decided to try for Wednesday of June, & make all arrangements to have new Govt. set up by beginning of next week. Malcolm will come in but I fear Sankey will have to go. The scene in my room of this gathering of the elders was queer. Baldwin sat as one troubled in spirit but almost dumb of tongue; Runciman stiff, palefaced, sharp eyed, very much like an elder; Thomas flushed, evidently wanting to say something but too troubled in mind for words to find a way out through the upset; Simon smooth in smile and attitude in his chair; Neville with an eye on Baldwin as though ready to pounce on him, like a man who sees things coming and knows that he need do nothing to help or hasten them.[66]

The remaining details were settled in the next few days. It was agreed that MacDonald should take Baldwin's old place as lord president of the council. Simon was to go to the Home Office, Hoare to the Foreign Office, Hailsham to the Woolsack and Malcolm MacDonald to the Colonial Office; Thomas stayed where he was, but Sankey was thrown to the wolves. On June 5th, MacDonald presided over the Cabinet for the last time. After he had thanked his colleagues for their 'splendid co-operation and friendship', Baldwin paid a tribute to his loyalty, courtesy, kindness and courage — 'not only his moral courage, but his physical courage in carrying on his work in circumstances of ill-health, especially when his eyesight was affected'.[67] That night MacDonald was dined by the Government P.P.Ss; the following night, he dined the National Labour ministers. In the afternoon of June 7th, he surrendered the seals of office; and Baldwin kissed hands as prime minister. A few hours later, MacDonald left for Lossiemouth on the night train; after he had arrived he described the events of the day in his notebook:

7 June. First thing of which awakening made me conscious was 'I die today'. But yet I knew nothing of the feelings of the condemned man following the same process of consciousness for I had cause to be cheerful. I listened to the birds singing in the trees, the dogs barking on the road, the cars rattling up — My last day and the sun rose brightly through the trees & my ears & eyes were full of joy ... 11. I had to go to the House and got a farewell cheer when I rose to answer a question; lunched there in due course; 2.30 took a discussion which Churchill raised on protection against air attack & refused to politely thank him for raising it, then got a second cheery farewell and at 3.30 rushed off to the Palace having captured Clive Wigram at No. 10 — 3.50 audience with King which in the end lasted for 50 minutes and he was ¼ hr late in seeing Mr Baldwin. He was most friendly. He said again looking sadly down to the floor with his right elbow on the arm of his chair: 'I hoped you might ha[ve] seen me through, but I now know it is impossible. But I do not think it will be very long. I wonder how you have stood it — especially the loss of your friends & their beastly behaviour'. Again: 'You have been the Prime Minister I have liked best; you have so many qualities, you have kept up the dignity of the office without using it to give you dignity'. 'You will see me as often as you like & of course you will come this year to Balmoral & as you now have nothing to do you will not merely stay a weekend'. And so. He made me doubly & trebly sorry to lay down my office. — Returned at once to Downing St and went back to Palace at 5.45 to be drilled in what I had to do at the Privy Council at 6. — 6. Privy Council. My first duty as Lord President was to call up Malcolm to be sworn in. (Note: his coat fitted badly). New Government sworn and left for Downing St by 6.30 p.m. to catch the 7.30 train for Lossiemouth — I left with feelings which mingled regret with relief, a sense of freedom with one of impotence. I might have been a memory disembodied. Dining with Lady Grant & Robbie & Malcolm in the train north I kept wondering who I was & how I would wake up next morning.

It was a dignified exit in the end, though a tragically belated one. An even greater tragedy was that it was not only belated, but incomplete. MacDonald was not the first or last old man in history to cling to power after he had lost the capacity to use it, or to cling to the shadow of power after he had lost the reality. Though evidence is scanty it is not difficult to guess what persuaded him to stay on as lord president after leaving Downing Street. As we have seen, he was under pressure from the King. As so often before, he persuaded himself that his presence was needed to maintain the Government's battered National image. At a deeper and less conscious level, he needed recognition and a role and feared the emptiness of retirement. But although his decision to stay in office is easy to forgive, and easier still to understand, there can be no doubt that it was mistaken. He had paid a high enough price for staying in Downing Street longer than he should have done; the price he was to pay for staying on as lord president was, in many ways, higher still.

V

After a fortnight in his new office, MacDonald noted hopefully that he was sleeping better.[68] The improvement does not seem to have lasted, however, and in a diary entry early in July 1935, only a few weeks after the end of his prime ministership, he confessed despairingly that although he wanted to guide the Cabinet on foreign policy, 'I am not able; my views, perfectly clear & definite, my brain will not express in effective speech.'[69] Increasingly, he felt excluded from the decisions that mattered: the Government's policy, he complained in another diary entry, later in the summer, was determined in private consultations 'amongst Tory Ministers who[m] I meet less & less except in Cabinet'.[70] The Abyssinian crisis, which was now entering an acute phase, brought a particularly cruel blow to his pride. In the middle of August, a special Cabinet was summoned to discuss the latest developments. MacDonald was afraid that the Foreign Office was driving Mussolini into a corner from which he would be unable to retreat and that if war resulted, Britain would be in no condition to fight; he arrived in London early, so as to put his doubts to Eden and Hoare, only to be fobbed off with the excuse that they had so many prior engagements that they could not spare the time to see him.[71] His attempts to influence his colleagues' election plans were equally unsuccessful. As soon as Baldwin took over as prime minister, the Conservatives began to press for an early election to capitalize on the change; though MacDonald dreaded the prospect, he did not feel strong enough to resist them. When he tried to persuade them to disgorge some of their seats in favour of their allies, however, his pleas went unheeded. As he put it in a bitter diary entry on July 25th:

> Important conference of Six to discuss political situation & election. Agreement that if possible election shd. be in November. I emphasised that [there were] too many Tory candidates & that Tories should stand down for more Liberals & Labour ... I cannot help feeling that Tories are willing to take Party advantage of the situation, rush us into the election ... & come back helped by our assistance but without our presence in the new Parliament beyond six or ten ... They did not appear to like my indicating that if I went into an election it was on condition of self-respect, & I almost

laughed aloud when one said that we ought not to consider party position in list of candidates. If that is a patriotic doctrine now it was equally so when their local associations were selecting candidates.[72]

The election itself brought much crueller blows. At the beginning of October, MacDonald spent two days in Seaham, spying out the land. He returned on the 9th, noting apprehensively, 'Chances of keeping seat not very good. I seem to have been regarded as the embodiment of wickedness.'[73] In spite of his apprehensions, however, he turned down the offer of a more promising constituency at Bosworth — explaining to Sir William Edge, the sitting National Liberal M.P., who had made the offer, that if he had decided not to contest Seaham again: 'all the neighbouring constituencies, and indeed right over the North East Coast, would have been pulled down ... So I am to stand my racket in order to try and save a few seats.'[74] On October 23rd, Baldwin announced that Parliament would be dissolved on the 25th and that polling day would be November 14th. On the 26th MacDonald noted privately that he was 'Beginning to feel the calm of the coming fight & the energy to go confidently through'.[75] On the 29th he left London to begin his campaign.

He did not remain calm or confident for long. He was old and ailing, and had rarely been seen in the constituency since the last election; his opponent was his old supporter, Emanuel Shinwell, a tough and vigorous campaigner in his mid-forties. The election had been called in the shadow of a dispute in the mining industry; in Seaham, as in other mining districts, the miners' traditional loyalty to the Labour Party was reinforced by their even fiercer loyalty to their union and to each other. In more fortunate parts of the country, Government candidates could point to signs of economic recovery since the last election: in the north-east region, nearly half-a-million insured workers were still unemployed,[76] and to thousands of Seaham voters the Government's chief monuments were the means test and the indignities associated with it. In 1931, MacDonald's platform had had two planks — patriotism on the one hand, and his own record of service to the Labour movement on the other. Now both planks seemed rotten. Seaham's patriotism in sending him to Westminster had been rewarded by four years of stagnation and neglect; the Government had become a Conservative one, in which MacDonald was little more than a passenger. Given the state of opinion over the country as a whole, it was almost inevitable that Seaham should have swung back to Labour in 1935. It swung all the harder because it felt that the trust it had shown in 1931 had been betrayed.

MacDonald's first meeting, at the Theatre Royal in Seaham Harbour, went well enough. 'Although there was a fairly strong hostile element, which gave vent at times to booing,' the *Durham County Advertiser* reported, 'the ex-Prime Minister easily held his own and was repeatedly applauded when he scored off his opponents.'[77] Next day he was less successful. He addressed audiences of 1,000 at Easington Colliery and Hordern, and in both places there was a good deal of booing and interruption.[78] Meanwhile, his own nerve was beginning to crack. 'Struck by blatancy and ignorance of many of people ... ,' he noted. 'The group laugh when you are serious is the most disconcerting form of interruption. Already feeling strain on a too slowly moving head.'[79] During the second week of the campaign, the strain became much heavier. At Shotton on November 6th, the *Durham County Advertiser* reported, 'a section of the audience shouted, hooted, hissed and jeered and drummed on the floor with their feet to such an extent that the ex-Premier could scarcely be heard above the din'; though MacDonald stood his ground, he was unable to make a connected speech and could only shout a few angry retorts at the crowd.[80] His reception at Deaf Hill was even worse. When he tried to speak, his voice was drowned by the strains of the 'Red Flag', followed, somewhat incongruously, by 'Pack Up Your Troubles', 'Tipperary' and 'Loch Lomond'; and after twenty minutes the meeting had to be abandoned.[81] On November 7th, he noted that there was 'Something uncomfortable in atmosphere to-day; feel as if demons were about.'[82] That night he and J. H. Thomas were shouted down at Murton, where, as the *Durham County Advertiser* put it, 'a large hostile crowd rendered speech-making impossible by scenes unparalleled in the Seaham Division.'[83]

To judge by the local press, the last week of the campaign passed more peacefully. As in 1931, however, MacDonald could not face the nervous strain of the count; and in the evening of November 14th he left for London by the overnight train. Next day, Shinwell was declared elected with 38,380 votes to MacDonald's 17,882. In Bassetlaw, Malcolm also lost his seat, having polled 20,764 votes to his Labour opponent's 21,903. As so often, MacDonald poured out his feelings in an anguished diary entry:

A heart-breaking day. Arrived early at King's Cross & saw first results. Not at all good for the Labour Opposition. Very tired: hardly able to walk. Buck joined me at lunch. In the middle Mita opened door & sobbed 'Malcolm is defeated' & before we finished, Dr Grant telephoned in a broken voice: 'I am heartbroken & have had to escape from the counting. You must be prepared for a defeat by at least 15,000'. Thus the cloud descended. My poor boy. Luck has been hard, & I cannot put my crushed feelings into thought. For myself, I care nothing. I was prepared for myself, but not for him. Alister & Ishbel, Malcolm & Sheila (who has made a fine beginning on the political platform) have been speaking to me over the telephone & it was hard to say anything. The miners have done it to both of us. – When I entered the fight for Seaham I knew that I could keep the seat only by a miracle, but I did not anticipate the bitterness and hysteria of the fight. I found myself up against an immovable wall. I talked to people whose minds had been poisoned by a previously conducted campaign of lies & calumny to regard me as the author of all their hardships. The Means Test applied to hundreds of families & the coal agitation did the rest. I had, in addition, an absolutely useless organisation which never began to work but was in confusion from beginning to end. Very soon there developed a wild and hysterical rowdyism, the persistent interruption of meetings which forbad connected & built up speeches and the actual break up of meetings. Some of the displays were absolutely bestial. Many of the faces of the women were lined with destitution; their eyes flamed and gleamed with hate & passion; their hair was dishevelled; their language filthy with oaths & some obscenity; they filled one with loathing & fear just like French Revolution studies. Night after night their misery was upon me. To this, the fact that I helped to save them has perversion brought both them and me.[84]

'You have shared the fate of the prophets and my heart is heavy for you,' wrote Baldwin in a graceful letter of commiseration. 'I know your own defeat will not cause you the sharp, piercing disappointment that Malcolm's will. But it is something to have a son who stands by his father's side at all times, good and bad ... I do know much of what you are feeling, if not all. And I give you my hand in enduring friendship.'[85] But no expression of sympathy, however graceful, could disguise the fact or the magnitude of MacDonald's defeat. In the country as a whole, the Government had done better than it had expected to do. In the new House of Commons it had 431 seats to Labour's 154 and a majority over all parties of 247. In votes its victory was not so overwhelming, but even in votes it was comfortably ahead. Labour's vote had increased by 1,600,000 and its share of the total vote had gone up from nearly 31 per cent to nearly 38 per cent, but, in spite of the virtual disappearance of the Liberals as a significant electoral force, it was scarcely any stronger than it had been in 1929. In Seaham the swing against the Government was much larger. MacDonald's vote was down by 11,000; Shinwell had polled 15,000 more votes than Coxon had polled in 1931; Labour's share of the vote had gone up from 45 per cent to 67 per cent. In 1931 MacDonald's victory in Seaham had given added force, both to the Government's claim to stand above party and class divisions and to his own claim to speak for a sizeable body of non-Conservative opinion which his Conservative colleagues would ignore at their peril. His defeat in 1935 underlined the fact that the Government was now, for all practical purposes, a Conservative one; that it could not only survive, but prosper, without his help; and that, in any case, he was in no position to help it.

At one level, he felt his humiliation keenly. 'Reflecting that the man who is out is like one drowning,' he noted sardonically on November 17th; 'makes a brave show at first as he slowly sinks; onlookers marvel and applaud; sinks below surface & person becomes vaguer & dimmer & is at last lost.'[86] Yet, as the tone of that entry implies, he had still not brought himself to recognize that all politics now had to offer him was more humiliation, of a more subtle kind. On November 19th, he had an audience with the King, who told him, according to a note in the MacDonald papers, that 'I must remain in Government. He would be greatly grieved and unhappy were it otherwise ... Did not expect to live more than five years and, as I would likely live after him, his death would free me.'[87] A few hours later, he had an interview with Baldwin, who asked him to stay on as lord president and to fight a by-election; according to his diary, he accepted, 'on condition that suitable provision shd. be made for Thomas and agreement re Malcolm'.[88] Next day, it was agreed that Thomas, whose breezy vulgarity had made him a number of enemies among the dominion prime ministers, should replace Malcolm as colonial secretary and that Malcolm should take Thomas's place as dominions secretary. Soon afterwards, the death of Noel Skelton, who had just been re-elected as one of the Unionist M.P.s for the Scottish Universities, made it necessary to hold a by-election there; and in spite of some opposition in Scottish university circles, the Association of Unionist Graduates agreed at the end of December to nominate MacDonald as their candidate.[89] Meanwhile, Sir Ian Macpherson, the National Liberal M.P. for Ross and Cromarty, had been given a peerage; and at the beginning of January 1936, Malcolm was nominated as the National Government candidate for Ross and Cromarty.

The Scottish Universities' result was declared at the beginning of February. MacDonald was returned with 16,393 votes to the Scottish Nationalist's 9,034 and the Labour candidate's 3,597, and took his seat on February 5th. According to Harold Nicolson, he was greeted with 'much booing' from the Labour benches and with 'only perfunctory cheers' from the Government side of the House;[90] according to *The Times*, there was loud and prolonged cheering on the Government benches, mingled with boos from the Opposition and cries of 'The Prodigal Son' and 'All the duchesses will be wanting to kiss me now.'[91] A week later, Malcolm was returned for Ross and Cromarty with a majority of 3,000. 'The House went on the boil with pleasure and [I] was surrounded with happy friends,' MacDonald noted, with unintended pathos. 'The feeling which has been taking possession of me that the MacDonald family was a burden went at once.'[92] When Canon Donaldson sent his congratulations on Malcolm's victory, 'in spite of Labour's defeat', MacDonald replied with an echo of his old pugnacity:

The only part of your letter with which I should very profoundly disagree is the phrase 'in spite of Labour's defeat'. Labour was not defeated in Ross and Cromarty. Labour was victorious; and a queer mixture which had neither principle nor political policy, now known as Opposition Labour, was defeated. The old friends of Labour, and those who were Socialists a quarter of a century ago who are still living, I believe unanimously voted for Malcolm ... So that I venture to flatter myself that it was not merely a personal friend of mine but an old Socialist who still sticks to his faith who congratulated me upon Malcolm's success.[93]

VI

MacDonald lingered on as lord president for another seventeen months – a forlorn and, as time went on, an almost forgotten figure, cruelly aware of his diminishing effectiveness, full of grievances against his colleagues and the world, and with no real influence on events. Of course, there were cheerful moments. In January 1936, Ishbel bought a pub in Buckinghamshire, called the Plough Inn; though MacDonald did not visit it until April, it is clear from his diary that he got considerable vicarious enjoyment from the venture and kept a careful eye on its progress.[94] He rejoiced in Malcolm's frequent successes as a minister, and approved strongly when Alister, whose first marriage had ended in divorce, married a second time. Though his relationship with Lady Londonderry seems to have been less close than it had been earlier, Marthe Bibesco was still a frequent visitor and an even more frequent correspondent. Ben Tillett still sent him a flood of encouraging letters, and he still kept in touch with Minnie Pallister and the ever-faithful Jim Middleton. But he was more isolated politically than he had ever been. Though he still served on the Committee of Imperial Defence and the Defence Requirements Committee, as well as on a number of less important Cabinet committees, Baldwin rarely consulted him informally, and when he tried to make sure that his views were heard in discussion outside the Cabinet he was very often snubbed. He scarcely ever appeared at the dispatch box, and the newspapers ceased to pay attention to him. He had no patronage, no future, and hardly any following; when he appeared in the lobbies, he seemed lost and helpless, like a ghost from a vanished era.[95]

Meanwhile, his eyesight, general health and ability to concentrate all continued to decline. In April 1936, he had to have a minor operation, and spent two weeks in a nursing home recovering from it. In May he had another eye examination – noting afterwards that it had shown that 'much of my trouble arises from an overtired brain & have been advised to take six months rest.' In July, he contracted an eye infection, which kept him out of action for half a week. In August, he complained in a sad diary entry that his golf was deteriorating badly – 'one reason being that my head & eyes refuse to concentrate. They refuse to think.'[96] At the beginning of November, he confessed to Sir Alexander Grant that he was 'having to work much slower than I used to';[97] a few days later he collapsed during a speech by Baldwin at the Lord Mayor's Banquet, and had to be carried out into the corridor.[98] His handwriting deteriorated too, and his diary entries were often marred by spelling mistakes and omitted words; in conversation he was increasingly apt to make slips of the tongue and to forget people's names, sometimes with bizarre results. In December 1936, after a lunch at the House of Commons for the American airman, Charles Lindbergh, at which MacDonald was one of the guests, Harold Nicolson noted that while they were talking about the Oxford by-election, MacDonald 'turns to Lindbergh. "Now mark my words", he says, "that Professor Lindbergh is no good at all – I know him – no good at all". "Lindemann?" I suggest. "Of course", Ramsay asserts with a cursing gesture, as when one has missed a putt at golf. "Of course I meant Linderbergh." '[99]

George V's death in January 1936, had been a heavy blow to MacDonald; it is clear from his diary that he must have taken some time to recover from it. On January 20th, a few hours before George V died, a special Privy Council was held at Sandringham, so that the royal assent could be given to the proclamation setting up a council of state. The King, MacDonald noted was

sitting up in chair with three pillows propping him up. He had changed greatly; his voice was fairly firm but his body weak. I read the business in its usual form and after a slight pause he answered 'Approved' in the same tones as usual at the P.C. He seemed detached from us all & weary. Then he had to sign the warrant (or whatever it is called)[.] His right hand was plainly useless and lay out of sight on his leg. Dawson knelt by the table in front of him & helped him to manipulate his left, the fingers of which he kept drumming upon the warrant in front of him. 'I cannot concentrate' he said with a sighing smile. Dawson suggested he should help him by supporting the pen which seemed to be difficult for him to do. He said 'No I shall sign myself'. We waited looking on. At length he began, Dawson supporting the pen. The first mark on the paper is his abortive attempt to write 'George', & second is the usual mark which he then made with Dawson's help. Watching the struggle he went through to write [? make] his clearly expressed desire affection moved me to tears. Then we began to walk out of the bedroom. At first the King took no notice but was told that we were going. He looked at us & smiled. I was the last out & I shall never forget the look illuminated by affection (his eyes looked rather large) which he gave me & continued it as I went & bowed a second time – my final farewell to a gracious & kingly friend and a master whom I have served with all my heart.[100]

'What a change to whole outlook is death of King ... ,' he noted two days later. 'I feel that the link binding me [to] public life & making all I have to endure tolerable has broken.'[101]

An even more distressing blow came at the end of May, when a tribunal appointed under the 1921 Tribunals of Inquiry Act concluded that J. H. Thomas had leaked certain budget secrets to the Conservative M.P. for Balham and Tooting, Sir Alfred Butt, and to an old friend and business associate, Alfred Cosher Bates. It is not at all clear that the tribunal was right. The evidence against Thomas was circumstantial, and some of it, at least, would have been disallowed in an ordinary court. If he had acted as the tribunal suggested, he had clearly committed an offence under the Official Secrets Act, but he was never charged with having done so — much less found guilty. If he had been properly tried, with the normal safeguards against hearsay evidence in operation, he might well have been found innocent. On the other hand, there could be no doubt that Butt and Bates had both behaved in a distinctly suspicious fashion — insuring themselves heavily against increases in taxation which were included in the Budget soon afterwards; doing so, for no obvious reason, wholly or partially through nominees; and on material points failing to satisfy the tribunal that they were telling the truth. There could also be no doubt that they were both close friends of Thomas, and that he had been in a position to disclose budget secrets to them had he wished to do so. More damningly still, it had emerged in the course of the hearings that Bates had paid him £15,000 as an advance on the proceeds of an autobiography which he had not even started to write, and that in 1935 Butt had acted for him when he had insured himself for £1,000 in the event of there being a general election during the year — a transaction on which he had made a profit of more than £600.[102] The tribunal's verdict put the seal on his disgrace, but the hearings had already disgraced him before the verdict was announced. He sent a letter to Baldwin resigning from the Cabinet a week before the verdict was known. Three weeks later, he resigned from the House of Commons as well.

MacDonald watched all this with a kind of helpless agony. Thomas was now his oldest friend in politics — the only member of the attenuated National Labour group whose roots in the Labour movement went almost as deep as did his own; the only figure of consequence in their generation of Labour leaders who had stayed with him through all the upheavals of the last five years. At first, he convinced himself that all would be well. 'Thomas' defence now in hand of solicitor,' he noted loyally on May 8th. 'I hope for a fine vindication ... I suspect other Cabinet quarters from whom leakages have come — wirepullers who are in constant touch with certain magnates of the press.'[103] Little by little, however, his hopes collapsed. By May 10th, he had to admit to himself that 'T's associates may be his undoing. I can see the public interest shifting from whether there was a leakage to what is the character of T's friends. On that the "jury of the street" may condemn him.'[104] By the 12th he was 'haunted by the feeling that J.H.T. is to be condemned'; by the 19th he was convinced that Thomas 'cannot now be saved'.[105] But although he reluctantly came to believe that Thomas probably had let some secrets slip, he refused to condemn him for doing so. Thomas's fault, he insisted, was merely 'his well known one of being unable to hold his tongue ... He will have profited nothing; he will have had no thought of anyone profiting; he just wanted to show that he carried great secrets.'[106] It was Thomas's friends who were at fault for abusing his confidence: Baldwin was to blame for holding the Budget Cabinet too long before the Budget statement. The revelation of Thomas's gamble on the date of the general election clearly came as a shock, but he was prepared to forgive even that.

FI

'He was a Cabinet Minister,' MacDonald noted sadly; 'but I can see how it was done over glasses. The pity, the pity of it all.'[107]

On May 20th, MacDonald and Thomas agreed that Thomas now had no alternative but to leave the Government. Afterwards MacDonald noted:

> Thomas, son & I lunched in Strangers' Room H. of C. & discussed the position. T. had drafted letter to Baldwin resigning. I approved; there is nothing else to do ... Later. The letter has been handed to Baldwin — Thomas did not attend Cabinet. To think of the H. of C. without Thomas is impossible; my Fides Achites, with whom I discussed every plan & move & project, the one who has stood with me from the beginning right up to now, surely this cruel ending is only a nightmare! I sat in my room at Privy Council & H. of C. & tried to understand what was happening and that from this week J.H.T.'s foot would never enter again. I felt widowed and crushed. Men who he has rescued & whose children he has helped leer when I pass them; Opposition Labour gloats; many Tories are pleased.[108]

The sequel was even more painful. The tribunal's findings were delivered to Simon, now home secretary, on May 27th, and on the 28th MacDonald was told what they were. He spent the Whitsun recess in Lossiemouth, in a state of acute distress. 'Thomas['s] condemnation broadcasted [sic] at 6 this evening,' he noted on June 2nd. 'I am stunned though I knew it was coming ... Feel no inclination to see anybody or speak to anybody. Every thought is of Thomas.'[109] For a while, he seems to have thought that Thomas might be prosecuted under the Official Secrets Act, and looked forward to giving evidence on his behalf — noting belligerently that he would be able to say 'that I, had I been a betting man, would have betted for at least a month before the Cabinet that income tax would be raised, and that I never knew that a present of necessity put me under obligations to the giver.'[110] But that prospect soon vanished. By June 9th, he was back in London, feeling 'crushed & heartless'.[111] Two days later Thomas made a personal statement in the House announcing his decision to leave Parliament. For MacDonald, it was a harrowing experience. The day, he noted, would

> be forever marked as that when Thomas ended (I shall not say 'for ever') his public life. One feels at such times that the implacable machines of the Gods have got one in their grip. Like a sacrificial victim, one feels drugged & paralysed and waits almost in a stupor the grinding out of event. The House was crowded: desported [sic] itself at question time and then pulled itself together for the 'execution'. Thomas, wife, family had met in my room & one after another walked out to find their seats in the gallery. His swan song was finely done — just a touch or two of the Thomas imperfections, like the overlooking of a few hs, but the tone in thought & cadence & the touch were admirable, & he walked out with his mss. held by a corner & flapping as he went slowly down to the Bar, moved the House. I

noticed a gleam of enmity & triumph in one or two noted for bitterness &
all unloveliness ... I sit in whilst the P.M. and Attlee spoke but my nerves
were so hammered upon that I could stand no more.[112]

MacDonald had been growing more and more alienated from his colleagues
even before Thomas's fall. In bitter diary entry after bitter diary entry he complained that they made the key decisions behind his back; that, although he made
it clear that he was available for consultation whenever it was needed, his advice
was never sought; that Baldwin was 'putty' in the hands of his party: that
Chamberlain was 'elbowing, elbowing' his way to the prime ministership and
had been allowed to make himself the dominant influence in the Cabinet.[113]
After Thomas's departure his complaints became even more frequent. Many of
them were fairly trivial, concerning such niceties as Baldwin's failure to write
to him during the summer recess and refusal to talk seriously when they met at
the end of it. Others had a deeper origin. Like many elderly men, MacDonald
found his thoughts turning more and more frequently to his past. He contemplated writing an autobiography, and began what he hoped would become the
opening chapter;[114] though he remained bitterly contemptuous of the official
Labour Party leadership, he became increasingly conscious of his roots in the
Labour movement. He filled his diary with references to internal Labour Party
politics, some of them savagely hostile, but others surprisingly sympathetic; in
more contemplative mood he noted, in the course of an entry on his seventieth
birthday, that the 1931 break 'has not been good for me ... my kith and kin are
the common folk.'[115] His Conservative colleagues had often grated on him in
the past. In such moods, they grated on him even more.

As time went on, his antipathy to them was strengthened by a more immediate difference. On the abdication crisis in December, 1936, MacDonald and the
rest of the Cabinet were at one. On the Spanish civil war — the great litmus test
of political attitudes in late 1936 and 1937 — their attitudes were very different.
At first MacDonald was torn. Though he was bitterly hostile to Franco, he was
afraid that the Republic might fall under Communist control and agreed that
the right policy for Britain was to remain neutral.[116] Once it had become clear
that Hitler and Mussolini were intervening heavily on the Fascist side, however, his sympathies swung towards the Republicans; and, as they did so, he
became more and more shocked by the contrary response of the rest of the
Cabinet. The Foreign Office's non-intervention policy, he noted at the end of
August 1936, 'has enabled the dictators to give the greatest help they can to
their fellow, Franco, and adds to an unfortunate impression that we are growing
weak and like Rome unable or unwilling to guard our frontiers'.[117] At the end
of November he complained, more succinctly, 'Enthusiasm for Franco growing
in Tory breasts'.[118] By early February 1937, he had detected a more fundamental
clash of loyalties. In Cabinet, he noted on February 3rd,

the casual & trifling remarks made (which generally reveal more of a person's mind than those more considered) are most revealing. The things said on the war in Spain are of the traditional Tory obscurantist tradition & the ignorance of Socialism[,] Bolshevism and Nazi-ism revealed makes me smile in grim wonder. The hard meaning of the European drift with Nazi-ism in the lead is not understood by the Cabinet, but the appalling thing to me [is] that it is democracy which I see to be breaking down.[119]

By now, his official life was almost over. Some time before, Baldwin had decided that he would leave office after George VI's coronation in May 1937; in late January or early February, after another warning from Duke-Elder that he needed six months' rest, MacDonald made up his mind to do the same. On March 10th, he discussed the coming changes with Chamberlain, who was to be Baldwin's successor. Chamberlain offered him a peerage, but he declined; they also discussed Malcolm's future, and Chamberlain gave an assurance that Malcolm would be included in the new Cabinet.[120] During the next few weeks, most of MacDonald's energies went into presiding over the coronation committee;[121] in the intervals he began to lay plans for a long holiday in South America. At the beginning of April he made his last appearance on an international stage as the head of the British delegation to the international sugar conference in London. On the 23rd, he arranged the details of his coming resignation with Baldwin; once again he was offered a peerage and once again he declined. On May 12th, George VI was crowned, and on the 26th MacDonald attended his last Cabinet. 'The P.M. sat with no life nor feeling,' he noted bitterly. 'At 5 asked him if I could go as agenda was finishing … He said I could. Felt awkward. Our companionship was ending: one of the most remarkable experiments in our history ending like an afternoon tea party! I lingered a minute: I went.'[122] Next day he had an audience with the King. For the third time he refused a peerage; as a sign of his appreciation the King gave him signed photographs of himself and the Queen. On the 28th, Baldwin formally tendered the Government's resignation and MacDonald ceased to be a minister.

The rest of the story is soon told. MacDonald spent most of the summer in Lossiemouth, noting when he arrived that his head had 'almost refused to work'.[123] After three months pottering about, he returned to London in mid-September to begin the preparation for his South American tour. At some stage during the summer or early autumn, the Robertons gave a small party for him at their home in Glasgow. With some difficulty, they managed to persuade most of their I.L.P. friends to come, even though few of them had spoken to MacDonald since 1931; to the great embarrassment of everyone present, MacDonald wound up the occasion with a speech insisting that he was still a socialist and always had been.[124] Early in November he gave a farewell party himself, at his house in Hampstead. Citrine, who was one of the guests, noticed that, although there were many people there, he could identify no one else as belonging to the Labour movement. As he and his wife were leaving, MacDonald put his hand on his shoulder and said, 'Don't go yet, Citrine.' They stayed and, as Citrine put it in his memoirs, found MacDonald 'Sitting at the top of the staircase, bending forward with his head between his hands'. MacDonald looked exhausted and said wearily, 'Oh, I am tired'; after a brief exchange about his coming holiday, the Citrines made their way downstairs. When they got to the bottom, MacDonald called out from the top stair, 'Why don't you get the T.U.C. to send you to South America with me, Citrine? It will do you good.'[125]

On November 4th, MacDonald and Sheila left London for Liverpool. There was a small crowd at the station to see them off, including some reporters. 'I have no plans,' MacDonald told them. 'I am in search of that most elusive of all forms of happiness — rest.'[126] On the 5th he and Sheila set sail in the liner, *Reina del Pacifico*. On the 6th, the ship called in at La Rochelle, where MacDonald was knocked down in the street by a bicycle.[127] On the 7th, he felt seasick after playing an energetic game of deck quoits, and went to his cabin early. On the morning of the 9th, he played deck quoits again, and after lunch he fell ill and sent for the ship's doctor. By the afternoon he felt better, and had tea with the Bishop of Nassau. At 6.30 he sent for the doctor again. At 7.45 he died of heart failure.[128]

The *Reina del Pacifico* arrived in Bermuda on November 15th. From there, MacDonald's body was taken back to England on the cruiser, H.M.S. *Apollo*. On the morning of the 25th it was landed at Devonport, and from there it was taken by train to London. At noon next day, a public funeral service was held at Westminster Abbey; during the afternoon, MacDonald's body was cremated after a private service in Golders Green. That night, the ashes were taken by train to Lossiemouth, where they were greeted by a party of MacDonald's boyhood friends. At 1.45 on November 27th a short service was held at the Hillocks. The Orpheus Choir sang 'I to the hills will lift mine eyes' and 'The Lord's My Shepherd'; Pipe-Major Reid of the Highland Light Infantry played the lament, 'The Flowers of the Forest'. Then MacDonald's ashes were taken to Spynie churchyard, and buried in the grave overlooking the Moray Firth in which Margaret's had been buried twenty-six years before.

Epilogue

ONLY part of the story ends in Spynie churchyard. As we have seen, the cloud of hostility and contempt which had enveloped MacDonald in his last years lingered on for almost a generation, obscuring his achievements and distorting even his failures; though the hatreds of the 1930s have since died down, his place in history remains unusually uncertain. It would be presumptuous to imply that it can now be established in some definitive sense, *sub specie aeternitatis*. The historian is not a kind of celestial chief justice, sentencing the guilty and setting free the innocent. He is part of the process he describes, and his judgments can never be more than provisional. Yet if we are to learn the lessons of Mac-Donald's career — and there is not much point in studying it if there are no lessons to be learned — a tentative assessment must be offered, if only as a contribution to a continuing debate.

The two charges most often brought against him are that he was a vain and snobbish social climber, who betrayed his party and ideals, and that he was an impractical dreamer, who could not cope with the problems of government. The truth is more complicated and, in an odd way, less comfortable. His political creed was undoubtedly utopian, and his platform rhetoric, like that of most of the great orators of his generation, strikes a modern ear as sentimental. But, as he showed at innumerable committee meetings and international conferences, he was quite capable of mastering formidable masses of detail, and his approach to economic problems was surprisingly hard-headed. He had personal weaknesses, of course, though snobbery was not among them. He was certainly vain, though no vainer than most successful politicians. He was also over-sensitive, suspicious and inclined to self-pity. At the same time, he was kindly, honourable, remarkably courageous and remarkably consistent. The MacDonald who watched in despair while 'the militarists poked out their heads' in the navy debate in March, 1934 was the MacDonald who had struggled unavailingly against Grey's foreign policy before 1914. The MacDonald who largely determined the Labour Party's 1929 election programme was the MacDonald who had written *Socialism and Society* a quarter of a century before. The same is true of his actions in August, 1931. The attitudes and beliefs which guided him during the disputes that broke the Labour Government were the attitudes and beliefs which had guided him for most of his political life. Once he had come to the conclusion that it would be a disaster for the country if the parity were abandoned, he had no choice but to act as he did. If he had acted differently, he would have been untrue to his convictions and untrue to himself.

But although he had only one choice then, he had had many more choices earlier. Given the state of economic knowledge at the time, among the opponents of economic orthodoxy as well as among its supporters, it is doubtful if any Government could have solved the problems facing Britain in 1930 and 1931: as we have seen, the notion that there was, even in embryo, a clear 'radical' alternative to the Government's economic policy, which it could have followed if only it had been more intelligent and more courageous, does not fit the facts. All the same, solutions could have been sought with more energy and imagination; if they had been, it is possible that the state of economic knowledge would have improved more rapidly than it did. More obviously still, the one, albeit only partial, solution which was already in existence could have been applied. That solution was, of course, protection – the only policy which, as Keynes pointed out, was both desirable in itself and calculated to please the business community, a revival of whose confidence was a precondition of recovery. It was also MacDonald's policy; and, even so, it was not applied. The 1929 Government faced an appalling crisis, unprecedented in scale and complexity, which no Government at the time knew how to solve. The fact remains that it failed: and that it failed with MacDonald at its head. Prime ministers usually get the credit when their Governments do well. They usually deserve at least a share of the blame when their Governments do badly. MacDonald is no exception.

His failures after 1929 can be understood, however, only against the background of his achievements before then. The part he played in building up the Labour Party before the First World War is now well known, and needs no discussion here. His role during and after the war is less familiar. In the fifteen years from 1914 to 1929 the Labour Party, against what most observers would at first have considered to be the odds, replaced the Liberals as the main anti-Conservative party in Britain. Partly because the process was completed so quickly, and partly because its beneficiaries often talked in this way themselves, it has sometimes seemed in retrospect that there was something inevitable about it: that the men and women who took part in it were, so to speak, the agents of a law of political sociology which could not have been successfully defied. The reality is more interesting. It is true that profound social forces were at work, and that these were bound to have an effect of some kind on the structure of politics. It does not follow that they were bound to have the effect which they actually had. British politics in this period were extraordinarily fluid: more fluid than they had been since the middle of the nineteenth century, and more fluid than they have ever been since. That they eventually settled down into the mould we have known for more than forty years was due, not to some mysterious manifest destiny, but to the skill, cunning and determination of those who struggled to ensure that they did so. And MacDonald was foremost in that struggle.

Whether or not it would have had the same outcome if he had not been there to take part in it can never be known. What is certain is that, in a number of critical episodes, Labour's approach to it was determined largely by him and that, to a remarkable degree, it followed the course which he wanted it to take. Given the social changes of the previous fifty years, the divisions in the Liberal Party and the extension of the suffrage which took place at the end of the First World War, it would have been almost impossible to prevent the Labour Party from establishing itself as a strong parliamentary force at some stage in the early 1920s. But it was one thing to become a strong parliamentary force: another to become, permanently and without question, the main anti-Conservative party in the country. As MacDonald pointed out *ad nauseum*, the ground which the Labour Party gained between 1918 and 1922 was vulnerable to counter-attack. If the Liberals had played their cards more skilfully and the Labour Party less so, they might have recaptured enough of that ground to push the Labour Party back into third place. If they had done so, the party system we know today might never have taken shape, and the course of British history might have been quite different. Similar considerations apply to the gains which the Labour Party made between 1922 and 1929. The notion that the Liberal Party of the late 1920s was a spent force, doomed to electoral extinction, does not stand up to serious examination. It had plenty of money and plenty of ideas; its leader was the greatest figure in twentieth-century British politics. It had lost much of its old support in the constituencies, particularly in industrial areas. But some of that support had been lost comparatively recently, and might have been won back. To assume that it was lost irrevocably because working-class voters in industrial seats could never again have been persuaded to vote across class lines is to beg one of the central questions in recent British history. Class is not the only influence on voting behaviour, even in Britain; in North America it is, notoriously, a weaker influence than it is here. What Lloyd George was trying to do in the late 1920s was, in effect, to push British politics along the North American road. The fact that he failed does not prove that he was bound to fail.

To become the main anti-Conservative party in Britain, the Labour Party had to come decisively ahead of the Liberals, not just in one election, but in several. It had to create a situation in which it was clear that the Liberals could not reasonably hope to form a Government themselves, and that the choice lay between itself and the Conservative Party. It had also to create a situation in which Liberals faced with that choice would vote for it rather than for the Conservatives. To do all these things, it had to win and hold the support, not just of class conscious trade unionists and convinced socialists, but of numbers of people who had normally thought of themselves as Liberals in the past or had been brought up in families which had normally thought of themselves as

Liberals. It had to convince such people that, although it was a working-class party, it was not an exclusively working-class party: that although it looked forward to the total transformation of society, it could run the society in which it found itself as competently as the other parties could. It had, in short, to transform itself from the 'Labour Alliance' of the pre-war years into the 'great progressive party', embracing the more radical sections of the old Liberal Party as well as the trade unions and the socialist societies, of which MacDonald had dreamed intermittently since the 1890s.

It would be wrong to suggest that he was solely responsible for that transformation. Henderson played an important part in it as well. So did Sidney Webb, and so, in a different way, did Snowden. So did such intellectual converts as Cole, Tawney, Hobson, Brailsford, Clifford Allen and a long list of others. So, for that matter, did the fastidious Asquithian grandees, who seemed incapable of realizing that times had changed since the setting of the Edwardian sun; so, too, did the less fastidious proclivities of Lloyd George, whose conduct in office might have been calculated to drive idealistic Radicals into Labour's arms. But there can be no doubt that MacDonald was the central figure. His stand during the war made him, so to speak, the obverse of Lloyd George. He was the man of integrity, who had upheld the principles of liberal internationalism when their old champions had deserted to the enemy, the natural leader of the dissenting Radicals who campaigned for a compromise peace during the war and for a revision of the Versailles settlement thereafter. His role after the war was more important still. Others did more to build up the party machine and to maintain the links between the machine and the trade unions which paid for it. No one did more to propagate the ideology which the machine was supposed to serve or to shape the image which it projected to the voters. He made bad mistakes, of course, particularly in his handling of his colleagues; and it was partly because of these that the anger and bitterness of 1931 went so deep and lasted so long. But his successes easily outweighed his failures. Under his leadership, the Labour Party seemed both adventurous and safe: a party of government which had not ceased to be a party of protest. It was because of this that it became the natural home for disaffected Liberals who had been shaken out of their old loyalties by the war and its aftermath, and went on to enrol most, if not all, of the 'Liberal England' of the past (to say nothing of Liberal Wales and Liberal Scotland) under its banner. His monument was the wide-ranging, heterogeneous Labour coalition that won the 1945 election: the lineal descendant of the Liberal coalition of 1906. Few of the bright young university men who found themselves elected as Labour members of Parliament in 1945 would have acknowledged a debt to MacDonald. They owed it even so.

That was his achievement: it was also his tragedy. By 1945 the Labour Party was ready to change society, and Britain was ready for a radical Labour Government. In the 1920s neither of these things was true. MacDonald's Labour Party was like a lanky schoolboy who has outgrown his strength – all reach, and no grasp. It had high ideals, but few ideas about how to put them into practice. It knew what it was against, but except in the most general terms it did not really know what it was for. It sought a new social order, but its attitudes on a large range of practical problems were shot through, often without its realizing the fact, with assumptions derived from the social order against which it was in revolt. It rejected deflation, but it also rejected protection, without which there could be no alternative to deflation. It had to appeal, moreover, to a profoundly conservative country, which was dimly aware that it had lost its old supremacy but was profoundly unwilling to recognize the fact explicitly, and which felt instinctively that all change was likely to be for the worse. It would be absurd to suggest that MacDonald was ahead of his party or his country: the real charge to be made against him is that he was not, and that he did too little to lead them along more radical paths. But it would be equally absurd to portray him as a brake on more adventurous colleagues. His greatest error was to reject Keynes's advice in August, 1931 and to try to stick to a parity which was already doomed. But, as we have seen, there is no evidence that that error was challenged by any member of the Cabinet. His opponents objected, not to holding the parity, but to the policies without which the parity could not be held. The same is true of the arguments over public works. MacDonald had been sceptical of the public-works solution to unemployment from the start, but so were most of his colleagues: so, for that matter, was the pamphlet which G. D. H. Cole had written for the Labour Party before the 1929 election. All the evidence suggests that, not only MacDonald, but the entire Cabinet, was convinced by the Ministry of Transport's objections to a big road programme. On protection, MacDonald was less orthodox than the Cabinet as a whole, and can be criticized, not for giving too little weight to his colleagues' views, but for giving them too much.

In their pain and anger after 1931 many Labour men and women came close to suggesting that the moral of MacDonald's career was merely that the Labour Party had had the misfortune to saddle itself for nine years with a weak and disagreeable leader. In doing so they belittled him, and also belittled themselves. In fact, he emerges from the record as a decent and likeable man, who, for most of his term of office, led his party with conspicuous skill. The true moral is less palatable. It is that a radical party requires, not merely high ideals and skilful leadership, but intellectual coherence and a willingness to jettison cherished assumptions in the face of changing realities. It is an easy moral to formulate. Half a century of British history bears witness to the fact that it is not so easy to practise.

A Note on Sources

THIS book is based primarily on the Ramsay MacDonald papers, which were deposited in the Public Record Office in London when I finished working on them. The collection consists of some 1600 files, divided by the P.R.O. into eight broad categories: Official-Public, Official-Private, Personal, Indices, Political-Party, Political-Public, Political-Constituency and Miscellaneous. Of these, the first, containing more than 600 files (the vast majority of which were maintained by MacDonald's Private Office staff while he was in office), is by far the largest. The material in the first two relates exclusively to MacDonald's periods in office; categories 3, 5, 6, 7 and 8 contain material spanning virtually the whole of his career, though the correspondence files from about 1915 to about 1922 are disappointingly thin. With the exception of the fourth, I have made extensive use of all of them; MacDonald's diary has been allotted by the P.R.O. to category 8. In my note references to the MacDonald papers, I have cited the P.R.O. classification numbers – the first referring to the category, and the second to a particular file or group of files within that category.

Next in importance to the material in the MacDonald papers come Mac-Donald's articles and books; and published reports of his speeches, of his election campaigns and of his activities at international conferences. A full bibliography of his political and literary writings would fill several pages; those which seem to me most significant are all referred to in the text or the notes. It is, however, worth mentioning that I found the files of *The Socialist*, *Seedtime*, the *Ethical World* and the *New Age* of particular value for the period before 1900; those of the *Echo*, the *Leicester Pioneer* and the *Socialist Review* of particular value for the period from 1900 to 1914; and those of *Forward*, the *Labour Leader*, the *New Leader* and the *Socialist Review* of particular value for the period from 1914 to 1929. For the period from 1919 to 1922, when the correspondence files in the MacDonald papers are thin, and when there are large gaps in his diary, his weekly columns in *Forward* and his monthly editorial in the *Socialist Review* are indispensable. For reports of his speeches, I have relied mainly on *Hansard*, the Labour Party and I.L.P. conference reports, and reports in *The Times*, the *Manchester Guardian* and a wide variety of local newspapers, all of which are mentioned in the notes. The local newspaper press is of particular importance for his various election campaigns — notably for his campaigns as candidate for Dover and Southampton in the 1890s, for Leicester in 1900, 1906 and 1918, for Woolwich in 1921, for Aberavon in 1922 and for Seaham Harbour in 1931 and 1935. His activities at international conferences from 1929 onwards can be traced in successive volumes of the published British diplomatic documents, edited by E. L. Woodward and Rohan Butler. My notes give full references to the sources I have used for his activities as foreign secretary in 1924 and for his role at conferences of the Socialist International from 1919 to 1922.

I have also made substantial use of the Cabinet and Cabinet committee minutes and papers at the P.R.O. — an indispensable source for his periods as prime minister. The Labour Party archives at Transport House were as indispensable for the period from 1900 to 1914, and for various episodes during the 1920s and the second Labour Government. I have relied heavily on the archives of the Labour and Socialist International at the International Institute for Social History in Amsterdam for my account of MacDonald's activities as secretary of the International, and rather less heavily on the minutes of the Fabian Society executive for my account of his career in the 1890s. I have also found useful material in the following private papers or collections of papers:

Baldwin papers (Cambridge University Library)
Bibesco papers (courtesy of Princess Bibesco)
Winston Churchill papers (courtesy of Mr Martin Gilbert)
Herbert Gladstone papers (British Museum)
Francis Johnson papers — correspondence of Keir Hardie and Bruce Glasier (courtesy of Mr Francis Johnson; transcripts, courtesy of Dr Kenneth Morgan and Dr Henry Pelling)
Londonderry papers (courtesy of Lady Mairi Bury; Northern Ireland Public Record Office)
Malcolm MacDonald diary (courtesy, Rt Hon. Malcolm MacDonald)
Middleton papers (courtesy, Mrs Lucy Middleton)
Morel papers (L.S.E. Library)
Mure papers (courtesy, Mrs Cecily Mure, née Gordon-Cumming)
Passfield papers (L.S.E. Library)
Ponsonby papers (Bodleian Library, Oxford)
Ponsonby diary (courtesy, Lord Ponsonby of Shulbrede)
Roberton papers (courtesy, Lady Helen Roberton)
Strauss diary (courtesy, Rt Hon. George Strauss, M.P.)
Ivor Thomas papers (courtesy, Mrs Sheila Lockhead)

The books and articles on which I have relied most heavily are all listed in my notes and do not need repeating here. It would, however, be churlish not to acknowledge the debt I owe to Dr Henry Pelling's still indispensable, *The Origins of the Labour Party*, to Bealey and Pelling's *Labour and Politics, 1900–1906*, to Dr Kenneth Morgan's *Keir Hardie* and to Clegg, Fox and Thompson's *A*

History of British Trade Unions since 1889, for the period before 1914; to Julius Braunthal's splendid *History of the International* for the period after the First World War; to Alan Bullock's *The Life and Times of Ernest Bevin*, Maurice Cowling's *The Impact of Labour, 1920–1924*, R. Page Arnot's *The Miners: Years of Struggle* and Stephen Roskill's *Hankey Man of Secrets* for the period from 1923 to 1929; to Dr W. H. Janeway's Cambridge Ph.D. Thesis, 'The Economic Policy of the Second Labour Government' and Dr R. J. Skidelsky's *Politicians and the Slump* for the second Labour Government; to Dr David Wrench's University of Wales Ph.D. thesis, 'Aspects of National Government Policy, 1931–1935' for the National Government; and to W. G. Runciman's *Relative Deprivation and Social Justice*, which has influenced my approach to the whole inter-war period more than any other single book on the subject. In a different category are the memoirs and published diaries of politicians, civil servants and writers active in the period. Of these, I have derived most benefit from Margaret Cole's *The Life of G. D. H. Cole* (not strictly a memoir, but it can be regarded as one), M. A. Hamilton's *Remembering My Good Friends*, Thomas Jones's *Whitehall Diary* (edited by Keith Middlemass), Harold Nicolson's *Diaries and Letters, 1930–1939*, edited by Nigel Nicolson, John Paton's *Left Turn*, Beatrice Webb's diaries edited by Margaret Cole, and Lord Vansittart's *The Mist Procession*. Last, but by no means least, I should mention Egon Wertheimer's *Portrait of the Labour Party*, which seems to me one of the most perceptive studies of its subject ever published.

Abbreviations

B.D.	*Documents on British Foreign Policy, 1919–1939* (ed. E. L. Woodward and Rohan Butler). Followed by series and volume numbers.
B.S.P.	British Socialist Party.
C.P.	Cabinet paper. Followed by Cabinet office serial number.
Cabinet	Cabinet conclusions (i.e. minutes). Followed by Cabinet office serial number.
CAB.	Other Cabinet records. Followed by P.R.O. classification number.
C.I.D.	Committee of Imperial Defence.
D.G.F.P.	*Documents on German Foreign Policy.*
D.R.C.	Defence Requirements Committee.
D.C. (M) (32)	Ministerial Committee on the 1932 Disarmament Conference, i.e. the Cabinet's Disarmament Committee.
Diary	MacDonald's diary. P.R.O. classification, 8/1.
F.O.	Foreign Office.
I.L.P.	Independent Labour Party.
I.L.P.C.R.	*Independent Labour Party Conference Report.*
I.S.B.	International Socialist Bureau.
King's letter	Daily letter sent to the King by the prime minister during parliamentary sessions reporting on the House of Commons sitting of that day.
L.C.C.	London County Council.
L.P.C.R.	*Labour Party Conference Report.*
L.P.L.F.	Labour Party Letter Files at Transport House.
L.R.C.	Labour Representation Committee.
L.S.E.	London School of Economics.
L.S.I.	Archives of the Labour and Socialist International at the International Institute for Social History, Amsterdam.
MDP	MacDonald papers. Followed by P.R.O. classification number.
N.A.C.	National Administrative Council (of the I.L.P.).
N.E.C.	National Executive Committee (of the Labour Party).

Notebook	MacDonald's notebook. Used as a diary when not in London. P.R.O. classification, 8/1.
P.P.S.	Parliamentary Private Secretary.
P.R.O.	Public Record Office.
S.D.F.	Social Democratic Federation.
S.D.P.	Social Democratic Party.
S.H.R.A.	Scottish Home Rule Association.
T.U.C.	Trades Union Congress.
U.D.C.	Union of Democratic Control.

Notes

Chapter 1   Lossiemouth

1 Harold Nicolson, *Diaries and Letters 1930–1939*, ed. Nigel Nicolson, vol. 1 (1966), p. 287.
2 Charles Loch Mowat, *Britain Between the Wars* (1955), p. 142.
3 Lord Elton, *The Life of James Ramsay MacDonald* (1939).
4 L. MacNeill Weir, *The Tragedy of Ramsay MacDonald* (1938). Other biographies and memoirs in this category are: Viscount Snowden, *Autobiography* (2 vols., 1934); M. A. Hamilton, *Arthur Henderson* (1938), and *Remembering My Good Friends* (1944); Fenner Brockway, *Inside the Left* (1942); Raymond Postgate, *Life of George Lansbury* (1951); Francis Williams, *Ernest Bevin* (1952); Hugh Dalton, *Call Back Yesterday* (1953); J. R. Clynes, *Memoirs* (particularly vol. 2, 1937); and M. I. Cole (ed.), *Beatrice Webb's Diaries, 1912–24* (1952) and *1924–32* (1956).
5 Labour Party, *The Rise of the Labour Party* (1946).
6 Labour Party, *Marching On* (1950).
7 See particularly Henry Pelling, *The Origins of the Labour Party* (1954); F. Bealey and H. Pelling, *Labour and Politics 1900–1906* (1958); A. J. P. Taylor, *The Troublemakers* (1964); D. C. Watt, *Personalities and Policies* (1965); R. Bassett, *1931: Political Crisis* (1958); Richard W. Lyman, *The First Labour Government 1924* (1957); A. J. P. Taylor, *English History 1914–1945* (1965).
8 Of particular interest is Wilson's reference to the 1931 crisis: 'Economically, the Labour Government of 1929 to 1931 ... was destroyed by doctrines and by policies which no-one of any Party would defend today. Yet in the final agony, I think we can all of us here, for that reason, only barely comprehend the urgency and compulsion of those outside pressures ...

'I believe — and it is hard even today to be objective — that he made that decision, in my view, because he sincerely felt that he was putting the survival of his country above the survival of his Party, but at the same time he felt that long-term and perhaps not so long-term, the Party would return to power.'

9 Extract from minute-book of Alves Free Kirk Session in possession of Mrs Ishbel Peterkin.
10 Interview, Allan Maclean.
11 Elton, op. cit., p. 17; MDP 3/49.
12 Interview, Allan Maclean.
13 Cf. particularly *Wanderings and Excursions* (1925), pp. 17–39.
14 Royal Commission on the Employment of children, young persons and women in Agriculture (1869), *Fourth Report*, Appendix, Part II, pp. 27–8.
15 Elton, op. cit., p. 17.
16 Interviews, Allan Maclean, William Sims.
17 Interview, Captain Dunbar; Charles Rampini, *A History of Moray and Nairn* (Edinburgh, 1897), pp. 333–40.
18 *New Statistical Account of Scotland*, vol. 13, Elgin, p. 147.
19 Ibid., p. 158.
20 Rampini, op. cit., pp. 279, 368–71.
21 Elton, op. cit., p. 34.
22 Royal Commission, *Fourth Report*, p. 35.
23 Ibid., p. 40.
24 Ibid., p. 34.
25 MacDonald to Lord Tweedsmuir (John Buchan), June 24th, 1937, MDP 6/102 green; 6/162.
26 Drainie School log-books.
27 Ibid., entries for 1875, March 2nd, 1878, 1882.
28 MacDonald, 'The Old Dominie', *Wanderings and Excursions*, pp. 21–8.
29 Elton, op. cit., pp. 29 and 37; 'The Old Dominie', pp. 22–3; MacDonald, 'The Top of the Knowe', *Wanderings and Excursions*, pp. 36–7.
30 MDP 3/58.
31 'The Old Dominie', p. 24.
32 Elton, op. cit., p. 28.
33 Ibid., pp. 25–6; MDP 3/57.
34 MDP 3/57.
35 Elton, op. cit., p. 36; MDP 3/57.
36 MDP 3/57.
37 *Elgin Courant*, November 20th, 24th, 27th, December 4th, 1885.
38 Ibid., July 9th, 1886.
39 MDP 3/57.
40 Elton, op. cit., pp. 33–4.
41 MDP 3/57.
42 Drainie School log-books.
43 Elton, op. cit., p. 39.
44 Interview, Allan Maclean; Elton, op. cit., p. 40.

Chapter 2 London

1 Samuel Bryher, *An Account of the Labour and Socialist Movement in Bristol* (1929).
2 *Justice*, October 31st, 1885.
3 Elton, op. cit., p. 44.
4 Ibid., p. 49.
5 Bryher, op. cit., p. 31.
6 Ibid., p. 30.
7 *Justice*, December 12th, 1885.
8 Bryher, op. cit.; Pelling, op. cit., p. 43.
9 MDP 3/63.
10 Elton, op. cit., p. 53.
11 Ibid.; Herbert Tracey, *J. Ramsay MacDonald* (1924), p. 29.
12 MDP 3/1.
13 *Christian Socialist* (February 1886).
14 Ibid. (May 1886).
15 *Socialist* (August 1886).
16 MDP 5/211.
17 MacDonald to Mr Stewart, September 18th, 1887, letter in the possession of Mrs Margaret Sutherland.
18 Elton, op. cit., p. 54.
19 MDP 3/63.
20 MDP 3/66.
21 Elton, op. cit., pp. 56–7.
22 Ibid., p. 57; interview with William Sims.
23 Elton, op. cit., p. 57.
24 Conor Cruise O'Brien, *Parnell and His Party* (1957), p. 275.
25 *Elgin Courant*, September 13th, 17th, 20th, 24th, 27th, October 1st, 4th, 11th, 1889.
26 MDP 5/9.
27 Minute-book of the London Section of the Scottish Home Rule Association, MDP 5/54.
28 S.H.R.A. minutes, April 7th, 1888, MDP 5/54.
29 Ibid., *passim*, MDP 5/54.
30 *Dover Telegraph*, December 7th and 14th, 1892; *Dover Express*, December 16th, 1892.
31 Gwyther to MacDonald, June 8th, 1890, MDP 5/1; February 25th, 1891, MDP 5/2; May 23rd, 1892, MDP 5/3; Permit to visit Mouten Hadley Common, September 7th, 1891, MDP 5/2; Accounts of Children's Fund left by Mrs Gwyther, MDP 5/56.
32 Cutting in MDP 6/195. This is dated March 24th, 1894; but in a speech at Dover in 1892 MacDonald said he joined the St Pancras Parliament 'some

six years ago'; *Dover Telegraph*, November 2nd, 1892.

33 Sidney Webb to MacDonald, January 22nd, 1890, MDP 5/1.

34 Webb to MacDonald, January 20th, 1890, MDP 5/1. Webb to Beatrice Potter, September 7th, 1891, Passfield papers.

35 Emily Troup to MacDonald, December 31st, 1891, MDP 5/2; Notice of South Place Ethical Society 5/215.

36 Pelling, op. cit., pp. 34–5; Edward R. Pease, *The History of the Fabian Society* (1925, reprinted 1963), pp. 28–36.

37 J. R. MacDonald, 'The New Fellowship', *Seedtime* (April 1892).

38 Edith Lees to MacDonald, February 3rd, 1890, MDP 5/1.

39 *Seedtime* (April 1890).

40 Elton, op. cit., pp. 64–5; Edith Lees to MacDonald, May 22nd, 1891, MDP 5/2.

41 Olivier to MacDonald, April 4th, 1892, MDP 5/3.

42 Lulman to MacDonald, March 17th, 1891, MDP 5/2.

43 Edith Lees to MacDonald, September 25th, 1891, MDP 5/2.

44 Edith Lees to MacDonald, September 27th, 1891, MDP 5/2.

45 Edith Lees to MacDonald, September 29th, 1891, MDP 5/2.

46 E. M. Ellis (*née* Lees) to MacDonald, April 6th, 1892, MDP 5/3.

47 *Seedtime* (April 1893).

48 Letters from 'Mary' to MacDonald, mostly n.d., MDP 5/1–4.

49 Gwyther to MacDonald, July 24th, 1891, MDP 5/2.

50 MacDonald to Gwyther, n.d., MDP 5/2.

51 Draft of novel in MDP 3A/103.

52 Ibid.

Chapter 3   Dover, Southampton and Bayswater

1 Acting Editor of *New Review* to MacDonald, August 19th, 1891, MDP 3A/2; W. Robertson Nicoll to MacDonald, February 10th, 1892; W. L. Courtney to MacDonald, January 15th, 1892, MDP 3A/3.

2 Competition Editor of Dundee *People's Journal* to MacDonald, October 17th, 1892, MDP 3A/3. Dundee *People's Journal*, Christmas number, November 29th, 1892.

3 Statements in MDP 3A/3.

4 Notices in MDP 5/216; Pease to MacDonald, October 4th, 5th and 7th, 1892, MDP 5/3.

5 *Dover Express*, June 17th, 1892, and August 12th, 1892.

6 Ibid., August 12th, 1892.

7 *Dover Telegraph*, October 12th, 1892.

8 Ibid.

9 Ibid.

10 F. Garrett to MacDonald, October 10th, 1892, MDP 7/1.
11 *Dover Express*, October 7th, 1892.
12 Ibid.
13 *The New Charter*, section I, MDP 7/39.
14 *Dover Telegraph*, June 28th, 1893.
15 *Southampton Times*, April 21st, 1894.
16 John Randolph to MacDonald, April 28th, 1894, MDP 7/40.
17 *Southampton Times*, May 21st, 1894.
18 Ibid., June 9th, 1894.
19 Anonymous article, almost certainly by MacDonald, in *Seedtime* (July 1894).
20 *Southampton Times*, July 21st, 1894.
21 Elton, op. cit., pp. 68–9.
22 MacDonald to Crisp, July 16th, 1894, published in *Southampton Times*, August 11th, 1894.
23 *Southampton Times*, July 21st, 1894.
24 Ibid., July 7th, 1894.
25 Ibid., August 4th, 1894.
26 Ibid., October 6th, 1894.
27 Ibid., July 6th, 1895.
28 Ibid., July 20th, 1895.
29 Ibid., November 30th, 1895.
30 Ibid., July 20th, 1895.
31 Ibid., August 31st, 1895.
32 Viscount Samuel, *Memoirs* (1945), pp. 26–7.
33 John H. Aldridge to J. H. Weber, copy in MDP 7/40.
34 H. Cobb to MacDonald, December 12th and 16th, 1895, MDP 7/40.
35 J. H. Weber to MacDonald, December 30th, 1895, MDP 7/40.
36 Envelope marked 'various', MDP 7/40.
37 Weber to MacDonald, January 8th, 1896, MDP 7/40.
38 D. Bicker-Caarten to MacDonald, January 15th, 1896, MDP 7/40.
39 Weber to MacDonald, January 15th, 1896, MDP 7/40.
40 Weber to MacDonald, February 6th, 1896, MDP 7/40.
41 *Southampton Observer*, February 8th, 1896.
42 Ibid., February 29th, 1896.
43 The phrase was Bernard Shaw's; quoted in Elton, op. cit., p. 21.
44 Fabian Society, executive minutes, March 15th, 1895.
45 Beatrice Webb, diary, October 18th, 1895, Passfield papers.
46 Cf. Sir Sydney Caine, *The History of the Foundation of the London School of Economics and Political Science* (1963); Fabian Society, executive minutes, October 5th, 1894, March 29th, 1895, June 21st, 1895; Beatrice Webb, diary, April 18th, 1896, Passfield papers.
47 Caine, op. cit., p. 61.

48 Pease to MacDonald, April 8th, 1896, MDP 5/6.

49 Pease to MacDonald, April 9th, 1896, MDP 5/6.

50 Fabian Society, executive minutes, April 17th, 1896.

51 Ibid., April 24th, 1896.

52 Beatrice Webb, diary, April 18th, 1896, Passfield papers.

53 Marjory Pease to MacDonald, May 21st, 1896, MDP 5/6.

54 Fabian Society, executive minutes, June 5th, 1896; Henry Macrosty to MacDonald, June 17th, 1896, MDP 5/6.

55 Fabian Society, executive committee minutes, April 9th, 1897.

56 Henry Macrosty to MacDonald, July 13th, 1896, MDP 5/6.

57 Fabian Society, Tract no. 70, *Report on Fabian Policy* (1896).

58 Henry Macrosty to MacDonald, July 13th, 1896, MDP 5/6; J. Fred Green to MacDonald, July 13th, 1896, MDP 5/6.

59 J. Fred Green to MacDonald, July 13th, 1896, MDP 5/6.

60 Fabian Society, executive minutes, July 24th, 1896.

61 Edward R. Pease, *The History of the Fabian Society* (3rd edn, 1963), p. 127; Fabian Society, executive minutes, October 9th, 1896.

62 J. Ramsay MacDonald, *Margaret Ethel MacDonald* (1920 edn), p. 100; Margaret Gladstone to MacDonald, July 2nd, 1896, MDP 3/65; J. H. Weber to Margaret Gladstone, June 28th, 1896, MDP 7/40; interview, Lily Montagu.

63 *Margaret Ethel MacDonald*, p. 17.

64 Ibid., p. 19.

65 Ibid., pp. 64–110; Elton, op. cit., pp. 75–8.

66 Margaret Gladstone to MacDonald, June 15th, 1896, MDP 3/65.

67 Margaret Gladstone to MacDonald, June 25th, 1896, MDP 3/65.

68 Margaret Gladstone to MacDonald, July 2nd, 1896, MDP 3/65.

69 Margaret Gladstone to MacDonald, July 11th, 1896, MDP 3/65.

70 Margaret Gladstone to 'Mrs. MacDonald' (i.e. Annie Ramsay), July 9th, 1896, MDP 3/61; Annie Ramsay to Margaret Gladstone, July 15th, 1896, MDP 3/61.

71 Margaret Gladstone to MacDonald, September 24th, 1896, MDP 3/65.

72 Margaret Gladstone to MacDonald, September 20th, 1896, MDP 3/65.

73 J. Angrave to MacDonald, n.d., MDP 5/6.

Chapter 4 Lincoln's Inn Fields

1 J. R. MacDonald, *Margaret Ethel MacDonald* (privately printed memoir, 1911), p. 14.

2 Ibid., pp. 23–4.

3 Margaret Gladstone to MacDonald, September 8th, 1896, MDP 3/65.

4 MDP 3/95.

5 MacDonald, *Margaret Ethel MacDonald* (memoir), p. 39.
6 Interview with Mrs Grace Paton.
7 Interview with Mrs Ishbel Peterkin.
8 MacDonald, *Margaret Ethel MacDonald* (biography), p. 216.
9 Interviews, Rt Hon. Malcolm MacDonald and Mrs Ishbel Peterkin.
10 Margaret Gladstone to MacDonald, July 2nd, 1896, MDP 3/65.
11 Elton, op. cit., p. 94.
12 MacDonald, 'What Lack We Yet', *Ethical World*, June 18th, 1898; 'Protestant Succession', *Ethical World*, July 2nd, 1898.
13 MacDonald, MS. lecture on 'Dogma', n.d., MDP 6/178.
14 Fabian Society, executive minutes, September 25th, 1896, September 30th, 1898, July 7th, 1899 and July 18th, 1899; Margaret MacDonald's engagement-book gives a good picture of MacDonald's provincial engagements, MDP 3/206.
15 Samuel, op. cit., p. 24.
16 Minutes of *Progressive Review* publishing company, MDP 5/67; Editorial, *Progressive Review* (October 1896).
17 Clarke to MacDonald, February 2nd, 1896 and n.d., probably early 1896, MDP 5/66.
18 Editorial, *Progressive Review* (October 1896).
19 Ibid.
20 Minutes of *Progressive Review* publishing company, MDP 5/67; Clarke to MacDonald, December 21st, 1896, MDP 5/66; Samuel to MacDonald, July 4th, 6th, 12th, 13th, 14th, 19th, and 20th, 1897, and MacDonald to Samuel (drafts), July 3rd, 4th and 12th, 1897, MDP 5/66.
21 MacDonald, articles in the *New Age*, September 2nd and September 9th, 1897.
22 MacDonald, ibid., November 25th, 1897.
23 Ibid.
24 Articles in *New Age*, December 9th, 1897 and January 27th, 1898.
25 *I.L.P.C.R.* (1896). In the first ballot MacDonald and H. R. Smart tied for bottom place, each receiving 47 votes. There was then a second ballot, in which MacDonald received 39 votes to Smart's 48.
26 *I.L.P. News* (May 1897).
27 MacDonald to Herbert Samuel, August 16th, 1895, quoted in Viscount Samuel, op. cit., p. 27.
28 'Whi i am Anarkist', n.d., MDP 5/68.
29 John Gerrie to MacDonald, September 21st, 1896, MDP 5/6.
30 Quoted in Elton, op. cit., p. 89.
31 Cuttings from *Daily News*, February 16th, 1898, and *Echo*, February 19th, 1898, MDP 6/195; election leaflet, MDP 7/41.
32 Quoted in *Labour Leader*, March 13th, 1897.
33 *I.L.P. News* (July 1897); *I.L.P.C.R.* (1898).

34 *I.L.P. News* (May 1898).
35 *Nineteenth Century* (January 1899).
36 N.A.C. Report, *I.L.P.C.R.* (1899).
37 MacDonald to Hardie, July 12th, 1899, Francis Johnson papers.
38 *Leicester Daily Mercury*, October 4th, 1899.
39 *Woolwich Herald*, February 16th, and 23rd, 1900.
40 *I.L.P.C.R.* (1900).
41 *I.L.P. News* (February 1900).
42 Article on 'The Propaganda of Civilization', *International Journal of Ethics* (July 1901), MDP 3A/52.
43 *I.L.P. News* (January 1898).
44 Shaw to MacDonald, November 20th, 1899, MDP 5/9.
45 Fabian Society, executive minutes, January 12th, February 23rd, and April 20th, 1900.
46 Introduction to William Stewart, *J. Keir Hardie* (1921), p. xxi.
47 Pelling, op. cit., p. 217.
48 N.A.C. Report, *I.L.P.C.R.* (1899); *Labour Leader*, April 18th, 1899.
49 Pelling, op. cit., p. 219.
50 *Ethical World*, December 30th, 1899.
51 *Clarion*, March 3rd, 1900.
52 *Ethical World*, March 10th, 1900, MDP 6/195.
53 Bealey and Pelling, op. cit., pp. 25–30.

Chapter 5   *Building a party*

1 Richard Whiteing, *Ring in the New* (1906), pp. 301–2.
2 *Labour Leader*, April 21st, 1900. The other was Brocklehurst.
3 *Leicester Daily Mercury*, n.d., quoted in *I.L.P. News* (April 1902).
4 Beatrice Webb, *Our Partnership*, ed. Barbara Drake and Margaret Cole (1948), pp. 229–30, 260–62.
5 MacDonald to Countess of Warwick, draft letter, n.d. but probably January 1905, MDP 5/15.
6 MacDonald to Margaret MacDonald, n.d., MDP 3/65.
7 Kenneth O. Morgan, *Keir Hardie* (1975), p. 142.
8 MacDonald to Margaret MacDonald, n.d., February or March 1904, MDP 3/65.
9 Bealey and Pelling, op. cit., p. 36.
10 Ibid.
11 L.R.C. executive minutes, January 10th, 1901.
12 Philip Poirier, *The Advent of the Labour Party* (1958), pp. 118–19.
13 Bealey and Pelling, op. cit., pp. 33–4.
14 Ibid., p. 40.

15 *Ethical World*, October 27th, 1900.
16 *Leicester Daily Post*, September 22nd, 1900.
17 Ibid., September 26th, 27th, and 29th, 1900.
18 MacDonald to Walter Hazell, October 13th, 1900, MDP 7/2.
19 Hazell to MacDonald, October 19th, 1900; MacDonald to Hazell, October 22nd, 1900, MDP 7/2.
20 *Leicester Daily Post*, October 3rd, 1900.
21 Lord Pethick-Lawrence, *Fate Has Been Kind* (1942), p. 58.
22 'Work and the Workers', *Echo*, July 25th, 1901.
23 *To the Trade-Unionists of Great Britain* (L.R.C. circular, November 1901).
24 L.R.C. circular, September 26th, 1902.
25 *I.L.P.C.R.* (1901).
26 'Work and the Workers', *Echo*, February 27th, 1902.
27 L.R.C. circular, September 1902.
28 L.R.C. executive minutes, January 10th, 1901.
29 'A New Party', *Echo*, October 17th, 1901.
30 Jesse Herbert to MacDonald, March 4th, 1901, MDP 5/11; Herbert to MacDonald, April 15th, 1902, MDP 5/12.
31 Ibid.
32 MDP 5/69.
33 *What I saw in South Africa* (1902), p. 47.
34 Ibid., pp. 50–51.
35 Ibid., p. 7.
36 MDP 3/83.
37 *What I saw in South Africa*, p. 118.
38 Ibid., p. 131.
39 Memorandum by Jesse Herbert dated March 6th, 1903, Gladstone papers, Add. MSS. 46025, ff. 127–36.
40 Correspondence between Herbert and MacDonald, MDP 5/13.
41 Bealey and Pelling, op. cit., p. 157.
42 Undated memorandum, MDP 5/81.
43 'Work and the Workers', *Echo*, January 27th, 1904.
44 George Banton to MacDonald, January 30th and June 11th, probably 1901; C. H. Wynn to MacDonald, March 19th, 1901, MDP 7/3.
45 George Banton to MacDonald, n.d., probably early in 1903; Fred W. Rogers to MacDonald, February 20th, 1903, MDP 7/5.
46 MacDonald to Alderman Wood, draft dated April 24th, 1903, MDP 7/5.
47 *Leicester Daily Post*, June 29th, 1903.
48 Ibid.
49 George Banton to MacDonald, June 18th, 1903, MDP 7/5.
50 Ibid.
51 *Leicester Daily Post*, June 30th, 1903.
52 Bealey and Pelling, op. cit., p. 156.

53 *Leicester Daily Post*, September 4th, 1903.

54 *Congrès socialiste international: compte-rendu analytique* (Brussels, 1904).

55 Bealey and Pelling, op. cit., p. 179.

56 *New Liberal Review* (September 1903).

57 'Work and the Workers', *Echo*, March 23rd, 1904.

58 Bealey and Pelling, op. cit., p. 141.

59 T.U.C. Conference Report (1903).

60 'Work and the Workers', *Echo*.

61 MDP 5/13.

62 L.R.C. executive minutes, February 11th, 1904.

63 Shaw to MacDonald, April 3rd, 1904, MDP 5/14.

64 'Work and the Workers', *Echo*, November 23rd, 1904.

65 'The Electorate and the Tariff Temptation', *New Liberal Review* (November 1903).

66 *The Zollverein and British Industry* (1903), p. 164.

67 Ibid., pp. 159–60.

68 J. R. MacDonald, *Socialism and Society* (1905), p. xiii.

69 Circular letter, signed by MacDonald and dated March 17th, 1905, MDP 5/15.

70 *Socialism and Society* (1905 edn), p. 16.

71 Ibid., pp. 11–12.

72 *Socialism and Government* (1909 edn), vol. 1, p. 11.

73 *Socialism and Society*, p. 31.

74 Ibid., pp. 15 and 37.

75 Ibid., p. 18.

76 Ibid., p. 42.

77 *The Socialist Movement* (Home University Library, 1911 edn), p. 16.

78 *Socialism and Society*, p. 97.

79 Ibid., p. xxi.

80 Ibid., p. 107.

81 Ibid., pp. 110–13.

82 Ibid., quoted in *Ramsay MacDonald's Political Writings*, ed. Bernard Barker (1972), pp. 91–3.

83 *Socialism and Government*, p. 91.

84 *Socialism and Society*, pp. 43–4.

85 Ibid., quoted in Barker, op. cit., p. 95.

86 *Socialism and Government*, vol. 2, p. 5.

87 *Socialism and Society*, p. 143.

88 Ibid., p. 154.

89 Ibid., pp. 128–9.

90 Ibid., p. 142.

91 Ibid., pp. 164–5.

92 Ibid., pp. 178–9.

93 Herbert to MacDonald, May 15th, 1905, MDP 5/15.
94 Bealey and Pelling, op. cit., pp. 290–92.
95 *Leicester Pioneer*, January 13th, 1906.
96 Ibid., January 6th, 1906.
97 *Leicester Daily Mercury*, January 6th, 1906.
98 Ibid.
99 *Leicester Pioneer*, January 13th, 1906.
100 Ibid., January 20th, 1906. This was, of course, a two-member constituency.

Chapter 6   Parliamentary apprenticeship

1 MacDonald to Margaret MacDonald, January 28th, 1906, MDP 3/65.
2 H. A. Clegg, Alan Fox and A. F. Thompson, *A History of British Trade Unions since 1889* (1964), vol 1, p. 388.
3 Bealey and Pelling, op. cit., pp. 276–7.
4 *Labour Leader*, May 10th, 1907.
5 Undated memorandum, MDP 5/81.
6 *Leicester Pioneer*, March 10th, 1906.
7 *Hansard* (1906), vol. 153, cols. 119–25.
8 G. Shaw Lefebvre to MacDonald, June 14th, 1906, MDP 5/16.
9 MacDonald to E. D. Morel, February 21st, 1906, Morel papers.
10 *Hansard* (1906), vol. 155, cols. 245–51.
11 Ibid. (1906), vol. 155, cols. 1051–7; vol. 156, cols. 1075–86.
12 Letters and resolution in MDP 5/79.
13 *Labour Leader*, August 10th, 1906.
14 *Margaret Ethel MacDonald* (memoir), p. 36.
15 Interview, Malcolm MacDonald.
16 MacDonald to Margaret MacDonald, August 3rd, 1906, MDP 3/65.
17 For a valuable discussion of MacDonald's views on the Empire, see Bernard Porter, *Critics of Empire* (1968), *passim.*
18 *Margaret Ethel MacDonald* (biography), pp. 233–5.
19 Morgan, op. cit., p. 160.
20 Ibid., p. 161.
21 MacDonald to Glasier, July 21st, 1906, Glasier papers.
22 MacDonald to Glasier, May 31st, 1907, Glasier papers.
23 For MacDonald's comments on Shackleton's decision not to stand and on the 'lobbying' which preceded Henderson's election, cf. *Leicester Pioneer*, January 11th, and January 24th, 1908.
24 Glasier to MacDonald, October 27th, and November 5th, 1908, MDP 5/18.
25 *Hansard* (1907), vol. 169, cols. 746–51.
26 Ibid. (1907), vol. 172, cols. 1593–1601.
27 Ibid. (1907), vol. 174, cols. 822–30.

28 José Harris, *Unemployment and Politics* (1972), p. 241.

29 E. Halévy, *History of the English People in the Nineteenth Century* (1952 edn), vol. 6, p. 256.

30 J. R. MacDonald, *The New Unemployed Bill of the Labour Party* (1907), copy in MDP 3A/52.

31 Glasier to MacDonald, March 12th, 1908, MDP 5/18.

32 John Lithiby to MacDonald, December 2nd, 1905, MDP 5/15; F. E. Johnson to MacDonald, October 7th, 1907, MDP 5/17.

33 *Hansard* (1908), vol. 186, cols. 19–28.

34 Ibid. (1909), vol. 5, col. 497.

35 J. R. Clynes, *Memoirs 1869–1924* (1937), vol. 1, p. 124.

36 His motto, he declared, was 'Lay on, Macduff! And damned be he who first cries: "Hold, enough!"' *Labour Leader*, August 10th, 1906.

37 *I.L.P.C.R.* (1907).

38 Labour Party, National Executive Committee minutes, minutes of emergency sub-committee, June 28th, 1907.

39 N.A.C. Report, *I.L.P.C.R.* (1908).

40 MacDonald to Glasier, n.d., probably July 20th or 21st, 1907, Francis Johnson papers.

41 *The Times*, August 1st, 1907.

42 Undated note in MacDonald's hand, headed 'Statement agreed to [by] Mr. Grayson and the Huddersfield & Colne Valley Rep's at the House of Commons on day of Mr. Grayson's introduction', MDP 5/18.

43 *I.L.P.C.R.* (1908).

44 Ibid.

45 Paul Campbell to Margaret MacDonald (signed 'Brother Paul'), April 22nd, 1908, MDP 5/18.

46 MacDonald to Margaret MacDonald, n.d., MDP 3/65.

47 MacDonald to Glasier, May 31st, 1907, Francis Johnson papers.

48 *Leicester Pioneer*, April 11th, 1908.

49 Laurence Thompson, *The Enthusiasts* (1971), p. 141; Glasier to MacDonald, April 9th, 1908, MDP 5/18.

50 Morgan, op. cit., p. 172.

51 Hardie to Glasier, n.d., Francis Johnson papers.

52 Morgan, op. cit., p. 219.

53 Snowden to MacDonald, September 21st, 1908, MDP 5/18.

54 Morgan, op. cit., p. 160; Thompson, op. cit., p. 148.

55 At the end of February 1908, there were 765 I.L.P. branches as against 545 at the beginning of March 1907; N.A.C. Report, *I.L.P.C.R.* (1908). The number of S.D.F. branches increased from 187 in December 1906 to 211 a year later; Chushiki Tsuzuki, *H. M. Hyndman and British Socialism* (1961), p. 164.

56 Tsuzuki, op. cit., pp. 163–70.

57 *Leicester Pioneer*, September 12th, 1908; Labour Party, N.E.C. minutes, September 10th, 1908.
58 Snowden to MacDonald, September 16th, 1908, MDP 5/18.
59 Anderson to MacDonald, September 24th, 1908, MDP 5/18.
60 MacDonald to Margaret MacDonald, n.d., MDP 3/65.
61 MDP, uncatalogued.
62 *Labour Leader*, October 2nd, 1908.
63 *Socialist Review* (November 1908).
64 M. McMillan to MacDonald, September 22nd, 1908, MDP 5/18.
65 Copy of letter from T. W. Earnshaw addressed to I.L.P. branches, September 16th, 1908, MDP 5/18.
66 Snowden, op. cit., vol. 1, p. 166.
67 *Leicester Pioneer*, November 7th, 1908.
68 B. H. Bates to MacDonald, October 30th, 1908, MDP 5/18.
69 R. C. Wallhead to MacDonald, November 3rd, 1908, MDP 5/18.
70 Glasier to MacDonald, November 5th, 1908, MDP 5/18.
71 N.A.C. Report, *I.L.P.C.R.* (1909).
72 B. Riley to MacDonald, January 25th, 1909, MDP 5/19.
73 'From Green Benches', *Leicester Pioneer*, November 28th, 1908.
74 MacDonald to Glasier, December 31st, 1908, Francis Johnson papers.
75 Snowden to MacDonald, February 5th, 1909, MDP 5/19.
76 *I.L.P.C.R.* (1909).
77 Ibid. The speech was reprinted, slightly expanded, as an I.L.P. pamphlet, *Socialism To-day*, MDP 3A/52.
78 'From Green Benches', *Leicester Pioneer*, April 24th, 1909.
79 *I.L.P.C.R.* (1909).

Chapter 7   Leader bereaved

1 'From Green Benches', *Leicester Pioneer*, May 8th, 1909.
2 'Outlook', *Socialist Review* (June 1909).
3 Ibid. (August 1909).
4 *Hansard* (1909), vol. 6, cols. 1608–9.
5 MacDonald to Margaret MacDonald, September 2nd, 1909, and n.d., probably August or September 1909, MDP 3/65.
6 *Leicester Pioneer*, October 2nd, 1909, and December 18th, 1909.
7 *The Awakening of India* (1910), p. 64.
8 Ibid., pp. 140–41.
9 Ibid., pp. 146–8.
10 Ibid., pp. 167–8.
11 Ibid., p. 189.
12 Ibid., pp. 117–19.

13 Ibid., popular edition, p. 187.
14 Ibid., popular edition, p. 168.
15 Ibid., popular edition, p. 187.
16 MacDonald to Hardie, February 3rd, 1910, Francis Johnson papers.
17 Henderson to W. C. Robinson, February 15th, 1910, L.P.L.F.
18 MacDonald to Hardie, n.d., early 1910, Francis Johnson papers.
19 Hardie to MacDonald, n.d., probably February 1910, MDP 5/20.
20 George Barnes to MacDonald, February 1st, 1910, MDP 5/20.
21 MacDonald to Margaret MacDonald, n.d., MDP 3/65.
22 MacDonald to Barnes, February 3rd, 1910, Francis Johnson papers.
23 Shackleton to MacDonald, February 8th, 1910, MDP 5/20.
24 Shackleton to MacDonald, February 11th, 1910, MDP 5/20.
25 Shackleton to MacDonald, October 31st, 1910, MDP 5/20.
26 Barnes to Hardie, February 19th, 1910, Francis Johnson papers.
27 *The Times*, February 18th, 1910.
28 Ibid., February 19th, 1910.
29 *Labour Leader*, March 18th, 1910.
30 Note by Hardie, dated March 7th, Francis Johnson papers.
31 'From Green Benches', *Leicester Pioneer*, March 12th, 1910.
32 Francis Johnson papers.
33 Ibid.
34 'Outlook', *Socialist Review* (November 1910).
35 Labour Party, N.E.C. minutes, September 29th, 1910.
36 Diary, MDP 8/1.
37 Carrington Diary, November 22nd, 1910. I am indebted to Professor Anthony King for this reference.
38 Labour Party, N.E.C. minutes, February 1910.
39 'Outlook', *Socialist Review* (September 1910).
40 Diary, June 9th, 22nd, July 4th, 12th, 27th.
41 Major-General J. E. B. Seely, *Adventure* (1930), p. 148.
42 Murray of Elibank to MacDonald, September 4th, 1912, MDP 5/22.
43 Lloyd George to MacDonald, September 8th, 1910, MDP 5/20.
44 Lord Riddell, *More Pages From My Diary, 1908–1914* (1934), pp. 21, 155, 163; Diary, June 9th, 1910, November 14th, and 22nd, 1911.
45 Lloyd George to MacDonald, September 22nd, 1913, MDP 5/23.
46 Roy Jenkins, *Asquith* (1964), p. 261.
47 Reported in *The Times*, February 1st, 1910.
48 H. Hackett to MacDonald, January 28th, 1910, MDP 5/20.
49 Quoted in *Leicester Pioneer*, January 11th, 1908.
50 *I.L.P.C.R.* (1910).
51 The phrase is C. L. Mowat's.
52 Diary.
53 'Outlook', *Socialist Review* (August 1910).

54 W. C. Anderson to MacDonald, August 3rd, 1910, MDP 5/20.
55 Barnes to MacDonald, n.d., MDP 5/21.
56 MacDonald to Margaret MacDonald, n.d., MDP 3/65.
57 Viscount Snowden, *An Autobiography* (1934), vol. 1, pp. 219–20.
58 Henderson to MacDonald, January 2nd, 1911, MDP 5/21. This is the source for Barnes's attacks on the parliamentary party.
59 *Labour Leader*, January 20th, 1911.
60 Benson to MacDonald, January 26th, 1911, MDP 5/21.
61 Elton, op. cit., pp. 189–91.
62 *The Times*, February 7th, 1911.
63 Snowden, op. cit., vol. 1, p. 220.
64 *Labour Leader*, February 10th, 1911.
65 *Leicester Pioneer*, February 11th, 1911.
66 Diary.
67 Interview, Malcolm MacDonald.
68 *Margaret Ethel MacDonald* (memoir), pp. 6–7.
69 Thompson, op. cit., p. 173.
70 Elton, op. cit., p. 197.
71 Middleton to MacDonald, September 9th, 1911, L.P.L.F.
72 Glasier to MacDonald, September 30th, 1911, MDP 5/21.
73 Katharine Bruce Glasier to MacDonald, October 4th, 1911, MDP 3/20.
74 *Margaret Ethel MacDonald* (memoir), pp. 54–5.
75 MDP 3/95.
76 Katharine Bruce Glasier to MacDonald, December 9th, 1912, MDP 3/21.
77 Interview, Malcolm MacDonald.

Chapter 8   Pressure group under pressure

1 Drake and Cole (eds), op. cit., p. 474.
2 Diary, November 14th, 1911.
3 *Hansard* (1911), vol. 25, cols. 654–7.
4 Ibid. (1911), vol. 26, cols. 718–36.
5 'Outlook', *Socialist Review* (June 1911).
6 Drake and Cole (eds), op. cit., p. 475.
7 *Labour Leader*, June 30th, 1911.
8 *Hansard* (1911), vol. 27, cols. 1441–9.
9 *Labour Leader*, July 14th, 1911.
10 Tom Fox to MacDonald, July 18th, 1911, MDP 5/21.
11 W. C. Robinson to MacDonald, July 19th, 1911, MDP 5/21.
12 'Outlook', *Socialist Review* (August 1911).
13 Ibid. (September 1911).
14 Henderson to MacDonald, September 30th, 1911, MDP 5/21.

15 'Outlook', *Socialist Review* (March 1911).
16 Ibid. (December 1911).
17 Ibid. (September 1911).
18 'From Green Benches', *Leicester Pioneer*, May 20th, 1911.
19 Ibid., August 5th, 1911.
20 Murray of Elibank to MacDonald, October 19th, 1911, MDP 5/21.
21 Richard Hawkin to MacDonald, July 24th, 1911, L.P.L.F.; translation of *Dépêche* article in MDP 6/14.
22 Diary.
23 'Outlook', *Socialist Review* (May 1911).
24 M. I. Cole (ed.), *Beatrice Webb, Diaries 1912–1924*, p. 218.
25 Tillett to MacDonald, July 5th, 1911, MDP 5/21.
26 This account of the 1911 railway dispute is based on Philip Bagwell, *The Railwaymen* (1963), chs xi and xii.
27 MacDonald, *The Social Unrest* (1913), p. 86.
28 'Outlook', *Socialist Review* (October 1911).
29 *The Social Unrest*, pp. 41–2, 75–6.
30 'Outlook', *Socialist Review* (September 1911).
31 Ibid. (October 1911).
32 *Hansard* (1911), vol. 29, col. 1951.
33 'Outlook', *Socialist Review* (October 1911).
34 *Labour Leader*, August 25th, 1911; undated note signed by G. H. Roberts, MDP 5/21.
35 Thompson, op. cit., p. 171.
36 *Labour Leader*, September 1st, 1911.
37 *Hansard* (1911), vol. 31, cols. 1209–23.
38 Ibid. (1912), vol. 34, col. 53.
39 *Labour Leader*, March 15th, 1912.
40 'From Green Benches', *Leicester Pioneer*, February 24th, 1912.
41 *Hansard* (1912), vol. 39, cols. 248–55.
42 'From Green Benches', *Leicester Pioneer*, June 8th, 1912.
43 *Socialism and Government*, vol. 1, pp. 65–76.
44 Catherine Marshall to MacDonald, October 19th, 1912, MDP 5/22; H. N. Brailsford to MacDonald, April 23rd, and October 14th, 1912, MDP 5/22.
45 'From Green Benches', *Leicester Pioneer*, March 9th, 1912.
46 *Margaret Ethel MacDonald* (memoir), pp. 27–30.
47 Lansbury to MacDonald, June 26th, 1912, MDP 5/22.
48 N.E.C. minutes, October 15th, 1912.
49 Ibid., November 13th and 14th, 1912.
50 Ibid., December 6th, 1912.
51 Ibid., January 31st, 1913.
52 Note dated 'July 30' in notebook of Birkbeck College lecture-notes, MDP 3/66.

53 Robert Gathorne-Hardy (ed.), *Ottoline at Garsington* (1974), p. 110; Wilfrid Scawen Blunt, *My Diaries* (1932 edn), pp. 469, 472, 588, 631, 642.
54 Letters from Lady Margaret Sackville to MacDonald, MDP 3/21; 3/23; 6/16.
55 Elton, op. cit., pp. 238–9.
56 Note dated 'Tuesday 23rd', MDP 3/66.
57 MDP 3/66.
58 W. C. Anderson to MacDonald, April 4th, 1911, MDP 5/21.
59 A. P. Nicholson to MacDonald, February 10th, 1912, MDP 5/22; note by MacDonald, dated 'July 30', MDP 3/66.
60 Henderson to MacDonald, August 20th, 1912, MDP 5/22.
61 'From Green Benches', *Leicester Pioneer*, July 20th, 1912.
62 Paul Campbell to MacDonald, October 11th, 1912, MDP 3/21.
63 L. S. S. O'Malley, *The Indian Civil Service 1901–1930* (2nd edn, 1965). pp. 221–2.
64 Elton, op. cit., p. 236.
65 *Leicester Pioneer*, May 9th, 1913.
66 *Labour Leader*, June 26th, 1913.
67 Reynolds to MacDonald, n.d., MDP 7/48.
68 Labour Party. N.E.C. minutes.
69 N.A.C. Report, *I.L.P.C.R.* (1914).
70 *Labour Leader*, June 26th, 1913.
71 Labour Party, N.E.C. minutes, June 19th, 1913.
72 N.A.C. Report, *I.L.P.C.R.* (1914).
73 Borrett to MacDonald, June 21st, 1913, MDP 7/48.
74 Draft letter headed 'Not sent', MDP 7/48.
75 MacDonald to Banton, June 25th, 1913, MDP 7/48.
76 Memorandum by MacDonald, MDP 7/48.
77 *Leicester Daily Post*, June 26th, 1913, MDP 6/197.
78 Labour Party, N.E.C. minutes, July 16th, 1913; N.A.C. Report, *I.L.P.C.R.* (1914).
79 *Labour Leader*, July 17th, 1913.
80 *L.P.C.R.* (1914).
81 *Labour Leader*, June 26th, 1913.
82 Ibid., July 10th, 1913.
83 *L.P.C.R.* (1914).
84 Labour Party, N.E.C. minutes, May 6th, 1914.
85 Cf. Ross McKibbin, *The Evolution of the Labour Party, 1910–1924* (1974), pp. 72–7.
86 Wedgwood to MacDonald, June 12th, 1913, MDP 5/23.
87 MDP 5/24.
88 MDP 8/1.
89 'From Green Benches', *Leicester Pioneer*, March 6th, 1914.

90 *Hansard* (1914), vol. 60, cols. 434–41.
91 'From Green Benches', *Leicester Pioneer*, March 27th, 1914.
92 *The Times*, March 24th, 1914, MDP 6/198.
93 Labour Party, N.E.C. minutes.
94 Brockway, op. cit., pp. 36–8.
95 *Labour Leader*, April 16th, 1914.
96 'From Green Benches', *Leicester Pioneer*, April 24th, 1914.
97 Ibid., May 29th, 1914.

Chapter 9   Voice of reason

1 Diary, September 23rd, 1914.
2 Ibid. *Lord Riddell's War Diary* (1933), pp. 3–6, gives a different account of the dinner. In particular, Riddell claimed that MacDonald said that, if Belgian neutrality were infringed, Britain would be justified in declaring war on Germany. This view was so contrary to the position MacDonald took up publicly, and to that expressed in his own diary, that it seems highly unlikely that he ever expressed it.
3 MDP 6/11.
4 'From Green Benches', *Leicester Pioneer*, March 20th, 1909.
5 N.E.C. minutes, January 30th, 1911; Henderson to Middleton, January 18th, 1911, L.P.L.F.
6 'Outlook', *Socialist Review* (March 1911).
7 Diary.
8 'Outlook', *Socialist Review* (December 1911).
9 'From Green Benches', *Leicester Pioneer*, December 2nd, 1911.
10 Ibid., July 20th, 1911.
11 Ibid., July 27th, 1912.
12 Ibid., July 25th, 1913.
13 *Leicester Pioneer*, January 23rd, 1914.
14 'From Green Benches', *Leicester Pioneer*, March 20th, 1914.
15 *Hansard* (1914), vol. 65, cols. 1829–31.
16 Labour Party, N.E.C. minutes, August 5th, 1914.
17 Diary, September 23rd, 1914.
18 *Labour Leader*, August 15th, 1914.
19 T. E. Merrifold to MacDonald, September 2nd, 1914; A. Nelson to MacDonald, August 9th, 1914; Devi I.L.P. to MacDonald, August 20th, 1914; B. R. Evans to MacDonald, August 19th, 1914; Sidney Palmer to MacDonald, August 25th, 1914; W. H. Ayles to MacDonald, August 7th, 1914, MDP 5/100. W. Leach to MacDonald, August 14th, 1914, MDP 5/24.
20 Diary, October 25th, 1914.

21 Ibid., September 23rd, 1914.
22 Morel papers.
23 MDP 5/24.
24 MDP 5/98.
25 Ibid.
26 Morel papers.
27 Ponsonby papers.
28 MDP 5/98.
29 MacDonald to Williams, August 26th, 1914, MDP 5/98.
30 MDP 5/98.
31 A. H. Reynolds to MacDonald, September 14th, 1914, MDP 5/98.
32 Diary, October 16th, 1914.
33 MDP 5/98.
34 Diary.
35 MDP 5/98.
36 Henderson to MacDonald, October 19th, 1914, MDP 5/98.
37 Henderson to MacDonald, October 19th, 1914, MDP 5/98.
38 MDP 5/98.
39 Ibid.
40 Diary.
41 Ibid.
42 *Labour Leader*, August 29th, 1914.
43 Diary.
44 *Labour Leader*, August 29th, 1914.
45 'A Refusal to Surrender', *Forward*, October 3rd, 1914.
46 MacDonald to Laidler, November 3rd, 1914, MDP 5/24.
47 Marvin Swartz, *The Union of Democratic Control in British Politics during the First World War* (1971), p. 42.
48 Diary.
49 Ponsonby diary, April 21st, 1915.
50 Leonard Woolf, *Beginning Again* (1965), pp. 217–26.
51 *Labour Leader*, March 16th, 1916.

Chapter 10   Public enemy

1 MacDonald to Morel, September 8th, 1914, Morel papers.
2 MDP 5/24.
3 Diary, October 18th, 1914.
4 Murray to MacDonald, n.d., and November 28th, 1914; Alexander McConnell to MacDonald, December 8th, 1914, MDP 5/101.
5 Elton, op. cit., pp. 269–71.
6 MDP 5/101.

7 Diary, December 10th, 1914.
8 Seely, op. cit., pp. 202–6.
9 Undated memorandum, MDP 5/101.
10 Swartz, op. cit., pp. 178–80.
11 Arthur Marwick, *Clifford Allen, the Open Conspirator* (1964), pp. 35–55.
12 Draft Statement headed 'Morning Post Attack', MDP 5/108.
13 Interview, Allan Maclean.
14 Interview, Lady Helen Roberton.
15 Personal information.
16 Diary, particularly November 30th, and December 14th, 1915; March 30th, and November 25th, 1916.
17 Gathorne-Hardy, op. cit., pp. 110, 249, 260.
18 Hamilton, *Remembering My Good Friends*, pp. 74–7.
19 Ronald W. Clark, *The Life of Bertrand Russell* (1975), pp. 252, 318.
20 Gathorne-Hardy, op. cit., pp. 249–50.
21 *John Bull*, February 13th, 1915.
22 Ibid., February 20th, 1915.
23 Scurr to MacDonald, September 15th, 1915; J. Syme to MacDonald, September 1st, 1915; Brockway to MacDonald, September 3rd, 1915; J. Young to MacDonald, September 3rd, 1915; N.U.R. to MacDonald, September 4th, 1915; Katharine Bruce Glasier to MacDonald, September 3rd, 1915; anon. to MacDonald, n.d., MDP 5/107.
24 Diary.
25 Requisition, August 20th, 1915; A. F. MacDonald to MacDonald, September 10th, 1915; MacDonald to A. F. MacDonald, September 16th, 1915, MDP 5/105.
26 Requisition, August 1st, 1916; cuttings from *Elgin Courant*; Robert Munro to MacDonald, August 24th, 1916; MacDonald to Cameron, October 4th, 1916; MacDonald to A. F. MacDonald, October 4th, 1916, MDP 5/105.
27 Diary, October 1st, 1914.
28 Diary.
29 Ibid., January 13th, 1916.
30 *Labour Leader*, June 29th, 1916.
31 Diary, September 12th, 1915.
32 N.E.C. minutes, May 19th, 1915.
33 Trevelyan to Ponsonby, May 27th, 1915, Ponsonby papers.
34 N.E.C. minutes, September 15th, 1915.
35 Ibid., September 27th, 1915.
36 Diary, September 28th, 1915.
37 N.E.C. minutes.
38 Ibid., January 5th, 1916.
39 *Labour Leader*, special conference edition, January 8th, 1916.
40 N.E.C. minutes, January 6th, 1916.

41 N.E.C. minutes.
42 Diary, January 13th, 1916.
43 Ibid., January 29th, 1916.
44 N.E.C. minutes, April 16th, 1916.
45 Ibid., April 26th, 1916.
46 Ibid., April 27th, 1916.
47 *Labour Leader*, May 25th, 1916.
48 Huysmans to MacDonald, January 16th, 1915, MDP 5/104.
49 MacDonald to Middleton, February 8th, 1915, MDP 5/104.
50 N.E.C. minutes, June 28th, 1915; James Middleton to MacDonald, September 10th, 1915, L.P.L.F.
51 British Section, International Socialist Bureau, minutes, August 13th, 1915.
52 N.E.C. minutes, September 15th, 1915; British Section, International Socialist Bureau, minutes, September 16th, 1915.
53 Diary, March 30th, 1916; N.E.C. minutes, March 30th, 1916.
54 *Labour Leader*, April 6th, 1916.
55 Ibid., May 18th, 1916.
56 Swartz, op. cit., p. 70.
57 Ponsonby papers.
58 *Hansard* (1916), vol. 82, cols. 2188–97.
59 MDP 5/115.
60 Pease to MacDonald, October 11th, 1916; MacDonald to Pease, October 12th, 1916, MDP 5/26.
61 Diary.
62 Ibid., December 24th, 1916.
63 Ibid., December 28th, 1916.
64 Ibid., December 31st, 1916.
65 Ibid., February 5th, 6th, 7th, 11th, 12th, 24th, 1917.
66 Ibid., January 2nd, 1917.
67 Ibid., January 9th, and 10th, 1917.
68 *National Defence* (1917), p. 28.
69 Ibid., p. 33.
70 Ibid., p. 39.
71 Ibid., pp. 40–43.
72 *Labour Leader*, December 14th, 1916.
73 *National Defence*, pp. 56–63.
74 Ibid., p. 77.
75 Ibid., p. 90.
76 Ibid., pp. 101–2.
77 Ibid., p. 115.
78 Ibid., pp. 14–15.
79 Ibid., p. 110.

Chapter 11   Defeat

1 Diary, March 15th, 1917.
2 Ibid., March 16th, 1917.
3 Ibid., March 29th, 1911.
4 Ibid., April 3rd, 1917.
5 Branko Pribićević, *The Shop Stewards' Movement and Workers' Control, 1910–1922* (1959), pp. 110–26.
6 'From a Labour Bench', *Forward*, March 31st, 1917.
7 Ibid.
8 *I.L.P.C.R.* (1917).
9 'From a Labour Bench', *Forward*, April 21st, 1917.
10 Ibid., April 28th, 1917.
11 Ibid.
12 *War Memoirs of David Lloyd George* (1938 edn), vol. 2, p. 1124.
13 Diary, May 7th, 1917.
14 *Daily Herald*, Leeds Conference number, June 9th, 1917.
15 Diary.
16 'From a Labour Bench', *Forward*, April 14th, 1917.
17 MacDonald to Kerensky, n.d. (draft), MDP 5/27.
18 Diary, April 25th, 1917.
19 MacDonald to Vandervelde, April 26th, 1917, MDP 5/27.
20 Diary.
21 N.E.C. minutes.
22 Diary, May 9th, 1917.
23 Ibid., May 10th, 1917.
24 *Hansard* (1917), vol. 93, cols. 1657–65.
25 Diary.
26 Ibid., May 24th, 1917.
27 CAB 24/14. GT 875, 334–6.
28 *Hansard* (1917), vol. 94, cols. 494–5.
29 Diary, June 8th, 1917.
30 Ibid., June 13th, 1917.
31 Diary.
32 MacDonald to Petrograd Workmen and Soldiers' Council, MDP 5/27.
33 MDP 5/27.
34 Diary.
35 *Hansard* (1917), vol. 96, cols. 1479–96.
36 Diary, July 26th, 1917.
37 MacDonald to W. H. Buckler, August 17th, 1917, MDP 5/27.
38 Lloyd George, op. cit., vol. 2, p. 1127.
39 N.E.C. minutes, July 25th, 1917.
40 N.E.C. report, *L.P.C.R.* (January/February 1918).

41 N.E.C. report, Ibid.
42 N.E.C. report, Ibid.
43 Diary, August 29th, and 30th, 1917.
44 Bernstein to MacDonald, September 30th, 1917, MDP 5/27.
45 Diary.
46 MDP 5/27.
47 N.E.C. minutes, September 26th, 1917.
48 N.E.C. International Joint Committee minutes, October 24th, 1917.
49 N.E.C. minutes of Joint Meeting.
50 N.E.C. report, *L.P.C.R.* (January/February 1918).
51 Diary, December 28th, 1917.
52 Ibid., December 29th, 1917.
53 *L.P.C.R.* (January/February 1918).
54 *Forward*, February 2nd, 1918.
55 N.E.C. International Joint Committee minutes, January 8th, 1918.
56 N.E.C. minutes, February 19th, 1918.
57 MacDonald to Henderson (draft), January 30th, 1918, MDP 5/28.
58 Henderson to MacDonald, January 31st, 1918, MDP 5/28.
59 MacDonald to Henderson, 'Thursday Night', MDP 5/28.
60 Henderson to MacDonald, February 2nd, 1918, MDP 5/28.
61 MacDonald to Henderson, February 5th, 1918; Henderson to MacDonald, February 6th, 1918, MDP 5/28.
62 Diary, February 18th, 1918.
63 Diary.
64 *Forward*, December 29th, 1917.
65 Ibid., January 12th, 1918.
66 Diary, January 14th, 1918.
67 Ibid., February 11th, 1918.
68 *Hansard* (1918), vol. 103, cols. 44–8.
69 Diary, May 14th, 1918.
70 Ibid., June 26th, 1918.
71 'Outlook', *Socialist Review* (October 1918).
72 N.E.C. minutes, September 18th, 1918.
73 Ibid., July 11th, 1918.
74 Ibid., August 8th, 1918.
75 *Socialism after the War*, p. 17.
76 *Labour Leader*, May 11th, 1916.
77 *Socialism after the War*, p. 3.
78 Ibid., pp. 17–18.
79 Ibid., pp. 18–19.
80 N.E.C. minutes, September 26th, 1917.
81 Ibid., October 16th, 1917.
82 G. D. H. Cole, *A History of the Labour Party From 1914* (1948), pp. 44–81.

83 Diary, October 7th, 1917.
84 Ibid., October 9th, 1917.
85 Ibid., October 15th, 1917.
86 Ibid., October 16th, 1917.
87 *Forward*, April 6th, 1918.
88 Cf. particularly *Forward*, January 1918 and 'Outlook', *Socialist Review* (April 1918).
89 MacDonald to 'Dear Sir', July 17th, 1918, MDP 5/28.
90 'Outlook', *Socialist Review* (January 1918).
91 Diary, December 27th, 1917.
92 Ibid., April 14th, 1918.
93 MacDonald to Michael, April 17th, 1918, MDP 5/28.
94 N.E.C. minutes, May 29th, and 30th, 1918.
95 MacDonald to Ponsonby, n.d., Ponsonby papers.
96 N.E.C. minutes, February 27th, 1918.
97 Ibid., April 24th, 1918.
98 Ibid., July 24th, 1918.
99 *Forward*, August 3rd, 1918.
100 N.E.C. minutes, August 27th, 1918.
101 *Forward*, July 27th, 1918.
102 N.E.C. minutes, July 31st, 1918.
103 Diary.
104 N.E.C. minutes.
105 *Leicester Daily Mercury*, December 2nd, 1918.
106 Ibid., December 10th, 1918.
107 MDP 7/51.
108 *Forward*, December 14th, 1918.
109 Ibid., December 21st, 1918.
110 *Leicester Daily Mercury*, December 12th, 1918.
111 Ibid.
112 Ibid., December 13th, 1918.
113 Diary, 'Christmas Day', 1918.
114 Diary.
115 Ibid.
116 Ibid., December 31st, 1918.

Chapter 12   Rebuilding a career

1 Diary, January 7th, 1919.
2 'Outlook', *Socialist Review* (January 1919).
3 *Forward*, January 25th, 1919.
4 Diary, January 21st, 1919.

5 Ibid., March 3rd, 1919.

6 Ibid., January 21st, 1919.

7 Ibid., March 2nd, 1919.

8 Ibid., May 18th, 1919.

9 Ibid., April 13th, 1919.

10 Interviews, Sir Alec Martin, Lady Helen Roberton, Mrs M. A. Hamilton.

11 Markwald to MacDonald, June 21st, October 7th, November 2nd, 8th, 12th, 19th, and 29th, December 21st, 1921, MDP 6/24; Robert Burton and Frost to MacDonald, January 2nd, 6th, and 16th, 1922, MDP 5/32; Markwald to MacDonald, December 12th, 1922, MDP 5/32.

12 Interview, Sir Alec Martin.

13 Diary, *passim*.

14 MacDonald to 'Your Laidieship' (probably Minnie Pallister), August 18th, 1920, Ivor Thomas papers.

15 Reprinted in *Wanderings and Excursions*, pp. 57–61.

16 Henry Pelling, *A History of British Trade Unionism* (1963), pp. 261–4.

17 Interview, Mrs Lucy Middleton.

18 Hamilton, *Remembering My Good Friends*, pp. 122–3.

19 Pelling, *A History of British Trade Unionism*, pp. 261–4.

20 Hamilton, *Remembering My Good Friends*, p. 128.

21 Diary, April 23rd, 1921.

22 Ibid., April 25th, 1921.

23 Ibid., March 3rd, 1919.

24 Ibid., March 20th, 1919.

25 Ibid., April 10th, 1921.

26 Interview, Captain Dunbar.

27 W. G. Runciman, *Relative Deprivation and Social Justice* (1966), esp. Part Two.

28 *Forward*, March 1st, 1919.

29 *Official Bulletin of the International Labour and Socialist Conference* (Berne), February 7th, 1919.

30 *Forward*, February 8th, 1919.

31 *Labour Leader*, February 27th, 1919.

32 *Forward*, April 12th, 1919.

33 Diary, April 1st, 1919.

34 Ibid.

35 Ibid., May 3rd, 1919.

36 *Labour Leader*, May 22nd, 1919.

37 'Outlook', *Socialist Review* (July 1919).

38 Diary, May 14th, 1919.

39 L.P.C.R. (1919).

40 *Forward*, July 12th, 1919.

41 Ibid., August 2nd, 1919.

42 This account is based primarily on Julius Braunthal, *History of the International*, vol. 2 (1967), chaps. 6 and 11.

43 *Labour Leader*, July 17th, 1919.

44 *Official Bulletin of the International Labour and Socialist Conference* (Berne), February 21st, 1919.

45 *Forward*, June 4th, 1920.

46 'Outlook', *Socialist Review* (October 1919). This, and *Forward*, August 16th, 1919, are the sources for this account of the Lucerne conference.

47 Longuet to MacDonald, December 16th, 1919, MDP 5/29.

48 *Forward*, December 6th, 1919.

49 Wallhead to MacDonald, January 15th, 1920, MDP 5/30.

50 R. E. Dowse, *Left in the Centre* (1966), p. 72.

51 'Outlook', *Socialist Review* (January 1921).

52 Ibid. (January 1920).

53 *Forward*, January 17th, 1920.

54 'Outlook', *Socialist Review* (July 1920).

55 *Forward*, January 24th, 1920.

56 Ibid., January 17th, 1920.

57 *Parliament and Revolution* (1919), pp. 87–8.

58 Ibid., p. 38.

59 Ibid., p. 44.

60 Ibid., p. 31.

61 Ibid., p. 26.

62 Ibid., pp. 27–31.

63 Ibid., p. 92.

64 'Outlook', *Socialist Review* (April 1920).

65 *I.L.P.C.R.* (1920).

66 Quoted in S. R. Graubard, *British Labour and the Russian Revolution* (1956), p. 193.

67 *Forward*, April 17th, 1920.

68 Braunthal, op. cit., pp. 230–32.

69 *Forward*, August 7th, and 14th, 1920.

70 Ibid., August 14th, 1920.

71 *Wanderings and Excursions*, pp. 164–70.

72 *Labour Leader*, October 21st, 1920.

73 Diary, November 10th, 1920.

74 Ibid., December 16th, 1920.

75 'Outlook', *Socialist Review* (January 1921).

76 MacDonald to Troelstra, December 29th, 1920, Troelstra papers.

77 N.E.C. report, *L.P.C.R.* (1921).

78 *Forward*, April 9th, 1921.

79 Verbatim notes of Caxton Hall conference, October 19th, and 20th, 1921, L.S.I.

80 Diary, October 20th, 1921.
81 *Forward*, April 15th, 1922.
82 Ibid., April 8th, 1922.
83 I.S.B., Executive Minutes, April 2nd, 1922, L.S.I.
84 *The Second and Third International and the Vienna Union. Official Report of the Conference between the Executives, held at the Reichstag, Berlin, on 2nd April, 1922 and following days.*
85 *Forward*, April 15th, 1922.
86 Roubanovitch to MacDonald, April 24th, 1922, L.S.I.
87 Otto Wels to MacDonald, April 22nd, 1922, L.S.I.
88 MacDonald to Radek, April 28th, 1922, L.S.I.
89 Wels to MacDonald, May 8th, 1922, L.S.I.
90 Minutes of committee of nine, May 23rd, 1922, L.S.I.
91 MacDonald to Adler, May 30th, 1922, L.S.I.
92 *Forward*, August 26th, 1922.

Chapter 13   Woolwich and after

1 Diary, July 7th, 1920.
2 Ibid., January 15th, 1919.
3 Ibid., April 9th, 1919.
4 Ibid., July 7th, 1920.
5 See above, p. 256.
6 Snowden, op. cit., p. 533.
7 Marwick, op. cit., esp. chap. IX; Emmanuel Shinwell, speech at Mac-Donald centenary lunch, October 12th, 1966.
8 Interviews, Rosslyn Mitchell and Lady Helen Roberton.
9 Diary, October 5th, 1915; June 18th, 1918. Cole's influence can be detected in *Socialism after the War*, esp. chap. II, and in MacDonald, *Socialism: Critical and Constructive* (see below, pp. 178-9).
10 Diary, April 3rd, 1919.
11 *Forward*, July 5th, 1919.
12 *Nation*, November 8th, 1919 (article dated September 15th).
13 *Labour Leader*, August 28th, 1919.
14 *Forward*, October 11th, 1919.
15 Ibid., May 22nd, 1920.
16 Ibid., August 28th, 1920.
17 Diary, April 13th, 1921.
18 *Forward*, April 2nd, 1920.
19 Diary, April 15th, 1921.
20 *Forward*, May 7th, 1921.
21 Ibid., May 14th, 1921.

22 Ibid., April 19th, 1919; August 2nd, 1919; October 18th, 1919; 'Outlook', *Socialist Review* (October 1919).
23 Diary, October 11th, 1921.
24 *Forward*, July 30th, 1921.
25 Ibid., July 10th, 1920.
26 Ibid., July 15th, 1922.
27 Richard W. Lyman, 'James Ramsay MacDonald and the Leadership of the Labour Party, 1918–1922', *Journal of British Studies* (November 1962); H. S. Lindsay to MacDonald, June 8th, 1920, MDP 5/30.
28 Lyman, 'James Ramsay MacDonald and the Leadership of the Labour Party, 1918–1922'.
29 Diary.
30 Ibid., January 31st, 1921 and February 2nd, and 5th, 1921.
31 Ibid., February 8th, 1921.
32 *Forward*, February 19th, 1921.
33 Woolwich *Pioneer*, February 18th, 1921.
34 *Forward*, February 26th, 1921.
35 Woolwich *Pioneer*, special election supplements, MDP 7/53; Lyman, 'James Ramsay MacDonald and the Leadership of the Labour Party, 1918–1922'.
36 *Communist*, February 19th, 1921.
37 *John Bull*, February 26th, 1921.
38 *Daily News*, February 26th, 1921.
39 *Woolwich Gazette*, March 1st, 1921; *Observer*, February 27th, 1921.
40 *National News*, February 27th, 1921; *Daily Herald*, February 26th, 1921.
41 *Daily Herald*, March 2nd, 1921.
42 *Daily Telegraph*, March 3rd, 1921.
43 Diary, March 2nd, 1921.
44 *Evening Standard*, March 3rd, 1921.
45 Diary, April 3rd, 1921.
46 Ibid., June 25th, 1921.
47 Lyman, 'James Ramsay MacDonald and the Leadership of the Labour Party, 1918–1922'.
48 MacDonald to Ponsonby, November 1st, 1921, Ponsonby papers.
49 MacDonald to Algernon Lee, August 30th, 1922, Lee papers.
50 Marwick, op. cit., pp. 73–83.
51 Ibid., pp. 78–9; Lyman, 'James Ramsay MacDonald and the Leadership of the Labour Party, 1918–1922'.
52 *Labour Leader*, November 11th, 1920.
53 *Socialism: Critical and Constructive* (1925 edn), pp. 65, 68.
54 Ibid., p. 68.
55 Ibid., p. 69.
56 Ibid., pp. 255–6.

57 Ibid., p. 265.
58 MacDonald to Ponsonby, June 2nd, 1922, Ponsonby papers.
59 Emrys Hughes, 'Ramsay MacDonald's Fight', *New Leader*, November 3rd, 1922; Memorandum by Ivor Thomas, March 6th, 1938, Ivor Thomas papers.
60 Thomas memorandum.
61 *New Leader*, August 3rd, 1922.
62 *Afan Sentinel* (March 1922); Thomas papers.
63 *New Leader*, November 3rd, 1922.
64 Interview, Len Williams.
65 Thomas memorandum; interview, Len Williams.
66 *Western Mail*, November 3rd, 1922.
67 *Labour Voice*, November 11th, 1922.
68 *New Leader*, November 17th, 1922.
69 W. L. Guttsman, *The British Political Elite* (1963), pp. 236–9.
70 Mowat, op. cit., p. 147.
71 Emanuel Shinwell, *Conflict Without Malice* (1955), p. 83.
72 Diary, May 1st, 1923.
73 *Daily Herald*, November 21st, 1922.
74 Snowden, op. cit., vol. 1, p. 574.
75 Diary, May 1st, 1923.
76 *Forward*, November 25th, 1922.
77 Ibid.
78 Shinwell, op. cit., p. 84.
79 *Manchester Guardian*, November 22nd, 1922.
80 Ibid.
81 *New Leader*, November 24th, 1922.
82 Diary, May 1st, 1923.
83 John McNair, *James Maxton: The Beloved Rebel* (1955), *passim*.
84 'Outlook', *Socialist Review* (June 1923).
85 *Socialist Review* (January 1923) (signed article).
86 *The Times*, June 28th, 1923.
87 Ibid., July 4th, 1923.
88 *Hansard* (1923), vol. 167, cols. 1312–15.
89 'Outlook', *Socialist Review* (September 1923).
90 *Hansard* (1922), vol. 159, cols. 3237–45.
91 'Outlook', *Socialist Review* (February 1923).
92 *Hansard* (1923), vol. 161, col. 326.
93 MDP 8/1.
94 *New Leader*, June 15th, 1923; 'Outlook', *Socialist Review* (July 1923).
95 *Hansard* (1923), vol. 167, cols. 1772–84.
96 Ibid. (1923), vol. 168, cols. 461–79.
97 Lyman, *The First Labour Government 1924*, esp. chap. IV.

98 *The Times*, November 17th, 1923.

99 *New Leader*, November 23rd, 1923.

100 *The Times*, November 21st, 22nd, 1923; H. A. Marquand, *Organised Labour in Four Continents* (1939), p. 146.

101 *New Leader*, November 30th, 1923.

102 Ibid.

103 Diary, December 8th, 1923.

Chapter 14   Prime minister

1 Maurice Cowling, *The Impact of Labour 1920–1924* (1971), pp. 331–40.

2 Lyman, *The First Labour Government 1924*, pp. 81–4; *The Times*, December 8th, 1923; Taylor, *English History 1914–1945*, p. 209.

3 Diary, December 9th, 1923.

4 Brailsford to MacDonald, December 10th, 1923, MDP 5/33.

5 Diary, December 9th, 1923.

6 Ibid., December 10th, 1923.

7 Sidney Webb, 'The First Labour Government', *Political Quarterly* (January–March 1961); *The Times*, December 14th, 1923.

8 *The Times*, December 14th, 1923.

9 Diary, December 12th, 1923.

10 Lyman, *The First Labour Government 1924*, p. 86.

11 MDP 5/124.

12 Webb, op. cit., p. 9.

13 Interview, Mrs Lucy Middleton.

14 Ponsonby to MacDonald, wrongly dated November 11th, 1923, MDP 5/124.

15 Diary, December 10th, 11th, 1923; Viscount Haldane, *An Autobiography* (1929), pp. 319–24; Lyman, *The First Labour Government 1924*, p. 101.

16 Olivier to MacDonald, January 4th and 7th, 1924, MDP 5/124.

17 Haldane to MacDonald, January 11th, 1924, MDP 5/124.

18 Hamilton, *Henderson*, p. 236.

19 Sidney Webb, op. cit., p. 14.

20 Hamilton, *Henderson*, p. 236.

21 MDP 1/196.

22 MacDonald to Henderson, December 22nd, 1923, MDP 5/35.

23 Quoted in H. Hessell Tiltman, *James Ramsay MacDonald* (1929), pp. 309–13.

24 Diary, January 19th, 1924.

25 Ibid., January 21st, 1924.

26 Harold Nicolson, *King George V* (1952), p. 386.

27 Diary, January 22nd, 1924.

28 Webb, op. cit., p. 19.

29 Cabinet 7 (24).
30 Diary, January 23rd, 1924.
31 Ibid., February 3rd, 1924.
32 Quoted in Nicolson, *King George V*, p. 386.
33 Diary, January 10th, 1924.
34 Ibid., January 19th, 1924.
35 Ibid., January 26th, 1924.
36 Ibid., February 3rd, 1924.
37 Ibid., March 2nd, 1924.
38 Ibid., April 28th, 1924.
39 MacDonald to Chelmsford, August 16th, 1924, MDP 1/190.
40 Diary, June 18th, 1924.
41 Cuttings of articles by Mrs Ishbel Peterkin, Middleton papers.
42 Interview, Sir Patrick Duff.
43 Sir Charles Petrie, *The Powers Behind The Prime Minister* (1958), p. 142; interview, Mrs Rose Hoenig (*née* Rosenberg).
44 Stephen Roskill, *Hankey Man of Secrets*, vol. 2 (1972), pp. 353–4.
45 Thomas Jones, *Whitehall Diary*, ed. Keith Middlemas, vol. 1 (1969), pp. 262–310.
46 Interview, Mrs Rose Hoenig; Petrie, op. cit., p. 143.
47 Diary, April 10th, 1924.
48 Joseph Brown to Rose Rosenberg, May 4th and 16th, 1924; Rose Rosenberg to Brown, May 6th, 1924; C. P. Duff to Brown, September 4th, 1924, MDP 1/176.
49 Brown to Rose Rosenberg, February 19th, 1924, MDP 1/176.
50 Brown to Rose Rosenberg, April 27th, 1924; Rosenberg to Brown, April 28th, 1924, MDP 1/176.
51 Brown to Rose Rosenberg, May 14th, 1924, MDP 1/176.
52 Brown to Rosenberg; Rosenberg to Brown, May 12th, 1924, MDP 1/176.
53 Correspondence in MDP 1/185.
54 Brown to MacDonald, June 29th, 1924, MDP 1/176.
55 Rosenberg to Brown, July 17th, 1924, MDP 1/185.
56 Diary, March 2nd, 1924.
57 Ibid., July 15th, 1924.
58 Haldane, op. cit., p. 327.
59 Webb, op. cit., p. 19.
60 Ponsonby diary, March 7th, 1924.
61 Ibid., April 17th, 1924.
62 *Hansard* (1924), vol. 169, cols. 749–74.
63 Nicolson, *King George V*, p. 392.
64 Cabinet 10 (24).
65 M. A. Hamilton ('Iconoclast'), *J. Ramsay MacDonald (1923–1925)* (n.d.), p. 41.

66 Diary, March 2nd, 1924.
67 Diary.
68 Childs to Gower, January 24th, 1924; Gower to Childs, January 30th, 1924, MDP 1/221.
69 Childs to Gower, February 2nd, 1924, MDP 1/221.
70 Reports in MDP 1/220.
71 R.S. (24) 1st minutes, MDP 1/86.
72 R.S. (24) 2nd minutes, MDP 1/86.
73 Cabinet 18 (24).
74 Ibid., 20 (24).
75 R.S. (24) 3rd minutes, MDP 1/86.
76 Hansard (1924), vol. 171, cols. 316–25.
77 C.I.D. papers 127-A, MDP 1/157.
78 Ibid., 92-A, 96-A, 122-A, 125-A, MDP 1/157.
79 Minutes in MDP 1/155.
80 Hansard (1924), vol. 175, cols. 1782–6.
81 Diary, July 1st, 1924.
82 Cabinet 13 (24); Alan Bullock, The Life and Times of Ernest Bevin, vol. 1 (1960), p. 237.
83 Cabinet 22 (24); Bullock, op. cit., vol. 1, pp. 237–42.
84 Webb, op. cit., p. 23.
85 Cabinet 23 (24).
86 Hansard (1924), vol. 171, cols. 1680–84.
87 Ponsonby diary, March 7th, 1924.
88 Ibid., April 17th, 1924.
89 Robert E. Dowse, 'The Left Wing Opposition during the first two Labour Governments', Parliamentary Affairs, vol. 14, p. 84.
90 Ponsonby diary, April 17th, 1924.
91 Diary, March 2nd, 1924.
92 Ibid.
93 Diary, May 9th, 1924.
94 Ibid.
95 Diary, June 26th, 1924.
96 MDP 1/228.
97 R. K. Middlemas, The Clydesiders (1965), pp. 152–3.
98 C.P. 212/24, MDP 1/56.
99 Webb Diaries (1924–1932), p. 19.
100 Hankey to MacDonald, April 3rd, 1924, MDP 1/56.
101 Hansard (1924), vol. 171, cols. 2212–16.
102 Note by Clynes, April 5th, 1924, MDP 1/56.
103 Hansard (1924), vol. 171, cols. 2256–61.
104 Ibid. (1924), vol. 171, cols. 2715–21.
105 MDP 1/56.

106 King's letter, April 8th, 1924, MDP 1/228.
107 *Hansard* (1924), vol. 172, cols. 97–105.
108 Ibid. (1924), vol. 172, cols. 244–5.
109 Hankey to MacDonald, April 3rd, 1924, MDP 1/56.
110 MDP 1/23.
111 Cabinet 27 (24).
112 *Webb Diaries (1924–1932)*, p. 13.
113 Ibid., p. 20.
114 Diary, April 28th, 1924.
115 *Webb Diaries (1924–1932)*, p. 28.
116 Dowse, 'The Left Wing Opposition', p. 85.
117 *Hansard* (1924), vol. 174, cols. 645–60.
118 Cabinet 11 (24).
119 Ibid., 27 (24).
120 Ibid., 35 (24).
121 Ibid., 40 (24).
122 *Hansard* (1924), vol. 176, cols. 2091–2114.
123 Cabinet 47 (24).
124 Ibid., 41 (24).

Chapter 15   Foreign triumphs

1 British Institute of International Affairs, *Survey of International Affairs, 1924*, pp. 348–9.
2 Memorandum by J. Sterndal Bennett (F.O. print C2028/1346/18), MDP 1/114.
3 Diary, February 3rd, 1924.
4 Lyman, *The First Labour Government 1924*, p. 160.
5 Cabinet 8 (24).
6 *The Times*, March 3rd, 1924.
7 Ibid.
8 Crewe to MacDonald, March 9th, 1924, MDP 1/202.
9 *Hansard* (1924), vol. 170, cols. 45–6.
10 Diary, April 10th, 1924.
11 Text of report in MDP 1/151.
12 MDP 1/120.
13 MDP 1/119.
14 Cabinet 26 (24).
15 Text in MDP 1/117.
16 British Institute of International Affairs, op. cit., p. 359.
17 Text in MDP 1/101.
18 MacDonald to Sir G. Grahame (F.O. print C6562/70/18), MDP 1/95.

19 Quoted in Foreign Office summary of negotiations (F.O. print C11114/70/ 18), MDP 1/130.

20 Text in MDP 1/101.

21 Crewe to MacDonald, May 9th, 1924, MDP 1/202.

22 Foreign Office record of talks between MacDonald, Theunis and Hymans, MDP 1/125.

23 Ibid.

24 Diary, May 5th, 1924.

25 Foreign Office record of Chequers talks, MDP 1/123.

26 Diary, July 9th, 1924.

27 Foreign Office record of Paris talks, MDP 1/124.

28 Text of agreement in Foreign Office print C11043/70/18, MDP 1/130.

29 H. L. Lindsay to MacDonald, July 4th, 1924, MDP 1/182.

30 Quoted in Lyman, *The First Labour Government 1924*, p. 164.

31 *Proceedings of the London Reparations Conference*. This was published as Cmd. 2270. The text I have used is confidential print 12530, MDP (unclassified); vol. 1, pp. 2–3.

32 Ibid., vol. 1, pp. 5–11; Diary, July 17th, 1924.

33 Cabinet 44 (24).

34 Conference, *Proceedings*, vol. 1, pp. 252–9.

35 Ibid., vol. 1, pp. 268–73.

36 Ibid., vol. 1, pp. 32–44.

37 Diary, August 2nd, 1924.

38 MDP 1/139.

39 Diary, August 5th, 1924.

40 Conference, *Proceedings*, vol. 2, pp. 160–63.

41 Ibid., vol. 2, p. 167.

42 Ibid., vol. 2, p. 174.

43 Ibid., vol. 2, pp. 175–9.

44 Diary, August 8th, 1924.

45 Cabinet 47 (24).

46 Diary, August 6th, 1924.

47 Ibid., August 7th, 1924.

48 MacDonald to Herriot and Theunis, August 9th, 1924, CP 441 (24), MDP 1/138.

49 Diary, August 11th, 1924.

50 Conference, *Proceedings*, vol. 2, pp. 185–92.

51 Diary.

52 Ibid.

53 MacDonald to Snowden, '2 a.m.', August 14th, 1924, MDP 8/1.

54 Unsigned note by MacDonald, August 14th, 1924, MDP 1/127.

55 Ibid.; Diary, August 14th, 1924.

56 Diary, August 14th, 1924.

57 Diary.
58 Conference, *Proceedings*, vol. 2, pp. 122–54.
59 Ibid., vol. 2, pp. 7–8.
60 MacDonald to Parmoor, August 11th, 1924.
61 MacDonald to Sir Ellis Hume-Williams, August 11th, 1924, MDP 1/183.
62 Diary, September 21st, 1924.
63 Quoted in Lyman, *The First Labour Government 1924*, p. 173.
64 League of Nations, *Official Journal, Records of the Fifth Assembly, Text of the Debates* (Geneva, 1924), pp. 41–5.
65 MS lent by Lord Stamford.
66 Quoted in M. A. Hamilton, *J. Ramsay MacDonald*, p. 109.
67 Unsigned note headed 'The Geneva Protocol', MDP 5/139.
68 League of Nations, *Fifth Assembly Debates*, pp. 57–64.
69 Diary, September 21st, 1924.
70 League of Nations Union, *Protocol for the Pacific Settlement of Disputes* (1924); a copy is in MDP 5/139.
71 Minutes in MDP 1/155.
72 C.P. 45√, 24).
73 Cabinet 51 (24).
74 MDP 1/200.

Chapter 16   Domestic setbacks

1 Diary.
2 Gower to Wigram, 1/97.
3 Diary, September 21st, 1924.
4 'Iconoclast', *MacDonald*, p. 116.
5 MacDonald to Thompson, February 4th, 1924, MDP 1/194.
6 MacDonald to Grant, February 5th, 1924, MDP 1/194.
7 Grant to MacDonald, February 8th, 1924, MDP 1/194.
8 Thompson to MacDonald, February 9th, 1924, MDP 3/32.
9 MacDonald to Thompson, February 11th, 1924, MDP 1/194.
10 Grant to MacDonald, April 18th, 1924, MDP 1/194.
11 Grant to MacDonald, September 15th, 1924, MDP 1/194.
12 Grant to MacDonald, December 4th, 1924, MDP 1/194.
13 MacDonald to Grant, December 17th, 1294, MDP 1/2.
14 'Iconoclast', *MacDonald*, p. 109.
15 Katharine Bruce Glasier to MacDonald, September 22nd, 1924, MDP 1/2.
16 Middleton to MacDonald, September 22nd, 1924, MDP 1/182.
17 Diary, September 21st, 1924.
18 *Hansard* (1924), vol. 169, cols. 768–9.
19 Ponsonby diary, 'Whitsuntide recess'.

20 Cabinet 44 (24).
21 Ponsonby diary, August 13th, 1924.
22 Lyman, *The First Labour Government 1924*, pp. 195-6; British Institute of International Affairs, op. cit., pp. 241-5.
23 *Hansard* (1924), vol. 176, cols. 3136-7.
24 MDP 1/2.
25 Lyman, *The First Labour Government 1924*, pp. 199-201.
26 Cabinet 51 (24).
27 Diary.
28 *The Times*, September 29th, 1924.
29 Diary, September 27th, 1924.
30 Lyman, *The First Labour Government 1924*, p. 204.
31 This account is based on Hastings's speech in the House of Commons in October (see below, p. 376), *Hansard* (1924), vol. 177, cols. 596-619.
32 See below, p. 366.
33 Nicolson, *King George V*, p. 398.
34 *Hansard* (1924), vol. 177, cols. 602-5.
35 *Whitehall Diary*, vol. 1, pp. 287-90.
36 Ibid., vol. 1, p. 287.
37 *Hansard* (1924), vol. 177, col. 5.
38 *Whitehall Diary*, vol. 1, pp. 290-92.
39 *Hansard* (1924), vol. 176, col. 3221.
40 Lyman, *The First Labour Government 1924*, p. 237.
41 F. H. Newark, 'The Campbell Case and the First Labour Government', *Northern Ireland Legal Quarterly*, vol. 20, no. 1, pp. 30-31. I should add that Professor Newark's interpretation of MacDonald's role in the Campbell case differs substantially from mine.
42 Newark, op. cit., p. 31.
43 *The Times*, September 25th, 1924.
44 *Whitehall Diary*, vol. 1, p. 292.
45 Diary, September 27th, 1924.
46 Ibid., September 29th, 1924.
47 *Hansard* (1924), vol. 177, cols. 8-15.
48 *Whitehall Diary*, vol. 1, p. 296.
49 *Hansard* (1924), vol. 177, col. 16.
50 Diary.
51 Ibid., October 1st, 1924.
52 Ibid., October 2nd, 1924.
53 *Whitehall Diary*, vol. 1, p. 296.
54 Diary, October 2nd, 1924.
55 *The Times*, October 6th, 1924.
56 Cabinet 52 (24).
57 *Whitehall Diary*, vol. 1, p. 293.

58 Diary, October 6th, 1924.
59 *Hansard* (1924), vol. 177, cols. 512–13.
60 *Manchester Guardian*, October 9th, 1924.
61 Cabinet 53 (24).
62 Ibid., 54 (24).
63 Diary, October 8th, 1924.
64 Ibid., October 9th, 1924.
65 Lyman, *The First Labour Government 1924*, pp. 255–7.
66 'Iconoclast', *MacDonald*, p. 122.
67 Middlemas, *Clydesiders*, p. 179.
68 'Iconoclast', *MacDonald*, p. 123.
69 This account of MacDonald's election tour is based partly on 'Iconoclast', *MacDonald*, pp. 123–9, and partly on Lewis Chester, Stephen Fay and Hugo Young, *The Zinoviev Letter* (1967), pp. 8–11.
70 *The Times*, October 18th, 1924.
71 'Iconoclast', *MacDonald*, p. 129.
72 Chester *et al.*, op. cit., p. 11.
73 *The Times*, October 24th, 1924.
74 Ibid., October 29th, 1924; Chester *et al.*, op. cit., p. 11.
75 Snowden, op. cit., p. 710.
76 *Manchester Guardian*, October 25th, 1924.
77 'Iconoclast', *MacDonald*, pp. 150–53.
78 Diary, October 31st, 1924.
79 *Manchester Guardian*, October 27th, 1924.
80 Chester *et al.*, op. cit., pp. 131–2.
81 *The Times*, October 25th, 1924.
82 Chester *et al.*, op. cit., esp. Chaps. 5 and 6.
83 Diary, October 28th, 1924.
84 *Daily Mail*, October 28th, 1924.
85 *The Times*, October 28th, 1924.
86 *Manchester Guardian*, October 28th, 1924.
87 Diary, October 31st, 1924.
88 *Whitehall Diary*, vol. 1, pp. 298–301.
89 Diary, November 3rd, 1924.
90 Cabinet 58 (24).
91 Diary, November 5th, 1924.
92 *Forward*, December 6th, 1924.
93 Diary, November 28th, 1924.

Chapter 17   Portrait of a sexagenarian

1 Diary.
2 Hamilton, *Henderson*, p. 256.

3 Shinwell, op. cit., pp. 98–9.
4 Hamilton, *Henderson*, pp. 256–7.
5 Bullock, op. cit., vol. 1, p. 258.
6 Marwick, op. cit., p. 93.
7 *Webb Diaries (1924–1932)*, p. 52.
8 Ibid., p. 51.
9 Hamilton, *Henderson*, pp. 256–7.
10 *Webb Diaries (1924–1932)*, p. 54.
11 Ibid., p. 51.
12 Diary, December 3rd, 1924.
13 For the minority movement see R. Martin, *Communism and the British Trade Unions* (1969).
14 *Wanderings and Excursions*, p. 13.
15 MacDonald to Trenchard, June 9th, 1925, MDP 6/28.
16 Rose Rosenberg to Ernest Bevin, April 26th, May 9th, 1927, MDP 5/38.
17 MacDonald to Villard, July 25th, 1927, MDP 3A/33.
18 Rose Rosenberg to Williams, April 22nd, 1926.
19 MacDonald to Shepherd, March 7th, 1927.
20 Brown to MacDonald, November 4th, 1925, MDP 7/26.
21 Brown to MacDonald, March 5th, 1927, MDP 7/28.
22 Brown to MacDonald, August 5th, 1927, MDP 7/28.
23 Brown to MacDonald, November 5th, 1924, MDP 7/25; MacDonald to Brown, November 18th, 1925, MDP 7/26.
24 MacDonald to Brown, December 6th, 1926, MDP 7/27.
25 N.E.C. finance sub-committee minutes, November 24th, 1924; Correspondence between Rose Rosenberg and Captain Hall, June–November 1925, MDP 5/36.
26 MacDonald to W. Miller, July 29th, 1925, MDP 6/28.
27 MacDonald to A. J. Russell, January 10th, 1927, MDP 3A/33.
28 Blackwood to MacDonald, November 18th, 1925, MDP 3/33; J. R. Jarvie to Rose Rosenberg, November 25th, 1925, MDP 3A/31; MacDonald to Roy Hopkins, March 9th, 1926, MDP 3A/32.
29 MacDonald to Mrs Dryhurst, May 18th, 1925, MDP 6/28.
30 MacDonald to R. Richards, November 10th, 1925, MDP 5/36.
31 MacDonald to Edward Cain, March 10th, 1926, MDP 5/37.
32 MacDonald to H. O. Coleman, December 8th, 1926, MDP 5/37.
33 Diary, June 6th, 1926.
34 Ibid., July 4th, 1926.
35 Ibid., April 3rd, 1927.
36 Ibid., January 20th, 1928.
37 MacDonald to William Frost, November 17th, 1925 MDP 3/33; Rose Rosenberg to Colonel L'Estrange Malone, April 16th, 1925, MDP 5/36.
38 Diary, April 11th, 1925.

39 MacDonald to Miss I. M. Drummond, December 16th, 1925, MDP 3/33.
40 Notebook.
41 MDP 6/29.
42 MacDonald to Reith, January 12th, 1927, MDP 6/30.
43 Reith to MacDonald, January 15th, 1927, MDP 6/30.
44 MacDonald to Reith, January 18th, 1927, MDP 6/30.
45 MacDonald to Hugo Allen, February 21st, 1928, MDP 6/31.
46 MacDonald to R. M. Cant, January 30th, 1928, MDP 6/31.
47 MacDonald to Peach, October 1st, 1928, MDP 5/39.
48 MacDonald to Martin, March 13th, 1928, MDP 6/31.
49 Diary, January 27th, 1928; correspondence with Sir A. Grant and J. L. Caw, MDP 6/28 and 3/33; correspondence with Alfred Mattison, May–October 1925, MDP 5/36; correspondence with J. D. Morgan, April–July 1925, MDP 5/36.
50 Diary, July 16th, 1926.
51 Ibid., November 6th, 1928.
52 Egon Wertheimer, *Portrait of the Labour Party* (1929), p. 175.
53 *Webb Diaries (1924–1932)*, pp. 117–18.
54 Interview, Mrs Rose Hoenig.
55 Nicolson, *Diaries*, vol. 1, pp. 67–8.
56 The Marchioness of Londonderry, *Retrospect* (1938), pp. 223–4.
57 Hugh Dalton, *Call Back Yesterday* (1953), pp. 175–6.
58 Interviews, Mrs Cecily Mure, Princess Bibesco, Mrs M. A. Hamilton, Lady Helen Roberton.
59 *Remembering My Good Friends*, p. 121.
60 *The Man of Tomorrow* (1923); *J. Ramsay MacDonald (1923–1925)* (1925).
61 *Remembering My Good Friends*, p. 128.
62 Diary, December 7th, 1924.
63 Ibid., September 26th, 1928.
64 Ibid., January 30th, 1929.
65 Bradley to MacDonald, March 23rd and November 30th, 1925, MDP 6/28.
66 MacDonald to Bradley, December 2nd, 1925, MDP 6/28.
67 Diary, April 12th, 1929.
68 Ibid., June 6th, 1926.
69 MacDonald to Cecily Gordon-Cumming, May 23rd, 1930, Mure papers.
70 'Iconoclast', *MacDonald*, p. 168.
71 *Webb Diaries (1924–1932)*, p. 13.
72 Brockway, op. cit., p. 152.
73 Ponsonby diary, August 13th, 1924
74 Ibid., August 14th, 1924.
75 'Iconoclast', *MacDonald*, p. 174.
76 Ivor Thomas to MacDonald, July 23rd, 1925, MDP 5/36.
77 MacDonald to Cole, December 24th, 1929, MDP 2/6.

78 See esp. MacDonald to Laski, June 14th, 1926, MDP 5/37; other correspondence in MDP 5/38 and 5/39.
79 See below, pp. 487–8.
80 *Remembering My Good Friends*, p. 125.
81 Margaret Cole, *The Life of G. D. H. Cole* (1971), pp. 167–8.
82 Wertheimer, op. cit., pp. 174–5.
83 Interviews, Mrs Rose Hoenig, Mrs Margaret Sutherland, James Margach, personal information.
84 MacDonald to Ivor Thomas, December 8th, 1927, MDP 5/38; February 20th, 1928, MDP 5/39.
85 Lord Dawson of Penn to MacDonald, December 2nd, 1924, MDP 1/2.
86 MacDonald to Macmillan, September 27th, 1927; memorandum by Conan Doyle, n.d., MDP 6/72.
87 MacDonald to Macmillan, September 12th and 27th, 1927; Macmillan to MacDonald, September 16th, 1927, MDP 6/72.
88 MacDonald to Gilmour, September 15th, 1927, MDP 6/72; Gilmour to MacDonald, September 23rd, 1927, MDP 6/30.
89 MDP 6/72.
90 MacDonald to Macmillan, September 23rd, 1927, MDP 6/72.
91 MDP 6/72.
92 Ibid.
93 Correspondence in MDP 6/30 and 6/72.
94 *Hansard* (1927), vol. 210, col. 380.
95 *The Times*, November 16th, 1927.
96 *Hansard* (1927), vol. 210, cols. 818–19.
97 MDP 6/31.

Chapter 18   Under fire

1 *Webb Diaries (1924–1932)*, p. 55.
2 MacDonald to Fenner Brockway, February 25th, 1925; notice issued by John Scurr and Fenner Brockway attached to it, MDP 5/136.
3 MacDonald to J. Wooley, February 25th, 1925, MDP 6/28.
4 MacDonald to W. J. Jupp, February 23rd, 1925, MDP 5/36.
5 MacDonald to Kerr, February 25th, 1925, MDP 5/36.
6 Correspondence in MDP 5/132 and 5/36.
7 MacDonald to Henderson, March 30th, 1925, MDP 5/36.
8 MDP 5/132.
9 *Hansard* (1925), vol. 182, cols. 338–47.
10 Diary, April 11th, 1925.
11 John Paton, *Left Turn!* (1936), p. 228.
12 *I.L.P.C.R.* (1925).

13 Spoor to MacDonald, April 24th, 1925, MDP 5/36.
14 MacDonald to Spoor, April 28th, 1925, MDP 5/36.
15 Correspondence in MDP 5/134.
16 *Webb Diaries (1924–1932)*, p. 60.
17 Grigor Vasileff to MacDonald, April 27th, 1925, MDP 5/36.
18 MacDonald to Vasileff, May 13th, 1925, MDP 5/36.
19 J. D. A. Law to MacDonald, June 1st, 1925, MDP 5/36.
20 MacDonald to Law, June 10th, 1925, MDP 5/36.
21 Law to MacDonald, June 15th, 1925, MDP 5/36.
22 George Howgate to MacDonald, June 19th, 1925, MDP 6/28.
23 *Webb Diaries (1924–1932)*, p. 63.
24 R. Page Arnot, *The Miners: Years of Struggle* (1953), pp. 226–393.
25 *Hansard* (1925), vol. 187, cols. 1598–9.
26 *Daily Mail*, August 4th, 1925.
27 *Webb Diaries (1924–1932)*, p. 16.
28 Spoor to MacDonald, August 11th, 1925, MDP 5/36.
29 Spoor to MacDonald, August 20th, 1925, MDP 5/36.
30 Thomas to MacDonald, August 18th, 1925, MDP 5/36.
31 Bullock, op. cit., vol. 1, pp. 283–4.
32 MacDonald to Snowden, September 26th, 1925.
33 *L.P.C.R.* (1925).
34 *Forward*, October 10th, 1925.
35 Kerr to MacDonald, n.d., MDP 5/36.
36 Jenkins to MacDonald, October 9th, 1925, MDP 5/36.
37 *Webb Diaries (1924–1932)*, p. 74.
38 *Hansard* (1925), vol. 188, cols. 1739–47.
39 Ibid. (1925), vol. 188, cols. 2075–86.
40 Rose Rosenberg to MacDonald, December 8th, 1925, MDP 5/36.
41 *Webb Diaries (1924–1932)*, p. 80; Dowse, *Left in the Centre*, pp. 118–19.
42 Bullock, op. cit., vol. 1, p. 282; Middlemass, *Clydesiders*, p. 196.
43 Bullock, op. cit., vol. 1, esp. Chaps. 10 and 11.
44 *Forward*, October 17th, 1925.
45 Marwick, op. cit., pp. 99–102.
46 Allen to MacDonald, November 2nd, 1925, MDP 5/36.
47 Kerr to MacDonald, October 3rd, 1925, MDP 5/36.
48 MacDonald to Kerr, October 6th, 1925, MDP 5/36.
49 MacDonald to Thomas, October 6th, 1925, MDP 5/36.
50 Kerr to MacDonald, November 11th, 1925, MDP 5/36.
51 MacDonald to Wake, November 12th, 1925, MDP 5/36.
52 *Forward*, November 14th, 1925.
53 Wake to MacDonald, November 13th, 1925, MDP 5/36.
54 N.E.C. minutes, December 16th, 1925.
55 Labour Party Organization sub-committee minutes, June 21st, 1926.

56 Peter Kelly to MacDonald, November 18th, 1925, MDP 5/36.
57 MacDonald to Kelly, November 19th, 1925, MDP 5/36.
58 Circular letter from Brockway to I.L.P. parliamentary group, February 16th, 1926; MacDonald to Brockway, February 17th, 1926, MDP 5/37.
59 MacDonald to George Martin, March 16th, 1926, MDP 5/37.
60 Account based on Bullock, op. cit., vol. 1, pp. 299–315; R. Page Arnot, op. cit., pp. 403–30; *Whitehall Diary*, vol. 2, pp. 24–35; Keith Middlemas and John Barnes, *Baldwin* (1969), pp. 394–410.
61 MacDonald to Cook, March 30th, 1926, MDP 5/37.
62 *Forward*, April 24th, 1926.
63 Lord Citrine, *Men and Work* (1964), p. 163.
64 Diary.
65 Bullock, op. cit., vol. 1, pp. 314–15.
66 *Hansard* (1926), vol. 195, cols. 104–16.
67 Citrine, op. cit., p. 175.
68 Diary, May 3rd, 1926.
69 Diary.
70 Ibid., May 10th, 1926.
71 *Hansard* (1926), vol. 195, col. 347.
72 *Whitehall Diary*, vol. 2, pp. 39–44.
73 Diary, May 7th, 8th and 9th, 1926.
74 Diary.
75 Ibid.
76 Ibid., May 12th, 1926.
77 Ibid., May 13th, 1926.
78 *Hansard* (1926), vol. 195, cols. 1042–5.
79 Ibid. (1926), vol. 195, cols. 1045–51.
80 Diary, May 14th, 1926.

Chapter 19   Regaining the initiative

1 MacDonald to Kerr, May 14th, 1926, MDP 6/29.
2 *Forward*, May 22nd, 1926.
3 Quoted in Bullock, op. cit., vol. 1, p. 349.
4 Ibid., pp. 349–50.
5 Diary.
6 Ibid.
7 Diary, June 10th, 1926.
8 Ibid., June 16th, 1926.
9 Ibid., June 21st, 1926.
10 *Forward*, July 3rd and 10th, 1926.
11 *Hansard* (1926), vol. 197, cols. 1056–68.

12 Ibid. (1926), vol. 198, cols. 1743–5.
13 Diary, September 3rd, 1926.
14 *Hansard* (1926), vol. 199, cols. 159–71.
15 Diary, September 3rd, 1926.
16 Churchill papers, 22/113.
17 Ibid.
18 Diary, September 3rd, 1926.
19 Page Arnot, op. cit., pp. 480–81.
20 Diary.
21 Page Arnot, op. cit., p. 481.
22 *Forward*, September 11th, 1926.
23 *Hansard* (1926), vol. 199, cols. 291–2.
24 Cook to MacDonald, January 13th, 1927, MDP 5/38.
25 MacDonald to Cook, January 14th, 1927, MDP 5/38.
26 MacDonald to Frank Lee, February 24th, 1927, MDP 5/38.
27 MacDonald to T. S. B. Williams, March 3rd, 1927, MDP 5/38.
28 MacDonald to Hicks, December 30th, 1926, MDP 5/37.
29 *Forward*, October 16th, 1926.
30 Ibid., January 29th, 1927.
31 Bullock, op. cit., vol. 1, p. 379.
32 *Forward*, September 17th, 1929.
33 *L.P.C.R.* (1927).
34 H. N. Brailsford, John A. Hobson, A. Creech Jones, and E. F. Wise, *The Living Wage* (1926), esp. pp. 27–41.
35 Dowse, *Left in the Centre*, p. 122.
36 Paton, op. cit., p. 236.
37 Dowse, *Left in the Centre*, pp. 117–51, 212–15.
38 MacDonald to Mosley, August 5th, 1925, MDP 5/36.
39 MacDonald to Strachey, November 23rd, 1925, MDP 6/28.
40 MacDonald to Niemeyer, March 16th, 1926, MDP 5/37.
41 *Forward*, March 27th, 1926.
42 MacDonald to W. Leach, April 13th, 1926, MDP 6/29.
43 MacDonald to Paton, April 22nd, 1926, MDP 6/29.
44 MacDonald to Bondfield, March 31st, 1926, MDP 5/37.
45 Hobson to MacDonald, October 7th, 1926, MDP 5/37.
46 MacDonald to Hobson, October 8th, 1926, MDP 5/37.
47 MacDonald to Brockway, June 11th and 17th, July 27th and August 2nd, 1926; Brockway to MacDonald, June 11th, 14th and 24th, July 26th and 29th, 1926, MDP 5/37.
48 *L.P.C.R.* (1926).
49 N.E.C. minutes, February 18th and December 21st, 1927.
50 MacDonald to Strachey, February 5th, 1927, MDP 3A/33.
51 Dowse, *Left in the Centre*, pp. 126–7.

52 MacDonald to Paton, April 8th, 1927, MDP 5/38.
53 *Forward*, April 16th, 1927.
54 MacDonald to Salter, April 8th, 1927, MDP 5/39.
55 Shinwell, op. cit., pp. 102–3.
56 Leach to MacDonald, January 17th, 1929, MDP 5/40.
57 MacDonald to Perriman, January 18th, 1929, MDP 5/40.
58 MacDonald to Allen, October 6th, 1926, MDP 5/37.
59 MacDonald to Newbold, May 13th, 1925, MDP 6/28.
60 *Forward*, March 19th, 1927.
61 Ibid., January 22nd, 1927.
62 Ibid., June 30th, 1928.
63 Ibid., April 16th, 1927.
64 Diary, June 20th, 1926.
65 *Forward*, January 28th, 1928.
66 Ibid., August 11th, 1928.
67 Ibid., September 3rd, 1927.
68 Ibid., December 1st, 1928.
69 Ibid., July 25th, 1927.

Chapter 20   Labour and the nation

 1 *Forward*, April 19th, 1927; March 17th, 1928; February 4th, 1928.
 2 MacDonald to Beneš, November 26th, 1928, MDP 5/39.
 3 MacDonald to Longuet, January 26th, 1928, MDP 5/39.
 4 MacDonald to Lady Courtney, October 20th, 1928, MDP 6/31.
 5 *Forward*, July 16th, 1927.
 6 *Hansard* (1927), vol. 202, cols. 409–16.
 7 MacDonald to Lampson, February 9th, 1927, MDP 5/38.
 8 Lampson to MacDonald, March 21st, 1927, MDP 5/38.
 9 *Forward*, October 29th, 1927.
10 Diary.
11 *Manchester Guardian*, September 14th, 1927.
12 MacDonald to Scott, September 13th, 1927, MDP 5/39.
13 Diary, September 16th, 1927.
14 Diary.
15 MDP 5/38.
16 Ibid.
17 *Hansard* (1927), vol. 210, cols. 2089–101.
18 *Forward*, March 31st, 1928.
19 MacDonald to Shotwell, April 22nd, 1928, MDP 6/31.
20 *Hansard* (1928), vol. 217, cols. 431–47.
21 *L.P.C.R.* (1928).

22 MacDonald to Baker, October 22nd, 1928, MDP 6/31.

23 *Forward*, October 27th, 1928.

24 *Hansard* (1928), vol. 222, cols. 755–64.

25 *Forward*, November 17th, 1928.

26 Ibid., December 22nd, 1928.

27 MacDonald to Warburg, January 31st, 1928, MDP 5/39.

28 MacDonald to Harrison Brown, November 22nd, 1928, MDP 5/39.

29 MacDonald to Sadler, November 27th, 1928.

30 MS. in MDP 3A/33.

31 Villard to MacDonald, December 6th, 1928, MDP 6/32.

32 MacDonald to Smith, November 14th, 1928, MDP 6/31.

33 Summary in *New York Literary Digest*, February 9th, 1929, MDP 5/40.

34 MDP 6/32.

35 MacDonald to House, April 8th, 1929, MDP 6/32.

36 N.E.C. minutes, July 27th, 1927; Dalton, op. cit., p. 171.

37 *L.P.C.R.* (1927).

38 Diary.

39 Dalton, op. cit., pp. 173–5, MacDonald to Graham, July 7th, 1927, MDP 5/38. Dalton states that Snowden was not consulted about the committee, but this is contradicted by MacDonald to Snowden, October 15th, 1927, MDP 8/1 (see below, p. 476).

40 *L.P.C.R.* (1927).

41 MDP 8/1.

42 Ibid.

43 *Forward*, October 22nd, 1927.

44 MDP 5/38.

45 Ibid.

46 N.E.C. minutes, October 26th, 1927.

47 Text in MDP 5/38.

48 Diary, dated '1928', obviously written at the start of the year.

49 N.E.C. minutes, February 29th, 1928.

50 Ibid., March 28th, 1928.

51 *L.P.C.R.* (1928).

52 *Forward*, October 13th, 1928.

53 Jack Rees to MacDonald, February 13th, 1928, MDP 7/29.

54 Brown to MacDonald, February 14th, 1928, MDP 7/29.

55 Claude Cummings to MacDonald, April 4th, 1928, MDP 7/29.

56 MacDonald to Brown, March 23rd, 1928, MDP 7/29.

57 MacDonald to R. Strange, April 18th, 1928.

58 *Webb Diaries (1924–1932)*, p. 169.

59 N.E.C. minutes, May 23rd, 1928.

60 Brown to MacDonald, July 16th, 1928, MDP 7/29.

61 MacDonald to Brown, June 29th, 1928, MDP 7/29.

62 MDP 7/29.
63 Ibid.
64 Ibid.
65 Ibid.
66 Diary.
67 Ibid.
68 Ibid.
69 Greenwood to MacDonald, n.d., enclosing Tawney to Henderson, MDP 5/40.
70 Trevor Wilson, *The Downfall of the Liberal Party* (Fontana edn, 1968), p. 373.
71 MDP 6/32.
72 *Forward*, March 9th, May 4th, 1929.
73 Ibid., March 16th, 1929.
74 Diary.
75 *The Times*, May 25th, 1929.
76 Ibid., May 29th, 1929.
77 Ibid.
78 MacDonald to Henderson, May 29th, 1929, MDP 5/40.
79 MacDonald to Tawney, April 9th, 1929, MDP 5/40.
80 *Forward*, May 25th, 1929.
81 Wertheimer, op. cit., pp. 176–7.

Chapter 21   Second innings

1 Dalton, op. cit., p. 212.
2 Tiltman, op. cit., pp. 229–30.
3 Diary, June 1st, 1929.
4 *The Times*, June 3rd, 1929.
5 Diary, June 4th, 1929.
6 Ibid., June 5th, 1929.
7 Ibid., April 14th, 1929.
8 Snowden, op. cit., pp. 760–64.
9 Nicolson, *George V*, p. 435.
10 Diary.
11 Ibid.
12 Ibid.
13 Ibid.
14 Wertheimer, op. cit., pp. 185–6.
15 Diary, April 14th, 1929.
16 Addison to MacDonald, June 9th, 1929, MDP 5/40.
17 Diary, June 20th, 1929.

18 Diary.
19 Lord Vansittart, *The Mist Procession* (1958), p. 371.
20 Wertheimer, op. cit., p. 174.
21 P. W. Wilson, 'The Man who talks for Britain', *New York Times*, September 29th, 1929 (cuttings in MDP 6/87).
22 *Whitehall Diary*, vol. 2, p. 208.
23 *Webb Diaries (1924–1932)*, p. 249.
24 See particularly MacDonald to Lady Londonderry, June 12th, August 29th and September 6th, 1930, Londonderry papers, D3099/3/10/30 44 and 46.
25 Londonderry papers, D3099/3/10/77, February 13th, 1931.
26 Ibid., D3099/3/10/66, December 20th, 1930.
27 Ibid., D3099/3/10/90, May 23rd, 1931.
28 Mure papers, n.d., postmarked June 5th, 1929.
29 Ibid., n.d., postmarked July 21st, 1929.
30 Ibid., n.d., postmarked July 30th, 1929.
31 Interview, Mrs Cecily Mure.
32 Mure papers, both n.d.
33 Interview, Mrs Cecily Mure.
34 Mure papers, n.d., postmarked March 5th, 1930.
35 Ibid., n.d.
36 Ibid., n.d., postmarked June 24th, 1930.
37 Ibid., postmarked or dated December 26th, 1929; May 7th, July 8th, July 15th, September 1st, October 29th, 1930.
38 Ibid., April 2nd, 1931.
39 Ibid., n.d.
40 See above, p. 484.
41 *Hansard* (1929), vol. 229, cols. 47–9.
42 Ibid. (1929), vol. 229, cols. 63–76.
43 P. W. Wilson, op. cit.
44 Raymond O'Connor, *Perilous Equilibrium: The United States and the London Naval Conference of 1930* (Lawrence, Kansas, 1960); note by R. L. Craigie dated June 10th, 1929, MDP 1/267.
45 Craigie note, MDP 1/267.
46 Diary, June 21st, 1928.
47 Note of meeting in MDP 1/267.
48 Note by MacDonald in MDP 1/267.
49 For American view see *B.D.* 2/I nos. 20, 32 and 37; for British, *B.D.* 2/I nos. 28 and 35 and memoranda by Alexander and Madden, both July 23rd, 1929, MDP 1/267.
50 Diary, July 14th, 1929.
51 MacDonald to Dawes, July 23rd, 1929, MDP 1/267.
52 *B.D.* 2/I no. 25.

H1

53 MacDonald to Alexander, July 30th, 1929, MDP 1/267.
54 MacDonald to Dawes, August 1st, 1929, MDP 1/267.
55 Report by MacDonald to Cabinet 33 (29), September 13th, 1929.
56 MacDonald to Dawes, August 8th, 1929, *B.D.* 2/I no. 28.
57 Dawes to MacDonald, n.d., *B.D.* 2/I no. 32.
58 MacDonald to Dawes, August 30th, 1929, *B.D.* 2/I no. 40.
59 Diary.
60 Ibid.
61 MacDonald to Dawes, August 30th, 1929, *B.D.* 2/I no. 41.
62 MacDonald to Dawes, September 9th, 1929, *B.D.* 2/I no. 49.
63 *B.D.* 2/I nos. 54 and 55.
64 MacDonald to Dawes, September 23rd, 1929, *B.D.* 2/I no. 67.
65 Diary.
66 *New York Times*, September 28th, 1929, MDP 6/87.
67 Notebook, September 27th, 1929.
68 This account of MacDonald's American visit is based mainly on cuttings from the *New York Times* in MDP 6/87. All quotations are taken from there unless otherwise stated.
69 *B.D.* 2/I no. 77; Roskill, op. cit., p. 492.
70 *B.D.* 2/I no. 77.
71 Diary.
72 *Hansard* (1929), vol. 231, cols. 885–92.
73 *Webb Diaries (1924–1932)*, p. 223.
74 Dalton, op. cit., p. 246.
75 Harold Nicolson, *Dwight Morrow* (1935), p. 378.
76 Ibid., p. 381.
77 *Documents of the London Naval Conference 1930* (1930), pp. 50–53.
78 Cabinet 1 (30).
79 Diary.
80 CAB 29/128.
81 Diary.
82 *B.D.* 2/I no. 123.
83 David Carlton, *MacDonald versus Henderson* (1970), pp. 126–7.
84 Account of conference based mainly on *B.D.* 2/I nos. 142–84, partly on Conference, *Documents*, partly on Carlton, op. cit., and O'Connor, op. cit., partly on Diary.
85 Diary, January 23rd, 1930.
86 Conference, *Documents*, pp. 515–18.
87 Diary, February 12th, 1930.
88 Diary.
89 *B.D.* 2/I nos. 153, 155 and 158; Diary, March 17th, 1930.
90 Diary.
91 Ibid., March 20th.

92 Meeting of British and American delegations, March 24th, 1930, *B.D.* 2/I no. 168.
93 Minutes of British delegation meeting, CAB 29/128.
94 Diary.
95 Cabinet 19 (30).
96 Meeting of French and British delegations, April 8th, 1930, *B.D.* 2/I no. 181.
97 *B.D.* 2/I no. 184.
98 Conference, *Documents*, pp. 261–4.

Chapter 22   Slump

1 Diary, September 26th, 1929.
2 Department of Employment, *British Labour Statistics, Historical Abstract 1886–1968* (1971), Table 162.
3 For the terms 'economic conservative' and 'economic radical' (and a contrary view of the alleged differences between them) cf. R. J. Skidelsky, *Politicians and the Slump* (1976).
4 W. H. Janeway, 'The Economic Policy of the Second Labour Government' (Cambridge Ph.D. thesis), Chaps. II, IV and V.
5 Memorandum, 'The Steps taken by the Lord Privy Seal in relation to rationalisation', MDP 1/418.
6 *Committee on Finance & Industry, Report* (1931), Cmd. 3897, p. vi.
7 MacDonald to Baldwin, July 30th, 1929, MDP 5/40.
8 MacDonald to Snowden, August 2nd, 1929, MDP 2/6.
9 Diary, December 2nd, 1929; *Whitehall Diary*, vol. 2, pp. 219–28.
10 *Whitehall Diary*, vol. 2, p. 226.
11 Skidelsky, op. cit., pp. 122–31.
12 Diary, December 3rd, 1929.
13 Ibid., December 17th, 1929.
14 Janeway, op. cit., pp. 129–33.
15 *Hansard* (1929), vol. 233, cols. 1751–2.
16 Diary.
17 Ibid.
18 Ibid., December 12th, 1929.
19 *Hansard* (1929), vol. 233, cols. 1245–1311.
20 *Hansard* (1929), vol. 233, cols. 1672–89, 1749–74.
21 *Annual Register* (1929), p. 114.
22 Diary, December 19th, 1929.
23 *Hansard* (1929), vol. 229, cols. 73–5.
24 *Annual Register* (1930), p. 2.
25 Cabinet 55 (29).
26 Diary.

27 Note dated February 4th, 1930, MDP 5/171.
28 Diary, February 20th, 1930.
29 *Annual Register* (1930), p. 13.
30 Diary, February 26th, 1930.
31 Diary.
32 Report by Lord Ullswater to prime minister, July 17th, 1930, Cmd. 3636.
33 MDP 1/330.
34 MDP 5/34 green.
35 N.d., MDP 5/34 green.
36 Diary.
37 N.E.C. minutes, May 20th, 1930.
38 Skidelsky, op. cit., p. 202.
39 Diary.
40 MDP 1/445.
41 MDP 1/446.
42 Cabinet 6 (30).
43 C.P. 134 (30); filed in MDP 1/446.
44 Diary, December 24th, 1929.
45 Ibid., February 9th, 1930.
46 Ibid., April 29th, 1930.
47 MacDonald to Newbold, June 2nd, 1930, MDP 6/33.
48 Note dated May 7th, 1930, MDP 1/456.
49 Diary, March 2nd, 1930.
50 Cabinet 26 (30).
51 *Whitehall Diary*, vol. 2, pp. 256–7.
52 Diary, May 19th, 1930.
53 *Whitehall Diary*, vol. 2, pp. 257–9.
54 Ibid., pp. 259–60.
55 Diary, May 20th, 1930.
56 Cabinet 29 (30).
57 Account by Rt. Hon. G. R. Strauss, quoted in Skidelsky, op. cit., pp. 185–6.
58 Diary, May 22nd, 1930.
59 *Hansard* (1930), vol. 239, cols. 1329–40, 1348–72.
60 Diary.
61 Ibid.
62 Cabinet 31 (30); *Hansard* (1930), vol. 240, cols. 432–4.
63 Thomas to MacDonald, June 13th, 1930, MDP 1/418.
64 Diary, June 16th, 1930.

Chapter 23   Looking for a policy

1 Diary, June 16th, 1930.

2 Ibid., June 24th, July 1st and 2nd, 1930.
3 Diary.
4 Ibid., July 17th, 1930.
5 Diary.
6 Notebook.
7 *Whitehall Diary*, vol. 2, p. 262.
8 Cabinet 31 (30).
9 *Annual Register* (1930), p. 59.
10 Diary, July 1930.
11 MDP 1/459.
12 Skidelsky, op. cit., p. 196.
13 Janeway, op. cit., pp. 65–6.
14 Memorandum by Hartshorn, August 18th, 1930, MDP 1/472.
15 Diary.
16 *British Labour Statistics*, Table 162.
17 Anderson to MacDonald, July 30th, 1930, MDP 1/462.
18 MDP 1/472.
19 Memoranda by Leith-Ross, n.d. and August 1st, 1930; MacDonald to Snowden, July 14th, 1930, MDP 1/257.
20 MDP 1/446.
21 MDP 1/454.
22 MacDonald to Anderson, July 12th, 1930, MDP 1/446.
23 Maybury memorandum, August 15th, 1930, MDP 1/472.
24 Official note of meeting on August 18th, 1930, MDP 1/472.
25 C.P. (30) 35; MDP 1/446.
26 *How to tackle Unemployment* (October 1930).
27 MDP 5/174.
28 Minutes of Cabinet 56 (30), September 25th, 1930, filed in CAB 23/90B.
29 Cabinet 56 (30), September 25th, 1930.
30 Hartshorn memorandum, August 18th, 1930, MDP 1/472.
31 *Whitehall Diary*, vol. 2, p. 235.
32 Snowden, op. cit., vol. 1, p. 923.
33 Diary, July 22nd, 1930.
34 Notebook, August 14th, 1930.
35 R. F. Harrod, *The Life of John Maynard Keynes* (1951), pp. 424–9.
36 Memorandum dated May 30th, 1930, MDP 1/455.
37 *Whitehall Diary*, vol. 2, p. 262.
38 Janeway, op. cit., p. 14.
39 Cabinet 14 (30).
40 Minute dated February 11th, 1930, MDP 1/244.
41 MDP 1/244.
42 Minutes of meeting in MDP 1/243.
43 Taylor to MacDonald, March 2nd, 1930, MDP 6/33.

44 Buxton to MacDonald, MDP 1/243.
45 Memorandum by Henderson, March 10th, 1930, MDP 1/243.
46 Cabinet 17 (30), March 26th, 1930.
47 Thomas to Buxton, April 25th, 1930, MDP 1/244; Addison to MacDonald, April 17th, 1930, MDP 2/10.
48 Adamson to MacDonald, April 24th, 1930, MDP 1/243.
49 MDP 1/243.
50 Snowden to MacDonald, April 28th, 1930, MDP 1/243.
51 Notes in MDP 1/243.
52 Attlee memorandum, June 9th, 1930, MDP 1/243.
53 See Cabinets 42 (30) and 45 (30).
54 Cabinet 47 (30), July 30th, 1930.
55 *Hansard* (1930), vol. 242, cols. 890–96.
56 See Cabinet 33 (30) and unnumbered Cabinet minutes on pp. 433–5 of CAB 23/64.
57 Cabinet 33 (30), June 24th, 1930.
58 CAB 23/64, pp. 433–5, no Cabinet number or date.
59 Notebook, August 26th and 29th, 1930.
60 Graham to MacDonald, September 3rd, 1930, MDP 1/420.
61 MacDonald to Thomas, August 31st, 1930, MDP 2/10.
62 Cabinet 50 (30), September 2nd, 1930.
63 Graham to MacDonald, September 3rd, 1930, MDP 1/420.
64 MDP 1/420.
65 Snowden to MacDonald, MDP 2/10.
66 Buchan to MacDonald, September 5th, 1930, MDP 6/33.
67 Bevin to MacDonald, August 27th, 1930, MDP 1/461.
68 Notebook, August 14th, 1932.
69 Addison to MacDonald, MDP 2/10.
70 MDP 5/174.
71 Lloyd George to MacDonald, September 14th, 1930, MDP 5/174.
72 MDP 5/174.
73 Ibid.
74 CAB 23/90B.
75 Diary, October 5th, 1930.
76 *L.P.C.R.* (1930).
77 McNeill Weir, op. cit., p. 237.
78 *L.P.C.R.* (1930).
79 *Manchester Guardian*, October 8th, 1930.
80 McNeill Weir, op. cit., p. 244.
81 *L.P.C.R.* (1930).
82 Diary, October 7th, 1930.
83 *L.P.C.R.* (1930).

Chapter 24   Marking time

1 Diary, October 12th, 1930.
2 Diary.
3 Ibid.
4 Ibid., October 9th, 1930.
5 Cabinets 64 (30) and 65 (30), October 28th and 29th.
6 Annex to Cabinet 65 (30), CAB 23/65 pp. 257–68.
7 Diary, October 16th, 1930.
8 *Hansard* (1930), vol. 244, cols. 5–7.
9 Ibid. (1930), vol. 244, cols. 45–56, 67–81, 226–34, 397–404.
10 Diary.
11 *Hansard* (1930), vol. 244, cols. 703–17.
12 Ibid. (1930), vol. 244, cols. 812–20.
13 Diary, November 4th, 1930.
14 By Robert Boothby, quoted in Skidelsky, op. cit., p. 69.
15 Sir Oswald Mosley, *My Life* (1968), pp. 264–82.
16 See particularly the *Observer*, November 23rd, 1930.
17 Skidelsky, op. cit., p. 279.
18 MacDonald to Buchan, September 8th, 1930, MDP 6/33.
19 MDP 2/7.
20 Ibid.
21 Diary.
22 Ibid.
23 MDP 8/1.
24 Ibid.
25 Diary, December 3rd, 1930.
26 Ibid., December 4th, 1930.
27 The Earl of Birkenhead, *Halifax* (1965), pp. 233–90; S. Gopal, *The Viceroyalty of Lord Irwin, 1926–1931* (1957), pp. 35–88.
28 Diary.
29 Ibid.
30 Ibid.
31 Ibid.
32 *Indian Round-Table Conference Proceedings* (1931), Cmd. 3778, pp. 331–54, 417–513.
33 *Hansard* (1931), vol. 247, cols. 637–50, 689–703, 744–8.
34 Diary, January 26th, 1930.
35 *Hansard,* (1929), vol. 231, cols. 1303–13; Diary, November 7th, 1929.
36 Diary, July 3rd, 1930.
37 *L.P.C.R.* (1930).
38 Lloyd George to MacDonald, October 9th and 23rd, 1930; MacDonald to

Lloyd George, October 10th, 1930, MDP 5/174.

39 Diary.

40 Ibid., October 20th, 1930.

41 *Hansard* (1930), vol. 244, col. 32.

42 Cabinet 68 (30).

43 Diary.

44 MDP 1/330.

45 Ibid.

46 Henderson to MacDonald, December 5th, 1930, MDP 1/330.

47 N.E.C. minutes, December 17th and 18th, 1930.

48 *Annual Register* (1931), pp. 9, 12.

49 Account based on Cabinet minutes, papers in MDP 1/440, and Janeway, op. cit., Chap. VI.

50 MDP 1/440.

51 C.P. 3 (31).

52 MacDonald to Snowden, December 30th, 1930, MDP 5/41.

53 Diary.

54 Ibid., January 14th, 1931.

55 Cabinet 6 (31).

56 C.P. 31 (31).

57 Cabinet 12 (31).

58 Hankey to MacDonald, February 10th, 1931, MDP 1/440.

59 Cabinet 13 (31).

60 Diary, February 11th, 1931.

61 MDP 5/177.

62 Note of interview between Bondfield and Sinclair, MDP 5/177.

63 Cabinet 13 (31).

64 *Hansard* (1931), vol. 248, col. 435–49.

65 CAB 24/223.

66 Cabinet 69 (30), November 19th, 1930.

67 Keynes to MacDonald, March 5th, 1931, MDP 2/11.

68 Diary, March 1st, 1931.

69 MDP 2/11.

70 Diary.

71 Janeway, op. cit., p. 221.

72 MDP 2/11.

73 Diary, March 3rd, 1931.

74 Thorne to MacDonald, March 3rd, 1931, MDP 5/42.

75 Taylor to MacDonald, March 4th, 1931, MDP 6/34.

76 Turner to MacDonald, March 7th, 1931, MDP 6/34.

77 MacDonald to Lloyd George, January 28th, 1931, MDP 5/175; Diary, February 2nd, 1931.

78 *Hansard* (1931), vol. 248, cols. 646–60.

79 Hartshorn to MacDonald, March 2nd, 1931, MDP 5/175; Sir John Alexander to MacDonald, March 19th, 1931, MDP 1/466; Johnston to MacDonald, April 1st, 1931, MDP 5/175.

80 Diary.

81 MDP 5/42.

82 Wilson, op. cit., p. 394.

83 *Webb Diaries (1924–1932)*, p. 269.

84 Diary, March 10th, 11th, 1931.

85 Ethel Snowden to MacDonald, March 27th, 1931, MDP 5/42.

86 Diary, March 29th, 1931.

87 MacDonald to Snowden, April 7th, 1930, MDP 5/179; Snowden to MacDonald, April 13th, 1930, MDP 5/42.

88 Janeway, op. cit., pp. 223–4.

89 Diary, April 16th, 1931.

90 Diary.

91 Ibid., May 20th, 1931.

92 Cabinet 72 (30), December 10th, 1930.

93 Cabinet 16 (31), March 4th, 1931; Cabinet 17 (31), March 11th, 1931.

94 Snowden to MacDonald, 'Easter Monday', 1931, MDP 5/179; Parmoor to MacDonald, April 13th, 1931, MDP 2/11.

95 MacDonald to Snowden, April 7th, 1931, MDP 5/179.

96 MacDonald to Addison, April 14th, 1931.

97 Cabinets 22 (31), 23 (31).

98 Cabinet 27 (31), May 6th, 1931.

99 Diary.

100 Ibid., April 30th, 1931.

101 Ibid., April 21st, 1931.

102 Ibid., May 20th, 1931.

103 MacDonald to Middleton, May 25th, 1930, Middleton papers.

104 Cabinet 31 (31).

105 Diary, June 11th, 1931.

106 Treasury note in MDP 1/259.

107 Diary.

108 Ibid.

109 MDP 5/177.

110 Diary, June 14th, 1931.

111 Ibid., June 16th, 1931.

112 Ibid.

113 Ibid.

114 MDP 5/177.

115 Cabinet 33 (31).

116 Diary, June 16th, 1931.

117 *Webb Diaries (1924–1932)*, p. 276.

118 Frank Owen, *Tempestuous Journey: Lloyd George, His Life and Times* (1954), p. 717.
119 MacDonald to Montagu Norman, June 18th, 1931, MDP 2/11.

Chapter 25   Crisis

1 For talks on June 6th, 1931, see Edward W. Bennett, *Germany and The Diplomacy of the Financial Crisis* (1962), p. 125; for continuation of the talks on June 7th, *B.D.* 2/II no. 51.
2 Diary, June 7th, 1931.
3 Bennett, op. cit., p. 141.
4 Diary, June 21st, 1931.
5 Bennett, op. cit., pp. 166–243; Goronwy Rees, *The Great Slump* (1970), pp. 141–5.
6 Cabinet 36 (31).
7 Bennett, op. cit., p. 253; Janeway, op. cit., p. 240.
8 Diary.
9 Ibid.
10 Cabinet 38 (31).
11 Carlton, op. cit., pp. 201–2; Bennett, op. cit., pp. 249–51; *B.D.* 2/II no. 194.
12 Diary, July 15th, 1931.
13 *B.D.* 2/II No. 193; Carlton, op. cit., pp. 202–3; Bennett, op. cit., pp. 253–5.
14 Diary, July 15th, 1931.
15 *B.D.* 2/II no. 193.
16 Diary, July 16th, 1931.
17 Bennett, op. cit., pp. 263–74.
18 *B.D.* 2/II Appendix I.
19 Diary.
20 Ibid., July 23rd, 1931.
21 Bassett, *Nineteen-Thirty-One*, p. 53; Janeway, op. cit., p. 241.
22 Advance copy in MDP 5/182.
23 Cabinet 40 (31).
24 Diary, July 31st, 1931.
25 Bennett to MacDonald, August 2nd, 1931, MDP 5/42.
26 MacDonald to Bennett, August 8th, 1931.
27 MDP 1/260.
28 *Committee on Finance & Industry, Report* (1931), Cmd. 3897, pp. 239–41.
29 MDP 1/260.
30 Janeway, op. cit., p. 243.
31 MDP 1/260.
32 Ibid.
33 Ibid.
34 Snowden to MacDonald, August 7th, 1931, MDP 1/260.

35 Diary, August 11th, 1931.
36 Ibid.
37 Janeway, op. cit., p. 246.
38 Diary, August 13th, 1931.
39 Skidelsky, op. cit., p. 356.
40 Diary, August 17th, 1931.
41 Ibid., August 18th, 1931.
42 Janeway, op. cit., pp. 247–9.
43 Skidelsky, op. cit., pp. 359–62.
44 C.P. 203 (31), Appendix to Cabinet 41 (31).
45 Note headed 'National Emergency', MDP 1/260.
46 Howarth note, 'National Emergency'; commentary on Henderson's speech headed 'The Financial Crisis of August, 1931', MDP 1/260.
47 Cabinet 41 (31).
48 Ibid.
49 Diary, August 19th, 1931; note initialled by C. P. Duff summarizing course of the crisis headed 'The Financial Crisis', MDP 5/182.
50 Cabinet 41 (31).
51 Reports to Cabinet 42 (31), August 20th, 1931, by MacDonald, Snowden and Graham.
52 Conclusion 2, Cabinet 42 (31).
53 T.U.C. record of meeting, MDP 1/260.
54 Diary, dated August 21st, but referring to August 20th, 1931.
55 Note headed 'Notes on the Economy Issue', dated August 27th, 1931, MDP 1/260. Though this was written *after* the fall of the Labour Government, there is no reason to believe that Henderson's opinions were any different when he wrote it from what they had been five or six days before.
56 In his note of August 7th, see above, p. 612.
57 See below, p. 626.
58 For Margaret Bondfield's position, see minutes of National Union of General and Municipal Workers National Executive, August 27th, 1931. I am grateful to Mr Giles Radice, M.P., for drawing this to my attention.
59 It is not clear who these were. According to Postgate, *The Life of George Lansbury*, p. 269, Lansbury was opposed from the start but had only three supporters at first. Dalton, op. cit., p. 275, says 'Greenwood, Johnston and Lansbury were opposed to any dole cut throughout. Others joined up only later.'
60 Diary, dated August 22nd, but referring to August 21st, 1931.
61 Cabinet 43 (31), August 21st, 1931.
62 Diary, dated August 22nd, but referring to August 21st.
63 Cabinet 43 (31).
64 Diary, dated August 22nd, but referring to August 21st. For time of meeting, Duff note, MDP 5/182.

65 Bassett, op. cit., pp. 106–7; report by MacDonald to Cabinet 44 (31), August 22nd, 1931.
66 Duff note, MDP 5/182.
67 Bassett, pp. 107–9.
68 Diary, dated August 22nd, referring to August 21st.
69 Cabinet 44 (31).
70 Cabinet 45 (31).
71 Duff note, MDP 5/182.
72 Nicolson, *King George V*, pp. 460–61.
73 Ibid., pp. 461–2.
74 Diary, August 23rd, 1931.
75 Note in possession of Mrs Sheila Lochhead.
76 Malcolm MacDonald diary.
77 Cabinet 46 (31).
78 Appendix to Cabinet 46 (31); CAB 23/67.
79 Cabinet 46 (31); note by Rose Rosenberg, MDP 5/182; Janeway, op. cit., p. 263.
80 Nicolson, *King George V*, p. 464.
81 Ibid.
82 Cabinet 46 (31).
83 Middlemas and Barnes, *Baldwin*, pp. 628–9.
84 Diary, August 23rd, 1931.
85 Malcolm MacDonald diary.
86 Nicolson, *King George V*, pp. 465–6; Middlemas and Barnes, op. cit., pp. 629–30.
87 Cabinet 47 (31).
88 Bassett, op. cit., p. 160.
89 Cabinet 47 (31).

Chapter 26   Split

1   See above, p. 637.
2   Snowden, op. cit., vol. 1, p. 954.
3   Dalton, op. cit., p. 273.
4   Diary, August 24th, 1931.
5   Both letters are in MDP 1/383.
6   Minute by C. P. Duff, August 25th, 1931, MDP 5/182.
7   Minute by C. P. Duff, August 26th, 1931, MDP 5/182.
8   MDP 5/180.
9   Shinwell, op. cit., p. 110.
10 Snell to MacDonald, August 26th, 1931, MDP 5/44.
11 MDP 5/180.

12 Bernard Donoughue and G. W. Jones, *Herbert Morrison* (1973), pp. 162–7.
13 Diary, August 26th, 1931.
14 Dalton, op. cit., pp. 273–4.
15 Dalton diary, August 24th, 1931 (p. 48), Dalton papers.
16 Bassett, op. cit., p. 169.
17 Ibid., pp. 173–4.
18 Ibid., pp. 182–3.
19 Ibid., pp. 185–7.
20 Note by Duff, dated August 27th, 1931, MDP 1/383.
21 MacDonald to Lindsay, August 27th, 1931, MDP 5/180.
22 Diary, August 27th, 1931; Bassett, op. cit., p. 189.
23 Interview, Rt. Hon. George Strauss, M.P.
24 Tillett to MacDonald, August 31st, 1931, MDP 5/181.
25 Malcolm MacDonald strongly dissents from this view and believes that his father deliberately stayed away from the party meeting because he thought it would damage the party if he went to it, and that he was right to stay away.
26 *Hansard* (1931), vol. 256, col. 28.
27 Letters from Parkinson, Arnott, and Gossling in MDP 1/383; from Ammon, Attlee, Lawson, Leach, Riley, Taylor, Turner and Welsh in MDP 5/181; from Dunnico in MDP 5/180.
28 Thomas to MacDonald, August 26th, 1931; Middleton, August 27th; Roberton, September 1st; Donaldson, September 4th; Lewis, Stibbs and Morgan, n.d.; all in MDP 5/180.
29 MacDonald to Lunn, September 1st, 1931, MDP 5/181.
30 MacDonald to Gordon MacDonald, September 2nd, 1931, MDP 5/181.
31 MDP 5/181.
32 Ibid.
33 MDP 5/180.
34 Ibid.
35 Ibid.
36 Coxon to MacDonald, September 3rd, 1931, MDP 5/180.
37 MDP 5/180.
38 Ibid.
39 Grant to MacDonald, September 1st, 2nd, 6th and 9th, 1931, MDP 5/180.
40 Grant to MacDonald, September 13th, 1931; Coxon to MacDonald, n.d., MDP 5/180.
41 MDP 5/180.
42 Coxon to MacDonald, n.d., MDP 5/180.
43 MacDonald to Coxon, September 15th, 1931, MDP 5/180.
44 MDP 5/180.
45 Diary.
46 Bassett, op. cit., pp. 196–7.

47 Diary.
48 MacDonald to Sutcliffe, September 2nd, 1931, MDP 5/181.
49 MacDonald to Mackenzie, September 5th, 1931, MDP 5/180.
50 Aitchison to MacDonald, August 29th, 1931, MDP 5/180.
51 MacDonald to Aitchison, September 2nd, 1931, MDP 5/180.
52 'Secretary's notes of a conversation between Sir Ernest Harvey and Mr. Peacock and Members of the Cabinet on Thursday, September 3rd, 1931 at 3 p.m.', CAB 23/68.
53 Church to MacDonald, September 6th, 1931, MDP 5/43.
54 MDP 5/180.
55 Ibid.
56 Diary, September 7th, 1931.
57 *Hansard* (1931), vol. 256, cols. 13–25.
58 Quoted in Bassett, op. cit., p. 222.
59 *Hansard* (1931), vol. 256, cols. 25–40.
60 Bassett, op. cit., p. 221.
61 *Hansard* (1931), vol. 256, cols. 419–41, 476–81.
62 Diary, September 9th, 1931.
63 Diary.
64 Strauss diary.
65 Diary.
66 Ibid.
67 Bassett, op. cit., pp. 187–9, 207–8, 217–18.
68 Diary, September 8th, 1931.
69 Diary.
70 Ibid.
71 Bassett, op. cit., p. 237.
72 Janeway, op. cit., pp. 305–7.
73 Ibid., p. 308; Diary, September 18th, 1931.
74 Diary, September 20th, 1931.
75 *Hansard* (1931), vol. 256, cols. 1299–1304.
76 Bassett, op. cit., p. 241.
77 Diary, September 25th, 1931.
78 MacDonald to Baldwin, September 23rd, 1931, MDP 5/186.
79 MDP 5/180.
80 Ibid.
81 Diary, September 25th, 1931.
82 C.P. 247 (31).
83 MDP 5/186.
84 Nicolson, *King George V*, p. 491.
85 Diary, September 28th, 1931.
86 Bassett, op. cit., p. 265.
87 A point made by Taylor, op. cit., p. 323.

88 Both letters in MDP 5/186.
89 Diary.
90 David Wrench, 'Aspects of National Government Policy, 1931-1935', University of Wales Ph.D. thesis, p. 42.
91 Ibid., p. 43.
92 Cabinet 68 (31).
93 MDP 5/186.
94 Thomas Jones, *A Diary With Letters* (1954), p. 56.
95 Cabinet 69 (31).
96 Nicolson, *King George V*, p. 493.
97 Cabinet 70 (31).
98 Wrench, op. cit., p. 53.
99 Diary, October 5th, 1931.
100 Ibid., October 7th, 1931.
101 Donoughue and Jones, op. cit., p. 169.
102 Interview, Len Williams.
103 See esp. Bassett, op. cit., Chap. XV.
104 Quoted in Bassett, op. cit., p. 286.
105 *The Times*, October 8th, 1931.
106 Ibid., October 26th, 1931.
107 MDP 6/34.
108 *Daily Herald*, October 7th, 1931.
109 Ibid., October 12th, 1931.
110 Dalton, op. cit., p. 294.
111 *Daily Herald*, October 13th, 1931.
112 *Durham County Advertiser*, October 16th, 1931.
113 *The Times*, October 13th, 1931.
114 *Daily Herald*, October 16th, 1931; *Durham County Advertiser*, October 23rd, 1931.
115 Unpublished MS. biography of Ramsay MacDonald by Ernest Stanford, p. 118.
116 *The Times*, October 13th, 1931.
117 Stanford MS., p. 121.
118 *The Times*, October 28th, 1931.
119 Stanford MS., pp. 127–8.

Chapter 27   *'Nae my ain hoose'*

1 Diary.
2 Quoted in Bassett, op. cit., p. 332.
3 See particularly MacDonald to Baldwin, October 7th, 1931, MDP 5/186; Church to MacDonald, October 9th, 1931, MDP 5/42; De La Warr to

MacDonald, October 13th, 1931, MDP 5/42; Stonehaven to MacDonald, October 23rd, 1931, MDP 1/388.

4 Diary.

5 Ibid., November 22nd, 1931.

6 MacDonald to Boltz, November 18th, 1931, MDP 5/42.

7 MacDonald to Tillett, November 3rd, 1931, MDP 5/42.

8 MacDonald to Diack, November 5th, 1931, MDP 6/34.

9 MacDonald to Archbishop of York, November 11th, 1931, MDP 6/34.

10 MacDonald to Haddow, December 26th, 1931, MDP 3/39.

11 Titler to MacDonald, December 29th, 1931, MDP 5/43.

12 MacDonald to Titler, December 30th, 1931, MDP 5/43.

13 MDP 5/43.

14 Peach to MacDonald, January 6th, 1932, MDP 5/43.

15 MacDonald to Peach, January 9th, 1932, MDP 5/43.

16 Notes headed 'Meeting held at No. 10 Downing Street on Friday 13th October, 1933', MDP 5/195.

17 Notebook, December 27th, 1932.

18 Diary, October 23rd, 1933.

19 Ibid., November 20th, 1933.

20 Notebook, July 15th, 1934.

21 *Webb Diaries (1924–1932)*, p. 294; Sidney Webb (Lord Passfield), 'What Happened in 1931: A Record', *Political Quarterly* (January–March 1932).

22 Issue of September 1932; copy in MDP 3/40.

23 Diary, January 8th, 1932.

24 MacDonald to Tillett, October 10th, 1932, MDP 5/43.

25 Campion to the author.

26 MacDonald to Morgan, November 14th, 1931, MDP 5/42.

27 Diary, March 31st, 1932.

28 Ibid., July 14th, 1932.

29 MacDonald to Allen, December 26th, 1932, MDP 3/40.

30 Welsh to MacDonald, September 19th, 1933, MDP 5/44.

31 Bullock, op. cit., vol. 1, pp. 197, 454–5.

32 Tillett to MacDonald, January 29th, 1932, MDP 5/43.

33 MacDonald to Tillett, February 3rd, 1932, MDP 5/43.

34 Tillett to MacDonald, April 15th, 1932, MDP 5/43.

35 MDP 3/40.

36 Rosenberg to MacDonald, April 30th, 1932, MDP 5/43.

37 Diary, November 25th, 1932.

38 Ibid., November 26th, 1932.

39 MDP 5/43.

40 Ibid.

41 Ibid.

42 MacDonald to Bromley, November 14th, 1933, MDP 5/44.
43 MacDonald to Evans, November 29th, 1933, MDP 5/44.
44 MacDonald to Allen, January 18th, 1932, MDP 5/43.
45 Diary, June 4th, 1933.
46 MacDonald to Tillett, March 8th, 1933, MDP 5/44.
47 Richardson to MacDonald, n.d., MDP 5/44.
48 MacDonald to Richardson, May 30th, 1933, MDP 5/44.
49 Diary, February 23rd, 1934.
50 Ibid., September 24th, 1933.
51 Notebook, January 12th, 1934.
52 Nicolson, *King George V*, p. 494.
53 Notebook, December 27th, 1932.
54 Diary, May 20th, 1934.
55 Ibid., September 21st, 1932.
56 Ibid., September 17th, 1933.
57 Ibid., January 24th, 1934.
58 Ibid., May 18th, 1934.
59 Interview, Princess Bibesco.
60 February 22nd, 1932, Bibesco papers.
61 March 20th, 1932, Bibesco papers.
62 November 11th, 1932, Bibesco papers.
63 June 17th, 1935, Bibesco papers.
64 June 29th, 1935, Bibesco papers.
65 Londonderry, op. cit., pp. 13–27, 97–124, 236–49; Eileen O'Casey, *Sean* (1973), pp. 50–53; Janet Adam Smith, *John Buchan* (1965), pp. 312–13, 330–32; H. Montgomery Hyde, *Baldwin* (1973), pp. 295–6.
66 Dated 9th July, MDP 3/46.
67 Dated October 12th, 1933, MDP 3/114.
68 MDP 3/114.
69 Londonderry papers, n.d., D 3099/3/10/124.
70 Ibid., n.d., D 3099/3/10/126.
71 Ibid., December 27th, 1931, D 3099/3/10/128.
72 Ibid., March 27th, 1932, D 3099/3/10/152A.
73 Ibid., May 21st, 1932, D 3099/3/10/165.
74 Londonderry papers, D 3099/3/10/165.
75 Ibid., May 28th, 1932, D 3099/3/10/168.
76 Ibid., October 9th, 1932, D 3099/3/10/215.
77 Ibid., 'December 1932', D 3099/3/10/238.
78 Ibid., March 24th, 1938, D 3099/3/10/255.
79 Ibid., September 26th, 1933, D 3099/3/10/281.
80 Diary, January 16th, 1933.
81 Ibid., July 28th, 1933.
82 MDP 3/117.

83 Interview, Mrs Grace Cooke; Grace Cooke, *The Plumed Serpent* (1942), pp. 70–80.
84 Diary, July 26th, 1933.
85 Diary.
86 Ibid.
87 MDP 6/143.
88 MacDonald to Princess Bibesco, n.d., postmarked February 29th, 1932, Bibesco papers.
89 MDP 3/40.
90 Communiqué dated March 13th, 1932, MDP 6/143.
91 Diary, March 31st, 1932.
92 Horder to MacDonald, March 28th, 1932, MDP 6/143.
93 April, 19th 1932, MDP 6/143.
94 Diary, May 1st, 1932.
95 Ibid., May 2nd, 1932.
96 MacDonald to Bella Ramsay, May 27th, 1932, in possession of Mr and Mrs Hett.
97 Horder to MacDonald, September 22nd and October 20th, 1932, MDP 3/40.
98 November 3rd, 1932, MDP 6/143.
99 MacDonald to Elliott, December 26th, 1932, MDP 5/43.
100 Diary, January 19th, 1933.
101 Ibid.
102 Ibid., March 29th, 1934.
103 Ibid., January 27th, 1934.
104 Notebook, August 9th, 1933.
105 Ibid., August 28th, 1933.
106 Hugh L'Etang, *The Pathology of Leadership* (1969), p. 71.
107 Major-General A. C. Temperley, *The Whispering Gallery of Europe* (1938), p. 240.
108 *Hansard* (1933), vol. 274, col. 1312.
109 Ibid. (1932), vol. 272, col. 37.
110 Ibid. (1933), vol. 276, cols. 511–12.
111 Ibid. (1933), vol. 277, cols. 1375–6.
112 Diary, March 22nd, 1933.
113 Ibid., March 23rd, 1933.
114 Ibid., March 24th, 1933.
115 Ibid., May 11th, 1933.
116 Ibid., October 2nd, 1933.
117 Notebook, January 5th, 1934.
118 Stanford MS., p. 160.
119 *Hansard* (1933), vol. 283, cols. 20–29.
120 Note by Rose Rosenberg, February 28th, 1934, MDP 5/195.

121 Diary, February 27th, 1934.
122 Ibid., March 18th, 1934.
123 Horder to MacDonald, June 21st, 1934, MDP 6/143.
124 Diary, June 19th, 1934.
125 Ibid., October 8th, 1934.
126 Roskill, *Hankey*, vol. 3, p. 162.
127 Notebook.
128 MDP 6/149.

Chapter 28   Crumbling coalition

1 Diary.
2 MDP 5/42.
3 Snowden, op. cit., vol. 1, pp. 998–9.
4 Middlemas and Barnes, op. cit., p. 655.
5 Ibid.
6 See below, pp. 709–13.
7 See particularly MacDonald to Betterton, November 5th, 14th, 19th, 21st, 1931, MDP 1/467.
8 C.P. 311 (31); draft in MDP 5/184.
9 Cabinets 87(31) and 88 (31), December 10th and December 11th, 1931.
10 Lady Londonderry nicknamed him the 'silk worm'.
11 Wrench, op. cit., pp. 176–89.
12 MacDonald to Willingdon, December 6th, 1931, MDP 2/32.
13 Diary, November 11th, 1931 (wrongly dated October 11th).
14 Wrench, op. cit., p. 190.
15 Ibid., pp. 191–2.
16 Diary, November 11th, 1931.
17 Ibid., November 23rd, 1931.
18 Wrench, op. cit., pp. 195–7.
19 Hoare to MacDonald (wrongly dated 'December 30'), MDP 2/32.
20 Wrench, op. cit., p. 201.
21 Ibid., p. 202.
22 MacDonald to Willingdon, December 6th, 1931, MDP 2/32.
23 Wrench, op. cit., p. 67.
24 Cabinet 76 (31), November 12th, 1931.
25 Cabinet 81 (31); Wrench, op. cit., p. 72.
26 Snowden, op. cit., p. 1006.
27 MDP 5/42.
28 *Annual Register* (1931), p. 104.
29 C.P. 311 (31), draft.

30 Note headed 'Chequers Jan 10/32', MDP 1/587.
31 Wrench, op. cit., pp. 77–8.
32 The committee's was C.P. 25 (32), Snowden's C.P. 31 (32) and Samuel's C.P. 32 (32).
33 Cabinets 5 and 6 (32) (both on January 21st).
34 Diary, January 22nd, 1932.
35 Wrench, op. cit., pp. 84–5.
36 Cabinet 7 (32).
37 Diary, January 22nd, 1932.
38 Diary.
39 See above, p. 694.
40 Christopher Thorne, *The Limits of Foreign Policy* (1972), p. 258. My account of the Shanghai crisis and of MacDonald's role in it is based on Thorne.
41 Diary, January 30th, 1932.
42 J. Wheeler-Bennett, *The Disarmament Deadlock* (1934), pp. 14–19.
43 Cabinet 90 (31), December 15th, 1931.
44 Diary, January 24th, 1932.
45 Ibid., April 7th, 1932.
46 DC (M) 32 1st meeting, March 21st, 1932, record in MDP 1/591.
47 Wheeler-Bennett, op. cit., p. 32.
48 Minutes of British Commonwealth delegations, MDP 1/501.
49 Diary, May 1st, 1932.
50 MDP 2/12.
51 Wrench, op. cit., p. 318.
52 Roskill, *Hankey*, vol. 3, p. 45.
53 Notebook, July 6th, 1932.
54 Account based on J. Wheeler-Bennett, *The Wreck of Reparations* (1933), and *B.D.* 2/III pp. 188–269.
55 Notebook.
56 Ibid., June 28th, 1932.
57 Ibid., June 30th, 1932.
58 Ibid., July 1st, 1932.
59 *B.D.* 2/III pp. 272–362.
60 *B.D.* 2/III no. 172.
61 *B.D.* 2/III no. 173.
62 *B.D.* 2/III no. 174.
63 Notebook, July 5th, 1932.
64 *B.D.* 2/III nos. 184 and 185.
65 Notebook, July 9th, 1932.
66 Ibid., July 10th, 1932.
67 Lamont to Rosenberg, July 12th, 1932, MDP 3/40.
68 Keynes to MacDonald, July 12th, 1932, MDP 2/12.
69 MacDonald to Keynes, July 13th, 1932, MDP 2/12.

70 Wheeler-Bennett, *The Disarmament Deadlock*, p. 51; *B.D.* 2/III no. 270.
71 Samuel to MacDonald, July 9th, 1932, MDP 2/12.
72 MacDonald to Baldwin, June 21st, 1932, MDP 2/12.
73 Wrench, op. cit., p. 100.
74 Samuel to MacDonald, July 17th, 1932, MDP 2/12.
75 MacDonald to Samuel, July 21st, 1932, MDP 2/12.
76 MDP 2/12.
77 Wrench, op. cit., pp. 103–4.
78 Cabinet 46 (32).
79 MDP 5/191.
80 See particularly Usher to Margesson, January 2nd, 1932, and MacDonald to Stonehaven, January 8th and 21st, 1932, MDP 5/43.
81 Rose Rosenberg to Glyn, July 22nd, 1932, MDP 5/43.
82 MacDonald to De La Warr, July 29th, 1932, MDP 5/43.
83 MacDonald to Snowden, July 29th, 1932, MDP 5/43.
84 MacDonald to Picton, July 30th, 1932, MDP 2/12.
85 MDP 2/12 (filed under 'Simon').
86 MDP 1/504.
87 Diary, September 9th, 1932.
88 MDP 5/191.
89 Diary, September 9th, 1932.
90 Samuel papers, quoted in Wrench, op. cit., p. 106.
91 MDP 5/191.
92 Ibid.
93 MacDonald to Snowden, September 14th, 1932, MDP 5/191.
94 Snowden to MacDonald, September 15th, 1932, MDP 5/191.
95 Cabinet 57 (32); MacDonald to Samuel, September 17th, 1932, MDP 2/12.
96 MDP 5/191.
97 Diary, September 23rd, 1932.
98 Cabinet 47 (32).
99 Cabinet 48 (32).
100 Diary, September 28th, 1932.

Chapter 29   Ebb tide

1 Wrench, op. cit., p. 114.
2 MacDonald to Baldwin, September 10th, 1932, Baldwin papers, 167/187.
3 Baldwin to MacDonald, September 12th, 1933, Baldwin papers, 167/189.
4 Diary, September 29th, 1932.
5 Ibid., October 11th, 1932.
6 MacDonald to Glyn, December 25th, 1932, MDP 5/43.
7 MacDonald to Thomas, January 2nd, 1933, MDP 5/44.

8 Diary, January 29th, 1933.

9 Wrench, op. cit., 129; Rose Rosenberg to Betterton, October 20th, 1932, MDP 2/12.

10 Cabinet 25 (33), April 7th, 1933.

11 Diary, April 7th, 1933.

12 Ibid., March 5th, 1933.

13 Notebook, April 23rd, 1933.

14 MacDonald to Betterton, August 4th, 1933, MDP 2/13.

15 MDP 5/196.

16 See MacDonald to Roberton, February 10th, 1933, MDP 3/41; MacDonald to Runciman, August 21st, 1933, MDP 2/12; Chamberlain to MacDonald, October 17th, 1933, MDP 2/13.

17 Earl of Avon, *The Eden Memoirs: Facing the Dictators* (1962), p. 23.

18 See below, pp. 743–4.

19 Op. cit., pp. 119–20.

20 Copy in MDP 1/256.

21 Diary, January 29th, 1933.

22 Cabinet 9 (33), February 15th, 1933; Diary, February 19th, 1933.

23 MDP 2/13.

24 Ibid.

25 MDP 1/600 and 1/601.

26 *Manchester Guardian*, March 16th, 1933.

27 MDP 2/13.

28 Chamberlain to MacDonald, March 31st, 1933, MDP 2/13.

29 Cabinet 24 (33).

30 Cabinet 25 (33).

31 Diary, April 7th, 1933.

32 Cabinet 30 (33).

33 Cabinet 33 (33).

34 Diary, May 21st, 1933.

35 Cabinet 36 (33).

36 Ibid.

37 Courthorpe to MacDonald, May 31st, 1933, MDP 5/44.

38 MacDonald to Glyn, May 27th, 1933, MDP 5/44.

39 MacDonald to Usher, June 1st, 1933, MDP 5/44.

40 MacDonald to Wigram, June 2nd, 1933, MDP 2/13.

41 MacDonald to Steel-Maitland, August 12th, 1933, MDP 5/44; National Labour minutes, October 13th, 1933, MDP 5/195.

42 Butler to MacDonald, August 23rd, 1933, MDP 1/366.

43 MDP 1/366.

44 Notebook, August 28th, 1933.

45 The memorandum is in MDP 5/196, and a handwritten draft is in MDP 8/1.

46 Diary, October 17th, 1933.

47 Ibid., November 23rd, 1933.
48 MacDonald to Chamberlain, April 26th, 1934, MDP 5/46.
49 Chamberlain to MacDonald, April 26th, 1934, MDP 5/46.
50 Diary.
51 Notebook, January 5th, 1934.
52 Diary.
53 Ibid.
54 MDP 2/14.
55 Ibid.
56 Diary.
57 Ibid.
58 Ibid.
59 See Cabinets 50 (32), 56 (32), 57 (32), 39 (32) and 64 (32), October 11th and 31st, and November 30th, 1932; minutes of meeting of ministers in MacDonald's room in the House of Commons, October 19th, 1932, MDP 1/504.
60 Notebook, December 1st–10th, 1932.
61 Interview, Malcolm MacDonald.
62 Diary, February 28th, 1933.
63 Ibid., March 2nd, 1933.
64 Ibid., October 22nd, 1933.
65 Ibid., November 30th, 1933.
66 Ibid., February 4th, 1934.
67 Ibid., February 13th, 1934.
68 Ibid., June 3rd, 1933.
69 Diary.
70 Roberton papers.
71 MacDonald to Londonderry, October 27th, 1934, MDP 8/1.
72 Diary, March 5th, 1933.
73 Ibid., March 2nd, 1933; D.C. (M) (32) minutes, MDP 1/591.
74 D.C. (M) (32) minutes, MDP 1/591.
75 Diary, March 2nd, 1933.
76 D.C. (M) (32) minutes, March 3rd, 1933, MDP 1/591.
77 D.C. (M) (32) minutes, March 5th, 1933, MDP 1/591.
78 Notebook, March 9th, 1933.
79 Ibid.
80 Minutes of meeting at French Ministry of War, March 10th, 1933, 'Paris visits' folder, MDP 1/520.
81 Notebook, March 10th, 1933.
82 MDP 1/520.
83 Cabinets 17 (33) and 18 (33), March 13th and 15th, 1933.
84 Notebook, March 16th, 1933.
85 Ibid., March 19th, 1933.

86 Roskill, *Hankey*, vol. 3, p. 87.
87 Diary, October 15th, 1933.
88 D.C. (M) (32) minutes, November 7th, 1933; Cabinet 61 (33), November 8th, 1933.
89 German Documents (*D.G.F.P.* Series C, Volume II).
90 Diary, November 17th, 1933.
91 Ibid., November 26th, 1933.
92 D.C. (M) (32) minutes, November 30th, 1933, MDP 1/591; Hankey's paper is in MDP 1/493.
93 Roberton papers.
94 Diary, February 23rd, 1934.
95 Ibid., March 13th, 1934.
96 MacDonald to Angell, March 13th, 1934, MDP 2/14.
97 C.P. 64 (34), copy in MDP 1/613.
98 MDP 1/493.
99 D.C. (M) (32) minutes, May 8th, 1934, MDP 1/494.
100 Diary, June 21st, 1934.
101 Cabinet 26 (34), June 27th, 1934.
102 D.C. (M) (32) minutes, June 25th, 1934, MDP 1/494.
103 Diary, June 29th, 1934.

Chapter 30   Return to Spynie

1 Notebook, August 8th, 1934.
2 Ibid., August 10th, 21st, 22nd, 1934.
3 Ibid., August 1st, 1934.
4 Ibid., August 18th, 1934.
5 Ibid., September 2nd, 1934.
6 Ibid., September 29th, 1934.
7 Ibid., October 1st, 1934.
8 Robert Rhodes James, *Memoirs of a Conservative* (1969), p. 402.
9 Diary, December 22nd, 1934.
10 Ibid., January 8th, 1935.
11 Ibid., January 29th, 1935.
12 Hankey diary, February 24th, 1935, quoted in Roskill, *Hankey*, vol. 3, p. 162.
13 Diary, February 23rd, 1935.
14 Ibid., February 27th, 1935.
15 Diary.
16 Ibid., January 1st, 1935.
17 Chamberlain to Baldwin, January 4th, 1935, Baldwin papers 170/31; Keith Feiling, *The Life of Neville Chamberlain* (1970), pp. 241-2.

18 Diary, January 28th, 1935.
19 Cabinet 6 (35), January 30th, 1935.
20 Diary, January 30th, 1935.
21 Diary.
22 Ibid.
23 Ibid., February 11th, 1935.
24 Ibid., February 12th, 1935.
25 Ibid., February 13th, 1935.
26 Diary.
27 Ibid., March 14th, 1935.
28 Ibid., March 21st, 1935.
29 Ibid., April 4th, 1936.
30 Cabinet 41 (34), November 21st, 1934.
31 Cabinet 42 (34), November 26th, 1934.
32 Diary.
33 Ibid., November 22nd, 1934.
34 Ibid., January 14th, 1934.
35 Roskill, *Hankey*, vol. 3, p. 148.
36 Cmd. 4827.
37 Diary.
38 Ibid., March 5th, 1935.
39 Ibid., March 16th, 1935.
40 Diary.
41 Cabinet 15 (35); Avon, op. cit., p. 129.
42 Diary, April 2nd, 1935.
43 Ibid., April 3rd, 5th, 7th, 1931.
44 Vansittart, op. cit., p. 519.
45 Cabinets 20 (35) and 21 (35), April 8th, 1935.
46 Notebook, n.d.
47 Text in MDP 1/552.
48 Diary.
49 Frank Hardie, *The Abyssinian Crisis* (1974) pp. 117-18.
50 Vansittart, op. cit., pp. 520-21.
51 Diary.
52 Ibid., April 23rd, 1935.
53 Diary.
54 MDP 2/15.
55 Diary.
56 Ibid.
57 Ibid.
58 Ibid., May 9th, 1935.
59 Diary.
60 Ibid., May 12th, 1935.

61 Ibid., May 13th, 1935.
62 Ibid., May 16th, 1935.
63 Diary.
64 Ibid., May 27th, 1935.
65 MDP 5/47.
66 Diary, May 28th, 1935.
67 Cabinet 32 (35).
68 Diary, June 19th, 1935.
69 Ibid., July 3rd, 1935.
70 Ibid., July 11th, 1935.
71 Notebook, August 21st, 1935.
72 Diary.
73 Ibid., October 9th, 1935.
74 MacDonald to Edge, October 23rd, 1935, MDP 7/36.
75 Diary.
76 *British Labour Statistics*, Table 162.
77 *Durham County Advertiser*, November 1st, 1935.
78 Ibid.
79 Notebook, October 30th, 1935.
80 *Durham County Advertiser*, November 8th, 1935.
81 Ibid.
82 Notebook.
83 *Durham County Advertiser*, November 15th, 1935.
84 Diary, November 15th, 1935.
85 Baldwin to MacDonald, November 15th, 1935, MDP 3/43.
86 Diary.
87 Note dated November 19th, 1935, MDP 8/1.
88 Diary, November 19th, 1935.
89 See correspondence in *The Times*, November 26th–29th, 1935.
90 Nicolson, *Diaries*, vol. 1, p. 242.
91 *The Times*, February 6th, 1936.
92 Diary, February 11th, 1936.
93 MacDonald to Donaldson, February 14th, 1936, MDP 5/48.
94 *The Times*, January 6th, 1936; Diary, April 11th, 1936.
95 Interview, Frank Barlow.
96 Diary, August 28th, 1936.
97 MacDonald to Grant, November 2nd, 1936, MDP 3/44.
98 *The Times*, November 10th, 1936.
99 Nicolson, *Diaries*, vol. 1, p. 283.
100 Diary, January 20th, 1936.
101 Ibid., January 22nd, 1936.
102 *Budget Disclosure Inquiry, Report of The Tribunal appointed under The Tribunals of Inquiry (Evidence) Act. 1921* (1936), Cmd. 5184.

103 Diary.
104 Ibid.
105 Ibid.
106 Ibid., May 12th, 1936.
107 Ibid., May 19th, 1936.
108 Ibid., May 20th, 1936.
109 Notebook, June 2nd, 1936.
110 Ibid.
111 Diary, June 9th, 1936.
112 Ibid., June 11th, 1936.
113 Ibid., March 7th, 16th; April 7th, 11th, 1936.
114 Ibid., April 13th, 1936.
115 Ibid., October 12th, 1936.
116 Ibid., July 29th, 30th, 1936.
117 Ibid., August 28th, 1936.
118 Ibid., November 25th, 1936.
119 Diary.
120 Ibid.
121 See MDP 1/648-1/650.
122 Diary.
123 Notebook, n.d., probably early July 1937.
124 Interview, Lady Helen Roberton.
125 Citrine, op. cit., p. 291.
126 *The Times*, November 10th, 1937.
127 Undated letter from MacDonald to Princess Bibesco, found among his papers on the *Reina del Pacifico*, Bibesco papers.
128 Account based on reports in *The Times*, November 1937.

Index

Index

I

DATE DUE

2-22-78			
GAYLORD			PRINTED IN U.S.A.

NATIONAL POLICY
UNITY AND SECURITY
SOCIALIST POLICY
Saved!
VOTE for the NATIONAL GOVERNMENT